THE BELFAST AGREEMENT

A practical legal analysis

Austen Morgan
BSc MA in Law PhD
of Lincoln's Inn, Barrister
and
Member of the Inn of Court of Northern Ireland

THE BELFAST PRESS
London 2000

First published in Great Britain 2000 by
The Belfast Press Limited
29 Ludgate Hill, London EC4M 7JE

British Library Cataloguing in Publication Data
A catalogue record for this book is available from the British Library

ISBN 0-9539287-0-5

Designed and produced for The Belfast Press by Chase Publishing Services
Printed in the European Union by Antony Rowe, Chippenham, England

Contents

Prologue

The 10 April 1998 – Good Friday in the Christian calendar – dawned cold and grey at Castle Buildings, a nondescript civil-service building at Stormont on the eastern edge of Belfast. Inside were the United Kingdom and Irish premiers, the Rt. Hon. Tony Blair MP and Bertie Ahern TD, and the leaders of eight Northern Ireland political parties; outside, there was a growing global media village. A midnight deadline had passed without any puffs of white smoke signalling agreement.

An astute observer would have spotted an invigorated John Hume MP MEP, leader of the nationalist Social Democratic and Labour Party (SDLP), touring the press tents, following a meeting in the early hours with the Rt. Hon. David Trimble MP, leader of the Ulster Unionist Party (UUP). The same person might have noticed the Sinn Féin leaders, Gerry Adams and Martin McGuinness (both abstentionist MPs[1]), avoiding media opportunities. There was no sign of the Rev. Dr Ian Paisley MP MEP, leader of the Democratic Unionist Party (DUP): he had walked out of the all-party negotiations, as they were then called, the previous July (with Robert McCartney QC MP of the United Kingdom Unionist Party (UKUP)); and had been banned overnight by the secretary of state, the Rt. Hon. Marjorie 'Mo' Mowlam MP, from the grey-hutted press centre in the car park at Castle Buildings.

Inside, the armies of advisers, supporters and others in the parties' rooms continued to watch the watchers, on the televisions supplied to the talks' participants by the Northern Ireland Office (NIO).

There was no sign of the two heads of government for much of the day. Then, in the late afternoon, Alistair Campbell, the prime minister's press secretary, came out to brief the media; a document had been agreed finally after nearly two years of talks, covering apparently – what were called – the Strand One (internal United Kingdom[2]), Strand Two (north-south) and Strand Three (east-west) institutions, plus constitutional issues and a miscellany of matters dealing with terrorism and democracy.

Inside Castle Buildings, in the fourth-level conference room (where a pooled television camera had been installed to broadcast a short ceremony), the United States chairman, Senator George Mitchell, with his colleagues, General John de Chastelain of Canada, and Prime Minister Harri Holkeri of Finland, opened the final plenary of the negotiations at 17.05. The prime minister and the taoiseach were also in attendance, with their government delegations.

The chairman asked if there were any amendments to the multi-party agreement, final copies of which had been distributed to all parties that morning. Sinn Féin

1 Application 39511/98: *McGuinness v United Kingdom* (8 June 1999, unreported), European Court of Human Rights.

2 Conceived originally as internal Northern Ireland relations.

stated it had a number of concerns, which were annexed subsequently to the summary record of the session.[3] The Northern Ireland Women's Coalition (NIWC) also had an issue of concern.[4]

Senator Mitchell then proceeded to a vote on the final agreement, under procedural rule 34. Sinn Féin stated that it would not be voting, as it had to report back to its ard chomhairle (or national executive). 'It said that it would let the Chairman know the outcome of its deliberations in due course.' The UUP explained that it would be reporting to the Ulster Unionist Council on 18 April 1998. The United Kingdom government, followed by the Irish government, assented to the multi-party agreement. Each party, in alphabetic order, was then asked to vote. The Alliance Party, Labour,[5] the NIWC and the Progressive Unionist Party (PUP) did so in favour. Sinn Féin said it would register its vote when instructed to do so. The SDLP, Ulster Democratic Party (UDP) and UUP (referring to its caveats) voted last in favour of the agreement. The chairman declared that sufficient consensus (under the rules of the talks) had been achieved.

The prime minister and taoiseach then thanked the independent chairmen. They thanked the Northern Ireland parties. And the party leaders paid tribute to the three chairmen and two heads of government. Senator Mitchell declared the plenary closed sine die.

The cameras, however, had started broadcasting earlier than intended, and there was live television coverage of the end of this final session of the talks.

It was at 17.36 that Senator Mitchell – commencing the brief ceremony – announced that 'the two Governments, and the political parties of Northern Ireland, ha[d] reached agreement'. He went on to address the people watching at home: 'If you support this agreement, and if you also reject the merchants of death and the purveyors of hate, if you make it clear to your political leaders that you want them to make it work, then it will.'[6]

It was next the turn of the party leaders (in order of electoral support). 'We rise from this table', David Trimble said, 'knowing that the Union is stronger than it was when we first sat down. We know that the fundamental act of union is there intact.'[7] 'There can be a new dawn in politics on this island', said John Hume. '... It will be a new agreed Ireland in which the rights and interests of both the nationalist and unionist traditions, and others, will be safeguarded and cherished.'[8] Gerry Adams stated: 'we remain absolutely committed to our Irish republican objectives ... British policy in Ireland has manifestly failed. Partition has failed. The decades of unionist rule in the north were exclusive and partisan.'

The Sinn Féin president announced that he would take the document back to

3 Summary Record of Final Plenary Session – Friday 10 April 1998 (17.05). The Sinn Féin comments are at Annex A.

4 Summary Record of Final Plenary Session – Friday 10 April 1998 (17.05). Annex B.

5 This is not part of the (British) Labour Party led by Tony Blair.

6 Statement, 10 April 1998, Office of the Independent Chairmen.

7 *Irish Times*, 11 April 1998. This report differs from the text David Trimble published subsequently: *Fordham International Law Journal*, 22, 4, April 1999, pp. 1169–70.

8 *Irish Times*, 11 April 1998.

his party: 'When we have democratically come to a conclusion we will let you know.'[9]

The parties were followed by the heads of government. At a table especially set up in the room, Tony Blair and Bertie Ahern (attended by officials) signed the two originals of the British-Irish Agreement, to which would be annexed the agreement reached in the multi-party negotiations. Marjorie 'Mo' Mowlam, and David Andrews, the Irish foreign minister, also signed.

The prime minister and taoiseach then held a joint press conference outside Castle Buildings (the photograph of them shaking hands appears on the cover of this book). 'I said when I arrived here that I felt the hand of history upon us.' The prime minister continued: 'Today I hope that the burden of history can at long last start to be lifted from our shoulders.'[10]

9 *Irish Times*, 11 April 1998; see also, Gerry Adams and Martin McGuinness's addresses, 18 April 1998. At its ardfhéis (conference) in Dublin on 18-19 April 1998, the leadership temporized; Gerry Adams said of the agreement: 'This is not a settlement. It is transitional. It is an accommodation. It can be a basis for advancement.' The ardfhéis was adjourned to 10 May 1998 in Dublin. The ard chomhairle (national executive) proposed two resolutions: the first amending the party's constitution, to allow successful candidates to take their seats in the Northern Ireland assembly; the second calling for 'yes' votes in the 22 May referendums. Sinn Féin continued to oppose the central concept of consent in the Belfast Agreement. (All relevant texts available at http://sinnfein.ie.)

10 *Irish Times*, 11 April 1998.

Preface

It would be Thursday, 2 December 1999 (over 600 days later), before the Belfast Agreement (or the Agreement) entered into force. On that day, power was devolved from London to Belfast. Devolution was suspended on 12 February 2000, due to the failure of the IRA to decommission; the institutions were restored on 30 May 2000, upon a promise to allow inspection of arms dumps.

History, Politics and the Law

The achievement of the Belfast Agreement, reached at Stormont on Good Friday 1998, is historic. It is an important event in Irish and British history. Senator George Mitchell has already published his – at times revealing – memoir of the multi-party negotiations.[1] Thomas Hennessy has written an account of the 1996–98 talks based upon collected documents.[2] Others will no doubt follow. This book is not a contribution to that literature; it is not about the personalities and politics of the Northern Ireland problem.[3]

Issues of history are touched upon in passing in the substantive parts of the book, where necessary to delineate the law – international and municipal – of this particular constitutional solution. Part 1 is introductory, and includes four historical chapters.[4] Otherwise, the normal protocols of legal analysis in international law and in the common law – involving narrative and a respect for chronology - are followed throughout this work.

The Belfast Agreement: a practical legal analysis is what the title says. It is about the Belfast Agreement, also referred to as the Stormont Agreement or the Good Friday Agreement.[5] This is a relatively short text (30 pages), drawn up by two governments and agreed by most – but not all – of Northern Ireland's political parties. Legally, the Belfast Agreement is an international agreement, or treaty (the consequences of which have not been appreciated generally). The Agreement has been incorporated variously in United Kingdom law, and in Irish law, as part of its implementation by the two governments. The Northern Ireland Act (NIA) 1998 is the principal consequence of the Belfast Agreement. But it is not the only statute in United Kingdom law, to say nothing of Irish law. Even where the Belfast Agreement has not been incorporated in one way or another, it may be of domestic relevance given respective rules of interpretation in the two jurisdictions in Ireland. The

1 *Making Peace*, London 1999.

2 *The Northern Ireland Peace Process: ending the troubles?* Dublin 2000.

3 These are being left in the Prologue, except where, in Parts 2 to 4, they become legally significant.

4 The standard student textbook takes an unarticulated internal historical approach: Brigid Hadfield, *The Constitution of Northern Ireland*, Belfast 1989.

5 See Chapter 1.

Belfast Agreement has also spawned a number of subsidiary international agreements, which are of considerable legal significance.

The book is structured by the contents of the Belfast Agreement, some 11 sections (as they are called in that text). These are dealt with consecutively in Chapters 8 to 23 (the additional chapters being required to deal mainly with annexes to several sections), plus Chapter 24 on the British-Irish Agreement. The focus throughout is the text. If the Belfast Agreement is to succeed historically and politically, it will have to work legally. I aim to give it a fair wind by respecting the document as drafted (regardless of well or badly), and bringing to it only the norms of rational argument and commitment to the rule of law.

The subtitle of the book – a practical legal analysis – is important, and distinguishes it from other possible works on the Belfast Agreement. The book provides the material of legal argument and submission. Lawyers may be distinguished professionally in several ways. Perhaps the most important is academic lawyers versus practitioners (another professional gulf is between international and domestic lawyers). Often, there is little interaction. And, in United Kingdom and Irish law, jurists are not as highly valued as they are in continental civil law systems.[6] There, legal analysis interacts more often with history, philosophy and the social sciences. Teaching and scholarship in these islands have their own protocols; occasionally, the work of academic lawyers is used in the courts (or in giving legal advice, or in the vast array of non-contentious work – the legal iceberg below the sea).

Practitioners, in contrast, comprise solicitors, barristers and judges (and, from time to time in private but mainly public international law, legal scholars). They are the actors upon the legal stage, not the legal critics in the academy. Some write texts for busy colleagues; but publication is not a qualification valued for high judicial office in United Kingdom or Irish law. Their law is case – that is, client – driven. One's duty is to the client, and to the court – domestic or international. In the common law, adversarialism reigns. Justice – criminal but also civil – is for the court, having heard contending views. The good lawyer is the one who correctly predicts the outcome of a particular action in a designated court or courts.

To any question about the meaning of the Belfast Agreement, I answer: that is a matter for the courts (which courts is a significant problem). If it is to work as an international agreement, variously incorporated in United Kingdom and Irish law, domestic judges will incrementally interpret the text, and other cases, as specific problems are brought before them by practising lawyers. The meaning of the Belfast Agreement could, of course, be sought directly from the International Court of Justice at The Hague, article 36(2) of the statute providing for inter alia the interpretation of a treaty. But that would probably give rise to problems of jurisdiction (discussed in Chapter 2).

Readership

This book has been written with four distinct professional groups in mind. First,

6 An exception in the United Kingdom, and in criminal law, is Glanville Williams: see, for example, *R v Director of Public Prosecutions, ex parte Kebilene* [1999] 3 WLR 972, 987 per Lord Cooke of Thorndon.

solicitors, barristers and judges in Northern Ireland, and in the Republic of Ireland. They will be involved in cases concerning the new institutions of government, internal to the United Kingdom state but also linking it internationally. This professional group has been engaged already in cases in Dublin and Belfast on other aspects of the Agreement. The likelihood is that this process will develop, and that landmark judgments – of considerable significance to the political actors – will spring from ordinary private, and public, law disputes.

Second, practitioners and constitutional scholars in Great Britain interested generally in United Kingdom devolution and human rights law – as part of the constitutional reform project of the labour government elected in May 1997.

Third, diplomats, political leaders and experts engaged in trying to solve persisting ethnic and other crises, particularly through the drafting of international instruments. The Oslo Accords (of 1993 and 1994), between Israel and the Palestinians, are a proximate non-legal comparator of the Belfast Agreement.[7] (Where peace is promised, international investors are never far behind.) This book, however, is not a comparative academic work. International comparisons have not always been used constructively in Northern Ireland. And genuine comparisons require equal treatment of different countries, not an accumulation of apparent analogies from abroad to back up an established local position.

Fourth, and finally, academic lawyers in both parts of Ireland, Great Britain and internationally. The Belfast Agreement will, no doubt, appear on undergraduate syllabi and be the object of postgraduate studies and research. Given its extraordinary political profile at home and abroad, this will happen sooner rather than later. It will also be the subject of academic publications – probably journal articles rather than full-scale studies (with advocacy never far below the surface of disciplinary debate).

Two cautions need to be entered about a home-grown literature on the Belfast Agreement. First, in Northern Ireland, academic culture is not free of nationalist-unionist rivalries, and there is no dominant community of local scholars – given an absent centre – professing a liberal-democratic discourse with thorough integrity. Analysis is occasionally the academic contribution to the local inter-communal struggle; politics by other means. Second, and related, some legal academics, mainly in Northern Ireland, precisely because of their alienation from the institutions of the law (permitted by academic freedom), engage in ideologically driven theoretical discussion rather than practical legal analysis.

Political and Academic Viewpoints

The Belfast Agreement is generating its own academic literature. One extremely useful scholarly work – including an important article by the then Irish attorney general, David Byrne SC, which will be referred to in subsequent chapters – appeared in the United States in April 1999, about the time of the first anniversary: book 4 of volume 22 of the *Fordham International Law Journal* (published by the

7 Israel-Palestinian Declaration of Priniciples, 13 September 1993, done at Washington, DC, and the Agreement on the Gaza Strip and the Jericho Area, 4 May 1994, done in Cairo. Oslo I and II are not, of course, treaties: http://www.israel-mfa.gov.il. See also, E. Cotran & C. Mallat, eds, *The Arab-Israeli Accords: legal perspectives*, The Hague 1996, based on a conference of mainly Arabs and Israelis in London in December 1994.

School of Law at Fordham University in New York). It will be cited throughout as *Fordham International Law Journal*. It was dedicated to Senator Mitchell, and to the Nobel laureates, David Trimble and John Hume. Reference was made to Northern Ireland's peace process.[8] Though the appended Belfast Agreement covers only 46 pages of the journal, 27 articles are spread over 724 pages – an indicator of the significance of this legal instrument (which had not then entered into force, and looked at the time of publication like it might never).

Though produced externally, it reproduced aspects of the internal intellectual culture of Northern Ireland. I discuss the *Fordham International Law Journal* here because it is an impressive beginning to debate about the Belfast Agreement.

A great deal of political advocacy is contained in this fat volume. Ulster unionism, essentially anti-terrorism, is represented with three articles.[9] One, by Ian Paisley, is fundamentally anti-Agreement. Ranked against them are five nationalists, though John Bruton TD would not be acceptable to republicans.[10] The article from the Women's Coalition is best characterized as anti-unionist if not pro-nationalist.[11]

Only one of the 11 political contributions (including Senator Mitchell's), that by the centrist Alliance Party, affirms coherently the norms of liberal democracy (as opposed to consociational democracy) which interrelate with individual legal rights and duties; the Alliance Party juxtaposes 'tribal dualism' – allegedly characteristic of the Belfast Agreement – to 'pluralism'.[12] Senator Mitchell's piece addresses Northern Ireland as an instance of peace making by a United States Democrat: 'the agreement does not, by itself, provide or guarantee a durable peace, political stability, or reconciliation'.[13] (And he was to be called back to conduct the Mitchell review of September to November 1999, which led eventually to devolution after approximately 18 months.)

The 16 academic viewpoints (as they were called by the editors) are predominantly pro-nationalist, and some pro-republican – though the latter may have been inspired by secular radicalism.[14] Singularly, Dennis Kennedy, of the Cadogan Group, who is neither an ethnic nor political unionist, critically discusses the Belfast Agreement from what he describes as a position of principle.[15] Many of the other academic contributors are enthusiastically pro-Agreement, some claiming they have directly and indirectly influenced the text put together by the two governments; 'The focus of those who wish to see society transformed as a result of

8 In the Middle East, Israel's peace process was launched effectively at the Madrid peace conference on 30 October 1991. In Northern Ireland, it was paradoxically Sinn Féin which raised the question (having always argued that the cause of violence is the British presence): *A Scenario for Peace* (May 1987); *Towards a Lasting Peace* (1992).

9 By David Trimble, Duncan Shipley-Dalton and Ian Paisley.

10 By John Hume, Gerry Adams, Bertie Ahern, John Bruton, David Byrne SC, then attorney general.

11 By Kate Fearon and Monica McWilliams (pp. 1258–9).

12 By Stephen Farry and Sean Neeson (p. 1242).

13 Page 1139.

14 I would not include Seamus Dunn and Jacqueline Nolan-Haley, Colin Harvey or John Morison in this generalization about nationalism, republicanism and radicalism.

15 'The analyst, or, for want of a better word, the intellectual, removed from the heat of negotiation, may be much more conscious of the contradictions involved, and of the bending, or setting aside, of truths and principles.' (p. 1462)

the Good Friday Agreement', ends one such contribution, 'will be to ensure that ... the major players in the peace process [who] picked up the human rights ball and ran with it ... [do] not drop[ped] it'.[16]

The interwoven themes of most of these early Fordham contributions on the Belfast Agreement (though they are rarely express) would appear to be: one, a constitutional weakening of Northern Ireland's position within the United Kingdom; two, a major all-Ireland institutional advance; and three, the centrality of unspecified human rights. The name 'Good Friday Agreement' (which came to be associated most closely with the Irish government[17]) is emblematic of such key principles. Nationalist Ireland is telling itself it has made a structural advance beyond the 1920–22 partition settlement.

The paradox of the Belfast Agreement is that the above three themes are accepted substantively by anti-Agreement unionists (29 of the 58 designated unionists elected to the Northern Ireland assembly on 25 June 1998). What Sinn Féin affirms, Ian Paisley accepts; indeed, it is sufficient proof. Anti-Agreement unionism (seemingly a growing constituency) is, therefore, represented ironically in these academic viewpoints, though not one author hails from anywhere near that political position.

Missing entirely from the academic viewpoints in this New York journal is the intellectual case for pro-Agreement unionism, a constituency which is barely recognized by most of the pro-nationalist and pro-republican contributors. Without that political position, led by David Trimble, there would have been no Belfast Agreement, nor devolution – nor the possibility of 'a new society' proclaimed by one of the Fordham contributors.[18] This has been confirmed most authoritatively by Senator Mitchell: the first chapter of his memoir opens with David Trimble telling him he was prepared to accept the Agreement, and his penultimate chapter poses the question: 'Why did Trimble take that fateful step?'[19]

This Preface is not the place to do justice to such a range of academic contributions, unbalanced though it be. No doubt the arguments will spill out into Northern Ireland politics. In terms of law, two points need to be made. One, the negotiation of the Agreement, which has a relevance for the interpretation of a treaty, and its implementation, was both more complicated and at times more prosaic than some of the Fordham contributors suggest.[20] Two, domestic and – where relevant – international courts are unlikely to have cause to view the Belfast Agreement in the radical light of such commentators writing in early 1999. The jurisprudence of the Belfast Agreement will evolve incrementally, perhaps dramatically given a particular legal problem, on the basis of the common law traditions in Northern Ireland and in the Republic of Ireland.

16 Paul Mageean and Martin O'Brien (p. 1538). See also, Christopher McCrudden, attributing a central role to the Committee on the Administration of Justice (p. 1742).

17 Compare the taoiseach introducing the second stage of the Nineteenth Amendment of the Constitution Bill 1999 (Dáil Éireann, *Official Report*, 21 April 1998) with the second stage of the British-Irish Agreement Bill 1999 (Dáil Éireann, *Official Report*, 9 March 1999).

18 Kieran McEvoy, p. 1575.

19 *Making Peace*, London 1999, pp. 3-5 & 180-1.

20 For example, Kevin McNamara MP had no more privileged insight than the Belfast authors who quote him (Paul Mageean and Martin O'Brien, p. 1538, referring to an article in the *Irish Times*, 29 October 1998).

Approach and Structure

The Belfast Agreement, as noted, is legally a treaty, the parties being the two states. There are distinct rules of interpretation in international law (discussed in Chapter 2). Interpretation is less literal and more purposive; perforce, it requires a contextualizing of each section of the Agreement in terms of this and previous attempts to find a solution – particularly on the Anglo-Irish plane – to the Northern Ireland problem.

The legal precedent for the Belfast Agreement is the 1985 Anglo-Irish Agreement (though the Northern Ireland Constitution Act (NICA) 1973 was replaced by the NIA 1998 – a major change in domestic law). That earlier international agreement gave the Irish government a right of consultation in the affairs of Northern Ireland. And Tom Hadden and Kevin Boyle's *The Anglo-Irish Agreement: commentary, text and official review*, Dublin and London 1989 was an inspiration for this book. After Part 1 (Introduction), each section forms a chapter, with the paragraphs (in bold) considered sequentially. The paragraphs of the Agreement are annotated using the statutory model, but modifying it for a treaty. (Annotations are printed in a smaller font.) When the text turns from legal and quasi-legal drafting in parts 2 and 3 to a more discursive style in part 4, annotation is replaced by legal commentary. This work, in comparison with Hadden and Boyle's pioneering effort, has had to be all-encompassing in scale, given the structure of the 1996–98 multi-party negotations, and the resultant agreement of Friday, 10 April 1998. It is a work of reference, rather than legal criticism, to be used on the basis of the Tables of Cases, Statutes and Other Domestic Legislation, and Treaties and Other Documents, plus the Index; specific points will be looked up, though the chapters in Part 1 (Introduction) – especially Chapters 3 and 4, and 5 and 6 – may be read as free-standing essays on the domestic, constitutional law of the two states parties. Elsewhere, the aim is to provide the most immediately practical information, so lawyers can argue a point about the meaning of a word or phrase in a paragraph or section.

Politics and history are involved in any analysis of the Belfast Agreement, but one's interest is only in the legal point being established. There may, of course, be no legal point, if the Belfast Agreement – a historic compromise between unionism and nationalism – is characterized exclusively (as is becoming the tendency) in terms of the advance of one political tradition – according to the logic of zero sum – at the expense of another.[21] In this case, it is of diminishing constitutional use; the Agreement becomes simply a new occasion for the old quarrel to be continued by tribal leaders using legal rhetoric and academic proxies. The Belfast Agreement is not transitional to a united Ireland (as is claimed increasingly by Sinn Féin). On the other hand, it does seek to make Northern Ireland attractive to the nationalist minority, for the foreseeable (and indefinite) future. In the latter context, the Belfast Agreement is a constitutional foundation[22] to the operation of locally specified democratic government. If it is not that, and nationalist Ireland seems unwilling to accept such a compromise, it is nothing legally useful.

21 See the organization, Friends of Ireland: Friends of the Good Friday Agreement, co-founded by Kevin McNamara MP, a former shadow secretary of state for Northern Ireland.

22 On 21 March 2000, the secretary of state said in Dublin: 'The Agreement gave us a framework for a new constitution and it laid the basis for a new Northern Ireland ...': Northern Ireland Information Service: http://www.nio.gov.uk.

The Belfast Agreement is a partitionist settlement: better, and less controversially, it is located firmly within the 1920–22 constitutional arrangements, whereby a new state was legally created in 26 of Ireland's 32 counties (see Chapter 5). It is entirely fanciful – and an instance of nationalist appropriation of the Agreement – to try and infer that it provides for joint sovereignty or authority in Northern Ireland. That process began, not in April 1998, but in September 1999 (following the publication of the Patten report on policing), and will be considered in Chapter 21. It broke into the political world after the suspension of the institutions by the United Kingdom government on Saturday 12 February 2000, with some extraordinary legal claims being made publicly and retrospectively from Dublin.[23]

The international law approach taken here is, I submit contrary to United Kingdom municipal lawyers, the most appropriate for the Belfast Agreement. Even when attention turns to the NIA 1998, by which some – not all – of the Agreement was incorporated into United Kingdom law, statutory interpretation does not supercede the treaty text. (The Republic of Ireland of course, as a separate sovereign state, has its own laws.) Specific paragraphs are incorporated directly in United Kingdom law. Parliamentary counsel was instructed substantially by the Belfast Agreement, mediated by the NIO, as is clear from the Notes on Clauses (which are not usually considered by the courts). In the case of statutory ambiguity, it is possible (indeed necessary), in United Kingdom law, to look at the international agreement for legal meaning. The Belfast Agreement, and subsidiary international agreements, deal with, as well as Strand One, Strands Two and Three of the multi-party negotiations, the Strands Two and Three institutions being international in legal character.

The structure of the book, as noted, is determined by the Belfast Agreement. It is in five parts.

The first part is an introduction, discussing concepts and legal materials used later in the analysis of the Agreement. This is to avoid cluttering annotations on successive paragraphs (Parts 2 and 3 and the discussion in Part 4) with necessary background information. Chapter 1 delineates the Belfast Agreement, deriving the idea of a text with a political and a legal face (an image yet to be advanced by any legal commentators). Chapter 2 is a necessary synopsis of relevant public international law topics. This is to counteract the normal bias of United Kingdom and Irish municipal lawyers, and the simplified and distorted reputation international law has acquired in Northern Ireland as a result of the troubles. This is not centrally a contribution to public international law scholarship. Chapters 3 to 6 (as noted) establish the two states parties to the Agreement: the United Kingdom, which dates from 1800, and the Irish state, legally created in 1922.[24] There is a great deal more scholarly study of the former than the latter, so I have had to compensate in the spirit of the principle of sovereign equality (this does not mean I endorse the ideological joint sovereignty or authority interpretation).

23 *Irish Times*, 14 February 2000.

24 This presentation is necessary, because the relationship between the two states has not been clarified adequately for present purposes; for example, while historians discuss the putative national revolution of 1916–23, virtually no attention is paid the Irish legal revolution of 1937. 'Probably more than any other discipline, history is an essential component of the study of law.' (Paul Sieghart, *The International Law of Human Rights*, Oxford 1983, p. 3)

Chapter 7 considers the names of the two states in three systems of law, and derives a working nomenclature for the rest of the book based on the principle of mutual respect.

Parts 2 to 4 follow the 11 sections of the Agreement, using the text distributed in Northern Ireland (and presented to parliament in April 1998). These 16 chapters contain annotations and discussion of the text of the Belfast Agreement. It is not just the Final Agreement (see Chapter 2) which is annotated. The unpubished Mitchell Draft Paper (see Chapter 2) is also legally analysed. The evolution of the Belfast Agreement between 6 and 10 April 1998 is shown by: deletions in square brackets; and additions in italics. The annotations (as noted, based on the statutory model modified for a treaty) are structured as follows: a historical introduction, where necessary, referring to the precise topic; the title of the section (in bold), followed by a short discussion with numbered paragraphs; each paragraph of the section (in bold), followed by comprehensive annotation in unnumbered paragraphs, the relevant words under discussion being rendered initially in quotation marks.

Part 2 is headed Constitution. It deals with the Declaration of Support (Chapter 8), and Constitutional Issues (Chapter 9) plus Annexes A and B (Chapters 10 and 11). This part involves a consideration of international law and municipal law. It is concerned essentially with constitutional theory, not working institutions. I argue – contrary to the first theme of the Fordham academic viewpoints (see above) – that the Part is characterized predominantly by the end of the Irish territorial claim to Northern Ireland.

Part 3 turns to Institutions. The provisions considered in Chapters 12 to 17 are constitutional, but they concern the working of the government of Northern Ireland. Chapters 12 and 13 deal with Strand One, the institutions whereby power is devolved from London to Belfast. Contrary to the second theme of the Fordham academic viewpoints, I submit that this is the most important dimension. The Belfast Agreement, as I have stated, is located legally within the historic partitioning of Ireland. Chapters 14 and 15 deal with Strand Two, north-south relations. These are balanced, unlike in the 1973 Sunningdale agreement, by Strand Three – east-west relations (Chapters 16 and 17).

Part 4 is a collection of discrete issues. I label it 'Rights, etc.' after the Rights Safeguards and Equality of Opportunity section (Chapter 18). This is not to endorse the third theme of the Fordham academic viewpoints, namely that the whole of the Belfast Agreement was influenced inordinately by the human rights community in Northern Ireland. I submit that the Human Rights Act 1998 – which was passing through parliament at the time of the Belfast Agreement (and is not mainly attributable to that community) – was, and will be, much more significant. Further, it was article 13 (ex article 6a) of the European Community treaty, inserted by the treaty of Amsterdam of 2 October 1997, which largely inspired the anti-discrimination and equality of opportunity provisions.

I suggest further that Chapters 19 to 22 contain a better unity for this part, best entitled 'from terrorism to democracy'. Chapters 19 ('Decommissioning') and 22 ('Prisoners') are about the progressive ending of terrorism. Chapters 20 and 21 ('Security' and 'Policing and Justice') are about the return to democracy. If the

Belfast Agreement approximates to a peace agreement (which is arguable), its cornerstone is the ending of paramilitary violence; without that, it cannot succeed as a constitutional arrangement.

'Validation, Implementation and Review' (Chapter 23 in Part 4) is about the legal face of the Belfast Agreement. It is the end of the text of the international agreement (less Annex 2), as is clear from the version presented to parliament in 1999.[25] However, I have created a Part 5 for the short load-bearing British-Irish Agreement of four articles, since this was annexed originally to the Multi-Party Agreement (Parts 2 to 4). This is discussed separately in Chapter 24.

Legal Materials

The materials used in the 24 chapters may be described as primary legal sources. I have concentrated upon statute and case law in several domestic jurisdictions, and international instruments and the practice of states (see further Chapter 2). Academic monographs and journal articles have been used where relevant, but I have not sought to join issue centrally in academic debate with this secondary literature. That will come.

The questions discussed are those which arise from each section of the Belfast Agreement. It is not possible – as a legal practitioner – to anticipate all likely areas of contention, and even litigation. Who would have predicted the resignation of the Deputy First Minister (designate) on 15 July 1999? And the refusal of the Northern Ireland assembly to accept his resignation on 29 November 1999? The first event was not fully informed legally;[26] and the second continues to strain the notion of the rule of law (see Chapter 12). The question of suspension of the institutions was possible (at least from July 1999), but who would have credited an argument – now of mythical proportions – that the United Kingdom government acted illegally on 12 February 2000?[27] The procession of possible legal issues and cases in however many jurisdictions is never predictable. Many problems lie latent in the text, awaiting judicial resolution in United Kingdom and Irish law, and maybe even in international law. I do, however, consider all aspects of the Agreement which have been raised already in the courts or in controversy, between 10 April 1998 and 2 December 1999 (and beyond) – when the Belfast Agreement, though often invoked, was perceived incorrectly as some sort of multilateral domestic agreement (akin to a contract) rather than a treaty in escrow, with a legal effect derived from its conditions precedent.

All legal practitioners are, or should be, committed to the rule of law. 'There have been important developments over the past twenty years', David Byrne SC, the Irish attorney general, said in August 1998, 'where democratic principles, consent, and the establishment of the rule of law have been the tools of legal and political change and not terrorism and violence. During this period, the lawyer has become a more effective champion of freedom and justice than the terrorist or urban

25 This is discussed in Chapter 1.

26 *Irish Times* 29 July 1999.

27 See my article rebutting this thesis, *Irish Times*, 10 March 2000. However, subediting removed the reference to the taoiseach's article in the same paper on 14 February 2000 (where it was argued that the Irish government was prohibited by the constitution from helping suspend the north-south implementation bodies).

guerrilla.'[28] This point was confirmed by Chris Patten in his report on policing in Northern Ireland on 9 September 1999: 'No one who believes in an open society and the rule of law can be neutral as between democracy and violence, the protection of human rights and their abuse, the recognition of the dignity of every individual and its denial.'[29] This is the spirit in which this book has been written, and is presented to practising lawyers and others.

It aims to state the law as of 1 August 2000, the Northern Ireland assembly, and executive, having exercised power from 2 December 1999 (less the period of suspension, 12 February 2000 to 30 May 2000).

Austen Morgan,
3 Temple Gardens,
Temple,
London EC4Y 9AU
020 7353 0832
austenmorgan1@compuserve.com

Note: These are the rules on the use of the *fada* accent in Irish followed in this book. I use it. When I am citing or quoting a United Kingdom source, I follow the practice of no Irish accents in English. In the case of an Irish source (in Irish or English), I use the accent if it was used originally.

28 *Fordham International Law Journal*, p. 1206.

29 *A New Beginning: policing in Northern Ireland: the report of the independent commission on policing for Northern Ireland*, paragraph 1.7.

Acknowledgements

A number of people helped make this book possible. First, the Alexander Maxwell Law Scholarship Trust, which granted me an award in January 1999. This allowed me to set aside a number of months to work full time researching and writing. Second, Chase Publishing Services, especially Ray Addicott and Tracey Day. Third, Jeremy Carver CBE, head of public international law at Clifford Chance in London. He was a good practical teacher and colleague. Fourth, officials – lawyers and non-lawyers – in the London, Belfast, Dublin triangle. I was kept well supplied with legal documents from both sides of the Irish Sea. Civil servants work normally out of the public spotlight, so cannot be thanked individually. Fifth, – is this a first? – the internet, already an indispensible tool of legal research, made possible by many independent endeavours. And sixth, a number of individuals to be thanked personally, including Stephen Barr, Graham Gudgin, Alex Kane, David Kerr, Elizabeth Meehan, David Richardson and Barry Whyte. None of the above (as usual) is responsible for anything here; hopefully, however, the arguments and debates in the following chapters will be seen to be presented comprehensively and fairly to the legal communities in Ireland, Great Britain and further afield.

Alexander Maxwell Law Scholarship Trust

Maurice W. Maxwell whose family founded Sweet & Maxwell, the law publishers, by his will established a charitable trust to be known as the Alexander Maxwell Law Scholarship Trust in memory of his great-great-grandfather. The Trust is committed to promoting legal research and writing at various levels by providing financial assistance to authors whether they are experienced legal practitioners, those in the early years of practice or at postgraduate level.

The author of this book received financial assistance from the Trust to enable him to complete the work.

The Trust generally makes awards on an annual basis and applicants are invited to submit an application by 31 August in the previous year. Further details of the Trust and how to apply for an award can be obtained from The Clerk to the Trustees, Alexander Maxwell Law Scholarship Trust, c/o Sweet & Maxwell, 100 Avenue Road, London NW3 3PF.

Table of Cases

United States of America

Table of Statutes and Other Domestic Legislation

England
Laws in Wales Act 1536 27 Hen 8 c 26 – 30
Union with Scotland Act 1706 6 Anne c 11 – 30, 148

European Community
Council Directive 76/207/EEC – 369
Council Directive 86/613/EEC – 369
Council Directive 97/80/EC – 369

France
Déclaration des droits de l'homme et du citoyen 1791 – 359

Great Britain
Act for the Dependency of Ireland on Great Britain 1719 6 Geo 1 c 15 – 31
Irish Appeals Act 1783 23 Geo 3 c 28 – 31
Yelverton's Act 1782 21 & 22 Geo 3 c 53 – 31
Union with Ireland Act 1800 39 & 40 Geo 3 c 67 – 30–1, 32, 92, 146, 148, 149

Ireland/ Irish Free state/ Éire/Ireland/ Republic of Ireland
Act of Union (Ireland) 1800 39 & 40 Geo 3 c 38 – 30–1, 32, 92, 146, 148
Adaptation of Enactments Act 1922 – 94, 96, 100, 124
Agreement with United Kingdom (Capital Sum) Act 1938 – 83, 95, 101
Aliens Act 1935 – 125
Aliens Order 1946 (SR&O 395) – 125
Aliens (Amendment) Order 1975 (SI No. 128) – 125
Anti-Discrimination (Pay) Act 1974 – 369
British-Irish Agreement Act 1999 – 13, 261, 262, 270, 274, 276, 287, 290, 294, 310, 313, 314, 417, 533
British-Irish Agreement (Amendment) Act 1999 – 262, 313, 533
Bunreacht na hÉireann (1937) – 76–85, 93, 100, 110, 111, 116, 133, 150–80, 189, 370, 402, 404, 472, 560
Preamble – 82, 97, 179, 370
Article 1 – 81, 82, 157, 161, 167,
Article 2 – 79, 81, 82–3, 85, 87–8, 100, 101, 112, 118, 120, 123, 125, 127, 150–80, 262, 271, 346, 530, 531, 561
Article 3 – 79, 81, 82–3, 85, 87–8, 97, 98, 100, 101, 112, 120, 122, 123, 125, 127, 145, 150–80, 346, 530, 531, 561
Article 4 – 82–3, 86, 87, 96, 101, 102, 153, 179
Article 5 – 82, 86, 87, 118, 153, 167, 179
Article 6 – 157, 160, 167, 176, 178, 226, 274, 370, 440
Article 7 – 82
Article 8 – 79, 82, 153, 168, 179, 415
Article 9 – 82, 125, 153, 172, 179, 490

Scotland

United Kingdom of Great Britain and Ireland/ Northern Ireland

Table of Treaties and Other Documents

Abbreviations

BIA	British-Irish Agreement (of 10 April 1998)
BIAA	British-Irish Agreement Act
BIC	British-Irish Council
BIIC	British-Irish Intergovernmental Conference
BIIPB	British-Irish Inter-Parliamentary Body
BNH	Bunreacht na hÉireann
CAJ	Committee for the Administration of Justice
CAPO	Committee to Advise on the Presiding Officer
CSCE	Conference on Security and Cooperation in Europe
DFM	Deputy First Minister
DUP	Democratic Unionist Party
EC	Equality Commission
EC	European Community
ECHR	European Convention on Human Rights
ECJ	European Court of Justice
ECNI	Equality Commission for Northern Ireland
ECtHR	European Court of Human Rights
EEC	European Economic Community
EPA	Emergency Provisions Act
EPC	European Political Cooperation
EU	European Union
FA	Final Agreement (of 10 April 1998)
FAIT	Families Against Intimidation and Terror
FCO	Foreign and Commonwealth Office
FM	First Minister
GOIA	Government of Ireland Act 1920
HRA	Human Rights Act 1998
IA	Ireland Act 1949
ICJ	International Court of Justice
IFI	International Fund for Ireland
IICD	Independent International Commission on Decommissioning
ILA	International Law Association
INLA	Irish National Liberation Army
IONA	Islands of the North Atlantic
IRA	Irish Republican Army

ISO	Initial Standing Order
JMC	Joint Ministerial Committee
LVF	Loyalist Volunteer Force
MDP	Mitchell Draft Paper (of 6 April 1998)
MoU	Memorandum of Understanding
MPA	Multi-Party Agreement (of 10 April 1998)
NATO	North Atlantic Treaty Organization
NGO	Non-Governmental Organization
NIA	Northern Ireland Act (1974; 1982; 1998; 2000)
NICA	Northern Ireland Constitution Act 1973
NIHCR	Northern Ireland Human Rights Commission
NIO	Northern Ireland Office
NITPA	Northern Ireland (Temporary Provisions) Act 1972
NIUP	Northern Ireland Unionist Party
NIWC	Northern Ireland Women's Coalition
NNIA	New Northern Ireland Assembly
NSMC	North/South Ministerial Council
OV	Orange Volunteers
PANI	Police Authority for Northern Ireland
PFNI	Police Federation for Northern Ireland
PfP	Partnership for Peace
PR(STV)	Proportional Representation (Single Transferable Vote)
PTA	Prevention of Terrorism Act
PUP	Progressive Unionist Party
RHD	Red Hand Commandos
ROI	Republic of Ireland
RUC	Royal Ulster Constabulary
SACHR	Standing Advisory Commission on Human Rights
SDLP	Social Democratic and Labour Party
SEA	Single European Act
SO	Standing Order
SOS	Secretary of State
TEC	Treaty establishing the European Community
TEU	Treaty on European Union
TSN	Targeting Social Need
TUAS	Totally Unarmed Strategy- Tactical Use of Armed Struggle
UDA	Ulster Defence Association
UDP	Ulster Democratic Party
UFF	Ulster Freedom Fighters
UKUP	United Kingdom Unionist Party
UNCLOS	United Nations Convention on the Law of the Sea
UUP	Ulster Unionist Party
UVF	Ulster Volunteer Force

PART 1

INTRODUCTION

This contains seven chapters. The reasons for such an Introduction are given in the Preface.

1

What is the Belfast Agreement?

1.1 This chapter deals with (a) the extant texts; (b) the relationship between politics and law; (c) the relationship between the Multi-Party Agreement (MPA) and the British-Irish Agreement (BIA) of 10 April 1998; and (d) the giving effect to the Belfast Agreement in United Kingdom and Irish law – in order to answer the question: what is the Belfast Agreement?

1.2 The answer is not self-evident or simple. And this is borne out by the public and political discussion of – usually – the Good Friday Agreement since 10 April 1998. There was no appreciation of before and after entry into force on 2 December 1999. Nor was there any apparent awareness of the relationship between international and municipal law in both states. This criticism applies to politically active lawyers in Northern Ireland and in the Republic of Ireland. And not one of the academic viewpoints in the *Fordham International Law Journal* contains an adequate discussion of the legal status of the Belfast Agreement.

The extant texts

1.3 The immediate origin of the Belfast Agreement was a 65-page typescript 'Draft Paper' (plus two pages of contents), circulated to the participants in the multi-party negotiations at Castle Buildings at approximately 00.30 on Tuesday 7 April 1998 (though dated 6 April 1998), under cover of a memorandum from the Office of the Independent Chairmen (Senator George J. Mitchell, General John de Chastelain and Prime Minister Harri Holkeri). This will be referred to as the Mitchell Draft Paper (MDP) of 6 April 1998 in the following chapters.

1.4 The Mitchell Draft Paper has never been published officially. However, a copy has been available on the internet, from the Newshound, since approximately Easter 1998, at: http://www.nuzhound.com.[1] I use this text here, to show legally the evolution of the Belfast Agreement.

1.5 The participants at Castle Buildings were next issued at approximately 12.00 on Friday, 10 April 1998 with a 67-page typescript 'Final Agreement' (plus two pages of contents) under cover of a memorandum from the independent chairmen. This actual typescript document will be referred to here as the Final Agreement (FA) of 10 April 1998. The independent chairmen indicated that the title meant it was to be a final agreement. The Final Agreement was the text before the last plenary at 17.05 on that day,[2] though the prime minister, in his letter to David

1 Plus articles by Ed Maloney (*Sunday Tribune*, 19 April 1998) and Gary Kent (*Newsletter*, 1 May 1998 and *Fortnight*, May 1998) on the differences between the Mitchell Draft Paper and the Final Agreement.

2 There is a photograph of Senator Mitchell holding this text after the final plenary, between pages 86 and 87 of his book: *Making Peace*, London 1999.

Trimble shortly before (see Chapter 20), indicated the legal intention of at least one of the BIA signatories.

1.6 There is – for a lawyer – a striking difference between the Mitchell Draft Paper and the Final Agreement. This is the four-article British-Irish Agreement (BIA), which was referred to in the Mitchell Draft Paper at several points[3] but was not circulated on 6 April 1998. On 10 April 1998, it turned up as part of the Final Agreement, annexed to what it called the multi-party agreement.[4] The Northern Ireland political parties had not been involved in its negotiation.

1.7 The document before the participants in that final plenary of 10 April 1998 became the Belfast Agreement.[5] It was also the effective text signed by Tony Blair and Bertie Ahern (though not presented as such to parliament and the Oireachtas until March 1999). This paradox – involving a delay of eleven months – will be explained presently.

1.8 The Belfast Agreement has been published officially[6] in the following hard copies:

- 30-page booklet, with coloured front cover, entitled *The Agreement: agreement reached in the multi-party negotiations*, published by the United Kingdom government (and distributed to Northern Ireland households);[7]
- 35-page booklet, in two columns, entitled *Agreement reached in the Multi-party Negotiations*, published by the Irish government (and distributed to Republic of Ireland households). This version included the Irish-language text of the proposed Irish constitutional amendments;
- 30-page document, entitled *The Belfast Agreement: an agreement reached at the multi-party talks on Northern Ireland*, Cm 3883, presented to parliament by the secretary of state for Northern Ireland on 20 April 1998, and published by the Stationery Office Limited;[8]
- an Irish-language version of the Irish government's booklet, available in the Republic of Ireland;
- the same Irish text and format, with the United Kingdom government's coloured cover (suitably translated), available in Northern Ireland;

3 Paragraph 1 of Constitutional Issues; Annex B; paragraph 1 of Strand Two; the first paragraph 1 and the second paragraph 1 of Strand Three; paragraph 1 of Validation, Implementation and Review.

4 First recital of the preamble of the BIA.

5 Typographical errors were mysteriously added subsequently: on what became page 16, the heading and subheading were altered; on what became page 29, an 'of Ireland' appeared below the full name of the United Kingdom state.

6 The Northern Ireland Office made the agreement available on the internet: http://www.nio.gov.uk. There were several newspaper versions, including by the *Irish Times* on 11 April 1998. This is available on the internet on a special page at http://www.nuzhound.com.

7 There is only one difference with the Irish government's version (other than the presence of the Irish-language text of the proposed Irish constitutional amendments): in Annex B of Constitutional Issues in the latter, the date of the BIA (10 April 1998) has been added. This difference applies to the Irish-language version in Northern Ireland, meaning there is a formal inconsistency between the two United Kingdom versions distributed in Northern Ireland. The difference has been corrected in the March 1999 blue-book version.

8 The number Cm 3883 had been included in paragraph 2 of the Validation, Implementation and Review section of the Mitchell Draft Paper.

- a 44-page blue book, under the title *Agreement between the Government of the United Kingdom of Great Britain and Northern Ireland and the Government of Ireland*, Cm 4292, Belfast, 10 April 1998, and headed Ireland No. 1 (1999), presented to parliament by the secretary of state for foreign and commonwealth affairs in March 1999, also published by the Stationery Office Ltd;[9]
- the above, printed as Treaty series No. 50 (2000), presented to parliament by the secretary of state for foreign and commonwealth affairs in May 2000 as Cm 4705, also published by the Stationery Office Ltd;
- and the 49-page[10] Irish version, entitled *Agreement between the Government of Ireland and the Government of the United Kingdom of Great Britain and Northern Ireland*, published in March 1999. This has a similar layout to the United Kingdom version (however, Annex 1 (the MPA) contains, as annex, the BIA).

1.9 In this book, I refer to the English-language edition distributed in Northern Ireland, which is exactly the same – less the typographical errors – as the command paper of 20 April 1998 (Cm 3883).[11] This is what the people of Northern Ireland voted upon on 22 May 1998. I cross-reference to the blue-book version presented to parliament by the foreign secretary in May 2000 (Cm 4705). I also give page references to the 1999 Irish version (it being impossible to cite a common United Kingdom/Irish edition because of different pagination and the annexing of the BIA to the MPA in the Irish version).

1.10 It has become customary to cite the Belfast Agreement by paragraph numbers within each named section as listed on the contents page, and that practice will be followed here. This will resolve the problem of quoting page numbers in different versions.

1.11 The name 'the Belfast Agreement' was given to the United Kingdom command paper, Cm 3883. It is also the term used in the Northern Ireland Act (NIA) 1998, and 'the Belfast Agreement' is defined in section 98.[12] But where did this title come from? The Mitchell Draft Paper – the origin of the text – had no title.

1.12 The Final Agreement was entitled 'AGREEMENT REACHED IN THE MULTI-PARTY NEGOTIATIONS' (though Annex 1 of the British-Irish Agreement referred to it as the 'Agreement reached in the Multi-party Talks). And the former title was used in the Northern Ireland and Republic of Ireland versions of the Belfast Agreement.

1.13 'The Belfast Agreement' – I will argue below – is the most appropriate title. But it has had to do battle with 'the Good Friday Agreement' and, to a lesser extent, 'the Stormont Agreement'.

9 This is the same as Cm 3883 with two differences: the MPA has been annexed to the BIA (and is structured as follows: BIA, pp. 1–6; MPA [Annex 1], pp. 7–43; Annex 2, p. 44); the layout has been improved, with each section starting on a new page.

10 The numbered pages relate only to Annex 1 (pp. 1–42).

11 This is similar to the version – the MPA with the BIA annexed – published under 'Treaties, Agreements and Related Documents', in volume XXXVII, number 4, of *International Legal Materials*, in July 1998. A composite was made from the NIO website (visited 13 April 1998) and that of the department of the taoiseach (visited 27 May 1998).

12 'The agreement reached at multi-party talks on Northern Ireland set out in Command Paper 3883.'

1.14 The originator of the 'Good Friday' name is most likely an unidentified Northern Ireland journalist. In his report in the *Irish Times* on 11 April 1998, Frank Millar – filing from Castle Buildings – reported a local broadcaster[13] as saying: 'Think of all the bad days we've known here ... This really will be Good Friday.' The Good Friday Agreement is a catchy journalistic tag. And it was applied spontaneously in a heavily religious culture in Northern Ireland.

1.15 There is an argument that Christian anniversaries should not become political clichés. There is also a view that, in Ireland, talk of Holy Week, and especially Easter Week, has a strong republican connotation – and is best avoided.[14]

1.16 When secretary of state Mo Mowlam presented the Belfast Agreement to parliament ten days afterwards, she chose to use the term 'the Good Friday Agreement'.[15] And so it has stuck (to the extent that, in the early spring of 1999, the anniversary of the Agreement was being proclaimed as 2 April, Good Friday that year[16]). The United Kingdom government still respects Cm 3883 and the NIA 1998, but, in July 1999, during the abortive attempt to form the Northern Ireland executive, the term 'Good Friday Agreement' was defined in a draft international agreement.[17]

1.17 The Stormont Agreement is of unionist provenance, and has developed in reaction to the nationalist Good Friday terminology.

The relationship between politics and law

1.18 The Belfast Agreement was made apparently by eight political parties – the Ulster Unionist Party, the Social Democratic and Labour Party, Sinn Féin, the Alliance Party, the Progressive Unionist Party, the Northern Ireland Women's Coalition, the Ulster Democratic Party and Labour[18] – and the United Kingdom and Irish governments.

1.19 Politics and law-making were intertwined in 1996–98. The political parties, however, were not assembled as a legislature, or constitutional convention. It was the two governments which played the preeminent legal (and political) role. The Belfast Agreement looks, from the circumstances of its making, very much like a political settlement imposed by the two governments on the political parties. And the text represents a political compromise which, under the Validation, Implementation and Review section, was to be legitimized in the separate referendums of 22 May 1998.[19]

13 Attempts to identify this individual have failed so far.

14 Thus, the *Irish Times* of 11 April 1998, playing with nationalist historiography, headed its front-page leader 'Easter 1998'.

15 House of Commons, *Hansard*, 6th series, 310, 479–82, 20 April 1998.

16 Even by the prime minister: *Belfast Telegraph*, 10 March 1999.

17 Schedule, containing *The Way Forward* joint statement of the United Kingdom and Irish governments of 2 July 1999, to a draft letter from the secretary of state for Northern Ireland to the Irish foreign minister, placed by the foreign and commonwealth office in the library of the house of commons on 13 July 1999. Interestingly, the Good Friday Agreement was defined as the MPA only.

18 This has no connection with the (British) Labour Party, which was elected to office in May 1997.

19 In the first, consultative, referendum on that date, on an 81.1 per cent turnout in Northern Ireland, 71.12 per cent voted 'yes' to the Agreement, and 28.88 per cent voted 'no';

1.20 The talks' participants – as they were called – were the political parties and the two governments (the Irish government did not participate formally in Strand One negotiations).[20] But the term 'participant' was used sometimes by the independent chairmen to mean only the political parties.[21]

1.21 Thus, the covering memorandum to the Mitchell Draft Paper of 6 April 1998, addressed as usual to 'All Participants', noted: 'many parts of this Draft Paper are based on work done by the two Governments, jointly except in the case of Strand One'. Invoking the participants to engage in intensive discussion and negotiation, the independent chairmen wrote: 'The Chairmen and the Governments will be available to take part in these discussions. You, the participants, are the owners of this process and it is you who must decide if there is to be an agreement, and, if so, what it is to provide.'

1.22 The organization of the multi-party negotiations, like that of the final plenary on 10 April 1998 (described in the Prologue), has an important bearing on the structure of the Belfast Agreement. Its legal meaning must be sought, not just in the text, but in the context of its production between June 1996 and April 1998.

The relationship between the Multi-Party Agreement and the British-Irish Agreement of 10 April 1998

1.23 The word 'agreement' festoons the document of 10 April 1998. First, there is the 'Agreement reached in the multi-party negotiations' (pp. 1–26), to which is annexed the 'Agreement between the Government of the United Kingdom of Great Britain and Northern Ireland and the Government of Ireland' (pp. 27–30). Second, there is the 'British-Irish Agreement' (pp. 27–30), which includes Annex 1, the agreement reached in the multi-party talks (pp. 1–26). (The latter term is clearly an inconsistency, most likely a drafting mistake in Castle Buildings, and I will refer here to the multi-party negotiations. This was corrected in the blue-book version of March 1999, and in the 1999 Irish version.)

1.24 The agreement reached in the multi-party negotiations will be referred to henceforth as the Multi-Party Agreement (MPA). This name stems from the BIA.[22] The annexed agreement will be referred to as the British-Irish Agreement (BIA). And this name stems from the MPA.[23] The two combined are the Belfast Agreement, as is clear from Cm 3883 – and more so from Cm 4705. However, the March 1999 Irish version confuses the matter. The first six pages – with the same layout as

676,966 electors to 274,879. The electorate was voting on the full text of the Belfast Agreement. The United Kingdom government hailed the result as a simple 71 per cent says 'yes'. Unfortunately, as was to be seen in the assembly elections, most of the 'no's came from the majority, unionist, community. The pro-nationalist (in many unionist eyes) nature of the Agreement was reinforced by a second referendum on 22 May, in the Republic of Ireland. In the Republic, people voted only on the constitutional amendment, though copies of the Agreement were distributed to households. On a 56.3 per cent turnout there, 94.39 per cent voted 'yes' to 5.61 per cent 'no'; 1,442,583 southern electors to 85,748.

20 *Ground Rules for Substantive All-Party Negotiations*, Cm 3232, 16 April 1996, rule 10.

21 Draft Record of Opening Plenary Session, Wednesday 12 June 1996, p. 2.

22 Preamble, first recital.

23 Paragraph 1 of Constitutional Issues; Annex B; paragraph 1 of Strand Two; the first paragraph 1 and second paragraph 1 of Strand Three; and paragraph 1 of Validation, Implementation and Review.

the United Kingdom version – are the BIA. Pages 1–37 (as numbered) are Annex 1. Again, the layout follows the United Kingdom version. But then, at pages 38–42, the BIA is annexed to the MPA (a mistake which may reveal uncertainty about what the Belfast Agreement is legally). There follows, on a final, unnumbered page, Annex 2.

1.25 There are two ways – I submit – of looking at the Belfast Agreement. One, as printed, pages 1–26, followed by pages 27–30. The MPA was accepted by seven of the eight political parties in the final plenary on 10 April 1998. But did the two governments also assent to this agreement? And were the political parties implicated in the BIA by virtue of the last-minute annexing in the FA? The answers are, respectively, yes and no.

1.26 But they can only be explained through the second way of looking at the Belfast Agreement; starting with pages 27–30, and then, through Annex 1, reading pages 1–26. This is the structure in the blue-book version of March 1999 (and also in the 1999 Irish version). The BIA is legally a treaty, or international agreement, made between two contracting states, and signed by the United Kingdom government and the Irish government. Annex 1 is, according to international law, part of the text of the BIA: article 31(2) of the 1969 Vienna convention on the law of treaties.

1.27 The Belfast Agreement then is a legal text, and it takes the form of an international agreement. The Belfast Agreement is the BIA. And it has two parties; the two states – not the political parties. This has consequences when it comes to construing the Belfast Agreement in United Kingdom or Irish courts. 'Acts which ratify a treaty or other international agreement, or give its provisions the force of law [as does the Northern Ireland Act 1998 among others], or otherwise relate to it, form a distinct class of growing importance akin to the class of constitutional Acts.'[24]

1.28 But what is the MPA, which, after all, is called an agreement? This is, at best, a political or moral agreement between the political parties (or at least those who assented on 10 April 1998). The two states are legal parties, but only through Annex 1, and only to the extent that the content of the MPA contains obligations binding on the states parties – after entry into force – in international law (as is clear from article 2 of the BIA).[25] Indeed, the MPA is characterized as 'a comprehensive political agreement' in paragraph 2 of Constitutional Issues.

1.29 The political parties are not parties to the BIA, since that is for contracting states alone. The MPA is, therefore, the political face of the Belfast Agreement (less the BIA).

1.30 Put differently, the Belfast Agreement – which comprises the MPA plus BIA – can be read two ways: politically (pp. 1–26 and pp. 27–30 – though the latter pages are redundant); and legally (pp. 27–30 and pp. 1–26 – where the former are crucial). When the Belfast Agreement is being referred to politically, it is the MPA

24 F.A.R. Bennion, *Statutory Interpretation*, 3rd edn, London 1997, p. 127. Ratification here is incorrect.

25 An instance of a Northern Ireland Civil Service misunderstanding is: an assembly member asked the minister for health, social services, and public safety to state the legal authority for the use of the Irish language in her department; the minister answered: 'The authority for this is derived from the Good Friday Agreement.' (Northern Ireland Assembly, *Official Report*, 9 June 2000, pp. WA5–6) This is an inadequate legal reply.

without the BIA. The legal face of the Belfast Agreement is the BIA, to which is annexed the MPA – or simply the BIA.

1.31 The Belfast Agreement has, since 10 April 1998, been disputed in the main by political parties. However, it has to be interpreted legally, if it is to be of any constitutional use. In this case, it is necessary to distinguish: obligations on one or both contracting states; text which is not legally binding in international law (but may, once incorporated in United Kingdom and or Irish law, bind a government or actual or potential office holder); and general principles of international law, which operate upon the text to become implied in the Belfast Agreement.[26]

1.32 David Byrne SC, the Irish attorney general at the time of the Belfast Agreement, discussed these issues in a wide-ranging address to the American Bar Association (International Law and Practice Section) in Toronto on 3 August 1998. (This was published subsequently in the *Fordham International Law Journal*, discussed in the Preface.)

1.33 'Lawyers for the parties, primarily the two governments', he wrote, 'reduced the matters agreed upon by the parties into two legally enforceable and interdependent agreements: the Multi-Party Agreement, to be signed by all parties, and the British-Irish Agreement, solely between the two governments.'[27] The drafting of the Belfast Agreement is admitted, but the political parties and the two governments have been elided as (legal?) parties. It is not explained that the MPA is only legally enforceable by virtue of its annexing to the BIA (and that the two states parties are not bound by everything therein: article 2 of the BIA). The reference to the signing of the MPA by all the parties is a slip.

1.34 Later, in a section headed 'Giving Legal Effect to the Agreement', the Irish attorney general describes the MPA correctly as 'a political agreement, expressed in the language of political negotiation'. 'We were, however, anxious to give the Agreement as authoritative a standing as possible ... Therefore, side-by-side at the multi-party negotiations, the governments framed an agreement between them.' This is the BIA. However, the relationship between the political and legal agreements is not adequately delineated: 'The Agreement reached in the multi-party talks forms an annex to the British-Irish Agreement, and conversely, the British-Irish Agreement was annexed to the Multi-Party Agreement.'[28]

1.35 To conclude generally, the Belfast Agreement comprises the MPA and the BIA: a political agreement (namely the MPA); and a legal agreement (the BIA) – with the latter containing a legal (in international law) annex. The two annexings are different.

26 As the Supreme Court of Canada said: 'The Constitution is more than a written text. It embraces the entire global system of rules and principles which govern the exercise of constitutional authority. A superficial reading of selected provisions of the written constitutional enactment, without more, may be misleading. It is necessary to make a more profound investigation of the underlying principles animating the whole of the Constitution, including the principles of federalism, democracy, constitutionalism and the rule of law, and respect for minorities. Those principles must inform our overall appreciation of the constitutional rights and obligations that would come into play in the event that a clear majority of Quebecers vote on a clear question in faviour of secession.' (*Reference re secession of Quebec* [1998] 2 SCR 217, 220)

27 Page 1207.

28 Pages 1208–14.

1.36 And that is why the Belfast Agreement is the most appropriate colloquial name for the legal text. The BIA was 'done in two originals at Belfast on the 10th day of April 1998'.[29] (The political parties signed nothing; the prime minister and secretary of state and taoiseach and Irish foreign minister, on behalf of their governments, signed on vellum.[30]) It is customary to use the place of adoption, or signing, of an international agreement for its name – for example, the 1990 Dublin convention of the European Community on refugees (though confusion may sometimes be caused by placenames).

1.37 Placename can be seen in the blue-book version of March 1999 (Cm 4292), where there is the heading 'Ireland No. 1 (1999)', and a reference to 'Belfast, 10 April 1998', followed by the phrase '[The Agreement is not in force]'. This was to remain the position until 2 December 1999.

The giving effect to the Belfast Agreement in United Kingdom and Irish law

1.38 Treaties are agreements in international law. And they bind states. How they are made is a matter of international law. But there is also a role for domestic law: determining the competence of governments (or ministers) to make such international agreements. Ratification, where applicable, is a process in international law.[31] However, there may well be domestic law dealing with the matter.

1.39 First, the United Kingdom state. The power to make treaties belongs to the crown. It is exercised by the executive using the royal prerogative. Ministers are generally accountable to parliament, but the legislature has no role in treaty making or ratification. However, under the Ponsonby rule,[32] where a treaty is awaiting ratification, parliament must be notified by the presentation of a command paper (the form in which the agreement is first published); ratification may not take place (except in cases of urgency) until the passage of 21 parliamentary days, time notionally to arrange and hold a (consultative) debate if so desired by parliament.

1.40 There was no provision for ratification in the BIA: article 4(2) is about conditions precedent. As noted above, Mo Mowlam presented the Belfast Agreement to parliament on 20 April 1998. Her short introduction – covering less than four columns of *Hansard* – took the form of a ministerial statement. Questions took less than 90 minutes.[33] There was no vote. This was compatible – whatever the inten-

29 It is interesting that the subtitle of the command paper – *an agreement reached at the multi-party talks on Northern Ireland* – used the phrase in Annex 1 of the BIA.

30 Neither the prime minister nor taoiseach, under article 7(2) of the 1969 Vienna convention on the law of treaties, had to produce full powers. The general practice with bilateral treaties today is to dispense with full powers if the other side has not requested them. It is not known if the secretary of state had full powers issued by the foreign secretary, but her signature added nothing to the prime minister's. The Irish foreign minister did not require full powers, and his signature added nothing to the taoiseach's.

31 Provided for in article 14(1) of the 1969 Vienna convention on the law of treaties.

32 House of Commons, *Hansard*, 5th series, 171, 2001–4, 1 April 1924. See also, House of Commons, Procedure Committee, *Second Report: parliamentary scrutiny of treaties*, HC 210, 19 July 2000, which argued for a role for select committees.

33 House of Commons, *Hansard*, 6th series, 310, 479–500, 20 April 1998.

tion of the government – with the Belfast Agreement being in United Kingdom law a treaty signed on 10 April 1998.[34]

1.41 However, there was a second presentation, this time by the secretary of state for foreign and commonwealth affairs, in March 1999. Following the signing of four supplementary treaties on 8 March 1999 in Dublin – dealing with the North/South Ministerial Council (NSMC), the British-Irish Council (BIC), the British-Irish Intergovernmental Conference (BIIC) and six implementation bodies – the BIA proper was presented to parliament, with the MPA annexed, in the blue-book version as Cm 4292 (the other four treaties being Cm 4293–6).[35] The explanatory memorandum accompanying the BIA described its purpose as 'to underpin the commitments made by the British and Irish Governments as participants in the multi-party negotiations concluded in Belfast on 10 April 1998'. Referring to the MPA annexed, the memorandum stated: 'the two Governments undertake in this Agreement [the BIA] to implement their commitments under the Multi-Party Agreement'.[36]

1.42 The entry into force of the BIA on 2 December 1999 went unnoticed in United Kingdom law.[37]

1.43 It is not clear why the United Kingdom government waited nearly a year before presenting the BIA proper to parliament. After all, it had been signed on 10 April 1998. The most likely explanation is that London (and Dublin?) wanted to legitimize the MPA as a multi-party agreement, and not advance politically the – correct – legal view that the only binding agreement was the treaty of 10 April 1998.

1.44 The United Kingdom state was bound in international law by the Belfast Agreement. It was not, of course, a part of United Kingdom law. The government, as a result of the state's international obligations, and before the Belfast Agreement entered into force, sought to implement it mainly, but not exclusively, through the NIA 1998 (this will be considered principally in Chapters 12 and 13).

1.45 Second, the Irish state. Article 29 of the 1937 constitution of Éire/Ireland, Bunreacht na hÉireann (BNH), deals with international relations. Section 5 covers international agreements:

> 1. Every international agreement to which the State becomes a party shall be laid before Dáil Éireann.

34 The 1985 Anglo-Irish Agreement, in contrast, was the subject of a two-day debate on a motion to approve, which was carried by 473 votes to 47 (House of Commons, *Hansard*, 6th series, 87, 749–830, 886–974, 26–27 November 1985). The upper house approved without a vote (House of Lords, *Hansard*, 5th series, 468, 797–887, 26 November 1985). This had been provided for in paragraph 6 of the joint communiqué; the agreement was not to enter into force – under article 13 – until afterwards. Article 13 did not amount to ratification.

35 All five command papers are dated March 1999.

36 Available on the FCO website: http://www.fco.gov.uk.

37 Domestic legislation referred to Cm 3883 not Cm 4292: Northern Ireland Act 1998 (Appointed Day) Order 1999, SI 1999/3208. The BIA was referred to by the secretary of state for Northern Ireland during the debate on the Order: House of Commons, *Hansard*, 6th series, 340, 254, 30 November 1999.

2. The State shall not be bound by any international agreement involving a charge upon public funds unless the terms of the agreement shall have been approved by Dáil Éireann.
3. This section shall not apply to agreements or conventions of a technical and administrative character.

Laying before and approving (where the terms of the agreement involve a charge upon public funds[38]) are the two necessary procedures.

1.46 On 21 April 1998, Dáil Éireann approved the Belfast Agreement. This met apparently the requirements in article 29 of the constitution.[39] The following day, Seanad Éireann also approved the Agreement.[40] However, the first decision (under the constitution, the second is not necessary) should be considered further. Was it the political face of the Belfast Agreement or the legal one that was approved?

1.47 The motion agreed on 21 April 1998 was that: 'Dáil Éireann hereby welcomes and approves the terms of the Agreement reached in the Multi-Party Negotiations in Belfast on 10 April, 1998, copies of which were laid before Dáil Éireann on 15 April 1998.' The 35-page Dublin text referred to above – the MPA plus BIA – was laid on 15 April 1998. But does 'the Agreement' specified in the motion refer to the MPA (to which was annexed the BIA), or to the BIA (to which the MPA was annexed)? There seems to be an ambiguity. In favour of the former interpretation is the fact that the taoiseach, in moving earlier the second stage of the constitutional amendment bill, had said: 'I am laying before the House a settlement for peace in Northern Ireland ... [t]he political Agreement concluded between all the participating parties on Good Friday, 10 April ... .'[41] In favour of the latter interpretation is the reference to terms of the Agreement in the motion. On balance, and despite the fact that the taoiseach in his speech ranged outside the constitutional amendment shortly to be put to the people (being taken simultaneously), it is most unlikely that Dáil Éireann approved the terms of the Belfast Agreement – understood legally – on 21 April 1998.

1.48 This is confirmed by parliamentary events nearly a year later. On 8 March 1999, the secretary of state, Mo Mowlam, and the Irish minister for foreign affairs, David Andrews, signed at Dublin Castle the four treaties (which have been mentioned above) supplementing the Belfast Agreement.[42] (These treaties will be considered in Chapters 15, 17 and 18.) It was at this point (8 March 1999), that the government chose to lay the Belfast Agreement (the BIA with the MPA annexed)

38 *The State (Gilliland) v Governor of Mountjoy Prison* [1987] IR 201, 236 per Finlay CJ.

39 Dáil Éireann, *Official Report*, 21 April 1998.

40 Seanad Éireann, *Official Report*, 22 April 1998.

41 Dáil Éireann, *Official Report*, 21 April 1998; see also, his speech the following day to the Seanad: Seanad Éireann, *Official Report*, 22 April 1998.

42 Agreement between the Government of the United Kingdom of Great Britain and Northern Ireland and the Government of Ireland establishing Implementation Bodies (Cm 4293);
Agreement between the United Kingdom of Great Britain and Northern Ireland and the Government of Ireland establishing a North/South Ministerial Council (Cm 4294);
Agreement between the United Kingdom of Great Britain and Northern Ireland and the Government of Ireland establishing a British-Irish Intergovernmental Conference (Cm 4295);
Agreement between the Government of the United Kingdom of Great Britain and Northern Ireland and the Government of Ireland establishing a British-Irish Council (Cm 4296).

before Dáil Éireann. The following day, all five treaties were approved by Dáil Éireann.[43] In a speech immediately afterwards, the taoiseach referred to the Good Friday Agreement (increasingly the preferred name in the Republic) as a treaty.[44] There was no similar laying before Seanad Éireann, even though the bill – called the British-Irish Agreement Bill – dealing with three of the treaties, was rushed there on 11 March 1999.

1.49 It is not clear why the Irish government waited eleven months to lay (what it called) the Good Friday Agreement before Dáil Éireann as required by article 29 of the constitution. It may have been part of the plan to legitimize the MPA, and avoid admitting that there was only one legal agreement with two parties. Perhaps Dublin was waiting for political agreement on the implementation bodies (the subject of the most extensive 8 March 1999 treaty). More likely, the Irish government made a legal mistake on 21 (and 22) April 1998 about 'the Agreement reached in the Multi-Party Negotiations'. This suspicion is reinforced by the argument that, at that point, no one in Dublin was thinking about further treaties,[45] so there was no possible combined future occasion for having the Belfast Agreement legally approved in accord with the constitution.

1.50 This mistake – about political and legal faces – may have been compounded by the preamble to the four supplementary treaties of 8 March 1999:

> Having regard to Article 2 of the Agreement between the Government of the United Kingdom of Great Britain and Northern Ireland and the Government of Ireland done at Belfast on 10th April 1998 (the British-Irish Agreement), and the Multi-Party Agreement reached at Belfast on 10th April 1998 (the Multi-Party Agreement), annexed to the British-Irish Agreement ...

This is the United Kingdom version only. The presence of the commas before and after the reference to the MPA (especially the second one) distinguish it from the BIA. (There are no commas in the Irish versions of the NSMC, BIIC and BIC treaties; they appear, however, in the implementation bodies treaty.) It may be implied by these preambles that the MPA is a separate legal agreement, with (legal) parties and legal obligations. This is suggested further by the way the MPA is specified separately in each treaty as if if were another legal agreement.[46]

1.51 This, admittedly, is countered with the reference in the preambles to the MPA being annexed to the BIA, which gives it legal effect.

1.52 The entry into force of the BIA on 2 December 1999 was noticed in Irish law. This was largely because of the constitutional changes consequent upon Annex B to the Constitutional Issues section (see Chapter 11).

1.53 Article 4(2) of the BIA (discussed in Chapter 24) required the United Kingdom and Irish governments to notify each other in writing of the completion of the

43 Dáil Éireann, *Official Report*, 9 March 1999. The title of the 10 April 1998 agreement was reversed, the government of Ireland being put first.

44 Dáil Éireann, *Official Report*, 9 March 1999.

45 Article 2 of the BIA established the NSMC, BIC and BIIC (and the implementation bodies). Paragraph 10 of Strand Two of the Belfast Agreement referred to the two governments making 'necessary legislative and other enabling preparations' after decisions about the bodies, suggesting that they were still seen in April 1998 as being of statutory origin: see the speech of the taoiseach to the Dáil and the Seanad.

46 NSMC, article 2; Implementation Bodies, article 3(2); BIC, article 2; BIIC, article 2.

requirements for the entry into force of the Belfast Agreement. Entry into force was to be upon the receipt of the later of the two notifications.

1.54 The United Kingdom government agreed to participate in a televised ceremony at Iveagh House in Dublin, the Irish department of foreign affairs. Peter Mandelson (who had replaced Mo Mowlam on 11 October 1999) attended early on 2 December 1999. He exchanged notifications with David Andrews, the Irish foreign minister. In his short address, the secretary of state referred to the new 'British-Irish Treaty'.[47] Shortly after 10.30, the taoiseach announced to the Dáil that the BIA had entered into force (this applied also to the supplementary agreements of March 1999).[48]

47 *Irish Times*, 3 December 1999.
48 Dáil Éireann, *Official Report*.

2

Public International Law

2.1 This chapter – as signalled in the Preface – deals synoptically with (a) the plane of international law; (b) states and governments; (c) territorial sovereignty; (d) human rights and self-determination; (e) the law of treaties; (f) the pacific settlement of international disputes; and (g) the relationship between international and municipal law in the United Kingdom and Irish states. Its modest purpose – this is not a book on international law – is to introduce to the readership specified in the Preface relevant, but little known, legal concepts deployed in Chapters 3–6, and the substantive parts of this work. It is an invitation to further reading.

2.2 This has become necessary given public, and even legal, discussion of the Belfast Agreement since 10 April 1998. It has been appropriated largely by one political tradition in Ireland; the concepts are used mainly politically. Mention was made in the Preface of rivalry between international and municipal lawyers. International law in Northern Ireland has been promoted inordinately by the local human rights community (see Chapter 18). Municipal lawyers, who do not have to deal generally with international issues, are disadvantaged – in Northern Ireland, doubly so by the political use of international law.

The plane of international law

2.3 All lawyers exist in one or more legal jurisdictions. Private international law – or conflict of laws – comprises systems of domestic law interacting. Public international law, in contrast, is a system in its own right. (It is a matter of law, in United Kingdom courts, unlike foreign legal rules which have to be proved as facts.) International law is normally thought of as an overarching set of rules; thus the image of a plane distinct form the domestic – or municipal – law below it. I will use the term 'international law' hereafter in this public sense.

2.4 International law is the law, not of nations, but of states. The so-called law of nations originated in the sixteenth and seventeenth centuries, in a western Europe unified by Christianity (though it is argued that state practice – especially in England – allows the tracing of international law from the middle ages). The term 'international law' was formulated by Jeremy Bentham. It developed in time and space during the age of the universalizing nation state, to the extent that the members of the global twentieth-century international organizations – the League of Nations and the United Nations – comprised states.

2.5 Most of today's states – the product constitutionally of peoples – originated in the twentieth century (the Republic of Ireland is an instance), very many since the end of the Second World War in 1945.

2.6 Article 1 of the 1933 Montevideo convention on rights and duties of states, adopted by the seventh International Conference of American States, provides:

'The State as a person of international law should possess the following qualifications: (a) a permanent population; (b) a defined territory; (c) government; and (d) capacity to enter into relations with other States.' This is considered to reflect the requirements for statehood in customary international law. There is no necessity for defined or undisputed borders: *North Sea Continental Shelf*, Judgment, ICJ Reports 1969, p. 32. Stable political organization[1] is probably a condition precedent for the creation of a new state, but a subsequent breakdown in public order does not diminish a state's legal existence.

2.7 Lawyers in the common-law world are familiar with judge-made law and parliamentary enactments. International law, in contrast, is a system of customary law, based upon the practice of states.[2] There is no doctrine of precedent in the jurisprudence of the world court – the Permanent Court of International Justice, which gave way to the International Court of Justice. And international instruments, bilateral but especially multilateral, are essentially of evidential value. The idea of the United Nations as the parliament of nations is not legally exact (nor is the Security Council a world government).

2.8 The sources of international law – according to article 38(1) of the 1945 Statute of the International Court of Justice (ICJ), 'the principal judicial organ of the United Nations' – are: (1) international conventions, whether general or particular (that is, multilateral and bilateral agreements); (2) international custom, as evidence of a general practice accepted as law; (3) the general principles of law recognized by civilized nations; and (4) judicial decisions and the teachings of the most highly qualified publicists of the various nations.

2.9 The first is only in the context of contesting states before the ICJ. The second, and perhaps third, have the character of formal sources. And the fourth is only a 'subsidiary means' for the determination of rules of law. This article does not provide a strict hierarchy of sources, 'and presumably a treaty contrary to a custom or to a general principle part of the *jus cogens* [certain overriding principles of international law] would be void or voidable'.[3]

2.10 Analogies with domestic statute and common law (treaties and customary international law) are not fully appropriate in the law of states. Text does not necessarily trump other rules. And ICJ cases (as noted) do not have the same authority. The establishment of a particular international law may involve a complex intellectual exercise, which remains less legally certain than might be the case in domestic law.[4]

1 'The shortest definition of a state ... is perhaps a stable political community, supporting a legal order, in a certain area. The existence of effective government, with centralized administrative and legislative organs, is the best evidence of a stable political community.' (Ian Brownlie, *Principles of Public International Law*, 4th edn, Oxford 1990, p. 73)

2 See Final Report of the Committee on Formation of Customary General International Law, chaired by Prof. M.H. Mendelson QC, presented to the International Law Association at its London Conference (2000).

3 Brownlie, *Principles*, p. 4.

4 For an appreciation of this in an otherwise passionate book, see Geoffrey Robertson QC, *Crimes against Humanity: the struggle for global justice*, London 2000, pp. 80–123.

States and governments

2.11 The principle subjects of international law – its legal persons – are independent, sovereign states. They have rights and duties, and the capacity to maintain rights by bringing international claims. In municipal law, the state is generally under the control of the government.[5] The government, in international law, acts invariably as the state, while, in municipal law, the government may be the executive branch with powers separate from the legislature and judiciary – looked at domestically, the state is not a unified entity.

2.12 The non-identity of state and government is related to the duality between international and municipal law.

2.13 The existence of states, in customary international law, is – historically – a matter of recognition. (This is the constitutivist theory, as opposed to the declaratory theory, whereby international legal personality is conferred by operation of law. But political non-recognition surely affects the requirements for statehood empirically, reducing the relevance of the doctrinal polarization.) A new state thrives or fails, according to the range and intensity of recognition by other states. Examples of entities not recognized generally at some point as states are: Taiwan (because it claims to be China), Western Sahara, North Korea, and Northern Cyprus – the three latter through failure to obtain sufficient recognition. The international club of states, which imposes no requirement as to size, is otherwise a difficult one to join.

2.14 Recognition, however, is often presumed. This is certainly the case for a long-established state such as England/Great Britain/the United Kingdom. It was the same for the Irish Free State, legally created within the British commonwealth of nations in 1922 (it was certainly recognized widely from 1931). And this recognition was transferred in 1937 to the putative successor state of Éire/Ireland, which became known as the Republic of Ireland when it quit the commonwealth in 1949.

2.15 No state from 1921 refused to recognize that the United Kingdom included, as an integral part, Northern Ireland. And no state from 1937 ever recognized Éire/Ireland as embracing all of Ireland.

2.16 The United Nations was held to have a degree of legal personality in 1949: *Reparations for Injuries Suffered in the Service of the United Nations*, Advisory Opinion, ICJ Reports 1949, pp. 187–8. International organizations, which range from the United Nations, to a body established by two or more states for even a finite period, may enjoy rights and bear obligations, under international law.

2.17 Individuals, or groups, it is thought (though Hersch Lauterpacht believed otherwise), cannot be subjects of international law, with international personality. However, they are potential beneficiaries of human rights protection provided for in treaties (and in customary international law). Individuals remain objects of international law, being related to one or more states through their nationality (however, an individual can make an application to the European Court of Human Rights against any member state of the Council of Europe).

5 Article 28.2 of Bunreacht na hÉireann reads: 'The executive power of the State shall, subject to the provisions of this Constitution, be exercised by or on the authority of the Government.'

Territorial sovereignty

2.18 The world is divided spatially into four legal regimes: the *res nullius* – land, etc., not yet under territorial sovereignty; the *res communis* – the high seas and outer space (not capable of being placed under state sovereignty); mandated and trust territories; and territorial sovereignty. Most of the land of the world is under the sovereignty of one or other state, territorial sovereignty meaning land, etc., within the exclusive jurisdiction of a state (or a condominium of two or more states).[6]

2.19 International law has delineated historically five (original or derivative) ways by which a state may acquire territory, based upon civil law modes for the transfer of real property *inter vivos*:

- *occupation* (from *occupatio* in Roman law), applying only to *res nullius*. Discovery by a state's agent, and a formal declaration of possession may establish a root of title. The state must continuously and peaceably administer the territory. Loss of sovereignty requires the intention to abandon the territory, combined with the failure to exercise state authority. There may well be competing claims, to be decided on the evidence;[7]
- *accretion* (or *avulsion*), usually by natural changes in internal or territorial seas;
- *cession*, whereby one state, by treaty, transfers territory to another. Sovereignty shifts either when the treaty comes into force, or when the territory is handed over. (This does not apply to the legal creation of a new state, as happened in Ireland in 1922. That remains a question about a new international legal person.[8]) Cession is to be distinguished from secession, where the seceding entity acts unilaterally, either to create a new state or to join an existing state;
- *conquest*, historically the most important, but prohibited by the United Nations Charter.[9] It requires intention. If followed by annexation (with or without a treaty of cession), this gives good title. (If there is acquiescence, title may still be acquired through recognition or prescription);
- *prescription*, through *de facto* exercise of authority, based upon the mistaken belief of ownership. No time is specified. It requires the absence of protest by the claiming state. (Prescription does not apply to *res nullius*.)

2.20 These five categories are not discrete, and international fora often avoid

6 It is not necessary for the state to control all of its territory: *Legal Status of Eastern Greenland*, Judgment, 1933, PCIJ, Ser A/B, No. 53, p. 50.

7 In the case of the Island of Rockall, possession was declared by a British naval officer on 18 September 1955 (in pursuance of a royal warrant of 14 September). The Island of Rockall Act 1972 purported to incorporate it into the district of Harris in the County of Inverness in Scotland (Scots law thereafter applying). Rockall, from a United Kingdom point of view, declined in significance, when the government announced in July 1997 its intention to ratify the 1982 United Nations Convention on the Law of the Sea (UNCLOS).

8 Sir Robert Jennings, *The Acquisition of Territory in International Law*, Manchester 1963, p. 7. Arguably, the legal creation of a new state should be a sixth mean of acquiring territory.

9 Article 2(4). The doctrine of intertemporal law applies the law of nations as it existed at the time of the conquest, otherwise titles would change with the law: *Island of Palmas Arbitration Case (United States v Holland)*, *Annual Digest*, 1927–28, Case no. 1, pp. 3–5.

plumping for one or other in deciding disputes. There is no problem in international law until two or more states claim jurisdiction over the same territory. Tribunals investigating titles are concerned with evidence of the exercise of sovereignty, at the critical date or dates (often chosen to make self-serving acts irrelevant). The question is: who has the better right? And the answer will be based invariably upon reasons which are substantially factual.

Human rights and self-determination

2.21 This topic is something of a – historical – innovation in international law. Here, one looks behind the state on the international plane to individuals and groups. The source of human-rights protection is mainly multilateral international agreements.[10] The concept of self-determination – based upon consent in municipal law in an age of democracy – has to do with the requirements of statehood. The basic legal rule in this general area, despite commitment to world governance, remains the principle of non-intervention in the domestic jurisdiction of states: article 2(7) of the United Nations Charter.

2.22 Humanitarian intervention in the nineteenth century (against mainly the Ottoman empire) and, associated with the League of Nations, the protection of national minorities by treaty, formed the basis of the post-1945 legal and social protection of human rights and fundamental freedoms.[11]

2.23 The non-binding Universal Declaration of Human Rights (1948) led eventually to the two 1966 covenants – one on economic, social and cultural rights,[12] and the other on civil and political rights[13] – which came into force in 1976. (It remains to be seen to what extent 'third-generation' collective, group rights[14] – being promoted especially by developing states – become part of international law.) The United Nations commission on human rights[15] eventually achieved its international bill of human rights,[16] including the protocol to the civil and political rights convention, allowing victims to communicate with the human rights committee of the United Nations.

10 There is also customary international law of human rights, based upon state policy; but no state claims the right to practice genocide, slavery, murder, torture, etc. 'Many overoptimistic international lawyers argue that everything in the Universal Declaration is by now part of international law, but this is the sort of wishful thinking that has made international human rights law such a fatuous academic exercise. If human rights are to have the force of law in the twenty-first century, we must abandon these norms of the imagination (which guarantee sophisticated rights to hundreds of millions of women and children who have no hope of possessing them) and concentrate on consolidating, and above all enforcing, the elemental rules which have already ripened into rules of international law.' (Geoffrey Robertson QC, *Crimes against Humanity: the struggle for global justice*, London 2000, pp. 81–2)

11 Preamble & Articles 1, 55 & 56, United Nations Charter.

12 The International Covenant on Economic, Social and Cultural Rights.

13 The International Covenant on Civil and Political Rights.

14 See, for example, the 1981 African Charter on Human Rights and Peoples' Rights, which also includes articles on duties.

15 Article 68 of the Charter.

16 The principal legal inspiration was Hersch Lauterpacht's *An International Bill of the Rights of Man*, published in New York in 1945, and republished as *International Law and Human Rights* in 1950.

2.24 The 1950 European Convention for the Protection of Human Rights and Fundamental Freedom, and the associated Commission and Court in Strasbourg, were of more practical use in Europe (there is also regional machinery in the Americans and in Africa.) Again, the Organization for Security and Co-operation in Europe, following the 1975 Helsinki Final Act (not a treaty in international law[17]), is an important institutional expression of the concern for human rights. It has emerged in Europe in the wake of the breakdown of bipolar cold-war certainties.[18]

2.25 International law remains otherwise largely unrevised by the insertion of post-Second World War human rights culture; general moral invocations of 'international law' – as during the Pinochet case[19] in the United Kingdom in 1998–99 – do not override what remains essentially the law of sovereign states; it is modified. 'The processes of promoting and protecting human rights', according to the Vienna declaration and programme of action of the 1993 world conference on human rights, 'should be conducted in conformity with the purposes and principles of the Charter of the United Nations and international law.'[20]

2.26 The right of self-determination has developed separately from human rights generally, though it is arguably the progenitor of third-generation rights of peoples (it owes much to the Soviet Union within the United Nations).

2.27 President Woodrow Wilson of the United States, drawing on nationalities in Latin America and in Europe in the nineteenth century, put forward ideas of international democracy – concerning peoples – during the First World War.[21] He popularized the notion of national self-determination, but failed to make it a part of international law through the League of Nations.[22]

2.28 Wilson treated 'nation' and 'people' as synonyms, but that is to beg the question. No such mistake has been by international law.[23] When self-

17 The International Helsinki Federation for Human Rights describes it as 'politically and morally binding': http://www.ihf-hr.org.

18 See especially Document of the Copenhagen Meeting of the Conference on the Human Dimension, 29 June 1990, 29 ILM 1305 (1990), and Charter of Paris for a New Europe, 21 November 1990, 30 ILM 190 (1991).

19 *R v Bow Street Metropolitan Stipendiary Magistrate, ex parte Pinochet Ugarte* [1998] 3 WLR 1456; *R v Bow Street Metropolitan Stipendiary Magistrate, ex parte Pinochet Ugarte (No. 2)*, [1999] 2 WLR 272; *R v Bow Street Metropolitan Stipendiary Magistrate, ex parte Pinochet Ugarte (No. 3)* [1999] 2 WLR 827.

20 UN Doc. A/CONF. 157/24 (Part 1) at 20 (1993).

21 In May 1916, he pronounced the principles: 'First, that every people has a right to choose the sovereignty under which they shall live ... Second, that the small states of the world have a right to enjoy the same respect for their sovereignty and for their territorial integrity that great and powerful nations expect and insist upon.' (Quoted in Dorothy Macardle, *The Irish Republic*, London 1968, pp. 180–1) Wilson's 14 points and four principles followed in 1918. 'Self-determination', wrote Alfred Cobban, 'was to Wilson almost another word for popular sovereignty ... The idealisation of democracy was an essential part of Wilsonian ideology.' (*The Nation State and National Self-Determination*, London 1969, p. 63)

22 Article X of the Covenant was a national sovereignty guarantee of territorial integrity and existing political independence for all member states.

23 The only suggestion contrary to this is: General Assembly resolution 637A (VII) of 16 December 1952, which refers to 'the principle of self-determination of all peoples and nations'. Even if 'nation' were permitted, as an alternative to 'people', it would have to be defined legally in a similar manner.

determination was put on the legal map by the United Nations Charter, it was in terms of peoples only.[24] And it is the self-determination of peoples which became part of the *jus cogens* in international law: *Barcelona Traction Co Ltd*, Second Phase, Judgment, ICJ Reports 1970, p. 304. Are so and so a people? is a reasonable factual question, in any particular case. And the most likely general answer is: a people is a community already formed in time and space.[25] (The Canadian supreme court thinks Quebecers share many of the characteristics of a people, but without any legal consequence: *Reference re Secession of Quebec* [1998] 2 RCS 216, 281–2.) As Judge Dillard said of the cardinal restraint imposed by the legal right of self-determination, in his separate opinion, in *Western Sahara*, Advisory Opinion, ICJ Reports, 1975 p. 122: 'It is for the people to determine the destiny of the territory and not the territory the destiny of the people.'[26]

2.29 The law on self-determination of peoples has to be constructed from all the material sources:

- United Nations Charter (1945): articles 1(2), 55;
- Declaration on the Granting of Independence to Colonial Countries and Peoples (1960), General Assembly Resolution 1514 (XV): paragraph 2;
- Principles which should guide Members in determining whether or not an obligation exists to transmit the information called for under Article 73 e of the Charter (1960), General Assembly Resolution 1541 (XV): principles VI to IX;
- International Covenant on Economic, Social and Cultural Rights (1966): article 1(1);
- International Covenant on Civil and Political Rights (1966): article 1(1);
- Declaration on Principles of International Law concerning Friendly Relations and Co-operation among States in accordance with the Charter of the United Nations (1970), General Assembly Resolution 2625 (XXV): the principle of equal rights and self-determination of peoples;
- Final Act of the Conference on Security and Co-operation in Europe, Helsinki 1975:[27] declaration on principles guiding relations between participating states: principle VIII;
- Jurisprudence of the International Court of Justice:

  Legal Consequences for States of the Continued Presence of South Africa in Namibia (South West Africa) notwithstanding Security Council Resolution 276 (1970), Advisory Opinion, ICJ Reports 1971, pp. 31–2;
  Western Sahara, Advisory Opinion, ICJ Reports 1975, pp. 31–3;

24 The purpose included: 'To develop friendly relations among nations based on respect for the principles of equal rights and self-determination of peoples, and to take other appropriate measures to strengthen universal peace.' (Article 1)

25 Sir Ian Sinclair, the legal adviser to the Foreign and Commonwealth Office, produced the following working definition, in evidence on the Falklands to the Foreign Affairs Committee: 'whether the people in a particular territory constitute a settled and self-sustaining community with its own institutions and civil administration being built up over many years'. (*British Yearbook of International Law, 1983*, Oxford 1984, p. 400)

26 Judge Dillard went on to say: '... It becomes almost self-evident that the existence of ancient "legal ties" ..., while they may influence some of the projected procedures for decolonization, can have only a tangential effect in the ultimate choices available to the people.'

27 This is expressly not a treaty. However, it is evidence of the practice of states.

East Timor (Portugal v Australia), Judgment, ICJ Reports 1995, p. 102.

2.30 These material sources have to be studied to ascertain the law on self-determination of peoples, this principle coexisting with a number of others. (There may also be customary rules of self-determination.) Not every self-styled nation may insist upon a right to independent statehood through secession (and certainly not by using violent means).[28] Self-determination today, after the end of post-war decolonization, has largely returned to its original association with sovereign equality. 'A right to *external* self-determination (which ... potentially takes the form of the assertion of a right to unilateral secession) arises in only the most extreme of cases and, even then, under carefully defined circumstances.'[29]

2.31 A number of hurdles has to be overcome before a right in international law may be established. First, the principle of United Nations non-intervention in the domestic jurisdiction of states, under article 2(7) of the Charter. Secondly, the association of the right with third-world decolonization, evident in the 1960 Declaration and the practice of the United Nations in the 1960s and 1970s. Thirdly, the crucial Resolution 1541 of 1960 (developed in the 1970 Principles of International Law), whereby self-determination is defined, not simply as sovereign, independent statehood, but as also allowing for free association, and even integration with another state (or – a phrase added in 1970 – any other political status freely determined by a people).[30] Fourthly, the transition from political statehood (a plebiscitary principle) to economic, social and cultural development (a self-government principle) in the two 1966 international covenants. Fifthly, the right to resist force (by non-violent means?), in the 1970 Principles of International Law, and to seek and receive support within the purposes and principles of the Charter. Sixthly, also in the same source, the immunity granted democratic states conducting themselves in compliance with the principle.[31] Seventhly, the principle of the inviolability of frontiers, in the 1975 Helsinki Final Act (which only precludes the threat or use of force by states).[32] Eighthly, a distinction between internal and external political status in the same source, suggesting a more gradualist approach to statehood (but also an extension of the principle of self-determination – but not a right of secession – to racial, national and other minorities in sovereign, independent states).[33] Ninthly, also in the same source, a development of the principle of non-intervention, requiring states to refrain from direct or indirect assistance to terror-

28 See the Austrian administrative court case, *George K v Ministry of the Interior* ILR 71 (1986), where it was held that self-determination did not allow an ethnic group (in the Italian South Tyrol) to use force.

29 *Reference re Secession of Quebec* [1998] 2 RCS 217, 282.

30 See the general definition of self-determination in Brownlie, *Principles*: 'the right of cohesive national groups ("peoples") to choose for themselves a form of political organization and their relations to other groups. The choice may be independence as a state, association with other groups in a federal state, or autonomy or assimilation in a unitary (non-federal) state.'(p. 595)

31 This point particularly impressed the Canadian supreme court: *Reference re Secession of Quebec* [1998] 2 RCS 217, 282–4.

32 From the 1970 General Assembly Declaration on the threat or use of force.

33 External self-determination has also been seen, not as a historical precursor of internal self-determination, but as a right – including the right to secede – consequent upon the absence of internal self-determination (in other words, democracy): *Reference re Secession of Quebec* [1998] 2 RCS 217, 285–7.

ist activities, or to subversive or other activities directed towards the violent overthrow of the regime of another participating state.

2.32 An important Canadian – and therefore common law – case illustrating some of the above points is *Reference re Secession of Quebec* [1998] 2 RCS 217. This was a reference by the governor in council of two main questions, dealing with secession by the national assembly, legislature or government of the province. The second question concerned whether there was a right of self-determination in international law allowing Quebec to formally effect a unilateral secession.[34] The Supreme Court held – assuming a clear democratic expression of support on a clear question for Quebec secession – that this people: one, did not constitute a people governed as part of a colonial empire; two, was not subject to alien subjugation, domination or exploitation; and possibly three, was not denied any meaningful exercise of its right to self-determination within the state of which its formed a part. 'In other circumstances, peoples are expected to achieve self-determination within the framework of their existing state. A state whose government represents the whole of the people or peoples resident within its territory, on a basis of equality and without discrimination, and respects the principles of self-determination in its internal arrangements, is entitled to maintain its territorial integrity under international law and to have that territorial integrity recognized by other states. Quebec does not meet the threshold of a colonial people or an oppressed people, nor can it be suggested that Quebecers have been denied meaningful access to government to pursue their political, economic, cultural and social development.'[35]

The law of treaties

2.33 The word 'treaty' is a synonym for international agreement, or simply agreement between states. Insofar as treaties may be classified, bilateral international agreements bear a resemblance to contracts in private law. Multilateral international agreements are sometimes described as law-making treaties. As international instruments, treaties have a flexibility – evident in the drafting – often not permitted in domestic (statute) law. This also means that statements of general principle may fail to contain adequate legal provisions.[36]

2.34 The meaning of a treaty is to be sought in the intention of the parties as expressed in the text.

2.35 The Belfast Agreement, read legally, is an international instrument, with only two parties. It has, of course, been incorporated variously in the laws of the two states. Even when this, and consequential, domestic law is due to be construed by the courts, the Belfast Agreement may still require – in the case of ambiguity[37] – interpretation as a treaty.

2.36 The law on the interpretation of treaties – based on the work of the International Law Commission – is to be found in the 1969 Vienna convention on the law

34 The Supreme Court used this terminology.

35 Page 295.

36 For the view that only treaties are legally binding, and that informal international instruments do not exist in comparable normative orders (politics, morality, religion, courtesy), see Jan Klabbers, *The Concept of Treaty in International Law*, The Hague 1996.

37 *R v Secretary of State for the Home Department, ex parte Brind* [1991] 1 AC 696, 747–8 per Lord Bridge of Harwich, 760, per Lord Ackner.

of treaties, which came into force on 27 January 1980.[38] (It has not been incorporated into United Kingdom law.) Particular articles are declaratory of general international law, but the convention in part involves a development of the law.[39] A recital in the preamble notes that 'the principles of free consent and of good faith and the *pacta sunt servanda* rule are universally recognized'. And article 26, headed '*Pacta sunt servanda*', reads: 'Every treaty in force is binding upon the parties to it and must be performed by them in good faith.'

2.37 Interpretation of treaties is dealt with in part III, articles 31–33. The first two are relevant here:

> Article 31
>
> General rule of interpretation
>
> 1. A treaty shall be interpreted in good faith and in accordance with the ordinary meaning to be given to the terms of the treaty in their context and in the light of its object and purpose.
> 2. The context for the purpose of the interpretation of a treaty shall comprise, in addition to the text, including its preamble and annexes:
>   (a) any agreement relating to the treaty which was made between all the parties in connexion with the conclusion of the treaty;
>   (b) any instrument which was made by one or more parties in connexion with the conclusion of the treaty and accepted by the other parties as an instrument relating to the treaty.
> 3. There shall be taken into account, together with the context:
>   (a) any subsequent agreement between the parties regarding the interpretation of the treaty or the application of its provisions;
>   (b) any subsequent practice in the application of the treaty which establishes the agreement of the parties regarding its interpretation;
>   (c) any relevant rules of international law applicable in the relations between the parties.
> 4. A special meaning shall be given to a term if it is established that the parties so intended.
>
> Article 32
>
> Supplementary means of interpretation
>
> Resource may be had to supplementary means of interpretation, including the preparatory work of the treaty and the circumstances of its conclusion, in order to confirm the meaning resulting from the application of article 31, or to determine the meaning when the interpretation according to article 31:
>   (a) leaves the meaning ambiguous or obscure; or
>   (b) leads to a result which is manifestly absurd or unreasonable.

There is clearly a general rule (the textual approach[40]) – not rules – and supplementary means of interpretation.[41]

2.38 The basic rule of interpretation is 'the ordinary meaning to be given to the terms of the treaty in their context and in the light of its object and purpose'. Ar-

38 See I. Sinclair, *The Vienna Convention on the Law of Treaties*, 2nd edn, London 1984.

39 Such parts constitute presumptive evidence of emergent rules of general international law.

40 To be distinguished from the intention approach and the teleological approach. Aspects of both are, of course, contained in the textual approach. The ECJ, however, has adopted a teleological approach to its treaties.

41 Anthony Aust, *Modern Treaty Law and Practice*, Cambridge 2000, pp. 184–206.

ticle 31(1) isolates the terms of a treaty, plus their context. Context is defined in article 31(2) as the text plus agreements and instruments made in connection with the conclusion of the treaty. Text is defined as the terms plus the preamble plus annexes. Article 31(3) also adds to the context, mainly subsequent agreements and practices concerning interpretation, but also 'any relevant rules of international law applicable in the relations between the parties'.

2.39 Supplementary means may be resorted to in two instances: to confirm an article 31 interpretation; or determine the meaning in the case of ambiguity or obscurity, or absurdity or unreasonableness. Such means include the preparatory work – generally known in international law as the *travaux préparatoires*[42] – and the circumstances of its conclusion.

The pacific settlement of international disputes

2.40 The first purpose of the United Nations is the maintenance of international peace and security,[43] and one of its principles is that members 'shall settle their international disputes by peaceful means in such a manner that international peace and security, and justice, are not endangered'.[44]

2.41 Chapter 6 of the United Nations Charter deals with the pacific settlement of disputes; parties to a dispute, likely to endanger the maintenance of international peace and security, are required first of all to 'seek a solution by negotiation, enquiry, mediation, conciliation, arbitration, judicial settlement, resort to regional agencies or arrangements, or other peaceful means of their own choice'.[45] This was reiterated in the 1970 Declaration of Principles of International Law, a new obligation of seeking 'early and just settlement' – which falls short of an obligation to reach a settlement – being added.

2.42 Chapter 14 of the Charter deals with the International Court of Justice at The Hague, article 92 annexing the Statute of the ICJ to the Charter. All members of the United Nations are *ipso facto* parties to that Statute.[46]

2.43 In the Statute, chapter 2 deals with the competence of the ICJ. Relevant articles are:

> Article 34
>
> 1. Only states may be parties in cases before the Court.
> 2. ...
>
> Article 35
>
> 1. The Court shall be open to the states parties to the present Statute.
> 2. ...
>
> Article 36
>
> 1. The jurisdiction of the Court comprises all cases which the parties refer to it and all matters specifically provided for in the Charter of the United Nations or in treaties and conventions in force.

42 R. Wetzel & D. Rausching, *The Vienna Convention on the Law of Treaties: Travaux Préparatoires*, Frankfort am Main 1978.

43 Charter, article 1(1).

44 Charter, article 2(3).

45 Article 33(1).

46 Charter, article 93(1).

2. The states parties to the present Statute may at any time declare that they recognise as compulsory ipso facto and without special agreement, in relation to any other states accepting the same obligations, the jurisdiction of the Court in all legal disputes concerning:
a. the interpretation of a treaty;
b. any question of international law;
c. the existence of any fact which, if established, would constitute a breach of an international obligation;
d. the nature or extent of the reparation to be made for the breach of an international obligation.
3. The declarations ... may be made unconditionally or on condition of reciprocity on the part of several or certain states, or for a certain time.
4. ...
5. ...
6. In the event of a dispute as to whether the Court has jurisdiction, the matter shall be settled by the decision of the Court.

...

Article 40

1. Cases are brought before the Court ... either by the notification of the special agreement or by a written application addressed to the Registrar ....

...

Article 53

1. Whenever one of the parties does not appear before the Court, or fails to defend its case, the other party may call upon the Court to decide in favour of its claim.
2. The Court must, before doing so, satisfy itself, not only that it has jurisdiction in accordance with Articles 36 and 37, but also that the claim is well founded in fact and law.

...

Article 59

The decision of the Court has no binding force except between the parties and in respect of that particular case.

Article 60

The judgment is final and without appeal ....

2.44 Article 36(1) founds jurisdiction on inter alia the agreement of the parties. Such a special agreement is known as a *compris*. Article 36(2) is about compulsory jurisdiction (states being said to accept the optional clause, as it was known in the time of the League of Nations[47]). According to the Manila Declaration on the Peaceful Settlement of International Disputes, adopted in 1982 by the General Assembly, 'recourse to judicial settlement of legal disputes, particularly referral to the International Court of Justice, should not be considered an unfriendly act between States'.[48]

2.45 The experiences of the United Kingdom and Irish states, as regards special agreements and especially the optional clause, contrast.

47 Pacific Settlement of International Disputes, General Act of League of Nations Assembly, 1928, chapter II, article 17.

48 Draft Declaration, 21 ILM 449 1982; GA Res 37/10 GAOR 37th session supp. 51 p. 261.

2.46 The United Kingdom, as an original member of the United Nations, accepted the compulsory jurisdiction of the ICJ from 1946. According to its current declaration of 1969, the United Kingdom accepts it for all disputes arising after 24 October 1945. Reservations – which are accepted in practice by the ICJ – were entered, the most important being disputes with a commonwealth country arising before 1969. The United Kingdom is today the only permanent member of the Security Council which makes itself liable in this way to being taken to the world court.

2.47 The Irish state – as a member of the commonwealth – signed the optional clause of the then Hague court in 1929 for a period of 20 years. In 1937, it was committed constitutionally – that is in Irish law – to 'the principle of the pacific settlement of international disputes by international arbitration or judicial determination'.[49] When the Republic joined the United Nations eventually in 1955, it did not make a declaration under article 36(2) of the Statute.

2.48 The issue has been raised rarely in Irish public life.[50] However, it now looks like the state might be willing to act finally on its constitutional, if not international, obligation.[51]

The relationship between international and municipal law in the United Kingdom and Irish states

2.49 It is common to distinguish monist from dualist systems of law. In the former, international law is part of municipal law. In the latter, they remain two separate legal orders. The doctrinal debate – which often involves rivalry between international and municipal lawyers – revolves around the state looked at externally and internally (with the possibility of international obligations not being acted upon in statute or common law).

2.50 The role of municipal law in international law – to look at the problem from one side – is generally non-existent (aside from the influence of the general principles of civilized nations). A state cannot invoke its constitution as a defence to a breach of an international obligation. Article 27 of the Vienna convention on the law of treaties, for example, states that 'a party may not invoke the provisions of its internal law as justification for its failure to perform a treaty'.[52]

49 Bunreacht na hÉireann, article 29.2.

50 At the 1958 Fianna Fáil ardfhéis, the last attended by Eamon de Valera, he baulked at a suggestion of taking the Irish constitutional claim to the ICJ: 'you know the way these tribunals are'. (Quoted in Enda Staunton, 'The Boundary Commission Debacle of 1925', *History Ireland*, Summer 1996, p. 45)

51 On 19 March 1997, the president of Ireland, Mary Robinson, who was to take up shortly the position of human rights commissioner at the United Nations, referred, during a visit to the ICJ at The Hague, to 'the desirability of wider acceptance of the compulsory jurisdiction of the Court'. (ICJ Communiqué) Shortly afterwards, the European Union, which includes the Irish state, required candidate countries seeking to accede 'to submit unconditionally to compulsory jurisdiction of the ICJ'. (*Agenda 2000*, European Commission Doc/97/6, Strasbourg, 15 July 1997, pp. 68–9) In January 1999, Bertie Ahern, the Irish taoiseach, addressing student supporters, stated that the Republic was thinking of making a declaration under article 36.2 (*Sunday Times*, 17 January 1999).

52 See also article 46, to the effect that competence to conclude treaties (a question of municipal law) is only relevant where there is manifest violation of a rule of fundamental importance.

2.51 The obverse of this problem – international law in municipal law – has been handled variously in the United Kingdom and Irish states.

2.52 Between 1737 and 1861, English courts took the view that customary international law was incorporated – automatically – in municipal law. That is, if it did not conflict with acts of parliament or decisions of the highest courts. Since 1876,[53] the common law has appeared to hold that international legal rules (contained increasingly in treaties) have to be transformed, by acceptance and recognition, into rules of municipal law through legislation, judicial decision or established usage.

2.53 The conundrum of incorporation/transformation is resolvable by distinguishing customary international law, where the court may require proof of the rules before directly applying them,[54] from treaties requiring consequential legislation (to avoid the crown in the United Kingdom substituting legislatively for parliament).[55]

2.54 Courts in the United Kingdom, faced with a conflict between a statute and international law, are bound – by parliamentary sovereignty – to apply the former at the expense of the latter. However, there is a rule of interpretation that judges, where possible, should construe a statute so that it does not conflict with a relevant rule of international law. Treaties may require, or imply, a change in municipal law. This can only happen through legislation. And treaties may be incorporated by parliament in a number of different ways.[56] Courts may only enforce the consequential statutes. There is also a rule of interpretation that, where there is evidence of parliamentary intention, statutes embodying treaties should be construed so as not to conflict with international obligations.[57]

2.55 Parliamentary sovereignty is not a doctrine of Irish law. The 1937 constitution addresses the question of the relationship between international and municipal law:

> INTERNATIONAL RELATIONS
>
> Article 29
>
> 1. Ireland affirms its devotion to the ideal of peace and friendly co-operation amongst nations founded on international justice and morality.
> 2. Ireland affirms its adherence to the principle of the pacific settlement of disputes by international arbitration or judicial determination.
> 3. Ireland accepts the generally recognised principles of international law as its rule of conduct in its relations with other States.
> 4. [dealing with the executive functions of the state]
> 5. [dealing with treaties]
> 6. No international agreement shall be part of the domestic law of the State save as may be determined by the Oireachtas.

53 *R v Keyn* (1876) 2 Ex D 63, 202, 203.
54 *Trendtex Trading Corp. v Central Bank of Nigeria* [1977] 1 QB 529, 569 per Stephenson LJ.
55 *The Parlement Belge* [1879] 4 PD 129, 154–5 per Sir Robert Phillimore; [1880] 5 PD 197. The rule applies to treaties affecting private rights or liabilities, or which lead to a charge on public funds, or require modification of statute or common law before they are enforced in municipal courts.
56 F.A. Mann, *Foreign Affairs in English Courts*, London 1986, pp. 97–102, discusses five ways.
57 *Salomon v Commissioners of Customs & Excise* [1967] 2 QB 116.

This article on international relations deals partly – and inadequately – with the relationship between international and municipal law. The text is part of municipal law, and a constitution is not necessarily the place for statements of international law.

2.56 Nevertheless, sections 1 and 2 affirm such principles (which become international obligations by virtue of statehood). Section 3 is best read in the same light: it does, after all, refer to a 'rule of conduct in its relations with other States'.[58] However, a tendency has developed to read it as: 'Ireland accepts the generally recognised principles of international relations'[59] – providing as it were for the incorporation of customary international law. Sections 4 and 5 deal properly with constitutional topics in the field of international relations. And so does section 6. The incorporation of treaties is a matter for the Oireachtas – which is the same rule as in the United Kingdom.

2.57 The Irish courts have not answered the question as regards customary international law. The emergent appreciation in the 1960s of article 29.3 as a statement of international law seems, in the 1990s, to have been reversed.[60] Nor have they considered the argument that the European convention on human rights may have been incorporated by article 29.4.4 of BNH and article 6 (ex article F) of the Treaty on European Union.[61]

58 *The State (Gilliland) v Governor of Mountjoy Prison* [1987] IR 201, 217 per Barrington J.

59 See *Report of the Law Enforcement Commission*, London May 1974, Cmnd. 5627, pp. 22–24 & 34–6, dealing with extradition. See also a submission by Clive R. Symmons, 'Suggestions for the Revision of Article 29.3', in order to provide correctly for the incorporation of customary international law, appendix 16 (pp. 580–3) of *Report of the Constitution Review Group*, Dublin May 1996, which stimulated a discussion of the article by the Group where there was at least a presumption of incorporation (pp. 106–8).

60 O'Byrne J in the Supreme Court, in *Saorstat and Continental Steamship Co v De Las Morenas* [1945] IR 291, 298 held that article 29.3 had incorporated the principle of the sovereign immunity of states. The Supreme Court took an opposite view of article 29.3 in *re Ó Laighléis* [1960] IR 93, 121–6, Maguire CJ stating that sections 1–3 'clearly refer only to relations between states' (124). And Henchy J in the High Court, in *The State (Sumers Jennings) v Furlong* [1966] IR 183, 190, in holding that the courts must give effect to a statute even where it conflicts with a principle of international law (as if parliamentary sovereignty applied), similarly downgraded the incorporation of customary international law. But O'Flaherty J, in *Government of Canada v the Employment Appeals Tribunal and Burke* [1992] 2 IR 484, 498 seemed to imply that the Oireachtas could only legislate, because of article 29.3, in accord with the generally recognised principles of international law. Finally, Barr J, in *ACT Shipping (PTE) Ltd v Minister for the Marine* [1995] 2 ILRM 30, held that a private litigant could invoke article 29.3 against the state.

61 *Kavanagh v Government of Ireland* [1996] 1 IR 321, 330 per Laffoy J, 351 per Barrington J. Article 29.4.4 relates of course to European Community law.

3

Domestic Law: The United Kingdom, 1800–1920

3.1 This chapter looks at the first party to the Belfast Agreement through (a) the union of 1800 and its vicissitudes; (b) the constitutional entrenchment of the United Kingdom state in domestic law?; (c) the Government of Ireland Act (GOIA) 1920; and (d) section 75 of the GOIA 1920. It is followed by a second chapter bringing the constitutional history of Northern Ireland up to 10 April 1998. This is a necessary consequence of the international law approach specified in the Preface. In these two chapters, the United Kingdom state is looked at internally in terms of Irish and British law. Such an introduction is relevant to Part 2 (Constitution), and in particular Chapter 10 (Annex A to Constitutional Issues). The constitutional status of Northern Ireland was a major issue in the multi-party negotiations. It is necessary – given the political approaches in Ireland to the history of the United Kingdom state – to stress that this is legal history only based upon constitutional texts.

The union of 1800 and its vicissitudes

3.2 In the beginning – from 1 January 1801 – was the United Kingdom of Great Britain and Ireland ('the United Kingdom'). On 1 January 2001 (the vacated start of the new millennium), the so-called British state will be able to celebrate its 200th birthday.[1]

3.3 Wales had been incorporated into England by Henry VII in the sixteenth century.[2] But it was the republican Oliver Cromwell's commonwealth of the 1650s which prefigured the later union of three kingdoms. The union, however, was to be less a case of coercion, and more a question of – parliamentary – consent. The union between Scotland and England – Great Britain – occurred in 1707.[3] And was followed by the union of 1800 between Ireland and Great Britain.[4] George III presided as a constitutional monarch over this new centralized United Kingdom state off the continent of Europe.

3.4 The two most important provisions of the 1800 acts of union are:

1 The United Kingdom government, however, in the form of Lord Falconer of Thoroton replying to Lord Laird in the house of lords, has been declining through 2000 to prepare to mark this anniversary of the origin of the state; for an example, see House of Lords, *Hansard*, 5th series, 612, 1364–5, 9 May 2000. The Irish government denied it had been responsible: *Sunday Times*, 23 April 2000.

2 Laws in Wales Act 1536 27 Hen 8 c 26 (England), a statute recent Welsh writers describe as the act of union of 1536.

3 Union with Scotland Act 1706 6 Anne c 11 (England); Act of Union (1706) c 7 APS XI 406 (Scotland).

4 Union with Ireland Act 1800 39 & 40 Geo 3 c 67 (Great Britain); Act of Union (Ireland) 1800 39 & 40 Geo 3 c 38.

Act of Union (Ireland) 1800

...

Article First

That it be the first article of the union of the kingdoms of Great Britain and Ireland, that the said kingdoms of Great Britain and Ireland shall, upon the first day of January, which shall be the year of our lord one thousand eight hundred and one, and for ever, be united into one kingdom, by the name of 'the united kingdom of Great Britain and Ireland' ...

...

Article Third

That it be the third article of union, that the said kingdom be represented in one and the same parliament, to be stiled 'The parliament of the united kingdom of Great Britain and Ireland.'

3.5 While the Irish parliament[5] seemed to want a state of two countries, the parliament of Great Britain was attached to the United Kingdom idea.[6] The new state had two – hardly equal – legislative parents. However, the acts of union – as acts, not of the United Kingdom parliament, but of the two predecessors – remain arguably the fundamental law of the state; in other words, beyond the reach of the Westminster parliament. The Irish act remains the law in Northern Ireland[7] (and possibly even survives in the Republic); and the British act applies in England and Wales, and Scotland.[8] There is no significant difference between the two texts.

3.6 In the case of the Scottish union, there had been the Treaty of Union 1706. There is an argument that a similar agreement between the Kingdoms of Ireland and Great Britain was made in 1800.[9] (This is a matter for the law of treaties as it stood in 1800; was Ireland then a person in international law?).[10] There was a union by formal consent of two parliaments (whatever of the political processes involved), and there can be no doubt that the two acts – in three if not four legal jurisdictions – remain good law.

3.7 The existence of two acts challenges the Diceyan legal historicism of Westminster, whereby England begat Great Britain which begat the United Kingdom (evident in the adjectival lingerings 'English' and 'British' at the expense of 'United Kingdom'[11]). In Scotland, there is legal authority for Great Britain being

5 This was established in 1297, and remained unrepresentative until its demise in 1800. It only achieved legislative autonomy in 1782: Poynings' Law 1495 10 Hen 7 c 4 (Ireland); Poynings' Law 1495 10 Hen 7 c 22 (Ireland); Act for the Dependency of Ireland on Great Britain 1719 6 Geo 1 c 15 (Great Britain); Yelverton's Act (Ireland) 1781–2 21 & 22 Geo 3 c 48 (Ireland); 1781-2 21 & 22 Geo 3 c 47 (Ireland); 1782 21 & 22 Geo 3 c 53 (Great Britain); Irish Appeals Act 1783 23 Geo 3 c 28 (Great Britain).

6 The Irish Act refers to 'the united kingdom of Great Britain and Ireland'; the other to 'the United Kingdom of Great Britain and Ireland'. The United Kingdom had been a description of the Scottish union in 1706, though the term 'United Kingdom of Great Britain' occurs in several articles.

7 *The Statutes Revised: Northern Ireland*, 2nd edn, Belfast 1982, citing 1951 c 1 (NI).

8 *Halsbury's Laws*, vol. 31, 1994 reissue, pp. 289–97.

9 Harry Calvert, *Constitutional Law in Northern Ireland*, London & Belfast 1968, p. 17 n 36. The evidence is to be found in the preambles to the acts of union, and also in article 4.

10 For a discussion of the Scottish case, see T.B. Smith, 'The Union of 1707 as Fundamental Law', [1957] PL 99. See also, *Lord Gray's Motion* [2000] 2 WLR 664, a decision of the committee for privileges, dealing with the House of Lords Bill.

11 See W.E.H. Lecky's *History of England in the Eighteenth Century*, 8 vols, London 1878–90, from which he extracted *The History of Ireland in the Eighteenth Century*, London 1892.

a new parliament.[12] Jurists in Ireland (regardless of their views on the union), could also appreciate better the United Kingdom's creation by two separate legislatures in 1800.

3.8 The United Kingdom was to be more centralized than integrated. The executive (and legislature) was concentrated in London. But Irish laws and courts continued. And departments remained devolved, with Dublin Castle continuing to run the administration under the Ireland Office in London. It was more self-government by a residual Irish protestant ascendancy, and less British rule. And the character of the union would stimulate nineteenth-century Irish nationalism.

3.9 This political movement owed its strength to evolving British democracy; the extension of the franchise between 1832 and 1929.[13] Daniel O'Connell's catholic emancipation and repeal in the 1830s and 1840s, and Charles Stewart Parnell's home rule in the 1880s, were significant popular movements in United Kingdom politics.

3.10 But democracy also frustrated the idea of Irish self-government within the United Kingdom, between the 1880s and early 1920s (the home rule era). The Irish nation, an eighteenth-century protestant concept, generated, in the hands of catholic nationalists, an oppositional Irish – mainly Ulster – unionism. Northern protestants accepted the union as the constitutional status quo, supported (like many southern catholics) the British empire,[14] and saw themselves as British subjects with a compatible, regional Irish identity. Irish unionists feared inter alia legal revolution; the eventual repeal of article 3 of the acts of union (which would have dissolved the United Kingdom parliament), and even the repeal of article 1, under which the two countries had been united.

3.11 Asquith's liberal government was forced to resort to the idea of partition in 1913–14, on the eve of the First World War. Carson's unionists came to accept it after the war, in 1918–19. And Irish nationalists – who became Sinn Féin republicans after the Dublin rising – divided between 1921 and 1925 on the question. This was in the context of a new state, the Irish Free State, a form of dominion home rule, which is discussed in Chapter 5.

The constitutional entrenchment of the United Kingdom state in domestic law?

3.12 Article first of the 1800 acts stated that the union of the two countries should be permanent.[15] The same acts dissolved the two parliaments, eradicating the possibility of constitutional amendment of the terms of the union. The United Kingdom parliament – in existence from 1 January 1801 on the basis of such fundamental law – was bound arguably not to dissolve the union.[16] But was there

12 *MacCormick v Lord Advocate* 1953 SC 396, 411 per Lord President Cooper.

13 For a similar legal analysis, deploying the Diceyan concept of convention, see Calvert, *Constitutional Law*, pp. 11–12.

14 See the preamble to the 1800 acts of union.

15 The Irish act said 'for ever', the British act 'for ever after'. Similar language had been used for the Scottish union. This was not uncommon in Scottish acts, and the words would probably be interpreted judicially as mere surplusage; all acts, in a sense, are for ever, unless they are expressly limited.

16 The same argument applies to the Scottish union.

constitutional entrenchment of the United Kingdom state in domestic law? (Alternatively, if it was a case in 1800 of the parliament of Great Britain taking over the Irish parliament, then, since English law does not recognize fundamental acts, Westminster had the power – under parliamentary sovereignty – to repeal the union.)

3.13 The question of parliamentary sovereignty, and whether it exists in Scots and Irish law, has been caught up with the problem of whether the acts of union are – unamendable – fundamental law.

3.14 The courts in Ireland, and Scotland by analogy, have had little to say about the constitutional permanence of the 1706 and 1800 unions. Non-justiciability has been the answer of the Scottish courts.[17] The partial severance of the Irish union in 1922 has never been considered in a reported United Kingdom case.

3.15 An indirect attempt at a review of the Irish Church Act 1869, disestablishing the Church of Ireland (otherwise protected by article fifth of the acts of union), had been rejected by Cockburn CJ in the Court of Queen's Bench in London in 1872: 'an act of the legislature [was] superior in authority to any court of law'.[18]

3.16 In 1966, the committee for privileges in the house of lords, reporting negatively on a petition from Irish peers for the continuing right to sit in the upper house under the acts of union, touched on the issue; Lord Wilberforce was reluctant to follow Lord Reid's argument of implied repeal of the acts of union: 'in strict law there may be no difference in status, or as regards the liability to be repealed, as between one Act of Parliament and another, but I confess to some reluctance to holding that an Act of such constitutional significance as the Union with Ireland Act is subject to the doctrine of implied repeal or of obsolescence – all the more when these effects are claimed to result from later legislation which could have brought them about by specific enactment'.[19]

17 In *MacCormick v Lord Advocate* 1953 SC 396, 410–13, where the petitioners objected to the new queen becoming Elizabeth II (when she was the first Elizabeth in the United Kingdom), it was held inter alia on appeal that the court had no jurisdiction to review this government action. Lord President Cooper, however, did say that 'the principle of the unlimited sovereignty of Parliament [was] a distinctly English principle which has no counterpart in Scottish constitutional law'. The union did create a new parliament, and the acts of union contained fundamental law (this was seemingly conceded by the lord advocate). The lord president mentioned the possibility of an advisory opinion by the International Court of Justice. In *Gibson v Lord Advocate* 1975 SLT 134, a Scottish fisherman sought declarator that European Economic Community regulations allowing other member states' vessels access were contrary to article 18 of the act of union. Lord Keith held that fishing was a matter of public law, and therefore not protected by article 18. Discussing the *MacCormick* case, he reserved his position on Westminster imposing English private law totally, and also on the abolition of the Church of Scotland and the Court of Session. Scottish courts – it would seem – are reluctant, despite speculating, to review the validity of constitutional legislation.

18 *Ex parte Canon Selwyn* (1872) 36 JP 54.

19 Committee for Privileges, *Report on the Petition of the Irish Peers*, 5 July 1966, House of Lords Session Papers 53, p. 73; also, *The Petition of the Earl of Antrim and Eleven Other Irish Peers* [1967] AC 691, 724. The committee comprised, other than the four law lords, a further 15 lords. This issue – it is not a decision of the judicial committee – is discussed further by Brigid Hadfield, 'The Belfast Agreement, Sovereignty and the State of the Union' [1998] PL 599, 605–7.

3.17 The argument about constitutional entrenchment, discussed by writers sympathetic to the union in Ulster and Scotland,[20] leads nowhere democratic; the idea of the royal assent being withheld rose briefly in 1914 before falling. The 1800 acts of union did not prevent church disestablishment in 1869, or the creation of the Irish Free State in 1922 – neither of which amounted to a legal revolution. Westminster, which sees itself as the contemporary manifestation of the sovereign English/Great Britain parliament, may – does – legislate in vain. The United Kingdom courts – I submit – would not make an ineffective stand against parliament in a political crisis, by declaring that the acts of union were fundamental law.[21] Most likely, following Lord Reid in 1966, they would accept express repeal in whole or in part in a Westminster statute.

The Government of Ireland Act 1920

3.18 Northern Ireland has never been a state (pejoratively, a statelet). Its constitutional roots are the 1800 acts of union, and it too will be 200 years old on 1 January 2001. It became a region of the United Kingdom, by devolution on the appointed day – 3 May 1921[22] – under the GOIA 1920, a normal act of the Westminster parliament.

3.19 Thus ended whatever integration had been achieved by the United Kingdom in the nineteenth century. Partition was driven by the desire to reduce London's involvement, while keeping both parts of Ireland within the state: Northern Ireland, unwanted by Ulster unionists, was paradoxically a concession to (constitutional) nationalism.[23] And the GOIA 1920 was not to be a precedent for federalism in the twentieth-century United Kingdom state; it was only a British answer to the Irish question.

3.20 The basic architecture of the GOIA 1920 – the partition act – was ambitious. Its long title was 'An Act to provide for the better Government of Ireland'. Section 1 established a parliament for Southern Ireland, and also one for Northern Ireland. The latter was defined expressly as six parliamentary counties plus two parliamentary boroughs, Southern Ireland being all the rest – 26 counties.

3.21 Section 2 provided for a Council of Ireland, which never came into existence.[24] It was to have a president nominated by the lord lieutenant, and 40 members drawn equally from the two houses of commons and two senates (though subsequent election was envisaged). The two parliaments could 'by identical Acts' – this was section 3 – replace the Council with a Parliament of Ireland (comprising the sovereign and two houses). It would require absolute majorities in the two

20 Harry Calvert, *Constitutional Law*, pp. 17–23; J.D.B. Mitchell, *Constitutional Law*, 2nd edn, Edinburgh 1968, pp. 73–4; Smith, 'The Union of 1707', pp. 108–15.

21 *AG v Guardian Newspapers (No. 2)* [1990] 1 AC 109 HL.

22 SR&O 1921, No. 533.

23 The GOIA 1920 originated with the cabinet's Irish committee on 4 November 1919; partition was seen as getting rid of 'the tap root of the Irish difficulty by providing for the complete withdrawal of British rule from the whole of Ireland in the sphere of its domestic government.' (Quoted in Nicholas Mansergh, *The Unresolved Question: the Anglo-Irish settlement and its undoing, 1921–72*, London 1991, p. 124)

24 One all-Ireland institution – the High Court of Appeal for Ireland in section 38 – did exist briefly.

houses of commons. These would be the constituent acts of 'Irish union', as it was called; there would be a government of Ireland, albeit still within the United Kingdom, achieved by the consent of the two parliaments.

3.22 Ulster unionists had no interest in such reunification. It was equally clear that home rule within the United Kingdom would not have satisfied Irish nationalists in 1921 (though a separate, united Ireland proved unobtainable by political or military means).

3.23 Meanwhile, the two parliaments were to have 'power to make laws for the peace, order, and good government of Southern Ireland and Northern Ireland'.[25] All powers were transferred, except those excluded expressly (section 4). There was another category of reserved matters (section 9). These were intended for the Irish parliament. In the meantime, they were equivalent to excluded matters. (However, the tripartite distinction survived, and reserved matters would become, in 1973, lesser excluded matters.) Section 5 prohibited the establishment or endowment of any religion directly or indirectly, or the imposition of any disability or disadvantage on account of religious belief or religious or ecclesiastical status – an anti-discrimination provision.

3.24 Executive power remained vested in the sovereign, with the lord lieutenant exercising any prerogative or other executive power as respects (what were called) Irish services. (Under section 12, the lord lieutenant, in assenting to bills, had the power to reserve for up to a year pending the signification of his majesty's pleasure.) Departments were to be established in both parts of Ireland by the lord lieutenant, until such time as the two parliaments took over. They were to be headed by ministers, who would constitute two executive committees of the Privy Council of Ireland. The governments of Southern and Northern Ireland, with their seats respectively in Dublin and Belfast, comprised the departments with their (and other) ministers – the name 'executive committee' being preferred to 'cabinet'. (The office of prime minister, in Northern Ireland, was to be an adoption of Westminster convention, though there would be a prime minister's department.)

3.25 These were clearly subordinate administrations in Dublin and Belfast. Section 19 provided for continuing representation at Westminster, with a new election to fill the 46 seats (reduced from 105); 33 were to be in Southern Ireland, 13 in Northern Ireland.

3.26 The continuing legislative supremacy of the United Kingdom parliament after 23 December 1920 (the date of royal assent) was clear from the following further provisions of the act (not dealing specifically with excluded or reserved matters):

- section 6 on conflict of laws (according to the marginal note), whereby neither parliament had the power to repeal or alter acts of the United Kingdom parliament passed after the appointed day;[26]
- section 19 on Irish representation in the United Kingdom house of commons,

25 This phraseology originated with the constitutions for New Zealand, Canada, Australia and South Africa. It was used consistently in the three previous home rule bills for Ireland.

26 This meant, of course, that Westminster, by legislating in a transferred area, was taking such power back. The problem was solved by including a 'pre-appointed day' clause in Westminster bills, deeming them to have been passed before 3 May 1921.

whereby the applicable electoral law would remain in force 'unless and until the Parliament of the United Kingdom otherwise determine[d]';

- section 51 allowing for constitutional questions arising in Ireland to be determined speedily by the judicial committee of the privy council (comprising mainly law lords);
- section 52 concerning appeals from the Joint Exchequer Board to the judicial committee of the privy council (ditto);
- section 53 on the finality of decisions by the house of lords or the judicial committee of the privy council on the validity of laws passed by either parliament in Ireland;
- section 61 on the continuation of existing laws, institutions, and authorities in Ireland, whether judicial, administrative, or ministerial, and all existing taxes in Ireland, subject to repeal, abolition, alteration, and adaptation by either parliament under the Act;
- section 75, (according to the marginal note) a saving for the supreme authority of the Parliament of the United Kingdom. This section, which was placed after the definitions section, and before the final section on short title and repeal read: 'Notwithstanding the establishment of the Parliaments of Southern Ireland and Northern Ireland, or the Parliament of Ireland, or anything contained in this Act, the supreme authority of the Parliament of the United Kingdom shall remain unaffected and undiminished over all persons, matters, and things in Ireland and every part thereof.'

Section 75 of the Government of Ireland Act 1920

3.27 Section 75 of the GOIA 1920 acquired belatedly in 1998 a reputation for being the site of the so-called British claim (in international law) to Northern Ireland.[27] This view is incorrect, confusing as it does domestic and international law.

3.28 First, section 75 is about parliamentary sovereignty in domestic law, not the territorial sovereignty of the United Kingdom state. The latter is a question of international law. And the issue of whether Northern Ireland belongs to the United Kingdom is a matter for research using the concepts of statehood, recognition, title and borders. The United Kingdom does not need to claim Northern Ireland. It is the sovereign power – and has been so recognized for well over 200 years. The state has not even had to defend its title against the 1937 Irish constitutional claim to Northern Ireland. No other state endorsed that claim.

3.29 Secondly, the continuing sovereignty of the Westminster parliament (a question solely of domestic or constitutional law) was inherent in the attempt to create self-government in Ireland from the 1880s. It was related historically to nationalism rather than unionism. This can be seen in (a) the three – failed – home rule bills/act, and (b) the particular legislative history of the GOIA 1920. Here it is

27 Robert McCartney QC MP, *The McCartney Report on the Framework Documents*, Bangor, Co. Down, early 1998(?), p. 15; United Kingdom Unionist Party, *An Analysis of the Castle Buildings Deal of 10 April 1998*, Bangor, Co. Down, May 1998, Section B, Question 3; Geraldine Kennedy, *Irish Times*, 18 April 1998; Martin McGuinness, address, Sinn Féin ardfhéis, Dublin, 18 April 1998, p. 4 (http://sinnfein.ie); David Byrne SC, *Fordham International Law Journal*, p. 1219.

necessary to analyse the relative legislative competences of the one/two parliaments in Ireland and the United Kingdom parliament (the latter of course being omnicompetent).

3.30 The year 1885, it should be noted, was when A.V. Dicey first published his *Introduction to the Study of the Law of the Constitution*, in which he characterized the English (sic) constitution in terms of the triptych of parliamentary sovereignty, the rule of law and unenforceable conventions. Parliamentary sovereignty in 1885, not surprisingly given the influence of John Austin,[28] and the global reach of the United Kingdom state, did have a territorial – rather than strictly constitutional – reach.

3.31 But parliamentary sovereignty was to be seriously constrained, not just by the loss of territory subsequently, and the 1931 Statute of Westminster, but by the theory and practice of international law, and the impossibility of enforcement outside the United Kingdom.[29]

3.32 At no stage from 1885–86, when Gladstone succumbed to Parnell, was the union legally at risk. (It was the rhetoric of nationalism[30] – when the model was merely Grattan's parliament of 1782–1800 – which ignited unionist fears. Devolution was not O'Connellite repeal.) However, there was a perceived risk, in 1886, that the United Kingdom parliament might have been superseded, because the first home rule bill contained a provision – clause 39(1) – allowing amendment by the Irish and United Kingdom parliaments.[31] No one appears to have considered reaffirming the 1800 acts of union (especially articles first and third) during the home rule era, the better to reassure unionists (no doubt because this would have had a contrary effect on Irish nationalists). The acts remained the law, whether fundamental or not; in the case of the latter, there was no repeal, express or implied during the home rule era.

3.33 The 1886 home rule bill – which did not pass the house of commons – contained two assertions of United Kingdom parliamentary sovereignty in the 'miscellaneous' part. The first (clause 36 dealing with the judicial function) retained the appellate jurisdiction of the House of Lords for Ireland (plus its jurisdiction over claims to Irish peerages). The second (clause 37, which was not well drafted) stated that 'the exclusive authority of the Imperial Parliament' would 'in nowise be diminished or restrained by anything herein contained'.

3.34 Both clauses had marginal notes: 'Saving of powers of House of Lords'; 'Saving of rights of Parliament'. These are significant.

3.35 The 1893 home rule bill – which fell in the house of lords – tried a different, and better, approach. The bill had a preamble: 'Whereas it is expedient that without impairing or restricting the supreme authority of Parliament, an Irish Legislature

28 *The Province of Jurisprudence Determined*, ed. Robert Campbell, London 1885, pp. 219–21.

29 On the theoretical nature of English parliamentary sovereignty, see Viscount Sankey LC in *British Coal Corporation v The King* [1935] AC 500, 520 PC.

30 'No man', said Parnell in January 1885 in Cork, 'has the right to fix the boundary to the march of a nation ... We have never attempted to fix the *ne plus ultra* to the progress of Ireland's nationhood, and we never shall.' (Quoted in F.S.L. Lyons, *Charles Stewart Parnell*, London 1978, pp. 260–1) This is inscribed on his monument in central Dublin.

31 W.R. Anson, 'The Government of Ireland Bill and the Sovereignty of Parliament', *Law Quarterly Review*, no. VIII, October 1886, p. 427.

should be created for such purposes in Ireland as in this Act mentioned.' There followed, in the 'miscellaneous' part of the bill, 'Supplemental provisions as to the powers of Irish Legislature' (the marginal note). Clause 33(1) addressed the question of Irish legislative autonomy economically. The Irish legislature could repeal or alter any provision of the parent act, where it was given that power expressly. It could also amend or alter acts in force in Ireland, which related to its devolved powers. Westminster would continue to legislate for Ireland, including in areas of devolved responsibility. Irish acts would be valid, except to the extent of repugnancy to United Kingdom legislation.

3.36 The 1912 bill – which became the Government of Ireland Act 1914[32] – adopted yet a third way. In the 'general' part of the bill, with the marginal note 'Concurrent legislation', clause 41 elaborated on legislative autonomy. Subclause 1 dealt with the limitations on the Irish parliament's ability to repeal or alter Westminster legislation. Subclause 2 required Irish laws to be read subject to acts of the United Kingdom parliament, and alluded to repugnancy. Subclause 3 was a proviso as regards the Irish parliament's power under the parent act to vary imperial taxation.[33]

3.37 Section 75 of the GOIA 1920, then, had a general legislative history dating from 1886. The idea of a saving clause came from the 1886 bill. The rights of the Westminster parliament also dated from that time. The 1893 bill contained the clearest approach: a preamble relating the Irish legislature to the supreme parliament; and a positive definition of Irish legislative powers. The 1914 enacted version was more grudging, no doubt to reassure Irish and British unionists about devolution.

3.38 There was never, at any point, an intention to give the Irish legislature the power to: repeal existing United Kingdom laws unconditionally; amend the parent act (outside permitted limits);[34] or legislate exclusively for Ireland – in other words legislative independence, which, in international law, might have led to separate statehood.

3.39 If some or all of this had been provided for, then Dicey's view of the Westminster parliament having the power to 'make or unmake any law whatever' throughout the kingdom – including the power to abolish the Irish parliaments – (combined with 'no person or body [being] recognised by the law of England [sic] as having a right to override or set aside the legislation of Parliament')[35] would have been at risk.

3.40 But, as long as articles first and third (especially the former) of the 1800 acts of union were still in force, there would not be any question of United Kingdom territorial sovereignty being under serious threat in domestic law.

3.41 All this was known presumably to the draftsman of the 1920 bill. He followed the saving provision idea of 1886, and placed – what became – section 75 as the penultimate clause of the bill. The text was new; but the ideas

32 This was repealed by section 76(2) of the GOIA 1920.

33 See also clause 1(2), which anticipated section 75 of the GOIA 1920.

34 Ireland followed Canada in having no general power to amend the parent act; Australia had been given such a power.

35 *An Introduction to the Study of the Law of the Constitution*, 10th edn, 1959, pp. 39–40.

were commonplace. 'Notwithstanding' referred to devolution, either the two parliaments (or one united parliament) and the home rule provisions in the act. It was then clearly asserted that 'the supreme authority of the Parliament of the United Kingdom' remained unaffected and undiminished over 'all persons, matters and things in Ireland and every part thereof'. Supreme authority is legislative supremacy. Why the draftsman chose a jurisdictional-type phrase – '... in Ireland ...' – is not known. He could have left it out without affecting the meaning of the clause. The explanation is presumably the political instructions he received.

3.42 It had certainly nothing to do with territorial sovereignty, and a British claim to Ireland/Northern Ireland.

3.43 The first draft clause survived six subsequent versions of the bill, as it wound its way through parliament. Section 75 was mentioned only once, on 28 June 1920, by Captain W. Benn, during the committee stage in the commons. He queried the absence of such a provision in the constitutions of Australia, South Africa and Canada. (All were still part of his majesty's dominions, but none had been part of the United Kingdom.) The conservative Walter Long, a former chief secretary for Ireland, but then the first lord of the admiralty, replied. He distinguished Australia and Canada (but not South Africa) as the coming together of separate states, before adding more helpfully: 'Here you are setting up two local Parliaments and reserving the supreme power of this Parliament, which is in no way diminished or interfered with[36] by anything in this Bill. It is in order to make the position perfectly clear that this Clause is inserted.'[37]

3.44 The sentence about making the position perfectly clear is legally significant. The marginal note to section 75 – though it is not strictly part of the act – read: 'Saving for supreme authority of the Parliament of the United Kingdom'. (And here lawyers – regardless of sympathies – should have paused at the word 'saving', before construing parliamentary sovereignty as identical to territorial sovereignty.) It signals that the act does not trespass on the rule specified in the marginal note.

3.45 Section 75, as it were, or the legal rule to which it refers, exists outside the GOIA.

3.46 Bennion, *Statutory Interpretation*, 2nd edn, explains: 'A saving is a provision the intention of which is to narrow the effect of the enactment to which it refers so as to preserve some existing legal rule or right from its operation ... Savings are regarded as unreliable guides to the provisions to which they are attached ... A saving is taken not to be intended to confer any right which did not exist already.'[38]

3.47 Or here, the GOIA has nothing to do with the supreme authority of the United Kingdom parliament in Ireland.

3.48 'Considerable caution', said Lord Simon of Glaisdale in a House of Lords judgment, 'is needed in construing a general statutory provision by reference to its statutory exceptions.' (Here, construing the GOIA by reference to section 75.) '"Savings clauses"', he continued, 'are often included by way of reassurance, for avoidance of doubt or from abundance of caution.'[39]

36 This is an interesting paraphrase of unaffected and undiminished.

37 House of Commons, *Hansard*, 5th series, 131, 147–8, 28 June 1920.

38 1992, pp. 494–5.

39 *Ealing LBC v Race Relations Board* [1972] AC 342, 363.

3.49 Section 75, it may be inferred, was added from an abundance of caution. The fight for its repeal – initiated by the Irish government in the early 1990s – will be considered in Chapter 10; a political gesture against unionism came to be seen as a substantive political goal for nationalism.

4

Domestic Law: Northern Ireland, 1921–1998

4.1 This chapter continues with the domestic law of Northern Ireland – following its establishment as a subordinate administration in 1921 – by looking at (a) constitutional developments concerning in particular Northern Ireland, 1921–23; (b) the United Kingdom's Ireland Act 1949; and (c) direct rule from London, 1972–1998 (less January to May 1974). This third part deals with the Northern Ireland (Temporary Provisions) Act (NITPA) 1972, mainly the Northern Ireland Constitution Act (NICA) 1973, the Northern Ireland Act (NIA) 1974 and the Northern Ireland Act 1982. It is concerned with United Kingdom devolution, in particular the Sunningdale power-sharing executive of 1974, which was the precedent for the devolved administration provided for in the Belfast Agreement. Such an introduction is relevant to Part 3 (Institutions), in particular Chapters 12 and 13 (on Strand One), but also Chapters 14 and 15 (on Strand Two) as qualified by Chapters 16 and 17 on Strand Three. Throughout those chapters, the 1974 executive will be compared with the one formed eventually on 2 December 1999 under the NIA 1998. Again, this introduction deals with constitutional issues only.

Constitutional developments concerning in particular Northern Ireland, 1921–1923

4.2 The – partitionist – GOIA 1920 worked in Northern Ireland (and even to some extent in Southern Ireland). Unionists then adopted a defensive strategy in Ulster, leaving the United Kingdom government (see Chapter 5) to solve the rest of the Irish question. Irish nationalists – under the sway of a revolutionary Sinn Féin in 1921 – continued to insisted that all of Ireland was theirs. But the Irish settlement of 1921–22, though it was not always clear at the time, was premissed on the already-existing border between six and 26 counties.

4.3 The GOIA had received the royal assent on 23 December 1920. On the day the constitution of the new Irish Free State was enacted at Westminster (see Chapter 5) – 5 December 1922 – the sovereign parliament also enacted the Irish Free State (Consequential Provisions) Act 1922 (Session 2). Section 1 dealt with the modification of the GOIA 1920:

> 1(1) Subject to the provisions of the First Schedule to this Act, the Government of Ireland Act, 1920, shall cease to apply to any part of Ireland other than Northern Ireland, and in the event of such an address as is mentioned in article 12 of the Articles of Agreement for a treaty between Great Britain and Ireland [see Chapter 5] ... being presented to His Majesty by both Houses of the Parliament of Northern Ireland within the time mentioned in that Article, the Government of Ireland Act, 1920, and the other enactments mentioned in the First Schedule to this Act, shall, as from the date of the presentation of such an address, have effect subject to the modifications set out in that Schedule.

The date of presentation of the address was 8 December 1922. Thus, less than two years after its enactment, the GOIA 1920 ceased to apply outside Northern Ireland. The first schedule included the following modifications: a governor for Northern Ireland (on a considerably reduced salary); a privy council for Northern Ireland; effective suspension of the Council of Ireland for five years; and abolition of the High Court of Appeal for Ireland. Further consequential provisions – outside the GOIA 1920 – were contained in the body of the act.

4.4 What happened to section 75, to the supreme authority of Westminster over 'all persons, matters, and things in Ireland and every part thereof'? The answer (for the reasons discussed already in Chapter 3) is that it remained; the rule existed outside the GOIA 1920. Theoretical parliamentary sovereignty over Ireland (and the world) survived the end of United Kingdom territorial sovereignty (to the extent that this happened through the creation of the Irish Free State, a point discussed in Chapter 5).

4.5 Failure to appreciate the distinction between domestic and international law has led writers to refer to implied amendment by section 1(1) of this 1922 Act, so that 'Northern' is square bracketed before 'Ireland' in section 75.[1] There was no such amendment, as should be evident from subsequent legislative history. Parliament twice expressly amended section 75, the first time by statutory revision in 1927; on neither occasion was Northern inserted before Ireland.[2] (And it was not inserted at any point up until repeal of the section on 2 December 1999.)

4.6 The Irish Free State (Consequential Adaptation of Enactments) Order 1923 presents a similar problem. This Order was made on 27 March 1923 under section 6 of the 1922 Act, allowing for 'adaptations of any enactments so far as they relate to any of His Majesty's Dominions other than the Irish Free State'. Even if the GOIA 1920 came under section 6 (which is arguable),[3] the saving contained in section 75 most certainly did not.

4.7 Section 2 of the 1923 Order (if this is wrong) reads in part.

> 2 ... references in any enactment passed before the establishment of the Irish Free State to 'the United Kingdom' or 'the United Kingdom of Great Britain and Ireland' or 'Great Britain and Ireland', or 'the British Islands' or 'Ireland' shall, in the application of the enactment to any part of Great Britain and Ireland other than the Irish Free State, be construed as exclusive of the Irish Free State ...

The GOIA 1920 was passed before the establishment of the Irish Free State. And 'Ireland' is referred to in section 75. Even if the GOIA 1920 is held to have applied to 'any part of Great Britain and Ireland other than the Irish Free State' (which is

1 *The Future of Northern Ireland: a paper for discussion*, NIO, October 1972, Annex 1; *Statutes Revised: Northern Ireland*, 2nd edn, Belfast 1982, vol. D, Acts of the United Kingdom Parliament, 1894–1920, p. 912 n 14; Brigid Hadfield, *The Constitution of Northern Ireland*, Belfast 1989, p. 66; Brigid Hadfield, 'The Belfast Agreement, Sovereignty and the State of the Union', [1998] PL 599, 601 (though here it is '(*sc.* Northern)').

2 Statute Law Revision Act 1927 s 1 schedule, part 1; Northern Ireland Constitution Act 1973 s 41(1), schedule 6 part 1. The first amendment removed 'the Parliament of Ireland'; the second 'the establishment of the Parliaments of Southern Ireland and Northern Ireland'.

3 Section 2 of the GOIA 1920 on the Council of Ireland still applied under paragraph 3 of the first schedule to the 1922 Act.

not the case), the rule on parliamentary sovereignty exists outside section 75 in the common law (to which the 1923 Order does not apply).

The United Kingdom's Ireland Act 1949

4.8 Northern Ireland's third constitutional milestone – after the 1800 acts of union and the GOIA 1920 – was the Ireland Act (IA) 1949. The title indicates that it dealt with both parts of Ireland. Its focus was mainly Éire/Ireland's departure from the commonwealth (Chapter 6), but this had consequences for Northern Ireland.

4.9 The long title of the act (long titles are rarely considered in statutory interpretation) included the phrase: 'to declare and affirm the constitutional position and the territorial integrity of Northern Ireland'. Section 1 on 'constitutional provisions' included:

> 1(2) It is hereby declared that Northern Ireland remains part of His Majesty's dominions and of the United Kingdom and it is hereby affirmed that in no event will Northern Ireland or any part thereof cease to be part of His Majesty's dominions and of the United Kingdom without the consent of the Parliament of Northern Ireland.

There had been no such declaration and affirmation in the GOIA 1920, under which Northern Ireland was established as a region of the United Kingdom.

4.10 But that solution to the Irish question had been incontrovertibly within the United Kingdom, at a time when the 'unitary state' theory (and *inter se* doctrine) of the British empire – his majesty's dominions – still prevailed. The creation of a new state – the Irish Free State – took place at the earliest in 1922, but, by 1931 at the latest, his majesty's dominions comprised – in international law – a number of sovereign, independent states.

4.11 Moreover, in 1937, Éire/Ireland had come into being (Chapter 6), claiming to be the state of a nation coterminous with the territory of Ireland. Section 1(2) of the IA 1949 was a response to a further nationalist development, namely the Irish state's unilateral departure from the commonwealth.

4.12 There is no doubt that the subsection was declaratory of existing law (confirmed by the use of the word 'remains'). This was United Kingdom municipal law, but it also reflected the position in international law. The declaration was to the effect that Northern Ireland was part of his majesty's dominions – the territories under the sovereignty of the crown – including the United Kingdom. His majesty's dominions were mentioned no doubt because of the nature of United Kingdom constitutional law. But also because Éire/Ireland was recognized as having ceased to be a part of his majesty's dominions in 1949 (the Irish Free State having left the United Kingdom in 1922).

4.13 Northern Ireland (though it did not exist as a region) had been part of his majesty's dominions from 1171 to 1972,[4] and of the United Kingdom since 1801.

4.14 The second part of the subsection was an affirmation, or legal entitlement. It is new, and was to be described – by unionists – as the constitutional guarantee. This is to the effect that in no event would Northern Ireland cease to belong to the state without an exercise of consent. Just as sovereignty had been associated with the English/Great Britain/United Kingdom parliament (rather than people), so

4 Alternatively, 1541 – when the kingdom of Ireland was created.

consent – the basis of democracy – was here ascribed to the subordinate Northern Ireland parliament.[5]

4.15 The sovereign parliament, however, did not – in United Kingdom law – fetter its option of expelling Northern Ireland without consent of the local parliament; the constitutional guarantee was not entrenched.

4.16 Self-determination was not yet part of the *jus cogens* in international law, but the history of the constitutional guarantee – or the consent principle (in the form of the Northern Ireland parliament) – would be coterminous with the development of that collective right in international law. This is discussed further in Chapter 9.

4.17 United Kingdom constitutional law in 1949 suggested that Northern Ireland would not be forced into a united Ireland without its consent. It was not possible to leave his majesty's dominions without quitting the United Kingdom, showing the former was dependent upon the latter. The long title of the act referred to 'constitutional position' and 'territorial integrity'. Constitutional position no doubt was a reference to Northern Ireland being an integral part of the United Kingdom. Territorial integrity – a principle of international law[6] – was probably used in the same way, though there was also a local use of the concept in the prohibition on 'any part' of Northern Ireland ceasing to belong without consent of its parliament.

Direct rule from London, 1972–1998 (less January–May 1974)

4.18 The Northern Ireland parliament was prorogued, and then abolished, in 1972–73. There followed, in 1974, the short-lived – power-sharing – Northern Ireland assembly. Direct rule resumed (and continued unaffected by another – non-legislative – assembly in 1982–86) – the Belfast Agreement taking 26 years to arrive. There are four key acts for this period (discussed below), the most important, the NICA 1973 – known as the Constitution Act – governing the January–May 1974 assembly, and remaining in force until repealed mainly by the NIA 1998.

5 Comprising the house of commons, senate and his majesty: GOIA 1920 s 1(1). A nationalist majority in the commons would not have been followed, because of electoral delays, by a nationalist majority in the senate for four years. Theoretically, the sovereign – on the advice of United Kingdom ministers – could have withheld the royal assent to a secessionist Northern Ireland act.

This is the way consent was understood in section 4 of the 1931 Statute of Westminster. Parliament was also implied in Malcolm MacDonald, the dominions secretary's, comment in 1937 about de Valera's new constitution: 'the bases of any political agreement [between London and Dublin] would [include] acquiescence by the Irish Free State Government in the present position whereby the consent of Northern Ireland is essential to the establishment of a United Ireland.' (Quoted in David Harkness, 'Mr de Valera's dominion: Ireland's relations with Britain and the Commonwealth, 1932–8', *Journal of Commonwealth Political Studies*, VIII, 3 November 1970, p. 215) MacDonald may have been relying upon section 3 of the GOIA 1920, even though it no longer applied in the territory of the Irish Free State. More likely, he was articulating a convention of the United Kingdom state, rooted of course in the political reality of the Ulster question.

6 Article 10 of the League of Nations Covenant; principle IV, 1975 Helsinki Final Act.

The Northern Ireland (Temporary Provisions) Act 1972

4.19 The Northern Ireland parliament was prorogued for a year on 30 March 1972 – early in the contemporary troubles – by section 1(3) and (5) of the NITPA 1972.[7] (It would be abolished on 18 July 1973 by section 31 of the Northern Ireland Constitution Act 1973.) Northern Ireland, however, was not to be returned to the position before partition.

4.20 Legislative power was treated on a purely temporary basis. Laws for Northern Ireland were to come from Westminster as orders in council for any purpose for which the parliament of Northern Ireland had power to make laws, (unamendable) drafts having been approved by each house of parliament (section 1). These orders in council were to be part of the Northern Ireland statute book as it was seen.

4.21 Executive power was similarly treated. The NITPA 1972 recognized there would be a secretary of state for Northern Ireland – created by exercise of the prerogative – in the United Kingdom cabinet. He was to take over as chief executive officer as respects 'Irish services' in place of the governor of Northern Ireland:

> 1(1) ...
>
> (a) all functions which apart from this Act belong to the Governor, or to the Governor in Council, or to the Government or any minister of Northern Ireland or head of a department of the Government of Northern Ireland, shall be discharged by the Secretary of State; and
>
> (b) all functions which belong to a department of the Government of Northern Ireland may be discharged by the Secretary of State or (except in so far as he otherwise directs) may, notwithstanding that there is no head of the department, be discharged by the department on behalf of the Secretary of State and subject to his direction and control.

These two paragraphs are of considerable constitutional significance, greater than might be expected in a temporary provisions act.

4.22 Paragraph (a) is not ostensibly exceptional. No doubt, the Westminster (?) draftsman was simply rounding up executive functions, by specifying the governor, the governor in council, the government of Northern Ireland, any minister or head of a department; all of whose functions were to be discharged by the secretary of state. But there is a problem with the minister/head of department distinction.

4.23 The governor was provided for in the GOIA 1920 (as the existing lord lieutenant), and the schedule to the Irish Free State (Consequential Provisions) Act 1922 (Session 2). The governor in council originated in that schedule, in the paragraph dealing with the new Privy Council of Northern Ireland. The government of Northern Ireland was provided for in the GOIA 1920 sections 2(1), 8(4) and (7): it comprised only the executive branch – including inter alia ministers and heads of department (and also surely – given paragraph (b) – departments).

4.24 Ministers and heads of department were defined in section 8(3)–(4) of what was called the principal act.[8] Under section 8(1)–(2), executive power, which was vested in the sovereign, could be delegated to the lord lieutenant (later, governor), or any chief executive officer or officers appointed in the latter's place. The

7 This was rushed through all parliamentary stages, 27–29 March 1972.
8 Irish Free State (Consequential Provisions) Act 1922 (Session 2) first schedule, para 1(1).

executive power – vested in the sovereign – was all executive power, since the lord lieutenant was responsible only for Irish services. Under section 8(3), delegated executive powers were to be exercised through (not by) departments established by either the governor or the Northern Ireland parliament. The heads of those departments (holding office during the pleasure of the governor) were, under section 8(4), ministers of Northern Ireland. But the governor had the power to appoint additional ministers, who would not be heads of department. One such might have been the prime minister (an office not created by the act). But this could also have covered junior ministers. The GOIA 1920, then, envisaged departmental and other ministers. (The legislative protocol in section 1(1)(a) of the NITPA 1972, given the practice from 1921,[9] should have been head of department followed by minister.)

4.25 The lord lieutenant (the governor did not exist before 5 December 1922) established, by notification in the *Belfast Gazette* of 7 June 1921, seven departments of the Northern Ireland government. The first was a prime minister's department. The local parliament also met for the first time that day, and Sir James Craig's cabinet was sworn into office. This was following Westminster practice, since the seven heads of department (there were no non-departmental ministers) were members of the Privy Council of Ireland (later Northern Ireland) – all chosen by the lord lieutenant. The establishment of departments coincided with the appointment of – accountable – ministers, though the simultaneous transfer of functions to the departments was to assume significance.[10]

4.26 The role of the lord lieutenant in creating departments (which the governor retained until 1973[11]), was subordinate to the power of the Northern Ireland parliament. But executive power flowed from the sovereign to the lord lieutenant to a 'chief executive officer[12] or officers for the time being appointed in his place' (section 8(2)). And the lord lieutenant – under section 8(3) – had the power to 'appoint officers [equivalent to political heads of departments] to administer those departments', such officers 'hold[ing] office during the pleasure of the Lord Lieutenant'.

4.27 This commonplace United Kingdom constitutional arrangement, however, has been misconstrued in Northern Ireland, seemingly on the basis of an early act of its parliament – the Ministries of Northern Ireland Act (Northern Ireland) 1921 – which received the royal assent on 14 December 1921.[13] It was drafted – like all

9 This is because the prime minister was a departmental head from 1921 to 1972.

10 Irish Free State (Consequential Provisions) Act 1922 (Session 2) first schedule, para 2(2). Two notices were published on 7 June 1921: '(No. 1.) Establishment of Departments and Appointment of Ministers of Northern Ireland'; '(No. 2.) Assignment of Functions to Departments'. (Sir Arthur S. Quekett, *The Constitution of Northern Ireland*, vol. 2, Belfast 1933, pp. 276–83)

11 Under s 1(1) of the NITPA 1972, the secretary of state took over the functions of the governor. The office was not abolished until 18 July 1973: Northern Ireland Constitution Act 1973 s 32.

12 Note the secretary of state is described as acting as chief executive officer as respects Irish services instead of the governor: NITPA 1972 s 1(1).

13 The only political discussion I have seen involved John M. Taylor MP and George Howarth MP, a NIO minister, in the second standing committee on delegated legislation, on 30 March 2000, dealing with the draft Equality ((Disability, etc.) (Northern Ireland) Order 2000: www.parliament.the-stationery-office.co.uk/.

Northern Ireland legislation between 1921 and 1945 – by Sir (as he became) Arthur S. Quekett, an Irish barrister who had succeeded his father as legal assistant to the Local Government Board in Dublin. Devolution in Northern Ireland (the first in the history of the United Kingdom) was to be given a legal form inspired by – statutory – local government in late Victorian Ireland. The bill was not studied by the new Northern Ireland cabinet.[14] It passed through the local parliament at the end of its first session with minimal debate. Lord Londonderry, who referred to section 8 of the GOIA 1920, told the senate incorrectly (as it turned out): 'all these powers are vested in Ministers who are under the control of Parliament'.[15] If that was the intention of the government, it is not what its draftsman constructed.

4.28 The purpose of the Northern Ireland act was to dissolve certain branches of government of 7 June 1921 (never actually created), and leave such functions to ministers for distribution (section 1). Section 2(1) went on to make the ministries – less the prime minister's department – bodies corporate, but the only capacity specified was 'to acquire and hold land'. It is not clear why this was thought necessary.[16] Quekett's *Constitution of Northern Ireland* (3 vols, 1928–46) throws no light on his reason, save his comment that that act does not apply to the prime minister's department.[17] The phrase 'powers or duties [otherwise functions] of a Ministry' was used. This also appeared in section 1 as a proviso: 'where any powers or duties of a Ministry have been assigned, their exercise or performance shall remain subject to the direction and control of the Minister'. These ministries were to have seals, authenticated by the minister or a senior official (section 2(2)), distinct from the great seal of Northern Ireland held by the governor.[18]

4.29 And this takes us back to the NITPA 1972, in particular section 1(1)(b). Paragraph (a) seemingly did not sweep up all functions, even given the reference to the government of Northern Ireland. It only reached those belonging to office holders. This is because paragraph (b) went on to refer 'all functions which belong to a department'. No doubt these were all statutory. But it is difficult to see how the architecture of section 8 of the GOIA 1920 can be reduced to either, departments leading constitutionally, or departments augmenting ministers.

4.30 Powers in the GOIA 1920 were to be exercised through departments (headed by ministers), not by departments (section 8(3)(b)) – an important distinction.

4.31 And this takes us back to the meaning of the proviso in section 1 of the Ministries of Northern Ireland Act (Northern Ireland) Act 1921. The minister was described as having 'direction and control' of the 'exercise or performance' of 'any powers or duties of a Ministry'. The context was the ministerial distribution of business of his ministry among the various officers. Direction and control, therefore, seems to relate to ministerial delegation. And not to the powers of the ministerial office, as suggested by the proviso. Again, this is inconsistent with the constitutional provisions of the GOIA 1920.

14 It was considered only on 28 November 1921: CAB/4/27, PRONI.

15 Senate, *Northern Ireland Hansard*, I, 138, 8 December 1921.

16 It was not considered necessary in the Irish Free State: Ministers and Secretaries Act 1924 ss 1 & 2. Ministers there were made corporations sole.

17 Vol. 2, pp. 289–90.

18 Irish Free State (Consequential Provisions) Act 1922 (Session 2), first schedule, para 2(4).

4.32 There is – or was – a question of vires.[19] The principal act was the GOIA 1920, in particular section 8 on executive powers. The Northern Ireland parliament did have powers to legislate for 'good government' (section 4), and its governmental institutions were clearly a transferred matter. But the Ministries of Northern Ireland Act (Northern Ireland) 1921 – I submit – went outside this, not in making ministries bodies corporate with the capacity to acquire and hold land, but in seemingly determining the ministry/minister relationship in terms of 'the powers and duties' of the former being exercised or performed 'subject to the direction and control of the Minister' (proviso to section 1).

4.33 The mistake was the legal shift of the powers and duties of the minister, under the GOIA 1920, to – apparently – the ministry, under the Ministries of Northern Ireland Act 1921. 'Direction and control' was poor compensation for this – ultra vires – constitutional revision.

4.34 The constitutional significance of paragraphs (a) and (b) in the NITPA 1972 lies in ministerial accountability. Until 1972, Northern Ireland ministries were accountable through their ministers to the local parliament. What happened with direct rule? Under paragraph (a), the functions went to the secretary of state, whose Northern Ireland Office (NIO), as a department of the United Kingdom government, was effectively answerable to the Westminster parliament. (This is aside from any question of conventions, the Westminster speaker having ruled in 1923 that transferred matters were not for the sovereign parliament.[20] In 1972, that convention was suspended.) Junior ministers in the United Kingdom act normally on behalf of their head of department, but, in the NIO in 1972, the secretary of state had to delegate responsibilities to junior ministers exceptionally. Under paragraph (b), so-called departmental functions were treated very differently. These were transferable to the secretary of state, and he would have been answerable presumably at Westminster. But the secretary of state could direct that such functions remained with the departments, even though they did have a (ministerial) head. This was clearly only justifiable as a temporary measure. It meant that Northern Ireland departments (without a head) were not answerable to a local parliament, while the secretary of state (who could have taken over the functions) did not have to account to the United Kingdom parliament.

4.35 The only influence the secretary of state had (over functions not appropriated), was 'direction and control' over Northern Ireland departments without a head. The 1921 meaning of direction and control related to ministerial delegation within a ministry; the power remained with the minister delegating. In 1972, in contrast, the secretary of state was exercising a lesser power over functions he did not delegate because he had chosen not to acquire them in the first place.

4.36 The expression is the same in 1921 and 1972. The contexts are different, and thus the legal meanings.

4.37 The NITPA 1972 was significant in a second way. With the prorogation of the Northern Ireland parliament, the constitutional guarantee in section 1 of the Ireland Act 1949 became voidable. The government therefore enacted a section 2

19 For an important example: *R (Hume) v Londonderry Justices* [1972] NI 91, corrected by the Northern Ireland Act 1972.

20 House of Commons, *Hansard*, 5th series, 163, 1623–5, 3 May 1923.

on the 'status of Northern Ireland as part of the United Kingdom':[21]

> Nothing in this Act shall derogate or authorise anything to be done in derogation from the status of Northern Ireland as part of the United Kingdom.

There was no reference to her majesty's dominions, but that was not necessary. Under the IA 1949, Northern Ireland was part of his majesty's dominions by virtue of being in the United Kingdom. Section 2 was a very clear definition of constitutional status (the first time the phrase had been used). Two guarantees were given: one, though the Northern Ireland parliament had been prorogued, the NITPA 1972 did not derogate from that status; and, two, the act did not authorize any such derogation.

4.38 But the focus had shifted to the Westminster parliament. The guarantee was strictly worthless – in domestic law – since the sovereign parliament could not bind itself. In the Northern Ireland (Border Poll) Act 1972 (which received the royal assent on 7 December), the United Kingdom government arranged for a border poll – or plebiscite – on (as the secretary of stated ordered later) 8 March 1973. This had been promised at prorogation. Two questions – essentially in the alternative – were asked: the first – for unionists – was, 'Do you want Northern Ireland to remain part of the United Kingdom?'; the second – for nationalists – was, 'Do you want Northern Ireland to be joined with the Republic of Ireland, outside the United Kingdom?' Nearly 60 per cent of the entire electorate of Northern Ireland voted in favour of Northern Ireland remaining part of the United Kingdom. This comprised 591,820 voting yes to the first question, while only 6,463 voted yes to the second. Approximately 41.3 per cent of the electorate – there was a nationalist boycott – did not vote.

4.39 The absence of a local parliament forced Westminster to go to the people in early 1973. The 1972 border poll act was a response to the prorogation of the local parliament.[22] Westminster had no choice, on the question of the consent of Northern Ireland to leaving the United Kingdom, to making the people there voting sovereign on at least the constitutional question of the border. This did not make the constitutional law of Northern Ireland distinctly different from that of the rest of the United Kingdom.

4.40 The transition from the NITPA 1972 – which was continued in force for a further year by order in council under section 1(5)[23] – continued with the Northern Ireland Assembly Act 1973. Under this, a 78-member Northern Ireland assembly – to replace the parliament – was elected by proportional representation (the single transferable vote) on 28 June 1973. Within three weeks, there would be a new constitution for Northern Ireland drawn up at Westminster.

The Northern Ireland Constitution Act 1973

4.41 This was based upon a NIO document, *The Future of Northern Ireland: a paper for discussion* (October 1972), and the white paper, *Northern Ireland Constitutional Proposals*, Cmnd 5259, March 1973.

21 This was proposed successfully by the labour opposition: House of Commons, *Hansard*, 5th series, 834, 646, 29 March 1972.

22 The Northern Ireland (Border Poll) Act 1972 was repealed by the Northern Ireland Constitution Act 1973 s 41(1) & sch 6 part 1.

23 Northern Ireland (Temporary Provisions) Act Extension Order 1973, SI 1973/602.

4.42 The NICA 1973 was a major piece of legislation, with 43 sections and six schedules. It received the royal assent on 18 July 1973, and some parts of it came into force immediately. The NICA 1973 repealed much of the GOIA 1920.[24] For the next 25 years or so, the partition act (which started with 76 sections and nine schedules) was a slim text of 14 sections (five dealing with financial provisions) and no schedules, many of them amended close to the point of repeal. Westminster could have reenacted easily the few remaining provisions in the new constitution act.

4.43 The first part – preliminary – included a new constitutional guarantee as section 1:

> Status of Northern Ireland as part of the United Kingdom (marginal note)
>
> It is hereby declared that Northern Ireland remains part of Her Majesty's dominions and of the United Kingdom, and it is hereby affirmed that in no event will Northern Ireland or any part of it cease to be part of Her Majesty's dominions and of the United Kingdom without the consent of the majority of the people of Northern Ireland voting in a poll held for the purposes of this section in accordance with Schedule 1 to this Act.

This was essentially the same text as in the IA 1949 (with a new comma separating the declaration from the affirmation, and 'thereof' changed to 'of it').

4.44 The only difference was the entity consenting. The parliament was gone. And the assembly was not substituted, no doubt because of the border poll several months earlier. There may also have been a fear over the legitimacy of the assembly. However, it was not 'the people' of democratic theory who would consent (perhaps out of a concern for the sovereignty of parliament). It was a simple majority in Northern Ireland voting in a poll. Schedule 1 dealt with the details. A poll was entirely within the discretion of the secretary of state, but not before 9 March 1983 and not within ten years subsequently. The secretary of state could make provision for the persons entitled to vote, the question or questions asked, and whether existing electoral law was to be followed.

4.45 Section 1 and schedule 1 were not to be used in the 25 years to the Belfast Agreement (when new arrangements were made subsequently). These are considered in detail – against this historical background – in Chapter 10.

4.46 Part II – legislative powers and executive authorities – replaced the NITPA 1972.[25]

4.47 Legislative powers were returned to Belfast for transferred matters (which were distinguished from excepted or reserved matters). (Orders in council were retained by sections 38 and 39 for elections and reserved matters and alterations in devolved responsibilities.) There was a unicameral assembly. And measures, as they were called, were enacted by being passed by the assembly and approved by her majesty in council.[26] The legislative competence of the assembly was addressed in a subsection:

24 Sch 6 parts I & II; A.J. Whysall, *The Northern Ireland constitutional legislation: a guide* (for official use only), 2nd edn, March 1996 reprint, p. 7.

25 Section 1 of this act expired: NICA 1973 s 2(4). The remainder was repealed by the Northern Ireland Act 1998 s 100(2) & sch 15.

26 Four measures were to be passed between 1 January and 29 May 1974, two of which remain partly in force. United Kingdom ministers could advise the sovereign not to approve a measure: Notes on Clauses, para 14, quoted in Whysall, *Northern Ireland*, p. 27.

> 4(4) This section does not affect the power of the Parliament of the United Kingdom to make laws for Northern Ireland but, subject to ... section 17 [making discriminatory legislation void], a Measure may amend or repeal any provision made by or under any Act of Parliament in so far as it is part of the law of Northern Ireland.

This was a simple statement of legislative competence. The first clause of the sentence acknowledged the sovereignty of the Westminster parliament. And the second clause stated the competence of the assembly to amend or repeal any law of Northern Ireland. This included any existing laws within the transferred areas. It also extended to any future Westminster legislation in the same areas.

4.48 The key concept was 'any law of Northern Ireland'. The assembly could not, for example, amend or repeal the NICA 1973.[27]

4.49 The sections dealing with executive authorities were more innovative. The NICA 1973 repealed most of section 8 of the GOIA 1920 from the appointed day (for the initial devolution of legislative and executive responsibility – which was 1 January 1974[28]). This meant that the internal constitution in the Ministries of Northern Ireland Act (Northern Ireland) 1921 – which inspired the direct rule provisions of the NITPA 1972 – was no longer arguably ultra vires. The ministries were renamed departments, to deny the heads of departments the title 'ministers'.[29]

4.50 The main provisions dealing with the executive were:

> Executive authorities in Northern Ireland (marginal note)
>
> 7 (1) The executive power in Northern Ireland shall continue to be vested in Her Majesty.
> (2) As respects transferred matters the Secretary of State shall ... exercise on Her Majesty's behalf such prerogative or other executive powers of Her Majesty in relation to Northern Ireland as may be delegated to him by Her Majesty.
> (3) The powers so delegated shall be exercised through the members of the Northern Ireland Executive established by this Act and the Northern Ireland departments.
> (4) ...
> (5) ...
> (6) The Secretary of State as Her Majesty's principal officer in Northern Ireland, the members of the Northern Ireland Executive, any other persons appointed under section 8 below and the Northern Ireland departments are in this Act referred to as Northern Ireland executive authorities.
>
> The Northern Ireland Executive (marginal note)[30]
>
> 8(1) The Northern Ireland Executive shall consist of –
> (a) the chief executive member;
> (b) the persons who are for the time being heads of the Northern Ireland departments; and
> (c) any other person appointed under subsection (3) below to be a member of the Executive.
>
> (2) The chief executive member shall preside over the Executive and act as Leader of the Assembly.

27 Section 2(2) & schedule 2, para 15.

28 Northern Ireland Constitution (Devolution) Order 1973, SI 1973/2162, made under section 2 of NICA 1973.

29 NICA 1973 s 7(5); Notes on Clauses, quoted in Whysall, *Northern Ireland*, p. 45.

30 The Northern Ireland Constitution (Amendment) Act 1973, which received the royal assent on 19 December 1973, amended section 8, to allow for up to 15 appointments (with not more than 11 members of the Northern Ireland Executive).

(3) The chief executive member and the heads of the Northern Ireland departments shall be appointed by the Secretary of State on behalf of Her Majesty and the Secretary of State may likewise appoint such number of additional persons (if any) as he thinks fit to discharge, whether as members of the Executive or otherwise, such functions as he may determine; but the total number of persons at any time holding appointments under this section shall not exceed twelve.

...

(8) Persons appointed under this section shall hold office at Her Majesty's pleasure ...

...

(10) Every person appointed under this section shall, on appointment, take the oath or make the affirmation set out in Schedule 4 to this Act.

4.51 These provisions were constitutionally consistent with section 8 of the GOIA 1920, though there were a number of changes. Executive authority was disaggregated into authorities. And the Northern Ireland Executive (section 8) was augmented by the secretary of state as her majesty's principal officer in Northern Ireland (in 1920, the lord lieutenant, later governor), other persons appointed under section 8 but not in the executive (a new idea), and the Northern Ireland departments (which did not, of course, come from the GOIA 1920) – to make up those executive authorities in Northern Ireland. The overall effect was the widening of the basis of the executive branch of government.

4.52 Section 7(1) was consistent with section 8(1) of the 1920 act.[31] Section 7(2) followed section 8(2) of the 1920 act. Section 7(3) altered the relationship in section 8(3) of the 1920 act, making departments equivalent to ministerial figures.

4.53 Section 8(1) represented a development of section 8(3)–(4) of the 1920 act, in that, as well as heads of departments, there could also be non-departmental ministers appointed by the secretary of state (the chief executive member but also junior ministers). Section 8(2) had no precedent in the 1920 act, where no provision had been made for a prime minister. Section 8(8) was consistent with section 8(3) of the 1920 act. And section 8(10) – oath or affirmation – was new, corresponding to the ending of appointments to the privy council of Northern Ireland (section 32(3)).[32]

4.54 Given that the secretary of state, defined as her majesty's principal officer in Northern Ireland, in section 7(2) and (6), appointed, under section 8(1), the members of the Northern Ireland executive and others, this suggests that they were her majesty's ministers[33] – though they no longer had to be privy counsellors. Under the then crown proceedings law in Northern Ireland[34] – based on section 53

31 'All executive power in Northern Ireland as in Great Britain will continue to flow from Her Majesty the Queen.' (*Northern Ireland Constitutional Proposals*, Cmnd 5259, March 1973, para 81) See the letters patent of the secretary of state for Northern Ireland, 20 December 1973, kept in the London office.

32 The Privy Council of Northern Ireland continues to exist. Privy counsellors took an oath of allegiance to the sovereign.

33 Though not a minister of the crown: NICA 1973 s 19(1). Minister of the crown is defined in Ministers of the Crown Act 1975 s 8(1) as 'the holder of an office in Her Majesty's Government in the United Kingdom, and includes the Treasury, the Board of Trade and the Defence Council'.

34 Northern Ireland (Crown Proceedings) Order 1949, SI 1949/1836; Northern Ireland (Crown Proceedings) (Amendment) Order 1971, SI 1972/212.

of the Crown Proceedings Act 1947 – the members of the Northern Ireland executive (and others appointed under section 8) were her majesty's government in Northern Ireland (the secretary of state being part of her majesty's government in the United Kingdom).

The Northern Ireland Act 1974

4.55 The Northern Ireland executive took office on 1 January 1974. It was to last less than five months. On 29 May 1974, the assembly was prorogued for four months;[35] prorogation was later extended, until dissolution on 28 March 1975.[36] Legislative functions stayed in Belfast, in suspension. So also, in a sense, did executive functions. They were transferred immediately, under section 8(6) of the NICA 1973, to four junior ministers in the NIO, who could hold office for no more than six months.

4.56 This was a – partial – return to the direct rule of 1972–73, while an attempt was to be made, which would later take the form of the Northern Ireland convention (8 May 1975 – 5 March 1976), to find another solution.

4.57 In July 1974, the secretary of state presented to parliament the white paper, *The Northern Ireland Constitution*, Cmnd 5675. It recommended a proper return to direct rule, and a constitutional convention.

4.58 The vehicle for the resumption of full direct rule was the Northern Ireland Act (NIA) 1974, which received the royal assent on 17 July 1974. This was notionally a temporary measure (until the convention reported), but it was to remain in force until the Belfast Agreement was implemented.[37] As with the NITPA 1972 (which had effectively expired on 1 January 1974),[38] there were no repeals; the NICA 1973 remained in force.

4.59 Section 1(3) of the NIA 1974 stated that schedule 1, headed temporary provisions for government of Northern Ireland, would have effect with respect to 'the exercise of legislative, executive and other functions ... in the interim period', this being defined as one year from enactment (though renewable annually by order (section 1(4)–(6)).[39]

4.60 The provisions for legislative functions in schedule 1 – in the transferred and reserved areas under the NICA 1973 – were similar to those in the NITPA 1972:

> 1(1) During the interim period –
>
> (a) no Measure shall be passed by the Assembly; and
>
> (b) Her Majesty may by Order in Council make laws for Northern Ireland and, in particular, provision for any matter for which the Constitution Act [NICA 1973] authorises or requires provision to be made by Measure.
>
> ...

35 The Northern Ireland Assembly (Prorogation) Order 1974, SI 1974/926, made under NICA 1973 s 27(6) 'and ... all other powers enabling Her in that behalf'.

36 Northern Ireland Act 1974 s 1(2); Northern Ireland Assembly (Dissolution) Order 1975, SI 1975/422, made under s 1(1).

37 Repealed by Northern Ireland Act 1998 s 100(2), sch 15.

38 Repealed by Northern Ireland Act 1998 s 100(2), sch 15.

39 Interim period orders subsequently extended the date each year until 16 July the following year.

(4) No recommendation shall be made to Her Majesty ... unless either –
(a) a draft of the Order has been approved by resolution of each House of Parliament; or
(b) the Order declares that it has been made to appear to Her Majesty that by reason of urgency the Order requires to be made without a draft having been so approved.

The NITPA 1972 section 1 had contained a proviso regarding orders in council undergoing the affirmative resolution procedure. The NIA 1974 introduced, in schedule 1, the concept of an urgency order (without resolution of each house), though subparagraph 5 required them to be laid subsequently before parliament. If there was no resolution within 40 days, they would cease to have effect (though without prejudice to anything done under the order).[40]

4.61 Under paragraph 1(7) of schedule 1 of the NIA 1974, references to measures are deemed to include such order in council, and, under section 4(3) of the NICA 1973 – a provision designed to deter judicial review in Northern Ireland – 'a Measure shall have the same force and effect as an Act of the Parliament of the United Kingdom'.[41] (Such orders were Northern Ireland legislation under the Interpretation Act 1978 sections 5, 23(4), 24(5) and schedule 1.) Thus, Northern Ireland primary legislation during direct rule, which, at Westminster, took the form of delegated – or secondary – legislation, with concomitant lack of scrutiny, had the full force of statute law.

4.62 The provisions for executive functions in schedule 1 of the NIA 1974 were even less accountable than under the NITPA 1972:

2(1) During the interim period –
(a) no person shall be appointed or hold office under section 8 of the Constitution Act [NICA 1973]; and
(b) any functions of the head of a Northern Ireland department may be discharged by that department and any functions of any other person appointed under that section may be discharged by the Secretary of State.

2(2) During the interim period any functions of a Northern Ireland department, including functions discharged by virtue of sub-paragraph (1)(b) above, shall be discharged by the department subject to the direction and control of the Secretary of State.

...

2(5) This paragraph shall not invalidate anything done before the beginning of the interim period [by the four junior ministers appointed to the NIO under section 8(6) of the NICA 1973 for up to six months][42] ...

4.63 The distinction in section 8(1) of the NICA 1973 – heads of departments and other appointed persons – was carried over into paragraph 2(1)(b). Functions of heads of departments, which, under the NITPA 1972, had gone to the secretary

40 Merlyn Rees introduced the practice in 1976 of publishing a proposal (a draft draft order) with an explanatory document, to counter the problem of unamendability.

41 Measures could still be ultra vires the NICA 1973. This does not affect the omnicompetence of Westminster.

42 Between 29 May 1974 and 17 July 1974, these four junior ministers were accountable, not to Westminster where they were members, but to the Northern Ireland assembly which was prorogued: *The Northern Ireland Constitution*, Cmnd 5675, July 1974, para 29.

of state, were now left in Northern Ireland with the departments.[43] It was only the functions of the other persons – including the chief executive (who was not considered a head of department)[44] – which went to the secretary of state. Though the word 'may' was used with reference to both departments and the secretary of state, the fact that all such functions had to go somewhere after prorogation made it more likely that they would go to the departments than the secretary of state. Executive power – unlike in 1972 – was left largely in Northern Ireland.

4.64 Paragraph 2(2) on departments meant that newly acquired functions, plus existing functions, would be under the secretary of state's direction and control. The same point can be made as above, with reference to the origin of this phrase in the Ministries of Northern Ireland Act (Northern Ireland) 1921, and its use in the NITPA 1972. Direction and control is a lesser responsibility than normally attaches to the office of minister. With no assembly in Northern Ireland, to hold the departments – with their existing and newly acquired functions – accountable, the secretary of state was not held accountable at Westminster to the same extent over functions which were not his responsibility.

4.65 This was only an interim provision on 17 July 1974. However, with renewal each year from 1975 to 1999 – a total of 25 times – such unaccountable government lasted over 25 years.[45]

The Northern Ireland Act 1982

4.66 Direct rule continued, while governments sought to find ways of returning to devolution. In the period 1974–98, a major legislative initiation was taken with the Northern Ireland Act (NIA) 1982, which received the royal assent on 23 July 1982. This provided for another Northern Ireland assembly, as in 1973. One was elected on 20 October 1982,[46] but it was boycotted by one community, and it was dissolved on 23 June 1986.[47] There were repeals to the Northern Ireland Assembly Act 1973, the NICA 1973 (and the NIA 1974),[48] but the Constitution Act (as it had been called first in 1974)[49] remained essentially the principal act.

4.67 The purpose of the NIA 1982 was the resumption of legislative and executive functions by the Northern Ireland assembly. The process was known as rolling devolution. It was to start with scrutinizing and consultative functions.

43 This has been characterized as virtually the abolition of heads of departments under direct rule: Whysall, *Northern Ireland*, p. 9.

44 Departments were the renamed ministries: NICA 1973 s 7(5). No new departments were established by measures.

45 The draft Northern Ireland Act 1974 (Interim Period Extension) Order 1999 was laid before both houses on 7 July 1999. The existing order was due to run out on 16 July 1999. Under the – ultimately unsuccessful – *Way Forward* plan of 2 July 1999, it was intended to transfer powers on 18 July 1999. The order was necessary for the two days' hiatus. It was to last until 16 July 2000. Devolution took place on 2 December 1999, under the Northern Ireland Act 1998 (Appointed Day) Order 1999, SI 1999/3208.

46 Northern Ireland Assembly (Day of Election) Order 1982, SI 1982/1078, made under s 27(7) of the NICA 1973, as applied by s 1(1) of the NIA 1974.

47 Northern Ireland Assembly (Dissolution) Order 1986, SI 1986/1036, made under s 5(1) of the NIA 1982.

48 Section 7(3) & sch 3.

49 Section 7(2).

Section 1 allowed the assembly (with certain majorities) to submit proposals to the secretary of state for the general or partial suspension of direct rule (the provisions of schedule 1 of the NIA 1974). Suspension – general or partial (under section 2) – was to be by orders in council at Westminster. General suspension, under part I of schedule 1, was to be achieved by having the (existing) interim period under NIA 1974 s 1(3) expire by order. Partial suspension, under part II of schedule 1, would allow the assembly to pass measures dealing only with specified departments, while the secretary of state could appoint under section 8(1) of the NICA 1973 heads – and deputy heads – to such departments. Section 6 and schedule 2 contained amendments to the NICA 1973 and the Northern Ireland Assembly Act 1973 to allow for such general or partial suspension.

4.68 While the process was couched in terms of the suspension (not the end) of direct rule, the government sought to do it on the legislative basis of the 1973 devolution provisions.

4.69 Section 3 allowed the assembly, pending the general suspension of direct rule, to consider Northern Ireland matters other than those excepted (unless referred by the secretary of state). And section 4 allowed the assembly to establish balanced (statutory) committees[50] overseeing the Northern Ireland departments under the control of the secretary of state, with chairmen and deputy chairmen. This was the area in which the assembly, despite its actual unrepresentative composition, performed reasonably well in its something less than four years' existence.

50 With parties sitting in the assembly.

5

Domestic Law: The Irish Free State, 1922–1937

5.1 This chapter turns to the second party to the Belfast Agreement and considers (a) from Southern Ireland to the Irish Free State, 1920–22; (b) a new state?; (c) whither Northern Ireland, 1921–25?; and (d) Eamon de Valera undermines the 1921 Anglo-Irish treaty, 1932–37. There is a second chapter dealing with the successor state of Éire/Ireland, which signed the Belfast Agreement. Such a historical introduction is relevant to both Parts 2 (Constitution) and 3 (Institutions). Chapters 5 and 6 involve a gradual shift from United Kingdom to Irish domestic law (plus international law). Devolution is internal to the United Kingdom, but, in 1998, unlike in 1973, that settlement, following the 1985 Anglo-Irish Agreement, took the form of an international agreement; this was necessary for the constitutional sections and the Strands Two and Three add-ons. The Irish state is, of course, much smaller, and more recent, than the other state party. But sovereign equality is a principle of international law.[1] Its constitutional history will, therefore, be examined as objectively as in Chapters 3 and 4. This is stated in full awareness of the disjuncture in Ireland between political and legal revolution (1916–23 and 1937), whereby its constitution is little appreciated inside or outside the country (thus the Irish state has had to be established at greater length).[2] But comity of nations, in the context of the end of the Irish territorial claim (Chapter 11), becomes necessary, having always been desirable, between United Kingdom and Irish lawyers.

From Southern Ireland to the Irish Free State, 1920–1922

5.2 Southern Ireland was not established successfully, as a devolved region of the United Kingdom under the GOIA 1920. However, it had a role in the transition to a 26-county Irish polity and administration. The post-1916 Sinn Féin, following the 1918 election, had set up the Dáil Éireann regime, along side the Irish Republican Army (IRA).[3] However, Dáil Éireann was never recognized by the United Kingdom government. On 6 December 1921, Irish representatives agreed the so-called

1 Article 2, United Nations Charter.

2 An important sign of the maturing of Irish intellectual and cultural life has been the shift in focus from nation to state, evident in Seán Ó Mordha's *Seven Ages: the story of the Irish state*, shown on RTE in February–April 2000.

3 The Irish republic, proclaimed in Dublin in 1916, failed to achieve recognition by any state in the world: *Irish Free State v Guaranty Safe Deposit Co* 129 Misc. NY 551, 557 (1927); 222 NYS 182 (1927) per Peters J (the Dail organization was ... simply an organization festering a rebellion or revolt against the British government in Ireland'). The name of the pretend state was Saorstát Éireann, though it did not appear in its constitution: Brian Farrell, 'A Note on the Dáil Constitution, 1919', *Irish Jurist*, n.s., IV, 1969, p. 127. Section 2 of the Interpretation Act 1923 described the First Dáil as having promulgated 'a provisional constitution for the said assembly as Dáil Éireann and Government of Saorstát Éireann'.

Anglo-Irish treaty with the United Kingdom government (whether this was an international agreement is discussed below). The Irish Free State – dominion home rule[4] – was established provisionally in 1922, and then through legal creation by the United Kingdom state; Dáil Éireann, as the parliament of Southern Ireland, drafted the new constitution.[5]

Southern Ireland

5.3 Southern Ireland was not quite – as would be implied judicially – 'a statutory abortion of December 1920'.[6] Elections for the new 26-county parliament were held on 19 May 1921 (Sinn Féin treating this, plus the Northern parliament, as the second Dáil). The four unionists elected turned up on 28 June 1921 and two on 13 July 1921, when the house of commons and senate adjourned without day named. Courts were established under sections 38–53 of the GOIA 1920, including the High Court of Appeal for Ireland[7] (the republican courts of 1920–22, used inter alia by defendants to enjoin plaintiffs in the official courts, are not legally significant whatever of their political import[8]).

5.4 The GOIA 1920 was mentioned in articles 10, 13 and 17 of the treaty of 6 December 1921. Article 17 provided for 'provisional arrangement for the administration of Southern Ireland' for up to 12 months. A meeting of the Southern house of commons was to be summoned to approve the treaty (article 18). 'The provisional Government of Southern Ireland' (article 15) was to be constituted by elected members of the Southern Parliament,[9] and powers transferred provisionally from London to Dublin when each member of the administration had signified in writing acceptance of the so-called treaty (article 17).

5.5 After the establishment of the Irish Free State, with its own courts, Meredith J (who had been president of the Dáil supreme court in 1920–22) held that all provisions of the GOIA 1920, not inconsistent with the 1922 constitution,

4 An idea which had originated in 1917–18 in the report of the Irish Convention chaired by Sir Horace Plunkett: Parliamentary Papers, 1918, X, *Report of the Proceedings of the Irish Convention 1918*. The Irish Free State was a vindication for the six constitutional nationalists elected in 1918 on a platform of dominion home rule.

5 See Lloyd George, House of Commons, *Hansard*, 2nd session, 5th series, 149, 42, 14 December 1921.

6 *Cogan v Minister for Finance* [1941] IR 389, 402 per Gavan Duffy J (Gavan Duffy – then a solicitor in London – had been one of the signatories of the treaty). John McColgan, *British Policy and the Irish Administration, 1920–22*, London 1983, appreciates the continuity as an administrative historian.

7 On 1 October 1921 (SR&O, 1921 No. 1527).

8 Dáil Eireann Courts (Winding Up) Act 1923, as amended in 1924. See Cahir Davitt, 'The Civil Jurisdiction of the Courts of Justice of the Irish Republic, 1920–1922', *Irish Jurist*, n.s., III, 1968, p. 112; James Casey, 'Republican Courts in Ireland, 1919–1922', *Irish Jurist*, n.s., V, 1970, p. 321, & 'The Genesis of the Dáil Courts', *Irish Jurist*, n.s., IX, 1974, p. 326; Brian Farrell, 'The Legislation of a "Revolutionary" Assembly: Dáil Decrees, 1919–1922', *Irish Jurist*, n.s., X, 1975, p. 112; *R (Kelly & Others) v Maguire & O'Sheil* [1923] 2 IR 58; *Hanrahan v Stapleton* [1928] 62 ILTR 11 Judge Roche; *O'Crowley v The Minister for Justice* [1935] IR 536 Johnston J; *ITGWU vTGWU* [1936] IR 471 Meredith J.

9 Article 17 referred indirectly to the house of commons (GOIA 1920 2nd & 5th schedules); article 18 directly.

remained part of Irish law under article 73 of the latter text: 'The Provisional Parliament never repealed the Act of 1920.'[10]

The treaty of 6 December 1921

5.6 Following a truce on 11 July 1921, Eamon de Valera entered into negotiations with Lloyd George (without the participation of Sir James Craig, the Northern Ireland prime minister). Irish plenipotentaries were in London between 11 October 1921 and 6 December 1921, when the Articles of Agreement for a Treaty between Great Britain and Ireland (the treaty') were signed by members of the United Kingdom government and Irish leaders.

5.7 Article 18 stated that the instrument would be submitted by his majesty's government for the approval of parliament (and by the Irish signatories to a meeting summoned for the purpose of the members elected to sit in the House of Commons of Southern Ireland). If approved, it would be ratified by the necessary legislation. This was legislation at Westminster, not in Dublin, since powers had yet to be transferred.

5.8 The treaty stated that the Irish Free State would have the same constitutional status within 'the Community of Nations known as the British Empire',[11] as Canada, Australia, New Zealand and South Africa.[12] It would have the power to make laws 'for the peace, order and good government of Ireland [sic]', and there would be an executive responsible to that parliament (article 1). Powers and duties were further elaborated: service of the public debt (article 5); Irish coastal defence (article 6); harbour and other facilities in peace and war (article 7); Irish military defence (article 8); access to ports in both countries (article 9). 'In form it connoted the conclusive recognition of Irish internal sovereignty.'[13]

Legal creation

5.9 On 16 December 1921, the Articles of Agreement for a Treaty (as it would continually be described in London) were approved by both houses of parliament at Westminster.

5.10 The treaty was scheduled to the Irish Free State (Agreement) Act 1922, being given the force of law from 31 March 1922. Powers were to be transferred to the provisional government by orders in council.[14] The parliament of Southern Ireland was to be dissolved within four months, and elections held for (effectively) the parliament of the Irish Free State. There would be no further byelections for Westminster seats outside Northern Ireland (a clear admission that the GOIA 1920 had not been superseded entirely by the treaty, through implied repeal or legal revolution).

5.11 The Irish Free State Constitution Act 1922 (Session 2) – which received the royal assent on 5 December 1922 (within the 12 months allowed by the treaty) – established the new dominion in United Kingdom law. The act had scheduled to it

10 *Cahill v A-G* [1925] 1IR 70, 77; see also, *Wigg v A-G* [1927] AC 674; [1927] IR 285 PC.
11 The oath in article 4 included reference to 'the British Commonwealth of Nations'.
12 Canada was mentioned further in articles 2 and 3.
13 Leo Kohn, *The Constitution of the Irish Free State*, London 1932, p. 50.
14 The Provisional Government (Transfer of Functions) Order 1922, SR&O 1922, No. 315, 1 April.

the constituent act, exactly as it had been passed by the provisional parliament in Dublin on 25 October 1922. The most important provisions were:

> Whereas the House of the Parliament ... sitting as a Constituent Assembly for the settlement of the Constitution of the Irish Free State has passed the Measure ... set forth in the Schedule to this Act, whereby the Constitution appearing as the First Schedule to the Constituent Act is declared to be the Constitution of the Irish Free State:
>
> ...
>
> The Constitution set forth in the First Schedule to the Constituent Act shall, subject to the provisions to which the same is by the Constituent Act so made subject as aforesaid, be the Constitution of the Irish Free State, and shall come into operation on the same being proclaimed by His Majesty in accordance with Article eighty-three of the said Constitution, but His Majesty may at any time after the proclamation appoint a Governor-General for the Irish Free State.
>
> ...
>
> Saving [marginal note]
>
> Nothing in the said Constitution shall be construed as prejudicing the power of Parliament to make laws affecting the Irish Free State in any case where, in accordance with constitutional practice, Parliament would makes laws affecting other self-governing Dominions.

5.12 The following day – 6 December 1922 – George V at Buckingham Palace did 'announce and proclaim that the Constitution of the Irish Free State as the same was passed and adopted by the said Constituent Assembly [had] been passed and adopted by Parliament'.[15]

The constitution

5.13 The power to make laws in Ireland – in United Kingdom (including Irish) law – dated from 31 March 1922, and was to become effective with the summoning of the provisional parliament of the Irish Free State.

5.14 The sources of Irish law – a separate jurisdiction – were: (1) English common law, from 1171 to 1800; (2) acts of the parliament of Ireland, 1495–1800 (legislative independence having been achieved in 1782); and (3) the common law from 1801, plus acts of the United Kingdom parliament (continuing) – as was made clear by section 4 of the Irish Free State Constitution Act 1922 (Session 2).

5.15 The events of 1916, 1918 and 1919–21, while politically significant, are only of legal consequence[16] to the extent that the GOIA 1920 was superseded in the 26 counties by the treaty, and the two 1922 Westminster acts. This is the view of the common law in Ireland; the constituent act of 1922 (to use the United Kingdom terminology) was 'an original source of jurisdiction': *Cahill v A-G* [1925] IR 70, 76 per Meredith J.[17]

15 SR&O 1922, No. 1353.

16 For instances of republican legalism, see the Plunkett case, which brought the Dáil courts to an end in 1922 (Davitt, 'Civil Jurisdiction', pp. 127–8, Casey, 'Republican Courts', pp. 338–40, but also Farrell, 'A Note', pp. 120–3, plus the affidavit of his father, Count Plunkett, DE 38/40, National Archives, Dublin); the case brought by Mrs Tom Clarke on 4 August 1922 (Davitt, 'Civil Jurisdiction', pp. 128–9 & Casey, 'Republican Courts', p. 340).

17 See also *R (Alexander) v Judge of the Circuit Court for Cork* [1925] 2 IR 165. Other aspects of Irish law suggest a legal revolution in, not 1916, but 1919: the Interpretation Act 1923

5.16 The 'root of title' of the new state in Irish law, under article 83 of the new constitution, dates (on the basis of the argument of Meredith J) from 6 December 1922.[18]

5.17 The second Dáil – turning to political history – had approved the treaty on 7 January 1922, by 64 votes to 57. Arthur Griffith summoned the Southern Parliament for 14 January 1922 (under articles 17 and 18 of the treaty), and Michael Collins became leader of the eight-strong provisional government. Its activities were circumscribed until 1 April 1922, when powers were transferred by order in council. This parliament was dissolved on 27 May 1922, and its successor was summoned by the provisional government under the Irish Free State (Agreement) Act 1922 to meet on 1 July 1922.

5.18 Sinn Féin failed to run an agreed slate of candidates in the election of 16 June 1922 (to keep out other political forces), and, on 28 June 1922, civil war broke out between anti-treaty and pro-treaty forces. The (revolutionary) third Dáil was not summoned for 30 June 1922, and the provisional parliament was postponed five times until it met eventually on 9 September 1922 (being called confusingly the third Dáil).

5.19 The Irish republic – affirmed by republicans – was killed off. With the deaths of Griffith and Collins, William Cosgrave became chairman of the provisional government (and later president of the executive council[19]).

5.20 On 18 September 1922, Cosgrave introduced the three-clause bill (with two schedules), which later became the constituent act. The first schedule comprised the constitution. This had been drafted by a committee under Collins in January to March 1922. There followed consultation. It was negotiated with London in June 1922 (and released in time for the election). It was revised in the constituent assembly in September and October 1922.[20] The second schedule was the treaty.

5.21 The bill was enacted on 25 October 1922 as the Constitution of the Irish Free State (Saorstát Eireann) Act 1922 (No. 1 of 1922). It provided:

> Dáil Eireann sitting as a Constituent Assembly in this Provisional Parliament[21], acknowledging that all lawful authority comes from God to the people and in the confidence that the National life and unity shall thus be restored, hereby proclaims the establishment of the Irish Free State (otherwise called Saorstát Eireann) and in the exercise of undoubted right, decrees and enacts as follows: -

(defining constitutional terms); the Indemnity Act 1924 (covering the period 21 January 1919 to 28 June 1922); *Fogarty v O'Donoghue* [1926] IR 531 per Murnaghan J (though the case was not based centrally on the legality of the revolutionary Dáil).

18 Other decisions prefer the date of enactment, 25 October 1922: *The State (Ryan) v Lennon* [1935] IR 170; *Lynham v Butler (No. 2)* [1933] IR 74, 94–5 per Kennedy CJ but also *In re Reade* [1926] IR 31, 47–9 per Kennedy J (31 March 1922 as the critical date); *In re Irish Employers' Mutual Insurance Association* [1955] IR 176 per Kingsmill Moore J; *The Criminal Law (Jurisdiction) Bill 1975* [1977] IR 129, 146–8 per O'Higgins CJ.

19 Under article 51 of the Irish Free State constitution.

20 Brian Farrell, 'The Drafting of the Irish Free State Constitution', in four parts, *Irish Jurist*, n.s., V, 1970, pp. 115 & 343 and VI, 1971, pp. 111 & 345; Thomas Towey, 'Hugh Kennedy and the Constitutional Development of the Irish Free State, 1922–1923', *Irish Jurist*, n.s., XII, 1977, p. 355.

21 The United Kingdom version was the House of the Parliament.

> The Constitution set forth in the First Schedule hereto annexed shall be the Constitution of the Irish Free State (Saorstát Eireann).
> The said Constitution shall be construed with reference to the Articles of Agreement for a Treaty between Great Britain and Ireland set forth in the Second Schedule hereto annexed (hereinafter referred to as 'the Scheduled Treaty') which are hereby given the force of law ...
> This Act may be cited for all purposes as the Constitution of the Irish Free State (Saorstát Eireann) Act, 1922.

5.22 The provisional parliament was a law-making body – in United Kingdom, and therefore Irish, law – and this was recognized in the second United Kingdom act of 5 December 1922. Article 83 of the new constitution read: 'The passing and adoption of this Constitution by the Constituent Assembly and the British Parliament shall be announced as may be, and not later than [6 December 1922], by Proclamation of His Majesty, and this Constitution shall come into operation on the issue of such Proclamation.'

5.23 The 1922 Irish act – number 1 of 1922 – was to be described, by Hugh Kennedy KC, one of the drafters of the constitution, when chief justice in 1932, as 'the fundamental instrument of the new State'.[22] The constitution was amendable under article 50. But amendments had to be 'within the terms of the Scheduled Treaty'. And that could only – as it transpired – be altered by agreement of the two governments and parliaments. The forefront of the act – the preamble and three sections – did not have a means of amendment; as the work of the constituent assembly, it could only be altered arguably by another such gathering.

5.24 Article 73 of the constitution provided for the continuation of – consistent – laws in force on 6 December 1922. (This is where the question of the Irish act of union of 1800 would be considered.) The Adaptations of Enactments Act 1922 – No. 2 of 1922 – was enacted on 20 December 1922, to adapt 'acts of the British [sic] Parliament' to the Irish Free State (British here can only mean United Kingdom). Under section 3, the name Ireland (even when used with Great Britain or by implication in the United Kingdom) was to mean Saorstát Eireann.

A new state?

5.25 This question is usually examined in United Kingdom and Irish law, but it is a problem of international law – with the creation of the Irish Free State evident in the former, and its existence traceable in the latter.

5.26 Did the Irish Free State become a legal person on 6 December 1922? Treating this as a question of law, and looking at the qualifications specified in the 1933 Montevideo convention (see Chapter 2) – population, territory, government, relations with other states – an answer may be attempted. There is no problem as regards a permanent population in the 26 counties. Nor is there a problem of territory, even given the references to 'Ireland' in the 1921 treaty.

5.27 Effective government is an important issue. The republican movement divided in December 1921 over the treaty (against the background of nationalist–unionist rivalry). There is an argument that the lack of democracy in 1922 – the cause or consequence of the civil war which broke out in June – means there was

22 Foreword to Kohn, *Irish Free State*, p. xii.

not effective government. But there is also a counter-argument (and a good one) that the pro-treaty forces, who succeeded in defeating the IRA by May 1923, managed the transition from anti-British lawlessness to Irish legality, sufficiently to guarantee the Irish Free State's prospects in its early years.

5.28 International relations is a more difficult issue, and one that requires a preliminary examination of United Kingdom and Irish law.

5.29 According to the constitution of the former, the crown[23] was the basis of the United Kingdom and the British Empire (or British Commonwealth of Nations).[24] The crown was indivisible, and his majesty's dominions therefore constituted a unity. This was a one-state view of the United Kingdom and dominions. Their relations were considered in 1920 part of municipal – not international – law; thus, the unitary theory, or *inter se* doctrine, whereby the government of the United Kingdom purported to speak for all his majesty's governments in international relations.

5.30 The dominions were self-governing, with their own constitutions and embryonic – independent – contacts with other states.[25] They had been bound by treaties made by the sovereign, but this would no longer be the case from the initialling of the treaty of Locarno on 16 October 1925.[26] The dominions – though founding members of the League of Nations – sat with Great Britain (as it was called), and the British Empire was permanently represented on the Council. They became generally recognized as independent states after the 1926 imperial conference held at Westminster.[27] This was partly because the Irish Free State had allied immediately with the other – white – dominions to assert commonwealth equality. Following the 1930 imperial conference, the Statute of Westminster 1931 was enacted at the request of the dominions. The Colonial Laws Validity Act 1865[28] no longer applied to new acts (section 2). Section 4 of the Statute stated that United Kingdom laws would not extend to a dominion, unless it was expressly declared that the dominion had so requested and consented.

23 Lloyd George told Griffiths and Collins on 1 June 1922: 'The Crown was a mystical term which, as they well knew, in the British Commonwealth simply stood for the power of the people.' (Quoted in Thomas Jones, *Whitehall Diary: Volume III: Ireland, 1918–1925*, ed. Keith Middlemass, London 1971, p. 207)

24 The former phrase was used in article 1 of the treaty; the latter in article 4 (it did not fully enter United Kingdom law until the Statute of Westminster 1931).

25 Lorna Lloyd & Alan James, 'The External Representation of the Dominions, 1919–1948', *British Year Book of International Law, 1996*, Oxford 1997, pp. 479–501.

26 Cmd 2525. The Final Protocol of the Locarno Conference, 1925 (and Annexes), contained, in Annex A, article 9: 'The present treaty shall impose no obligation upon any of the British dominions, or upon India, unless the Government of such dominion, or of India, signifies its acceptance thereof.'

27 Arthur Balfour described the members as 'autonomous communities within the British Empire, equal in status, in no way subordinate one to another in any aspect of their domestic or external affairs, though united by a common allegiance to the Crown and freely associated as members of the British Commonwealth of Nations.' (Quoted in F.S.L. Lyons, *Ireland since the Famine*, London 1973, p. 508)

28 This did not apply to Ireland before 1922. It is unlikely that it applied to the Irish Free State. This dominion had its own agreed repugnancy provisions (in Irish, and United Kingdom, law).

5.31 In Irish (as well as United Kingdom) law, the Irish Free State, under article 2 of the treaty, was to follow the 'law, practice and constitutional usage ... [of] the Dominion of Canada'. Anglo-Irish, but not other, relations were specified in other articles. As for the 1922 constitution, there were no provisions for external relations. Article 51 on executive authority concerned only internal relations. Insofar as it may be interpreted as also applying to external relations, the central role of the king was only slightly mitigated by the law, practice and constitutional usage of Canada.[29]

5.32 To conclude, doubt must be cast on the proposition – as a question of international law – that a new state entered the community of nations on 6 December 1922. Certainly, self-government was achieved in much of Ireland. But the Irish Free State did not have sufficient capacity to enter into relations with other states.

5.33 On the other hand, it did have – increasingly voluntary – relations with, and through, the British commonwealth. It joined the League of Nations in 1923. It also signed an international agreement with Canada, dealing with the exchange of money orders.[30] The following year, it achieved independent diplomatic representation in the United States. It must have had some – irrevocable – legal personality. It was probably a state in international law by 1925–26. (By 1929, its initiative – without reservations – led commonwealth members to sign the optional clause of the statute of the world court.)

5.34 Looking at the existence of states alternatively in terms of recognition, the problem of the Irish Free State is related to that of the United Kingdom. Recognition of the latter was presumed. The existence of the Irish Free State from 1922 would have been acknowledged. But would that have been recognition of a state? Probably not. This may have altered in 1925–26. Or in 1930. But, more likely, the Statute of Westminster 1931 (which received the royal assent on 11 December) would have aided greatly recognition of the Irish Free State as a member of the community of nations.

The treaty

5.35 So what about the treaty? Treaties, in customary international law, are agreements between states (which does not preclude other international agreements having legal force).[31] The United Kingdom was a state in December 1921. But the five Irish signatories, whatever they maintained about Ireland being a nation, were not competent – in international law (or really Irish law) – to conclude a treaty.

5.36 The United Kingdom government clearly intended something different, when it signed the Articles of Agreement for a Treaty. (It would continue to use the full title throughout the 1920s.) Lloyd George described it as 'an Agreement in the nature of a Treaty', when commending it to parliament shortly afterwards, adding confusingly: 'exactly in the same way as the "Articles of Agreement"

29 The provisional government added an external affairs section to the constitution, but it did not survive the negotiations in London (Farrell, 'The Drafting', VI, pp. 123–4 & p. 359).

30 League of Nations, *Treaty Series*, general index no. 1, vols I–XXXIX.

31 Articles 1–4, 1969 Vienna convention on the law of treaties.

entered into by the Act of Union was called a Treaty by both parties in this House [in 1800]'.[32]

5.37 A treaty was clearly the Irish objective in 1921, for reasons of nationalist assertion. The word spawned the popular descriptions of the contesting parties in 1922: pro-treaty and anti-treaty. Even though the full title was used in the second schedule to the Constitution of the Irish Free State (Saorstát Eireann) Act 1922, this was referred to – as noted – as 'the Scheduled Treaty'. By this stage – the eve of the creation of the Irish Free State – such language was used rhetorically to promote recognition as a state.

5.38 The United Kingdom and the Irish Free State clashed over registration of the treaty as number 636 at the League of Nations on 11 July 1924.[33] The Irish won.[34] But registration does not make an agreement a treaty if it is not one in international law.[35] There was a further clash over the registration of the 1925 agreement (see below) as number 1088 on 8 February 1926.[36]

5.39 Arguably – and this accords with the title of the text – there was an agreement on 6 December 1921. This was a political agreement. And it was not an international agreement. It was internal to the United Kingdom, between the government and the leaders of Irish republicanism. But – continuing the argument – the intention was to have a treaty. (And, it could be argued, when the Irish Free State became, in international law, a state, in 1925–26 or 1931, the articles of agreement were transformed into such an international instrument.)[37]

5.40 This, however, requires proof that the United Kingdom was prepared to abandon the unitary theory (or *inter se* doctrine) in general, and to see dominion home rule in Ireland lead to separate statehood. Neither is credible in the circumstances of 1921 (and it did not acquiesce in 1924 over the registration of the treaty at the League of Nations).

5.41 Most likely, then, Lloyd George and his colleagues, for reasons of statecraft, played along with the Sinn Féin representatives' characterization of their political agreement as a treaty in international law. Thus, the references to 'Great Britain' (only part of the state) and 'Ireland' – a term used politically, not legally, in the title of the treaty.

5.42 The fact that the Irish leaders – and consequently Irish history – called it the 1921 (or Anglo-Irish) treaty, does not make it a treaty. Reviewing (in 1963) de Valera's exchanges with Lloyd George in the summer of 1921, Professor Robert Jennings coined the phrase 'the Irish doctrine of self-recognition' to theorize Sinn Féin's assertions about the right to statehood.[38]

32 House of Commons, *Hansard*, 2nd session, 5th series, 149, 128, 15 December 1921.

33 League of Nations, *Treaty Series*, XXVI, 10 & XXVII, 449–50. A footnote recorded: approved by Dáil Éireann on 7 January 1922 and ratified by the 'British Parliament' on 31 March 1922, entering into force on the latter date.

34 David Harkness, *The Restless Dominion: the Irish Free State and the British Commonwealth of Nations, 1921–31*, London 1969, pp. 59–62.

35 No more than does subsequent listing in the United Kingdom treaty series: Clive Parry & Charity Hopkins, *An Index of British Treaties, 1101–1968*, London 1970, p. 181 (though it is categorized as '[political]').

36 League of Nations, *Treaty Series*, XLIV, 263, 266.

37 But, the whole purpose of the treaty was – in sympathetic Irish eyes – the creation of a state.

38 *The Acquisition of Territory in International Law*, Manchester 1963, p. 8 n 2.

5.43 Though it was not – and did not become – a treaty, the 1921 treaty (as it will continue to be known) was to be respected – and amended – by the London and Dublin governments and their parliaments. This was because it was the law in the United Kingdom, and separately in the Irish Free State. It was part of two systems of domestic law, but not of international law. London would seek to hold the Irish Free State to the treaty, until the Statute of Westminster 1931 changed the United Kingdom-law view of relations with the dominions (it also changed the laws of the dominions).

5.44 But Dublin was to respect the treaty as fundamental Irish law. The pro-treatyites in government (1922–32) would accept it could only be amended by agreement, even after 1931. The anti-treatyite Eamon de Valera, in striking contrast, was prepared to run domestic legal risks to undermine the treaty in 1932–37 (this is discussed below).

Whither Northern Ireland, 1921–1925?

Articles 11–15 of the treaty

5.45 Five of the 18 articles of the treaty related to Northern Ireland, whose government continued to develop under the GOIA 1920. Lloyd George freely used a political 'Ireland'[39] in the text, and, by inference, 'Irish Free State' and 'Irish Government' (Sinn Féin continuing to deceive itself). Nevertheless, it was legally clear that the treaty, and the associated provisional parliament and government, applied only to the 26 counties.[40]

5.46 Article 11 of the treaty introduced what became known as the Ulster month concept. Under this, Northern Ireland had to consent to join the Irish Free State (despite the opening 'Ireland' in article 1). The month was to date from, not the first 1922 United Kingdom act, but the second (the constituent act) – that is, 5 December 1922 (and gave Northern Ireland effectively 13 months from the date of the treaty to – inevitably – consolidate further).[41]

5.47 Article 11 provided that the GOIA 1920 was 'to remain of full force and effect' in Northern Ireland. It would require a resolution of both houses of parliament there, for Northern Ireland to participate in an election for the parliament of the Irish Free State (the inevitable result amounting to another unionist safeguard). There was no promise to repeal the GOIA 1920. During the Ulster month, 'the powers of the Parliament and the Government of the Irish Free State [were] not [to] be exercisable as respects Northern Ireland'. This implied politically – but not legally – that the Irish Free State had some right to Northern Ireland. But partition was acknowledged expressly in the treaty.

39 And indeed, 'Great Britain', sometimes used internationally as the name of the state.

40 The Ulster clauses of the treaty were construed in only one case: *DPP v McNeill* [1975] NI 177 per Lowry LCJ; see also C.R. Symmons, 'Who owns the territorial waters of Northern Ireland?' [1976] NILQ, 27, 1, 48 & 'A Rejoinder', (1984) 33 ICLQ 1064; T. Towey, 'Who owns the territorial waters of Northern Ireland?: the *McNeill* case: another view' (1983) 32 ICLQ 1013; also C.R. Symmons, *Ireland and the Law of the Sea*, Blackrock, Co. Dublin 1993, pp. 43–7.

41 Irish Free State (Agreement) Act 1922 s 1(5); Irish Free State Constitution Act 1922 (Session 2) s 5. The concept of ratification here does not imply a treaty. It refers to legalization of a political agreement. See also article 18: article 11 indicates that only the Westminster parliament was involved.

5.48 The pretence of one Ireland was carried through to article 14. This provided for the consequences of Northern Ireland consenting to join the Irish Free State. The parliament and the government there would continue to operate under (seemingly) the GOIA 1920. And the parliament and government of the Irish Free State would have, in Northern Ireland, in the non-transferred areas, the powers it had in the rest of Ireland, 'subject to such other provisions as may be agreed in manner hereinafter appearing' (in article 15). This may be seen as a transfer of (most but not all) powers from London to Dublin, but, given that the GOIA 1920 was to continue apparently in Northern Ireland, it is difficult to see how it could be united (albeit federally) with a dominion outside the United Kingdom. Article 14 makes it difficult to argue for the creation of a new state.

5.49 Article 15 continued this scenario (a federal Ireland), allowing Belfast and Dublin (as a transitional administration) to discuss provisions including: safeguards with regard to patronage, revenue collection, duties and minorities in Northern Ireland; the settlement of financial relations between north and south; the relation of defence forces in Northern Ireland and the Irish Free State.

5.50 Article 12 – returning to the partition option – switched from consent to a united Ireland (as in article 11) to an act of negative consent. Thus, during the Ulster month, the two houses of the Northern Ireland parliament had to present an address to the sovereign, if they wanted the GOIA 1920 to 'continue to be of full force and effect'. In such an eventuality, 'the powers of the Parliament and Government of the Irish Free State [would] no longer extend to Northern Ireland'. Again, this seems to suggest an Irish Free State right, but the reference to the GOIA 1920 continuing is decisive of the issue.

5.51 (Article 13 transferred the powers of the Southern Ireland parliament as regards the Council of Ireland to the Irish Free State parliament. Again, a Council of Ireland between a dominion and a region of the United Kingdom, militates against a new state being created.)

5.52 Article 12 contained a proviso which helped make the treaty, namely the idea of a boundary commission. In the eventuality of Northern Ireland opting within the month to stay within the United Kingdom, a three-person commission was to determine the boundaries between Northern Ireland and the rest of Ireland, 'in accordance with the wishes of the inhabitants, so far as may be compatible with economic and geographic conditions'. This was not a simple plebiscitary test, and Sinn Féin – at a time when such commissions were operating under the treaty of Versailles in Europe – engaged in wishful thinking about gaining a united Ireland by encroaching incrementally upon unionist territory.

The address

5.53 Did Northern Ireland – in United Kingdom (and Irish) law – have to vote itself into the United Kingdom after 5 December 1922? This is suggested by a reading of the treaty based on 'Ireland' in article 1, and the references to the address in articles 12 and 14. But articles 14 and 15 are dependent upon article 11, where the Northern Ireland parliament had to vote to participate in an Irish Free State election. Northern Ireland – in Irish (and United Kingdom) law from 25 October 1922 – had, under the treaty, the right not to join the Irish Free State. It would only have been after the resolution specified in article 11 (and a nationalist election victory), that the 'no such address' scenario of articles 14 and 15 would have bitten. If Northern Ireland had done nothing after 5 December 1922, it would have continued to be part of the United Kingdom.

5.54 On 7 December 1922 (the day after the royal proclamation), the two houses of the Northern Ireland parliament, without dissent and for the avoidance of doubt, agreed to present – through Irish privy councillors who were also MPs at Westminster, and Lord Londonderry – the article 12 address to the sovereign. It was presented on 8 December 1922. And, following the text of article 12, it requested that the powers of the parliament and government of the Irish Free State should no longer extend to Northern Ireland. This does not mean they had so extended on 6 December 1922.

The boundary commission

5.55 In early 1922 – and this was not envisaged in the treaty – Churchill as colonial secretary promoted cooperation between Craig and Collins over Northern Ireland. In this context, the two leaders agreed that they might dispense with the boundary commission.

5.56 Such a strategy, however, could not supplant the logic of partition. It became, and remained, Craig's position, that he would not nominate his member of the boundary commission. Following the civil war in the south, Cosgrave tried to negotiate, but, on 26 April 1924, he formally requested the United Kingdom to establish the commission. London nominated an English-born, South African judge, Feetham J. Dublin's nominee was a member of the government, Eoin MacNeill.

5.57 The question of the Ulster member was referred to the judicial committee of the privy council.[42] It ruled that the royal prerogative (exercised by the governor or United Kingdom ministers) did not extend to such a statutory appointment;[43] and that the Northern Ireland government could, under the Irish Free State (Agreement) Act 1922, effectively veto the commission being brought into existence. (The commission, however, if established, could reach a majority decision.)[44]

5.58 London and Dublin, therefore, had to amend the treaty, in particular the proviso to article 12. The method chosen confirms that the 1921 treaty was not a (legally binding) international agreement.

5.59 On 4 August 1924, Cosgrave and the United Kingdom prime minister, Ramsay MacDonald, agreed, 'subject to the confirmation' of their two legislatures, that Northern Ireland's power of appointment would be transferred to the United Kingdom government. This political agreement was to supplement – not strictly to amend – article 12 of the treaty, 'to which the force of law was given' by the first 1922 United Kingdom act and the 1922 Irish act. This 1924 text was a political agreement to change Irish and United Kingdom law. The United Kingdom

42 It was done by an order in council of 25 June 1924, an exercise presumably of the royal prerogative.

43 *Attorney-General v De Keyser's Royal Hotel Ltd* [1920] AC 511 HL.

44 Irish Free State (Agreement) Act 1922: report of the judicial committee of the privy council, as approved by order of his majesty in council, of 31 July 1924, on the questions connected with the Irish boundary commission referred to the said committee, Cmd 2214.

parliament enacted on 9 October 1924,[45] and the Oireachtas on 25 October 1924.[46] Both legislatures confirmed the supplementary agreement, enacting that the 1921 treaty 'shall have effect accordingly'.

5.60 London appointed J.R. Fisher (a unionist newspaper editor from Belfast), and the commission began work on 6 November 1924. Feetham J was forced to construe the article 12 proviso, and concluded that there had been no intention to radically alter either Northern Ireland or the Irish Free State.[47] Adjustments were drafted using confessional data from the 1911 census, but contemporary economic and geographic surveys. The three commissioners agreed a first draft of an award (of net benefit in terms of acres and persons to the Irish Free State) on 5 November 1925. But, two days later, this appeared in the *Morning Post* (Fisher being most likely responsible).

The 1925 agreement

5.61 The question of the border was back on the political agenda, and, on 3 December 1925, Cosgrave signed an agreement with Craig and Stanley Baldwin. It took a similar form to the 1924 supplemental agreement, namely a political decision to alter Irish and United Kingdom law (Craig had no such power, though the agreement was approved by his parliament).

5.62 The title and relevant paragraphs are:

> AGREEMENT AMENDING AND SUPPLEMENTING THE ARTICLES OF AGREEMENT FOR A TREATY BETWEEN GREAT BRITAIN AND IRELAND TO WHICH THE FORCE OF LAW WAS GIVEN BY THE IRISH FREE STATE (AGREEMENT) ACT, 1922, AND BY THE CONSTITUTION OF THE IRISH FREE STATE (SAORSTÁT EIREANN) ACT, 1922.
>
> ...
>
> And WHEREAS the British Government and the Government of the Irish Free State being united in amity in this undertaking with the Government of Northern Ireland, and being resolved mutually to aid one another in a spirit of neighbourly comradeship, hereby agree as follows: -
>
> The powers conferred by the proviso to Article 12 of the said Articles of Agreement on the Commission therein mentioned are hereby revoked, and the extent of Northern Ireland for the purposes of the Government of Ireland Act, 1920, and of the said Articles of Agreement shall be such as was fixed by sub-section (2) of section one of that Act.
>
> ...
>
> This Agreement is subject to confirmation by the British Parliament and by the Oireachtas of the Irish Free State, and the Act of the British Parliament confirming this Agreement shall fix the date as from which the transfer of the powers of the Council of Ireland [provided for in paragraph 5] under this Agreement is to take effect.

5.63 This political agreement finally sealed the 1921 treaty. The title shifted the emphasis from putative parties to the Articles of Agreement for a Treaty, to existing Irish and United Kingdom law. Paragraph 6 showed it was a political agreement dependent upon parliamentary confirmation, and was designed to amend

45 Irish Free State (Confirmation of Agreement) Act 1924.

46 Treaty (Confirmation of Supplemental Agreement) Act 1924.

47 See chairman's memorandum, annexed to chapter III: G.J. Hand, ed., *Report of the Irish Boundary Commission, 1925*, Shannon, 1969, pp. 32–65.

domestic law in the Irish Free State and the United Kingdom. Its main provision was paragraph 1, which revoked the 1921 boundary commission solution and acknowledged the GOIA 1920 status quo (6 and 26 counties). (This acceptance was aided by a United Kingdom concession on the public debt: article 5 of the treaty.) The settling of the border was accompanied by the transfer of the powers of the Council of Ireland (which had not been established, and could not have worked legally) to Northern Ireland (depriving the Irish Free State of any institutional link[48]).

5.64 This political agreement of 3 December 1925 was scheduled to a United Kingdom act[49] (10 December), and to an Irish Free State act[50] (17 December). Thus, Irish and United Kingdom law were separately, but consistently, altered. The mechanism, again, was not strictly an amendment of the treaty (which again was described as having been given the force of law in the first 1922 United Kingdom act and the 1922 Irish act). This is in spite of the two 1925 acts purporting to confirm an agreement 'amending and supplementing' the treaty. It was, rather, that the references to the treaty in section 2 of the constituent act/the Constitution of the Irish Free State (Saorstát Eireann) Act 1922 would have effect accordingly.

5.65 The 1921 treaty, as argued, was not a treaty, and did not become a treaty. But what about this 1925 political agreement? Contrary to the two acts – purporting to amend the 1921 treaty – it can be read as a free-standing agreement. Three heads of government agreed to accept the 1920 border (referring to the GOIA). But can that be turned into international law? Certainly, it is possible to detect two contracting states – the United Kingdom and the Irish Free State – in the political agreement (their governments were distinguished from Sir James Craig's). And Northern Ireland would be bound by United Kingdom international obligations.

5.66 The point turns on whether the Irish Free State was legally a state – or was so recognized – on 3 December 1925. This was three years after the dominion had been created in municipal law. It was also more than two weeks after the United Kingdom, initialling the 1925 treaty of Locarno, had expressly not included the Irish Free State and the other dominions. Had it acquired – irrevocable – legal personality in international law? The discussion above suggests that 1925–26 or 1931 may be critical dates. It is therefore possible – if the first critical date can be established – that the Baldwin/Cosgrave/Craig agreement embodies the first treaty entered into by the Irish Free State.

5.67 If this argument is correct, it means that the Irish Free State undertook – in international law – to recognize the United Kingdom of Great Britain and Northern Ireland. It did so by accepting the pre-1920 administrative boundary, which, on 3 May 1921, became the border between two United Kingdom subordinate administrations, on 6 December 1922 the border between the United Kingdom and

48 Paragraph 5: '... the Governments of the Irish Free State and of Northern Ireland shall meet together as and when necessary for the purpose of considering matters of common interest arising out of or connected with the exercise and administration of the said [Council of Ireland] powers.' It was to be 40 years – 1965 – before the two premiers met again.

49 Ireland (Confirmation of Agreement) Act 1925.

50 Treaty (Confirmation of Amending Agreement) Act 1925.

the new Irish Free State dominion and, arguably in December 1925, an international frontier.

5.68 It also means that this possible international obligation, which was respected by the Cosgrave government, was subsequently breached by de Valera after he came to power in 1932.

5.69 There is evidence of the post-1925 view of the Irish government (insofar as this is relevant), during the passage in the United Kingdom parliament of the Statute of Westminster bill. On Friday, 18 November 1931, Winston Churchill, then a conservative backbench opponent of MacDonald's national government, claimed that the Irish Free State would be able to repudiate the 1921 treaty. This was reported by the press.

5.70 Cosgrave, as president of the executive council, wrote to MacDonald on 21 November 1931, and his letter was read to the commons the following Thursday: 'I need scarely impress upon you that the maintenance of the happy relations which now exist between our two countries', he wrote, 'is absolutely dependent upon the continued acceptance by each of us of the good faith of the other ... We have reiterated time and again that the Treaty is an agreement which can only be altered by consent. I mention this particularly, because there seems to be a mistaken view in some quarters that the solemnity of this instrument in our eyes could derive any additional strength from a [United Kingdom] Parliamentary law [such as the Statute of Westminster].'[51]

5.71 Cosgrave, as I have argued, was wrong about the 1921 treaty in international law, though not about its status as fundamental Irish law (as a result of the 1922 constituent assembly). But was he not correct about the 1925 agreement, which, in Irish law, was described as amending the 1921 treaty, but was – arguably – Irish Free State acceptance, in international law, of the border as an international frontier?[52]

Eamon de Valera undermines the 1921 Anglo-Irish treaty, 1932–1937

5.72 The Statute of Westminster 1931 had a paradoxical effect in Anglo-Irish relations.

5.73 London refused to save – that is, exclude – the two 1922 acts (as it did with Canada, Australia and New Zealand, but not South Africa) during the passage of the bill. This meant that, in United Kingdom law (extending to the Irish Free State?), the treaty was unilaterally amendable under section 2(2). But, from the Irish law point of view, the Constitution of the Irish Free State (Saorstát Eireann) Act 1922 was amendable in two ways: as regards the first schedule, by the

51 House of Commons, *Hansard*, 5th series, 260, 311, 24 November 1931.

52 There is published evidence that the Irish Free State government, then or subsequently, considered the 1925 agreement to be an obligation in international law. 'The basic principle of respect for treaties (*pacta sunt servanda*)', read a department of external affairs memorandum of 26 October 1969 (dealing with the implications for the 1925 agreement of the 1937 constitutional claim to Northern Ireland), 'means that they must not be unilaterally terminated. International relations would be very haphazard and unstable if changes of government or unilateral acts by governments were to mean a termination of their international commitments.' (Quoted in Enda Staunton, 'The Boundary Commission Debacle 1925', *History Ireland*, summer 1996, p. 45)

Oireachtas, under article 50 (the period of eight years being extended to 16 years by a 1929 act[53]); as regards the second schedule – 'the Scheduled Treaty' – only by agreements of the two governments confirmed by the two parliaments. (Cosgrave enacted 17 amendments under article 50, and, as noted, there were two changes under the treaty.) The forefront – as noted – was only amendable by another constituent assembly, if such could be summoned constitutionally.

5.74 The Irish Free State was legally, at the point at which power transferred to the anti-treatyite Fianna Fáil party on 9 March 1932, more pro-treaty than the United Kingdom. Eamon de Valera (who believed in the Irish republic proclaimed in Dublin in 1916) had, during the 1921 treaty negotiations, advanced the idea of 'external association' – voluntary membership of a commonwealth headed by a divisible sovereign.

5.75 From 1932, he set out as the new president of the executive council – using article 50 of the Irish Free State constitution (as amended by Cosgrave) – to change dominion home rule into external association by:

- one, removing the oath for members of the Oireachtas, in article 4 of the treaty, and articles 17 and 55 of the constitution, by section 1 of the following enactment;
- two, removing the treaty from Irish law, through section 2 of the Constitution (Removal of Oath) Act 1933, by repealing section 2 of the Constitution of the Irish Free State (Saorstát Eireann) Act 1922 (and schedule 2), and amending article 50 of the constitution;
- three, removing the right of appeal – 'special leave' – to the privy council, through the Constitution (Amendment No. 22) Act 1933, by repealing the proviso to article 66 of the constitution, this also applying to judgments pronounced by the Supreme Court before enactment;
- four, the downgrading of the governor-general, by appointment of Domhnall Ua Buachalla (Donal Buckley), and by the removal of his article 37 and 41 powers, through the twentieth and twenty-first constitutional amendments in 1933 (the governor-general survived until 11 December 1936);
- five, changing citizenship law, through the twenty-sixth constitutional amendment providing for extra-territoriality,[54] and the Aliens Act 1935 and the Irish Nationality and Citizenship Act 1935, enacted under article 3 of the constitution;
- six, abolition of Seanad Eireann, through the twenty-fourth constitutional amendment in 1936;
- seven, the twenty-seventh – and final – constitutional amendment of 11 December 1936 (required seemingly under the preamble to the Statute of Westminster 1931, whereby the abdication of Edward VIII was a matter legally for all dominion parliaments), which removed all references to the sovereign (and the governor-general) in the constitution by amending ten articles;[55]

53 The Constitution (Amendment No. 16) Act 1929. According to Leo Kohn, Cosgrave acted in deference to the opposition (*Constitution*, p. 257).

54 Permitted by section 3 of the Statute of Westminster 1931.

55 The Executive Powers (Consequential Provisions) Act 1937 had to be enacted on 8 June

- and eight, the enactment of the Executive Authority (External Relations) Act 1936, the following day (which did relate to the abdication), but also recognized the king as the head of the commonwealth, with the power – on advice of the Irish Free State government – to appoint diplomatic and consular representatives, and conclude international agreements.

5.76 After nearly five years, the Irish Free State was still a dominion (albeit – in Irish eyes[56] – externally associated with the British Commonwealth of Nations), but the crown – of symbolic importance to Lloyd George in 1921–22 – had been removed from the internal government of the state. The sovereign remained the head of the Irish Free State for the purposes of (some) external relations only.

5.77 De Valera had been extremely lucky not to have met with the opposition of the Irish Free State courts, under articles 65, 66 and 69 of the constitution.[57] He exploited – without acknowledgement – a judgment of the privy council following the Statute of Westminster 1931.

5.78 Among the legal risks he ran were:

- one, the abolition of the oath on 3 May 1933 (after a general election). Articles 17 and 55 of the constitution could be amended under article 50, but all amendments had to within the terms of the scheduled treaty, and article 4 of the treaty also contained the oath (this is why de Valera had to relate the abolition of the oath to the following change);
- two, the removal of the treaty from Irish law on 3 May 1933, by repeal of section 2 of the Constitution of the Irish Free State (Saorstát Eireann) Act 1922 (plus schedule 2). The Oireachtas did not have the power, under the constitution, to repeal the treaty. This was contrary to Irish law. And the Statute of Westminster 1931, if recognized as part of Irish law, applied to only the two 1922 United Kingdom acts (insofar as they applied in Ireland), not the (Irish) constituent act of 1922. Further, the forefront of the 1922 act was not part of United Kingdom law, and was not amendable in Irish law. (Seanad Eireann had tried to impose a condition precedent of a further agreement with the United Kingdom government in 1932–33, but de Valera overcame their delaying power);
- three, the removal of the right of appeal to the privy council on 16 November 1933, by the twenty-second constitutional amendment. Article 66 was amendable under article 50. But article 2 of the treaty (now supposedly expunged from Irish law) tied the Irish Free State to the law, practice and

1937 to deal with outstanding matters. Section 2 swept up any remaining powers of the king and governor-general and transferred them to the executive council. Section 7 allowed for retrospective effect.

56 But section 3(2) of the Executive Authority (External Relations) Act 1936 gave effect to the instrument of abdication upon the passing the act. The instrument scheduled referred to 'Edward the Eighth, of Great Britain, Ireland, and the British Dominions beyond the Seas, King, Emperor of India'.

57 The Irish Free State judges, who learned their law in the days of the old United Kingdom, were not inclined generally to use the powers of constitutional judicial review in the 1920s and the 1930s; a public safety measure of 1923 was held to be incapable of immediate application.

constitutional usage in Canada.[58] And there was binding privy council authority from 1926 for special leave being the law in Canada and therefore the Irish Free State.[59] Both states had failed politically to get changes in 1926 and 1930 at the imperial conferences. There was no longer repugnancy of dominion law to 'the law of England',[60] but this privy council case could have been followed, through the common law, by an Irish court.

5.79 De Valera was otherwise fortunate in the following judgments:

- one, *The State (Ryan) v Lennon* [1935] IR 170 (judgment on 19 December 1934), an Irish case on article 2A of the constitution (a public safety measure), enacted by Cosgrave in 1931 – the seventeenth constitutional amendment – but implemented by de Valera in 1933, which raised inter alia the question of the constitutionality of the sixteenth amendment (of article 50). (The prosecutors – as republicans – did not take a point about repugnancy to the treaty.) The government won the case, but not before Kennedy CJ dissented most powerfully, finding against the sixteenth and seventeenth amendments. There were troubling dicta. Fitzgibbon J, one of the majority of two, fired a shot across the bows of the executive on the question of the treaty,[61] and on the proposed citizenship act.[62] The treaty, the Supreme Court implied, had not been repealed in Irish law;
- two, *Moore v A-G* [1935] IR 472 PC (advice given on 6 June 1935), an Irish case which went to the privy council, six days before enactment of the twenty-second constitutional amendment on 16 November 1933. A preliminary point on the validity of the Irish act (the petitioners having been refused the record of proceedings by the Supreme Court in Dublin) was heard on 3 and 4 December 1934. The case was then adjourned in favour of a Canadian petition for special leave: *British Coal Corporation v R* [1935] AC 500 PC. Viscount Sankey LC advised that the Canadian petition was incompetent after the Statute of Westminster 1931;[63] the dominion had the right to end special leave for criminal cases. As for the Irish case, the lord chancellor advised that the Statute of Westminster 1931 was again decisive. Section 2 disapplied the Colonial Laws Validity Act 1865, and the Irish Free State had the power to repeal or amend any act of the United Kingdom parliament insofar as it was part of the law of the dominion. He gave short shrift to the – then unreported – *Ryan*'s case, and the submissions of Wilfrid Greene KC, on the root of title in Irish law, to the effect that the Constitution (Removal of Oath) Act 1933 and the twenty-second constitutional amendment were both invalid (the lord chancellor referred to 'what is called Irish law'[64]).

58 *Performing Rights Society v Bray Urban District Council* [1930] AC 377, 394–6 per Viscount Sankey LC.

59 *Nadan v R* [1926] AC 482 PC.

60 Section 2(2) of the Statute of Westminster 1931.

61 He stated section 3 of the Constitution (Removal of Oath) Act 1933 was 'totally ineffective', and that the Oireachtas had no power to amend (the forefront of) the constituent act (p. 227).

62 Pages 227 & 236–7.

63 Sections 2(1), 3 and 7(1).

64 Page 485.

5.80 De Valera was vindicated by the lord chancellor of England and Wales, though he never sought to use this Westminster-centred view. The treaty, as part of United Kingdom law, was repealable by the Irish Free State (according to the lord chancellor). The treaty as a political or international agreement – 'any contractual obligation' – was disregarded by the privy council. And no credence was paid the – Irish – point that the treaty had been given legal form, in Irish law, by the constituent assembly.

5.81 *Ryan*'s case in the Supreme Court (which was about the 1931 public security measure) – it is submitted – contains in part the correct answer to de Valera's unconstitutional incremental undermining of the treaty (not reflected in the final majority decision), even if Kennedy CJ and Fitzgibbon J were unwilling to acknowledge article 83 of the Irish constitution.[65] *Moore*'s case (which was about the privy council), even if it is correct on United Kingdom law (the applicability of the Colonial Laws Validity Act 1865 is doubted), does not address the question of the treaty in the Irish Free State being part of Irish law.[66]

5.82 The majority in *Ryan*'s case (plus Kennedy CJ) erred in refusing to admit more than Irish law, while Viscount Sankey LC, in *Moore*'s case, made exactly the opposite mistake, considering only United Kingdom law – while this may be the logic of jurisdiction, the interrelationship between Irish law and United Kingdom law was constitutionally significant given the legal creation of one state by the other.[67]

5.83 De Valera was not satisfied with his external association of late 1936, having had the idea of a new constitution in mind for some time; Kennedy CJ died in office on 12 December 1936 aged 57 years. The reason de Valera gave for going even further is interesting: 'The Courts [in the Irish Free State] have expressed certain opinions in dealing with certain cases and made certain suggestions as to their views about the powers [in the Oireachtas] to pass Acts in relation to the terms of the Treaty. We were not going to risk a[n Irish Free State] Constitution like this ... being enacted here and being operated with such possible views held by the courts.'[68]

5.84 The judiciary was bound by the declarations made on appointment, under article 68 of the constitution and section 99 of the Courts of Justice Act 1924, to 'uphold the Constitution ... as by law established'. De Valera now had to mastermind a legal revolution (involving changes to the High and Supreme Courts).

65 Murnaghan J did mention it, while declining to go into the adoption of the constitution (p. 238).

66 This was refuted by an analysis of the two 1922 United Kingdom acts: Viscount Sankey LC held that the first act had not given the provisional parliament the power to enact a constitution; the constituent act was ratified by the second United Kingdom act: 'The Treaty received the force of law, both in the United Kingdom and in Ireland by reason of the passing of an Act of the Imperial Parliament; and the Constituent Act owed its validity to the same authority ... The [1931] Statute alone gives to the Oireachtas power to repeal or amend the Constituent Act, which has the force of an Imperial enactment.' (pp. 479 & 486)

67 For a discussion of the two jurisdictions, see O. Hood Phillips, '*Ryan's Case*' (1936) 206 LQR 241.

68 Dáil Éireann, *Official Reports*, col. 416, 13 May 1937.

6

Domestic Law: Éire/Ireland, 1937–1998

6.1 This chapter continues with the domestic law of the Irish state by looking at (a) the enactment of Bunreacht na hÉireann (BNH), 1937; (b) Éire/Ireland a new state?; (c) *Hibernia Irredenta*, the Irish constitutional claim to Northern Ireland; and (d) constitutional developments, 1937–1998. The use of the name Éire/Ireland (for the years 1937–1949) is explained in Chapter 7, dealing with nomenclature in general. This chapter, along with Chapter 5, is a necessary historical introduction to Part 2 (Constitution) and also Part 3 (Institutions). The idea of state succession in 1937 has not been canvassed directly in United Kingdom or Irish law hitherto. This chapter's principal focus is the Irish territorial claim to Northern Ireland. The relationship between nation and state in Irish law became a problem in 1937, which impacted negatively in Northern Ireland and Great Britain. It was an important topic in the 1996–98 multi-party negotations, and the significance of the Belfast Agreement solution will be assessed in Chapter 11. Here, the background to the Irish government's case is considered.

The enactment of Bunreacht na hÉireann, 1937

6.2 The legal revolution in Ireland took place in 1937 not in 1919 or 1922.[1] De Valera decided to go to the people, who had not been involved in the constitution of the Irish Free State.[2] The Fianna Fáil leader, having achieved external association unexpectedly, needed a new – internal – republican constitution (this had been announced first in May 1935). Its cornerstone was the already-existing Executive Authority (External Relations) Act 1936. And the directly elected president who was to replace the governor-general would not be described expressly as head of state.[3]

6.3 The draft constitution was published on 1 May 1937, and only approved by Dáil Éireann on 14 June 1937. On 2 June 1937, the Oireachtas had enacted the Plebiscite (Draft Constitution) Act. There was provision for a plebiscite coinciding with the next general election, and de Valera is thought to have selected the date of 1 July 1937 the previous March. The question was whether voters favoured the draft constitution approved by the Dáil. The draft constitution was to be voted upon 'throughout Saorstát Éireann', defined in Irish law as the 26 counties.[4]

1 *Commissioners of Public Works v Kavanagh* [1962] IR 216, 225–6 per Ó Dálaigh J; *The Criminal Law (Jurisdiction) Bill, 1975* [1977] IR 129, 147 per O'Higgins CJ.

2 Articles 2, 12, 14, 47 (amended), 48 (amended), 50 (amended) & 51 of the Irish Free State constitution; Dáil Éireann, *Official Reports*, 416, 13 May 1937; BNH, article 49.

3 The British Commonwealth of Nations was to be hidden away in article 29.4.2 as 'any group or league of nations'. The All-Party Oireachtas Committee on the Constitution has advised against calling the Irish president head of state: *Third Progress Report: The President*, Pn 6250, Dublin Stationery Office, 1998, pp. 3–4.

4 Section 1 of the Treaty (Confirmation of Amending Agreement) Act 1925. De Valera told

6.4 De Valera was bound by the Irish Free State constitution, but he avoided enactment of his 1937 draft by the Oireachtas. The treaty was still extant in Irish law, and Dáil Éireann (there was no Seanad Éireann) did not have the power under article 12 to enact a new constitution. That was for a new constituent assembly only. The plebiscite on 1 July 1937 (as opposed to its organization) was not constitutional, which is why enactment by the people (as it was dubbed) was a legal revolution.

6.5 It was only enacted narrowly, by 685,105 votes to 526,945 – a majority of 158,160. The turnout was less than in the simultaneous general election, and the 86,065 who voted for the constitution but not Fianna Fáil as first preference, were outnumbered by the nearly 10 per cent who spoiled their vote. There were majorities against in Dublin Townships, West Cork, Co. Dublin, Co. Sligo and Co. Wicklow.[5] 'The people', de Valera intimated to the United States minister, 'had not understood the importance of the fundamental measure.'[6]

6.6 Article 48 provided for the repeal of the Irish Free State constitution, from the date of coming into operation. Under article 62, this was either after an interval of 180 days, or sooner if the Dáil so decided. De Valera did not let the Dáil (operating under the Irish Free State constitution) decide,[7] and Bunreacht na hÉireann came into operation on 29 December 1937 (without legal challenge to its validity).

6.7 Bunreacht na hÉireann means literally constitution of Ireland. However, the version voted upon by the people, and published by the Stationery Office (in the series of Irish acts) has a gaelic heading above the preamble on the English and Irish texts.[8] It is for this reason that Bunreacht na hÉireann, abbreviated to BNH, is the correct way to refer to the constitution of Ireland.[9] This was not discussed by the Constitution Review Group in its *Report* of 1996. But the All-Party Oireachtas Committee on the Constitution appears to be following the practice.[10] The first published version had '(Constitution of Ireland)' on a title page (not part of the constitution), but this was merely an aid to non-Irish speakers.

6.8 De Valera had reduced the High Court from seven to five, and increased the Supreme Court from three to five (though the Irish Free State courts would continue until 1961 under article 58[11]). He made Timothy Sullivan chief justice. De Valera's first attorney-general, Conor A. Maguire KC, was promoted to president of the High Court. His successor, James Geoghegan KC, was one of the new Supreme Court appointees. Finally, George Gavan Duffy KC (the treaty signatory

the Dáil that 'the majority of the people' (in the 26 counties) would be acting 'on behalf of the whole' (in the 32 counties) (Dáil Éireann, *Official Reports*, 1912–13, 4 June 1937).

5 *Iris Oifigiúil*, 16 July 1937.

6 Quoted in Deirdre McMahon, *Republicans and Imperialists: Anglo-Irish relations in the 1930s*, London 1984, p. 221.

7 The clerk to the Dáil insisted successfully that he be responsible for transmission of BNH (though it was not legislation) to the Supreme Court for enrolment.

8 This is the position with the most recently published edition.

9 The English referent is used in the Interpretation Act 1937 s 1 and the Constitution (Consequential Provisions) Act 1937 s 1.

10 *Third Report: The President*, Pn 6250, Dublin Stationery Office 1998, p. 10.

11 Courts (Establishment and Constitution) Act 1961.

turned Free State critic) – who would become the leading interpreter of BNH – was made a High Court judge.

6.9 Article 58 required the judiciary to make and subscribe a declaration (in article 34.5) to 'uphold the Constitution and the laws', any judge or justice declining or neglecting to do so immediately or as soon as may be thereafter being deemed to have resigned. A new judicial oath was symptomatic of a legal revolution.

6.10 Dáil Éireann had had no role in the enactment of BNH. However, two pieces of legislation were necessary before 29 December 1937.

6.11 The Interpretation Act 1937 (enacted on 8 December) disapplied the 1923 act as regards the new Oireachtas. De Valera dispensed with the lineage of the first, second and third Dáils (though the numbering remained); this was to be year zero under his new constitution. Seanad Éireann was also a new upper house.

6.12 The Constitution (Consequential Provisions) Act 1937 (enacted on 17 December) included such things as the construing of 'Irish Free State' as Ireland, excluding 'any area which is, for the time being, not within the area and extent of application of the laws enacted by the Oireachtas' (section 2); and the waiving of punishments of the constitution (special powers) tribunal[12] by the government, 'except in capital cases' (section 13).

6.13 BNH was more than twice the length of the 1922 constitution (as I will now refer to it); it was also better drafted with clearer layout. Much of the old constitution, however, was adopted. That had the English text on the recto page, but BNH (article 63 stated that the Irish text prevailed in cases of conflict) had the Irish version – in gaelic type which would be amended in roman – on the recto page.

6.14 I use the 1937 Stationary Office edition in the series of public general acts of the Irish Free State and Éire/Ireland. It is the one closest to the draft constitution (which had the national language in roman type) on which the people voted,[13] though amendments have to be followed in later editions. Dáil Eireann, for example, appears without the second fada, as in the 1938 enrolled copy.

6.15 Under article 63, 'conclusive evidence of the provisions of th[e] Constitution' is provided by the copy enrolled in the office of the registrar of the Supreme Court. A certified copy[14] – signed by the taoiseach, the chief justice and the chairman of Dáil Éireann – was enrolled on 18 February 1938. Article 25.5 (inserted by the legislature in 1941) empowered the taoiseach 'from time to time as occasion appears to him to require' to enroll a new definitive version, authenticated by the taoiseach and chief justice and signed by the president. This happened on 25 March 1942, again on 24 December 1980, and most recently on 23 March 1990. The latter is the definitive version. Articles 51.4 and 52.1 envisage published editions without the transitory provisions (which are present only in the 1937 edition[15]). Unfortunately, there are differences: 'alteration of

12 Set up under article 2A of the Irish Free State constitution.

13 The draft constitution had been passed by Dáil Éireann on 14 June 1937.

14 The clerk of the Dáil certified on 31 January 1938 that the copy corresponded to that passed as the draft constitution.

15 They were published separately as *Forálltí Sealadacha de Bhunreacht na hÉireann*, Dublin Stationery Office, 1984, PP 63/9.

typography, standardisation of spelling, grammatical modernisations, correction of mistakes, and a variety of heterogenous grammatical alterations'.[16]

6.16 In his 1935 St Patrick's day broadcast to the United States, de Valera had described 'Ireland ... [as] a Christian and a Catholic nation'.[17] 'This historic document', began a draft teaching guide to BNH produced by official sources, 'asserts in clear terms that it has been conceived for the governing of a people both Catholic and Irish'.[18]

6.17 BNH began with a preamble by 'the people of Éire'. There followed articles 1–3 on the nation. The next part was the state (articles 4–11). The state was then configured: the president (articles 12–14); the national parliament, known as the Oireachtas (articles 15–27); the government (a modest article 28, but with 12 sections); international relations (article 29); various offices of state (articles 30–33); courts and justice (articles 34–39); fundamental rights (articles 40–44) plus directive principles of social policy (article 45); amendment (articles 46–47); repeal of the 1922 constitution and continuance of laws (articles 48–50); and transitory provisions (articles 51–63, being omitted subsequently).

6.18 There were considerable institutional continuities, but the main constitutional innovations were:

- a Christian (trinitarian) ethos in the preamble and the fundamental rights articles, including the 'special position' of the catholic church in article 44;
- the fundamental concept of the Irish nation – what de Valera called otherwise 'the Irish people'[19] – legitimizing the state;
- the idea of a 'national territory' – the island of Ireland – in articles 2 and 3, called, in article 4, Éire or Ireland;
- the superiority of the 'national language' (Irish) to English (article 8);
- a directly elected president along side the sovereign recognized by the dominions[20];
- greater constitutional judicial review (articles 34.3.2 and 34.4.4 & 5 plus 28.2 and 29.4.1), including presidential referral of bills to the supreme court (articles 26);
- a government with more powers than the United Kingdom cabinet, with a head called the taoiseach;
- provisions for international relations, though the Executive Authority (External Relations) Act 1936 still governed external relations;
- the fundamental rights articles, and the general guidance on social policy;

16 Richard F. Humphrey, 'The Constitution of Ireland: the forgotten textual quagmire', *Irish Jurist*, n.s., XXII, part I, summer 1987, p. 169 at 171. Humphrey compared the 1938 enrolled copy with a 1978 edition.

17 Quoted in J. Bowyer Bell, *The Irish Troubles: a generation of violence, 1967–92*, Dublin 1993, p. 24.

18 S10108, Dept. of the Taoiseach, National Archives, Dublin. See also, Sean T. O'Kelly, a future president of Ireland, on 24 June 1937, quoted in J.J. Lee, *Ireland, 1912–1985: politics and society*, Cambridge 1989, p. 206.

19 See, for example, his speech outside Leinster House, on 10 December 1925, at the time of the recognition of Northern Ireland (Dorothy Macardle, *The Irish Republic*, London 1974, p. 816).

20 Section 3(1) of the Executive Authority (External Relations) Act 1936.

- after three years, amendment by referendum only.[21]

Éire/Ireland a new state?

6.19 There is no doubt that the Irish Free State was, in the 26 counties, the successor state to the United Kingdom of Great Britain and Ireland.[22] (Northern Ireland was neither a state, nor a successor.) Given that there is little doubt about statehood in Ireland in 1937, was Éire/Ireland a successor to the Irish Free State? The answer would appear to be yes.

6.20 State succession refers to a set of historical facts, and is not a presumption about the transmission of legal rights and duties. It is the permanent transfer of territorial sovereignty within international law, and the means by which it occurs include the total dismemberment of an existing state. Problems concerning treaties, nationality and international claims may be preempted in international and municipal law by a number of mechanisms: treaty, acquiescence or estoppel.

6.21 The Irish Free State came to an end on 29 December 1937, under article 48 of BNH. There was no United Kingdom law contradicting this, though Éire/Ireland was considered to be still a dominion.[23] There is no reason in international law to query Irish municipal law.

6.22 Éire/Ireland came into existence on the same day. Was it a new legal person? It replaced the Irish Free State at the League of Nations, but that was a matter under the constitution of this international organization. There seems to have been no question of a new state as such in international law (or of recognition *de novo*). Éire/Ireland was treated as a successor state in its international relations.

6.23 BNH, and the associated legislation, addressed the question in municipal law. The Executive Authority (External Relations) Act 1936 was, of course, an act of the Irish Free State, which, under article 50 of BNH, continued to be the law where it did not conflict with the constitution.

6.24 BNH, in article 49.3, described the government as 'the successors of the Government of Saorstát Eireann as regards all property, assets, rights and liabilities'. There were many changes: of name, from Irish Free State to Éire/ Ireland; of territory, from 26–32 counties; of the basis of executive authority, from the king to the people; of political culture, from liberal democracy towards catholic nationalism. There was – as the late Professor Kelly,[24] after K.C. Wheare,[25] wrote – a supplanting of a disputed (United Kingdom versus Irish) *Grundnorm* by a new one.

21 Article 51 allowed the Oireachtas to amend BNH until 25 June 1941. There were two acts, on 2 September 1939 and 30 May 1941. There were no changes by referendum until 1962, this being a phenomenon of the 1970s (five), 1980s (three) and 1990s (eight). There have been 17 successful amendments, the two most important areas being Europe and personal rights.

22 *Irish Free State V Guaranty Safe Deposit Co* 129 Misc. NY 551, 562–3, 565 (1927); 222 NYS 182 (1927) per Peters J. Article 80 of the 1922 constitution described the government of the Irish Free State as 'the successors' to the provisional government (which existed, of course, in United Kingdom law).

23 *The Times*, 30 December 1937; *Murray v Parkes* [1942] 2 KB 123.

24 John Maurice Kelly, *Irish Constitution*, 3rd edn, by Gerard Hogan & Gerry Whyte, Dublin 1994, p. 3.

25 *The Constitutional Structure of the Commonwealth*, London 1961, p. 94.

6.25 Subsequent legislation bears out the new *Grundnorm*. The Interpretation Act 1937, in breaking the connection with the Irish Free State, also cut Éire/Ireland off from the revolutionary Dáil regime. The Constitution (Consequential Provisions) Act 1937, as noted, provided for the general adaptation of Saorstát Éireann in existing laws. It was to be construed and have effect: as meaning the 26 counties before 29 December 1937; and as meaning 'Ireland' afterwards, though – following article 3 of BNH – Ireland would not include any area outside the jurisdiction of the Oireachtas.

6.26 State succession raises the problem of existing treaties. The general rule – in the law of treaties – is one of non-transmissibility; the new state starts with a clean slate. The 1978 Vienna convention on succession of states in respect of treaties[26] (though it applies only to successions after entry into force) partly codifies customary international law. Article 11 on boundary regimes reads: 'A succession of States does not as such affect: (a) a boundary established by a treaty; or (b) obligations and rights established by a treaty and relating to the rEgime of a boundary.'[27]

6.27 The 1921 treaty, in Irish law, was repealed from 29 December 1937. And the United Kingdom had, in its law, given this power to the Irish Free State in the Statute of Westminster 1931. It was not in any case a treaty in international law.

6.28 The 1925 treaty, discussed above, is another matter. Most likely, it did not disappear with the Irish Free State. There is an argument that de Valera, in advancing a new constitution in 1935–37 (which claimed Northern Ireland), was breaching the Irish state's international obligations. The 1925 treaty continued to apply after 29 December 1937. Éire/Ireland was from its creation out of step with international law in this regard.

Hibernia Irredenta, the Irish constitutional claim to Northern Ireland

6.29 J.J. McElligott, head of the civil service, had advised de Valera on 23 March 1937, against giving 'a permanent place in the Constitution to a claim to "Hibernia Irredenta"'. Articles 1–3 were criticized as embodying the fiction of an Irish nation, as being offensive to 'neighbouring countries' and as setting back the practical prospects of unity.

6.30 He also offered legal advice: 'From the point of view of international law, it is not clear whether we are on safe ground in claiming sovereignty and jurisdiction over land recognised internationally, de jure and de facto, as belonging to another country. The doctrine of repugnance finds a place in our Constitution [a reference to the treaty], and this doctrine may be used against use ... and may expose us to the risk of adverse judgment from international bodies such as the League of Nations or the Hague Court.'[28]

26 Presented to Parliament, January 1980, Cmnd 7760.

27 See also *Case Concerning the Frontier Dispute (Burkina Faso-Mali)*, ICJ Reports 1986, p. 554 at 566.

28 S 9715A, Dept. of the Taoiseach, National Archives, Dublin; quoted in Ronan Fanning, *The Irish Department of Finance, 1922–58*, Dublin 1978, p. 267, & John Bowman, *De Valera and the Ulster Question, 1917–1973*, Oxford 1989, p. 148. Similar advice came from Diarmuid O'Crowley, the disenchanted republican judge of 1920–22, in the *Irish Independent*, 10 May

6.31 BNH was front loaded with nation-state pretension,[29] including the specific territorial claim to Northern Ireland in articles 2 and 3. The key innovations were:

- the preamble, containing a catholic nationalist historiography;
- article 1, an affirmation of national sovereignty;
- article 2, a definition of the national territory: 'The national territory consists of the whole island of Ireland, its islands and the territorial seas';
- article 3, jurisdiction: 'Pending the re-integration of the national territory, and without prejudice to the right of the Parliament and Government established by this Constitution to exercise jurisdiction over the whole of that territory, the laws enacted by that Parliament shall have the like area and extent of application as the laws of Saorstát Eireann and the like extra-territorial effect';
- article 4, naming the state Éire or Ireland;
- article 5: 'Ireland is a sovereign, independent, democratic state';
- article 7, a national flag: the green, white and orange tricolour (a republican emblem);
- article 8, treating Irish – the national language – as the first official language, and English as a (sic) second official language;
- article 9, on 'citizen of Ireland', requiring 'fidelity to the nation' and 'loyalty to the State'.[30]

The United Kingdom law view

6.32 London had given up defending the 1921 treaty, and it was embroiled in an economic war with de Valera when he enacted BNH. The government's Irish situation committee considered – and rejected – doing nothing: 'If we were to accept the change *sub silentio*', advised Malcolm MacDonald, the dominions secretary, 'would not our action be tantamount to a recognition of the claim set forth in Clauses 2 and 3 of the Constitution ... to the whole of the island!'[31]

6.33 BNH – despite its presentation as an 'internal' constitution – was met with the immediate response of a press statement in *The Times* (parliament was in recess) on 30 December 1937. The United Kingdom government associated Canada (listed first), Australia, New Zealand and South Africa with its response to articles 2, 3 *and* 4:

> His Majesty's Government in the United Kingdom ... cannot recognize that the adoption of the name Eire or Ireland, or other provisions of those Articles, involves any right to territory or jurisdiction over territory forming part of the United Kingdom of Great Britain and Northern Ireland, or affects in any way the position of Northern Ireland as

1937. The original of the document has the phrase 'this doctrine may be used against us ...' underlined, with a manuscript exclamation mark in the margin (the hand was probably de Valera's).

29 In 1919–21, Dáil Éireann referred to the United Kingdom government as a pretender.

30 Other variations mainly on the theme of 'Ireland' are: 'a President of Ireland (*Uachtarán na hÉireann*)' (article 12.1); 'Constitution of Ireland' and 'the welfare of the people of Ireland' (article 12.8); 'National Parliament' (heading to articles 15–27); 'the people' (taken from the preamble and used in articles 27, 30.3, 46.2, 47.1, 47.2.1–2); 'Ireland' in article 29; the exclusion of non-belief in the definition of religion (article 44).

31 CP 300/37, Cab 24/273, PRO.

> an integral part of the United Kingdom of Great Britain and Northern Ireland. They therefore regard the use of the name Eire or Ireland in this connexion as relating only to that area which has hitherto been known as the Irish Free State.

There could be a 26-county Éire or Ireland (a historical name associated with the island). That was the only way to coexist with the United Kingdom of Great Britain and Northern Ireland.

6.34 The Eire (Confirmation of Agreement) Act 1938 – which returned the ports retained under articles 6 and 7 of the treaty,[32] and implemented financial and trade agreements of 25 April 1938[33] – stated in section 1: 'The territory which, in accordance with the provisions of the Irish Free State (Agreement) Act, 1922, and the Irish Free State Constitution Act, 1922 (Session 2) was required to be styled and known as the Irish Free State shall be styled and known as Eire, and accordingly, references in any enactment to the Irish Free State shall be construed as references to Eire.'

6.35 This was a change in United Kingdom law. The Statute of Westminster 1931 allowed the United Kingdom to legislate for a dominion, only if it was expressly declared that the dominion had so requested and consented. This was not Westminster purporting to legislate for the 26 counties; it was the United Kingdom parliament legislating to defend Northern Ireland (following BNH) and construing references to the Irish Free State in its own laws. The United Kingdom could live with the name Eire, precisely because it was not – for English speakers – geographical Ireland.

6.36 In international law, the United Kingdom was not able – because of Éire meaning Ireland – to follow the practice of not naming other states. In any case, the United Kingdom treated Éire as still part of the commonwealth, and de Valera – committed to external association – did not negate this in any way. Just as there was an Irish-law name for the successor to the Irish Free State, so there was from 17 May 1938 a new name in United Kingdom law.

The Irish law view

6.37 The jurisprudence produced by judicial interpretation of BNH is, on the basis of Kennedy CJ's canonical legal historiography of the 1922 constituent act,[34] remarkably uncritical of the Ireland-a-nation aspiration. The common law on the territorial claim developed as follows:

32 Indicating it was still good law in the United Kingdom: section 2(2). Éire, in contrast, did not legislate. Query: did the government have the terms approved under article 29.5.2 of BNH?

33 The status of these agreements is uncertain. Query: did the Éire government have the terms approved under article 29.5.2 of BNH? It is unlikely. The Executive Authority (External Relations) Act 1936, which referred to treaty-making powers, required the sovereign to act on the advise of the executive council (section 3(1)). But George VI could not make an international agreement with himself. Instead, the Éire government legislated consequentially: Agreement with United Kingdom (Capital Sum) Act 1938; Finance (Agreement with United Kingdom) Act 1938. As for the United Kingdom, there was an attempt to follow the 1924 and 1925 precedents, having the overall agreement confirmed by Westminster. It seems that the United Kingdom government's 'subject to Parliamentary confirmation' means it was not signing a treaty.

34 *The State (Ryan) v Lennon* [1935] IR 170, 203–12.

- (of dicta on the preamble and article 1, *Byrne v Ireland* [1972] IR 241, 296 per Budd J[35] located sovereignty in the people: 'Article 1 itself underlines that it is the nation, which can only be a reference to the People, which has the sovereign right to choose its form of government.' But this people, under section 2 of the Plebiscite (Draft Constitution) Act 1937, were the electors of the 26 counties only);
- *People (AG) v Ruttledge* [1978] IR 376, 379–80 per O'Byrne J (other members of the Supreme Court agreeing) – a case decided in 1947 – where it was held that 'the whole of Ireland is included in the national territory of the State', but 'the laws enacted by the Oireachtas do not purport and are not intended to bind the six counties of Northern Ireland';
- *Boland v An Taoiseach* [1974] IR 338, a Supreme Court case on the 1973 Sunningdale agreement, in particular a draft joint declaration on the status of Northern Ireland, where the Irish government secured a Pyhrric legal victory (because it was seen to be politically irredentist[36]) by adopting a minimalist legal position of denying all allegations. O'Keefe P stated that it would have been unconstitutional for the Irish government to have acknowledged that it did not have a legitimate claim to Northern Ireland (363–4);
- *The Criminal Law (Jurisdiction) Bill 1975* [1977] IR 129, another Supreme Court case, an article 26 – presidential – referral,[37] where O'Higgins CJ held that articles 2 and 3 were aspirational: 'It is true that the Constitution is a legal document, but it is a fundamental one which establishes the State and it expresses not only legal norms but basic doctrines of political and social theory ... The Constitution contains more than legal rules: it reflects, in part, aspirations and aims and expresses the political theories on which the people acted when they enacted the Constitution ... Th[e] national claim to unity exists not in the legal but in the political order ...' (147)
- *McGimpsey v Ireland* [1988] IR 567; [1990] IR 110, the case (after *Boland*) brought by two Northern Ireland unionists following the 1985 Anglo-Irish Agreement, where Barrington J in the High Court tended to followed O'Higgins CJ's judgment of 1976 on 'a nationalist constitution' (583),[38] but Finlay CJ in the Supreme Court (the other four judges agreeing) – following Hederman J's dictum about 'a constitutional imperative' in *Russell v Fanning* [1988] IR 505, 537 – chose to apply O'Byrne J's judgment of 1947 and the *Boland* case of 1974 to the effect that article 2 was a claim of legal right (119) ('an unequivocal claim of legal right', per McCarthy J (125)), but – a point

35 Also, Walsh J (264).

36 Garret FitzGerald, *All in a Life*, London 1989, pp. 222 & 226–7.

37 There was also a Sunningdale connection. The 1974 *Report of the Law Enforcement Commission* on extradiction had recommended extra-territorial jurisdiction. The United Kingdom parliament enacted on 7 August 1975: Criminal Jurisdiction Act 1975 s 5(1) and Schedule 4. The Oireachtas followed on 3 March 1976. Following the case, it was enacted as the Criminal Law (Jurisdiction) Act 1976.

38 See also *McGlinchey v Ireland (No 2)* [1990] 2 IR 220, where Costello J, before the *McGimpsey* appeal in the Supreme Court, followed O'Higgins CJ and Barrington J (plus *The State (Gilsenan) v McMurrow* [1978] IR 360), holding that there was no constitutional restriction on the Oireachtas enacting so that a citizen might be handed over to the RUC.

little noted – article 3 was a disclaimer of acquiescence, prescription or estoppel (in international law) as regards 'the frontier at present existing between the State and Northern Ireland ... [being] conclusive of the matter' (119);

- (dicta to the effect that the English-language name of the state – in Irish law – is 'Ireland': *People (AG) v Ruttledge* [1978] IR 376, 379 per O'Byrne J; *Byrne v Ireland* [1972] IR 241, 261 per Walsh J; *Ellis v O'Dea* [1989] IR 530, 539–40 per Walsh J.)

6.38 In the more than six decades of BNH, the major judgments were produced during the Northern Ireland troubles which commenced in the late 1960s. O'Higgins CJ's aspirational view of articles 2 and 3 of 1976 did not liberalize Irish constitutional law.[39] Finlay CJ's strong nationalist reassertion – in the political context of 1990 – meant that the end of the territorial claim was likely to come sooner rather than later.

Constitutional developments, 1937–1998

6.39 Despite the 60-plus years of de Valera's constitution, most of the developments under this head were not brought to fruition.

The 1949 declaration of the Republic of Ireland

6.40 Why did de Valera not have the people enact a republican constitution after 1936? Aside from any question of United Kingdom opposition (probably exaggerated), the most likely reason is that the Irish republic of 1916 could not be realized in a 26-county state; the desire to maintain good relations with the six counties – de Valera's proffered reason for staying in the commonwealth – is not particularly convincing.

6.41 Before losing power in 1948, difficulties over diplomatic appointments led de Valera to consider repealing his 1936 act. But it was Sean MacBride,[40] the new minister of external affairs in John A. Costello's coalition government, who pushed for a definitive quitting of the commonwealth. The result was the – short – Republic of Ireland Act 1948;[41]

> 1 The Executive Authority (External Relations) Act, 1936 ... is hereby repealed.
> 2 It is hereby declared that the description of the State shall be the Republic of Ireland.
> 3 The President, on the authority and on the advice of the Government, may exercise the executive power or any executive function of the State in or in connection with its external relations.
> 4 ...
> 5 ...

The act's coming into operation was delayed, because the United Kingdom raised its own legal vulnerability internationally at the hands of most-favoured-nation states (desiring similar trade and citizenship privileges to Éire). Eventually, the

39 Hon. Mr Justice John Kenny, 'The advantages of a written constitution incorporating a bill of rights', NILQ, 30, 2, autumn 1977, pp. 189–206, 203–6.

40 See the article by Dick Walsh – 'MacBride's spinning set up a Taoiseach on tour' – in the *Irish Times*, 5 April 1999.

41 The Irish title – Acta Phoblacht na hÉireann 1948 – took precedent under article 25.4.6 (added in 1941) since the act had been passed in both official languages.

Republic of Ireland was declared – on the appointed day – on Easter Monday (18 April), 1949. (I will henceforth refer to the Republic of Ireland [ROI] for the period from 1949.)

6.42 Article 5 of BNH described 'Ireland [as] a sovereign, independent, democratic state', and remained unchanged. So did the constitutional name, Éire/Ireland, in article 4. The new statutory name, the ROI, according to the 1948 act (it was agreed only five days before presentation to the Dáil), was a 'description' of the state.

6.43 This second declaration of a republic was much less significant than the final departure from the commonwealth. Hitherto, membership had been thought to be mutual; the United Kingdom now accepted that a member state could leave of its own volition. Costello, leader of a pro-commonwealth party, and cognizant of the practical difficulties, had hoped for some sort of associate membership.

6.44 Éire/Ireland, under article 29.4.2 of BNH, had remained within the commonwealth, while legally describing the relationship as external association (the United Kingdom government accepting there had been constitutional change in 1936–37). In 1948, de Valera's political opponents – by repealing the Executive Authority (External Relations) Act 1936 – cut the last ties with the commonwealth.

6.45 This was recognized subsequently by the United Kingdom parliament on 2 June 1949, in the Ireland Act 1949:

> 1(1) It is hereby recognized and declared that the part of Ireland heretofore known as Eire ceased, as from the eighteenth day of April, nineteen hundred and forty-nine, to be part of His Majesty's dominions.
>
> 1(2) ...
>
> 1(3) The part of Ireland referred to in subsection (1) of this section is hereafter in this Act referred to, and may in any Act ... after the passing of this Act be referred to, by the name attributed thereto by the law thereof, that is to say, as the Republic of Ireland.

The United Kingdom parliament, of course, in responding to the Republic of Ireland Act 1948, did not take account of the constitutional name in the preamble and article 4 of BNH (which was also the United Kingdom law name). It is possible to construe section 1(3) of the Ireland Act 1949 as allowing for the name Republic of Ireland or Eire.

6.46 The rest of the Ireland Act 1949 went on to provide for ROI not to be a foreign country for the purposes of law (section 2);[42] the operation of the British Nationality Act 1948 to allow for reciprocal citizenship (section 5); a three-month residence qualification for electors in Northern Ireland (section 6).

The proposed constitutional reforms of 1967

6.47 Sean Lemass had not been keen on a new constitution in the 1930s, and, when he succeeded de Valera in 1959, he hinted at reform. Shortly before resigning

42 London continued to handle relations with Dublin through the Commonwealth Relations Office, until it merged with the Foreign Office in October 1968.

in 1966, he appointed an informal, all-party committee on the constitution (which he joined as a back bencher), chaired by George Colley.[43]

6.48 The unanimous *Report of the Committee on the Constitution*[44] of December 1967 made no recommendations as regards article 2. However, it recommended amending – on the basis of a draft by Prof. John Kelly – article 3:

> 1 The Irish nation hereby proclaims its firm will that its territory be re-united in harmony and brotherly affection between all Irishmen.
>
> 2 The laws enacted by the Parliament established by the Constitution shall, until the achievement of the nation's unity shall otherwise require, have the like area and extent of application as the laws of the Parliament which existed prior to the adoption of this Constitution. Provision may be made by law to give extra-territorial effect to such laws.[45]

While the territorial claim would still have remained, the reference to reuniting Ireland 'in harmony and brotherly affection between all Irishmen' presaged a cultural revolution against de Valeraism.

6.49 Other proposed changes included: 'Ireland' as the English-language name of the state (article 4); adding the description 'republic' to article 5; the right to divorce for non-catholics (article 41.3.2 – the constitutional ban – would be removed in 1995); and removing the reference to the 'special position' of the catholic church (and all other churches) in article 44.1.2–3 (which was done in 1972).

6.50 This interim report was overtaken by the outbreak of the Northern Ireland troubles in October 1968. It represented a high point of thinking about reform. The milestones of relative failure over the following 30 years were:

- an inter-party committee on the implications of Irish unity, established by Jack Lynch (1972–73);
- an all-party committee on lasting reconciliation, established by Liam Cosgrave (1973–75);
- a constitution review body chaired by the attorney general in 1982, following Garret FitzGerald's call for a constitutional crusade;
- the new Ireland forum of 1983–84, which came up with the solutions of a unitary state, a federal/confederal state or joint authority and talked about 'a new Ireland ... requir[ing] a new constitution';[46]
- an exception: the Progressive Democrats' *Constitution for a New Republic* (1988), which emphasized the concept of consent;
- the defeat of Proinias de Rossa's private member's bill, on amending articles 2 and 3,[47] by 74 votes to 66 (on second reading) in December 1990;[48]

43 Prof. John Kelly had called for constitutional revision, especially of articles 2 and 3, in the legal periodical he edited (*Irish Jurist*, 1966, pp. 1–15 & 1967, pp. 296–8).

44 Pr 9817, Dublin Stationery Office. One of its members was David Andrews, in 1998 the Irish minister for foreign affairs. Lemass also appointed a legal committee chaired by the attorney general, but its draft report of August 1968 was not completed.

45 This arguably was the article construed by Finlay CJ in *McGimpsey v Ireland* [1990] IR 110, 119.

46 New Ireland Forum, *Report*, Dublin May 1984, pp. 31–8, 23 & 31.

- the – Dublin – forum for peace and reconciliation of 1994–96, which adjourned sine die when Sinn Féin failed to accept the principle of consent;
- the all-party Oireachtas committee on the constitution, established in July 1996 – following the formidable May 1996 *Report of the Constitution Review Group*[49] chaired by T.K. Whitaker, which failed to include the separation of nation and state in its full review of the constitution.[50]

The 1973 Sunningdale agreement

6.51 This emerged from a four-day conference of the United Kingdom and Irish governments, plus the parties in the Northern Ireland executive (designate), on 9 December 1973. An agreed communiqué was issued, which, according to paragraphs 6 and 20, was intended to lead to an international agreement on the status of Northern Ireland in early 1974.

6.52 It led instead to the *Boland* case, and the collapse of the Northern Ireland executive in May 1974.

6.53 All that remained was paragraph 5 as a draft, where the two governments tried to agree a joint declaration:

The Irish Government fully accepted and solemnly declared that there could be no change in the status of Northern Ireland until a majority of the people of Northern Ireland desired a change in that status.	The British Government solemnly declared that it was, and would remain, their policy to support the wishes of the majority of the people of Northern Ireland. The present status of Northern Ireland is that it is part of the United Kingdom. If in the future the majority of the people of Northern Ireland should indicate a wish to become part of a united Ireland, the British Government would support that wish.

The Irish government, while it alluded to consent ('a majority of the people'),[51] did not define the status of Northern Ireland. This the United Kingdom government did

47 De Rossa went further than the 1967 proposals. He proposed, as article 2, the existing text plus (suggested by Mary Robinson in the *Irish Times* of 21 April 1990): 'This shall not be held to mean that there will be any change in the status of Northern Ireland other than with the consent of a majority of the people of Northern Ireland.' Some changes were made to O'Kelly's 1967 draft of article 3: from 'Irish nation' to 'the people of the state'; from 'territory' to 'the people of Ireland'; from 'brotherly affection ...' to 'peace and consent'. O'Kelly's 3.2 (which was largely adopted) had already become the law by virtue of *McGimpsey v Ireland* [1990] IR 110, 119.

48 Dáil Éireann, *Official Reports*, 994–1032, 4 December 1990; 1303–38, 5 December 1990; 1969–2004, 11 December 1990; 2277–318, 12 December 1990. The workers' party secured the support in the lobbies of labour and Fine Gael; the progressive democrats, however, were in coalition with Fianna Fáil.

49 Pn 2632, Dublin Stationery Office.

50 *First Progress Report*, Pn 3795, Dublin Stationery Office 1997; *Second Progress Report: Seanad Éireann*, Pn 3835, Dublin Stationery Office 1997; *Third Progress Report*, Pn 6250, Dublin Stationery Office 1998. Page 23 of the latter refers to future work on the people of Northern Ireland and emigrants. This is believed to have resulted from a letter of comfort from the taoiseach to Sinn Féin at Castle Buildings before or on 10 April 1998.

51 Paragraph 3, containing the view of the taoiseach, embodied the ideas of aspiration and

in the right-hand column. It also made it clear that it was formally neutral as between the union or a united Ireland.[52] It is difficult to see how Dublin and London – on the basis of these two columns – could have produced an agreed text in 1974.[53]

6.54 The unqualified commitment of Irish nationalists to consent – judging by the new Ireland forum *Report* (1984) – must be doubted. That presumed liberal reassessment of the tradition characterized section 1 of the Northern Ireland Constitution Act 1973, as 'an effective unionist veto on any political change affecting the exercise of nationalist rights and on the form of government for Northern Ireland'.[54]

The 1985 Anglo-Irish Agreement[55]

6.55 This agreement was a treaty, signed by Margaret Thatcher and Garret FitzGerald at Hillsborough on 15 November 1985. It established an inter-governmental conference (and a secretariat), where ministers and officials from London and Dublin would met to discuss: political matters; security and related matters; legal matters, including the administration of justice; and the promotion of cross-border cooperation.

6.56 It was a consultation plus agreement.[56] While there was no derogation from sovereignty, the Irish government was recognized as the guarantor of 'the minority community' in Northern Ireland.[57] Rhetoric from the new Ireland forum *Report* (1984) was adopted.

6.57 Article 1 contained a joint declaration on the status of Northern Ireland:

> The two Governments:
> (a) affirm that any change in the status of Northern Ireland would only come about with the consent of a majority of the people of Northern Ireland;
> (b) recognise that the present wish of a majority of the people of Northern Ireland is for no change in the status of Northern Ireland;
> (c) declare that, if in the future a majority of the people of Northern Ireland clearly wish for and formally consent to the establishment of a united Ireland, they will introduce and support in the respective Parliaments legislation to give effect to that wish.

This declaration was notable for having no reference to the status of Northern

unity by consent. The latter had been accepted in the ROI by Fine Gael and labour, but not yet by Fianna Fáil.

52 United Kingdom neutrality dated from 15 November 1971, when the prime minister, Edward Heath, said in a speech in the Mansion House in London: 'If at some future date the majority of the people of Northern Ireland want unification and express that desire in the appropriate constitutional manner, I do not believe any British Government would stand in the way.' This was quoted in *The Future of Northern Ireland: a paper for discussion*, NIO, October 1972, para. 34.

53 FitzGerald, *Life*, p. 222 states that the Irish government, following *Boland*, was able to acknowledge 'the factual position of Northern Ireland within the United Kingdom'.

54 Page 17; also p. 25.

55 Agreement between the Government of the United Kingdom of Great Britain and Northern Ireland and the Government of the Republic of Ireland, Cmnd 9657, November 1985, with joint communiqué stating that the exchange of notifications of acceptance would not be completed until the agreement had been approved by the two parliaments (paragraph 6).

56 Brigid Hadfield, 'The Anglo-Irish Agreement 1985', (1986) NILQ 37, 1, p. 1 at 14.

57 Articles 4(c) and 5(c).

Ireland.[58] It built on the 1973 commitment to consent, the Irish government gaining a negotiating advantage in article 1(a).[59] This was also the case in the United Kingdom governments's commitment to democracy/self-determination, especially article 1(c) – which envisaged mechanisms for a legal cession.

6.58 London – having abandoned the attempt in the negotiations to get rid of the territorial claim – had to protect Dublin from constitutional challenge.[60] Nevertheless, article 1 was the one and only joint declaration in international law about the status of Northern Ireland. That still remained a matter of United Kingdom constitutional law,[61] distinct from any pretence in Irish constitutional law.

6.59 The Anglo-Irish Agreement was challenged in English (not Northern Ireland) law, as well as Irish law. *Ex parte Molyneaux* [1986] 1 WLR 331 was an unsuccessful application in London for leave to apply for judicial review. The making of treaties is not generally reviewable,[62] though the court – in an *ex tempore* judgment – characterized it as only akin to a treaty. [63] *McGimpsey v Ireland* [1988] IR 567; [1990] IR 110 had a much greater impact, in Irish law, because of constitutional judicial review in that jurisdiction. The Supreme Court, however, held that article 1 of the 1985 agreement involved only recognition of the *de facto* position of Northern Ireland; it did not affect the claim of legal right in international law.

6.60 The three-year review under article 11 of the Anglo-Irish Agreement of the working of the conference had been published on 24 May 1989.[64] The two governments reaffirmed their full commitment to all of the provisions of the agreement. This was before the Supreme Court decision in *McGimpsey*, which was handed down on 1 March 1990. By then – given attempts to construct another political solution – it was too late to attempt to review with the Irish government the joint declaration on the status of Northern Ireland.

Political talks, 1988–1998

6.61 The negotiations which led to the Belfast Agreement can be traced from 1988. There is a tendency to see this in terms of a pan-nationalist consensus initiated by Sinn Féin.[65] A better view is the initiatives for talks of three strands taken by the United Kingdom government, during the time of Peter Brooke (1989–1992) and Sir Patrick Mayhew (1992–97).

6.62 London – partly at the behest of Dublin – made an offer to the republican

58 This includes one of the recitals in the preamble.

59 'Could' in 1973 became 'would' in 1985, seemingly as a result of the meeting between Margaret Thatcher and Charles Haughey on 21 May 1980.

60 The *Boland* case was treated as still good law.

61 Section 1 of the Northern Ireland Constitution Act 1973.

62 *Council of Civil Service Unions v Minister for the Civil Service* [1985] AC 374, 418 per Lord Roskill.

63 Using section 2 of the Ireland Act 1949 to answer a point taken about article sixth of the 1800 acts of union.

64 Tom Hadden & Kevin Boyle, *The Anglo-Irish Agreement: commentary, text and official review*, Dublin & London 1989, containing in chapter 7 the text of the official review.

65 Eamonn Mallie & David McKittrick, *The Fight for Peace: the secret story behind the Irish peace process*, London 1997.

movement in public in late 1993: give up violence, and there would be a place for democrats in Northern Ireland. Sinn Féin had not been involved in the 1991–92 talks, but, following the Mitchell report containing six principles of democracy and non-violence,[66] it was admitted belatedly (in September 1997) to the 1996–98 talks (its complete cessation of August 1994 – broken with the Docklands bomb in February 1996 – having been restored in July 1997).

6.63 This inclusive – alternatively, all-party (later multi-party) – process was marked by a number of historic (political) documents, all of which referred to constitutional questions:

- the *Downing Street Declaration*[67] of 15 December 1993, issued by John Major and Albert Reynolds. Written largely in Dublin, it announced 'a peace process designed to culminate in a political settlement'. The United Kingdom and Irish governments, responding to the Hume/Adams talks, addressed the question of self-determination for the first time. The Irish government, advancing the concept of 'a balanced constitutional accommodation', referred to constitutional changes reflecting the principle of consent;
- the *Framework Documents*[68] of 22 February 1995 (Parts I and II), issued by John Major and John Bruton in London. Written entirely in Dublin (at least as regards Part II) by Seán Ó hUigínn, a senior department of foreign affairs official, these texts expanded the ideas in the *Downing Street Declaration*. The United Kingdom government, in Part I, referred to the 'Union of Great Britain and Northern Ireland',[69] but also to a 'shared understanding of the constitutional issues, which achieved a balanced accommodation'.[70] The two governments referred, in Part II, in eight paragraphs on constitutional issues, to the possible replacement of the GOIA 1920 and the end of the Irish territorial claim;
- the nine-paragraph Heads of Agreement[71] of 12 January 1998, negotiated by the two governments (and the eight parties?) at a turning point in the talks. The Heads of Agreement effectively drew a line under the *Downing Street Declaration* and *Framework Documents*. The short text also anticipated the final shape of the Belfast Agreement.[72] It referred to a new British-Irish Agreement, and what later became the British-Irish Council (BIC).

66 Report of the International Body (Senator George Mitchell, General John de Chastelain, Prime Minister Harri Holkeri), Dublin & Belfast, 22 January 1996. John Major and John Bruton had announed a twin-track initiative (negotiations and decommissioning) on 28 November 1995.

67 Entitled, *Joint Declaration: Downing Street*, 15 December 1993. It was evocative of the *Downing Street Declaration* of 1969: *Text of a Communiqué and Declaration issued after a meeting held at 10 Downing Street on 19 August 1969*, Cmnd 34154, which had proclaimed: 'The border is not an issue.'

68 Entitled, *Frameworks for the Future* (nd but 22 February 1995), and comprising (as Part I) *A Framework for Accountable Government in Northern Ireland*, and (as Part II) *A New Framework for Agreement*. Part I was the work of the United Kingdom government; Part II was jointly with the Irish government. They came to be referred to as the *Framework Documents*.

69 Page 14.

70 Page 18.

71 Entitled, 'Propositions on Heads of Agreement'. It was accompanied by a joint statement by the two governments. Both were published in the *Irish Times* of 13 January 1998.

72 The joint statement referred to 'only the outline of an acceptable agreement'.

7

The Two States

7.1 This chapter – which ends Part 1 (Introduction) – revisits an important question of legal terminology through (a) the domestic law name of the United Kingdom state; (b) the view of the Irish; (c) the domestic law name of the Irish state; and (d) the view in the United Kingdom – before (e) proposing a working solution. International law is discussed where relevant. The problem of how to refer to the London and Dublin governments in different jurisdictions was not, as the Irish government, and maybe the United Kingdom government, hopes, resolved in the Belfast Agreement. This is in spite of the ending of the Irish territorial claim.

The domestic law name of the United Kingdom state

7.2 The starting point is the 1800 acts of union passed by the parliaments of Ireland and Great Britain.

7.3 As noted, the Irish act[1] envisaged a union of two countries, Great Britain and Ireland. Thus, article first stated that the name of the union of the two kingdoms would be 'the united kingdom of Great Britain and Ireland'. The sovereign, by proclamation, would be responsible for royal style and titles. Article third provided for 'The parliament of the united kingdom of Great Britain and Ireland'.

7.4 The act of the Great Britain parliament, in contrast, drawing on the description united kingdom from the 1707 union, provided for 'the United Kingdom of Great Britain and Ireland'.[2]

7.5 The country names – England, Scotland, Wales, Ireland – survived 1800, especially in adjectival form. But the British view of 'the United Kingdom' prevailed over the Irish one. However, this new state – the United Kingdom of Great Britain and Ireland – was not, in its domestic law, a unified entity.[3] It had – reflecting the struggles of the seventeenth century – a sovereign and a parliament: a sort of bipolar state.

7.6 The sovereign had been empowered to fashion the name of the imperial crown (plus ensigns, armorial flags and banners) as he chose. On 1 January 1801, he became 'George the Third by the Grace of God of the United Kingdom of Great Britain and Ireland King, Defender of the Faith'.[4] (The new union flag also came into existence.) Queen Victoria – following legislation – added 'Empress of India'[5]

1 Act of Union (Ireland) 1800 39 & 40 Geo 3 c 38.
2 Articles first and third, Union with Ireland Act 1800 39 & 40 Geo 3 c 67 (Great Britain).
3 There is strictly no concept of the state in United Kingdom law: *Entick v Carrington* (1765) 19 St Tr 1030; *Chandler v Director of Public Prosecutions* [1964] AC 763.
4 Proclamation, SR&O and SI revised to 31 December 1948, pp. 789–91.
5 Proclamation, SR&O and SI revised to 31 December 1948, pp. 798–9.

in 1876. And Edward VII – also following legislation – added to his kingship, 'and of the British dominions beyond the Seas'[6] in 1901.

7.7 The Royal and Parliamentary Titles Act 1927 permitted George V – following the 1926 imperial conference – to change his kingship to 'Great Britain, Ireland and the British Dominions beyond the Seas'. He was still – in United Kingdom and Irish law – king of Ireland (a geographical entity no longer existing politically). The term 'United Kingdom' was dropped, to avoid having to add the Irish Free State (or have it assumed in the British Dominions beyond the Seas).[7] However, the same act renamed Westminster as the parliament of the United Kingdom of Great Britain and Northern Ireland. The change took effect in mid session, and there was provision for construing 'United Kingdom' in future legislation as comprising Great Britain and Northern Ireland.

7.8 To the uncertainty of 1922–27 (when the United Kingdom of Great Britain and Ireland persisted[8]) was added a king of Great Britain, Ireland, etc. from 13 May 1927 with a parliament of the United Kingdom of Great Britain and Northern Ireland from 12 April 1927. Was the kingdom – that is the state – still the United Kingdom? The answer depends upon whether the government, which acted in the name of the crown, looked to the nomenclature of the sovereign or of the parliament.

7.9 The preamble to the Statute of Westminster 1931 declared that royal style and titles was a matter for the dominions. There was no change in 1937, when BNH was enacted. Nor in 1949, when Éire left the commonwealth. George VI had dropped 'Emperor of India' the previous year, and a republic in the commonwealth – India – presented a problem for the crown.

7.10 The crown was divided following the accession of Elizabeth II in 1952, and the commonwealth conference in December. Under the Royal Titles Act 1953 – and her proclamation of 28 May 1953 – the sovereign became 'Elizabeth II, by the Grace of God of the United Kingdom of Great Britain and Northern Ireland and of Her other Realms and Territories Queen, Head of the Commonwealth, Defender of the Faith'.[9]

7.11 It had taken Northern Ireland 33 years before it was recognized in the royal style and titles, and the Westminster parliament 26 years before its name became effectively that of the state. But the United Kingdom of Great Britain and Northern Ireland of 1953 onwards had to compete culturally with the surviving names: England from before 1707 and (Great) Britain from before 1801.

7.12 The international law name of the United Kingdom state – the name the Foreign Office chose to use abroad – was a matter of practice. The United Kingdom of Great Britain and Ireland, lawyers advised, had ceased to exist on 6 December

6 Proclamation, SR&O and SI revised to 31 December 1948, pp. 799–800.

7 United Kingdom ministers and officials – and only Kevin O'Higgins ultimately – were responsible for the comma between Great Britain and Ireland: R.F. Shinn Jr, 'Changing the King's Title, 1926: an asterisk to "O'Higgins' Comma"', *Irish Jurist*, 1981, pp. 114–40.

8 Even though section 6 of the Irish Free State (Consequential Provisions) Act 1922 allowed adaptations of enactments.

9 Appendix – Instruments not SI, pp. 2973–4.

1922, because Ireland was no more.[10] The term 'United Kingdom' – according to the Irish Free State – gave the impression that, because they had once been a part of that state, they could still be bound in international law. But why not simply truncate the United Kingdom to its new geographical area? Treaties were made by the British Empire, the United Kingdom and Great Britain (all three names being used variously). In 1924, in the treaty recognizing the Soviet Union, the foreign office referred to the government of 'Great Britain and Northern Ireland'. The treaty of Locarno 1925 was the first in which the dominions were not bound by the sovereign. While the sovereign as king of the United Kingdom of Great Britain and Ireland (sic) was invoked with fellow heads of states in Annex A, the contracting state bound was described as Great Britain (with no reference to Northern Ireland).

7.13 London seems to have shortened Great Britain and Northern Ireland in the 1920s. Though it was His Majesty's Government in the United Kingdom which signed the optional clause at the world court in 1929, Great Britain had been used consistently there as the name of the state from 1922; this would continue through the inter-war period.

The view of the Irish

7.14 The Irish Free State – from 1922 – took against the name United Kingdom. It was a slight, so it was considered, to the new Irish state seeking recognition. And truncation to Northern Ireland was no solution, certainly before the December 1925 agreement.

7.15 The Adaptation of Enactments Act 1922 and the Interpretation Act 1923, which had to deal inter alia with 'British Statute[s]' before 6 December 1922, referred to 'the Parliament of the late United Kingdom of Great Britain and Ireland'. 'Late', if it was appropriate in Irish law, was certainly not correct in international law.

7.16 In Irish constitutional law, the 1921 treaty terminology of 'Great Britain' and 'Ireland' was reaffirmed in the 1924 boundary commission agreement and again in 1925. London was prepared to continue using 'British Government' in Irish matters after 6 December 1921.[11]

7.17 At the 1926 imperial conference – turning to international law and practice – the Irish Free State, seeking to change belatedly the sovereign's style and titles, proposed 'King of the United Kingdom of Great Britain and of Canada, Australia, New Zealand, South Africa and the Irish Free State, Emperor of India'.[12] The United Kingdom of Great Britain suggestion – nearly a year after the December 1925 agreement – casts some doubt on Irish Free State recognition of Northern Ireland. The placing of the names indicates the Irish Free State was seeking to distance itself from the United Kingdom, but not beyond India!

10 Sir Cecil Hurst to Ramsay MacDonald, 8 August 1924, RA GV M1950/1, quoted in Shinn, 'King's Title', p. 121 n 20.

11 But not in the treaty. Lloyd George and his colleagues signed as 'the British delegation'. Article 18 referred to 'His Majesty's Government' in – implicitly – the United Kingdom of Great Britain and Ireland.

12 Shinn, 'King's Title', p. 135. But Fitzgerald, the external affairs minister, had already proposed 'King of Great Britain, of Ireland, and of the British Dominions beyond the Seas' in April 1926 (p. 131).

7.18 Things became no clearer under de Valera. While the Interpretation Act 1937 continued to define British statutes in terms of the late United Kingdom, the Executive Powers (Consequential Provisions) Act 1937 had defined (Irish) statutes as including acts passed by 'the Parliament of the former United Kingdom of Great Britain and Ireland'.[13] There was only one parliament of the United Kingdom between 1801 and 1922 (and it continued), but 'former' seems to have been used to refer to Irish acts during the union while 'late' referred to United Kingdom-wide acts of the same period. (There was no provision for United Kingdom acts – before 1931, much less after – applying in the jurisdiction of the Irish state).

7.19 Something surprising happened following the 1938 United Kingdom-Éire agreement – as it was called – on the ports, finance and trade. The Irish final settlement of £10m was provided for by the Agreement with United Kingdom (Capital Sum) Act 1938. That act then defined the United Kingdom as comprising 'Great Britain and Northern Ireland'. The trade agreement – dealing with customs duties – was enacted as the Finance (Agreement with the United Kingdom) Act 1938 on the same day. There, the Channel Islands and Isle of Man were added to the definition of the United Kingdom. No reference was made subsequently to these two statutes, dating from that final agreement between de Valera and the United Kingdom.

7.20 Irish jurists have tended to the view that Éire/Ireland did not recognize Northern Ireland, and certainly not as part of the – continuing – United Kingdom. Thus, in the *Boland* case in 1974, counsel for the state (T.K. Liston SC) listed the statutes which referred to Northern Ireland, thereby – he argued – giving it *de facto* recognition: Erne Drainage and Development Act 1950 section 1; Foyle Fisheries Act 1952 section 2; Irish Nationality and Citizenship Act 1956 section 7; Great Northern Railway Act 1958 section 2; and Extradition Act 1965 section 41.[14] Judicial notice of Northern Ireland was taken belatedly in *The State (Joachim Gilsenan) v Peter A. Murrow* [1978] IR 360, 365–6 per Gannon J, 370–1 per Henchy J.

7.21 The Oireachtas had had no difficulty referring to Northern Ireland (or, in the Extradition Act 1965, England and Wales, Scotland, the Isle of Man and the Channel Islands). *De facto* recognition – the argument used to defend, if not Sunningdale, then the 1985 Anglo-Irish Agreement – was acceptable to the Irish courts. (Incidentally, the Anglo-Irish Agreement used the term 'United Kingdom government' consistently.) It is therefore strange that the executive branch should have remained particularly irredentist; a 1996 foreign affairs white paper, for example, *Challenges and Opportunites Abroad*, was still using the terminology of 'Ireland' and 'Great Britain', especially when discussing 'the still unresolved question of Northern Ireland'.[15]

The domestic law name of the Irish state

7.22 The foundation act of the Irish state contained its name: Constitution of the Irish Free State (Saorstát Eireann) Act 1922 (No. 1 of 1922). Though the national

13 This was repeated in the Interpretation Act 1937.

14 He could have added: Great Northern Railway Act 1953 section 2. See also, the Criminal Law (Jurisdiction) Act 1976.

15 Pages 52–3. This, it is important to note, was coterminous with the 1996–98 political talks.

language was referred to in article 4, the English name of the state was given precedence in the constitution. (The Stationery Office in Dublin, however, in publishing the acts of the Oireachtas each year, was to imprint Saorstát Eireann on the spine.)

7.23 Section 2 of the forefront of the foundation act referred to repugnancy between the constitution and the 1921 treaty. As noted, the treaty was deemed to be between 'Great Britain' and 'Ireland'. And, while 'Ireland' was used in article 1, the new administration was to be 'styled and known as the Irish Free State' (there was no provision for an Irish name). Also as noted, the Northern Ireland articles caused a problem for the new Irish state.

7.24 This erupted in a transitory provision in the constitution (article 74), dealing with (continuing domestic) trade in 1922–23 between the state and 'any part of Great Britain or the Isle of Man'. It had to be cured at Westminster in section 4 of the Irish Free State (Consequential Provisions) Act 1922 (Session 2), which allowed the (United Kingdom) Customs and Excise to regulate 'importation and exportation ... into and from Northern Ireland otherwise than by sea or air' – that is, trade across the land frontier. (Section 13 of the Adaptation of Enactments Act 1922, in empowering the minister for finance of the Irish Free State to regulate imports and exports 'by land', contained an ackowledgement of this new political frontier.) The Irish Free State (Consequential Adaptation of Enactments) Order 1923, of 27 March 1923, provided in article 4(1) that 'the Irish Free State [should], in relation to any part of Great Britain or Northern Ireland, be deemed to be parts beyond the seas for customs purposes ...'.

7.25 Dublin appears to have been content to use the Irish Free State in its external relations. The French name (État Libre d'Irlande) – and especially the French language – were used at international gatherings, to distinguish the new member of the community of nations from the Anglophone dominions. It is not surprising that Irlande/Ireland – at the same time as Grande Bretagne/Great Britain – was used by others at the world court in the inter-war period.

7.26 The problems in Irish law begin on 29 December 1937. Article 4 of BNH reads in Irish: 'Éire is ainm don Stát nó, sa Sacs-Bhéarla, *Ireland*.' (It is not clear whether the printer of the 1937 version was unable to italicize in the Irish language given the use of gaelic type.) The Irish text is translated literally in BNH – with the three commas in the 1937 version (one of which was dropped later) – to read: 'The name of the State is *Éire*, or, in the English language, *Ireland*.' (Here, the Irish and English names are italicized.[16]) There is no conflict between the Irish and English versions, so article 63 of BNH does not apply. All the words have been translated from Irish to English, except for the proper names Éire and Ireland; one English name has been used in the Irish version; and one Irish name in the English one.

7.27 (Alternatively, if there is conflict between the two versions, it is not clear that the Irish version prevailing may be translated differently. There is a problem with the word 'Ireland' in the Irish version. To properly construe the Irish version, it is necessary to read the English one. 'Ireland is the name of the state, or, in the English language, Ireland.' is not coherent enough to be interpreted judicially.)

16 This was the position in the article 63 enrolled copy of 1938.

7.28 The word nó/or, it may be observed, is used rather than agus/and, suggesting possible alternatives in the English language.

7.29 What does article 4 mean? One answer is the English text should be drafted to read: 'The name of the State is *Ireland*, or, in the Irish language, *Éire*.' This is an acceptable translation of an Irish sentence containing an English word. However, the draftsman must be considered to have rejected it. Another answer is that article 4 reads essentially: '*Éire* is ainm don Stát./The name of the State is *Ireland*.' This was proposed by the Constitution Review Group in May 1996 as a simplication.[17] But again, the draftsman must be considered to have rejected it.

7.30 The meaning of article 4 – in its English and Irish versions – is to be found in its drafting history (which is, arguably, admissible in Irish law).

7.31 And here we need to begin with the first reference to Éire in BNH. The preamble, as noted, contains the enactment phrase: '*We, the people of Éire, ... Do hereby adopt, enact, and give to ourselves this Constitution.*' 'People of Éire' is a translation of 'muintear na hÉireann'. And these people – recognizing the reality of a legal revolution in a 26-county state – were, under section 2 of the Plebiscite (Draft Constitution) Act 1937, the electors of Saorstát Éireann.

7.32 Éire – I submit – was chosen deliberately as the English-language name, not simply to encourage the use of Irish, but because 'the people of Ireland' were not enacting the new constitution.[18]

7.33 Such a point was painfully obvious to de Valera. The word Éire in the preamble was debated during the committee stage in the Dáil (on the motion to approve the draft constitution) on 4 June 1937. 'I am using Éire for the State.', said the then president of the executive council (using state geographically as in the Irish Free State). 'When we are talking about the people of Éire', he said shortly afterwards, 'it is obvious that it must be only the part [of Ireland] which we can effectively control.'[19]

7.34 Article 4 had been considered earlier in the committee stage. De Valera's draft – BNH was actually an English text translated into Irish – read: 'The name of the State is Éire.' There were two criticisms from opposition deputies. One, the Irish name was used in English, to which de Valera countered it was like the use of 'taoiseach'. Two, the state was known as Ireland (which was not entirely the case), de Valera's response being to accept 'The name of the State is Ireland' in his draft.

7.35 But he produced a new version – the current English one – for the recommittal stage, commenting: 'It is as well that we should have it [the name in Irish], not simply in English, seeing that the Irish text is the fundamental text, that "Éire" is used here and there.'[20] It was approved by the Oireachtas and put to the people for enactment.

17 It originated with the all-party Oireachtas committee in 1967 (Pr 9817, Dublin Stationery Office, p. 6).

18 See the anonymous legal opinion in the working papers of the 1982 attorney general's committee on the constitution, in 1 *Preamble*, published by the Constitution Review Group, May 1996, pp. 52–8, especially pp. 54–5 & 58.

19 Dáil Éireann, *Official Reports*, 1912–13, 4 June 1937, quoted in Michael Conlon's research paper, in *1 Preamble*, published by the Constitution Review Group in May 1996, p. 7.

20 Dáil Éireann, *Official Reports*, 954 & 971, 25 May 1937, quoted in Michael Conlon's

7.36 De Valera clearly wanted Éire for the 26 counties in the English-language version. And Éire was the name the state would choose to use from 29 December 1937 (without any outside interference).

7.37 Even the Stationery Office took to using Éire (without Ireland) on published acts of the Oireachtas from 1938 to 1950 (though Éire was dropped from the title page of the annual volume in 1947, the Irish harp thereafter symbolizing the state). To the argument that Éire was consistent with the use of Saorstát Éireann up to 1937, I would reply: de Valera wanted an Irish-language name used by English speakers at home and abroad.

7.38 The particular English version of article 4 enacted – I submit – must be interpreted in the context of the preamble, and an examination of the drafting history of BNH.[21] A knowledge of de Valera's distinction between the 1916 republic and his external association of 1936 is vital. The meaning of article 4 (even given the Irish version) is that, as long as partition lasts, Éire is the name of the 26-county state, but, once Ireland is reunited (and the republic restored), then the name of the state – reconciling geography and politics – becomes Ireland.

7.39 This construction has not emerged from the dicta in several cases in the Irish courts. In *People (AG) v Ruttledge* [1978] IR 376, 379 – decided in 1947 – O'Byrne J, turning to the constitution, said: 'The name of the State in the English language is Ireland (Article 4) ... .' This paraphrase was not part of the ratio decidendi, since the Supreme Court only interpreted article 3. In *Byrne v Ireland* [1972] IR 241, 261, Walsh J said: 'under Article 4 the name of the State in the English language is "Ireland"'. Again, this is only a paraphrase, with the ratio decidendi relating to article 5. The same judge made the same point later in *Ellis v O'Dea* [1989] IR 530, 539–40: 'In the English language the name of this State is "Ireland" and is so prescribed by Article 4 of the Constitution.' But this occasionally cited sentence relates only to a brief excursus on foreign courts drawing up warrants using the – the United Kingdom law – name of the Republic of Ireland, which Walsh J wanted sent back by the Irish authorities for amendment.

7.40 None of these dicta on article 4 amounts to judicial interpretation (such as exists on articles 2 and 3).

7.41 In conclusion, BNH named the 26-county state Éire (alternatively, it allowed a choice of Éire or Ireland). Article 4 of the constitution has never been amended. So, in Irish law, the name of the state – I submit – is Éire (either absolutely in the English language, or as an alternative to Ireland). There is no disagreement about it being Éire in Irish.

7.42 The Republic of Ireland Act 1948 – with the marginal note to section 2: 'The Republic of Ireland' – killed off the domestic use of Éire in 1949. There was no amendment of the constitution. But there was a change in government practice. Éire was replaced by the Republic of Ireland, even on postage stamps. This had a great deal to do with anti-de Valera sentiment on the part of the Costello coalition government (1948–51).

research paper, in *2 The Nation and the State*, published by the Constitution Review Group in May 1996, pp. 16–17.

21 *Attorney General v Hamilton* [1993] 2 IR 250, 268 per Finlay CJ.

7.43 Fianna Fáil was back in office in 1951–54 and 1957–73 (its second 16-year term). Éire was still the name of the state under the constitution, but the British had been keen to use it to refer to the 26 counties from 1938. Sean MacBride had had the Republic of Ireland redeclared, but de Valera saw this statutory description – the status republic and the name Ireland – as drawing attention twice to the unsolved problem of partition. Moreover, the British had switched from Éire to the Republic of Ireland following Easter Monday, 1949.

7.44 His solution, Éire, had been trampled upon at home, and the alternative, Republic of Ireland, only added to the injury.

7.45 It was, therefore, in the 1950s, that the Irish government resolved the dilemma by calling itself the government of Ireland.[22] This had the virtue of going back to the constitution, but not to Éire. It also represented a compromise with the 1948 statutory name, being seen to be a shortened version of the Republic of Ireland (though this – Irish and British – name appealed to Irish liberals as a modern solution to the terminological problem[23]).

7.46 The main impetus for the change in state practice – not domestic law (because the Republic of Ireland remained unrepealed) – was Ireland's reaching out to the outside world. This raises the question of international practice. The Irish Free State had given way to Éire (which was probably the state's most successful name). But there seems to have been a reaction in Dublin to its use by the United Kingdom from 1938. The government of Ireland – on analogy with the president of Ireland – was the name used on treaties. Éire, of course, was translated into French as Irlande (even in British texts), coming back as Ireland in English. The Costello government then disrupted the practice to some extent by insisting upon the Republic of Ireland (though it is not clear if this applied also to treaties). When the name was shortened in the 1950s (still within the English language), it tapped the Ireland that had been used internationally in a geographical rather than political sense.

7.47 The Irish state joined the United Nations in 1955 as 'Ireland'. The British protested, but ineffectually – though it encouraged the expansive United Kingdom of Great Britain and Northern Ireland after 1953. The state subsequently joined the then European Economic Community in 1973, again as 'Ireland'.[24] The United Kingdom protested some more, but it was losing – in international popularity – the match against a small state with an anti-colonial reputation.

7.48 It was such a combination of domestic and international events (seasoned with historic Anglophobia), which made Ireland the name of the state even though, under the constitution, it was Éire, and, in its statutory law, it was the

22 Diplomatic accreditation to the president seems to have been a stimulus. Between 1937 and 1949, representatives of foreign states were accredited to the sovereign. From 1949, the President of Ireland (sic) took over this function. The change in domestic practice seems to have come from article 12 of BNH.

23 Irish Theological Association, Working Party Report, 16 May 1972, in *1 Preamble*, published by the Constitution Review Group in May 1996, pp. 26–34, especially p. 29; *The State (Gilsenan) v McMurrow* [1978] IR 360, 370–1 per Henchy J.

24 The full name of the United Kingdom was used in the 1972 treaty of accession: *Documents concerning the accessions to the European Communities*, Luxembourg, Office for Official Publications of the European Communities 1988.

Republic of Ireland description. Judicial dicta – most recently from 1989 – were as much a response to political consensus, though such judgments have been cited to legitimize – if not legalize – the name 'Ireland'.

7.49 The consequence – if the judicial dicta are accepted at common law – is that the Irish state, which has continued to use Ireland after the Belfast Agreement entered into force, has invented a 26-county 'Ireland' through BNH; a political Ireland as distinct from the geographical one. The government of Ireland cannot be that literally, if the territorial claim in its law has been ended by constitutional amendment.

7.50 Ireland was treated as a geographical expression (including islands), along side England, Wales and Scotland in section 3 of the Interpretation Act 1923 (which did not apply to the 1922 constitution). Northern Ireland was also defined therein, as the part of Ireland not under the jurisdiction of Saorstát Éireann. Ireland had already been defined – for the purpose of construing British statutes (sic) – in section 3 of the Adaptation of Enactments Act 1922 as Saorstát Éireann (which was *de facto* 26 counties and would become *de jure* only a part of geographical Ireland).

7.51 Section 5 of the Interpretation Act 1937 (which does apply to BNH) disapplied the 1923 act from enactments of the new Oireachtas. And the Interpretation Act applying from 29 December 1937 contains no definition of Ireland, or reference to Northern Ireland (Great Britain, however, is defined as not including the Isle of Man or the Channel Islands).

7.52 Articles 2 and 3 of BNH (as noted) required the Constitution (Consequential Provisions) Act 1937 to be enacted before the constitution came into operation. Section 2 provided for the general adaptation of the expression Irish Free State/Saorstát Éireann in existing legislation. From 29 December 1937, the term was to 'be construed and have effect (unless the context otherwise requires) as meaning Ireland ...'. 'Ireland' was not defined in the act, but the Interpretation Act 1923 applied. The Adaptation of Enactments Act 1922 did not. Subsection (2) of the 1937 act, however, went on to state that no adaptation would be permitted 'to extend the meaning of such expression as to include therein any area which is, for the time being, not within the area and extent of application of the laws enacted by the Oireachtas'. Thus – incontrovertibly – the 32-county Ireland in Irish statutes and statutory instruments by adaptation meant, under articles 2 and 3 of BNH, a 26-county Ireland.

The view of the United Kingdom

7.53 This – unlike the domestic law name of the United Kingdom state – may be presented summarily:

- between 1801 and 1922, the geographical entity Ireland was an integral part – albeit slightly separately administered – of the United Kingdom of Great Britain and Ireland;
- in 1921–22, the United Kingdom – partly through the provisional parliament – created the Irish Free State within its own law;
- it used the name Irish Free State from 6 December 1922 until 29 December 1937, but recognized an Irish bilingual propensity for Saorstát Éireann, or even État Libre d'Irlande in external relations;

- the Irish Free State was a 26-county state (leaving aside any questions of international law) from 6 December 1922, and this was settled finally in the agreement of 3 December 1925 recognizing Northern Ireland;
- the United Kingdom took exception on 29 December 1937 to article 4 of Bunreacht na hÉireann (as well as articles 2 and 3), seeing Éire/Ireland as symbolizing the new territorial claim. Northern Ireland was stated to be an integral part of the United Kingdom. And London expressed the view that the name Éire or Ireland (it stated no preference) related only to the 26-county territory of the former Irish Free State;[25]
- the problem was solved in United Kingdom law on 17 May 1938, when section 1 of the Eire (Confirmation of Agreements) Act 1938 stated that the former Irish Free State would now be styled and known as Eire. This was repealed by part V of Schedule I of the Statute Law (Repeals) Act 1981;
- Eire, rather than Ireland, was a friendly British response.[26] The Irish name was that preferred by Eamon de Valera. (The three international agreements of 25 April 1938 had been between the government of the United Kingdom and the government of Eire, though Dublin insisted apparently upon the government of Ireland and the government of the United Kingdom – which it would subsequently define fully in its domestic legislation);
- when Éire quit the commonwealth finally on 18 April 1949, the United Kingdom law solution was to, first, allow the continuing use of Eire (which continued as an option until 1981), and then, secondly, offer the name Republic of Ireland as an alternative. The question of Irish law – a description printed as a name in the 1948 act – would be an issue requiring expert evidence in a United Kingdom court, any criticism of the British draftsman being most unlikely to affect the impact of section 1(3);
- the Republic of Ireland has been the preferred name of the Irish state in United Kingdom law since Eire was repealed in 1981;
- it is also the name in Northern Ireland law, that parliament having simply shifted from the Irish Free State (as defined in United Kingdom law) to the 26-county Republic of Ireland: Interpretation Act (NI) 1954 section 46(1);
- internationally, since the 1950s, the United Kingdom has not been able to prevent recognition of Ireland as the name of the Irish state. Resistance has encouraged the use of the full title: United Kingdom of Great Britain and Northern Ireland – showing the need to defend a Northern Ireland obscured by a widely recognized geographical Ireland;
- the United Kingdom has perceived the use of Ireland as related to the territorial claim in articles 2 and 3 of the constitution. It is a paradox that de Valera came up with the acceptable solution of Éire, but others – excluding liberals who see the sense in Irish and United Kindom law of the Republic of Ireland – insist upon Ireland (as a better alternative or the only English-language name). The United Kingdom has difficulty comprehending that, with the end of the territorial claim when the Belfast Agreement entered into

25 *The Times*, 30 December 1937.

26 See Malcolm MacDonald's reply to a parliamentary question on 15 February 1938: House of Commons, *Hansard*, 5th series, 331, 1676–7.

force, the current Irish government is even more energetically committed to the symbol.

Proposing a working solution

7.54 There is a post-modernist propensity to want to embrace everybody's view, even when it comes to naming states. (Éire is still used by many pro-Irish people in the United Kingdom wanting to show respect for the national language, even though nationalists in Ireland tend to see 'Éire' as being used contemporaneously by the likes of the *Daily Telegraph* much in the way it uses 'Persia'.)

7.55 Here we are dealing with two states, on the plane of international law, and also in two systems of municipal law. The proposed working solution – which has been followed hitherto – has been to refer to the United Kingdom state and the Irish state (and to use these adjectives to refer to territory, government, law, jurisdiction, etc. – where there is no particular term of art, such as 'citizen of Ireland' or 'British citizen').

7.56 United Kingdom – not British: partly because British is not accurate; and partly because it plays into the Britain/Ireland duality of Irish nationalism (where the problem of Northern Ireland is obscured). There is less of a problem using Irish state; there is only one state wholly within geographical Ireland (and a term such as southern Irish, or Southern Ireland, has been superseded constitutionally).

7.57 There are further problems in the two systems of municipal law, which are not resolvable – because of the international plane – by following domestic propensities.

7.58 In United Kingdom law (how does English or British law apply to Ireland?), I will call the state the United Kingdom (short version) or the appropriate long version from 1801 to the present (even through the hiatus of 1922 to 1927 or 1953). The geographical entities (Great) Britain, Ireland, Northern Ireland will be adjectived on the basis of the appropriate political entity at that time.

7.59 The main problem with United Kingdom law is the absence of a state, reflected in a nineteenth-century universalism, followed by the unitary state concept – the *inter se* doctrine – of the inter-war years, when the British empire centred on London gave way to a number of dominions and the Indian and Irish republics (followed by post-Second World War global decolonization).

7.60 There is no problem with Irish law, there having been law in Ireland from the middle ages. The same cannot be said for Irish nationalist historiography, and the historic foe – England, later Britain (but not the United Kingdom). A succession of names will have to be used for the Irish state (leaving aside when it came into existence in international law). Ireland was part of the United Kingdom until 1922. Northern Ireland had been treated separately from 1920. The Irish Free State existed between 1922 and 1937. Thereafter, I will use the composite Éire/Ireland, to follow article 4 of BNH (but without prejudice to the argument – after de Valera – that the English-language name of the 26-county state is only Éire) for the period from 1937. When it comes to 1949, I will use the Irish statutory name and the United Kingdom law name, the Republic of Ireland. This is simply to distinguish it from Northern Ireland.

PART 2

CONSTITUTION

Part 2 turns to the text of the Belfast Agreement, to the constitutional principles at the beginning of the MPA. These include article 1 of the BIA.[1] Interpreting the MPA means looking at the political face of the Belfast Agreement. However, for the purposes of legal analysis, the MPA is read as Annex 1 of the BIA (that is, the legal face of the Belfast Agreement). Chapter 8 looks at the Declaration of Support by the participants. Chapter 9 turns to Constitutional Issues, which endorses article 1 of the BIA. Chapter 10 is Annex A to Constitutional Issues, namely proposed changes in United Kingdom statutory law. These are now sections 1 (plus schedule 1) and 2 of the Northern Ireland Act ('NIA') 1998. They were brought into force on 2 December 1999.[2] Chapter 11 is Annex B, which deals with the proposed amendments to the 1937 Irish constitution. These were enacted by the Nineteenth Amendment of the Constitution Act 1998, and took effect under article 4(3) of the BIA on 2 December 1999.[3] To the view that there has been a constitutional weakening of Northern Ireland's position within the United Kingdom, I argue in this part of the book – as stated in the Preface – that the constitutional changes brought about by the Belfast Agreement are characterized predominantly by the end of the Irish territorial claim to Northern Ireland.

1 The relevant page numbers are pp. 1–4 and 27–8 of Cm 3883; pp. 2–3 and 9–13 of Cm 4705 (and, in the 1999 Irish version, two unnumbered pages and pp. 3–7).
2 Northern Ireland Act 1998 (Commencement No. 5) Order 1999, SI 1999/3209.
3 The United Kingdom and Irish governments had fulfilled by 19 November 1998 the two respective requirements under article 4(1)(a) and (b) for entry into force.

8

Declaration of Support

8.1 The Declaration of Support is the first section of the Belfast Agreement, at page 1 of Cm 3883 and page 9 of Cm 4705 (page 3 of the 1999 Irish version). It is in particular the first section of the MPA.

TITLE: DECLARATION OF SUPPORT

8.2 This statement of six paragraphs appeared first in the MDP of 6 April 1998. It was, therefore, the work of the United Kingdom and Irish governments.[1] It underwent several changes before appearing in the FA of 10 April 1998. I show [deletions] and *additions* thus.

1. **We, the participants in the multi-party negotiations, believe that the agreement we have negotiated offers a truly historic opportunity for a new beginning.**

8.3 ANNOTATIONS

'We, the participants'. The participants are listed nowhere in the Belfast Agreement. The term 'participant' was defined in the *Ground Rules for Substantive All-Party Negotiations*, Cm 3232, 16 April 1996, as embracing the two governments and the elected political parties in Northern Ireland.[2] However, the term also tended to be used in the talks, by the three independent chairmen,[3] to mean the political parties only.[4] The term 'participant' is used here most likely in this latter sense (as is also suggested by paragraph 5 below).

'in the multi-party negotiations,'. The negotiations commenced as nearly all-party talks on 10 June 1996.[5] When Dr Paisley's DUP and Robert McCartney QC's UKUP walked out in July 1997, they were renamed the multi-party talks. Sinn Féin only joined the talks in September 1997, following the restoration of the IRA ceasefire. The term 'multi-party talks' was used erroneously in the first recital of the preamble, and in Annex 1, of the BIA (Cm 3883), though it was corrected (as regards the latter) in Cm 4705 to multi-party negotiations. This is the term which inspired the generic agreement reached in the multi-party negotiations, used in the popular United Kingdom and Irish versions of the Belfast Agreement in April 1998.

'believe that the agreement we have negotiated offers a truly historic opportunity for a new beginning.' The agreement negotiated – given the definition of participants – can only be the MPA. It cannot be the BIA, to which the MPA is annexed. Nor do the two states parties appear to be bound by the content of the Declaration of Support. A truly historic opportunity is rhetoric referring, less to the two referendums, and more to the successful implementation of the Belfast Agreement. A new beginning was stated to be the objective of the negotiations in April 1996.[6]

1 Covering memorandum from the Independent Chairmen, 6 April 1998.
2 Rule 10.
3 Senator George J. Mitchell; General John de Chastelain; Prime Minister Harri Holkeri.
4 See Chapter 1.
5 Sinn Féin was excluded because the IRA had broken its ceasefire in February 1996.
6 *Ground Rules for Substantive All-Party Negotiations*, Cm 3232, rule 1.

2. **The [failures]** ***tragedies*** **of the past have left a deep and profoundly regrettable legacy of suffering. We must never forget those who have [been injured or who have] died** ***or been injured,*** **and their families. But we can best honour them through a fresh start, in which we firmly dedicate ourselves to the achievement of reconciliation, tolerance, and mutual trust, and to the protection and vindication of the human rights of all.**

8.4 ANNOTATIONS

'The tragedies of the past'. Failure was used in the first draft of the so-called Hume-Adams declaration on 6 October 1991.[7] 'Tragedy and suffering' was used in the *Downing Street Declaration* of 15 December 1993.[8] It may be surmised that failure was unacceptable to unionists.

'have left a deep and profoundly regrettable legacy of suffering.' The victims of the troubles warrant separate inclusion, in the context of reconciliation, in the Human Rights subsection of the Rights, Safeguards and Equality of Opportunity section.[9]

'We must never forget those who have died or been injured, and their families.' Those who have died or been injured are the victims of the troubles. No doubt the change of order between injury and death is to reflect the greater crime, but also – generally – the loss experienced by families.

'But we can best honour them through a fresh start,'. A fresh start is similar to a new beginning in paragraph 1.

'in which we firmly dedicate ourselves to the achievement of reconciliation, tolerance, and mutual trust,'. 'Reconciliation' is included, under Human Rights, in the Rights, Safeguards and Equality of Opportunity section.[10] 'Tolerance' is also mentioned there. 'Mutual trust' is not addressed in that subsection, but mutual understanding and respect are.

'and to the protection and vindication of the human rights of all.' 'Human Rights' is the first part of the Rights, Safeguards and Equality of Opportunity section. Human rights for all is an inclusive phrase.

3. **We are committed to partnership, equality and mutual respect as the basis of [the] relationships within Northern Ireland, between North and South, and between these islands.**

8.5 ANNOTATIONS

'We are committed to partnership, equality and mutual respect'. Partnership is a political concept, dating from the mid-1970s, when it became a synonym for power-sharing. 'Equality' is a different matter. This must be a reference to equality of opportunity, part of the title of the Rights, Safeguards and Equality of Opportunity section. 'Mutual respect' appears in association with mutual understanding, in the first paragraph 13 of the Rights, Safeguards and Equality of Opportunity section.

'as the basis of relationships within Northern Ireland, between North and South, and between these islands.' This triptych is deeply rooted in London-Dublin diplomacy, and was the basis of the structure – three interlocking strands – of the 1996–98 negotiations.

Its was used first in public by Charles Haughey on 8 December 1980, when – in a joint communiqué with Margaret Thatcher – he referred to commissioning joint studies for a

7 Eamonn Mallie & David McKittrick, *The Fight for Peace: the inside story of the Irish peace process*, London 1997, p. 118.

8 Paragraph 1.

9 First paragraphs 11–13.

10 First paragraphs 11–13.

'special consideration of the totality of relationships within these islands'.[11] The idea of three interlocking strands was used to fashion the unsuccessful political talks of 1991–92. This diplomatic approach to a problem has a certain efficacy, but the number and the character of those relationships has not been consistently clear.

Within Northern Ireland is taken to be the ethnic/political relationship between catholics and protestants, or nationalists and unionists. But, as a result of unionist criticism, a fourth set of relations was added to this strand in 1996, namely that between Belfast and London.[12] Between North and South is an inelegant rendition of 'within the island of Ireland'[13]. These geographical entities avoid the political terminology of Northern Ireland and the Republic of Ireland. The North, however, is a nationalist referent. The South – which does not conjure up memories of Southern Ireland (1920–22) – is not to the same extent a unionist term for the Republic of Ireland. Between these islands is the so-called east-west dimension, the term 'British Islands' – in United Kingdom law, the United Kingdom, the Channel Islands and the Isle of Man – being no longer appropriate.[14] The idea originated in Charles Haughey's totality of relationships within these islands.

There are two related problems with the three interlocking strands. First, do they refer only to interstate or intergovernmental relations, or to relations between peoples as well?[15] The answer would seem to be both. Secondly, does the totality of relationships encompass the internal and north-south dimensions? It should if we are talking about interstate relations. Both problems are evident in the respective references to the BIA in Strands Two and Three: 'the totality of relationships';[16] 'the totality of relationships among the peoples of these islands'.[17]

4. **We reaffirm our total and absolute commitment to exclusively democratic and peaceful means of resolving differences on political issues, and our opposition to any use or threat of force by others for any political purpose, whether in regard to this agreement or otherwise.**

8.6 ANNOTATIONS

This paragraph has its origin in the decision of the United Kingdom government, at the behest of the Irish government, following the unsuccessful talks in 1991–92, to try and include Sinn Féin in an agreement on the basis of the IRA having given up violence.[18]

11 Reported in *Irish Times*, 9 December 1981. For Margaret Thatcher's view, see *The Downing Street Years*, London 1995, p. 390.

12 *Ground Rules for Substantive All-Party Negotiations*, Cm 3232, 16 April 1996, rule 2.

13 *Ground Rules for Substantive All-Party Negotiations*, Cm 3232, 16 April 1996, rules 2 & 3.

14 The term dates from 1889, when of course it included Ireland. This remained the position until 1 January 1979: Interpretation Act 1978 s 22(1), sch 2, part 1, para 4(2).

15 *Ground Rules for Substantive All-Party Negotiations*, Cm 3232, 16 April 1996, rules 1 & 2.

16 Paragraph 1 of Strand Two.

17 First paragraph 1 of Strand Three.

18 'The British and Irish governments reiterate that the achievement of peace must involve a permanent end to the use of, or support for, paramilitary violence. They confirm that, in these circumstances, democratically mandated parties which establish a commitment to exclusively peaceful methods and which have shown that they abide by the democratic process, are free to participate fully in democratic politics and to join in dialogue in due course between the Governments and the political parties on the way ahead.' (Paragraph 10, *Downing Street Declaration*, 15 December 1993) There are four preconditions for paramilitary parties engaging in talks: a permanent end to the use of or support for violence; a democratic mandate; establishing a commitment to exclusively peaceful methods; showing they abide by the democratic process.

The requirement of decommissioning prior to talks was dropped effectively in November 1995 with the adoption of the twin-track approach,[19] of talks about talks and an international body on the decommissioning issue.

The Mitchell report of 22 January 1996[20] – which stated that the paramilitaries wanted to decommission[21] – outlined six principles of democracy and non-violence.[22] Mitchell proposed parallel decommissioning, that is during all-party negotiations.

'We reaffirm our total and absolute commitment to exclusively democratic and peaceful means of resolving differences on political issues,' This is Mitchell's first principle, but with democratic and exclusively peaceful means changed to exclusively democratic and peaceful means.

'and our opposition to any use or threat of force by others for any political purpose, whether in regard to this agreement or otherwise.' This was based on Mitchell's fourth principle. It left out to renounce for themselves. It also did not include any effort by others. It did, however, extend the principle beyond the course or outcome of all-party negotiations. The agreement is the Belfast Agreement. Or otherwise is widely drawn.

However, the paragraph does not – as might be expected – endorse the Mitchell principles. This had been a condition precedent of all the parties participating in the negotiations. If endorsement was necessary for the talks, so – the argument goes – it should have been integral to the Belfast Agreement (the paragraph does after all contain the widely drawn or otherwise).

The Mitchell principles not reaffirmed expressly by the Declaration of Support are: the total disarmament of all paramilitary organizations (number two); verification by an independent commission (number three); pre-agreement to accept the terms of any agreement, and a commitment to use only democratic means to alter any aspect of that outcome (number five); and taking effective steps to end punishment killings and beatings (number six). With the exception of number five, which had been superseded partly and was otherwise covered by the first principle, this means that the Declaration of Support did not endorse three of Mitchell's six principles. Decommissioning is, however, a separate section. And the Independent Commission is dealt with in the Decommissioning section. That leaves punishment killings and beatings without a reference in the Belfast Agreement.

> **5. We acknowledge the substantial differences between our continuing, and equally legitimate, political aspirations.** ***However, we will endeavour to strive in every practical way towards reconciliation and rapprochement within the framework of democratic and agreed arrangements.*** **[However,] [w]*We* pledge that we will, in good faith, work to ensure the success of each and every one of the arrangements to be established under**

19 Joint communiqué, John Mayor and John Bruton, 10 Downing Street, 28 November 1995.

20 Report of the International Body (Senator George J. Mitchell, General John de Chastelain and Prime Minister Harri Holkeri), Dublin and Belfast.

21 Paragraphs 24–32, especially 25.

22 'We recommend that the parties to ... negotiations affirm their total and absolute commitment: to democratic and exclusively peaceful means of resolving political issues; to the total disarmament of all paramilitary organisations; to agree that such disarmament must be verifiable to the satisfaction of an independent commission; to renounce for themselves, and to oppose any effort by others, to use force, or threaten to use force, to influence the course or the outcome of all-party negotiations; to agree to abide by the terms of any agreement reached in all-party negotiations and to resort to democratic and exclusively peaceful methods in trying to alter any aspect of that outcome with which they may disagree; and, to urge that "punishment" killings and beatings stop and to take effective steps to prevent such actions.' (Paragraph 20)

this agreement. It is accepted that all of the institutional *and constitutional* arrangements – an Assembly in Northern Ireland, a North/South Ministerial Council, implementation bodies, a British-Irish Council, and a British-Irish Intergovernmental Conference *and any amendments to British Acts of Parliament and the Constitution of Ireland* – are interlocking and *interdependent* [mutually supportive and that all will enter into force at or around the same time] *and that in particular the functioning of the Assembly and the North/South Council are so closely inter-related that the success of each depends on that of the other.*

8.7 ANNOTATIONS

This paragraph could embrace all participants, the eight parties and the two governments. However, it is drafted more in the second sense of participants, namely the parties being pushed towards an agreement by the United Kingdom and Irish governments. While the Irish government may be deemed to have aspirations of unity, the United Kingdom has never similarly affirmed an aspiration of continuing the union.

The paragraph was expanded substantially between the MDP and the FA, making the longest one longer still.

'We acknowledge the substantial differences between our continuing, and equally legitimate, political aspirations.' Acknowledge the substantial differences refers to the continuing divide in Ireland between nationalism and unionism, as that is expressed in Northern Ireland. This divide is managed – not transcended – by the Belfast Agreement. Continuing and equally legitimate relates loosely to paragraph 1(i) of Constitutional Issues, where legitimacy is derived from consent. Political aspirations is a reference to the alternatives of the union or a united Ireland in the same paragraph.

A recital in the preamble to the 1985 Anglo-Irish Agreement referred to 'the two major traditions that exist in Ireland', defining these as unionism and nationalism. Another recital referred to 'the identities of the two communities in Northern Ireland'. These, however, were not related to the two major traditions. It went on to refer to the right of each community 'to pursue its aspirations by peaceful and constitutional means'. However, article 4(a)(i) referred to 'the two traditions which exist in Northern Ireland' and to their 'rights and identities'. And article 7(c) used the term 'nationalist community'.

'However, we will endeavour to strive in every practical way towards reconciliation and rapprochement within the framework of democratic and agreed arrangements.' Clearly the first sentence was considered too negative, condemning Ireland to continuing difference over aspirations (even if the means were democratic). The original juxtaposition was working the institutions of the Belfast Agreement. This added sentence suggests a different political trajectory. We will endeavour to strive in every practical way is highly aspirational. Reconciliation is provided for, along with victims of violence, in the Rights, Safeguards and Equality of Opportunity section. It is not clear what rapprochement adds. Democratic arrangements is presumably a reference to Strand One. Again, it is not clear what agreed adds.

'We pledge that we will, in good faith, work to ensure the success of each and every one of the arrangements to be established under this agreement.' Pledge involves only a political commitment. In good faith was used in the *Ground Rules for Substantive All-Party Negotiations*, Cm 3232, 16 April 1996.[23] It suggests article 26 of the 1969 Vienna convention on the law of treaties ('*Pacta sunt servanda*'), but the political parties are not bound by the law of treaties. Work to ensure the success of is another commitment to the

23 Rule 16.

Belfast Agreement. Each and every one of the arrangements to be established under this agreement relates to the principle in the negotiations that nothing was agreed until everything was agreed.[24] Arrangements suggests institutions. And this was the meaning in the MDP. However, constitutional was added. The reference to British Acts of Parliament and to the Constitution of Ireland is definitely the Irish government It is similar to paragraph 2 of Constitutional Issues (and is discussed there).

The institutions listed – the assembly, the North/South Ministerial Council, implementation bodies, the British-Irish Council and the British-Irish Intergovernmental Conference – are the main ones in the Belfast Agreement. The paragraph read in draft that the institutions were interlocking and mutually supportive and all would enter into force at around the same time. In fact, under article 4 of the BIA, institutional and constitutional changes were due to take effect at the point at which that treaty entered into force. (See also paragraph 3 of the Validation, Implementation and Review section.) The phrase above was deleted, and replaced with a particular instance of interdependence: namely that between the assembly and the North/South Council (the word ministerial is missing).

6. **Accordingly, in a spirit of concord, we strongly commend this agreement to the people, North and South, for their approval.**

8.8 ANNOTATIONS

'Accordingly, in a spirit of concord,'. This is the language of treaties. However, given paragraph 5, the spirit refers most likely to the political parties and not the two governments.

'we strongly commend this agreement'. This was the parties anticipating the two referendums – one in Northern Ireland, the other in the Republic of Ireland – scheduled for 22 May 1998, under paragraph 2 of the Validation, Implementation and Review section.

'to the people, North and South, for their approval.' This 'people' has no constitutional status in United Kingdom or Irish law (after the end of the territorial claim). However, paragraph 1(iv) of Constitutional Issues refers to 'the people of the island of Ireland'. North and South is the inelegant terminology used in paragraph 3. Approval refers to the importance of legitimacy, in order to give the Belfast Agreement prospects of success after the simultaneous referendums. It was approved in the Northern Ireland referendum. That in the Republic of Ireland dealt only with amendments to BNH (see Chapter 11).

24 *Ground Rules for Substantive All-Party Negotiations*, Cm 3232, 16 April 1996, rule 23.

9

Constitutional Issues

9.1 Constitutional Issues is the second section of the Belfast Agreement, to which are attached Annexes A and B (though without reference).[1] The section (less the two annexes) is at page 2 of Cm 3883 and pages 10–11 of Cm 4705 (pages 4–5 of the 1999 Irish version). It is in particular the second section of the MPA.

9.2 Paragraph 1 is based on article 1 of the BIA.[2] There, the United Kingdom and Irish governments returned to their 1973 draft declaration, and article 1 on the status of Northern Ireland in the 1985 Anglo-Irish Agreement.[3] Paragraph 2, in contrast, does not relate to the BIA. It does, however, introduce Annexes A and B indirectly.

Constitutional history

9.3 Some constitutional history is necessary, drawing on Chapters 3 and 4, and especially 5 and 6. Chapter 2 (Public International Law) is also an essential foundation for the following analysis.

9.4 There has never been any problem in international law about the existence of the United Kingdom and Irish states (in spite of the Irish territorial claim). The latter – from whenever it became a state – had a 26-county territory, and, in Bunreacht na hÉireann, article 3 maintained this jurisdiction from 1937.

9.5 In United Kingdom law, the existence – and names – of the Irish state are clear from 1922 to the present (see Chapter 7). The problem is Irish constitutional law since 1937, in particular the territorial claim resting on the concept of 'national territory' in article 2 (though this in turn is based upon the – unquestioned – concept of 'the Irish nation' in article 1).

9.6 The nationalist nature of BNH was explained clearly by O'Higgins CJ in *Criminal Law (Jurisdiction) Bill, 1975* [1977] IR 129, 147: 'One of the theories held in 1937 by a substantial number of citizens was that a nation, as distinct from a State, has rights; that the Irish people living in what is now called the Republic of Ireland and in Northern Ireland together formed the Irish Nation; that a nation has a right to unity of territory in some form, be it as a unitary or federal state; and that the Government of Ireland Act, 1920, though legally binding, was a violation of that national right to unity which was superior to positive law.'

9.7 The solution to this legal problem was, of course, the withdrawal of the claim, by constitutional amendment in Irish law. That is the purpose of Annex B to Constitutional Issues. Annex A – as will be seen – is largely reciprocal cover for the

1 Chapters 10 and 11.

2 Pages 27–8 of Cm 3883 and pp. 2–3 of Cm 4705 (2 unnumbered pages & pp. 38–9 of the 1999 Irish version).

3 See Chapter 6.

unilateral Irish legal act. But the problem of Northern Ireland from 1972 had required an interim solution, namely a London-Dublin agreement in international law as to its constitutional status. It never got beyond the concept of consent and into recognition (the only joint declaration agreed between London and Dublin was article 1 of the 1985 Anglo-Irish Agreement). Such a statement, of course, fell far short of the sort of agreement two neighbouring sovereign states should have, even if there is a problem of national minorities.[4]

9.8 But, and this is the crucial point, this interim solution had to be constructed in such a way as not to contradict the Irish territorial claim (even though the United Kingdom had resisted it from 29 December 1937). London could only extract so much by way of international agreement, because its main concern was to defend the Irish government with which it was negotiating from its own Supreme Court. Articles 2 and 3 came to permit *de facto* recognition of Northern Ireland (so it was thought in Irish law), but there was always a fear that an Irish government might be dragged over the line into unconstitutionality by the United Kingdom.

9.9 The 1973 joint declaration was never constructed. The Irish government 'fully accepted and solemnly declared' at Sunningdale, and appeared to be legally bound by the use of the word 'could'. But it only agreed in paragraph 5 of the draft what it had already affirmed (on behalf of nationalists) in paragraph 3, namely its commitment to unity by consent. (The United Kingdom got no further than the draft in defining the status – in international law – of Northern Ireland. It morally trumped the Irish government with its democratic position, in the distinction between present pro-union consent and – a possibly future – pro-united Ireland consent.)

9.10 The 1985 joint declaration had to be an advance on 1973, even if important aspects of paragraph 5 were not adopted by the two governments. (Article 1 of the Anglo-Irish Agreement did not reassure unionists that the Irish government – in effect – endorsed section 1 of the Northern Ireland Constitution Act 1973.[5]) The Irish affirmation (unity by consent) was more political than legal,[6] while the recognition (no consent for a change) did not specify the status of Northern Ireland. However, the declaration (about consent for a united Ireland) legally bound the United Kingdom government.[7] (John Hume misconstrued the meaning of article 1(c), believing that Britain so-called, having shifted apparently from unionism to 'neutrality', could be pushed to become a persuader for unity.[8])

9.11 Whether the Irish territorial claim has been ended, and at what price to the United Kingdom (if any), will be answered in the next two chapters. *A priori*, one

4 See Chapter 19.

5 For nationalist views, see the new Ireland forum *Report* (1984), pp. 17 & 25.

6 The nationalist goal was defined, in the new Ireland forum *Report* (1984) as: 'a united Ireland in the form of a sovereign, independent Irish state to be achieved peacefully and by consent'. (p. 28)

7 Tom Hadden & Kevin Boyle reviewed critically article 1 (outside their terms of reference), in *The Anglo-Irish Agreement: commentary, text and official review*, Dublin & London 1989, pp. 18–22. They recommended that current status and minority aspiration should be articulated in both Irish and United Kingdom constitutional law.

8 The United Kingdom had been prepared to 'support' a united Ireland from 1971. But this was on the basis of consent.

would have expected that, if the territorial claim was going, there was no need for a joint declaration developing (arguably) the 1985 article. Clearly, the Irish government, in removing the claim from its constitution (in a minimalist manner I will argue), extracted two prices. The first was the so-called balanced constitutional accommodation, which is not a balance (see Chapter 10). The second is the 1998 attempt to update the 1985 declaration, which is what paragraph 1 of Constitutional Issues is about. The very project is suspect *ab initio*.

The right of self-determination?

9.12 The origins of the updated constitutional statement in 1998 – in article 1 of the BIA – lie in the so-called Hume-Adams declaration of 1992, in which the international law concept of self-determination figured prominently.

9.13 The so-called Irish peace process started as a Sinn Féin confection,[9] based upon an appreciation of the IRA's inability to achieve a united Ireland by violence alone. The goal became a pan-nationalist consensus – in which Sinn Féin hoped to mobilize the Irish government, the SDLP, Irish-America and sympathetic elements in Britain – to achieve so-called national self-determination in the shortest time possible. This has been described as the totally unarmed strategy (TUAS), following discovery of a 1994 IRA document, but TUAS is also interpreted – more literally – as the tactical use of armed struggle;[10] this is compatible with the IRA ceasefire of 1994–96, resumed in 1997.

9.14 The first Hume-Adams dialogue of 1988 collapsed, the SDLP leader stressing agreement on the exercise of self-determination in Ireland. That of 1992–93 bore fruit in a succession of (Dublin-influenced) draft declarations, including the crucial Sinn Féin text of June 1992 where it toyed with consent.[11]

9.15 After the rejection of the idea of Britain as a persuader for unity,[12] self-determination turned up in the *Downing Street Declaration* of 15 December 1993, and again – slightly modified – in the *Framework Documents* of 22 February 1996. London and Dublin, however, could only produce separate statements of its application to Ireland.[13]

9.16 The United Kingdom government had been slow to adopt the right of self-determination in its foreign policy (even though the 1966 covenants entered into force in international law in 1976). But this did not prevent it granting

9 See references to the Irish peace initiative in communications of 7 January, 29 January and 26 October 1992 and 14 June 1993, in *Setting the Record Straight*, Sinn Féin's record of communications with the British government, October 1990 to November 1993, released on 5 January 1994.

10 The former title is used by Eamonn Mallie & David McKittrick, *The Fight for Peace: the inside story of the Irish peace process*, London 1997, pp. 421–4. But they acknowledge the shift in meaning (pp. 396 & 398)

11 Mallie & McKittrick, *Fight*, pp. 415–17.

12 Joint statement of John Major and Albert Reynolds, 29 October 1993, paragraph 5.

13 'The British Government recognise that it is for the people of Ireland alone, by agreement between the two parts respectively and without external impediment, to exercise their right of self-determination on the basis of consent, freely and concurrently given, North and South, to bring about a united Ireland, if that is their wish; the Irish Government accept that the democratic right of self-determination by the people of Ireland as a whole must be achieved and exercised with and subject to the agreement and consent of a majority of the the people of Northern Ireland.' (*Framework Documents*, part II, para 16)

independence to 28 states between 1960 and 1982.[14] In this juxtaposition is revealed the gulf – reflected in the common and civil law traditions – between English empiricism and the theoretical propensity of other European cultures; words appeal to theorists and ideologues; pragmatists are happiest with actions.

9.17 Self-determination was invoked invariably by the United Kingdom when national interests were at stake: Gibraltar from the 1960s; the Falklands after the Argentinian invasion in 1982; but not Hong Kong in the 1990s (because of the treaty with China). Foreign policy cooperation in Europe, however, was the main stimulant: Afghanistan, following the Soviet involvement in 1979; Palestine in the 1980 Venice declaration; Cambodia, after the Vietnamese intervention; East Timor against Indonesia; South Africa from 1984 (an absence of internal self-determination);[15] and Namibia – the last major colony.

9.18 Self-determination has been bandied about by United Kingdom ministers and officials since the early 1980s, in a politically effusive rather than legally accurate sense. It was only a matter of time before London was likely to be persuaded to use the concept in a non-legal manner in its dealings with the two parts of Ireland.

9.19 The right of self-determination – based upon the discussion in Chapter 2 – has to be applied to Ireland carefully. The question has never been considered by the House of Lords or the Irish Supreme Court (or the ICJ). Sinn Féin – on the basis of the following argument – is most unlikely to be able to appropriate it for Irish republicanism.[16]

9.20 First, Ireland lies outside the time and space of the right in international law: Irish statehood dates from the 1920s, and self-determination did not become a legal right until after 1945; separatism (Sinn Féin's only understanding of self-determination) was transcended after the relative failure of this national strategy in the 1920s–1950s; the country has been part of Europe since 1973, and was never part of the third world.

9.21 Secondly, since the people of Ireland has been divided historically, there is no possibility of that (geographical, not political) entity having a right to self-determination in international law.

9.22 Reference was made in Chapter 2, in the discussion of self determination of peoples, to an important Canadian case: *Reference re Secession of Quebec* [1998] 2 RCS 216.[17] The Supreme Court discussed the legality of self-determination as a principle in international law: 'a right to secession only arises under the principle of self-determination of people at international law where "a people" is subject to alien subjugation, domination or exploitation; and possibly where "a people" is denied any meaningful exercise of its right of self-determination within the state of which it forms a part. In other circumstances, peoples are expected to achieve self-determination within the framework of their existing state. A state whose

14 Sir Ian Sinclair, legal adviser to the Foreign and Commonwealth Office, still described it as a political principle: *British Yearbook of International Law, 1983*, Oxford 1984, p. 400.

15 Also Uganda and Cambodia.

16 For an attempt, see *Towards a Lasting Peace in Ireland*, Dublin & Belfast, 1992, pp. 5–6 & 16.

17 See also A.F. Bayefsky, *Self-Determination in International Law: Quebec and lessons learned*, The Netherlands 2000.

government represents the whole of the people or peoples resident within its territory, on a basis of equality and without discrimination, and respects the principles of self-determination in its international arrangements, is entitled to maintain its territorial integrity under international law and to have that territorial integrity recognized by other states.' (222) Applying that case, through the common law, it is most unlikely that, in United Kingdom or in Irish law, there would be a finding of the right of the Irish people to national self determination.

9.23 The Irish attorney general, David Byrne SC, referred to 'national self-determination' in his address to the American Bar Association (International Law and Practice Section) in Toronto on 3 August 1998.[18] The Canadian Supreme Court had heard the above case on 16 to 19 February 1998, but judgment was not delivered until 20 August 1998. The Irish attorney general, therefore, was unable to comment on any possible Irish significance.

9.24 In contradistinction, the people of the Republic of Ireland, and the people of the United Kingdom (not Northern Ireland[19]), have had a separate (unincorporated) right in international law to self-determination since 1976, in the sense of continuing self-government. (And the Republic's territorial claim was an infringement in international law of the right extended to the people of the United Kingdom.) The United Kingdom's so-called constitutional guarantee to Northern Ireland, while coterminous with the right to self-determination, is a matter of consent in municipal law. The idea of internal self-determination (which might be extendable to unionists and nationalists separately) has no bearing on state formation; it evolved in antithesis to the concept of external self determination.[20]

9.25 Thirdly, the international law on minorities – for catholics in Northern Ireland – is very applicable. Historically, self-determination has had little to offer minorities. There was treaty protection after the First World War. Article 27 of the 1966 covenant on civil and political rights refers to 'ethnic, religious or linguistic minorities'.[21] Racial discrimination has been a major problem. Though the concept of minority appeared in the 1985 Anglo-Irish Agreement,[22] this was not prototypical of bilateral treaties protecting minorities.[23] The Council of Europe's 1995 Framework Convention for the Protection of National Minorities[24] – specified in the Belfast Agreement[25] – codifies state practice. This is considered in Chapter 18.

18 *Fordham International Law Journal*, p. 1215.

19 This was asserted by unionists in 1972. However, the United Kingdom government avoided granting the right to the people of Northern Ireland: *The Future of Northern Ireland: a paper for discussion*, NIO, October 1972, paras. 27(vi) & 75.

20 Robert McCorquodale, 'Negotiating Sovereignty: the practice of the United Kingdom in regard to the right of self-determination', *British Yearbook of International Law, 1995*, Oxford 1996, p. 283.

21 See also the United Nations General Assembly Declaration on the Rights of Persons belonging to National or Ethnic, Religious and Linguistic Minorities of 18 December 1992, 32 ILM 911 (1993).

22 Articles 4(c) and 5(c).

23 The 1996 Hungary/Romania Treaty on Understanding, Cooperation and Good Neighbourhood, articles 14–15 & annex.

24 34 ILM 351 (1995).

25 First paragraph 9 of the Rights, Safeguards and Equality of Opportunity section.

9.26 Fourthly, the most appropriate legal principle for Ireland is *uti possidetis*.[26] In the two great waves of state creation – south America in the nineteenth century and Africa in the twentieth – it has been uppermost. Self-determination was qualified, and minority rights were not invoked. *Uti possidetis* means that it is better to work with existing borders than to risk a new state being created in politically adverse circumstances. The Government of Ireland Act 1920 provided for an internal border within the United Kingdom. When it came to the creation of the Irish Free State subsequently, it achieved viability behind what became an international frontier. If the pro- or anti-treatyites had reopened the question of partition in the 1920s, nationalism might not have been so successful. The Irish Free State, established in the 26 counties, would not, if it had sought to unite Ireland by force, have entered the community of nations in the 1920s. Irish history – though no one is aware of it – proves the efficacy of the principle of *uti possidetis* in Ireland.

TITLE: CONSTITUTIONAL ISSUES

9.27 Constitutional refers undoubtedly to Annex B, the amendment to Bunreacht na hÉireann. Annex A, changes to United Kingdom statute law, may also be said to be constitutional. But this does not accurately describe paragraph 1, where six points are made. Their precedent is the 1973 draft declaration, and article 1 of the 1985 Anglo-Irish Agreement, on the constitutional status of Northern Ireland. A declaration in international law does not, of course, change municipal law; it is a substitute for it. Paragraph 1 – the main content of Constitutional Issues – is a further declaration by the two states, which avoids the domestic law of the United Kingdom and Irish states. It is described as 'embodying understandings on constitutional issues', in paragraph 1 of the Validation, Implementation and Review section.

9.28 Given that three of the points are related to self-determination, it would seem that, whereas the United Kingdom government sought in the 1970s and 1980s to pull Dublin towards consent as a substitute for the recognition of Northern Ireland *de jure*, in this declaration of 1998 seemingly the Irish government has pulled London towards the right of the Irish people to national self-determination.

1. **The participants endorse the commitment made by the British and Irish Governments that, in a new British-Irish Agreement replacing the Anglo-Irish Agreement, they will:**

9.29 ANNOTATIONS

'The participants'. Here, participants can only refer to the political parties. This confirms the point made in Chapter 8 about paragraphs 1 and 5 of the Declaration of Support.

'endorse'. This is a cross-reference to article 1 of the British-Irish Agreement, the joint

26 Malcolm Shaw, 'The Heritage of States: the principle of *uti possidetis* today', *British Yearbook of International Law, 1996*, Oxford 1997; Declaration on the Granting of Independence to Colonial Countries and Peoples (1960), General Assembly Resolution 1514 (XV), paragraph 6; *Western Sahara*, Advisory Opinion, ICJ Reports 1975, p. 12; *Frontier Dispute*, Judgment, ICJ Reports 1986, pp. 564–7; *Land, Island and Maritime Frontier Dispute (El Salvador/Honduras)*, Judgment, ICJ Reports 1992, pp. 386–9.

declaration by the United Kingdom and Irish governments. The text in the MPA follows that in the BIA. It was not in fact open to amendment by the political parties, having been agreed by the two states parties. The MDP, since it was drawing on a BIA, neither listed in the contents, much less annexed, correctly anticipated the FA.

'the commitment made by the British and Irish governments that,'. Commitment refers to the declaration in article 1 of the BIA. But it also indicates that both governments have accepted – in that treaty – a series of obligations, in subparagraphs (i)–(vi). British government has been the practice in Anglo-Irish relations since at least the 1924 amendment of the 1921 treaty. However, the term 'United Kingdom government' was used consistently in the 1985 Anglo-Irish Agreement (even if the accompanying joint communiqué referred to 'the British Parliament'). Irish government is generally uncontroversial.

'in a new British-Irish Agreement replacing the Anglo-Irish Agreement,'. This is the first reference to the BIA in the MPA (the contents page gives the full title). That international agreement is entitled: *Agreement between the Government of the United Kingdom of Great Britain and Northern Ireland and the the Government of Ireland.* (The Irish version reverses the names.) BIA is therefore the MPA name, given by the political parties; it may, however, be more of a description. The BIA is also referred to similarly in paragraph 1 of Strand Two, the first paragraph 1 and second paragraph 1 of Strand Three and paragraph 1 of Validation, Implementation and Review.

'replacing' is a reference to article 3(1) of the BIA, which states clearly that the Anglo-Irish Agreement 'shall cease to have effect on entry into force of' the BIA. The Anglo-Irish Agreement was the name, or description, given to the 1985 international agreement, which was entitled: *Agreement between the Government of the United Kingdom of Great Britain and Northern Ireland and the Government of the Republic of Ireland.*[27] The accompanying joint communiqué of 15 November 1985 was headed: Anglo-Irish Summit Meeting.

'they will:'. They of course refers to the United Kingdom and Irish governments.

(i) recognise the legitimacy of whatever choice is freely exercised by a majority of the people of Northern Ireland with regard to its status, whether they prefer to continue to support the Union with Great Britain or a sovereign united Ireland;

9.30 ANNOTATIONS

'recognise the legitimacy'. The preamble to the 1985 Anglo-Irish Agreement recognized 'the need for continuing efforts to reconcile and to acknowledge the rights of the two major traditions that exist in Ireland'. Here it is now a question of legitimacy. But the legitimacy is not about the political right to be for or against the union. The legitimacy refers to the goal of maintaining the union or replacing it with a united Ireland.

The United Kingdom government, as was inferred by John Hume in 1985, would appear – only appear – to have adopted a neutral position (acceptance of the consent principle does not mean the abandonment of all constitutional duties). Neutrality, however, was suggested in a speech in London by Peter Brooke MP, the secretary of state for Northern Ireland – who later acknowledged prompting by Hume – in November 1990: 'The British government has no selfish strategic or economic interest in Northern Ireland: our role is to help, enable and encourage. Britain's purpose ... is not to occupy, oppress or exploit, but to ensure democratic debate and free democratic choice. That is our way.'[28]

27 The Irish version: *Agreement between the Government of Ireland and the Government of the United Kingdom.*

28 Original text, 9 November 1990, Whitbread restaurant, London. The phrase 'no selfish strategic or economic interest' resurfaced without any commas in the *Downing Street Declaration*, paragraph 4, and in the *Framework Documents* (part II, paragraph 20).

'of whatever choice is freely exercised'. This can only be a reference to United Kingdom law, in particular to the draft clauses and schedule in Annex A. The idea of a free choice was implicit in the United Kingdom contribution to the 1973 draft declaration. It was developed in the 1985 Anglo-Irish Agreement: 'clearly wish for and formally consent' being the two conditions precedent in article 1(c).

'by a majority of the people of Northern Ireland with regard to its status,'. This is again a reference to Annex A. There its status is defined as part of the United Kingdom, with the alternative being part of a united Ireland.

'whether they prefer to continue to support the Union with Great Britain or a sovereign united Ireland;'. Prefer clearly relates to the union or a united Ireland. But there is no such equivalence. The constitutional status quo is the union. Those who prefer it include so-called unionists (who have proved resistant to abandoning that allegiance), but also democrats unattracted by the blandishments of nationalists. The latter might be reluctant to say they prefer the union, or are unionists. Preferring a united Ireland, on the other hand, is purely aspirational. There is no democratic basis for it at present (and it has been the objective of republican terrorists for nearly three decades). To continue to support the union suggests that it rests only upon the will of unionists. That might be the case politically; it is not legally. The union rests upon United Kingdom and international law. That will only give way (under the Belfast Agreement), if and when unionists are overwhelmed democratically by nationalists, and other conditions in Annexes A and B are fulfilled. The Union with Great Britain phrase differs from the 1973 draft declaration, where London referred to Northern Ireland being part of the United Kingdom. Its status was missing totally from article 1 of the 1985 Anglo-Irish Agreement, and from the preamble.[29] A 'sovereign united Ireland' is evocative of article 5 of Bunreacht na hÉireann, where Ireland is described as 'a sovereign, independent, democratic state'. The term sovereign united Ireland was used in the preamble to the 1985 Anglo-Irish Agreement, but it was qualified with: 'achieved by peaceful means and through agreement'; the aspiration was confined to essentially so-called constitutional nationalists.

(ii) recognise that it is for the people of the island of Ireland alone, by agreement between the two parts respectively and without external impediment, to exercise their right of self-determination on the basis of consent, freely and concurrently given, North and South, to bring about a united Ireland, if that is their wish, accepting that this right must be achieved and exercised with and subject to the agreement and consent of a majority of the people of Northern Ireland;

9.31 This is the first of three subparagraphs on self-determination. Subparagraph (ii) is a joint declaration by the two governments. The separate statements in the 1993 *Downing Street Declaration* and the 1995 *Framework Documents* have been combined. Subparagraph (iii) – for the purpose of identifying context – is about present consent, self-determination for the union. And subparagraph (iv) deals with possible future consent, self-determination favouring a united Ireland. The treatment of self-determination, in this application to Ireland, is so legally incoherent that it is difficult to resist the conclusion that the United Kingdom government was engaged only in a defensive political exercise.

29 The *Downing Street Declaration* had only 'the Union' (paragraph 4) as did the *Framework Documents* (part II, paragraph 20).

9.32 ANNOTATIONS

'recognise that it is for the people of the island of Ireland alone,'. The right of self-determination turns on people. People is not defined in international law. That is because any putative beneficiary of the right has to prove itself historically. It is a very high threshold. Irish nationalists talk about the Irish people as an entity, but this is not equivalent to the people of Ireland. The people of geographical Ireland do not, given the division over self-government since the 1880s, constitute a people in international law. The United Kingdom has either made a fundamental legal mistake, or it was engaged principally, following Hume-Adams in 1992–93, with the Irish government in creating a mood for all-inclusive political talks.

The island of Ireland comes from the definition of the national territory in article 2 of Bunreacht na hÉireann. It reappeared in article 2(a) of the 1985 Anglo-Irish Agreement (island being totally superfluous). Its use from 1993 by Dublin, to refer to geographical Ireland, betrays the problem with the government of Ireland terminology (discussed in Chapter 7). Alone adds nothing, though it invokes the self-reliance of Sinn Féin nationalism. It was the fourth draft of Hume-Adams, by John Hume and Dublin officials in April 1992, which made self-determination a British commitment. The phrase then used was 'the Irish people collectively', which has a nationalist pedigree similar to the Irish people as a whole.[30] The people of the island of Ireland alone first appeared in the 1993 *Downing Street Declaration*, and was repeated in the 1995 *Framework Documents* – less the reference to the island of.

'by agreement between the two parts respectively and without external impediment,'. By agreement comes from John Hume's concept of self-determination. Treating it as a synonym for all-Ireland self-government (occluding the plebiscitary principle), he argued that the 'exercise' of self-determination could only be 'achieved' with 'the agreement of the people of Northern Ireland'.[31] As such, it is a statement about political viability. Agreement here relates to the Republic of Ireland and Northern Ireland. These are the two parts to which reference is made. Respectively seems to contribute nothing given the earlier use of between. And without external impediment was added in the 1995 *Framework Documents*, no doubt to conciliate nationalist suspicion.

'to exercise their right of self-determination'. Exercise comes from John Hume. More appropriately related to the plebiscitary principle; in his view it seems to mean effective Irish self-government. The right of self-determination is the core of the subparagraph, but – I submit – the surrounding text distorts the application of the legal right. The key issue is whether the so-called people of the island of Ireland alone constitutes a group in international law. If they do, they have fulfilled one condition for an unqualified right; if they do not, they have no right.

'on the basis of consent, freely and concurrently given, North and South,'. Self-determination in international law is related to 'consent' in muncipal law. The idea of internal democracy, long applied on the international plane (sovereign equality), was extended to peoples. Self-determination, whether plebiscitary or self-government (alternatively, external or internal), is democracy in action. Freely and concurrently given, North and South refers to Annex B, in particular draft article 3.1 and the idea of two referendums (first advanced in 1994 to the surprise of United Kingdom officials). North and South are once again the inelegant referents.

'to bring about a united Ireland, if that is their wish,'. Self-determination is about a people determining collectively. Only Irish nationalists see it in terms of a united Ireland. If that is

30 Sinn Féin, *Lasting Peace*, p. 5.

31 'The traditional objective of Irish nationalism – the exercise of self-determination by the people of Ireland as a whole – cannot be achieved without the agreement of the people of Northern Ireland.' (Mallie & McKittrick, *Fight*, p. 119)

their wish shifts the concept from that goal to the question of democratic means.

All the above was the original United Kingdom statement (slightly modified) in the 1993 *Downing Street Declaration* and the 1995 *Framework Documents*. It has clearly been accepted now by the Irish government, which raises the question: why not earlier? The remainder – in turn – is based on the original Irish government statement, and it too has been accepted by the United Kingdom government. The same question may be posed. Sticking together two texts hardly suggests a common understanding.

'accepting that this right must be achieved and exercised'. The right is self-determination. Achieved and exercised are John Hume's concepts in reverse order. Putting achieved first suggests an Irish struggle to get United Kingdom acceptance. This phrase – and the one below – follow the 1993 and 1995 London-Dublin texts.

'with and subject to the agreement and consent of a majority of the people of Northern Ireland;'. With and subject makes all that goes before in the subparagraph dependent upon all that remains. What remains is a condition subsequent. Agreement is again John Hume. Consent is the old United Kingdom principle of 1973 and 1985, and adds nothing. A majority of the people of Northern Ireland relates to the electoral outcome under Annex A.

(iii) acknowledge that while a substantial section of the people of Northern Ireland share the legitimate wish of a majority of the people of the island of Ireland for a united Ireland, the present wish of a majority of the people of Northern Ireland, freely exercised and legitimate, is to maintain the Union and, accordingly, that Northern Ireland's status as part of the United Kingdom reflects and relies upon that wish; and that it would be wrong to make any change in the status of Northern Ireland save with the consent of a majority of its people;

9.33 This subparagraph is about present – pro-union – consent. It is not strictly about self-determination as a right. Its origins are the status of Northern Ireland sentence in the United Kingdom contribution to the 1973 draft declaration, as diluted in article 1(b) of the 1985 Anglo-Irish Agreement.

9.34 ANNOTATIONS

'acknowledge that while a substantial section of the people of Northern Ireland share the legitimate wish of a majority of the people of the island of Ireland for a united Ireland,'. This was a development of the recognition of northern nationalists in the 1985 Anglo-Irish Agreement[32] (and first appeared in the 1995 *Framework Documents*). But it is not clear on what this is based. In the only border poll there has been (1973), there were only 6,463 votes in favour of a united Ireland. Admittedly, 41.3 per cent of the entire electorate – including nationalist boycotters – did not vote.

A substantial section of the people of Northern Ireland is conjecture, even if it may be inferred from political alignment. Opinion poll evidence is one thing, the political views of elected representatives another, and a prediction as to how people would vote on a specific question an entirely different matter. The legitimate wish refers back to legitimacy in subparagraph (i). Wish was used in 1973 and 1985 to mean pre-plebiscitary opinion. A majority of the people of the island of Ireland for a united Ireland is again conjecture. Given the disjuncture between the well-established Irish state, and Northern Ireland violence, any argument based on inference must be less than convincing. The percentage turnout on 22 May 1998 in the referendum on articles 2 and 3 was only 56.3 per cent. A mere 5.61 per cent of that figure – 85,748 voters – endorsed the Irish terrritorial claim. The island of Ireland has been discussed in subparagraph (ii).

32 Indirectly in the preamble and articles 4(c) and 5(c), and directly in article 7(c).

'the present wish of a majority of the people of Northern Ireland, freely exercised and legitimate,'. Present wish may be taken from the 1 May 1997 general election in the United Kingdom, when Northern Ireland returned 13 unionists to 5 nationalists. Or from the 25 June 1998 assembly elections, when 58 unionists and 42 nationalists were elected (along with 8 others). But a majority of the people of Northern Ireland sounds more plebiscitary. Freely exercised must mean in accordance with appropriate electoral law. Legitimate is again about a goal (the maintenance of the constitutional status quo) rather than democratic means.

'is to maintain the Union'. The union has been mentioned in subparagraph (i), but there is no reference here to with Great Britain.

'and, accordingly, that Northern Ireland's status as part of the United Kingdom reflects and relies upon that wish;'. Accordingly has the effect of diminishing the following statement, which suggests that present consent leads to status. Northern Ireland's status as part of the United Kingdom is the Irish admission the United Kingdom failed to obtain in 1973 and 1985. (This is the only reference to the United Kingdom in paragraph 1, and only the shortened version is used.) But it is not an unqualified recognition. Reflects and relies upon that wish is a second attempt to diminish the acknowledgement of Northern Ireland *de jure*. (It first appeared in the 1995 *Framework Documents.*) Wish is of course present consent. Reflects that wish suggests that consent causes the constitutional position. This is not the case. The status of Northern Ireland is a question of United Kingdom constitutional law, and of international law. It is fixed, until the Westminster parliament, and the practice of states, should alter it. Consent is a variable on the basis of this constitutional status. But, even if consent turns against the union, it is not dissolved until there has been a change in the law. And relies is less inaccurate than reflects. But here it can only be interpreted as reinforcing the incorrect idea conveyed by reflects.

'and that it would be wrong to make any change in the status of Northern Ireland save with the consent of a majority of its people;'. The first semi-colon attaches this clause to the above sentence. Wrong suggests a moral rather than legal liability. It was first used in the 1995 *Framework Documents.* To make any change in the status of Northern Ireland requires reversion to the previous sentence, where the statement about status is pressed fore and aft into an inaccuracy. Save with the consent of a majority of its people is back to the United Kingdom concept the Irish government accepted as long ago as 1973.

(iv) affirm that if, in the future, the people of the island of Ireland exercise their right of self-determination on the basis set out in sections (i) and (ii) above to bring about a united Ireland, it will be a binding obligation on both Governments to introduce and support in their respective Parliaments legislation to give effect to that wish;

9.35 In 1973, the United Kingdom government was prepared to 'support' a wish for a united Ireland. In 1985, both governments undertook to 'introduce and support in the respective Parliaments legislation to give effect to that wish'. The subparagraph adds little if anything to what has gone before, and is overshadowed by the marginal changes in United Kingdom law in Annex A.

9.36 ANNOTATIONS

'affirm that if, in the future, the people of the island of Ireland exercise their right of self-determination'. Such a future was envisaged also in 1973 and 1985. People of the island of Ireland and their right of self-determination have been discussed above.

'on the basis set out in sections (i) and (ii) above to bring about a united Ireland,'. It is not clear why subparagraph (i) is mentioned, and subparagraph (iii) is excluded. A reference to subparagraph (ii) would have sufficed. It seems to be an appropriation of references to a united Ireland. Sections is not the correct terminology, either for paragraph 1 of Constitutional Issues or article 1 of the BIA: Annex 2 refers to it as comprising paragraphs. This problem has arisen since paragraph 1 is seemingly part of domestic law, while article 1 is definitely international law. Section is correct for the latter; and subparagraph for the former.

'it will be a binding obligation on both Governments to introduce and support in their respective Parliaments legislation to give effect to that wish;'. Binding obligation is upon the states in international law. It is strange that this subparagraph (unlike Annex A), does not mention the need for legal cession. Neither government has so far committed itself to this essential legal stage. This would have been the place to do so.

(v) **affirm that whatever choice is freely exercised by a majority of the people of Northern Ireland, the power of the sovereign government with jurisdiction there shall be exercised with rigorous impartiality on behalf of all the people in the diversity of their identities and traditions and shall be founded on the principles of full respect for, and equality of, civil, political, social and cultural rights, of freedom from discrimination for all citizens, and of parity of esteem and of just and equal treatment for the identity, ethos, and aspirations of both communities;**

9.37 This subparagraph implies continuity after a united Ireland, with the United Kingdom and Irish states administering Northern Ireland similarly. It was trailed in speeches of Dublin ministers,[33] and first appeared in the 1995 *Framework Documents*. After the Belfast Agreement, David Byrne SC, the Irish attorney general, said: 'the commitments in the British-Irish Agreement to equality of treatment and parity of esteem, and to the dual citizenship rights of the people of Northern Ireland, are explicitly to apply irrespective of the status of Northern Ireland'.[34]

9.38 ANNOTATIONS

'affirm that whatever choice is freely exercised by a majority of the people of Northern Ireland,'. This refers back to subparagraph (i).

'the power of the sovereign government with jurisdiction there shall be exercised with rigorous impartiality'. The concept of sovereignty was used in subparagraph (i), but only with reference to a united Ireland. Here, it is generic, containing an implied recognition of United Kingdom sovereignty over Northern Ireland. Sovereignty and jurisdiction were used first together in article 2(b) of the 1985 Anglo-Irish Agreement. The two, however, are not identical. Northern Ireland and the Republic of Ireland are two separate jurisdictions; Northern Ireland also belongs to a different state. Northern Ireland and Scotland are two separate jurisdictions; however, they belong to the same state. Irish governments, on the basis of article 3 of BNH, have never exercised jurisdiction over Northern Ireland. They claimed that the United Kingdom had jurisdiction without sovereign right. Rigorous impartiality is the core of the subparagraph.

'on behalf of the people in the diversity of their identities and traditions'. This is obviously the people of Northern Ireland. Diversity, identities and traditions turns this people into a plurality. Diversity was first used in the 1993 *Downing Street Declaration*.[35] Identity and tradition first appeared in the new Ireland forum *Report* of 1984.[36] Identities was used in the

33 Dick Spring's idea of a covenant, put forward in an Irish Association address on 5 March 1993.

34 *Fordham International Law Journal*, p. 1219.

35 Paragraph 6.

36 Dublin Stationery Office, p. 28 (para 5.4).

preamble to the 1985 Anglo-Irish Agreement to refer to the two communities. Traditions were then all-Ireland, namely unionism and nationalism. But article 4(a)(i) linked tradition and community in Northern Ireland.

'and shall be founded on the principles of full respect for, and equality of, civil, political, social and cultural rights, of freedom from discrimination for all citizens, and of parity of esteem and of just and equal treatment for the identity, ethos, and aspirations of both communities;'. These principles have been drawn from a comprehensive set of sources (and appeared first in the 1995 *Framework Documents*). Full respect for, and equality of, addresses the bicommunal nature of Northern Ireland. Human rights are strangely missing, given their inclusion in the Rights, Safeguards and Equality of Opportunity section. Civil and political rights suggests the 1966 covenant. Social and cultural rights also refers forward to the Economic, Social and Cultural subsection of Rights, Safeguards and Equality of Opportunity, though economic is absent here. They are evocative of the second 1966 covenant. Freedom from discrimination for all citizens refers probably to the ground of religious belief or political opinion, which was addressed in part III of the NICA 1973. Discrimination is dealt with more widely in part VII of the NIA 1998. Parity of esteem – based on a proposal for 'recognition of the nationalist community in a legal sense [in domestic law?]' – is the principal legacy of the informal Opsahl commission of 1992–93.[37] Just and equal treatment refers back to rigorous impartiality. But it is confined here to identity, ethos and aspirations – which makes it a rather cultural, parity-of-esteem-type obligation.

(vi) recognise the birthright of all the people of Northern Ireland to identify themselves and be accepted as Irish or British, or both, as they may so choose, and accordingly confirm that their right to hold British and Irish citizenship is accepted by both Governments and would not be affected by any future change in the status of Northern Ireland.

9.39 This is a completely new principle – citizenship. It originated in the 1995 *Framework Documents*, where the removal of the territorial claim was mooted. The governments – it was promised – would 'maintain[ing] the existing birthright of everyone born in either jurisdiction in Ireland to be part as of right, of the Irish nation'.[38] (Nationality, of course, while it is used adjectively in United Kingdom law, and, in Irish law, in association with citizenship, has no legal effect in either state.)

9.40 Paragraph 1(vi) was clearly an attempt to reassure Sinn Féin. Its belated call for a 'yes' vote in the 22 May 1998 referendums, where articles 2 and 3 of BNH were amended in the Republic of Ireland, was conditional on inter alia no 'dilut[ion of] the citizenship rights in the north'.[39]

9.41 However, at some point after the two governments agreed in 1995 to birthright to dual nationality in Northern Ireland, they discovered the law on citizenship was more complex. Thus a second annex had to be added to the BIA, heavily qualifying subparagraph – or section – (vi) of article 1. It is therefore appropriate to also consider this joint understanding here (just as paragraph 1 of

37 *A Citizens' Inquiry: the Opsahl report on Northern Ireland*, ed. Andy Pollak, Dublin 1993, pp. 112–13.

38 Part II, paragraph 21.

39 Ard Chomhairle paper to 1998 (resumed) ardfhéis, 10 May, dealing with emergency resolution no. 2: http://sinnfein.ie.

Constitutional Issues could be discussed in Chapter 24). Annex 2, however, has tended to be ignored in Irish government discussions of paragraph:1(vi) of Constitutional Issues:

ANNEX 2

Declaration on the Provisions of Paragraph[40] (vi) of Article 1 In Relationship to Citizenship

The British and Irish Governments declare that it is their joint understanding that the term 'the people of Northern Ireland' in paragraph (vi) of Article 1 of this Agreement means, for the purposes of giving effect to this provision, all persons born in Northern Ireland and having, at the time of their birth, at least one parent who is a British citizen, an Irish citizen or is otherwise entitled to reside in Northern Ireland without any restrictions on their period of residence.

9.42 This major qualification of birthright – completely undermining the idea – indicates a clash between rhetoric and law. It is therefore necessary to look at the law on citizenship (the term of art) in Northern Ireland. It is not a straightforward topic.

9.43 The people of Northern Ireland, I submit, did not acquire Irish citizenship by birth, unlike those born in the United Kingdom before 1 January 1983 (who have a birthright in that state's citizenship law). There was no birthright to Irish citizenship on 10 April 1998, and, arguably, there may well be a problem in Irish law with the citizenship provision from 2 December 1999, under the partly retrospective Irish Nationality and Citizenship Bill when enacted.

Nationality law

9.44 In international law,[41] this is substantially a matter for two domestic jurisdictions (with extra-territorial effect), though the problem has been compounded by European citizenship – for Irish or United Kingdom nationals – since 1992.[42]

9.45 Up until 1922, the people of Ireland were generally natural-born British subjects.[43] With the creation of the Irish Free State, there came a limited form of internal citizenship. This was unique in the sovereign's dominions. Everyone domiciled in the Irish Free State on 6 December 1922[44] – on the basis of birth or descent in Ireland (sic),[45] or residence in the 26 counties – became a citizen of Saorstát Eireann (a status persons[46] could elect not to accept).[47]

40 Paragraph 1(iv) refers to sections, as does article 1(iv). In keeping with the Belfast Agreement as a whole, I am referring to the two paragraphs of Constitutional Issues. This means that section (vi) is a subparagraph. In terms of article 1, subparagraph (vi) is a section. Either way, it is not a paragraph.

41 1930 Hague Convention Concerning Certain Questions Relating to the Conflict of Nationality Laws.

42 1997 treaty of Amsterdam, article 17 (ex article 8) of the European Community treaty.

43 Clive Parry, *Nationality and Citizenship Laws of the Commonwealth and of the Republic of Ireland*, London 1957, p. 925; British Nationality and Status of Aliens Acts 1914 to 1943.

44 See *In re Logue* [1933] 67 ILTR 253 per Judge Moonan, for a decision interpreting the 1921 treaty. This case was mentioned in the explanatory memorandum to the 1956 Irish act.

45 Section 3 of the Adaptation of Enactments Act 1922 does not apply.

46 It is arguable whether this included British subjects.

47 Constitution of the Irish Free State (Saorstát Eireann) Act 1922, first schedule, article 3: but see also article 17 and second schedule, article 4.

They travelled abroad, including in Northern Ireland, as British subjects under United Kingdom law: the British Nationality and Status of Aliens Acts 1914 to 1943.

9.46 De Valera ended the restriction on extra-territoriality in 1935 with the twenty-sixth constitutional amendment.[48] Irish passports – an administrative matter, there is no law – followed.[49] He also made provisions (in the Aliens Act 1935) for the exclusion by order of British subjects in Northern Ireland and Great Britain from the category of alien.[50] His Irish Nationality and Citizenship Act 1935 – the first in the history of the Irish Free State – which created 'natural-born citizens of Saorstát Eireann', had only a minimal impact upon Northern Ireland.[51] Irish nationality was not a term of art. In 1937, Bunreacht na hÉireann, while it gave the Oireachtas the power to legislate on citizenship in article 9, did nothing to alter the law.[52]

9.47 Articles 2 and 3 are not the basis of a right to an Irish passport, and the removal of the territorial claim does not directly diminish rights to Irish citizenship under the law.

9.48 It was the British Nationality Act 1948 – of the United Kingdom parliament – which recognized dual nationality in Éire/Ireland: British subject (not commonwealth citizen[53]) and citizen of Éire. Persons in Northern Ireland became citizens of the United Kingdom and Colonies (plus commonwealth citizens). When the Irish state quit the commonwealth, becoming the Republic of Ireland, the United Kingdom – in the Ireland Act 1949 – deemed it not to be a foreign country. Its citizens could not be aliens in United Kingdom law.

9.49 Reciprocal citizenship rights – based on the 1949 United Kingdom act[54] and the 1935 (later 1956) Irish act[55] – became the practice, though differences were to remain.[56] In 1971, Ireland and Great Britain – for the purposes of passport controls – became a common travel area.[57] (Common travel area issues are a subject for consideration by the new British-Irish Intergovernmental Conference.[58])

48 Amending article 3 in the first schedule of the Constitution of the Irish Free State (Saorstát Eireann) Act 1922.

49 They were in existence by early 1937: Spanish Civil War (Non-Intervention) Act 1937 s 6(1).

50 Aliens Act 1935 s 5; Aliens Order 1946 (SR&O 395); Aliens (Amendment) Order 1975 (SI No. 128).

51 The contrary argument depends upon defining the jurisdiction of the Irish Free State on 6 December 1922 as geographical Ireland: Dáil Éireann, *Official Reports*, 997–9, 29 February 1956; *In re Logue* [1933] 67 ILTR 253 per Judge Moonan.

52 *Murray v Parkes* [1942] 2 KB 123, 131: 'a national character as an Irish citizen within the wider British nationality' per Viscount Caldecote CJ.

53 The United Kingdom anticipated Éire/Ireland's withdrawal from the commonwealth.

54 Section 2(1).

55 Respectively, sections 23 and 26.

56 *Anglo-Irish Joint Studies; joint report and studies*, Cmnd 8414, November 1981, pp. 14–23.

57 Immigration Act 1971 section 1(3); there does not appear to be an equivalent provision in Irish law.

58 Communiqué of inaugural summit meeting, 17 December 1999.

9.50 The heavily retrospective[59] Irish Nationality and Citizenship Act 1956 (amended in 1986 and 1994) – the source of the law on 10 April 1998 – purported to make all those born in Ireland Irish citizens from birth.[60] Sections 6 and 7 are politically driven legal drafting. Éire/Ireland was concerned not to provoke the United Kingdom, but it also wanted to affirm Ireland a nation in the Republic and among northern nationalists. (Irish citizenship brought with it subsequently, through the common law, a – constitutional[61] – right to an Irish passport.)

9.51 An apparent withholding of major extra-territorial effect in section 7(1), requiring persons born in Northern Ireland after 6 December 1922 to declare their citizenship, actually allowed the Irish government to offer citizenship to northerners by descent. 'Not otherwise an Irish citizen' was the key phrase, bringing in existing citizenship law plus sections 6(2) and 6(4) (and 7(2)) of the then new act. This – seemingly – was as long as they had at least one grandparent born in Ireland before 6 December 1922.[62]

9.52 Irish officials, however, contrary to what was suggested in Dáil Éireann in 1956,[63] maintain that this two-descents rule is an endlessly recurring descent rule. If that were the position (and there are no cases on the issue), the Oireachtas would have provided in its nationality law for birth in the jurisdiction of the state to be eclipsed from the second generation by the descent rule. A two-descents rule, however, relates descent in Northern Ireland to that outside Ireland, where arguably the third and last generation had to be registered under section 7(2).

9.53 Was Northern Ireland given its uniquely recurring descent rule by sections 6 and 7? This was certainly not express, and it is difficult to imply it from those sections. It is impossible to distinguish descent in Éire/Ireland from that in Northern Ireland. An endless descent rule is a curiosity in the law of citizenship; one descent is the norm. Even more perplexing is the deeming of the descent rule in Northern Ireland as a birth rule.[64]

9.54 Persons in Northern Ireland acquired their Irish citizenship (which was otherwise retrospective) on 17 July 1956. But they remained also citizens of the United Kingdom and Colonies, as well as commonwealth citizens/British subjects. Successive United Kingdom governments acquiesced in this dual nationality.

59 Sections 6(1) and 7(1), taken with s 6(2), have the effect of making everyone born in Ireland before 6 December 1922 – alive or dead – an Irish citizen from birth. This was also applied to the Irish Free State from 6 December 1922.

60 Section 6(1).

61 *The State (M) v Attorney General* [1979] IR 73, 80–1 per Finlay P; article 40.3.1 of BNH.

62 Sections 6(2) & (4); see questions 1(a) to (c) in section 5 of the Republic's passport application form, PAS 1. Question 1(b) confirms a grandparent, but question 1(c) extends this by another two generations. PAS 4 (issued by the Irish embassy in London) has the same questions in section 5, though there has been a shift from Irish to Ireland. The note to section 5 is also the same, with the change from Irish to Ireland. The publication of the Citizenship Section of the Department of Justice, Equality and Law Reform, *Irish Citizenship*, available on the internet, sticks to the grandparent rule: http://www.irlgov.ie/justice/Publications/Citizenship.

63 Dáil Éireann, *Official Reports*, 997–1001, 29 February 1956; 1056, 22 March 1956. See also the explanatory memorandum on the bill, under Citizenship by Birth and Descent and Part II Citizenship.

64 Sections 6(1) and 7(1). The latter suggests that s 6(1) shall apply to someone who acquires citizenship other than under that section!

9.55 In the absence of complete harmony between citizenship law in every state (an impossible ideal), there will perforce be instances of extra-territorial jurisdiction.

9.56 The dual nationality of 1948 still applies to the Republic, but not to those born there after 1 January 1949.[65] Those over 50 years are entitled to apply for a United Kingdom passport. The 1956 dual nationality in Northern Ireland continues (though, on 1 January 1983, in United Kingdom law, persons there became British citizens[66]).

9.57 Irish citizenship in Northern Ireland on 10 April 1998 stemmed from the Irish Nationality and Citizenship Act 1956, and was unaffected by amendment of articles 2 and 3 of BNH on 2 December 1999. However, the constitutional amendments required consequential changes to sections 2 and 7 of the 1956 act. No provision was made for this in the Belfast Agreement. But, on 2 December 1999, the Irish Nationality and Citizenship Bill 1999 was published.[67] Its long title is: An Act to Amend and Extend the Irish Nationality and Citizenship Acts, 1956 to 1994.

9.58 As noted in Chapter 7, the definition of Ireland in terms of the former article 2 of BNH is being replaced with 'the island of Ireland', which is defined as including 'its islands and seas' (section 2(d)). In some places, Ireland is being redefined as 'the State' (section 8(c) and (f)[68] – confirming the two Irelands of Irish law. The principal amendments – in section 3 (which will come into operation retrospectively on 2 December 1999[69]) – are to sections 6 and 7 of the 1956 act, with section 6 now dealing with 'birth in the island of Ireland' and section 7 'citizenship by descent' (the distinction having not been clear hitherto.[70] The Irish state would appear to be adopting a normal two-generation descent rule[71]).

9.59 As for the birth rule, 'every person born in the island of Ireland is entitled to be an Irish citizen' (section 6(1)). The concept of entitlement is presented as significant.[72] But section 6(2)(a) states: 'a person born in the island of Ireland is an Irish citizen from birth if he or she does ... any act which only an Irish citizen is entitled to do.' There is similar retrospection in the 1956 act. The desire not to

65 British Nationality Act 1948 s 2(1)–(2); British Nationality Act 1981 s 31(3)–(4).

66 British Nationality Acts 1981 and 1983 as amended.

67 It was introduced in Seanad Éireann, and had a second stage debate on 8 December 1999. The committee stage followed on 26 January 2000. Second stage in the Dáil was taken on 13 April 2000. Nothing more was heard of the bill up until 30 June 2000.

68 The minister for justice, equality and law reform announced that this would be retrospective to 2 December 1999: Seanad Éireann, *Official Reports*, 8 December 1999.

69 Section 9(3).

70 'The present sections 6 and 7 of the 1956 Act deal with citizenship by birth in Ireland and by descent in an intertwined way.' (Minister for justice, equality and law reform, Dáil Éireann, *Official Reports*, 13 April 2000)

71 The explanatory and financial memorandum, however, claims that the descent rule is only being restated (paragraph 7 plus 15–16).

72 Austin Currie TD, who was born in Northern Ireland, alluded inadvertently to entitlement being an aspect of right, when he said: 'I did not ever apply for a British passport [in Northern Ireland], despite the fact that I was legally entitled to do so.' (Dáil Éireann, *Official Reports*, 13 April 2000)

impose Irish citizenship on all in Northern Ireland is evident,[73] but section 6(1)–(2) – if coherent law – may have a major extra-territorial effect in Northern Ireland through the extension of the birth rule. It would seem that the right to citizenship is latent (as many rights are). The bill does not specify what acts amount to evidence of exercise of the right. The explanatory and financial memorandum, however, states: '(Such acts include, for instance, applying for an Irish passport.)'[74] But a departmental press release made reference inter alia to getting an Irish passport, suggesting the Irish government will decide who is a citizen (on the basis of a birth certificate).[75] Section 6 approximates to a tautology: Irish passports are granted only to Irish citizens; Irish citizenship is a conditional precedent for an Irish passport.

9.60 Introducing the bill in Seanad Éireann, John O'Donoghue, the minister for justice, equality and law reform, referred to paragraph 1(vi) of the BIA, without reference to Annex 2,[76] as the basis for the change in citizenship law as regards Northern Ireland. Paragraph 1(vi), however, imposed no such obligation on the Irish government (other than to deal with consequential amendments). The review of citizenship law, and in particular the birth rule, was not required by the Constitutional Issues section.

9.61 ANNOTATIONS

'recognise the birthright of all the people of Northern Ireland [but see Annex 2 to the BIA] to identify themselves and be accepted as Irish or British, or both, as they may so choose,'. This text – even in the absence of Annex 2 – can have no legal effect, not even in international law. It would appear to be about nationality (without using the term). But nationality, despite the use of the phrase nationality law, is not a term of art in United Kingdom or Irish law.

The idea of 'birthright' originated in 1956, when the minister for justice, proposing that the Irish Nationality and Citizenship Bill be read a second time, said of the people of Northern Ireland: 'Citizenship is, in our opinion, their birthright.'[77] This was rhetoric. It was inconsistent with the bill, because section 7(1) – as enacted – disapplied the birth rule in section 6(1); it was not possible to acquire Irish citizenship by birth in Northern Ireland

73 However, Irish law cannot deprive a person in Northern Ireland suitably qualified of British citizenship.

74 Paragraph 9. The note continues: 'An effect of the new section 6(2)(a) is to relieve a person born in Northern Ireland of the necessity, when (say) applying for an Irish passport, to go through the additional procedure (not required of a person born in the State) of either making a declaration of citizenship or showing citizenship anyway by descent, by the production of birth certificates of antecedents.' Irish citizens from Northern Ireland do not have to make a declaration. And the passport application form, PAS 1 (for those resident in the state), requires only the birth certificate of applicants born in Ireland. The minister for justice, equality and law reform also referred to applying for a passport: Seanad Éireann, *Official Report*, 8 December 1999.

75 Department of Justice, Equality and Law Reform, 2 December 1999. The minister for justice, equality and law reform elaborated at the second stage in the Dáil: 'I can ... apply for an Irish passport and, as soon as I do, the law will recognise that I am exercising my entitlement to be an Irish citizen. Furthermore, if I apply for an Irish passport, all I have to do is to produce the birth certificate which shows that I was born on the island of Ireland ... .' (Dáil Éireann, *Official Reports*, 13 April 2000).

76 See also the explanatory and financial memorandum, paragraph 3.

77 Dáil Éireann, *Official Reports*, 1000, 29 February 1956.

'pending the re-integration of the national territory'. And the deeming in section 7(1) – whereby a person born in Northern Ireland is excluded from the birth rule only to have his descent deemed as a birth rule (because of a distant ancestor) – distorts the distinction between birth and descent.

Birthright – contrary to what Irish and seemingly United Kingdom officials thought originally – does not mean here a legal right acquired by birth.

All the people of Northern Ireland introduces Annex 2, and I will now turn to that:

'The British and Irish Governments declare that it is their joint understanding that the term "the people of Northern Ireland" in paragraph (vi) of Article 1 of this Agreement means, for the purposes of giving effect to this provision, all persons born in Northern Ireland and having, at the time of their birth, at least one parent who is a British citizen, an Irish citizen or is otherwise entitled to reside in Northern Ireland without any restriction on their period of residence.' The British and Irish Governments is reversion to pre-1985 terminology, London insisting in the Anglo-Irish Agreement upon the United Kingdom government. Declare makes this in line with the international law declarations, attempted in 1973 and achieved in 1985. Joint understanding again keeps this in international law. The two states cannot – in United Kingdom or Irish law – bind their courts with this shared interpretation, though account may be taken variously of pronouncements of effectively the executive on the international plane. The term the people of Ireland is being construed as referring to all persons. This means that all in paragraph (vi) adds nothing. In paragraph (vi) of Article 1 of this Agreement should be a reference to section (vi) for consistency with section (iv). In international law, Annex 2 is qualifying Article 1 of the BIA. An annex, under article 31(2) of the 1969 Vienna convention on the law of treaties, is part of the text of the treaty. Thus, the apparent right in Article 1 is taken back immediately by Annex 2. This can only be because the idea of birthright – as is suggested by the 1995 *Framework Documents* – was accepted diplomatically without legal investigation. Means, for the purposes of giving effect to the provision, is a clear reference to legal right.

All persons born in Northern Ireland makes the all in subparagraph (vi) superfluous. And having, at the time of their birth, makes it clear there is no birthright, either in Irish law or – apparently – in United Kingdom law.

At least one parent who is a British citizen reinforces the idea of the absence of a birthright. This was not always the position. Under the British Nationality and Status of Aliens Acts 1914 – 1943, birth within 'His Majesty's dominions and allegiance' made one a 'natural-born British subject'.[78] Under the British Nationality Acts 1948 to 1965, citizenship of the United Kingdom and Colonies could also be acquired by birth only.[79]

From 1921 to 1982, there was a birthright in Northern Ireland to be a British subject or (later) citizen of the United Kingdom and Colonies. (The Immigration Act 1971[80] introduced – from 1 January 1973 – the restrictive concept of right of abode in the United Kingdom. This was the point at which the immigration legislation started to influence the law on citizenship.)

It was the British Nationality Act 1981 which abolished the birth rule from 1 January 1983. A person born in the United Kingdom from that date had to have at least one parent a British citizen 'or settled in the United Kingdom'.[81] Settled is redefined in section 33 (2A) of the Immigration Act 1971[82] as 'ordinarily resident there without being

78 Section 1(1)(a).

79 Section 4.

80 Sections 1 & 2. Amended by the British Nationality Act 1981 s 39(2).

81 Section 1(1).

82 Originally, Immigration Act s 2(3)(d). Amended by British Nationality Act 1981 s 39(6) sch 4 para 7.

subject under the immigration laws to any restriction on the period for which he may remain'.

(Only British citizenship granted the right of abode in the United Kingdom, but the right of abode – under section 2 of the 1971 act as amended in 1981 – applies also to commonwealth citizens who had retained the right from 1971.)

But query those born in Northern Ireland, whose nationality status as British subject or citizen of the United Kingdom and Colonies, under the acts of 1914 to 1943 (repealed 1948), or those of 1948 to 1965 (repealed 1981), continues? They retain their birthright, even if, under the British Nationality Act 1981, they lost the ability to pass it on – through citizenship law – to their descendants.

An Irish citizen takes us to Irish law. It is the case that Irish citizens born in Northern Ireland do not have a birthright. This was the position on 10 April 1998, and it is not clear what change there will be (retrospectively) from 2 December 1999. They acquired their citizenship only by descent. The descent rule was contained in section 6 of the Irish Nationality and Citizenship Act 1956, in particular subsections (2) and (4).

Or is otherwise entitled to reside in Northern Ireland without any restriction on their period of residence is back again to United Kingdom law (it cannot be Irish law). It is part of the definition of the United Kingdom birth rule, for a person born there from 1 January 1983 to a parent who is 'settled in the United Kingdom': this being defined as 'ordinarily resident there without being subject under the immigration laws to any restriction on the period for which he may remain'.[83]

Returning to paragraph 1(vi):

To identify themselves and be accepted as Irish or British, or both, as they may so choose, has no legal effect. To identify raises the concept of identity. Themselves means it is entirely subjective. And hardly the basis of a legal right. And be accepted does not even have political effect, since that depends upon the subjectivity of others. And this cannot be provided for legally, in international or municipal law. Irish or British are the two identities, which were not specified in the preamble to the 1985 Anglo-Irish Agreement. British is the correct word, but only with reference to those acquiring citizenship from 1 January 1983. There is no equivalence between identity, or nationality, and citizenship. As they may so choose reinforces the point about subjectivity. Being Irish or British is, in this text, of no legal or political effect.

'and accordingly confirm that the right to hold British citizenship and Irish citizenship is accepted by both Governments and would not be affected by any future change in the status of Northern Ireland.' And accordingly makes the remainder of this subparagraph dependent upon what has gone before. Since the subparagraph is turning from nationality – of no particular legal effect – to the law on citizenship, it was necessary to have Annex 2 delimiting all the people of Northern Ireland. Confirm that their right to hold both British and Irish citizenship is accepted by both Governments is strange wording. Usually, governments through parliaments grant rights. British citizenship is correct since 1 January 1983. And Irish citizenship also, since the 1956 Irish Nationality and Citizenship Act came into operation. (Dual nationality – the right to be both a British citizen and an Irish citizen – has no implications for passports; indeed, both administrations endeavour to prevent persons holding two passports simultaneously.) And it would not be affected by any future change in the status of Northern Ireland is the only legally binding part of the subparagraph. Change of status can only be – under the Belfast Agreement – from an integral part of the United Kingdom to part of a united Ireland. Here, the two governments, in international law, have undertaken to maintain the existing dual nationality. Obviously, an Irish government would wish to have Irish citizens throughout its territory. But here, it has accepted that British citizenship can continue. (This was first conceded in the new Ireland forum *Report*

83 Immigration Act 1971 s 33(2A), added by British Nationality Act 1981 s 39(6), sch 4, para 7.

(1984).[84]) The Irish state has admitted the likelihood that United Kingdom law will have an extra-territorial effect in Northern Ireland indefinitely.[85]

This is surely the major significance of paragraph 1(vi), a concession by the Irish government to the effect that British citizenship will continue in a united Ireland. However, David Byrne SC has made the point about the BIA that 'there is for the first time an explicit acceptance by the British Government of the right of the people of Northern Ireland to hold Irish citizenship'.[86] Again, it is the difference between saying and doing. Having introduced dual nationality to the Republic of Ireland in 1949, successive United Kingdom governments tolerated without apparent diplomatic protest the extra-territorial effects of the Irish Nationality and Citizenship Act 1956 in a part of the United Kingdom.

The Treacy and Macdonald *case*

This subparagraph – which is really article 1 of the BIA, and therefore an international law provision – is believed to have inspired the *Treacy and Macdonald case*.[87] It was brought in late 1999 by two Northern Ireland junior barristers, Seamus Treacy and Barry Macdonald, following successful applications to be appointed queen's counsel. They were due to be called to the inner bar of Northern Ireland by the lord chief justice, the decision having been made by the sovereign on the advice of the lord chancellor (rather than by the secretary of state), along with ten other barristers, on 21 December 1999.

However, having applied, and succeeded, the two barristers objected to what they appear to have considered an oath of allegiance: counsel were required to declare that they would 'well and truly serve Her Majesty Queen Elizabeth II and all whom [they] may lawfully be called upon to serve in the office of one of Her Majesty's Counsel'. This apparently was considered incompatible with the Belfast Agreement (which of course had entered into force on 2 December 1999). There was also a point about the bar council of Northern Ireland having proposed a new declaration for senior counsel,[88] following an earlier challenge by a junior barrister – Philip Magee – in 1995 to an actual oath of allegiance.[89]

On 20 December 1999, the two applicants, represented by Michael Lavery QC, secured leave from Kerr J to apply for judicial review of the lord chancellor's decision to insist upon the United Kingdom declaration (accepted in Northern Ireland in 1996). On 10 January 2000, Kerr J gave leave to join the lord chief justice as co-respondent. The bar council of Northern Ireland intervened on behalf of the applicants, as did the Northern Ireland Human Rights Commission.

On 2 May 2000, Kerr J found in favour of the applicants. However, the judgment was not the legal victory perceived by some commentators.[90] The application for judicial review, as regards the lord chief justice, was dismissed, largely it seems because he only advised the lord chancellor. The court found that Lord Irvine of Lairg had acted unreasonably (in the *Wednesbury* sense) in the way he decided to retain the English and Welsh declaration in Northern Ireland; given the proposal for reform by the bar council, and possible uncertainty as to the views of the Northern Ireland judges, he should have appreciated that his decision would be controversial.[91]

84 Page 32. It is not clear whether the descent rule was two generations or for ever.
85 See *Framework Documents*, part II, paragraph 19.
86 *Fordham International Law Journal*, p. 1217.
87 The applicants' undated skeleton argument claimed that the Belfast Agreement 'brought into being a novel approach to citizenship and constitutionalism for this part of the United Kingdom'. (Paragraph 13)
88 The Elliott report of May 1997.
89 This was found by the government to be contrary to the Promissory Oaths Act 1868; section 12(4) substituted a declaration for QCs.
90 *Irish Times*, 3 May 2000.
91 This judgment would not have precluded the lord chancellor making the same decision

The applicants, and their supporters, were unsuccessful on all other points taken. These included, from Treacy and Macdonald, paragraph 1(vi) of the Constitutional Issues section of the Belfast Agreement (actually article 1(vi) of the BIA, as Kerr J appreciated, to which is attached Annex 2). This was framed in terms of relevant considerations in judicial review litigation, the argument being seemingly that the Belfast Agreement gave new rights to Irish citizens in Northern Ireland (or, at least, the lord chancellor, should have considered this). There does not appear to have been any extensive consideration of the legal status of the Belfast Agreement, which only entered into force in international law after the queen had signed, and the lord chancellor counter-signed, the royal warrant. The court appears not to have been addressed substantively on nationality law.[92]

On 23 June 2000, the lord chancellor decided not to appeal the judgment. The bar council of Northern Ireland had reaffirmed its decision after 2 May 2000, and this may have been a major consideration. The lord chancellor decided also to accept the Elliott amendment to the declaration. But the government, in particular the secretary of state for Northern Ireland, also appears to have been involved. Political fallout from any appeal seems to have been a factor. Finally, the lord chief justice, whose stand had been supported originally by the executive, was reported, by the lord chancellor, following consideration by the government, to be now supporting the declaration Treacy and Macdonald had demanded originally.[93]

> **2. The participants also note that the two Governments have accordingly undertaken in the context of this comprehensive political agreement, to propose and support changes in, respectively, the [Irish] Constitution *of Ireland* and in British legislation relating to the constitutional status of Northern Ireland.**

9.62 This second paragraph in Constitutional Issues is legally very different. Paragraph 1 – with six subparagraphs – is a joint understanding in international law. The second paragraph, in contrast, is not part of the BIA, not even through Annex 1 (the MPA). If it were, it would mean the two states announced agreed changes to their constitutional law on 10 April 1998, the prerogative, in the United Kingdom state, of parliament, and, in the Irish state, of the Oireachtas and then the people. (Both governments, however, subsequently advocated the changes on the grounds that they formed part of the Belfast Agreement. In fact, they were conditions precedents for entry into force under article 4(1) of the BIA.) Annexes A and B are, of course, attached to Constitutional Issues, suggesting a degree of distance (the original intention was to annex them simply to the MPA). While paragraph 2 refers to constitutional changes, the Annexes are not expressly specified. Paragraph 2 appeared first in the MDP, though it was amended – most likely by the Irish government – in time for the FA.

again, taking into account the views of the bar council and those of the judiciary (whether altered or not): *Electronic Telegraph*, 3 May 2000, quoting 'one senior QC'.

92 The judgment refers to Ronald Wetherup QC making two points: the Belfast Agreement did not enter into force until after the decision; it did not allow particular groups or individuals to opt out of their citizenship duties. 'I do not need to reach a decision on Mr Wetherup's first point on the effect of the Good Friday Agreement because I am satisfied that he is correct on the second.' Quoting article 1(vi) of the BIA, Kerr J concluded: 'There is nothing in the declaration which infringes the right of the applicants to identify themselves as Irish or which compromises their claim to assert that they are Irish citizens.'

93 House of Lords, *Hansard*, 5th series, 614, 622–3, 26 June 2000.

9.63 ANNOTATIONS

'The participants also note that the two Governments have accordingly undertaken in the context of this comprehensive political agreement, to propose and support changes in, respectively, the Constitution of Ireland and in British legislation relating to the constitutional status of Northern Ireland.' The participants refers back to paragraph 1. Again, these participants are the political parties only. Also note is much weaker than endorse in paragraph 1. This is probably because the participants in this sense included parties in the United Kingdom parliament,[94] who would have the opportunity to consider the question of legislative changes at Westminster. The two Governments refers back to the phrase the British and Irish Governments in paragraph 1. Have accordingly undertaken in the context of this comprehensive political agreement is strange wording. The accordingly appears to make the constitutional changes dependent upon the comprehensive political agreement. But the two governments – not otherwise participants – can hardly do something in the context. Essentially, this is a separate state-to-state undertaking, which is not here binding in international law. There is no agreement to change their constitutions, much less in the manner suggested in Annexes A and B. To propose refers to the powers of the executive in each state vis a vis the legislature. And support means actively promote, this having been used first in the United Kingdom contribution to the 1973 draft declaration. The use of the word respectively means that each government has a duty to propose and support in its own jurisdiction. The Irish Constitution, the term used first, was correct, though the upper-case 'C' is not strictly necessary. If 'the Constitution of Ireland' is titular, it is incorrect. Bunreacht na hÉireann would have been the correct title. Constitution of Ireland recalls paragraph 5 of the Declaration of Support (the term also being added to the MDP to appear in the FA). A similar point may be made – returning to Constitutional Issues – about the juxtaposition of Ireland and British legislation relating to the constitutional status of Northern Ireland. This is the Irish nationalist dualism, not correct terminology.

94 Plus Sinn Féin in Dáil Éireann, though it is not clear when the party 'signed up' to the Belfast Agreement.

10

Annex A

10.1 Annex A is attached to Constitutional Issues, the second section of the Belfast Agreement. It is at page 3 of Cm 3883 and page 11 of Cm 4705 (page 5 of the 1999 Irish version). Annex A became, during implementation of the Belfast Agreement, section 1 plus schedule 1 and section 2 of the NIA 1998; these were brought into force on 2 December 1999.[1]

10.2 There is no reference to changes in United Kingdom statutory law in article 1 of the BIA.[2] And paragraph 2 of Constitutional Issues – which introduced the idea of draft legislation – makes no reference to Annex A.[3] Nor is there any reference to Annex A in paragraph 2 of the Validation, Implementation and Review section. Annex A, however, is referred to in article 4(1) of the BIA: the enactment of legislation at Westminster for the purpose of implementing the provisions of Annex A was a requirement for entry into force of the BIA.

10.3 The United Kingdom government did not enter directly into a binding international agreement to change its constitutional law on a reciprocal basis. There was no agreement as a result of paragraph 2 of Constitutional Issues plus Annex A, and the MPA being annexed to the BIA. (This is borne out by paragraph 2 of the Validation, Implementation and Review section.) The reason no doubt is parliamentary sovereignty. But the government proposed and supported legislative changes at Westminster, insisting that, as part of a Belfast Agreement endorsed by the people of Northern Ireland on 22 May 1998, they were unamendable. This contradicted the idea of a sovereign parliament in domestic law; referendums are always only consultative in the United Kingdom. Even taking the BIA – which did not enter into force until 2 December 1999 – into account, article 4(1)(a) distinguished the legislation enacted and the provisions of Annex A; limited amendment was possible (and was indeed necessary).

10.4 The content of Annex A is relatively insignificant. It deals with the United Kingdom's so-called statutory guarantee as to the constitutional status of Northern Ireland.[4] There are some further insignificant provisions in clause 2. The total effect is very little: the option of a united Ireland, in United Kingdom law (not politics), having been implied, now becomes express in section 1 of the NIA 1998.

10.5 The context of Annex A was the ending of the 1937 Irish territorial claim. Not only did the Irish government join issue on an international declaration (countering United Kingdom concern for consent with an Irish commitment to national self-determination), but it also extracted the price of a – so-called –

1 Northern Ireland Act 1998 (Commencement No. 5) Order 1999, SI 1999/3209.
2 Section (iv) refers only to legislating for a united Ireland.
3 It had been intended to annex Annex A simply to the MPA.
4 *Notes on Clauses* (Northern Ireland Office, October 1998) describes clause 1 as 'the statutory embodiment of the principle of consent'.

balanced constitutional accommodation – an idea promoted by the Irish government in 1993–95.

10.6 In the 1993 *Downing Street Declaration*, the taoiseach confirmed that, 'in the event of an overall settlement, the Irish Government [would], as part of a balanced constitutional accommodation, put forward and support proposals for change in the Irish Constitution ...'.[5] The 1995 *Framework Documents* referred to 'an agreed new approach to the traditional constitutional doctrines': 'This new approach for Northern Ireland ... will be enshrined in British constitutional legislation ... either by amendment of the Government of Ireland Act 1920 or by its replacement by appropriate new legislation, and appropriate new provisions entrenched by Agreement.'[6]

10.7 Annex A was included in the MDP. Though it was not for the political parties at Castle Buildings, two amendments were made (there was a third later). The amendments, and the final legislation, are discussed here. Sections 1 (plus schedule 1) and 2 of the Northern Ireland Act 1998 are to be interpreted in United Kingdom law, but, in the case of ambiguity, recourse may be had to Annex A to the Constitutional Issues section; however, this part of the Belfast Agreement was not binding in international law.

Constitutional history

10.8 This has been considered above in Chapters 3 and especially 4. The constitutional guarantees of the United Kingdom parliament are given here again for the purpose of comparison (Article 1 of the 1985 Anglo-Irish Agreement – which exists in international law only – has been added for completeness):

IRISH FREE STATE (AGREEMENT) ACT 1922

SCHEDULE

11. Until the expiration of one month from the passing of the Act of Parliament for the ratification of this instrument [which was to take place on 5 December 1922], the powers of the Parliament and Government of the Irish Free State shall not be exercisable as respects Northern Ireland ... and no election shall be held for the return of members to serve in the Parliament of the Irish Free State for constituencies in Northern Ireland, unless a resolution is passed by both Houses of the Parliament of Northern Ireland in favour of the holding of such elections before the end of the said month.
12. If before the expiration of the said month, an address is presented to His Majesty by both Houses of the Parliament of Northern Ireland to that effect, the powers of the Parliament and Government of the Irish Free State shall no longer extend to Northern Ireland ...
    (From the 1921 treaty, still in force)

IRELAND ACT 1949

1(2) It is hereby declared that Northern Ireland remains part of His Majesty's dominions and of the United Kingdom and it is hereby affirmed that in no event will Northern Ireland or any part thereof cease to be part of His Majesty's dominions and of the United Kingdom without the consent of the Parliament of Northern Ireland.
(Repealed, Northern Ireland Constitution Act 1973 s 41(1))

5 Paragraph 7.
6 Part II, paragraphs 15 & 20.

NORTHERN IRELAND (TEMPORARY PROVISIONS) ACT 1972

2 Nothing in this Act shall derogate or authorise anything to be done in derogation from the status of Northern Ireland as part of the United Kingdom.

(Repealed, Northern Ireland Act 1998 s 100(2))

NORTHERN IRELAND CONSTITUTION ACT 1973

1 It is hereby declared that Northern Ireland remains part of Her Majesty's dominions and of the United Kingdom, and it is hereby affirmed that in no event will Northern Ireland or any part of it cease to be part of Her Majesty's dominions and of the United Kingdom without the consent of the majority of the people of Northern Ireland voting in a poll held for the purposes of this section in accordance with Schedule 1 to this Act.

[Also Schedule 1]

(Repealed, Northern Ireland Act 1998 s 100(2))

1985 ANGLO-IRISH AGREEMENT

ARTICLE 1

The two Governments

(a) affirm that any change in the status of Northern Ireland would only come about with the consent of a majority of the people of Northern Ireland;

(b) recognise that the present wish of a majority of the people of Northern Ireland is for no change in the status of Northern Ireland;

(c) declare that, if in the future a majority of the people of Northern Ireland clearly wish for and formally consent to the establishment of a united Ireland, they will introduce and support in the respective Parliaments legislation to give effect to that wish.

(This was replaced by article 1 of the BIA on 2 December 1999)

10.9 Northern Ireland became a part of the United Kingdom as a result of the 1800 acts of union. The GOIA 1920, which provided for the devolved administration, did not affect that constitutional position. Nor did the 1921 treaty affect Northern Ireland; the princple of consent was enshrined in United Kingdom law.

10.10 The Ireland Act 1949 statutory guarantee – to the parliament of Northern Ireland – was a response to Éire/Ireland leaving the commonwealth. Section 1(2), it is rarely noted, envisaged the possibility of a united Ireland (albeit by implication). But the guarantee was more a political gesture than the granting of a legal right. The United Kingdom parliament could not bind itself – in municipal law – to always accept the wishes of a subordinate parliament.

10.11 The position in international law (the 1949 act reiterated the position of the United Kingdom government) was probably different. Expulsion of the people of Northern Ireland against their wishes, was surely contrary to customary international law on human rights. And the emerging legal right of self-determination (to be applied to the people of the United Kingdom as a whole) reinforces this point.

10.12 The NICA 1973 guarantee was cast in similar terms. But now it was the people of Northern Ireland. And the means for ascertaining their consent – following the 1973 border poll – was provided for in schedule 1 of the act. The municipal law guarantee had the same status. But the international law obligation of the United Kingdom state (not to expel the people of Northern Ireland against their wishes) was commensurately stronger, given the right of self-determination was now part of the *jus cogens*.

10.13 This is where article 1 of the 1985 Anglo-Irish Agreement comes in. The Irish government affirmed unity by consent, and committed itself to legislate for a united Ireland. The United Kingdom obtained (at most) *de facto* recognition for Northern Ireland.

TITLE: ANNEX A: DRAFT CLAUSES/SCHEDULES FOR INCORPORATION IN BRITISH LEGISLATION

10.14 'Draft' suggests preliminary text. This can only have been a courtesy towards parliament, before the presentation of the Northern Ireland Bill. 'Clauses' refers to a bill at Westminster. It is not clear why 'schedules' is in the plural when there is only one. 'For incorporation' is intriguing; most likely, it is not here a term of art. 'British legislation' is, again, the nationalist duality, rather than the appropriate adjective for the parliament of the United Kingdom of Great Britain and Northern Ireland.

1. (1) **It is hereby declared that Northern Ireland in its entirety remains part of the United Kingdom and shall not cease to be so without the consent of a majority of the people of Northern Ireland voting in a poll held for the purposes of this section in accordance with Schedule 1.**

10.15 This is the constitutional guarantee in section 1(1) of the NIA 1998, designed to replace those of 1972 (spent) and 1973. The 1949 and 1973 guarantees took the form of a declaration followed by an affirmation.[7] Here, the affirmation is included in the declaration.

10.16 ANNOTATIONS

'It is hereby declared' makes this declaratory of existing United Kingdom law. The declaration refers to the entire subsection. Section 1 of the NICA 1973 was repealed by section 100(2) of the NIA 1998 on 2 December 1999. On the same day, section 1 and schedule 1 of the NIA 1998 were brought into force under section 101(3).[8] Northern Ireland's status as part of the United Kingdom is primarily a question of international law. This is arguably incorporated – as a point of law and fact? – in municipal law.[9] The absence of section 1(1) of the NIA 1998 would make no difference to the constitutional position.

'that Northern Ireland in its entirety' is a new formulation. Northern Ireland is, and will continue to be defined geographically, by section 1(2) of the Government of Ireland Act 1920.[10] (It has also been further defined by section 98 of the NIA 1998, dealing with internal waters and territorial sea.) In its entirety has been taken from the affirmation in section 1 of the NICA 1973.

'remains part of the United Kingdom' follows the 1949 and 1973 declarations.

7 *Notes on Clauses* (NIO, October 1998) refers to reenactment 'with greater economy of language'.

8 Northern Ireland Act 1998 (Commencement No. 4) Order 1999, SI 1999/2936.

9 Thus the 1995 *Framework Documents* contained the following: 'the present reality, in fact and international law, of the Union of Great Britain and Northern Ireland, affirmed in the Northern Ireland Constitution Act 1973'. (p. 14)

10 *Halsbury's Statutes*, 41, London 1995 reissue, pp. 550–1; Interpretation Act 1978 s 20(2); David Trimble appears to have been reassured on this point by Paul Murphy in a letter of 9 April 1998: *Irish Times*, 18 May 1998.

'and shall not cease to be so' relates the declaration and affirmation of 1973, to the extent that they become one. The affirmation of 1973 has been declared in 1998. The wording also does away with the necessity of repeating: part of the United Kingdom.

'without the consent of a majority of the people of Northern Ireland' follows the 1973 affirmation, though the majority has been altered to a majority.

'voting in a poll held for the purposes of this section in accordance with Schedule 1.' follows the text of 1973 (less: to this Act). Section is correct given that the poll is referred to in clause 1(2) in Annex A.

It is implied that the poll under section 1(1) would produce a pro-union majority. This is the meaning of 'But' which begins section 1(2).

1. (2) **But if the wish expressed by a majority in such a poll is that Northern Ireland should cease to be part of the United Kingdom and form part of a united Ireland, the Secretary of State shall lay before Parliament such proposals to give effect to that wish as may be agreed between Her Majesty's Government in the United Kingdom and the Government of Ireland.**

10.17 The text of this subsection is completely new. However, it picks up from article 1(c) of the 1985 Anglo-Irish Agreement. That in turn was based on the 1973 draft declaration.[11]

10.18 On 8 March 1973, as a result of the Northern Ireland (Border Poll) Act 1972, the United Kingdom government asked the people: 'Do you want Northern Ireland to be joined with the Republic of Ireland, outside the United Kingdom?' The answer was no; few if any expected a yes vote, not least the nationalists boycotting the poll. On 9 December 1973, in the United Kingdom contribution to paragraph 5 of the Sunningdale communiqué, the government stated that, if the people of Northern Ireland wished to become part of a united Ireland, 'the British government would support that wish'.

10.19 What does support that wish mean? The United Kingdom government had already arranged an act of formal consent. It was prepared implicitly – from at least December 1973 – in both international and municipal law,[12] to allow the people of Northern Ireland to vote to leave the United Kingdom (and it was the Irish government – unwilling to change its constitution – which ensured it did not become an international obligation of the United Kingdom's in early 1974).

10.20 In article 1(c) of the 1985 Anglo-Irish Agreement – 12 years later – the United Kingdom declared – along with the Irish government – that if a majority 'cleared wish[ed] for and formally consent[ed] to the establishment of a united Ireland', it would 'introduce and support in ... Parliament[s] legislation to give effect to that wish'.

10.21 Section 1(2) of the NIA 1998 simply incorporates part of article 1(c) into United Kingdom law. The United Kingdom government – as the executive of the state – was bound in international law. It is now bound in municipal law to do something it agreed to do first in 1985.

11 *Notes on Clauses* (NIO, October 1998) describes it as 'the other side of the principle of consent'.

12 Northern Ireland Constitution Act 1973 s 1 & sch 1, which came into force on 18 July 1973, under s 43(5).

10.22 'clearly wish for' (which draws on the 1973 draft declaration) is some political assessment of public opinion, either an election result or – a series of – commercial poll results. This then triggers a border poll, which is a matter of secretary of state discretion. The border poll is the act of formal consent. What then happens? In 1985, the United Kingdom government undertook to 'introduce and support ... legislation', to presumably allow for a legal cession of Northern Ireland. But that would have required a pre-agreement with the Republic of Ireland, and coordination with its legislation – after its poll – to allow for the same legal cession. There would then be an international agreement transferring Northern Ireland from one state to the other.

10.23 Legal cession involving two democracies is a complicated sequence. And it has not been provided for fully in Annex A.

10.24 ANNOTATIONS

'But if the wish expressed by a majority in such a poll is that Northern Ireland should cease to be part of the United Kingdom and form part of a united Ireland,'. But has been considered above, under section 1(1). The rest of the phrase simply repeats the point made in section 1(1). This is to the effect that Northern Ireland would not cease to be part of the United Kingdom 'without the consent of a majority of the people of Northern Ireland voting ...'. The only addition is the limitation of the alternative to the status quo being a united Ireland.

This may be politically realistic. But it means legally – just as it did under the Northern Ireland (Border Poll) Act 1972 – that support for consent in United Kingdom law, cannot be translated readily into support for self-determination in international law. The United Kingdom arguably has granted the right of internal self-determination to the people of Northern Ireland: that is the meaning of devolution. It has certainly not granted the right of external self-determination to that section of its people only. The exercise of such a right could include a united Ireland, but it could also, in international law, mean a continuation of the union, or independence, or some other constitutional arrangement.

'the Secretary of State shall lay before Parliament such proposals to give effect to that wish as may be agreed between His Majesty's Government in the United Kingdom and the Government of Ireland.' The secretary of state, it may be assumed, is the secretary of state for Northern Ireland. But, under section 5 and schedule 1 of the Interpretation Act 1978, secretary of state means one of her majesty's principal secretaries of state (and this phrase is used in commencement orders).

Shall lay before parliament is weaker than introduce and support in parliament from 1985, and even arguably support in 1973.

Such proposals to give effect to that wish: wish refers back to the first wish in section 1(2). Wish then clearly embraces consent, and is not simply a trigger for a border poll. Such proposals is not, it would appear, legislation. And this explains the absence of support.

As may be agreed between indicates that section 1(2) is dealing, not with legislation at Westminster, but with an international agreement. This is a new conception of legal cession as regards Northern Ireland. The role of parliament is commensurately less, and that of the Irish government greater than was envisaged in 1985. One possible explanation is: what would happen if Northern Ireland voted to leave the United Kingdom, and the Republic of Ireland did not – under Annex B – vote to accept Northern Ireland, or at least not immediately? Legislation at Westminster would not get rid of Northern Ireland. Section 1(2) leaves open the option.

This dovetails with an important decision of the Canadian Supreme Court mentioned in Chapters 2 and 9, which – through the common law – could be highly persuasive in United

Kingdom law. Between 16 and 19 February 1998, as a result of a reference by the governor in council, the supreme court considered a possible future secession of Quebec: *Reference re Secession of Canada* [1998] 2 RCS 217. The date of the judgment is 20 August 1998 (four months after the Belfast Agreement).

The first main question considered related to the constitutionality of unilateral secession by the national assembly, legislature or government of Quebec.[13] The Canadian Supreme Court held that this would be unconstitutional. This was because the constitution was more than a written text. It embraced other principles, including federalism, democracy, constitutionalism, the rule of law and respect for minorities. 'Those principles must inform our overall appreciation of the constitutional rights and obligations that would come into play in the event of a clear majority of Quebecers votes on a clear question in favour of secession.'[14] The Supreme Court held that such a vote required a principled negotiation. There was a reciprocal duty – following such an expression of popular will – on the other participants in the Canadian confederation to engage in discussions to address any legitimate initiative to change the constitutional order. (A unilateral secession, the Supreme Court held, even if politically successful, and ultimately legal in international law through recognition,[15] could not be retrospectively legalized in Canadian law.)

It is highly arguable that *Reference re Secession of Canada* is applicable to Northern Ireland. The principles of democracy, constitutionalism, the rule of law and respect for minorites are just as much a part of United Kingdom law. The house of lords, or the judicial committee of the privy council, could well consider them relevant to the principled negotiation of the London-Dublin agreement envisaged by section 1(2) of the NIA 1998, in the event of the people of Northern Ireland, in a poll held under schedule 1, voting in favour of joining the Republic of Ireland.

'Her Majesty's government in the United Kingdom' is an unusual phrase. The British government is the one favoured by the Irish government. (That is the term in the BIA, and is used adjectively in the Declaration of Support and directly in Constitutional Issues.) The United Kingdom government was the one insisted upon in the 1985 Anglo-Irish Agreement, but that is not the phrase used here. The answer may lie in a distinction in United Kingdom legislation on inter alia crown proceedings, between her majesty's government in the United Kingdom and her majesty's government in Northern Ireland.[16] The Northern Ireland executive committee constitutes the latter. The Northern Ireland Office is part of the former. The phrase was used before the suspension of Stormont, when 'the two Governments' meant London and Belfast. In the 1969 *Downing Street Declaration*, following the introduction of troops on to the streets of Northern Ireland, reference was made to 'the Northern Ireland Government' and to 'Her Majesty's Government in the United Kingdom'.[17] The point can only be that any Northern Ireland government would not have a say in any London-Dublin agreement.[18]

The Government of Ireland – Irish law terminology – has been discussed already in Chapter 7. Its appearance here on 10 April 1998, in draft United Kingdom legislation, was surprising.

It was revealed subsequently at Westminster that, as part of the multi-party negotiations,

13 The court used this terminology.
14 Page 292.
15 Though recognition might be influenced by the legality of the unilateral succession.
16 The Crown Proceedings (Northern Ireland) Order 1981, SI 1981/233.
17 Paragraph 4. The term used otherwise was 'the United Kingdom government'.
18 Her Majesty's Government in the United Kingdom and the Government of Ireland have been used again, the draftsman following section 1 of the NIA 1998 in sections 1 and 2 of the Northern Ireland (Location of Victims' Remains) Act 1999.

the two governments had agreed to recognize each other's name.[19] Thus, the BIA is between the Government of the United Kingdom of Great Britain and Northern Ireland and the Government of Ireland (the order was later reversed by the Irish government). The Irish government, if there was such an understanding reached during the talks, evidently considered it did not apply during the multi-party negotiations.[20] Nor has the Irish government referred to the United Kingdom of Great Britain and Northern Ireland since 10 April 1998. The United Kingdom government, however, has stuck by the secret agreement, dropping all references to the Republic of Ireland in its draft legislation and replacing them with Ireland tout court.[21]

But ministers and their advisers failed to distinguish between international law – where the Belfast Agreement exists – and United Kingdom law.

Here, under section 1(3) of the Ireland Act 1949, the domestic-law name of the neighbouring state is the Republic of Ireland (the 'may' refers to the existing name in 1949, Eire, which survived until 1981[22]). It is not normal to name other states in United Kingdom law, but: one, Ireland is a special case given its origins; two, the name intrudes upon part of the United Kingdom; and three, London and Belfast have to communicate about the neighbouring state. During the passage of the Northern Ireland Bill, there was a risk of implied repeal of section 1(3) of the Ireland Act 1949. Attempts to amend clause 1(2) in the commons and the lords failed.[23] But the name Ireland in schedules 2 and 3 – dealing with extradition between Northern Ireland and Ireland (sic) – was changed back to the Republic of Ireland.[24] Thus, there is no possibility of the NIA 1998 having impliedly repealed section 1(3) of the Ireland Act 1949.

The Republic of Ireland remains the United Kingdom law name of the neighbouring state. It is the name by which the Northern Ireland assembly is required to refer to its neighbour. This will continue to be the position, even if the United Kingdom government decides to continue using the government of Ireland in its international dealings.

Despite this, parliamentary draftsmen have continued to try and abolish the Republic of Ireland terminology. When the Disqualifications Bill was published on 21 December 1999, the long title used the term 'Government of Ireland' and even 'the legislature of Ireland (the Oireachtas)'. However, the explanatory notes (of the same date) prepared by the home office referred to 'Irish legislature' and 'the Irish Republic'. And the home office minister who took the bill through the house of commons also used Irish Republic.[25]

19 House of Commons, *Hansard*, 6th series, 316, 1219–20, 22 July 1998, 317, 574, 30 July 1998, 574; House of Lords, 5th series, 593, 1188, 19 October 1998. Bertie Ahern referred to the end of the nomenclature wars in a lecture at the Irish Studies Centre, University of North London, on 15 April 1999: http://www.irlgov.ie/taoiseach/press. He – like United Kingdom ministers – failed to distinguish municipal from international law. He also dated the wars incorrectly from 1949.

20 Paragraph 5 of Declaration of Support; paragraphs 1 and 2 of Constitutional Issues.

21 The United Kingdom law name, the Republic of Ireland, appears in schedule 2, paragraph 3(a), schedule 3, paragraph 9(f) and schedule 14, paragraph 20 of the NIA 1998.

22 Eire (Confirmation of Agreements) Act 1938 s 1; Statute Law (Repeals) Act 1981 schedule I part V.

23 House of Commons, *Hansard*, 6th series, 316, 1217–23, 22 July 1998, 317, 572–8, 30 July 1998; House of Lords, 5th series, 593, 1185–90, 19 October 1998, 594, 635–41, 10 November 1998.

24 Respectively paragraphs 3(a) and 9(f); *Notes on* Clauses (NIO, October 1998), schedule 2, paragraph 3; House of Lords, *Hansard*, 5th series, 593, 1831–3, 27 October 1998.

25 *Hansard*, 6th series, 343, 25, 24 January 2000 (Mike O'Brien).

TITLE: SCHEDULE 1: POLLS FOR THE PURPOSE OF SECTION 1

10.25 Section 2 will be considered below. Since schedule 1 relates to section 1, I consider it here.

10.26 Schedule 1 refers of course to the NIA 1998. This was not made clear at Castle Buildings, where the shape of the settlement bill – as it was then called – was not disclosed. Section 1 and schedule 1 also refer back to the Northern Ireland Constitution Act 1973. There, the schedule was entitled 'Polls for Purposes of Section 1'. In the Belfast Agreement, the phrase above was retained; a definite article was added, and purpose rendered in the singular. When it came to the bill, the definite article was retained, but purposes was put back into the plural.

10.27 This was an unnoticed change to Annex A, which the United Kingdom government argued was otherwise unamendable.[26] This argument prevailed even though paragraph 4 of schedule 1 (see below) had not been drafted by the time of the Belfast Agreement.

1. **The Secretary of State may by order direct the holding of a poll for the purposes of section 1 on a date specified in the order.**

10.28 This is exactly the same text as in paragraph 1 of schedule 1 of the NICA 1973, with 'of this Act' deleted and the rest of the paragraph – dealing with the frequency of polls – omitted (to be dealt with in paragraph 3).

10.29 ANNOTATIONS

'The secretary of state' is presumably the secretary of state for Northern Ireland, but, under section 5 and schedule 1 of the Interpretation Act 1978, it may be any one of her majesty's principal secretaries of state. This paragraph gives to the secretary of state the discretionary power to hold a poll under section 1. There is no legal requirement in this paragraph to so do. The secretary of state, of course, is bound by cabinet collective responsibility, and is individually responsible to parliament.

2. **Subject to paragraph 3, the Secretary of State shall exercise the power under paragraph 1 if at any time it appears likely to him that a majority of those voting would express a wish that Northern Ireland should cease to be part of the United Kingdom and form part of a united Ireland.**

10.30 This is a totally new provision. The power given by paragraph 1 of schedule 1 of the NICA 1973 was never used. The secretary of state, however, does not have the power to fetter his discretion. It may be doubted to what extent paragraph 2 is doing anything more than making this explicit.

10.31 ANNOTATIONS

'Subject to paragraph 3,' relates to the frequency of polls.

'the Secretary of State shall exercise the power under section 1' is mandatory.

'if at any time it appears likely to him that a majority of those voting would express a wish that Northern Ireland should cease to be part of the United Kingdom and form part of a united Ireland.' is the test. The secretary of state, therefore, has to anticipate broadly the result, at least as to whether it is yes or no. It is a personal decision, though he will have the benefit of advice.

26 The first Irish government version had: Polls for the purpose of selection (sic) 1. This was corrected in the 1999 Irish version.

Given that paragraph 3 requires a gap of seven years between polls, it is implied that the power will not be used on a whim. The secretary of state could hold a poll one year, which produced a slight no majority. Yes campaigners would then – in the absence of a change in the law by Westminster – be prevented from proving the strength of their wish for another seven years.

It is by no means easy to predict the result of such a consultative referendum. Professional pollsters have during general elections incorrectly predicted the result. There is, in the case of consenting to cession or secession, a further unpredictability (which may be described as the Quebec effect – there, though separatists won general elections, they lost referendums called to bring about a break up of Canada).

The paragraph does not specify conditions precedent for the secretary of state's exercise of judgment. It could be a political event, or demand by a party or parties. More likely, given the reference to a poll, it would be an election result. But there is nothing to distinguish local government, assembly, Westminster or European elections; or some other consultative referendum held under a different act.

Refusal to exercise discretion under paragraph 2 – apparently doing nothing – would be judicially reviewable. But so also would be any substantive moves towards holding such a poll. Such legal challenges – requiring the courts to second guess the secretary of state on how a putative wish would affect the result of a poll – are unlikely to be successful.

> **3. The Secretary of State shall not make an order under paragraph 1 earlier than [five]** ***seven*** **years after the holding of a previous poll under this Schedule.**

10.32 This paragraph originates in paragraph 1 of schedule 1 of the NICA 1973. There, the secretary of state was precluded from holding a poll before 9 March 1983, that is ten years after the poll held on 8 March 1973 under the Northern Ireland (Border Poll) Act 1972. This is the origin of the ten-year rule, applied to the subsequent frequency of polls.

10.33 ANNOTATIONS

'The Secretary of State shall not make an order under paragraph 1' is clear.

'earlier than seven years' is an amendment to the 1973 provision. The MDP – no doubt at the behest of the Irish government – had halved the ten-year rule to five years. By the time of the FA, it had been increased to seven years. This may be considered as a result of unionist pressure.

'after the holding of a previous poll under this Schedule.' means, given the last poll was on 8 March 1973, that the secretary of state may hold a poll at any time after section 1 of the NIA 1998 – with schedule 1 – was brought into force under section 101(3) on 2 December 1999.

> **4. (Remaining paragraphs along the lines of paragraphs 2 and 3 of existing Schedule 1 to 1973 Act.)**

10.34 The rest of schedule 1 to the NIA 1998 was not drafted by the time of the Belfast Agreement. Paragraphs 2 and 3 of schedule 1 to the NICA 1973 dealt with the details of the order for a poll, and its approval by the positive resolution procedure. They were redrafted for the legislation, but only the existing paragraph 2 went into the new schedule:

NORTHERN IRELAND ACT 1998

SCHEDULE 1

...

4 (1) An order under this Schedule directing the holding of a poll shall specify –
(a) the persons entitled to vote; and
(b) the question or questions to be asked.
(2) An order –
(a) may include any other provision about the poll which the Secretary of State thinks expedient (including the creation of criminal offences); and
(b) may apply (with or without modification) any provision of, or made under, any enactment.

10.35 Paragraph 4(1) follows paragraph 2 of 1973, though the express reference to 'the conduct of the poll' has been dropped. This may be considered to be included in paragraph 4(2)(a), where the creation of criminal offences is a new instance. Paragraph 4(2)(b) is a new, wider – more than electoral law – provision. The original paragraph 3 has not been included in the new schedule 1. It provided for the power to vary or revoke a previous order, and the positive resolution procedure. The power to vary or revoke is now contained in section 14 ('implied power to amend') of the Interpretation Act 1978. It is not therefore strictly necessary in the NIA 1998. There is a reference to schedule 1 in section 96 on orders and regulations, subsection (2) providing for made by statutory instrument after a draft of the order has been laid before and approved by resolution of each house of parliament.

The legal cession of Northern Ireland

10.36 This has been mentioned above, and it is also relevant as regards Annex B. However, it may be summarized here as a series of steps. While the absence of consent in Northern Ireland is all that stands politically in the way of a united Ireland (not taking into account the wishes of the people of the Republic of Ireland), the legal process is more complicated and not yet provided for finally:

- one, some event (including an election) leads nationalists to call for a border poll. This political process may trigger the following legal sequence;
- two, the secretary of state, under paragraph 1 of schedule 1 of the NIA 1998, directs the holding of a poll under section 1. This decision is potentially subject to judicial review in Belfast or London, the test – in paragraph 2 – being the appearance at that time of a likely nationalist victory (though the court might consider it under irrationality rather than illegality);
- three, the order, under section 96(2)(b), receives the approval of each house of parliament. Alternatively, it may not;
- four, the order may be amended, under section 14 of the Interpretation Act 1978, by the secretary of state going back to each house of parliament;
- five, such an order may be made after the NIA 1998 comes into force, but, under paragraph 3 of schedule 1, there can be no further poll for another seven years (without amendment of the act);
- six, a date for the poll is specified under paragraph 1 of schedule 1. It is up to the secretary of state, and ultimately each house of parliament, under

paragraph 4 of schedule 1, to specify the voters and the question/questions. The secretary of state may specify further provisions he considers expedient, and apply electoral and other law (there is no legal precedent from 1973). Under United Kingdom constitutional law, all referendums are only consultative because of the doctrine of parliamentary sovereignty;

- seven, a poll is held. If the nationalists lose, they have to wait seven years for another poll (or amend the NIA 1998). If they win, they may still have to wait:
- eight, events now turn to the Republic (if they have not already), and the provision in the amended article 3 of BNH of a separate plebiscite before Northern Ireland can be incorporated into the Irish state. That is a matter of Irish law (which has not been provided for in the Belfast Agreement). It may be that the Oireachtas will have to specify a tougher electoral test for the Republic,[27] and the Supreme Court might even rule – interpreting 'the consent of a majority of the people, democratically expressed, in both jurisdictions in the island'[28] – that the Northern Ireland result is not adequate;
- nine, (if there are no difficulties in Irish law) the secretary of state is then required, under paragraph 2 of schedule 1 of the NIA 1998, to enter into an international agreement with the Irish government. Under paragraph 1(iv) of Constitutional Issues (or article 1(iv) of the BIA), there is 'a binding obligation on both Governments to introduce and support in their respective Parliaments legislation to give effect to that wish [for a united Ireland].';
- ten, this returns the matter to the Oireachtas and Westminster. There is no requirement in the Belfast Agreement on the United Kingdom and Irish states to agree legal cession in international law.

2. The Government of Ireland Act 1920 [shall cease to have effect] *is repealed*; and this Act shall have effect notwithstanding any other previous enactment.

10.37 The amendment to the MDP has no legal significance. Shall cease to have effect is common practice for the body of an act.[29] The word repealed is used to refer to a schedule of repeals (as in section 100(2) of the NIA 1998). This short sentence – with a semi-colon – contains, according to nationalists, the balance, on the United Kingdom side, for the end of the territorial claim in Annex B.

10.38 Thus, on Saturday, 18 April 1998, Geraldine Kennedy, the *Irish Times*'s political correspondent, wrote: 'The Union, as it stands in British constitutional terms, will be changed, changed utterly,[30] by the Northern Ireland Agreement.' Sinn Féin – as everybody knew – was due to hold its ardfhéis that weekend.

10.39 The party's chief negotiator, Martin McGuinness, told delegates in Dublin the same day: 'We fought for and got the repeal of the Government of Ireland Act which underpinned the union, and insisted that other relevant legislation,

27 Tougher than 'the consent of a majority of the people of Northern Ireland voting in a poll held for the purposes of ... section [1]'.

28 The amended article 3.1.

29 The practice of double repeal.

30 A reference to Yeats' 'Easter, 1916' (1916).

including the Act of Union and the NI Constitution Act 1973 must also be altered, repealed or rendered inoperable by any new Act ... The union has undoubtedly been weakened as a result of the inclusion of a clause limiting the life of the union to the will of a majority in the Northern state ... There is now no absolute commitment, no raft of parliamentary acts to back up an absolute claim, but only an agreement to stay until the majority decides otherwise.'[31]

10.40 The following Tuesday (21 April 1998), the taoiseach told the Dáil: 'Any British territorial claim of sovereignty, made without reference to consent, going back to the Government of Ireland Act, 1920, the Act of Union or for that matter to 1170, will be superseded in the British Act, and becomes irrelevant for the future.'[32]

10.41 On Friday 8 May 1998, Geraldine Kennedy,[33] quoting 'political and legal sources' in Dublin as pointing to clause 2 of Annex A as the key constitutional provision in the Belfast Agreement, described it as 'go[ing] to the core of Britain's statutory chain of title to the sovereignty of both parts of Ireland, North and South ... The replacement of Section 75 with the principle of consent is revolutionary in British constitutional terms. Northern Ireland will have a unique status within the United Kingdom because, for the first time, the people, rather than the Parliament, will be sovereign and supreme.' The resumed Sinn Féin ardfhéis was that weekend.[34]

10.42 On 3 August 1998, David Byrne SC, the Irish attorney-general, told the American Bar Association (International Law and Practice Section) in Toronto: 'It is now clear, through the repeal of the Government of Ireland Act 1920, and a British declaration that their new legislation is to have effect notwithstanding any other previous enactment, that there is no longer any vestige of a British claim to jurisdiction over Northern Ireland other than in explicit fulfillment of the wishes of its people.'[35]

10.43 ANNOTATIONS

'The Government of Ireland Act 1920 is repealed:'. This has already been considered at length in Chapters 3 and 4. Section 75 – I argued there – is not a British claim to Northern Ireland. Its repeal does nothing in international law. Section 75, a saving provision, remains part of the constitutional law of the United Kingdom. The legislative supremacy of Westminster was reaffirmed in paragraph 33 of Strand One of the Belfast Agreement (and was reenacted in section 5(6) of the NIA 1998).

It is not clear why the Government of Ireland Act 1920 was not repealed earlier. The NICA 1973 was intended as a new basis for devolution. (An explanation may be hazarded: the then government, aware of the symbolism of the 1920 act for unionists, decided against reenacting surviving provisions in a new statutory form.)[36]

31 http://sinnfein.ie. Gerry Adams claimed: 'the new Act will supersede all other British constitutional legislation including the Act of Union.'

32 Press release, http://www.irlgov.ie/taoiseach.

33 David Trimble, leader of the Ulster Unionist Party, replied in the *Irish Times* on 18 May. He repeated his claim of 10 April 1998 that the union had been strengthened at Castle Buildings, and asked of Martin McGuinness: 'Is he being conned? Or is he conning others? Or both?'

34 See Gerry Adams' speech of 10 May 1998: http://sinnfein.ie.

35 *Fordham International Law Journal*, pp. 1218–19.

36 The idea for repeal of the whole 1920 act probably came from unionists. This was to prevent Dublin redrafting section 75.

There is nothing in Annex A to state when the act was to be repealed. It was therefore reasonable to assume this would be when the NIA 1998 achieved the royal assent on 19 November 1998. However, during the committee stage in the commons, Paul Murphy, the minister of state in the NIO, surprised anti-Agreement unionists on 22 July 1998, by telling them there would be a quid pro quo for the delay in the constitutional amendments in Annex B.

The secretary of state would only repeal the 1920 act[37] when the BIA entered into force, using – what became – section 101(3) of the NIA 1998.[38] It was indeed repealed on 2 December 1999.[39]

Since the act has been repealed, it is worth recording the remaining few sections and their destinations:

- section 1(2), on the definition of Northern Ireland. This survived repeal, since it is referred to in article 1 of the schedule to the Ireland (Confirmation of Agreement) Act 1925. Northern Ireland is also defined further in section 98 of the NIA 1998;
- section 8(7), on Belfast as the seat of the government of Northern Ireland. Section 93 of the NIA 1998 deals with government buildings;
- section 20(3), on the Exchequer and Consolidated Fund of Northern Ireland. There is no longer a separate Exchequer; it was abolished in 1973. Section 57 of the NIA 1998 provides for the continuation of the Fund;
- section 21(4), on customs forms for intra-United Kingdom trade. Duties are an excepted matter under paragraph 9(a) of schedule 2 of the NIA 1998;
- section 26(1)–(3) and (5), on land purchase annuities. Section 94 of the NIA 1998 now applies;
- section 27, on existing public loans (before the appointed day). This is spent;
- section 29, on provisions against double stamp duties. Stamp duty was transferred to the inland revenue in 1974. It is now provided for in section 150 of the Finance Act 1998;
- section 41(1), on the application of existing enactments and rules as regards the courts. This is now dealt with in paragraph 12 of schedule 12 of the NIA 1998;
- section 61, on continuation of existing laws, etc. Section 95(2) of the NIA 1998 provides that those laws shall continue to have effect subject to the act;
- section 65(1), on special provisions as to freemasons. Section 77 (unlawful oaths, etc.) of the NIA 1998 does not affect this;
- section 68(1), on provisions as to certain officers of local authorities. This is reenacted in section 95(3) of the NIA 1998;
- section 75, on the saving for the supreme authority of the Parliament of the United Kingdom. This has been considered in Chapters 3 and 4. It has been reenacted as section 5(6) of the NIA 1998.

37 Section 100(2) and schedule 15.

38 House of Commons, *Hansard*, 6th series, 316, 1227.

39 Northern Ireland Act 1998 (Commencement No. 5) Order 1999, SI 1999/3209.

10.44 ANNOTATIONS

'and this Act shall have effect notwithstanding any other previous enactment.' The main part of this sentence refers to the repeal of a specific act. The phrase after the semi-colon should grammatically refer to some aspect of the GOIA 1920. However, as became clear with the publication of the Northern Ireland Bill, it referred to the new devolution act for Northern Ireland (the NIA 1998).

The subject matter appears to be repeal. And the suggestion – according to nationalists – is that the NIA 1998 has impliedly repealed the 1800 acts of union and the NICA 1973 (and any other measures still in force). This is reinforced apparently by the explanation in *Notes on Clauses*: 'in order to underline that the Bill sets out to be a new start as respects the constitutional and Governmental arrangements of Northern Ireland'.[40] New start is evocative of new beginning and fresh start in the Declaration of Support.[41] The use of constitutional and governmental does not disguise its rhetorical character.

This suggestion is legal nonsense. The 1920 act has been repealed expressly by section 2 of the NIA 1998, as have all those listed in schedule 15 as a result of section 100(2). None of these repeals affects the constitutional position. There has been no implied repeal of the 1800 acts of union or the NICA 1973 (which has been expressly repealed in part). Repeal – as every lawyer knows – is a legal process which acts backwards in time. The phrase after the semi-colon refers to the opposite of repeal, to the surviving effects of previous enactments.[42]

Section 37 of the Scotland Act 1998 contains a – correct – statement of implied repeal (though it is most unlikely that there could be any): 'The Union with Scotland Act 1706 and the Union with England Act 1707 have effect subject to this Act.'

The rules on repeal belong to the common law, and they apply to all statutes in United Kingdom law. 'A repeal revokes or abrogates an Act or part of an Act.'[43] A repeal may be either express or implied.[44]

'There is no special wording required [for express repeal], and the one word "repeal" will delete the provision as effectively as any verbal jumping on its bones or scattering of its ashes.'[45] 'Repeal by implication is only effected where the provisions of a later enactment are so inconsistent with or repugnant to the provisions of an earlier one that the two cannot stand together.'[46]

'Where a later enactment does not expressly repeal an earlier enactment which it has power to override, but the provisions of the later enactment are contrary to those of the earlier, the later by implication repeals the earlier in accordance with the maxim *leges posteriores priores contrarias abrogant* (later laws abrogate earlier contrary laws). This is subject to the exception embodied in the maxim *generalia specialibus non derogant* [a general provision does not abrogate an earlier specific one].'[47]

'The courts presume that Parliament does not intend an implied repeal ... The presumption against implied repeal is stronger where modern precision drafting is used. It is also stronger the more weighty the enactment said to have been repealed. Lord Wilberforce said extra-

40 NIO, October 1998.
41 Paragraphs 1 and 2.
42 Though the annotator for *Halsbury's Statutes* has assumed it is about repeal: *Halsbury's Statutes Services: Issue 87*, pp. 173 & 185.
43 F.A.R. Bennion, *Statutory Interpretation*, 3rd edn, London 1997, p. 221.
44 *Re Williams, Jones v Williams* (1887) 36 Ch D 573, 578 per North J.
45 Bennion, *Statutory Interpretation*, p. 222.
46 *Halsbury's Statutes*, 41, London 1995 reissue, p. 546; *Churchwardens and Overseers of West Ham v Fourth City Mutual Building Society* (1891) 1 QB 654, 658 per A.L. Smith J; Kutner v *Phillips* [1891] 2 QB 267, 271–2 per A.L. Smith J.
47 Bennion, *Statutory Interpretation*, p. 225.

judicially that he was reluctant to hold that an Act of such constitutional significance as the Union with Ireland Act 1800 is subject to the doctrine of implied repeal.'[48]

If the draftsman – incorporating the Belfast Agreement – had wanted to repeal the acts of union 1800 and the NICA 1973, etc., he could – and should – have done it expressly; by putting it in section 2 of the NIA 1998, and again in schedule 15 (following the double repeal rule).

That he did not is conclusive of the argument that Northern Ireland's constitutional position remains as it was before, whatever of changes in the institutions of government consequent upon devolution.

The parliamentary draftsman did amend the definition of 'the constitutional laws of Northern Ireland' in section 46(2) of the Interpretation Act (Northern Ireland) 1954, by repealing the reference to the Government of Ireland Act 1920.[49] The draftsman left: 'the statutory provisions relating to or affecting the legislative powers of Parliament'. This includes now and principally the NIA 1998. But it must also refer – as it has always done – to the 1800 acts of union. Article third created the parliament of the United Kingdom of Great Britain and Ireland (later Northern Ireland).

48 Bennion, *Statutory Interpretation*, pp. 225–6. The reference is to: Committee for Privileges, *Report on the Petition of the Irish Peers*, 5 July 1966, House of Lords Session Papers 53, p. 73; also, *The Earl of Antrim Petition and Eleven Other Irish Peers* [1967] AC 691, 724. Lord Wilberforce is quoted in Chapter 3. Also, *In re Parliamentary Privilege Act 1770* [1958] AC 331 PC, 350 per Viscount Simonds; *Kariapper v Wijesinha* [1968] AC 717 PC, 744 per Sir Douglas Menzies.

49 Section 100(2) & sch 15.

11

Annex B

11.1 Annex B is similarly attached to Constitutional Issues, the second section of the Belfast Agreement. It is at pages 3–4 of Cm 3883 and pages 12–13 of Cm 4705 (pages 6–7 of the 1999 Irish version). Annex B became, during implementation of the Belfast Agreement, article 29.7 of BNH; the new articles 2 and 3 plus article 29.8 emerged, when the BIA entered into force on 2 December 1999 – the Irish government having no discretion, under article 4(3), as regards the changes in the constitution.

11.2 There is no reference to changes in Irish constitutional law in article 1 of the BIA.[1] And paragraph 2 of Constitutional Issues – which introduced the idea of constitutional changes – makes no reference to Annex B.[2] Annex B, however, is referred to in paragraph 2 of the Validation, Implementation and Review section (without any reciprocal reference to Annex A). It is also referred to in article 4(1) of the BIA: the approval of the amendments in Annex B in a Republic of Ireland referendum was a requirement for entry into force of the BIA (Annex B is also referred to in article 4(3), dealing with the effect of the international law obligation in Irish domestic law).

11.3 The Irish government did not enter directly into a binding international agreement to change its constitutional law on a reciprocal basis. There was no agreement as a result of paragraph 2 of Constitutional Issues plus Annex B, and the MPA being annexed to the BIA. However, paragraph 2 of the Validation, Implementation and Review section contradicts this apparently, given that the United Kingdom's consultative referendum was related to an Irish government bill for a constitutional referendum. It might be better to state that the Irish government agreed to unilaterally change the constitution. The governmment proposed and supported constitutional amendments in the Oireachtas, and argued for a 'yes' vote in the referendum of 22 May 1998, insisting that, as part of the Belfast Agreement, they had to be supported by the people of the Republic of Ireland.[3]

11.4 The content of Annex B is of major significant. The territorial claim in articles 2 and 3 – as was made clear during the referendum – was being removed. This is in spite of the attempt by the Irish government to suggest that articles 2 and 3 were simply being updated. The idea of two referendums in article 3 is an extraordinary concession (which came as a surprise to the United Kingdom

1 Subparagraph (iv) refers only to legislating for a united Ireland.

2 It had been intended to annex Annex B simply to the MPA.

3 The Oireachtas took the second stage of the Nineteenth Amendment of the Constitution Bill and the motion to approve the Belfast Agreement together: in Dáil Éireann on 21 April 1998; and in Seanad Éireann on 22 April 1998.

government).[4] Other nationalist gains are more apparent than real: the north/south bodies – articles 3.2 and 29.7.2 – have led to the Republic of Ireland sharing its sovereignty with the United Kingdom state; the constitutional right to citizenship – in article 2 – is no such thing; the extra-territoriality provision in article 29.8 is unnecessary; and the conditional nature of the amendments (article 29.7.3–5) was unnecessarily provocative to anti-Agreement unionists.

11.5 Annex B was included in the MDP. But it was more a matter for the two governments at Castle Buildings, than the eight political parties. By the time of the FA, further changes – in structure and substance – had been made, seemingly by the Irish government. Those amendments are discussed here. I show [deletions] and *additions* thus. Annex B – after the inclusion of the Irish-language text – went on to become part II of the schedule to the Nineteenth Amendment of the Constitution Act 1998 (promulgated on 3 June 1998).

Constitutional history

11.6 This has been considered above in Chapter 6. There, BNH was described as being front-loaded with nation-state pretension; the preamble and articles 1 to 9 (less article 6). McElligott's internal critique of 1937 (quoted in Chapter 6) – I submit – has been vindicated partly by the Belfast Agreement after 61 years.

Separating nation and state in BNH

11.7 Returning to the spirit of McElligott's Irish official mind, it is possible – as a preliminary to reviewing the 1998 changes to articles 2, 3 and 29 – to separate nation and state in BNH in a drafting exercise. Separating nation and state was apparently the intention of the Irish government, though this must be doubted.[5] This exercise provides a context for judging the actual amendments; it has no other status. It shows remarkably how little surgery would be necessary in a constitution of 63 original articles, to leave the Republic of Ireland in the main as a 26-county liberal nationalist polity aspiring to unity by consent, and, equally importantly, doing so perceived by Ulster unionists (possible amendments are italicized):

> Preamble
>
> In the name of *Almighty God*, from Whom is all authority and to Whom, as our final end, all actions both of men and States must be referred,
>
> We, the people,
>
> *Affirming our inalienable, indefeasible and sovereign right to choose our own form of Government, to determine our relations with other nations, and to develop our life, political, economic and cultural, in accordance with our own genius and traditions,*
>
> *Acknowledging the Christian values cherished by the majority of the people,*
>
> *Recognising the diverse traditions, ideals and allegiances of those who share the whole island of Ireland, its islands and seas,*
>
> And seeking to promote the common good, with due observance of Prudence, Justice and

4 Dublin made this concession in 1994, when it was still hanging on to 'national territory' and its 're-integration'. Its origins may lie in the new Ireland forum *Report*, Dublin Stationery Office, 1984, p. 27 (para 5.2).

5 'We have drawn a clearer distinction between the jurisdiction of the State on the one hand and the membership of the nation on the other hand.' (David Byrne, *Fordham International Law Journal*, p. 1218)

Charity, so that the dignity and freedom of the individual may be assured, social order attained, Ireland united, and concord established with other nations,

Do hereby adopt, enact, and give to ourselves this Constitution.

Article 1

The Irish nation consists of all persons of Irish nationality. Irish nationality is the birthright of all persons born in the whole island of Ireland, its islands and seas.

Article 2

1. *The people affirm their aspiration to unite both parts of Ireland.*
2. *It is hereby declared that Ireland may be united only by peaceful means and with the consent of the people of the State established by this Constitution and of the people of Northern Ireland, expressed in separate votes.*

Article 3

The laws enacted by *the Parliament established by this Constitution* shall have the like area and extent of application as the laws of *the Parliament which existed prior to the adoption of this Constitution.*

Article 4

The name of the State is *Ireland.*

Article 5

Ireland is a sovereign, independent, democratic *Republic. The State may be referred to as the Republic of Ireland.*

Article 8

1. *The Irish language and the English language are the official languages of the State.*

2.1. *The Irish language is a distinctive and unique expression of human culture.*

2.2. *The State, therefore, pledges to take special care to foster and increase the use of the Irish language.*

3. Provision may, however, be made by law for the exclusive use of either of the said languages for any one or more official purposes, either throughout the State or in any part thereof.

Article 9

1.1 On the coming into operation of this Constitution any person who was a citizen of Saorstát Éireann immediately before the coming into operation of this Constitution shall become and be a citizen of Ireland.

1.2 The future acquisition and loss of Irish nationality and citizenship shall be determined in accordance with law.

1.3 No person may be excluded from Irish nationality and citizenship by reason of the sex of such person.

1.4 *No person may be excluded from Irish nationality and citizenship by reason of the place of birth in either part of Ireland of such persons.*

2. *Allegiance to the State and observance of the laws of the State* are fundamental political duties of all citizens.

Article 29

4.2 *The State as a member of the United Nations confirms its determination to comply with its obligations under the Charter of the United Nations.*

11.8 This exercise definitely separates nation and state in BNH. Not only is the territorial claim removed, but it is seen to have been removed in these nine changes: articles 2 and 3 have been largely scrapped; essential changes have been made to the preamble, and especially article 1; some tidying up has been done to articles 4 and 5; articles 8, 9 (partly to grant the constitutional right to citizenship) and 29 complete the process.

11.9 The catholic nationalist historiography of the preamble has been replaced by an article 1 which becomes a democratic claim to statehood. Éire has also been killed off (in the preamble and article 4). The new article 1 – in 29 words – relates nation, nationality, birthright and Ireland (without using the word territory). Article 2 has been replaced entirely with an aspirational section and a peaceful means and consent section. Article 3 has been abbreviated to a simple statement of jurisdiction (dropping the reference to Saorstát Éireann), extra-territoriality being unnecessary. The new article 5 deals with the Republic of Ireland problem. The new article 8 has two official languages. And the new article 9 gives a constitutional right to citizenship (9.1.4), and modernizes the duties of fidelity and loyalty. Article 29.4.2 replaces the old 'commonwealth' provision, with a confirmation – in fundamental municipal law – of the state's international obligations.

11.10 Annex B, in contrast, emerged from a reluctant nationalist political process: 'Sinn Féin opposes changes that would dilute the definition of the territory of the nation, weaken the imperative to unity or dilute the citizenship rights in the north and incorporate the "consent" clause. Sinn Féin does not accept the legitimacy of the six county statelet.'[6] The Irish government – following a minimalist strategy rather than legal principle – chose to put its amendments through article 29 ('International Relations'), partly to avoid constitutional challenge to the Belfast Agreement after *Crotty v An Taoiseach* [1987] IR 713, partly to portray the north/south bodies as having a jurisdictional effect,[7] partly to diminish the impact of the changes to articles 2 and 3, and partly to make the changes – uniquely – conditional on the BIA coming into force.[8]

TITLE: ANNEX B: IRISH GOVERNMENT DRAFT LEGISLATION *TO AMEND THE CONSTITUTION*

11.11 Annex A made no reference in the title to the United Kingdom government. Here, the authorship of Annex B is identified as the Irish government. Draft legislation – as in Annex A – is presumably a recognition of the prerogative of the Oireachtas under article 15.2.1. 'To amend the constitution' was added in Castle Buildings, to make clear that constitutional amendments were part of the Belfast Agreement.

Add to Article 29 the following sections:

6 Ard Chomhairle paper on emergency resolution number 2, resumed ardfhéis, 10 May 1998: http://www.sinnfein.ie.

7 Ard Chomhairle paper on emergency resolution number 2, resumed ardfhéis, 10 May 1998: http://www.sinnfein.ie.

8 Geraldine Kennedy, *Irish Times*, 18 April 1998, comparing Annex B in the MDP with the transitory provisions of BNH (articles 51–63).

11.12 Article 29 of BNH deals with international relations. It has been considered in Chapters 1 and 2. Article 29 began with six sections. The first three deal with international law, and are not strictly constitutional. Sections 5 and 6 are concerned properly with treaties in Irish law. Section 4 is about the executive power of the state in external relations (including international agreements); in 1937, it had two subsections:

> 1. The executive power of the State in or in connection with its external relations shall in accordance with Article 28 of this Constitution ['The Government'] be exercised by or on the authority of the Government.
>
> 2. For the purpose of the exercise of any executive functions of the State in or in connection with its external relations, the Government may to such extent and subject to such conditions, if any, as may be determined by law, avail of or adopt any organ, instrument, or method of procedure used or adopted for the like purpose by the members of any group or league of nations with which the State is or becomes associated for the purpose of international co-operation in matters of common concern.

11.13 Article 29.4.1 is to the effect that, just as the government execises executive power domestically, under article 28.2 subject to the provisions of the constitution, it also does so in the international field. But does this mean that the Irish state internationally is subject to a domestic rule of law? Since international and municipal law have been confused in article 29, it would appear that the government has fundamentally little discretion on the international plane. But this is contrary to the separation of powers in article 6 – plus 15.2.1, 28.2, 29.4.1, 34.1 and 37 – of the constitution. The Irish courts, alert to the dangers (for them) of repeated constitutional review of the executive, developed in the 1970s the idea of foreign policy being generally non justiciable unless the rights of a citizen were at stake: *Boland v An Taoiseach* [1974] IR 338.[9]

11.14 The conduct of government policy abroad may be held to be unconstitutional in Irish law. Article 29.4.1 – like article 28.2 – is a basis for judicial review (on analogy with articles 34.3.2 and 34.4.4–5) by the High Court and Supreme Court.

11.15 The leading case is now *Crotty v An Taoiseach* [1987] IR 713, where the Supreme Court, by three to two (with the chief justice in the minority), held that, while the conduct of foreign policy was generally non justiciable, the ratification of Title III of the 1986 Single European Act, providing for foreign policy cooperation in Europe, would be an alienation of the powers of government or a fettering of the sovereignty of the state, and therefore unconstitutional in the absence of a specific amendment to BNH.

11.16 A nationalist concept of the fatal loss of sovereignty, rather than democratic notions of pooling or sharing sovereignty in the interests of international cooperation, may be detected in the majority judgment. 'Sovereignty ... is the unfettered right to decide: to say yes or no', said Finlay CJ.[10] But was the

9 Also, *Buckley and Others (Sinn Féin) v Attorney General* [1950] IR 67.

10 Article 30(6)(c) made reference to the Western European Union and the Atlantic Alliance. Summary of plaintiff's case (745–50). Per Finlay CJ (769), per Walsh J (781, 783), per

power of the Irish state to act in the interests of the people – Irish and other – not increased by the Single European Act?[11] The common good in the preamble seemed not to extent outside the state. The judgment certainly came as a surprise to the political elite, the major parties having been advised seemingly that a constitutional amendment was not required for the ratification of the Single European Act under article 29.4.2 of the constitution.

11.17 The Supreme Court majority appears to have elided the idea of a separate state – whose (internal) constitution is provided by BNH – with the politics of separatism; historically, they were related – legally, they are not identical.

11.18 The relative lack of discretion in international relations is confirmed by subsection 2 of article 29.4. Ostensibly, it seems to be giving constitutional permission for Éire/Ireland to be a member of the league of nations. In reality, it was about the commonwealth. It is the point at which de Valera's republican constitution, paying cognizance indirectly to the Executive Power (External Relations) Act 1936 (but not to the United Kingdom view of continuing membership), articulated his external association: Éire/Ireland – according to de Valera – was an independent state, which had chosen voluntarily to associate externally with the commonwealth. This was not the position in international law in 1937. The existence of the Executive Power (External Relations) Act 1936 has led Irish courts to interpret 'subject to such conditions, if any, as may be determined by law' to mean legislative permission for the executive to act abroad.

11.19 Did article 29.4.2 cover other international relations? Arguably, it deals with multilateral, but not bilateral, agreements. The Republic of Ireland joined the United Nations in 1955 without amending its constitution. In doing so, it accepted obligations under the Charter to act on Security Council decisions.[12] In contrast, the following actions were deemed to require constitutional amendments:

- one, joining the European Communities in 1973, which required a new subsection 3 in article 29.4 (the third constitutional amendment in 1972) plus what became article 29.4.5 in 1992 (part of the eleventh constitutional amendment);
- two, ratifying the Single European Act in 1987, which required an additional sentence in subsection 3 of article 29.4 (the tenth constitutional amendment). This was provoked by the successful constitutional challenge: *Crotty v An Taoiseach* [1987] IR 713;
- three, ratifying the (Maastricht) Treaty on European Union in 1992, which required a new article 29.4.4 (plus taking a sentence from 29.4.3 and making it 29.4.5) (part of the eleventh constitutional amendment);
- four, ratifying the (1989) Agreement relating to Community Patents in 1992, which required a new article 29.4.6 (part of the eleventh constitutional amendment);
- five, ratifying the Treaty of Amsterdam in 1998, which required new article 29.4.5–6 and the renumbering of existing subsections 5 and 6 as 7 and 8 (the

Henchy J (787, citing article 1 of the constitution). Hederman J argued that the organs of state were 'the guardians of these powers – not the disposers of them' (794).

11 Finlay CJ went on to make precisely this point, but only with reference to qualified majority voting (769).

12 Article 25.

eighteenth constitutional amendment, held on the same day – 22 May 1998 – as the nineteenth constitutional amendment referendum).

11.20 ANNOTATIONS

'Add to Article 29 the following sections:'. This is incorrect. Annex B in the MDP originally contained the text of article 29.7–8 – two sections (see below). This was corrected in the FA to one section: article 29.7; the intention was to have article 29.7–8 added to the constitution, along with the new articles 2 and 3, but all the changes were being put through one section initially. (This has not been corrected in paragraph 2 of the Validation, Implementation and Review section.) The complexity of Annex B stems simply from the constitutional amendments being made conditional on the entry into force of the BIA.

> **7.1 [In this section and in section 8 of this Article 'the Agreement' means the British-Irish Agreement done at Belfast on the [blank] day of [blank] 1998.]**
>
> **[7.2 The State may ratify the Agreement.]** ***The State may consent to be bound by the British-Irish Agreement done at Belfast on the [blank] day of [blank] 1998, hereinafter called the Agreement.***

11.21 Obviously, major rethinking was done by the Irish government at Castle Buildings. First, the decision to have two new sections in article 29 – 7 and 8 – survived, but Annex B was restructured (seemingly because of a mistake over section 8). Section 7 was to be ratification of the BIA, and provision for the north/south bodies; section 8, the changes to articles 2 and 3, and the new provision on extra-territoriality. Secondly, a statutory style of drafting – the definition in section 7.1 – gave way to something more appropriate to a constitution. Thirdly, the BIA was identified correctly as a treaty by the reference in section 7.2 of the MDP to ratification. This, however, was changed to 'consent to be bound' in the new section 7.1 in the FA. The BIA was a bilateral agreement which did not require ratification.[13] The blanks – for the date of signing – appeared in the FA, and in Cm 3883. The first Irish version (which was available on 15 April 1998) filled in the full date of the BIA. So did Cm 4292 (and the 1999 Irish version).

11.22 ANNOTATIONS

'The State may consent to be bound'. This is an unprecedented provision in an Irish constitutional amendment, given the meaning of article 29 of BNH (discussed above). It raises the question of the Irish state's treaty-making powers. On 3 August 1998, David Byrne SC, the Irish attorney general, told the American Bar Association (International Law and Practice Section) in Toronto that 'the people of the State, while they were asked to agree to other specific constitutional changes, were also asked to approve the Agreement as a whole'.[14] This is most unlikely. First, there is no basis, in articles 46 and 47 of BNH, for a consultative referendum such as occurred in Northern Ireland. Second, the drafting of the constitutional amendments suggests only a concern to avoid a *Crotty*-type challenge over Strand Two, if not articles 2 and 3. (Paragraph 2 of the Validation, Implementation and Review section still bears this out.) Third, article 29.6 envisages all international agreements having effect in domestic law through legislation by the Oireachtas (not constitutional amendment by the people).

13 Ratification, however, had been envisaged in an agreed paper by the British and Irish governments, 'CONSTITUTIONAL ISSUES', circulated to the parties in the multi-party negotiations on 24 March 1998; this – and other evidence – suggests Irish authorship.

14 *Fordham International Law Journal*, p. 1216.

States are legal persons in international law. However, in Irish constitutional law (stemming from the Irish Free State), the word state is sometimes a synonym in domestic law for the government.[15] But even if government is meant in draft article 29.7.1 (and it was the government which signed the BIA), the state has an international law connotation. The phrase consent to be bound occurs in article 46.1 of the 1969 Vienna convention on the law of treaties (to the effect that municipal law on competence to conclude treaties cannot be used as a defence to a breach of an international obligation). Consent to be bound refers there to states in international law. But the phrase is used here within the constitution, and can only mean the government acting within Irish law.

At no point in the history of the Irish state, either the Irish Free State or Éire/Ireland, did an Irish government go to the people in this manner on an international agreement. (The Single European Act, and the Treaty on European Union, were not about 'consent' but about 'ratification'.[16]) If, however, it is held that the people of the Republic voted for the Belfast Agreement, then article 29.7.1 of BNH could become the constitutional basis of the Irish state's treaty-making powers in areas where sovereignty is being fettered.

Article 29.5–6 acknowledges that the government, on behalf of the state, may make treaties. The issue is their effect in municipal law. Article 29.6 expressly states that international agreements may only be incorporated in Irish law by the Oireachtas. Article 29.4.2 – dealing covertly with the commonwealth in 1937 – required the government to act in accord with the law 'if any' (that is, acts of the Oireachtas and the common law), when it availed of or adopted 'any organ, instrument or method of procedure used or adopted for the like purpose by the members of any group or league of nations'.

The Irish government was not asking here in advance for constitutional licence. The taoiseach and the minister for foreign affairs signed the BIA on 10 April 1998. From that moment of consent, in international law, the government on behalf of the state was bound, even though the treaty was not due to come into force until the two governments had variously fulfilled the conditions precedent in article 4.

The view of the Irish attorney general quoted above had encouraged Geraldine Kennedy to speculate earlier about the difficulty of amending the BIA generally, given its putative incorporation in BNH – which can only be amended by the people of Éire/Ireland under articles 46 and 47.[17] (This, unwittingly, raises the argument about the 1921 treaty in the Irish Free State constitution, considered in Chapter 5.) It also ignores the review procedures in the MPA, and the sovereign ability of the two states parties to amend the BIA or replace it altogether. It is fanciful to suggest that the people of Éire/Ireland appropriated the BIA legally through article 29.7.1 for Irish municipal law, consequently denying the continuing existence of the Belfast Agreement in international law, and the right of the political parties in Northern Ireland to influence the United Kingdom government.

The most likely explanation for section 7.1 (looking at the drafting) is that the Irish government – fearful of *Crotty* – tried to follow the Single European Act and Treaty on European Union precedents. Thus the reference to ratification in the MDP (which survives in paragraph 2 of the Validation, Implementation and Review section). However, those were multilateral agreements with provisions in international law for ratification. The Belfast Agreement is a bilateral agreement without a ratification provision. When it became clear that there would be no ratification, the Irish draftsman switched to 'consent'. In doing so, the complexity of Irish constitutional and common law (article 29.4.2 and 29.5–6 and *Crotty*) on domestic competence to make international agreements, including those affecting the sovereignty of the state, was apparently overlooked.

15 Articles 1 (where government is used for state) and 6 (government and rulers of the state).

16 This was also the case with accession to the 1972 European Communities treaties.

17 Geraldine Kennedy, *Irish Times*, 18 April 1998 & 8 May 1998.

'by the British-Irish Agreement done at Belfast on the [blank] day of [blank] 1998, hereinafter called the Agreement' is uncontroversial. This shows that the Irish government was accepting the British-Irish Agreement name (which also occurs in paragraph 1 of Constitutional Issues, the first paragraph 1 of Strand Two, the first paragraph 1 and second paragraph 1 of Strand Three and paragraph 1 of Validation, Implementation and Review). Done at Belfast shows the Irish government accepted the practice of referring to international agreements by their place or places of signing (the basis of the Belfast Agreement name). Hereinafter called the Agreement – that is, the BIA – is referred to twice below, in section 7.2 and section 7.3.

> **7.2 Any institution established by or under [this]** ***the*** **Agreement may exercise the powers and functions thereby conferred on it in respect of all or any part of the island of Ireland notwithstanding any other provision of [the]** ***this*** **Constitution conferring [the exercise of] a like power or function on another person or organ of State appointed under** ***or created*** **or established by** ***or under*** **this Constitution. Any power or function conferred on such an institution in relation to the settlement** ***or resolution*** **of disputes** ***or controversies*** **may be in [lieu of]** ***addition to or in substitution for*** **any like power or function conferred by this Constitution on any such other person or organ of State as aforesaid.**

11.23 Evidently, the Irish government was still drafting at Castle Buildings; the draftsman had to shift focus from the BIA to his own constitution. There are two problems with section 7.2. Why was it considered necessary? And why was the same subject dealt with in the new article 3.2 in section 7.3?

11.24 Draft article 3.2 (see below) adds nothing to the constitution. Its existence – it may be inferred – is political, designed to compensate for the loss of 'the re-integration of the national territory' in article 3. The answer to the first question is again *Crotty*.

11.25 The case therefore needs further examination. Only title III of the Single European Act (SEA) is relevant.

11.26 The SEA treaties had been signed at Luxembourg and The Hague in February 1986. They were partly incorporated in Irish law by the European Communities (Amendment) Act 1986, amending the European Communities Act 1972. The people – it was held by the Supreme Court – had in 1972 allowed the state to join dynamic and developing entities, and to amend the treaties so long as such amendments did not alter the essential scope or objectives of the Communities. This was under the first sentence of article 29.4.3 of BNH. It could have been argued that, under the then second sentence, the 1986 act was 'necessitated by the obligations of membership of the Communities'. But this point – according to Finlay CJ – would not have covered ratification of the SEA (which was still outstanding). The validity of the 1986 act was upheld by the Supreme Court (Finlay CJ giving the only opinion under article 26.2.1 of the constitution).

11.27 It is difficult to understand this – majority or unanimous – decision, on the one hand, along with the contrary three to two decision[18] on title III. Part of an unratified treaty, despite article 29.5–6 (plus 29.4.2), was easier to effectively strike down than an act of the Oireachtas under article 15.4.2.

18 Hederman J agreed with Walsh J and Henchy J (794).

11.28 Article 30 of the SEA (with 12 subarticles) – 'Treaty provisions on European Cooperation in the sphere of foreign policy' – fell outside the existing treaties. There was to be a framework of European Political Cooperation (EPC),[19] with a secretariat of diplomats in Brussels. The Supreme Court was taken by the preambular references to European Union. But this would not be brought into being until the Treaty on European Union in 1992. '*Crotty* is best regarded as a unique case [wrote Gerard Hogan at the time], turning on a very unusual set of facts.'[20]

11.29 Section 7.2 of Annex B is about Strand Two. That is entitled 'North/South Ministerial Council' (NSMC), which was to be established – according to paragraph 1 – under the BIA (article 2(i)). This makes the NSMC a treaty body. The Council was to comprise members of the Northern Ireland executive committee,[21] and Irish government ministers (paragraphs 1 and 2 of Strand Two). The functions of the NSMC – paragraphs 1 and 5 – are arguably executive, but within a framework of cooperation across an international frontier. Paragraph 11 makes the NSMC a policy-making body.

11.30 But article 2(ii) of the BIA also refers to the creation of implementation bodies, provided for in paragraph 9(ii) of Strand Two. The functions of these bodies are defined also in paragraph 11: 'the implementation bodies will have a clear operational remit'. Under the BIA, these were to be treaty bodies also. However, under paragraph 10 of Strand Two, there is reference to the two governments making 'necessary legislative and other enabling preparations'. This suggests they might be statutory bodies created by Westminster and the Oireachtas; in which case there would be two and not one. And article 4(3) of the BIA refers to 'such legislation shall have been enacted as may be required to establish the institutions referred to in Article 2 of this Agreement.'

11.31 The meaning of section 7.2, though it was destined for BNH, must be sought, because of the express reference to the BIA in section 7.1, in Strand Two. Section 7.2 certainly applies to the NSMC. It is less certain that it covers the implementation bodies; however, the word institution is generic in article 2 of the BIA. (The Irish government's Referendum Commission had difficulty explaining articles 3.2 and 29.7.2 to the voters: the former was for 'cross border bodies', the latter for the institutions in article 2 of the BIA, including the NSMC.[22])

11.32 One returns again to the necessity of section 7.2. Practical cooperation has taken place across the border in Ireland since the early 1950s. Joint bodies were purported to have been created. Transnational cooperation has involved a sovereign state and a regional administration of the United Kingdom. The Anglo-Irish Intergovernmental Council (an east-west arrangement) did not require a constitutional amendment in 1981. Nor did the Intergovernmental Conference (a more north-south arrangement) established by the 1985 Anglo-Irish Agreement.

19 EPC had existed from October 1970. This was given a formal legal basis in articles 1 and 3 of title I. Title I was not mentioned in the Supreme Court.

20 Gerard Hogan, 'The Supreme Court and the Single European Act', *Irish Jurist*, n.s., XXII, part I, summer 1987, p. 55 at 69.

21 Paragraph 17 of Strand One.

22 Referendum on Northern Ireland, *Your Time to Decide*, Dublin Stationery Office, 1998, pp. 3 & 5.

11.33 Both of these institutions (the latter with cross-border cooperation functions) were created before the *Crotty* case in 1986–87.

11.34 But the Intergovernmental Conference, within the framework of the Anglo-Irish Council,[23] survived judicial challenge in *McGimpsey v Ireland* [1988] IR 567, [1990] 1 IR 110. And *Crotty* was argued unsuccessfully on behalf of the plaintiffs in that case.[24] It is difficult to see how *Crotty* – an evenly balanced decision much influenced by Walsh J – could still be a threat to the Strand Two institutions, whether the NSMC or the implementation bodies. (Gerard Hogan had been of the opinion in 1989 that: 'It is likely that the reasoning of the majority will be narrowly interpreted in future cases and there have already been indications that judicial review of the executive's treaty-making powers should be kept to a bare minimum.'[25])

11.35 The Belfast Agreement was more than 12 years after the SEA, and the Irish government and courts – it may be surmised – have learned better how to operate the separation of powers in article 6 of BNH.

11.36 The best argument against the need for section 7.2 has to do with types of international cooperation. That in Ireland is bilateral (and involving only the Northern Ireland part of the United Kingdom). This applies to the NSMC, and also to the implementation bodies. The European Communities, however, is not only multilateral, it is also sui generis. The European Communities – to which the *Crotty* decision refers – is an entirely different order of commitment. It also has supranational characteristics, not least the supremacy of European law (according to the European Court of Justice) in each member state.

11.37 In the spring of 1999, the Irish attorney general advised the government that it could participate in NATO's Partnership for Peace programme (PfP)[26] without seeking constitutional licence. (The reference to the Atlantic Alliance in the SEA – which did not apply to Éire/Ireland – was commented upon adversely by one of the Supreme Court majority in *Crotty*.[27]) The attorney distinguished political commitments from obligations in international law.[28] It is true that Irish neutality – meaning effectively non-membership of NATO, originally because of the United Kingdom – is not a provision of BNH,[29] even though the Irish government sees NATO membership as requiring a constitutional amendment. But is participation in NATO's PfP, however tailored to look like a bilateral

23 Article 2(a) of the 1985 Anglo-Irish Agreement.

24 At 121–2. Again a nationalist interpretation is evidence: it is in the national interest to cooperate with the United Kingdom (to get a united Ireland), but cooperation in Europe, extending into political areas, is against Irish national interests – understood in isolationist terms.

25 *Irish Jurist*, n.s., XXII, part I, summer 1987, p. 55 at 69. He cited Barrington J in the *McGimpsey* case in the High Court.

26 Plus the Euro-Atlantic Partnership Council.

27 Title III, article 30(6)(c). *Crotty v An Taoiseach* [1987] IR 713, 782 per Walsh J.

28 Letter, private secretary, minister for foreign affairs, to librarian, Dáil Éireann, 8 April 1999, annex 7 to Department of Foreign Affairs, *Ireland and the Partnership for Peace: an explanatory guide*, Dublin 1999, pp. 24, 74–7.

29 Article 15.6.1–2, often seen in terms of a monopoly on the use of force vis a vis foreign forces, refers in fact to the illegitimacy of republican violence; it is an anti-private army provision. Similar comments apply to article 28.3.1–3 on war and peace, and invasion; note the 'armed rebellion' in subsection 3.

relationship,[30] not a form of multilateral cooperation, which qualifies national sovereignty every bit as much as EPC within the then European Communities?

11.38 The 1997 treaty of Amsterdam, which was ratified after a constitutional amendment in 1998 (but did not enter into force until 1 May 1999), provides, in title V, for a common foreign and security policy including the progressive framing of a common defence policy.[31]

11.39 ANNOTATIONS

'Any institution established by or under the Agreement may exercise the powers and functions thereby conferred on it in respect of all or any part of the island of Ireland'. Any institution established by or under the Agreement relates to Strand Two (because of the later reference to the island of Ireland). The institutions are the NSMC and the implementation bodies. But doubt must be cast over the inclusion of the latter, given paragraph 10 of Strand Two (and article 4(3) of the BIA). The NSMC is undoubtedly a treaty body under article 2(i) of the BIA. But the implementation bodies, taking paragraph 10 of Strand Two with article 2(ii) of the BIA, would seem to have been envisaged as statutory bodies.

These may arguably be included as having been established under – if not by – the BIA.

Section 7.2 is clearly dealing with Strand Two. But why not a constitutional provision for the Strand Three institutions, the British-Irish Council, the British-Irish Intergovernmental Conference and possible east-west – multilateral or bilateral – implementation bodies under the first paragraph 10 of Strand Three? If *Crotty* was seen as problematic for north-south cooperation (arguably permitted by article 1 of BNH), east-west cooperation – including through bodies – has surely more of the character of alienating powers and fettering sovereignty?

'may exercise the powers and functions thereby conferred on it in respect of all or any part of the island of Ireland' is suggestive of the implementation bodies only.

Powers and functions may be a term of art in Irish law. However, section 1 of the Ministers and Secretaries Act 1924 refers to 'the powers, duties and functions' of departments of state. Duties has been dropped here. The NIA 1998 – which has a bearing because of part V of the act – defines functions as including powers and duties (section 98). And functions is the term of art used after the Belfast Agreement to refer to both departments and implementation bodies.[32]

Thereby conferred on it refers to by or under the BIA. In respect of all or any part of the island of Ireland suggests territory, and the distinction between cross-border and all-Ireland activity. This is evident in paragraph 9(ii) of Strand Two. It is less evident in paragraph 11. Cross-border had a localized meaning in the 1985 Anglo-Irish Agreement,[33] and this appears to have been carried over into the Belfast Agreement. The island of Ireland – which reveals difficulty with the government of Ireland term – originates in article 2 of BNH.

'notwithstanding any other provision of this Constitution conferring a like power or function on another person or organ of State appointed under or created or established by or under this Constitution.' The purpose of section 7.2 is to enable functions of Irish government to be performed under Strand Two. This implies cooperation given that the

30 Through a presentation document in accord with the principle of self–differentiation.

31 Recital in preamble TEU; articles 11 (ex J.1) to 28 (ex J.18). The WEU and NATO are mentioned in article 17 (ex J.7). Paragraph 2 states: 'Questions referred to in this Article shall include humanitarian and rescue tasks, peacekeeping tasks and tasks of combat forces in crisis management, including peacemaking.'

32 New Northern Ireland Assembly, *Report from the First Minister (Designate) and the Deputy First Minister (Designate)*, NNIA 6, 18 January 1999, annexes 2 & 5.

33 Articles 9 & 10.

jurisdiction of the Republic of Ireland is only 26 counties. These functions of government are provided for in BNH, in principally article 28 ('The Government'). Article 28.2 deals with the executive power of the state internally. And article 28.12 provides that the organization of and distribution of business amongst departments of state, etc., shall be regulated in accordance with law.

Notwithstanding makes clear that existing constitutional provisions are not to override those in section 7.2. Any other provision of this Constitution conferring a like power or function must be a reference to article 28. However, article 28.12 makes powers and functions a matter of law. Power and function has been discussed above. On another person or organ of State may be simply wide drafting. But it suggests that section 7.2 could involve an officer of state specified in the constitution. This would be very far from the transnational cooperation envisaged in Strand Two. Organ of state also suggests more than ordinary administration business in a department of state. Appointed under or created or established by or under this Constitution sweeps up everything administrative.

'Any power or function conferred on such an institution in relation to the settlement or resolution of disputes or controversies may be in addition to or in substitution for any like power or function conferred by this Constitution on any such person or organ of State as aforesaid.' This sentence refers to dispute resolution. It must also be taken as a reference to articles 34–37 of the constitution dealing with the courts. The only reference in Strand Two is to disagreements in paragraphs 3(iii) and 14.

Power or function has been discussed above. Conferred on such an institution is a reference back to institution at the beginning of the section. In relation to the settlement or resolution of disputes or controversies is widely drafted. Settlement suggests judicial or arbitral processes. Resolution is more mediation. Disputes or controversies is strange; disputes should suffice. Though disagreements is used in Strand Two. Controversies suggests public political differences. May be in addition to or in substitution for any like power or function is strange. It can only be a reference to the courts. In addition to means the courts do not have a monopoly of dispute resolution in the 26 counties, even though the Strand Two bodies are by definition transnational. In substitution for suggests new institutions appropriating functions of the courts. But this is more than is envisaged in paragraphs 3(iii) and 14 of Strand Two. Any like power or function conferred by this Constitution on any such other person or organ of State as aforesaid makes clear it is referring back to the first sentence of the section.

[8.1] *7.3* **If the Government declare that the State has become obliged, pursuant to the Agreement, to give effect to the amendment of this Constitution referred to therein, then, notwithstanding Article 46 hereof, this Constitution shall be amended as follows:**

11.40 This is where the numbering mistake was made in the MDP, no doubt because of the complexity of Annex B. Section 8 of article 29 is a substantive amendment to the constitution (and is located within section 7.3). Section 7.3 – along with 7.4 and 7.5 – relates only to the modality of changing the constitution. In order to create greater clarity, sections 7.3, 7.4 and 7.5 will be considered sequentially, the substantive amendments to articles 2, 3 and 29 (continuing) being taken afterwards.

11.41 ANNOTATIONS

'If the Government declare that the State has become obliged, pursuant to the Agreement,'. If indicates the conditional nature of the substantive constitutional amendments – articles 2, 3, 29.7.1–2 and 29.8. The Government is defined in article 28 ('The Government'), in particular in section 2.[34] The government is a synonym for the executive. This is the first reference to the government in Annex B. The state occurs in section 7.1. And section 7.2 uses institution, person or organ of State, most likely because of the overlap between executive and judiciary.

Declare is – apparently – the key to the substantive constitutional amendments. A declaration is mentioned in sections 7.4 and 7.5. But the meaning of declaration is not defined in Annex B. The government would appear to have complete discretion under the constitution, as to when it makes the declaration. The rest of the phrase – that the State has become obliged – resolves the matter. This is a reference to the BIA, and in particular to article 4(3). There, the Irish government is required, immediately at the point at which the BIA enters into force, to ensure that Annex B takes effect. The Irish government is required – when the BIA enters into force – to make the declaration referred to in sections 7.3, 7.4 and 7.5. Failure to do so would be a breach of an international obligation.

On 1 December 1999, the taoiseach told the Dáil that he would be laying before the Oireachtas the following day: the Irish and United Kingdom notifications under article 4(2) of the BIA (discussed in Chapter 1) bringing the British-Irish Agreement into force; and the declaration by the government under article 29.7.3, that the state had become obliged to give effect to the substantive constitutional amendments in articles 2, 3 and 29.[35]

The BIA entered into force at Iveagh House early on 2 December 1999, at a ceremony attended by the secretary of state for Northern Ireland and the foreign minister (see Chapter 1).[36] Attention then shifted to the cabinet room in Government Buildings, where another televised ceremony at 09.30 – involving the taoiseach, his government colleagues and the attorney general, Michael McDowell SC – took place. It was over in ten minutes. The attorney confirmed that the BIA had entered into force, and that, under article 4(3), the government was immediately thereafter obliged to ensure that the Annex B constitutional amendments took effect. Michael McDowell SC advised that the (written) declaration under article 29.7.3 should be made. As the taoiseach told the Dáil at 10.30, in the third televised set of proceedings that morning: 'this was done. The Government has made the declaration that the State has become obliged, pursuant to the Agreement, to give effect to the amendments.'[37]

Pursuant to the Agreement refers back to section 7.1, where the Agreement is defined as the BIA.

'to give effect to the amendment of this Constitution referred to therein, then, notwithstanding Article 46 hereof, this Constitution shall be amended as follows:'. To give effect to the amendment (singular) of this Constitution referred to therein means the amendment referred to in article 4(3) of the BIA. The amendment is Annex B; however, in article 4(3), Annex B is defined as 'the amendments to the Constitution of Ireland'. The amendment (namely Annex B) is therefore the amendments contained in Annex B.

Then indicates that the preceding phrase is a condition precedent.

Notwithstanding article 46 hereof is a reference to BNH. Article 46 deals with amending the constitution.[38] Annex B is distinguished apparently from the normal rules by this phrase.

34 'The executive power of the State shall, subject to the provisions of this Constitution, be exercised by or on the authority of the Government.' See also paragraph 11 of the schedule to the Interpretation Act 1937.

35 He did not mention article 29: Dáil Éireann, *Official Report*, 1 December 1999.

36 Those – like Eoghan Harris – who believe they witnessed the end of the territorial claim as invited guests were in the wrong place: *Sunday Times*, 5 December 1999.

37 Dáil Éireann, *Official Report*, 2 December 1999.

38 The procedure for a constitutional amendment is as follows: a bill passed by both houses of the Oireachtas, expressed to be 'An Act to amend the Constitution' (sections 2 and 3); such

This is because, under article 46, all amendments take effect immediately. Article 29 was amended in accord with article 46. But the amendment of articles 2 and 3, and article 29 substantively, did not follow the normal pattern. However, given the sovereignty of the people, it did not mean that they were contrary to article 46, and therefore unconconstitutional. Article 29.7 took effect immediately. Within it, in article 29.7.3 (governed by article 29.7.3–5), lay the conditional amendments to articles 2 and 3 plus the new article 29.8 (see further the *Riordan* case discussed below).

This Constitution shall be amended as follows introduces the four sets of changes, indicated by i., ii., iii., and iv in section 7.3. The four specific amendments will be considered below, following sections 7.4 and 7.5.

> [8.3] *7.4* **If [such] a declaration *under this section* is made, this *sub*section *and subsection 3*, other than the amendment *of this Constitution* effected thereby, *and subsection 5 of this section* shall be omitted from every official text of this Constitution published thereafter, but notwithstanding such omission this section shall continue to have the force of law.**

> [8.2] *7.5* **If *such* a declaration [under this section] is *not* made within twelve months of this section being added to this Constitution or such longer period as may be [determined] *provided for* by law, *this* section [7 of this Article] shall cease to have effect and shall be omitted from every official text of this Constitution published thereafter.**

11.42 Again, the MDP has been redrafted by the Irish government. Significantly, the order has been reversed. Section 8.2 was about no declaration after 12 months; and section 8.3 about the timing envisaged in the Belfast Agreement. Section 7.4 in the FA now deals with – what was – the desired objective, and section 7.5 with the eventuality of delay (which occurred).

11.43 The precedent for article 29.7.3–5, of course, is the transitionary provisions of BNH in 1937, which were removed from subsequent published editions; these are articles 51–63.

11.44 Article 51 – which no longer has the force of law – dealt with amendments by the Oireachtas in the first three years after the first president has entered upon his office. Article 51.4 read: 'This Article shall be omitted from every official text of this Constitution published after the expiration of the said period.'

11.45 Article 52 deals with the mechanism of essentially hidden articles. According to section 1: 'This Article and the subsequent Articles shall be omitted from every official text of this Constitution published after the date on which the first President shall have entered upon his office.' And section 2 provides: 'Every Article of this Constitution which is hereafter omitted ... shall notwithstanding such omissions continue to have the force of law.'

11.46 ANNOTATIONS

'If a declaration under this section is made, this subsection and subsection 3, other than the amendment of this Constitution effected thereby, and subsection 5 of this section shall be

> proposal having been 'duly approved' by the people under article 47.1, the bill is signed by the president 'forthwith upon his being satisfied that the provisions of ... Article [46] have been complied with in respect thereof'; due promulgation by the president as law.

omitted from every official text of this Constitution published thereafter, but notwithstanding such omission this section shall continue to have the force of law.' This succinctly turns Annex B into a substantive amendment of articles 2, 3 and 29.8 of BNH (within a 12-month deadline determined by section 7.5).

If a declaration under this section is made refers back to section 7.3. This would suggest that the declaration is defined above. But it only links to the BIA, where there is no reference to a declaration. This subsection and subsection 3 ... and subsection 5 of this section shall be omitted: that is, sections 7.3, 7.4 and 7.5 shall be omitted. Their contribution is purely transitory. Other than the amendment of this Constitution effected thereby refers to the substantive changes in section 7.3. The amendment – singular as in section 7.3 – is listed as i., ii., iii., and iv. There are, then, four substantive amendments in Annex B plus sections 7.1 and 7.2. From every official text of this Constitution published thereafter follows articles 51.4 and 52.1. Official text refers to Stationery Office editions. The successive enrolled copies of the constitution contain all the transitory provisions. But not withstanding such omission this section shall continue to have the force of law tracks article 52.2 exactly (less the word but).

This raises an interesting question. Presumably article 52 was included in order to simplify the constitution, and improve its accessibility. But lawyers and courts may need the full 63 articles, in order to perform properly their legal business. It is for this reason that, in 1984, the transitory provisions were published separately, after several years of campaigning by Professor John Kelly. A new edition will be required to deal with sections 7.3, 7.4 and 7.5.

'If such a declaration is not made within twelve months of this section being added to this Constitution or such longer period as may be provided for by law, this section shall cease to have effect and shall be omitted from every official text of this Constitution published thereafter.' Section 7.5 turns to what would happen if there had been no declaration – that is, the BIA had not entered into force – within 12 months.

If such a declaration refers back to section 7.4, which refers back to section 7.3. Both those deal with the making of the declaration. However, if there is no declaration, and 12 months have passed, and there is no legislation, then Annex B (even given the 22 May 1998 referendum) would never have the force of law. There were, therefore, three conditions subsequent to the referendum necessary to make the successful result a nullity.

Is not made within twelve months is the first reference to a deadline in the Belfast Agreement. (There is another – two years – in the Decommissioning section[39] and in the Prisoners section.[40]) This 12 months exists only in Annex B, but it set a notional target date for the implementation of the whole Agreement. On the other hand, section 7.5, in providing for after 12 months – entirely within the discretion of the Irish government – shows this is not a final date.

Of this section being added to this Constitution requires a return to the constitution and the specific legislation. The idea that section 7.5 started to bite on 23 May 1999 – 12 months after the referendum[41] – is incorrect. Articles 46 and 47 lay out the stages of a constitutional amendment. Section 5 of article 46 refers to the president signing the bill – expressed to be 'An Act to amend the Constitution' (article 46(3)) – and this 'shall be duly promulgated by the President as a law'. The Nineteenth Amendment of the Constitution Act 1998 was promulgated under the constitution on 3 June 1998.

Or such longer period as may be provided for by law refers to the ability of the Irish government to legislatively extend the 12-month period. There was no public discussion – in the year from 22 May 1998 – of the Irish government playing a constitutional amendment

39 Paragraph 3.
40 Paragraph 3.
41 There is no rule relating to time in the Interpretation Act 1937.

card, to the effect that the referendum result would be rendered worthless with a negative declaration on or after 2 June 1999 (and the absence of legislative proposals). According to reports, the cabinet was told on 18 May 1999, that legislation extending the period for a further 12 months would be introduced in time to be promulgated by the president.[42]

The Declaration under Article 29.7 of the Constitution (Extension of Time) Bill 1999 – comprising two sections – was rushed through all its Oireachtas stages on 26 May 1999. It was promulgated by the president (under article 25.2.1) on 3 June 1999. The reference to a declaration under article 29.7 is, of course, to a declaration under subsections 3 and 4; no declaration is made under article 29.7.5. Section 1 of the bill changed the 'twelve months' period in article 29.7.5 to effectively '24 months'. However, the Oireachtas cannot amend the constitution. It simply used the power provided by article 29.7.5 (in the constitution from 3 June 1998), to enact that the declaration in article 29.7.3 need not be made until 3 June[43] 2000. The government considered a number of dates: one month, three months and 12 months from 3 June 1999. One month – associated with the target of 30 June 1999 for the transfer of powers to Northern Ireland – was proposed unsuccessfully by the Sinn Féin member, Caoimhghin Ó Caoláin TD. Three months meant a risk of the Oireachtas having to be recalled during the summer recess. Twelve months was selected on the basis of the first 12 months, but it was stressed that this was permissive of a declaration at any point after 3 June 1999.

This section shall cease to have effect is unprecedented in Irish constitutional law. This section is of course section 7. It includes sections 7.1 and 7.2, and the substantive amendments – articles 2 and 3 and 29.8. Whatever of the legality of this provision (see below), no Irish government has hitherto ignored a constitutional amendment referendum result.

And shall be omitted from every official text of this Constitution published thereafter (which has also been used in section 7.4) refers back to articles 51.4 and 52.1 (with a legalistic thereafter added).

The *Riordan* case on Annex B

11.47 The first challenge to the Belfast Agreement – even before the 22 May 1998 referendums – took place in the Irish High Court, over Annex B – in particular the conditional amendment of articles 2 and 3 through article 29: *Riordan v An Taoiseach*, unreported.

11.48 The applicant – a lay litigant – was Denis Riordan, a Limerick college lecturer. On 20 May 1998, he sought an injunction in the High Court from Kelly J to restrain the holding of the referendum, on the ground that section 1 of the Nineteenth Amendment of the Constitution Bill was repugnant to the constitution. This application for judicial review (No. 1998/213 JR) was refused in an ex tempore judgment.[44] He appealed on 19 July 1998 (Appeal No. 202/98), but the Supreme Court refused, on 19 November 1998, to allow him to amend his proceedings – to take account of the successful referendum. 'Th[e] Court did, however, attempt to isolate what it understood to be the Appellant's real grievances and to indicate that it considered them to be without foundation.'[45]

42 *Irish Times*, 17 May 1999.

43 Section 7.5 refers to 'within twelve months of this section being added to this Constitution'. The calculation is 12 months from 4 June 1998, giving 3 June 1999. The taoiseach, however, referred to 2 June 1999: Dáil Éireann, *Official Reports*, 26 May 1999.

44 Leave had been granted on 19 May 1998.

45 Barrington J, Supreme Court, 20 May 1999, unreported, p. 4 of (unapproved) judgment.

11.49 The appellant continued with his appeal against the original order. (Meanwhile, he sought – having issued a plenary summons – to enjoin the government from making the declaration in article 29.7.3 of BNH (No. 1992/2897P). On 25 March 1999, O'Sullivan J in the High Court dismissed in an ex tempore judgment what was described as a fourth application as an abuse of process; Mr Riordan was restrained from bringing further proceedings without leave of the court.[46]) The original appeal was rejected by Barrington J – on behalf of the Supreme Court (Hamilton CJ, Denham J, Keane J and Murphy J) – on 20 May 1999.

11.50 The appellant's concern was that articles 46 and 47 had not been complied with in the nineteenth amendment to the constitution. He objected in particular to the draft section 7.3 of article 29, taking three points: articles 2 and 3 were being amended indirectly through article 29; section 7.3 ignores article 46; it also allows the government to amend the constitution, without reference to the people.[47] The Supreme Court upheld the conditional assent of the people to the amendment of articles 2 and 3, in the context of the implementation of the Belfast Agreement by all the parties.[48] It relied mainly upon the argument of popular sovereignty (without specific citation): 'This Court has repeatedly stated that under our constitutional system the people are sovereign. Provided the appropriate procedures are complied with there are no circumstances in which this Court could purport to sit in judgment on an authentic expression of the people[']s will or an amendment of the Constitution made in accordance with article 46.'[49]

11.51 There is an argument that, under article 46.1, which allows constitutional amendments to be 'by way of variation, addition, or repeal', there is no provision for conditional amendment (the transitory provisions applying only to the coming in to operation of the constitution under article 62). However, under articles 46.1 and 47.1, the people may amend any provision of the constitution. The people, under articles 5 and 6 (plus the preamble) are sovereign (article 1 being associated by virtue of: *Byrne v Ireland* [1972] IR 241, 296 per Budd J). Thus, under the constitution, enacted by the people, the people, in amending the constitution, can do so conditionally without breaching articles 46 and 47.[50]

46 An appeal against O'Sullivan J was expected. On 29 June 2000, the Supreme Court struck out, as an abuse of process, motions by Riordan that the Supreme Court had made serious errors in its judgment; leave of the Supreme Court would be required for any further motions.

47 A point on article 15.4 had been rejected separately on 19 November 1998 (in appeal no 381.97) as not applying to constitutional amendments: 'There can be no question of a constitutional amendment properly placed before the people and approved by them being itself unconstitutional.' (p. 6)

48 No distinction was made between political and legal parties, between the political and legal faces of the Belfast Agreement. See in particular the judgment of Kelly J, 20 May 1998, p. 5, dealing with two conditions precedent.

49 Barrington J, Supreme Court, 20 May 1999, unreported, p. 7 of (unapproved) judgment.

50 A point could have been taken – but was not – about article 51 (the first transitory provision). It began: 'notwithstanding anything contained in article 46 hereof' (this inspired section 7.3), which would have been useful to the Supreme Court. The appellant could have argued that articles 46 and 51 were isolated as being unamendable by the Oireachtas in 1938–41; the former were therefore more fundamental. However, article 46 was qualified by article 51, albeit only for three years.

[8.1.i] *7.3.i* **[by the substitution of the following Articles for Articles 2 and 3]** ***the following Articles shall be substituted for Articles 2 and 3 of the Irish text:***

'2. [Irish text to be inserted here]

3. [Irish text to be inserted here]'

11.52 The changes to the MDP again show the underpreparedness of the Irish government. In particular, it points up the nature of the national language under the Irish constitution. The amendments were drafted in English (and these were the versions shown to Sinn Féin). There was no recognition in Annex B of the significance of Irish in the constitutional law of the Republic.

11.53 BNH was enacted (by the people) in English and Irish, with the Irish text on the recto page (unlike the bilingual text of the 1922 constitution). Under article 8.1, Irish is the first official language. Under article 63, where there is conflict between the Irish and English versions, the Irish text shall prevail. (Article 25.5.4 applies to copies enrolled subsequent to 1938.)

11.54 Because the constitution was enacted in the two official languages,[51] the view has been taken that each language text must be amended separately. Thus, an Irish text of a constitutional amendment is given along with the English text (the order of precedent being determined by Irish being the national language). Constitutional amendments are initiated in Dáil Éireann as bills, but expressed to be acts to amend the constitution.[52]

11.55 Under the constitution, while there is no general requirement to legislate in Irish and English in articles 20–27 ('Legislation'), the president is required to sign the English and/or Irish texts passed or deemed to have been passed by the Oireachtas.[53] The text or texts is/are then enrolled in the office of the registrar of the supreme court.[54] If only one text has been signed, an official translation (invariably in Irish) is required to be issued.[55] Finally, if there are two enrolled texts, and a conflict between the Irish and English, the text in the national language shall prevail (article 25.4.6).

11.56 Because of the rule that Irish prevails where there is a conflict, acts to amend the constitution have a quadripartite structure. It is not simply a case of Irish to amend Irish and English to amend English (that applies only to additions, such as the eighteenth amendment of the constitution to ratify the treaty of Amsterdam in 1998).

11.57 The Nineteenth Amendment of the Constitution Act 1998 – consequent upon Annex B – is in both Irish and English (with Irish on the recto – or unevenly numbered – pages). Section 1 states article 29 is hereby amended, and section 2 deals with citation. Section 1 – in Irish and then English – refers to the schedule containing parts I and II. Part I relates to the Irish-language text of the constitution; part II to the English. But – and this flows from the use of a bill to

51 Article 8.1–2.
52 Article 46.2–3.
53 Article 25.4.3.
54 Article 25.4.5.
55 Article 25.4.4.

amend the constitution – part II (in English) gives additions (and repeals)[56] in English, but actual variations[57] in first Irish and then English. (Part I – the Irish text of the bill/act – gives additions in Irish, and variations also in Irish and English. Needless to say, the Irish and English in parts I and II have to be consistent.[58])

11.58 ANNOTATIONS

'i. the following Articles shall be substituted for Articles 2 and 3 of the Irish text: "2. [Irish text to be inserted here] 3. [Irish text to be inserted here]"'. The FA contained no Irish text, despite the significance of Irish in the draft amendments to the constitution. However, the need for it was recognized in the changes introduced to the MDP at Castle Buildings.

Thereafter, things developed. The United Kingdom version distributed in Northern Ireland reproduced the FA, but without any Irish text. (This also applies to Cm 3883, presented to parliament on 20 April 1998.) The Irish government version distributed in the Republic (which was the version laid before the Oireachtas on 15 April 1998) did contain Irish text. However, it was only that necessary to change the English-language version of the constitution.

The Irish-language versions (including articles 2 and 3 in English) were published in the Republic and Northern Ireland separately (the NIO simply adding a different cover to the text). These did contain the Irish-language text for the constitutional amendment. The Irish was in roman type, this applying to the 1998 variations/additions to articles 2, 3 and 29 (when article 29 had been enacted originally in gaelic type).

No differences have been detected yet between this translation, and that in the nineteenth amendment to the constitution. (Query whether amendments are treated as statute from the point of enrolling, in order to avail of article 25.4.6 of the constitution, pending the enrolling of a new copy of the constitution, at which point article 25.5.4 requires the Irish version to prevail when there is conflict?)

The United Kingdom blue book (Cm 4292), presented to parliament in March 1999, contains the English-language amendments to the constitution in its Annex 1, as indeed does the Irish version of the British-Irish Agreement (which was laid before Dáil Éireann on 8 March 1999, under article 29.5.1, and approved under article 29.5.2 the following day).

11.59 Since this is an English-language book, there will be no further discussion of Irish text in Annex B. That may become necessary in the future if there are conflicts between Irish and English (assuming the Irish is consistent) arising in litigation. Whatever of Irish constitutional law, this authorial decision recognizes the practicality that, just as BNH was drafted and debated in English, so also with the 1998 amendments to articles 2, 3 and 29.

ii. the following Articles shall be substituted for Articles 2 and 3 of the English text:

11.60 This was added to the MDP. It simply introduces the main part of Annex B, namely the amendment of articles 2 and 3. The 1937 text has been considered in Chapter 6, but it it worth reproducing the two articles here for the purposes of comparison:

> Article 2
>
> The national territory consists of the whole island of Ireland, its islands and the territorial seas.

56 Articles 46.1 & 51.1 (spent).

57 Articles 46.1 & 51.1 (spent).

58 In theory, there might be a conflict between the two Irish versions of the English text.

Article 3

Pending the re-integration of the national territory, and without prejudice to the right of the Parliament and Government established by this Constitution to exercise jurisdiction over the whole of that territory, the laws enacted by that Parliament shall have the like area and extent of application as the laws of Saorstát Eireann and the like extra-territorial effect.

Article 2

It is the entitlement and birthright of every person born in the island of Ireland, which includes its islands and seas, to be part of the Irish nation. That is also the entitlement of all persons *otherwise* qualified in accordance with law to be citizens of Ireland. Furthermore, the Irish nation cherishes its special affinity with people of Irish ancestry living abroad who share its cultural identity and heritage.

11.61 Again, the Irish government was still working on the constitutional amendments. A crucial 'otherwise' has been added to the MDP, linking nationality and citizenship. (The Referendum Commission, however, did not properly explain this point in its literature.[59])

11.62 The former articles 2 and 3 – as they may be referred to after 2 December 1999 – constituted a unity. The key concept was 'national territory'. National comes of course from nation. And a defined territory – though it does not have to be completely delineated – is a necessary aspect of statehood.[60] States have territorial sovereignty in international law; nations are defined usually in terms of culture and identity. The issue was confused in BNH: the nation was treated as having the characteristics of a state. And it has not been resolved definitively by the new amendments.[61]

11.63 The words national territory, and, I submit, also the concept, are missing from the articles 2 and 3 in Annex B. Former article 2 – contrary to Irish government representations about 'reformulating'[62] it – was in fact replaced. Article 2 is now about three different subjects: nationality; citizenship and the Irish diaspora. The first and second could have been dealt with better elsewhere (respectively, in articles 1 and 9). The third is unnecessary in a constitution. Clearly, the Irish government, finding it impossible finally to keep any of article 2 – national territory is the substance – decided to fill the space with nationalist political rhetoric.

11.64 The important question is: has the territorial claim been removed from the constitution? This requires answers to subordinate questions: one, has it been removed from the new articles 2 and 3?; two, is *McGimpsey v Ireland* [1988] IR 567; [1990] IR 110 still good law?; three, is a territorial claim lurking in the untouched preamble, articles 1, 4, 5, 8 and 9?; four, what did the people vote for in the

59 The Referendum on Northern Ireland, *Your Time to Decide*, Dublin Stationery Office, 1998, p. 3.

60 Article 1 of the 1933 Montevideo convention on rights and duties of states.

61 Desmond M. Clarke, 'Nation, State and Nationality in the Irish Constitution', *Irish Law Times*, no. 16, 1998, p. 252: 'the proposed amendments suggest the need for more care, in constitutional discussions, of what we mean by a nation or a state'. (252) Also, the same author's article in *Fortnight*, June 2000.

62 Bertie Ahern, Nineteenth Amendment of the Constitution Bill, second reading, Dáil Éireann, *Official Reports*, 21 April 1998.

nineteenth amendment to the constitution? (These questions will be answered below after detailed consideration of the new articles 2 and 3.)

11.65 ANNOTATIONS

'It is the entitlement and birthright of every person born in the island of Ireland, which includes its islands and seas, to be part of the Irish nation.' This is the first of three sentences. The subject is undoubtedly nationality. Nationality is a legitimate political concept, not least in a state which was created by Irish nationalism. It is not – despite its use in United Kingdom and Irish law – a legal concept; nationality law – which has a United Kingdom pedigree – is not a term of art in the domestic law of either state.

The drafting exercise at the beginning of this chapter shows how nationality could be acknowledged in the constitution – in a new article 1: 'The Irish nation consists of all persons of Irish nationality. Irish nationality is the birthright of all persons born in the whole island of Ireland, its islands and seas.' This defines the Irish nation in terms of people, and makes nationality a question of consciousness. It is therefore voluntary. The second sentence makes nationality a birthright (to no particular legal effect), the relevant territory – but not the word – being that in the former article 2.

It is the entitlement and birthright is a strange beginning. Entitlement is legally sounding, but probably of no effect. The use of two words suggests entitlement is different from birthright. Birthright is evocative of paragraph 1(vi) of Constitutional Issues, which has been discussed above in Chapter 8. There, it was argued, insofar as citizenship law was concerned on 10 April 1998, that Irish citizens in Northern Ireland did not have a birthright (in Irish law), but that British subjects and citizens of the United Kingdom and Colonies, born before 1 January 1983, did have a birthright (in United Kingdom law). The origin of paragraph 1(vi), and also of the heavily qualifying Annex 2 of the BIA, as well as draft article 2, is no doubt the 1995 *Framework Documents*: 'maintaining the existing birthright of everyone born in either jurisdiction in Ireland to be part, as of right, of the Irish nation'.[63]

Of every person born in the island of Ireland, which includes its islands and seas is awkward. Born is obviously the basis, from which birthright has been derived. The island of Ireland again appears, to distinguish the geographical entity from the political Ireland, whose seat of government is in Dublin. The former article 2 used 'the whole island of Ireland'. From the point of view of continuity, this would have been perfectly serviceable – as long as the national territory was being excised. Which includes its islands and seas is peculiar. It is difficult to think of an island (Ireland) – a geographical concept – as includings islands and seas. The islands and seas surround Ireland. Islands and seas is an attempt to preserve part of the former article two. However, and crucially, the word territory has been dropped from in front of seas. The term of art in international law is territorial sea. A state (if not land locked) has territorial sea, even if geographically these are different seas.[64]

To be part of the Irish nation is the crucial part of the sentence. However, it does not define Irish nation. It is still implied that the Irish nation is a teleological entity located in Ireland (which is what Irish nationalists believe). The draftsman of the constitutional amendment, having begun with the 1995 *Framework Documents*, and having no instructions to define Irish nation in article 1 (and relocate the popular sovereignty claim to the preamble), has done his best to try and say the people of Ireland – but only if they are born there – may belong to the Irish nation. Birth in a particular geographical entity is unduly restrictive for nationality. Surely it can be acquired by descent and residence or even by affinity?

'That is also the entitlement of all persons otherwise qualified in accordance with law to be citizens of Ireland.' This second sentence attempts to relate nationality and citizenship, which are always associated in Irish citizenship law – to no particular legal effect. It contains

63 Part II, paragraph 21.

64 Ian Brownlie, *Principles of Public International Law*, 4th edn, Oxford 1990, p. 180.

– allegedly – the so-called constitutional guarantee to northern nationalists about their right to Irish citizenship.

The obvious place to put a citizenship provision is in article 9, which deals with that subject (under the general heading of 'THE STATE'). In the drafting exercise at the beginning of the chapter, this point was addressed as section 1.4: 'No person may be excluded from Irish nationality and citizenship by reason of the place of birth in either part of Ireland of such persons.' This formulation does give a – constitutional – guarantee to the right to Irish citizenship, which is then provided for by the Oireachtas under article 9.1.2.

That in article 2 is an ugly beginning to the sentence. It must refer to the end of the nationality provision only, namely to be part of the Irish nation.

Is also the entitlement relates back to entitlement in the first sentence. But this time birthright – in the citizenship provision – is being avoided. Is this the consequence of paragraph 1(vi), which is part of the BIA, being read together with Annex 2? It is obvious that birthright is being used in connection with nationality, to no particular legal effect, and being kept out of citizenship law.

Of all persons otherwise qualified in accordance with law to be citizens of Ireland is a reference to article 9 (without a proper cross-reference as is normal in BNH). The otherwise was only added to the MDP. Without it, the sentence suggests that membership of the Irish nation – through birth in Ireland – is also the entitlement of Irish citizens. This suggests there may not be an equivalence, contrary to Irish citizenship law. With otherwise, nationality and citizenship are again identified, when the legal task should be to relate them: all Irish citizens have the right to Irish nationality (though not all may choose to affirm it); Irish nationality alone does not entitle one to citizenship.

In accordance with law simply repeats the wording in article 9.1.2.

Citizens of Ireland is strange. This is the term used in article 9.1.1. But sections 2 and 5(2) of the Irish Nationality and Citizenship Act 1956 make clear that, on 17 July that year, the correct legal term became 'Irish citizen'. Irish citizenship is what is delineated in sections 6 and 7 of the act. And the constitution says that is a matter for legislation. Irish citizen has been used in the Irish Nationality and Citizenship Bill 1999.

'Furthermore, the Irish nation cherishes its special affinity with people of Irish ancestry living abroad who share its cultural identity and heritage.' This third separate provision is distinct from nationality (which has always had a territorial connotation in Ireland) and from citizenship (which de Valera was keen to extend further to the Irish diaspora).

It is difficult to know why the diaspora became constitutionally important in 1998. It was a theme of Mary Robinson's presidency (1990–97), but one with which Irish liberal admirers felt uncomfortable.[65] Tourism – particularly but not exclusively by those of Irish ancestry – was a buoyant industry of the decade. The Irish government might have been amenable to some particular pressure, but the main reason for the diaspora achieving constitutional recognition – to no particular legal effect – may well have been to fill the empty article 2.

Sinn Féin is highly nation-bound like all nationalists, but Irish-America was one of the components of the pan-nationalist consensus it isolated (another – though not as close – was British sympathizers, not necessarily of Irish origin).

Nineteenth-century Irish nationalists were heavily dependent upon their kin in the United States. However, just as the latter always put their American interests first, so the real Irish nationalists distinguished the ethnic group. The Irish race – which found institutional expression in the United States in the Irish race conventions of 1916 and 1919 – embraced the Irish at home and abroad (mainly the latter). Identification as a racial group helps explain the culture of Irish nationalism. The Irish nation in contrast – in which nationalists

65 She never – judging by her legal work before assuming the presidency – sought to put the diaspora into the constitution: *Irish Times*, 21 April 1990.

believed – was located only in Ireland, and was therefore defined territorially.

There was no room in this race for the Scotch-Irish of North America, and the Ulster Scots at home were elided by Irishness. If they were Irish, they belonged to the nation; if they were Ulster-Scots, or British, the were not real Irish people.

Furthermore shows the diaspora is being added to article 2, contrary to the general drafting principles of BNH (which improved the 1922 constitution by breaking it down further).

The Irish nation is the second use of the term in the article. However, it has become the subject of the sentence, suggesting an – undefined – entity.

Cherishes its special affinity is not the language of a constitution, though it might be appropriate for a preamble.

With people of Irish ancestry living abroad is about those who identify with Irish nationalism, invariably catholic nationalists. Bringing in the diaspora cuts against the traces of Irish pluralism in article 3. Living suggests temporary migrants.

Who share its cultural identity and heritage makes it clear that, despite common traits, the Irish nation and the diaspora are different.

Article 3

1. **It is the firm will of the Irish nation, in harmony and friendship, to unite all the people who share the territory of the island of Ireland, in all the diversity of their identities and traditions, recognising that a united Ireland shall be brought about only by peaceful means with the consent of a majority of the people, democratically expressed, in both jurisdictions in the island. Until then, the laws enacted by the Parliament established by this Constitution shall have the like area and extent of application as the laws enacted by the Parliament that existed immediately before the coming into operation of this Constitution.**
2. **Institutions with executive powers and functions that are shared between those jurisdictions may be established by their respective responsible authorities for stated purposes and may exercise powers and functions in respect of all or any part of the island.**

11.66 Article 3 – in two sections – deals with four separate subjects: the aspiration to unity; consent and peaceful means; jurisdiction; and north/south implementation bodies. This again is contrary to the drafting spirit of BNH, which improved much of the Irish Free State constitution.

11.67 The drafting exercise at the beginning of this chapter did three things: firstly, it put the aspiration to unity, expressed clearly, as the first section of a draft article 2; secondly, the peaceful means and by consent conditions were made the second section. That draft article 3 remained what it was, a simplified statement about jurisdiction. There is no need – given the new article 29.7.2 – to revisit the question of implementation bodies in article 3 (unless the intention was to politically compensate for the loss of the 're-integration of the national territory' phrase).

11.68 ANNOTATIONS

'It is the firm will of the Irish nation, in harmony and friendship, to unite all the people who share the territory of the island of Ireland, in all the diversity of their identities and traditions,'. This proposition – which is only part of the first sentence of article 3.1 – is the unity by consent provision.

Unity by consent was expressed in the drafting exercise above as: 'The people affirm their aspiration to unite both parts of Ireland' (article 2.1). The people – who in the preamble enacted BNH – are the subject of the sentence. Affirm and aspiration are the correct words for the goal of a united Ireland, even if this may gloss the politics of the Republic. To unite both parts of Ireland is clear, everyone knowing – and sharing – the word Ireland, without specifying an island status.

The inspiration for article 3.1 was the Kelly-inspired draft recommended in the 1967 *Report of the Committee on the Constitution*[66] (discussed above in Chapter 6). That report did not of course seek to remove the territorial claim. The – unsuccessful – draft for article 3.1 was: 'The Irish nation hereby proclaims its firm will that its territory be re-united in harmony and brotherly affection between all Irishmen.'

It is the firm will of the Irish nation is from 1967, though the order has been reversed. However, this makes no difference. Given the deep historic difference in Ireland about separate statehood (and three decades of violence), it is difficult to know who are the people who express this firm will. It applies realistically to the republicans but few others. We are in the political realm of the nationalist ideal. The Irish nation remains the subject of this partial sentence, since the firm will rests on the pre-existing nation. Irish nation was used twice in article 2, first as an object (which people might choose to affirm), and secondly as a subject relating to the diaspora. Here it is again predetermining the answer: to what do the people of the Republic, and the people of Northern Ireland, aspire?

In harmony and friendship is inspired by the Kelly draft. But, in 1967, Ireland was to be reunited in harmony and brotherly affection between all Irishmen. This specified the means to unity. No doubt brotherly was not adopted in the 1990s because of potential accusations of sexism. Harmony and friendship, however, is not unambiguously about the means to reunification. The phrase has been placed after: it is the firm will of the Irish nation.

To unite all the people who share the territory of the island of Ireland: to unite refers to the aspiration or the goal of reunification. All the people is unnecesary emphasis for the people. Who share is ambiguous. To an Irish nationalist, much taken with the territory of Ireland, all those on the island do in a sense share it; they are resident there. But share surely connotes an element of agreement. This is missing in the main between the peoples of the two parts of Ireland. The territory is strangely present in article 3.1. Having removed the offensive 'national territory' in article 2, and continued this work in article 3, it is almost as if the word territory had to be restored. It has been located to no particular effect. Island of Ireland, having been used in article 2, is again deployed to no particular legal effect.

In all the diversity of their identities and traditions is the first constitutional glimpse of pluralism, first articulated by Kelly as harmony and brotherly affection. (It also appears in paragraph 1(v) of Constitutional Issues.) This may be politically necessary if nationalism is to transcend its fundamentalist framework. It is not legally necessary for BNH to deal with unionists, located in the main – as article 3.1 makes clear – outside the jurisdiction of the state. They are of another state and territory. Identities and traditions first surfaced in the new Ireland forum *Report* of 1984.[67] They then appeared in the preamble to the 1985 Anglo-Irish Agreement, though there was no clear relationship between tradition (nationalism or unionism) and identity (catholics and protestants in Northern Ireland). However, article 4(a)(i) suggests they are synonyms. Diversity first surfaced in the 1993 *Downing Street Declaration.*[68]

'recognising that a united Ireland shall be brought about only by peaceful means with the consent of a majority of the people, democratically expressed, in both jurisdictions in the island.' This is the crux of the constitutional amendment in Annex B. After the withdrawal of the territorial claim, it states the conditions – plural – under which a united Ireland can be achieved.

66 Pr 9817, Dublin Stationery Office, pp. 5–6.

67 Dublin Stationery Office, p. 28 (paragraph 5.4).

68 Paragraph 6.

The draft article 2.2 in the exercise above tackled peaceful means and consent in the one section: 'It is hereby declared that Ireland may be united only by peaceful means and with the consent of the people of the State established by this Constitution and of the people of Northern Ireland, expressed in separate votes.' The statement is a declaration. And a united Ireland is permissive. The exercise of consent – national self-determination for nationalists – takes place separately in Irish and United Kingdom law.

Recognising is here a political word. It suggests, not a legal position which is being declared, but a statement of the historically inevitable;[69] like the use of 'would' in article 1(a) of the 1985 Anglo-Irish Agreement.

That a united Ireland shall be brought about is mandatory. Though the shall refers on to peaceful means and consent, brought about refers to a united Ireland.

Only by peaceful means is a clear disavowal of violence. This does not mean that physical-force Irish republicanism cannot produce political change. It means that constitutional nationalists will only ally with republicans – despite their past deeds – when they are using peaceful means. Peaceful, certainly since 1994, has been defined as the absence of violence. And that absence need not be permanent, as the resumed IRA campaign of 1996–97 shows. The absence of an 'and' after peaceful means may have significance. Peaceful means and consent are two separate conditions. The absence of the conjunction has the effect of making it appear one condition only.

With the consent of a majority of the people, democratically expressed, in both jurisdictions in the island sounds more like paragraph 1 of Constitutional Issues. This is part of an amendment of a constitution of a state, which – under article 3.1 – has jurisdiction in 26 counties of Ireland. It is hardly for BNH to provide apparently for Northern Ireland. With the consent makes clear the consent principle applies to a united Ireland. Of a majority of the people, given that people is used earlier to refer to those who share the territory of the island of Ireland, might appear to an all-Ireland poll. However, it must be read with the following: democratically expressed, in both jurisdictions in the island. The use of the word both indicates that a majority is required in Northern Ireland, and in the Republic. Thus, Annex B dovetails with Annex A, on United Kingdom constitutional provisions. But, given that article 3.1 of the Irish constitution falls to be interpreted by the Irish High and Supreme Courts, it is theoretically possible that a majority of the people (in Northern Ireland), democratically expressed, could for example be taken to be a majority of electors rather than a majority of voters in a border poll. There is no organic legal connection between section 1 and schedule 1 of the NIA 1998 and article 3.1, other than their proximity in Annexes A and B. More significant is the absence of any meaning to a majority of the people (in the Republic of Ireland), democratically expressed. People must mean all people. This is qualified by democratically expressed. But does that refer to electoral law? And does it refer to electors or to voters? Or, alternatively, does it refer to BNH, where there are provisions for referendums. The first, in article 47.1 refers to constitutional amendments (which a border poll might or might not be) under article 46. A majority of votes cast is required. The second, in article 47.2, is for proposals other than constitutional amendments. This refers to article 27, reference of bills to the people. There seems to be no possibility of a border poll under article 47.2 (where, in subsection 1, a proposal is vetoed by a majority of voters if it constitutes more than a third of electors, and certainly not under subsection 2, where article 27 proposals are otherwise approved). Jurisdictions is inspired by the former article 3. The Republic of Ireland is a state, and Northern Ireland is part of another state. Talking about jurisdictions allows nationalists to acknowledge a border, but not the question of two distinct territorial sovereignties. Jurisdictions is inadequate. Northern Ireland and Scotland

69 The late Cardinal Conway said: 'you cannot bomb a million Protestants into a united Ireland'. This may be simply a statement of political practicality, or it may contain an ethical – and democratic – prohibition.

are, for example, two jurisdictions – within the United Kingdom state. In the island is the second use in the sentence, chosen as an alternative to Ireland.

'Until then, the laws enacted by the Parliament established by this Constitution shall have the like area and extent of application as the laws enacted by the Parliament that existed immediately before the coming into operation of this Constitution.' This sentence – the third subject in article 3 – is about 26-county Irish Free State jurisdiction continuing in Éire/ Ireland. It was not strictly necessary in 1937, but for the 'national territory of articles 2 and 3, and the 'without prejudice' phrase, which suggested then – though Finlay CJ in *McGimpsey* did not so construe in 1990 – that the Irish state might exercise jurisdiction in Northern Ireland short of full territorial sovereignty.

The drafting exercise above – seeking to keep a jurisdiction article – suggested for article 3: 'The laws enacted by the Parliament established by this Constitution shall have the like area and extent of application as the laws of the Parliament which existed prior to the adoption of this Constitution.' This was based upon the third phrase in the existing article 3, changed the reference to Saorstát Éireann (long since gone), and dropped the reference to extra-territoriality.

The inspiration for this part of article 3.1 was Kelly's 1967 draft article 3.2: 'The laws enacted by the Parliament established by this Constitution shall, until the achievement of the nation's unity shall otherwise require, have the like area and extent of application as the laws of the Parliament which existed prior to the adoption of this Constitution. Provision may be made by law to give extra-territorial effect to such laws.' The reference to the nation's unity related to the territorial claim surviving in article 2. Extra-territoriality has, in Annex B, been placed in article 29.

Until then comes from 1967. It refers here to a united Ireland in the preceding sentence. This is in accord with the apparent mandatory nature of that objective.

The laws enacted by the Parliament established by this Constitution is from Kelly's draft. So also is: shall have the the like area and extent of application as the laws of the Parliament. Which existed prior to the adoption of this Constitution has been altered to: that existed immediately before the coming into operation of this Constitution. Operation was the term used to refer to BNH's coming into effect on 29 December 1937.

'Institutions with executive powers and functions that are shared between those jurisdictions may be established by their respective responsible authorities for stated purposes and may exercise powers and functions in respect of all or any part of the island.' This relates to the paragraph 9(ii) bodies in Strand Two. It does not cover the NSMC, also in Strand Two. But the bodies – under the same name of institution – have been provided for in article 29.7.2. There can be no legal reason for this second visitation.

Institutions with executive powers and functions seems similar to article 29.7.2. There, the subject is any institution. Here, it is in the plural. Powers and functions is similar, and the comments above on functions meaning powers and duties (in United Kingdom law at least) apply. However, the word executive intrudes here. This was noticeably absent in article 29.7.2. Executive exists in the constitution in a number of places: in article 6, as a branch of government, exercising some powers, and in article 28.2, where the executive power of the state (in internal affairs[70]) is exercised by or on the authority of the government. The word executive tended to be avoided in the talks to play down any constitutional significance. This section of article 3, to say nothing of the word's presence, gives the bodies a constitutional significance.

That are shared between those jurisdictions is legally less than exact. Shared relates back to article 3.1, and the comment there applies. Jurisdiction also relates back, and the comment there also applies.

70 See article 29.4.1.

May be established by their respective responsible authorities is extraordinary. BNH empowers the government of the 26 counties within that jurisdiction. The constitution has no effect in Northern Ireland, and it is unusual to refer to areas outside the state – other than through article 29. Respective responsible authorities is a strange phrase for government. Government is what is required by the Irish constitution. No doubt it was not used to cover a number of Northern Ireland options: direct rule; devolution; the collapse of the assembly.

For stated purposes would seem to be a reference to paragraph 11 of Strand Two, in particular 'clear operational remit'.

And may exercise powers and functions in respect of all or any part of the island is also extraordinary. It is not for the Irish constitution to determine how institutions may function throughout Ireland. BNH may permit organs of the state to do things at home and abroad. The implementation bodies are not, however, institutions of the Irish state. Here, the word executive has not been used before powers and duties. This is consistent with article 29.7.2. In respect of all or any part refers to the distinction between cross-border and all-Ireland, commented upon with reference to article 29.7.2. Of the island is the third use of this substitute for Ireland in article 3 (and the fourth use in articles 2 and 3).

[ii.] ***iii.*** **[by the addition of the following section to this Article:]** ***the following section shall be added to the Irish text of this Article:***

'8. [Irish text to be inserted here]'

and

iv. the following section shall be added to the English text of this Article:

'8. The State may exercise extra-territorial jurisdiction in accordance with the generally recognised principles of international law.'

11.69 The comments above about the Irish and English language versions of articles 2 and 3 apply to this article 29.8.

11.70 It was necessitated – in the eyes of the Irish government – by the 'like extra-territorial effect' in the former article 3. Instead of understanding that jurisdiction, and its reason for inclusion in 1937, a new section was created in the international relations article to state apparently a rule of international law in the constitution.

11.71 Extra-territoriality is not centrally a matter of international law.[71] This is in spite of state territory being a principal concept in the law of nations. The sovereignty of a state extends beyond its land territory and its internal seas to its territorial sea.[72] Extra-territorially refers to the jurisdiction of a state being exercised externally in specific areas such as criminal[73] or nationality law or

71 'Lotus', Judgment No. 9, 1927, PCIJ, Series A, No. 10, at pp. 18–19. This case, however, holds that a state, in order to maintain its peace, order and good government may legislate in its criminal law extra-territorially.

72 Article 2 of the 1982 United Nations Convention on the Law of the Sea (UNCLOS).

73 Home Office, *Review of Extra-Territorial Jurisdiction: steering committee report*, July 1996. This report by an interdepartmental committee described extra-territoriality as a safety net, to be exercised only where extradition – as a result of treaties – was not available (1). The European Committee on Crime Problems (of the Council of Europe), in *Extra-territorial Criminal Jurisdiction*, a report of 1990, described six principal bases of jurisdiction, including the principle of universality (authorized usually by a multilateral agreement); piracy is an example of a universal crime.

diplomatic and consular rights. It is a matter of municipal law in the main.[74]

11.72 Principles of territorial sovereignty serve to restrict direct or indirect incursions into other jurisdictions. 'Usually the coexistence of overlapping jurisdiction is acceptable and convenient; and forbearance by states in the exercise of their jurisdictional powers avoids conflict in all but a small (although important) minority of cases.'[75] Extra-territoriality persists without legal regulation.

11.73 The reason is the difficulty of formulating general principles. In 1988, the International Law Association (ILA) established a committee on extra-territoriality under Sir Ian Sinclair. Some progress was made in the areas of export controls and anti-trust law.[76] Other topics were discussed at a symposium in Dresden in 1993, and at the ILA conferences in Buenos Aires in 1994 and Helsinki in 1996. The committee reported 'that a consensus on the international law of jurisdiction [was] not within easy reach', and recommended its own dissolution.[77]

11.74 Extra-territoriality existed in the Irish Free State from its creation: *R (Alexander) v Judge of the Circuit Court for Cork* [1925] 2 IR 165, 193 per FitzGibbon J. In 1931, the Statute of Westminster declared – throughout the empire but not in the Irish Free State(?) – that dominions could legislate extra-territorially (section 3). The reference to extra-territoriality in article 3 was presumably for the avoidance of doubt in 1937, given that BNH was claiming a right to include Northern Ireland in its jurisdiction while choosing not to legislate for it. The use of the word 'like' may have been necessary for the succession of states. But it risked restricting the development of extra-territoriality in following years. In *The Criminal Law (Jurisdiction) Bill 1975* [1977] IR 129, 148 per O'Higgins CJ, the Supreme Court upheld the validity of the bill on the basis that the Oireachtas was able to legislate with extra-territorial effect because this power had existed in Saorstát Éireann in 1937.

The Irish state had no legal need to insert an extra-territoriality provision in article 29 of the constitution. It existed in its domestic law, and there was nothing in international law preventing it. The United Kingdom had encouraged extra-territoriality (in Northern Ireland) in criminal law, and tolerated it in Irish nationality law from 1956. Article 29.8 serves politically to reinforce anti-Agreement views about the territorial claim not having been removed from BNH.

11.75 ANNOTATIONS

'The State may exercise extra-territorial jurisdiction in accordance with the generally recognised principles of international law.'

The subject of the sentence is the state, so article 29 would seem to be the most appropriate place in the constitution. However, that article still confuses municipal and international law. The former article 3 stated that the laws of the Oireachtas were to have the like extra-territorial effect as those of Saorstát Éireann. Jurisdiction may be legislative, curial or executive. In article 3, it was only legislative. In article 29, it is now legislative, curial and executive. By attributing extra-territoriality to the state – which embraces legislative, executive and judicial powers of government under article 6 – article 29.8 has greatly

74 *Oppenheim's International Law*, 9th edn, London 1994, Sir Robert Jennings & Sir Arthur Watts, eds, vol. 1, *Peace*, p. 457 n 2.

75 Jennings and Watts, *Oppenheim's International Law*, vol. 1, p. 457.

76 Karl Meessen, ed., *International Law of Export Control: jurisdictional issues*, The Hague 1992.

77 Karl Meessen, ed., *Extraterritorial Jurisdiction in Theory and Practice*, The Hague 1996.

increased its range. There is a risk of the Irish government claiming an extra-territorial right, under article 29.8, to interfere in Northern Ireland.

May exercise extra-territorial jurisdiction is permissive, but unnecessary.

In accordance with the generally recognised principles of international law adds nothing. If anything, the principle of a state's title to exercise jurisdiction resting in its sovereignty,[78] and – the United Kingdom's – supreme authority within its state territory, combine to deny any extra-territorial effect vis a vis Northern Ireland.

Has the territorial claim been removed?

11.76 This question was posed above, and four subordinate questions presented.

11.77 The first is: has the territorial claim been removed from articles 2 and 3? This lay in the concept of national territory. The nation for Irish nationalists has always been associated with Ireland. And territory is a defining characteristic of a state. Despite the return of the word territory to article 3.1 (to no particular effect), national territory has been removed from the constitution.

11.78 Article 2 now deals with nationality, citizenship and the diaspora. Article 3 with the aspiration to unity, peaceful means and consent, jurisdiction and extra-territoriality. However confusing, and offensive to unionists, there is nothing in the completely new article 2 and the much-amended article 3 to constitute a territorial claim.

11.79 The second subordinate question is: is *McGimpsey v Ireland* [1988] IR 567; [1990] IR 110 still good law? It was this landmark decision which interpreted articles 2 and 3 as containing the territorial claim; the former was a claim of legal right, and the latter – an international law point – a disclaimer of acquiescence, prescription or estoppel in terms of United Kingdom territorial sovereignty. There was a constitutional imperative to unite Ireland. The text of article 2 has gone. So has the 'without prejudice' phrase in article 3, on which Finlay CJ based his little-noticed international law point. *McGimpsey* has nothing on which to bite in the articles 2 and 3 which will take effect when the BIA comes into force. The constitutional imperative has been relegated to an aspiration.

11.80 The third subordinate question is: is there the same, or another, territorial claim lurking in other articles? Despite the problem of article 1 (the undefinable Irish nation), and the catholic nationalist preamble, the difficulty over the Irish-law name (the preamble and articles 4 and 5), and the irritants of the national language (article 8) and Irish citizenship law (based on article 9), there is not enough here to constitute a full-blown territorial claim. (While Finlay CJ did not have to look further than articles 2 and 3, it is probable that he would have used other articles to reinforce the Supreme Court's interpretation.) Any new embryonic claim would have to be interpreted harmoniously[79] with the new articles 2 and 3 (identified with the BIA): with peaceful means and the consent of the majority of the people in both jurisdictions in article 3.1.

11.81 The fourth subordinate question is: what did the people of the Republic vote for on 22 May 1998? Fortunately, the eighteenth and nineteenth amendments

78 'Lotus', Judgment No. 9, 1927, PCIJ, Series A, No. 10, at p. 19.

79 *Dillane v Attorney General* [1980] ILRM 167, 170 per Henchy J; *Information (Termination of Pregnancies) Bill, 1995* [1995] 1 IR 1, 32 per Hamilton CJ.

of the constitution, as a result of *McKenna v An Taoiseach (No 2)* [1995] 2 IR 10, were conducted under the aegis of the Referendum Commission. This statutory body was required by section 3 of the Referendum Act 1998 to present the arguments for and against the amendments to articles 2, 3 and 29 (not the Belfast Agreement[80]), in order to ensure a fair and informed vote.

11.82 The literature distributed to households, and reproduced in the national and local press, would appear to have been at least vetted by the chairman, Mr Justice Tom Finlay, the former Chief Justice.[81] In *Arguments For and Against*, the people were told that a reason for voting 'no' was the 'surrender [of] our claim to Northern Ireland'[82]. Of those who voted, 85,748 persons voted 'no' – 5.61 per cent of those voting; 1,442,583 voted 'yes' – 94.39 per cent of those voting. There was a turnout of 56.3 per cent, with 17,064 spoiled votes. The interpretation of a constitutional provision involves a number of different rules.[83] Given the Referendum Commission, it will be possible to argue – as evidence of the intention of the people[84] – that Mr Justice Tom Finlay and his colleagues presented the argument that a 'no' vote would preserve the constitutional claim to Northern Ireland.

80 The question asked in the referendum was: 'Do you approve of the proposal to amend the Constitution contained in the undermentioned Bill?: Nineteenth Amendment of the Constitution Bill, 1998.' However, in the Referendum in Northern Ireland booklet, *Your Time to Decide*, Dublin, the Referendum Commission, 1998, the following was stated: 'The proposed amendment must be considered in the context of the agreement reached in the Multi-Party negotiations which has annexed to it the text of the British/Irish Agreement, and which is being or will soon be delivered to your home.'

81 Thus, in the Referendum in Northern Ireland booklet, *Your Time to Decide*, Dublin, the Referendum Commission, 1998, articles 2 and 3 are described thus: 'It constitutes a legal claim by the State ...'; 'the provisions of article 3 do not in any way delimit or reduce the claim made in Article 2 to the entire national territory.'

82 In *Your Time to Decide*, the Referendum Commission stated: 'The proposed new Article 2 no longer makes a claim as a legal right to the territorial area of the whole of the island of Ireland.' (p. 3)

83 See the essay 'Constitutional Interpretation', in John M. Kelly, *The Irish Constitution*, Gerard Hogan & Gerry Whyte, eds, Dublin 1994, pp. xcviii–cxxii, where the Irish judiciary is described as favouring an eclectic approach. However, the so-called 'broad' approach, essentially purposiveness, is concerned with the 'intentions of the people as embodied therein'. (xcix)

84 *Attorney General v Hamilton* [1993] 2 IR 250, 289–90 per McCarthy J.

PART 3

INSTITUTIONS

Part 3 addresses the main aspect of the Belfast Agreement, the new institutions of government for Northern Ireland.[1] Chapter 12 deals with the Strand One proposals, for Democratic Institutions in Northern Ireland (some 36 paragraphs). Chapter 13 on the Annex to that chapter follows, dealing with the Pledge of Office and the (ministerial) Code of Conduct. Chapter 14 covers Strand Two, the North/South Ministerial Council (some 19 paragraphs). There follows another short chapter, Chapter 15, on the Annex to that chapter, on the work programme during the transition. Chapters 16 and 17 turn to Strand Three (some 21 paragraphs). Chapter 16 examines the British-Irish Council; Chapter 17 the British Irish Intergovernmental Conference. Strand One has been incorporated in United Kingdom law principally by the NIA 1998. Strand Two has given rise to two subsidiary treaties,[2] and legislation at Westminster and in the Oireachtas. And Strand Three has also led to two subsidiary international agreements. The United Kingdom and Irish governments had fulfilled their obligations under article 2 of the BIA by 8 (alternatively, 22) March 1999, meeting the third requirement for entry into force under article 4(1)(c). To the view that there has been a major all-Ireland institutional advance, I argue in this part of the book – as stated in the Preface – that the institutional changes brought about by the Belfast Agreement are characterized predominantly by the significance of Strand One, with the Strand Two and Three add-ons complementing each other.

1 The relevant page numbers are: pp. 5–16 of Cm 3883; pp. 14–28 of Cm 4705 (and, in the 1999 Irish version, pp. 8–22).

2 Plus an exchange of notes of 18 June 1999.

12

Strand One: Democratic Institutions in Northern Ireland

12.1 Strand One is the third section of the Belfast Agreement. It is at pages 5–9 of Cm 3883 and pages 14–20 of Cm 4705 (pages 8–14 of the 1999 Irish version). At 36 paragraphs, it overshadows Strands Two and Three (19 and 21 paragraphs respectively). This is the longest chapter in the book, dealing as it does with the core of the Belfast Agreement. I show [deletions] to the MDP, and *additions* thus.

12.2 Strand One is about devolution. It was described as involving 'relationships and arrangements within Northern Ireland, including the relationship between any new institutions there and the Westminster Parliament'.[1] The participants in this part of the talks were the United Kingdom government and the political parties (the United Kingdom government chairing). 'The Irish Government [was to] be kept informed ... through liaison arrangements agreed between the two Governments following consultation with the parties.'[2]

The history of devolution to Northern Ireland

12.3 There are two precedents for United Kingdom devolution of powers to Northern Ireland. The first – under the GOIA 1920 – was the parliament of Northern Ireland; this lasted from 1921 until 1972. What remains of the GOIA 1920 has been repealed by the NIA 1998.[3] The second is the Northern Ireland assembly, under the NICA 1973. This lasted for the first five months of 1974. Much of the NICA 1973 has been repealed by the NIA 1998[4] (the remaining sections could have been reenacted;[5] the reason this was not done may have been because they were not dealt with in the Belfast Agreement).

12.4 The NIA 1998, therefore, was drafted on a not quite clean legal sheet. This is distinct from the point about Northern Ireland remaining an integral part of the United Kingdom under the 1800 acts of union (see Chapters 3, 4 and 10).

12.5 Devolution remained United Kingdom policy after 1974. In the 1985 Anglo-Irish Agreement, this was reiterated in article 4(b)–(c); devolution and transcendance of the the agreement were related.[6] The 1993 *Downing Street Declaration*'s reference to 'institutions and structures',[7] however, seemed to be more concerned with Strands Two and Three. The 1995 *Framework Documents*

1 *Ground Rules for Substantive All-Party Negotiations*, Cm 3232, 16 April 1996, rule 2.
2 *Ground Rules for Substantive All-Party Negotiations*, Cm 3232, 16 April 1996, rule 19.
3 Sections 2, 100(2) & schedule 15.
4 Section 100(2) & schedule 15.
5 They are: 10 (attorney-general for Northern Ireland); 33(2) (pensions for former members and ministers); 34 (director of public prosecutions for Northern Ireland); 35 (crown solicitor for Northern Ireland); 36 (less subsection 1(d)) (other Northern Ireland officers); 37(2)–(4) (consolidated funds); 41–43 & sch 6 (repeals, savings, interpretation).
6 Articles 2(b), 5(c) & 10(c).
7 Paragraph 9.

contained, in contrast, as part I, 'A Framework for Accountable Government in Northern Ireland' (the blue pages). This was the work entirely of London, and discussed a form of devolution (not actually achieved).[8] The true progenitor of Strand One was the Heads of Agreement of 12 January 1998, which envisaged 'democratically-elected institutions in Northern Ireland'.

12.6 Devolution in Northern Ireland, as a consequence of the Irish question of Victorian politics, never led to home rule all-round much less a federal United Kingdom. Though it was not part of new labour's project to 'modernise British politics'[9] following its election in May 1997, the Belfast Agreement of 10 April 1998 came to merge with plans for Scottish and Welsh devolution.

12.7 In referendums on 11 and 18 September 1997 respectively, Scotland and Wales (by the narrowest of margins) had voted for devolution. There followed the Government of Wales Act 1998 (which received the royal assent on 31 July), and the Scotland Act 1998 (19 November). The latter was passed on the same day as the NIA 1998. The Scottish parliament and Welsh assembly were elected on 6 May 1999.[10] And the transfer of powers took place on 1 July 1999.

12.8 The impasse over decommissioning in Northern Ireland meant that it dropped behind, devolution not taking place until 2 December 1999.

12.9 The three 1998 acts constitute a set on United Kingdom devolution.[11] Scotland, Wales and Northern Ireland have similar provisions for the determination of devolution issues by the judicial committee of the privy council (in addition, the Human Rights Act 1998 – to apply throughout the United Kingdom – received the royal assent on 9 November 1998; it was brought into force partly for each of the three administrations upon devolution). Devolution in Northern Ireland is, therefore, regulated in an integrated legal context, with the courts in London, Edinburgh, Cardiff and Belfast likely to balance centrifugal and centripetal tendencies.

12.10 The Belfast Agreement – looked at legally – is of course a treaty. It has been incorporated mainly in United Kingdom law by principally the NIA 1998. Thus, the *Notes on Clauses* contains for each clause an 'Agreement reference' (which is sometimes specified as not relevant). Of the act's nine parts, seven – I

8 The prime minister, John Major, wrote in a foreword: 'For reasons that are unique to Northern Ireland, devolution of significant legislative and executive powers has always been a central plank of Government policy for Northern Ireland alone.' (p. iii)

9 The origin of labour's programme of constitutional reform lay in the new clause IV adopted in 1995: 'An open democracy, in which the government is held to account by the people, decisions are taken as far as practicable by the communities they affect; and where fundamental human rights are guaranteed.' (Quoted in John Rentoul, *Tony Blair*, London 1996, p. 488) The phrase quoted appeared in the prime minister's prefaces to the following white papers: *Scotland's Parliament*, Cm 3658, July 1997; *A Voice for Wales*, Cm 3718, July 1997; *Rights Brought Home: the human rights bill*, Cm 3782, October 1997. The other aspects of the programme are: a mayor and strategic authority for London; freedom of information; a referendum on the voting system; and house of lords reform.

10 On 10 May 1999, BBC television relaunched its television evening news, stressing the United Kingdom and the regional capitals Belfast, Edinburgh and Cardiff.

11 There is no relationship between powers devolved and the length of the act: Scotland, 132 sections and 9 schedules (109 pp); Northern Ireland (101 sections and 15 schedules (100 pp); Wales (159 sections and 18 schedules (183 pp).

(preliminary), II (legislative powers), III (executive authorities), IV (the Northern Ireland assembly), VI (financial provisions), VIII (miscellaneous), IX (supplemental) – deal centrally with devolution.

12.11 Here I will reference the relevant sections of the NIA 1998 in discussing each paragraph of Strand One. Reference will also be made to standing orders: the initial standing orders (ISOs), made by the secretary of state under paragraph 10(1) of the schedule to the Northern Ireland (Elections) Act 1998, in June[12] and November[13] 1998 and July[14] and November[15] 1999; and the standing orders (SOs), under section 41 and schedule 6 of the NIA 1998, approved by the assembly with cross-community support on 9 March 1999[16] (but determined by the secretary of state prior to devolution[17]). These standing orders were amended slightly by the assembly on 6 December 1999.[18]

12.12 There is a view that devolution in 1999 substantially follows the precedents of 1921–72 and 1974. This is so, and the three administrations may be compared across time. But the conclusion drawn by some municipal lawyers about legal texts is not valid. The GOIA 1920 was the constitutional foundation for 1921–72; and the NICA 1973 underpinned legally the 1974 assembly and executive. However, the NIA 1998 does not stand in exactly the same position – and statutory annotation does not exhaust the task of practical legal commentary on the 10 April 1998 settlement.

12.13 The 1985 Anglo-Irish Agreement marked a new departure, determining the legal shape of the Belfast Agreement. While the Irish government was not integrally involved in Strand One, it nevertheless remains the position that the NIA 1998 may have to be interpreted in terms of an international agreement. During the legislative process, the United Kingdom government cited the Belfast Agreement continually.

12.14 Further, concentrating upon the NIA 1998, at the expense of the Belfast Agreement, ignores the most controversial aspects of the 1998 settlement: the changes mainly in the Irish constitution; the north-south aspect in Strand Two; Strand Three on east-west; and the plethora of discrete issues: rights, etc., decommissioning, security, policing and justice and prisoners. These have generated a host of subsequent international agreements and domestic legislation. They cannot be ignored, even – especially – in Northern Ireland law.

TITLE: DEMOCRATIC INSTITUTIONS IN NORTHERN IRELAND

12.15 Strand One should have been entitled the Northern Ireland Assembly for

12 Letter, secretary of state to initial presiding officer (Lord Alderdice), 29 June 1998, New Northern Ireland Assembly, *Official Report*, vol. 1, p. 1, 1 July 1999. ISOs 1–19 were produced.

13 ISOs 20–21 followed: New Northern Ireland Assembly, *Official Report*, vol. 1, p. 194, 26 October 1998; *Report of the Committee on Standing Orders*, NNIA 9(i), p. 6, 8 March 1999.

14 ISOs 22–25 (8 July 1999), and a new ISO 22 (15 July 1999).

15 A new ISO 14.

16 New Northern Ireland Assembly, *Report of the Committee on Standing Orders*, NNIA 9(ii), 8 March 1999; Northern Ireland Assembly, *Standing Orders*, NNIA 10, ordered to be printed by the Assembly on 9 March 1999.

17 Northern Ireland Assembly, *Official Report*, vol. 4, no. 1, p. 1, 6 December 1999.

18 Northern Ireland Assembly, *Official Report*, vol. 4, no. 1, pp. 1–7, 6 December 1999.

reasons of consistency. Strand Two is the North/South Ministerial Council. And Strand Three is the British-Irish Council and the British-Irish Intergovernmental Conference. The Heads of Agreement of 12 January 1998, in announcing 'democratically-elected institutions', went on to refer to 'provisions to ensure that all sections of the community can participate and work together successfully in the operation of these institutions and that all sections of the community are protected.' The only democratic institution in Strand One is the assembly. The civic forum (paragraph 34) is not a directly elected body. The reference to democratic institutions in the title is therefore to an assembly characterized by safeguards.

1. **[The following is intended to]** ***This agreement*** **provide*s* for a democratically elected Assembly in Northern Ireland which is inclusive in its membership, capable of exercising executive and legislative authority, and subject to safeguards to protect the rights and interests of all sides of the community.**[19]

12.16 The full text of the 12 January 1998 Heads of Agreement on Strand One read: 'Democratically-elected institutions in Northern Ireland, to include a Northern Ireland assembly, elected by a system of proportional representation, exercising devolved executive and legislative responsibility over at least the responsibilities of the six Northern Ireland departments and with provisions to ensure that all sections of the community can participate and work together successfully in the operation of these institutions and that all sections of the community are protected.'

12.17 The relevant parts of the NIA 1998 are I, II, III, IV, VI, VIII and IX.

12.18 ANNOTATIONS

'This agreement provides for a democratically elected Assembly in Northern Ireland which is inclusive in its membership,'. This agreement is the MPA. It refers back to paragraphs 1 and 6 of the Declaration of Support. Strand One is the only section in Part 3 of this book to refer to the MPA. Strands Two and Three refer to the BIA in their opening paragraphs.

A democratically elected Assembly in Northern Ireland follows the Heads of Agreement (dropping the ungrammatical hyphen). Under section 4(5) of the NIA 1998, the assembly was defined as 'the New Northern Ireland Assembly, which after the appointed day [defined in section 3(1)] shall be known as the Northern Ireland Assembly'.

The New Northern Ireland Assembly was established by section 1(1)[20] of the Northern Ireland (Elections) Act 1998 (which received the royal assent on 7 May). It is this measure – and not the NIA 1998 – which governed the assembly during the transition, or shadow phase. It is also the Northern Ireland (Elections) Act 1998 which governed assembly initial standing orders; under section 1(6) and paragraph 10(1) of the schedule, the secretary of state determined the standing orders and notified the presiding officer – on one occasion with a handwritten order.[21]

The Northern Ireland assembly came into legal existence at (arguably) one minute past midnight on 2 December 1999.[22]

19 The words 'inclusive', 'executive and legislative authority' and 'safeguards' were unusually underlined in the MDP.

20 'There shall be an Assembly called the New Northern Ireland Assembly, for the purpose of taking part in preparations to give effect to the agreement reached at the multi-party talks on Northern Ireland set out in Command Paper 3883.'

21 New Northern Ireland Assembly, *Official Report*, vol. 2, p. 319, 15 July 1999.

22 Northern Ireland Act 1998 (Appointed Day) Order 1999, SI 1999/3208. This was an order

Which is inclusive in its membership is a strange phrase. The assembly has been described as democratically elected. This is provided for further in paragraph 2. The assembly is therefore as inclusive as the appropriate electoral law requires. The 1995 *Framework Documents* referred to 'local institutions of government that are directly accountable to the people – all the people – and to which they can give their wholehearted commitment and support'.[23] Inclusiveness came to apply, during the transition (1 July 1998 to 1 December 1999), not to the assembly, but to its executive. Sinn Féin, which has the same rights as all other political parties, by virtue of the election of 25 June 1998, argued that the executive had to be all-inclusive regardless of the provisions on decommissioning (see Chapter 19).

'capable of exercising executive and legislative authority'. This comes from the 12 January 1998 Heads of Agreement, where executive is listed before legislative. The Northern Ireland (Elections) Act 1998 gave no powers to the transitional or shadow assembly. These came from section 3 of the NIA 1998, which provided for a devolution order specifying the appointed day. The appointed day was 2 December 1999.[24] This is the day when parts II and III of the act came into force – part II (sections 5–15) is legislative powers; part III (sections 16–30), executive powers.

'and subject to safeguards to protect the rights and interests of all sides of the community.' This phrase distinguishes the Northern Ireland assembly from other United Kingdom elected bodies. The 1921 Northern and Southern Ireland Parliaments were modelled on that of Westminster; they were simple majoritarian bodies (taking no formal account of the party system). The 1974 Northern Ireland assembly was premissed on 'government by consent'; the executive, 'having regard to the support it command[ed] in the Assembly and to the electorate on which that support [was] based, [was required to be] widely accepted throughout the community'.[25] (There was no provision for legislative safeguards.) Safeguards are further specified in paragraph 5. To protect the rights and interests is the reason for the safeguards. It is not clear what rights are involved. Are these human rights, which are usually individual? This is possible from the context, but there seems to be a suggestion of group rights. The meaning of rights is further elaborated by the reference to interests. Interests is an entirely different concept. Presumably, the individual or, more likely, the group defines its interests. They can – and often are – in conflict with the interests of other individuals and groups. However, the use of all mitigates this to some extent. All sides of the community is the key phrase, suggesting only compatible rights and interests. In the preamble to the 1985 Anglo-Irish Agreement, there was a reference to 'the two communities in Northern Ireland'. These are best defined as catholics and protestants (ethnic groups), though there is a connection with nationalism and unionism – which were traditions in the 1985 preamble. The two are connected in article 4(a)(i). Community is different. It must refer to all the people of Northern Ireland. Thus, the phrase 'thoughout the community' was used in section 2 of the NICA 1973. All sides may be a reference to the aforementioned two communities, but it is likely to be more general – a plurality of sides, or – better – groups or interests.

Subheading: The Assembly

12.19 This is the first of eight – what must be called – subsections to the Strand One section. Subsections have paragraphs numbered sequentially throughout the section.

in council, made at a special privy council on 1 December 1999. It had been debated and voted upon in parliament on 30 November 1999: House of Commons, *Hansard*, 6th series, 340, 253–76, 30 November 1999 (318 votes to 10); House of Lords, 5th series, 607, 723–52, 30 November 1999.

23 Part I, paragraph 3.

24 Northern Ireland Act (Appointed Day) Order 1999, SI 1999/3208.

25 Section 2.

2. **A[n] *108-member* Assembly will be elected by PR(STV) from existing Westminster constituencies.**

   [[Note from the Independent Chairmen: There is disagreement among participants as to the size of the Assembly and as to whether the election system should provide greater opportunity to smaller parties to be represented in the Assembly. We believe that it should.

   Options for your consideration include, but are not limited to:

   (a) increasing the number of seats per constituency from 5 to 6; and/or
   (b) providing a top-up of 10 or 20 additional seats.]]

12.20 The relevant sections of the NIA 1998 are 31–38. As can be seen, it was the independent chairmen who recommended a 108-member assembly in order to help smaller parties.

12.21 This paragraph defines the size of the unicameral assembly and its electoral system. The 1921–72 parliament of Northern Ireland had 52 members in the house of commons and 26 in the senate.[26] (There were also 13 – later 12 – MPs in the Westminster parliament, a figure reduced from that in 1918.) Elections were originally by proportional representation (though this was changed in 1929 by the Northern Ireland parliament to the Westminster first past the post system).[27] The 1974 assembly – which was unicameral – had 78 members. They too were elected by proportional representation.[28] In 1995, the number of Northern Ireland constituencies at Westminster was increased from 17 to 18 (the number elected in May 1997).[29]

12.22 The assembly, of course, was established legally – as the New Northern Ireland Assembly – under section 1(1) of the Northern Ireland (Elections) Act 1998, which received the royal assent on 7 May. Section 1(1) came into force on 28 May 1998.[30] Under section 4(5) of the NIA 1998, it became the Northern Ireland Assembly on the appointed day (or devolution day) – as defined in section 3. This was 2 December 1999.[31]

12.23 Section 40 (and schedule 5) provide for a Northern Ireland assembly commission, a body corporate (40(1)). This comprises the presiding officer and a number of members (initially five) appointed under standing orders.[32] The commission provides the assembly with property, staff and services, and allows the assembly to sue or be sued. Paragraph 6 of schedule 6 provides that – by order in council – the commission may be treated as a crown body for the purposes of any enactment. On 2 December 1999, the Commission began to be treated as a crown

26 GOIA 1920 ss 13(2), 14(2), schs 3 & 5.
27 GOIA 1920 s 14(3); House of Commons (Method of Voting and Redistribution of Seats) Act 1929.
28 Northern Ireland Assembly Act 1973 ss 1(2) & 2(3)–(5) schedule; NICA 1973 ss 28(1) & 29.
29 Parliamentary Constituencies (Northern Ireland) Order 1995, SI 1995/2992.
30 Northern Ireland (Elections) Act 1998 (Commencement) Order 1998, SI 1998/1338.
31 Northern Ireland Act 1998 (Appointed Day) Order 1999, SI 1999/3208.
32 There is no relevant SO. On 6 December 1999, it was reported to the assembly that the commission comprised the Speaker, Eileen Bell, Gregory Campbell, Rev. Robert Coulter, John Fee and Dr Dara O'Hagan (Northern Ireland Assembly, *Official Report*, vol. 4, no. 1, p. 8, 6 December 1999).

body, defined as 'a body which is the servant or agent of the Crown'.[33] This has implications for Parliament Buildings at Stormont; in particular, it may mean that the commission is required to fly the union flag on designated days.

12.24 The Scotland Act 1998 established a Scottish parliament (section 1(1)). Section 21(1) (and schedule 2) provided for a Scottish parliament corporate body – similar to the Northern Ireland assembly commission. The Government of Wales Act 1998, in contrast, established a national assembly for Wales (section 1(1)). Under section 1(2), this was to be a body corporate in its own right. And the exercise of assembly functions was to be regarded as done on behalf of the crown (section 1(3)).

12.25 ANNOTATIONS

'A 108-member Assembly will be elected by PR(STV) from existing Westminster constituencies.' A 108-member assembly is more than twice the size of the old Northern Ireland house of commons, and 30 stronger than the 1974 assembly. The 1995 *Framework Documents* envisaged 'about 90 members',[34] that is five-seat constituencies. By the time of the MDP (6 April 1998), no decision had been made on the number. The independent chairmen recommended increasing the number of seats from five to six per constituency (from 90 to 108), or having a top-up of ten to twenty seats. The purpose was specified as 'provid[ing] greater opportunity to small parties to be represented'. It is believed that the principal loser of the increase from 90 to 108 was the UUP. It is not clear that small parties benefited. The Ulster Democratic Party, for example, which had been in the talks, never made it into the assembly. 108 seats means six per Westminster constituency. And this is what is provided for in section 33(1)–(2) of the NIA 1998.

Will be elected by PR(STV). The use of initials indicates that this electoral system was familiar to the political parties in Northern Ireland in 1998.

Electoral reformers in pre-partition Ireland – campaigning against the first past the post system – pointed to the existence of the protestant/unionist minority.[35] Proportional representation was included in the Government of Ireland Act 1914. This was also the case with the GOIA 1920, for both parliaments.[36] The 1921 treaty envisaged, only if there was a united Ireland, 'safeguards for minorities in Northern Ireland'.[37] The constitution of the Irish Free State provided for election 'upon principles of Proportional Representation,[38] but it was the Electoral Act 1923 which specified the single transferable vote.[39] Proportional representation by means of the single transferable vote (in multi-member constituencies) became the system in both parts of Ireland. While it was abolished in Northern Ireland in 1929 by the local parliament, it was put into BNH in 1937[40] (Fianna Fáil, as the largest party, tried in 1959, at the behest of Eamon de Valera, and again in 1968, to abolish it, but was unsuccessful.)[41] PR(STV) returned to Northern Ireland for the 1973 assembly

33 Northern Ireland Assembly Commission (Crown Status) Order 1999, SI 1999/3145, made 24 November 1999. This is subject to the negative resolution procedure.

34 Part I, paragraph 5.

35 1918 general election, 2 seats in University of Dublin; 1919, Sligo corporation election.

36 Section 14(3). PR(STV) was defined according to the Representation of the People Act 1918.

37 Article 15.

38 Article 26.

39 Section 17(1).

40 Articles 16.2.5 & 18.5.

41 Third Amendment to the Constitution Bill, 1959; Fourth Amendment to the Constitution Bill, 1968.

election.[42] It has remained for local, assembly and European elections; but not those for Westminster, which continue on the first past the post system.

PR(STV) was specified in the Northern Ireland (Elections) Act 1998.[43] And reenacted in the NIA 1998.[44]

From existing Westminster constituencies. These were increased from 17 to 18 as a result of the Parliamentary Constituencies (Northern Ireland) Order 1995, SI 1995/2992.

3. **The Assembly will exercise full legislative and executive authority in respect of those matters currently within the responsibility of the six Northern Ireland Government Departments, with the possibility of taking on responsibility for other matters as detailed elsewhere in the agreement.**

12.26 The relevant sections of the NIA 1998 are 3 and 4.

12.27 This paragraph of Strand One refers to the powers devolved. The – United Kingdom – model in 1920 was powers to make laws for 'the peace, order and good government' of Northern Ireland, with an express list of excluded matters (which remained the responsibility of the government in London).[45] There was also a list of reserved matters, which was included under executive authority.[46] They were reserved pending agreement to an Irish parliament by the two parliaments in Ireland. In 1973, this was modified to: all matters were transferred, except those which were excepted (in a schedule), and those which were reserved (in another schedule).[47]

12.28 The distinction between transferred and non-transferred matters gave rise at Westminster to the speaker's ruling of 1923, on what Northern Ireland questions could be asked in the sovereign parliament. This was constitutionally a convention. It provided for: if the question related to a devolved power, the Northern Ireland parliament was the place to raise it; otherwise, Westminster would be interfering in the business of a subordinate parliament's minister; there was no minister at Westminster with the responsibility.[48] This remained the position until prorogation in 1972.

12.29 The transfer of powers to Scotland and Wales on 1 July 1999 necessitated a new speaker's ruling. This arose following questions to the secretary of state for Wales on 7 July 1999. On 12 July 1999, the speaker ruled: 'I do not wish the rules relating to questions to become unduly restrictive, but a fundamental rule relating to questions is that they must relate to matters for which Ministers in this House are responsible ... Where matters have been clearly devolved to the Scottish Parliament or to the Welsh Assembly, questions on the details of policy or expenditure would not be in order. Where Secretaries of State have a residual, limited or shared, role, questions should relate to that role.'[49]

42 Northern Ireland Assembly Act 1973 s 2(3).
43 Sections 1(3)–(5), 2(3)–(4).
44 Section 34(1)–(2). The Northern Ireland (Elections) Act 1998 is repealed by s 100(2) & sch 15.
45 GOIA 1920 s 4.
46 GOIA 1920 ss 4(14), 8(2) & (8), 9.
47 NICA 1973 ss 2 & 3 & schs 2 & 3.
48 House of Commons, *Hansard*, 5th series, 163, 1624–5, 3 May 1923. The Northern Ireland house of commons had a similar ruling: *Hansard*, 8, 490, 29 March 1927.
49 House of Commons, *Hansard*, 6th series, 335, 21–2, 12 July 1999.

12.30 ANNOTATIONS

'The Assembly will exercise full legislative and executive authority'. The order in paragraph 1 has been reversed, legislative now leading. This follows section 2 of the NICA 1973, both as to marginal note and to the designating of powers. And it has been applied in 1998.[50] In section 4(1) of the NIA 1998, transferred matter 'means any matter which is not an excepted or reserved matter'. Excepted matter 'means any matter falling within a description specified in Schedule 2'. Reserved matter 'means any matter falling within a description specified in Schedule 3'.

'in respect of those matters currently within the responsibility of the six Northern Ireland Government Departments'. This means that the existing powers (whether in Belfast or London) – and only those – were to pass to the assembly on the appointed day.[51] The legislative powers of the former Northern Ireland parliament, under the GOIA 1920, passed, under section 1(3) of the Northern Ireland (Temporary Provisions) Act 1972, to Westminster. They were returned under the NICA 1973. And reverted again to Westminster, under section 1(3) and paragraph 1(1)(b) of schedule 1 of the Northern Ireland Act 1974. The respective provisions dealing with executive powers are: section 1(1) of the 1972 act, and section 1(3) and paragraph 2 of schedule 1 of the 1974 act. The definition of transferred matters in section 4 of the NIA 1998 – not an excepted or reserved matter – establishes the powers of the six Northern Ireland departments. The use of the word 'government' is not strictly necessary. This suggests that the term Northern Ireland government may be applied to the assembly's executive authority.[52] The six departments at the time of the Belfast Agreement were agriculture; economic development; environment (Northern Ireland); education; health and social services; finance and personnel.

'with the possibility of taking on responsibility for other matters as detailed elsewhere in this agreement.' The Heads of Agreement of 12 January 1998 had referred to 'at least' the six Northern Ireland departments. Section 4 of the NIA 1998 deals with reserved matters becoming transferred matters, and vice versa. The secretary of state has to amend schedule 3 by order in council. A condition precedent is an assembly resolution passed with cross-community support (see below). This is similar to the provision in section 3 of the NICA 1973 (without of course the cross-community requirement), though the assembly could only resist the loss of power then. Detailed elsewhere in this agreement refers to paragraph 7 of the Policing and Justice section. There, the United Kingdom government is stated to be ready in principle to devolve 'policing and justice issues'. These are reserved under paragraphs 9–12 of schedule 3 of the NIA 1998. However, whereas in 1973 this would have been for the secretary of state alone, the assembly now has to agree to accept such powers on a cross-community basis.

4. The Assembly – operating where appropriate on a cross-community basis – will be the prime source of authority in respect of all devolved responsibilities.

12.31 This paragraph adds little to this subsection or the following one. It contains a careful political balance. The concept of cross-community support is introduced in paragraph 5 (and is considered there). Devolved responsibilities have been dealt with in paragraph 3. It also has a bearing on the subsection below on executive authority (paragraphs 14–25).

50 The Scotland Act 1998, in contrast, has only transferred powers and reserved powers: sections 29(2)–(4) and 30(1)–(2), schedules 4 & 5.

51 The 1995 *Framework Documents* envisaged 'legislative and executive responsibility over as wide a range of subjects as in 1973'. (Part I, paragraph 5)

52 The GOIA 1920 referred to the parliament and government of Northern Ireland: section 2(1).

Subheading: Safeguards

5. There will be safeguards to ensure that all sections of the community can participate and work together successfully in the operation of these institutions and that all sections of the community are protected, including:

[[Note from the Chairmen: There is disagreement among participants as to whether the executive heads of departments should be titled 'Assembly Secretaries' or 'Ministers'. Throughout this text the position will be titled 'Assembly Secretary/Minister'.]]

(a) allocations of Committee Chairs, [Assembly Secretaries/]Ministers and Committee membership in proportion to party strengths;

(b) the European Convention on Human Rights (ECHR) and any Bill of Rights for Northern Ireland supplementing it, which neither the Assembly nor public bodies can infringe, together with a Human Rights Commission;

(c) arrangements to provide that key decisions and legislation are proofed to ensure that they do not infringe the ECHR and any Bill of Rights for Northern Ireland;

(d) arrangements to ensure key decisions are taken on a cross-community basis;

[[Note from the Chairmen: There is disagreement among the participants as to the nature of such arrangements. Options for your consideration include, but are not limited, to the following:

(a) That this might require that any key decision would only pass if it is supported by:

either[53] a majority of those members present and voting which includes majorities of those who identify themselves (at the outset) as Nationalist and Unionist respectively

or a weighted majority (two thirds) of those members present and voting.

In this alternative key decisions requiring cross-community support would be designated in advance (eg election of presiding officer, standing orders, budget allocations, employment equality, cultural issues) and/or be triggered by a right of petition exercised by a significant minority of Assembly members, (___%); or

(b) Some combination of parallel consent and a weighted majority; or

(c) Another alternative would be to give to the Chair and Deputy Chair of the Executive/Liaison Committee (see paragraph 17 below) joint authority over key decisions; this would ensure cross-community support. Obviously, its effectiveness would depend on the definition of what are key decisions.]]

(i) either parallel consent, i.e. a majority of those members present and voting, including a majority of the unionist and nationalist designations present and voting;

53 The words either and or were uncharacteristically underlined.

(ii) or a weighted majority (60%) of members present and voting, including at least 40% of each of the nationalist and unionist designations present and voting.

Key decisions requiring cross-community support will be designated in advance, including election of the Chair of the Assembly, the First Minister and Deputy First Minister, standing orders and budget allocations. In other cases such decisions could be triggered by a petition of concern brought by a significant minority of Assembly members (30/108).

(e) an Equality Commission to monitor a statutory obligation to promote equality of opportunity in specified areas and parity of esteem between the two main communities, and to investigate individual complaints against public bodies.

12.32 The reason for this paragraph may be stated simply: nationalist experience of unionist government in Northern Ireland from 1921 to 1972. It is ironic that the precedent for 'safeguards' – in article 15 of the 1921 treaty – was in the context of a unionist minority in a united Ireland.[54] The 1974 assembly – recalled as something of a nationalist success – did not involve such controls on the legislature; power-sharing was provided for in the composition of the executive ('government by consent'[55]).

12.33 The 1995 *Framework Documents*, in part I, put forward 14 (not entirely consistent) 'characteristics' of internal government, including: 'to provide all the constitutional political parties with the opportunity to achieve a role at each level of responsibility, and to have a position proportional to their electoral strength in broad terms'.[56] This may be termed the proportionality principle, one that extends the relationship between voters and representatives (proportional representation) to that between representatives and legislative/executive offices. However, the system envisaged in 1995 of 'detailed checks and balances' – based on a three-person panel (like a collective presidency) – was much less ambitious than paragraph 5 of Strand One.

12.34 This contains five separate ways of essentially preventing one-party, unionist government (even though nationalism is a more united force): one, proportionality in appointments; two, human rights provisions for public administration; three, ditto for legislation; four, cross-community voting on key decisions; and five, equality of opportunity provisions. Of these, the first and the fourth give the legislature specific characteristics. As can be seen, the independent chairmen kept open the question of assembly secretaries, or ministers (which was resolved in favour of the latter but with a trace of the former). They had the task of trying to define cross-community voting. Of the three options offered, (b) and (c) were rejected. The adoption of option (a) required the new paragraph 6 on designation of identity in the FA.

54 The safeguards in Northern Ireland had to do with: patronage; collection of revenue; import/export duties; for minorities; settlement of the financial relationship betweeen north and south; a local militia and defence forces.

55 NICA 1973 s 2.

56 Paragraph 3.

12.35 ANNOTATIONS

'There will be safeguards to ensure that all sections of the community can participate and work together successfully in the operation of these institutions and that all sections of the community are protected, including:'. There will be safeguards (as noted above) is a new development in Northern Ireland government.

To ensure that all sections of the community can participate and work together successfully in the operation of these institutions is the first objective. All sections of the community is similar to all sides of the community in paragraph 1. Can participate is the proportionality principle. And work together successfully in the operation of these institutions is a very different criterion. It suggests the efficiency test in Strand One reviewing under paragraph 36.[57]

And that all sections of the community are protected is a second objective. All sections of the community is more pluralist than the more adversarial all sides. Protected raises the question: who from whom? The implication is nationalist protection from unionists, though many of the latter would point to the presence of Sinn Féin in the chamber. The use of the word including suggests that this list of five is not exhaustive.

'(a) allocations of Committee Chairs, Ministers and Committee Membership in proportion to party strengths;'. This is a major configuration of Northern Ireland government. It has been provided for in the NIA 1998 and in standing orders. Paragraphs 8 and 16 deal further with proportionality, specifying the d'Hondt[58] system. Used in the European parliament, it allocates seats among parties on the basis of (what is called) the largest average. The d'Hondt method – based on the formula S/1 + M (where S = seats and M = members) – favours larger parties.

Committee chairmen (sic) – and deputy chairmen[59] – are dealt with in section 29 of the NIA 1998 (statutory committees). The section specifies the nature of elections under standing orders. (Statutory committees are to advise and assist one or more ministers.) Under section 29(2)–(4), chairmen and deputy chairmen are to be elected using the d'Hondt formula, S/1 + C, where S = the number of seats[60] and C = the number of chairmen/deputy chairmen (in the case of a tie, C is replaced by V, which is the number of first preference votes obtained by the party on 25 June 1998). Subsection 7 deals with resignation and dismissal. Statutory committees are covered by SOs 44–47 (standing orders refer to chairs and deputy chairs.) The standing orders follow section 29 of the act, adding – in SO 41(4) – one time limit of 15 minutes, for the nominating officer of the party selected to make a nomination, and the person nominated to affirm the terms of the pledge of office and take up the selected office (though the assembly may extend a particular time limit if reasons are given and approved). SO 48 deals with non-statutory committees (standing committees and ad hoc committees), the chairs and deputy chairs of the former being elected as in SO 45.

Ministers are considered below in the subsection Executive Authorities.

Committee members are dealt with indirectly in section 41 of the NIA 1998 (standing orders). Subsection 3 refers to schedule 6, where paragraph 4 deals with committees: '(1) The standing orders shall include provision for ensuring that, in appointing members to committees, regard is had to the balance of parties in the Assembly.' SO 46 deals with membership of statutory committees. Each is to have eleven members. Seats are to be allocated 'on a proportionate basis' in accordance with a number of stated principles by the business committee.[61] This applies – under SO 48(4) – to standing committees.

57 The 1995 *Framework Documents* included the characteristic 'able to function effectively, efficiently and decisively within clearly defined areas of responsibility'. (Part I, paragraph 3)
58 Viktor d'Hondt, a Belgian mathematician, in the University of Ghent.
59 Paragraph 8.
60 On the day the assembly first met, that is 1 July 1998.
61 This is a Standing Committee.

'(b) the European Convention on Human Rights (ECHR) and any Bill of Rights for Northern Ireland supplementing it, which neither the Assembly nor public bodies can infringe, together with a Human Rights Commission;'. This safeguard is concerned essentially with administration by public bodies plus the assembly. It is dealt with extensively in the Human Rights part of the Rights, Safeguards and Equality of Opportunity section (and will be considered there).

Construing this safeguard, the ECHR has been – since the Belfast Agreement – incorporated in United Kingdom law by the Human Rights Act (HRA)1998.

Any Bill of Rights for Northern Ireland supplementing it suggests that such a bill of rights may not come into being, or at least not immediately. This must be read along with paragraph 4 in the Human Rights part referred to above. The phrase also suggests that the bill of rights only supplements what has now become the HRA 1998. Under section 22(6), the act extends to Northern Ireland. Supplementing is consistent with paragraph 4, but the idea of a freestanding bill of rights for Northern Ireland (embracing the ECHR) would seem no longer to be viable.

Which neither the Assembly nor public bodies can infringe specifies the areas where human rights law will apply. The reference to the assembly here must be distinguished from safeguard (c). It would seem to be the assembly acting other than legislatively, namely as an executive authority. However, subordinate legislation is a matter for the executive. Under section 24(1)(a) of the NIA 1998, a minister or department cannot make, confirm or approve any subordinate legislation, or do any act, incompatible with convention rights. Public bodies would seem to be the same as public authorities, the term used in part VII of the NIA 1998.

Together with a Human Rights Commission. This is specified further in paragraph 5 of the Human Rights part of the Rights, Safeguards and Equality of Opportunity section. It is also provided for in part VII and schedule 7 of the NIA 1998.

'(c) arrangements to provide that key decisions and legislation are proofed to ensure they do not infringe the ECHR and any Bill of Rights for Northern Ireland;'. Key decisions and legislation refer to the assembly. The definition of key decisions in safeguard (d) would seem to relate to procedures. There is no reference here to the assembly's executive authority. Under section 6 (legislative competence) of the NIA 1998, the assembly cannot legislate contrary to convention rights. SO 32 deals with human rights issues in the legislative process. This involves asking the Human Rights Commission to advice on compatibility, a function given the commission under section 69(4)(a) of the NIA 1998; paragraph (b) allows the commission to advise the assembly as it thinks appropriate.

'(d) arrangements to ensure key decisions are taken on a cross-community basis;

(i) **either** parallel consent, i.e. a majority of those members present and voting, including a majority of the unionist and nationalist designations present and voting;

(ii) **or** a weighted majority (60%) of members present and voting, including at least 40% of each of the nationalist and unionist designations present and voting.

'Key decisions requiring cross-community support will be designated in advance, including election of the Chair of the Assembly, the First Minister and Deputy First Minister, standing orders and budget allocations. In other cases such decisions could be triggered, by a petition of concern brought by a significant minority of Assembly members (30/108).' After safeguard (a), this is the most significant of the five listed in paragraph 5. This was not agreed by the time of the MDP. The independent chairmen put forward parallel consent, a weighted majority of 66 per cent with a right of petition, a combination of the two, or leaving it to the chair and deputy chair of the executive committee. As noted above, option (a) was accepted. This had implications for the designation of identity (see paragraph 6 below). The weighted majority was also altered.

'arrangements to ensure key decisions are taken on a cross-community basis;'. This requires all key decisions to be taken on a cross-community basis.

Key decisions, however, are not defined fully. Examples only are given: 'including election of the Chair of the Assembly, the First Minister and Deputy First Minister, standing orders and budget allocations'.[62] What is a key decision must be a matter for the discretion of the chair/deputy chair specified further in paragraph 7. In section 39(1) of the NIA 1998, the assembly is under the control of 'a Presiding Officer and deputies'. (The same terminology was used in the ISOs.) This individual may be referred to as the Speaker (or a deputy speaker) under standing orders. And, on 2 December 1999, the initial presiding officer became the speaker.[63] Under ISO 2(1) and SO 1(2), 'the Speaker's ruling shall be final on all questions of procedure and order'.

Cross-community basis in relation to a vote on any matter is defined in section 4(5) of the NIA 1998: '(a) the support of a majority of the members voting, a majority of the designated Nationalists voting and a majority of the designated Unionists voting; or (b) the support of 60 per cent of the members voting, 40 per cent of the designated Nationalists voting and 40 per cent of the designated Unionists voting;'. This is based on paragraph 5(d). The legal definition is the one in the act, though the Belfast Agreement may be looked at for the purposes of interpretation.

The first form of cross-community support – parallel consent – has been redrafted in the act (probably because it could be construed as a simple majority[64]). The requirement of present is implied in voting. There is no minimum required (though there must be a quorum of ten members including the speaker under SOs 9(1) and 25(5)). As long as there is a majority of nationalists and a majority of unionists – the majority of the assembly follows given the relative designations – there will be cross-community support. Parallel consent figured early in the transition or shadow phase for the election of the First Minister and Deputy First Minister on 1 July 1998.[65] It is presumably for the speaker to decide between paragraph 5(d)(i) or (ii) under SO 1(2), where this is not otherwise specified. Cross-community support in the sense of weighted majority has been redrafted in the act; 'present' has disappeared again. The quorum provision is as above. The weighted majority is 60 per cent (rather than a simple 51 per cent). But this cannot be achieved by nationalists or unionists predominating. It requires 40 per cent of the other communal bloc (referred to as 'designation'). Designated Nationalist and Unionist (upper case has been used in the act) are defined also in section 4(5) of the NIA 1998, there being a cross reference to standing orders. Under ISO 3(1) and SO 3(3)–(7), members take their seats at the first, or subsequent, meeting of the assembly by signing the assembly's roll of membership. They may enter the designation nationalist, unionist or other; under SO 3(7), the absence of a designation being deemed to be other. A member may change his designation no more than once in each assembly, this taking effect

62 The list in the MDP was: 'election of presiding officer, standing orders, budget allocations, employment equality, cultural issues'.

63 Not everyone was aware of this: Northern Ireland Assembly, *Official Report*, vol. 4, no. 1, pp. 1 and 3–4, 6 December 1999.

64 The MDP had used the word 'respectively'.

65 This was under the secretary of state's initial standing orders: ISO 12(2)(c): New Northern Ireland Assembly, *Official Report*, vol. 1, pp. 6–23, 1 July 1998. The Rt. Hon. David Trimble MP and Seamus Mallon MP were proposed as First Minister (designate) and Deputy First Minister (designate) by the Rt. Hon. John Taylor MP and John Hume MP. They were elected by 61 votes to 27: the 61 comprised 24 nationalists, 30 unionists, and 7 others; the 27 were all unionists. The initial presiding officer, Lord Alderdice, recorded that the 24 nationalist yes votes represented 100 per cent (Sinn Féin abstained in the vote), and the 30 unionist yes votes represented 52.63 per cent. He also recorded that 61 of 88 votes was 69.3 per cent (p. 23).

30 days after notification to the speaker (SO 3(8)). There are 58 designated unionists, 42 designated nationalists and eight others in the assembly.[66]

The two options – (i) parallel consent or (ii) weighted majority – have been discussed above.

'Key decisions requiring cross-community support will be designated in advance,' must be a reference to the speaker under SO 1(2).

'election of the Chair of the Assembly' is dealt with in paragraph 7.

'the First Minister and Deputy First Minister' are capitalized thus in the Belfast Agreement. And that is how I will refer to them, or by the abbreviations FM and DFM. In the NIA 1998, DFM is rendered as deputy First Minister. I will use that formulation when referring to the act.

'standing orders' were provided for in paragraph 10(1) of the schedule to the Northern Ireland (Elections) Act 1998 (for the transition), and in section 41 of the NIA 1998 for the Northern Ireland assembly from the appointed day (2 December 1999). Standing orders, under section 41(2), require cross-community support. On 8 March 1999, the committee on standing orders reported to the assembly with a compendium of orders.[67] These were approved – after amending – on 8 and 9 March 1999.[68] SO 25 deals with voting in general. All decisions are to be by simple majority, other than as mentioned in paragraph (2), required under the NIA 1998, or under SO 70 (suspension of standing orders). Paragraph (2) refers only to appropriation of sums and taxation.

'budget allocations.' is covered by SO 25(2). (This phrase was in the MDP, and may be one of the Americanisms which have passed into the Belfast Agreement.)

'In other cases such decisions could be triggered by a petition of concern brought by a significant minority of Assembly members (30/108).' Also relevant is paragraph 13. Cross-community support is required under SO 25(2), the NIA 1998, and SO 70.[69] This provides for a significant minority of 30 petitioning for a cross-community support vote. It is dealt with in section 42 of the NIA 1998. Under subsection (1), it would seem that it requires 30 members (not at least 30[70]); no doubt, the speaker could choose to accept the first 30 names in such a petition.[71] Subsection (2) refers to the standing orders. SO 27 deals with petitions of concern: there must be 'at least 30 members'; and at least one day before a a vote is held. The first petition of concern was on 6 June 2000, dealing with a motion on the union flag. The speaker ruled that the petition received the previous day – copies of which were available in the business office – was valid. It was used at the end of the debate.[72]

'(e) an Equality Commission to monitor a statutory obligation to promote equality of opportunity in specified areas and parity of esteem between the two main communities, and to investigate individual complaints against public bodies.' An Equality Commission is dealt with further in the Human Rights part of the Rights, Safeguards and Equality of Opportunity section. It is provided for in part VII of the NIA 1998 (sections 73–78 on equality of opportunity) plus schedules 8 and 9. It replaces existing bodies dealing with fair employment, women, race and disability. There is also provision in standing orders for

66 New Northern Ireland Assembly, *Official Report*, vol. 1, pp. 4–5, 78 (1 July & 14 September 1998).

67 NNIA 9(i) and 9(ii).

68 New Northern Ireland Assembly, *Official Report*, vol. 2, pp. 197–235, 237–89, 291–309, 8–9 March 1999.

69 It is not clear that standing orders can be suspended: section 41 of NIA 1998.

70 Compare SO 24(2).

71 On 4 July 2000, a motion proposing the exclusion of Sinn Féin from the executive was debated by the assembly. It was proposed by the DUP, which had tried unsuccessfully on a number of earlier occasions to have such a debate. Northern Ireland Assembly, *Official Report*, vol. 5, no. 11, pp. 426–62, 4 July 2000.

72 Northern Ireland Assembly, *Official Report*, vol. 5, no. 2, pp. 43 & 44, 6 June 2000.

referral of draft legislation to a special (or standing) committee on conformity with equality requirements (SOs 33 and 55).

To monitor a statutory obligation to promote equality of opportunity in specified areas is dealt with in section 75 of the NIA 1998. Public authorities are required to have due regard to the need to promote equality of opportunity. The marginal note reads: 'statutory duty on public authorities'. But this duty is exercised within the discretion of public authorities. It may be considered to be less than 'a statutory obligation to promote equality of opportunity'. In specified areas is developed in subsection (1): persons of different religious belief, political opinion, racial group, age, marital status or sexual orientation; (2) men and women generally; (3) persons with a disability and persons without; and (4) persons with dependants and persons without. Subsection (2) requires public authorities to have regard to the desirability of promoting good relations between persons of different religious belief, public opinion or racial group.

And parity of esteem between the two main communities is a recent addition to Northern Ireland's language of equality. It originated in a proposal from 'a prominent Catholic nationalist lawyer' to the informal Opsahl commission of 1992–93. This was that there should be 'recognition of the nationalist community in a legal sense'.[73] Presumably, the proposal relates to domestic law. The nationalist minority was, after all, recognized in the 1985 Anglo-Irish Agreement. The commission recommended that '"parity of esteem" between the two communities ... ought to be given legal approval, promoted and protected, in various ways ... We recommend that the government moves to examine the feasibility of drafting ... legislation explicitly to recognize Irish nationalism in Northern Ireland in relevant ways.'[74] But it also went on to refer to international law. Query whether legal recognition of Irish nationalism requires a similar response to Ulster unionism?[75]

There is no reference to parity of esteem in part VII of the NIA 1998, where equality of opportunity is addressed. It also occurs within the Human Rights part of the Rights, Safeguards and Equality of Opportunity section. The Human Rights Commission is required to consider including parity of esteem in a possible future bill of rights for Northern Ireland.[76]

And to investigate individual complaints against public bodies. This is also mentioned in the Human Rights part of the Rights, Safeguards and Equality of Opportunity section.[77] Section 74 of the NIA 1998 refers to the functions of four existing bodies being transferred to the new Equality Commission. Section 75 on the statutory duty refers to schedule 9 (enforcement of duties). Paragraphs 10 and 11 deal with complaints and investigations.

Subheading: Operation of the Assembly

12.36 This third subsection of Strand One deals – in eight paragraphs – with a number of assembly activities, principally its system of committees. Its legislative role is considered in a later subsection.

73 *A Citizens' Inquiry: the Opsahl report on Northern Ireland*, ed. Andy Pollak, Dublin 1993, pp. 112–13.

74 Pollak, *A Citizens' Inquiry*, pp. 112–13.

75 The commission stated: 'It should be stressed that if this parity of esteem is to be achieved, the legal recognition of Irish nationalism should not mean the diminution of "Britishness" for unionists.' (p. 113)

76 Paragraph 4.

77 Paragraph 4.

6. ***At their first meeting, members of the Assembly will register a designation of identity – nationalist, unionist or other – for the purposes of measuring cross-community support in Assembly votes under the relevant provisions above.***

12.37 This was a new paragraph in the FA, necessitated by the adoption of the independent chairmen's option (a) for cross-community voting in paragraph 5. It was Senator Mitchell and his two colleagues who introduced the idea of designation of identity. This, however, was not developed in the MDP, there being only a reference to designation 'at the outset'. Designation of identity has, however, led to this example of devolution being characterized as 'tribal dualism'.[78]

12.38 ANNOTATIONS

'At their first meeting'. This was on Wednesday 1 July 1998. It was held in Castle Buildings at Stormont, in the conference room where the Belfast Agreement was accepted on 10 April 1998. The reason was the unavailability of the former house of commons in Parliament Buildings, which was awaiting fitting out following repairs after a fire in 1995.

'members of the Assembly will register a designation of identity – nationalist, unionist or other – '. This was provided for in the secretary of state's initial standing orders, notified on Monday 29 June 1998. ISO 3 dealt with taking seats in the assembly. This duly happened on 1 July 1998. At 14.15, 105 members (including the initial presiding officer, Lord Alderdice, appointed by the secretary of state) signed the roll of membership (two registers) on tables in the conference room. The initial presiding officer then checked the roll of membership during an adjournment, announcing that 'some changes have been made'. The two members of the Women's Coalition changed their designation from 'other Unionist/ Nationalist' to 'Inclusive other'.[79] Lord Alderdice stated that he had taken legal advice that morning: 'The precise wording can be flexible, but the designation has to be absolutely clear.'[80] Three members – two of them from Sinn Féin – signed the roll of membership at the next meeting, in Parliament Buildings, on 14 September 1998.[81]

'for the purposes of measuring cross-community support in Assembly votes under the relevant provisions above.' The provisions above are in paragraph 5(d). The concept of cross-community support is discussed above under that paragraph. The first assembly vote – using the designation of identity – was the election of the First Minister designate and the Deputy First Minister designate later that day.[82]

[6.] *7.* **[Note from the Chairmen: The Parties are in disagreement as to the allocation of the position of Chair of the Assembly and as to whether there should be a Deputy Chair. Options for your consideration include, but are not limited to, the following:**

(a) The Chair and Deputy Chair of the Assembly will be elected on a cross-community basis, as set out in paragraph 5(d) above.

(b) There will be a Chair of the Assembly, elected from among those who are not aligned with either of the two major communities.]]

The Chair and Deputy Chair of the Assembly will be elected on a cross-community basis, as set out in paragraph 5(d) above.

78 *Fordham International Law Journal*, p. 1242.

79 It seems that the Alliance Party members described themselves as 'Centre'.

80 New Northern Ireland Assembly, *Official Report*, vol. 1, pp. 4–5, 1 July 1998.

81 New Northern Ireland Assembly, *Official Report*, vol. 1, p. 78, 14 September 1998.

82 New Northern Ireland Assembly, *Official Report*, vol. 1, pp 22–3, 1 July 1998.

12.39 Here, option (a) was accepted.

12.40 ANNOTATIONS

'The Chair and Deputy Chair of the Assembly will be elected'. This was only decided in the FA, the independent chairmen having proposed also a chair of the assembly elected by those designated other.

On 29 June 1998, the secretary of state, Mo Mowlam, in a letter printed with the record of proceedings, appointed Lord Alderdice – until then the leader of the Alliance party – initial presiding officer. This was done under paragraph 3(1) of the schedule to the Northern Ireland (Elections) Act 1998. However, the duty under paragraph 3(1) included also an initial deputy presiding officer. This did not happen. Lord Alderdice was told he would remain in post, if there was no proposal from the assembly or no election was successful. ISO 13(5) was to the same effect. There were no proposals on 1 July 1998, so Lord Alderdice remained initial presiding officer.[83] This was the position throughout the transition (1 July 1998 to 1 December 1999). On 2 December 1999, the secretary of state's initial standing orders were replaced by the assembly's standing orders.[84] Under paragraph 13 of Schedule 14 of the NIA 1998, Lord Alderdice was deemed to have been elected under section 39 (thus satisfying SO 1(1)). There was no provision in standing orders for the election of a speaker, other than after a dissolution or when the office becomes vacant. Lord Alderdice became known as speaker. Three deputy speakers were elected on 31 January 2000, in accord with SO 5.[85]

'on a cross-community basis, as set out in paragraph 5(d) above.' This has been discussed at paragraph 5(d) above.

> [7.] *8.* **There will be a committee for each of the main executive functions of the Northern Ireland Administration. The Chairs and Deputy Chairs of the Assembly Committees will be allocated proportionally, using the d'Hondt system. Membership of the Committees will be in broad proportion to party strengths in the Assembly to ensure that the opportunity of Committee places is available to all members.**

12.41 This is the first of four paragraphs dealing with assembly committees. Statutory committees – so-called – are provided for in section 29 of the NIA 1998. SOs 43–58 deal with the totality of assembly committees.

12.42 ANNOTATIONS

'There will be a committee for each of the main executive functions of the Northern Ireland Administration.' Northern Ireland had six departments when the Belfast Agreement was concluded. Paragraph 14 of Strand One allows for up to ten departmental ministers plus the First Minister and Deputy First Minister. 'Each of the main executive functions' needs to be construed. It is implied – but only implied – that this means a committee per minister. It leaves open whether there should be a committee for the First Minister and Deputy First Minister. (Paragraph 9 resolves the matter, associating committees with departments.) Section 29(1) of the NIA 1998, in contrast, provides for a statutory committee for each minister (paragraph (a)), or in relation to more than one minister (paragraph (b)). Minister, according to section 7(3),[86] 'unless the context otherwise requires', means the First Minister, deputy First Minister or a Northern Ireland minister. It is arguable that section 29 is not a

83 New Northern Ireland Assembly, *Official Report*, vol. 1, pp 5–6, 1 July 1998.

84 These would appear to have been determined by the secretary of state prior to devolution: Northern Ireland Assembly, *Official Report*, vol. 4, p. 1, 6 December 1999.

85 Donovan McClelland (SDLP), Sir John Gorman (UUP) and Jane Morrice (Women's Coalition): Northern Ireland Assembly, *Official Report*, vol. 4, no. 7, pp. 267–70, 31 January 2000.

86 And section 98.

context requiring the dropping of the First Minister and deputy First Minister. Paragraph 9 again resolves the matter, requiring minister to be read as departmental minister. However, in the Departments (Northern Ireland) Order 1999,[87] under article 3(1)(a) and schedule 1, there is created an office of the First Minister and deputy First Minister. (This is permitted under section 21(3) and paragraph 6 of schedule 14 of the NIA 1998.) As a consequence, minister is defined in article 2(2) – for the purposes of the order – as including the First Minister and deputy First Minister acting jointly.

There was a battle to establish a committee of the centre under paragraph 8. On 6 December 1999, the assembly had voted – by 68 votes (34 nationalists, 27 unionists and 7 other) to 3 (all unionists) – to establish a standing committee on European affairs, and another on equality, human rights and community relations. These were all functions located in the office of the First Minister and Deputy First Minister.[88] Eight days later, the First Minister and Deputy First Minister moved an amendment to an Alliance party motion for a third scrutiny committee, for one consolidated committee of the centre covering all the discrete policy areas, but not the institutional functions, dealt with in their office. Twelve functions were listed. The First Minister explained: 'the amendment was tabled at such short notice ... largely because we were able to focus on this matter only last night, when we started to look at it and its implications and evolved this amendment after consultations with some Members'.[89] The amended motion was passed by 52 votes (22 nationalists, 26 unionists and 4 others) to 33 (9 nationalists, 22 unionists and 2 others).

The phrase Northern Ireland Administration suggests the word administration is preferable to government.

'The Chairs and Deputy Chairs of the Assembly Committees will be allocated proportionally, using the d'Hondt system.' This has been discussed above under paragraph 5(a).

'Membership of the Committees will be in broad proportion to party strengths in the Assembly to ensure that the opportunity of Committee places is available to all members.' This has been discussed above under paragraph 5(a). 'Broad porportion' suggests something less than mathematical proportionality. The reason is given: to ensure that the opportunity of Committee places is available to all members. This is not expressly guaranteed in section 29 of the NIA 1998, though SO 45(2) – seemingly construing SO 46 – states each non-ministerial member must be offered a place on a statutory committee.

On the evening of 29 November 1999, following the appointment of ministers designate, the assembly appointed chairmen and deputy chairmen to ten shadow statutory committees (one for each department less the centre) under section 29 of the NIA 1998.[90] ISO 23 applied. Neither post could be filled by a member from the same party as the minister.[91] Robert McCartney QC MP intimated that he would not be nominating on behalf of the UKUP, or the breakaway NIUP of four members.[92] Ten committee chairmen were then nominated: Danny Kennedy; Denis Haughey;[93] Rev. Dr Ian Paisley; Pat Doherty; Fred Cobain; Joe Hendron; Rev William McCrea, Dr Esmond Birnie; Francie Molloy and Eamonn O'Neill. This reflected the party balance of ministers. Deputy chairmen were then nominated: George Savage; Sam Wilson; Sean Neeson; Michelle Gildernew; Tommy Gallagher; Alan McFarland;

87 SI 1999/283. This was made on 10 February 1999. It came into operation on 1 December 1999: Departments (1999 Order) (Commencement) Order (Northern Ireland) 1999, SR 1999/480.
88 Northern Ireland Assembly, *Official Report*, vol. 4, no. 1, pp. 1–7, 6 December 1999.
89 Northern Ireland Assembly, *Official Report*, vol. 4, no. 2 (reissue), p. 61, 14 December 1999.
90 Through paragraph 9 of schedule 14.
91 NIA 1998 s 29(5)–(6); ISO 23(12).
92 Because of section 29(3) of the NIA 1998; but see ISO 23(8).
93 Replaced by Alban Maginness sometime before 17 January 2000, following his appointment as a junior minister: Northern Ireland Assembly, *Official Report*, vol. 4, no. 4, p. 89, 17 January 2000.

Mervyn Carrick; Carmel Hanna; James Leslie and Mary Nelis. Because of the continuation of d'Hondt, the SDLP lost a seat to the Alliance Party leader; Sinn Féin benefited from Robert McCartney's refusal to participate. There was no prohibition on the chairman and deputy chairman being from the same party.[94] The assembly met at 10.30 the following day, and promptly adjourned to 16.06, during which suspension the party whips agreed nine additional members for each of the ten committees (not including ministers, chairmen or deputy chairmen); 90 positions for 76 members (eight of whom did not put themselves forward). ISO 23(2)(b) required the whips to have regard to the balance of parties in the assembly, and in such a way to ensure an opportunity of membership to all non-ministerial members. Lord Alderdice played a prominent role in the negotiations.[95] Taking into account ministers, chairmen and deputy chairmen, there were 57 unionists, 44 nationalists and 9 others (mainly Alliance) nominated or appointed to the 10 committees.[96]

[8.] 9. The Committees will have a scrutiny, policy development and consultation role with respect to the Department with which each is associated, and will have a role in initiation of legislation. They [should] ***will*** **have the power to:**

- **[agree]** ***consider and advise on*** **Departmental budgets and Annual Plans** ***in the context of the overall budget allocation*****;**
- **approve relevant secondary legislation and take the Committee stage of relevant primary legislation;**
- **call for persons and papers;**
- **initiate enquiries and make reports[.];**
- ***consider and advise on matters brought to the Committee by its Minister.***

12.43 This is one of the most important provisions – after paragraph 5 – in Strand One (a third being paragraph 16). The treatment of assembly committees in the NIA 1998 is modest. The role – scrutiny, policy development and consultation – has been interpreted by parliamentary counsel as 'to advise and assist each ... Minister in the formulation of policy ...' (section 29(1)(a)). This – pro-ministerial – concept has been followed in standing orders.[97] But section 29 (statutory committees) directly incorporates paragraph 9 through subsection (1)(c) in conferring powers. Standing orders follows suit; SO 45(2) refers directly to paragraph 9 (and section 44(1) of the NIA 1998[98]). The text of the Belfast Agreement – on the powers of committees – is legally binding in Northern Ireland law.

12.44 ANNOTATIONS

'The Committees will have a scrutiny, policy development and consultation role with respect to the Department with which each is associated, and will have a role in initiation of legislation.'

The Committees follows from the first sentence of paragraph 8. But the meaning must be taken from 'with respect to the Department with which each is associated'. The intention of

94 This came as a surprise to some assembly members.

95 Northern Ireland Assembly, *Official Report*, vol. 3, no. 2, p. 35, 30 November 1999.

96 Two small unionist parties – the UKUP and NIUP – declined to participate. A member of the latter, however, Roger Hutchinson, lost the whip when he decided to participate.

97 SO 45(1)(a).

98 This was added after devolution: Northern Ireland Assembly, *Official Report*, vol. 4, no. 1, pp. 1–7, 6 December 1999.

the draftsman would appear to have been committees for the – up to ten – departments. The NIA 1998 originated the idea of statutory committees, not because of their legislative role, but because they were provided for in that act. Unfortunately, section 29 refers to ministers and not to departments, raising the question of whether the First Minister and Deputy First Minister are ministers in that context. Standing orders follow the act. But the Departments (Northern Ireland) Order 1999[99] resolves the matter. It includes an office of the First Minister and deputy First Minister in article 3(1) and schedule 1, and defines minister – for the purpose of the order – in article 2(2) as including the First Minister and deputy First Minister.

Will have a scrutiny, policy development and consultation role is in fact three separate roles. These are potentially powerful committees, more ambitiously conceived than committees at Westminster or in Edinburgh or Cardiff.[100] Scrutiny refers to the traditional legislative role vis a vis the executive. How successful this will be will depend partly upon the powers of the committees, but mainly upon the play of party interests in the involuntary coalition. Policy development suggests a degree of power-sharing with ministers. However, the initiative seems to be with the department. Consultation is a weak word, conjuring up images of departments adding committees to their list of consultees.

And will have a role in initiation of legislation. This is normally for the executive. Or – at Westminster – occasionally for back benchers. Part II of the NIA 1998 (legislative powers) makes no reference to statutory committees. Nor do standing orders, though there is provision for members introducing public bills and private members' bills.[101] There is provision for taking the committee stage of a public bill (see below).

'They will have the power to:' was changed from should in the MDP.

'consider and advise on Departmental budgets and Annual Plans in the context of the overall budget allocation;'. This was changed from agree Departmental budgets and Annual Plans in the MDP; a considerable weakening of a potential power. Consider and advise allows statutory committees to comment only. Departmental budgets and Annual Plans in the context of the overall budget allocation may allow debate at critical points, such as when the departmental budget is being set.

'approve relevant secondary legislation and take the Committee stage of relevant primary legislation;'. This power indicates that the statutory committees have a role in the legislative process. The use of 'relevant' twice may simply be to distinguish one committee from another. Approve relevant secondary legislation is a limited power. The NIA 1998 makes no express provision for secondary – Northern Ireland – legislation, other than through section 29(1)(c) incorporating paragraph 9. Standing orders do, in SO 40 (statutory rules of Northern Ireland). Rules or draft rules before the assembly are to be referred to the appropriate statutory committee. The committee may deal with the matter itself or delegate it to the examiner of statutory rules as it sees fit. The committee is required to report to the assembly on rules its considers. And take the Committee stage of relevant primary legislation is more important legislatively. There is no express provision in the NIA 1998, other than through section 29(1)(c) legislating for the powers in paragraph 9. Standing orders, however, do provide in SO 31 (public bills: committee stage). A bill is referred to the appropriate committee unless the assembly orders otherwise. The committee may recommend amendments be taken at the consideration stage.

99 SI 1999/283.

100 The Government of Wales Act 1998 provides also for – balanced – statutory committees (sections 56–61): an executive committee (essentially the government) (section 56); subject committees (for each member of the executive committee) (section 57); a subordinate legislation scrutiny committee (sections 58–59); an audit committee (section 60); and regional committees (section 61).

101 SO 28(1)–(2).

'call for persons and papers;' is the power (along with the following one) which might see the statutory committees become like Westminster select committees. (The consultative committees in the NICA 1973 were excluded expressly from having access to departmental papers.[102]) This power is provided for in section 44 (power to call for witnesses and documents) in the NIA 1998, plus sections 45 (offences) and 46 (oaths). The penalty – after summary conviction – is a fine or up to three months' imprisonment for a refusal to respond to a committee summons.

'initiate enquiries and make reports;' sets the context for the above power. There is no express reference in the NIA 1998 (other than through section 29(1)(c)), nor in standing orders – other than through SO 43(2).

'consider and advise on matters brought to the Committee by its Minister.' This was added to the MDP. It is entirely within the discretion of the minister. There is no requirement that he – in the words of the first sentence of paragraph 9 – consults the committee.

[9.] *10.* Standing Committees other than Departmental Committees may be established as may be required from time to time.

12.45 ANNOTATIONS

'Standing Committees'. There is no reference in the NIA 1998. Standing orders, however, provide in SO 48 for non-statutory committees. These comprise standing committees and ad hoc committees (which, under SO 48(7), have 'specific time-bounded terms of reference'[103]). Standing committees are defined as permanent committees, and are appointed in the same manner as statutory committees under SOs 45 and 46. The standing committees specified in standing orders are: the committee on procedures (SO 52); the business committee, chaired by the speaker (SO 53); a special committee on conformity with equality requirements (SO 54); the public accounts committee – specified in section 60(3) of the NIA 1998 – (SO 55); the committee on standards and privileges (SO 56); and the audit committee – to exercise the functions in section 66 of the NIA 1998[104] – (SO 57). On 14 December 1999, following an earlier decision of 6 December 1999, a committee of the centre was agreed (SO 58).[105]

'other than Departmental Committees'. This suggests that paragraphs 8 and 9 are about departmental committees (the phrase is used also in paragraph 12). Presumably, parliamentary counsel wanted to distinguish them from committees of officials and chose the term statutory committee. Standing committees have the same status in the Belfast Agreement, and at least two – the public accounts committee and the audit committee – are specified in the NIA 1998 (making them statutory!).

'may be established as may be required from time to time.' Standing (and ad hoc) committees are a matter for the assembly under standing orders, which may be altered with cross-community support.

11. The Assembly may appoint a special Committee to examine and report on whether a measure or proposal for legislation is in conformity with equality requirements, including the ECHR/Bill of Rights. The Committee shall have the power to call for people and papers to assist in its consideration of the matter. The Assembly shall then consider the report of the Committee and can determine the matter in accordance with the cross-community consent procedure.

102 Section 25(7).
103 They are not specified further.
104 These relate to the expenses of the Northern Ireland Audit Office.
105 Northern Ireland Assembly, *Official Report*, vol. 4, no. 2 (reissue), pp. 53–63, 14 December 1999.

12.46 This – and paragraphs 12 and 13 – were added to the MDP. The drafting shows signs of having been rushed; the word 'procedure' is confusingly used in two different ways. The three paragraphs concern equality of opportunity, not human rights – which are dealt with in the NIA 1998 under legislative competence[106] and stages of bills[107] (plus standing orders[108]). Section 13(3)(a) – part of stages of bills – states that standing orders shall include provision for establishing a committee under paragraph 11. They may include provision for a bill to be considered by the committee (but this seems not to be mandatory).

12.47 ANNOTATIONS

'The Assembly may appoint' makes appointment discretionary. Appointment would seem to refer to consideration of a bill.

'a special Committee' relates only to the legislative process. Thus, it is mentioned in SO 33 (public bills: equality issues). Any member of the executive committee, or the chairman of an appropriate statutory committee, may move that the assembly refer a bill to the special committee on conformity with equality requirements. The committee is dealt with further in SO 54.

'to examine and report on whether a measure or proposal for legislation'. This has been incorporated in SO 54(1), with 'measure' altered to 'bill'.

'is in conformity with equality requirements,' is not defined. The sections and schedules of the NIA 1998 dealing with the equality commission are not relevant. The phrase 'in conformity with the requirements for equality and observance of human rights' occurs in SO 33(5). And indeed 'including rights under the European Convention on Human Rights or any Northern Ireland Bill of Rights' has been added parenthetically to SO 54(1). It is not clear what equality requirements flow from the convention, now incorporated partially by the Human Rights Act 1998.[109] The question of a bill of rights remains open. The human rights commission – under paragraph 4 of the Human Rights part of the Rights, Safeguards and Equality of Opportunity section – is to advise on further rights, reference being made to 'the principles of mutual respect for the identity and ethos of both communities and parity of esteem'. These would seem to be the only possible relevant equality requirements.

'The Committee shall have the power to call people and papers to assist in its consideration of the matter.' This puts the committee – initially a special standing committee, later an ad hoc committee – on a par with the statutory committees, which have the power to call for persons and papers under paragraph 9. The full phrase has been included in SO 54(2).

'The Assembly shall then consider the report of the Committee and can determine the matter in accordance with the cross-community consent procedure.' This has been rewritten in SO 54(3): 'The Assembly shall consider any reports of the Committee and determine the matter in accordance with the procedures on cross-community support within the meaning of the Northern Ireland Act 1998.' Cross-community support is referred to in paragraph 5(d) above as parallel consent or a weighted majority. The relevant section of the NIA 1998 is 4(5). 'Consent procedure' is a synonym for cross-community support.

It does not relate to special procedure in paragraphs 12 and 13. Special procedure refers to special committee.

106 Section 6(2)(c).
107 Section 13(4).
108 SO 32 (human rights issues).
109 Article 14 (prohibition of discrimination) relates to the rights in the convention. This is not equality of opportunity.

12. ***The above special procedure shall be followed when requested by the Executive Committee, or by the relevant Departmental Committee, voting on a cross-community basis.***

12.48 ANNOTATIONS

'The above special procedure' is strange wording, not least since consent procedure occurs in paragraph 11. It can only be a reference to the special committee on conformity with equality requirements (leading possibly to a determination by the assembly on a cross-community basis). Special procedure is not a reference to cross-community support.

'shall be followed when requested by the Executive Committee,' has now been written into SO 33(2). SO 32(2) goes further and states 'any member of the Executive Committee'.

There is a conflict here, which is not resolvable by looking at section 13(3)(a) of the NIA 1998. The United Kingdom and Irish governments are bound in international law to follow paragraph 12. The assembly has its standing orders, and, under section 41(1) of the NIA 1998, 'the proceedings of the Assembly shall be regulated by standing orders'.

'or by the relevant Departmental Committee,' is a reference to the statutory committees provided for in section 29 of the NIA 1998. However, the term departmental committee has been used above in paragraph 10.

There is another conflict. Paragraph 12 refers to the committee requesting the special procedure (that is, appointment of a special committee). But SO 33(2) refers to the chairman of the committee. Again, the United Kingdom and Irish governments are bound by paragraph 12; the assembly must follow standing orders.

'voting on a cross-community basis.' This cannot mean that the executive committee, or statutory committee, votes on a cross-community basis. This is inconsistent with paragraph 5(d). And with section 4(3) of the NIA 1998. Only the assembly can so vote. The phrase is superfluous.

13. ***When there is a petition of concern as in 5(d) above, the Assembly shall vote to determine whether the measure may proceed without reference to this special procedure. If this fails to achieve support on a cross-community basis, as in 5(d)(i) above, the special procedure shall be followed.***

12.49 Paragraph 13 relates only to paragraphs 11 and 12, dealing with the special committee on conformity with equality requirements. It is far from clear. (It is not about petitions of concern generally, which are dealt with in section 42 of the NIA 1998 and SO 27.)

12.50 ANNOTATIONS

'When there is a petition of concern as in 5(d) above,'. This might appear to refer to the assembly considering the report of the committee under paragraph 11. A significant minority of 30 members – provided for in paragraph 5(d) – can with a petition of concern trigger a key decision. But why is this necessary when paragraph 11 provides for cross-community support? Petitions of concern – in general – are provided for in section 42 of the NIA 1998. And subsection 3 refers to petitions of concern leading to a referral to the special committee on conformity with equality requirements. The petition of concern begins the process.

The construction put on the phrase by the standing orders committee in March 1999 – in SO 54(4) – is consistent with section 42(3): a petition of concern about the measure (bill or proposal) is presented initially; there is then a parallel consent vote on whether to proceed; if this is unsuccessful, the measure (bill or proposal) is referred to the committee.

'the Assembly shall vote to determine whether the measure may proceed without reference to this special procedure.' This is a reference to a cross-community vote (on what basis?) to proceed, without reference to the special committee.

'If this fails to achieve support on a cross-community basis, as in 5(d)(i) above, the special procedure shall be followed.' If this fails to achieve support on a cross-community basis, as in 5(d)(i) is a reference to a failed parallel-consent vote on the measure (bill or proposal) proceeding. The special procedure shall be followed is a reference to a referral to the special committee.

SO 54 of 9 March 1999 originally made the special committee on conformity with equality requirements a standing committee of the assembly. On 14 December 1999, the assembly decided (without a vote) to make this a special ad hoc committee, to be appointed as and when necessary. This was after a dispute between Sinn Féin, which maintained that paragraph 11 referred to a permanent committee, and the SDLP; Mark Durkan MLA claimed to have had a considerable hand in drafting paragraphs 11–13.[110]

Subheading: Executive Authority

[[Note from the Chairmen: There is disagreement among the participants as to whether executive authority should be vested in an Executive Committee or a Liaison committee. Throughout this text the Committee will be titled 'Executive/Liaison Committee'.]]

12.51 This is the fifth subsection of Strand One. Paragraphs 14–25 deal with executive authority (singular); and they do so before legislative powers. In the NIA 1998, legislative powers are part II and executive authorities (plural) – following the 1920 and 1973 precedents – are part III (divided into authorities, functions and miscellaneous). Executive authority was the term used in the GOIA 1920 (sections 8–10); in the NICA 1973, this became executive authorities (sections 7–11). The independent chairmen left open the option of an executive or a liaison committee, which was resolved in favour of the former (without – I submit – any connotation of the latter idea).

[10.] ***14.*** **Executive authority to be discharged on behalf of the Assembly by [up to [ten] Assembly Secretaries/Ministers, with posts allocated to parties on the basis of the d'Hondt system by reference to the number of seats each party has in the Assembly.]** ***a First Minister and Deputy First Minister and up to ten Ministers with Departmental responsibilities.***

12.52 The idea of a First Minister and Deputy First Minister was not agreed in the MDP; the independent chairmen proposed an executive committee chair and deputy chair in paragraph 17 (with an independent chairmen's note attached). Direct election by the assembly is provided for in paragraph 15 below. Also, the number of ten ministers was square bracketed. But the suggestion of a maximum quickly became considered as a right (with consequences for the organization of the Northern Ireland departments). The hypothetical figure of ten was to have included the executive/liaison committee chair and deputy chair in paragraph 17 of the MDP. The consequence of specifying here the offices of First Minister and Deputy First Minister (and associating them with the assembly in paragraph 15

110 Northern Ireland Assembly, *Official Report*, vol. 4, no. 2 (reissue), pp. 51–3, 14 December 1999.

below) was to inflate the size of the executive/liaison committee from up to ten to (up to) twelve; it was eventually twelve (plus two junior ministers).

12.53 The relevant sections of the NIA 1998 are 16 (First Minister and deputy First Minister), 17 (ministerial offices) and 18 (Northern Ireland ministers); mention should also be made here of section 19 (junior ministers).

12.54 ANNOTATIONS

'Executive authority to be discharged on behalf of the Assembly' makes constitutionally for an executive in the government of Northern Ireland.

Executive authority was the phrase used in 1920, when 'executive power ... continue[d] vested in His Majesty the King' (section 8(1)). The sovereign could delegate prerogative and other executive powers to the lord lieutenant (later governor). Those powers were to be exercised through departments (established by the governor or the local parliament), their ministerial heads – who had to be privy councillors – being appointed by the governor.[111]

Much the same applied in 1973. Executive power continued vested in her majesty under section 7(1). Again, her majesty delegated prerogative and other executive powers to the secretary of state (section 7(2)). These were to be exercised by members of the executive and the departments (section 7(3)). Under section 8, the secretary of state, on behalf her majesty, appointed the chief executive member, heads of departments and persons to discharge other functions. Section 8(10) provided for the oath/affirmation in schedule 4.

Section 7(6) listed the executive authorities as: the secretary of state; executive members, and others appointed under section 8; and the departments. The use of executive authority in paragraph 14, therefore, emphasizes the unitary – rather than disaggregated – nature of executive power in Northern Ireland.

This was altered in part III (sections 16–30) of the NIA 1998. But the rhetoric of pluralism does not affect the basis of the executive authorities. Section 23(1) – which does not begin 'authorities', but is located under 'functions' – states: 'The executive power in Northern Ireland shall continue to be vested in Her Majesty' (section 22 deals with statutory functions). There is constitutional continuity with 1920 and 1973. But there is no reference to delegation to the secretary of state of prerogative and executive powers in the transferred area, nor of these powers being exercised by ministers and departments. This is because the secretary of state – who transferred powers on the appointed day under section 3 – was no longer to appoint the executive committee. Nor was there any oath or affirmation (unlike in Scotland and Wales[112]). The executive responsible for transferred matters, which emerges under the d'Hondt rule from the assembly, appears – but only appears – to be running a republican polity (thus the attempt to distinguish statutory functions from prerogative and executive powers in sections 22 and 23). Under section 23(2)–(4) – the flow again being obscured – her majesty's prerogative and executive powers are exercised by the First Minister and deputy First Minister, other ministers or departments.

'by a First Minister and Deputy First Minister'. The idea of a – joint – head of the executive (almost colloquially a joint presidency) was absent from the MDP. This is in spite of there having been a chief executive member in the 1974 assembly, who had a (nationalist) deputy – filling a post unspecified in the NICA 1973.[113]

A First Minister and Deputy First Minister was an evolution of the panel idea in the 1995 *Framework Documents*. This executive – of three – was envisaged as being elected from a

111 GOIA 1920s 8(2)–(4).

112 Scotland Act 1998 s 84 (oath of allegiance for MSPs; plus the official oath under the Promissory Oaths Act 1868 for members of the executive). Government of Wales Act 1998 s 20 (oath of allegiance – or affirmation – in Promissory Oaths Act 1868 s 2 for assembly members).

113 Brian Faulkner and Gerry Fitt.

single Northern Ireland constituency (like the three members of the European parliament). The panel was to have powers over the assembly, constituting 'a system of detailed checks and balances'.[114]

The terminology – and capitalization – of First Minister and Deputy First Minister is evocative of president and vice-president (the latter, certainly in the United States, often being more of an understudy). Though the two offices are mentioned in paragraphs 14–18 and 23, at no point is any distinction made.[115] When parliamentary counsel came to incorporate the Belfast Agreement in the NIA 1998, he changed the capitalization to First Minister and deputy First Minister (section 7(3)). This implies a unified office – First Minister – in which the second joint holder is a deputy, but without any apparent distinct – or inferior – responsibilities. There is even a subheading in schedule 10: 'Delegation by First Ministers'.

The NIA 1998 does not reveal any difference between the two offices. Section 16 deals with their joint election by the assembly. Section 17 deals with the joint determination of ministerial offices. Section 19 deals with the joint determination of junior ministers. And section 20 provides that they shall be chairmen of the executive committee (which requires agreement on how that role is to be performed).

Standing orders of the assembly – the legislature – do not cover the joint head of the executive, not even their election within six weeks of each assembly meeting, though they are mentioned in SOs 11, 14 and 42.

'and up to ten Ministers with Departmental responsibilities.' This was incorporated by section 17(4) of the NIA 1998, but the secretary of state was given the power – not in the Belfast Agreement – to provide by order for a greater number.

On 18 December 1998, the First Minister and Deputy First Minister agreed to reorganize the six Northern Ireland departments into ten: agriculture and rural development; environment; regional development; social development; education; higher and further education, training and employment; enterprise, trade and investment; culture, arts and leisure; health, social services and public safety; finance and personnel. There was also to be an office of the First Minister and Deputy First Minister, comprising an economic policy unit and responsibility for equality. (Under section 21(3) of the NIA 1998, a department under the First Minister and deputy First Minister is not – for the purposes of sections 17(2)–(3) and 18(4) [and despite section 7(3)] – to be included in the up to ten ministers figure.)

This amounted substantively – under section 17 of the NIA 1998 and ISO 21 – to the determination of ministerial offices (designate). But for the determination to have effect under section 17(5) and ISO 21(4), it required approval by the assembly.

A report was presented to the assembly on 18 January 1999; however, a number of functions remained to be allocated.[116] The initial presiding officer ruled that it was not a determination requiring cross-community support.[117] Presumably, though it was not argued, he was relying upon the reference to 'each of the functions' in ISO 21(2). The report was approved on a simple majority of 74 votes to 27.[118]

114 Part I, paragraph 5; also, paragraphs 18–22.

115 Two offices are stated in section 16(2), (6)–(8) of the NIA 1998.

116 New Northern Ireland Assembly, *Report from the First Minister (Designate) and Deputy First Minister (Designate)*, NNIA 6, pp. 4 & 9, 18 January 1999. Section 17(3) and ISO 21(2) required all functions to be allocated. (The latter described functions exercisable 'by the heads of the different Northern Ireland departments existing at the date of the determination'. Under paragraph 2(1)(b) of schedule 1 to the Northern Ireland Act 1974, functions of the heads of departments were to be discharged by the departments.)

117 New Northern Ireland Assembly, *Official Report*, vol. 1, pp. 416–17, 18 January 2000.

118 New Northern Ireland Assembly, *Official Report*, vol. 1, pp. 474–5, 18 January 2000.

It was represented (with amendments) on 15 February 1999.[119] Annex 1a was the expanded list of functions; Annex 1b the 18 December 1998 agreement on departments. The formal determination – simply a list of ministers and departments[120] – was included as Annex 2. The list of ministerial offices (column 1) referred to departments. But the list of departments (column 2) did not have the relevant functions included. Each office holder would 'exercise the functions of Minister of that Department'.[121] (ISO 21(4) refers to 'a determination under paragraph (1)', and this is also referred to in paragraph (2). The determination before the assembly made no reference to any document containing the expanded list of functions.[122] And the functions of minister begs the question about the functions of a department.) After a two-day debate, the formal determination was approved by the assembly on 16 February 1999, on a cross-community basis, by 77 (41 nationalists, 29 unionists and 7 others) votes to 29 (all unionists).[123]

The vote on 18 January 1999 – to summarize – had not been a determination under ISO 21(4), because the list of functions was not complete. The vote on 16 February 1999, on a determination which made no reference to the expanded list of functions, amounted – it is claimed – to legal approval to the ten ministerial offices. There is uncertainty that, under the transition provision (paragraph 3 of schedule 14 of the NIA 1998), the 'functions to be exercisable by the holder of each such office' were determined properly.

Meanwhile, an order in council under the Northern Ireland Act 1974, the Departments (Northern Ireland) Order 1999, SI 1999/283, had been made at the privy council on 10 February 1999. This created five new departments: office of the First Minister and deputy First Minister; culture, arts and leisure; higher and further education, training and employment, regional development; and social development (article 3(1)). Three were given new names: agriculture and rural development; enterprise, trade and investment; health, social services and public safety (article 3(4)–(7)). Education and finance and personnel retained the same names. Article 8 gave the First Minister and deputy First Minister acting jointly the power to transfer or assign functions. In the transition, this was a matter for the secretary of state: through a transfer of functions order under section 4 of the Ministries Act (Northern Ireland) 1944. On 30 November 1999, the secretary of state made the Departments (Transfer and Assignment of Functions) Order (Northern Ireland) 1999, SR 1999/481; it came into operation on 1 December 1999. The order transferred functions from the six existing departments, to the ten new departments plus the office of the First Minister and deputy First Minister. It also assigned new functions to the latter. Also on 30 November 1999, the secretary of state made the commencement order bringing the Departments Order into operation on 1 December 1999.[124] Excluded was article 8 (power to transfer or assign functions) and the repeal of section 4 of the Ministries Act (Northern Ireland) 1944. Under article 1(3) of the Departments Order, they were to come into operation the day after devolution, that is on 3 December 1999.

But the Departments (Northern Ireland) Order 1999 went further. The Northern Ireland

119 New Northern Ireland Assembly, *Report from the First Minister (Designate) and the Deputy First Minister (Designate)*, NNIA 7, 15 February 1999.

120 It stated that there would be ten ministerial offices, the holders of which would be in charge of departments 'exercis[ing] the functions of Minister of that Department.'

121 See the Departments (Northern Ireland) Order 1999 article 4(1). This means that the minister has only one function: direction and control of the department.

122 The First Minister informed the assembly that this had been done on the basis of legal advice: New Northern Ireland Assembly, *Official Report*, vol. 2, p. 9, 15 February 1999.

123 New Northern Ireland Assembly, *Official Report*, vol. 2, pp. 4–63, 68–110, 15–16 February 1999.

124 Departments (1999 Order) (Commencement Order) (Northern Ireland) 1999, SR 1999/480.

Office decided to consolidate Northern Ireland legislation, beginning with the repeal of the Ministries Act (Northern Ireland) 1921.

Reference has been made already to this, in Chapter 4. Section 2(1) made ministries – less the prime minister's department – bodies corporate. This has been reenacted in the 1999 order as article 5 (with the marginal note 'Status of department, etc.'). The office of the First Minister and Deputy First Minister is included as a department. The proviso to section 1 in the 1921 act used the phrase 'subject to the direction and control of the Minister', but only seemingly in the context of delegation under section 1(3). Section 1 also – I submit – referred, contrary to the GOIA 1920, to 'any powers or duties of a Ministry'. (See also section 2(1) and (4), where it is suggested the minister gets his power from the ministry.) In 1921, 'any power or duty of the Ministry' could be exercised by the minister or a secretary or assistant secretary (section 2(4)). In 1999, any functions of a department may be exercised by the minister or a senior officer (article 4(3)), who is defined in article 2(3) as a member of the Northern Ireland civil service so designated for the purposes of the order. The phrase 'direction and control' – which was adopted for the 1972 and 1974 Westminster direct rule acts – is now in the 1999 order used to define the relationship between minister and department (article 4(1)).

In 1921–72, when the unionists ran Stormont, ministries had powers and duties. In 1972–73, and again since 1974, with direct rule from London, functions have belonged to Northern Ireland departments. Under the Belfast Agreement, with devolution on a basis of political proportionality, the departments will retain all their functions. Regardless of political change, there is significant continuity constitutionally and in terms of power: senior Northern Ireland officials remain the permanent government of the region. The permanent secretaries even meet weekly.

If direct rule involved many powers and duties remaining in Belfast (with departments), devolution – there will still be a secretary of state – could well be more of the same, with an ineffective political class deadlocked in the assembly and its committees.

Parliament, however, has given the assembly the power to correct this constitutional anomaly, unprecedented anywhere else in the United Kingdom or in the Republic of Ireland. Section 22 (statutory functions) of the NIA 1998 gives the assembly the power to confer functions on a minister or department. Subsection (2) states that: 'Functions conferred on a Northern Ireland department by an enactment passed or made before the appointed day shall, except as provided by an Act of the Assembly or other subsequent enactment, continue to be exercisable by that department.' The assembly could take powers away from the departments and give them to ministers.

[17.] *15.* **[Two Assembly Secretaries/Ministers will be selected as chair and deputy chair respectively, on a basis which ensures that between them they represent both main parts of the community in Northern Ireland.]**

[Note from Chairmen: There is disagreement among the participants as to the nature of such arrangements. An option for your consideration is that this could be achieved by requiring the Committee's nominations to be endorsed by the Assembly on a cross-community basis.]

[The Chair and Deputy Chair will be given ex-officio titles of First Secretary/Minister and Deputy First Secretary/Minister. Duties would, inter alia, include dealing with, and co-ordinating, the response of the Northern Ireland Administration to external relationships.]

The First Minister and Deputy First Minister shall be jointly elected into office by the Assembly voting on a cross-community basis, according to 5(d)(i) above.

12.55 This was a completely new paragraph in the FA. The offices of First Minister and Deputy First Minister (as noted) originated in paragraph 17 of the MDP. They were, however, the chair and deputy chair of the proposed executive/liaison committee. While selection was specified, some sort of election would have been necessary. It was the independent chairmen's note which suggested endorsement by the assembly. A leap was then made to election by the assembly.

12.56 The relevant section of the NIA 1998 is 16. But paragraph 2 of schedule 14 (transitional provisions) applied to the transition between 1 July 1998 and the transfer of powers on the appointed day under section 3. ISO 14 governed joint elections in the period; however, in circumstances that will be considered below, the secretary of state determined a revision to ISO 14 on 29 November 1999.

12.57 ANNOTATIONS

'The First Minister and the Deputy First Minister shall be jointly elected into office by the Assembly voting on a cross-community basis, according to 5(d)(i) above.' Voting on a cross-community basis, according to 5(d)(i) above is a reference to parallel consent, a majority of unionists plus a majority of nationalists (see above).

The First Minister and Deputy First Minister shall be jointly elected into office by the Assembly. Under section 1(2) of the Northern Ireland (Elections) Act 1998, the secretary of state was given the power to refer to the assembly: '(a) specific matters arising from th[e Belfast] agreement, and (b) such other matters as he thinks fit.' In a letter of 29 June 1998 to the initial presiding officer (appointed under paragraph 3(1) of the schedule by an earlier letter of the same date), Mo Mowlam stated that the first matter – of four – was 'the basic structures of the Assembly'. The assembly was to meet on 1 July 1998.

The first tiret of the first matter was the election of the First Minister-designate and the Deputy First Minister-designate. Under the initial standing orders (which had accompanied the first 29 June 1998 letter), there was an Annex A providing an initial agenda for the first meeting of the New Northern Ireland Assembly; item 2(c) was 'consideration of any proposals regarding the election of a First Minister (designate) and Deputy First Minister (designate)'.

The Rt. Hon. John Taylor MP, deputy leader of the UUP, moved – shortly after 15.30 on 1 July 1998 – that the Rt. Hon. David Trimble MP, his party leader, be First Minister (designate), and Seamus Mallon, deputy leader of the SDLP (and Taylor's member of parliament), be Deputy First Minister (designate). John Hume, leader of the SDLP, seconded the motion. Both nominees accepted the nomination.

There followed a debate in which 15 members spoke. Seamus Mallon, in reply to a question about decommissioning, affirmed that he was in favour. David Trimble quoted from the manifesto of the UUP: 'Ulster Unionists will not sit in Government with unreconstructed terrorists.'[125] Shortly after 17.30, David Trimble and Seamus Mallon were elected jointly by 61 votes (24 nationalists and 30 unionists) to 27 (all unionists).

The Rt. Hon. David Trimble MP, followed by Seamus Mallon MP, then made an affirmation in a form prescribed, based upon the second sentence of paragraph 35 below. Under ISO 14(6), the election would have been void without the affirmations.

The Belfast Agreement made no provision for resignation by the First Minister or Deputy

125 New Northern Ireland Assembly, *Official Report*, vol. 1, pp. 19–21, 1 July 1998; the full debate is pp. 6–24.

First Minister. During the transition beginning on 1 July 1998, it was the Northern Ireland (Elections) Act 1998 – and ISO 14 – which applied. This remained the position after the NIA 1998 received the royal assent on 19 November 1998, even though section 16(6)–(9) deals with resignation; it was not brought into force until 2 December 1999.[126]

On 15 July 1999, following an abortive attempt to form the executive (see Chapter 19), the Deputy First Minister made a personal statement to the assembly. He indicated that he wanted to also bring down the First Minister: 'it is now necessary that I resign ... I wish to inform the Assembly that, accordingly, I offer my resignation now, with immediate effect.'[127] This was accepted at the time by the initial presiding officer, and the party leaders who spoke on the statement in the assembly. The resignation was announced to the house of commons by the secretary of state while the assembly was still sitting.[128]

However, at the next meeting of the assembly on 29 November 1999, the initial presiding officer announced the receipt of a new ISO 14 from the secretary of state, dealing with an offer of resignation by the First Minister or Deputy First Minister.[129] The leader of the Alliance party had put down a motion stating that the assembly wished Seamus Mallon to hold office as Deputy First Minister. The initial presiding officer stated that such a motion required only a simple majority (unless there was a petition of concern). Lord Alderdice also stated that 'the validity of Mr Mallon's resignation [wa]s a matter of law and not of common sense.' He had received legal advice afterwards that, in the absence of a standing order, one could not be sure that the offer of resignation had been effective. 'Subsequent [unsolicited] legal advice took different turns. Some agreed with the initial advice while others stated that the resignation was full and complete as it was given in good faith and recognised by others.'[130]

After nearly three hours of debate, the assembly voted by 71 votes to 28 (all unionists), to effectively decline Seamus Mallon's offer of resignation of 15 July 1999. An anti-Agreement unionist queried whether this would have succeeded on parallel consent. (It would not: only 24 unionists voted for the motion.) Nevertheless, Seamus Mallon, when asked under ISO 14(9) whether he assented to the wish of the assembly, said: 'I do, and I regard this as cross-community support, which is the touchstone by which I had to measure the vote.' The initial presiding officer ruled: 'The outcome of the election of July last year to the office of First Minister and Deputy First Minister remains in effect.'[131]

There is no doubt that the secretary of state was able to introduce new ISO 14. But paragraph (8) is premissed on: 'where the First Minister or the Deputy first Minister has offered his resignation from office'. That presumes that 15 July 1999 was not legally effective. But the initial presiding officer did not so rule at the beginning of the debate: 'Whether the position is satisfactory from a legal point of view is not for me to judge: I am not a judge in a court.'[132]

It is difficult to avoid the conclusion that, a joint reelection for the First Minister and Deputy First Minister being unlikely with cross-community support under the original ISO 14, the NIO helped orchestrate a political arrangement for the assembly of less than perfect legality.[133]

126 Northern Ireland Act 1998 (Appointed Day) Order 1999, SI 1999/3208.

127 New Northern Ireland Assembly, *Official Report*, vol. 2, p. 325, 15 July 1999. Seamus Mallon MP explained his resignation in the *Sunday Times* of 18 July 1999: he had sought a suspension of the institutions unsuccessfully from London and Dublin.

128 House of Commons, *Hansard*, 6th series, 335, 563, 15 July 1999.

129 It contained new paragraphs (8)–(11).

130 New Northern Ireland Assembly, *Official Report*, vol. 3, no. 1, p. 3, 29 November 1999.

131 New Northern Ireland Assembly, *Official Report*, vol. 3, no. 1, p. 22, 29 November 1999.

132 New Northern Ireland Assembly, *Official Report*, vol. 3, no. 1, p. 3, 29 November 1999.

133 Seamus Mallon MP subsequently told parliament that he had resigned on 15 July 1999:

[10.] *16.* **[Executive authority to be discharged on behalf of the Assembly by up to [ten] Assembly Secretaries/Ministers, with]** ***Following the election of the First Minister and Deputy First Minister, the posts of Ministers will be*** **allocated to parties on the basis of the d'Hondt system by reference to the number of seats each party has in the Assembly.**

12.58 Paragraph 10 in the MDP was the basis of paragraph 14 of the FA (first minister and deputy first minister, and up to ten departmental ministers). However, part of it also ended up in this paragraph. Thus, the implied simultaneous appointment of all ten assembly secretaries/ministers was broken. No connection was made between the First Minister and Deputy First Minister being elected by the assembly, and the up to ten ministers being selected by the d'Hondt system.

12.59 This was the third tiret of the secretary of state's first matter ('basic structures of the Assembly') in her letter of 29 June 1998. But it was dependent upon the determination of ministerial offices. This did not occur, until the 18 December 1998 agreement was approved by the assembly on 16 February 1999. The running of d'Hondt, in order to elect Northern Ireland's ten departmental ministers, was delayed by the need to get agreement on the departments but mainly by the impasse over decommissioning.

12.60 The relevant section of the NIA 1998 is 18, plus paragraph 4 of schedule 14. The initial standing orders of 29 June 1998 did not provide for the election of ministers, though ISOs 20 and 21 (nominating officers, and determination of ministerial offices) were notified by the secretary of state in November 1998.[134] Following the 16 February 1999 determination, draft orders 22–25 were circulated (22 dealing with the appointment of ministers [designate]).[135] They were further amended at the time of the Hillsborough Declaration on decommissioning of 1 April 1999. ISOs 22–25, dated 8 July 1999, were issued to the assembly following the 2 July 1999 *Way Forward* proposals for establishing the executive. An amended ISO 22, which had been drafted on 14 July 1999, was issued the following day, when d'Hondt was being run in the assembly.

12.61 The UUP did not attend the meeting of the assembly on 15 July 1999. All the other unionists refused to nominate ministers. As a result, a nationalist/republican executive committee, comprising six SDLP and four Sinn Féin ministers, was elected. However, under ISO 22(15) (as amended), the ten assembly members were not permitted to continue to hold (shadow?) ministerial office.[136]

House of Commons, *Hansard*, 6th series, 344, 174, 8 February 2000. This was repeated in the Northern Ireland assembly: 'Mr Dodds: Did you resign or not, Seamus? The Deputy First Minister: I did – like a man.' (Northern Ireland Assembly, *Official Report*, vol. 5, no. 10, p. 380, 3 July 2000)

134 New Northern Ireland Assembly, *Official Report*, vol. 1, p. 194, 26 October 1998.

135 Draft orders 22–24 had been circulated originally on 5 August 1998.

136 New Northern Ireland Assembly, *Official Report*, pp. 319–23, 15 July 1999. Northern Ireland's first all-nationalist government comprised: Mark Durkan (finance and personnel); Bairbre de Brún (enterprise, trade and investment); Sean Farren (regional development); Martin McGuinness (agriculture and rural development); Brid Rodgers (higher and further education, training and employment); Pat Doherty (education); Dr Joe Hendron (health, social services and public safety); Denis Haughey (social development); Mary Nelis (culture, arts and leisure); Alban Maginness (environment).

12.62 ANNOTATIONS

'Following the election of the First Minister and Deputy First Minister,'. This took place on 1 July 1998. No time scale is mentioned in paragraph 16. A condition precedent of course was the determination of ministerial offices, under section 17 of the NIA 1998 (which received the royal assent on 19 November), plus paragraph 3 of schedule 14, and ISO 21 (which was made by the secretary of state in November 1998). The determination, based on the 18 December 1998 agreement, was approved by the assembly on 16 February 1999. The delay from mid-February 1999 was due entirely to the impasse over decommissioning.

'the posts of ministers' refers to the ten in the 16 February 1999 determination: ministers of: agriculture and rural development; culture, arts and leisure; education; enterprise, trade and investment; the environment; finance and personnel; health, social services and public safety; higher and further education, training and employment; regional development; social development.

'will be allocated to parties on the basis of the d'Hondt system'. This has been discussed above under paragraph 5(a).

'by reference to the number of seats each party has in the Assembly.' Under section 18(5) of the NIA 1998 the number of seats – S in the d'Hondt formula – relates to the first meeting of the assembly, on 1 July 1998. At the election on 25 June 1998, the following seats were gained by the parties:

Party	Seats
Ulster Unionist Party[137] (UUP)	28
Social Democratic and Labour Party (SDLP)	24
Democratic Unionist Party (DUP)	20
Sinn Féin (SF)	18
Alliance Party	6
United Kingdom Unionist Party[138]	5
Progressive Unionist Party	2
Northern Ireland Women's Coalition	2
Independent Unionists[139]	3

The d'Hondt formula – in section 17(5) of the NIA 1998 – is S/1 + M, where M = the number of ministerial offices held by the party. The ten ministerial offices had to be allocated under the d'Hondt formula as follows:

Party	1st round	2nd round	3rd round	4th round
UUP	28	14	9.33	7
SDLP	24	12	8	6
DUP	20	10	6.66	5
SF	18	9	6	4.5

Only four parties – UUP, SDLP, DUP and SF – are competing for the ten seats (since all ten are filled before the mathetical calculation drops to Alliance's 6 seats and the United Kingdom Unionist Party's 5). In the first round, all four parties take a seat each. In the second round, three parties take a second seat. This is because SF's 9 is less than the UUP's 9.33 in the third round; the UUP picks up its third seat. SF follows with its second in the third round. Then the SDLP with its third. At this point, all ten ministerial offices have been filled.

The UUP takes the first, fifth and eighth seats. The SDLP the second, sixth and tenth seats. The DUP the third and seventh. And SF the fourth and ninth. This gives an executive committee of: three UUP; three SDLP; two DUP; and two SF. (If there were twelve seats to fill,

137 One member, Peter Weir, subsequently lost the whip, but this does not affect the Ulster Unionist Party's entitlement to ministerial offices based upon 28 seats.

138 This party split later, in November 1998; the leader, Robert McCartney QC MP, remaining on his own. His four colleagues formed the Northern Ireland Unionist Party.

139 Later, the United Unionist Assembly Party.

the UUP would take the eleventh and the DUP the twelfth. And, if there were fourteen, the SDLP would take the thirteenth and SF the fourteenth – because, under section 18(6) of the NIA 1998, the SDLP obtained more first preference votes than SF, and SF obtained more than the Alliance party.)

D'Hondt was run successfully for the selection of ministers on 29 November 1999, after the motion dealing with the Deputy First Minister. The departments, and the ministers nominated, in order, were: enterprise, trade and investment (Sir Reg Empey); finance and personnel (Mark Durkan); regional development (Peter Robinson); education (Martin McGuinness); environment (Sam Foster); higher and further education, training and employment (Sean Farren); social development (Nigel Dodds); culture, arts and leisure (Michael McGimpsey); health, social services and public safety (Bairbre de Brún); agriculture and rural development (Brid Rodgers).[140]

Mention may be made here parenthetically of junior ministers. There is no provision for them in the Belfast Agreement. However, they are provided for in section 19 of the NIA 1998. Junior ministers are not subject to the d'Hondt rule. They are appointed jointly through a determination by the First Minister and Deputy First Minister, which is subject to approval by the assembly (by a simple majority). On 14 December 1999, the First Minister and Deputy First Minister presented to the assembly a draft determination on junior ministers. They proposed to appoint two to the office of the centre, on the ground of the burden carried by the joint head of the executive. The two junior ministers would be under the joint supervision of the First Minister and the Deputy First Minister, though they were to have functions delegated to them. The determination was opposed by the DUP and Sinn Féin, and by the smaller parties. It was, however, approved by 49 votes to 38 on a simple majority.[141] Under SO 42, all procedures were to be completed within seven days of the determination being made. The following day, two names were announced: Dermot Nesbitt (who resigned as a committee member); and Denis Haughey, who stood down as chairman of a statutory committee. As the speaker later told the assembly, he had met with the First Minister and the Deputy First Minister (on apparently 15 December 1999) and the two nominees, upon taking the pledge of office, were appointed to the office of the First Minister and deputy First Minister.[142]

[16.] *17.* The [Assembly Secretaries/] Ministers will constitute an *Executive*[/ Liaison] Committee, *which will be convened, and presided over, by the First Minister and Deputy First Minister.*

12.63 This is the paragraph in which executive committee was chosen over liaison committee, the alternatives having been noted by the independent chairmen under the subtitle Executive Authority in the MDP. Also, the role of First Minister and Deputy First Minister was boosted. This paragraph is based upon paragraphs 16 and 17 of the MDP (the latter containing a note from the independent chairmen).

12.64 The relevant section of the NIA 1998 is 20. Paragraphs 18–20 also deal with the executive committee.

12.65 The name executive committee comes from the GOIA 1920. Under section 8(4), heads of department were ministers. Ministers formed an executive committee of the privy council, 'to be called the Executive Committee of Northern Ireland' (section 8(5)). In 1973, there was a Northern Ireland executive. This

140 New Northern Ireland Assembly, *Official Report*, vol. 3, no. 1, pp. 23–7, 29 November 1999.

141 Northern Ireland Assembly, *Official Report*, vol. 4, no. 2 (reissue), pp. 33–47, 14 December 1999.

142 Northern Ireland Assembly, *Official Report*, vol. 4, no. 4, p. 89, 17 January 2000.

comprised the chief executive member; heads of departments; and any other members appointed by the secretary of state (section 8 of NICA 1973).

12.66 ANNOTATIONS

'The Ministers' would appear to be a reference to the departmental ministers mentioned in paragraph 16. It must, however, be read as including the First Minister and the Deputy First Minister, if the paragraph is to make sense. Section 20(1) of the NIA 1998 defines the executive committee as 'the First Minister, the deputy First Minister and the Northern Ireland ministers [who are dealt with separately in section 18]'.

'will constitute an Executive Committee' is the key phrase, requiring ministers to include the joint head of the executive. The nature of this executive committee, against the background of the 1921–72 executive committee (or cabinet), and the 1974 executive, will be considered below under paragraphs 19 and 20.

'which will be convened, and presided over, by the First Minister and Deputy First Minister.' This is an instance of the joint nature of the separate offices of First Minister and Deputy First Minister. They alone have the power to convene the executive committee. There is no indication how they are to preside over the executive committee, though it is implied that this is to be by agreement. Section 20(2) of the NIA 1998 states: 'The First Minister and the deputy First Minister shall be chairmen of the Committee.'

> [17.] *18.* **[Two Assembly Secretaries/Ministers will be selected as chair and deputy chair respectively, on a basis which ensures that between them they represent both main parts of the community in Northern Ireland.]**
>
> **[Note from the Chairmen: There is disagreement among the participants at to the nature of such arrangements. An option for your consideration is that this could be achieved by requiring the Committee's nominations to be endorsed by the Assembly on a cross-community basis.]**
>
> **[The Chair and Deputy Chair will be given ex-officio titles of First Secretary/Minister and Deputy First Secretary/Minister.]** *The d*[**D**]**uties** *of the First Minister and Deputy First Minister will* **[would, inter alia,] include,** ***inter alia,*** **dealing with[,] and co-ordinating[,]** *the work of the Executive Committee and* **the response of the Northern Ireland Administration to external relationships.**

12.67 Other than chairing the executive committee, this is the only paragraph specifying the duties of the joint executive head. The origin of this paragraph was the second paragraph in paragraph 17 of the MDP (which also included a note from the independent chairmen). The first paragraph of paragraph 17 of the MDP – which originated the idea of First Minister and Deputy First Minister – was of course the basis of paragraph 15 above.

12.68 In the report of the First Minister and Deputy First Minister of 15 February 1999 (which led to the 16 February determination), there is an office of the First Minister and Deputy First Minister. This was envisaged as a possibility in ISO 21(2). And also in section 21(3) and paragraph 6 of schedule 14 of the NIA 1998.[143] The central department or office had 26 functions listed (increased from 11 on 18 December 1998).

143 Section 18(7) – FM or DFM may hold a ministerial office – would seem to prevent this being construed as FM/DFM jointly being in charge of a department.

12.69 These functions were: economic policy unit; equality unit; liaison with NSMC including secretariat; liaison with BIC; civic forum (administrative and other arrangements, including secretariat support); liaison with secretary of state (excepted or reserved); European affairs/international matters/Washington bureau; liaison with IFI;[144] information services; community relations; executive committee secretariat; legislation progress unit; office of the legislative counsel; public appointments policy; visits; honours; freedom of information; victims; Nolan standards; public service office; machinery of government; emergency planning; women's issues; policy innovation unit; cross-departmental co-ordination; assembly ombudsman (liaison and appointment issues).

The Departments (Northern Ireland) Order 1999, SI 1999/283 had legislatively created the office of the First Minister and Deputy First Minister on 10 February 1999. It came into operation on 1 December 1999 (except for article 8, which came into operation on 3 December 1999).[145] The latter was to give time for the Departments (Transfer and Assignment of Functions) Order (Northern Ireland) 1999, SR 1999/481, made by the secretary of state and coming into operation on 1 December 1999. Under article 9, specified functions were assigned to the office of the First Minister and Deputy First Minister: the coordination of policy; liaison with other bodies, persons and authorities (both within and outside Northern Ireland); supporting the Executive Committee; information services; the legislative programme; policy in relation to public appointments; the economic policy unit; standards in public life; and other functions heretofore exercisable by the Central Secretariat.[146]

12.70 ANNOTATIONS

'The duties of the First Minister and the Deputy First Minister will include, inter alia,' indicates that no comprehensive definition is being given. In 1920, there was no provision for a prime minister. However, the lord lieutenant established a department of the prime minister in June 1921.[147] In 1973, provision was made for a chief executive member. But there was no definition of the functions then either.

'dealing with and co-ordinating the work of the Executive Committee' is clearly a central role. This follows from the paragraph 17 provision of chairing. Dealing with is not entirely clear. Coordinating is generally the work of a head of government. The work of the executive committee relates presumably to all business which is, or should be, brought to the executive committee. It does not allow direct interference in the work of departmental ministers. This function has been picked up in article 8 of the Departments (Transfer and Assignment of Functions) Order (Northern Ireland) 1999, SR 1999/481: supporting the Executive Committee, which is something less than coordination.

'and the response of the Northern Ireland administration to external relationships.' Response is a strange word. It suggests Northern Ireland only reacts. The use of administration (in lower case) follows the upper-case use in paragraph 8. Northern Ireland administration is generic; it may not become the name of the regional government. External relationships raises a problem. The Irish precedent is Dublin's department of external affairs (which became foreign affairs in 1971). External affairs – given Northern Ireland's position

144 International Fund for Ireland.

145 The Departments (1999 Order) (Commencement) Order (Northern Ireland) 1999, SR 1999/480; article 1(3) of the Departments (Northern Ireland) Order 1999.

146 This was a part of the department of finance and personnel, but it operated within the Northern Ireland Office.

147 *Belfast Gazette*, 7 June 1921.

in the United Kingdom – relate strictly to Strand Two business, the NSMC. However, external relationships may have a geographical meaning, in which case they include the region's relationship with the rest of the United Kingdom state. This would involve relations with the secretary of state over excepted and reserved matters. It would also include Strand Three, the BIC and BIIC – which embrace two states – involving an international relationship. This function has been picked up in article 8 of the Departments (Transfer and Assignment of Functions) Order (Northern Ireland) 1999, SR 1999/481: liaison with other bodies, persons and authorities (both within and outside Northern Ireland).

[18.] *19.* The Executive[/Liaison] Committee will provide a forum for the discussion of, and agreement on, issues which cut across the responsibilities of two or more [Assembly Secretaries/]Ministers, for prioritising executive and legislative proposals and *for* recommending a common position where necessary (e[.]g[.] in dealing with external relationships).

12.71 This is the first of two paragraphs defining the functions of the executive committee. The relevant section of the NIA 1998 is 20(3), which states: 'The Committee shall have the functions set out in paragraphs 19 and 20 of Strand One of the Belfast Agreement.'

12.72 There was no such specification of executive committee functions in 1920; nor of the executive's functions in 1973. The 1995 *Framework Documents* proposed the three-person panel, and government by proportionate assembly committees. Nationalists had tended to favour an executive approaching joint authority by London and Dublin; unionists an executive located in the legislature (much like the Welsh assembly[148]).

12.73 ANNOTATIONS

'The Executive Committee will provide a forum for the discussion of, and agreement on,'. This does not sound like a command and control centre for executive authority. The word forum is evocative of the new Ireland forum of 1983–84, and the 1994–96 forum for peace and reconcilation, on the one hand, and of the – elected – Northern Ireland forum for political dialogue of 1996–98[149] (boycotted subsequently by nationalists). Discussion has the same connotation. Agreement, at least, implies a collective body.

'issues which cut across the responsibilities of two or more Ministers,' suggests a highly Balkanized system of government, with vertical departments operating in relative isolation. The image of silo has come to be used. Governments do not function like that, even if vested departmental interests are frequently uppermost. The source of funding is central. And policy has, at least, to be coordinated (as is clear from paragraphs 18 and 20).

The compromise between a strong external executive (nationalism), and a weak internal one (unionism), has left the Northern Ireland executive committee dangerously underspecified. The resolution of how a body of political opponents will operate – in an involuntary coalition – lies in the permanent government of Northern Ireland: continuing rule by civil servants under – indirect – secretary of state control (with room for Dublin interference).

There is no alternative to individual, and collective, responsibility of ministers: individual responsibility – accountability – to the assembly: and collective responsibility through the executive committee. This is the secret of cabinet government in the United Kingdom.

148 Some of the functions of the secretary of state were transferred to the assembly: Government of Wales Act 1998 s 22 and schedules 2 and 3.

149 Set up under section 3 and schedule 2 of the Northern Ireland (Entry to Negotiations, etc) Act 1996.

Historically, it is how parliament supplanted the sovereign. Politically, the responsibility of ministers to the assembly individually and collectively is the only way to establish regional government.

'for prioritising executive and legislative proposals' is a toughening of collective action. Executive proposals must be administrative acts. Legislative proposals are where departments are required to seek powers from the Assembly. Prioritising suggests a pattern of expectation, which implies strong integrative tendencies.

'and for recommending a common position where necessary (e.g. in dealing with external relationships).' This suggests that a common position is the exception to the rule of Balkanized departmental government. It is justified feebly by an instance – external relations. But the Northern Ireland government can only function in the BIC, BIIC and NSMC, to say nothing of relations with the secretary of state, on the basis of an agreed position. To allow internal ministerial individualism to spill over into east-west, or particularly north-south, relations would be to bring about the joint authority (mediated by the Northern Ireland civil service) which unionists fear and dread.

[19.] *20.* **The Executive[/Liaison] Committee will seek to agree each year, and review as necessary, a programme incorporating an agreed budget linked to policies and programmes, subject to approval by the Assembly, after scrutiny in Assembly Committees, on a cross-community basis.**

12.74 In contrast to the cautious tone of paragraph 19, this is more robust. It deals with a programme of government.

12.75 ANNOTATIONS

'The Executive Committee will seek to agree each year,' is a modest ambition. If there is no agreement, there is no devolved government in any meaningful sense.

'and review if necessary,' adds dynamic to centralizing tendencies.

'a programme incorporating an agreed budget linked to policies and programmes,' is loose drafting. A programme can only be a programme of government. This is especially if its incorporates an agreed budget; it is more than a set of financial permissions. Linked to policies and programmes is more defensive departmentalism. If there is a programme at all, it can only absorb by ordering the policies and programmes of departments (consequent upon the break up of six and rebuilding as ten).

'subject to approval by the Assembly, after scrutiny in Assembly Committees, on a cross-community basis.' This is necessary accountability, but it adds to one lengthy process – getting four parties to agree a programme – a second potentially extensive process of assembly legitimization. However, with up to 90 assembly members supporting the executive committee through their parties, opposition may be muted among the remaining 18 members (not least when eight are anti-agreement).

[11.] *21.* **A party may decline the opportunity to nominate a person to serve as a[n Assembly Secretary/]Minister['] or may subsequently change its nominee.**

12.76 This paragraph may have been to provide for a hesitant party (most likely the DUP), without driving it into complete opposition. As things turned out, the DUP announced, and acted upon, a policy of complete opposition to the Belfast Agreement, but acceptance of ministerial positions, though without participation in the executive committee. There is no punishment for refusing to join an involuntary coalition. And there is no apparent sanction for ministers declining to attend the executive committee. This paragraph was originally the second paragraph under Executive Authority in the MDP. It has now been moved well down that subsection of Strand One.

12.77 The relevant section of the NIA 1998 is 18(3). While this requires the nominating officer of the party to nominate within a period specified in standing orders, and the nominated person to take up the selected ministerial office, there is no sanction – other than the opportunity passes to the next party. In standing orders, time limits have been specified by SO 41. The nomination must be made, and accepted, within a period of 15 minutes, unless the assembly approves an extension (it is unclear whether for a particular member or for the whole executive committee). Again, no sanction – other than loss to another party – is specified.

On 15 July 1999, during the running of d'Hondt when the UUP, DUP and Alliance party declined to participate, and an all-nationalist set of ministers was selected, John Hume had nominated Eddie McGrady MP, only to have him decline. The SDLP leader then successfully nominated Dr Joe Hendron as minister of health, social services and public safety.[150] Under section 18(3) of the NIA 1998, the initial presiding officer should have moved on to the next party, that is Sinn Féin. However, under ISO 22(6), made on 8 July 1999, he should have disregarded the SDLP entirely and left Sinn Féin to fill the remaining ministerial positions. (This was corrected subsequently by the secretary of state.[151]) At the next meeting of the Assembly on 29 November 1999, the initial presiding officer stated that he had following the act and not the initial standing orders (in fact, he had incorrectly followed the act in giving John Hume a second chance[152]).

12.78 ANNOTATIONS

'A party may decline the opportunity to nominate a person to serve as a Minister'. The party can only do this through its nominating officer. Nominating officer is defined in section 18(13) (and again in section 29(10)). This is either the registered nominating officer, under the Registration of Political Parties Act 1998,[153] or a member of the assembly nominated by him. Or – if the party chooses not to be registered – the person who appears to the presiding officer to be the leader, or his nominee.

'or may subsequently change its nominee.' This is an entirely different principle. Instead of the party refusing to participate in government, it takes control of its minister or ministers. Under section 18(9) of the NIA 1998, there are three ways a minister shall cease to hold office (distinct from section 30) – resignation, loss of assembly seat (other than at dissolution), and dismissal. The latter is the prerogative of the nominating officer at the time. This means that ministers, which the assembly may find difficult to sack, are under the control of their party leader (if he is the nominating officer).[154]

150 New Northern Ireland Assembly, *Official Report*, vol. 2, p. 322, 15 July 1999.

151 ISOs, as revised up to 26 November 1999.

152 Section 18(3).

153 This act, which received the royal assent on 19 November 1998, extends to Northern Ireland. It provides for a United Kingdom-wide register (with sanctions against non-registration). The party's nominating officer is a registered officer, who may be the party leader, with responsibility for the arrangement for 'the submission by representatives of the party of lists of candidates for the purpose of elections', and 'the approval of descriptions and emblems used on nomination and ballot papers at elections'. (paragraph 5 of schedule 1)

154 A separate nominating officer is unlikely to be able to remove his party leader without an internal political crisis.

[13.] *22.* [Assembly Secretaries/Ministers will be political Heads of the Northern Ireland Departments,] *All the Northern Ireland Departments will be headed by a Minister.* [and] *All Ministers* will liaise regularly with their respective Committee.

12.79 This contains two distinct provisions; heads of departments and statutory committees. The relevant sections of the NIA 1998 are 17(3) and 29. There are no relevant standing orders. The changes to the MDP have the effect of dropping the term head of department.

12.80 ANNOTATIONS

'All the Northern Ireland Departments will be headed by a Minister.' Under section 8(4) of the GOIA 1920, the heads of departments were the ministers. This changed in 1972, when functions where transferred to the secretary of state, but departments without heads were also left with functions.[155] Under section 8(1)(b) of the NICA 1973, heads of departments were – once again – members of the executive (though there could be non-departmental members). In 1974, while there was a transfer to the secretary of state, functions were again left with departments who lacked (politically accountable) heads.[156] This first sentence of paragraph 22 restores the position to that in 1920 and 1973, without addressing the question of the minister/department relationship. Under the Departments (Northern Ireland) Order 1999, SI 1999/283, which keeps departments bodies corporate,[157] but does not provide a constitutional status for ministers, the direct rule legal language of 1972 and 1974 of 'subject to the direct and control of the Minister' – misappropriated from 1921[158] – has effectively abolished the position of head of department.[159] This is evident in the Departments (Transfer and Assignment of Functions) Order (Northern Ireland) 1999, SR 1999/481. Article 2 (interpretation), which defines transferor and transferee in terms of departments, states that transferor includes 'the head of the department', and transferee 'the Minister of the department'. Minister in this first sentence above is clearly departmental minister, as in paragraph 14. Aside from the point about whether it includes the First Minister and Deputy First Minister (and whether either of those office holders can have a department under section 18(7) of the NIA 1998), it is possible – under section 19 – to have a non-departmental junior minister (a modification of the position in 1973); the functions, under section 19(1)(b), may or may not be part of a department, including the office of the First Minister and deputy First Minister.

'All Ministers will liaise regularly with their respective Committee.' All Ministers raises again the question of whether this includes the First Minister and Deputy First Minister (as in paragraph 17). Here, ministers have committees. And, under paragraphs 9 and 10, but not paragraph 8, committees are associated with departments. The ministers are departmental ministers.

Liaising regularly with their respective Committee was first addressed in section 7(4) of the NICA 1973. This provided that, in formulating policy, the executive member was to 'consult so far as practicable with the consultative committee established in relation to his

155 Northern Ireland (Temporary Provisions) Act 1972 s 1(1)(a)–(b).

156 Northern Ireland Act 1974 s 2(1)(b).

157 Article 5(1)–(2).

158 Ministries of Northern Ireland Act (Northern Ireland) 1921 s 1.

159 Article 2(2)(b) defines ministers as being 'in charge' of departments. This concept comes from section 17(3) of the NIA 1998 (which suggests no minister may have more than one department). Given the transitional provision in paragraph 3 of schedule 14, it may be argued that the minister is 'in charge' in the way the permanent secretary was under the NIA 1974.

department under section 25'.[160] There was a duty upon the executive member. The relationship has been redrawn in section 29 of the NIA 1998 (statutory committees) to read: 'to advise and assist each Northern Ireland Minister [defined indirectly in sections 7(3) and 18 as a departmental minister]'. This is the function of the statutory committee. (The powers, under section 29(1)(c), are those specified in paragraph 9 above.)

[14.] ***23.*** **As a condition of appointment, [Assembly Secretaries/]Ministers,** ***including the First Minister and Deputy First Minister,*** **will affirm [their readiness]** ***the terms of a Pledge of Office (Annex A) undertaking*** **to discharge effectively and in good faith all the responsibilities attaching to their** ***office*** **[posts, provided, however, that refusal to serve as an Assembly Secretary/Minister will not be grounds for removal from the Assembly].**

[20. Code of Practice]

[A Code of Practice will be drawn up by the Assembly on the basis of a cross-community vote. Any amendments to the Code will be made on a cross-community basis. The Code would codify and build upon the provisions of this agreement.]

12.81 The MDP had envisaged a code of practice drawn up by the assembly. Paragraph 20 suggests it was for the executive committee. Paragraph 14 of the MDP developed the point in paragraph 11 about declining nomination. However, there was no reference in paragraph 14 to the code of practice. This paragraph is important for containing the pledge of office provision (which required Annex A to be added to Strand One at Castle Buildings). It greatly altered paragraph 14 from being permissive of refusal to serve as an assembly secretary/minister.

12.82 The relevant sections of the NIA 1998 are 16(4) and (10), 18(8) and schedule 4. The are no relevant standing orders. However, ISO 14(6), and paragraph 2 of schedule 14, dealt with election of the First Minister and Deputy First Minister during the transition.

12.83 ANNOTATIONS

'As a condition of appointment' makes the taking of the pledge of office a condition precedent. The NIA 1998 states that each minister 'shall not take up office until he has affirmed the terms of the pledge of office' (section 18(8)[161]). ISO 14(6) – dealing with a modification for the transition – goes further, stating that if the First Minister and Deputy First Minister do not so affirm 'the election shall be void'.[162]

'Ministers, including the First Minister and the Deputy First Minister'. Here, ministers refers to all members of the executive committee (as in paragraph 17).

'will affirm the terms of the Pledge of Office (Annex A)'. The Pledge of Office is contained in Annex A (there is no Annex B) to Strand One. It comprises seven points – (a)–(g) – but point (g) refers to the Ministerial Code of Conduct. There follows a Code of Conduct – with nine tirets – applying to Ministers. The pledge of office is defined in section 16(10) of the NIA 1998 as the pledge of office, together with the code of conduct to which it refers. The text of annex A to Strand One is set out in schedule 4 to the act. (It is not clear why this was thought necessary. It does, however, resolve any ambiguity about the Code of Conduct – which

160 Subsections (4)–(7).

161 Section 16(4)(a) is in similar terms.

162 They means either the First Minister or the Deputy First Minister. Under ISO 14(1), they can only be elected jointly.

includes a reference to the Committee on Standards in Public Life (the Nolan – later Neill – committee) – being part of the required pledge of office.)

'undertaking to discharge effectively and in good faith all the responsibilities attaching to their office.' This is an inadequate paraphrasing of the pledge of office. It originated of course in paragraph 14 of the MDP. To discharge effectively is nowhere mentioned in Annex A. On the other hand, to discharge in good faith all the duties of office is the first of the seven pledges.

Though Annex A was part of the Belfast Agreement, and would be a schedule to the NIA from 19 November 1998, the secretary of state did not follow the pledge of office strictly in ISO 14(6) (even though it was annexed). This was because the second sentence of paragraph 35 was taken to require a modification of the pledge for the transition. The first term affirmed – non-violence – corresponds to (b) in the pledge of office. The second – opposition to the use or threat of force – does not occur in the pledge of office, though it may be implied from (b). The third term – to work in good faith – corresponds to (a), but it specifies the implementation of the MPA. And the fourth – observing the spirit of the pledge of office – lies by definition outside the letter of Annex A.

On 1 July 1998, immediately following the election of the Rt Hon. David Trimble MP and Seamus Mallon MP, the initial presiding officer asked them to come forward. Each in turn made an affirmation in the form prescribed, namely the four points in ISO 14(6).[163]

There is no provision in the standing orders dealing with the appointment of the First and Deputy First Minister, or departmental ministers.

On 15 July 1999, during the abortive running of d'Hondt, when the initial presiding officer asked each nominee if he or she was willing to take up the office, he or she replied: 'Yes. I affirm the Pledge of Office as set out in Schedule 4 to the Northern Ireland Act 1998.'[164] This same formula was used on 29 November 1999, though the nominee was asked to first confirm before making the affirmation. The initial presiding officer then said immediately afterwards: X is now Minister (Designate) for Y.

Paragraph 4 of schedule 14 refers to any nomination of a Northern Ireland minister having effect from the appointed day as if it had been made under section 18. This implies that ministers cannot be elected legally under d'Hondt – in the absence of a relevant ISO – before the transfer of powers (it does not preclude shadow ministers). *Notes on Clauses* bears this out, when it states that 'ministers will however still be obliged to take the pledge of office after the appointed day as a condition of formal appointment'.[165] This, however, did not happen.

[15.] *24.* **[Assembly Secretaries/]Ministers will have full executive authority in their respective areas of responsibility, within any broad programme agreed by the Executive[/Liaison] Committee [(see below)] and endorsed by the Assembly as a whole. [on a cross-community basis; or in accordance with budgetary policy or legislative proposals approved, on a cross-community basis, after scrutiny by the Departmental Committee and by the Assembly. In the event of any dispute between an Assembly Secretary/Minister and the Committee, the**

163 'I, ... , affirm to the Assembly my commitment to non-violence and exclusively peaceful and democratic means, my opposition to any use or threat of force by others for any political purpose, my commitment to work in good faith to bring into being the arrangements set out in the Agreement reached in the multi-party negotiations on 10 April 1998, and my commitment to observe the spirit of the Pledge of Office set out in Annex B to the initial standing orders.' (New Northern Ireland Assembly, *Official Report*, vol. 1, p. 23, 1 July 1998)

164 New Northern Ireland Assembly, *Official Report*, vol. 2, pp. 320–3, 15 July 1999.

165 NIO, October 1998, note to clause 15.

Assembly as a whole to have the power of decision exercised on a cross-community basis.]

12.84 Paragraph 15 of the MDP was reduced considerably. It diluted the role of assembly secretary/minister by emphasizing the constraints, including cross-community support (mentioned three times). All these have been removed in this paragraph.

12.85 There is no relevant section in the NIA 1998, nor relevant standing orders.

12.86 This paragraph is the other face of paragraphs 19 and 20 on the functions of the executive committee (incorporated by section 20(3) of the NIA 1998).

12.87 ANNOTATIONS

'Ministers will have full executive authority in their respective areas of responsibility,'. Ministers here may refer to all ministers, as in paragraphs 17 and 23. Will have full executive authority in their respective areas of responsibility is otherwise wordy. Executive authority refers back to the subheading of Strand One, and to the use of that concept in the GOIA 1920 and the NICA 1973 (in the plural). In their respective areas of responsibility, if it also includes the First Minister and Deputy First Minister, covers their joint responsibilities, plus those of departmental ministers.

The Departments (Northern Ireland) Order 1999, SI 1999/283 – in the absence of anything in the NIA 1998 – addresses (albeit inadequately) the powers of ministers. Minister, in the case of the office of First Minister and deputy First Minister, means the two 'acting jointly'. 'In the case of any other department, the Minister [is] in charge of that department'[166] (article 2(2)). The 1999 order – consolidating the 1921 Northern Ireland act (and subsequent local legislation) – attributes all functions to the departments, these being exercised subject to the direction and control of the minister (article 4(1)).

The determination of the First Minister and Deputy First Minister, under ISO 21, was approved by the assembly on 16 February 1999. Column 1 listed the ministerial offices in column one. It referred to the ten reorganized departments in column 2. But there was no reference, directly or indirectly, to the agreed allocation of functions to the departments. The functions to be exercised by the holder of each ministerial office were stated to be the 'exercise [of] the functions of Minister of that Department'.

This does not clarify what are the functions – that is powers and duties – of ministers under this constitution of Northern Ireland. Nor does it seem likely that a determination under ISO 21 – an initial standing order made under paragraph 10(1) of the schedule to the Northern Ireland (Elections) Act 1998 by the secretary of state – was approved properly by the assembly. On 30 November 1999, the secretary of state, under section 4 of the Ministries Act (Northern Ireland) 1944, made the Departments (Transfer and Assignment of Functions) Order (Northern Ireland) 1999, SR 1999/481, coming into operation on 1 December 1999. This transferred – some – functions from the existing six departments to most of the ten new departments. Functions were assigned singularly to the office of the First Minister and Deputy First Minister. Under articles 1(3), 8 and 9(2) plus schedule 3 of the Departments (Northern Ireland) Order 1999, SI 1999/283, section 4 of the Ministries Act (Northern Ireland) 1944 was repealed on 3 December 1999, and the power to transfer and assign functions given to the First Minister and Deputy First Minister.

[12.] 25. An individual may be [excluded or] removed from office [by] *following* a decision of the Assembly taken on a cross-community basis, [when] *if* (s)he loses the confidence of the Assembly, voting on

166 See also section 17(3) of the NIA 1998.

> **a cross-community basis, [either] for failure to meet his *or her* responsibilities [or because the Assembly believes, on a cross-community basis, that his retention of office is incompatible with democratic expectations and constraints.] *including, inter alia, those set out in the Pledge of Office. Those who hold office should use only democratic, non-violent means, and those who do not should be excluded or removed from office under these provisions.***

12.88 This was originally the third paragraph in the Executive Authority subsection of Strand One. Its status has been enhanced by being placed at the end of the subsection. The text has also been toughened up considerably.

12.89 The relevant section of the NIA 1998 is 30. There is no relevant standing order; nor initial standing order.

12.90 This is the most important paragraph of Strand One, indeed of the three sections of the Belfast Agreement dealing with institutions. It guarantees the rule of law, that those with private armies should not be allowed to become, or remain, members of the executive committee.

12.91 I am also including the letter of 10 April 1998, from the prime minister to David Trimble (which has been published by Senator Mitchell[167]). This is believed widely to have led finally to the MPA. Tony Blair (and Mo Mowlam) were two of the signatories of the Belfast Agreement. The letter was sent shortly before the final plenary (not afterwards as stated increasingly). And it is inconceivable that the other two signatories, Bertie Ahern and David Andrews, did not see it before signing the BIA (the Irish government has never claimed that it was unaware of the prime minister's undertaking). It therefore has a bearing on the meaning of paragraph 25 of Strand One.

12.92 Under article 31(1) of the 1969 Vienna convention on the law of treaties, the letter is arguably part of the context of the BIA for the purpose of interpretation. This may be established factually under article 31(2)(b). Secondly (and alternatively), – and here the letter is not so central – there should be taken into account, under article 31(3)(c), a principle of legality (by analogy with United Kingdom[168] and Irish law[169]) in international law.[170] Thirdly and alternatively, I submit that, under article 32, the letter is part of the preparatory work of the treaty, and/or the circumstances of its conclusion, and recourse may be had to it as a supplementary means of interpretation.

12.93 The prime minister wrote to the leader of the UUP: 'I understand your problem with paragraph 25 of Strand 1 is that it requires decisions on those who should be excluded or removed from office in the Northern Ireland Executive to be taken on a cross-community basis.[171] [new paragraph] This letter is to let you

167 *Making Peace*, London 1999, pp. 179–80. The letter was reported widely in the press, including (in part) in the *Irish Times* of 11 April 1998.

168 A.V. Dicey, *An Introduction to the Study of the Law of the Constitution*, 10th edn, 1965, pp. 202–3.

169 Articles 6.2, 15.2.1, 15.6.1–2, 28.3.1 & 3 of BNH.

170 Article 38(1)(c), Statute of the International Court of Justice: 'the general principles of law recognized by civilized nations'.

171 David Trimble was concerned presumably that the SDLP would not support the UUP against Sinn Féin.

know that if, during the course of the first six months of the shadow Assembly or the Assembly itself [that is, 1 July 1998 to 31 December], these provisions have been shown to be ineffective, we will support changes in these provisions to enable them to be made properly effective in preventing such people from holding office. [new paragraph] Furthermore, I confirm that in our view the effect of the decommissioning section of the agreement ... is that the process of decommissioning should begin straight away.'

12.94 ANNOTATIONS

'An individual may be removed from office'. Individual is initially strange in this context. Why not minister, given the reference to office? Minister includes the First Minister and Deputy First Minister in paragraphs 17 and 23. And junior ministers – who are provided for in section 30 of the NIA 1998 – were not envisaged on 10 April 1998. The MDP shows that the proposal was originally exclusion or removal; a member of the assembly might be prevented from becoming a minister. This first amendment – the exclusion of 'excluded or' – could have been crucial, denying the assembly the power to prevent a member becoming a minister. However, exclusion was reinstated, probably by unionists, in the last sentence. The power covers exclusion as well as removal (as may be seen from the prime minister's first paragraph). Indeed, the marginal note to section 30 of the NIA 1998 is 'Exclusion of Ministers from office'.

'following a decision of the Assembly taken on a cross-community basis,'. This requires a specific motion on exclusion/removal, a no-confidence resolution. Cross-community basis is a reference to paragraph 5(d). Nothing there states whether it should be by parallel consent or a weighted majority. ISO 12 specified three circumstances requiring cross-community support; the only possible relevant one is when a petition of concern (by at least 30 members) is presented. Parallel consent applies seemingly only to the election of the First Minister and Deputy First Minister. It must be inferred from the initial standing orders then that, if a petition of concern is involved, a weighted majority is required.

The issue has been dealt with extensively in section 30 of the NIA 1998. Exclusion – removal has not been incorporated – now applies to ministers or junior ministers (30(1)) or political parties (30(2)). The reference to political parties is consistent with exclusion; ministers or junior ministers with removal. Two circumstances justify exclusion when the assembly has no confidence in ministers or parties: one, not committed to non-violence and exclusively peaceful and democratic means (30(1)(a) and 30(2)(a)). This is (b) in the pledge of office, two, failure to observe any other terms of the pledge of office. Breach of the terms of the pledge of office then is the test, whether it has been affirmed or not. The act introduced the new idea of exclusion for 12 months (30(1) and 30(2)), extendable – indefinitely – by 12-month periods (30(3), though an assembly can vote to bring the exclusion to an end (30(4). There are three circumstances in which a motion for exclusion may be moved (30(5)): one, it is supported by at least 30 members (that is, there is a petition of concern); two, it is moved by the First Minister and the deputy First Minister; or three, the presiding officer moves the motion at the request of the secretary of state (whose involvement is provided for in 30(6)–(7)). Section 30(8) states that a resolution shall not be passed without cross-community support (parallel consent or weighted majority not being specified).

'if (s)he loses the confidence of the Assembly, voting on a cross-community basis,'. The gender alternative (s)he appears for the first – and last – time in Strand One in paragraph 25. The exclusion motion is characterized as a no-confidence resolution. This adds nothing to the paragraph (or to section 30 of the NIA 1998). The second reference to voting on a cross-community basis would appear to be superfluous. There is no suggestion of, first, a no-confidence vote, followed by a motion to exclude. The MDP contained a third reference to voting on a cross-community basis, equally superfluous.

'for failure to meet his or her responsibilities including, inter alia, those set out in the Pledge of Office,' is the test for exclusion. For failure to meet his or her responsibilities is not defined. It has been dropped in section 30 of the NIA 1998. Conceivably, it could become relevant again construing the act, if some action or inaction was not inconsistent with the pledge of office, but was otherwise a failure to meet his or her (ministerial) responsibilities. Including, inter alia, those set out in the Pledge of Office appeared for the first time in the FA. The MDP alternatives, of failure to meet responsibilities, or retention of office as incompatible with democratic expectations and constraints, were unlikely to be operational in what may be seen as a quasi-judicial process. The amendment of paragraph 25, the idea of a pledge of office, which adds substantially, required the drafting of Annex A to Strand One. (This is considered in Chapter 13.)

'Those who hold office should use only democratic, non-violent means, and those who do not should be excluded or removed from office under these provisions.' This new sentence (added to the MDP) contributes little, except in one very important respect. It is generally exhortatory, and not appropriate for a legal text, even one produced in a political context. Those who hold office should use only democratic, non-violent means is simply a reiteration of (b) in the pledge of office (slightly weakening the impact of that pledge). And those who do not should be excluded or removed from office under these provisions is more than the corollary of the first part of the sentence. And those who do not refers – not to holding office – but to democratic, non-violent means. Should be excluded or removed from office is the key to paragraph 25. It reinstates exclusion, and gives it equal status with removal – countering the argument that certain members should be given a chance as ministers. Under these provisions is strange. It must refer to the first sentence. But it has to refer also to the second, if exclusion is to be valid under the Belfast Agreement.

The prime minister's letter

12.95 (See pp. 226–7). This is essentially a political document, but it has an important bearing on the principle of legality in the governance of Northern Ireland.

12.96 The first paragraph suggests that David Trimble posed the question: paragraph 25 makes clear that members of the assembly in breach of the pledge of office can be excluded or removed from office, but what if – to take the most obvious example[172] – the SDLP backs Sinn Féin in resisting a motion to exclude? The SDLP might weigh the evidence differently, or, in accord with its stated policy, give Sinn Féin a chance in office in the hope that the republican movement would finally abandon the armed struggle, by fulfilling the decommissioning obligation of the Belfast Agreement.

12.97 The prime minister – on behalf of the United Kingdom state in international law – addressed this political possibility in his second paragraph. In doing so, he revealed the imperative of the rule of law domestically.

12.98 First, he specified a time scale beginning with the shadow assembly (which met first on 1 July 1998). This suggests that even shadow ministers who did not accord with the letter and spirit of the pledge of office[173] were not acceptable.

12.99 Secondly, he imposed a deadline – on the United Kingdom government – of six months. The deadline was for action if paragraph 25 was proved to be ineffective. (While the shadow executive was not formed by 31 December 1998, the

172 The paramilitary party, the PUP, with two members, does not figure in the d'Hondt calculations; Sinn Féin is the only relevant party to which paragraph 25 could apply.

173 Under ISO 14(6).

provisions allow for exclusion of a party – and Sinn Féin was pressing throughout for an inclusive executive regardless of decommissioning.)

12.100 Thirdly, the prime minister undertook to support changes, in presumably a review of paragraph 25 under possibly paragraph 36 (or the Validation, Implementation and Review section of the MPA). The word support indicates that the Irish government remained to be persuaded, to amend this aspect of Annex 1 of the BIA.

12.101 Fourthly, he reiterated the objective as 'preventing such people from holding office', which covers both exclusion and removal. The principle of legality is further apparent in the third paragraph on decommissioning. The prime minister stated – in accord with the unacceptability of illegal weapons held by illegal organizations – that decommissioning 'should begin straight away'.[174]

Subheading: Legislation

12.102 The assembly is a legislature, albeit a subordinate one. It is therefore strange that this subsection of four paragraphs is not located higher up in Strand One. The GOIA 1920, NICA 1973 and NIA 1998 all deal first with legislative powers. The reason presumably was the decision to lead with Safeguards, and following that logic through executive functions.

12.103 The relevant sections of the NIA 1998 are 5 –15. SOs 28–40 also apply (there are no relevant ISOs).

[21.] *26.* **The Assembly will have authority to pass primary legislation for Northern Ireland in devolved areas, subject to:**

(a) the ECHR and any Bill of Rights for Northern Ireland supplementing it which, if the courts found to be breached, would render the relevant legislation null and void;
(b) decisions by simple majority of members voting, except when decision on a cross-community basis is required;
(c) detailed scrutiny and approval in the relevant Departmental Committee;
(d) mechanisms, based on arrangements proposed for the Scottish Parliament, to ensure suitable co-ordination, and avoid disputes, between the Assembly and the Westminster Parliament;
(e) option of the Assembly seeking to include Northern Ireland provisions in United Kingdom-wide legislation in the Westminster Parliament, especially on devolved issues where parity is normally maintained (e.g. social security, company law).

12.104 The structure of this paragraph is similar to paragraph 5. There, five safeguards – d'Hondt, human rights, proofing, cross-community support, and equality – were listed. Proofing of legislation anticipates this paragraph. Here, legislative powers are subject to five similar restrictions: human rights, cross-community support; statutory committees; legislative competence; Westminster legislation.

174 This is in spite of his having just referred to the decommissioning schemes promised for June 1998.

12.105 The nature of devolution under the NIA 1998 may be recalled. Under section 4(1), a transferred matter 'means any matter which is not an excepted or reserved matter'. In other words, all is transferred (or devolved), unless it is excepted or reserved. Excepted 'means any matter falling within a description specified in Schedule 2'. Schedule 2 contains 22 paragraphs. Reserved 'means any matter falling within a description specified in Schedule 3'. Schedule 3 has 42 paragraphs. Section 4(2)–(4) allows for the amending of schedule 3 (reserved matters) by order in council, in order to add to or subtract from the transferred matters. This is a responsibility of the secretary of state, but a condition precedent is cross-community support in the assembly.

12.106 ANNOTATIONS

'The Assembly will have authority to pass primary legislation for Northern Ireland in devolved areas, subject to:'. The Assembly will have authority has been rendered as 'the Assembly may make laws, to be known as Acts' in section 5(1) of the NIA 1998.

'to pass primary legislation for Northern Ireland in devolved areas,'. Primary legislation – to be distinguished from delegated (or secondary or subordinate) legislation – is law made by a legislature. There is Westminster primary legislation, and there is Northern Ireland primary legislation. Since 1974, the latter has passed through the sovereign parliament as delegated legislation.[175] The order in council system applied only to the transferred area under the NICA 1973.[176] Excepted and reserved matters continued to be dealt with in Westminster primary legislation. In devolved areas is transferred matters under section 4 of the NIA 1998. Devolution is not a term of art, though the marginal note to section 3 is 'Devolution order'.

The assembly can legislate generally in the transferred area. And those matters are determined negatively by schedules 2 and 3 of the NIA 1998. But Westminster retains its legislative supremacy, and this is made clear in section 5(6).[177] Section 5(6) must be read with section 7 (entrenched enactments). These are entrenched enactments from the point of view of Northern Ireland; they cannot be entrenched generally in United Kingdom law. They are: the European Communities Act 1972; the Human Rights Act 1998; and sections of the NIA 1998.[178]

'subject to:' introduces the five restrictions, (a)–(e).

'(a) the ECHR and any Bill of Rights for Northern Ireland supplementing it which, if the courts found to be breached, would render the relevant legislation null and void;'.

The ECHR and any Bill of Rights for Northern Ireland supplementing it refers back to paragraph 5(b), and on to the Human Rights part of the Rights, Safeguards and Equality of Opportunity section. The 1950 European Convention on Human Rights has been incorporated – to the extend of the remedies – in the Human Rights Act 1998. This was due to come into force generally on 2 October 2000. There is as yet no bill of rights for Northern Ireland. That is a matter – initially – for the human rights commission in Northern Ireland. Section 5(1) of the NIA 1998 states that acts of the assembly – in the transferred area as defined in section 4 – are subject to sections 6 to 8. Section 7 (entrenched enactments) includes the Human Rights Act 1998. But that only prevents the assembly (or a minister or department through subordinate legislation) amending the act in Northern Ireland. Of

175 Paragraph 1(1) of schedule 1 (and section 1(3)) of the Northern Ireland Act 1974.

176 Some excepted and reserved matters were included: NIA 1974, sch 1 para 1(2); NICA 1973 s 5(1).

177 'This section does not affect the power of the Parliament of the United Kingdom to make laws for Northern Ireland, but an Act of the Assembly may modify any provisions made by or under an Act of Parliament in so far as it is part of the law of Northern Ireland.'

178 Sections 43(1)–(6) & (8), 67, 84–86, 95(3)–(4), & 98.

more relevance is section 13 (stages of bills). Under subsection (4), standing orders are to provide for: one, the presiding officer sending a copy of each bill, as soon as reasonably practicable after introduction, to the human rights commission; two, enabling the commission, where the assembly thinks fit, to advise on whether the bill is compatible with human rights (presumably as enacted[179]). The first is dealt with in similar terms in SO 28(6); SO 32 (human rights issues) covers the second. The text of a motion requesting advice is included. It only requires a simple majority.[180] SO 32(6) requires the advice to be circulated to all members, and published in a manner determined by the speaker. There is provision for the commission giving unsolicited advice to the assembly under section 69(4)(b).[181]

'which, if the courts found to be breached, would render the relevant legislation null and void;'. This phrase makes clear that the rights in the first part of the sentence must be part of Northern Ireland law. This means largely the convention rights specified in section 1(1) of the Human Rights Act 1998, which is due to come into force in Northern Ireland under section 22(3). However, under paragraph 1 of schedule 14 (transitional provisions) of the NIA 1998, sections 6(2)(c), 24(1) and 71 and schedule 10 of the Human Rights Act 1998 shall have effect as if that act were so in force.[182] The first relevant section as regards the courts is section 3 (interpretation of legislation). Section 3(1) reads: 'So far as it is possible to do so, primary legislation and subordinate legislation must be read and given effect in a way which is compatible with the Convention rights.' Acts of the Northern Ireland assembly are, under section 21(1), subordinate legislation. Section 3 does not affect the validity, continuing operation or enforcement of any incompatible subordinate legislation if primary legislation prevents removal of the incompatibility (subsection (2)(c)). The NIA 1998 does not do this. In section 6(1), it states: 'A provision of an Act is not law if it is outside the legislative competence of the Assembly.' Under section 6(2)(c), a provision is outside that competence if it is incompatible with any of the Convention rights.[183] However, under section 71(1), for a person to bring proceedings alleging incompatibility, and rely upon Convention rights, he must be a victim under article 34 of the Convention if proceedings were brought in Strasbourg.[184] (There may also be a defence under section 71(3) of the NIA 1998, introducing section 6(1)–(2) of the Human Rights Act 1998.) The effect of section 6(1) dates arguably from the determination of incompatibility (all appeals having been exhausted). Acts of the assembly, therefore, may be struck down – rendered invalid (to the extent of the incompatibility) under section 83 – by the courts.

'(b) decisions by simple majority of members voting, except when decision on a cross-community basis is required;'. This is more a description of the legislative process than a safeguard. The reference to cross-community support in paragraph 5(d) refers only to key decisions; none of the instances refers to legislating. ISO 12 on voting stated that every decision of the assembly was to be by a simple majority of those voting, except as provided in subparagraphs (2) and (3). (2) is: the election of the presiding officer and deputy presiding officer; standing orders; and where a petition of concern has been presented. (3) is the election of the First Minister and Deputy First Minister (by parallel consent). The NIA 1998 specifies cross-community support for the following: a change between transferred and reserved matters (section 4(3)); election of the First Minister and Deputy First Minister by parallel consent (16(3)); exclusion of ministers from office (30(8)); election of presiding officer and deputies (39(7)); standing orders (41(2)); petition of concern (42(1)); a special

179 Human rights is defined in section 69(11)(b) as including Convention rights. Paragraph 26(a) could well be crucial in construing the phrase 'human rights' – as defined – in section 69(4).

180 SO 25.

181 It seems it may publish the advice under section 69(9).

182 Schedule 14 of the NIA 1998 came into force partly on 1 June 1999: Northern Ireland Act 1998 (Commencement No. 1) Order 1999, SI 1999/340.

183 As defined in the Human Rights Act 1998.

184 See also section 7(7) of the Human Rights Act 1998.

standing committee on conformity with equality requirements (42(3)); appropriations and taxation (63)(3)); draft budgets (64(2)). In this list, the only legislative activity is the equality requirements committee (under paragraphs 11–13 of Strand One, and sections 13(3) and 42(3) of the NIA 1998). Standing orders follow the act. SO 25 states that every decision of the assembly is to be by simple majority of those voting. There are three exceptions: one, in paragraph (2) – appropriations and taxation; two, provided for in the NIA 1998 (on which see above); and three, SO 70 (suspension of standing orders).

'(c) detailed scrutiny and approval in the relevant Departmental Committee;'. This refers back to paragraphs 8 and 9. The term departmental committee (see paragraph 10) was clearly intended. Section 29 of the NIA 1998, however, uses the term statutory committee.

Detailed scrutiny is implied in paragraph 9. The legislative role there is: a role in initiation of legislation; approve relevant secondary legislation; committee stage of relevant primary legislation. Approval must therefore refer to secondary legislation. Section 29(1)(c) of the NIA 1998 (as noted) incorporates the paragraph 9 powers.

However, part II of the act (legislative powers, sections 5–15) has very little to say about the statutory committees. Under Scrutiny and stages of Bills, the roles of ministers, the presiding officer, the judicial committee of the privy council, and the European Court of Justice are specified. Section 13 (stages of bills) – which mentions the equality committee and the human rights commission – makes no reference to the statutory committees.

Standing orders (Legislation, SOs 28–40) do specify the committees. The stages for public bills are: introduction and first stage (SO 28); second stage (SOs 29 and 30); committee stage (SOs 29 and 31); consideration stage (SOs 29 and 34); and final stage (SOs 29 and 36); there is also a provision for reconsideration (SO 37). SO 39 (special scheduling requirements) includes provision for accelerated passage.

The role of the statutory committees is less than that implied in paragraph 9 of Strand One (even given the juxtaposition between 'approve' and 'take'). The committee stage in Northern Ireland is additional to Westminster's stages of a bill. Under SO 29(b), the committee stage involves 'detailed investigation by a Committee, followed by report to the Assembly.' SO 31(1) on committee stage reads: 'On the Second Stage of a Bill being agreed to, the Bill shall stand referred to the appropriate Statutory Committee, unless the Assembly shall order otherwise.' It is not automatic. And the committee does not vote on amendments. It may take evidence, and report its opinion (SO 31(2)). The report to the assembly may include proposals for amendments (SO 31(3)). The role of the human rights commission (SO 32), and the equality committee (SO 33), is potentially much more significant. Amendments are taken, on the floor of the assembly, at the consideration stage. Under accelerated passage (SO 39), the committee stage is dropped. SO 40 (statutory rules of Northern Ireland) does provide that secondary legislation is referred to the appropriate statutory committee. It may either deal with the rules or draft rules, or refer them to the examiner of statutory rules. However, the committee only considers the rules and reports to the assembly. This is less than the 'approve' in paragraph 9.

'(d) mechanisms, based on arrangements proposed for the Scottish Parliament, to ensure suitable co-ordination, and avoid disputes, between the Assembly and the Westminster Parliament;'. This is the least clear of the five conditions to which Northern Ireland primary legislation is subject in paragraph 26. It would seem to be a question of legislative competence, which relates to much more than Belfast/London – or Edinburgh/London – legislative disputes.

The date of this reference to mechanisms is 10 April 1998. In the white paper, *Scotland's Parliament*, Cm 3658, July 1997, it was stated there would 'be arrangements for resolving disagreements about whether legislation is within the powers of the Scottish Parliament' (p. x). Paragraphs 4.15–17 (pp. 14–15) included the following procedures: presiding officer checks draft legislation is intra vires before introduction; ditto for amendments; United

Kingdom government check as to vires before royal assent; in the event of a dispute, referral to the judicial committee of the privy council.

The Scotland Act 1998 contains the following provisions (in Legislation, sections 28–36): legislative incompetence in reserved matters (29(2)(b); ditto for schedule 4 (enactments protected from modification) (29(2)(c); scrutiny by the presiding officer on or before the introduction of a bill (31(2)); presiding officer may withhold submission of bills for royal assent in certain circumstances (32(2)–(3)); scrutiny by the judicial committee of the privy council (33); European Court of Justice references (34); secretary of state intervention if incompatibility with international obligations, interests of defence or national security or modification of the law on reserved matters (35(1)).

The NIA 1998 has the following provisions: legislative incompetence in excepted matters not ancillary to other provisions dealing with reserved or transferred matters (section 6(2)(b)); entrenched enactments (7); consent of secretary of state necessary to legislate on an excepted matter which is ancillary to other provisions dealing with reserved or transferred matters, or a reserved matter (8); scrutiny by the presiding officer on introduction of a bill and before its final stage (10); scrutiny by the judicial committee of the privy council (11); reconsideration when reference to the European Court of Justice (12 and 13(5)); secretary of state withholds submission of bills for royal assent in certain circumstances (14); parliamentary control where consent given by the secretary of state under section 8 (15).

These Westminster – and Whitehall – controls operate through the presiding officers, law officers and the judicial committee. The power of the secretary of state may be greater in Scotland, but that is a measure of its greater devolution.

'(e) option of the Assembly seeking to include Northern Ireland provisions in United Kingdom-wide legislation in the Westminster Parliament, especially on devolved issues where parity is normally maintained (e.g. social security, company law).'

Option of the Assembly seeking to include Northern Ireland provisions in United Kingdom-wide legislation in the Westminster Parliament is diplomatic phrasing, a gesture towards legislative integrationism (all acts to apply throughout the United Kingdom, unless there is a reason for not including Northern Ireland[185]). The word provisions is misleading and unnecessary. The provisions for Northern Ireland might be modified (in the United Kingdom context), but they would not originate – as it were – as suggestions of the assembly. It is most unlikely that London, having transferred a matter, would then legislate on behalf of a subordinate at its request. In the Westminster Parliament is superfluous. The assembly – outside the existing parity areas – is unlikely to be willing to make a concerted request. Asking is one thing; getting, another. There is no provision for such a request in standing orders, probably a recognition of the relative unimportance of the issue.

'especially on devolved issues where parity is normally maintained'. The word especially suggests more a continuation of the status quo than a development of this practice. Devolved issues is superfluous; it is otherwise implied. Parity refers to similar or identical legislation in Northern Ireland and Great Britain. United Kingdom-wide legislation – with a bearing on the Northern Ireland departments – is done in different ways. Occasionally, under the Northern Ireland parliament, there was a section stating simply that the act applied to Northern Ireland; more often, there were separate acts for Northern Ireland. Under direct rule, similar or identical legislation has been put on the so-called Northern

185 Under the English and Great British parliament, with a parliament in Ireland, there was a legal presumption that Westminster acts did not apply to Ireland. With the union, the presumption became that acts extended throughout the United Kingdom. While this survived partition (as regards Northern Ireland), devolution meant that Northern Ireland had to be expressly included. Parts of the United Kingdom are expressly excluded by extent clauses or even impliedly.

Ireland statute book – under the Interpretation Act (NI) 1954 – by order in council at Westminster. Occasionally, it is done by separate act.[186] Very rarely, there is a United Kingdom act.[187] Integration – even where parity justifies it – has been avoided by successive United Kingdom governments.

'(e.g. social security,'. Social security legislation, mainly since the second world war, has been the principal constituent of parity provision. Though the services are generally the same, Westminster puts the legislation on the Northern Ireland 'statute book'.[188] Subordinate legislation is dealt with by parliamentary counsel in Belfast. (There are of course administrative differences.)

In part VIII of the NIA 1998 (miscellaneous), under social security, child support and pensions, there are the following sections: consultation and co-ordination (87); the joint authority (88); industrial injuries advisory council (89). Section 28 also provides for agency arrangements between United Kingdom and Northern Ireland departments (which need not be reciprocal); one instance is child support. From a perusal of schedules 2 and 3, social security, child support and pensions are all generally transferred matters. Paragraph 11 of schedule 2 makes the appointment and removal of social security, and child support, commissioners an excepted matter. Paragraphs 17, 18 and 22 of schedule 3 make the following reserved matters: functions of the social security, and child support, commissioners; the social security advisory committee and industrial injuries advisory council; certain sections of the Pension Schemes Act 1993. Section 87(1) affirms the objective of 'single systems of social security, child support and pensions for the United Kingdom'. This is to be pursued through consultation between the secretary of state and the Northern Ireland social security minister.[189] Paragraph (a) of section 87(2) refers to arrangements for coordinating the operation of legislation, and paragraph (b) to reciprocal arrangements for coordinating the operation of legislation which operates differently. Section 87(4)(a) allows the secretary of state, by regulations, to adapt[190] legislation for the time being in force in Great Britain. A similar power is given to the Northern Ireland social security department in section 87(5). Section 88 deals with the social security, child support and pensions joint authority (a body corporate), comprising the secretary of state, the Northern Ireland social security minister and the chancellor of the exchequer. It has the power to give effect to arrangements under section 87(2). Section 89 makes changes pertaining to the social security advisory committee, and the industrial injuries advisory council, in the Social Security Administration (Northern Ireland) Act 1992.

'company law).' From a perusal of schedules 2 and 3, this is a transferred matter. There are seven main United Kingdom statutes. The first three consolidate the companies acts 1948 to 1983. The provisions they make for Northern Ireland are as follows: section 745 of the Companies Act 1985 (application only when expressly provided; act does not extend generally to Northern Ireland); section 9 of the Business Names Act 1985 (act does not extend to Northern Ireland); section 33 of the Companies Consolidation (Consequential Provisions) Act 1985 (except insofar as it has effect for maintaining the continuity of the

186 Examples are the Social Security Contributions and Benefits (Northern Ireland) Act 1992; the Social Security Administration (Northern Ireland) Act 1992; the Pensions Schemes (Northern Ireland) Act 1993.

187 For example, the Disability (Grants) Act 1993.

188 A list of the United Kingdom acts and equivalent Northern Ireland orders is contained in section 87(6) of the NIA 1998. See also Northern Ireland Act 1998 (Modification) Order 2000, SI 2000/741.

189 Minister of health, social services and public safety.

190 *Notes on Clauses*, NIO October 1998 states that s 87(4) 'allows the secretary of state to make any amendments that are necessary to give effect to arrangements made under subsection (2)'.

law, the act does not extend to Northern Ireland). Most of the Insolvency Act 1986 (section 441) does not extend, the Company Directors Disqualification Act 1986 does not extend to Northern Ireland (section 24). Financial services are a reserved matter (paragraph 23(a) of schedule 3). And the Financial Services Act 1986 – which ended the transferred matter[191] – does extend to Northern Ireland. Finally, the Companies Act 1989 extends to Northern Ireland in so far as it amends Northern Ireland law (section 213). Section 214 provides for the making of a corresponding provision for Northern Ireland (subject, not to affirmative resolution of both houses, but only to annulment of either).

[22.] *27.* The Assembly will have authority to legislate in reserved areas with the approval of the Secretary of State and subject to Parliamentary control.

12.107 Reserved matters were dealt with under executive authority in the GOIA 1920 (section 9). The Northern Ireland government had no say at all. This was because they were reserved pending Irish union under section 3; until then, they resembled the excepted matters specified in section 4(1).

12.108 In the NICA 1973, section 5 provided for the secretary of state's consent to legislate in the excepted and reserved areas, and section 6 for parliamentary control. The test for a provision dealing with an excepted matter was: ancillary to other provisions dealing with reserved or transferred matters (section 9(1)). The secretary of state had a discretion as regards reserved matters. Section 6 provided for such proposed measures being laid before parliament for 20 days (subject to annulment); provisions ancillary to reserved matters were excused.

12.109 Sections 8 and 15 of the NIA 1998 now deal with consent and control for legislation dealing with other than transferred matters. Section 8 makes secretary of state consent mandatory in two circumstances: a provision dealing with an excepted matter which is ancillary to provisions dealing with reserved or transferred matters; a provision which deals with a reserved matter. This is similar to, but more clearly expressed than, the provisions in the NICA 1973. The assembly can legislate on a reserved matter with consent of the secretary of state.

12.110 Where there has been secretary of state consent, section 15 requires that the Northern Ireland bill is laid before parliament for 20 days (subject to annulment); provisions ancillary to transferred matters are excused. This is similar to the NICA 1973 provision. There is therefore parliamentary control.

[23.] 28. Disputes over legislative competence to be decided by the Courts.

12.111 In the GOIA 1920, there was no express provision for the judicial settlement of such disputes. That does not mean the courts in Northern Ireland and Great Britain could not decide whether a local act was within legislative competence; 'the peace, order, and good government of ... Northern Ireland' in section 4(1). No act of the dominions had ever been found to be ultra vires such a grant of power, and this was also the case under the GOIA 1920.[192] The courts also had another approach: to ask if the Northern Ireland parliament had legislated on an excepted or reserved matter. But they were not troubled with constitutional cases on legislative competence between 1921 and 1972.

191 Section 209(2).

192 In *R (Hume) v Londonderry Justices* [1972] NI 91, the point was taken but not decided.

12.112 The NICA 1973 contained no provision for judicial settlement, and the assembly was short-lived.

12.113 In the NIA 1998 – as in the Scottish and Welsh acts – there is provision for judicial scrutiny. Section 11 provides for scrutiny by the judicial committee of the privy council during the legislative process in the assembly.[193] The scrutiny is for legislative competence, which is defined in section 6. A provision of a local act is not law if: one, it is extra-territorial; two, it deals with an excepted matter and is not ancillary to provisions dealing with reserved or transferred matters; three, it is incompatible with convention rights; four, it is incompatible with European law; five, it is discriminatory; or six, it modifies an entrenched enactment. Under section 11, the attorney-general for Northern Ireland[194] may refer a question of legislative competence to the judicial committee for decision, within four weeks of its passing. Legislative incompetence is dealt with more extensively in sections 79 to 83 (judicial scrutiny in part VIII) plus schedule 10.[195] These are referred to as devolution issues (section 79). And devolution issues – which may be considered in Northern Ireland, England and Wales or Scotland – are defined in the schedule as: one, legislative incompetence; two, invalid exercise of a function by a minster or department (under section 24); three, whether a minister or department has failed to comply with convention rights, European law or any order under section 27; and four, any question about excepted or reserved matters. Section 80 allows the secretary of state to remedy ultra vires acts by order (this power also applies to actions by ministers or departments). Section 81 allows a court finding a provision to be ultra vires to suspend its decision on any conditions to allow a defect to be corrected. Section 82 makes provisions for the judicial committee. And section 83 on statutory interpretation requires acts and bills to be read within legislative competence in cases of doubt, and subordinate legislation to be held similarly valid.

[24.] 29. Legislation could be initiated by an individual, a Committee or a[n Assembly Secretary/]Minister.

12.114 There was no express provision in the GOIA 1920 dealing with the legislative process. This was also the position in the NICA 1973.

12.115 In the NIA 1998, in scrutiny and stages of bills (in part II), it is assumed that a bill is in the charge of a minister (section 9(1)). Section 29 (statutory committees) provides the powers in paragraph 9 of Strand One. These include a role in initiation of legislation. However, it is not clear that a committee had equal status with a minister in this regard. Standing orders assume a minister and a member (presumably as an individual, not on behalf of a committee) have equal status in this regard. SO 28(1) refers to a minister or a member introducing a public bill. Though SOs 28 to 39 all refer to public bills, SO 28(2) deals with a member in charge of a private member's bill: he is required to follow the procedure in section 9(1) of the NIA 1998 (scrutiny by ministers): namely a statement that the bill is within the legislative competence of the assembly.

193 Scotland Act 1998 s 33; Wales of course has only responsibility for subordinate legislation.

194 Who remains the attorney-general for England and Wales under section 10 of the NICA 1973 (which is not repealed by the NIA 1998). The NIA 1998, however, refers to the attorney-general for Northern Ireland in the alternative (schedule 10).

195 Scotland Act 1998 ss 98–103 plus schedule 6; Government of Wales Act 1998 schedule 8.

Subheading: Relations with other institutions

12.116 This subsection of five paragraphs turns from the internal government of Northern Ireland to – what are called in paragraph 18 – external relationships (though the civic forum in paragraph 34 is entirely domestic). Paragraphs 31–33 deal with Strand One issues, particularly in terms of Belfast-London relations. Strands Two and Three are addressed in paragraph 30. The civic forum is presumably located here, so as not to encroach upon the assembly as legislature and executive.

> [25.] *30.* **Arrangements to represent the Assembly as a whole, at Summit level and in dealings with other institutions, will be in accordance with paragraph [17.]** ***18, and will be such as to ensure cross-community involvement.*** **[Otherwise, representation to be by the Assembly Secretary/Minister of the relevant departmental committee.]**

12.117 Paragraph 25 of the MDP contained the principle of an assembly secretary/minister representing, effectively, the government of Northern Ireland. This has been removed totally from this paragraph. The original referred to paragraph 17 of the MDP, the embryonic text of two paragraphs with a note from the chairmen in between. The first paragraph referred to the executive/liaison committee selecting a chair and deputy chair 'on a basis which ensures that between them they represent both main parts of the community in Northern Ireland'. The note referred to possible endorsement of nominations by the assembly. (And the second paragraph went on to proffer ex officio titles for the First Minister and Deputy First Minister, as they became.) This paragraph now refers to an amended, and renumbered, paragraph dealing with the duties of the First Minister and Deputy First Minister (paragraph 18 above). The principle of the MDP quoted above, I submit, has been carried over in the added phrase: and will be such as to ensure cross-community involvement.

12.118 This paragraph provides the linkage between Strand One and Strands Two and Three (which are dealt with in Chapters 14, 15, 16 and 17). North/south and east/west relations (less those internal to the United Kingdom) are treated identically.

12.119 There is no precedent for Strand Three; that is a completely new aspect of the Belfast Agreement. However, Strand Two concepts are as old as Northern Ireland devolution.

12.120 In the GOIA 1920, section 3 contained a power to establish a parliament for the whole of Ireland. Given that Irish union – as it was called – was dependent upon the consent of the northern and southern parliaments being established, this was most unlikely. However, the means were specified as 'by identical Acts' (section 3(1)). In the interim, and this was an essential part of the partition settlement, there was to be a council of Ireland (section 2). Its constitution could be varied from time to time also by identical acts (section 2(3)).

12.121 The council of Ireland failed to come into existence, because only Northern Ireland was prepared to work the GOIA 1920. Identical acts were eclipsed, in the Ireland Act 1949, by a different approach to north/south cooperation. In section 3(1), reference was made – in the context of the ROI leaving the commonwealth – to Northern Ireland acts giving effect to 'agreements or arrangements' between Belfast and Dublin. This concept of agreements or arrangements reappeared in section 12 of the NICA 1973, under 'Relations with the Republic of Ireland'. (See also section 53 of the NIA 1998.)

12.122 ANNOTATIONS

'Arrangements to represent the Assembly as a whole,' shows a transcendence of the parliament/government distinction of 1920,[196] and that between the assembly and executive in 1973.[197] The assembly is not just a legislature, as in paragraphs 26–29 above; it also contains executive authority (paragraphs 14 to 25). Though the national assembly of Wales is not strictly a legislature (subordinate legislation is an executive responsibility), it has a similar unity to the Northern Ireland assembly; thus, functions of ministers of the crown in relation to Wales have been transferred to the Cardiff assembly.[198] As a whole is superfluous.

'at Summit level and in dealings with other institutions,'. Summit level is a reference to paragraph 3(i) of Strand Two (though the term plenary is used). Summit is used in the first paragraph 3 of Strand Three. Other institutions refers back to the subheading. Institutions generally means all those created in Strands One, Two and Three. Here, the institutions are only those involving external relations (Belfast-London relations being internal to the United Kingdom).

'will be in accordance with paragraph 18,'. This paragraph is not readily intelligible without reference to the MDP. Paragraph 18 above is about the duties of the First Minister and Deputy First Minister (in connection with the executive committee, 'and the response ... to external relationships'). In accordance with paragraph 18, however, introduces meaning, when it is compared with the MDP text in paragraph 25. The joint nature of the offices of First Minister and Deputy First Minister, through the reference to external relationships, is the principle of paragraph 30.

'and will be such as to ensure cross-community involvement.' From the principle of a joint head of the executive is derived the idea of cross-community involvement. Cross-community has been used, in paragraph 5(d), as regards voting on key decisions in the assembly. Here, cross-community involvement means, in the context of Strands Two and Three, joint participation by Northern Ireland ministers. It may be considered a confidence-building measure: no unionist can operate alone, without an opposite nationalist minister being involved, in the British-Irish Council. Similarly, no nationalist can work the North/South Ministerial Council, without effectively a unionist minister shadowing. This relationship is not specified further in Strands Two and Three. But paragraph 30, by appropriating the principle of paragraph 18, and applying it to representing the assembly, introduces a major aspect of external relationships in Strand One.

This has been recognized in part V of the NIA 1998, which deals with the Strands Two and Three institutions (plus – out of a desire to keep it away from Strand One – the civic forum). Section 52 treats the North-South Ministerial Council and the British-Irish Council similarly. Subsection (1) requires the First Minister and the deputy First Minister acting jointly to nominate ministers and junior ministers to ensure 'such cross-community participation ... as is required by the Belfast Agreement'. Paragraph 30 has been incorporated in United Kingdom law.

[26.] *31.* Terms will be agreed between appropriate Assembly representatives and the Government of the United Kingdom to ensure effective co-ordination and input by [Assembly Secretaries] *Ministers* to national policy-making, including on EU issues.

196 GOIA 1920 s 2(1).
197 NICA 1973 ss 4 & 7–8.
198 Government of Wales Act 1998 part II.

12.123 This, and the two following paragraphs, deal with the aspect of Strand One which had to be added to the reference to internal relations: 'including the relationship between any new institutions there and the Westminster Parliament'.[199] Devolution within the United Kingdom state always meant that Belfast-London relations would be as significant as 'relationships within Northern Ireland'.

12.124 This paragraph addresses the centripetal aspect of United Kingdom government, following the centrifugal devolution of power to Scotland, Wales and Northern Ireland. It is similar to paragraph 26(d) above, dealing with relations between Westminster and the assembly, the sovereign parliament and a subordinate legislature. The intended mechanism for executive coordination between London and Edinburgh, Cardiff and Belfast is a series of central department to regional department (bilateral) functional concordats.

12.125 In October 1999, the lord chancellor, as chairman of the devolution policy committee of the cabinet, presented to parliament a memorandum of understanding and supplementary agreements (the MoU) between London, Edinburgh and Cardiff (Belfast being represented by the secretary of state pending devolution).[200] (Following devolution, the executive committee considered the memorandum of understanding on 11 January 2000 and on two following occasions. With the restoration of the institutions, it was debated by the assembly on 5 June 2000, and noted by 52 votes to 23.[201]) The document comprises: a non-legally binding memorandum of understanding (to be construed so as not to conflict with the Belfast Agreement[202]); a supplementary agreement on a joint ministerial committee (JMC), meeting at head of administration level and in functional formats; a concordat on European Union policy; another on financial assistance to industry; a third concordat on international relations; and a fourth one on statistics. The United Kingdom government is administratively in the driving seat, and the MoU envisages London departments having separate bilateral relations with (effectively) subordinate departments in the three devolved administrations. The Northern Ireland executive committee agreed the documents, securing an addition dealing with Strand Two of the Belfast Agreement.[203]

12.126 ANNOTATIONS

'Terms will be agreed'. Terms will be agreed is a reference presumably to the MoU.

Its intended existence was first revealed by Baroness Ramsay, a junior Scottish minister, in the house of lords, in the early hours of 28 July 1998, during debate on the Scotland bill. She announced, first, there would be a (non-statutory) joint ministerial committee, comprising the United Kingdom government and the devolved administrations. Its purpose was described as the consideration of reserved matters impinging on devolved responsibilities. Secondly, she referred to bilateral concordats between the Scottish executive and United Kingdom departments (seemingly department to department).[204] While Baroness Ramsay declined to commit a not-yet-existing Scottish executive, she did say that a great deal of thought – presumably in London – had gone into the new relationship.

199 *Ground Rules for Substantive All-Party Negotiations*, 16 April 1996, Cm 3232, rule 2.
200 *Memorandum of Understanding and supplementary agreements*, Cm 4444.
201 Northern Ireland Assembly, vol. 5, no. 1, *Official Report*, pp. 24–40, 5 June 2000.
202 Paragraph 2.
203 Northern Ireland Assembly, *Official Report*, vol. 5, no. 1, pp. 25 & 36, 5 June 2000.
204 *Hansard*, col. 1488.

'between appropriate Assembly representatives and the Government of the United Kingdom'. Appropriate assembly representatives is unspecific, reflecting the general ambiguity of Strand One. Is it the First Minister and Deputy First Minister, the executive committee, assembly statutory committees, or the whole assembly? There is no doubt about the Government of the United Kingdom, the executive of a centralized, unitary state. It is interesting that the term United Kingdom is being revised, in the context of devolution to Scotland, Wales and Northern Ireland, as a domestic name/description of the state.

'to ensure effective co-ordination and input by Ministers to national policy-making,' embraces two distinct processes: United Kingdom coordination and regional participation at the centre. These are now covered by the MoU. Effective coordination suggests something more federal. The MoU makes it clear that the United Kingdom government is taking the lead, including internally in its relations with the devolved administrations.[205] Input to national policy-making is dealt with in the particular supplementary agreements.

'including on EU issues.' is most likely the rationale for input by Ministers to national policy-making. Input relates largely to the European Union, which is also mentioned effusively in paragraph 17 of Strand Two.

The Union, it is important to remember, comprises member states, which have shaped its trajectory through treaties. This is in spite of preambular references to peoples of Europe, and a citizenship common to nationals of their countries. The – advisory – committee of the regions,[206] comprising representatives of regional and local bodies (proposed by the member states), and provided for in the 1992 Maastricht treaty, taps regionalism, without in any way passing over the member states to their constituent parts; it is not an institution of the European Community.[207] It is the case that the 1992 Maastricht treaty, in providing for the council, allowed representation 'at ministerial level, authorised to commit the government of that Member State'.[208] This permits regional ministers to represent their state. This is possible in the case of Belgium, Germany, Austrian and Spain, given their internal constitutions. A Northern Ireland minister could be part of the United Kingdom delegation (as in agriculture), but he would never represent Northern Ireland on the council.

EU relations are specified along with international relations in Part 1 of the MoU (the memorandum of understanding proper). 'The UK Government', it states, 'recognises that the devolved administrations will have an interest in international and European policy making in relation to devolved matters, notably where implementing action by the devolved administrations may be required'. This is minimal input to national policy making on EU issues. And is confirmed by the following undertaking: 'The UK Government will involve the devolved administrations as fully as possible in discussions about the formulation of the UK's policy position on all EU and international issues which touch on devolved matters. This must, obviously, be subject to mutual respect for the confidentiality of those discussions and adherence to the resultant UK line, without which it would be impossible to maintain such close working relationships.'[209] The concordat on EU policy issues – the responsibility of the Foreign and Commonwealth Office – elaborates. Ministers and officials of the devolved administrations are to be fully involved in discussions 'on all issues which touch on matters

205 The JMC met six times in the first six months of 2000, being chaired twice by the prime minister and four times by the chancellor of the exchequer. The prime minister's meetings in April and June dealt with health, confounding any quasi-federal notions of, say, a council of health ministers. 'So far the JMC has been used to promote the agenda of senior UK ministers.' (*Monitor*, Constitution Unit Bulletin, issue 11, June 2000, p. 4)

206 1997 Amsterdam treaty, articles 263–265 (ex 198a–c).

207 Nor is the Economic and Social Committee: 1997 Amsterdam treaty, articles 257–262 (ex 193–198).

208 Article 203 (ex 146).

209 *Memorandum of Understanding and supplementary agreements*, Cm 4444, paras. 17 and 19.

which fall within the responsibility of the devolved administrations'. For ministers, there will be the JMC in European format (with an EU official sub-committee). Attendance at relevant council meetings will be determined by the lead UK minister on a case-by-case basis: 'The role of Ministers and officials from the devolved administrations will be to support and advance the single UK negotiating line which they will have played a part in developing.'[210]

[27.] *32.* Role of the Secretary of State:

(a) to remain responsible for NIO matters not devolved to the Assembly, subject to regular consultation with the Assembly and [Assembly Secretaries/]Ministers;

(b) to approve and lay before the Westminster Parliament any Assembly legislation on reserved matters;

(c) to represent Northern Ireland interests in the United Kingdom Cabinet;

(d) to have the right to attend the Assembly at their invitation.

12.127 This is the second of three paragraphs on Belfast-London relations: paragraph 31 deals with ministers but more likely departments; this paragraph is about the secretary of state as a member of the United Kingdom executive; and paragraph 33 deals with legislation.

12.128 ANNOTATIONS

'Role of Secretary of State:'. Under the GOIA 1920, there was a lord lieutenant, and later a governor of Northern Ireland. The governor's functions were transferred to the secretary of state (SOS) for Northern Ireland with direct rule in 1972.[211] The office of governor was abolished, but that of SOS retained, in the NICA 1973. During the 28 years of the office, the SOS has been involved as a direct-rule governor (providing the legislation from Westminster, but leaving the administration to the Northern Ireland departments).

'(a) to remain responsible for NIO matters not devolved to the Assembly, subject to regular consultation with the Assembly and Ministers;'. Devolved matters are all those not excepted or not reserved: schedules 2 and 3 of the NIA 1998. The SOS is therefore responsible, individually or collectively through the cabinet, for excepted and reserved matters. Northern Ireland remains a part of the United Kingdom, and, given the limited nature of devolution, the office of secretary of state – which has always been more important than governor – is likely to continue. There have been suggestions that Scotland, Wales and Northern Ireland might become one secretaryship, with territorial junior ministers. The fact that Northern Ireland is somewhat exceptional may count against any merger of cabinet positions. Subject to regular consultation with the Assembly and Ministers is nothing new. Consultation is entirely within the discretion of the SOS. It is also part of the practice of the United Kingdom state, though occasionally waived for one reason or another. Consultation rarely satisfies the consultees, while the consultor remains free to do what he wants.

'(b) to approve and lay before the Westminster parliament any Assembly legislation on reserved matters;'. This has been discussed above under paragraph 27. The consent – not approval – of the SOS is necessary if the Assembly legislates on a reserved matter, under section 8(2) of the NIA 1998. Section 15 provides for parliamentary control: laid before parliament for 20 days (subject to annulment).

'(c) to represent Northern Ireland interests in the United Kingdom Cabinet;'. This is a formal statement of an aspect of the SOS's responsibility. However, there is nothing in the Belfast Agreement, nor in the NIA 1998, to indicate how Northern Ireland could express an

210 *Memorandum of Understanding and supplementary agreements*, Cm 4444, para. B3.14.
211 Northern Ireland (Temporary Provisions) Act 1972 s 1(1)(a).

interest: through the First Minister and Deputy First Minister, the executive committee, the Assembly? At the same time, the SOS is required to participate in decision-making in the United Kingdom executive, taking into account a wide range of matters. Given the remaining powers of the SOS, and the much greater significance of the United Kingdom government, it is just as likely that the the SOS will represent greater United Kingdom interests to the Northern Ireland administration.

'(d) to have the right to attend the Assembly at their invitation.' This role is contradictory. If the SOS has a right, then it must rest somewhere. There is nothing in the NIA 1998 granting such a right. (Section 76 of the Government of Wales Act 1998, in contrast, states that the Welsh secretary shall be entitled to attend and participate in any proceedings of the assembly.) Nor is there anything in standing orders. At their (its?) invitation cancels out any notion of a right. On the other hand, the assembly may invite – it cannot compel.

[28.] ***33.*** **The Westminster Parliament (whose power to make legislation for Northern Ireland would remain unaffected) will:**

(a) legislate for non-devolved issues, other than where the Assembly legislates with *the* approval of the Secretary of State and subject to *the* control of Parliament;

(b) to legislate as necessary to ensure *the* United Kingdom's international obligations are met in respect of Northern Ireland;

(c) scrutinise, including through the Northern Ireland Grand and Select Committees, the responsibilities of the Secretary of State.

12.129 This third paragraph deals with legislation, principally the powers of the sovereign parliament.

12.130 ANNOTATIONS

'The Westminster Parliament (whose power to make legislation for Northern Ireland would remain unaffected) will:'. This is a statement of parliamentary sovereignty, or the legislative supremacy of parliament. Section 75 of the GOIA 1920 was due for repeal under Annex A of Constitutional Issues. But this opening phrase of the paragraph – by virtue of the MPA being Annex 1 of the BIA (and article 2 thereof) – indicates that the United Kingdom government, and the Irish government, were affirming Westminster legislative supremacy. They were more agreed on paragraph 33 of Strand One than on Annex A. But this did not reassure critics of the Belfast Agreement, who believed that the repeal of section 75 – with what is left of the GOIA 1920 – ended United Kingdom sovereignty over Northern Ireland. As noted in Chapter 3, the GOIA 1920 was not repealed until the BIA, including this paragraph, entered into force on 2 December 1999. Furthermore, section 5(6) of the NIA 1998, which came into force on devolution day under section 3(1), states in part: 'This section does not affect the power of the Parliament of the United Kingdom to make laws for Northern Ireland ... .' Further, in the MoU of October 1999, the four adminstrations agreed: 'The United Kingdom Parliament retains authority to legislate on any issue, whether devolved or not. It is ultimately for Parliament to decide what use to make of that power. However, the UK Government will proceed in accordance with the convention that the UK Parliament would not normally legislate with regard to devolved matters except with the agreement of the devolved legislature. The devolved administrations will be responsible for seeking such agreement as may be required for this purpose on an approach from the UK Government.'[212]

'(a) legislate for non-devolved issues, other than where the Assembly legislates with the approval of the Secretary of State and subject to the control of Parliament;'. The Westminster parliament, by virtue of parliamentary sovereignty, can legislate for Northern

212 *Memorandum of Understanding and supplementary agreements*, Cm 4444, para. 13.

Ireland – full stop. It does not need the opening of this paragraph, or section 5(6) of the NIA 1998, or the MoU. It can therefore legislate for non-devolved issues, the excepted and reserved matters under the NIA 1998. This part of this paragraph is saying that Westminster – which passed the NIA 1998 – will not legislate for transferred matters (that is what devolution is about). But it is going slightly further, and reaffirming paragraph 27 above, which specifies assembly legislation on reserved matters, with SOS consent and parliamentary control (sections 8 and 15 of the NIA 1998). Does this mean that Westminster has given up the right to legislate for such reserved matters, as well as all the transferred matters? On the former, the SOS can withhold consent, and parliament can exercise control even if there is consent. On the latter, Westminster can only amend or repeal the NIA 1998, to bring back some or all transferred matters (most easily by adding them to schedule 3 listing the reserved matters). But, as the sovereign parliament, it has full powers to do so. Devolution did not see the end of orders in council in 1973,[213] and sections 84–86 of the NIA 1998 reenact these; section 84 deals with district council elections and boundaries, section 85 with reserved matters (paragraphs 9–17 of schedule 3), and section 86 with consequential provisions.

'(b) to legislate as necessary to ensure the United Kingdom's international obligations are met in respect of Northern Ireland;'. The United Kingdom state, by virtue of international law, has obligations. Some of these stem from the rule of law internationally; others – most – from agreements entered into by the state. (By virtue of article 2 of the BIA, the United Kingdom accepted an obligation to implement the MPA in Annex 1, mainly by incorporating the Belfast Agreement by means of the NIA 1998; Strands Two and Three of the MPA are also international obligations of the United Kingdom state.) Obligations belong to the state, and therefore apply – as it were – to all parts. A specific international agreement – like the BIA – may deal with one part of the state. But it is not a Northern Ireland obligation; it is a United Kingdom one: and it binds all devolved administrations.

This part of this paragraph is strangely drafted. It seems to be referring to legislation in general – 'as necessary' – to fulfil an international obligation respecting Northern Ireland. Meeting an obligation may, or may not, require legislation. It can only mean that the existence of international obligations is to be written into the devolution legislation, with the consequence that the United Kingdom government has to do certain things in Northern Ireland to fulfil international obligations.

Sections 26 and 27 of the NIA 1998 deal with international obligations (in terms much stronger than apply to Scotland[214] and Wales[215]). There was nothing like this in the GOIA 1920 and the NICA 1973. But Westminster had the power to legislate – if a minister did not have it – to compel or restrain the Northern Ireland administration. (*Notes on Clauses*[216] admits this does not exist in the Belfast Agreement, but states that the need for the powers flows from the fact that 'international relations etc.' are not a devolved responsibility; note the etc.) Though the comment may not apply to devolution legislation (because Westminster remains sovereign), the powers given the secretary of state – under the guise of international agreements – certainly resemble the so-called Henry VIII clauses criticized by the courts from the second half of the nineteenth century.[217]

Section 26 (international obligations) gives the SOS the power by order to direct a minister or department not to take a proposed action, if it 'would be incompatible with any international obligations [as defined in section 98], with the interests of defence or national

213 NICA 1973 ss 38 & 39.
214 Scotland Act 1998 s 58 (power to prevent or require action).
215 Government of Wales Act 1998 s 108 (international obligations).
216 NIO October 1998.
217 *R v Minister of Health, ex parte Wortley Rural District Council* [1927] 2 KB 229, 236 per Lord Hewart CJ.

security or with the protection of public safety or public order'. There is also a power to direct that a minister or department does take action to comply. These powers – especially the latter – are considerable, and give the SOS a potentially powerful role in Northern Ireland government.[218] He can direct that a bill be introduced in the assembly, and that subordinate legislation be not made (or, if made, revoked).

This section may have been modelled on that in the Scottish act. However, there, the SOS has to have 'reasonable grounds'. Further, there is no similar reference to the interests of defence or national security,[219] or to the protection of public safety or public order. These are not international obligations (though they may have a bearing).

Section 27 (quotas for purposes of international, etc., obligations[220]) allows a minister of the crown to specify a Northern Ireland quota contribution to a United Kingdom international obligation or obligation under European law.

'(c) scrutinise, including through the Northern Ireland Grand and Select Committees, the responsibilities of the Secretary of State.' Scrutiny is one of the functions of the Westminister parliament. The secretary of state, as a member of the United Kingdom government, is accountable to parliament.

The Northern Ireland grand committee – Scotland and Wales also have one each – is a house of commons standing committee (which generally debate and consider public bills at the committee stage). The Scottish committee comprises all 72 MPs from Scotland. The Welsh one has the 40 MPs plus up to five others. The Northern Ireland committee, while it has all 18 MPs, also has up to 25 other members of parliament. It deals with bills relating exclusively to Northern Ireland. Following consultations, the then secretary of state, Sir Patrick Mayhew, informed Northern Ireland MPs in February 1997 that their grand committee would have a similar legislative role to the Scottish committee. Northern Ireland orders and orders in council, it was suggested, were to be taken from the standing committee on delegated legislation (which had only one local MP). Sir Patrick envisaged a dimunition in the role of the committee in the eventuality of devolution. A new government was elected on 1 May 1997. There has been little resort to the Northern Ireland grand committee in the 1997 parliament. The Northern Ireland affairs committee (a select committee) has 13 members, four of them from Northern Ireland. The current chairman is the Rt. Hon. Peter Brooke MP, a former secretary of state for Northern Ireland. It examines the expenditure and administration of the NIO, and associated public bodies. It publishes its minutes of evidence, reports and special reports – plus responses of government.

> **[29.] *34.* A consultative Civic Forum will be established. It will [be] comprise[d of] representatives of the business, trade union and voluntary sectors, and such other sectors as agreed by the First [Secretary/]Minister and Deputy First [Secretary/]Minister. It will act as a consultative mechanism on social, economic and cultural issues. The First [Secretary/]Minister and Deputy First [Secretary/]Minister will by agreement provide administrative support for the Civic Forum and establish guidelines for the selection of representatives to the Civic Forum.**

12.131 This paragraph has been added at the end of the relations with other institutions subsection. Strands One, Two and Three all have distinct institutions. Paragraph 30 deals with Strands Two and Three. Paragraphs 31–3 take up the Strand One issues not covered in the first five subsections (essentially the Belfast-

218 There is a similar power to allow the SOS not to submit a bill for royal assent.

219 They are specified in s 58(4)(a).

220 There is no equivalent in the Scotland Act 1998; there is in the Government of Wales Act 1998 – section 108.

London relations which were overshadowed initially by reference to internal relations). The civic forum is part of internal relations. But, having no formal role in the government of Northern Ireland, it was not dealt with as a Strand One institution. It sits uneasily at the end of this subsection as another institution of the Belfast Agreement.

12.132 ANNOTATIONS

'A consultative Civic Forum will be established.' This is purely a consultative body; the word is used again later with reference to its function. It was strangely referred to in the transition as the consultative civic forum, when Civic Forum would seem to have been the intended name. This first sentence states simply that it will be established. Given that the Belfast Agreement is a treaty, the obligation belongs to one or both states parties. It is a United Kingdom government responsibility, since the civic forum is internal to Northern Ireland.

The civic forum was not established by the Belfast Agreement. Nor is it to be established by the NIA 1998. (The assembly, of course, was established – as the New Northern Ireland Assembly – by the Northern Ireland (Elections) Act 1998. Under section 4(5) of the NIA 1998, it became the Northern Ireland Assembly on the appointed day.)

The civic forum is not a statutory body. This is in spite of its inclusion in the NIA 1998 (oddly, following the Belfast Agreement, in part V, dealing with Strands Two and Three – though it is not listed in the title). Section 56(1) refers to it as 'the Forum', but subsection (4) defines it as 'the consultative Civic Forum established in pursuance of paragraph 34 of Strand One of the Belfast Agreement by the First Minister and the deputy First Minister acting jointly'. Section 56 transfers the obligation to the First Minister and Deputy First Minister. This section did not come into force at royal assent. It only happened on 2 December 1999.[221] Schedule 14 (transitional provisions) provides in paragraph 15 for section 56(1) arrangements (for obtaining from the forum its views) made and approved before commencement of that section having effect as if they had been made under the section. This proved unnecessary given that the civic forum had not been established by devolution day.

The secretary of state wrote on 29 June 1998, when referring matters to the assembly under section 1(2) of the Northern Ireland (Elections) Act 1998 (of the fourth and last matter): 'during the Assembly's shadow phase I am anxious to consult the First Minister and Deputy First Minister (and the Assembly more widely) so that arrangements can be put in place to secure the earliest appropriate establishment of the Civic Forum.'[222] Official advice was submitted relatively early on 18 August 1998 to the First Minister and Deputy First Minister. In their interim report of 14 September 1998, they set the goal of the civic forum being 'fully representative of society in Northern Ireland'.[223] On 18 January 1999, they reported that they 'had received considerably more correspondence on this topic that any other matter referred to [them]'.[224] On 15 February 1999, the First Minister and Deputy First Minister reported finally to the assembly. The civic forum was to have 60 members, plus a chairperson appointed by the First Minister and Deputy First Minister (it was also to be under their office). They are to nominate six members. Business and trade unions have seven each; the voluntary/community section 18 (30 per cent). The other sectors (sharing 22 seats) are: agriculture/fisheries; churches, culture, arts and sport; victims; community relations; and education. There are arrangements for securing nominations from consortia and other sectors, with gender, community background, geographical and age balance. A target date

221 Northern Ireland Act 1998 (Commencement No. 5) Order 1999, SI 1999/3209, article 2 and schedule.

222 New Northern Ireland Assembly, *Official Report*, vol. 1, p. 2, 1 July 1998.

223 New Northern Ireland Assembly, *Interim Report from the First Minister (Designate) and Deputy First Minister (Designate)*, NNIA 1, 14 September 1998, p. 8.

224 New Northern Ireland Assembly, *Report from the First Minister (Designate) and the Deputy First Minister (Designate)*, NNIA 6, 18 January 1999, p. 8.

of six months after the appointed day was set, and a formal review promised to report by the end of the following twelve months.[225] The assembly, on 16 February 1999, approved the proposals in relation to establishing the consultative civic forum by 78 votes to 28 on a simple majority.[226] Little action appears to have been taken after devolution on 2 December 1999. Any work on the civic forum was a victim of suspension on 12 February 2000.[227] Following restoration on 30 May 2000, the Deputy First Minister announced to the assembly on 19 June 2000 that the members would be appointed in September 2000 and the first plenary held in October 2000.[228]

'It will comprise representatives of the business, trade union and voluntary sectors, and such other sectors as agreed by the First Minister and the Deputy First Minister.' Details of the composition of the civic forum are given in the paragraph above.

'It will act as a consultative mechanism on social, economic and cultural issues.' This is the only definition of the function of the civic forum. Consultative has been repeated, having been used descriptively in the first sentence. The civic forum is the consultee. Section 56(1) of the NIA 1998 requires the First Minister and Deputy First Minister to make arrangements for obtaining from the forum its views. This is within their joint discretion. However, section 56(2) requires those arrangements to be approved by the assembly. Social, economic and cultural matters is the remit of the civic forum. This clearly rules out politics as such.

'The First Minister and the Deputy First Minister will by agreement provide administrative support for the Civic Forum and establish guidelines for the selection of representatives to the Civic Forum.' Administrative support for the civic forum was provided for in the joint report of 15 February 1999: 'The Civic Forum should operate under the aegis of the Office of the First Minister and Deputy First Minister, which will provide administrative support consisting of a secretariat and operating expenses, including members' expenses and consultancy fees.'[229] It had been intended originally to have liaision with the civic forum in the secretariat of the executive committee, but this was altered to 'Civic Forum (administrative and other arrangements, including secretarial support)' in the Office of the First Minister and Deputy First Minister.[230] The guidelines for the selection of representatives were listed in the report to the Assembly.[231] The word representative cannot be analogous to the members of the Assembly, all of whom were elected on 25 June 1998. The members of the civic forum will only be representative in the sense that arrangements for securing nominations from the consortia and other sectors – subject to review – were presented by the First Minister and Deputy First Minister and approved by the assembly.

Subheading: Transitional Arrangements

12.133 This subsection is the only one in the Belfast Agreement dealing with the transition between the assembly meeting for the first time and powers being devolved. Section 1(1) of the Northern Ireland (Elections) Act 1998 stated that the New Northern Ireland Assembly was established for 'the purpose of taking part in preparations to give effect to the agreement reached at the multi-party talks on

225 New Northern Ireland Assembly, *Report from the First Minister (Designate) and the Deputy First Minister (Designate)*, NNIA 7, 15 February 1999, pp. 8–14.

226 New Northern Ireland Assembly, *Official Report*, vol. 2, pp. 108–9, 16 February 1999.

227 Northern Ireland Act 2000 schedule para. 4(d).

228 Northern Ireland Assembly, *Official Report*, vol. 5, no. 5, p. 173, 19 June 2000.

229 New Northern Ireland Assembly, *Report from the First Minister (Designate) and the Deputy First Minister (Designate)*, NNIA 7, 15 February 1999, p. 13.

230 New Northern Ireland Assembly, *Report from the First Minister (Designate) and the Deputy First Minister (Designate)*, NNIA 7, Annexes 1a and 1b.

231 New Northern Ireland Assembly, *Report from the First Minister (Designate) and the Deputy First Minister (Designate)*, NNIA 7, p. 10.

Northern Ireland set out in Command Paper 3883'. Preparations were the transition. In the first letter of 29 June 1998 to the initial presiding officer, the secretary of state referred to 'the work of the new Assembly in both its "shadow" and substantive phases'. The second letter of the same date (drawing on paragraphs 7 and 8 of Strand Two) referred to 'the Northern Ireland transitional (or shadow) administration'.[232] Shadow is used only in paragraph 34 with reference to ministers; otherwise, the correct concept is of a transition. I will therefore refer to the transition to devolution in this book.

[30.] *35.* **The Assembly will meet first for the purpose of organisation, without legislative or executive powers, to resolve its standing orders and working practices and make preparations for the effective functioning of the Assembly, the British-Irish Council, and the North/South Ministerial Council and associated implementation bodies.** ***In this transitional period, those members of the Assembly serving as shadow Ministers shall affirm their commitment to non-violence and exclusively peaceful and democratic means and their opposition to any use or threat of force by others for any political purpose; to work in good faith to bring the new arrangements into being; and to observe the spirit of the Pledge of Office applying to appointed Ministers.***

12.134 The second sentence was added to the MDP.

12.135 ANNOTATIONS

'The Assembly will meet first for the purpose of organisation, without legislative or executive powers, to resolve its standing orders and working practices'. Without legislative or executive powers refers to the period leading up to the devolution order. Section 3(1) of the NIA 1998 states that if it appears to the secretary of state that sufficient progress has been made in implementing the Belfast Agreement, he shall lay before parliament the draft of an order in council appointing a day for the commencement of parts II and III (legislative powers and executive authorities). The assembly met first on 1 July 1998. It met thereafter on: 14 and 15 September, 5 October, 26 October, 9 November 14 and 15 December 1998; and 18 January 1999, 1 February, 15 and 16 February, 22 February, 1 March, 8 and 9 March – a total of 16 sitting days (as defined in standing orders). Devolution, however, did not come as intended on 10 March 1999. The Assembly met subsequently on 15 July 1999, but there was no devolution then either. Following meetings on 29 and 30 November, devolution ensued on 2 December 1999.

The word first does not imply any particular number of meetings of the assembly.

The purpose of organisation seems to refer generally to the transition. It encompasses all that follows.

To resolve its standing orders involved: appointment on 1 July 1998 by 76 votes to 27 of an 18-member standing orders committee (under ISO 15, plus the initial agenda in annex A);[233] an interim report to the assembly on 14 September 1998,[234] and a motion carried without division (ruled as meeting the cross-community requirement) granting leave for the presentation of the full report on 26 October 1998;[235] presentation of a progress report on

232 New Northern Ireland Assembly, *Official Report*, vol. 1, pp. 1–2, 1 July 1998.
233 New Northern Ireland Assembly, *Official Report*, vol. 1, pp. 24–33, 1 July 1998.
234 New Northern Ireland Assembly, *Interim Report from the Committee on Standing Orders*, NNIA 2, 14 September 1998.
235 New Northern Ireland Assembly, *Official Report*, vol. 1, pp. 86–93, 14 September 1998.

26 October 1998,[236] which was noted;[237] presentation eventually of the final report on 8 March 1999,[238] followed by two days of debate and voting to approve the standing orders.[239] Nothing more was heard from the standing orders committee. However, on 6 December 1999, after devolution, the two former chairmen, Fred Cobain and Denis Haughey, proposed a number of amendments to standing orders. These were agreed with cross-community support: 68 votes for (34 nationalists, 27 unionists and 7 other); and 3 against (all unionists).[240]

And working practices is not clear. Among the other preparations made by the assembly were: decision on 1 July 1998 to appoint a committee to advise the presiding officer – which came to be known as CAPO[241] – in accord with ISO 16; appointment of a six-member shadow commission on 14 September 1998,[242] whose report[243] was approved by the assembly on 22 February 1999;[244] appointment of an ad hoc committee on procedural consequences of devolution (under ISO 15), in response to a request for representations from the procedure committee of the house of commons;[245] presentation of an interim report on 5 October 1998,[246] and a final report on 9 November 1998,[247] the assembly taking note of the former,[248] and approving the final report;[249] agreement on 22 February 1999 to accept recommendations of the senior salaries review body in respect of ministers and members' salaries and allowances;[250] regulation of all-party assembly groups;[251] presentation of a code of conduct plus guide to the rules,[252] including provision for a register of members' interests, agreed by the assembly on 1 March 1999;[253] publication of the register of members' interests on 1 June 1999[254] (with a second edition in June 2000[255]); publication on 22 July 1999 of the report of the ad hoc committee on the port of Belfast[256] (which was agreed retrospectively by the Assembly).[257]

236 New Northern Ireland Assembly, *Progress Report from the Committee on Standing Orders*, NNIA 4, 26 October 1998.

237 New Northern Ireland Assembly, *Official Report*, vol. 1, pp. 195–207, 26 October 1998.

238 New Northern Ireland Assembly, *Report of the Committee on Standing Orders*, NNIA 9(i) and (ii), 8 March 1999.

239 New Northern Ireland Assembly, *Official Report*, vol. 2 pp. 197–235, 237–89 and 291–309, 8 and 9 March 1999.

240 Northern Ireland Assembly, *Official Report*, vol. 4, no. 1, pp. 1–7, 6 December 1999.

241 New Northern Ireland Assembly, *Offical Report*, vol. 1, pp. 37–8, 1 July 1998.

242 New Northern Ireland Assembly, *Official Report*, vol. 1, pp. 78–80, 14 September 1998.

243 New Northern Ireland Assembly, *Report of the Shadow Assembly Commission*, NNIA 8, 22 February 1999.

244 New Northern Ireland Assembly, *Official Report*, vol. 2, pp. 121–46, 22 February 1999.

245 New Northern Ireland Assembly, *Official Report*, vol. 1, pp. 81–6, 14 September 1998.

246 New Northern Ireland Assembly, *Interim Report of the Ad Hoc Committee on the Procedural Consequences of Devolution*, NNIA 3, 5 October 1998.

247 New Northern Ireland Assembly, *Report of the Ad Hoc Committee on the Procedural Consequences of Devolution*, NNIA 5, 9 November 1998.

248 New Northern Ireland Assembly, *Official Report*, vol. 1, pp. 155–62, 5 October 1998.

249 New Northern Ireland Assembly, *Official Report*, vol. 1, pp. 257–73, 9 November 1998.

250 New Northern Ireland Assembly, *Official Report*, vol. 2, pp. 146–8, 22 February 1999.

251 New Northern Ireland Assembly, *Official Report*, vol. 2, pp. 149–52, 22 February 1999.

252 New Northern Ireland Assembly, *The Code of Conduct together with The Guide to the Rules Relating to the Conduct of Members*, NIA 1, 1 March 1999.

253 New Northern Ireland Assembly, *Official Report*, vol. 2, pp. 169–84, 1 March 1999.

254 New Northern Ireland Assembly, *Register of Members' Interests as at 21st May 1999*, NNIA 11, 1 June 1999.

255 Northern Ireland Assembly, *Register of Members' Interests*, 2nd edn, 27 June 2000.

256 New Northern Ireland Assembly, *Report of the Ad Hoc Committee (Port of Belfast)*, NNIA 12, 22 July 1999.

257 New Northern Ireland Assembly, *Official Report*, vol. 3, no. 2, p. 36, 30 November 1999.

'and make preparations for the effective functioning of the Assembly, the British-Irish Council and the North/South Ministerial Council and associated implementation bodies.' Preparations is the word used in section 1(1) of the Northern Ireland (Elections) Act 1998. Effective functioning implies that these four institutions are to operate on devolution day. The word function is used of the implementation bodies in paragraph 10 of Strand Two. The Assembly is the principal institution in Strand One; the British-Irish Council in Strand Three (see further in Chapter 16); and the North/South Ministerial Council and the implementation bodies in Strand Two (see further in Chapters 13 and 14).

'In this transitional period, those members of the Assembly serving as shadow Ministers shall affirm their commitment to non-violence and exclusively peaceful and democratic means and their opposition to any use or threat of force by others for any political purpose; to work in good faith to bring the new arrangements into being; and to observe the spirit of the Pledge of Office applying to appointed Ministers.'

This second sentence was added to the MDP. Under transitional arrangements, there was no reference to forming the executive committee. (And the only reference to ministers in the transition in Strand One is paragraph 16, which does not expressly state that there should be shadow ministers before devolution.) The idea of shadow ministers does exist in the second sentence. But the context is imposing the controls that would apply after devolution.

'In this transitional period,' is referring to the first sentence, and defining it as a transition.

'those members of the Assembly serving as shadow Ministers' introduces the concept of shadow ministers. They are not required for the transition, though there was the option of a shadow executive committee if sufficient progress was made.

'shall affirm their commitment to non-violence and exclusively peaceful and democratic means' is (b) in the pledge of office (Annex A to Strand One). Clearly, the fear had to do with Sinn Féin taking one or more ministerial offices. Thus, the application – by this sentence – of the pledge of office to the transition.

'and their opposition to any use or threat of force by others for any political purpose;' reinforces the point above. However, opposition to use or threat of force is not an express term of the pledge of office. This only strengthens the point that the possibility of Sinn Féin shadow ministers was an important issue at Castle Buildings.

'to work in good faith to bring the new arrangements into being;' is a modification to the transition of the pledge in paragraph 5 of the Declaration of Support.

'and to observe the spirit of the Pledge of Office applying to appointed Ministers.' This confirms that the concern was the non-applicability of the pledge of office in the transition. This paragraph applies the spirit from the point at which paragraph 16 produces a d'Hondt nomination.

This sentence inspired ISO 14(6), whereby, upon the election of the First Minister and Deputy First Minister, they had to affirm – separately[258] though this is not stated – (a) commitment to non-violence and exclusively peaceful and democratic means; (b) opposition to any use or threat of force by others for political purposes; (c) commitment to work in good faith to bring into being the arrangements set out in agreement reached in the multi-party negotiations on 10 April 1998; and (d) commitment to observe the spirit of the pledge of office (which was annexed to the initial standing orders).

Subheading: Review

12.136 The idea of review exists in the last section of the Belfast Agreement, Validation, Implementation and Review (paragraphs 5–8). (This is also the last section of the MPA.) Paragraph 5 provides for each institution reviewing itself, consulting the relevant government or governments. 'It will be for each institution

258 New Northern Ireland Assembly, *Official Report*, vol. 1, p. 23, 1 July 1998.

to determine its own procedures for review.' Thus the Review subsection of Strand One is arguably a restatement of a general principle. However, review – in the transition – is also dealt with in Validation, Implementation and Review. Paragraph 4 reads: 'In the interim, aspects of the implementation of the multi-party agreement will be reviewed at meetings of those parties relevant in the particular case (taking into account, once Assembly elections have been held, the results of those elections), under the chairmanship of the British Government or the two Governments, as may be appropriate; and representatives of the two Governments and all relevant parties may meet under independent chairmanship to review implementation of the agreement as a whole.'

12.137 Did paragraph 36 apply to the transition? If it did, it has to be read along with paragraph 4 in Validation, Implementation and Review. There is no basis – given there is no reason to restrict paragraph 36 of Strand One to devolution – for reading only paragraph 4 of Validation, Implementation and Review. That would be to ignore paragraph 36 in a Strand One which deals extensively with the transition.

[31.] *36.* **After a specified period there will be a review of these arrangements, including the details of electoral arrangements and of the Assembly's procedures, with a view to agreeing any adjustments necessary in the interests of efficiency and fairness.**

12.138 ANNOTATIONS

'After a specified period' says nothing. A period is any length of time.

'there will be a review of these arrangements,' suggests a freestanding Strand One review. The word will in a treaty is mandatory. Paragraph 4 of Validation, Implementation and Review suggests a different procedure in the interim. Paragraph 36 has to be read arguably with that transition provision. These arrangements embrace the totality of Strand One as specified in the above 35 paragraphs.

'including the details of electoral arrangements and of the Assembly's procedures,'. These are instances, but review is not confined to either or both. Electoral arrangements must refer to members of the assembly. Section 3 of the Northern Ireland (Elections) Act 1998 provides for vacancies following the 25 June 1998 election, the secretary of state doing this by order by reference to byelections or substitutes or such other method as he thinks fit. This has been reenacted in section 35(1)–(2) of the NIA 1998. The act provides further for: dates of elections and dissolutions (section 31); extraordinary elections (section 32); constituencies and numbers of members (section 33); elections and franchise (section 34). However, under paragraph 12 of schedule 2, elections, including the franchise, to inter alia the assembly, are an excepted matter. The assembly's procedures must be a reference to standing orders. The introduction to the 9 March 1999 set states: 'It is the Committee [on Standing Orders'] intention that Standing Orders will undergo further development in the future ... . '

'with a view to agreeing any adjustments necessary in the interests of efficiency and fairness.' With a view to agreeing is the purpose of a review. Any adjustments necessary is as vague as electoral arrangements and Assembly procedures, though there is an argument that adjustments is modification and not major surgery. In the interests of efficiency and fairness are two wide-ranging justifications.

13

Annex A

13.1 Annex A is attached to the Strand One section of the Belfast Agreement (there is no annex B). It is not, however, listed in the table of contents. It is at page 10 of Cm 3883 and pages 20–21 of Cm 4705 (pages 14–15 of the 1999 Irish version).

13.2 This annex is related to paragraph 23 in Strand One (discussed in Chapter 12). It was added to the MDP at Castle Buildings, replacing the idea of a code of practice – to be drawn up by the assembly on a cross-community basis – to 'codify and build upon the provisions of this agreement [that is, the MPA.]'.[1] The Pledge of Office (including Code of Conduct) is also mentioned in paragraphs 25 and 35 of Strand One.

13.3 Annex A has been incorporated directly into the NIA 1998, at schedule 4. The Pledge of Office is mentioned in sections 16(4)(a) and (10), 18(8) and 19(2)(b), dealing with the appointment of the First Minister and Deputy First Minister, the Northern Ireland ministers and any junior ministers.

13.4 The Pledge of Office was also included, as annex B, in the initial standing orders of 29 June 1998. (ISO 14(6) was based on paragraph 35 of Strand One.) It was not included in the 9 March 1999 edition of standing orders.

13.5 There are two related problems with the Pledge of Office: one, what is the status of the Code of Conduct appended?; two, is this the Ministerial Code of Conduct referred to at (g)? The solutions help answer the question about the drafts of a Northern Ireland ministerial code, produced by the NIO in the early months of 1999. Following devolution, this was considered by the executive committee at its first meeting on 2 December 1999. On 19 June 2000 – after suspension – the Deputy First Minister told the assembly, in reply to a question, that the executive committee had adopted a ministerial code.[2]

13.6 The answer to the first problem is in section 16(10) of the NIA 1998: 'In this Act the "pledge of office" means the pledge of office which, together with the code of conduct to which it refers, is set out in Annex A ... reproduced in Schedule 4 ... .' The Code of Conduct is not part of the Pledge of Office, but it is attached. A court would most likely construe Annex A to Strand One in the Belfast Agreement similarly.

13.7 The answer to the second problem requires Annex A to be construed. Point (g) in the Pledge of Office refers to 'the Ministerial Code of Conduct'. There follows a text headed: 'Code of Conduct', the opening words of which are: 'Ministers must at all times:'. This Code of Conduct is the Ministerial Code of Conduct. There is no

1 Paragraph 20 of the MDP.

2 Northern Ireland Assembly, *Official Report*, vol. 5, no. 5, p. 174, 19 June 2000.

reference in the Belfast Agreement to any additional text to be drawn up subsequently.

13.8 Doubt must be cast on the NIO's draft ministerial code. This would seem to be the code of practice for ministers in the MDP – to be drawn up by the assembly – which never made it into the Belfast Agreement. It may be desirable to have such a document; the point is simply that the NIO cannot invoke the Belfast Agreement, and cite section 16(10) of the NIA 1998, to legitimize its work.

13.9 The United Kingdom *Ministerial Code*, published by the cabinet office in July 1997, is both a code of conduct (similar to code of practice in the MDP) and guidance on procedures for ministers. Paragraph 1 (ministers of the crown) follows the terms of a house of commons resolution on ministerial accountability of 19 March 1997. It is the most appropriate source for any Northern Ireland ministerial code, suitably adapted to take account of the devolved administration provided for in the Belfast Agreement.

13.10 Paragraph 1 requires 'the highest standards of constitutional and personal conduct in the performance of [ministerial] duties'. There follow nine principles of conduct: collective responsibility; parliamentary accountability; not knowingly misleading parliament; a public interest defence for resisting openness; officials required to be as helpful as possible to parliamentary committees; no conflict between public duties and private interests; restrictions on gifts and hospitality; separation of the roles of minister and constituency member; no use of resources for party political purposes. 'These notes should be read [states the *Ministerial Code*] against the background of the duty of Ministers to comply with the law, including international law and treaty obligations, and to uphold the administration of justice, the general obligations listed above; and in the context of protecting the integrity of public life.'

Subheading: PLEDGE OF OFFICE

13.11 This is the first text in Annex A. It is introduced in paragraph 23 of Strand One, and mentioned in paragraphs 25 and 35.

To pledge:

- **(a) to discharge in good faith all the duties of office;**
- **(b) commitment to non-violence and exclusively peaceful and democratic means;**
- **(c) to serve all the people of Northern Ireland equally, and to act in accordance with the general obligations on government to promote equality and prevent discrimination;**
- **(d) to participate with colleagues in the preparation of a programme for government;**
- **(e) to operate within the framework of that programme when agreed wtihin the Executive Committee and endorsed by the Assembly;**
- **(f) to support, and to act in accordance with, all decisions of the Executive Committee and Assembly;**
- **(g) to comply with the Ministerial Code of Conduct.**

13.12 There are seven separate pledges here. They will be referred to as pledges (a)–(g).

13.13 ANNOTATIONS

'(a) to discharge in good faith all the duties of office;'. In good faith is not expressly required in the United Kingdom *Ministerial Code*. Northern Ireland – it is implied – has little experience of proper self-government. No doubt nationalists believe it is necessary to require unionists to operate in good faith. Unionists – given the inclusion of Sinn Féin in the involuntary coalition – certainly require a good faith pledge. All the duties of office are not specified. Those of the First Minister and Deputy First Minister are stated in paragraph 18 of Strand One to include coordinating the executive committee and responding to external relationships. Ministers are described in paragraph 14 of Strand One as having departmental responsibilities. And junior ministers – who appeared for the first time in the NIA 1998 – have their functions determined by the First Minister and Deputy First Minister. The United Kingdom *Ministerial Code* refers to the highest standards of constitutional and personal conduct in the performance of ministerial duties (without specifying the latter).

'(b) commitment to non-violence and exclusively peaceful and democratic means;'. This originated in the 1996 Mitchell principles of democracy and non-violence. Senator Mitchell and his two colleagues required 'total and absolute commitment' to six separate principles. The first was: 'to democratic and exclusively peaceful means of resolving political issues'. (The fifth principle also used this terminology.) The fourth principle was: 'to renounce for themselves, and to oppose any effort by others, to use force, or threaten to use force, to influence the course of the outcome of all-party negotiations'. The Mitchell international body juxtaposed democracy and violence. It reinforced – in the first principle – democracy with exclusively peaceful. And it isolated the threat or use of force in the fourth principle. Both principles ended up in paragraph 4 of the Declaration of Support: exclusively democratic and peaceful means; opposition to any use or threat or threat of force. Pledge (b) has abbreviated Mitchell. Thus, his title of democracy and non-violence has been shortened to non-violence. And his first principle has been rearranged to exclusively peaceful and democratic means. The second sentence of paragraph 35 of Strand One – with or without the text of pledge (b) – rendered Mitchell more faithfully. There is commitment to non-violence and exclusively peaceful and democratic means, but also opposition to the use or threat of force. ISO 14(6) required both the commitment to non-violence and the opposition to force.

'(c) to serve all the people of Northern Ireland equally, and to act in accordance with the general obligations on government to promote equality and prevent discrimination;'. This third pledge is the most general, containing the essence of ministerial duty. To serve all the people of Northern Ireland equally contains the basic notion of public service. However, this is particularized for Northern Ireland with 'all' and 'equally'; all means including the minority community, and equally taps the concept of equality. And to act in accordance with the general obligations on government must be a reference to the Northern Ireland assembly. (Government is also mentioned in pledge (d).) To promote equality and prevent discrimination refer to the Human Rights part of the Rights, Safeguards and Equality of Opportunity section. Equality is provided for in the United Kingdom Legislation and New Institutions in Northern Ireland subsections. Anti-discrimination legislation is specified in the Economic, Social and Cultural Issues part. The first anti-discrimination measure – based upon that in the first amendment to the constitution of the United States – was section 5 of the GOIA 1920 (prohibition of laws interfering with religious equality, taking property without compensation,[3] etc.). Laws enacted by the Northern Ireland parliament were to be void to the extent of contravention. No law was held to be discriminatory between 1921 and 1972, or subsequently. Section 8(6) also prohibited religious discrimination in the exercise

3 Northern Ireland courts interpreted this as referring to all property. This was the principal basis for challenging the validity of local acts: *O'Neill v NIRTB* [1938] NI 104; *Robb v Electricity Board for NI* [1937] NI 103.

of administration power. The NICA 1973 contained a part III, prevention of religious and political discrimination. This prohibited legislative discrimination 'against any person or class of persons' on the ground of 'religious belief or political opinion' (section 17). The secretary of state could refer legislation to the judicial committee of the privy council (section 18). Section 19 prohibited discrimination by public authorities. The standing advisory commission on human rights (SACHR) was established by section 20, to advise the secretary of state on the law against discrimination. These provisions – plus those on equality – have been extended in part VII of the NIA 1998 (sections 76–78).

'(d) to participate with colleagues in the preparation of a programme for government;'. This fourth pledge refers to paragraph 20 of Strand One – the second of two making for collegiality – but with greater force. The executive committee was only to seek to agree a programme incorporating an agreed budget linked to policies and programme. This has become, in the Pledge of Office, 'the preparation of a programme for government'. 'To participate with colleagues' does not specify achieving a programme of government, but the word colleagues suggests otherwise. This is confirmed by the next pledge.

'(e) to operate within the framework of that programme when agreed within the Executive Committee and endorsed by the Assembly;'. This relates to paragraph 19 of Strand One, the first paragraph on collegiality. However, that is considerably less certain: 'a forum for the discussion of, and agreement on, issues which cut across the responsibilities of two or more Ministers'; 'prioritising executive and legislative proposals'; 'recommending a common position where necessary'. The fifth pledge reinforces the fourth; a programme of government is the condition precedent. To operate within the framework of that programme is the principal constraint on ministers. Framework is the key word. If the programme reinforces this idea, then arguably ministers cannot operate outside the programme. But this raises the problem of departments – which are not specified in the Pledge of Office – having functions, and effectively the Northern Ireland civil service being the constraint upon ministers. When agreed within the Executive Committee means no agreement no programme; and nothing for ministers to do. And endorsed by the Assembly is the hurdle an executive committee agreement has to overcome. Endorsed is weaker than the approved the assembly has practised during the transition. Given a programme of government (certainly as defined in paragraph 20 of Strand One) must involve a budget, then under SO 25(2) (appropriations and taxation), a cross-community vote will be required at the legislative stage.

'(f) to support, and to act in accordance with, all decisions of the Executive Committee and Assembly;'. This sixth pledge reinforces collegiality – following the fourth and fifth – though the reference to the assembly undermines to some extent the idea of an executive branch of government. This is much stronger than paragraphs 19 and 20 of Strand One. To support, and to act in accordance with requires a minister, not only to avoid single-mindedness, but to follow a collective position. The idea of support implies a degree of affirmation, not merely desisting from acting contrary to a decision. All decisions of the Executive Committee makes for a cabinet – whether the executive committee comes to be called the executive, the government or something else. And Assembly embraces two ideas: executive committee decisions – like the programme of government – which need to be approved by the Assembly; and decisions initiated by the Assembly. Given, of course, that 90 members of the Assembly belong to the four parties comprising the executive committee, the remaining 18 – who include eight anti-agreement unionists – are unlikely to be able to carry through successfully an assembly initiative.

'(g) to comply with the Ministerial Code of Conduct.' This seventh pledge is of considerable significance. It incorporates by reference in the Pledge of Office, the Ministerial Code of Conduct. That is why Annex A is the Pledge of Office plus the Code of Conduct: section 16(10) of the NIA 1998. There is little doubt that the Code of Conduct – the text following – is the Minsterial Code of Conduct; it begins: 'Ministers must at all times:'. While it refers to other documents,[4] there is no basis in Annex A for the ministerial code developed by the Northern Ireland civil service (the eighth tiret refers to any rules that might be offered, though it is not specified by whom).

Subheading: CODE OF CONDUCT

13.14 The concept in the MDP was a code of practice, so-called quasi-legislation – rules, statutory and non-statutory, drawn up by government departments. The idea of a code of practice – for departments, committees and chairmen, and the assembly – first appeared in the United Kingdom contribution to the 1995 *Framework Documents.*[5] The code was to be 'reflected' in the standing orders.

13.15 The idea of codes of conduct – including a ministerial code – stems from the appointment of the committee on standards in public life chaired by Lord Nolan (the Nolan committee) in October 1994. This followed concerns about unethical conduct by politicians at Westminster, including taking cash for asking parliamentary questions.

13.16 The Nolan committee's first report[6] – in May 1995 – looked at MPs, ministers, civil servants and quangos. Its recommendations included a parliamentary commissioner for standards, and a new committee on standards and privileges. Nolan concluded that the entire public service needed: seven principles of public life, codes of conduct incorporating those principles, independent scrutiny and education (in standards).

13.17 Ministers and civil servants – the executive – were considered together. Nolan noted a recently announced code of conduct for civil servants. It appeared in January 1996. Ministers then had *Questions of Procedure for Ministers,*[7] a document which had remained confidential until 1992. It was the Nolan committee which recommended amending the crucial paragraph 1 discussed above: principles of ministerial conduct. Nolan also recommended a free-standing code of conduct for ministers. The *Ministerial Code* published on the instructions of the prime minister in the summer of 1997 was subtitled: *a code of conduct and guidance on procedures for ministers.*

Ministers must at all times:

- **observe the highest standards of propriety and regularity involving impartiality, integrity and objectivity in relationship to the stewardship of public funds;**
- **be accountable to users of services, the community and, through the Assembly, for the activities within their responsibilities, their stewardship of public funds and the extent to which key performance targets and objectives have been met;**
- **ensure all reasonable requests for information from the Assembly, users of services and individual citizens are complied with; and that Departments and their staff conduct their dealings with the public in an open and responsible way;**

4 The first report of the committee on standards in public life and the register of interests.

5 Part I, paragraph 17.

6 First Report of the Committee on Standards in Public Life, *Standards in Public Life*, Volume 1: Report, Cm 2850-I, May 1995.

7 Cabinet Office 1992.

- **follow the seven principles of public life set out by the Committee on Standards in Public Life;**
- **comply with this code and with rules relating to the use of public funds;**
- **operate in a way conducive to promoting good community relations and equality of treatment;**
- **not use information gained in the course of their services for personal gain; nor seek to use the opportunity of public service to promote their private interests;**
- **ensure they comply with any rules on the acceptance of gifts and hospitality that might be offered;**
- **declare any personal or business interests which may conflict with their responsibilities. The Assembly will retain a Register of Interests. Individuals must ensure that any direct or indirect pecuniary interests which members of the public might reasonably think could influence their judgement are listed in the Register of Interests; [sic]**

13.18 ANNOTATIONS

'Ministers must at all times:'. It is not initially clear whether ministers includes the First Minister and Deputy First Minister. The Executive Authority subsection of Strand One does not provide absolute guidance. However, section 35 adapted the pledge of office to the transition. And, on 1 July 1998 – in accordance with ISO 14(6) – the First Minister and Deputy First Minister affirmed inter alia commitment to observe the spirit of the Pledge of Office (to which is attached the Code of Conduct). Section 16(4)(a) of the NIA 1998 requires the First Minister and Deputy First Minister to affirm the terms of the pledge of office (from their first election after devolution); this is defined in subsection (10) as including the Code of Conduct. Ministers includes the First Minister and Deputy First Minister; any alternative view would have the joint head of the executive governing without affirming a pledge of office.

'observe the highest standards of propriety and regularity involving impartiality, integrity and objectivity in relationship to the stewardship of public funds;'. Observe the highest standards follows from ministers must at all times. It is probably inspired by 'Ministers of the Crown are expected to behave according to the highest standards of constitutional and personal conduct': *Ministerial Code*, paragraph 1. Of propriety and regularity has been appropriated from paragraph 57 on accounting officers: 'The essence of the role is a *personal* responsibility for the propriety and regularity of the public finances for which he or she is responsible.' Propriety – conformity with convention in language and conduct – is unproblematic in the context of Northern Ireland. Regularity – a state of being regular – is more perplexing. It would seem to be an aspect of propriety, alluding to equal treatment. Involving impartiality, integrity and objectivity relates to the seven principles of public life restated by the Nolan committee. Impartiality, however, is not listed. The closest would seem to be the first sentence of the first principle, selflessness: 'Holders of public office should take decisions solely in terms of the public interest ... .' The public interest may be a difficult concept to apply in Northern Ireland (it means as defined by the NIO under direct rule). Integrity and objectivity are Nolan's second and third principles. Integrity is defined as: 'Holders of public office should not place themselves under any financial or other obligations to outside individuals or organisations that might influence them in the performance of their official duties.' Objectivity is defined as: 'In carrying out public business, including making public appointments, awarding contracts, or recommending individuals for rewards and benefits, holders of public office should make choices on merit.' In relationship to the stewardship of public funds is the first of two uses of this phrase. The first tiret of the Code of Conduct avoids the question of honour in paragraph 1 of the *Ministerial Code*, and reduces the principles of ministerial conduct to a question of propriety in the use of public finances.

'be accountable to users of services, the community and, through the Assembly, for the activities within their responsibilities, their stewardship of public funds and the extent to which key performance targets and objectives have been met;'. The key concept of this second tiret is accountability. This is the fourth of Nolan's principles of public life: 'Holders of public office are accountable for their decisions and actions to the public and must submit themselves to whatever scrutiny is appropriate to their office.' Accountability is also the second principle of ministerial conduct in paragraph 1 of the *Ministerial Code*: 'Ministers have a duty to Parliament to account, and be held to account, for the policies, decisions and actions of their Departments and Next Step Agencies;'. Accountability is defined more widely, and rhetorically, here. Be accountable to users of services has a connotation of local government (in keeping with the general constitutional view of the government of Northern Ireland not being run on central government principles). The community embraces users of services. It is also the one community of paragraph 1 of Strand One. Accountability to the community comes through elections. The New Northern Ireland Assembly was elected on 25 June 1998. Under section 31(2) of the NIA 1998, the next election is scheduled for 1 May 2003 (making a nearly five-year assembly). Thereafter, there are to be fixed assemblies of four years' duration. And, through the Assembly, takes us to the proper arena of accountability in a representative democracy. For the activities within their responsibilities recalls paragraph 24 of Strand One. Their stewardship of public funds is repeated from the first tiret. This is the first thing for which ministers are accountable. And the extent to which key performance targets and objectives have been met is the second area of ministerial responsibility. Key performance targets and objects relates to public sector management (throughout the United Kingdom). Each Northern Ireland department – as a substitute for a mission statement – has to set aims and also objectives. The latter are medium-term goals. Each year, a number of key challenges is set, and progress monitored.

'ensure all reasonable requests for information from the Assembly, users of services and individual citizens are complied with; and that Departments and their staff conduct their dealings with the public in an open and responsible way;'. This refers to openness, Nolan's fifth principle of public life: 'Holders of public office are accountable for their decisions and actions to the public and must submit themselves to whatever scrutiny is appropriate to their office.' It is also the fourth principle of ministerial conduct: 'Ministers should be as open as possible with Parliament and the public, refusing to provide information only when disclosure would not be in the public interest, which should be decided in accordance with relevant statute and the Government's Code of Practice and Access to Government Information (Second Edition, January 1997)'. This, of course, was in July 1997. The government was committed to freedom of information, and it is legislating.[8] Ensure all reasonable requests for information imposes a test – or defence – of reasonableness. This will be specified in the freedom of information act. From the Assembly is similar to the second tiret. The Assembly is simply another entity alongside civil society. SO 19 makes provision for oral and written questions to members of the executive committee in the Assembly. This includes the First Minister and Deputy First Minister, though there is no precedent in Strand One of the Belfast Agreement. However, it is consistent with section 21(3) of the NIA 1998, and the Departments (Northern Ireland) Order 1999, SI 1999/283. SO 20 deals with private notice questions. Users of services is the phrase already used in the second tiret. Users of services usually have statutory rights in the legislation dealing with the service in question. And individual citizens refers to public information, including freedom of information. And that Departments and their staff conduct their dealings with the public in

8 On 9 February 2000, the executive committee in Belfast agreed that the freedom of information bill should be extended to Northern Ireland: *Irish Times*, 10 February 2000. Freedom of information is a transferred matter. Paragraph 26(e) of Strand One allows the assembly to request inclusion in United Kingdom-wide legislation.

an open and responsible way is a rare reference to the Northern Ireland civil service in the Belfast Agreement (departments have been mentioned in Strand One with reference to ministers). This provision exists in a code for ministers given their formal responsibility for officials. It is another aspect of openness in the seven principles of public life. In addition, principle five of paragraph 1 of the *Ministerial Code* states that ministers should require their officials to be 'as helpful as possible' when giving evidence to parliamentary committees.

'follow the seven principles of public life set out by the Committee on Standards in Public Life;'. The Nolan committee has been discussed above; in November 1997, Lord Neill of Bladen QC took over as chairman of this standing body. It was the committee on standards in public life, in its first report in 1995, which laid down the seven principles of public life. These are held to apply across the entire public service. Though the seven principles of public life are specified at this tiret (without being listed), they are scattered thoughout the Code of Conduct without attribution.

'comply with this code and with rules relating to the use of public funds;'. Code is a reference to the Code of Conduct. Comply reinforces the other eight specific requirements. Rules relating to the use of public funds is the third reference to money. The location of the rules is not identified.

'operate in a way conducive to promoting good community relations and equality of treatment;'. This tiret has no counterpart in the seven principles of public life or paragraph 1 of the *Ministerial Code*. This is because it is of purely Northern Ireland provenance. Bad community relations had led the last prime minister of Northern Ireland, Brian Faulkner, to set up a department of community relations (there was also a commission at one remove from Stormont). The commission survived as a council; the department's functions were absorbed under direct rule by the department of finance and personnel. The central community relations unit (part of central secretariat) was due, under the 18 December 1998 agreement, to go to the office of the First Minister and Deputy First Minister. This became the position on 2 December 1999. Promoting good community relations has been an activity of government since 1971. It relates mainly to cultural and educational work. Ministers are required to operate in a way conducive to promoting good community relations; this includes not doing anything to make relations even more difficult. Equality of treatment is dealt with in the Human Rights part of the Rights, Safeguards and Equality of Opportunity section of the Belfast Agreement. Article 14 of the European convention on human rights – a convention right under the Human Rights Act 1998 – is not a provision for equality of treatment; it relates solely to discrimination in the enjoyment of convention rights. Part VII of the NIA 1998 provides for an equality commission (sections 73 and 74), dealing with equality of opportunity. Section 75 imposes a statutory duty on public authorities to have due regard to the need to promote equality of opportunity. Section 76 reenacts the anti-discrimination provisions of 1973.

'not use information gained in the course of their service for personal gain; nor seek to use the opportunity of public service to promote their private interests;'. This seventh tiret is an anti-corruption provision. Its source is most likely the second part of Nolan's first principle of public life: selflessness – '... [Holders of public office] should not [take decisions] in order to gain financial or other material benefits for themselves, their family, or their friends.' The Code of Conduct contains a strong anti-corruption provision. Not use information gained in the course of their service for personal gain also contains an element of confidentiality. Nor seek to use the opportunity of public service to promote their private interests reinforces the first point.

'ensure they comply with any rules on the acceptance of gifts and hospitality that might be offered;'. This accords with the seventh principle of ministerial conduct in paragraph 1 of the Ministerial Code: 'Ministers should avoid accepting any gift or hospitality which might, or might reasonably appear to, compromise their judgement or place them under an improper obligation;'. The eighth tiret does not specify any rules. The test in the *Ministerial*

Code is: might reasonably appear to compromise judgment or place a minister under an improper obligation. It is dealt with twice in the *Code*: one, in paragraph 85, under ministers' visits; two, in detail, in paragraphs 126–128. The reference to 'any rules' is the only point at which the Code of Conduct leaves open the possibility of a further text. However, no provision is made for it in Annex A.

'declare any personal or business interests which may conflict with their responsibilities. The Assembly will retain a Register of Interests. Individuals must ensure that any direct or indirect pecuniary interests which members of the public might reasonably think could influence their judgement are listed in the Register of Interests;'. This corresponds to the sixth principle of public life: honesty – 'Holders of public office have a duty to declare any private interests relating to their public duties and to take steps to resolve any conflicts arising in a way that protects the public interest.' The sixth principle of ministerial conduct in the *Ministerial Code* is: 'Ministers must ensure that no conflict arises, or appears to arise, between their public duties and their private interests;'. Declare any personal or business interests which may conflict with their responsibilities leaves it to the minister. This sentence must be interpreted along with the second: 'The Assembly will retain a Register of Interests.' Individuals must ensure that any direct or indirect pecuniary interests which members of the public might reasonably think could influence their judgement are listed in the Register of Interests makes its mandatory. Indirect pecuniary interests includes presumably members of a minister's family. The test is as in the *Ministerial Code* for gifts or hospitality, which members of the public might reasonably think could influence their judgement. The 9 March 1999 standing orders contains a section on standards and privileges. SO 62 deals with members' interests. SO 62(1) provides for a register of members' interests, listing the categories in the guide to the rules relating to the conduct of members. (This accompanied the code of conduct for members.[9] approved by the assembly without a vote on 1 March 1999.[10] This code of conduct for members incorporates all seven of the Nolan principles of public life. Members are required to fulfil conscientiously the requirements of the assembly in respect of the registration of interests. The rules are enforceable by the assembly. On 14 December 1999, following devolution, the assembly, in the absence of a transitional provision in schedule 14 of the NIA 1998, endorsed the 1 March 1999 decision; the speaker explained that the register of members' interests was now – under section 43 – mandatory.[11]) The register is open for public inspection. SO 62(2) requires each member to inform the clerk of standards of the details of his interests, changes being notified within four weeks. SO 62(3) requires members to declare any relevant pecuniary interest or benefit before participating in assembly or committee proceedings. 'An immediate relative' is expressly covered. SO 62(4) contains the paid advocacy (really non-advocacy) rule, included in the house of commons response of 6 November 1995 to Nolan's first report. Arranging or going as part of delegations, however, is not included in the standing order.[12] On 1 June 1999, Denis Arnold, the clerk of standards, published the *Register of Members' Interests as at 21st May 1999*.[13] This contained responses by only 68 of the 108 members: 17 of the 28 UUP members; 21 of the 24 SDLP; 15 of the 20 DUP; no Sinn Féin members; 5 of the 6 Alliance members; all 4 of the NIUP, all 3 of the UUAP; the 2 NIWC members; 1 of the 2 PUP members; and not the 1 UKUP member. The second edition of the *Register of Members'*

9 New Northern Ireland Assembly, *The Code of Conduct together with the Guide to the Rules relating to the Conduct of Members*, NIA 1.

10 New Northern Ireland Assembly, *Official Report*, vol. 2, pp. 169–84, 1 March 1999.

11 Northern Ireland Assembly, *Official Report*, vol. 4, no. 2 (reissue), pp. 148–9, 14 December 1999.

12 It is, however, covered by the 1 March 1999 assembly resolution, approving the code of conduct and guide to the rules relating to the conduct of members.

13 New Northern Ireland Assembly, NNIA 11. This is to be published annually. The updated register is available at: www.ni-assembly.gov.uk.

Interests was ordered to be printed by the committee on standards and privileges on 27 June 2000; all 108 members completed returns.

13.19 The Code of Conduct for ministers in the Belfast Agreement is an unacknowledged adaptation of the seven principles of public life. It contains the following: selflessness in the first and seventh tirets; integrity in the first tiret; objectivity again in the first tiret; accountability in the second tiret; openness in third tiret; and honesty in the ninth tiret. In addition, the seven principles of public life were cited in the fourth tiret. The only principle missing from the Code of Conduct is leadership: 'Holders of public office should promote and support these principles by leadership and example.'

14

Strand Two: North/South Ministerial Council

14.1 Strand Two is the fourth section of the Belfast Agreement. It is at pages 11–13 of Cm 3883 and pages 22–5 of Cm 4705 (pages 16–19 of the 1999 Irish version). The Annex will be considered in the next chapter (along with the – largely aspirational – history of practical cooperation[1]). At 19 paragraphs, Strand Two is overshadowed by Strand One (36 paragraphs); Strand Three (21 paragraphs) is also larger. [Deletions] to the MDP, and *additions* are shown thus.

14.2 Strand Two – along with Strand Three – is provided for in part V of the NIA 1998. Section 52 deals with the North-South Ministerial Council[2] and the British-Irish Council together. Section 53 covers any agreement or arrangement entered into by a Northern Ireland minister or junior minister. The British-Irish Intergovernmental Conference is dealt with in section 54. And implementation bodies – to be agreed by the NSMC before the appointed day – were provided for in section 55. (Section 56 on the civic forum has nothing to do with Strands Two or Three.)

14.3 The key legal instrument is the agreement between the United Kingdom and Irish governments establishing the North/South Ministerial Council (again?), done at Dublin on 8 March 1999[3] – one of the supplementary agreements relating to the BIA. This was presented to parliament by the foreign secretary in March 1999 as Cm 4294. The agreement was approved by Dáil Éireann (under article 29.5.2 of BNH) on 9 March 1999.[4] (Further provision was made in Irish law by section 3 of the British-Irish Agreement (BIA) Act 1999, promulgated on 22 March 1999.)

14.4 To this must be related the agreement during the transition on implementation bodies. On 18 December 1998, the First Minister and Deputy First Minister agreed six areas for cooperation and six implementation bodies. This was approved by the assembly on 18 January 1999 (the assembly took note subsequently of the same agreement, on 15 February 1999).[5]

1 This term occurs in article 10(c) of the 1985 Anglo-Irish Agreement. It was used by the prime minister, John Major, in his foreward to the 1995 *Framework Documents* (p. iv).

2 The Belfast Agreement refers to the North/South Ministerial Council, the NIA 1998 to the North-South Ministerial Council. The latter is more grammatical and more consistent. However, later legislation at Westminster and in the Oireachtas has reverted to the former convention.

3 Agreement between the Government of the United Kingdom of Great Britain and Northern Ireland and the Government of Ireland establishing a North/South Ministerial Council, Cm 4294, Ireland No. 3 (1999).

4 *Official Report.*

5 New Northern Ireland Assembly, *Report from the First Minister (Designate) and Deputy First Minister (Designate)*, NNIA 6, 18 January 1999 and NNIA 7, 15 February 1999.

14.5 This was followed by the international agreement between the United Kingdom and Irish governments establishing implementation bodies, done at Dublin again on 8 March 1999[6] – a second of the agreements supplementing the BIA. This was presented to parliament by the foreign secretary in March 1999 as Cm 4293. The agreement was approved by Dáil Éireann (under article 29.5.2 of BNH) on 9 March 1999.[7]

14.6 On 18 June 1999, by an exchange of notes,[8] the secretary of state and Irish foreign minister, referring to Part 4 of Annex 1 and Part 4 of Annex 2 (Special EU Programmes), agreed that, by community initiatives, they had intended to include any successor to the PEACE programme.[9] This agreement followed the Berlin European Council decision in March 1999 to categorize the successor programme as mainstream structural funding. The attorney general's office, and 'the British-Northern Ireland legal advisers', had raised a possibility of ultra vires if the point was not clarified.[10]

14.7 Provision was made in United Kingdom law by the North/South Co-operation (Implementation Bodies) (Northern Ireland) Order 1999, SI 1999/859 of 10 March 1999. This was made under section 55 of the NIA 1998, which had come into force on 19 November 1998. (See also the North/South Co-operation (Implementation Bodies) (Amendment) (Northern Ireland) Order 1999, SI 1999/2062, made on 19 July 1999, adding Schedule 1A to the original order.) Corresponding provision was made in Irish law by the British-Irish Agreement Act 1999, promulgated on 22 March 1999. (See also the British-Irish Agreement (Amendment) Act 1999, adding an interpretative schedule to the original act, which the president was requested to sign early under article 25.2.2 of BNH.)

14.8 Strand Two – in the typology of the talks – was about relationships 'within the whole island of Ireland'.[11] This phrase, of course, comes from article 2 of BNH. That Ireland is an island is an unremarkable geographical fact. The island of Ireland, however, is to be distinguished from the Ireland whose government ended the territorial claim (see Chapter 7). The Strand Two negotiations involved the United Kingdom and Irish governments, and the political parties; they were chaired by Senator Mitchell.

14.9 Given that Ireland had been an administrative entity until 1920, it is not surprising that practical cooperation between Belfast and Dublin remained an issue. It was, however, implicated in the political disagreement over partition; a strong nationalist cutting edge was to be given to what might have developed more naturally between neighbouring democracies.

6 Agreement between the Government of the United Kingdom of Great Britain and Northern Ireland and the Government of Ireland establishing Implementation Bodies, Cm 4293, Ireland No. 2 (1999).

7 *Official Report*.

8 But not under article 5, as the international agreement had not entered into force.

9 Schedule of the North/South Co-operation (Implementation Bodies) (Amendment) (Northern Ireland) Order 1999, SI 1999/2062, made on 19 July 1999. The agreement, under article 29.5.3 of Bunreacht na hÉireann, was not laid before Dáil Éireann.

10 It is not obvious that the problem has been solved; the issue is whether the successor programme was intended (not whether it was defined as a community initiative).

11 *Ground Rules for Substantive All-Party Negotiations*, Cm 3232, rule 2. Rule 1 uses the phrase 'the island of Ireland'.

An Irish dimension

14.10 Section 1 of the GOIA 1920 partitioned Ireland, giving it two regional parliaments within the United Kingdom. Section 3 provided for a power to reunite Ireland with an Irish parliament (so-called Irish union). It was to comprise his majesty and two houses. The means were identical acts, agreed by absolute majorities of the two houses of commons. These would be the constituent acts. Devolution is a relationship initiated by the centre; but the GOIA 1920 transferred the power to merge two regions on the basis of consent. It provided for a parliament – and government – of Ireland within the United Kingdom.

14.11 In the – foreseeable – interim, there was to be a council of Ireland. This was 'with a view to the eventual establishment of a Parliament for the whole of Ireland, and to bringing about harmonious action between the parliaments and governments of Southern Ireland and Northern Ireland, and to the promotion of mutual intercourse and uniformity in relation to matters affecting the whole of Ireland, and to providing for the administration of services which the two parliaments mutually agree should be administered uniformly throughout the whole of Ireland ...' (section 2(1)). These objectives, as the drafting indicates, were neither distinguished nor properly interrelated.

14.12 The council of Ireland was to comprise a president, nominated by the lord lieutenant, and 40 members, drawn from the two houses in both Belfast and Dublin (section 2(2)). Its constitution could be varied by identical acts of the two parliaments; direct election to the council of Ireland was a possibility (section 2(3)).

14.13 The idea of reserved matters (section 8) related to: one, the council of Ireland ceasing to exist on the date of Irish union; and two, a further transfer of powers from London to the new Irish parliament and government (section 3(2)). Reserved matters included principally the police (for three years), the post office and land purchase. Some could be transferred to the council of Ireland. The council was given immediately – by virtue of section 10(2) – all-Ireland powers in the areas of railways, fisheries and the contagious diseases of animals (but not at the expense of domestic jurisdiction). The two parliaments could also, by identical acts, delegate other powers to the council (section 10(1)). There was also a power to make orders respecting private bill legislation affecting Southern Ireland and Northern Ireland (section 7).

14.14 The idea of identical acts is fundamental to the GOIA's Irish dimension (to use a later term). In all the scenarios of 1920, all-Ireland relations were to be within the United Kingdom. There was no council of Ireland, because Southern Ireland declined to implement the act. Needless to say, there was no Irish union.

14.15 A new state was created in 1922, though, as a dominion, it took a number of years to become independent. In 1949, Éire/Ireland quit the commonwealth, and became the Republic of Ireland. There had been no identical acts – or legal possibility of such measures – between 1921 and 1949.

14.16 The Ireland Act 1949, which declared the Republic of Ireland to be not a foreign country (section 2(1)), proffered a new conception of an Irish dimension. Section 3(1)(a)(ii) referred to 'agreements or arrangements' between the Republic of Ireland and Northern Ireland. (Also included was the United Kingdom and the

Republic of Ireland, the east/west dimension.) This provision was retrospective to 1922 (and there was reference to any agreements or arrangements made after this act). Section 3 was about the continuing operation of statutes of the United Kingdom. Acts of the Northern Ireland parliament, giving effect to agreements or arrangements with the Irish Free State and/or Éire/Ireland, were unaffected – the Ireland Act 1949 purported – by the leaving of the commonwealth.

14.17 The high point of practical cooperation between Belfast and Dublin – despite the Irish cold war – was in the early 1950s. The legal means, however, seemed to follow the redundant identical acts model; acts of the Northern Ireland parliament and the Oireachtas. Insofar as (which is unlikely) this was the agreements and arrangements model, which Westminster considered the only one applicable given the formation of the Irish Free State in 1922, it was far from being legally appropriate for relations between two states; Northern Ireland had no power, in United Kingdom law, to enter into international agreements.

14.18 The principal instances of cooperation were:[12]

(1) **drainage of the river Erne.** A draft agreement was drawn up by the ministry of finance for Northern Ireland and the electricity supply board in the Republic of Ireland for works on both sides of the border. This looks like a contract in private international law. While provision was made for a United Kingdom or Irish arbitrator,[13] the law of the contract is not specified. Under the Erne Drainage and Development Act 1950, the board was authorized to enter into the agreement. There does not appear to have been related Northern Ireland legislation;

(2) **the Foyle Fisheries Commission.** Under the Foyle Fisheries Act (Northern Ireland) 1952, and an apparently identical act of the Republic of Ireland (seemingly drafted in Belfast), the ministry of commerce for Northern Ireland and the minister for agriculture in the Republic of Ireland, were permitted to purchase jointly fisheries and land. Conservation boards in both jurisdictions were dissolved. And the above commission established, to preside over a lough and other areas without the territorial sea being determined. The commission purported to be a body corporate. And the administrations in Belfast and Dublin appointed the members. It was required to have an office in Northern Ireland and in the Republic of Ireland;[14]

(3) **the Great Northern Railway.** Under the Great Northern Railway Act 1953, and a similar act in Northern Ireland, the minister for industry and commerce in the Republic of Ireland and the ministry of commerce for Northern Ireland, were permitted to purchase jointly the Great Northern Railway Company (Ireland), which ran a number of cross-border routes.

12 Paragraph 6 of Annex 2 to the NIO document, *The Future of Northern Ireland: a paper for discussion*, October 1972. For a fuller administrative account, see Michael Kennedy, *Division and Consensus: the politics of cross-border relations in Ireland, 1925–69*, Dublin 2000.

13 The terms 'United Kingdom of Great Britain and Northern Ireland' and 'the Republic of Ireland' were used in the second schedule to the draft agreement.

14 Paragraph 10 of the third schedule of the Irish act. It was in fact administered from Derry/Londonderry.

There was to be an office in Dublin and another in Belfast. The two ministers jointly appointed the board, and could jointly direct its members. The board again purported to be a body corporate. The 1953 agreement was terminated in 1958. Under the Transport Act (Northern Ireland) 1958, and a similar measure in the Republic, the undertaking was divided between the Ulster transport authority and Córas Iompair Éireann.

14.19 The legality of these three activities must be doubted. There is no clear distinction between private international law and public international law (the latter seems to be non existent). Nor is there any awareness of the relationship between international law and domestic law in the United Kingdom and Irish states. A United Kingdom perception of the Republic of Ireland as not foreign (and therefore not another state?), and an Irish view of Northern Ireland as somehow part of the nation state, appear to have combined to confuse the 1920 identical acts model and the 1949 agreements or arrangements one – while excluding the only model, the international organization, which could have worked given that the border in Ireland was an international frontier.

14.20 The term 'Irish dimension' emerged in the NIO document, *The Future of Northern Ireland: a paper for discussion*, October 1972. It was juxtaposed to 'the United Kingdom interest': 'The United Kingdom Government has three major concerns in Northern Ireland. First, that it should be internally at peace ... Second, that it should prosper ... Third, that Northern Ireland should not offer a base for any external threat to the security of the United Kingdom.'[15] The following reasons were given for an Irish dimension: one, Northern Ireland is part of the geographical entity of Ireland; two, 'an element of the minority in Northern Ireland has hitherto seen itself as simply a part of the wider Irish community'; three, 'the problem of political terrorism ... has always had manifestations throughout the island'.[16]

14.21 The idea in section 3(1)(a)(ii) of the Ireland Act 1949 reappeared in the NICA 1973. Section 12 provided for consultation, agreements or arrangements with the Republic of Ireland.[17] Agreements or arrangements came from 1949. Consultation – making a triptych – was added in 1973.[18] Section 12(1) permitted a Northern Ireland executive authority (defined in section 7) to do any of the three with an authority of the Republic of Ireland. Section 12(2) declared[19] that the assembly could give effect to any agreement or arrangement, 'including provision for transferring to any authority designated by or constituted under the agreement or arrangement any function which would otherwise be exercisable ... in Northern Ireland'. This allowed for a transfer of functions between Northern Ireland and the Republic of Ireland. Section 12(2) went on to provide for the reverse: 'or for transferring to an authority in Northern Ireland any functions which would

15 Paragraph 74.

16 Paragraph 76.

17 The Republic of Ireland was – in the opinion of parliamentary counsel – the United Kingdom-law name in 1973.

18 It seems that according to Notes on Clauses (not made available), section 12 'permitted the establishment of an (sic) similar body to the Council of Ireland envisaged in the 1920 Act (but never in the event set up), responsible for administering certain services on both sides of the border'. (Alan Whysall, *Northern Ireland constitutional legislation: a guide*, 2nd edn, March 1996, p. 51)

19 Declared because of the Ireland Act 1949 s 3.

otherwise be exercisable by an authority elsewhere [presumably in the Republic]'.

14.22 Section 12 of the NICA 1973 was never used, either by the assembly in 1974, or under direct rule in the following 25 years. The points made above about the 1949 agreements or arrangements model apply. The 1973 idea added nothing new; indeed, the agreements or arrangements (there seems to be no difference) had apparently the effect of either diminishing or restoring United Kingdom sovereignty, by the transfer of functions into or out of Northern Ireland. This point is confirmed by the fact that consultation, agreements and arrangements were with any authority of the Republic of Ireland, meaning a transfer of sovereignty between neighbouring states.

14.23 The constitution act had received the royal assent on 18 July 1973. The Sunningdale conference – involving the United Kingdom and Irish governments, and the parties involved in the Northern Ireland executive designate – met from 6 to 9 December 1973.

14.24 The communiqué issued at the end included provision for a council of Ireland in paragraphs 7–9 (of the 20).

14.25 Paragraph 7 stated there would be a council of ministers, 'with executive and harmonising functions and a consultative role'. It would comprise seven members of the Irish government, and the same number from the Northern Ireland executive (with additional non-voting members); it would act by unanimity. There would also be a consultative assembly, 'with advisory and review functions'. This was to have 60 members, 30 from Dáil Éireann and 30 from the Northern Ireland assembly; they would be elected by PR(STV). The council of Ireland would have a secretariat, servicing the institutions; it was to be headed by a secretary-general, would have permanent headquarters and would employ its own staff.

14.26 Paragraph 8 dealt with particular functions (see Chapter 15). It also alluded to legalization. The Oireachtas and the assembly would legislate from time to time to transfer functions to the council of Ireland. (No reference was made to how this would be established; the council of Ireland model in the GOIA 1920 had long been superseded.) 'Where necessary, the British Government w[ould] cooperate in this devolution of functions.' None of this of course happened. The formal conference agreed for early 1974 – which would have translated the provisions of the communiqué into presumably an international agreement – was never convened.

14.27 The 1985 Anglo-Irish Agreement, an attempt by the United Kingdom to harness the Irish state to the process of managing Northern Ireland, envisaged practical cooperation; the term occurred in article 10(c). Part F provided for cross-border cooperation on security, economic, social and cultural matters. Article 9 dealt exclusively with security, a major United Kingdom responsibility.

14.28 Article 10(a) referred to cooperation 'to promote the economic and social development of those areas of both parts of Ireland which have suffered most severely from the consequences of the instability of recent years'. This was a reference to the border counties, and cross-border came in time to have this particular geographical meaning. The two governments were to consider 'the possibility of securing international support for this work'. Most immediate attention focused on this latter aspect. On 18 September 1986, the two governments agreed to establish the International Fund for Ireland (IFI)[20] as an international organization.[21] The Irish government did not get much from article 10(a) in the first three years, leading up to the review under article 11.[22] However, cross-border – and even all-Ireland – economic and social cooperation became a regular item at meetings of the intergovernmental conference from the early 1990s.

14.29 Article 10(b) provided – in the absence of devolution – for 'the promotion of co-operation between the two parts of Ireland concerning cross-border aspects of economic, social and cultural matters' within the responsibility of the secretary of state. Article 10(c) looked to devolution taking place. At that point, 'machinery [would] need to be established by the responsible authorities in the North and South for practical co-operation in respect of cross-border aspects of these issues'. The raison d'être for Strand Two stems from the Anglo-Irish Agreement.

The international dimension

14.30 The international order comprises states. And international law provides for relations between them.

14.31 Article 1(2) of the charter states that the second purpose of the United Nations is 'to develop friendly relations among nations based on respect for the principles of equal rights and self-determination of peoples'. Chapter 9 provides for international economic and social cooperation, 'with a view to the creation of conditions of stability and well-being which are necessary for peaceful and friendly relations among nations ...' (article 55).

14.32 The 1975 Helsinki Final Act, of the conference on security and cooperation in Europe (while not a treaty[23]), contains, as one of the ten principles guiding relations between participating states, number IX on cooperation among states: 'They will endeavour, in developing their co-operation as equals, to promote mutual understanding and confidence, friendly and good-neighbourly relations among themselves, international peace, security and justice.'

Towards the Belfast Agreement

14.33 The Sunningdale blueprints were dusted off in Dublin in the early 1990s after nearly 20 years.

14.34 The 1993 *Downing Street Declaration*, an agreed framework for peace, concentrated upon principles. However, reference was made to Europe requiring new approaches to serve interests common to both parts of the island of Ireland, and to Ireland and the United Kingdom as partners in the European Union.[24]

20 Agreement between the Government of the United Kingdom of Great Britain and Northern Ireland and the Government of the Republic of Ireland concerning the International Fund for Ireland, Cmnd 9908, London and Dublin 18 September 1986.

21 Article 5(1).

22 Tom Hadden & Kevin Boyle, *The Anglo-Irish Agreement: commentary, text and official review*, Dublin & London 1989, pp. 42–6; the IFI is considered separately in chapter 3 there (pp. 49–56).

23 Section: Follow-Up to the Conference. It is an official document of the United Nations.

24 Paragraph 3. The European Economic Community was mentioned in the Sunningdale communiqué.

14.35 In the United Kingdom contribution to the 1995 *Framework Documents*, a comprehensive settlement was said to include 'a new North/South body or bodies', an interparliamentary forum, administrative support, and day-to-day cooperation and communication between departments and those with executive authority. 'The source of their authority would stem from the administrations in Belfast and Dublin.'[25]

14.36 Part II – the shared understanding, but mainly the work of Dublin – contained 15 paragraphs on North/South Institutions (there were two paragraphs on Northern Ireland government): 'with clear identity and purpose, to enable representatives of democratic institutions, North and South, to enter into new, co-operative and constructive relationships; to promote agreement among the people of the island of Ireland; to carry out on a democratically accountable basis delegated executive, harmonising and consultative functions over a range of designated matters to be agreed; and to serve to acknowledge and reconcile the rights, identities and aspirations of the two major traditions'.[26]

14.37 Again, the decisive precursor of the Belfast Agreement was the 12 January 1999 Heads of Agreement. It anticipated a North-South ministerial council, and implementation bodies. The council was to comprise those with executive responsibilities in Northern Ireland and the Republic of Ireland. 'Each side [was to] consult, co-operate and take decisions on matters of mutual interest within [their] mandate.' The implementation bodies (plus other unspecified mechanisms) were to be 'in meaningful areas and at an all-island level'. Meaningful is a strange word to be used of government.[27]

Legislation at Westminster

14.38 Despite – because of – the non-use of section 12 of the 1973 act, parliamentary counsel reenacted agreements or arrangements in section 53 of the NIA 1998 (section 12 of the 1973 act is repealed by section 100(2) and schedule 15 of the 1998 act):

(1) This section applies to any agreement or arrangement entered into by a Minister or junior Minister participating ... in a meeting of the North/South Ministerial Council ... .

(2) Provision may be made by Act of the Assembly for giving effect to any agreement or arrangement to which this section applies, including provision –

(a) for transferring to any body designated by or constituted under the agreement or arrangement any functions which would otherwise be exercisable by any Minister or Northern Ireland department;

(b) for transferring to a Minister or Northern Ireland department any functions which would otherwise be exercisable by any authority outside Northern Ireland.

(3) ...

25 Part I, Annex B, paragraph 1.

26 Part II, paragraph 13(b).

27 It was to be used of the north-south implementation bodies, by the Deputy First Minister, at the inaugural meeting of the NSMC, in Armagh, on 17 December 1999.

14.39 This is exactly the same as in 1973, with one difference. Section 53(2)(a) refers, not to 'any authority [of the Republic] designated by or constituted under the agreement or arrangement', but to 'any body'. Any body is closer to constituted under the agreement or arrangement, but the possibility of designated still remains. It is not clear what this body is. It is not necessarily equivalent to the implementation body in section 53(4) and (5). It could therefore still be an authority of the Republic of Ireland.

TITLE: NORTH/SOUTH MINISTERIAL COUNCIL

14.40 This title, while inconsistent with Strand One, is consistent with Strand Three. The North/South Ministerial Council – the Belfast Agreement uses an inelegant and ungrammatical oblique stroke – or NSMC (the abbreviation in part V of the NIA 1998), is the lead institution.

1. **Under a new British/Irish Agreement dealing with the totality of relationships, and related legislation at Westminster and in the Oireachtas, a North/South Ministerial Council to be established to bring together those with executive responsibilities in Northern Ireland and the Irish Government, to develop consultation, co-operation and action within the island of Ireland – including through implementation on an all-island *and cross-border* basis – on matters of mutual interest within the competence of the *A*[a]dministrations, North and South.**

14.41 Paragraph 1 provides for the establishment and purposes of the NSMC, as the basis of north-south practical cooperation. Its remit is circumscribed by: one, matters of mutual interest; two, within the competence of the two administrations. The NSMC is an international organization, a cooperation body; while it may share sovereignty, it does not detract from the sovereignty of the United Kingdom and add to that of the Republic of Ireland (or vice versa).

14.42 ANNOTATIONS

'Under a new British/Irish Agreement dealing with the totality of relationships,'. The new British-Irish Agreement is, of course, the BIA. The Strand Two section of the Belfast Agreement forms part of Annex 1. The name of the treaty of 10 April 1998 is given by paragraph 1 of Constitutional Issues (and the first paragraphs of Strands Two and Three and Validation, Implementation and Review). The oblique stroke is singular to this section, inspired no doubt by the title. The totality of relationships is used here (and in the second paragraph 1 of Strand Three) to refer to the scope of the BIA. In the first paragraph 1 of Strand Three, it is 'the totality of relationships among the peoples of these islands'. Its origins lie in the December 1980 meeting in Dublin, between the Irish and United Kingdom premiers, which began the contemporary phase in Anglo-Irish diplomacy. They commissioned joint studies,[28] as the basis of 'a [future] special consideration of the totality of relationships within these islands'. It has never been clear whether these are government to government relationships, or between the civil societies of both states. The meaning in 1980–81 was much more the former, and 'the totality of relationships among the peoples of these islands' is a later development. The basis of the 1996–98 talks was: 'to achieve a new beginning for relationships within Northern Ireland, within the island of Ireland and between the peoples of these islands, and to agree new institutions and structures to take

28 Anglo-Irish Joint Studies, *Joint Report and Studies*, Cmnd 8414, November 1981. The areas were: possible new institutional structures; citizenship rights; security matters; economic cooperation; and measures to encourage mutual understanding.

account of the totality of relationships'.[29] This is a third meaning to totality, corresponding to the scope of the BIA in article 2: the MPA, which includes Strand One, plus the international institutions (Strands Two and Three).

'and related legislation at Westminster and in the Oireachtas,' is a confusing phrase. Its origins are the nationalist idea that, given unionist unwillingness to construct a strong Irish dimension, Dublin can effectively pressure London to make decisions for Northern Ireland. Westminster legislation is perceived ironically as the means to realizing nationalist aspirations.

The 1920 council of Ireland – which was never established – was a creature of Westminster legislation. The legal mechanism for the 1973 council of Ireland (which never reached formal agreement), was unspecified in the Sunningdale communiqué. The 1995 *Framework Documents*, in suggesting 'a North/South body involving Heads of Departments on both sides', went on to describe this embryonic NSMC as 'duly established and maintained by legislation in both sovereign Parliaments'.[30] (Why maintained?) Dublin may have had some faith in the identical acts model, thinking of the the Foyle fisheries commission of 1952 as a precedent. But it was stated both governments agreed. London can only have failed to remember, or chosen to forget, its 1949 statutory view (reenacted in 1973) of agreements or arrangements as the way to construct north/south institutions. The NSMC was to be established under article 2 of the BIA, an international agreement. 'In particular there shall be established', reads the second sentence, 'in accordance with the provisions of the Multi–Party Agreement immediately on the entry into force of this agreement ... (i) the North/South Ministerial Council'. This would have been enough to create an international organization called the NSMC under the BIA. The passive tense was used to spare Northern Ireland blushes; it was actually the United Kingdom government which was helping establish the NSMC. 'Established ... on the entry into force of this Agreeement' is the key phrase.

The supplementary agreement of 8 March 1999 (referred to above) was probably unnecessary. Cm 4294 is entitled 'agreement between the government of the United Kingdom of Great Britain and Northern Ireland and the government of Ireland establishing a North/South Ministerial Council'. The first recital of the preamble begins: 'Having regard to Article 2 of the [BIA]'. And article 1 commences: 'Under and in furtherance of Article 2 of the [BIA] ... there is hereby established a North/South Ministerial Council.' Under article 2 of the BIA makes this supplementary agreement a duplicate. In furtherance of does not add anything, since there is nothing in article 2 requiring a second agreement. The most likely explanation is that 'there shall be established' in article 2 was open to interpretation by Irish government advisers as requiring precisely this (it contrasts with 'there is hereby established' in the supplementary agreement).[31] Further, since the implementation bodies did require a supplementary agreement (they were only decided upon subsequently), Dublin requested – and London acceded to – a set of four new international agreements done on 8 March 1999.

The role of legislation was not as specified. There was no Westminster enactment establishing the NSMC. Sections 52 and 53 in part V of the NIA 1998 take the council as already existing. This is also the case with the Oireachtas legislation. Section 3 of the BIA Act 1999 – promulgated on 22 March 1999 – related only to participation of Irish ministers. Under interpretations (section 2), the NSMC is defined in Irish law as having been established by the supplementary agreement on 8 March 1999.

29 *Ground Rules for Substantive All-Party Negotiations*, Cm 3232, April 1996, rule 1.

30 Part II, paragraph 25. 'Both Governments believe', the paragraph read, 'that the legislation should provide for a clear institutional identity and purpose for the North/South body. It would also establish the body's terms of reference, legal status and arrangements for political, legal, administrative and financial accountability.'

31 'Shall' here may sound like legislative rather than treaty language.

It remains unclear whether related legislation at Westminster and in the Oireachtas was simply the influence of the *Framework Documents*, or that the two governments intended something on 10 April 1998 on which they subsequently revised their view jointly.

'a North/South Ministerial Council to be established' has been discussed in the above annotation.

'to bring together those with executive responsibilities in Northern Ireland and the Irish Government,'. The 1920 council of Ireland was to comprise members of the two legislatures. This suggests a representative body, though, since the two regional governments were to be drawn from the parliaments (section 8(4)(b)), it could have included ministers as members. The 1973 council of Ireland comprised two institutions. The council of ministers was obviously a meeting of executive members from the two administrations. The consultative assembly was more like the GOIA 1920 idea. The 1995 *Framework Documents* envisaged heads of departments, then a term of art in Northern Ireland law[32] (equivalent to minister in Irish law). The members of the NSMC are specified further in paragraph 2.

'to develop consultation, co-operation and action within the island of Ireland' is the NSMC triptych of purposes. This originates with the council of ministers' 'executive and harmonising functions and consultative role' in the 1973 Sunningdale communiqué. This was picked up by the Irish government in the 1995 *Framework Documents*. The North/South body was to have 'delegated executive, harmonising or consultative functions'.[33] (The word function appears to be slipping.) It was also revealed that there was a 'scale' starting with consultation, proceeding to harmonization and finishing with executive action.[34] The idea of a scale – to which was related that of an embryonic government of Ireland (predicted by the Irish foreign minister, David Andrews, during the multi-party talks[35]) – is totally absent from paragraph 1. Consultation leads the list. But it is followed by co-operation, the generic term for north/south activity. And followed by action. This is similar to executive action from 1995, but there was clearly a desire not to use the word executive. The island of Ireland has been noted above. Its inspiration is article 2 of BNH, though the United Kingdom government may have been attracted by the geographical precision of the term.

' – including through implementation on an all-island and cross-border basis – '. This parenthesis was in the MDP. However, cross-border was added. No doubt, this was to convey that north/south could be confined to the border counties, as under the 1985 Anglo-Irish Agreement, and did not need to be coextensive with the two administrations. The parenthesis introduces the concept of implementation, which reappears in paragraph 5(iii) and (iv) (and is developed further in paragraphs 8 and 9). There is also a definition in paragraph 11: of implementing policies 'on an all-island and cross-border basis'.

'on matters of mutual interest' is a major condition precedent. Before an issue may be considered by the NSMC, it should be tested as meeting the criterion of mutual interest. Given that the Irish dimension has been implicated in nationalist aspiration, and appears to be a down-payment while waiting for the tide of consent to shift, it is likely that Dublin will proffer issues which have a great deal to do with nationalist politics, and very little to do with practical cooperation. Given, further, that Northern Ireland is part of a much larger state, which subsidizes the region to a considerable extent, it might be difficult to find a practical interest perceived by unionists. This is to hypothesize without taking account of any unionist hostility to such an Irish dimension at all.

'within the competence of the Administrations, North and South.' is a second major condition precedent. The Republic of Ireland is a sovereign state, and it has full competence

32 NICA 1973 s 8(1)(b), amended to s 8(1)(a).

33 Part II, paragraph 25.

34 Part II, paragraph 28.

35 George Mitchell, *Making Peace*, London 1999, pp. 167–8.

in all matters. Northern Ireland, in contrast, is a devolved administration. It has transferred matters, but there is still considerable secretary of state influence. This phrase means that the competence of the lesser administration, Northern Ireland, determines the range of issues which may be addressed by the NSMC. Administrative has been given an upper-case first letter in this section of the Belfast Agreement. North and South have been discussed above in Chapter 8.

> **2. All Council decisions to be by agreement between the two sides. Northern Ireland to be represented by [[executive members of the Northern Ireland Administration]]** ***the First Minister, Deputy First Minister and any relevant Ministers,*** **the Irish Government by the Taoiseach and relevant Ministers, all operating in accordance with the rules for democratic authority and accountability in force in the Northern Ireland Assembly and the Oireachtas respectively. Participation in the Council to be one of the essential responsibilities attaching to relevant posts in the two Administrations.** ***If a holder of a relevant post will not participate normally in the Council, the Taoiseach in the case of the Irish Government and the First and Deputy First Minister in the case of the Northern Ireland Administration to be able to make alternative arrangements.***

14.43 This – along with paragraph 6 – is the major constitutional prescription for the NSMC, even though the legal status of the council is nowhere defined in Strand Two.

14.44 ANNOTATIONS

'All Council decisions to be by agreement between the two sides.' The 1920 council of Ireland (40 members plus the president) was to operate apparently by simple majority, with a quorum of 15; the president had a casting vote only.[36] The 1973 council of ministers (seven from each administration) was to act by unanimity. The 60-strong consultative assembly was not a decision-making body. The 1995 *Framework Documents* stated: 'both Governments envisage that all decisions within the body would be by agreement between the two sides'.[37] All Council decisions means all; there is no provision for majority voting – qualified or otherwise – on the NSMC. To be by agreement is the same as the unanimity rule in the Sunningdale communiqué. Between the two sides is adversarial terminology. The Irish government, of course, is bound by collective responsibility. Once again, as with competence in paragraph 1, the NSMC must move at the speed of the slowest; namely the Northern Ireland delegation: if there is no agreement in Belfast, there is no prospect of a NSMC decision. Checks and balances, characteristic of Strand One, exist – less obtrusively – in Strand Two.

'Northern Ireland to be represented by the First Minister, Deputy First Minister and any relevant Ministers, the Irish Government by the Taoiseach and relevant Ministers,'. This is an important provision, which had a bearing during the transition.

Northern Ireland may be represented by the First Minister and Deputy First Minister. Paragraph 18 of Strand One describes their duties as including 'the response of the Northern Ireland administration to external relationships'. This applies to the transition, and to devolution. The First Minister and Deputy First Minister were elected by the assembly on 1 July 1998. They formed – under paragraph 8 – the Northern Ireland transitional administration. The Rt. Hon. David Trimble MP and Seamus Mallon MP were eligible to attend any shadow NSMC that might have been held. They were also empowered, under the

36 GOIA 1920 s 2.
37 Part II, paragraph 35.

Belfast Agreement, to reach the 18 December 1998 agreement with the Irish government; section 55 of the NIA 1998 – the final part of the legal process – had come into force on 19 November 1998. This point about the transitional administration – as regards after the appointed day – is not contradicted by section 52 of the NIA 1998. Section 52(1) leaves it to the First Minister and Deputy First Minister to 'make such nominations ... as they consider necessary ... to ensure ... such cross-community participation ... as is required by the Belfast Agreement'. While ministers and junior ministers are likely nominees, they are not strictly necessary on all occasions.

This point is borne out by the next phrase: and any relevant Ministers. The use of the word any – there is none with reference to the Irish government – leaves open the possibility of the joint head of the executive, certainly during the transition, and even at points after devolution, constituting the Northern Ireland administration's delegation.

The idea of cross-community participation in section 52 of the NIA 1998 is important. It originates in paragraph 30 of Strand One, where the term 'cross-community involvement' is used. The First Minister and Deputy First Minister, under paragraph 18, exemplify cross-community participation. Cross-community participation, when ministers and junior ministers are eligible for nomination under section 52, can only involve one office holder being accompanied by another from the other tradition. Participation is defined in section 52(9)(a) as in accordance with paragraphs 5 and 6 of Strand Two (which includes decision-making). Since Strands Two and Three are dealt with together in the NIA 1998, this would be a confidence-building provision since it applies equally to unionists and nationalists in their preferred strand.

A system of shadowing would seem to be a necessary minimum, with ministerial private secretaries liaising. Codetermination, however, involving joint decision-making, is required arguably by the NIA 1998. It is not clear what practice has been followed since devolution. Certainly, each minister who had attended a NSMC in sectoral format, has reported to the assembly on behalf of him/herself and another minister from the opposite tradition.

The inaugural meeting of the NSMC took place in Armagh on 13 December 1999. The following day, the First Minister and Deputy First Minister reported to the assembly, as required under section 52(6)(b) and (7) of the NIA 1998. (No advance notice of the meeting had been given to the assembly, as required under section 52(5).[38]) The First Minister[39] listed ministers attending (in addition to himself and the Deputy First Minister): Bairbre de Brún, Mark Durkan, Sir Reg Empey, Sean Farren, Sam Foster, Michael McGimpsey, Martin McGuinness and Brid Rodgers. This was all the members of the executive committee, less the two DUP ministers who were abstaining from the executive. The First Minister stated: 'This report has been approved by all Ministers who attended that meeting and is made on behalf of all by the First Minister and Deputy First Minister.'[40] In reply to a question about the abstaining ministers, he stated that they had both been asked to participate, but declined; they were not then nominated, avoiding breach of the Pledge of Office.

On 24 January 2000, the minister for enterprise, trade and investment, Sir Reg Empey, accompanied by Sean Farren, attended a NSMC in sectoral format in Newry. Sir Reg reported to the assembly on behalf of both ministers on 31 January 2000.[41] On 3 February 2000, the minister for education, Martin McGuinness, accompanied by Dermot Nesbitt, attended a NSMC in sectoral format in Dublin. Martin McGuinness reported to the assembly on behalf

38 The agenda had been circulated in advance: Northern Ireland Assembly, *Official Report*, vol. 4 no. 2 (reissue), p. 22, 14 December 1999.

39 On this occasion, the Rt. Hon. David Trimble MP sat beside Seamus Mallon MP: Northern Ireland Assembly, *Official Report*, vol. 4 no. 2 (reissue), p. 21, 14 December 1999.

40 Northern Ireland Assembly, *Official Report*, vol. 4 no. 2 (reissue), p. 21, 14 December 1999.

41 Northern Ireland Assembly, *Official Report*, vol. 4 no. 7, p. 256, 31 January 2000.

of both ministers, after suspension, on 5 June 2000.[42] On the same day, Brid Rodgers, who had been accompanied by Dermot Nesbitt to an agricultural NSMC on 9 February 2000 (just before suspension), reported to the assembly on behalf of herself and Dermot Nesbitt.[43] A health NSMC had been held in Belfast on 4 February 2000. Bairbre de Brún had been accompanied by Sir Reg Empey. She reported to the assembly on behalf of them both on 12 June 2000.[44] On 16 June 2000, a finance sectoral meeting was held in Dublin. Mark Durkan reported to the assembly on 26 June 2000, on behalf of himself and Sam Foster.[45] Michael McGimpsey had attended a NSMC sectoral meeting in Belfast on 21 June 2000, accompanied by Bairbre de Brún. He reported to the assembly on behalf of them both on 3 July 2000.[46] Also that day, Brid Rogers reported, on behalf of herself and Dermot Nesbitt, attendance at a second agricultural NSMC in Dublin on 26 June 2000.[47]

'the Irish Government by the Taoiseach and relevant Ministers,' means that the taoiseach must attend meetings of the NSMC. Paragraph 3(i) below suggests this applies only to meetings in plenary format. The taoiseach may, however, attend alone. Relevant Ministers is a matter for Irish law. This could in theory be none. Section 3 of the BIA Act 1999, incorporating the Belfast Agreement in part, states that NSMC meetings may be attended by one or more of the following: the taoiseach, other ministers of the government and ministers of state.

'all operating in accordance with the rules for democratic authority and accountability in force in the Northern Ireland Assembly and the Oireachtas respectively.' This, along with paragraph 6, determines how the NSMC functions. Two point are important. One, it is implied that the rules are different each side of the border. Two, those in the Republic of Ireland will not be the focus of any attention.

The Irish government, the executive of a sovereign state, has a foreign policy towards Northern Ireland. Articles 6 and 29 of Bunreacht na hÉireann govern that relationship. (The new article 29.7.2 is unnecessary for the NSMC; no constitutional amendment was necessary for the 1981 Anglo-Irish intergovernmental council, nor for the intergovernmental conference – a treaty body – set up in 1985. And article 3.2 does not apply to the NSMC.) All operating in accordance with refers to the executive members attending meetings of the NSMC.

The rules for democratic authority and accountability suggests democratic authority and accountability are different, and even that there may be more than one rule for each. The rules for the 1920 council are contained in section 2 of the GOIA; its constitution could be changed by identical acts of the two parliaments in Ireland. There are no such rules for the 1973 council of ministers in the 1973 Sunningdale communiqué. The 1995 *Framework Documents* envisaged that heads of departments ('on each side'), 'would exercise their powers in accordance with the rules for democratic authority and accountability for this function in force in the Oireachtas and in new institutions in Northern Ireland'.[48]

Democratic authority must refer to the totality of rules bearing on a member of the executive. In the case of Northern Ireland, this would have to be ascertained by reading the Belfast Agreement against the background of the United Kingdom unwritten constitution, and through its incorporation by the NIA 1998. Part – but only part – of that democratic authority is expressed in section 52(5): the First Minister and Deputy First Minister are required, before each NSMC meeting, to notify the executive committee and the Assembly of

42 Northern Ireland Assembly, *Official Report*, vol. 5 no. 1, pp. 14–20, 5 June 2000.
43 Northern Ireland Assembly, *Official Report*, vol. 5 no. 1, pp. 21–4, 5 June 2000.
44 Northern Ireland Assembly, *Official Report*, vol. 5 no. 3, pp. 81–9, 12 June 2000.
45 Northern Ireland Assembly, *Official Report*, vol. 5 no. 7, pp. 279–82, 26 June 2000.
46 Northern Ireland Assembly, *Official Report*, vol. 5 no. 10, pp. 387–94, 3 July 2000.
47 Northern Ireland Assembly, *Official Report*, vol. 5 no. 10, pp. 395–9, 3 July 2000.
48 Part II, paragraph 35.

the following: the date of the meeting; the agenda; and the nominations of ministers and junior ministers made. If democratic authority may be considered before participation, accountability can be seen as after the event. Accountability is an important principle of the United Kingdom constitution, but it does not always require active disclosure.[49]

Accountability relates to individual and collective responsibility of ministers. Part – but again only part – of that accountability is expressed in section 52(6) of the NIA 1998: any minister having attended the NSMC must report, first to the executive committee, and secondly to the assembly. The latter is to be oral, unless standing orders provide otherwise. The standing orders of 9 March 1999 make no provision for the NSMC.

In force in the Northern Ireland Assembly and the Oireachtas respectively provides cover for the real issue. There can be no doubt that the Irish government will run its Northern Ireland policy, including economic, social and cultural cooperation, the way it runs domestic policy. The emphasis, however, is upon encouraging unionists to embrace an Irish dimension, reassurances being given about mandates or democratic authority and accountability or scrutiny.[50]

'Participation in the Council to be one of the essential responsibilities attaching to relevant posts in the two Administrations.' Again, this is actually about Northern Ireland. There was nothing like this in the plans for the 1920 council or the 1973 council. Its origins are the 1995 *Framework Documents*, where the idea of a duty of service was advanced.[51] Participation in the Council helped introduce the idea of cross-community participation in section 52(1) of the NIA 1998. To be one of the essential responsibilities attaching to relevant posts is incorporated through section 52(2): 'It shall be a Ministerial responsibility of a Minister or junior Minister nominated ... to participate in the Council ... in such meetings or activities as are specified in the nomination.' However, there are no obvious sanctions for declining a nomination (other than the political loss consequent upon non attendance). The Pledge of Office requires ministers to discharge in good faith all the duties of office. But is participation in the NSMC a duty of office? It is not described as such. The Pledge of Office also requires ministers to act in accordance with decisions of the executive committee and the assembly (and this point is reinforced by section 52(3)). Nominations are not – though they could become – decisions of (most likely) the executive committee. This absence of sanctions is confirmed by section 52(4): 'A Minister may in writing authorise a Minister or junior Minister who has been nominated ... to enter into agreements or arrangements in respect of matters for which he is responsible.' It is possible to delegate, or transfer, ministerial powers in Strand Two.

'If a holder of a relevant post will not participate normally in the Council, the Taoiseach in the case of the Irish Government and the First and Deputy First Minister in the case of the Northern Ireland Administration to be able to make alternative arrangements.' Again, this concerns Northern Ireland only. The sentence was added to the MDP. The eventuality envisaged is that of the DUP, which was entitled to two ministerial seats, refusing to participate in the NSMC, or refusing to engage in any ceding of United Kingdom sovereignty (understood – incorrectly – by that party as having bodies with executive functions). If a holder of a relevant post will not participate normally in the Council embraces refusing a nomination under section 52(1) of the NIA 1998. It also includes refusing to participate, under section 52(2), participation being defined in section 52(9)(a), as that specified in paragraphs 5 and 6 of Strand Two. The First Minister and the Deputy First Minister ... to be able to make alternative arrangements contains no notion of sanctions. The power of nomination in section 52(1) includes the power to renominate. The sanction is only political; if a minister forgoes an opportunity of participation, another minister may be given the opportunity.

49 It is the second principle in paragraph 1 of the United Kingdom *Ministerial Code*.

50 1995 *Framework Documents*, part II, paragraph 35.

51 Part II, paragraph 25.

3. The Council to meet in different formats:

(i) in plenary format twice a year, with Northern Ireland representation led by the [First Secretary and Deputy Secretary] ***First Minister and Deputy First Minister*** **and the Irish Government led by the Taoiseach;**

(ii) in specific sectoral formats on a regular and frequent basis with each side represented by the appropriate Minister [[Assembly Secretary]];

(iii) in an appropriate format to consider institutional or cross-sectoral matters (including in relation to the EU) and to resolve disagreement.

14.45 This paragraph deals with the number and types of meetings of the NSMC. It may be considered part of the constitution of the NSMC (a concept from the GOIA 1920).

14.46 ANNOTATIONS

'The Council to meet in different formats:' is probably mandatory.

'(i) in plenary format twice a year, with Northern Ireland representation led by the First Minister and Deputy First Minister and the Irish Government led by the Taoiseach;' must be read with paragraph 2. Paragraph 2 would suggest there can only be plenary meetings of the NSMC. This subparagraph must be considered to qualify that provision. In plenary format twice a year follows the cycle of the European council.[52] Northern Ireland representation led by the First Minister and Deputy First Minister allows – reading this with paragraph 2 – for the joint head of the executive alone. And the Irish government led by the Taoiseach, again read with paragraph 2, could require at least one other. But section 3 of the BIA Act 1999 allows the taoiseach to attend on his own.

'(ii) in specific sectoral formats on a regular and frequent basis with each side represented by the appropriate Minister;' refers to most of the meetings which are not plenaries. In specific sectoral formats is not defined. Sectoral conjures up the idea of the economy or society segmented, and run as a command economy, or with a high degree of regulation. More likely, the meaning comes from the word Minister. Specific sectoral formats would seem to relate to departments of government, allowing for a combination or – less likely – a fracturing of departmental responsibilities. On a regular and frequent basis is not defined either. It may be inferred that something more than twice a year is expected. However, that would require a highly institutionalized view of practical cooperation. Practical cooperation, as a process, is likely to throw up requirements, including meetings and other contacts and communications. With each side represented by the appropriate Minister again uses the adversarial side of paragraph 2. The reference to Minister relates to a department, and therefore to a range of public responsibilities.

'(iii) in an appropriate format to consider institutional or cross-sectoral matters (including in relation to the EU) and to resolve disagreement.' In an appropriate format means essentially an ad hoc meeting. To consider institutional or cross-sectoral matters (including in relation to the EU) is the first reason. It is not clear what institutional matters are. Under article 2 of the BIA, the NSMC is an institution. So also are the implementation bodies. Institutional may refer only to the NSMC. The implementation bodies, under paragraph 11, are under the policy direction of the NSMC (seemingly in plenary format but conceivably in sectoral format). Cross-sectoral matters refers to (ii). Obviously, the fewer sectors, then the less need there is for cross-sectoral meetings in an appropriate – ad hoc – format. Including in relation to the EU refers to paragraph 17. Europe is considered clearly to overlap sectors. But, again,

52 1997 Amsterdam treaty, TEU article 4 (ex article D).

that depends upon the definition of sector. And to resolve disagreement is the second reason given. This refers to paragraph 14, where disagreements are dealt with slightly more fully.

4. Agendas for all meetings to be settled by prior agreement between the two sides, but *it will be* open to either to propose any matter for consideration or action.

14.47 This is another constitutional aspect of the NSMC. Given the first sentence of paragraph 2, it is hardly necessary. Such a matter could have been dealt with better in rules of procedure for the NSMC, leaving substantive points for Strand Two. The 1920 and 1973 plans contained no such proposal.

14.48 ANNOTATIONS

'Agendas for all meetings to be settled by prior agreement between the two sides,' is an aspect of the first sentence of paragraph 2. It also relates more practically to paragraph 16. Nevertheless, there is a principle involved; neither administration can set the agenda on its own. Between the two sides continues with the adversarial terminology of paragraph 2.

'but it will be open to either to propose any matter for consideration or action.' sets up a preceding or subsequent principle: either administration can put items on the agenda. Any matter for consideration or action allows for, at one end, consultation, and, at the other, executive action. The phrase does not impose any obligation on the other party, such as seriously considering the request for an item.

5. The Council:

(i) to exchange information, discuss and consult with a view to co-operating on matters of mutual interest within the competence of both [a]Administrations, *North and South*;

(ii) to use best endeavours to reach agreement on the adoption of common policies, in [the] areas [listed in Annex A,] *where there is a mutual cross-border and all-island benefit, and which are within the competence of both Administrations, North and South,* making determined efforts to overcome any disagreements;

(iii) [in specified areas set out in Annex B] to take decisions *by agreement on policies* [on action] for implementation separately in each jurisdiction, *in relevant meaningful areas within the competence of both Administrations, North and South*;

(iv) [in other specified meaningful areas set out in Annex C] to take decisions *by agreement* on *policies and* action at an all-island and cross-border level *to be* [through] implement[ation]*ed by the* bodies to be established as set out in paragraphs [7] 8 and [8] 9 below.

14.49 This is one of the most important paragraphs in Strand Two. This and paragraph 6 are directly incorporated in United Kingdom law, by section 52(9)(a) of the NIA 1998 construing participation.

14.50 This paragraph deals formally with the functions of the NSMC, but actually with the scope of Strand Two in the Belfast Agreement. There was no such conceptual delineation in 1920, merely the institution and the areas under the council of Ireland. The 1973 Sunningdale communiqué began the process: the council of ministers was intended to have 'executive and harmonising functions and a consultative role'.[53] The latter was related seemingly to the second institution, the consultative assembly (with advisory and review functions).

14.51 The 1995 *Framework Documents*, in theorizing North/South Institutions at considerable length, came up with 'the scale between consultation, harmonisation and executive action'.[54] These designated functions were then separately analysed.[55] Mutual understanding or common or agreed positions was the general goal of consultation. Under harmonization, there would be 'an obligation on both sides to use their best endeavours to reach agreement on a common policy' even though implementation might be separate. Executive action was conceived as joint implementation; crucially, a distinction was drawn between existing bodies 'acting in an agency capacity, whether jointly or separately', and 'new bodies specifically created and mandated for this purpose'. Existing/new was confused – fatally from the point of view of the Irish government – with separate/ joint.

14.52 While the areas of cooperation are considered in Chapter 15, it is necessary to appreciate the considerable difference between the MDP and the FA. In the former, there were three annexes to Strand Two listing administrative matters. They were related to paragraph 5. Paragraph 5(i) – consultation – had no annex. Annex A related to paragraph 5(ii), and dealt with harmonization. Paragraph 5(iii) was related to Annex B: this was implementation separately in each jurisdiction. Annex C, related to paragraph 5(iv), comprised desired implementation bodies. In the negotiations, Annexes A, B and C were scrapped. As a result, the tripartite definition of consultation, harmonization and executive action, and the distinction within the latter between existing and new bodies (generating paragraphs 5(i)–(iv)) became garbled in the amending of the text.

14.53 ANNOTATIONS

'The Council:' begins the paragraph listing the four functions of the NSMC, based upon a nationalist reasoning of practical cooperation.

'(i) to exchange information, discuss and consult with a view to co-operating on matters of mutual interest within the competence of both Administrations, North and South;'. This passed from the MDP into the FA with only minimal amendment. Consultation had been conceived in the *Framework Documents* as: 'a forum where the two sides would consult on any aspect of designated matters on which either side wished to hold consultations'. To exchange information, discuss and consult is a weakening of Dublin's desired duty to exchange information in 1995. With a view to co-operating is similar to 'there would be no formal requirement that agreement would be reached or that policy would be harmonised or implemented jointly'. On matters of mutual interest refers back to the condition precedent in paragraph 1. Within the competence of both Administrations, North and South, refers to the second condition precedent in paragraph 1. Given the word both survived, the addition North and South was unnecessary.

'(ii) to use best endeavours to reach agreement on the adoption of common policies, in areas where there is a mutual cross-border and all-island benefit, and which are within the competence of both Administrations, North and South, making determined efforts to overcome any disagreements;'. With the scrapping of Annex A, this subparagraph required redrafting. Harmonization in 1995 was conceived as 'an obligation on both sides to use their

53 Paragraph 7.

54 Part II, paragraph 28.

55 Part II, paragraph 29.

best endeavours to reach agreement on a common policy and to make determined efforts to overcome any obstacles'. To use best endeavours to reach agreement on the adoption of common policies is the *Framework Documents*. Where there is a mutual cross-border and all-island benefit, and which are within the competence of both Administrations, North and South was added in compensation for the loss of Annex A. Mutual cross-border and all-island benefit repeats the mutual interest point of paragraph 5(i). It is of course the first condition precedent of paragraph 1. Cross-border and all-island is also from paragraph 1, cross-border having been added to the MDP. Making determined efforts to overcome any disagreements is from the *Framework Documents*.

'(iii) to take decisions by agreement on policies for implementation separately in each jurisdiction, in relevant meaningful areas within the competence of both Administrations, North and South;'. Subparagraphs (iii) and (iv) turn to the third function, executive action. The distinction in the *Framework Documents* between existing bodies – 'jointly or separately' – and new bodies (joint), explains the two subparagraphs.

However, this conceptual subtlety, with the reference forward to paragraph 9, undermines the provision on implementation bodies other than during the transition.

Paragraph 5(iii) was the hook for Annex B, which was also scrapped. To take decisions by agreement on policies for implementation separately in each jurisdiction is the substitute for Annex B. The word action was dropped, and replaced with policies. This makes subparagraph (iii) very similar to subparagraph (ii). For implementation separately in each jurisdiction is particular, but what is the point of agreed policies in (ii) if they are not to be implemented? In relevant meaningful areas is a rare resort to the language of the 12 January 1998 Heads of Agreement, taken from the text dropped in subparagraph (iv). Within the competence of both Administrations, North and South is repeated for the third and last time, having been taken from paragraph 1, where it is a condition precedent.

'(iv) to take decisions by agreement on policies and action at an all-island and cross-border level to be implemented by the bodies to be established as set out in paragraphs 8 and 9 below.' This is the second subparagraph dealing with implementation, and therefore with bodies. We turn from existing bodies and separate implementation – the two concepts become intertwined – to new bodies and joint implementation.

Annex C was the casualty here. To take decisions by agreement on policies and action returned to the policies of subparagraph (ii) and subparagraph (iii), where it replaced action. Action survives here, but it is overshadowed by policies. At an all-island and cross-border level returns to subparagraph (ii), and ultimately to paragraph 1. To be implemented is the second use of the concept, showing the distinction between existing and new.

By the bodies to be established as set out in in paragraphs 8 and 9 below is the most crucial phrase in Strand Two. The problem did not exist in the MDP; it arose through drafting at Castle Buildings between 6 and 10 April 1998.

The text in the MDP is: implementation bodies to be established as set out in paragraphs 7 and 8 below. The change in numbering came about partly because of the addition of the FA paragraph 7 (dealing with the transition). Paragraphs 7 and 8 in the MDP dealt with the Annex C bodies (to be created in the transition), and any further bodies. They correspond to FA paragraphs 10, 11 and 12. Annexes A to C were replaced with the idea of a work programme during the transition, requiring the drafting of paragraphs 8 and 9. The error – from the point of view of the Irish government – was to change 7 and 8 in paragraph 5(iv) to 8 and 9 (and not 10, 11 and 12). This was compounded by the drafting of paragraph 9 under the influence of Annexes B and C (see below under paragraph 9).

6. **Each side to be in a position to take decisions in the Council within the defined authority of those attending, through the arrangements in place for co-ordination of executive functions within each jurisdiction. Each side**

to remain accountable to the Assembly and Oireachtas respectively, whose approval, through arrangements in place on either side, would be required for decisions beyond the defined authority of those attending.

14.54 This paragraph returns to paragraph 2, and the ideas of democratic authority and accountability. It also anticipates paragraph 12. However, the distinction between democratic authority (before the event) and accountability (afterwards) is elided with the notion of power to take decisions. The Northern Ireland ministers are accountable to the assembly, and it is a matter of United Kingdom constitutional law as to what decision-making powers they have in dealings with a neighbouring state.

14.55 ANNOTATIONS

'Each side to be in a position to take decisions in the Council within the defined authority of those attending,'. Each side is again cover for Northern Ireland. Defined authority is the democratic authority discussed under paragraph 2. To be in a position to take decisions in the Council makes this paragraph about decision-making by Northern Ireland ministers.

A number of factors has to be considered together. The determination by the First Minister and Deputy First Minister of 15 February 1999 under ISO 21 – a list of ten departments – stated that the holder of each ministerial office 'shall exercise the functions of Minister of that Department'.[56] No reference was made to the functions of each department, and the functions of a minister were specified only as 'in charge of'.[57] This was also the definition in article 2(2)(b) of the Departments (Northern Ireland) Order 1999, SI 1999/283 of 10 February 1999. Article 4(1) went on to describe 'the functions of a department ... [being] exercised subject to the direction and control of the Minister'. The NIA 1998 does not resolve the question of the relationship, referring to functions exercised by departments and ministers (section 22(1)–(2)). Section 53 on agreements or arrangements entered into on the NSMC raises the question of the (1949) agreements and arrangements reenacted in 1973 – but never used. These could only be international agreements,[58] and they can only be made under the royal prerogative (which is dealt with in section 23). Paragraph 3 of schedule 2 (excepted matters) includes international relations. Excluded from this exception, under subparagraph (b), are the legislative powers, provided for in section 53. The agreements or arrangements still remain problematic.[59] There is nothing in the BIA addressing this question. The supplementary agreement on the NSMC (Cm 4294) states that it shall be constituted and shall operate in accordance with the MPA (article 2), and that 'each side acting in accordance with the appropriate arrangements in its jurisdiction' shall share responsibility for its operation (article 3).

'through the arrangements in place for co-ordination of executive functions within each jurisdiction.' This adds little if anything to the first phrase. Again, the issue is Northern Ireland. Co-ordination of executive functions refers back to paragraph 18 of Strand One. On one view, this requires the participation of the First Minister and Deputy First Minister for a decision to be made on the NSMC. Further, paragraph 19 of Strand One would seem to

56 New Northern Ireland Assembly, *Report from the First Minister (Designate) and Deputy First Minister (Designate)*, NNIA 7, 15 February 1999.

57 See also, NIA 1998 s 17(1)(b) & (3), sch. 14 para. 3.

58 For a contrary view, see Anthony Aust, *Modern treaty law and practice*, Cambridge 2000, p. 51, who sees them as informal arrangements.

59 This does not apply to the paragraph 9(ii) implementation bodies. The – necessary – supplementary agreement of 8 March 1999 stated: 'The North/South Ministerial Council may propose to the two Governments amendments to Annexes 1 and 2 hereto. Such amendments may be made by the two Governments by exchange of notes.' The royal prerogative is retained by the United Kingdom government. See also article 7.

require a prior executive committee decision. Under the Pledge of Office, all ministers are bound to act in accordance with all decisions of the executive committee (and the assembly).

'Each side to remain accountable to the Assembly and Oireachtas repectively,' simply repeats the point in paragraph 2. Accountability is only meaningful if there are procedures governing a minister's appearances before the assembly, statutory committees and non-statutory committees. The former – reporting to the assembly – is provided for in section 52(6) of the NIA 1998. The standing orders of 9 March 1999, while they provide for statutory committees, do not cover the summoning of ministers on NSMC matters under paragraph 9 of Strand One (especially the power to initiate enquiries and make reports, which is incorporated through section 29(1)(c)). Standing orders has also provided for non-statutory committees, but not for a standing committee on the NSMC (nor possibly a separate one on implementation bodies).

'whose approval, through the arrangements in place on either side, would be required for decisions beyond the defined authority of those attending.' This phrase relates to the first phrase of the first sentence. Paragraph 6 could have been drafted to read: 'Ministers from Northern Ireland may take decisions in the Council within their defined authority; Assembly approval is necessary for decisions beyond that defined authority.' The meaning of this phrase is dependent upon the interpretation of the first phrase of the first sentence. It does indicate that there is a limit to ministerial authority, and that the assembly then takes responsibility. This is a question for the assembly to answer through the mechanisms of accountability it puts in place. It could for example preclude any decision on the NSMC that was not made subject to assembly approval, like the United Kingdom's – and Denmark's – parliamentary reserves in the European Union.[60]

> **7.** ***As soon as practically possible after elections to the Northern Ireland Assembly, inaugural meetings will take place of the Assembly, the British/Irish Council and the North/South Ministerial Council in their transitional forms. All three institutions will meet regularly and frequently on this basis during the period between the elections to the Assembly, and the transfer of powers to the Assembly, in order to establish their modus operandi.***

14.56 This paragraph applies generally to the Belfast Agreement; it is not principally a Strand Two matter. It was not in the MDP. And it deals with the important transition from 1 July 1998.

14.57 Strand One, as noted, contains a subsection on Transitional Arrangements (paragraph 35). That was concerned with the assembly during the transition, though reference was made also to the BIC, the NSMC and the implementation bodies. (There was a reference to shadow ministers having to observe the spirit of the Pledge of Office, which was added along with Annex A to Strand One.)

14.58 Paragraph 7 of Strand Two deals with the transition more centrally.

14.59 ANNOTATIONS

'As soon as practically possible after elections to the Northern Ireland Assembly,' specifies no times. The assembly elections were held on 25 June 1998. As soon as practically possible resembles legislative language: reasonably practicable. That is for judicial interpretation in each particular case.

60 This point was made by Lord Cope of Berkeley, a former NIO minister, during the committee stage of the Northern Ireland Bill in the house of lords: House of Lords, *Hansard*, 5th series, 593, 1449, 21 October 1998.

'inaugural meetings will take place of the Assembly, the British/Irish Council and the North/South Ministerial Council in their transitional forms.' This defines in the most general terms that there is to be a transition, and that the three principal institutions of Strands One, Two and Three will move forward in order to prepare for devolution. The assembly met first on 1 July 1998. Subsequent meetings took place on (in 1998) 14 and 15 September; 5 October, 26 October, 9 November, 14 and 15 December; (in 1999) 18 January, 11 February, 15 and 16 February, 22 February, 1 March, 8 and 9 March – a total of 16 sitting days. The abortive attempt to form the executive led to the meeting of 15 July 1999. And devolution followed the meetings of 29 and 30 November 1999. The second institution mentioned is the British/Irish Council, as was the case in paragraph 35 of Strand One (the oblique stroke is particular to the Strand Two text). No meeting of the BIC took place during the time the assembly was meeting. The inaugural meeting took place in London on 17 December 1999. The third institution is the NSMC. It did meet belatedly in shadow form, on 1 December 1999 – on the eve of devolution, to agree the work under paragraphs 8 and 9.[61] Its inaugural meeting was in Armagh on 13 December 1999. It is not known why the BIC did not meet before devolution. Obviously, there may have been a desire to link the two: they are so treated in section 52 of the NIA 1998; when the implementation bodies were agreed on 18 December 1998, there was a reason for convening the NSMC – and therefore the BIC – in its transitional form.

There was an argument that the formation of the executive committee was a condition precedent for the NSMC meeting. Taking paragraph 35 of Strand One (which does mention shadow ministers in the context of the Pledge of Office) together with this paragraph on transitional forms, it would seem that there was an imperative to convene meetings of the BIC and NSMC along side the assembly. There is no express reference to the executive committee, nor to this being a condition precedent for – singularly – the NSMC. This argument about a condition precedent sits uneasily with a widely accepted view that the Belfast Agreement requires all participants to fulfil their obligations; through advances on all fronts – the idea was espoused by Mo Mowlam, the secretary of state – the appointed day was to be achieved: there were no preconditions.

'All three institutions will meet regularly and frequently on this basis during the period between the elections to the Assembly, and the transfer of powers to the Assembly, in order to establish their modus operandi.' All three institutions treats the assembly, the BIC and the NSMC as complementary. Emphasis upon any one risks unbalancing the Agreement. Will meet regularly and frequently recalls paragraph 3(ii). The 16 sitting days of the assembly are given above. The BIC and NSMC did not meet in that period. On this basis is a reference to their transitional form. During the period between the elections to the assembly, and the transfer of powers to the assembly, is the period from 25 June 1998. Devolution was envisaged originally as taking place in February 1999. The first target date was 10 March 1999, by which time sufficient progress had been made for the secretary of state to be likely to transfer powers. There had been no meeting of the BIC and NSMC. And the only decommissioning had been from the Loyalist Volunteer Force, on 18 December 1998; the LVF had not been involved in the talks. On Saturday, 15 May 1999, the prime minister set unilaterally[62] 30 June 1999 – the eve of devolution day in Scotland and Wales – as the new target. In order to establish their modus operandi must be interpreted literally and in the context of the assembly. Modus operandi is Latin for method of working. It is implied that the

61 The meeting was held in Parliament Buildings. It was attended by the First Minister and the Deputy First Minister, and John O'Donoghue TD and Liz O'Donnell TD of the Irish government.

62 This date had been mentioned the previous day at Downing Street, in the one-page (draft?) agreement – seemingly a working document – on decommissioning: 'All parties anticipate, without prejudice to their clear positions on this issue, a devolution of powers by 30th June.' (*Irish Times*, 17 May 1999)

object was to get the institutions into proper working order by devolution day. The work of the assembly has been detailed in Chapter 12. Something commensurate must have been intended for the BIC and NSMC.

> **8.** ***During the transitional period between the elections to the Northern Ireland Assembly and the transfer of power to it, representatives of the Northern Ireland transitional Administration and the Irish government operating in the North/South Ministerial Council will undertake a work programme, in consultation with the British Government, covering at least 12 subject areas, with a view to identifying and agreeing by 31 October 1998 areas where co-operation and implementation for mutual benefit will take place. Such areas may include matters in the list set out in the Annex.***

14.60 Paragraphs 8 and 9 were added to the MDP. This is because Annexes A, B and C were a major casualty of the last days of the talks. The very many concrete proposals therein (considered in Chapter 15) were scrapped in favour of a time-limited work programme.

14.61 ANNOTATIONS

'During the transitional period between the elections to the Northern Ireland Assembly and the transfer of power to it,' is a repetition of the phrase in paragraph 7. While powers are used there, here is is power. The elections were on 25 June 1998. And devolution ensued on 2 December 1999.

'representatives of the Northern Ireland transitional Administration and the Irish Government operating in the North/South Ministerial Council' is the third reference to transition, after paragraph 35 of Strand One and paragraph 7 above. Representatives, under paragraph 18 of Strand One, may be the First Minister and the Deputy First Minister. There was no requirement for shadow ministers, nor an executive committee. The term Northern Ireland transitional Administration summarizes the transition provisions. It was a transitional executive. This confirms the point made above that a transitional administration is a condition precedent for the NSMC meeting, but the formation of the executive committee was not. The Irish Government is the other party.

'will undertake a work programme,' is the essence of paragraphs 8 and 9. The idea came from unionists in Castle Buildings as an alternative to Annexes A, B and C.

'in consultation with the British Government,' is the United Kingdom's view of its role, as the sovereign power, in north/south relations. The GOIA 1920 contained no such reservation. However, the 1973 Sunningdale communiqué referred to 'appropriate safeguards for the British Government's financial and other interests'. There was no reservation in section 12 of the NICA 1973, though the agreements or arrangements – in keeping with devolution – were restricted to transferred matters. The 1995 *Framework Documents* had the United Kingdom government expressing an interest at the end of an apparently limitless offer: 'The British Government believe that, in principle, any function devolved to the institutions in Northern Ireland could be so designated, subject to any necessary savings in respect of the British Government's powers and duties, for example to ensure compliance with EU and international obligations.'[63] This concern with international obligations was general to United Kingdom devolution, though it took a particularly pronounced form as regards Northern Ireland – and not because of Strand Two in the Belfast Agreement. Thus the extraordinary powers in section 26 of the NIA 1998, dealing with much more than international obligations.

63 Part II, paragraph 28.

It may be considered that the United Kingdom government was concerned to ensure that the Northern Ireland transitional administrative did not 'give away' too much. That is not correct. The old 1985 Anglo-Irish Agreement logic – despite the Belfast Agreement – remained to the fore during the transition. The Irish government continued to see the Dublin-London axis as crucial. Northern nationalists resorted to Dublin, and the Irish government negotiated with London. The United Kingdom government became implicated in a pan-nationalist consensus against unionists.

'covering at least 12 subject areas,' was the substitute for the Annexes A, B and C (which are considered in Chapter 15). Subject areas seems to be a reference to effectively departments; as in agriculture, education, etc., in the annex to Strand Two. Subject areas are to be distinguished from matters, which are discussed below.

'with a view to identifying and agreeing by 31 October 1998' makes this date a target. The date of the agreement – 10 April 1998 – means that this was a little over six months later. The referendum and the assembly elections had yet to come. The First Minister and Deputy First Minister were not elected until 1 July 1998. Taking the holiday period into account, there was a period of about two months to engage in the work programme. The date of 31 October 1998 was not met. The First Minister and Deputy First Minister did not reach agreement until 18 December 1998.

In the background was the United Kingdom government. The assent of the Irish government was expressed through the Deputy First Minister. The assembly was told on 18 January 1999 that the agreement 'follow[ed] consultation with the British and Irish Governments'.[64]

'areas where co-operation and implementation for mutual benefit will take place.' relates to paragraph 9. Co-operation derives from paragraph 5. It might seem to refer to subparagraph (i), the *Framework Documents*' concept of consultation. Alternatively, the reference to co-operation in paragraph 1 would suggest it means harmonization. However, paragraph 9 makes it clear it is paragraph 5(iii), separate implementation. It is therefore in the *Framework Documents*' concept of executive action. Implementation should refer to paragraph 5(iii) and (iv), but implementation body has now come to mean new body. This is again clear from paragraph 9. For mutual benefit is the first condition precedent in paragraph 1, with interest replaced by benefit.

'Such areas may include matters in the list set out in the Annex.' Such areas refers to the 12 subject areas above. Matters, however, are different. They are expressly stated to be listed in the annex. If subject area is the first category, then matter presumably is animal and plant health, etc. (the actual topic for agreement as an implementation body). This is the only reference to the annex in Strand Two. The may made it discretionary. The annex (see Chapter 15) had no status other than possible suggestions, alongside any other options.

> 9. ***As part of the work programme, the Council will identify and agree at least 6 matters for co-operation and implementation in each of the following categories:***
>
> ***(i) Matters where existing bodies will be the appropriate mechanisms for co-operation in each separate jurisdiction;***
>
> ***(ii) Matters where the co-operation will take place through agreed implementation bodies on a cross-border or all-island level.***

14.62 This is the main paragraph of Strand Two as regards implementation bodies. It (along with paragraph 8) is related to paragraph 5(iv) above – the fourth function of the NSMC; executive action through new implementation bodies. It relates entirely to the transition, being part of the work programme provisions.

64 New Northern Ireland Assembly, *Report from the First Minister (Designate) and Deputy First Minister (Designate)*, NNIA 6, 18 January 1999, p. 5.

14.63 This means that paragraph 5(iv) has no existence after devolution, and that paragraph 12 does not include further implementation bodies.

14.64 ANNOTATIONS

'As part of the work programme,' refers to paragraph 8, to be achieved by 31 October 1998.

'the Council will identify and agree' makes it clear the NSMC is a condition precedent for agreement. The 18 December 1998 agreement was between the First Minister and the Deputy First Minister only. Identify and agree is used in paragraph 8, though with a view was added before the phrase. This could make 31 October 1998 a target; alternatively or in addition, it makes identification and agreement conditional.

'at least 6 matters for co-operation and implementation in each of the following categories:'. Paragraph 8 referred to at least 12 subject areas. It then refers to the matters in the annex to Strand Two. The word matters is used again here. The at least 6 is the at least 12 from paragraph 8, since the phrase is disjunctive; it is each of the following categories. But is co-operation and implementation one or two concepts? Co-operation and implementation – which have appeared in paragraph 8 – take their separate meanings from subparagraphs (i) and (ii). They are juxtaposed, though there is considerable conceptual confusion. Co-operation is defined in paragraph 9(i) as 'matters where existing bodies will be the appropriate mechanisms for co-operation in each separate jurisdiction'. This is the separate jurisdictions (and existing bodies) of paragraph 5(iii), derived from the *Framework Documents*' concept of executive action through separate implementation. The related Annex B (now scrapped) was described as a 'list of specified areas in which Council is to take decisions on action for implementation separately in each jurisdiction [para 5(iii)]'. Despite that, implementation – by the time of the FA – had nothing to do with existing bodies. Implementation was now defined in paragraph 9(ii) as 'matters where the co-operation will take place through agreed implementation bodies on a cross-border or all-island level'. Though co-operation is repeated, the point is implementation. Agreed implementation bodies is the new bodies of the *Framework Documents*. On a cross-border or all-island level is the phrase used first in paragraph 1, and then in paragraph 5(ii). However, in both of those the word and is used. Here it is or. It must be assumed that when it came to the definition of the paragraph 9(ii) bodies, the draftsman chose to alter and to or. It occurs with an and in paragraph 11. Or means that an implementation body can exist for the border counties, rather than be an all-island institution. Annex C (now also scrapped) was headed: 'list of Implementation Bodies in specified areas in which the Council is to take decisions on action at an all-island and cross-border level (paras 5(iv) and 7.)'.

The actual text of the 18 December 1998 agreement between the First Minister and the Deputy First Minister confirms the developing distinction between co-operation and implementation in paragraphs 8 and 9.

It is headed: 'Statement – 18 December 1998'. Paragraph 6 reads: 'The Agreement required a "work programme" on at least 12 matters, six being new implementation bodies, and six being matters for co-operation. The six implementation bodies (Annex 2) are … .' Paragraph 7 begins: 'The six areas for co-operation (Annex 3) include some aspect of … .' Annex 2 is headed: 'IMPLEMENTATION BODIES'. And Annex 3: 'MATTERS FOR CO-OPERATION'.[65]

However, this 18 December 1998 text was not presented to the assembly on 18 January 1999, when members voted to approve the agreement. Approval was given to a report from the First Minister designate and the Deputy First Minister designate of that date. They referred to 'six areas as suitable for co-operation through existing bodies', and to 'six areas as suitable for the establishment of implementation bodies'. Annex 4 was subtitled: 'Areas

65 New Northern Ireland Assembly, *Report from the First Minister (Designate) and Deputy First Minister (Designate)*, 15 February 1999, no page numbers.

Identified for Co-operation Using Existing Bodies', and Annex 5: 'Areas Identified as Suitable for Implementation Bodies'.[66]

The 18 December 1998 agreement was presented eventually, as an annex – 1b – to the report of the First Minister and Deputy First Minister of 15 February 1998 (though the Strand Two decisions were not introduced – only Strand One). The assembly took note of the 15 February 1999 report the following day. The First Minister and Deputy First Minister stated therein they had 'reported on the outcome on 18 January, following our agreement on 18 December.' Reference was made to 'the Assembly's approval of our agreement'. The agreement, and the approval, were 'subject to formal, joint endorsement with the Irish Government in the North/South Ministerial Council'.[67]

The paragraph 5(iv) problem needs revisiting from the perspective of paragraphs 8 and 9.

Paragraph 5 is the functions of the NSMC. Their inspiration is the scale of consultation, harmonization and executive action from the *Framework Documents* (though harmonization was changed to co-operation and executive dropped in paragraph 1 after the 12 January 1998 Heads of Agreement). In the context of Annexes A, B and C (consultation did not have an annex), executive action was distinguished – following the *Framework Documents* – between separate implementation with existing bodies, and joint implementation through new bodies. Paragraph 5(iv) is the joint, new implementation bodies – or implementation bodies for short. It refers to paragraphs 8 and 9 below. Paragraph 5(iv) may have been intended to refer to paragraph 9(ii) (and paragraph 12); it does neither, though the former is included in paragraphs 8 and 9. Sense therefore has to be made of paragraphs 5, 8 and 9 together. Paragraph 5(iv) introduces the implementation bodies (which are joint and new). The reference to paragraphs 8 and 9 – the work programme – means that there can only be implementation bodies created during the transition. This means that paragraph 12 – 'any further development' – cannot involve implementation bodies. Alternatively, construing paragraph 9: this is introduced by paragraph 5(iv). However, paragraph 9(i) relates to 5(iii) and not 5(iv) (which refers to paragraphs 8 and 9). One has to either ignore paragraph 5(iii) – a general function – or paragraph 9(i), six matters during the transition. Both cannot exist under the Belfast Agreement. Since six areas for cooperation were agreed on 18 December 1998, that means there is no need to agree paragraph 5(iii) activity after devolution.

There is no problem with paragraph 9(ii). It is compatible with paragraph 5(iv). But it affects the meaning of paragraph 12.

> **[7.] *10.* [For the areas listed in Annex C, where it is agreed that new implementation bodies are to be established, [t]*T*he two Governments [to] *will* make [all] necessary legislative and other *enabling* preparations to ensure, *as an absolute commitment, that these bodies, which have been agreed as a result of the work programme,* [the establishment of these bodies] *function at the time of* [at] the inception of the British-Irish Agreement [or as soon as feasible thereafter, such that these bodies function effectively as rapidly as possible.] *and the transfer of powers, with legislative authority for these bodies transferred to the Assembly as soon as possible thereafter. Other arrangements for the agreed co-operation will also commence contemporaneously with the transfer of powers to the Assembly.* [The bodies to have a clear operational remit. To implement,**

66 New Northern Ireland Assembly, *Report from the First Minister (Designate) and Deputy First Minister (Designate)*, 18 January 1999, pp. 5–6, 18 & 21.

67 New Northern Ireland Assembly, *Report from the First Minister (Designate) and Deputy First Minister (Designate)*, 15 February 1999, p. 3.

on an all-island and cross-border basis, policies agreed in the Council. To report to the Council while remaining subject to normal accountability to the Northern Ireland Assembly and the Oireachtas, through the Council.]

14.65 This paragraph – along with paragraphs 8 and 9 – finishes off provision for the work programme. Its purpose – it appeared in the MDP in a slightly different version – was to reassure nationalists that bodies agreed in the work programme would be created by the United Kingdom government, behind the backs of unionists. The earlier version (dealing with Annex C) saw the bodies being created at the inception of the BIA, or as soon as feasible thereafter.

14.66 The origin of the idea of United Kingdom action (associated with that of legislation), is the *Framework Documents.*[68]

14.67 ANNOTATIONS

'The two Governments will make necessary legislative and other enabling preparations' is a commitment binding on London and Dublin. Necessary legislative preparation repeats the point in paragraph 1 regarding the NSMC. In fact, the two governments did not take this legislative road. The six implementation bodies (see Chapter 15) were created by one of the supplementary treaties of 8 March 1999. This agreement was presented to parliament in March 1999 as Cm 4293. It was approved by Dáil Éireann (under article 29.5.2 of Bunreacht na Éireann) on 9 March 1999. The implementation bodies stood created as international organizations (with the agreement due to enter into force on the same day as the BIA).

The two states then transferred functions out of their domestic jurisdictions. This was the role for legislation: North/South Co-operation (Implementation Bodies) (Northern Ireland) Order 1999, SI 1999/859, made on 10 March 1999; and parts II–VIII of the BIA Act 1999, promulgated on 22 March 1999. The secretary of state used the power in section 55 of the NIA 1998, which had come into force at royal assent on 19 November 1998. And other enabling preparations is not clear. If it had been intended to create international organizations by treaty, then the phrase should have read: all necessary legal preparations.

'to ensure, as an absolute commitment, that these bodies, which have been agreed as a result of the work programme,' is again a binding undertaking. As an absolute commitment is among the strongest language in the Belfast Agreement. These bodies, which have been agreed as a result of the work programme is a reference only to paragraph 9(ii). The work programme is dealt with in paragraphs 8 and 9.

'function at the time of the inception of the British-Irish Agreement and the transfer of powers,'. At the time of the inception of the British-Irish Agreement is the date, under article 4(2), on which the BIA enters into force. The conditions precedent are: the Annexes A and B to Constitutional Issues changes; and the legislation necessary to establish article 2 institutions, including the implementation bodies (plus the rest of the MPA). It is not clear whether article 4(1)(c) was drafted with the view that legislation was the legal means to the creation of the six bodies. It is a matter for interpretation whether legislation or required to establish are the operative words. I submit that the latter is the better view: thus, the argument is whether creation by treaty amounts to establishment (in the context of article 4(1)(c)). And the transfer of powers refers to the devolution order under section 3 of the NIA 1998. This was a matter for the secretary of state: the test is sufficient progress having been made in implementing the Belfast Agreement. (The United Kingdom and Irish governments were required to coordinate the day of entry into force of the BIA, with the appointed day for the commencement of parts II and III of the NIA 1998, under paragraph 3 of the Validation,

68 Part II, paragraph 28.

Implementation and Review section). Function is the most important word in this phrase. In the MDP, the phrase was: such that these bodies function effectively as rapidly as possible. The verb function may be related to the noun functions. The six bodies were created by treaty, but it took the legislation to transfer the functions to them. The undertaking to have bodies which functioned on devolution day would seem to imply after legislation, contrary to the interpretation possible of article 4(1)(c) of the BIA. (However, the MDP did not envisage the bodies being necessarily ready on devolution day; function there must have had a meaning closer to operation.)

'with legislative authority for these bodies transferred to the Assembly as soon as possible thereafter.' is perplexing. The bodies could only be constructed out of transferred matters. The functions were destined, under the NIA 1998, to come under the assembly on devolution day. There is a further problem. The bodies, as international organizations created by two states, belong to London and Dublin. Under article 5 of the supplementary agreement of 8 March 1999, the two governments by exchange of notes – at the request of the NSMC – will amend the international agreement. This indeed happened on 18 June 1999 (see above). The bodies do not belong to the assembly (and the Oireachtas). Legislative authority for these bodies can mean only the power to transfer functions out of, and into, Northern Ireland under section 53(2) of the NIA 1998. Of course, the ministers in the NSMC are accountable to the assembly, so – through committees – the assembly could control the bodies. However, standing orders of 9 March 1999 make no such provisions. The NSMC met eventually in shadow form at Parliament Buildings in Belfast on 1 December 1999. 'The Council agreed that the functions and structures of the implementation bodies, and the common arrangements applying to them, should be as specified' in the 8 March 1999 agreement between London and Dublin.[69]

'Other arrangements for the agreed co-operation will also commence contemporaneously with the transfer of powers to the Assembly.' is a reference only to paragraph 9(i). The agreement of the First Minister and the Deputy First Minister of 18 December 1998 (approved by the assembly on 18 January 1999) listed six areas of cooperation. No legal preparation was necessary. This sentence means that, on devolution day, administrative work would commence in these areas; a decision of the NSMC, whether during the transition or after, would be a necessary condition precedent.

> **[7.] *11.* [...] The *implementation* bodies will have a clear operational remit. [To] *They will* implement[,] on an all-island and cross-border basis[,] policies agreed in the Council. [...]**

14.68 These two sentences were part of a larger paragraph in the MDP. Paragraph 11 is the one cited in sections 53(5) and 55(3) of the NIA 1998 by way of definition of an implementation body. This contrasts with the argument that, during the transition, an implementation body is as defined in paragraph 9(ii), and, after devolution, is defined in paragraph 12. No doubt the key words of paragraph 11 were 'clear operational remit'. The focus on paragraph 11 may indicate the legal impossibility of implementation bodies under paragraph 12.

14.69 ANNOTATIONS

'The implementation bodies will have a clear operational remit.' It is not evident what clear operational remit means. Government is structured by functions. Some functions have been transferred to implementation bodies. Under the second sentence of this paragraph, the NSMC has a policy responsibility. Operational remit cannot relate to functions; they are either domestic or shared. It must therefore relate to policy. But that is a matter for ministerial discretion, under paragraph 2.

69 Press release: http://www.northernireland.gov.uk.

'They will implement on an all-island and cross-border basis policies agreed in the Council.' They will implement refers to the implementation bodies. The adjective implementation and the verb implement stem from the juxtaposition of cooperation and implementation in paragraph 8 (repeated in 9), and the designation of the paragraph 9(ii) bodies as implementation bodies. (The existing bodies in paragraph 9(i) are just as much implementation bodies.) On an all-island and cross-border basis stems from paragraphs 1 and 9(ii). This phrase was first used in the *Framework Documents* with reference to subsidiary bodies administering designated functions on an all-island or cross-border basis.[70] This is the sense in which it is used in paragraph 9(ii). However, the term all-island and cross-border arose in paragraph 1, due to the addition of and cross-border to the MDP. This has been followed here. It would seem that, since paragraph 9(ii) defined the bodies to be created in the transition, it is a case of them being cross border or all island. They can only implement on an all-island and cross-border basis under paragraph 11, if they have been created under paragraph 9(ii) on an all-island as opposed to cross-border basis. Policies agreed in the Council makes the NSMC the executive institution in Ireland responsible for the six paragraph 9(ii) bodies, with the members accountable respectively to the assembly and Oireachtas. There is no role for departments in Northern Ireland or the Republic of Ireland controlling the bodies, on the basis of where the functions originated. The bodies are different from departments, and this paragraph locates them constitutionally under the NSMC.

[8.] *12.* Any further [bodies in addition to those specified in the Annexes and other] development[s] of these arrangements[,] to be by agreement in the Council and with the specific endorsement of the Northern Ireland Assembly and Oireachtas, subject to the extent of the competences and responsibility of the two Administrations.

14.70 There was a version of this paragraph in the MDP. Paragraph 5(iv) there – equivalent to 5(iv) in the FA – referred to implementation bodies in paragraphs 7 and 8. Paragraph 7 related to Annex C. And paragraph 8 to any further bodies and other developments in the future. This is not the position here. Paragraph 5(iv) – which defines implementation bodies in general, under functions of the NSMC – refers onwards to paragraphs 8 and 9. But these, as noted, deal only with the work programme in the transition. Paragraph 5 does not provide for any further implementation bodies, and the change in paragraph 12 from the MDP bears this out.

14.71 ANNOTATIONS

'Any further development of these arrangements'. These arrangements refers to the other arrangements in the second sentence of paragraph 10. It is not clear that the word other means that the first sentence of paragraph 10 is also arrangements. Arrangements may refer only to the cooperation of paragraph 8, which leads to paragraph 9(i). Alternatively, these arrangements refers to paragraph 9(i) and (ii). The earlier version in the MDP, in distinguishing any further bodies from other developments of these arrangements, bears out the former interpretation. Any further development refers to devolution, and is derived from other developments of these arrangements in the MDP, confirming the interpretation above.

'to be by agreement in the Council' is required already by paragraph 2.

'and with the specific endorsement of the Northern Ireland Assembly and the Oireachtas,' distinguishes devolution from the transition. Section 53(4) of the NIA 1998 states that implementation bodies agreed after the appointed day cannot come into operation without the approval of the assembly. It does not say the assembly has the power to create further

70 Part II, paragraph 25.

implementation bodies (and the assembly could not do it the way it was done on 8 March 1999). In the case of ambiguity about section 53(4), it is therefore necessary to refer to the Belfast Agreement – where any doubt about bodies after the appointed day would be resolved negatively. The government of the Republic of Ireland, a sovereign state, did not need to provide for a similar power in the BIA Act 1999.

'subject to the extent of the competences and responsibility of the two Administrations.' repeats the second condition precedent in paragraph 1. This is repeated also in paragraph 5(i)–(iii). Responsibility, in the singular, adds nothing.

13. It is understood that the North/South Ministerial Council and the Northern Ireland Assembly are mutually inter-dependent, and that one cannot successfully function without the other.

14.72 This was added to the MDP. The paragraph links Strands One and Two. But it is a repetition of an aspect of a general point – interlinkage – in paragraph 5 of the Declaration of Support. Linkage in the Belfast Agreement derives from the rule of the talks that 'nothing [would] be finally agreed ... until everything [was] agreed'.[71]

14.73 Paragraph 5 of the Declaration of Support (see above) – building on that in the MDP – interlinks much, but not all, of the Belfast Agreement. Specified are all of the institutional and constitutional arrangements, seemingly those mentioned in article 4 of the BIA. Paragraph 5 of the Declaration of Support seems to be – but only seems – equivalent to article 2: 'It is accepted that all of the institutional and constitutional arrangements – an Assembly in Northern Ireland, a North/South Ministerial Council, implementation bodies, a British-Irish Council and a British-Irish Intergovernmental Conference – are interlocking and inter-dependent and that in particular the functioning of the Assembly and the North/South Council are so closely inter-related that the success of each depends on that of the other.' In paragraph 5 of the Declaration of Support, the assembly is an institution; in article 2 of the BIA, the institutions specified are only the international organizations.

14.74 Strand One is included, however, in the interlinkage by reference to the provisions of the Multi-Party Agreement in article 2 of the BIA. Also included – in the BIA if not paragraph 5 of the Declaration of Support – by virtue of the reference to the provisions of the Multi-Party Agreement, are sections six to ten[72] of the Belfast Agreement (though a distinction needs to be made between bodies corporate and other – non-legal – entities).

14.75 ANNOTATIONS

'It is understood' suggests that what follows is provided for elsewhere. This is indeed the case: paragraph 5 of the Declaration of Support.

'that the North/South Ministerial Council and the Northern Ireland Assembly are mutually inter-dependent, and that one cannot successfully function without the other.' Paragraph 13 has been taken from the Declaration of Support. There are two differences of emphasis. One, the earlier refers to the NSMC and the Assembly as being closely inter-related. Here, it is mutually inter-dependent, which is a general term in paragraph 5. Two, the earlier refers to the success of each depending on that of the other. Here, it is about successfully functioning.

71 *Ground Rules for Substantive All-Party Negotiations*, Cm 3232, 16 April 1996, rule 23.

72 Rights, Safeguards and Equality of Opportunity, Decommissioning, Security, Policing and Justice, and Prisoners.

Does paragraph 13 – after paragraph 5 of the Declaration of Support – imply that, if the assembly goes, so does the NSMC (and the implementation bodies)? This is an aspect of a more general question: if the Belfast Agreement collapses, does everything go? The answer has to do with the BIA (it provides for the institutions and the constitutional changes; it also provides for everything else in the MPA which is legally binding on the two states parties).

If the BIA – having entered into force – comes to an end (through termination or suspension[73]), then neither government would be obliged to implement, or continue implementing, any aspect of the Belfast Agreement. However, the constitutional changes could only be reversed, respectively by parliament and by a referendum. The north-south and east-west institutions – as specified in article 2 of the BIA – would no longer have any legal foundation (the supplementary agreements are related to the BIA). The rest of the Belfast Agreement, mainly Strand One but also the remaining aspects of the MPA outside the three strands, would remain a matter for a United Kingdom government freed of any obligations in international law.

However, just as parliament may theoretically change the law at any point, the two states could negotiate a new international agreement.[74]

Each particular question – about for example the NSMC or the implementation bodies – must be answered, on a case-by-case basis, against this general legal background. There is no legal – as opposed to political – argument that, just because the aspects were interlinked when they were created, they must also all fall together. That depends upon the fate – and terms, if they survive – of the BIA.

A domino effect was implied – but without ultimate legal conviction – by the second recital of the preamble of the four supplementary agreements of 8 March 1999 (including the NSMC one): 'Recalling that the participants in the multi-party negotiations pledged that they would work in good faith to ensure the success of each and every one of the arrangements to be established under the Multi-Party Agreement, and that it was accepted that "all of the institutional and constitutional arrangements – an Assembly in Northern Ireland, a North/South Ministerial Council, implementation bodies, a British-Irish Council, and a British-Irish Intergovernmental Conference and any amendments to British Acts of Parliament and the Constitution of Ireland – are interlocking and interdependent and that in particular the functions of the Assembly and the North/South Council are so closely inter-related that the success of each depends on that of the other".'

This was to repeat paragraph 5 of the Declaration of Support in the Belfast Agreement (by paraphrasing and quotation), to no particular – additional – legal effect. Part of the preamble is not a term of the international agreement. However, each of the four agreements is supplementary to the BIA, and article 8 of the implementation bodies agreement makes express that it shall be read with that parent agreement. Annex 1 of the BIA – the MPA – contains paragraph 5 of the Declaration of Support, and paragraph 13 of Strand Two. They exist legally, and do not need to be repeated in the implementation bodies supplementary agreement.

73 Article 60 of the 1969 Vienna convention on the law of treaties.

74 This can be the only explanation for Paul Murphy's comment during the debate on the implementation bodies' order: 'It is clear that the implementation bodies could not continue to function as envisaged in the agreement. Arrangements for the Executive functions that they carried out would have to be reviewed. For example, the Foyle Fisheries Commission has been operated as a cross-border body for many years, and doubtless will continue to do so.' As a result of an intervention from an anti-agreement unionist, the minister of state went on to say: '... The North-South Ministerial Council, to which the bodies are accountable, would disappear if there were no Assembly. Similarly, the bodies envisaged in the agreement would disappear.' (House of Commons, *Hansard*, 6th series, 327, 137, 8 March 1999)

Article 62 of the 1969 Vienna convention on the law of treaties – in part V dealing with invalidity, termination and suspension of the operation of treaties – provides for the fundamental change of circumstances known as frustration. The basic rule is that a fundamental change of circumstances, which was not foreseen by the parties at the time of agreement, may not be invoked as a ground for terminating or withdrawing from a treaty. There is one exception: '(a) the existence of those circumstances constituted an essential basis of the consent of the parties to be bound by the treaty; and (b) the effect of the change is radically to transform the extent of obligations still to be performed under the treaty'. There are therefore two factual questions to be answered with evidence: did the parties – namely the two states – enter into the Belfast Agreement on the basis that all aspects would rise together?; would the collapse of the assembly radically transform the performance of the BIA? The evidence for the answer 'yes' to both questions is strong.[75]

If the assembly were to collapse, what would happen to the NSMC? The answer is simple – factual rather than legal. The NSMC includes ministers from Northern Ireland. They would go with the assembly. It would not then be possible for the NSMC to meet much less make decisions.

If the assembly were to collapse, what would happen to the implementation bodies? Again, the answer is simple – and factual. The bodies are dependant entirely upon the NSMC for policy. No NSMC, no policy. No policy, no (living) bodies.

Terminating or suspending the BIA is, of course, different from the United Kingdom government suspending some or all of the institutions agreed on 10 April 1998. United Kingdom sovereignty over Northern Ireland remained unaffected. Arguably, London can do what it wishes with the assembly, without even consulting Dublin. (The Irish government was not a party to the Strand One negotiations.) However, for diplomatic rather than legal reasons, the United Kingdom government has envisaged suspension of the NSMC (and implementation bodies) and the BIC – but not the BIIC – through an international agreement with the Irish government.

The draft agreement of 13 July 1999, associated with the aborted *Way Forward* plan of 2 July 1999 to establish the executive, addressed the question of Strands Two and Three suspension. The draft agreement envisaged the implementation bodies surviving for four months. No attempt would be made by the two governments to change radically their nature. At the end of that period, the functions – if there was still suspension – would be transferred back to the two administrations. However, – a curiosity – 'the Bodies may retain such functions as were exercised by a single body in both jurisdictions prior to the entry into force of the Implementation Bodies Agreement'.[76] This raises the question: what single bodies?

Suspension after devolution was revisited in the Northern Ireland Act (NIA) 2000, which received the royal assent on 10 February 2000. This followed the failure of the IRA to begin decommissioning by 31 January 2000, in accord with an apparent understanding[77] reached in the Mitchell review of September to November 1999. The NIA 2000 was brought into force by order of the secretary of state on 12 February 2000.[78] Section 5 (implementation bodies) required the secretary of state to transfer functions back to Northern Ireland during a suspension, and to return the functions to the implementation

75 There is evidence that the prime minister intended 'a mutual destruction' provision: Mitchell, *Making Peace*, pp. 175–6. The end of the assembly was to lead apparently to the end of the NSMC and the implementation bodies.

76 Annex, Part B, Section three, paragraphs 1–4.

77 Rt. Hon. Peter Mandelson MP: House of Commons, *Hansard*, 6th series, 344, 131–2, 8 February 2000.

78 Northern Ireland Act 2000 (Commencement) Order 2000, SI 2000/396, 11 February 2000.

bodies following any restoration order. This section made reference to an international agreement between the United Kingdom and Irish government. However, there was no such agreement. And the Irish government continued to refuse to make one with the United Kingdom government. Thus, what the Irish government had been prepared to do in July 1999, it was unwilling to do the following February. The argument, such as it was, emanating from Dublin, was that article 29.7.1 of BNH prevented the government suspending the North-South implementation bodies (there was no problem with the NSMC). This is not credible.[79]

[9.] *14.* Disagreements within the Council to be addressed in the format described at paragraph 3(iii) above or in the plenary format. By agreement between the two sides, experts could be appointed to consider a particular matter and report.

14.76 This paragraph deals with dispute resolution.

14.77 ANNOTATIONS

'Disagreements within the Council' is a change from resolve disagreement in paragraph 3(iii).

'to be addressed in the format described at paragraph 3(iii) above' is not very helpful. Paragraph 3(iii) states simply that disagreements will be resolved in an appropriate – that is, ad hoc – format. There has also been a change from resolve to address.

'or in the plenary format.' does add to paragraph 3(iii), if appropriate format there is interpreted as not including the plenary format in 3(i).

'By agreement between the two sides,' is superfluous given paragraph 2.

'experts could be appointed to consider a particular matter and report.' is permitted already under paragraph 2. However, it is the substantive point – after plenary format – in this paragraph. Presumably, the experts are not those in paragraph 16. They are independent consultants. The terms of reference are confined to a particular matter, the word used in paragraphs 8 and 9.

[10.] *15.* [The necessary costs of the Council and the funding of the implementation bodies to be agreed within the Council, subject to normal procedures in the Oireachtas and the Northern Ireland Assembly.] Fund[s]*ing* to be provided by the two Administrations on the basis that the Council and the implementation bodies are a necessary public function.

[11. The Council's expenditure to be audited jointly by the Comptroller and the Auditor-General's Office and by the Northern Ireland Audit Office. Their joint report to be submitted simultaneously to the Oireachtas and to the Assembly.]

14.78 This is the only paragraph relating to finance. Paragraph 11 of the MDP was not included, no doubt because the idea of transnational auditing was a considerable advance on the principle of practical cooperation.

14.79 The practice in Anglo-Irish relations originally followed the principle of joint funding.[80] That, however, has given way to subsequent agreements on finance outside the establishing treaty.[81]

79 See my article, *Irish Times*, 10 March 2000.

80 Article 10 of the International Fund for Ireland agreement, Republic of Ireland No. 1 (1986), Cmnd 9908, 18 September 1986.

81 Article 7 of the agreement Establishing the Independent International Commission on

14.80 Funding had been addressed in paragraph 9 of the 1973 Sunningdale communiqué. In the initial period, the two administrations would provide grants to the council 'towards agreed projects and budgets, according to the nature of the service involved'. There would be further studies of funding for the longer term. The cost of the secretariat was to be shared, 'and other services would be financed broadly in proportion to where expenditure or benefits accrue'.

14.81 The NSMC (and dependent implementation bodies) are, of course, shared by a regional administration of the United Kingdom and the Irish state – not two states.

14.82 ANNOTATIONS

'Funding to be provided by the two Administrations' refers initially to the NSMC – a cooperation council. There is no express provision for funding, or administration generally, in the 8 March 1999 supplementary agreement. However, article 3 states that both sides are responsible for the operation of the council. This does not necessarily imply joint funding of the NSMC.

After the NSMC comes the six implementation bodies, and the areas for cooperation. The – necessary – 8 March 1999 supplementary agreement establishing the implementation bodies states, in article 3(2), that each body shall be funded in accordance with the provisions of the MPA – which does not answer the question of proportion, much less whether there should be particular ratios for each body. Annex 2 of the agreement – which was not approved by the assembly – makes reference to the finance departments (in Belfast and Dublin), and, in part 7 (common arrangements), has a section on financial arrangements. The bodies were to receive grants initially under the Appropriations (Northern Ireland) Order 1999, SI 1999/658 (made on 10 March 1999), and from money voted by Dáil Éireann (not the Oireachtas). The finance ministers have the power to override NSMC decisions; this is not specified in the Belfast Agreement. There is also provision for the bodies being subject to departments in Belfast and Dublin; which again is not in the Belfast Agreement. The North/South Co-operation (Implementation Bodies) (Northern Ireland) Order 1999, SI 1999/859, incorporates this agreement as schedule 1. Named departments in Northern Ireland – under section 55(2)(c) of the NIA 1998 – are specified as the grant-making authority, but only with the approval of the finance department. There is no reference to proportions. Part VIII of the BIA Act 1999, dealing with common provisions, includes section 42 (grants to bodies). Here, a minister, with the approval of the minister for finance, may make a grant to a body. There is no reference to proportions.

'on the basis that the Council and the implementation bodies constitute a necessary public function.' adds nothing. The NSMC is an international organization. It rests on the BIA. It is for the two members – the United Kingdom and Irish states – to determine its future. That is not a matter for the two administrations. As a treaty body, it is of course a necessary public function under the Belfast Agreement. Much the same applies to the implementation bodies. They begin as functions in departments in two administrations (or as new functions). When the functions were transferred to the body, an international organization, they become the responsibility of the NSMC under Strand Two. But again, given the 8 March 1999 supplementary agreement, the question of there being continuing necessary public functions rests with the United Kingdom and Irish states.

[12.] *16.* **The Council to be supported by a standing joint Secretariat, staffed by members of the Northern Ireland Civil Service and the Irish Civil Service.**

Decommissioning, Treaty Series No. 54 (1997), Cm 3753, 26 August 1997; article 4(2) of the agreement Establishing the Independent Commission for the Location of Victims' Remains, Ireland No. 7 (1999), Cm 4344, 27 April 1999.

14.83 The inspiration for this is the Anglo-Irish secretariat, set up under article 3 of the 1985 Anglo-Irish Agreement. It was located at Maryfield outside Belfast. As a result of an undertaking given by the United Kingdom prime minister at Castle Buildings, it was closed down at the end of 1998. The secretariat – comprising United Kingdom and Irish officials – then relocated to Windsor House in central Belfast.

14.84 There was a very different concept in the 1973 Sunningdale communiqué. The council of Ireland was to have a secretariat, 'which would be kept as small as might be commensurate with efficiency in the operation of the Council'. The secretariat was to service the council of ministers, and the consultative assembly. It would also 'supervise the carrying out of the executive and harmonising functions and the consultative role of the Council'. No bodies were envisaged. The council of ministers was to appointed a secretary-general, and decide upon the location of the permanent headquarters (the plans for such headquarters being drawn up by the secretary-general) – suggesting an ambitious body. The council of ministers was also to make arrangements for the recruitment of staff, 'in a manner and on conditions which would, as far as practicable, be consistent with those applying to public servants in the two administrations'.

14.85 ANNOTATIONS

'The Council to be supported by a standing joint Secretariat,' is similar to the 1985 Anglo-Irish secretariat: 'A Secretariat shall be established by the two Governments to service the Conference on a continuing basis ... .' The absence of a date (either hereby or upon entry into force) suggests this was not a treaty body. Much the same applies to the standing joint Secretariat; it has no existence in international law.

'staffed by members of the Northern Ireland Civil Service and the Irish Civil Service.' The Anglo-Irish secretariat was a United Kingdom/Irish joint unit. The United Kingdom officials were drawn from the NIO; the Irish mainly from the department of foreign affairs. This secretariat will have (relatively inexperienced) Northern Ireland officials, side by side with Irish officials with an institutional memory of nearly 14 years at Maryfield.

No reference is made in the Belfast Agreement to a location for the secretariat; Belfast and Dublin are the seats of the two administrations. On 15 February 1999, the First Minister and the Deputy First Minister reported to the assembly that, following consultation with other parties, Armagh in Northern Ireland has emerged as a favoured venue, at least for the inaugural meeting of the NSMC – the council, not the secretariat.[82] The inaugural meeting was indeed held in Armagh on 13 December 1999. Armagh was favoured traditionally by the SDLP as the alternative capital of Northern Ireland; it is also considered a possible seat of the embyro government of Ireland.[83] Officials – the First Minister and Deputy First Minister reported – had been asked 'to look at options for a permanent location for the Council in Armagh', without prejudice to other Northern Ireland locations. No reference was made to a location for the secretariat.[84] This is unusual for a cooperation council, and unprecedented

82 However, the Deputy First Minister, at the inaugural meeting, referred to Armagh as 'the administrative centre of this new North South institution'.

83 Armagh was announced as the likely location for the NSMC secretariat (sic) by David Andrews in the Dáil on 9 March 1999. Two days later, Dr Maurice Hayes, a former Northern Ireland civil servant, told the senate that, in 1974, Armagh was being considered as the seat of the council of Ireland (Seanad Éireann, *Official Report*). At the inaugural meeting of the NSMC in Armagh on 13 December 1999, the Deputy First Minister said, having referred to the European Union: 'let Armagh become the Strasbourg of Ireland'.

84 New Northern Ireland Assembly, *Report from the First Minister (Designate) and Deputy First Minister (Designate)*, pp. 4–7.

in Ireland. The 1973 Sunningdale communiqué stated that the location of meetings would be left to the council of ministers. It is customary to rotate venues between administrations, and even to seek to cover principal and symbolic locations. To have a fixed location, and in Northern Ireland – with the Irish government agreeing – means Strand Two will look less like practical cooperation and more like the embyro government of Ireland.

[13.] *17.* **The Council to consider the European Union dimension of relevant matters, including the implementation of EU policies and programmes and proposals under consideration in the EU framework. Arrangements to be made to ensure that the views of the Council are taken into account and represented appropriately at relevant EU meetings.**

14.86 This paragraph is a companion to paragraph 31 in Strand One.

14.87 Europe has long fascinated Irish governments, and supporters of a united Ireland. This aspiration, seemingly, is an aspect of European integration, even though the reformation of the old United Kingdom could be just as easily espoused. There is no logical connection between the former aspiration, and the fact that the United Kingdom and the Republic of Ireland are both member states of a supranational body. The impact of European Economic Community membership – less than one year after joining – was mentioned in the 1973 Sunningdale communiqué.

14.88 In 1992, the Irish government published *Ireland in Europe: a shared challenge: economic co-operation on the island of Ireland in an integrated Europe,*[85] a set of independent consultants' reports on the all-Ireland aspect of the single European market. Also in 1992, the SDLP – in the aborted talks – grafted on to the joint authority model of the 1983–84 Dublin forum, the idea of a European protectorate – Northern Ireland would be run by three internal, and three external, commissioners (the latter from London, Dublin and Brussels).[86]

14.89 ANNOTATIONS

'The Council to consider the European Union dimension of relevant matters,'. Relevant matters presumably refers to the matters in paragraph 9, both cooperation and implementation. However, it is the European Union, and not the NSMC, which determines whether those matters are relevant – and have a European dimension.

'including the implementation of EU policies and programmes and proposals under consideration in the EU framework.' Each member state has a two-way relationship with the EU institutions, particularly the council and commission. There is policy formulation, a process of decision making by the member states collectively. And there is policy implementation by the European commission, through not just the member states, but also sub-state regional administrations.

Proposals under consideration in the EU framework relates to the former, policy formulation. Here, the points made with reference to paragraph 31 of Strand One may be repeated. The United Kingdom has national interests to consider, which it advances in Brussels. It is most unlikely that any regional administration – Scotland, Wales or Northern Ireland – could change central government policy, if it was not so minded. Regional ministers could (but are

85 Dublin, 1992.

86 Paul Bew, Henry Patterson & Paul Teague, *Northern Ireland: between war and peace: the political future of Northern Ireland*, London 1997, pp. 76–83.

unlikely to) represent the United Kingdom, but it would not be on behalf of their regional administration. They are more likely to be included in a United Kingdom ministerial delegation (with commensurate arrangements for officials). The Irish government is considered under the second sentence of this paragraph.

Implementation is another matter, particularly when it comes to spending European funds in the regions. This would seem to be the context for the implementation of EU policies and programmes (it is unlikely that the United Kingdom or Irish states would agree to cooperate on European law).[87]

The relevant structural funds – LEADER, INTERREG and SSPPR (the 1995–2000 peace and reconciliation fund) – are rooted in treaty-based regional policy and cohesion. The objective is less integration, in the sense of harmonization or equalization, and more the mitigation of socio-economic extremes across geographical Europe.[88] Thirteen existing community initiatives were to be reduced to three according to Agenda 2000, the European plan preoccupied with the absorption of former communist states. The first of the three community initiatives was to be cross-border, transnational and inter-regional cooperation. Thus, north-south cooperation will be related integrally to east-west cooperation, and even to the relationship between the two islands and the European mainland. There may be a role for the NSMC, as an agent of Brussels, but equally for the BIC, which might be better placed to deal with the islands/mainland relationship.

'Arrangements to be made to ensure that the views of the Council are taken into account and represented appropriately at relevant EU meetings.' The NSMC has no standing within the EU. This will remain the position even if it becomes involved in implementation of aspects of regional policy. It comprises the Northern Ireland administration (which is only a part of the United Kingdom) but also the Irish government. The Republic of Ireland is a member state. And it will no doubt advance its national interests, both in the NSMC (its Northern Ireland policy) and in Europe. Whether its Northern Ireland policy is adopted by the NSMC is a matter ultimately for the two sides in Northern Ireland. Even if it is, it is not unlikely that this could conflict with other Irish policy, or vested interests in the Republic. It is not clear what arrangements can achieve the point of the second sentence. The views of the Council may be ascertainable on north-south matters, but less easily on any European aspect (since Europe is a separate area of policy). Taken into account involves making them known. It is entirely another matter whether they are adopted by one or other member state. Represented appropriatedly indicates that the member state or states will make that decision.

The meaning of this paragraph from the point of view of Northern Ireland has been circumscribed by the memorandum of understanding and supplementary agreements (MoU), presented to parliament by the lord chancellor in October 1999 (Cm 4444). With these documents, London is seeking to coordinate relations with Edinburgh, Cardiff and Belfast after devolution to the three regions. The memorandum proper, plus the concordat on the coordination of European Union policy issues, subordinates the devolved adminstrations to central government. While the BIC and NSMC are acknowledged,[89] it is most unlikely that Northern Ireland – given this modernization of the United Kingdom's constitution – will be able to do very much through the NSMC in Europe.

[14.] *18.* The Northern Ireland Assembly and the Oireachtas to consider developing a joint parliamentary forum, bringing together equal numbers from both institutions for discussion of matters of mutual interest and concern.

87 But see the joint statement issued by London and Dublin before the Lisbon European Council in March 2000.

88 1997 Amsterdam treaty, TEU, title XVII (ex title XIV), economic and social cohesion, articles 158–162 (ex 130a–e).

89 Paragraph 18.

14.90 The 1920 council of Ireland was intended to be an inter-parliamentary body. It was to comprise a president appointed by the lord lieutenant, and 40 members. They were to be elected – 20 from Southern Ireland and 20 from Northern Ireland – in the proportion 7 to 13 from the two senates and houses of commons. The 1973 council of Ireland included a consultative assembly, comprising 30 members from Dáil Éireann and 30 from the Northern Ireland assembly; they were to be elected by proportional representation using the single transferable vote.

14.91 However, an inter-parliamentary body was constructed on the east-west axis. This was first suggested in the 1981 joint studies, the product of London-Dublin diplomacy.[90] Article 12 of the 1985 Anglo-Irish Agreement stated that it was for parliamentary decision at Westminster and in Dublin, though the two governments would support it if it were established. The British-Irish Inter-parliamentary Body was set up eventually, in 1990.

14.92 The origin of the north-south parliamentary body in this paragraph is the 1995 *Framework Documents*. It was stated that the two governments expected there would be a parliamentary forum.[91] The MDP stated that the two legislatures were to be encouraged to form the joint parliamentary forum.

14.93 ANNOTATIONS

'The Northern Ireland Assembly and the Oireachtas to consider developing' cannot be one of the MPA proposals to which the two governments, by virtue of article 2 of the BIA, are bound to implement. It is a matter entirely for the two legislatures. To consider developing leaves this option entirely open. It is not part of the Belfast Agreement. The 1920 council of Ireland was to include the senate and house of commons of Southern Ireland. But the 1973 consultative assembly, as envisaged, included only Dáil Éireann. Here, the reference to the Oireachtas means that the seanad in Dublin is to participate.

'a joint parliamentary forum,' uses the terminology of the *Framework Documents*. Forum has been used frequently in both parts of Ireland: in the Republic of Ireland, the 1983–84 forum (comprising nationalists revising the means to a united Ireland);[92] and the 1995 forum for peace and reconciliation, set up after the 1993 *Downing Street Declaration*;[93] and the 1996–98 forum, set up under section 3 and schedule 2 of the Northern Ireland (Entry to Negotiations, etc) Act 1996, to promote dialogue and understanding in Northern Ireland.

'bringing together equal numbers from both institutions' does not specify election. It is more likely that a system or systems of nomination is involved. If the assembly were to have say X members, the Dáil would have to have less than X to allow for the participation of the seanad.

'for discussion of matters of mutual interest and concern.' is the purpose of the joint parliamentary forum. The *Framework Documents* envisaged 'a wide range of matters of mutual interest' being considered.[94] It is not clear whether matters relates to paragraph 9 (cooperation and implementation) or is wider. Is the joint parliamentary forum to be like the 1973 consultative assembly, or more like the British-Irish Interparliamentary Body? Mutual interest comes from paragraph 1, the first condition precedent to the work of the NSMC. And concern would seem to add nothing.

90 *Anglo-Irish Joint Studies: joint report and studies*, Cmnd 8414, November 1981, pp. 4, 11–12.
91 Part II, paragraph 36.
92 New Ireland Forum, *Report*, Dublin, May 1984.
93 Paragraph 11.
94 Part II, paragraph 36.

[15.] ***19.*** **Consideration to be given to the establishment of an independent consultative forum appointed by the two A[a]dministrations, representative of civil society, comprising the social partners and other members with expertise in social, cultural, economic and other issues.**

14.94 The inspiration for this is the civic forum in paragraph 34 of Strand One. This forum is to be distinguished from the joint parliamentary forum. It is a second all-Ireland institution augmenting the NSMC and the implementation bodies.

14.95 ANNOTATIONS

'Consideration to be given to the establishment of' is similar to paragraph 18. The Northern Ireland civic forum was to be established. This is purely hypothetical. It cannot therefore be a shared obligation of the two governments under article 2 of the BIA.

'an independent consultative forum' differs from the Northern one, which is described as a consultative civic forum. This has had independent added, perhaps because of the experts concept. Civic has been dropped, probably because the Republic of Ireland is not prepared to give the same weight to civil society as Northern Ireland appears to do.

'appointed by the two Administrations,' is the Northern Ireland executive committee and the Irish government. Appointed is less democratic than the term representative used of the Northern Ireland forum. There is no apparent intention that the Northern Ireland forum should become one half of the all-Ireland body.

'representative of civil society' uses those concepts of representation and civil society. However, they have not been used in the same way to structure the independent consultative forum.

'comprising the social partners' is European terminology. It is used in the Republic of Ireland, and to a considerably lesser extent in the United Kingdom. The social partners are management and trade unions, who are the first two sectors mentioned in paragraph 34 of Strand One. However, here, there is no provision for the voluntary sector.

'and other members with expertise in social, cultural, economic and other issues.' is a new idea. The idea of expertise is probably drawn from the consultees on various committees which the Irish government uses for the discussion of policy. Social, cultural, economic resembles the economic, social and cultural matters of title F of the 1985 Anglo-Irish Agreement. It is not clear what other issues are: politics are presumably excluded.

15

Annex

15.1 This Annex is attached to Strand Two of the Belfast Agreement. It is not, however, listed in the table of contents. It is at page 13 of Cm 3883 and page 25 of Cm 4705 (page 19 of the 1999 Irish version). The Annex is referred to in paragraph 8 of Strand Two, paragraphs 8 and 9 dealing with the work programme during the transition. The Annex lists 12 possible areas of practical cooperation between the Northern Ireland assembly and the Irish government.

History of practical cooperation

15.2 Given that Ireland was once an administrative unit within the United Kingdom, one might have expected a degree of continuing economic, social and even cultural integration after 1920.[1] This, however, would be to reckon without the consequences of the creation of an Irish state; all-Ireland activity, attractive to nationalists, was commensurately unappealing to unionists: they had in any case more appropriate access to a much more significant United Kingdom state.

The Government of Ireland Act 1920

15.3 A council of Ireland was provided for in section 2(1). Two of its four purposes were: to provide for the administration of services which the two parliaments mutually agree should be administered uniformly throughout the whole of Ireland, or which by virtue of this Act are to be so administered; to promote mutual intercourse and uniformity in relation to matters affecting the whole of Ireland.[2]

15.4 There was no mutual agreement, because, even though Southern Ireland was set up in 1922, it was destined – under the 1921 treaty – to become the dominion Irish Free State, within the commonwealth but outside the United Kingdom.

15.5 A number of all-Ireland matters was provided for in section 10 (powers of council of Ireland). Subsection (2) listed:

- railways,
- fisheries; and
- the Diseases of Animals Acts.

With a view to the uniform administration throughout Ireland of these public services, the powers of the United Kingdom would be transferred on the appointed

1 This is ignoring the social divergence of nineteenth-century Ireland which underpinned partition.

2 The third and fourth were: to bring about harmonious action between the parliaments and governments of Southern Ireland and Northern Ireland; with a view to the eventual establishment of a Parliament for the whole of Ireland.

day to the council of Ireland. It would be, in a sense, a third government in Ireland (not including the continuing sovereignty of the Westminster parliament). The council of Ireland was even to have law-making powers in these three areas (which helps explain its structure as an interparliamentary body). However, under a proviso, Southern Ireland and Northern Ireland could deal with the construction, extension or improvement of railways wholly within their jurisdictions.

15.6 All-Ireland administration did not come to pass. Under section 1(1) and paragraph 3 of the first schedule of the Irish Free State (Consequential Provisions) Act 1922 (Session 2), the council of Ireland – now to link Northern Ireland and the Irish Free State (a putative new state) – was envisaged as continuing. (This – a variation of the 1921 treaty[3] – had been agreed in discussions between London, Dublin and Belfast.[4]) Paragraph 3(1) amounted to a reenactment of section 2(3) of the GOIA 1920, with the Southern Ireland parliament replaced by that of the Irish Free State; the constitution of the council of Ireland could be amended by identical acts. As for the powers to be transferred from United Kingdom departments to the council of Ireland, paragraph 3(2) provided for postponement as regards Northern Ireland: identical acts could lead to a transfer by order in council, otherwise it would not happen for five years.

15.7 There were no identical acts after 1922. In 1925, under the tripartite agreement accepting the border, the powers being held for the council of Ireland were transferred to Northern Ireland. The council was effectively killed off. The Belfast and Dublin governments were to 'meet together as and when necessary for the purpose of considering matters of common interest arising out of or connected with the exercise and administration of the said powers'.[5]

The Ireland Act 1949

15.8 There were no such meetings dealing with railways, fisheries, contagious diseases of animals – or any other matter. The Second World War, during which Éire/Ireland asserted neutrality successfully, divided Ireland fundamentally. The welfare state accentuated the contrast. And this continued to the beginning of the troubles in 1968.

15.9 Section 3(1)(a)(ii) of the Ireland Act 1949 had introduced the idea of agreements or arrangements between the two governments, with legal effect being given by Northern Ireland statutes. Whatever of the legality of the few instances of north-south activity in the early 1950s, they represent the high point of practical cooperation:

- drainage of the river Erne;
- the Foyle Fisheries Commission;
- joint purchase of the Great Northern Railway (later split up).

15.10 There was a thaw in the Irish cold war in 1965, when the two premiers, Sean Lemass and Captain Terence O'Neill, exchanged visits. When the Irish taoiseach travelled north on 17 January 1965, he was carrying a shopping list of demands. No significant progress was made on the question. However, the matters

3 The treaty was silent on the council of Ireland.
4 House of Commons, *Hansard*, 5th series, 159, 388–9, 27 November 1922.
5 Paragraph 5 of the schedule to Ireland (Confirmation of Agreement) Act 1925.

are presented here as a matter of record:

- the abolition of barriers to tourism;
- the facilitation of education exchanges;
- sharing health facilities where urgent and necessary;
- trade matters;
- the joint development of nuclear power where this proves economic;
- joint agricultural research projects;
- reciprocal practising rights for lawyers;
- joint administration of certain charities.[6]

Lemass' difficulty at home had not been huge aspirations; he found the Irish state most reluctant to countenance the loss of control which practical cooperation across a frontier entailed. (This would also be the case in the 1970s and even 1980s.)

The 1973 Sunningdale communiqué

15.11 The *locus classicus* of north-south cooperation was the work done between 6 and 9 December 1973, in the civil-service college in Berkshire. It was ambitious given the absence of precedents; and this remains the position even given Strand Two of the Belfast Agreement.

15.12 The institutions were a council of ministers, a consultative assembly and a secretariat led by a secretary-general located in permanent headquarters. The council of ministers was to have 'executive and harmonising functions and a consultative role', the consultative assembly 'advisory and review functions'. The communiqué is silent on the legalization of this Irish dimension, though there was to be a formal conference early in 1974 to sign – an international – agreement. The text does refer to legislation in Belfast and Dublin to devolve functions to the council of Ireland.

15.13 Considerable attention was given to matters. 'In the context of its harmonising functions and consultative role, the Council of Ireland would undertake important work relating, for instance, to the impact of EEC membership.' This was towards the end of the first year of United Kingdom and Irish membership.

15.14 As for executive functions, there was no agreed list, but there would be 'studies' (just as there would be a work programme 25 years later). Decisions on executive decision-making by the council of ministers were to be made at the formal conference early in the new year.

15.15 The objectives to be borne in mind in the studies were:

- to achieve the best utilisation of scarce skills, expertise and resources;
- to avoid, in the interests of economy and efficiency, unnecessary duplication of effort; and
- to ensure complementary rather than competitive effort where this is to the advantage of agriculture, commerce and industry.

This was extremely general, and much more than a specification for interstate

6 John Horgan, *Sean Lemass: the enigmatic patriot*, Dublin 1997, p. 279.

cooperation in the early 1970s. A modified version of these objectives was included in the 1995 *Framework Documents*.[7]

15.16 There was the equivalent of the 1998 annex in the 1973 communiqué, the studies being directed to identifying 'suitable aspects of activities in the following broad fields':

- exploitation, conservation and development of natural resources and the environment;
- agricultural matters (including agricultural research, animal health and operational aspects of the Common Agricultural Policy), foresty and fisheries;
- co-operative ventures in the fields of trade and industry;
- electricity generation;
- tourism;
- roads and transport;
- advisory services in the field of public health;
- sport, culture and the arts.

This list of eight broad fields was extremely general. And the categories would reappear in the 1990s.

The 1995 Framework Documents

15.17 They did so as illustrations in the *Framework Documents* of executive, harmonising and consultative functions:

executive:

- sectors involving a natural or physical all-Ireland framework;
- EC programmes and initiatives;
- marketing and promotion activities abroad; and
- culture and heritage;

harmonising: aspects of

- agriculture and fisheries;
- industrial development;
- consumer affairs;
- transport;
- energy;
- trade;
- health;
- social welfare;
- education; and
- economic policy.

Further examples were given of three of the above ten categories. 'The Governments also expect', the document read, 'that a wide range of functions would be designated at the consultative level.'[8]

7 Part II, paragraph 25. However, there was a new idea: 'the achievement of economies of scale ...'. This suggests a nationalist view of Ireland rather than an objective concept of state relations; the Republic of Ireland cannot generally rival the United Kingdom on economies of scale.

8 Part II, paragraph 34.

The Mitchell Draft Paper of 6 April 1998

15.18 This was the draft of the Belfast Agreement: it is available on the internet[9] at: http://www.nuzhound.com. The area changed most in the last days at Castle Buildings was Strand Two, in particular the matters designated for practical cooperation. There were three annexes in the MDP:

- Annex A, attached to paragraph 5(ii). This was described as common policies; it was harmonization from the *Framework Documents*. A total of 25 matters was listed, in the following categories: agriculture (3); education and training (6); health (2); industrial and trade matters (5); marine and waterways (4); energy and transport (3); and environment (2);
- Annex B, attached to paragraph 5(iii). This was referred to as separate implementation, and had been so conceived in the *Framework Documents*. By the time of the FA, it was being called cooperation. A total of 16 matters was listed: agriculture (2); education and youth (1); social welfare/community activity (2); the environment (3); culture, heritage and the arts (2); health (3); marine and waterways (1); sport (1); and science and technology (1);
- Annex C, attached to paragraph 5(iv). This was described as implementation bodies. It was the joint implementation of the *Framework Documents*. Eight bodies were listed, three (*) not having been agreed with the United Kingdom government:[10]
  (1) tourism;
  (2) environmental protection;
  (3) EU programmes;
  (4) transport planning;
  (5) inland waterways;
  (6) Irish language promotion;*
  (7) trade promotion and indigenous company development;*
  (8) arts.*

15.19 There were altogether 49 matters, including eight implementation bodies. This was reduced in the talks to the Annex of 12 subject areas and/or matters.

ANNEX

Areas for North/South co-operation and implementation may include the following:

1. **Agriculture – animal and plant health.**
2. **Education – teacher qualifications and exchanges.**
3. **Transport – strategic transport planning.**
4. **Environment – environmental protection, pollution, water quality, and waste management.**
5. **Waterways – inland waterways.**

9 Reference is made there to two articles comparing the MDP to the FA: by Ed Moloney, in the *Sunday Tribune* of 19 April 1998; by Gary Kent in the *Belfast Newsletter* of 1 May 1998 and *Fortnight* of May 1998.

10 It is not clear why three bodies were put into the MDP without the assent of the responsible government. Senator Mitchell gives his version in *Making Peace*, London 1999, pp. 149–65.

6. **Social Security/Social Welfare – entitlements of cross-border workers and fraud control.**
7. **Tourism – promotion, marketing, research, and product development.**
8. **Relevant EU Programmes such as SPPR, INTERREG, Leader II and their successors.**
9. **Inland Fisheries.**
10. **Aquaculture and Marine Matters.**
11. **Health: accident and emergency services and other related cross-border issues.**
12. **Urban and rural development.**

Others to be considered by the shadow North/South Council.

15.20 ANNOTATIONS

'Areas for North/South co-operation and implementation may include the following: ... Others to be considered by the shadow North/South Council.' The combination of the discretionary opening line, and the mandatory closing one, diminishes the significance of the 12 matters listed. Areas is the word used in paragraph 8 of Strand Two, where there is reference to 12 subject areas. However, it gives way to matters in paragraphs 8 and 9. There would appear to be no difference between subject area and matter, even though the list of 12 starts (as regards items 1–7 and 11) with a departmental area of responsibility (or part of a department), and then apparently specifies a particular matter. North/South is taken from the NSMC. However, in the closing line North/South Council is used without Ministerial, as in paragraph 5 of the Declaration of support. Co-operation and implementation is the juxtaposition, based on paragraph 5(iii) and (iv) (and attempted in paragraph 9(i) and (ii)), between originally separate implementation and implementation jointly. It settled down in paragraphs 8 and 9 to be cooperation, including possibly harmonization but more like common policies, and implementation – meaning a new, all-Ireland or cross-border body. The word shadow in the closing line is a late addition to the text, as is the reference to shadow ministers in paragraph 35 of Strand One.

All 12 subject areas originated in Annexes A, B or C; they were selected from the 49. From Annex A (common policies) there is: teacher qualifications and exchanges; inland fisheries; accident and emergency services and other related cross-border issues; and urban and rural development (4). From Annex B (separate implementation) there is: animal and plant health; (part of) environmental protection, pollution, water quality, and waste management; entitlements of cross-border workers and fraud control; and aquaculture and marine matters (4). From Annex C (implementation bodies) there is: strategic transport planning; (part of) environmental protection, pollution, water quality, and waste management; inland waterways; tourism – promotion, marketing, research, and product development; relevant EU Programmes such as SPPR, INTERREG, LEADER II and their successors (5).

After the Belfast Agreement

The agreement of 18 December 1998

15.21 The work programme specified in paragraphs 8 and 9 of Strand Two was the second of four matters referred by the secretary of state on 29 June 1998 to the assembly.[11] This was done under section 1(2) of the Northern Ireland (Elections) Act 1998.

15.22 The BIA of course was not in force, though, under article 4(1)(c), the

11 New Northern Ireland Assembly, *Official Report*, vol. 1, pp. 2 & 34–7, 1 July 1998.

institutions in article 2 – including the implementation bodies – were a condition precedent of entry into force. If the two governments did not discharge their obligations under the treaty, there would be no BIA – and therefore no devolution. The Northern Ireland (Elections) Act 1998 empowered the secretary of state to refer matters to the assembly. Under paragraph (1) of the schedule, the secretary of state directed the times and places of meeting. The New Northern Ireland Assembly was defined in section 1(1) as 'for the purpose of taking part in preparations to give effect to the' Belfast Agreement. It did not have any legislative powers under this act, and it did not acquire them before devolution under the NIA 1998. However, referral of matters had a constitutional role, understood in terms of the transition. The secretary of state cited paragraph 35 of Strand One in her letter of 29 June 1998. Assembly approval was implied arguably by the Northern Ireland (Elections) Act 1998, even in areas where it was not specified in the initial standing orders.

15.23 The assembly could not overrule a decision of the two governments under the BIA. But, under legislation incorporating the Belfast Agreement, including the Northern Ireland (Elections) Act 1998, assembly approval was an integral part of the preparations giving effect to the Agreement.

15.24 The First Minister and Deputy First Minister made an interim report to the Assembly on 18 September 1998. They stated they had received 'a technical assessment of possible areas for co-operation under the auspices of the North-South Ministerial Council, submitted on 24 August 1998' (co-operation would appear to be used here generically).[12] They announced that the NSMC would meet in the near future;[13] the First Minister specified late September or early October 1998.[14] On 26 October 1998 – following return from the United States – the Deputy First Minster, in a statement to the assembly, reported that a small working group had been established by the SDLP and UUP. He stated that detailed assessments had been requested from the civil service; those available were to be placed in the library of the assembly. It was stated that Northern Ireland officials had been meeting with officials from the Republic of Ireland as regards the NSMC.[15]

15.25 Agreement was reached between the First Minister and Deputy First Minister on 18 December 1998. There had been no meeting of the NSMC, though the Irish (and United Kingdom) government was involved.[16] The Strand Two aspect of the agreement was reported to the assembly on 18 January 1999. There was agreement on six areas for cooperation and six implementation bodies:

cooperation:

- transport;
- agriculture;
- education;

12 This assessment was published in part in the *Irish News* on 8 September 1998.

13 New Northern Ireland Assembly, *Interim Report from the First Minister (Designate) and Deputy First Minister (Designate)*, 14 September 1998, pp. 2 & 7.

14 New Northern Ireland Assembly, *Official Report*, vol. 1, p. 96, 14 September 1998.

15 New Northern Ireland Assembly, *Official Report*, vol. 1, p. 211, 26 October 1998.

16 The report stated agreement was 'following consultation with the British and Irish governments'. (p. 5)

- health;
- environment;
- tourism.

implementation bodies:[17]

- inland waterways;
- food safety;
- trade and business development;
- special EU programmes;
- language (Irish and Ulster Scots);
- aquaculture and marine matters.

Details of each cooperation area were specified. As for the implementation bodies, the full functions were also listed in the report.[18] The assembly voted by 74 to 27 to approve the report.[19]

15.26 For reasons unexplained, the agreement of 18 December 1998 was not presented to the assembly on 18 January 1999 (though it was mentioned[20]). The six cooperation matters and the six implementation bodies were accompanied by reporting by officials. However, when the First Minister and Deputy First Minister reported further on 15 February 1999, the whole of the 18 December 1998 agreement was included unedited as annex 1b. The six cooperation matters were described as 'includ[ing] some aspects of' the listed areas[21] (which had not been the case on 18 January 1999).

15.27 This 15 February 1999 report was only noted, as part of an approval of another matter by 78 votes to 28 on 16 February 1999.[22]

Necessary legislative and other enabling preparations

15.28 According to paragraph 10 of Strand Two, following the work programme – where the target date of 31 October 1998 slipped to 18 December 1998 – the two governments would make necessary legislative and other enabling preparations.

15.29 Things did not go according to this plan, judging by the subsequent preparations. First, the six implementation bodies were created by treaty,[23] not by

17 The origin of these six is interesting: four of the six – EU programmes, inland waterways, language, and trade and business development – had been in Annex C of the MDP, albeit in different forms; the two latter had not been accepted by the United Kingdom government.

18 New Northern Ireland Assembly, *Interim Report from the First Minister (Designate) and Deputy First Minister (Designate)*, 18 January 1999, pp. 5–6, 18–26.

19 New Northern Ireland Assembly, *Official Report*, vol. 1, pp. 474–5, 18 January 1999.

20 New Northern Ireland Assembly, *Official Report*, vol. 1, p. 3, 18 January 1999.

21 New Northern Ireland Assembly, *Interim Report from the First Minister (Designate) and Deputy First Minister (Designate)*, 15 February 1999, no page numbers.

22 New Northern Ireland Assembly, *Official Report*, vol. 2, pp. 108–9, 16 February 1999. The Rt. Hon. David Trimble MP, the First Minister, told parliament on 8 March 1999: 'the order and the associated treaty give effect to agreements that were made between the parties in the Northern Ireland Assembly on 18 December, although they were not formally approved until 15 [16] February because of some outstanding business'. (House of Commons, *Hansard*, 6th series, 327, 124, 8 March 1999)

23 The precedent is the International Fund for Ireland, set up by international agreement in 1986. The international tin council litigation in London in the late 1980s is important for

domestic legislation.[24] Secondly, the functions agreed by the First Minister and Deputy First Minister (and approved by the assembly), were augmented by provisions regarding arrangements for the bodies.

The international agreement

15.30 On 8 March 1999, in Dublin, Marjorie Mowlam, the secretary of state for Northern Ireland, and David Andrews, the Irish foreign minister, signed four supplementary agreements (related to the BIA). One of those agreements, and the only one strictly necessary, concerned implementation bodies. It was presented to parliament as Cm 4293 in March 1999, and approved by Dáil Éireann (under article 29.5.2 of Bunreacht na hÉireann) on 9 March 1999.[25]

15.31 The implementation bodies agreement comprises nine articles, plus Annex 1 and Annex 2 (respectively in Cm 4293, pages 2–4, 5–12 and 13–50). Annex 1 was the only part of the text which had been approved by the assembly (on 18 January 1999).[26]

15.32 Article 1 – under and in furtherance of article 2 of the BIA – establishes the six implementation bodies. They are named:

- Waterways Ireland;
- The Food Safety Promotion Board;
- The Trade and Business Development Body;
- The Special EU Programmes Body;
- The North/South Language Body;
- The Foyle, Carlingford and Irish Lights Commission.

15.33 Article 2 introduces Annexes 1 and 2: Annex 1 is the functions as they relate to matters within the competence of Northern Ireland ministers; Annex 2 is described thus: 'Each Body shall exercise its functions and be structured in accordance with the arrangements ... [in] Annex 2 ... .' Article 3 refers to the MPA. While article 4 deals with Irish Lights. Article 5 introduces a new principle. Under Strand Two, the NSMC is meant to belong to the two administrations. However, the NSMC has to request the two states to amend – by exchange of notes – any of the provisions of Annexes 1 and 2.[27] Article 6 relates to legal capacity, in Northern Ireland and separately in the Republic of Ireland. Article 7 is also a strange principle. The United Kingdom and/or Irish foreign ministers may direct a body –

the relationship between international and municipal law: *J.H. Rayner (Mincing Lane) v Dept. of Trade and Industry* [1988] 3 All ER 257 CA, 275 per Kerr LJ; [1990] 2 AC 418, 482–3 per Lord Templeman HL. See also: *Arab Monetary Fund v Haskim* [1990] 3 WLR 139; [1991] 2 WLR 729, 732 & 735 per Lord Templeman (contra Lord Lowry).

24 The Rt. Hon. David Trimble MP told parliament on 8 March 1999: 'There was difficulty with the particular legal concepts used and I am glad that, following much discussion, we got it right.' (House of Commons, *Hansard*, 6th series, 327, 124, 8 March 1999)

25 The agreement had been laid before Dáil Éireann on 8 March 1999.

26 The Rt. Hon. David Trimble MP told parliament on 8 March 1999: 'Most of the documentation [referring to the order and the treaty], which is lengthy and detailed, simply fleshes out the detail of what was agreed on 18 December.' (House of Commons, *Hansard*, 6th series, 327, 124, 8 March 1999)

27 This is arguably contrary to paragraph 10 of Strand Two, interpreting legislative authority to mean legal responsibility.

over the head of the NSMC – to ensure compliance with other international obligations. Article 8 states that the agreement is to be read with the BIA. And article 9 provides for its entry into force on the same date as the BIA.

15.34 Annex 1 is uncontroversial. It is the functions agreed on 18 December 1998, and approved by the assembly on 18 January 1999.

15.35 In contrast, Annex 2 – which dominates the agreement – would appear to be more than technical details. Since article 2.2 (exercise of functions and structured arrangements) is partly dependent upon article 2.1 (functions), it is likely that Annex 2 will be construed in terms of Annex 1.

15.36 There certainly seems to have been a desire to inflate Annex 1 without referral to the assembly. To take an example, Waterways Ireland is to have waterways added 'progressively thereafter' according to Annex 1. In Annex 2, all this was to happen on 1 April 2000. Further, in Annex 1, the body is to take over the 'functions' of a related company. In Annex 2, this becomes 'take over the control' of the company. No doubt, many such examples could be detected in each of the six bodies. Most likely then, the meaning of Annex 2 will be subject to considerable interpretation subject to Annex 1.

15.37 Part 7 (common arrangements) of Annex 2 raises a different order of problems. Each body, having been created in international law by article 1, is further specified in accord with article 6. This is done in such a way that the two civil services, which – under Strand Two – are only meant to constitute the NSMC secretariat, have a considerable role in north-south relations.

15.38 Thus, the two finance departments (and grant-giving departments) are entrusted with drawing up a financial memorandum. This will specify 'the accounting year and currency' of the bodies. Northern Ireland and the Republic of Ireland have different accounting years, and different currencies. Further, the comptroller and auditor general for Northern Ireland, and the Irish comptroller and auditor general are to cooperate in examining and certifying accounts. There was a provision for joint auditing in the MDP. It was taken out, and does not form part of the Belfast Agreement. No doubt, other points of conflict with what is – effectively – a fundamental agreement in international law will emerge.

15.39 In essence, the six implementation bodies, despite the work of the First Minister and Deputy First Minister, and the approval of the assembly, have been treated, less like international organizations with unique legal personality, and more as shared domestic clients of two systems of administration. The functions have been transferred; but civil service control continues.

Legislation

15.40 There was separate legislation in London and in Dublin.

15.41 At Westminster, the North/South Co-operation (Implementation Bodies) (Northern Ireland) Order 1999, SI 1999/859 was made on 10 March 1999. It had been debated, in the house of commons, at 22.00 on 8 March 1999 (the day the international agreement was signed). The debate lasted less than 90 minutes. The order was approved by the house of lords the following day, in about 30 minutes. It was made by the secretary of state under section 55 of the NIA 1998 on 10 March 1999. (The direct-rule order in council powers were not used.)

15.42 Though the order met the target date for devolution, this did not occur as a consequence.

15.43 In the Oireachtas, the Irish government took the four supplementary agreements (plus the BIA) – not just that on the implementation bodies – with the legislation. This was called the British-Irish Agreement (BIA) Bill; while it dealt mainly with the implementation bodies, it also provided for the NSMC and the BIC (but not the BIIC). The BIA was approved by Dáil Éireann (under article 29.5.2 of Bunreacht na hÉireann) on 9 March 1999, on a motion from the minister for foreign affairs, David Andrews. This was nearly a year after 10 April 1998. The four supplementary agreements – signed the previous day, on 8 March 1999 – were also approved. The taoiseach then moved the second reading debate of the bill. The committee and remaining stages were taken on 10 March 1999. Seanad Éireann took all the stages on 11 March 1999. The BIA Act was promulgated, by the president under the constitution, on 22 March 1999 (as number 1 of 1999). This was an ordinary act of the Oireachtas, but one that had been expedited considerably.

15.44 The London order and Dublin act have in common the implementation bodies' agreement of 8 March 1999, respectively as schedule 1 (pp. 9–25) and as the only schedule (pp. 27–53). The United Kingdom and Irish legislation is consequential upon article 6 of the implementation bodies' agreement: 'Each Body shall have legal personality.' The two governments were transferring domestic functions to six international organizations, created simultaneously in Northern Ireland (not United Kingdom[28]) and Irish law. However, the order and act differ considerably. This is to be expected given the different styles of drafting (and statute books).

15.45 The order has an introductory part (articles 1–3), followed by six parts (one for each body) (articles 4–24), and then seven schedules (of which the first is, of course, the international agreement). Article 2 (interpretation) refers to the agreements or arrangements in the NSMC under part V of the NIA 1998 (without further specifying them). Article 3 (the agreement) refers to that establishing the implementation bodies in international law.

15.46 Each of parts II to VII is similarly structured: the implementation body; transfer of functions; grants; and annual report and accounts. This is based no doubt on section 55(2) of the NIA 1998, under which the secretary of state may: (a) confer on the body the legal capacities of a body corporate; (b) confer functions; (c) confer grant-making powers on a Northern Ireland department; (d) make provision for accounting and auditing; (e) make consequential or supplementary provisions.

15.47 Paragraph (a) is covered by paragraph 2 of schedule 2 to the order. Paragraph (b) is covered by defining the functions as those in Annex 1 of the international agreement (Annex 2 is referred to as simply arrangements). Paragraph (c) is covered by the designation of a lead department, not the finance

28 Section 55 of the NIA 1998 was part of a United Kingdom-wide statute. There was no intention to create the bodies in Great Britain (not even the Foyle, Carlingford and Irish Lights Commission). Article 1(3) of the order states it does not extend to England and Wales or Scotland.

department[29] (which was not provided for in the Belfast Agreement[30]). Paragraph (d) is covered by a designated minister (again not provided for in the Belfast Agreement) presenting annual reports and accounts to the assembly. And paragraph (e) is covered by schedules 6 and 7.

15.48 The Irish bill has a preliminary and general part.[31] This is followed by parts II to VII (one for each body). A part VIII deals with other provisions. And the schedule is of course the international agreement.

15.49 Part I of course makes provision for the NSMC and the BIC (sections 3 and 4), but is otherwise attempting to replicate in Irish law what the order does in Northern Ireland law; this is in spite of the long title. Section 2 (interpretation) refers to both the BIA and the implementation bodies' agreement. A Northern Ireland minister is defined as a minister or a department, of which a minister is head (even though that term is no longer used in United Kingdom legislation[32]). Section 2(2) provides that the act shall be construed with due regard to the MPA, the BIA and the implementation bodies' agreement.[33]

15.50 Parts II–VII deal with the six implementation bodies similarly. (There is of course no parent provision, as with section 55 of the NIA 1998). The NSMC is defined strangely in part II: 'when performing functions in relation to the Body, functions of the Body or the waterways'.[34] This statutory definition is at variance with the NSMC's international status, otherwise recognized in the BIA Act 1999. Each part then defines the status of the body as a body corporate, including perpetual succession. Functions and arrangements follow the United Kingdom order. Again, Strand Two of the Belfast Agreement is incorporated in whole or in part. Finally, repeals of relevant legislation are located within each part. A relevant minister is defined for the inland waterways body,[35] but not for the other five (in contrast to the United Kingdom order) in parts III–VII. This, however, is done in section 39. Finally, the Commissioners of Irish Lights are dissolved, under section 37 (like the Foyle Fisheries Commission by section 35), but there is no comparable provision in United Kingdom law; this is because of article 4 of the international agreement (and paragraph 7.1 of part VI of Annex 2).[36]

29 Finance department approval is required.

30 Reference is made in the order to article 3.1 of the international agreement. This refers to the MPA. The effect is to incorporate some or all of Strand Two of the Belfast Agreement in Northern Ireland law.

31 'We need not fool ourselves', an opposition member told the senate, 'that we are giving this Bill strict parliamentary scrutiny but what we are endorsing is a direct outcome of the Good Friday Agreement.' (Seanad Éireann, *Official Report*, 11 March 1999)

32 The Departments (Northern Ireland) Order 1999, SI 1999/283, articles 2(2)(b) & 4(1).

33 This was criticized by John Bruton, the Irish opposition leader, as muddying the separation of powers by requiring the judiciary to interpret a political agreement. The Belfast Agreeement has, of course, a political face and a legal one. The major problem is likely to be varying United Kingdom and Irish interpretations of the BIA, to which the MPA is annexed.

34 See also part VI on the language body.

35 There is a reference to the minister in part VI (the language body).

36 Under paragraph 3 of schedule 3 of the NIA 1998, the following is reserved: navigation, including merchant shipping, but not harbours or inland waterways. If this covers aids to navigation (which is not necessarily the position), then section 4(2)–(4) would allow responsibility for Irish Lights to be transferred to the assembly.

15.51 Part VIII covers other provisions in 18 sections. Section 39 (as noted) defines appropriate ministers, generally one for each body.[37] Section 40 provides for the transfer of staff, which is not covered in the United Kingdom order.[38] Section 42 allows for grants to the bodies. Section 47 allows for the article 7 direction by the minister for foreign affairs.[39] Section 50 allows for ombudsman cooperation in both parts of Ireland, which is not covered similarly in the United Kingdom order (though this is in Annex 2 of the international agreement). Section 55 refers to the areas of cooperation under paragraphs 8 and 9(i) of Strand Two. Public bodies concerned are to have such functions as are necessary or expedient in order to cooperate. Finally, section 56(1) – referring to paragraph 2.5 of part 7 of Annex 2 of the international agreement – deems it to be an audit (which confirms the point made above about the United Kingdom order: joint auditing is in the agreement, even though it was taken out of the MDP).

The role of the English[40] and Irish attorneys-general

15.52 An international agreement, an order at Westminster, and an act of the Oireachtas were not apparently sufficient. On 8 March 1999, the secretary of state and the Irish foreign minister exchanged letters. (There is no United Kingdom source on this; it was made public through the Dáil and Seanad.[41]) The two governments agreed that the attorneys-general would consult and cooperate as necessary, to address any problems which may arise concerning the interpretation and application of Northern Ireland and Irish domestic legislation in regard to the implementation bodies. This, seemingly, is to be after judicial decisions, construing the international agreement, which will have an effect in the other jurisdiction. The Irish foreign minister referred to it as dispute resolution. However, the two law officers would report on the legislation – regardless of cases – within six months of the BIA entering into force; that is, by 2 May 2000.

15.53 This important development was not in the Belfast Agreement; nor had it been included in the implementation bodies' agreement. Neither parliament saw fit to empower its government's chief legal adviser to perform this constitutionally innovative role. The letters exchanged were drafted by the attorneys. It emerged subsequently that the secretary of state had suggested that the two attorneys-general should bring forth any necessary additional refinements of the legislation within six months.[42]

Amending the international agreement

15.54 On 18 June 1999, by an exchange of notes,[43] the secretary of state and

37 The language body has two ministers.
38 Annex 2 of the international agreement provides for staffing by 'open recruitment, temporary secondment and the transfer of staff' (paragraph 3.2). The use of 'and' rather than 'or' may cause problems of interpretation.
39 The United Kingdom equivalent is paragraph 3 of schedule 2 of the order.
40 Under section 10(1) of the NICA 1973, the attorney-general for England and Wales also became the attorney-general for Northern Ireland (following temporary provisions in 1972). This section is not repealed by the NIA 1998, though it allows for a separate attorney-general of Northern Ireland.
41 By David Andrews, on 9 March 1999.
42 The Irish government preferred to rely upon the BIA and the supplementary agreement.
43 But not under article 5, as the international agreement had not entered into force.

Irish foreign minister, referring to Part 4 of Annex 1 and Part 4 of Annex 2 (Special EU Programmes), agreed that, by community initiatives, they had intended to include any successor to the PEACE programme.[44] This agreement followed the Berlin European Council decision in March 1999 to categorize the successor programme as mainstream structural funding. The attorney general's office, and 'the British-Northern Ireland legal advisers', had raised a possibility of ultra vires if the point was not clarified.[45]

15.55 Provision was made in United Kingdom law by the North/South Co-operation (Implementation Bodies) (Amendment) (Northern Ireland) Order 1999, SI 1999/2062, made on 19 July 1999, adding Schedule 1A to the original order. The secretary of state acted under section 55 of the NIA 1998. The Irish foreign minister, unable to use section 5 of the British-Irish Agreement Act 1999 (regulations to remove difficulties), had to seek primary legislation. The British-Irish Agreement (Amendment) Act 1999 added an interpretative schedule to the original act. The president was requested to sign the bill early under article 25.2.2 of BNH.

44 Schedule of the North/South Co-operation (Implementation Bodies) (Amendment) (Northern Ireland) Order 1999, SI 1999/2062, made on 19 July 1999. The agreement, under article 29.5.3 of BNH, was not to have been laid before Dáil Éireann.

45 It is not obvious that the problem has been solved; the issue is whether the successor programme was intended (not whether it was defined as a community initiative).

16

Strand Three: British-Irish Council

16.1 Strand Three is the fifth section of the Belfast Agreement. It comprises two separate institutions, the BIC and the BIIC. The BIC is considered in this chapter; the BIIC in the following one. Strand Three is at pages 14–16 of Cm 3883 and pages 26–8 of Cm 4705 (pages 20–2 of the 1999 Irish version). At 21 paragraphs (12 for the BIC and 9 for the BIIC), Strand Three is overshadowed by Strand One (36 paragraphs); but it is longer than Strand Two (19 paragraphs). I show [deletions] to the MDP, and *additions* thus.

16.2 Strand Three – along with Strand Two – is provided for in part V of the NIA 1998. Section 52 deals with the North/South Ministerial Council and the BIC, as complementary institutions. Section 53 covers any – north-south or east-west – agreement or arrangement, entered into by a Northern Ireland minister or junior minister. Functions may be transferred to a body under section 53(2). The BIIC is dealt with in section 54. And (north-south) implementation bodies created before the appointed day are provided for in section 55. (Section 56 on the civic forum has nothing to do with Strands Two or Three.)

16.3 The devolved administration in Northern Ireland would appear to have the power, under the NIA 1998, to form east-west implementation bodies, either within the United Kingdom (plus the Isle of Man and the Channel Islands), or even on an international basis, involving the Republic of Ireland. This flows from section 53(1)–(3) of the NIA 1998. Subsection (4) requires assembly approval. While this was inspired by paragraph 12 of Strand Two, section 53 relates equally to the BIC and the NSMC. Subsection (5), apparently qualifying subsection (4), cannot be understood to mean that BIC implementation bodies are not possible.

16.4 The key legal instrument is the agreement between the United Kingdom and Irish governments establishing the British-Irish Council (again?), done at Dublin on 8 March 1999[1] – one of the supplementary agreements relating to the BIA.[2] (There are some textual differences between the United Kingdom and Irish versions.[3]) This international agreement was presented to parliament by the foreign secretary in March 1999 as Cm 4296. It was approved by Dáil Éireann (under article 29.5.2 of BNH) on 9 March 1999.[4] (Further provision was made in Irish law by section 4 of the British-Irish Agreement Act (BIAA) 1999, promulgated on 22 March 1999.)

1 Agreement betweeen the government of the United Kingdom of Great Britain and Northern Ireland and the government of Ireland establishing a British-Irish Council, Cm 4296, Ireland No. 5 (1999).

2 See the memorandum on procedural guidance, agreed at the inaugural meeting in London on 17 December 1999.

3 The first recital in the preamble in the Irish version is missing two commas, distinguishing the MPA from the BIA. The British/Irish Agreement is also used in article 1 of this version.

4 *Official Report*.

16.5 Strand Three – in the typology of the talks – was about relationships 'between the two Governments, including their relationship with any new institutions in Northern Ireland'.[5] However, under the basis of the all-party negotiations, reference was made to achieving a new beginning 'between the peoples of these islands'.[6] Strand Three was negotiated between the two governments, though there was provision for consultation with the political parties.

16.6 Given that Great Britain and Ireland had constituted the United Kingdom state until 1922, it should not be surprising that an east-west dimension figures in the Belfast Agreement. But this would be to reckon without the consequences of the formation of an Irish state. A 'these islands' perspective was anathema to proponents of national self-reliance; southern unionism was largely vanquished, and Ulster unionists – rejoicing in differences in Ireland – relied upon their region being an integral part of the United Kingdom (even if many in Britain considered them simply Irish).

The British-Irish dimension

16.7 There was no east-west dimension in the GOIA 1920, because Southern Ireland and Northern Ireland remained part of the United Kingdom. Nor was there one in the NICA 1973, the only precedent for devolution on a basis of power-sharing. The Sunningdale communiqué, heavy with an Irish dimension, was silent on relations between the two states.

16.8 The inspiration for Strand Three was twofold, and contradictory: Irish policy on Northern Ireland from 1980, and the response of selected unionists to the emerging Irish dimension.

16.9 On 8 December 1980, the United Kingdom and Irish premiers, meeting in Dublin, commissioned joint studies covering a number of discrete policy areas,[7] 'in order to assist them in their special consideration of the totality of relationships within these islands'.[8] Northern Ireland was not central to this development, though the Irish government presented it as a significant constitutional advance.[9] It was an attempt at a bilateral relationship between two states within Europe, with Northern Ireland unspecified centrally as a common problem.

16.10 In November 1981, the Anglo-Irish intergovernmental council was established; there was no international agreement. It was to deal with 'matters of common interest and concern, with particular reference to the achievement of peace, reconciliation and stability and the improvement of relations between the two countries and their peoples'.[10] The council was not a great success, though there were meetings of ministers, and episodic Anglo-Irish summits involving heads of government.[11]

5 *Ground Rules for Substantive All-Party Negotiations*, Cm 3232, 16 April 1996, rule 2.
6 *Ground Rules for Substantive All-Party Negotiations*, Cm 3232, 16 April 1996, rule 1.
7 They were: possible new institutional structures; citizenship rights; security matters; economic cooperation; and measures to encourage mutual understanding.
8 Anglo-Irish Joint Studies, *Joint Report and Studies*, Cmnd 8414, November 1981, p. 4.
9 Margaret Thatcher, *The Downing Street Years*, London 1995, p. 390.
10 Anglo-Irish Joint Studies, *Joint Report and Studies*, Cmnd 8414, November 1981, p. 4.
11 It was at the third summit meeting that the Anglo-Irish agreement was signed: joint

16.11 This was partly because of the diversion of the new Ireland forum, which met in Dublin in 1983–84. Its *Report* came up with three solutions to the Irish question: a unitary state; a federal/confederal state, and joint authority. While the United Kingdom government was conceived as a facilitator/persuader for Irish unity,[12] there was also proposed (but only for the united Ireland option) 'an Irish-British Council with intergovernmental and interparliamentary structures which would acknowledge the unique relationship between Ireland and Britain and which would provide expression of the long-established connnections which unionists have with Britain'.[13]

16.12 The Anglo-Irish intergovernmental conference was established, as a result of the international agreement signed at Hillsborough in Co. Down on 15 November 1985, within the framework of the Anglo-Irish intergovernmental council. It was 'concerned with Northern Ireland and with relations between the two parts of the island of Ireland'.[14] And it would deal on a regular basis with: political matters; security and related matters; legal matters, including the administration of justice; and the promotion of cross-border cooperation.

16.13 The 1985 Anglo-Irish Agreement, and the conference, foreshadowed the BIIC aspect of Strand Three (considered in the next chapter). It was the involvement of the Republic of Ireland in helping run Northern Ireland – on a basis perceived as approaching practical joint authority – which led unionists to emphasis an alternative British-Irish dimension.

16.14 A principal proponent was Sir John Biggs-Davison MP, who advocated the Islands of the North Atlantic, or IONA. The Council of the (British) Isles idea – of Scottish provenance – was adopted by Ulster unionists in the early 1990s.

16.15 The 1993 *Downing Street Declaration* referred to 'institutional recognition of the special links that exist between the peoples of Britain and Ireland as part of the totality of relationships, while taking account of newly forged links with the rest of Europe'.[15]

16.16 The 1995 *Framework Documents* contained a significant difference of emphasis.

16.17 In part I, the United Kingdom government, outlining its approach to a comprehensive settlement, envisaged replacing the Anglo-Irish Agreement with a new and more broadly based one 'reflecting the totality of relationships'. There would be bilateral liaison through an intergovernmental council. There would also be an intergovernmental conference, with suitable rights of attendance and consultation for appropriate Northern Ireland representatives.[16]

16.18 In part II, the shared understanding drafted in Dublin, paragraphs 39–49

communiqué, 15 November 1985. This document also noted that there had been more than 20 meetings of ministers in the previous year.

12 'It would be for the British and Irish governments to create the framework and atmosphere within which such negotiations [embodying Irish unity] could take place.' (*Report*, Dublin 1984, p. 30)

13 *Report*, Dublin 1984, p. 32.

14 Article 2(a) of the 1985 Anglo-Irish Agreement, Cmnd 9657, Republic of Ireland No. 1 (1985).

15 Paragraph 9.

16 Annex B, pp. 17–18; see also paragraph 27 of part I.

dealt with east-west structures. This envisaged the intergovernmental conference as a continuing institutional expression of Dublin involvement in Northern Ireland. Paragraph 43 referred to bilateral matters of mutual interest not covered by other specific arrangements, either through the intergovernmental council, the conference or otherwise.[17]

16.19 Subsequently, the Irish government acceded to the unionists' idea of a council.[18] However, the Irish government which negotiated the Belfast Agreement subsequently sought to play down the BIC during the referendum in the Republic of Ireland.[19]

16.20 The Heads of Agreement of 12 January 1998 had promised a new British-Irish Agreement to replace the existing Anglo-Irish Agreement, and help establish close cooperation and enhance relationships. The first of four institutions was to be an intergovernmental council: 'to deal with the totality of relationships, to include representatives of the British and Irish governments, the Northern Ireland administration and the devolved institutions in Scotland and Wales, with meetings twice a year at summit level'.

The Nordic Council: an analogy?

16.21 The BIC has been compared[20] to another regional organization, in northern Europe or *Norden*[21] – the Nordic Council linking Denmark, Finland, Iceland, Norway and Sweden (plus the self-governing territories, the Aland Islands, the Faeroe Islands and Greenland); a total of eight members with a joint population of 23 million.[22]

16.22 The Nordic Council was established in 1952 by Denmark, Iceland, Norway and Sweden. Finland joined in 1955; the Faeroes and Aland in 1970, and Greenland in 1984. There was no proper legal basis[23] to the Nordic Council in 1952, due to the Soviet Union. This was provided by the 1962 Helsinki treaty of cooperation between the five states parties. It was revised in 1971, when the council of ministers was established. Amendments in 1993 allowed for greater participation by the Nordic countries in the process of European cooperation.

16.23 Article 1[24] defines the purpose of the Nordic Council as endeavouring to maintain and develop further cooperation between the Nordic countries in the

17 Part II, paragraph 43.

18 Bertie Ahern, address at the Irish Studies Centre, University of North London, 15 April 1999: http://www.irlgov.ie/taoiseach.

19 Leaflet, 'Vote Yes for Peace', issued by the Fianna Fáil party: this sought to emphases the BIIC at the expense of the BIC; the latter was described as 'a purely consultative British-Irish Council'.

20 The idea was first raised, only to be dismissed effectively, in the Anglo-Irish Joint Studies, *Joint Report and Studies*, Cmnd 8414, November 1981, p. 9. It was raised after the Belfast Agreement in Mads Qvortrup & Robert Hazell, *The British-Irish Council: Nordic lessons for the council of the isles*, London, The Constitution Unit, n.d. but 1998. Bertie Ahern toyed with the idea in a lecture, 'The Western Isles of Europe', in Edinburgh on 29 October 1998: http://www.irlgov.ie/taoiseach.

21 Address: http://www.norden.org.

22 Its symbol (since 1985) is a white swan – with eight-toothed wing – on a blue background.

23 Members had to rely upon their domestic law.

24 Redrafted in 1993.

legal, cultural, social and economic fields as well as in those of transport and communications, and environmental protection. The Nordic countries are to hold joint consultations on a permanent basis, and, where necessary, take coordinated measures.[25]

16.24 Cooperation is to take place through the Nordic Council, in the council of ministers, at meetings between prime ministers, foreign ministers and other ministers, in special cooperative bodies as well as between specialized public authorities.[26]

16.25 The Nordic Council – with a plenary assembly, praesidium[27] and standing committees – comprises the parliaments and governments of the eight members; 87 elected members plus any number of government representatives. It has the power to initiate proposals, and to give advice on matters pertaining to cooperation between all or some of the members.[28] It makes recommendations and statements, addressed to the council of ministers or national governments. Government representatives do not vote.[29] The Nordic Council is governed by rules of procedure.[30]

16.26 The council of ministers, in contrast, comprises the national and other governments. Each is represented by the prime minister, or the minister for cooperation. Decisions are by unanimity, the five Nordic countries only voting. They are binding on the states parties, though any one may enter a parliamentary reserve.[31] (The three sub-state members are bound, insofar as they accede to the decision in accordance with their statutes of self-government.) The budget is proportionately based on gross national product. The council of ministers determines its own rules of procedure.[32]

16.27 There are a number of stark contrasts between the Nordic Council and the BIC. One, its evolution as a bottom-up movement, starting with the civil-society Norden association in 1918, leading to the Nordic Council in 1952 and the council of ministers in 1971 (a period of 53 years). The BIC is a top-down body, and one that has come out of a Northern Ireland settlement. Two, the Nordic Council comprises five nation states, and three sub-state entities. The BIC is a mini-commonwealth of these islands, with one large state (and all the sub-state entities) from the United Kingdom; also, the small nation state was created out of that state. Three, the Nordic Council was an alternative to European cooperation, which is increasingly overshadowing *Norden*. Four, the Nordic Council members have a common tradition of Lutheran monarchism,[33] and social democracy. The BIC, in contrast (while it is not an attempt to recreate the old United Kingdom), is related principally to ending Northern Ireland violence. Five, the Nordic Council drives the council of ministers; the BIC, on the other hand, is a ministerial body.

25 Article 39.
26 Article 40.
27 There is a 20-strong international council secretariat in Copenhagen, sharing premises with the council of ministers' 80-strong international secretariat.
28 Article 44.
29 Article 49.
30 Article 59.
31 Article 63.
32 Article 66.
33 Finland became a republic in 1918, Iceland in 1940.

United Kingdom devolution

16.28 The BIC was agreed on 10 April 1998. At that point, Westminster and Whitehall were engaged in the constitutional reform of devolution throughout the United Kingdom.

16.29 Northern Ireland's devolution had been an aspect of the Irish question. It dated from 1920; there was also a failed attempt at power-sharing in 1974. Scotland and Wales also had failed attempts at devolution in the late 1970s. From the early 1990s, Northern Ireland was once again being considered actively for devolution by London.[34]

16.30 It was an accident of history that the Northern Ireland assembly came to overlap with the plans for a Scottish parliament and the Welsh assembly, following the election of a new government on 1 May 1997. Nevertheless, the project of devolution became integrated to some extent as bills for Northern Ireland, Scotland and Wales were drafted and turned into acts at much the same time during 1998.

16.31 One common feature was the proposal for a joint ministerial committee in the United Kingdom, plus concordats between departments. The source of this idea was the constitution unit of the cabinet office in London (headed by Sir Quentin Thomas CB, formerly of the NIO). These proposals were revealed by Baroness Ramsay, in the house of lords, after midnight on 29 July 1998 (during a debate on the Scotland Bill). The joint ministerial committee – she said – was to deal with reserved matters which impinge on devolved responsibilities, and probably also with devolved matters in the different parts of the United Kingdom.

16.32 All was revealed for the first time in October 1999, when the lord chancellor, Lord Irvine of Lairg, as chairman of the cabinet's devolution policy committee, presented a draft memorandum of understanding and supplementary agreements (MoU) to parliament (Cm 4444).[35] The MoU comprised a memorandum of understanding in part 1, between the United Kingdom government and the regional administrations in Scotland, Wales and Northern Ireland (this was before devolution to Northern Ireland on 2 December 1999, and its executive committee was square bracketed in part 1).

16.33 The memorandum of understanding proper sets out principles governing the relations between the centre and the devolved regions. The guiding principles are good communication; cooperation; exchange of information, statistics and research; and confidentiality. The memorandum is described as not legally binding. Paragraph 2 states: 'Nothing in this Memorandum should be construed as conflicting with the Belfast Agreement.'[36] The memorandum provides for a joint

34 John Major, in his foreword to the 1995 *Framework Documents*, wrote: 'For reasons that are unique to Northern Ireland, devolution of significant legislative and executive powers has always been a central plank of Government policy for Northern Ireland alone.'

35 *Memorandum of Understanding and supplementary agreements between the United Kingdom Government, Scottish Ministers and the Cabinet of the National Assembly of Wales.*

36 This was defined in footnote 2 as the BIA 'done at Belfast on 10 April 1998' and the MPA reached on the same date and annexed thereto. This contrasts with the definition of the Good Friday Agreement attached to the joint statement, *The Way Forward*, 2 July 1999, as the MPA only: schedule to the draft agreement between the government of the United Kingdom of Great Britain and Northern Ireland and the government of Ireland, placed in the library of the house of commons by Geofrey Hoon MP, foreign office minister of state, on 13 July 1999.

ministerial committee (JMC) (shadowed by officials under the cabinet secretary), which is the subject of a supplementary agreement.

16.34 The terms of reference of this consultative body are: the interfaces between devolved and non-devolved matters; devolved matters across the three regions; to keep liaison under review; and to consider disputes. There is to be a plenary meeting once a year, and meetings in functional formats (following European council practice) but chaired always by United Kingdom ministers. The supplementary agreement mentioned already also provides for a JMC secretariat, comprising staff from the cabinet office and the devolved administrations (initially located in their respective capitals).

16.35 International relations and relations with the European Union remain the responsibility of the United Kingdom government. Mention is made in the memorandum proper of bilateral and multilateral arrangements, including with the Republic of Ireland, through the BIC; and of Northern Ireland's relations with the neighbouring state through the NSMC. 'The UK Government', reads the crucial paragraph, 'will involve the devolved administrations as fully as possible in discussions about the formulation of the UK's policy on all EU and international issues which touch on devolved matters. This must, obviously, be subject to mutual respect for the confidentiality of those discussions and adherence to the resultant UK line, without which it would be impossible to maintain such close working relationships.'[37]

16.36 Part 2 of the document is mainly four centre/region overarching concordats: on coordination of European policy; on financial assistance to industry; on international relations; and on statistics. In the case of European policy and international relations, there is a text for each devolved administration (less, in October 1999, Northern Ireland) plus a common annex. The financial assistance to industry and statistics concordats are general. The first two are the responsibility of the foreign office; the second two, the treasury. Reference is also made to forthcoming bilateral concordats, between each United Kingdom department, and its opposite in each devolved region. Further, the four administrations may prepare concordats, or other less formal arrangements, on the handling of procedural, practical or policy matters.

16.37 Clearly, the centrifugal effect of administrations in Edinburgh, Cardiff and Belfast had been concerning central government. The solution was a counteracting centripetal pull back towards London based on the JMC and concordats. This would be in addition to the controls resulting from continuing United Kingdom parliamentary sovereignty, and continuing secretaries of state with new express powers under the devolution legislation. Counteracting fissiparious tendencies in the United Kingdom is a responsibility of central government.

16.38 It is not known if the BIC – also known as the council of the isles – was considered seriously after 10 April 1998 as a suitable framework for an autonomous JMC. The BIC includes the United Kingdom, plus Scotland, Wales and Northern Ireland. The fact that the Republic of Ireland (and other administrations), is a member should not affect how the United Kingdom relates to its devolved administrations. The first part of Strand Three of the Belfast Agreement – an important treaty after all – allows for bilateral and multilateral relations

37 Paragraph 19.

between members; the first paragraph 10 provides for multilaterals relations operating independently of the BIC (this is discussed further below).

16.39 Reference is made in one of the supplementary agreements to liaison between the JMC secretariat and the joint secretariat of the BIC (with the latter described as provided jointly by the British and Irish governments in coordination with officials from the other administrations).[38] In the former secretariat, the cabinet office leads the devolved administrations, in keeping with the ethos of the JMC. In the latter, the devolved administrations – it would seem – are effectively excluded, their place being taken by officals of the neighbouring state (seemingly still based in Dublin). The cabinet office is at the centre of the JMC with its concordats, and simultaneously taking a leading role in the BIC.

TITLE: BRITISH-IRISH COUNCIL

16.40 This title, while inconsistent with Strand One, is consistent with Strand Two, and with the second part of Strand Three. It is, more accurately, one of two titles in Strand Three. The British-Irish Council – there are no oblique strokes in Strand Three – is the first of two intergovernmental organizations dealing with east-west relations (but not, in the case of the BIC, on a more normal state-to-state basis).

16.41 The BIC was negotiated by the two governments. Nevertheless, the MDP text was amended crucially in a number of ways. It is compared most usefully with the provisions for the NSMC in Strand Two.

1. **A British-Irish Council (BIC) will be established under a new British-Irish Agreement to promote the harmonious and mutually beneficial development of the totality of relationships among the peoples of these islands.**

16.42 Paragraph 1 provides for the establishment and purpose of the BIC, as the basis of east-west practical cooperation involving all the administrations. Its remit is circumscribed only by mutuality. The BIC is another international organization, a cooperation body; while it may share sovereignty, it does not detract from the sovereignty of the United Kingdom or the Republic of Ireland.

16.43 ANNOTATIONS

'A British-Irish Council will be established under a new British-Irish Agreement'. The British-Irish Agreement is of course the BIA, the legal face of the Belfast Agreement. Strand Three forms part of Annex 1. The name of the treaty of 10 April 1998 is given by paragraph 1 of Constitutional Issues (and the first paragraphs of Strands Two and Three and Validation, Implementation and Review.) Article 2 of the BIA states that, in particular, there shall be established immediately on its entry into force, a number of institutions in accordance with the MPA. The third of the four listed is the BIC. This would have been enough to create an international organization called the BIC under the BIA. The passive tense was used to spare Northern Ireland blushes over particularly the NSMC. 'Established ... on the entry into force of this Agreement' is the key phrase in article 2 of the BIA.

The supplementary agreement of 8 March 1999 (referred to above) was probably unnecessary. Cm 4296 is entitled 'agreement between the government of the United Kingdom of Great Britain and Northern Ireland and the government of Ireland establishing a British-Irish Council'. The first recital of the preamble begins: 'Having regard to Article 2

38 Paragraph A2.4.

of the [BIA]'. And article 1 commences: 'Under and in furtherance of Article 2 of the [BIA] ... there is hereby established a British-Irish Council'. Under article 2 of the BIA makes this supplementary agreement a duplicate. In furtherance of does not add anything, since there is nothing in article 2 requiring a second agreement. The most likely explanation for the supplementary agreement is that 'there shall be established' in article 2 was open to interpretation by Irish government advisers as requiring precisely this (it contrasts with 'there is hereby established' in the supplementary agreement).[39] Further, since the north-south implementation bodies did need a supplementary agreement (they were only decided upon subsequently) Dublin requested – and London acceded to – a set of four new international agreements done on 8 March 1999.

'to promote the harmonious and mutually beneficial development of the totality of relationships among the peoples of these islands.' This is the purpose of the BIC. It contrasts with the purposes of the NSMC: to develop consultation, co-operation and action within the island of Ireland – including through implementation on an all-island and cross-border basis – on matters of mutual interest and within the competence of the Administrations, North and South.

To promote may be weaker than to develop. Promote suggests facilitate. The harmonious and mutually beneficial development of ... crosses with the NSMC's matters of mutual interest. There is therefore a condition precedent of mutually beneficial development. Development here may equate with to develop in Strand Two. Harmonious does not add a great deal. The second condition precedent in Strand Two – within the competence of the Administrations – is not stated here; it is, however, implied.

'the totality of relationships among the peoples of these islands.' This is different from the use of the totality of relationships in paragraph 1 of Strand Two, and in the second paragraph 1 of Strand Three. In both of those, the totality of relationships refers to the range of issues covered by the BIA.

The origins of totality of relationships lie in the December 1980 meeting in Dublin, between the Irish and United Kingdom premiers, which began the contemporary phase in Anglo-Irish diplomacy. They commissioned joint studies,[40] as the basis of 'a [future] special consideration of the totality of relationships within these islands'. It has never been clear whether these are government to government relationships, or between the civil societies of both states. The meaning in 1980–81 was much more the former, and the totality of relationships among the peoples of these islands is a later development.

However, the basis of the 1996–98 talks was 'to achieve a new beginning for relationships within Northern Ireland, within the island of Ireland and between the peoples of these islands, and to agree new institutions and structures to take account of the totality of relationships'.[41] This is a third meaning to totality, after government to government and civil society to civil society – and is now the one embodied generally in the BIA (though not in this paragraph).

> **2. Membership of the BIC will comprise representatives of the British and Irish Governments, devolved institutions in Northern Ireland, Scotland and Wales, when established, and, if appropriate, elsewhere in the United Kingdom, together with representatives of the Isle of Man and the Channel Islands.**

16.44 Paragraph 2 defines the membership of the BIC.

39 'Shall' here may sound like legislative rather than treaty language.

40 Anglo-Irish Joint Studies, *Joint Studies and Reports*, Cmnd 8414, November 1981. The areas were: possible new institutional structures; citizenship rights; security matters; economic cooperation; and measures to encourage mutual understanding.

41 *Ground Rules for Substantive All-Party Negotiations*, Cm 3232, April 1996, rule 1.

16.45 ANNOTATIONS

'Membership of the BIC will comprise' implies equality of members. Unlike the NSMC, which is described in paragraph 2 of Strand Two as comprising 'two sides', this is an open-ended body; the list is not closed.

'representatives of the British and Irish governments,' is different from the provisions in the second part of Strand Three for the BIIC. That is clearly a government to government body. Here, it is only representatives. No level is specified, unlike in paragraph 2 of Strand Two, where head of administration/government is stated. However, the memorandum of procedure, agreed at the inaugural meeting on 17 December 1999 in London, states, under paragraph 3, that the summit-level meetings will be attended by heads of administration.

British and Irish is the Irish nationalist duality. The name of the state (that of the sovereign and parliament) is the United Kingdom of Great Britain and Northern Ireland. This should be adjectived to the United Kingdom government, though there has been a practice of using British for embassy and citizen, for example. In Anglo-Irish relations, there has been an attempt to use the term 'United Kingdom government'. British and Irish was used in the 1973 Sunningdale communiqué. United Kingdom was used in the 1981 Anglo-Irish Joint Studies, albeit in a context of Anglo-French, Anglo-Irish, etc.[42] In the 1985 Anglo-Irish Agreement (a term implied from the joint communiqué[43]), United Kingdom government was used consistently. However, in the joint communiqué, British parliament was allowed to intrude. The Belfast Agreement represents a return to Irish nationalist terminology; United Kingdom is absent from the text, and Britain is adjectived against the noun Ireland.[44] Irish government is acceptable, given the Irish state is the only one wholly within Ireland.

'devolved institutions in Northern Ireland, Scotland and Wales, when established,' refers to the second rank of members after the two sovereign states. All three are part of the United Kingdom, so it is a case of a central government and three devolved administrations. It would seem to be that it is the executive and not legislature which is the member.[45] No devolved administrations existed at the time of the Belfast Agreement, 10 April 1998. It was approved in a referendum on 22 May 1998. The Northern Ireland assembly was elected on 25 June 1998. And powers were devolved under section 3 (devolution order) of the NIA 1998 (royal assent, 19 November 1998) on 2 December 1999. Scottish devolution had been approved in a referendum on 11 September 1997. The Scottish parliament was elected on 6 May 1999. Devolution took place on 1 July 1999, under section 130 (commencement) of the Scotland Act 1998 (royal assent, 19 November 1998). Welsh devolution had been approved narrowly on 18 September 1997. The national assembly for Wales was elected on 6 May 1999. Devolution took place on 1 July 1999, under section 158 (commencement) of the Government of Wales Act 1998 (royal assent, 31 July 1998).

'and, if appropriate, elsewhere in the United Kingdom,' would seem to refer to possible devolved administrations in England. The government elected on 1 May 1997 promised 'more accountability in the regions of England'.[46] On 19 November 1998, the Regional Development Agencies Act 1998 received the royal assent. This provides for agencies in each of the nine English regions, modelled upon those in Scotland and Wales. Regional

42 *Joint Report and Studies*, p. 9.

43 Entitled 'Anglo-Irish Summit Meeting'. It was also by implication that Anglo-Irish was added to intergovernmental conference.

44 Paragraph 5 of the Declaration of Support; paragraph 2 of Constitutional Issues.

45 According to the memorandum on procedural guidance of 17 December 1999, the members are the Irish government, the British government, the Northern Ireland executive committee, the Scottish executive (which should be Scottish ministers); the cabinet of the national assembly for Wales; the government of the Isle of Man; the bailiwick of Guernsey; and the bailiwick of Jersey.

46 Home Office, *Rights Brought Home: the Human Rights Bill*, Cm 3782, October 1997, p. 1.

development agencies – and local government bodies[47] – would seem not to be eligible for membership of the BIC. This may be implied from the members listed in this paragraph, starting with two states and moving on to three devolved administrations. However, the issue is not definitive. The government has made clear that it will not legislate for English devolution before the next general election. A condition precedent – as in Northern Ireland, Scotland and Wales – will be a referendum in the region.

'together with representatives of the Isle of Man and the Channel Islands.' The Isle of Man and the Channel Islands are not – in domestic law – part of the United Kingdom. This is defined in the Interpretation Act 1978 as Great Britain and Northern Ireland.[48] (However, the British Islands – from 1889 – are the United Kingdom, the Channel Island and the Isle of Man; the Republic of Ireland was included until 1 January 1979.[49]) Nor are they colonies of the United Kingdom of Great Britain and Northern Ireland. The Isle of Man and the Channel Islands are, however, crown possessions (the sovereign being a successor, in the case of the Channel Islands, to the dukes of Normandy). The Isle of Man is not the subject of a statutory definition. The name refers to the Island of Man in the Irish sea plus smaller islands appertaining. It has its own legislature, the Tynwald. However, its foreign relations are conducted by the United Kingdom on behalf of the Isle of Man. The Channel Islands – Jersey, Guernsey, Alderney and Sark and their respective dependencies – are not the subject of a statutory definition. Jersey has a legislature, the assembly of the states. Guernsey's is called the states of deliberation. Their foreign relations are also conducted by the United Kingdom on their behalf. European treaties apply only for certain purposes. The crown acts through the privy council, on the recommendation of privy councillors in the United Kingdom government; the home secretary is the minister principally responsible. However, the United Kingdom may be construed in some instances as including the Isle of Man and the Channel Islands,[50] and some United Kingdom legislation may also be extended by orders in council.[51] The Isle of Man is one further possible member of the BIC. The Channel Islands count as two: the bailiwick of Jersey, and the bailiwick of Guernsey (incorporating the interests of the islands of Alderney and Sark).

The second matter referred by the secretary of state in her letter of 29 June 1998 to the assembly included the BIC: 'participation by representatives of the Northern Ireland transitional (or shadow) administration in inaugural meetings of the Shadow British-Irish Council and the shadow North/South Ministerial Council and in regular and frequent meetings of these bodies'.[52]

On 14 September 1998, the First Minister and Deputy First Minister reported to the assembly that the first meeting of the BIC was expected to take place around the same time as the NSMC. 'Much will depend on the availability of the Prime Minister and the Taoiseach at that time.' Reference was made to an initial work programme.[53]

The BIC was the theme of the Encounter conference, held at Wilton Park in Sussex, on 4–6 December 1998, attended by some 50 delegates (including United Kingdom and Irish officials). Encounter had been established in 1983 by the United Kingdom and Irish governments, as a result of the 1981 Anglo-Irish Joint Studies. Its remit is the improvement

47 These are excluded in the memorandum on procedural guidance, agreed at the inaugural meeting in London on 17 December 1999.
48 Schedule 1 (dating from the Royal and Parliamentary Titles Act 1927 s 2).
49 Interpretation Act 1978, s 22(1), schedule 1, schedule 2, part I, paragraph 4(2).
50 British Nationality Act 1981 s 50(1).
51 Though under the Westminster parliament, there is a convention that they legislate for themselves.
52 New Northern Ireland Assembly, *Official Report*, 1 July 1998, p. 2.
53 New Northern Ireland Assembly, *Interim Report from the First Minister (Designate) and Deputy First Minister (Designate)*, 14 September 1998, pp. 7–8.

of relations between peoples in the interests of peace, reconciliation and stability.[54] The BIC was described by the joint chairmen, Sir Nicholas Fenn and Professor Terence Brown, as 'an institution of potentially enormous significance which has not yet attracted the private thought and public debate which it will deserve'. Sir Nicholas, in setting eight questions for consideration, posed the danger of the two governments dominating the BIC. The report of the conference includes, as the last of four propositions requiring further debate, a suggestion that the presidency should rotate between all members, 'and that it should have its own budget and a permanent, free-standing secretariat. Some difficulty was foreseen in negotiating the site of the secretariat. Bids were advanced for Cardiff, Glasgow, Belfast and the Isle of Man.'[55]

The report of the First Minister and Deputy First Minister of 18 January 1999 (containing Strand One and Strand Two decisions) included further information. The first meeting was scheduled for London, at approximately the same time as the first NSMC. Reference was also made to a draft memorandum of understanding, which was described as an international instrument to bring the BIC into being. Memoranda of understanding may be used by states,[56] but they are not international agreements. As noted above, the BIC was created by treaty: by the BIA, and the supplementary agreement of 8 March 1999. Reference was made also to a draft paper on procedural guidance. Rules of procedure are normal for such an international body. The two governments were reported to be working on suggestions for a work programme. The secretary of state was reported to have held meetings with her opposite numbers in Scotland and Wales, and with the minister of state in the department of the environment, transport and the regions.[57] On 27 May 1999, the Irish government opened consulates-general in Edinburgh and Cardiff, which were described as active in preparations for the BIC.

The report of the First Minister and Deputy First Minister of 15 February 1999 repeated much of the above. However, there was now reference to a draft treaty to bring the BIC formally into being. Compared with the activity there had been in connection with Strands One and Two, Strand Three – or at least the BIC – gives all the impression of having been overshadowed.

The BIC met finally after devolution on 2 December 1999, in London. Representatives of the United Kingdom and Irish governments, the Northern Ireland executive committee, the Scottish executive, the cabinet of the national assembly for Wales, the Isle of Man government, and the bailiwicks of Jersey and Guernsey attended the inaugural meeting at Lancaster House on 17 December 1999. Northern Ireland was represented by the First Minister and Deputy First Minister, plus a minister from each of the four parties in the executive committee: Bairbre de Brún; Mark Durkan and Sir Reg Empey (the DUP declining to participate).

This meeting agreed a memorandum on procedural guidance, an informal understanding which was not legally binding, based on the first part of Strand Three. Little was added to the Belfast Agreement text, though the dominance of the United Kingdom and Irish governments was suggested. The BIC also agreed a future programme of work. Five areas were selected, with one member leading in each: drugs (Irish government); social inclusion (Scotland and Wales); transport (Northern Ireland); environment (United Kingdom government); knowledge economy (Jersey). The next BIC summit was arranged for Dublin in June 2000, with drugs the principal item for discussion.

54 It was noted in New Northern Ireland Assembly, *Interim Report from the First Minister (Designate) and Deputy First Minister (Designate)*, 18 January 1999, pp. 6–7.

55 Encounter, *Strand III: The British-Irish Council*, report of the conference by rapporteur Tom Collins, foreword & pp. 3 & 28.

56 Anthony Aust, 'The Theory and Practice of Informal International Instruments' (1986) 35 ICLQ 787.

57 This was Richard Caborn. One meeting was on 16 December 1998.

3. **The BIC will meet [twice a year at]** ***in different formats: at*** **summit level,** ***twice per year;*** **[with other meetings on sectoral issues comprising appropriate representatives of the revelant members to be convened as necessary.]** ***in specific sectoral formats on a regular basis, with each side represented by the appropriate Minister; in an appropriate format to consider cross-sectoral matters.***

16.46 This is closely modelled on paragraph 3 of Strand Two. The FA version is significantly different from the MDP.

16.47 ANNOTATIONS

'The BIC will meet in different formats:' is very similar to the NSMC provision.

'at summit level, twice per year;' is similar to the NSMC. However, the term summit level is used here, while it is plenary in Strand Two. Twice per year is the same frequency. However, the representatives – as in paragraph 2 – are not specified. According to the report of the First Minister and Deputy First Minister to the assembly on 14 September 1998, it would seem that the summits were to be at head of administration level, including the prime minister and the taoiseach.[58] This is confirmed by the memorandum on procedural guidance of 17 December 1999, agreed at the inaugural meeting in London.

'in specific sectoral formats on a regular basis, with each side represented by the appropriate Minister;' is also similar to paragraph 3 of Strand Two. It was a significant addition to the MDP. The only difference is 'regular and frequent' is used of the NSMC in sectoral format. This would suggest a difference, though it could not be implied that the BIC had to meet regularly but infrequently.

'in an appropriate format to consider cross-sectoral matters.' is similar to paragraph 3 of Strand Two. However, there is no reference to institutional matters, nor to dispute resolution.

4. **Representatives of members will operate in accordance with whatever procedures for democratic authority and accountability are in force in their respective elected institutions.**

16.48 This is similar to paragraphs 2 and 6 of Strand Two.

16.49 ANNOTATIONS

'Representatives of members' repeats the two terms from paragraph 2.

'will operate in accordance with' is similar to operating in accordance with in paragraph 2 of Strand Two.

'whatever procedures for democratic authority and accountability are in force' is similar to rules for democratic authority and accountability in force in paragraph 2 of Strand Two. The comments there, as regards the Northern Ireland administration, apply here: democratic authority must refer to the totality of rules bearing on a member of the executive. In the case of Northern Ireland, this would have to be ascertained by reading the Belfast Agreement against the background of the United Kingdom unwritten constitution, and through its incorporation by the NIA 1998. Part – but only part – of that democratic authority is expressed in section 52(5): the First Minister and Deputy First Minister are required, before each BIC meeting, to notify the executive committee and the assembly of the following: the date of the meeting; the agenda; and the nominations of ministers and junior ministers made. If democratic authority may be considered before participation, accountability can be seen as after the event. Accountability is an important principle of the United Kingdom

58 New Northern Ireland Assembly, *Interim Report from the First Minister (Designate) and Deputy First Minister (Designate)*, 14 September 1998, pp. 7–8.

constitution, but it does not always require active disclosure.[59] Accountability relates to individual and collective responsibility of ministers. Part – but again only part – of that accountability is expressed in section 52(6) of the NIA 1998: any minister having attended the BIC must report, first to the executive committee, and secondly to the assembly. The latter is to be oral, unless standing orders provide otherwise. The standing orders of 9 March 1999 make no provision for the BIC.

'in their respective elected institutions.' has to cover two sovereign states, three, or possibly more, devolved administrations, and three United Kingdom dependencies.

5. The BIC will [consider, and will promote, consultation and] ***exchange information, discuss, consult and use best endeavours to reach agreement on*** **co-operation on matters of [common]** ***mutual*** **interest [falling] within the competence of [its members]** ***the relevant Administrations.*** **Suitable issues for early discussion in the BIC could include transport links,** ***agricultural issues,*** **environmental issues, cultural issues, [minority languages]** ***health issues, education issues*** **and approaches to [European Union (EU)] issues.** ***Suitable arrangements to be made for practical co-operation on agreed policies.***

16.50 This paragraph on functions of the BIC corresponds to paragraph 5 of Strand Two, where the NSMC was configured in terms of the *Framework Documents*' consultation, harmonization, separate implementation and joint implementation. The MDP text was altered significantly, making Strand Three more like Strand Two. However, the memorandum on procedural guidance, agreed at the inaugural meeting in London on 17 December 1999, refers only to a work programme to be adopted at the first summit-level meeting in elaborating upon this paragraph.

16.51 ANNOTATIONS

'The BIC will exchange information, discuss, consult and use best endeavours to reach agreement on co-operation' is consultation and harmonization from the *Framework Documents*. Paragraph 5(i) of Strand Two is: exchange information, discuss and consult with a view to co-operating .... Paragraph 5(ii) is: to use best endeavours to reach agreement on the adoption of common policies ... making determined efforts to overcome any disagreements. The phrase use best endeavours to reach agreement has been appropriated from paragraph 5(ii). The argument about harmonization – and even implementation – depends upon the final sentence of this paragraph. Agreement on co-operation raises the question of whether this is the generic cooperation (embracing all relations), or cooperation as opposed to implementation. I submit that the former is the better view. Since implementation is not used in this paragraph, the duality co-operation/implementation from paragraphs 8, 9 and 10 of Strand Two cannot be read into Strand Three.

'on matters of mutual interest' was changed from matters of common interest. It now corresponds to the first condition precedent in paragraph 1 of Strand Two, repeated in paragraphs 5 and 8.

'within the competence of the relevant Administrations.' was changed from its members. This brings it into line with the second condition precedent in paragraph 1 of Strand Two, repeated in paragraph 5. Relevant has been added to take account of the variable geometry provided for in paragraph 10; cooperation on a particular issue involving two or more members but not all. This suggests that the correct interpretation of paragraph 10 (despite a possible construction of the last sentence) is that all this activity takes place under the aegis of the BIC.

59 It is the second principle in paragraph 1 of the United Kingdom *Ministerial Code*.

'Suitable issues for early discussion in the BIC could include' came over unchanged from the MDP. Suitable issues could include is similar to the reference to the Annex to Strand Two in paragraph 8. For early discussion in the BIC precludes any delay in getting started. East-west cooperation would have to begin with discussion, given the innovative nature of this part of Strand Three. It does not suggest that the BIC is only a body for discussion.

'transport links, agricultural issues, environmental issues, cultural issues, health issues, education issues and approaches to EU issues.' This is not an exhaustive list of areas or sectors. Could include above makes that clear. Minority languages in the MDP was dropped, but there is no prohibition on bringing it back under cultural issues or even as minority languages. The additions are significant – agricultural issues, health issues, education issues – and suggest a considerable fattening up of the work of the BIC. European Union was changed to EU presumably to conform with the use of initials in paragraphs 3 and 17 of Strand Two plus the Annex.

'Suitable arrangements to be made for practical co-operation on agreed policies.' was added to the MDP. Suitable arrangements is unspecified. It is derived arguably from suitable issues in the sentence above. There is no inherent restriction on the meaning of suitable arrangements. Arrangement is used in paragraphs 10 and 12 of Strand Two to cover cooperation and implementation. To be made for practical co-operation can only be a reference to generic cooperation. Practical co-operation was used by John Major, then prime minister, in his foreword to the 1995 *Framework Documents*.[60] There, practical co-operation was used with reference to north-south relations in Ireland. This was elaborated further in part II, paragraphs 24–38. On agreed policies reinforces the point made above that this paragraph embraces consultation and harmonization, since paragraph 5(ii) of Strand Two is about common policies. But does this paragraph include implementation, either separately or jointly? Though the word is not used, and not juxtaposed to cooperation, suitable arrangements and practical co-operation in this sentence arguably allow for separate implementation and certainly for implementation bodies (though a distinction would have to be made between intra-United Kingdom bodies and international bodies). Agreement on policies exists in paragraph 5(iii) of Strand Two (separate implementation), and also in paragraph 5(iv) (joint implementation). Agreed policies is the wording in this last sentence. The answer can only be – taking account of internal versus external frontiers – that what is possible in north-south relations is also possible in east-west relations. This point is reinforced by the next paragraph.

6. It will be open to the BIC to agree common policies or common actions. Individual members may opt not to participate in such common policies and common action.

16.52 This is one of the most important paragraphs in the first part of Strand Three. It passed over from the MDP unamended. It makes the BIC similar to the NSMC, with the difference that the former is a multilateral body and the latter a bilateral body. However, the memorandum on procedural guidance, agreed at the inaugural meeting in London on 17 December 1999, referring to paragraphs 6 and 7, emphasizes the right of members to opt out.

16.53 ANNOTATIONS

'It will be open to the BIC to agree common policies or common actions.' defines the remit of the council. The purposes of the NSMC are defined in paragraph 1 of Strand Two as: to develop consultation, co-operation and action, including through joint implementation. This was clearly derived from the *Framework Documents*' consultation, harmonising and

60 Practical co-operation had been used first in this north-south context in article 10(c) of the 1985 Anglo-Irish Agreement.

executive functions. Here, common policies or common actions replicates the NSMC's functions. Policies are defined further in paragraph 5 of Strand Two: common policies is used in subparagraph (ii), which was derived from harmonization. Common actions is derived from common policies. However, action is used in Strand Two to cover paragraph 5(iii)–(iv), implementation or executive action. Further, in paragraph 5(iv), the phrase agreement on policies and action at an all-Ireland and cross-border level is used with reference to joint implementation.

'Individual members may opt not to participate in such common policies and common action.' This is the second principle in this paragraph. It relates to the BIC as a multilateral body. It is another way of saying that BIC decisions must be by unanimity, which follows from paragraph 7. The point is dealt with more fully in paragraph 10, dealing with variable geometry; two or more may still proceed under the aegis of the BIC, unanimity applying only to them.

This seems to be to allow for greater flexibility than is permitted within the Nordic Council. The council of ministers comprises five sovereign states (Denmark, Finland, Iceland, Norway and Sweden), and three sub-state entities (the home rule governments of the Faeroe Islands and Greenland and the regional government of the Aland Islands). It is here that cooperation between the Nordic countries is decided, under the Helsinki treaty and other agreements.[61] The quorum of the council of ministers is the five Nordic countries, though, on matters of exclusive concern, only the relevant administrations need participate. Each country – that is state – has one vote, and decisions are required to be by unanimity; abstention does not impede a decision.[62] Decisions of the council of ministers are binding on each of the five countries. However, any state may enter a parliamentary reserve. Decisions do not bind until that parliament has approved the decision. The three sub-state entities take part in the work of the council of ministers. They are only bound – through their national laws, not the council of ministers – insofar as they accede to the decision in accordance with their statutes of self-government.

> **7. The BIC normally will operate by consensus. In relation to decisions on common policies or common actions, including their means of implementation, it will operate by agreement of all members participating in such policies or actions.**

16.54 This paragraph is about decision-making. It is not equivalent to paragraph 6 of Strand Two. That is because it is dealing with the problem of a multilateral body. It refers back to paragraph 6 above (confirming the possibility of implementation bodies), and on to paragraph 10 on variable geometry. The draft in the MDP passed into the FA unamended.

16.55 ANNOTATIONS

'The BIC normally will operate by consensus.' is intriguing. Paragraph 2 of Strand Two requires all NSMC decisions to be by agreement between the two sides. And the council of ministers of the Nordic Council operates by unanimity. However, procedural matters there may be settled by a simple majority of those voting (with a casting vote by the presidency if necessary). By consensus is equivalent to unanimity, though it refers more to process than to outcome only. The BIC will operate by consensus has a clear meaning. So what does normally add? It can only mean that there may be circumstances in which less than by consensus suffices. This is not quite qualified majority voting in defined areas, but it does allow for consensus to be interpreted more loosely. Most likely, something resembling the council of ministers of the Nordic Council provision was envisaged. Presumbly, by consensus is equivalent to unanimity with abstention not affecting the decision.

61 Article 60.
62 Article 62.

'In relation to decisions on common policies or common actions, including their means of implementation,' was in the MDP. It relates back to the purpose of the BIC in paragraphs 1 and 6. Common policies or common actions is from paragraph 6. It has the same meaning as the functions of the NSMC. The interpretation of paragraph 6 above is confirmed by the phrase: including their means of implementation. Common policies or actions includes implementation.

'it will operate by agreement of all members participating in such policies or actions.' both applies the consensus rule to less than the full complement of members, and makes clear that decisions by two or more members are BIC decisions. This resembles article 62 of the 1962 Helsinki treaty, whereby, in the council of ministers of the Nordic Council, when there are matters of exclusive concern to certain countries, only those countries need be represented: the unanimity rule – allowing for abstention – applies.

8. The members of the BIC, on a basis to be agreed between them, will provide such financial support as it may require.

16.56 This is the only provision as regards finance. It is equivalent to paragraph 15 of Strand Two, where funding is to be provided by the two administrations (on no specified basis). The memorandum on procedural guidance, agreed at the inaugural meeting in London on 17 December 1999, elaborates; the host member of any meeting will provide the facilities, while travel and subsistence is the responsibility of each member.

16.57 ANNOTATIONS

'The members of the BIC, on a basis to be agreed between them,' refers impliedly to all members. The nature of the agreement would be governed by paragraph 7. A consensus would not be necessary. However, on a matter such as financial contribution, each member would practically be able to exercise a veto. Most of the putative members were not involved in the Belfast Agreement, and, in the case of the United Kingdom administrations and dependencies (less Northern Ireland), their participation will most likely be on their financial terms.

'will provide such financial support as it may require.' needs to be interpreted carefully. Paragraph 15 of Strand Two defines the NSMC and the implementation bodies as a necessary public function. Such a term is absent here, but that is of little or no significance. The problem here is what does the funding cover. The word it is used with reference to the BIC. Does that cover both the operation of the BIC, and the implementation of decisions on common policies or common actions? This is unlikely, but only because of the variable geometry nature of the BIC. The funding is to cover the work of the BIC alone.

9. A secretariat for the BIC will be provided by the British and Irish Governments in co-ordination with officials of each of the other members.

16.58 This paragraph on the BIC secretariat would appear to have been misinterpreted. It relates to paragraph 16 of Strand Two, and the second paragraph 8 of Strand Three.

16.59 ANNOTATIONS

'A secretariat for the BIC will be provided by the British and Irish governments' is consistent with paragraph 16 of Strand Two. There, a standing joint secretariat is provided for, staffed by officials of the Northern Ireland and Republic of Ireland administrations. It is also consistent with the second paragraph 8 of Strand Three: a standing joint secretariat of officials of the two governments. The British and Irish government is, of course, the nationalist duality, which has been used above in paragraph 2. The absence of the word standing – and no upper-case S – is of little significance. The BIC secretariat is not described as joint, because the BIC has more than two members. And this leads to the meaning of the remainder of the sentence. According to the memorandum on procedural guidance, agreed at the inaugural meeting in London on 17 December 1999, the Irish officials in the BIC secretariat will be based in Dublin.

'in co-ordination with officials of each of the other members.' has to have some meaning. If the two governments, who signed the BIA, had intended to keep the secretariat to themselves, then they should have stopped at the word Governments. It is the case that secretariats have functions, and these include coordination. But this paragraph is not about functions. It is about defining the secretariat, and the subject of the sentence is: A secretariat for the BIC. In co-ordination with officials of each of the other members has to mean more than London and Dublin telling the other administrations what is happening. This paragraph means that the other administrations – presumably on a basis to be agreed – have a right to participate in the secretariat. Not all, of course, may wish to do so. But, conceivably, the Northern Ireland administration might be keen to participate.

10. In addition to the structures provided for under the agreement, it will be open to two or more members to develop bilateral or multilateral arrangements between them. Such arrangements could include, subject to the agreement of the members concerned, mechanisms to enable consultation, co-operation and joint decision-making on matters of mutual interest; and mechanisms to implement any joint decisions they may reach. These arrangements will not require the prior approval of the BIC as a whole and will operate independently of it.

16.60 This paragraph originated in the MDP. It returns to the functions of the BIC, dealt with in paragraph 5, but also 6 and 7 above. It addresses centrally the question of a multilateral body, which has been touched upon in paragraphs 6 and 7.

16.61 ANNOTATIONS

'In addition to the structures provided for under this agreement,' has a bearing on the overall architecture of the Belfast Agreement. This agreement is the MPA. The structures is a new concept. In article 2 of the BIA, reference is made to institutions. Structures may be taken to be equivalent to institutions. The problem is: is it the institutions in Strands One and Two (and the second part of Strand Three), or all the institutions under the MPA? According to the former meaning, north-south cooperation in Strand Two stands alone. It is not an aspect of the BIC multilateral process. According to the latter, the NSMC might well be an aspect of the BIC, but – according to this view – the paragraph deals with bilateral and multilateral cooperation outside the main Strands One, Two and Three institutions. The former view, I submit, is better, because this paragraph is located in the first part of Strand Three. Also, paragraphs 6 and 7 allow for variable geometry under the aegis of the BIC.

'it will be open to two or more members to develop bilateral and multilateral arrangements between them.' It will be open is in accord with the second sentence of paragraph 6; here, the wording is positive. To two or more members suggests this is BIC activity. There is no need to provide for other relations under the first part of Strand Three. North-south relations are dealt with separately in Strand Two. Government to government east-west relations are covered in the second part of Strand Three. Other potential relationships exist outside the context of the Belfast Agreement; most are domestic to the United Kingdom, including the relationships with the Isle of Man and Channel Islands. Bilateral and multilateral arrangements is implicit in paragraphs 6 and 7. The word arrangements appears in paragraphs 10 and 12 of Strand Two: in the former, it covers cooperation and implementation in the transition; in the latter, cooperation and implementation after the appointed day. Arrangements is therefore a portmanteau word.

'Such arrangements could include, subject to the agreement of the members concerned,' repeats the word arrangements, and the principle in the second sentence of paragraph 6.

'mechanisms to enable consultation, co-operation and joint decision-making on matters of mutual interest;' returns to the question of functions addressed in paragraph 5 above. The word mechanisms first appeared in the 12 January 1998 Heads of Agreement, in the phrase suitable implementation bodies and other mechanisms. It then appeared in paragraph 9(i) of Strand Two, as mechanisms for co-operation. Whether mechanisms here means cooperation as distinct from implementation (policies as opposed to bodies), must be ascertained from the rest of the phrase. Consultation, co-operation and joint decision-making is redolent of consult, co-operate and take decisions, which was used in the Heads of Agreement of the NSMC. The word joint is strange. Usually it refers to bilateral relations. But here, multilateral relations are being addressed also. Consultation, co-operation and joint decision-making confirms further that the remit of the BIC is identical to that of the NSMC. On matters of mutual interest was also used first in the Heads of Agreement, of the NSMC. It then appeared in paragraphs 1 and 5 of Strand Two. This further confirms the point about identical functions.

'and mechanisms to implement any joint decisions they may reach.' The word mechanisms here is different from that above. Here, it is related to implementation. And the implementation has to do with joint decisions, taken from above and indirectly from the Heads of Agreement on the NSMC.

'These arrangements will not require the prior approval of the BIC as a whole and will operate independently of it.' must be read with the second sentence of paragraph 6. That stated that common policies and actions under the BIC might not embrace all members. Here, bilateral and multilateral relations – short of the full BIC – are being provided for positively. These arrangements repeats the word from the first sentence of this paragraph; a portmanteau word. Will not require the prior approval of the BIC as a whole is the other way of expressing the principle in paragraph 6. The BIC permits bilateral and multilateral relations under its aegis.

'and will operate independently of it.' does not mean that the bilateral and multilateral relations are outside the BIC. That would mean that the NSMC is provided for in this paragraph as an instance of bilateral relations. But this latter interpretation has been rejected above. The key word is operate. It does not mean that the relationship is not under the aegis of the BIC. The memorandum on procedural guidance, agreed at the inaugural meeting in London on 17 December 1999, states that bilateral and multilateral arrangements will not be supported normally by the secretariat, except with the approval of the United Kingdom and Irish governments – an indication of how they see the secretariat, and, indeed, the BIC.

11. The elected institutions of the members will be encouraged to develop interparliamentary links, perhaps building on the British-Irish Interparliamentary Body.

16.62 This paragraph is similar to paragraph 18 of Strand Two, but is altogether more realistic. The precedent is mentioned here.

16.63 ANNOTATIONS

'The elected institutions of the members' repeats the concepts used respectively in paragraphs 4 and 2.

'will be encouraged to develop interparliamentary links,' is stronger than in Strand Two. There, paragraph 18 reads that the Northern Ireland assembly and the Oireachtas are to consider developing a joint parliamentary forum. To consider and developing are not definite concepts. Will be encouraged here is much stronger. Those being encouraged are the legislatures of the members. But who does the encouraging? On one view, this is the two governments, the signatories of the BIA. On the other, the so-called signatories of the MPA, the political parties assenting to the Belfast Agreement. Yet, the membership of the BIC is much wider. However, if the United Kingdom government – accepting the former interpretation – is considered to be able to influence Scotland and Wales, and the Isle of Man and the Channel Islands, then this is a serious undertaking by London, supported by Dublin. The memorandum on procedural guidance, agreed at the inaugural meeting in London on 17 December 1999, states that, at an early summit-level meeting, the BIC will consider how it might address this issue in conjunction with the elected institutions involved.

'perhaps building on the British-Irish Interparliamentary Body.' is the precedent. Perhaps building implies that a good foundation has been laid. It would be difficult to ignore this precedent in order to start from scratch. The British-Irish Inter-Parliamentary Body (BIIPB) – with an address at the Inter-Parliamentary Union in the Palace of Westminster – may be traced from 1983. The 1981 Anglo-Irish Joint Studies referred to meetings of an Anglo-Irish parliamentary group every two years; however, the United Kingdom and Irish governments[63] differed on an inter-parliamentary body.[64] The 1985 Anglo-Irish Agreement made clear it was a matter for the two parliaments.[65] The BIIPB was established eventually in 1990, with a steering committee, and plenary conferences in both countries. It has no legal basis. It comprises 25 members from each of the Westminster and Irish parliaments. The BIIPB, which was conceived at the time of the Anglo-Irish intergovernmental council, but not created until more than four years after the Anglo-Irish intergovernmental conference, is not a creature of the 1985 Anglo-Irish Agreement; nevertheless, it was – and remains – boycotted by Ulster unionists. Four committees were also established in 1990: political and security; European and International affairs; economic and social; and culture, education and the environment. The Body – aside from meeting in committee and plenary formats – publishes reports, plus the responses of both governments.[66]

The BIIPB would be faced – in the context of the BIC – with two major changes. One, attracting the Ulster unionists. Two, reconfiguring the body to embrace all the elected institutions of the members. The former might be achievable if the latter is tackled. But this would amount to a very different BIIPB.

12. The full membership of the BIC will keep under review the workings of the Council, including a formal published review at an appropriate time after the Agreement comes into effect, and will contribute as appropriate to any review of the overall political agreement arising from the multi-party negotiations.

16.64 This provides for a review of the BIC. Paragraph 36 of Strand One also provides for review. There is no review clause in Strand Two. However, there are general review provisions in the Validation, Implementation and Review section of the Belfast Agreement, dealing with both the transition and devolution. There is also provision for a review of the BIIC in the second part of Strand Three. The memorandum on procedural guidance, agreed at the inaugural meeting in London on 17 December 1999, states that the BIC will publish an annual report, compiled by the secretariat and approved by the members.

63 The Irish government wanted such a body to have consultative, advisory and review functions, taken no doubt from the council of Ireland idea in the 1973 Sunningdale communiqué.

64 *Joint Report and Studies*, Cmnd 8414, November 1981, pp. 9 & 11–12.

65 Article 12.

66 Nick Taylor & Clive Walker, 'The British-Irish Interparliamentary Body' (1997) NILQ, 48, 4, p. 338.

16.65 ANNOTATIONS

'The full membership of the BIC' is the first reference to all the members. This may be implied in paragraphs 2, 4, 6 and 8.

'will keep under review the workings of the Council,' is a normal provision for such a body. It means continuing review.

'including a formal published review at an appropriate time' refers to a future review but without setting a time. Article 11 of the 1985 Anglo-Irish Agreement set a review for three years from signature (which was on 15 November 1985). Either government could request it earlier. The working of the conference – not article 1 on the status of Northern Ireland – was subject to review. It duly took place, seemingly shortly after 15 November 1988. It was published on 24 May 1989 (and is included – without commentary – in Tom Hadden and Kevin Boyle, *The Anglo-Irish Agreement: commentary, text and official review*, London and Dublin 1989[67]).

'after the Agreement comes into effect,' is a reference to the BIA, which is mentioned in paragraph 1. It is to be distinguished from this agreement in paragraph 10, which is the MPA – which is of course Annex 1 of the BIA. Article 4 refers to the entry into force of the BIA. Entry into force and coming into effect are the same. However, it is usual to refer to an international agreement entering into force, and to a statute coming into force.[68] Coming into effect, or taking effect, more usually refers to a specific provision. Dating the review from entry into force, and not from signature as in 1985, suggests a significant transition was envisaged. The BIA entered into force on 2 December 1999.

'and will contribute as appropriate to any review of the overall political agreement arising from the multi-party negotiations.' This is an entirely different principle. It allows all members of the BIC to contribute as appropriate. As appropriate suggests not all members will wish, or be able, to participate equally. Given that the BIC emerges out of a solution to the Northern Ireland problem, this is realistic. To any review refers to the other review provisions: during the transition, under paragraph 4 of the Validation, Implementation and Review section; and subsequently under paragraphs 5–8 of the same section. Of the overall political agreement is a rare admission that the MPA is not a legal text;[69] until, that is, it is annexed by the two states parties to the BIA. Arising from the multi-party negotiations is a reference to the 1996–98 talks. The MPA was entitled 'The Agreement: agreement reached in the multi-party negotiations'.

67 Chapter 7. This commentary was part of the review, and was submitted to the two governments.

68 See for example section 101(2) of the NIA 1998.

69 See also paragraph 2 of Constitutional Issues.

17

Strand Three: British-Irish Intergovernmental Conference

17.1 Strand Three is the fifth section of the Belfast Agreement. It comprises two separate institutions, the BIC and the BIIC. The BIC was considered in the previous chapter; the BIIC in this one. Strand Three is at pages 14–16 of Cm 3883 and pages 26–8 of Cm 4705 (pages 20–2 of the 1999 Irish version). At 21 paragraphs (12 for the BIC and 9 for the BIIC), Strand Three is overshadowed by Strand One (36 paragraphs); but it is longer than Strand Two (19 paragraphs). I show [deletions] to the MDP, and *additions* thus.

17.2 Given that the BIC and BIIC are rooted in east-west relations, some of the material in this chapter corresponds to paragraphs in the preceding chapter.

17.3 Whereas the BIC is a new, multilateral body for these islands, the BIIC is a bilateral – state to state (London and Dublin) – body, a successor to the 1985 intergovernmental conference. However, it is more like the 1981 Anglo-Irish intergovernmental council (which it also absorbs). In addition, Northern Ireland ministers will be involved as of right for the first time. There is continuity with 1981, rather than simply 1985 (the desire by the Irish government[1]), but the role of Northern Ireland ministers may well transform the BIIC.

17.4 Section 54 of the NIA 1998 deals with the BIIC. It incorporates the second paragraph 7 of Strand Three (attendance of Northern Ireland ministers for excepted and reserved matters). The principle of cross-community attendance is also enshrined (based on paragraph 30 of Strand One), similar to that for the NSMC and BIC under section 52 of the NIA 1998

17.5 The key legal instrument is the agreement between the United Kingdom and Irish governments establishing the British-Irish Intergovernmental Conference (again?), done at Dublin on 8 March 1999[2] – one of the supplementary agreements relating to the BIA. (There are some textual differences between the United Kingdom and Irish versions.[3]) This international agreement was presented to parliament by the foreign secretary in March 1999 as Cm 4295. It was approved by Dáil Éireann (under article 29.5.2 of BNH) on 9 March 1999.[4] No provision was made in Irish law – as it was for the NSMC and BIC – for the participation of their ministers in the BIIC.

1 See 'Vote Yes for Peace', a Fianna Fáil leaflet issued during the referendum in the ROI: it referred to 'continued existence of a British-Irish Intergovernmental Conference, meeting frequently to consult on matters such as security, justice, policing and prisons issues'; this was compared favourably to the 'purely consultative British-Irish Council'.

2 Agreement betweeen the government of the United Kingdom of Great Britain and Northern Ireland and the government of Ireland establishing a British-Irish Intergovernmental Conference, Cm 4295, Ireland No. 4 (1999).

3 The first recital in the preamble in the Irish version is missing two commas, distinguishing the MPA from the BIA. The British/Irish Agreement is also used in article 1 of this version.

4 *Official Report*.

17.6 Strand Three – in the typology of the talks – was about relationships 'between the two Governments, including their relationship with any new institutions in Northern Ireland'.[5] However, under the basis of the all-party negotiations, reference was made to achieving a new beginning 'between the peoples of these islands'.[6] Strand Three was negotiated between the two governments. However, there was provision for consultation with the political parties. No distinction was made between the BIC and the BIIC in 1996, it not being settled between the two governments whether there was to be one or two international organizations; simply a bilateral one, or a multilateral one as well.

17.7 Given that Great Britain and Ireland had constituted the United Kingdom state until 1922, it should not be surprising that an east-west dimension figures in the Belfast Agreement. But this would be to reckon without the consequences of the formation of an Irish state. A 'these islands' perspective was anathema to proponents of national self-reliance; southern unionism was largely vanquished, and Ulster unionists – rejoicing in differences in Ireland – relied upon their region being an integral part of the United Kingdom (even if many in Britain considered them simply Irish).

The British-Irish dimension

17.8 There was no east-west dimension in the GOIA 1920, because Southern Ireland and Northern Ireland remained part of the United Kingdom. Nor was there one in the NICA 1973, the only precedent for devolution on a basis of power-sharing. The Sunningdale communiqué, heavy with an Irish dimension, was silent on relations between the two states.

17.9 The inspiration for the second part of Strand Three is Irish policy on Northern Ireland from 1980.

17.10 On 8 December 1980, the United Kingdom and Irish premiers, meeting in Dublin, commissioned joint studies covering a number of discrete policy areas,[7] 'in order to assist them in their special consideration of the totality of relationships within these islands'.[8] Northern Ireland was not central to this development, though the Irish government presented it as a significant constitutional advance.[9] It was an attempt at a bilateral relationship between two states within Europe.

17.11 In November 1981, the Anglo-Irish intergovernmental council was established; there was no international agreement. It was to deal with 'matters of common interest and concern, with particular reference to the achievement of peace, reconciliation and stability and the improvement of relations between the two countries and their peoples'.[10] The council was not a great success, though

5 *Ground Rules for Substantive All-Party Negotiations*, Cm 3232, 16 April 1996, rule 2.
6 *Ground Rules for Substantive All-Party Negotiations*, Cm 3232, 16 April 1996, rule 1.
7 They were: possible new institutional structures; citizenship rights; security matters; economic cooperation; and measures to encourage mutual understanding.
8 Anglo-Irish Joint Studies, *Joint Report and Studies*, Cmnd 8414, November 1981, p. 4.
9 Margaret Thatcher, *The Downing Street Years*, London 1995, p. 390.
10 Anglo-Irish Joint Studies, *Joint Report and Studies*, Cmnd 8414, November 1981, p. 4.

there were meetings of ministers, and occasional Anglo-Irish summits involving the heads of government.[11]

17.12 This was partly because of the diversion of the new Ireland forum, which met in Dublin in 1983–84. Its *Report* came up with three solutions to the Irish question: a unitary state; a federal/confederal state, and joint authority. While the United Kingdom government was conceived as a facilitator/persuader for Irish unity,[12] there was also proposed (but only for the united Ireland option) 'an Irish-British Council with intergovernmental and interparliamentary structures which would acknowledge the unique relationship between Ireland and Britain and which would provide expression of the long-established connnections which unionists have with Britain'.[13]

17.13 The Anglo-Irish intergovernmental conference – the precursor of the BIIC – was established, as a result of an international agreement signed at Hillsborough in Co. Down on 15 November 1985, within the framework of the Anglo-Irish intergovernmental council. It was 'concerned with Northern Ireland and with relations between the two parts of the island of Ireland'.[14] And would deal on a regular basis with political matters; security and related matters; legal matters, including the administration of justice; and the promotion of cross-border cooperation.

17.14 The 1993 *Downing Street Declaration* referred to 'institutional recognition of the special links that exist between the peoples of Britain and Ireland as part of the totality of relationships, while taking account of newly forged links with the rest of Europe'.[15]

17.15 The 1995 *Framework Documents* contained a significant difference of emphasis.

17.16 In part I, the United Kingdom government, outlining its approach to a comprehensive settlement, envisaged replacing the Anglo-Irish Agreement with a new and more broadly based one 'reflecting the totality of relationships'. There would be bilateral liaison through an intergovernmental council (similar to the 1981 body?). There would also be an intergovernmental conference, with suitable rights of attendance and consultation for appropriate Northern Ireland representatives.[16] This was to anticipate the final shape of Strand Three in the Belfast Agreement.

17.17 In part II, the shared understanding drafted in Dublin, paragraphs 39–49 dealt with east-west structures. This envisaged the intergovernmental conference as a continuing institutional expression of Dublin involvement in Northern

11 It was at the third summit meeting that the Anglo-Irish agreement was signed: joint communiqué, 15 November 1985. This document also noted that there had been more than 20 meetings of ministers in the previous year.

12 'It would be for the British and Irish governments to create the framework and atmosphere within which such negotiations [embodying Irish unity] could take place.' (*Report*, Dublin 1984, p. 30)

13 *Report*, Dublin 1984, p. 32.

14 Article 2(a) of the 1985 Anglo-Irish Agreement, Cmnd 9657, Republic of Ireland No. 1 (1985).

15 Paragraph 9.

16 Annex B, pp. 17–18; see also paragraph 27 of part I.

Ireland: 'The Conference will be the principal instrument for an intensification of the co-operation and partnership between both Governments, with particular reference to the principles contained in the Joint [Downing Street] Declaration, in this Framework Document and in the new [British-Irish] Agreement, on a wide range of issues concerned with Northern Ireland and with the relations between the two parts of the island of Ireland.'[17] Paragraph 43 referred to bilateral matters of mutual interest not covered by other specific arrangements, either through the intergovernmental council, the conference or otherwise.[18]

17.18 The Heads of Agreement of 12 January 1998 promised a new British-Irish Agreement to replace the existing Anglo-Irish Agreement, and help establish close cooperation and enhance relationships. The last of four institutions was to be standing intergovernmental machinery between the Irish and British governments, 'covering issues of mutual interest, including non-devolved issues for Northern Ireland, when representatives of the Northern Ireland administration would be involved'.

The Nordic Council: an analogy?

17.19 The BIC has been compared[19] to another regional organization, in northern Europe or *Norden*[20] – the Nordic Council linking Denmark, Finland, Iceland, Norway and Sweden (plus the self-governing territories, the Aland Islands, the Faeroe Islands and Greenland); a total of eight members with a joint population of 23 million.[21]

17.20 However, the Nordic Council – particularly from the formation of the council of ministers in 1971 – may be contrasted with the 1985 intergovernmental conference, on which the BIIC is meant to be based.

17.21 The Nordic Council was established in 1952 by Denmark, Iceland, Norway and Sweden. Finland joined in 1955; the Faeroes and Aland in 1970, and Greenland in 1984. There was no proper legal basis[22] to the Nordic Council in 1952, due to the Soviet Union. This was provided by the 1962 Helsinki treaty of cooperation between the five states' parties. It was revised in 1971, when the council of ministers was established.

17.22 Amendments in 1993 allowed for greater participation by the Nordic countries in the process of European cooperation.

17.23 Article 1[23] defines the purpose of the Nordic Council as endeavouring to maintain and develop further cooperation between the Nordic countries in the legal, cultural, social and economic fields as well as in those of transport and

17 Part II, paragraph 42.

18 Part II, paragraph 43.

19 The idea was first raised, only to be dismissed effectively, in the Anglo-Irish Joint Studies, *Joint Report and Studies*, Cmnd 8414, November 1981, p. 9. It was raised after the Belfast Agreement in Mads Qvortrup & Robert Hazell, *The British-Irish Council: Nordic lessons for the council of the isles*, London, The Constitution Unit, n.d. but 1998. Bertie Ahern toyed with the idea in a lecture, 'The Western Isles of Europe', in Edinburgh on 29 October 1998: http://www.irlgov.ie/taoiseach.

20 Address: http://www.norden.org.

21 Its symbol (since 1985) is a white swan – with eight-toothed wing – on a blue background.

22 Members had to rely upon their domestic law.

23 Redrafted in 1993.

communications, and environmental protection. The Nordic countries are to hold joint consultations on a permanent basis, and, where necessary, take coordinated measures.[24]

17.24 Cooperation is to take place through the Nordic Council, in the council of ministers, at meetings between prime ministers, foreign ministers and other ministers, in special cooperative bodies as well as between specialized public authorities.[25]

17.25 The Nordic Council – with a plenary assembly, praesidium[26] and standing committees – comprises the parliaments and governments of the eight members; 87 elected members plus any number of government representatives. It has the power to initiate proposals, and to give advice on matters pertaining to cooperation between all or some of the members.[27] It makes recommendations and statements, addressed to the council of ministers or national governments. Government representatives do not vote.[28] The Nordic Council is governed by rules of procedure.[29]

17.26 The council of ministers, in contrast, comprises the national and other governments (and this is where the Nordic Council becomes relevant to the BIC and BIIC). Each government is represented by the prime minister, or the minister for cooperation. Decisions are by unanimity, the five Nordic countries only voting. They are binding on the states parties, though any one may enter a parliamentary reserve.[30] (The three sub-state members are bound, insofar as they accede to the decision in accordance with their statutes of self-government.) The budget is proportionately based on gross national product. The council of ministers determines its own rules of procedure.[31]

17.27 There are a number of stark contrasts between the Nordic Council and the BIIC. One, its evolution as a bottom-up movement, starting with the civil-society Norden association in 1918, leading to the Nordic Council in 1952 and the council of ministers in 1971 (a period of 53 years). The BIIC is a top-down body, and one that has come out of an attempt to manage the Northern Ireland problem – in 1985 under the Anglo-Irish Agreement, and in 1998 with the Belfast Agreement. Two, the Nordic Council comprises five nation states, and three sub-state entities. The BIIC is a simple bilateral body between two states; the smaller nation state was created out of the larger. Its origin is the Irish attempt from 1980 to influence United Kingdom policy on Northern Ireland. Three, the Nordic Council was an alternative to European cooperation, which is increasingly overshadowing *Norden*. The United Kingdom and the Republic of Ireland have been in Europe since 1973, though the reluctance of the former contrasts with the enthusiasm of the latter. Four, the Nordic Council members have a common tradition of Lutheran

24 Article 39.
25 Article 40.
26 There is a 20-strong international council secretariat in Copenhagen, sharing premises with the council of ministers' 80-strong international secretariat.
27 Article 44.
28 Article 49.
29 Article 59.
30 Article 63.
31 Article 66.

monarchism,[32] and social democracy. The BIIC, in contrast, is related principally to ending Northern Ireland violence. It comprises the government currently responsible, and the one that aspires to preside over a united Ireland. Five, the Nordic Council drives the council of ministers; the BIIC, on the other hand, is a ministerial body.

The prime minister's speech to the Oireachtas, 26 November 1998

17.28 The Belfast Agreement was concluded on 10 April 1998. There followed the referendums on 22 May 1998, and the Northern Ireland assembly elections on 25 June 1998. The First Minister and Deputy First Minister were elected on 1 July 1998.

17.29 While the transitional administration in Belfast addressed the matters referred by the secretary of state, the United Kingdom and Irish governments – the signatories of the BIA – continued to work on their relationship. The United Kingdom prime minister – the first in the history of Anglo-Irish relations – was invited to address the Oireachtas on 26 November 1998.

17.30 Strand Three – though there had been no meetings of the BIC (as required by paragraph 7 of Strand Two) – was evidently under active consideration. The prime minister mentioned the BIC (the new ingredient in the Belfast Agreement), and referred to transport, education and illegal drugs as possible areas of cooperation: transport and drugs did become issues on 17 December 1999.

17.31 However, the climax of his speech was the BIIC. The prime minister announced the launch of a new intensive process between London and Dublin. Three areas were mentioned: revitalized and modernized bilateral relations; close consultation on European issues; and working together on international issues.

17.32 It is perhaps significant that the prime minister – talking solely about bilateral relations – was configuring the BIIC more like the 1981 Anglo-Irish intergovernmental council than the 1985 intergovernmental conference: 'after keeping us apart for so long, Northern Ireland is now helping to bring us closer together. But I do not believe Northern Ireland can or should any longer define that relationship between us.'[33] There is evidence of such intent on the part of the United Kingdom government,[34] though it remains to be seen whether the Irish government will revert in the new form to the old content of trying to codetermine Northern Ireland.

17.33 An instance of this new vision is a joint statement by the United Kingdom prime minister and Irish taoiseach of 16 March 2000, when London and Dublin were divided over the suspension of the institutions in Northern Ireland. This joint statement referred to the forthcoming special European Council at Lisbon on 23–24 March 2000. They welcomed the presidency's ten-year reform strategy to make the EU the world's most dynamic and competitive area. The two heads of government presented a joint paper to their colleagues highlighting three broad areas where they would work together at the summit to secure progress: education and lifelong learning; innovation and enterprise; and social exclusion.

32 Finland became a republic in 1918, Iceland in 1940.

33 10 Downing Street press notice, p. 8.

34 This interpretation was repeated by the United Kingdom ambassador, Sir Ivor Roberts, in the *Irish Independent*, 4 July 2000.

TITLE: BRITISH-IRISH INTERGOVERNMENTAL CONFERENCE

17.34 This title, while inconsistent with Strand One, is consistent with Strand Two, and with the first part of Strand Three. It is, of course, one of two titles in Strand Three. The British-Irish Intergovernmental Conference – there are no oblique strokes in Strand Three – is the second of two intergovernmental organizations dealing with east-west relations (in the case of the BIIC, on a more normal state-to-state basis).

17.35 The BIIC was negotiated between the two governments. The MDP text was amended significantly in two ways (discussed below). The BIIC under the Belfast Agreement may be compared most usefully with the intergovernmental conference under the 1985 Anglo-Irish Agreement.

1. **There will be a new British-Irish Agreement dealing with the totality of relationships. It will establish a standing British-Irish Intergovernmental Conference, which will subsume both the Anglo-Irish Intergovernmental Council and the Intergovernmental Conference established under the 1985 Agreement.**

17.36 This paragraph replaces the 1981 and 1985 bodies with the BIIC.

17.37 ANNOTATIONS

'There will be a new British-Irish Agreement' is strangely located. Paragraph 1 of Constitutional Issues (the substance of which forms article 1 of the BIA) refers to a new British-Irish Agreement replacing the Anglo-Irish Agreement. Paragraph 1 of Strand Two and the first paragraph 1 of Strand Three then refer to this British-Irish Agreement (so also does paragraph 1 of Validation, Implementation and Review). It is therefore strange that the second paragraph 1 of Strand Three then (re)introduces the legal text. One possible explanation is that the provisions dealing with the BIIC were intended originally to be overarching in the Belfast Agreement. This point is reinforced by paragraph 9 (discussed below).

'dealing with the totality of relationships.' has been used in paragraph 1 of Strand Two, and the first paragraph 1 of Strand Three (though among the peoples of these islands has been added there). The totality of relationships is used here (as in paragraph 1 of Strand Two) to refer to the scope of the BIA. In the first paragraph 1 of Strand Three, in contrast, it is 'the totality of relationships among the peoples of these islands'. The origins of the phrase lie in the December 1980 meeting in Dublin, between the Irish and United Kingdom premiers, which began the contemporary phase in Anglo-Irish diplomacy. They commissioned joint studies,[35] as the basis of 'a [future] special consideration of the totality of relationships within these islands'. It has never been clear whether these are government to government relationships, or between the civil societies of both states. The meaning in 1980–81 was much more the former, and 'the totality of relationships among the peoples of these islands' is a later development. The basis of the 1996–98 talks was: 'to achieve a new beginning for relationships within Northern Ireland, within the island of Ireland and between the peoples of these islands, and to agree new institutions and structures to take account of the totality of relationships'.[36] This is a third meaning to totality, corresponding to the scope of the BIA in article 2: the MPA, which includes Strand One, plus the international institutions (Strands Two and Three).

35 Anglo-Irish Joint Studies, *Joint Report and Studies*, Cmnd 8414, November 1981. The areas were: possible new institutional structures; citizenship rights; security matters; economic cooperation; and measures to encourage mutual understanding.

36 *Ground Rules for Substantive All-Party Negotiations*, Cm 3232, April 1996, rule 1.

'It will establish a standing British-Irish Intergovernmental Conference,' states that the BIA establishes the BIIC. Standing is used uniquely of the BIIC, though the NSMC secretariat is to be standing (paragraph 16 of Strand Two), as is the secretariat in paragraph 8 below. Article 2 of the BIA states that, in particular, there shall be established immediately on the entry into force of the BIA, a number of institutions in accordance with the MPA. The fourth and last listed is the BIIC. This would have been enough to create an international organization called the BIIC under the BIA. The passive tense was used to spare Northern Ireland blushes over particularly the NSMC. 'Established ... on the entry into force of this Agreement' is the key phrase in article 2 of the BIA.

The supplementary agreement of 8 March 1999 (referred to above) was probably unnecessary. Cm 4295 is entitled 'agreement between the government of the United Kingdom of Great Britain and Northern Ireland and the government of Ireland establishing a British-Irish Intergovernmental Conference'. The first recital of the preamble begins: 'Having regard to Article 2 of the [BIA]'. And article 1 commences: 'Under and in furtherance of Article 2 of the [BIA] ... there is hereby established a British-Irish Intergovernmental Conference'. Under article 2 of the BIA makes this supplementary agreement a duplicate. In furtherance of does not add anything, since there is nothing in article 2 requiring a second agreement. The most likely explanation for the supplementary agreement is that 'there shall be established' in article 2 was open to interpretation by Irish government advisers as requiring precisely this (it contrasts with 'there is hereby established' in the supplementary agreement).[37] Further, since the north-south implementation bodies did need a supplementary agreement (they were only decided upon subsequently) Dublin requested – and London acceded to – a set of four new international agreements done on 8 March 1999.

'which will subsume both the Anglo-Irish Intergovernmental Council and the Intergovernmental Conference established under the 1985 Agreement.' Subsume here means absorb. The Anglo-Irish Intergovernmental Council was established in November 1981. There was no international agreement. However, it was recognized by article 2(a) of the 1985 Anglo-Irish Agreement, as constituting the framework within which the conference was being established. The Anglo-Irish Intergovernmental Council ceased to exist under this paragraph when the BIA entered into force on 2 December 1999, the MPA constituting Annex 1. The intergovernmental conference was different. It was a treaty body. Under article 3(1) of the BIA, the 1985 Anglo-Irish Agreement ceased to have effect on entry into force of the BIA on 2 December 1999.[38] Article 3(2) states – unnecessarily – that the conference shall cease to exist on entry into force of the BIA.

2. The Conference will bring together the British and Irish Governments to promote bilateral co-operation at all levels on all matters of mutual interest within the competence of both Governments.

17.38 This paragraph deals with membership, and with purpose. However, the latter is drafted oddly.

17.39 ANNOTATIONS

'The Conference will bring together the British and Irish Governments' is not normal treaty drafting. Paragraph 2 of Strand Two refers to Northern Ireland and the Irish government (the two members of the NSMC) being represented by various ministers. The first paragraph 2 of Strand Three states that membership of the BIC will comprise representatives of various administrations. This text does not refer to representatives. Nor does it refer to members. The 1985 Anglo-Irish Agreement was between the same parties who made the BIA. The intergovernmental conference was established in article 2, it being implied that the

37 'Shall' here may sound like legislative rather than treaty language.

38 Paragraph 1 of Constitutional Issues has the BIA replacing the Anglo-Irish Agreement.

two governments were the members. The strange text here no doubt derives from the MPA, a political agreement being given legal form by the two governments, by being annexed. Thus, the second part of Strand Three is drafted almost as a commentary directed at the political parties. Bring together is the language of politics, not law. The British and Irish governments is, yet again, the nationalist duality, characteristic of the Belfast Agreement (paragraph 5 of the Declaration of Support, paragraph 2 of Constitutional Issues, the first paragraph 2 of Strand Three).

'to promote bilateral co-operation at all levels on all matters of mutual interest within the competence of both Governments.' is the purpose of the BIIC. This may be distinguished from the 1985 Anglo-Irish Agreement: article 2(a) stated that the conference was 'concerned with Northern Ireland and with relations between the two parts of the island of Ireland, to deal ... on a regular basis with ... .' There is no reference to Northern Ireland in the purpose of the BIIC. It reads much more like a normal bilateral cooperation council, as the 1981 intergovernmental council was conceived (though that referred particularly to the achievement of peace, reconciliation and stability[39]). To promote bilateral co-operation at all levels is a straightforward statement of state to state bilateralism. Cooperation is the guiding concept, which is the obligation in international law. At all levels is not specified. However, given that summit level is used in the first paragraph 3 of Strand Three, and also (below) in the second paragraph 3, level would seem to relate to head of government, ministers, officials, etc.

'on all matters of mutual interest' is strange for a state to state relationship. Matters of mutual interest occurs in paragraph 1 of Strand Two (and also in paragraphs 5 and 8; the term mutual benefit also occurs). This is also the case with the first paragraphs 1 and 5 of Strand Three. The addition of all is singular to the BIIC. Does this mean that not all mutual interest or benefit may be pursued in the NSMC and the BIC?

'within the competence of both Governments.' is extraordinary for a state to state relationship. In originates in paragraph 1 of Strand Two (and is carried on in paragraphs 5 and 12). The same concept appears in the first paragraph 5 of Strand Three. The United Kingdom and the Republic of Ireland are sovereign states. They can do what they choose, within international law; that is the meaning of state sovereignty. Their governments may well be – are most certainly – constrained constitutionally in, respectively, United Kingdom and Irish law. But that does not mean they have a limited competence, like the Northern Ireland administration – a creature of powers devolved by statute (plus part of the royal prerogative).

The purpose of the BIIC has been drafted politically to fit into the MPA, not legally as part of a BIA replacing the 1985 Anglo-Irish Agreement.

3. **The Conference will meet as required at Summit level (Prime Minister and Taoiseach). Otherwise, Governments will be represented by appropriate Ministers. Advisers, including police and security advisers, will attend as appropriate.**

17.40 This corresponds to paragraph 3 of Strand Two, and the first paragraph 3 of Strand Three. It is about formats.

17.41 ANNOTATIONS

'The Conference will meet as required at Summit level (Prime Minister and Taoiseach).' Paragraph 3 of Strand Two refers to a plenary format, with the First Minister and Deputy First Minister and the taoiseach. The first paragraph 3 of Strand Three refers to summit level. This term is repeated here, with an upper-case S. There follows a parenthesis, explaining this as the prime minister and the taoiseach. (There is an argument as regards the first

39 Anglo-Irish Joint Studies, *Joint Report and Studies*, Cmnd 8414, November 1981, p. 4.

paragraph 3 of Strand Three, that summit level must mean heads of administration. Countering this is the argument that the level has not been specified; but this is probably because of the variety of offices involved. This is borne out by the memorandum on procedural guidance, agreed at the inaugural meeting in London on 17 December 1999.) As required is different from paragraph 3 of Strand Two (twice a year), and the first paragraph 3 of Strand Three (twice per year). As required leaves it to the initiative of either member of the BIIC, namely either government. This was also the position in article 3 of the Anglo-Irish Agreement.

In his speech to the Oireachtas on 26 November 1998, the prime minister stated that he and the taoiseach (with key ministerial colleagues) would meet in London the following spring. This can only have been intended as a meeting of the BIIC, after devolution – which was then expected in February 1999. There was no requirement in paragraph 7 of Strand Two, for meetings of the BIIC in shadow mode. The prime minister stated that the heads of government would meet at least once a year to review progress. This is the only indication of the frequency of meetings of the BIIC at summit level. The supplementary procedural arrangements, agreed at the inaugural meeting in London on 17 December 1999, state that the conference will normally meet at summit level at least twice a year (paragraph 3.2). The communiqué after the meeting envisaged the next summit-level meeting in the first half of 2000.

'Otherwise, Governments will be represented by appropriate Ministers.' Paragraph 3 of Strand Two refers to specific sectoral formats with the appropriate minister, meeting regularly and frequently. The first paragraph 3 of Strand Three has a similar formulation, meeting regularly. Here, there is not reference to regularly, much less frequently. Appropriate Ministers is, however, used, suggesting sectoral formats. But, again, this is left entirely to the initiative of either government. The supplementary procedural arrangements, agreed at the inaugural meeting in London on 17 December 1999, states that the two governments will decide on an initial schedule of meetings (paragraph 3.1). The conference will also remit to be considered by appropriate Ministers or officials, including the Secretariat, any matter coming before it (paragraph 3.3). The communiqué of this meeting referred only to meetings on other than Northern Ireland issues being arranged as necessary.

'Advisers, including police and security advisers, will attend as appropriate.' There is no reference to advisers in Strand Two, nor in the first part of Strand Three. This is related partly to paragraph 6 below. In the Anglo-Irish Agreement, the second of the four functions of the intergovernmental conference was security and related matters. The first article in the cross-border co-operation section dealt with security. Reference was made to a work programme for the chief constable of the Royal Ulster Constabulary and the commissioner of the Garda Síochána, though it was clear operational responsibilities remained with the two police forces. Article 3 dealt with format and frequency. It was stated that ministers could be accompanied by their official and professional advisers. The article went on to give an example: 'when questions of security policy or security co-operation are being discussed, they may be accompanied by the Chief Constable of the Royal Ulster Constabulary and the Commissioner of the Garda Siochana'. The word advisers here is broader. It allows for ministerial advisers. Including police and security advisers is probably taken from the 1985 agreement. However, security advisers are also officials, who were dealt with separately in article 3 of the Anglo-Irish Agreement. Will attend as appropriate is similar to appropriate ministers, and consistent with the unspecified nature of BIIC meetings. This contrasts with article 3 in 1985: 'Regular and frequent Ministerial meetings shall be held'. The supplementary procedural arrangements, agreed at the inaugural meeting in London on 17 December 1999, state that, because of the presence of Northern Ireland ministers, meetings would begin normally with a bilateral session between the appropriate ministers, their official and advisers. Where security-related matters were under discussion, such meetings might include police and security advisers and might be in restricted format.

4. **All decisions will be by agreement between both Governments. The Governments will make determined efforts to resolve disagreements between them. There will be no derogation from *the* sovereignty of either Government.**

17.42 This deals with decision-making, and corresponds to paragraphs 2 and 6 of Strand Two, and the first paragraph 7 of Strand Three.

17.43 ANNOTATIONS

'All decisions will be by agreement between both Governments.' Article 2(b) of the 1985 agreement contained the following: 'The United Kingdom Government accept that the Irish Government will put forward views and proposals on matters relating to Northern Ireland within the field of activity of the Conference in so far as these matters are not the responsibility of a devolved administration in Northern Ireland.' This made the intergovernmental conference a consultation body. However, the article goes on to state: 'In the interests of promoting peace and stability, determined efforts shall be made through the Conference to resolve any differences.' Differences refers to public or private disagreements, rather than to differences over a decision. The BIIC therefore represents a qualitative shift from a consultation body to a decision-making one. This may have arisen because of the commonality between the NSMC, the BIC and the BIIC in the MPA. Paragraph 2 of Strand Two states that all NSMC decisions are to be by agreement between the two sides. The first paragraph 7 of Strand Three refers to consensus, given the BIC is a multilateral body. All decisions will be by agreement between both Governments is similar to the first sentence in paragraph 2 of Strand Two. However, the will and the both are different. Will may be legally better. Both is syntactically unnecessary.

'The Governments will make determined efforts to resolve disagreements between them.' The origin of this is in article 2(b) of the Anglo-Irish Agreement (quoted above). However, that does not refer to decision making. Here, there is in a paragraph on decision making, a statement of determined efforts. It is similar to paragraph 5(ii) of Strand Two: 'making determined efforts to overcome any disagreements'.

'There will be no derogation from the sovereignty of either Government.' The origin of this is article 2(b) of the Anglo-Irish Agreement: 'There is no derogation from the sovereignty of either the United Kingdom Government or the Irish Government, and each retains responsibility for the decisions and administration of government within its own jurisdiction.' Note the change from is to will be. However, there is a basic problem. It is states – not governments – which are sovereign in international law. In United Kingdom law, parliament is sovereign; in Irish law, the international law position is recognized in article 5 of BNH: 'Ireland is a sovereign ... state.' The supplementary procedural arrangements, agreed at the inaugural meeting in London on 17 December 1999, makes no reference to decisions, other than any statements issued at the close of the conference (paragraph 4.5).

5. **In recognition of the Irish Government's special interest in Northern Ireland and of the extent to which issues of mutual concern arise in relation to Northern Ireland, there will be regular and frequent meetings of the Conference concerned with non-devolved Northern Ireland matters, on which the Irish Government may put forward views and proposals. These meetings, to be co-chaired by the Minister for Foreign Affairs and the Secretary of State for Northern Ireland, would also deal with all-island and cross-border co-operation on non-devolved issues.**

17.44 The 1985 intergovernmental conference was concerned with Northern Ireland. This is not the position with the BIIC; as can be seen from its purpose in paragraph 2 above. This Northern Ireland paragraph, however, does something to keep the work of the former intergovernmental conference going in the new bilateral BIIC. Under direct rule, the Irish government was entitled to put forward views and proposals on all non-devolved matters; with devolution, the range of matters is narrowed.

17.45 ANNOTATIONS

'In recognition of the Irish Government's special interest in Northern Ireland' is a major statement. It follows the last sentence in paragraph 4 above about there being no derogation from sovereignty.

This special interest was defined first in 1985, when the aspirational view of articles 2 and 3 of BNH was in the ascendant: *The Criminal Law (Jurisdiction) Bill 1975* [1977] IR 129. In the Anglo-Irish Agreement, the United Kingdom government envisaged two roles for the Irish government. First, in the attempt to bring devolution to Northern Ireland, the Irish government could, under article 4(c), put forward views and proposals on modalities 'in so far as they relate to the interests of the minority community'. Secondly, if devolution did not succeed, the Irish government could, under article 5(c), put forward views on proposals for major legislation and on major (Northern Ireland) policy issues, 'where the interests of the minority community are significantly or especially affected'.

The former was more generous than the latter, but direct rule was to run for more than 12 years until the Belfast Agreement. Political and legal thinking on minority rights, and the role of guarantor states, was developing in 1985. With the collapse of communism from 1989, it would become an important issue in Europe. In 1990, however, the Irish supreme court reaffirmed the territorial claim to Northern Ireland: *McGimpsey v Ireland* [1988] IR 567; [1990] IR 110. By then, London and Dublin were embarked – separately and together – on the process that led to the Belfast Agreement. The United Kingdom was unable to react fully to *McGimpsey* after 1990, though removal of the territorial claim became a political imperative for London. This was achieved with Annex B of Constitutional Issues.

The Irish Government's special interest in Northern Ireland cannot be construed in terms of the 1985 Anglo-Irish Agreement (much less the work of the intergovernmental conference). That treaty has been replaced by the BIA. The changes to BNH must be taken as the constitutional foundation of the Irish state's position – as regards Northern Ireland – in international law. Further, this phrase must be interpreted along with the Irish government's undertaking, in its part of the Rights, Safeguards and Equality of Opportunity section, to ratify as quickly as possible the Council of Europe's framework convention on national minorities. (This is discussed in Chapter 18.)

'and of the extent to which issues of mutual concern arise in relation to Northern Ireland,' is recognition that the BIIC is more like the 1981 inter-governmental council than the 1985 intergovernmental conference. In other words, Northern Ireland may become involved in this bilateral cooperation, because it is part of the United Kingdom. It is not suggestive of joint sovereignty or joint authority.

'there will be regular and frequent meetings of the Conference' originates in article 3 of the Anglo-Irish Agreement. Regular and frequent was used in paragraph 3(ii) of Strand Two, and, of the institutions (less the BIIC) during the transition, in paragraph 7. It was modified for the first paragraph 3 of Strand Three, and now appears in the full regular and frequent form here. Regular and frequent is used in the supplementary procedural arrangements, agreed at the inaugural meeting in London on 17 December 1999 (paragraph 3.1).

'concerned with non-devolved Northern Ireland matters,' is traceable from the Anglo-Irish Agreement. Article 2(b) allowed the Irish government to put forward views and proposals, in so far as the matters were not the responsibility of a devolved administration in Belfast. The NICA 1973 was then the constitution act (even though there was direct rule); it distinguished transferred, excepted and reserved matters. Non-devolved matters were the two latter. The NIA 1998 is the new constitution act. It contains a similar distinction in section 4.

'on which the Irish Government may put forward views and proposals.' is the same as in article 2(b) of the Anglo-Irish Agreement.

'The meetings, to be co-chaired by the Minister for Foreign Affairs and the Secretary of State for Northern Ireland,' is similar to article 3 of the Anglo-Irish Agreement. There, it was stated that, when the intergovernmental conference met at ministerial level, the secretary of state, and an Irish minister designated as the permanent Irish ministerial representative, would be joint chairmen. However, there was also a possibility of other ministers holding or attending meetings within the framework of the conference. There is no provision for other United Kingdom or Irish ministers under this paragraph.

'would also deal with all-island and cross-border co-operation on non-devolved issues.' All-island and cross-border cooperation on devolved matters is dealt with in Strand Two. It is the preserve of the NSMC, the Northern Ireland administration and the Irish government. Cross-border cooperation on security, economic, social and cultural matters was provided for in section F of the Anglo-Irish Agreement. Article 10 – dealing with economic, social and cultural matters – covered the range of non-devolved activities. Those devolved now come under the NSMC (under article 10(c)). The non-devolved remainder – hitherto under article 10(b) – are picked up by this phrase.

The inaugural meeting of the BIIC took place on 17 December 1999, in Downing Street, following the inaugural meeting of the BIC at Lancaster House. It was chaired jointly by the United Kingdom and Irish heads of government. The prime minister was supported by the secretary of state. The taoiseach was accompanied by three ministers. The First Minister and the Deputy First Minister were present for the entire proceedings.

The BIIC agreed a programme of work, under bilateral cooperation: asylum and immigration, including common travel area issues; European Union and international issues; social security, including methods of fraud detection; education; policy on misuse of drugs, combating organized crime and associated money laundering; and fiscal issues. Under Northern Ireland, the work programme would include: rights, policing, including implementation of the Patten report; criminal justice; normalization of security arrangements and practices; cross-border security cooperation; victims of violence; prisons issues; drugs and drug trafficking; broadcasting. Though the communiqué does not indicate this, bilateral cooperation, and not non-devolved Northern Ireland, matters were discussed.

The first meeting on non-devolved Northern Ireland matters, chaired jointly by the secretary of state and the Irish foreign minister, was anticipated for January 2000. It appears not to have taken place (and certainly not before suspension of devolution on 12 February 2000). The next meeting at summit level was envisaged as taking place in the first half of 2000; no venue was specified.

Though it is not mentioned in the communiqué, the First Minster told the assembly, on 17 January 2000, that he and the Deputy First Minister had raised the matter of fuel duty and its impact on the Northern Ireland economy. It appears that this was raised under bilateral cooperation, and would be considered under fiscal issues in the work programme. The First Minister commented: 'It was an interesting experience, both for myself and for the Deputy First Minister, to be present throughout the meeting ... and to be able to observe and to make observations on all matters which were handled ... We would not have had the opportunity to raise issues in that way under the *ancien regime*.'[40]

6. Co-operation within the framework of the Conference will include facilitation of co-operation in security matters. The Conference also will

40 Northern Ireland Assembly, *Official Report*, vol. 4, no. 4, pp. 91–7, 17 January 2000.

address, in particular, the areas of rights, justice, prisons and policing in Northern Ireland (unless and until responsibility is devolved to a Northern Ireland administration) and will intensify co-operation between the two Governments on the all-island and cross-border aspects of these matters.

17.46 This paragraph keeps alive an important function of the 1985 Anglo-Irish Agreement; security and related matters, including cross-border cooperation. It suggests that the Belfast Agreement is not itself a peace agreement.[41]

17.47 Security and related matters was the second function of the 1985 intergovernmental conference.[42] This covered security policy, relations between the security forces and the community, and prisons policy. The security situation – in keeping with United Kingdom intent – was to be considered at the regular meetings. There was to be a programme of 'making the security forces more readily acceptable to the nationalist community'.[43] One of the two articles on cross-border cooperation was devoted to security: there was to be a programme of work, involving the Chief constable of the Royal Ulster Constabulary and the commissioner of the Garda Síochána.[44]

17.48 ANNOTATIONS

'Co-operation within the framework of the Conference' is not consistent with paragraph 3. Under the Anglo-Irish Agreement, the intergovernmental conference was to be within the framework of the intergovernmental council.[45] Paragraph 3 above defines the format of the BIIC. Within the framework suggests another area of activity under this paragraph.

'will include facilitation of co-operation in security matters.' is weaker than in 1985. Then, the nature of the cooperation was prescribed. Now, it is assumed. Facilitation of co-operation removes security cooperation from the BIIC. Security matters are not defined; presumably, existing practical cooperation between the two police forces will continue.

'The Conference will also address, in particular, the areas of rights, justice, prisons and policing in Northern Ireland' builds on article 7 of the Anglo-Irish Agreement. That covered security policy, relations between the security forces and the community (where rights, justice and policing are located), and prisons policy. All these issues are dealt with at considerable length in the sixth to eleventh sections of the Belfast Agreement: rights in Rights, Safeguards and Equality of Opportunity; justice in Policing and Justice; prisons in Prisoners; and policing in (again) Policing and Justice. (They are all dealt with in Chapters 18–22 in Part 4 of this book.)

'(unless and until responsibility is devolved to a Northern Ireland administration)' is consistent with the Anglo-Irish Agreement. There, the Irish government had its consultation role in non-devolved matters (which were all the functions of government in 1985). Article 2(b) defined the role in 1985. Article 4(c) gave the Irish government a role in achieving devolution. And article 5(c), its role if direct rule continued. The matters transferred under the NIA 1998 are all those not excepted or reserved (section 4). Excepted matters are listed in schedule 2; reserved in schedule 3. Schedule 2 refers to: human rights obligations (paragraph 3(c)); judicial appointments (11); special powers and other provisions for dealing with terrorism and subversion (17); and some provisions of the NICA 1973 and the NIA 1998. These will never be transferred. Schedule 3 refers to criminal law (paragraph 9); public order (10); the police (11); firearms and explosives (12); some

41 See also paragraph 3 of the Security section.
42 Article 2(a).
43 Article 7.
44 Article 9.
45 Article 2(a).

emergency powers (14); the courts (15); some provisions of the NIA 1998. Section 4 of the NIA 1998 provides for reserved matters being transferred (and vice versa). Paragraph 7 of the Policing and Justice section states that the United Kingdom government would be willing, in certain circumstances, to devolve responsibility for policing and justice to the Northern Ireland assembly. Annex B of that section, containing the terms of reference for a review of the criminal justice system, refers to the option of devolution (and even the possibility of a department of justice in Belfast).

'and will intensify co-operation between the two Governments on the all-island or cross-border aspects of these matters.' is based on article 9 of the Anglo-Irish Agreement. But there appears to be a shift from security cooperation to cooperation on rights, justice, prisons and policing. Will intensify co-operation is the strongest commitment in the paragraph. Between the two Governments suggests this will be at the level of all-Ireland policy. In 1985, the cooperation was between the two police forces (with a background of security). On the all-Ireland or cross-border aspects is the terminology of the Belfast Agreement: all-island and cross-border in paragraphs 1, 5 and 11 of Strand Two; all-island or cross-border in paragraph 9. In 1985, cross-border was used of economic and social development in a border counties sense (article 10(a)). However, it was also used to mean all-Ireland (article 10(b)–(c)). This is probably the meaning in article 9 (cross-border cooperation on security matters), though there is also a local – border counties – sense of security cooperation. Of these matters shifts the meaning of the last sentence from security to rights, justice, prisons and policing.

7. **Relevant executive members of the Northern Ireland Administration will be involved in meetings of the Conference, and in the reviews referred to in paragraph 9 below to discuss non-devolved Northern Ireland matters. [The Northern Ireland administration will be given advance notice of what is to be discussed at such meetings of the Conference, and will be invited to express views to both Governments in advance. Representatives of the Northern Ireland Administration will attend meetings of the Conference as and when appropriate. The two Governments will meet on their own as and when necessary.]**

17.49 If the first major change between the 1985 intergovernmental conference and the BIIC is the shift from a concentration upon Northern Ireland to bilateralism, the second is the involvement of the Northern Ireland administration. This was enhanced considerably between the MDP and the FA, and it has been extended further since 10 April 1998.

17.50 The origin of this idea was the 1995 *Framework Documents*, in the United Kingdom's outline of a comprehensive settlement.[46] and in paragraph 48 of the joint understanding.[47] The text in the MDP was consistent with the *Framework Documents*, revealing an Irish desire to keep its contact with the United Kingdom government as private as possible. This paragraph was greatly – and simply – altered; the first sentence was retained, the second, third and fourth dropped.

46 Part I, Annex B, paragraph 1.

47 'Both Governments envisage that representatives of agreed political institutions in Northern Ireland may be formally associated with the work of the Conference, in a manner and to an extent to be agreed by both Governments after consultation with them. This might involve giving them advance notice of what is to be discussed in the Conference, enabling them to express views to either Government and inviting them to participate in various aspects of the work of the Conference. Other more structured arrangements could be devised by agreement.'

17.51 ANNOTATIONS

'Relevant executive members of the Northern Ireland Administration'. The Northern Ireland Administration is not a term used in Strand One; the assembly is used to refer to the executive as well as legislature. It is only in Strand Two that Northern Ireland Administration – with an upper-case A – occurs.[48] The term is only implied in the first part of Strand Three. Under paragraphs 14–25 of Strand One, provision is made for the assembly's executive authority. It is called the executive committee in paragraph 17. The executive comprises the First Minister and Deputy First Minister and up to ten ministers (confirmed as ten in the agreement of 18 December 1998[49]). Relevant is not defined.

It is, however, defined in section 54 of the NIA 1998. Subsection (1) – incorporating partly the second part of Strand Three – states that the section applies where excepted or reserved matters relating to Northern Ireland are being discussed by the BIIC. Any argument about remaining discretion – which would be weak after comparing the MDP text with the FA – is resolved definitely by the NIA 1998. Northern Ireland attendance is a right. Conceivably, an emergency session of the BIIC would not be possible, if the First Minister and Deputy First Minister – under paragraph 18 of Strand One – were not informed. The supplementary procedural arrangements, agreed at the inaugural meeting in London on 17 December 1999, state that failure to attend or non-participation will not prevent the holding of a meeting (paragraph 4.1). However, this text is not legally binding. Section 54(2) of the NIA 1998 states that the First Minister and Deputy First Minister acting jointly shall ensure 'such cross-community attendance by Ministers and junior Ministers ... as is required by the Belfast Agreement': attendance, not participation, because Northern Ireland is not a member of the BIIC. Involved in paragraph 7 has been so altered in the incorporation in United Kingdom law. Section 54 is similar to section 52 (dealing with the NSMC and the BIC), though participation is defined there with reference to paragraphs 5 and 6 of Strand Two and the first paragraph 5 of Strand Three. This leaves cross-community undefined. Cross-community must be interpreted by reading paragraphs 18 and 30 of Strand One together. I submit that it means joint participation by Northern Ireland ministers, most likely the First Minister and Deputy First Minister under paragraph 18 of Strand One; alternatively, pairs of nationalist and unionist ministers or junior ministers.

The supplementary procedural arrangements, agreed at the inaugural meeting in London on 17 December 1999, has a whole section on the Northern Ireland Administration (paragraph 4). Paragraph 4.1 (mentioned above) is about cross-community attendance. Paragraph 4.2 deals with the important role of reviewing the BIA (discussed under paragraph 9 below). Paragraph 4.3 deals with items deleted from the paragraph under consideration: advance notice and agendas to the First Minister and Deputy First Minister; the right of Northern Ireland ministers to suggest agenda items. Paragraph 4.4 (discussed above) distinguishes the bilateral session from the conference meeting in plenary session. And paragraph 4.5 allows Northern Ireland representatives to participate in discussions of all issues considered in the sessions which they attend.

In the draft international agreement of 13 July 1999, consequent upon *The Way Forward* plan of 2 July 1999, provision was made for the suspension of the institutions of governmment. This applied to the assembly, the NSMC, even the implementation bodies (after four months) and the BIC. No reference was made to the BIIC. Suspension is not provided for expressly in the Belfast Agreement. There is an argument that it is inconsistent not to suspend the BIIC. However, as noted, the – non binding – supplementary procedural arrangements, agreed at the inaugural meeting in London on 17 December 1999, do not, in paragraph 4.4, make a meeting of the BIIC dependent upon the attendance of Northern

48 Paragraphs 2 & 8 (transitional).

49 New Northern Ireland Assembly, *Report from the First Minister (Designate) and the Deputy First Minister (Designate)*, NNIA 6, 18 January 1999, pp. 3–5.

Ireland ministers. Even if this is a correct interpretation of paragraph 7, there is still the argument that non-devolved Northern Ireland matters should not be discussed without Northern Ireland attendance. This point appears to be strengthened by section 54 of the NIA 1998: subsection (1) states that 'this section applies where excepted or reserved matters ... are to be discussed'. Subsection (2) requires the First Minister and deputy first Minister to ensure cross-community attendance. However, subsection (1) does not make the excepted or reserved matters dependent upon such attendance.

'will be involved in meetings of the Conference,' has been discussed above. There is no restriction to items dealing with non-devolved Northern Ireland matters. Involved in meetings has been legislated as the right to attend all meetings.

'and in the reviews referred to in paragraph 9 below' extends the principle of a right of attendance to all the reviews under the BIA (see below). This is stronger than the principle in paragraph 9 (which probably survived deletion inadvertently). Involvement in reviews has not been legislated in the NIA 1998. This means this phrase has to be interpreted as part of an international agreement.

'to discuss non-devolved Northern Ireland matters.' would appear to be inelegantly located or meaningless. The text of this first sentence in the MDP passed into the FA. However, the phrase – which defines that part of the remit of the BIIC provided for in paragraph 5 – is better located after the word Conference. The Northern Ireland executive committee only has a right of attendance for non-devolved Northern Ireland matters, not for the range of bilateral matters expressed as the purpose in paragraph 2 above. There is no logical association between the paragraph 9 reviews (of the entire BIA) and non-devolved Northern Ireland matters. However, the supplementary procedural arrangements, agreed at the inaugural meeting in London on 17 December 1999, clearly states that, while non-devolved matters have to be on the agenda before the First Minister and deputy First Minister secure attendance, 'Northern Ireland administration representatives may participate in discussion of all issues considered in the sessions which they attend' (paragraph 4.5).

8. The Conference will be supported by officials of the British and Irish Governments, including a standing joint Secretariat of officials dealing with non-devolved Northern Ireland matters.

17.52 This paragraph corresponds to paragraph 16 of Strand Two and the first paragraph 9 of Strand Three. The precedent is the provision in article 3 of the Anglo-Irish Agreement: 'A Secretariat shall be established by the two Governments to service the Conference on a continuing basis in the discharge of its functions ... .'

17.53 The Anglo-Irish secretariat was located at Maryfield outside Belfast (beside Palace barracks in Hollywood). As a result of an undertaking given by the United Kingdom prime minister at Castle Buildings, it was closed down at the end of 1998. The secretariat – comprising United Kingdom and Irish officials – then relocated to Windsor House in Bedford Street in central Belfast. It appeared to be on its way out with the Anglo-Irish Agreement, which was not of course superseded until 2 December 1999.

17.53 ANNOTATIONS

'The Conference will be supported by officials of the British and Irish Governments,' is the first reference to officials in this part of Strand Three. The Anglo-Irish Agreement in contrast emphasised: meeting at Ministerial or official level; officials meeting in subordinate groups; ministers being accompanied by officials and professional advisers (article 3). The phrase appears axiomatic. However, it would seem to be a reference to a quasi-secretariat, located in London and Dublin.

'including by a standing joint Secretariat of officials dealing with non-devolved Northern Ireland matters.' means that the BIIC does not – it would seem – have a standing secretariat as such. This distinguishes it from the NSMC and the BIC. It only has a formal secretariat for that area of its activity under paragraphs 5 and 6 above. Since these paragraphs represent the work of the 1985 intergovernmental conference, this implies the continuation of Maryfield – at a new location. Standing joint Secretariat is the term – with the upper-case S – used in paragraph 16 of Strand Two. The upper-case S was possibly appropriated from article 3 of the Anglo-Irish Agreement. The secretariat for the BIC is simply a secretariat, in the first paragraph 9 of Strand Three.

The inaugural meeting of the BIIC, following devolution, took place in London on 17 December 1999. It approved a memorandum of understanding on supplementary procedural arrangements, which would not be legally binding nor override the MPA. This document signalled the establishment of the Joint Secretariat '[to] operate in accordance with arrangements to be determined from time to time by the two Governments'. Contrary to the impression given in paragraph 8, 'the Secretariat will provide support for the Conference, as appropriate, across its full remit to enable the Conference to carry out its functions'. It is then stated that the secretariat will be based in Northern Ireland, but that the two governments will designate officials in London and Dublin 'to support the work of the Secretariat, co-ordinate arrangements for Summit level meetings of the Conference and promote bilateral co-operation at all levels on matters of mutual interest' (paragraph 6). According to an Irish government press release of 8 December 1999,[50] citing only the BIA, the Anglo-Irish secretariat had become the British-Irish intergovernmental secretariat, also at Windsor House, with devolution on 2 December 1999, with a responsbility for non-devolved Northern Ireland matters. The joint secretaries in charge initially were Peter Bell[51] (from London) and Donal Hamill (Dublin).

9. **The Conference will keep under review the workings of the new British-Irish Agreement and the machinery and institutions established under it, including a formal published review three years after the Agreement comes into effect. Representatives of the Northern Ireland Administration will be invited to express views to the Conference in this context. The Conference will contribute as appropriate to any review of the overall political agreement arising from the multi-party negotiations *but will have no power to override the democratic arrangements set up by this Agreement.***

17.55 The origin of this paragraph is article 11 of the Anglo-Irish Agreement, which provided for a review of the working of the intergovernmental conference three years after signature. Review is referred to in paragraph 36 of Strand One, not specifically in Strand Two, in the first paragraph 12 of Strand Three, and here at the end of the second part of Strand Three. In addition, review is dealt with in the Validation, Implementation and Review section: in paragraph 4, dealing with the transition; and paragraphs 5–8, dealing with review procedures following implementation.

17.56 ANNOTATIONS

'The Conference will keep under review the workings of the new British-Irish Agreement' is a broad, general statement. The British-Irish Agreement is of course the BIA. Annex 1 is the MPA. The workings therefore refers to the totality of the Belfast Agreement. Keep under review means a continuing process.

50 Department of Foreign Affairs: http://www.irlgov.ie/information.
51 Peter Bell retired early in 2000.

'and the machinery and institutions established under it,'. Machinery and institutions would appear to be an aspect of workings, and not something juxtaposed. Institutions is used in paragraph 5 of the Declaration of Support, to cover Strands One, Two and Three. The word is also used in article 2 of the BIA. While it appears to refer only to Strands Two and Three, the words in particular suggest there are other institutions. Arguably, given the reference to the MPA, institutions refers to all governmental institutions under the Belfast Agreement. A case may be made out for institutions being indefinite as opposed to finite. If this is the position, then machinery would refer to those provisions of the Belfast Agreement which require organization but are not institutions of government for Northern Ireland.

'including a formal published review three years after the Agreement comes into effect.' indicates that keeping under review is a continuing process. The Anglo-Irish Agreement was reviewed in late 1988, the review being published on 24 May 1989. (It is available as chapter 7 in Tom Hadden and Kevin Boyle, *The Anglo-Irish Agreement: commentary, text and official review*, London and Dublin 1989.) This clearly is the model. After the Agreement comes into effect means from the point at which the BIA entered into force under article 4. This was on 2 December 1999, so it is intended that the review will be commenced, or completed, in December 2002.

This sentence refers to the workings of the new British-Irish Agreement (the BIA includes the MPA), and not centrally to the working of the BIIC. It is therefore difficult to reconcile it with paragraph 8 of the Validation, Implementation and Review section. That refers to a conference after four years, convened by the two governments and the (political) parties, to review and report on the operation of the MPA.

'Representatives of the Northern Ireland Administration will be invited to express views to the Conference in this context.' is strange. Under paragraph 7, Northern Ireland ministers have a right to attend all discussions of excepted and reserved matters. That is when the BIIC is considering Northern Ireland under paragraphs 5 and 6. Also under paragraph 7, they are to be involved in the reviews (plural) referred to in this paragraph.

Yet this paragraph states that, when the two governments are reviewing the BIA (as in 1988), the Northern Ireland executive will be invited to express views. But this was similar to the provision in paragraph 7 of the MDP – 'will be invited to express views to both Governments in advance' – which was dropped. I submit that this sentence should have been removed along with the second, third and fourth sentences of paragraph 7 of the MDP, which were removed. Its removal means reliance entirely upon paragraph 7 for the role of the Northern Ireland administration (with its peculiar non sequitur in the second clause of the sentence).

'The Conference will contribute as appropriate to any review of the overall political agreement arising from the multi-party negotiations' is the text in the MDP. It is clearly the second review of this paragraph. But it is difficult to see how the two coexist, even if this review is slightly more compatible with paragraph 8 of the Validation, Implementation and Review section.

The Conference is the two governments, but this may be to ignore the Northern Ireland administration (attending under paragraph 7). Will contribute as appropriate suggests a wider review, as in the conference after four years. To any review seems to ignore this provision. Of the overall political agreement arising from the multi-party negotiations is a rare recognition of the political face of the Belfast Agreement (see also paragraph 2 of Constitutional Issues). The MPA is entitled 'The Agreement: agreement reached in the multi-party negotiations'. This sentence in the MDP was clearly felt to be inadequate, judging by the addition made.

'but will have no power to override the democratic arrangements set up by this Agreement.' was added. The context suggests a fear that the conference (the two governments) would rewrite the MPA. This, of course, is how the MDP originated in the main. But will have no power is an impotent gesture. This statement in Annex 1 of the BIA does not detract from the sovereignty of either state. The United Kingdom and the Irish state do have the power. To override the democratic arrangements must be a reference to Strand One, entitled Democratic Institutions in Northern Ireland. There is an argument that the safeguards detract considerably from simple majoritarian democracy (without creating a vital pluralist democracy). Set up by this Agreement is perplexing. Elsewhere – paragraph 1 of the Declaration of Support and paragraph 1 of Strand One – agreement (with a lower-case a) is used to refer to the MPA. It is notionally the document agreed by the participants in the multi-party negotiations. Here, however, the BIA has been referred to in the first sentence, and Agreement in this third sentence must be the BIA. This confirms further that the second part of Strand Three was drafted originally in some sort of overarching manner, with reference to the BIA, which gives the Belfast Agreement the only legal form it can take.

PART 4

RIGHTS, ETC.

Part 4 contains a miscellany of issues.[1] The first five sections of the Belfast Agreement were dealt with in Parts 2 and 3 (constitution and institutions). There remain six sections, which are difficult to categorize. Here, I have used the title 'Rights, etc,'; rights is the first section, but it is followed by other rule of law issues. One observer has characterized these sections as: 'from Terrorism to Democracy'.[2] Whereas the constitution and institutions parts were drafted like legal text, these six sections are written at times more discursively. Chapter 18 deals with Rights, Safeguards and Equality of Opportunity. Chapter 19 turns to the question of the Decommissioning of paramilitary arms. Chapter 20 addresses (internal) Security in Northern Ireland. Chapter 21 looks at Policing and Justice, and Chapter 22 at the release of terrorist Prisoners. Chapter 23 deals with Validation, Implementation and Review of the MPA, but really of the BIA. To the view that human rights, as espoused by that community in Northern Ireland, characterizes the Belfast Agreement, I argue in this part of the book – as stated in the Preface – that the Human Rights Act 1998 and the 1997 Amsterdam treaty are, and will be, much more significant; further, that Chapters 19–22 contain a better unity, best described as from terrorism to democracy.

1 The relevant page numbers are pp. 16–26 of Cm 3883; pp. 29–43 of Cm 4705 (and, in the 1999 Irish version, pp. 23–37).

2 Duncan Shipley-Dalton, 'The Belfast Agreement', *Fordham International Law Journal*, 1999, 22, 2601, pp. 2619–20.

18

Rights, Safeguards and Equality of Opportunity

18.1 This sixth section of the Belfast Agreement deals with rights in general (using rights politically or colloquially, and not necessarily legally). It is divided into two subsections: human rights; and economic, social and cultural issues – not rights.[1] The first subsection is divided further into five parts, each with its own title. The second subsection is undivided. Rights, Safeguards and Equality of Opportunity is at pages 16–20 of Cm 3883 and pages 29–34 of Cm 4705 (pages 23–8 of the 1999 Irish version). There are 13 paragraphs under Human Rights, and five under Economic, Social and Cultural Issues. I will refer to the section as 'Rights, etc.', and to the two subsections by their subtitles (the paragraphs being separately numbered). I show [deletions] to the MDP, and *additions* thus.

18.2 The introductory material is not intended to be a general discussion of human rights, on which there is a large, advocatory academic literature. It is to provide sufficient background for the discussions on each paragraph below; there is less relative emphasis upon the Republic of Ireland, since only one paragraph in the Human Rights subsection deals with Irish law, and there is no reference in the second subsection.

18.3 A new – more wordy – style of drafting has been adopted in this section. However, since the MPA is Annex 1 of the BIA, the text may contain legal obligations of the states parties in international law. These, however, have to be extracted from the text (by analysis); not everything on the face of the section is binding (this is discussed under each paragraph). The annotation deployed in Parts 2 and 3 is replaced in this chapter with substantive discussion of each paragraph in Human Rights and Economic, Social and Cultural Issues.

Human rights in general

18.4 This topic has been discussed in Chapter 2 above on public international law. Human rights – as noted there – is something of an exception in the law of states.[2] And it exists mainly because multilateral international agreements, in the post-Second World War world, have been the means by which individuals and groups have come to benefit from human rights protection.

18.5 Humanitarian intervention in the nineteenth century (against mainly the Ottoman empire), and, associated with the League of Nations, the protection of national minorities by treaty, formed the basis of the post-1945 legal and social

1 This was not evident in the MDP and FA, given layout and titles. The mistakes were present in the 30-page booklet, with coloured front cover, distributed to Northern Ireland householders. They were corrected in the Republic of Ireland 35-page version. Cm 3883 only partly corrected the problem. Cm 4705 is correctly laid out.

2 There is also customary international law of human rights, based upon state policy; but no state claims the right to practice genocide, slavery, murder, torture, etc.

protection of human rights and fundamental freedoms.[3]

18.6 Following the signing of the United Nations Charter in San Francisco in 1945, the commission on human rights[4] (chaired by Eleanor Roosevelt) was entrusted with drawing up an international bill of rights. On 10 December 1948, the general assembly adopted the Universal Declaration of Human Rights. It was not legally binding.[5] Conflicts between the first, second and third worlds delayed work. It was only at the end of 1966 (after 20 years), that the two United Nations covenants – one on economic, social and cultural rights,[6] and the other on civil and political rights[7] – were ready for signing by states. It took a further ten years – until 1976 – before the two covenants came into force. (The United Kingdom ratified them in 1976; the Irish state in 1989–90.) Together with the Universal Declaration, the economic, social and cultural rights covenant, and the civil and political rights covenant, plus the optional protocol to the latter (allowing victims to communciate with the human rights committee of the United Nations) constitute the international bill of human rights; it includes legal as well as moral obligations.

Human rights in the United Kingdom and Irish states

The United Kingdom state

18.7 While post-Second World War multilateral treaties are the source of what we call human rights today, the notion of human rights and fundamental freedoms has deep roots in the (originally English) common law. (Human rights has also been effectively a term of art in Northern Ireland statutory law since 1973. This is discussed separately below.)

18.8 The idea of fundamental rights was derived from natural law. It was dominant in early modern England, and is evident as early as Magna Carta of 1215 and the Petition of Rights of 1628. Common lawyers were the protectors of such (legislative) fundamental rights, including what came to be called the – unenumerated – liberties of the subject; these are traceable from Magna Carta.

18.9 All that changed in the civil war in the seventeenth century. The common lawyers allied with parliament, to supplant the prerogative right of the sovereign. The outcome was the doctrine of parliamentary sovereignty, enshrined in article 9 of the 1688–89 bill of rights. This constitutional text also includes individual rights.

18.10 That bill of rights has had a particular Irish meaning. It was an aspect of the struggle between William of Orange and James II: 'the war of the two kings in Ireland (1688–91) was a conflation of three issues: between William and James as the new and deposed king of England; between the grand alliance and France; and between the protestants and catholics of Ireland'.[8]

3 Articles 1, 55 & 56, United Nations Charter.
4 Established under article 68, United Nations Charter.
5 There is an argument that it may have become so subsequently: the 1968 Teheran conference.
6 The International Covenant on Economic, Social and Cultural Rights.
7 The International Covenant on Civil and Political Rights.
8 T.W. Moody, in Seamus Deane, gen. ed., *The Field Day Anthology of Irish Writing*, vol. III, Derry 1991, p. 575.

18.11 Some unionist intellectuals continue to affirm the bill of rights of 1688–89 (and the 1700–1 act of settlement[9]). Clifford Smyth – discussing the Belfast Agreement – has recently stressed that the majority community in Northern Ireland derives its identity from that key event in the history of these islands.[10] That identity (to the extent that it exists) would appear to require to be respected under the first paragraph 9 of this section of the Belfast Agreement.

18.12 Parliamentary sovereignty (alternatively, a constitutional monarchy[11]) – and the 1688–89 bill of rights – had a number of consequences. First, the people could never be sovereign; they remained subjects of the monarch.[12] Second, there was no longer any fundamental law; only – private – statute law, with parliament able to override the common law. Third (and a partial continuation of pre-bill of rights law), English/British/United Kingdom subjects were deemed to have a range of – unspecified residual – rights, except where parliament or the courts impinged on certain personal freedoms.[13]

18.13 The jurisprudence of the United Kingdom, through the eighteenth, nineteenth and well into the twentieth century, focused on the unenumerated liberties of the subject. These were guaranteed in practice, not by the courts or parliament (through a written constitution), but by the benign paternalism of public officials observing the conventions of an uncodified constitution. Burke and Bentham were philosophically important. But Austin, Dicey and Jennings professed this unique (English) constitutional law (which has formed the staple educational diet of the judiciary throughout the twentieth century).

18.14 Austin, Dicey and Jennings opposed eighteenth-century American and French ideas of a written constitution (which had appealed to republicans among the protestant nation in Ireland[14]), and – separately – any (pre-1688–89) notion of fundamental rights, even of a secular, democratic character: such as the American bill of rights of 1789, and the French déclaration des droits de l'homme et du citoyen of 1791.

18.15 This remained the position at home, even as the empire gave way to the commonwealth. Written constitutions, and, much later, charters of rights, became the norm for the dominions (including the Irish Free State); this was also the position subsequently with the colonies.

9 This has come under attack from within the Scottish parliament: *Electronic Telegraph*, 4 November 1999.

10 'David Trimble was trapped into an agreement within very narrow confines which effectively excluded the cultural interests of his own people – not only the folk culture of Orangeism, but the rising interest and demand for Ulster-Scots and Ulster's sense of "Britishness" in general ... Nationalists and British New Labour ministers knew what they were talking about but unionists did not. And no wonder: the linguistic shift signalled an abandonment of Britain's Glorious Revolution of 1688–89 and the adaption of a European impetus provided by the French Revolution 100 years later, with its commitment to the Enlightenment and human rights.' (*Irish Times*, 11 June 1999)

11 Symbolized as the king in parliament.

12 Though the term 'citizen' was adopted in United Kingdom nationality law in 1949: British Nationality Act 1948.

13 The corollary is that the state had powers, except where expressly limited: *Malone v Metropolitan Police Commissioner* [1979] Ch 344.

14 And later to catholic nationalists.

18.16 The preamble to the 1945 Charter of the United Nations – and here I turn to international law – opened with 'the scourge of war, which twice in our lifetime has brought untold sorrow to mankind'.

18.17 It went on to reaffirm faith in 'fundamental human rights'. (These were taken to be part of the general principles of law recognized by civilized nations.) The third purpose of the United Nations (international cooperation) in article 1 includes 'respect for human rights and for fundamental freedoms for all without distinction as to race, sex, language, or religion'. And this phrase recurs in article 55 of chapter 9 (international economic and social cooperation). In article 56, the members pledged themselves to take joint and separate action for the achievement of the purposes in article 55. There followed the 1948 Universal Declaration of Human Rights, adopted by the general assembly.

18.18 Meanwhile, the United Kingdom helped establish the Council of Europe in 1949. In 1950, the Convention for the Protection of Human Rights and Fundamental Freedoms (the Convention) was agreed.

18.19 Its principal drafter was Sir Oscar Dowson (retired from the home office). Common law concepts were his inspiration. The Convention provided for a European commission of human rights, as well as the European Court of Human Rights (ECtHR) at Strasbourg. The lord chancellor, Lord Jowitt, had sought particularly to defend the common law (especially at home): 'we were not prepared [he wrote to a cabinet collegue] to encourage our European friends to jeopardise our whole system of law, which we have laboriously built up over the centuries, in favour of some half-baked scheme to be administered by some unknown court'.[15] The United Kingdom was forced to go along with the Convention for general foreign policy reasons, but only after the right of individual petition was made voluntary to contracting states, and the ECtHR was given no jurisdiction in such cases. The United Kingdom could keep its citizens out of the ECtHR.

18.20 It was the first state to ratify, on 8 March 1951 – the Convention entering into force on 23 September 1953.

18.21 Much is made of the (English) common law concept of effectively negative freedoms (the liberties of the subject respected by parliament and the courts). These civil liberties are contrasted with the so-called positive rights of multilateral agreements. However, since it was the common law which inspired the Convention, and United Kingdom jurists continued to imply that those European rights could be found in domestic, non-statutory law, the distinction may not be as great as is suggested.[16] The right to life, article 2 of the Convention, for example, is

15 Anthony Lester QC, 'Fundamental Rights: the United Kingdom isolated?' [1984] PL 46, 51–2.

16 'The Convention, for the most part, speaks the language of negative liberty, of freedom *from* unjustified interference ... The Convention has generally struck a harmonious note with the British constitutional tradition. The substance of the rights set out in in the Convention was not "progressive" or "radical", although the decision to set them within a court-based institutional framework was at the time it was taken, nearly 50 years ago. In many cases, U.K. judges have found, after examining the Convention, that it and the common law are consistent with each other.' (Peter Duffy QC & Paul Stanley, annotators to the HRA 1998, *Current Law Statutes*, vol. 3, London & Edinburgh 1999, p. 42) See also the view of Lord Lester of Herne Hill QC, *Counsel*, December 1999, pp. 20–2. Anthony Aust, *Modern Treaty Law and Practice*, Cambridge 2000, who argues that the United Kingdom has legislated

not quite a fundamental freedom: the article allows for deprivation of life by the use of – state – force which is no more than absolutely necessary.[17]

18.22 Whatever of the idea of human rights and fundamental freedoms, the modern concept – in multilateral international agreements – was a response to the conduct of the German state (and its allies) in the 1930s and 1940s. States – the main legal persons of international law – were assumed to be the only abusers of human rights.

18.23 This was a reasonable presumption in 1950; equally reasonably, 50 years later, we now know that sub-state actors – internal opponents of a regime – can also abuse human rights; the problem of terrorism has been experienced among Council of Europe member states most intensively in Northern Ireland by the United Kingdom (which is not to underestimate the internal security threats experienced by France, Germany, Italy and especially Spain in the 1970s and 1980s).[18]

18.24 The United Kingdom continued to resist individual petition throughout the 1950s: 'States are the proper subject of international law and if individuals are given rights under international treaties effect should be given to those rights through the national law of the States concerned.'[19] Incorporation was not on the mind of anyone within government. Then, at the end of 1965, Harold Wilson, the labour prime minister, without referring the issue to the cabinet, announced that the United Kingdom would accept the right of individual petition, and the compulsory jurisdiction of the ECtHR (for an initial period of three years).[20]

18.25 The first call for incorporation (though transformation would have been a better concept) of the Convention came from the junior barrister, Anthony Lester, in a Fabian pamphlet, *Democracy and Individual Rights*, in November 1968.

18.26 There followed a series of developments over the next 30 years including: one, the establishment of law commissions for England and Wales and Scotland, to promote law reform; two, entry into the European Economic Community in 1973, with important consequences for United Kingdom law; anti-discrimination legislation in 1970, 1973 (concerning Northern Ireland), 1975, 1976 and 1995 (and, again concerning Northern Ireland, 1976, 1989, 1997 and 1998); three, judicial activism in Strasbourg in the 1970s and 1980s, with the United Kingdom

consistently to implement treaty obligations, concedes that the ECHR is a special case (p. 157).

17 It also allows for the death penalty. This was abolished (though not for wartime) by protocol no. 6 in 1983. Articles 1 and 2 are Convention rights under section 1(1) of the HRA 1998.

18 'It is well established in the case-law of the Court that the Convention must be interpreted and applied in the light of present-day conditions. The existence of organised terrorism is a feature of modern life whose emergence since the Convention was drafted cannot be ignored any more than the changes in social conditions and moral opinion which have taken place in the same period.' (*McVeigh v UK* (1981) 5 EHRR 71, 88, ECHR)

19 Selwyn Lloyd, quoted in Anthony Lester QC, 'Fundamental Rights: the United Kingdom isolated?' [1984] PL 46, 58.

20 *Declarations recognising the competence of the European Commission of Human Rights to receive individual petitions and recognising as compulsory the jurisdiction of the European Court of Human Rights*, Cmnd 2894, February 1966. One of the reasons for the delay had to do with the War Damages Act 1965 (which came into force on 2 June 1965), to counteract *Burma Oil Co (Burma Trading) Ltd v Lord Advocate* [1965] AC 75.

state subjected disproportionately to over 50 adverse judgments; four (a variant of the point above), the Northern Ireland troubles contributing particularly to this range of individual versus state cases (nine Northern Ireland cases since 1966); five, procedural changes to judicial review in 1977, allowing for the development of administrative law; six, moves for general constitutional reform (including Charter 88), and attempts in both houses of parliament to incorporate the Convention; seven, growing support among the senior judiciary; eight, the conversion of the labour party in opposition, leading to its 1996 consultation paper, *Bringing Rights Home*;[21] and nine, the government white paper of October 1997, *Rights Brought Home*.[22]

18.27 An instance of growing support (or opposition?) among the senior judiciary, in addition to the (marginal) use of the Convention in United Kingdom law (see above), was the discovery in the common law – after submissions by Anthony Lester QC – of rights similar to those in the Convention (here, article 10): *Derbyshire County Council v Times Newspapers* [1993] AC 534, 551 per Lord Keith of Kinkel.

The Convention

18.28 On 1 November 1998, as a result of protocol no. 11 (ETS No. 155), done at Strasbourg on 11 May 1994 (following the Vienna declaration of 9 October 1993), there was a restructuring of the control machinery established under the Convention (due largely to increasing numbers of cases and members of the Council of Europe). The European commission of human rights was abolished. And the European Court of Human Rights became a full-time body. The articles were renumbered. The Human Rights Act (HRA) 1998 takes account of this in section 21(2)–(4). The protocol applies mainly to sections II–IV (articles 19–56) plus protocol no. 2, which become articles 19–51 in a new section II. Headings are also added throughout the Convention (meaning the convention rights may be specified by other than number).

18.29 The Convention was, and is, a multilateral agreement. The fact that it deals with human rights makes it no different from any other treaty; it was agreed by the members of the Council of Europe as contracting states. The fact that it provided for a European commission and court of human rights does distinguish the Convention (in terms of other courts, Strasbourg – which was not established until 1959 – is more a regional, and human rights only, version of the ICJ, than a companion to the ECJ, created by the member states of the European Community).[23]

18.30 The differences and similarities between these international courts can be seen in the types of cases provided for in the Convention, which may be heard by the ECtHR.

18.31 The subjects of international law are states, and state versus state litigation was specified in the Convention. Article 24 dealt with interstate cases: any high contracting party could refer – to the commission through the secretary-

21 18 December, published in [1997] EHRLR 71.

22 Cm 3782.

23 Strasbourg is resistent to European Union attempts to develop a draft charter of fundamental rights of the European Union.

general – 'any alleged breach of the provisions of the Convention by another High Contracting Party'. But article 44 also gave the high contracting parties the right to bring a case before the court (a right also held by the commission). Both applicant and respondent states had to have accepted compulsory jurisdiction under article 46, which allowed for conditions of reciprocity. All member states have accepted compulsory jurisdiction, for varying periods of time.

18.32 Under protocol no. 11 of 1994 (ETS No. 155), article 33 (interstate cases) reads: 'Any High Contracting Party may refer to the Court any alleged breach of the provisions of the Convention and the protocols thereto by another High Contracting Party.'

18.33 The fact that there has been only one interstate case decided finally by the court[24] – *Ireland (Republic of) v United Kingdom* [1978] 2 EHRR 25 – does not detract from this jurisdiction. Between 1955 and 1966, the United Kingdom (by virtue of its rights under the Convention) did not have to respond to individual petitions; only another member of the Council of Europe – accepting compulsory jurisdiction on a reciprocal basis – could have taken it to Strasbourg.[25]

18.34 However, the Convention also provided for individual petitions, now called individual applications. And this is where the confusion (deliberate or otherwise) about human rights abusers has arisen.

18.35 Article 25 allowed the commission to receive petitions addressed to the secretary-general 'from any person, non-governmental organisation or group of individuals claiming to be the victim of a violation by one of the High Contracting Parties of the rights set forth in this Convention, provided that the High Contracting Party against which the complaint has been lodged has declared that it recognises the competence of the Commission to receive such petitions. Those of the High Contracting Parties who have made such a declaration undertake not to hinder in any way the effective exercise of this right.'

18.36 This has now been replaced by article 34 under protocol no. 11: 'The Court may receive applications from any person, non-governmental organisation or group of individuals claiming to be the victim of a violation by one of the High Contracting Parties of the rights set forth in the Convention or the protocols thereto. The High Contracting Parties undertake not to hinder in any way the effective exercise of this right.'

18.37 This jurisdiction (the individual applications) was agreed by the contracting states. However, it was initially voluntary: each state party had to opt in with a declaration (which could be made for a specific period). The fact that there is no reference to a specified period in article 34 does not alter the underlying position; it is simply that all the signatories to protocol no. 11 accepted the right of individual petition without limit of time[26] (and this will bind any new members of the Council of Europe who become signatories to the Convention).

18.38 Mention should also be made – in parenthesis – of article 36 (third-party

24 A second case, concerning the Northern Ireland Act 1972, was struck off the list of the commission in October 1972.

25 It was possible for a non-United Kingdom national, of a state which accepted individual petition, to bring a case against the United Kingdom.

26 Individual petition was only accepted by all member states in 1987.

intervention). This allows a high contracting party to intervene in a case where one of its nationals is an applicant against presumably another high contracting party.

18.39 Three points have to be made about article 25, and now article 34, none of which has altered as regards the Convention as an international agreement.

18.40 One, who may make an application to Strasbourg? This is the same under the old article 25 and the new article 34: 'any person, non-governmental organisation or group of individuals'. 'Person' refers to natural person, legal persons (in United Kingdom law) being considered under 'non-governmental organisation' or even possibly 'group of individuals'. A company, for example, may allege breach of some – not all – rights as a non-governmental organization.[27]

18.41 Two, what is a victim? While applicants are defined essentially as all those who are not part of government (understood as the state), 'victim' is a term of art under the Convention. One becomes a claimant victim by making an application under article 34 (alternatively, upon having it admitted). What makes an actual victim in international law, within the jurisdiction of the ECtHR, is a final judgment by the court that one or more Convention rights of an individual have been violated.

18.42 A claimant victim is not (yet) an actual victim. But an actual victim – according to the ECtHR – has had his or her (or its) human rights violated. It is a factual – not legal – question as to who the abuser was.

18.43 Three, who is the respondent? This is easy to answer: 'one of the High Contracting Parties'. But that is a function of the Convention being governed by the law of treaties (which is a part of international law). The interstate jurisdiction is state versus state. The individual applications jurisdiction is individual versus any relevant member state of the Council of Europe.

18.44 But that does not mean that that state is the abuser in each and every incident of abuse. The state has been found legally to have violated one or more Convention rights of an individual applicant. But violation can be – and often is – a breach of article 1: 'The High Contracting Parties shall secure to everyone within their jurisdiction the rights and freedoms defined in Section 1 [now 'Rights and freedoms'] of this Convention.' It may also be a breach of any particular individual right or freedom containing express restrictions, violation arising – in addition to an act – from an omission or excessive restriction.

18.45 Take an example. If a civilian, or member of the security forces, has been killed by a paramilitary organization in Northern Ireland, his or her right under article 2 (right to life) has been abused and also violated – potentially.

18.46 The alleged victim becomes an actual victim through a Strasbourg judgment.

18.47 The abuser is the killer. But, under the Convention as an international agreement, his or her right to life has been violated by a state party, the United Kingdom (it could just as easily be the Republic of Ireland if the killing had been across the border).

18.48 This does not make either state the killer (and therefore abuser). It means

27 *Observer Ltd and Guardian Newspapers Ltd v United Kingdom* (1991) 14 EHHR 153, ECtHR (article 10). Article 8 cannot apply to a company.

simply that the relevant state – which has a domestic responsibility for law and order – has failed, in international law, to secure to one person within its jurisdiction their right to life. The state may not have killed him or her; but it should have protected the victim.

18.49 The Convention, as should be clear, is victim based. It provides for a court to which, first, a member state may resort, and second, an individual may have recourse. The emphasis is upon the abuse of a human right, and a just remedy from the only subject under the Convention – a state.

18.50 In the context of the holocaust, it was natural to think of violations by a state as being (direct) factual abuse, not simply that the state had indirectly violated – in international law – a Convention right.

18.51 But what if the state is demonstrably not the abuser (though in international law the violator), as has been the case predominantly in Northern Ireland for the past 30 years? The jurisprudence of the ECtHR, starting from the premise of just satisfaction to the injured party, has developed a notion – by analogy with Community law – of horizontal effect (individual to individual). Though this operates to implicate the state,[28] logically it recognizes the factual cause of abuse as a specific individual or institution (whatever of the overall – domestic – responsibility of the state in international law).

18.52 Terrorism as a phenomenon began to be addressed in international instruments in the 1970s: the 1975 Helsinki Final Act (which is not a treaty) includes, in the declaration on principles guiding relations between participating states, in particular the sixth principle on non-intervention in internal affairs: 'The participating States ... will, *inter alia*, refrain from direct or indirect assistance to terrorist activities, or to subversive or other activities directed towards the violent overthrow of the régime of another participating State.'

18.53 Mention should also be made of extradition, which is governed by international and municipal law, and in particular the political offences defence (in international law).[29] Terrorism came to be recognized in international law as not a political offence, for the purposes of extradition agreements between states.

18.54 The 1957 European convention on extradition, which entered into force on 18 April 1960, had been signed and ratified by the Irish state on 2 May 1966; the United Kingdom, in contrast, did not do so until 21 December 1990 and 13 February 1991. Extradition arrangements between the two states, however,

28 *Young, James and Webster v United Kingdom* (1981) 4 EHRR 38, 52 (the cause was a 'closed shop' industrial agreement, but domestic law permitted it); *X and Y v Netherlands* (1985) 8 EHRR 235, 239–42 (a sexual abuse case under article 8, where it was held that there was a positive obligation on the state to secure respect for private or family life through the criminal law); *Costello-Roberts v United Kingdom* (1993) 19 EHRR 112, 132–3 (an unsuccessful case of corporal punishment in an independent school, where it was stated that the state could not delegate its obligation under article 2 of protocol 1 [right to education] to a private body or individuals); *Tolstoy v United Kingdom* (1995) 20 EHRR 442 (under the Convention, an award of damages for defamation by a jury must bear a reasonable relationship of proportionality to the injury to reputation suffered); *A v United Kingdom* (1998) 5 BNIHRC 137, 141–2.

29 'Extradition shall not be granted if the offence in respect of which it is requested is regarded by the requested Party as a political offence or as an offence connected with a political offence.' (article 3(1) of the 1957 Convention)

remained a matter of domestic law in each state: Extradition Act 1965; Backing of Warrants (Republic of Ireland) Act 1965. The report of the 1974 United Kingdom/ Irish law enforcement commission,[30] on extradition and alternatives (part of the Sunningdale agreement), failed to agree an effective legal response to Northern Ireland terrorism (the – United Kingdom – Criminal Jurisdiction Act 1975, and the – Irish – Criminal Law (Jurisdiction) Act 1976, only allowed fugitive political offenders to be tried in either part of Ireland for terrorist crimes committed in the other.)

18.55 The 1977 European Convention on the Suppression of Terrorism (a response to Palestinian terrorism in Europe), which entered into force on 4 August 1978, and specified a list of offences committed by terrorists which were not to be considered political, produced an opposite reaction in London and Dublin. London signed on 27 January 1978, and ratified on 24 July 1978. Dublin only promised to do so when it signed the 1985 Anglo-Irish Agreement. It signed on 24 February 1986, but did not ratify until 21 February 1989. The Oireachtas, however, legislated: Extradition (European Convention on the Suppression of Terrorism) Act 1987 (plus the Extradition (Amendment) Acts 1987 and 1994). The act came into operation on 1 December 1987 (before the Irish Supreme Court, in *Finucane v McMahon* [1990] IR 165, did a great deal to restore the political offences defence for earlier cases).

18.56 On 12 January 1998, the United Nations Convention for the Suppression of Terrorist Bombings was opened for signature at New York. Part VI of the terrorism bill, introduced in the house of commons on 2 December 1999, and designed to put all anti-terrorism legislation on a permanent basis, included provisions on extra-territorial jurisdiction and extradition. The United Kingdom will be able to ratify the United Nations convention after enactment. Under article 3, the 'Convention shall not apply where the offence is committed within a single State, the alleged offender and victims are nationals of that State, the alleged offender is found in the territory of that State and no other State has a basis ... to exercise jurisdiction ...'.[31]

18.57 If the relationship between factual abuse and legal violation – under the Convention – is not entirely satisfactory from the point of view of addressing violence by sub-state actors, this is likely to be altered with the operation of the HRA 1998. This received the royal assent on 9 November 1998, and is due to enter into force throughout the United Kingdom on 2 October 2000.

The HRA 1998

18.58 The HRA 1998 – following the New Zealand bill of rights of 1990 – does not, of course, strictly incorporate the Convention; the rights remain in international law, subject to possible derogation and reservation. It is the remedies – not the rights – which have been brought home metaphorically. Domestic courts will now replace Strasbourg to a considerable extent, though the ECtHR will survive as effectively the final level of appeal. The HRA 1998 is largely an interpretative

30 *Report of the Law Enforcement Commission*, Cmnd 5627, presented to parliament May 1974.

31 Adopted by the general assembly, 15 December 1997. See also International Convention for the Suppression of the Financing of Terrorism, adopted by the general assembly 9 December 1999, opened for signature on 10 January 2000.

measure; the jurisprudence of Strasbourg will now infuse United Kingdom law, and, a point made much of in 1997, United Kingdom judges will be able to help shape human rights legal culture in Europe. It has been described as 'the most significant constitutional measure since the Bill of Rights of 1688–89 (apart from the European Communities Act in the areas where it reigns supreme)'.[32]

18.59 Under the HRA 1998, in private-law litigation between parties, the court now has to take account of Convention rights.

18.60 This is because of section 6 (acts of public authorities). Subsection (1) states: 'It is unlawful for a public authority to act in a way which is incompatible with a Convention right.' Subsection (3)(i) defines a public authority as including a court or tribunal (or a person exercising functions of a public nature), but neither house of parliament. Thus, a court, whether civil or criminal, is required by the HRA 1998, to act in a way which is compatible with a Convention right. (Section 2 requires the court, in interpreting the Convention right, to take into account inter alia the jurisprudence of the ECtHR.)

18.61 Section 7(1)(b) states that a person may rely upon a Convention right in any legal proceedings. It is possible – given this express (albeit indirect) horizontal effect[33] – to proceed against a non-state human or legal person in private law, and have the court find a breach of a Convention right (this is possible in the United Kingdom; not in Strasbourg.)[34]

18.62 Section 8(1) allows the court to grant such relief or remedy, or make such order, within its powers as it considers just and appropriate.[35] 'English law', as Lord Wilberforce once said, 'fastens not on principles but on remedies.'[36]

18.63 The former master of the rolls, Lord Woolf, has written recently of the creation of human rights torts in both public and private law: 'These torts will redefine the relationship between the individual and the State but will go beyond this by operating "horizontally" to influence the rights of individuals as well. The interests of minorities will be protected in a way which, up to now, has not been possible.'[37]

18.64 The impact of the HRA 1998 in the United Kingdom is expected to be considerable; it will transform civil and especially criminal law in the three jurisdictions. Nevertheless, legal radicals have seen the incorporation of the Convention being followed – in an unspecified timescale – by a constitutional bill of rights for the United Kingdom (either as a prelude to, or part of, a written constitution).[38]

32 Lord Lester of Herne Hill QC, *Counsel*, December 1999, pp. 20–2.

33 Murray Hunt, 'The "Horizontal Effect" of the Human Rights Act' [1998] PL 423.

34 See also s 22(4).

35 Query: if there is a private defendant, could damages be awarded against a public authority?

36 *Davy v Spelthorne BC* [1983] 3 All ER 278, 285.

37 Lord Lester of Herne Hill QC & David Pannick QC, *Human Rights Law and Practice*, London 1999, p. vii.

38 Decision of 1993 labour party conference; Lord Lester of Herne Hill QC & David Pannick QC, eds, *Human Rights, Law and Practice*, London 1999, p. 13; Michael Lavery QC, presenting to the secretary of state the 22nd report of SACHR, *Report for 1996–1997*, Belfast 1997, p. iv. The most influential set of recommendations remains Scarman LJ's *English Law–the new dimension*, London 1974. Robert Blackburn's *Towards a Constitutional Bill of Rights for the United Kingdom: commentary and documents*, London 1999 deals, however, with a home-grown bill of rights, building on the Convention, and not a written constitution as such.

18.65 Something of the judiciary's response to human rights law, internationally if not domestically, may be anticipated from a Court of Appeal case heard in June 1999: *Williams v Cowell* [2000] 1 WLR 187, 198, 202.[39] This was an interlocutory appeal from the employment appeal tribunal (Morison J), by a Welsh speaker seeking adjournment to Wales or a hearing in London in Welsh. Counsel for the applicant (Robin Allen QC) took inter alia breaches of articles 3, 6, 10 and 14 of the Convention. Rejecting the appeal, Mummery LJ (Nourse LJ agreeing) declined to give a 100-page judgment dealing with two lever arch files of human rights authorities: 'Perhaps there is a lesson here for the future ... When human rights points are taken there is a temptation to impress (and to oppress) the court with the bulk and to turn a judicial hearing of a particular case into an international human rights seminar. This temptation should be resisted. There should only be put before the court that part of the researched material which is reasonably required for the resolution of the particular appeal.'

European Community law

18.66 Equally important is European Community law – the law of the European Economic Community (EEC), later the European Community (EC) (and, where justiciable, the European Union (EU)). The European Court of Justice (ECJ) in Luxembourg is an institution of the EC, which is of course the foundation of the EU.

18.67 The treaty on European Union (TEU) acknowledges human rights.[40] It also makes reference to fundamental social rights.[41] This is not the position with the treaty establishing the European Community (TEC), though human rights points have been taken in Luxemburg cases.[42]

18.68 The EU is also perceived to be seeking to supplant the Council of Europe with its own draft charter of fundamental rights.[43] The aim is to make this part of one or other European treaty. The idea was proposed at the Cologne European Council in June 1999, and is due to be agreed in December 2000. An ad hoc body established to draft the charter held its first meeting on 17 December 1999. It is envisaged that the European council will propose to the parliament and commission that they should solemnly proclaim the European charter of fundamental rights. Consideration would then be given to whether, and, if so, how,

39 See also, *R v North West Lancashire Health Authority, ex parte A* [2000] 1 WLR 977, 995–6 per Auld LJ, 1000–3 per Buxton LJ, 1003 per May LJ (case heard 24–25 June 1999). Perhaps more importantly, Lord Woolf, then MR, intervened with a practice note: *Daniels v Walker* [2000] 1 WLR 1382, 1386–7 per Lord Woolf, 1388 per Latham J.

40 TEU, preamble, and articles 6 (ex article F) and 7 (ex F.1). But see article 46 (ex article L) preventing justiciability. Article 7 (ex article F.1) allows the council, acting by unanimity (not including abstentions and the member state), to determine the existence of a serious and persistent breach by a member state of principles mentioned in article 6(1) (ex article F). Following such a determination, the council may, acting by a qualified majority, decide to suspend certain of the member state's treaty rights.

41 TEU, preamble: 1961 European social charter and 1989 Community charter of the fundamental social rights of workers.

42 Gerald Barling QC & Mark Brealey, eds, *Practitioners' Handbook of EC Law*, London 1998, pp. 635–7.

43 See also the draft European citizens' charter, of the permanent forum of civil society, of 18 May 1997: http://eurplace.org/orga/forumsoc.

the charter should be integrated into the treaties. It is most unlikely to have the same legal status as the Convention, in international and municipal law,[44] and there is an alternative suggestion that the EU should sign up to – as opposed to simply respect – the Convention and the Strasbourg court. The issues were discussed extensively in the report of the house of lords select committee on the European Union (in particular, sub-committee E on law and institutions), *EU Charter of Fundamental Rights*, published on 16 May 2000.[45]

18.69 A founding principle of the EEC/EC was non-discrimination on the basis of nationality, which became, in the 1992 Maastricht treaty, citizenship of the EU (complementing national citizenship). This is now covered in articles 17 to 22 (ex articles 8–8e) of the TEC, plus articles 12 and 39. Article 8(2) (ex article 8(2)) states: 'Citizens of the Union shall enjoy the rights conferred by this Treaty and shall be subject to the duties imposed thereby.'

18.70 But the EEC/EC has also been the inspiration for anti-discrimination, and equal opportunities, legislation throughout the member states. Article 2 (ex article 2) states that part of the task of the EC is 'equality between men and women'. Article 3 (ex article 3) sets out the 21 activities of the EC. Article 3(2) (ex article 3(2)) states: 'In all the activities referred to in this Article, the Community shall aim to eliminate inequalities, and to promote equality, between men and women.' (Article 141 [ex article 119]) also deals with equal pay for male and female workers for equal work or work of equal value.)

18.71 Equal treatment between men and women – largely in employment[46] – was the principle of Council Directive 76/207/EEC of 9 February 1976.[47] Directives, secondary European legislation, have to be implemented by the member states to which they are addressed. This directive has direct effect against emanations of the state (where there is a private sector employer, an employee may be able to claim damages against the state for non-implementation of the directive). Employment tribunals are the appropriate court, though judicial review proceedings may be brought for incompatibility between domestic and European Community law. Directives are fully justiciable before the ECJ, and European Community law on men and women (not women) has shaped the national laws of the United Kingdom and Irish states. Discrimination on the ground of gender was made illegal in, respectively, 1975 and 1977.[48] The United Kingdom also legislated in the areas of religious belief or political opinion (uniquely in Northern Ireland) in 1976[49] (fair employment); race in 1976; and disability in 1995.

18.72 Article 13 (ex article 6a) – under principles – of the TEC, as a result of the treaty of Amsterdam agreed on 2 October 1997, permitted the Commission to

44 COM 1999/C 369/03, OJ C 21 December 1999.
45 HL Paper 67, 8th Report of 1999–2000 Session.
46 Access to employment, vocational training and promotion, and working conditions.
47 Also, council directive 86/613/EEC, for men and women engaged in an activity, including agriculture, in a self-employed capacity, and on the protection of self-employed women during pregnancy and motherhood, and council directive 97/80/EC, on the burden of proof in cases of discrimination based on sex.
48 Also, Equal Pay Act 1970 (United Kingdom) and Anti-Discrimination (Pay) Act 1974 (Republic of Ireland).
49 This followed part III of the NICA 1973 dealing with discriminatory legislation and discrimination by public authorities.

'take appropriate action to combat discrimination based on sex, racial or ethnic origin, religion or belief, disability, age or sexual orientation'.

18.73 On 25 November 1999, the Commission presented two proposed equal treatment directives (equal treatment being defined as no direct or indirect discrimination): council directive establishing a general framework for equal treatment in employment and occupation, plus COM (1999) 565 final; and council directive implementing the principle of equal treatment between persons irrespective of racial or ethnic origin, plus COM (1999) 566 final. These will be referred to as the two European proposed directives of 25 November 1999, the first dealing with employment and occupation and the second with racial or ethnic origin. The intended date of implementation of both is 31 December 2002. Neither affects the equal treatment between men and women directive of 1976.

18.74 The first proposed directive – the employment and occupation one – applies to all persons irrespective of racial or ethnic origin, religion or belief, disability, age or sexual orientation (article 1). The latter category is to be distinguished from sexual behaviour. The proposed directive covers: access to employment and occupation, including promotion, vocational training, employment conditions and membership of certain organizations (article 4). The second proposed directive – the racial or ethnic origin one – deals with the principle of equal treatment between individuals irrespective of racial or ethnic origin (they have been distinguished, confusingly, as respectively horizontal and vertical) (article 1). Its material scope is as in the first draft directive, plus social protection, social advantages, education, and access to and supply of goods and services.

18.75 The effects in United Kingdom, including Northern Ireland, law, and in Irish law, should be the same.

The Irish state

18.76 Irish law is part of the common law world. When the Irish Free State was legally created by the United Kingdom in 1922 (see Chapter 5), provision was made for a written constitution for the new dominion (drawn up by the constituent assembly in 1922).[50] Articles 6 to 10 contained rights for, variably, persons and citizens: liberty of the person (article 6), with a proviso for military actions during a state of war or armed rebellion; inviolability of the dwelling of a citizen (article 7); freedom of conscience, and the free profession and practice of religion for citizens (article 8); the right of free expression and the right to assemble peaceably and without arms (for persons?) (article 9); the right to free elementary education for citizens (article 10).[51]

18.77 Eamon de Valera brought about the successor state, Éire/Ireland, with Bunreacht na hÉireann in 1937 (see Chapter 6). There was a natural law inspiration[52] (though Irish courts deny this is part of the constitution[53]). On the western edge of Europe, de Valera headed articles 40–44 of his new constitution 'fundamental rights' (13 years, and a world war, before the European Convention).

50 Constitution of the Irish Free State (Saorstát Eireann) Act 1922.

51 In the 15 years of the 1922 constitution, only two items of legislation were declared to be unconstitutional.

52 Preamble, articles 6(1), 40.1.1, 42.1 & 5, 43.1.1 and 44.1.1.

53 *Information (Termination of Pregnancies) Bill, 1995* [1995] 1 IR 1, 38–43 per Hamilton CJ.

These are personal rights, including equality before the law (article 40);[54] the family, including recognition of the role of women within the home (article 41); education, including the right not to use state schools (article 42); private property, including a reference to social justice (article 43); and religion, including – until 1972 – recognition of the special position of the catholic church (article 44) (article 45, in addition, contains directive principles of social policy, for the general guidance of the Oireachtas).

18.78 Article 40.1, containing the principle of equality before the law, is, however, qualified, apparently allowing statutory (if not other) discrimination on the grounds of physical and moral capacity, and social function.[55]

18.79 The doctrine of unenumerated (or latent) rights, based on article 40.3.1, has, since the landmark decision of Kenny J, in *Ryan v Attorney General* [1965] IR 241, seen Irish courts recognize as many as 20 additional rights.[56] These are not express in the constitution; they have been deemed by the courts to be constitutional rights. 'As a result', noted the *Report of the Constitution Review Group* in 1996, 'we have a disparate set of rights which does not correspond to the broadly expressed and wide-ranging fundamental rights recognised in international conventions.'[57]

18.80 The Republic of Ireland – under Sean MacBride – had joined the Council of Europe in 1949. It was an early signatory of the 1950 Convention (on 4 November 1950), and ratified it on 25 February 1953 before entry into force. Along with Sweden, it allowed petitioning from the beginning and the compulsory jurisdiction of the ECtHR in this regard. It was the defendant in the first case of the Strasbourg court: *Lawless v Ireland (No. 3)* (1961) 1 EHRR 15, ECtHR. And it was the plaintiff in the only state to state case decided finally by the court:[58] *Ireland (Republic of) v United Kingdom* (1978) 2 EHRR 25, ECtHR. Nevertheless, the Republic of Ireland declined consistently to incorporate the Convention. It was the only state party to the Convention – following the United Kingdom's enactment of the HRA 1998 – not to have incorporated it in its domestic law.[59]

Human rights in Northern Ireland

18.81 The Northern Ireland administration was set up under the GOIA 1920, before the Irish Free State. That constitution act contained no fundamental human

54 Article 40 includes most of the rights of the 1922 constitution.

55 The *Report of the Constitution Review Group* in 1996 recommended replacement with a relevant differences provision, and an addition prohibiting unfair discrimination, directly or indirectly, on any ground (p. 242).

56 The *Report of the Constitution Review Group* in 1996 lists 18 (p. 246).

57 Page 247.

58 A second case, concerning the Northern Ireland Act 1972, was struck off the list of the commission in October 1972.

59 This was discussed in the *Report of the Constitution Review Group* in 1996 (p. 219). The Group did not favour direct incorporation into the constitution (necessary to make it fundamental); instead, it favoured drawing on the Convention, and other human rights instruments where: one, the right was not expressly protected; two, the standard of protection was higher in the Convention or other instrument; or three, the wording of the constitution might be improved. However, this is hardly consistent with the claim that every substantive right of the Convention exists in the constitution, either expressly or through article 40.3.1 (p. 218).

rights, or rights at all. However, section 5 prohibited discriminatory legislation (this applied also to Southern Ireland) on the basis essentially of religious belief; it was described as interfering with religious equality (seemingly a right). A series of instances was given; including the taking of any property without compensation (though Northern Ireland courts interpreted this as a separate right[60]).

18.82 Various calls for a bill of rights were made during the civil rights years of 1968–72 (a movement, modelled on the civil rights movement in the United States, subsequently styled as concerned with human rights,[61] which was unable to prevent communalism and nationalist assertion[62]). In the NIO document, *The Future of Northern Ireland: a paper for discussion*, October 1972, a bill of rights was suggested by inter alia the Ulster Unionist Party, the Alliance Party and the Northern Ireland Labour Party. The issue was not then central for nationalists. The United Kingdom government expressed general sympathy. However, it raised a number of legal problems: the rights to be enshrined; protection through the courts or a special body; remedies and relief; 'and how to deal with those [presumably the IRA] who consistently and deliberately infringe the rights of others'. 'What is essential is that any provisions which might be incorporated in legislation should have a practical and not just a declaratory effect.'[63]

18.83 The white paper, *Northern Ireland Constitutional Proposals*, Cmnd 5259, March 1973, discussed seemingly the idea of a charter of human rights in part IV. However, it was particularized to: 'provisions [to] supplement existing safeguards with specific statutory restraints against the abuse of legislative and executive powers, with a commitment to establish effective machinery to deal with job discrimination and with the establishment of a Standing Advisory Commission on Human Rights which will keep the whole field under continuous surveillance.'[64]

18.84 The NICA 1973 contained no fundamental human rights. However, part III dealt with the prevention of religious and political discrimination.[65] Section 17 prohibited legislation which discriminated against any person or class of persons on the ground of religious belief or political opinion. Legislation could be referred by the secretary of state to the judicial committee of the privy council for a decision on validity (section 18). Section 19 made such discrimination by public authorities unlawful (the Northern Ireland courts have had nearly three decades of experience interpreting section 19, drawing upon gender and race discrimination where relevant).

18.85 Section 20 established the standing advisory commission on human

60 *O'Neill v NIRTB* [1938] NI 104; *Robb v Electricity Board for NI* [1937] NI 103.

61 Caoimhghin Ó Caoláin TD, Dáil Éireann, *Official Report*, 25 November 1999.

62 Bob Purdie, *Politics in the Streets: the origins of the civil rights movement in Northern Ireland*, Belfast 1990. The leading advocate of a bill of rights was C. Desmond Greaves.

63 Paragraph 64.

64 Page 24.

65 Northern Ireland acts dealing very broadly with this issue – according to the Fair Employment Commission – are: Electoral Law Act (NI) 1969; Ministry of Community Relations Act (NI) 1969; Parliamentary Commissioner Act (NI) 1969; Commissioner for Complaints Act (NI) 1969; Prevention of Incitement to Hatred Act (NI) 1970; Police Act (NI) 1970; Rising Executive Act (NI) 1972; Rising Government Act (NI) 1972; Prosecution of Offences (NI) Order 1972, SI 1972/538. These were reforms achieved as a result of the the civil rights movement.

rights (SACHR). It was only to advise the secretary of state on preventing discrimination, and providing redress. This commission survived the end of the 1974 assembly, and secretaries of state administratively received advice on a range of human rights. In 1977, SACHR advised that there should be a bill of rights in Northern Ireland.[66] The commission (to which Anthony Lester was a consultant) recommended United Kingdom-wide legislation, though Robert Cooper dissented.

18.86 The 1973 Sunningdale agreement stated that the council of Ireland would be asked to consider in what way the principles of the Convention 'would be expressed in domestic legislation in each part of Ireland'.[67] There was only a passing mention of human rights in the 1981 Anglo-Irish Joint Studies.[68] The new Ireland forum *Report* of 1984 suggested incorporation of the Convention in the constitution of a united Ireland.[69] The 1985 Anglo-Irish Agreement referred, under political matters, to protecting human rights and preventing discrimination.[70]

18.87 The United Kingdom government in the 1980s was opposed to the incorporation of the Convention, and the Irish government was content with its constitutional fundamental rights. Another way had to be found in the preparations for the all-party, later multi-party, negotiations.

18.88 The 1993 *Downing Street Declaration* referred to respect for the 'civil rights and religious liberties of both communities'. It then went on to list six apparent rights, of no definite provenance. These were to be reflected in any future political and constitutional arrangements, emerging from a new and more broadly based agreement. These six rights inspired paragraph 1 of the Human Rights part below, and are discussed more fully there.

18.89 The six rights – according to the leading historians of, what they call, the Irish peace process – stemmed from an association between the Irish taoiseach, Albert Reynolds, and an east Belfast minister, Roy Magee, in touch with loyalist paramilitaries. There ensued an 'almost comic misunderstanding', according to Eamonn Mallie and David McKittrick. Loyalists had drafted the six points (it is not known who may have advised them), as an indication of the freedoms for republicans they respected. This would appear to have been a serious democratic offer. The taoiseach, however, endorsed the text, believing it was what the loyalists were demanding of him. Mallie and McKittrick provide no information on how the taoiseach intended such rights to be introduced into Irish law, and how the United Kingdom would reciprocate.[71]

18.90 Part I of the 1995 *Framework Documents* included a paragraph by the United Kingdom government on rights. Protection for specified civil, political, social and cultural rights was to be considered. 'The means of such protection would accord with the constitutional arrangements of the United Kingdom, and

66 *The Protection of Human Rights by Law in Northern Ireland*, Cmnd 7009, November 1977.

67 Paragraph 11.

68 *Joint Report and Studies*, Cmnd 8414, 1981, pp. 15–16 (in the report on reciprocal citizenship rights).

69 Page 31.

70 Article 5(a).

71 Eamonn Mallie & David McKittrick, *The Fight for Peace: the inside story of the Irish peace process*, London 1997, p. 224.

could build on existing safeguards.'[72] Greater formal protection for civil rights was mentioned in the United Kingdom's outline of a comprehensive settlement.[73]

18.91 The shared understanding of the United Kingdom and Irish governments in part II referred to the protection and guarantee of fundamental human rights. Each government would promise effective protection of common specified civil, political, social and cultural rights in its part of Ireland. In addition, democratic representatives would be encouraged to adopt an all-Ireland charter or covenant. (This apparently would be based upon the six points entered under misunderstanding in the 1993 *Downing Street Declaration*.)

18.92 Mention should also be made of the Dublin forum for peace and reconciliation in 1994–96, chaired by Judge Catherine McGuinness. On 31 March 1995, leading members of the human rights community in both parts of Ireland made a presentation to the forum.[74] A study of human rights protection was also commissioned, and published by the forum.

TITLE: RIGHTS, SAFEGUARDS AND EQUALITY OF OPPORTUNITY

18.93 According to the contents page, this is the title of the section comprising two subsections: Human Rights, and Economic, Social and Cultural Issues. This was only clarified subsequently with correct layout and headings. Rights in the title must be a reference to the subsection on Human Rights (13 paragraphs). It does not cover apparently Economic, Social and Cultural Issues, since these are expressly not considered rights. Safeguards is a concept used in paragraph 5 of Strand One. The safeguards there include the Convention, plus any bill of rights for Northern Ireland, a human rights commission; and an equality commission. These are dealt with also in the Human Rights subsection. But there are other safeguards in paragraph 5 of Strand One, such as cross-community voting, which have no connection with rights. Equality of opportunity is the third concept in the title. It too is dealt with in the Human Rights subsection. Equality of opportunity – as between persons of different religious beliefs – is defined in articles 2(2) and 5 of the Fair Employment and Treatment (Northern Ireland) Order 1998, SI 1998/3162.[75] Mention should also be made of the two equal treatment European proposed directives of 25 November 1999, following article 13 of the 1997 Amsterdam treaty, which are required to be implemented by 31 December 2002 (discussed above). The lengthy equality of opportunity in the title, when human rights and equality might have been suggested (as with the Decommissioning, Security, Policing and Justice, and Prisoners sections) indicates that no reference was intended to equality of outcome[76]. The elusive unity of this section of the Belfast Agreement is reflected in the titular difficulty. Three distinct things have been run together: while the third may be an aspect of the first (which requires to be demonstrated), it is not clear what the second has to do with them – other than

72 Paragraph 12.

73 Annex B, paragraph 1.

74 Forum for Peace and Reconciliation, *Report of Proceedings: volume 12: Friday, 31 March 1995*.

75 'in any circumstances the same opportunity of a kind mentioned in paragraph (4) as that other person has or would have in those circumstances, due allowance being made for any material difference in their suitability'. (article 5(2))

76 This remains contrary to EC law: *Kalanke v Frie Hansestadt Bremen* (Case 450/93) [1995] ECR I-3051; *Marschall v Land Nordrhein-Westfalen* (Case C-409/95) [1997] ECR I-6363.

the apparent beneficiary of assembly safeguards, the nationalist minority, has come to express its interests in terms of human rights and (simply) equality.

Subtitle: Human Rights

18.94 The meaning of this concept – heading the first subsection – is not clear. Does it refer to aspirations based upon non-legal sources? Or is it about rights in international law, such as the vertical rights guaranteed by the European Convention? Or is it about the rights in Northern Ireland law, including horizontal ones, which will ensue when the HRA 1998 is brought into force?

18.95 While Human Rights is the first of two subsections, comprising the first paragraphs 1–13 of Rights, etc., paragraph 1 stands alone, each of the other twelve being in one of the five parts separately entitled.

1. **The parties affirm their commitment to the mutual respect, the civil rights and the liberties of everyone in the community. Against the background of the recent history of communal conflict, the parties affirm in particular:**
    - **the right of free political thought;**
    - **the right to freedom and expression of religion;**
    - **the right to pursue democratically national and political aspirations;**
    - **the right to seek constitutional change by peaceful and legitimate means;**
    - **the right to freely choose one's place of residence;**
    - **the right to equal opportunity in all social and economic activity, regardless of class, creed, *disability*, gender or [colour] *ethnicity*;**
    - **the right to freedom from sectarian harassment[.]; *and***
    - ***the right of women to full and equal political participation.***

18.96 This paragraph appeared in the MDP in a slightly different form. It is a development of paragraph 5 of the 1993 *Downing Street Declaration*. Its origins, as noted above, lie in an Irish government misreading of a set of six points in 1993.

18.97 A great deal turns on whether this paragraph binds the United Kingdom and Irish states. The *Downing Street Declaration* was the work of the two governments. However, this paragraph begins: 'The parties' (and the term is used in the second sentence also). That is unlikely to be a reference to the states parties to the Belfast Agreement; they are usually identified. Most likely, the parties is equivalent to the participants (less the two governments), which has been used in the Declaration of Support. If this paragraph contains any new rights (and that is considered below), they have not been created by the two states parties in a British-Irish legal space.[77]

18.98 The opening two sentences are similar to the Declaration of Support. Mutual trust occurs there in paragraph 2. 'Civil rights and religious liberties' is from the *Downing Street Declaration*. 'The recent history of communal conflict' is more prosaic than the tragedies of the past in paragraph 2 of the Declaration of Support.

77 As apparently suggested by Christine Bell & Kathleen Cavanaugh, drawing seemingly on paragraph 1(vi) of Constitutional Issues (or article 1 of the BIA, which has to be read with annex 2): *Fordham International Law Journal*, p. 1366.

18.99 The six loyalist 'rights' of 1993 have been expanded to eight. The first four are exactly the same. The first and second relate to article 9 of the Convention. The third and fourth, in contrast, have a bearing on Annex A of Constitutional Issues. The fifth has been redrafted,[78] and may have been inspired by article 13(1) of the Universal Declaration. The sixth is an equal opportunity provision (related to human rights by a prohibition on discrimination). The text has been altered from 'class, creed, sex or colour' to 'class, creed, disability, gender or ethnicity'. The seventh was new to the MDP. It is a freedom, though it is described as a right. Its provenance may only be guessed. The eighth was added, one presumes by the Women's Coalition, at Castle Buildings. The idea of women's rights – as opposed to human rights enjoyed by women – raises difficult legal issues. Some of these 'rights' exist already in the Convention. Others may apply in international law. And yet others are purely aspirational.

18.100 This paragraph, I submit, has no significance for the protection of human rights in Northern Ireland, as a result of it being an integral part of the United Kingdom. In 1993, the latter was against incorporation of the Convention. The Irish state believed its constitutional fundamental rights were sufficient. There was talk of a non-binding charter for Ireland (which is mentioned in paragraph 10). By the time of the Belfast Agreement, which includes a commitment by the Irish government as regards the Convention (paragraph 9 below), the Human Rights Bill was passing through parliament. Paragraph 1 has no legal effect in international, much less, municipal law; it is purely aspirational as between the political parties.

Subheading: United Kingdom Legislation

18.101 This subheading is self explanatory. It covers the first paragraphs 2–4, dealing respectively with human rights, equality of opportunity and a possible bill of rights for Northern Ireland. The use of the term 'United Kingdom' adjectively here contrasts with its avoidance in paragraph 5 of the Declaration of Support and paragraph 2 of Constitutional Issues. This part brings generalizations about human rights to its legal core.

2. **The British Government will complete incorporation into Northern Ireland law of the European Convention on Human Rights (ECHR), with direct access to the courts, and remedies for breach of the Convention, including power for the courts to overrule Assembly legislation on grounds of inconsistency.**

18.102 The date of the white paper, *Rights Brought Home*, was October 1997. The human rights bill was introduced in the house of lords the same month. It was debated there between November 1997 and February 1998.[79] Thereafter, it passed through the commons.[80] Second reading took place on 16 February 1998, that is three months before the Belfast Agreement. Left was the committee stage (May to

78 From: the right to live wherever one chooses without hindrance; to: the right to freely choose one's place of residence.

79 1R, 23 October 1997; 2R, 3 November 1997, Cttee., 18, 24 & 27 November 1997; Report, 19 & 29 January 1998; 3R, 5 February 1998; Commons amendments, 29 October 1998.

80 1R, 6 February 1998; 2R, 16 February 1998; Cttee., 20 May, 3, 17 & 24 June & 2 July 1998; Report, 21 October 1998; 3R, 21 October 1998.

June 1998) and report and third reading (October 1998). Royal assent was on 9 November 1998.

18.103 The bill did not incorporate the Convention rights, only the remedies. The use of the term 'Northern Ireland law' is interesting. Section 22(6) of the HRA 1998 extends it expressly to Northern Ireland. This would have been the position in any case, given the presumption about Westminster legislation extending throughout the United Kingdom.

18.104 Section 6 includes in the definition of public authorities, courts. Section 7 allows proceedings to be brought by a victim of an unlawful act. Section 8 provides for judicial remedies. Section 9 (judicial acts) allows for appeals. Section 21(1) makes acts of the Northern Ireland assembly subordinate legislation. Section 6(3)–(4) recognizes the sovereignty of Westminster. Under section 6(1), it is unlawful for a public authority – including the Northern Ireland assembly – to act in a way which is incompatible with a Convention right.

18.105 Safeguard (b) in paragraph 5 of Strand One refers to the Convention, and any bill of rights for Northern Ireland, which neither the assembly nor public bodies may infringe, and a human rights commission. Safeguard (c) is the proofing of decisions and legislation to ensure compatibility. Section 6 of the NIA 1998 states that an act of the assembly is not law if it is outside legislative competence, including if it is incompatible with any of the Convention rights. The question of whether a bill is within the legislative competence of the assembly may be referred to the judicial committee of the privy council by the attorney-general (section 11). Section 24 deals with subordinate legislation and acts incompatible with, inter alia, Convention rights.

> 3. ***Subject to the outcome of public consultation underway,* [T]*the* British Government [has proposed] *intends*, as a particular priority, [the creation of] *to create* a statutory obligation on public authorities in Northern Ireland to carry out all the*ir* functions with due regard to the need to promote equality of opportunity in relation to religion and political opinion; gender; race; disability; age; marital status; dependants; and sexual orientation. Public bodies would be required to draw up statutory schemes showing how they would implement this obligation. Such schemes would cover arrangements for policy appraisal, *including an assessment of impact on relevant categories*, public consultation, public access to *information and* services, monitoring and timetables.**

18.106 This is a commitment by the United Kingdom government to legislate further for equality of opportunity. It is not as such part of the Belfast Agreement. Accompanying developments in anti-discrimination law and practice in Britain from the 1990s, the United Kingdom government established successively in Northern Ireland: the fair employment agency (later commission) for Northern Ireland;[81] the equal opportunities commission for Northern Ireland;[82] the commission for racial equality for Northern Ireland;[83] and the Northern Ireland disability council.[84]

81 Fair Employment (Northern Ireland) Acts 1976 and 1989. The fair employment agency originated in the proposals of the Van Straubenzee committee in 1973–74.

82 Sex Discrimination (Northern Ireland) Order 1976, SI 1976/1042.

83 Race Relations (Northern Ireland) Order 1997, SI 1997/869.

84 Disability Discrimination Act 1995.

18.107 In June 1997, the SACHR report, *Employment Equality: building for the future*, Cm 3684, was published after a comprehensive review of the Fair Employment Acts 1976 and 1989 (described as 'the most robust anti-discrimination measures in the UK').[85] Since it focuses on disadvantage and inequality, much of the review now falls outside the terms of this section of the Belfast Agreement.[86] In the subsequent white paper, *Partnership for Equality*, Cm 3890, presented to parliament in March 1998 (referred to below in the second paragraph 2), the government announced its commitment to a statutory obligation on public bodies in Northern Ireland in those areas covered by the existing policy appraisal and fair treatment (PAFT) administrative guidelines (covering the eight categories of religion and political opinion; gender; race; disability; age; marital status; having dependants; and sexual orientation).

18.108 The first change to the MDP text should have been unnecessary. Public consultation on the work of the three commissions and one council was already under way in April 1998; it was due to conclude on 12 June 1998. It is surprising that this was not mentioned in the MDP. It was added to the FA. 'In the consultation process on this proposal, the principle of a statutory obligation broadly found favour, though there were considerable reservations about the mechanisms for its oversight and enforcement.'[87]

18.109 The paragraph states that the United Kingdom government intended as a particular priority to create a statutory obligation on public authorities to carry out all their functions with due regard to the need to promote equality of opportunity.[88] This is done by section 75 of the NIA 1998. Subsection (1) states: 'A public authority shall in carrying out its functions relating to Northern Ireland have due regard to the need to promote equality of opportunity.' Have due regard means equality of opportunity has to be considered along side the other responsibilities of the public authority. This does not mean that public authorities must become campaigning organizations for equality of opportunity. Section 75 was brought into force incrementally: section 75(3)(a) and (d) on 1 March 1999, and 7 July 2000;[89] section 75(4) on 2 August 1999;[90] section 75 (for all other purposes) on 1 January 2000.[91]

18.110 The relevant categories are ordered differently in the NIA 1998. Paragraph (a) covers religious belief, political opinion, racial group, age, marital

85 Page 77.

86 There were also three volumes of research published in 1996. A covering letter from the chairman of SACHR, Michael Lavery QC, acknowledged that legislation had brought about significant progress in recruitment practices. Equality of opportunity had been enhanced. While he stated that legislation could not deal with long-term unemployment (and especially differential unemployment), the review after five years of the legislation was designed to effect change within a reasonable period of time. The report contains a note of dissent by Dermot Nesbitt (pp. 97–108).

87 *Notes on Clauses*, NIO October 1998, note to then clause 60.

88 This was announced finally on 10 July 1998 in a parliamentary answer.

89 Northern Ireland Act 1998 (Commencement No. 1) Order 1999, SI 1999/340, art 2(4); Northern Ireland Act 1998 (Designation of Public Authorities) Order 2000, SI 2000/1787.

90 Northern Ireland Act 1998 (Commencement No. 2) Order 1999, SI 1999/2204, art 3, as regards para. 1(b) of sch. 9.

91 Northern Ireland Act 1998 (Commencement No. 2) Order 1999, SI 1999/2204, art 4.

status or sexual orientation. Paragraphs (b)–(d) deal respectively with men and women; persons with a disability; and persons with dependants. It is not clear why parliamentary counsel chose to do it this way. Subsection (2) imposes a further obligation of having regard to the desirability of promoting good relations between persons of different religious belief, political opinion or racial group. This is additional to promoting equality of opportunity, but only three of the nine categories are involved; religious belief and political opinion relate legally in Northern Ireland to catholic/protestant ethnic relations.

18.111 Subsection (4) refers to schedule 9 (enforcement of duties). This consolidates the existing functions of the four equality bodies, merged in a new equality commission by section 74, under the headings: equality schemes; complaints; investigations; and certain exceptions for government departments. The statutory schemes in the paragraph are the equality schemes of the schedule. These are dealt with in paragraphs 2–9. Policy appraisal (including assessment of impact on relevant categories) is dealt with in paragraph 9. Public consultation is covered in paragraph 4(2)(b). Public access to information and services is provided for in paragraph 4(2)(f), monitoring in paragraph 4(2)(c), and timetables in paragraph 4(3)(b).

18.112 Under section 75(3)(a) of the NIA 1998, the NIO brought into force on 7 July 2000 the Northern Ireland Act 1998 (Designation of Public Authorities) Order 2000, SI 2000/1787. This designated a further 16 public authorities required to promote equality of opportunity. Most were United Kingdom government bodies, including the NIO. Also listed was the Northern Ireland Human Rights Commission (NIHRC) (which, at the time, employed ten staff – all female.[92] On 1 July 2000, fair employment legislation had also been applied to the NIHRC as a specified public authority.[93]).

18.113 The NIO had published its own draft equality scheme on 7 April 2000, with consultation ending on 2 June 2000 – within the six months allowed by paragraph 2 of schedule 9 of the NIA 1998 (the deadline being 1 July 2000). The NIO stated it would assess over three years its functions, policies and duties in terms of their impact on the promotion of equality of opportunity and good relations.[94] A comprehensive review after five years was promised, with a possible input from independent consultants. However, on 30 June 2000, the NIO issued a revised draft of its equality scheme.[95] Consultation was to run until 29 September 2000. The target of 22 December 2000 was set for the screening of policies, functions and duties in consultation with representatives of affected groups. The Committee on the Administration of Justice and the Northern Ireland Human Rights Commission declined to meet the NIO, either because they had submitted written comments or were unavailable before 30 June 2000.

> **4. The new Northern Ireland Human Rights Commission (see paragraph 5 below) will be invited *to consult and* to advise on the scope for defining, in**

92 The Northern Ireland Human Rights Commission: Background Information, n.d. but c. mid-2000.

93 Fair Employment (Specification of Public Authorities) Order (Northern Ireland) 2000, SR 2000/1999, made 25 May 2000 by J.A. Canavan.

94 Paragraph 2.1.

95 An Equality Scheme for the Northern Ireland Office: a document for public consultation.

Westminister legislation, rights supplementary to those in the European Convention on Human Rights, to reflect the particular circumstances of Northern Ireland, ***drawing as appropriate on international instruments and experience*****. These additional rights to reflect the principles of mutual respect for the identity and ethos of both communities and parity of esteem, and – taken together with the ECHR – to constitute a Bill of Rights for Northern Ireland. Among the issues for consideration by the Commission will be:**

- **the formulation of a general obligation on government and public bodies fully to respect, on the basis of equality of treatment, the identity and ethos of both communities in Northern Ireland;** ***and***
- **a clear formulation of the new rights not to be discriminated against and to equality of opportunity in both the public and private sectors.**

18.114 This paragraph must be read with paragraph 5(b) and (c) of Strand One, where references are made to 'any Bill of Rights for Northern Ireland'. Further, any bill of rights only supplements the Convention.[96] Paragraph 26(a) of Strand One also refers to 'the ECHR and any Bill of Rights for Northern Ireland supplementing it'.

18.115 The human rights commission (NIHRC) is dealt with below. This paragraph also refers to the bill of rights supplementing Convention rights. However, it goes on to state that the Convention and the supplementary rights are to constitute a bill of rights for Northern Ireland.

18.116 This concept of a bill seems different from that described above as advocated by legal radicals in Great Britain (a home-grown – domestic – bill of fundamental rights approaching a written constitution[97]). Is it supplementary rights, or a new, comprehensive bill of rights (but only for Northern Ireland)? The fact that the Convention has not been incorporated in the HRA 1998 – which must be the starting point once it comes into force – tells against the latter interpretation. Further, a bill of rights for Northern Ireland, unlike one for the United Kingdom, is most unlikely to be comprehensive.

18.117 The letter of this paragraph does not say there will be a bill of rights. The NIHRC is to be invited to, first, consult. This was added to the MDP. Secondly, it is to be asked to advise on – precisely – the scope for defining supplementary rights in Westminster legislation. It would appear that the NIHRC has anticipated the nature of its advice, plus the likely response of the United Kingdom government. Section 69(7) states that the secretary of state shall request such advice. This was done on 24 March 1999, but no time was specified. Thirdly, that will be ultimately a matter for parliament, based upon a decision of the United Kingdom executive. A bill of rights for Northern Ireland alone is not inevitable (even if the NIHRC continues to interpret the NIA 1998 in this manner[98]). The HRA 1998 – which post-dates the Belfast Agreement – has altered radically the terms of the debate.

96 Reference is also made in paragraph 11 to 'the ECHR/Bill of Rights'.

97 Robert Blackburn, *Towards a Constitutional Bill of Rights for the United Kingdom*, London 1999.

98 Northern Ireland Human Rights Commission, *Draft Strategic Plan, 1999–2002*, published in Belfast on 30 September 1999. Consultation ceased on 15 November 1999.

The Belfast Agreement, in any case, never promised a bill of rights for Northern Ireland, as long argued for by the human rights community there.

18.118 As to the content of a possible bill of rights, this is to reflect the particular circumstances of Northern Ireland. What these are is not specified.

18.119 The most obvious fact about Northern Ireland in the last three decades, has not been proven consistent gross violations by the state – allowing for derogations[99] and reservations[100] – of human rights (outside permitted limitations, which, in articles 8–11 of the Convention, include variously national security, public safety or the protection of public order, and the Strasbourg doctrine of margin of appreciation). The rule of law, of course, requires that there should be no breaches, ever. The United Kingdom has been found by the ECtHR to have been in breach of Convention rights in over 50 cases since 1966. There have been nine cases before the court concerning Northern Ireland (including one involving Gibraltar). The United Kingdom was exonerated in only two of those cases (which contrasts with the overwhelming majority of applications to Strasbourg from Northern Ireland, as elsewhere, being unsuccessful).

18.120 The Northern Ireland cases are: *Ireland v United Kingdom* (1978) 2 EHRR 25 (the only interstate case under article 24); *Dudgeon v United Kingdom* (1981) 4 EHRR 149; *Brogan v United Kingdom* (1988) 11 EHRR 117; *Fox, Campbell and Hartley v United Kingdom* (1990) 13 EHRR 157; *Brannigan and McBride v United Kingdom* (1993) 19 EHRR 539 (where the applicants were unsuccessful); *Margaret Murray v United Kingdom* (1994) 19 EHRR 193 (where the applicants failed); *John Murray v United Kingdom* (1996) 22 EHRR 29; *McCann v United Kingdom* (1996) 21 EHRR 97; *Tinnelly and McElduff v United Kingdom* (1998) 27 EHRR 249. Of the seven successful applications, two (*Dudgeon* and *Tinnelly*) concerned forms of discrimination. One (*McCann*) involved article 2 (the Gibraltar case). The remaining four had to do with emergency arrest and detention powers. Seven adverse findings in over 50 cases, while unacceptable, shows that the need to deal with Northern Ireland terrorism did not dominate the United Kingdom's relatively poor human rights record (if the Convention had been incorporated in 1966, this international reputation would have been different, partly because the abuses might not have happened and partly because, if they had, it would have been United Kingdom courts most likely which would have resolved the issue[101]).

18.121 The greatest abusers of human rights in Northern Ireland in that period – particularly of article 2 (the right to life) – have been republicans and loyalists. (It has been the failure to implement the Convention which has prevented such findings in domestic courts, through the development of a horizontal effect.) It is possible to answer the question, who killed whom?, using data published by the Cost of the Troubles Study, for the period 1969 to seemingly the end of February 1998, when some 3,593 people are recorded as having been killed in political violence. The largest category is people killed by republican paramilitaries: 2001,

99 Article 15.

100 Article 57.

101 It was argued in the early 1980s, on the basis of a study of how the Convention applied in the domestic law of signatory states, that individual petition, and the compulsory jurisdiction of the ECtHR, was more effective than the various forms of automatic incorporation: Andrew Z. Drzemczewski, *European Human Rights Convention in Domestic Law: a comparative study*, Oxford 1983.

or 56 per cent. The second largest is killings perpetrated by loyalist paramilitaries: 983, or 27 per cent. The security forces combined were responsible for 382 deaths, or 11 per cent. It is therefore the position that the vaste majority of deaths – 83 per cent – are attributable to illegal paramilitary organizations; just over 10 per cent were the responsibility of the state.[102] Not all of the latter will have been as a result of force which was no more than was absolutely necessary (on which there is only one Northern Ireland-connected ECtHR case). Almost all, if not all, of the former will have amounted to the abuse of the right to life under article 2 of the victim. The fact that a verdict against the actual perpetrator was virtually impossible at Strasbourg is likely to be cured by the HRA 1998 within a reasonable period of time.

18.122 The United Kingdom state has been found by Strasbourg to be in breach of Convention rights (principally article 5); but the IRA, along with other republican and loyalist paramilitary organizations, has escaped censure – and even criticism – for its considerably greater human rights abuses.[103] The Northern Ireland Human Rights Commission, set up under the Belfast Agreement (see paragraph 5 below), has yet to rule on whether sub-state actors can commit human rights abuses.[104] It is customary to refer to the Convention of 1950 as historically dated; 50 years later, it is just as appropriate to expect human rights culture to address problems of the day in the round realistically. The ECHR anticipated the Convention becoming historically dated in the practice of treating it as a 'living instrument which must be interpreted in the light of present-day conditions'.[105] An abuse is an abuse, regardless of who carries it out.

18.123 'Drawing as appropriate on international instruments and experience' defines the work on a possible bill of rights widely. It is not simply a question of compiling provisions in multilateral agreements (many oppressive states have exemplary constitutional provisions). The phrase as appropriate is used. And the United Kingdom traditionally has preferred to do rather than say; pragmatism rather than rhetoric. The question will – or should – be practical rather than simply declaratory effect.[106]

102 Marie-Therese Fay, Mike Morrissey & Marie Smyth, *Northern Ireland's Troubles: the human costs*, London 1999, p. 170 (table 6.13). The total of 3,601 is given on p. 130. Republican and loyalist organizations both killed more republicans and loyalists respectively.

103 This is slowly changing. In Algiers, in February 1999, there was established the International Federation of Associations of Victims of Terrorism. The founding members included Families Against Intimidation and Terror (FAIT). Senator Saida Benhabyles of Algeria was reported: 'There have been some doubts about who is killing who. Is this not the same in other countries? Amnesty International are continually supporting the rights of those associated with terrorist groups. They are supposed to defend human rights, but they defend the terrorists' rights. That is why we need an International Federation.' (*New Dialogue News*, no. 73, June 1999, p. 5)

104 Minutes, 11 October 1999. In contrast, Michael Lavery QC, the last chairman of SACHR, made it clear in his last report: 'I would wish to make it clear on SACHR's behalf, that, not for a moment, was SACHR unaware of the terrible violations of human rights suffered by the people of Northern Ireland on a daily basis as a result of terrorism.' (*Report for 1998–1999*, HC 265, p. v) He should have said abuse, not violation.

105 *Loizidou v Turkey* (1995) 20 EHRR 99, para. 71.

106 *Cruz Varas v Sweden* (1991) 14 EHRR 1, para. 99; *Aydin v Turkey* (7 March 1996, unreported) para. 212.

18.124 'These additional rights to reflect' seems to mean that the principles are to be included in advice to the United Kingdom government, not that all the rights must be an emanation of what follows in the paragraph.

18.125 The first principle is: 'mutual respect for the identity and ethos of both communities'. Mutual respect appears in paragraph 3 of the Declaration of Support. The identities of the two communities (related to the two major traditions of nationalism and unionism) was used first in the preamble to the 1985 Anglo-Irish Agreement. Ethos is a new addition. The identity, ethos and aspirations of both communities is used in paragraph 1(v) of Constitutional Issues (this also being article 1(v) of the BIA).

18.126 The second principle is parity of esteem. This was popularized following the 1993 *Opsahl Report*.[107] A prominent catholic nationalist lawyer submitted there should be 'recognition of the nationalist community in a legal sense' in seemingly domestic law. (No reference seems to have been made to recognition in international law, through the 1985 Anglo-Irish Agreement, and to this being the appropriate means.) The Opsahl commission recommended that 'parity of esteem' between the two communities should be given legal approval, promoted and protected: 'we recommend that the government moves to examine the feasibility of drafting such legislation explicitly to recognize Irish nationalism in Northern Ireland in relevant ways'. But the commission went on to refer to constitutional and international law, without making its recommendation clear. It concluded by saying that parity of esteem should not mean the diminution of Britishness for unionists. Parity of esteem is used in paragraph 1(v) of Constitutional Issues (article 1(v) of the BIA).

18.127 Two ideas for consideration by the NIHRC are given. The first is a statutory obligation on public bodies to respect the identity and ethos of the two communities. This is in addition to the obligation in the first paragraph 3, which was incorporated by section 75 of the NIA 1998: due regard to promoting equality of opportunity. The two communities are provided for there in terms of persons of different religious belief or different political opinion. Moreover, there is also a statutory obligation to have regard to the desirability of promoting good relations between persons of different religious belief or different political opinion. The bill of rights seemingly is to include – or at least the NIHRC is to consider – the possibility of a collective or group right of respect for the two ethnic communities.

18.128 The second idea for consideration is a clear formulation of non discrimination, and equality of opportunity, in the public and private sectors. Discrimination by public authorities against a person or class of persons on the ground of religious belief or political opinion is prohibited by section 76 of the NIA 1998. Under section 76(4), this does not apply to any unlawful act or omission under the Fair Employment (Northern Ireland) Act 1976 (which has now been repealed, and replaced, by the Fair Employment and Treatment (Northern Ireland) Order 1998, SI 1998/3162). The 1976 act covered discrimination in employment in both the private and public sectors. Missing was discrimination in the private sector in areas other than employment. This has been filled partly by the 1998

107 Andy Pollak, ed., *A Citizens' Inquiry: the Opsahl Report on Northern Ireland*, Dublin 1993, pp. 112–13. For earlier uses, see Tom Hennessy & Robin Wilson, *With All Due Respect: pluralism and parity of esteem*, Belfast, Democratic Dialogue, No. 7 (n.d.), p. 14.

order, which prohibits discrimination in the provision of goods, facilities and services. Anti-discrimination law, however, will be significantly reshaped from 31 December 2002, with the extension in European law of the principle of equal treatment, from as between men and women (and no discrimination on the basis of nationality), to the categories of racial or ethnic origin, religion or belief, disability, age or sexual orientation, in mainly, but not exclusively, employment. Public authorities are to have due regard to the promotion of equality, under section 75 of the NIA 1998. This leaves the possibility of a similar statutory duty being imposed on the private sector.

Subheading: New Institutions in Northern Ireland

18.129 This relates largely but not entirely to the United Kingdom legislation above. The three institutions mentioned are the Northern Ireland Human Rights Commission (NIHRC); the Equality Commission for Northern Ireland (ECNI); and a possible department of equality in the Northern Ireland government.

18.130 The use of the word institution is interesting. This is used in paragraph 5 of the Declaration of Support to mean the assembly and the Strands Two and Three bodies. Article 2 of the BIA, on the other hand, refers to the institutions of Strands Two and Three. However, these are arguably only instances, as there are institutions in Strand One. The use of institutions here indicates that the term also includes the NIHRC and the ECNI.

18.131 Part VII of the NIA 1998 deals with human rights and equal opportunities. Under Human Rights, there is: section 68, establishing the NIHRC (plus schedule 7); section 69 giving it functions; section 70, providing for assistance to litigants; section 71 incorporating the article 34 definition of a victim; and section 72, dissolving SACHR. Under Equality of Opportunity (note the change), there is: section 73, establishing the EC (plus schedule 8); section 74 giving it functions; section 75, imposing statutory duties on public authorities (plus schedule 9); section 76 prohibiting discrimination against a person or class or persons by public authorities on the ground of religious belief or political opinion; section 77, prohibiting unlawful oaths; and section 78, applying sections 76 and 77 to complaints alleging maladministration.

18.132 Under paragraph 22 of schedule 2, part VII of the NIA 1998 is generally an excepted matter (under the control of the secretary of state). However, there are exceptions: section 73 (the Equality Commission); section 74(1)–(4) (functions of the Equality Commission); section 75 (statutory duty on public authorities); section 77 (unlawful oaths); schedules 8 and 9. Equality of opportunity was envisaged always as a Northern Ireland government matter, and comes under the assembly.

5. **A new Northern Ireland Human Rights Commission,** ***with membership from Northern Ireland reflecting the community balance,*** **will be established by Westminster legislation, independent of Government, with an extended and enhanced role beyond that currently exercised by the Standing Advisory Commission on Human Rights, to include keeping under review the adequacy and effectiveness of laws and practices, making recommendations to Government as necessary; providing information and promoting awareness of human rights; considering draft legislation**

referred to them by the new Assembly; and, in appropriate cases, bringing court proceedings or providing assistance to individuals doing so.

18.133 A new Northern Ireland Human Rights Commission is provided for in section 68 of the NIA 1998 plus schedule 7. The NIHRC was to be a body corporate, with a chief commissioner (holding office for up to five years[108]) and commissioners (up to three years) appointed by the secretary of state. Section 68 was brought into force by the Northern Ireland Act 1998 (Commencement No. 1) Order 1999,[109] SI 1999/340 on 15 February and 1 March 1999.

18.134 'With membership from Northern Ireland reflecting the community balance' was added to the MDP. Presumably, the fear was that the secretary of state would select unionists or nationalists disproportionately. Section 68(3) requires the secretary of state as far as practicable, to secure that the commissioners as a group are representative of the community in Northern Ireland. Community is used in Northern Ireland in two ways: one, to refer to catholics or protestants, as in the preamble to the 1985 Anglo-Irish Agreement; two, to mean all the people of Northern Ireland, as in paragraph 1 of Strand One. Community balance in the Belfast Agreement suggests the former; representative of the community in the NIA 1998, the latter. The word representative – with connotations of politics – would indicate that the commission has to reflect the unionist/nationalist divide.[110] This was the view taken by the government during the passage of the bill through parliament: 'I think that all the world knows [said Paul Murphy MP, minister of state, on 27 July 1998] what traditions and communities we are considering: the broad Unionist community and the broad nationalist community ... When we discussed the matter, I have not the slightest doubt that we referred to the nationalist and Unionist communities.'[111]

18.135 On 18 January 1999, Prof. Brice Dickson was announced as the chief commissioner. The nine part-time commissioners followed on 1 March 1999, when the NIHRC met first: Christine Bell, Margaret-Ann Dinsmore QC, Tom Donnelly, Rev. Harold Good, Prof. Tom Hadden, Angela Hegarty, Patricia Kelly, Inez McCormack, and Francis McGuinness (five men and five women). Three had been associated with SACHR.[112] The commission includes four academic lawyers, one practising lawyer, and one non-practising lawyer; the other four are a person in business, a minister of religion, an official of UNISON and a charity

108 The first chief commissioner has been appointed for three years: *Irish Times*, 27 May 1999.

109 11 February 1999.

110 Attempts were made to construe the Belfast Agreement and the NIA 1998. Prof. Brice Dickson of the University of Ulster, in a SACHR paper of May 1998, 'Creating an Effective Human Rights Commission for Northern Ireland', proposed three principles: one, representatives from other bodies (especially the EC); two, persons from a human rights NGO (the Committee for the Administration of Justice [CAJ] is the leading one in Northern Ireland); three, persons familiar with international human rights standards. (pp. 21–2) In an undated briefing on the bill, SAHCR, quoting the Paris Principles to the effect that there should be a pluralist representation of the social forces involved in the promotion and protection of human rights, argued for a broad interpretation of the clause: 'to command the confidence of the entire community in Northern Ireland and should include a pluralist representation of a broad range of groups'. ('Briefing on the Human Rights and Equality Provisions of the Northern Ireland Bill', summary & p. 5)

111 House of Commons, *Hansard*, 6th series, 317, 59–60, 27 July 1998.

112 Seven other members of the outgoing SACHR had applied unsuccessfully.

worker. The chief commissioner and one other were publicly identified with the Committee for the Administration of Justice (CAJ) (though at least another two admitted membership).[113] Together with Inez McCormack (whose union, UNISON, is closely involved with the CAJ), that means that one pressure group has been granted half the positions on the NIHRC. The dominance is even greater when the lawyers are distinguished from the non-lawyers. The latter are: a person in business (Donnelly), a minister of religion (Good), a trade unionist (McCormack) and a charity worker (McGuinness). The other six are all lawyers. However, four of these are academic lawyers (Dickson, Bell, Hadden and Hegarty). A fifth is a non-practising lawyer running a law centre (Kelly). There is only one practising lawyer – albeit senior counsel – on the NIHRC (Dinsmore).

18.136 The announcement of the commissioners caused significant public comment in Northern Ireland.[114] A number of failed applicants identified themselves. There were in fact 154 applicants, of whom 23 were interviewed for the 9 commissioners posts (8 had been interviewed for the chief commissioner post). The government appears to have interpreted representative of the community in terms of religious background (there is said to be a 60/40 balance[115]), though it admitted that there was not a member of a unionist party on the NIHRC.[116] The Irish government had endorsed 5 candidates, of whom 2 were successful.[117]

18.137 SACHR was dissolved by section 72 of the NIA 1998 on 1 March 1999.[118] The functions of the new NIHRC are contained in section 69. Section 69(1)–(3) and (6)–(11) came into force on 1 March 1999, and section 69(5) on 1 June 1999;[119] section 69(4) came into force on 2 December 1999.[120]

113 Angela Hegarty, vice-chairman of the SDLP in 1989–91, made a presentation on behalf of the CAJ to the Dublin forum for peace and reconciliation on 31 March 1995: *Report of Proceedings*, vol. 12. She based her case on international law, and opposition to derogation: called for the dismantling of the legal framework which caused human rights abuses; stated there was no emergency; opposed emergency law as leading to abuse and harassment; called for fundamental reform of the police and the judiciary (pp. 12–17). (A colleague referred to children surrendering to paramilitaries for beatings for fear of the police p. 35). A former chairman of the CAJ, Steve McBride, posed the question of the CAJ: 'Do they recognize that the greatest abuse of human rights in Northern Ireland in the last twenty five years is that carried out by paramilitary groups and do they recognize that the principal obstacle in the dismantling of emergency legislation is the continuing existence of terrorist groups stockpiling weapons and indulging in violent intimidation?' (p. 27) Similar comments were made by inter alia Dr John Alderdice (p. 30), Mary Harney (p. 43) and senator Gordon Wilson (p. 56).

114 The *Irish Times* report on 2 March 1999 was headed: 'Nationalists welcome human rights appointeees.' It included a quotation from Sam Cushnahan, of Families Against Intimidation and Terror (FAIT): 'the list had not one person who "made their reputation by agitating on behalf of the victims of violence"'.

115 *Irish Times*, 27 May 1999.

116 Two have been associated with the SDLP.

117 House of Commons, *Hansard*, 6th series, 327, 284–7, 10 March 1999. The Rt. Hon. Paul Murphy MP, replying on 9 April 1999 to a letter from the Rt. Hon. John Taylor MP, relied upon the as far as practicable provision: 'This can only be achieved if there are suitable candidates of the calibre required.'

118 Northern Ireland Act 1998 (Commencement No. 1) Order 1999, SI 1999/340, article 2(3), schedule, part 3.

18.138 Section 69(11)(b) defines '"human rights" [as] includ[ing] the Convention rights' for the purposes of that section (Convention rights being defined in section 98(1) as those in the HRA 1998). But are the non-Convention rights those in Northern Ireland statute[121] and common law? Or are they all putative human rights in international law?

18.139 Parliament has not stated that the latter is the position. And parliamentary counsel is unlikely to have specified all human rights so imprecisely.

18.140 The draftsman in the Republic of Ireland, in that state's Human Rights Commission Bill of 1999, defined human rights in two ways (section 1). In section 2, human rights meant 'the rights, liberties and freedoms conferred on, or guaranteed to persons by the Constitution' plus 'the rights, liberties or freedoms conferred on, or guaranteed to persons by any agreement, treaty or convention to which the State is a party'.[122]

18.141 However, in section 11, dealing with domestic legal proceedings, the latter phrase was qualified by: 'and which has [sic] been given the force of law in the State or by a provision of any such agreement, treaty or convention which has been given such force'.

18.142 Reading sections 2 and 11 together, section 2 read: 'the rights, liberties or freedoms conferred on, or guaranteed to persons by the Constitution'.

18.143 Returning to section 69 of the NIA 1998, the *Notes on Clauses*[123] for the House of Lords said of subclause (1): 'The Bill does not attempt to restrict the meaning of "human rights" – it is deliberately intended to be wide, enabling the Commission itself to identify what it considers to constitute such rights.'[124] Implied in this surely is: in Northern Ireland law (given that rights – often unspecified – do exist in the common law, while anti-discrimination law has been identified with human rights since 1973[125]).

18.144 The term 'human rights' occurs first in section 69. Subsection (1) – the review function – uses the phrase: 'law and practice relating to the protection of human rights'. This must be existing rights in Northern Ireland law. (The same phrase is used in section 70(1)(a), dealing with legal proceedings.) Section 69(3) – the executive advisory function – uses the phrase: 'legislative and other measures which ought to be taken to protect human rights'. Obviously, these rights do not

119 Northern Ireland Act 1998 (Commencement No. 1) Order 1999, SI 1999/340, article 2(3) & (5), schedule, parts 3 & 4.

120 Northern Ireland Act 1998 (Commencement No. 5) Order 1999, SI 1999/3209, article 3, schedule.

121 These include the 'right' not to be discriminated against under section 76 of the NIA 1998.

122 The source of this idea would appear to have been Prof. Brice Dickson: NIHRC, minutes of 2nd meeting, 8 March 1999, and minutes of 7th meeting, 2 July 1999.

123 Northern Ireland Office, October 1998. See also Lord Williams of Mostyn in House of Lords, *Hansard*, 5th series, 593, 1512, 1529,1533, 1537, 21 October 1998: 'We want [the Commission] to develop organically with its own sense of purpose and priorities in a very difficult situation.' (1533); but '[The NIHRC] will see all proposed Assembly Bills and will be able to offer an opinion on whether they are compatible with the European Convention on Human Rights.' (1529) Also, House of Lords, *Hansard*, 5th series, 594, 706, 10 November 1998.

124 Of clause 54; see also subclause (8).

125 Northern Ireland Constitution Act 1973 s 20.

exist yet in Northern Ireland law. Subsection (4) – the assembly advisory function – refers to whether a bill 'is compatible with human rights'. These, given section 6(2)(c), must be the Convention rights only.[126] Section 69(5)(a) – the assistance function – again uses 'law and practice relating to the protection of human rights'. And subsection (6) – the education function – refers to 'promot[ing] understanding and awareness of the importance of human rights in Northern Ireland'. This could refer to international human rights; however, the word 'in' rather than 'to' has been used (suggesting already existing in Northern Ireland law).

18.145 Thus, subsection (3) alone refers to non-Convention rights (in domestic and/or international law). The NIHRC may advise the secretary of state, and the executive committee of the assembly, that – arguably – an international law right should be incorporated.

18.146 There is presumably no limit to the advice as regards the secretary of state, whose functions are of course limited in practice to Northern Ireland.

18.147 This is not the position as regards the executive committee. What can the assembly do as a devolved legislature? It can legislate on transferred matters only under section 4. Schedule 2 (excepted matters) includes international relations. This includes international agreements, which are governed by the law of treaties.

18.148 However, one of the three exceptions to this exception includes: 'observing and implementing international obligations, [and] obligations under the Human Rights Convention ...'.[127] This is defined as the 1950 Convention plus all the subsequent protocols ratified by the United Kingdom. Does this mean that the assembly can incorporate a human right from one of the protocols not included in the HRA 1998? The answer is clearly no. Observing international obligations refers to what the Northern Ireland administration does as an integral part of the United Kingdom when it acts on the international plane.

18.149 Implementing international obligations is a concept of international law; it is not the same as incorporation – a concept in United Kingdom law.

18.150 The NIA 1998, therefore, does not give the NIHRC the power to define human rights globally, as comprising mainly all putative international law rights (simply on the basis of finding a text). The meaning of human rights depends upon the function assigned to the commission by the NIA 1998. The functions of the NIHRC – as noted – are specified in section 69. And schedule 7 contains supplementary provisions, about the Commission established by section 68(1).

6. ***Subject to the outcome of public consultation currently under way, t*[T]he British Government *intends* [has proposed] a new statutory Equality Commission to replace the Fair Employment Commission, the Equal Opportunities Commission (NI), the Commission for Racial Equality (NI) and the Disability Council [- s]. *S*uch a unified Commission will advise on, validate and monitor the statutory obligation and will investigate complaints of default.**

126 This is confirmed on page 46 of the Strategic Plan.

127 Paragraph 3(c). This was added to HL Bill 158 (as amended in committee). It was government amendment No. 226. There was no debate: House of Lords, *Hansard*, 5th series, 593, 2833, 27 October 1998.

18.151 Subject to the outcome of public consultation currently under way was added to the MDP. Consultation was due to end on 12 June 1998. This corresponds to the addition at the beginning of the first paragraph 3: a reference to the consultation subsequent to the white paper, *Partnership for Equality*, Cm 3890, March 1998. And the comments above apply here also. The Equality Commission is not as such part of the Belfast Agreement (unlike the NIHRC).

18.152 A working party was announced by the NIO – to coincide with the decision to proceed with a unified commission – on 10 July 1998, to comprise representatives of the existing agencies, plus individuals with an interest in other aspects of equality. This was because of objections by various groups, who, while not opposing seemingly integrated anti-discrimination legislation (a matter for the assembly), were hostile to the consolidation of enforcement organizations.

18.153 Subsequently (in November 1998), the government asked a working group, chaired by Dr Joan Stringer of Edinburgh,[128] to report on the structure, priorities and functioning of the ECNI. The other members were the chairs and chief executives of the four existing bodies, plus a representative of the staff of each. On 2 February 1999, it announced it was seeking public comments on a consultation paper. Over 100 people attended a seminar on 19 February 1999. The working group reported belatedly in May 1999.

18.154 The new statutory Equality Commission is provided for in section 73 of the NIA 1998 plus schedule 8. The ECNI is to be a body corporate, with a chief commissioner (holding office for up to five years), between 13 and 19 commissioners (holding office for up to three years), including at least one deputy chief commissioner. Section 73 in part was brought into force by the Northern Ireland Act 1998 (Commencement No. 1) Order 1999, SI 1999/340 on 15 February 1999 for the purposes of appointing commissioners (sections 73(1), 74 and 75(4) were brought into force on 2 August 1999[129], and the remaining sections on 2 December 1999[130]).

18.155 Though it is not specified in this paragraph, section 73(4) of the NIA 1998 requires the secretary of state as far as practicable to secure that the commissioners, as a group, are representative of the community in Northern Ireland.

18.156 The ECNI members were announced finally on 22 July 1999. The chief commissioner is Joan Harbison (who was involved in SAHCR's employment equality review), and the deputy chief commissioner is Bronagh Hinds. There are a further 18 members, all appointed for three years from 2 August 1999.[131] They took over responsibility for the three existing commissions and one council on 1 October 1999.

18.157 The dissolution of the Fair Employment Commission, the Equal Opportunities Commission, the Commission for Racial Equality and the Disability

128 A member of the Equal Opportunities Commission in Great Britain.

129 Northern Ireland Act 1998 (Commencement No. 3) Order 1999, SI 1999/2204.

130 Northern Ireland Act 1998 (Commencement No. 5) Order 1999, SI 1999/3209.

131 They are: Jeremy Bryson, Harry Coll, Rosemary Connolly, Paul Donaghy, Alan Henry, John Heron, Ann Hope, Ruth Lavery, Stephen Livingstone, Margaret Logue, Shahid Malik, Harry McConnell, Robert Mullan, Bob Osborne, Richard Steele, Anna Watson, Monica Wilson and Noreen Wright.

Council was provided for in section 74.[132] Of the nine parts to the NIA 1998, most of the lobbying of parliament during passage of the bill was directed at part VII; the NIHRC was of considerable concern, but the ECNI attracted even greater attention. There had been over 120 responses to the white paper, *Partnership for Equality*. On 10 July 1998, the secretary of state announced – following consultation – that there would be a unified equality commission. However, there would be consultative councils on particular aspects of equality. Section 74(1) effectively merges the three commissions and one council in the ECNI. Section 74(3) refers to an appropriate division of resources between the functions previously exercised by separate bodies. There is to be a consultative council, defined in section 74(4) as a group of persons selected by the ECNI to advise in relation to the functions of one of the former bodies, or in relation to schedule 9. On or after 1 October 1999, the existing bodies became directorates of the new ECNI.[133]

18.158 Schedule 9 relates to section 75 (statutory duty on public authorities), and deals with enforcement by the ECNI. This has been discussed above under the first paragraph 3. These cover the various functions for the new ECNI listed in this paragraph: advice under paragraph 1(b) of schedule 9; validation under paragraph 6; monitoring under paragraphs 1(a) and 11; and investigation of complaints under paragraph 10.

18.159 The SACHR report, *Employment Equality: building for the future*, Cm 3684, June 1997, recommended, in chapter 6 ('Fair Employment Law and Institutions'), the consolidation of fair employment legislation in a fair treatment act. In the white paper, *Partnership for Equality*, Cm 3890, March 1998, the government offered to consider this. On 16 December 1998, parliament made the Fair Employment and Treatment (Northern Ireland) Order 1998, SI 1998/3162. It came into operation on 1 March 1999 and 16 August 1999.[134]

18.160 It deals mainly with discrimination in the employment field. However, the 1998 order adds other fields: bodies in charge of further and higher education; good, facilities, services and premises (with the exception for small dwellings); and barristers.

18.161 The order consolidates the legislation, repealing and reenacting the Fair Employment (Northern Ireland) Act 1976 and the Fair Employment (Northern Ireland) Act 1989.[135] Fair employment legislation – in keeping with the devolved nature of the Equality Commission for Northern Ireland – has been transferred from the United Kingdom to the Northern Ireland statute

132 This was opposed by SACHR. It called for further research, and a thorough review. (*Briefing on the Human Rights and Equality Provisions of the Northern Ireland Bill*, n.d.)

133 See also the Equality Commission for Northern Ireland (Supplementary Provisions) (Northern Ireland) Order 1999, SI 1999/1804, made under s 74(5) and (6) of the NIA 1998: this transferred the property, etc., of the dissolved bodies to the new ECNI on 20 July 1999.

134 Fair Employment and Treatment (1998 Order) (Commencement No. 1) Order (Northern Ireland) 1999, SR 1999/81 and Fair Employment and Treatment (1998 Order) (Commencement No. 2) Order (Northern Ireland) 1999, SR 1999/355.

135 Also repealed are the Fair Employment (Amendment) (Northern Ireland) Order 1991; the Fair Employment (Amendment) (Northern Ireland) Order 1995; (parts of) the Employment Rights (Northern Ireland) Order 1996.

book, this being the effect of using paragraph 1 of schedule 1 to the Northern Ireland Act 1974.[136]

18.162 But the order in council has also been used to effectively amend the existing Westminster acts. The principal amendments are: one, the extension of unlawful discrimination to the provision of good, facilities, services and premises on the ground of religious belief or political opinion (articles 28–31); two, making it lawful for a person to recruit specifically from the unemployed, and offering religion-specific training to persons not already in his employment (articles 75 and 76); three, providing a right of appeal against national security certificates (article 96) (further to sections 90–92 of the NIA 1998[137]); and four, making provision in relation to the arbitration and settlement of complaints (articles 88 and 89).

18.163 The order also, in part II, further specifies the principal functions of the Equality Commission for Northern Ireland: general duty (article 7); education and advisory functions (8); codes of practice (9); identification of patterns and trends of employment etc. (10); investigation of practices (11). Equality of opportunity is defined in article 5(5) as including affirmative action (which is defined in article 4 as 'action designed to secure fair participation in employment by members of the Protestant, or members of the Roman Catholic, community[138]). The general duty of the commission in article 7 is to: promote equality of opportunity; promote affirmation action (even though that is defined as included in equality of opportunity); to work for the elimination of unlawful discrimination; and to keep the working of the order under review. Article 10 requires the commission to identify and keep under review patterns and trends of employment and occupations. The principal purpose of this is to consider whether they reveal the existence or absence of equality of opportunity.[139]

18.164 Equality was one of the first items considered after devolution. On 18 January 2000, the executive committee considered its first legislative programme. Included was the Equality (Disability, etc.) Bill (Northern Ireland), a measure containing a number of reserved matters.[140] This was a parity measure, to coincide with the Disability Rights Commission Act 1999[141] at Westminster (due to come into force in Great Britain on 25 April 2000). First stage in the assembly was taken early on 24 January 2000. The Northern Ireland bill strengthens the legal rights of disabled people (non-discrimination, equality of opportunity, information and advice) by providing for enforcement through the ECNI. Additional commissioners were to be appointed. The secretary of state consented, under section 10(2) of the

136 It also amends the Sex Discrimination (Northern Ireland) Order 1976, SI 1976/1042; and the Race Relations (Northern Ireland) Order 1997, SI 1997/869.

137 See also, Northern Ireland Act Tribunal (Procedure) Rules 1999, SI 1999/2131, made on 28 July 1999 and coming into force the following day.

138 These terms are not defined in article 1(2). Article 52(11) defines community as regards part VII. Under article 52(2), monitoring returns are to include such information as may be prescribed. Regulations are dealt with in article 53. Under paragraph (3), an employer may be required to determine which community (if any) an employee/applicant belongs to, using the principal or a residuary method prescribed.

139 While the commission may interpret the data as it chooses, it would not be correct to assume that evidence of economic disadvantage proves there is not equality of opportunity.

140 Northern Ireland Assembly, *Official Report*, vol. 4, no. 7, pp. 262–7, 31 January 2000; para. 42 of sch. 3 of NIA 1998.

141 Royal assent, 27 July 1999.

NIA 1998, to the bill being considered on 26 January 2000. The second-stage debate took place on 7 February 2000.[142] The bill was then a victim of suspension by the secretary of state on 12 February 2000. The secretary of state then reverted to Westminster, with a draft order in council laid before parliament under paragraph 2(1)(a) of the schedule to the Northern Ireland Act 2000: Equality (Disability, etc.) (Northern Ireland) Order 2000, SI 2000/1110; this was made on 19 April 2000. Part II (disability discrimination) was to come into operation under order of the Office of the First Minister and deputy First Minister;[143] this happened – despite suspension – on 25 April 2000.[144]

18.165 On Thursday, 29 June 2000, the executive committee decided upon an agenda for government, seemingly an early – agreed – draft of a programme of government. The Deputy First Minister told the assembly on 3 July 2000 that this would include a new equality act: 'work will commence ... to extend protection to groups not already covered by anti-discrimination legislation and, where appropriate, to harmonise protection upwards'.[145]

7. ***It would be open to a new Northern Ireland Assembly to consider bringing together its responsibilities for these matters into a dedicated Department of Equality.***

18.166 This was added to the MDP.

18.167 On 29 June 1998, the secretary of state referred specific matters arising from the Belfast Agreement to the assembly under section 1(2) of the Northern Ireland (Elections) Act 1998. The first was the basic structures of the assembly. The second of four items was agreement on the number of ministerial posts and the distribution of executive responsibilities, by primarily the First Minister and the Deputy First Minister.[146]

18.168 In the agreement of 18 December 1998, the First Minister and Deputy First Minister – in providing for ten departments – added an office of the First Minister and Deputy First Minister (envisaged in section 21(3) of the NIA 1998). Equality and an economic policy unit were located especially at the centre (in addition to other central functions). The joint heads of the transitional administration stated later: 'We gave careful consideration to some Parties' concerns to establish a separate Department of Equality, but we concluded that this important function, given its cross-Departmental nature, would be best placed from a strategic point of view in the Office of the First Minister and Deputy First Minister.'[147] This report was approved by the assembly by 74 votes to 27 on 18

142 Northern Ireland Assembly, *Official Report*, vol. 4, no. 9, pp. 352–8, 7 February 2000.

143 The law was defined, with reference to article 4 (general functions of the Commission) as 'includ[ing] Community law and the international obligations of the United Kingdom'. This originated in the Disability Rights Commission Act 1999 section 2(5).

144 Equality (Disability, etc.) (2000 Order) (Commencement No. 1) Order (Northern Ireland) 2000. The Order was made by J.A. Canavan, a senior officer in the Office.

145 Northern Ireland Assembly, *Official Report*, vol. 5, no. 10, p. 370, 3 July 2000.

146 New Northern Ireland Assembly, *Official Report*, vol. 1, p. 1, 1 July 1998.

147 New Northern Ireland Assembly, *Report from the First Minister (Designate) and Deputy First Minister (Designate)*, 18 January 1999, pp. 4–5. See also the report of 15 February 1999, Annex 1b.

January 1999.[148] There followed approval of the determination by the First Minister and Deputy First Minister of the number of ministerial offices and the functions exercised by the holder of each by 77 votes (41 nationalists, 29 unionists and 7 others) to 29 (all unionists) on 16 February 1999.[149] Following the appointment of two junior ministers on 15 December 1999 (Dermot Nesbitt and Denis Haughey) in the office of the First Minister and Deputy First Minister, equality was assigned practically to them. An equality unit, part of the office of the First Minister and Deputy First Minister, is located at Queen's Court in Belfast.[150] However, following a meeting in London of the human rights task force (under the home office), attended by both junior ministers, Dermot Nesbitt referred to a new directorate responsible for taking forward the equality and human rights agenda within all departments.

[7.] 8. **These improvements will build on existing protections in Westminster legislation in respect of the judiciary, the system of justice and policing.**

18.169 'These improvements' must be a reference to the NIHRC, the EC and a possible department of equality, the two/three institutions dealing with human rights and equality of opportunity. 'Existing protections in Westminster legislation' must be a reference to United Kingdom, or Northern Ireland, law. But why protections? The insinuation is that the judiciary, the justice system and the police are a threat to human rights and equality of opportunity. The meaning of the judiciary is clear. It is bound by section 6(1) of the HRA 1998, being a public authority under section 6(3)(a) of that act. On 7 July 2000, the Northern Ireland Courts Service became one of 16 designated public authorities under section 75(3)(a) of the NIA 1998, required to have due regard to the need to promote equality of opportunity. It is unlikely that this relates specifically to the judiciary. The meaning of the system of justice is not clear. It may be all those involved, less the judiciary. The police is a reference to the Royal Ulster Constabulary. It is bound by the HRA 1998. It is also bound by section 75 of the NIA 1998. No new primary legislation is envisaged by this paragraph as regards the judiciary, the justice system and the police.

18.170 The judiciary, in Great Britain, and in Northern Ireland, is, and will continue to be, the agent of advance on human rights and equality of opportunity. With the HRA 1998, and part VII of the NIA 1998, considerable attention will focus on the courts. The civil judiciary (which will mainly address these questions) is not otherwise mentioned in the Belfast Agreement, though the criminal judiciary and magistracy is referred to in Annex B of the Policing and Justice section. The system of (criminal) justice is of course specified in these terms of reference of the United Kingdom government's review. And the – independent – review of policing, in Annex A of the Policing and Justice section, included in its terms of reference, the legislative and constitutional framework of impartial policing.

148 New Northern Ireland Assembly, *Official Report*, vol. 1, pp. 474–5, 18 January 1999.
149 New Northern Ireland Assembly, *Official Report*, vol. 2, p. 110, 16 February 1999.
150 This was visited by the Deputy First Minister alone on 8 December 1999, shortly after devolution.

Subheading: Comparable Steps by the Irish Government

18.171 This is an important aspect of the Rights, Safeguards and Equality of Opportunity section. It has been observed from time to time that the Irish government, invited by the United Kingdom government – under the 1985 Anglo-Irish Agreement – to comment on Northern Ireland affairs, has criticized there what it is not prepared to address in its own state. Article 2(b) granted the right to 'put forward views and proposals': 'The Conference will be mainly concerned with Northern Ireland; but some of the matters under consideration will involve co-operative action in both parts of the island of Ireland, and possibly also in Great Britain. Some of the proposals considered in respect of Northern Ireland may also be found to have application by the Irish Government.'[151]

18.172 Comparable Steps by the Irish Government – the first paragraph 9 – delivers on this Irish part of the 1985 agreement for the first time, and in a significant way.

> [8.] *9.* **The Irish Government will also take steps to further strengthen the protection of human rights in its jurisdiction. The Government will, taking account of the work of the All-Party Oireachtas Committee on the Constitution and the Report of the Constitution Review Group, bring forward measures to strengthen and underpin the constitutional protection of human rights. These proposals will draw on the European Convention on Human Rights and other international legal instruments in the field of human rights** ***and the question of the incorporation of the ECHR will be further examined in this context. The measures brought forward would*** **[and will] ensure at least an equivalent level of protection of human rights as will pertain in Northern Ireland. In addition, the Irish Government will*****:***
>
> - **establish a Human Rights Commission with a mandate and remit equivalent to that within Northern Ireland;**
> - **proceed with arrangements** ***as quickly as possible*** **to ratify the Council of Europe Framework Convention on National Minorities (already ratified by the UK);**
> - **implement enhanced employment equality legislation; [and]**
> - **introduce equal status legislation[.]** ***and***
> - ***continue to take further active steps to demonstrate its respect for the different traditions in the island of Ireland.***

18.173 The first sentence of this paragraph is an admission that human rights could be protected further in the Republic of Ireland. The second sentence is a broad undertaking to do this by means of constitutional amendment; if the Irish government were to legislate to protect human rights, it would not be fundamental in Irish law.

18.174 The Constitution Review Group was set up by the Irish government on 27 April 1995. The chairman was Dr T.K. Whitaker. Its purpose was to establish those areas where constitutional change might be desirable or necessary. Articles 2

151 See also article 5(b).

and 3 of BNH (and certain other areas) were excluded from consideration. Reliance was placed upon the 1995 *Framework Documents* (though they had no legal status). In May 1996, the Group published the formidable (701 pages) report, *Report of the Constitution Review Group*.[152] It is the most extensive study and discussion of the Irish constitution as it applies to the Republic of Ireland. There is an article by article examination, plus a series of notes on particular topics in a set of appendices.

18.175 In July 1996, the All-Party Oireachtas Committee on the Constitution was established. It had the work of the Constitution Review Group to rely upon. The first chairman was Jim O'Keeffe TD; the second is Brian Lenihan SC TD. Two reports followed in 1997.[153] There were a further two in 1998.[154]

18.176 The third sentence of this paragraph was amended at Castle Buildings. Originally, the Irish government offered to draw upon the Convention and other international instruments. It then agreed to examine the question of incorporation of the Convention (in the constitution). By the time it published the human rights commission bill on 5 July 1999, it had not decided on the question of incorporation.[155] A decision was reported as likely to coincide with the state's assumption of the chair of the Council of Europe in November 1999,[156] but it never came. The government had still not made a decision by 25 November 1999, when the second stage of the human rights commission bill was taken in the Dáil (nor when it was resumed on 1 March 2000). The minister for justice, equality and law reform stated that the matter had been considered in his department for a year or so. An interdepartmental committee of officials, including from the attorney general's office, had considered options: 'The matter is a complex one, raising difficult constitutional, legal and technical questions.'[157] The minister hinted at a legislative solution, while admitting difficulties, and concluded by stating his personal view that, with the Republic of Ireland the only one of the 41 members of the Council of Europe not to have incorporated, it was difficult to justify. He hoped to put proposals to the government consistent with the state's obligations under the Belfast Agreement.[158] The government is thought to have agreed to legislate for human rights – not propose a constitutional amendment – on 18 April 2000, with entry into force in October 2000 (though the bill would not be published until the beginning of the autumn session).[159] October 2000 was reaffirmed in the joint letter of Tony Blair and Bertie Ahern, issued in Belfast on 5 May 2000.

152 Pn 2632, Dublin, Stationery Office.

153 *First Progress Report*, 1997, Pn 3795, Dublin, Stationery Office; *Second Progress Report: Seanad Éireann*, 1997, Pn 3835, Dublin, Stationery Office.

154 *Third Progress Report: The President*, 1998, Pn 6250; Michael Laver, *A New Electoral System for Ireland?*, Studies in Public Policy, 2, Dublin, the Policy Institute in association with the All-Party Oireachtas Committee on the Constitution, 1998.

155 The review continues: explanatory and financial memorandum, note to section 11.

156 *Irish Times*, 27 October & 1 November 1999.

157 According to a press report, the government was faced with pressure from catholic groups, concerned about the possibility of abortion, and adoption by homosexual couples, as well as resistance from within the legal system: *Irish Times*, 1 November 1999.

158 Dáil Éireann, *Official Report*, 25 November 1999.

159 Press release, 20 April 2000; *Irish Times*, 21 April 2000.

18.177 Incorporation in Irish law, however, accords neither with the advice of the Constitution Review Group, nor with the Irish government's obligation under the Belfast Agreement.

18.178 The Constitution Review Group had considered fundamental human rights in 1995–96. Incorporation would have to be into the constitution. Two methods were discussed: direct incorporation of rights into articles 40–44; or the Swedish method, a constitutional provision stating that no law may be enacted contrary to the state's international obligations under the Convention.[160]

18.179 While the Constitution Review Group asserted that every substantive right of the Convention existed in the constitution, either expressly or through article 40.3.1 (the unenumerated rights), it went on to favour drawing upon the Convention and other human rights instruments where: one, the right was not expressly protected; two, the standard of protection was higher in the Convention or other instrument; or three, the wording of the constitution might be improved.[161]

18.180 The obligation in this paragraph – in the fourth sentence – is precise: at least an equivalent level of protection of human rights as will pertain in Northern Ireland. The is the problem to be addressed. It is solved if the level of protection is higher. It gives rise to two subordinate problems: the means of incorporation; and the development of jurisprudence. First, the easiest way to achieve an equivalent level of protection is to incorporate the Convention (in either of the two ways discussed by the Constitution Review Group). It would be exceedingly difficult to adopt the Constitution Review Group's recommendation, and seek to hit or surpass the target of equivalence. Secondly, there is the problem of jurisprudence. Under the HRA 1998, the common law of the United Kingdom must take into account ECtHR jurisprudence.[162] The Convention rights will mean what the United Kingdom courts come to say they are as the law develops (and the government envisages the decisions of the United Kingdom judges infusing legal learning throughout Europe). The Irish courts can keep on track, either by relating directly to Convention jurisprudence (which would require at least legislation), or by drawing inter alia on the United Kingdom through the common law.

18.181 The fifth, and last, sentence makes a series of five commitments, again to ensure equivalence between the Republic of Ireland and Northern Ireland. As stated above, equivalence is best obtained by aiming for a superior level of provision.

18.182 The first additional commitment is a human rights commission. The Irish government has had the benefit of studying the United Kingdom legislation, and observing the establishment of the NIHRC in Northern Ireland. As noted above, it even had its own candidates for the commission in Northern Ireland.

18.183 On 26 June 1999, Prof. Dickson, speaking at the second annual NGO forum on human rights at Dublin Castle (at which over 350 human rights activists were expected), regretted that the Irish government had not yet established its

160 This was ruled out by the minister for justice, equality and law reform: Dáil Éireann, *Official Report*, 1 March 2000.

161 *Report of the Constitution Review Group*, Pn 2632, 1996, Dublin, Stationery Office, pp. 213–19.

162 Section 2.

commission. He called for powers greater than those of the NIHRC in Belfast. Michael Farrell, a human rights activist in Dublin, criticized the criteria for members of the commission as being legally, and socially, exclusive.[163]

18.184 The human rights commission bill was presented on 5 July 1999.[164] It proposed a commission of nine members, including a president; who was likely to be a High or Supreme Court judge; there would also be a chief executive. Members must have relevant qualifications, though the government is required to have regard to the need to ensure the inclusion of men and women and broadly reflect the nature of Irish society.[165] Human rights – as noted – are defined apparently widely, as emanating from the constitution, or from any international agreement to which the state is a party (though, not being incorporated, they are not justiciable).[166] The functions of the commission are: to review law and practice; to consult with national and international bodies; to make recommendations to the government; to promote understanding and awareness; to conduct enquiries (with the power to send for papers or persons) and publish reports; to apply to appear as *amicus curiae*, or to institute legal proceedings on its own behalf for declaratory relief; and to provide legal assistance to litigants.

18.185 The second stage was not taken in the Dáil until 25 November 1999. The bill did not reappear in Dáil Éireann until 1 March 2000, when the second stage was resumed. Report and final stages were on 10 May 2000, and the bill went to the Seanad on 19 May 2000. It was promulgated on 31 May 2000 as the Human Rights Commission Act 2000. In the joint letter of the prime minister and the taoiseach of 5 May 2000, they had stated that the human rights commission would be established in July 2000. On 20 July 2000, more than two years after the Belfast Agreement, the Irish government announced that the former Supreme Court judge, the 72-year-old Judge Barrington, would preside over the new human rights commission. Donal Barrington, as a junior lawyer in 1959, had written a seminal pamphlet, *Uniting Ireland*. He served as a judge between 1979 and 2000, including the Court of First Instance at Luxembourg in 1989–96. The Irish Council for Civil Liberties, citing the views of 15 human rights NGOs, immediately criticized the appointment for lack of transparency. No other names were announced for the eight commissioners during that month: the minister for justice, equality and law reform stated he would be setting up a high-level selection committee to advise the government.

18.186 While human rights are defined in section 2 of this act as including the rights, liberties or freedoms conferred on or guaranteed by international agreements, in section 11 (legal proceedings instituted by the commission) these human rights must be given the force of law in the state before they are justiciable.

18.187 There seems to have been confusion about this in Dublin in 1998–99. Originally, the department of justice, equality and law reform appears to have

163 *Irish Times*, 28 June 1999.

164 The minister for justice stated the government intended to take full account of the 1993 Paris principles as regards the human rights commission.

165 The explanatory and financial memorandum states: 'members will be drawn from the widest possible background so as to ensure pluralist representation of the social elements involved in the promotion and protection of human rights in the State'. (Note on section 5)

166 The explanatory and financial referendum refers to them as 'perceived rights'.

defined human rights as those in domestic and international law.[167] Heads of a bill were agreed by the government on 10 February 1999. Head 14 (definition of human rights) referred only to domestic law.[168] No reference was made to the Convention.

18.188 The bill was then referred to the joint committee on justice, equality and women's rights (plus the all-party Oireachtas committee on the constitution). The joint committee's report includes at appendix 6 a departmental memorandum on the definition of human rights and incorporation of the Convention, which had been requested by the joint committee. The memorandum, citing article 29.6 of BNH, favoured only Irish-law rights, arguing that the attorney general (the adviser of the government in matters of law and legal opinion under article 30) had the responsibility to take account of international human rights obligations. Under 'related issues', the memorandum referred to giving effect to international instruments, other than through legislation – presumably by administrative means.

18.189 The definition was attacked by members of the human rights community, who gave evidence to the committee on 8 April 1999:[169] 'There are no international human rights instruments which have been given the force of law within the State at present, therefore, that is meaningless.'[170] The committee recommended the wider definition of human rights: 'this would permit the Commission to act as an advocate in relation to the development of the concept of human rights in Irish law ... the difficulties referred to arising from the fact that this might include rights contained in international instruments which are neither cognisable nor justiciable before Irish Courts at present would not arise in practice as the Commission could be expected to have regard to existing Irish domestic law where this is appropriate to the discharge of its functions.'

18.190 The response of the department was to use both definitions, with the effect explained above that it is the narrower definition which contains the meaning of human rights. A further complication was added by the minister towards the end of his speech on 25 November 1999: 'the issue of human rights is about much more than law in the pure legal sense. As a concept, it has more to do with the natural law, it is transcendent. Human rights are not just what international rules in conventions, treaties or agreements say they are.'[171]

18.191 At report stage, the labour party proposed an amendment (based on an

167 The source is Michael Farrell, giving evidence to the joint committee on justice, equality and women's rights on proposals for legislation by the minister for justice, equality and law reform for a human rights commission bill on 8 April 1999, *Report*, appendix 2: http://www.irlgov.ie/committees-99.

168 'for the purposes of this Bill, the term "human rights" shall be taken to mean the human rights and fundamental freedoms guaranteed by the Constitution or embodied in international human rights instruments which have been given the force of law in the State, or such other international human rights instruments as may be prescribed by the Minister by order under this Head to which the State is or may become a party, the provisions of which have been given the force of law in the State.'

169 The organizations who gave evidence were: Amnesty International; the Combat Poverty Agency; the Free Legal Advice Centres; the Irish Council for Civil Liberties, Pavée Point.

170 Michael Farrell, of the Irish Council for Civil Liberties.

171 Dáil Éireann, *Official Report*.

earlier proposal at committee stage) whereby the state would, within six months of enactment, ratify four international agreements. The minister for justice, equality and law reform resisted the amendment, by arguing that the doctrine of separation of powers in the constitution precluded the legislature from instructing the executive: 'Ireland, in so far as the adoption of international treaties and obligations is concerned, takes a dual approach because of the effect of Article 15 ..., which provides that exclusive power for making laws for the State is vested in the Oireachtas.'

18.192 The second additional commitment goes to the heart of the Irish government's involvement in Northern Ireland. As noted in Chapter 17, the second paragraph 5 of Strand Three refers to a 'special interest'.

18.193 This can be traced from the 1985 Anglo-Irish Agreement. In the preamble, reference was made to the two major traditions (unionism and nationalism), but also to the two communities in Northern Ireland; while these are best defined ethnically, using the religious labels, protestant and catholic, there is a relationship between the concepts. Thus, the term nationalist community is used in article 7(c), with reference to making the security forces more acceptable. Elsewhere, in articles 4(c) and 5(c), the term minority community – meaning the catholics – is used. In article 4(c), the Irish government is permitted to put forward views and proposals on the modalities of bringing about devolution, 'in so far as they relate to the interests of the minority community'. Given the no derogation from sovereignty in article 2(b), this must be some sort of guarantor role. Even though statute law would have difficulty with a concept of a minority community[172] (as would involuntary members), in international law it is possible to provide for such relationships. Similarly, in article 5(c), the Irish government – in the eventuality of devolution not being possible – is permitted to put forward views on proposals for major legislation and on major policy issues, 'where the interests of the minority community are significantly or especially affected'.

18.194 The 1985 Anglo-Irish Agreement – I submit – is not prototypical of the emerging international law on minorities.[173] This is because the guarantor role coexisted with a territorial claim (clarified by the Irish courts in the first five years of the agreement). Such a role may be an alternative to such a claim; the former is not a legitimate extension of the latter.

18.195 The 1966 international covenant on civil and political rights, ratified by the United Kingdom[174] and by the Irish state,[175] provided for minority rights in article 27: 'In those States in which ethnic, religious or linguistic minorities exist, persons belonging to such minorities shall not be denied the right, in community with the other members of their group, to enjoy their own culture, to profess and practise their own religion, or to use their own language.'

172 The terms 'protestant community' and 'roman catholic community' are used in article 4(1) of the Fair Employment and Treatment (Northern Ireland) Order 1998; however, this is in the context only of affirmative action.

173 As suggested by Clive R. Symmons, 'The Anglo-Irish Agreement and International Precedents: a unique experiment in inter-state co-operation on minority rights', *Irish Jurist*, XXII, n.s., part I, summer 1987, p. 71.

174 In 1976.

175 In 1990.

18.196 The protection of national minorities was addressed in the 1993 Vienna declaration,[176] made by the heads of state and government at the first summit of the Council of Europe. Two conditions were laid down: assuring the protection of the rights of persons belonging to national minorities within the rule of law; respecting the territorial integrity and the national sovereignty of States. The declaration stressed the importance of bilateral agreements protecting national minorities. Close cooperation with the high commissioner for national minorities of the Conference on Security and Cooperation in Europe (CSCE)[177] was promised. The council of ministers of the Council of Europe was instructed to inter alia assist with bilateral treaties, draft a framework convention and finally draft a protocol to the Convention.

18.197 The framework convention for the protection of national minorities (Framework Convention) was done at Strasbourg on 1 February 1995. The United Kingdom and Irish states were signatories. The United Kingdom ratified the Framework Convention on 15 January 1998 (in time for the Belfast Agreement). The Irish state ratified – on foot of the obligation entered into at Castle Buildings – on 7 May 1999, 13 months later. The phrase as quickly as possible had been added to the MDP, most likely at the behest of unionists.

18.198 The Framework Convention – a model for the Irish government's special interest in Northern Ireland vis a vis the minority community – is the Council of Europe's response to the problem of national minorities. Article 1 states that the protection of national minorities forms an integral part of the international protection of human rights, and is thus part of international cooperation. Article 3(1) allows every member of a national minority 'the right freely to choose to be treated or not to be treated as such'. Article 4(2) provides for full and effective equality between persons belonging to a national minority and those belonging to the majority, in all areas of economic, social, political and cultural life. Article 5(1) refers to maintaining and developing culture, and preserving the essential elements of identity, namely religion, language, traditions and cultural heritage. Article 17 allows national minorities to establish and maintain free and peaceful contacts across frontiers with persons lawfully in other states. Article 18 deals with bilateral and multilateral agreements, in particular between neighbouring states. And article 21 prohibits any act contrary to the fundamental principles of international law, in particular sovereign equality, territorial integrity and political independence.

18.199 In – particularly post-communist – Europe, there have been a number of attempts to deal with national minorities in bilateral agreements.[178] One

176 The signatories included Lord Mackay of Clashfern, the lord chancellor, and Albert Reynolds TD, the Irish taoiseach.

177 Document of the Copenhagen meeting of the conference on the human dimension, 29 June 1990, paras. (30)–(39), 29 ILM 1305 (1990). See also, charter of Paris for a new Europe and supplementary document to give effect to certain provisions of the charter, Paris, 21 November 1990 (supplementary document, II.B), 30 ILM 190 (1991).

178 An important bilateral agreement, following the collapse of East Germany, was the 1990 border agreement between Germany and Poland: 31 ILM 1292 (1992). This did not deal with minorities. And it did make the border permanent, on the basis of cold-war agreements between East Germany and Poland. It was part of the CSCE process. Articles 2 and 3 declared the border 'inviolable at any time now or in the future', both states renouncing any

instance is the 1996 Hungary-Romania treaty on understanding, cooperation and good neighbourhood (sic), especially articles 14 and 15 and the annex. Such agreements may be reciprocal (with each state having an interest in a national minority on the other's territory), but more often they are not: the host state benefits from the recognition and respect extended by the neighbouring state.

18.200 The third additional commitment of the Irish government's is enhanced employment equality legislation. This was in the pipeline at the time of the Belfast Agreement, and would seem to anticipate the first of the two proposed directives of the EC (see above) consequent upon the 1997 treaty of Amsterdam.[179]

18.201 An Employment Equality Bill of 1996 had been considered by the Council of State on 1 April 1997. The president (Mary Robinson) referred it to the Supreme Court, which pronounced it unconstitutional on 15 May 1997. There were three reasons: while positive discrimination (?) on the ground of disability was not unconstitutional, the effect of providing treatment and facilities on especially small employers was so; the vicarious criminal liability of employers related to more than regulatory offences; and the acceptance of a certificate by the director of equality investigations as *prima facie* true was contrary to trial in due course of law.[180] The bill went back to the Oireachtas in 1997. The Employment Equality Act 1998 was promulgated on 19 June 1998 (though the commencement order was not to be signed until 18 October 1999). The Act repealed the Anti-Discrimination (Pay) Act 1974, and the Employment Equality Act 1977. It gives protection to employees in the public and private sectors, as well as applicants for employment and training. It makes unlawful discrimination in collective agreements, in advertising and in vocational training. Discrimination is outlawed on nine grounds: gender, age, race, marital status, family status, sexual orientation, religious belief, disability, or membership of the traveller community (three – marital status, family status, membership of the traveller community – are in addition to likely EC law). It also provides for positive action measures on gender, plus people over 50 years, people with disabilities and members of the traveller community. Under the act, the Oireachtas approved the Employment Equality Act, 1998 (section 12) (Church of Ireland College of Education Order), 2000, allowing this institution to reserve 32 places in its first year for protestants. On 8 March 1999, the minister for justice, equality and law reform had announced there would be an Equality Authority (replacing the Employment Equality Agency), and an Office of Director of Equality Investigations. The latter is to hear cases – under both the Employment Equality Act and the Equal Status Act (see below) – and issue legally binding decisions, or mediation settlements. New offices in Clonmel Street in Dublin, with separate entrances, were opened by the taoiseach on 18 October 1999 (one of the guests being Joan Harbison, chief commissioner of the Equality Commission for Northern Ireland). The chairperson and vice chairperson of the

territorial claims for all times. Minority agreements, I submit, while they do not expressly include such border provisions, are nevertheless premised on such a vision – except where they state otherwise.

179 This opinion was given by Niall Crowley, chief executive officer of the Equality Authority, in an interview: *Irish Times*, 18 October 1999.

180 *Employment Equality Bill 1996* [1997] 2 IR 321.

Authority are, respectively, Kate Hayes[181] and Leonard Hurley.[182] It chief executive officer is Niall Crowley. Melanie Pine is director of equality investigations. On 27 June 2000, the equality authority statistics were released: of 4,585 queries since October 1999, 1,784 had related to employment equality issues; the largest categories were gender/sexual harassment/pregnancy and disability. On 27 July 2000, the minister for justice, equality and law reform launched the first annual report of the office of the director of equality investigations. It included the new logo, two intertwined Es, representing two parties in a dispute finding a solution through state intervention.

18.202 The fourth additional commitment is equal status legislation, which relates to non-work areas of possible discrimination (essentially services and property). This too antedated the Belfast Agreement, and would appear to implement the second proposed directive of the EC consequent upon the 1997 treaty of Amsterdam.[183]

18.203 An Equal Status Bill of 1997 had been considered by the Council of State on 6 May 1997. The president (Mary Robinson) referred it to the Supreme Court, where, on 19 June 1997, the chief justice ruled there was no justiciable issue. Two provisions – the vicarious criminal liability of employers, and certification by the director of equality investigations – were repugnant to the constitution, and there was therefore no presumption of constitutionality. This did not make the bill unconstitutional. A new Equal Status Bill was published on 19 April 1999. The minister for justice, equality and law reform promised on 18 October 1999 that it would be enacted and brought into operation in the first half of 2000. It was sent to the president for signature on 19 April 2000. On 27 June 2000, the minister for justice, equality and law reform announced that he had set a target of October 2000 for commencement. The bill is necessary to allow the state to ratify the United Nations convention on the elimination of all forms of racial discrimination, and lift its reserve on the United Nations convention on the elimination of all forms of discrimination against women. 'The basic principle underlying the legislation', according to the minister, 'is people should be judged on their merits as individuals rather than by reference to the group to which they belong'.[184] It covers the nine grounds of the Employment Equality Act 1998, plus colour, nationality and national or ethnic origin. Anti-discrimination cases (other than registered clubs) will be dealt with by the Director of Equality Investigations. The Equality Authority will deal also with equal status matters.

18.204 The fifth and final additional commitment – added to the MDP – is respect for the different traditions in Ireland. Given that BNH has been described as 'a nationalist constitution',[185] and the Irish government which signed the Belfast Agreement had a policy of representing northern nationalists only, this must be a reference to the unionist tradition, largely but not exclusively located in Northern

181 Chair of the Employment Equality Agency.

182 The members are Shane Broderick; Noreen Byrne; Dr Anne Clune; Carol Fawsitt; Thomas McCann; Anne Arthur-O'Brien; Ultan Courtney and Marie Moynihan (IBEC); plus two ICTU nominees.

183 This opinion was given by Niall Crowley, chief executive officer of the Equality Authority, in an interview: *Irish Times*, 18 October 1999.

184 Press release, 19 April 1999.

Ireland. Its appearance in the Belfast Agreement may be attributed to the unionist parties at Castle Buildings.

18.205 As noted above, this obligation would most likely require respect for Ulster unionist commitment to the 1688–89 bill of rights (if not the 1700–1 act of settlement), insofar as it exists among the majority community in Northern Ireland.[186]

18.206 The Irish government has specified two particular projects, which it believes discharge this particular obligation. One, the memorial to Irish soldiers killed in the First World War, which was unveiled by the United Kingdom and Irish heads of state at Messines in late 1998. Two, the development of the site of the battle of the Boyne, which is in the Republic of Ireland, as part of the state millennium programme. This is being done in consultation with elements of the Orange Order.

Subheading: A Joint Committee

18.207 This proposed body has no legal existence, in domestic or international law. It remains to be seen whether and when it is practically achieved. Its inclusion here suggests nationalism[187] rather than human rights internationalism.

[9.] *10.* **It is envisaged that there would be a joint committee of representatives of the two Human Rights Commissions, North and South, as a forum for consideration of human rights issues in the island of Ireland. The joint committee will consider, among other matters, the possibility of establishing a charter, open to signature by all democratic political parties, reflecting and endorsing agreed measures for the protection of the fundamental rights of everyone living in the island of Ireland.**

18.208 'It is envisaged that there would be' is not the language of international or municipal law. However, this is contradicted to some extent by the beginning of the second sentence: 'The joint committee will consider'.

18.209 The Belfast Agreement is legally a treaty. The MPA is Annex 1 of the BIA. The two states parties are bound in international law to fulfil their obligations under the agreement. However, there is no agreement here to create a joint committee, which would have to be done as an international organization. It is left by the two governments to the two bodies; the word 'forum', which resembles the Strands One and Two forums, is suggestive of this.

18.210 Under section 69(10) of the NIA 1998, the NIHRC (in Northern Ireland) has the function, which means either a power or a duty,[188] to do all that it can to ensure the establishment of the joint committee. Do all that it can is because the NIHRC, a Northern Ireland body created under the NIA 1998, has no jurisdiction in the Republic of Ireland. The human rights commission bill, presented on 5 July 1999, enacted in 2000, listed as one of the functions of

185 *McGimpsey v Ireland* [1988] IR 567, 583 per Barrington J.
186 The former, however, contains four references to the fate of protestants under James II.
187 Caoimhghin Ó Caoláin, Dáil Éireann, *Official Report*, 25 November 1999.
188 Section 98(1).

the southern body, to take whatever action is necessary to establish and participate in the joint committee.[189]

18.211 'a joint commmittee of representatives of the two Human Rights Commissions, North and South', makes absolutely no provisions. This joint committee is equivalent to any relationship the NIHRC (in Northern Ireland) might choose to have with any similar body, including in Great Britain, if one were to be established there, or with another member state of the European Union.[190]

18.212 The NIHRC (in Northern Ireland) has major implications for the goal of a human rights commission in the United Kingdom. There was no such commitment in the manifesto of the labour party in 1997. The white paper, *Bringing Rights Home*, suggested that, if parliament establishes a human rights committee, one of its main tasks might be to conduct an enquiry into whether a human rights commission is needed and how it should operate. The government stated it was not opposed to a non-statutory, privately financed body, but it could not be given the functions of existing equality bodies.[191]

18.213 If the NIHRC (in Northern Ireland) concentrates inordinately upon this joint committee, it will be less able to nurture a statutory United Kingdom body; it will be seen as an 'Irish' organization only. If, on the other hand, the NIHRC establishes good relations with legal and other interests in Scotland, England and Wales, then any achievements in Northern Ireland will be proclaimed in the United Kingdom debate.

18.214 'a forum for consideration of human rights issues in the island of Ireland' makes the joint committee little more than a talking shop; this would surely be achieved naturally without this paragraph.

18.215 The second sentence contains one instance of human rights issues, which is to be considered by the joint committee: the idea of a charter. As noted above, a charter, or covenant, is contained in the 1995 *Framework Documents*, related apparently to the misunderstood list of rights in the 1993 *Downing Street Declaration*. In 1993, and 1995, the United Kingdom government was opposed to incorporation of the Convention. So were the Irish governments of the time (though perhaps for different reasons). The charter was a human rights gesture, of no legal import.

18.216 The first point changed with the election of the labour government in 1997; the second surely with the Irish government's obligations under the first paragraph 9 above. It is therefore difficult to see what life is left in the charter idea. It was always a poor substitute for the proper protection of human rights. It can have no legal effect, and would seem to exist in the Belfast Agreement as simply another instance of sweeping up ideas of the 1990s. At best, it amounts to political endorsement by democratic parties of the human rights protection created otherwise. It is not clear whether the agreed measures (drawn up presumably by the joint committee) would be the same as, or more, than provisions legislated by Westminster and provided for in BNH (assuming incorporation of the Convention into the constitution).

189 Section 8(h).

190 The commission in the Republic is given the express function of consulting with national or international bodies or agencies (section 8(b)).

191 Cm 3782, October 1997, pp. 14–15.

Subheading: [Victims of Violence and Reconciliation] ***Reconciliation and Victims of Violence***

18.217 This subheading had a very different meaning in the MDP. It implied that the victims of violence (or their families) were required to engage in reconciliation. Altering the order makes the first paragraphs 11 to 13 about reconciliation, in which the victims of violence are to be remembered (as is clear from the first sentence of the first paragraph 11). However, though a new paragraph was added to the MDP (the first paragraph 12), the logical structure of this part still remains victims followed by reconciliation.

[10.] ***11.*** **The participants believe** ***that*** **it is essential to acknowledge and address the suffering of the victims of violence as a necessary element of reconciliation. [Sufficient resources, including statutory funding as necessary, should be allocated to victims' treatment and support programmes.]** ***They look forward to the results of the work of the Northern Ireland Victims Commission.***

18.218 The first sentence puts the victims of violence first, and makes them the object of reconciliation. The concept of victim would seem to include, not just a surviving casualty, but the relatives of those injured or killed.[192] There is nothing here to distinguish the victims of terrorist organizations or the security forces, as is correct for a victim-focused reconciliation. Reconciliation implies drawing a line under history, declining effectively to pursue the perpetrators of the original crimes.[193] This is consistent with the Prisoners section, and also with that on Decommissioning.

18.219 The MDP envisaged statutory funding for victims' treatment and support. This was deleted and replaced with a reference to the Northern Ireland Victims' Commission. However, the question of statutory funding is taken up in the following paragraph. The failure to mention the Victims' Commission suggests its existence may have been unknown to the Irish and United Kingdom drafters of the MDP.

18.220 This commission comprised Sir Kenneth Bloomfield KCB, former head of the Northern Ireland civil service. It had been announced on 24 October 1997, by the secretary of state (with the encouragement of the prime minister). The victims were to include 'those who had died or been injured in the service of the community'. The terms of reference were: 'those who have become victims in the last thirty years as a consequence of events in Northern Ireland'. Sir Kenneth worked alone during the last months of the Castle Buildings talks. His report was presented to the secretary of state on 29 April 1998, and published the following month by the NIO under the title, *We will remember them.*

18.221 The victims' commissioner referred to the 'painful privilege' he had been given, a reference to both the suffering he heard about directly and indirectly and the courage of the victims. He advised the secretary of state to consider not only his recommendations, but also the community's reaction to them. To the original idea of a new memorial, he countered with an emphasis upon areas

192 Sir Kenneth Bloomfield refers to living victims associated with the dead: *We will remember them*, May 1999, paragraph 2.10–13.

of policy and service provision, and possible memorial schemes distinct from physical projects. Twelve of the twenty recommendations were of a practical nature, including that victims must be as a barest minimum as well served as former prisoners (released under the Prisoners section).[194] The possibility of a truth and reconciliation commission at some stage in the future was mentioned. Similarly, a Northern Ireland memorial – a beautiful and useful building, with a peaceful and harmonious garden – should be considered at an appropriate time (Sir Kenneth refused to make any assumptions about the definitive end of the troubles.)

18.222 Sir Kenneth Bloomfield raised the question of the disappeared (and exiles).[195] The disappeared are victims of republican terrorist organizations, whose bodies have never been retrieved. There are thought to be as many as 20 disappeared, though only 15 have been identified. The killings by the IRA took place in Northern Ireland between 1972 and 1981 (though there was one by another republic group in France in 1986). The victims include members of the IRA, one army officer and a widowed mother of ten children from Belfast.

18.223 In *We shall remember them*, the victims' commissioner appealed for information on the disappeared: 'I realise that many of those in possession of such information may fear the risk of inculpating themselves, but I am sure cast-iron arrangements could be made, if necessary through trusted intermediaries, to report such information anonymously and in confidence.'[196]

18.224 On 29 March 1999, during talks at Hillsborough, outside Belfast on decommissioning, the IRA announced that it had located the graves of nine of its victims (less than half of the disappeared).[197] The information would only be handed over to the authorities, if the perpetrators were granted immunity. It was admitted that the NIO and the Irish government had been considering a response.[198]

18.225 On 27 April 1999, at Dublin, the two governments signed an agreement establishing the Independent Commission for the Location of Victims' Remains (the Commission).[199] It was to enter into force on 28 May 1999 (though the secretary of state and the justice minister were only due to exchange notifications that morning). The objective of the Commission was to facilitate the location of the remains of victims of violence, by receiving and disclosing information.[200]

193 An exception is the inquiry by Lord Saville of Newdigate into the events of 'Bloody Sunday' in Derry in 1972, which was announced by the labour government on 29 January 1998 – under pressure from the Irish government – before the Belfast Agreement (Dermot P.J. Walsh, *Bloody Sunday and the rule of law in Northern Ireland*, Dublin 2000, p. 296).

194 Sir Kenneth Bloomfield went on to chair the independent review of criminal injuries compensation, reporting on 2 July 1999. The secretary of state gave his response to this in parliament on 26 July 2000. He accepted the majority of the 64 recommendations, with some amendments. A new scheme was promised for 2002.

195 Both issues had been mentioned in the Mitchell report of 22 January 1996 (paragraph 52).

196 Paragraph 5.38.

197 *An Phoblacht*, 1 April 1999.

198 Statement of secretary of state, 29 March 1999, Northern Ireland Information Service: http://www.nio.gov.uk.

199 Ireland No. 7 (1999), Cm 4344.

200 Article 3(1).

18.226 On 26 May 1999, the Northern Ireland (Location of Victims' Remains) Act 1999 received royal assent; it entered into force on 28 May 1999. The Oireachtas enacted similarly the Criminal Justice (Location of Victims' Remains) Act 1999. (This act purported to give the commission an Irish-language name – An Coimisiún Neamhspleách um Aimsiú Taisi Iospartach – even though this was not provided for in the international agreement.) Both legislatures granted effectively immunity. There are major restrictions on the admissibility in any future criminal proceedings of evidence acquired in the location, searching for and recovery of remains for burial by the victims' relatives. Section 6 of the United Kingdom act allows the police to enter and search premises. This power had to be granted, because existing powers in Northern Ireland and Great Britain applied only to entry and search in the course of a criminal investigation.[201]

18.227 Sir Kenneth Bloomfield was appointed the United Kingdom member of the Commission; his Irish opposite number was John Wilson, a former tánaiste, who had performed a similar role in the Republic of Ireland.[202] The Northern Ireland memorial fund (see below) had written earlier to the families of the nine identified disappeared, offering them £4,000 each to help with burial expenses.[203]

18.228 At dawn on 28 May 1999, a body in a coffin was found unburied in a graveyard just over the border from Northern Ireland. Irish police started digging the following day, at six identified sites in Counties Louth, Monaghan, Meath and Wicklow.[204] No bodies were found as expected that weekend. After a month, one of the sites gave up what were proved subsequently to be the remains of two men. The search for the other named six victims was suspended – effectively cancelled – after seven weeks (though there were reports subsequently that digging might be resumed).[205] Digging was resumed the following year, for three weeks in May, but no further bodies were found.[206]

18.229 The searches for the disappeared delayed the report of the Republic's victims' commissioner, John Wilson, *A place and a name*. It was published eventually on 5 August 1999; it recommended three months for consultations, and a further three months for the department of justice, equality and law reform to draw up an implementation plan.

18.230 However, on 29 September 1999, the taoiseach acted on two recommendations urgently, dealing with unsolved crimes in the Republic of Ireland. He announced that an eminent legal person – subsequently identified as the outgoing lord chief justice, Liam Hamilton – would investigate privately the Dublin/Monaghan bombings of 1974, the Dundalk bombings and the case of Seamus Ludlow. On 12 October 1999, the minister for justice, equality and law reform, answering questions in the Dáil, stated that a public enquiry had not been ruled out following the eminent legal person's report.

201 A point made in the explanatory notes to the bill, provided by the Northern Ireland Office.

202 The review was announced on 21 May 1998. Reference was made to the family of the late Detective Garda Frank Hand. The terms of reference are given in Dáil Éireann, *Official Report*, 2 July 1998 (speech of minister for justice).

203 Press release, 17 May 1999: http://www.nio.gov.uk.

204 Press release, 4 June 1999.

12. *It is recognised that victims have a right to remember as well as to contribute to a changed society. The achievement of a peaceful and just society would be the true memorial to the victims of violence. The participants particularly recognise that young people from areas affected by the troubles face particular difficulties and will support the development of special community-based initiatives based on international best practice. The provision of services that are supportive and sensitive to the needs of victims will also be a critical element and that support will need to be channelled through both statutory and community-based voluntary organisations facilitating locally-based self-help and support networks. This will require the allocation of sufficient resources, including statutory funding as necessary, to meet the needs of victims and to provide for community-based support programmes.*

18.231 This paragraph was added to the MDP, no doubt to compensate for the sentence removed from the paragraph above. That is now the fifth and last sentence of this paragraph. The first sentence includes the idea of victims' right to remember (presumably within the context of reconciliation). The second sentence states that a true memorial to all the victims would be a peaceful and just society. The third sentence introduces a further idea; that young people in troubled areas are in a sense victims also. The fourth sentence anticipates the fifth, and is concerned with practical help to victims and their families.

18.232 The secretary of state accepted Sir Kenneth Bloomfield's report of 29 April 1999.

18.233 She had appointed one of her junior ministers, the Rt. Hon. Adam Ingram MP, minister for victims. It was the first time this responsibility had been accepted by the NIO.[207] In June 1998, the minister for victims established the victims liaison unit, located in the Stormont House Annexe, to support the implementation of the Bloomfield report. On 1 September 1998, he anounced the early release information scheme; victims and their families would be informed about the release of prisoners under the Belfast Agreement.[208] The United Kingdom government allocated £5 million to implement the 20 recommendations in the Bloomfield report. It went out to consultation on 30 June 1998, the period being extended to 30 November 1998. In January 1999, the parties in the assembly each appointed a spokesperson for victims. On 28 June 2000, Adam Ingram MP launched an information pack for families of homicide victims (seemingly non-terrorist murders), at the headquarters of Victim Support Northern Ireland. It had been prepared by inter alia the RUC and NIO. Significantly, the minister of state referred to 'in the event of further outbreaks of politically

205 *Belfast Telegraph*, 2 September 1999; *Observer*, 23 January 2000. The utilitarian calculus is: three sets of relatives may grieve properly; 12 – and possibly 17 – sets of relatives have had their hopes raised and dashed.

206 Victims Liaison Unit, *Newsletter*, issue 3, May 2000.

207 Adam Ingram talked about inheriting a blank sheet from the previous administration: House of Commons, *Hansard*, 6th series, 335, 242, 13 July 1999.

208 This was required under section 15 of the Northern Ireland (Sentences) Act 1998.

motivated crime, although he added that there were additional organisations which dealt specifically with this issue.'[209]

18.234 The sum of £1 million was devoted to a Northern Ireland memorial fund, announced on 23 December 1998. The idea originated with Sir Kenneth, for children and young people affected by the death of a parent. However, this was expanded to become a living memorial for victims/survivors. The fund is to seek donations in Northern Ireland, and from outside. It is chaired by Prof George Bain, president and vice-chancellor of Queen's University. There are 13 other trustees, including the spouses of the two Nobel laureates: the Rt. Hon. David Trimble MP; and John Hume MP – Daphne Trimble and Pat Hume.

> [11.] *13.* **The participants recognise and value the work being done by many organisations to develop reconciliation and mutual understanding and respect between *and within* communities and traditions, in Northern Ireland and between North and South, and they see such work as having a vital role in consolidating peace and political agreement. Accordingly, they pledge their continuing support to such organisations and will positively examine the case for enhanced financial assistance for the work of reconciliation. *An essential aspect of the reconciliation process is the promotion of a culture of tolerance at every level of society, including initiatives to facilitate and encourage integrated education and mixed housing.***

18.235 This third and final paragraph follows the original structure: victims of violence followed by reconciliation. The first sentence endorses programmes of reconciliation and mutual understanding. The participants – the political parties (with or without the two governments) – see reconciliation as having a role in consolidating peace and political agreement. 'Within communities and traditions' was added to the MDP.

18.236 More work has been done within Northern Ireland, than between there and the Republic of Ireland. It has been a response to the troubles; and has not, on its own, stopped the violence.

18.237 The second sentence is a promise of continuing funding. This is certainly an undertaking on behalf of the parties in the negotiations. Depending upon the meaning of partiticipants, it could be argued that the two governments also made this commitment.

18.238 The third sentence would appear to have been added by a centrist party. Most of the other parties would not object to a culture of tolerance, but integrated education and mixed housing are not mainstream causes in Northern Ireland.

Subtitle: ECONOMIC, SOCIAL AND CULTURAL ISSUES

18.239 This second subsection of the Rights, Safeguards and Equality of Opportunity section is even more discursive than the first one. In the MDP and the FA (plus the published version distributed in Northern Ireland), the section heading was repeated above the subtitle, contrary to the contents page. This gave the impression that this second subsection had something to do with rights. This is

209 Northern Ireland Information Service, 28 June 2000.

reinforced by the subtitle, which is evocative of the (first) 1966 international covenant on economic, social and cultural rights.[210] This subsection, however, has little to do with rights. The word issues is used, one must infer deliberately. There is a great deal on economic policy (the second paragraphs 1 and 2), very little on social issues (the second paragraph 2(iii)), and the cultural provision (the second paragraphs 3–5) is dominated seemingly by the Irish language. The only legal text – an international instrument – is that referred to in the second paragraph 4.[211]

1. ***Pending the devolution of powers to a new Northern Ireland Assembly,* [T]*the* British Government will pursue broad policies for sustained economic growth and stability in Northern Ireland, and [will reduce] *for promoting* social [ex]*in*clusion, [pending devolution of powers to a new Northern Ireland Assembly] *including in particular community developmenrt and the advancement of women in public life.***

18.240 This relates only to the period before devolution, the transition – which came to an end on 2 December 1999. As a statement of continuing United Kingdom government policy, it has little relevance to a devolution agreement. London intended presumably to pursue broad policies for sustained economic growth, and for promoting social inclusion, regardless of the Belfast Agreement. The additions to the MDP – community development, and the advancement of women in public life – are presumably aspects of continuing United Kingdom policy. There is no evidence that London did anything different as regards Northern Ireland after May 1998 as a result of this second paragraph 1.

2. ***Subject* [In the light of reactions] to *the* public consultation currently under way, the British Government will make rapid progress with:**
   (i) **a new regional development strategy for Northern Ireland, for consideration in due course by a *the* [sic] [new Northern Ireland] Assembly, [which would go beyond conventional land use and planning issues] [•] tackling the problems of a divided society and social cohesion *in urban, rural and border areas*[;], [•] [• generating a dynamic region and promoting sustainable developments;] [•] protecting and enhancing the environment[;], [•] [•deciding on major new development;] [•] producing new approaches to transport issues[;], [•] strengthening the physical infrastructure of the region[;], [•] developing the advantages and resources of rural areas[;] and [•] rejuvenating major urban centres;**

210 If this part dealt with economic, social and cultural rights, the Irish government would be at risk of embarrassment. According to a recent report of the UN committee on economic, social and cultural rights (referred to by Mary Robinson, the UN high commissioner for human rights), the 1966 covenant had not been incorporated fully in Irish law, it was cited rarely before the courts, and article 40.1 was inconsistent with principles of non discrimination (*Irish Times*, 17 May 1999).

211 The preamble to the Charter derives the right to use a regional or minority language from the covenant on civil and political rights (not that on economic, social and cultural rights), and from the spirit of the Convention; article 27 of the civil and political rights covenant deals with ethnic, religious or linguistic minorities.

(ii) **a new economic development strategy for Northern Ireland, for consideration in due course by a** ***the*** **[sic] [new Northern Ireland] Assembly, which would provide for short and medium term economic planning linked as appropriate to the regional development strategy[.]*; and***

(iii) **measures on employment equality[,] includ[ing]*ed in the recent White Paper ("Partnership for Equality") and covering*[:] [•] the extension** ***and strengthening*** **of anti-discrimination legislation [to the supply of goods, facilities and services;], [•] [• the strengthening of other aspects of existing fair employment laws;] [•] [• at the earliest possible time,] a review of the national security aspects of the present fair employment legislation** ***at the earliest possible time*****[;], [•] a new more focused Targeting Social Need initiative [to combat deprivation defined objectively;] and [•] a range of measures aimed at combating unemployment[, in particular youth and long-term unemployment,] and [at] progressively eliminating the differential in** ***un*****employment rates between the two communities by targeting objective need.**

18.241 This paragraph was significantly amended at Castle Buildings, and shortened. Nevertheless, it remains relatively long. It binds the United Kingdom government, subject to consultation then under way.

18.242 Subparagraphs (i) and (ii) deal respectively with regional development and economic development. Under direct rule, these were the ministerial reponsibility of the NIO. The three Northern Ireland departments of regional development, environment and enterprise, trade and investment became responsible with devolution. The obligations of the London government under subparagraphs (i) and (ii) then ceased. This is clear from the references to the assembly. These two paragraphs contain no policy commitments, and resemble departmental mission statements. Important phrases were removed from the regional development strategy subparagraph. No doubt, the programme of government referred to in paragraphs 20 and 24 of Strand One, and in the Pledge of Office in Annex A, will contain the results of any work carried out by the United Kingdom government between 10 April 1998 and 2 December 1999.

18.243 Subparagraph (iii), in contrast, contains a general commitment to develop policy in the area of employment equality. This is binding upon the United Kingdom government, but only to the extent that responsibility for equality was not devolved under the NIA 1998.[212] The white paper, *Partnership for Equality*, Cm 3890, March 1998, has been referred to above in the first paragraphs 3 and 6. It is referred to in this subparagraph expressly. The reference at the beginning of this paragraph to public consultation also applies to employment equality measures. This means that these policies were already under consideration, and that the United Kingdom was reserving its position here until after consultation. Four commitments applied conditionally to the transition; only the second – involving national security[213] – would appear to apply after devolution.

212 Excepted: ss 74(5), 76 & 78; reserved: ss 73, 74(3)–(4), 75, 77(1)–(2) & (4)–(8), schs. 8 & 9; transferred: ss 74(1)–(2), 77(3)–(4).

213 NIA 1998, sch. 2, para. 17.

18.244 The first two commitments in the MDP were combined into one, and amount to the extension and strengthening of anti-discrimination legislation. However, there is no express commitment to cover the supply of goods, facilities and services; this may be because it had been promised in the white paper then out to consultation.[214] Section 76 of the NIA 1998 – dealing with the public authorities defined in subsection (7) – makes unlawful discrimination against a person or class of persons on the ground of religious belief or political opinion. This widens the anti-discrimination by public authorities provision in section 19 of the NICA 1973. Section 76 of the NIA 1998 is an excepted matter,[215] and remains a responsibility of the central government.

18.245 Section 76(4) excludes discrimination caught by the Fair Employment (Northern Ireland) Act 1976 (just as section 19(4) of the NICA 1973 did). This was reenacted (and expanded) in the Fair Employment and Treatment (Northern Ireland) Order 1998, SI 1998/3162 on 16 December 1998 (which also amended the Sex Discrimination (Northern Ireland) Order 1976, SI 1976/1042 and the Race Relations (Northern Ireland) Order 1997, SI 1997/869). These orders are considered to be part of the Northern Ireland statute book. The Fair Employment and Treatment (Northern Ireland) Order 1998 deals further with the ECNI in part II (given it is the successor, under section 74(2) of the NIA 1998, to the Fair Employment Commission for Northern Ireland). The fact that the United Kingdom government decided to proceed under paragraph 1 of schedule 1 of the NIA 1974 suggests that anti-discrimination legislation dealing with public and private employment (and the ground of religious belief or political opinion), plus the provision of goods, facilities and services, was envisaged as a matter for the assembly. These responsibilities have not been transferred under the NIA 1998. However, the ECNI – under sections 73, 74(3)–(4), 75, 77(1)–(2) and (4)–(8) plus schedules 8 and 9 – is a reserved matter. And, this may become a transferred matter, under section 4(2)–(3), with cross-community support in the assembly. Alternatively, under section 8(b), the assembly may legislate on a reserved matter with the consent of the secretary of state.

18.246 The second commitment was a review of the national security aspects of the then existing fair employment legislation: the Fair Employment (Northern Ireland) Acts 1976 and 1989. National security was in the context of alleged discrimination by public authorities on the ground of religious belief or political opinion (rather than employment discrimination as such). Under section 42 of the 1976 act, the secretary of state was able to intervene effectively in any relevant proceedings by providing a defence: the act specified in the certificate was done for the purpose of safeguarding national security or protecting public safety or public order.

18.247 This had been criticized by SACHR in its report, *Employment Equality: building for the future*, Cm 3684, June 1997, 87–8. SACHR, however, did not propose the solution adopted in the NIA 1998, which would be endorsed by Lord Lester of Herne Hill QC.

214 This was recommended by the SACHR report, *Employment Equality: Building for the Future*, Cm 3684, June 1997, pp. 80–1. Premises were also included. The government promised to extend the law against religious discrimination to goods, facilities, services and premises in the white paper in March 1998: *Partnership for Equality*, Cm 3890, March 1998, pp. 43–4.

215 Sch. 2, para. 22(f).

18.248 Section 42 of the 1976 act was, at the time of the Belfast Agreement, under consideration in a case before the ECtHR at Strasbourg. The applicants – catholic contractors – had failed to secure building work from public authorities, the government rejecting their tenders on – as emerged after complaint – grounds of national security. On 8 April 1997, the United Kingdom government had failed before the European commission of human rights. On 10 July 1998, the ECtHR held, in *Tinnelly and McElduff v United Kingdom* [1998] 27 EHHR 249, that the United Kingdom had violated article 6.1 (a fair and public hearing by an independent and impartial tribunal). The ECtHR was sympathetic to the security considerations at stake, disagreeing simply with an aspect of the section 42 certificates.

18.249 Sections 90–92 of the NIA 1998 (discrimination: certificates by secretary of state) purported to correct the fault in section 42 of the Fair Employment (Northern Ireland) Act 1976. These apply to proceedings under sections 24 and 76 of the NIA 1998.[216] Section 91 and schedule 11 establish a tribunal – the Northern Ireland Act tribunal[217] – to which claimants in proceedings may appeal if the defendant proposes to rely upon a certificate.[218] The chairman, and any deputy chairman, of the tribunal is to be an existing or retired holder of high judicial office.[219] A claimant and his legal representatives may be excluded; in this eventuality, the attorney-general may appoint a Northern Ireland barrister to represent his interests (without being responsible to that party). Further appeal to the Court of Appeal of Northern Ireland may also be possible.

18.250 The inspiration for the Northern Ireland Act tribunal is the Special Immigration Appeals Commission Act 1997 (which extends to Northern Ireland). This set up a commission to hear appeals in immigration cases, where a person had been detained under the Immigration Act 1971 on national security grounds.

18.251 Article 80 of the Fair Employment and Treatment (Northern Ireland) Order 1998, SI 1998/3162 deals further with national security certificates.[220] It applies to proceedings where discrimination is alleged under parts III–V of the order (mainly but not exclusively employment). These are also brought under the Northern Ireland Act tribunal.

18.252 Under sections 91 and 92 of the NIA 1998, the lord chancellor made rules dealing with tribunal procedure on 28 July 1999: Northern Ireland Act Tribunal (Procedure) Rules 1999, SI 1999/2131. These impose a general duty on the tribunal to secure that information is not disclosed, contrary to the interests of national security, public safety or public order or in any other circumstances where disclosure is likely to harm a public interest (rule 3(1)). Upon receiving a notice of appeal through the tribunal, the secretary of state is required to inform the attorney-general, who may then appoint a special advocate (a Northern Ireland barrister) to represent the interests of the appellant, and/or the defendant

216 These sections exclude the Fair Employment (Northern Ireland) Act 1976.

217 Northern Ireland Act Tribunal (Procedure) Rules 1999, SI 1999/2131.

218 Under section 90(4), the secretary of state may also appeal.

219 Paragraph 3(3) of schedule 11.

220 So also do: article 53ZA of the Sex Discrimination (Northern Ireland) Order 1976, SI 1976/1042; article 41A of the Race Relations (Northern Ireland) Order 1997, SI 1997/869.

proposing to rely upon the certificate (if not the secretary of state). The appellant and his (normal) representative may be excluded from the tribunal, and there are restrictions upon the special advocate communicating with the party whose interests he has been appointed to represent (rule 9).

18.253 The third and fourth commitments are again general statements of policy. These bind the United Kingdom government only, during the transition. They are not commitments made on behalf of the assembly.

18.254 The third commitment is a new, more focused targeting social need initiative. A new targeting social need programme (new TSN) was introduced by the NIO during the transition. Draft new TSN action plans were published before devolution, as *Vision into Practice*, the first new TSN annual report, it being left to ministers in the executive to decide their future.

18.255 The fourth commitment includes progressively eliminating the differential in unemployment between the two communities (in the MDP, this was the differential in employment rates). Unfortunately, scholarly analysis in Northern Ireland has tended to be influenced inordinately by political conviction, national and unionist.[221] The argument – on the part of such critics – has tended to be that uneven unemployment is due to past and present (state?) discrimination against catholics, and is therefore correctable by fair employment law and practice. The subparagraph makes reference to a range of measures, without specifying the relationship between combating unemployment generally, and tackling the differential between the two communities. However, an economic hypothesis of a higher rate of population growth of catholics (incontrovertible), combined with catholic out-migration being less responsive to high unemployment (to be measured), has been advanced to explain minority overrepresentation among the unemployed (a phenomenon which has got worse under direct rule when anti-discrimination law and practice has been driven by London).[222] This remains to be scientifically assessed.

18.256 The assembly will no doubt address the differential question, though not necessarily on the basis of this subparagraph. It remains to be seen whether the four-party involuntary coalition in the executive committee will respond the way the NIO has done under pressure from SACHR and the human rights community.

> 3. **All participants recognise the importance of respect, understanding and tolerance in relation to linguistic diversity, *including in Northern Ireland,***

221 The following is an example of a unionist alleging, and a nationalist denying, discrimination: on 26 June 2000, Derek Hussey MLA raised the question of Strabane grammar school, which had been underallocated places seemingly, with the minister of education, Martin McGuinness. The latter replied: 'I do not agree that it is a discriminatory decision ... The situation in Strabane is that grammar school places are available in Strabane, Derry and Omagh, and the general policy parameters have been met within the area.' (Northern Ireland Assembly, *Official Report*, 26 June 2000, p. 265)

222 Graham Gudgin, 'Discrimination against Catholics during the Stormont regime', draft paper (August 1998), p. 18, subsequently published in Patrick J. Roche & Brian Barton, eds, *The Northern Ireland Question: nationalism, unionism and partition*, Aldershot, Hampshire 1999. A similar argument applies to changes in catholic over/under representation in employment: though catholics may benefit disproportionately from new jobs created, a rising catholic population can show this as growing disadvantage. Graham Gudgin's work was mentioned in the assembly: Northern Ireland Assembly, *Official Report*, 6 June 2000, pp. 74–5.

> ***the Irish language, Ulster-Scots and the languages of the various ethnic communities, all of* which *are* [is] part of the cultural wealth of [the people of] the island of Ireland.**

18.257 This is a general commitment to linguistic diversity in both parts of Ireland. While all the participants includes the Northern Ireland political parties, the paragraph is principally an agreement between the two governments; note the 'all'. The MPA, through annex 1, is part of the BIA.

18.258 Linguistic diversity is less of a problem for the United Kingdom state, given its practical experiences in Wales (bilingualism) and Scotland (a minority language) and increasingly in England with ethnic minority languages.

18.259 However, this obligation of the Irish state's in international law comes up against article 8 of BNH. That says nothing about linguistic diversity, or cultural pluralism.[223] Irish is defined as the national language (without any reference to actual people and their linguistic practices), and made the first official language; English is a second official language. There could be – but there are not – other official languages. The Irish government, then, through the BIA, has signed up to one principle in international law (linguistic diversity), while, in its domestic law, it enshrines an entirely different one (not because of the idea of official languages,[224] but because Irish is deemed to be the national language and consequently is the first official language).

18.260 This paragraph must be read with the following one (and indeed with the second paragraph 5). Paragraphs 3 and 4 were originally the one paragraph in the MDP. The changes to the MDP are significant. The European Charter for Regional or Minority Languages (the Charter) was added; however, it was located not in this general paragraph, but in the following particularization (below) of the principle of linguistic diversity in Northern Ireland.

18.261 The European Charter for Regional or Minority Languages was agreed at Strasbourg on 2 October 1992. It entered into force on 1 March 1998. The United Kingdom had (of 28 February 2000) neither signed nor ratified the Charter. Nor had the Irish state. However, the United Kingdom government stated its preparedness to sign, and apparently ratify, the Charter.[225] No such commitment has been evident from the Irish government. The Charter, by virtue of article 1(a)(ii), cannot apply to Irish or English in the Republic of Ireland. However, its ratification – as regards Ulster-Scots (and ethnic minority languages) – is required by this paragraph (read with the paragraph below), and, as regards Ulster-Scots, by the 8 March 1999 supplementary agreement (discussed in Chapter 15 above). At Hillsborough, on 5 May 2000, the United Kingdom government undertook to ratify the Charter by September 2000, and publish an action plan within six months of that date. The Irish government made no such undertaking.

223 There is nothing resembling the original article 44.1.2–3, which recognized the special position of the catholic church but also other minority churches.

224 Another recital of the preamble states: 'Stressing the value of interculturalism and multilingualism and considering that the protection and encouragement of regional or minority languages should not be to the detriment of the official languages and the need to learn them.'

225 House of Commons, *Hansard*, 6th series, 313, 350, 4 June 1998; 318, 603, 4 November 1998.

18.262 The Charter has five parts (the fourth and fifth not being relevant here). Part I is general provisions. Article 1 defines regional or minority languages as 'traditionally used within a given territory of a State by nationals of that State who form a group numerically smaller than the rest'. There is no distinction between a regional and a minority language. Nationals of that state is a condition precedent. A distinction is drawn between territorial and non-territorial languages: the former means the geographical area where the language is 'the mode of expression of a number of people justifying the ... various protective and promotional measures'; the latter, languages that cannot be identified with a particular area.

18.263 Article 2 (undertakings) introduces parts II and III.

18.264 Under article 2(1), part II is applied to all the regional and minority languages spoken within its territory. Part II (article 7 on objectives and principles) distinguishes between territorial and non-territorial languages. As regards the latter, the principles of paragraphs 1–4 are to be applied in a flexible manner. Paragraph 1 outlines nine objectives and principles, to be applied according to the situation of each language. The first is: 'the recognition of the regional or minority language as an expression of cultural wealth'. The seventh is: 'the provision of facilities enabling non-speakers of a regional or minority language living in the area where it is used to learn it if they so desire'. Paragraph 3 refers to the promotion of 'mutual understanding between all the linguistic groups of the country and ... respect, understanding and tolerance in relation to regional or minority languages ... [in] education and training ...'.

18.265 Article 1(2) states that, in respect of a language specified at ratification, each state party will apply a minimum of 35 paragraphs or subparagraphs from part III (including at least three from each of articles 8 and 12, and one from each of articles 9, 10, 11 and 13). The word paragraph would appear to be superfluous; it is a minimum of 35 subparagraphs.

18.266 Part III – articles 8–14 – covers education (8); judicial authorities (9); administrative authorites and public services (10); media (11); cultural activities and facilities (12); economic and social life (13); transfrontier exchanges (14). The seven articles comprise only 19 paragraphs, confirming the point above about the minimum being 35 subparagraphs. Each article has appropriate conditions: according to the situation of each language (used widely), and without prejudice to the teaching of official languages (8); not considered by the judge to hamper the proper administration of justice (9); where the number of users justifies, and as far as reasonably possible (10); to the extent of competence of public authorities (11) and (12). Article 14 (transfrontier exchanges) is particularly appropriate to Ireland. It requires the application or conclusion of bilateral agreements (such as the Belfast Agreement). However, this is where 'the same language is used in identical or similar form'.

18.267 On 4 June 1998 (two months after the Belfast Agreement), the United Kingdom government announced that the Scots language would be recognized under part II. Under part III, Welsh in Wales, Gaelic on Scotland and Irish in Northern Ireland ('at an early date') would be specified.[226] However, on 4 November 1998, the government stated that it proposed to commission

226 House of Commons, *Hansard*, 6th series, 313, 350, 4 June 1998.

independent academic research on whether Ulster-Scots was a language under the Charter.[227] This statement was superseded by the 8 March 1999 supplementary agreement, in which Ulster-Scots was defined as 'the variety of the Scots language traditionally found in parts of Northern Ireland and Donegal'.[228] On 4 June 1999, Paul Murphy, the political development minister, announced that Ulster-Scots would be recognized.

18.268 To this paragraph was added a significant phrase: 'including in Northern Ireland, the Irish language, Ulster-Scots and the languages of the various ethnic communities'. This is at variance with the principle of a national language in the Irish constitution, though the territorial claim was withdrawn upon the entry into force of the BIA. The added text arguably treats Irish, Ulster-Scots and the various ethnic community languages in Northern Ireland with the same esteem. This is certainly consistent with the Charter; one of the recitals of the preamble reads: 'Considering that the protection of the historical regional and minority languages of Europe, some of which are in danger of eventual extinction, contributes to the maintenance and development of Europe's cultural wealth and traditions.' All human culture is valued, even – especially – when threatened with extinction.

18.269 Evidence of this new administrative practice in language policy may be derived from one of the implementation bodies agreed by the First Minister and Deputy First Minister on 18 December 1998,[229] and approved by the Assembly on 18 January 1999: Language (Irish and Ulster-Scots).

18.270 Under one of the supplementary international agreements of 8 March 1999,[230] the two governments agreed to The North/South Language Body. It came into existence on 2 December 1999. It has a name in Irish: An Foras Teanga, and one in Ullans (Ulster-Scots): Tha Boord o Leid.[231] The Irish language agency is based in Dublin, with a regional office in Belfast; the Ullans agency in Belfast, with a regional office in Co. Donegal. This was agreed at the inaugural meeting of the NSMC on 13 December 1999, and reported to the assembly the following day.[232] Provisions for transfer of functions from Northern Ireland and the Republic of Ireland were made respectively under the North/South Co-operation (Implementation Bodies) (Northern Ireland) Order 1999, SI 1999/859 made on 10 March 1999, and the British-Irish Agreement Act 1999, promulgated on 22 March 1999.

18.271 The title, and two translations, indicates that minority languages are being promoted, with parity of esteem between Irish and Ulster-Scots (there are no regional languages in Northern Ireland, or in the Republic of Ireland,[233] and

227 See also an answer from John McFall: House of Commons, *Hansard*, 6th series, 319, 460, 17 November 1998.

228 Annex 2, part 5, paragraph 1.7.

229 New Northern Ireland Assembly, *Report from the First Minister (Designate) and Deputy First Minister (Designate)*, NNIA 6, 18 January 1999, pp. 6 & 25, and NNIA 7, 15 February 1999, Annex 1b.

230 Agreement between the government of the United Kingdom of Great Britain and Northern Ireland and the government of Ireland establishing Implementation Bodies, Cm 4293.

231 Article 1(e).

232 Northern Ireland Assembly, *Official Report*, vol. 4 no. 2 (reissue), p. 21, 14 December 1999.

233 At least in Irish constitutional law.

presumably one or more ethnic community languages could be added). But there is a problem since the Irish government has transferred all its existing Irish language functions to the international organization.[234] This means that the implementation body will have to work under article 8 of BNH in the Republic of Ireland, and, in Northern Ireland, under the Charter.

18.272 This may be aided by the provision in the 18 December 1998 agreement: 'One body, with two separate parts, with the following functions'; the functions are then specified for Irish and Ulster-Scots separately. There is a reference to Ulster-Scots in Northern Ireland, and 'throughout the island'. However, given the legal difference between the two regimes for language protection, two separate parts could have been construed as Irish in the Republic of Ireland under article 8 of BNH (the national language); and Irish and Ulster-Scots in Northern Ireland (plus Ulster-Scots in the Republic) under the Charter.

18.273 This interpretation is reinforced by the decision of the two governments – in delineating the exercise of functions in Annex 2 of the international agreement – to have an Irish language agency under its own chief executive.[235] (There is an Ulster-Scots agency,[236] the principle of language apartheid[237] being managed by having the chairpersons of the two agencies serve as joint chairpersons of the body.[238]) Each agency decides its own title, subject to the implementation body. The working language of the Irish language agency is Irish (subject to the financial memorandum in Annex 2, part 7, paragraph 2.2). There is no equivalent provision for the Ulster-Scots agency.

18.274 An Irish language agency made up of former Republic of Ireland institutions, and operating an Irish language policy (especially in Northern Ireland), will look more like a 26-county body operating in 32 counties than an international organization. The international agreement requires the agency to operate two separate regimes: 'In carrying out the Body's functions, the Irish language agency will have regard to the positions of the Irish language in the two jurisdictions. In Northern Ireland this position will be the British Government's commitments in respect of the Rights, Safeguards and Equality of Opportunity section of the Multi-Party Agreement and any relevant legislation. In Ireland, this position will be the constitutional and legal position of the Irish language, Irish government policy and the measures and practices built up to foster and promote the language.'[239]

18.275 The issue of the Irish language has been raised in the assembly. Though this has no bearing on the nature of the obligations of the United Kingdom state, it may indicate how the executive committee might choose to act. Under section 26 of the NIA 1998, the secretary of state may direct a minister or Northern Ireland department to act – or not to act – to give effect to international obligations.

234 A body to be established in accordance with section 31 of the Education Act 1998 is not provided for: Annex 2, part 5, paragraph 1.2(d).
235 Annex 2, part 5, paragraphs 1.4 & 2.10.
236 Annex 2, part 5, paragraph 1.8.
237 The two agencies will have separate budgets: Annex 2, part 5, paragraph 1.11–12.
238 Annex 2, part 5, paragraph 2.4.
239 Annex 2, part 5, paragraph 1.4.

18.276 From the first meeting on 1 July 1998, some members of Sinn Féin, by speaking partly in Irish, sought bilingual status for the Irish language with simultaneous translation facilities. One or two members of the SDLP leant support.[240] They met with repeated vocal opposition from mainly the DUP. There was no provision for Irish speaking in the initial standing orders of 29 June 1998, nor in the revised edition of 26 November 1999. However, the standing orders agreed by the assembly on 9 March 1999, and applying from 2 December 1999, include: 'Members may speak in the language of their choice (SO 71)'. During the transition, the speaker had available simultaneous translation, so he could monitor members when they spoke in Irish; presumably, if a member chose to use another language, the speaker would also have to have the facility to comprehend what was being said. (On 9 November 1998, Ian Adamson of the UUP spoke – using Irish and Ulster-Scots but mainly English – in an adjournment debate, advocating an Ulster-Scots academy[241]).

18.277 Bilingual practice – without any legal sanction – was given a boost when two Sinn Féin ministers took office on 2 December 1999. Martin McGuinness, who does not speak Irish, did not make an issue of the language in his first weeks in charge of the department of education.[242] Bairbre de Brún, however, the minister for health, social services and public safety, who is a committed Irish speaker, insisted successfully upon equal status for Irish and English in the work of her department. Thus, within the first few weeks, departmental advertisements were appearing in the two languages.[243] This may accord with article 8 of BNH, which of course has no application in Northern Ireland (though the practice of the Irish state has not been totally bilingual).

18.278 There was a minor confrontation between the executive and the assembly on 31 January 2000. The minister for health, social services and public safety answered questions for the first time that afternoon. Each answer was given first in Irish, and then in English, in what was a fixed time for oral answers (a practice not followed by her party colleague, Martin McGuinness, when he answered questions immediately beforehand). The speaker had cause to admonish the minister, and, after question time, took a number of points of order: he promised to deal with the matter in due course. There followed a debate on a motion dealing with maternity services in Belfast, where the advice of the relevant statutory committee had not been accepted by the minister. When she rose to respond in Irish, she said after a few moments (in English): 'Having spoken briefly in Irish now, I will speak only in English for the rest of this debate.'[244]

> **[3.] 4.** ***In the context of the active consideration currently being given to the UK signing the Council of Europe Charter for Regional or Minority Languages,*** **[T]*the* British Government will in particular[,] in relation to**

240 New Northern Ireland Assembly, *Official Report*, vol. 2 (part 2), pp. 296–7, 9 March 1999.

241 New Northern Ireland Assembly, *Official Report*, vol. 1, pp. 297–8, 9 November 1998; see also the comment of John Kelly on p. 299.

242 Northern Ireland Assembly, *Official Report*, vol. 4, no. 5, p. 218, 24 January 2000.

243 This was criticized by Dennis Kennedy, in an article in the *Belfast Telegraph*, 28 January 2000.

244 Northern Ireland Assembly, *Official Report*, vol. 4, no. 7, pp. 275–87, 300, 31 January 2000.

the Irish language, ***where appropriate and where people so desire it*** **[pending the transfer of responsibility to a new Northern Ireland Assembly]:**

- **take resolute action to promote the language;**
- **facilitate** ***and encourage*** **the use of the language in speech and writing in public and private life[,] where there is appropriate demand;**
- **seek to remove, where possible, restrictions which would discourage or work against the maintenance or development of the language;**
- ***make provision for liaising with the Irish language community, representing their views to public authorities and investigating complaints*** **[continue to take into consideration the needs and wishes expressed by users of the language in determining policy];**
- ***place*** **[impose] a statutory duty on the Department of Education for Northern Ireland to encourage and facilitate Irish medium education** ***in line with the current provision for integrated education;*** **[and]**
- **explore urgently with the relevant British authorities, and in co-operation with the Irish broadcasting authorities, the scope for achieving more widespread availability of Teilifis na Gaelige in Northern Ireland;[.]**
- ***seek more effective ways to encourage and provide financial support for Irish language film and television production in Northern Ireland; and***
- ***encourage the parties to secure agreement that this commitment will be sustained by a new Assembly in a way which takes account of the desires and sensitivities of the community.***

[The parties will seek to secure agreement that this commitment will be sustained by a new Northern Ireland Assembly.]

18.279 This paragraph is on the Irish language. However, paragraphs 3 and 4 were the one paragraph in the MDP. This paragraph is where the Charter was added to the MDP. But reference is made here to in particular; by virtue of that Charter, the undertakings here have to be construed in terms of its principles.

18.280 The paragraph binds the United Kingdom government. In the MDP, this was until devolution; in the FA, the commitment is to encourage the parties in the assembly. It does not directly bind the Irish state. That is done by reading this paragraph with the previous one.

18.281 The Charter entered into force on 1 March 1998. On 4 June 1998, the United Kingdom government announced it was willing to sign. On 4 November 1998, it stated it was willing to accede to – ratify – the Charter. On both occasions, ministers referred to specifying the Irish language[245] at an early date. Nothing ensued. It was only – as noted – at the time of the proposed restoration of the institutions, in the joint letter of the prime minister and taoiseach of 5 May 2000,

245 Under articles 1(2) and 3(1).

that the United Kingdom government announced it would ratify by September 2000, and publish an action plan within a further six months.

18.282 The conditions 'where appropriate' and 'where people so desire' are in accord with the Charter. Article 7(1) (objectives and principles) refers to 'according to the situation of each language'.[246] Subparagraph (g) refers to the provision of facilities for non-speakers 'if they so desire'.

18.283 There are eight specific undertakings, the last two having been added to the MDP. Some are derived from article 7 (objectives and principles) of the Charter; others have to be construed under the Charter.

18.284 The first is from paragraph (1)(c): 'the need for resolute action to promote regional or minority languages in order to safeguard them'. Safeguard has been dropped. The second is from paragraph (1)(d): 'the facilitation and/or encouragement of the use of regional or minority languages, in speech and writing, in public and private life'. Encourage was added to the MDP. Where there is appropriate demand was in the MDP.

18.285 The third is not from article 7 of the Charter. It is not in keeping with its spirit, the implication being that Irish is directly or indirectly restricted by unspecified means.

18.286 The fourth would seem to have been inspired by paragraph (1)(e): 'the maintenance and development of links ... between groups using a regional or minority language and other groups in the State employing a language used in identical or similar form, as well as the establishment of cultural relations with other groups in the State using different languages'. Groups does not necessarily mean language enthusiasts. And the principle is one of links within civil society. Here, the relationship is between the United Kingdom government and language activists. It is not clear how London, or the NIO, represents their views to public authorities under devolution. Investigating complaints suggests the devolved institutions will not function properly.

18.287 The fifth is contrary to the spirit of the Charter. The language of imposing, or placing, a statutory duty on a Northern Ireland department is also contrary to the spirit of devolution. (These concerns do not apply to the Republic of Ireland.) Irish medium education is the secondary sector, between primary and further education. The statutory duty is provided for in article 89 of the Education (Northern Ireland) Order 1998, SI 1998/1759, made on 21 July 1998. The objective could, of course, have been met by encouraging integrated education, as required by the first paragraph 13 of this section. On 31 January 2000, in a written answer, the minister for education stated that he hoped to establish a council for Irish-medium education in February 2000.[247] This – Comhairle Na Gaelscolaíochta – was announced in a written answer on 30 June 2000. The minister for education stated his department responded to parental demand: '[it] funds Irish-medium schools which are robust, do not involve unreasonable public expenditure, and meet specified criteria.'[248]

18.288 The sixth relates to a long-running disagreement in the Anglo-Irish

246 This is repeated also in articles 8(1), 9(1), 10(1) & 11(1).

247 Northern Ireland Assembly, *Official Report*, vol. 4, no. 7, p. 307, 31 January 2000.

248 Northern Ireland Assembly, *Official Report*, vol. 5, no. WA 4, p. WA 5, 30 June 2000.

conference, about Irish language broadcasting from the Republic to Northern Ireland. It would appear that the United Kingdom government blames the 'relevant British [broadcasting?] authorities'. Transfrontier broadcasting is a matter of international regulation. A recital to the Charter states that the protection and promotion of regional or minority languages is 'an important contribution to the building of a Europe based on the principles of democracy and cultural diversity within the framework of national sovereignty and territorial integrity'.[249]

18.289 Article 11 (media) deals with the matter. Paragraph 2 guarantees freedom of direct reception of radio and television broadcasts from a neighbouring country. This is a freedom to receive; not a freedom to broadcast internationally. However, there is a major set of restrictions: 'The exercise of the above-mentioned freedoms, since it carries with it duties and responsibilities, may be subject to such formalities, conditions, restrictions or penalties as are prescribed by law and are necessary in a democratic society, in the interests of national security, territorial integrity or public safety, for the prevention of disorder or crime, for the protection of health or morals, for the protection of the rights of others, for preventing disclosure of information received in confidence, or for maintaining the authority and impartiality of the judiciary.'

18.290 At the time of the restoration of the institutions in May 2000, the prime minister, in his joint letter with the taoiseach, dated 5 May 2000, stated: 'Technical discussions on the steps required further to extend TG4 reception in Northern Ireland will continue.'

18.291 The seventh was added to the MDP. Article 11 (media) deals also with audiovisual works in a regional or minority language.[250] Paragraph (1)(f) states that, where the law provides for assistance in general for the media, additional costs for media using regional or minority languages will be met. Alternatively, existing measures for financial assistance will be applied to audiovisual productions in the regional or minority languages. In the joint letter of the prime minister and the taoiseach of 5 May 2000, other measures were announced 'including a two year Irish language TV and film production pilot scheme which will start by April 2001'.

18.292 The eighth originated in the MDP, as a statement about the United Kingdom government's commitment passing to the assembly. This has been diluted to a continuing government commitment, to encourage the parties to sustain the commitment. 'In a way which takes account of the desires and sensitivities of the community' is a prohibition on gesture politics.

> **[4.] 5. All participants acknowledge the sensitivity of the use of symbols and emblems for public purposes, and the need in particular in creating the new institutions to ensure that such symbols and emblems are used in a manner which promotes mutual respect rather than division.**

249 Article 5 states: 'Nothing in this Charter may be interpreted as implying any right to engage in any activity or perform any action in contravention of the purposes of the Charter of the United Nations or other obligations under international law, including the principle of the sovereignty and territorial integrity of States.'

250 Paragraph 1(d) is: 'to encourage and/or facilitate the production and distribution of audio and audio-visual works in the regional or minority languages'.

Arrangements will be made to monitor this issue and consider what action might be required.

18.293 Northern Ireland is part of the United Kingdom. The monarch is the head of state. And the ensigns armorial, flags and banners – which date from 1801, and are part of the royal prerogative[251] – are as in Great Britain. The union flag so called – which originated in 1606 after the union of the kingdoms of Scotland and England under James I/VI – is the flag of the state.[252] The national flag, as it is regarded, may also be flown on land by British citizens.[253] The crown is an excepted matter under paragraph 1 of schedule 2 of the NIA 1998, though, under section 23, in the case of transferred matters, the royal prerogative may be exercised by a Northern Ireland minister or department. The view was taken by the NIO in May 2000 that the power had been devolved. Official flag days throughout the United Kingdom, however, remain a matter for the sovereign: a royal command by her majesty issued on the royal prerogative. This is sent to the department of culture, media and sport, which notifies other departments including the NIO. *Whitaker's Almanac* lists some 20 occasions or anniversaries for 2000, 15 of which are general to the United Kingdom. St David, St George and St Andrew are all celebrated regionally, but not St Patrick.[254] However, Northern Ireland appears to have added certain days from the 1920s. On Europe day, the European flag should be flown with the union flag, which retains precedence. The Flags and Emblems (Display) Act (Northern Ireland) 1954 had prohibited the flying of any emblem there that might occasion a breach of the peace. This prevented effectively the flying of the Irish tricolour as a party, or communal, symbol (emblem was defined in the act as not including the union flag[255]). However, the use of flags and emblems was listed in article 5(a) of the 1985 Anglo-Irish Agreement as a problem for the conference; the Flags and Emblems Act was repealed in 1987,[256] meaning that, just as the union flag was being used communally, so the Irish tricolour – hitherto an emblem – could be used in territorial segregation.[257]

18.294 This paragraph does not provide for the abolition of symbols and emblems (flags are not even mentioned). It does refer to sensitivity about their use. The reference to creating new institutions would appear not to mean the two states parties, but the transitional – and then devolved – administration in Northern Ireland. The goal in the use of symbols and emblems (flags – and there is only one flag in United Kingdom law – are not mentioned) is the promotion of mutual respect, rather than division. The second and last sentence – monitoring and consideration of action – suggests very little was agreed in this paragraph.

251 Article first, Act of Union (Ireland) 1800.

252 Proclamation dated January 1, 1801, as to the royal style and titles and as to the ensigns armorial, standard, and union flag, SR&O and SI revised to December 31, 1948, pp. 789–91.

253 House of Lords, *Hansard*, 4th series, 192, 579–80, 14 July 1908 (Earl of Crewe).

254 London also marks the opening and proroguing of parliament.

255 Section 1 referred to 'a Union flag (usually known as the Union Jack)'. Section 2(4) defined an emblem as including 'a flag of any kind other than the Union flag'. The offence in section 2(1) referred to emblems.

256 Public Order (Northern Ireland) Order 1987.

257 On the consequences of repeal, see Brigid Hadfield, 'Order in the Law of Public Order?', *Northern Ireland Law Quarterly*, spring 1987, pp. 93–6.

18.295 The paragraph was relatively uncontroversial immediately after 10 April 1998. The NIA 1998 made no reference to symbols and emblems. Section 41 (and schedule 6) deal with standing orders, but make no reference to symbols etc. The union flag was not a matter for devolution. Under ISO 19 – submitted by the secretary of state on 29 June 1998 – 'no political symbols, emblems or flags [were to] be displayed in the Assembly'. This initial standing order used symbols and emblems, but it also added flag. (It referred to in the assembly only, and, indeed, during the transition, the secretary of state flew the union flag from Parliament Buildings.) The initial presiding officer had complete discretion in the matter otherwise. The shadow assembly commission (established on 14 September 1998) came up with an emblem for the Northern Ireland assembly: the motif of the linen or flax plant (six blue flowers), once the basis of Northern Ireland's linen industry.[258] This was used in the assembly. (The commission, however, could not agree on the union flag, disagreement apparently resulting in its not being flown.[259]) The Standing Orders agreed by the assembly on 9 March 1999 do not contain any provision regarding symbols, emblems or flags.

18.296 It looked like the issue might remain uncontroversial, until the publication, on 9 September 1999, of the report of the independent commission on policing for Northern Ireland, chaired by Chris Patten: *A New Beginning: policing in Northern Ireland* (discussed in Chapter 21). In a chapter, 'Culture, Ethos and Symbols' (taken from the terms of reference), in which Patten recommended the abolition of the Royal Ulster Constabulary (RUC) name, the replacement of the force's badge and symbols, the end of the flying of the union flag from police buildings, and its replacement by a new police service flag, reference was made to symbols 'free from association with the British or Irish states'.[260] The report itself is crown copyright. Patten clearly – judging by subsequent attempts to justify his report – misinterpreted the constitutional nature of the Belfast Agreement settlement. In particular, he did not consider the one paragraph – this one – where the question of symbols was addressed. He simply drew an inference from the assembly's linen plant motif. Attention focussed subsequently on the practical and theoretical delegitimization of symbols of the United Kingdom state, and the equating, by Patten, of his own and the Irish states.

18.297 The question of the union flag on police buildings had been solved apparently on 24 July 1998, shortly after the Patten commission began its work. The Police Act (Northern Ireland) 1970 had transferred RUC estates, crown buildings, from the ministry of home affairs, to the new police authority. The Police (Northern Ireland) Act 1998 deemed police authority property not to be property of or property held on behalf of the crown. This provision was brought into force on 1 April 1999.[261] The chief constable, therefore, decided to no longer fly the union flag on designated bank holidays from police buildings. Two issues remain:

258 It was used first on the New Northern Ireland Assembly, *Official Report*, 15 February 1999, and on the New Northern Ireland Assembly, *Report of the Shadow Assembly Commission*, NNIA 8, 22 February 1999.

259 House of Commons, *Hansard*, 6th series, 350, 275–8, 16 May 2000 (speech of Rev. Dr Ian Paisley).

260 Paragraph 17.6.

261 Schedule. 1 para. 1; Police (1998 Act) (Commencement No. 3) Order (Northern Ireland) 1999, SR 1999/176/art. 3.

whether the chief constable was addressing all designated flag days, or only the extra Northern Ireland ones; whether the chief constable retains the power to fly the union flag on such relevant days on all police buildings.[262]

18.298 However, in the wake of Patten, and with two Sinn Féin ministers, attempts were made to use the Belfast Agreement to eradicate all symbols of the United Kingdom state in the work of the devolved administration, the alternative suggestion being parity of esteem between the union flag and the Irish tricolour.[263] After 2 December 1999, the minister for education, and the minister for health, social services and public safety, declined to fly the union flag from departmental buildings on the designated days.

18.299 This was noticed over the holiday period. At some point, the matter was referred to the First Minister and Deputy First Minister.[264] (The secretary of state referred subsequently to an initial attempt having been made to resolve the issue during the early stages of the executive.[265]) On 17 January 2000, a written answer from Bairbre de Brún was published: 'until the matter is resolved I have decided to suspend the flying of the British national flag alone at Department ... buildings'.[266] A week later, in a written answer, the minister for education said: 'My policy is that no flags should be flown from departmental buildings.'[267] On 7 February 2000, Sean Farren, the SDLP minister for higher and further education, training and employment, replied that he would have full regard to any executive committee decision. In the meantime, he would review the flying of the union flag in line with the second paragraph 5 of Rights, Safeguards and Equality of Opportunity.[268]

18.300 The issue was debated in the assembly on 17 January 2000, on a motion from the DUP condemning the minister for health, social services and public safety. The term 'national flag' was used in the motion. An SDLP amendment, condemning 'the abuse of national flags and other symbols and emblems ... as party political, or sectarian symbols', and referring to the mutual respect rather than division point in the second paragraph 5, was defeated by 63 votes to 24. Speaking in the debate, the First Minister said: 'Great care should be taken not to offer any insult to Her Majesty, who is sovereign and is the only Sovereign in this land.' He went on to cite section 23(1) of the NIA 1998. The First Minister explained the position about official flag days, but raised a query about additional

262 Under clause 50(2)(b) of the Police (Northern Ireland) Bill, published on 16 May 2000, the secretary of state is to be empowered to make regulations, after consultation with the policing board, the chief constable and the police association, 'regulating the flying or carrying of [a flag for the police force] or any other flag'.

263 Speech of Michelle Gildernew, Northern Ireland Assembly, *Official Report*, vol. 4, no. 4, p. 128, 17 January 2000; speech by Alban Maginness, Northern Ireland Assembly, *Official Report*, vol. 4, no. 9, p. 379, 7 February 2000.

264 Sam Foster, the minister for the environment, stated he raised it: Northern Ireland Assembly, *Official Report*, vol. 4, no. 4, p. 131, 17 January 2000. This was most likely at the executive committee meeting on 11 January 2000.

265 House of Commons, *Hansard*, 6th series, 350, 266, 16 May 2000.

266 Northern Ireland Assembly, *Official Report*, vol. 4 no. 2, p. 144, 17 January 2000. See also, Northern Ireland Assembly, *Official Report*, vol. 4 no. 10, pp. 406–7, 8 February 2000. As for the minister of education, see Northern Ireland Assembly, *Official Report*, vol. 4 no. 5, p. 217, 24 January 2000.

267 Northern Ireland Assembly, *Official Report*, vol. 4, no. 5, pp. 217–18, 24 January 2000.

268 Northern Ireland Assembly, *Official Report*, vol. 4, no. 9, p. 398, 7 February 2000.

days.[269] The DUP motion was carried by 51 votes to 32, the UUP voting with the DUP.

18.301 The issue arose again on 7 February 2000, on an Alliance party motion to make St Patrick's day (17 March) a full public holiday. The UUP moved an amendment that it should be added to the list of official flag days.[270] The amendment was carried by 50 votes to 32 (the DUP supporting the UUP), and the amended motion was accepted without a vote.

18.302 During suspension, and following the attempt at Hillsborough to restore the institutions, the secretary of state, in a private letter to the Rt. Hon. David Trimble MP[271] of 16 May 2000, made two relevant points: the government would recognize in visible ways that Northern Ireland was legitimately part of the United Kingdom, but these would be sensitive to the views of both traditions; on flag flying he wrote: 'I do not want this to become a running sore.'[272]

18.303 Late that evening, in the house of commons, and without the normal consultation, the secretary of state introduced the Flags (Northern Ireland) Order 2000, SI 2000/1347.[273] This was to allow the secretary of state to make regulations regulating the flying of flags (sic) at government buildings in Northern Ireland after the restoration of the institutions. However, the order required a further order for it to come into operation.[274] The regulations were to be referred in draft to the assembly, and the secretary of state was to have regard to the Belfast Agreement in drawing them up. The regulations were to be approved by the houses of parliament.[275] The secretary of state was taking a reserve power only, using paragraph 1(1) of the schedule to the Northern Ireland Act 2000 while he could during suspension (after restoration it might have required an act of parliament). Flag flying would be a matter for the executive, in the first instance, if and when it was restored under that Westminster legislation. This, however, appears nowhere on the face of the order.

18.304 The relationship with the NIA 1998 is important. If flag flying comes under the crown in paragraph 1 of schedule 2 (excepted matters), the order was unnecessary. The secretary of state has the power to make regulations under the royal prerogative during suspension or after restoration. However, the consensus among those who spoke seemed to be that it came under section 23(2); presumably

269 Also: 'I believe that it is possible to have a completely neutral environment that respects the sovereignty which exists here. I am well aware that the flag is, at times, used in a provocative way. But no real objection can be taken to things that fall within the normal course of events.'

270 The proposer of the motion stated it was unnecessary as 17 March was already an official flag day.

271 He argued later that day for United Kingdom-wide legislation on flying the union flag: 'The existence of the flag and the occasions on which it is flown are matters of custom, practice and administrative procedures, not of law.' (House of Commons, *Hansard*, 6th series, 350, 272–4, 16 May 2000)

272 *Irish Times*, 17 May 2000.

273 It had been debated earlier in the house of lords (House of Lords, *Hansard*, 5th series, 613, 200–9, 16 May 2000). Lord Falconer of Thoroton explained that the order was being made under paragraph 1(1) of the schedule to the Northern Ireland Act 2000.

274 Article 1(2).

275 Article 4.

because it was not specified adequately in schedules 2 or 3. In that case, if it was a transferred matter, the secretary of state should have sought normally to make it a reserved matter by amending schedule 3, under section 4(2). However, under section 4(3), a condition precedent is an assembly resolution with cross-community support. During suspension, it was not therefore possible to make a transferred matter a reserved matter (other than by primary Westminster legislation, amending the NIA 1998). Paragraph 1(1) of the schedule to the Northern Ireland Act 2000, however, allowed Westminster to legislate by order in council in place of the assembly. But could the assembly, if it had not been suspended, legislate to give the secretary of state the power to make regulations? The answer lies in paragraph 1(2): 'A provision which would be outside the legislative competence of the Assembly may not be included in such an Order.' The assembly cannot amend section 4 of the NIA 1998.[276] It is a more difficult question whether section 6 (legislative competence), read with section 4, allows the transfer of regulation-making powers from the assembly to the secretary of state.

18.305 The order made reference to 'government buildings', defined as 'wholly or mainly occupied by members of the Northern Ireland Civil Service'. This excludes – as emerged in the debate – Parliament Buildings at Stormont (which would be a matter for the assembly commission after restoration). It also excludes the police force.

18.306 The secretary of state sought to give the impression that, if Sinn Féin, with or without the SDLP, sought to oppose the union flag, he would step in. The tone of several parliamentary contributions was that his order would not solve such a problem. And the contribution of Lord Falconer of Thoroton, introducing the order in the house of lords, and posing questions to be answered by the regulations, confirms this.[277]

18.307 Following the restoration of the institutions, the assembly returned to the issue on 6 June 2000. The DUP moved a motion that the union flag should fly on executive buildings on designated days, and additionally on Parliament Buildings during each sitting day. However, the SDLP and Sinn Féin had submitted a petition of concern the previous day,[278] under SO 27, requiring a cross-community vote. A total of 53 unionists voted for the motion; 34 nationalists voted against (7 others also voted against). The motion was not carried.

276 Paragraph 22 of schedule 2.

277 'If, at the end of the day, there is a need to exercise this reserve power there are a number of questions which will need to be answered. What arrangements for flag flying are suitable for government buildings in Northern Ireland and which respect the provisions of the Good Friday agreement? Is it right that the Union flag should be flown from government buildings in Northern Ireland on more days than is the case elsewhere in the United Kingdom? Is it necessarily helpful to require the flag to fly from every government building, wherever it is located and however significant or insignificant it may be? What other arrangements should be in place for flag flying?' (House of Lords, *Hansard*, 5th series, 613, 201, 16 May 2000)

278 This was suggested and supported by the Alliance party (Northern Ireland Assembly, *Official Report*, p. 48, 6 June 2000).

19

Decommissioning

19.1 This is one of the shortest sections of the Belfast Agreement. It was also the most important from 1 July 1998 (when the First Minister and Deputy First Minister were elected by the assembly). The decommissioning issue largely explains the delay in devolution until 2 December 1999. And its non-appearance led to the suspension of the institutions by the secretary of state between 12 February 2000 and 30 May 2000. The section is at page 20 of Cm 3883 and page 35 of Cm 4705 (page 29 of the 1999 Irish version). It is five paragraphs long, though decommissioning – I submit – is implied elsewhere in the agreement reached on 10 April 1998 (see below). The MDP is important for construing the FA; I indicate [deletions] and *additions* thus.

19.2 Decommissioning is one of a quartet of related issues in the Belfast Agreement. It is about terrorists[1] becoming democrats. Security is interrelated, representing the response of the state to a diminishing threat. Policing and Justice is about good government. The fourth section, Prisoners, demonstrates most clearly the truly historic opportunity for a new beginning (proclaimed in paragraph 1 of the Declaration of Support). This section promised the decommissioning of all paramilitary arms within two years from 22 May 1998 – unconditionally in the context of the implementation of the overall settlement.

Attempts to solve the Northern Ireland problem

19.3 From 1969, the United Kingdom government (and the Irish government when consulted) was to seek to exclude republican (and loyalist) terrorists from a political solution. The problem, of course, became more intractable with time; ironically, when the IRA was at its strongest, in 1972, it was execrated by London and Dublin.

19.4 Key landmarks in the process of terrorist exclusion are:

- the 1969 *Downing Street Declaration* (of 19 August), of the United Kingdom and Northern Ireland governments ('the two Governments'), following the introduction of troops on to the streets, when London stated 'the border is not an issue', Northern Ireland was described as 'a matter of domestic jurisdiction', it was 'emphasise[d] again that troops [would] be withdrawn

1 Terrorism was defined first as regards Northern Ireland as 'the use of violence for political ends and includes any use of violence for the purpose of putting the public or any section of the public in fear' (Detention of Terrorists (Northern Ireland) Order 1972, SI 1972/1632, art 2(2)). It was redefined as a result of Lord Lloyd of Berwick's report, *Inquiry into legislation against terrorism*, of October 1996, Cm 3420 – as: 'the use or threat, for the purpose of advancing a political, religious or ideological cause, of action which – (a) involves serious violence against any person or property, (b) endangers the life of any person, or (c) creates a serious risk to the health or safety of the public or a section of the public' (Terrorism Bill, clause 1(1)). See now Terrorism Act 2000 s1(1).

when law and order [had] been restored', and Belfast promised to take into the fullest account at all times London's views on 'matters affecting the status of citizens of that part of the United Kingdom and their equal rights and protection under the law';[2]

- the 1973 Sunningdale communiqué, where the Irish government stated that 'the people of the Republic, together with a minority in Northern Ireland represented by the SDLP delegation[, believed] ... the only unity they wanted to see was a unity established by consent'. 'It was agreed by all parties [a term seemingly including the two governments] that persons committing crimes of violence, however motivated, in any part of Ireland should be brought to trial irrespective of the part of Ireland in which they [we]re located';[3]
- the new Ireland forum of 1983–84, which 'was open to all democratic parties which reject violence and which have members elected or appointed to either House of the Oireachtas or the Northern Ireland Assembly';[4]
- the 1985 Anglo-Irish Agreement, in which one of the recitals of the preamble read: 'Reaffirming their total rejection of any attempt to promote political objectives by violence or the threat of violence and their determination to work together to ensure that those who adopt or support such methods do not succeed.'

19.5 London, and Dublin, remained of the view that, whether one was talking about Northern Ireland within the United Kingdom, or a united Ireland, there was no room for political violence. (This is not to deny the historical effects of republican and loyalist terrorism.) It was only when the republicans, if not the loyalists, started to put out feelers in the late 1980s (following their entry into Northern Ireland politics at the beginning of the decade), that the two governments, independently, began to look to incorporating the extremes.

19.6 Following the abortive Hume-Adams dialogue of 1988, and outside the context of the 1991–92 political talks on the future of Northern Ireland, the Hume-Adams dialogue of 1992–93 (assisted this time by the Irish government), led to a change in United Kingdom government policy. A concern with the democratic centre (evident at Sunningdale) was supplanted by a preoccupation with the paramilitary extremes; all-inclusive political talks became the shared goal of London and Dublin from late 1993 – given an end to violence.

19.7 This preoccupation was to continue through the Belfast Agreement and devolution and even into suspension.

19.8 What about the IRA's armed struggle, championed by Sinn Féin? This question was not to be answered sufficiently clearly – after five years – by the time of the election of the First Minister and Deputy First minister on 1 July 1998. The republican acronym TUAS, said to mean totally unarmed strategy, was also interpreted, or became, the tactical use of armed struggle.[5]

2 Cmnd 4154, August 1969.

3 Paragraphs 3 & 10.

4 *Report*, 1984, p. 1. Sinn Féin had been elected to the assembly in 1982; like the SDLP, it was boycotting it.

5 Eamonn Mallie & David McKittrick, *The Fight for Peace: the inside story of the Irish peace process*, London 1997, pp. 311–12, 396, 398–9, 421–4.

The imperative of decommissioning (December 1993–)

19.9 In paragraph 10 of the 1993 *Downing Street Declaration*, the United Kingdom and Irish governments explained how Sinn Féin (the point also applied to loyalists) could enter politics: 'The British and Irish governments reiterate that the achievement of peace must involve a permanent end to the use of, or support for, paramilitary violence. They confirm that, in these circumstances, democratically mandated parties which establish a commitment to exclusively peaceful methods and which have shown that they abide by the democratic process, are free to participate fully in democratic politics and to join in dialogue in due course between the Governments and the political parties on the way ahead.'

19.10 London and Dublin, therefore, laid down four conditions precedent to participation in political negotiations on 15 December 1993: one, a permanent end to the use of, or support for, paramilitary violence; two, a democratically mandated party; three, establishing a commitment to exclusively peaceful methods; and four, showing that they abide by the democratic process. The second was the least difficult; though Gerry Adams – the abstentionist MP – had lost his Westminster seat in 1992 (and would not regain it until 1997).

19.11 But the first, third and fourth required more than Sinn Féin simply characterizing its pan-nationalist strategy as an Irish peace initiative. There were two clear stages: (using later terminology) a – permanent – ceasefire; followed by a commitment to exclusively peaceful methods. Implied in paragraph 10 of the *Downing Street Declaration* was a start to the decommissioning of paramilitary weapons – something which would become of considerable symbolic importance.

19.12 This was not – as would later be claimed (and believed apparently)[6] – a belated thought of Sir Patrick Mayhew, the secretary of state, in his Washington DC speech of 7 March 1995. Decommissioning had been put forward first by the Irish government. On 1 June 1994 (before the IRA ceasefire), Dick Spring, the foreign minister, was asked a question in the Dáil by Michael McDowell SC TD (now the attorney general), about whether the IRA would have to disarm for Sinn Féin to be involved in talks. The foreign minister replied: 'The key to Sinn Fein-IRA being part of the political discussion is a permanent cessation of violence. It has to be permanent and there can be no equivocation about that. There will have to be verification of the handing over of arms. As I said publicly on many occasions, there is little point in attempting to bring people into political dialogue if they are doing so on the basis of giving it a try ... .'[7]

19.13 The Irish government resiled from this position on 12 December 1994. The United States government, however, reaffirmed the need for decommissioning, after Washington three, on 9 March and 4 April 1995.

19.14 A republican movement – as would become clear – refusing to decommission any weapons, while inferring that it had crossed the bridge from terrorism to democracy, would have a difficult task building confidence within the unionist community. If this was not evidence at the time of devolution on 2 December 1999, it was perceived – almost universally – to be the case on 12 February 2000 when the institutions were suspended.

6 See Tony Blair's Stranmillis speech of 15 June 1999.

7 Dáil Éireann, *Official Report*, 1 June 1994; Paul Bew & Gordon Gillespie, *Northern Ireland: a chronology of the troubles, 1968–1999*, Dublin 1999, p. 290.

19.15 The IRA announced 'a complete cessation of military operations' from 31 August 1994. The loyalists followed on 13 October 1994, their ceasefires being dependent only upon the IRA's.[8] The IRA broke its ceasefire on 9 February 1996, with the London Docklands bomb (followed by major explosions in Manchester, and Lisburn in Northern Ireland). The loyalists, like the republicans, continued (from 1994 to the present) with so-called punishment beatings and expulsions, killing of selected targets and paramilitary activity short of all-out war. On 20 July 1997 (after 15 months), the IRA resumed its complete cessation of violence. Subsequently, it would discount this breach when assessing the duration of its ceasefire.[9]

The Mitchell international body (December 1995–January 1996)

19.16 The reason for the IRA breaking its complete cessation had to do with the Mitchell report;[10] but this led to the United Kingdom government dropping the condition precedent of actual decommissioning before entry into talks.

19.17 The Mitchell report originated in a joint communiqué of the United Kingdom and Irish governments of 28 November 1995, proposing a twin-track process to make progress in parallel.[11] One track was to be talks about talks (with a target for all-party negotiations of the end of February 1996). The other was to be an – advisory – international body, to provide an independent assessment of the decommissioning issue by the middle of January 1996. Decommissioning – after almost two years – was taken out of the talks process as a result of this initiative by London and Dublin.[12]

19.18 The international body, with addresses in Dublin and Belfast, comprised Senator George J. Mitchell (chairman) of the United States, General John de Chastelain of Canada, and Mr Harri Holkeri, former prime minister of Finland. Its terms of reference were contained in the joint communiqué, and there was no international agreement establishing it. The international body began work on 9 December 1995 and reported on 22 January 1996.

19.19 The Mitchell report put forward six 'fundamental principles of democracy and non-violence'; the participants in all-party negotiations were to affirm their total and absolute commitment:

- to democratic and exclusively peaceful means of resolving political issues;
- to the total disarmament of all paramilitary organisations;

8 The two ceasefires influenced the 1995 *Framework Documents*. Annex A of part I (by the United Kingdom government) referred to parties with a democratic mandate, that have established a commitment to exclusively peaceful means (paragraph 4). The shared understanding in part II referred to the profound desire for a permanent end to violence (paragraph 3; see also paragraph 56).

9 On 16 November 1999, Sinn Féin referred to 'almost four years'; on 1 February 2000, the IRA referred to its cessation 'entering its fifth year'.

10 Senator Mitchell refutes the Sinn Féin interpretation of the United Kingdom's response: George Mitchell, *Making Peace*, London 1999, pp. 39–40.

11 The imminent visit of the United States president to Ireland was crucial in this policy change.

12 The joint communiqué reaffirmed paragraph 10 of the *Downing Street Declaration*. It also referred to arrangements necessary for the removal from the political equation of arms silenced by the ceasefires.

- to agree that such disarmament must be verifiable to the satisfaction of an independent commission;
- to renounce for themselves, and to oppose any effort by others, to use force, or threaten to use force, to influence the course of the outcome of all-party negotiations;
- to agree to abide by the terms of any agreement reached in all-party negotiations and to resort to democratic and exclusively peaceful methods in trying to alter any aspect of that outcome with which they may disagree; and
- to urge that 'punishment' killings and beatings stop and to take effective steps to prevent such actions.

19.20 The first particular question the two governments had asked of the international body was to identify and advise on a suitable and acceptable method for full and verifiable decommissioning. The three members recommended an independent international commission on decommissioning, and provided guidelines on the modalities.[13]

19.21 The second question was whether there was a clear commitment on the part of the paramilitary parties (as they came to be called) to decommission. The Mitchell report answered in the affirmative.[14] However, this was qualified: not prior to negotiations (the Mitchell principles were intended to fill this vacuum.) The international body went on – seeking a compromise between the United Kingdom government and Sinn Féin views[15] – to suggest the parties should consider 'some decommissioning ... during the process of all-party negotiations'.[16] This was seen as contributing to 'a progressive pattern of mounting trust and confidence' in the talks.

19.22 The Mitchell report was published on 24 January 1996. The prime minister, John Major, accepted the report in a statement in the house of commons.[17] The United Kingdom government welcomed and fully endorsed the Mitchell principles. It also stated it was ready to implement the recommendations on the modalities of decommissioning. As to parallel decommissioning, the prime minister did not reject that advice.[18] He went on to support the idea upon which Mitchell and his colleagues had commented – which had been mentioned in the joint communiqué of 28 November 1995[19] – of an elected body: 'If it were broadly acceptable, with an appropriate mandate, and within the three-strand structure, an elective process could contribute to the building of confidence.'[20]

13 These were: neither victory nor defeat; satisfaction of an international commission; complete destruction of armaments; fully verifiable; no risk of prosecution; mutual decommissioning.

14 Paragraph 25. However, Mitchell seems not to have been so sure: *Making Peace*, pp. 40–1.

15 This idea originated with Michael Ancram, a NIO minister: Mitchell, *Making Peace*, pp. 33–4.

16 Paragraph 34. The analogy was with El Salvador.

17 House of Commons, *Hansard*, 6th series, 280, 353–8, 357–70, 24 January 1996.

18 'Although the body makes no formal recommendation on this point, it suggests an approach under which some decommissioning would take place during the process of all-party negotiations.' (col. 353) The relevant paragraph in the report is 34. The prime minister quoted paragraph 34 later, saying: 'That is precisely the way I see it.' (col. 366)

19 Paragraph 3.

20 Paragraph 56. The clear implication was that Sinn Féin could gain entry to the all-party negotiations, if elected, and without prior IRA decommissioning.

19.23 The IRA's Docklands bomb followed on 9 February 1996 (having been in preparation from October 1995).[21] The prime minister and the taoiseach met in London on 28 February 1996, to review progress in preparatory talks for all-party negotiations[22] (this had been intended from 28 November 1995). They set the date for the start of all-party negotiations – 10 June 1996. 'Whether those negotiations', the prime minister told the house of commons, 'will include Sinn Féin will depend on whether the ceasefire has been restored.'[23] Elections for 110 delegates to the Northern Ireland forum for political dialogue were held on 30 May 1996; 17 were from Sinn Féin.[24] The date for the beginning of talks was met. The IRA's ceasefire was not restored. And Sinn Féin was not admitted as one of the elected political parties.

19.24 New governments took office in London and Dublin following elections in the late spring of 1997: Tony Blair's after 1 May 1997; and Bertie Ahern's after 6 June 1997. On 20 July 1997, the IRA restored its complete cessation of military operations. Sinn Féin entered the all-party negotiations on 9 September 1997 (but not before two unionist parties had walked out in the summer).

The Independent International Commission on Decommissioning

19.25 The two governments had moved slowly to implement Mitchell's January 1996 proposals for full and verifiable decommissioning. The (Irish) Decommissioning Act 1997 was promulgated on 26 February 1997; the (United Kingdom) Northern Ireland Arms Decommissioning Act 1997 received the royal assent the following day. Boths acts referred to an international commission – but did not purport to create it. The United Kingdom act provided for decommissioning schemes drawn up by the secretary of state (section 1(1)), and also for arrangements (section 10(2)[25]). The Irish act, in contrast, provided for regulations made by the minister, and arrangements (made by the commission pursuant to regulations[26]) (sections 1(1), 2(1), 4(1) and (2)(g)(i)–(ii)).

19.26 The agreement establishing the independent international commission on decommissioning was signed on 26 August 1997, by the secretary of state for Northern Ireland and the Irish foreign minister.[27] It entered into force on 24 September 1997 – after the entry of Sinn Féin into the multi-party negotiations – when three commissioners were appointed: General John de Chastelain of Canada, Brigadier Tauno Nieminen of Finland and Ambassador Donald C. Johnson of the United States of America;[28] it was given offices in Dublin and Belfast.

21 Toby Harnden, *'Bandit Country'*, London 1999, p. 24; it was the work of the south Armagh brigade of the IRA.
22 Joint communiqué, paragraph 12.
23 House of Commons, *Hansard*, 6th series, 272, 900, 28 February 1996. See also, *Ground Rules for Substantive All-Party Negotiations*, Cm 3232, 16 April 1996, rules 8 and 9.
24 Under the Northern Ireland (Entry to Negotiations, etc.) Act 1996, which received the royal assent on 29 April 1996.
25 The United Kingdom decommissioning scheme of 29 June 1998 refers to arrangements in paragraphs 12–14.
26 Regulation 8 of the Decommission Act 1997 (Decommissioning) Regulations 1998, SI 1998/216.
27 Cm 3753, Treaty Series No. 54 (1997).
28 He was to be replaced by Andrew Sens – a United States staff member of the commission,

19.27 It is not clear why the legislation preceded the international agreement; most likely, the two governments sought to control when the IICD – an independent international commission – began to function in parallel with the multi-party negotiations. References in the international agreement to mechanisms on decommissioning, appear to have meant only consulting the political parties in the multi-party negotiations.[29]

19.28 The subordinate legislation was not in fact in place until after the Belfast Agreement was concluded. On 29 June 1998, the NIO[30] published a booklet, entitled decommissioning scheme, based on section 3(1)(c) and (d) of the Northern Ireland Arms Decommissioning Act 1997; it came into force on 30 June 1998.[31] Also on 29 June 1998, the Irish government prepared to bring the remaining sections of its act into operation on the following day.[32] It also published its regulations (under sections 2(1) and 4(2)(g) of the Decommissioning Act 1997[33]); these came in operation on 30 June 1998.[34]

19.29 From the Mitchell report of 22 January 1996, it took over 29 months to get the IICD up and running fully on 30 June 1998; in that time, the multi-party negotiations had taken place, Sinn Féin had been incorporated into the talks process and the Belfast Agreement had been achieved.

19.30 The objective of the IICD, under article 3 of the international agreement, is to facilitate the decommissioning of arms,[35] in accord with the Mitchell report, any United Kingdom decommissioning schemes and any Irish regulations or arrangements.[36] I submit that the decommissioning scheme and the regulations (and any arrangements made by the commission) must fall within the definition: to facilitate the decommissioning of arms. Otherwise, there would be a risk of the two governments defining the objective of the commission differently. Further, any arrangements made by the commission have to be within, not just the regulations of the Irish legislature, but also the decommissioning scheme of the United Kingdom parliament.

and former State Department official – from 3 July 1999. Donald Johnson had informed the two governments in May 1999 that he wished to resign for career reasons.

29 The fourth recital in the preamble to the international agreement refers to a joint communiqué of 29 July 1997, when Dublin and Belfast decided to proceed with the IICD 'in order that the mechanisms on decommissioning would be capable of being launched simultaneously with substantive political negotiations'. Mechanisms is used in article 4(d), on reporting to the two governments, with reference to the other participants in political negotiations.

30 Under the signature of Adam Ingram MP.

31 It was made under sections 1(1) (including 2 and 3).

32 Decommissioning Act 1997 (Sections 5 and 6) (Commencement) Order 1998, SI 1998/215.

33 However, the explanatory note states the regulations are in accordance with sections 2 and 4(2)(g). If the latter is correct (and some of the regulations appear to relate to functions of the commission), this would suggest there are no section 4(1) regulations or section 4(2)(h) regulations.

34 Decommissioning Act 1997 (Decommissioning) Regulations 1998, SI 1998/216.

35 Defined as firearms, ammunition, explosives and explosive substances.

36 The former, under section 2(1) of the United Kingdom act, was a condition precedent. The latter, under section 2(1), was not a condition precedent, but it was under section 4(1); however, these regulations appear to have been anticipated legally by the international agreement.

19.31 Article 4 lists the functions: (a) to consult 'on the type of scheme or schemes for decommissioning including the role it might play in respect of each scheme';[37] (b) to present proposals for schemes to the two governments 'having due regard to the views expressed by those it has consulted'; (c) 'to undertake ... such tasks that may be required of it to facilitate the decommissioning of arms, including observing, monitoring and verifying decommissioning and receiving and auditing arms';[38] and (d) to report periodically to the two governments and the political parties.[39]

19.32 These are the only possible functions of the IICD. The United Kingdom act is silent on the functions of the commission. The Irish act, however, in addition to providing for regulations in relation to decommissioning (section 2), goes on to provide for regulations generally in relation to the commission in section 4: subsection (2)(g) relates to the functions of the IICD, there being functions (i) to (vi).[40]

19.33 It is not possible to unilaterally provide for the functions of an international organization established by agreement. If this has been attempted in the Irish government's regulations of 30 June 1998 (as a result of section 4(2)(g)), and this does not correspond to the international agreement, there is a strong possibility that Westminster and the Oireachtas have created two decommissioning commissions. The fact that the United Kingdom decommissioning scheme is similar to the Irish regulations, only raises the relationship between the United Kingdom act, the international agreement and the decommissioning scheme; while effective under the act, the scheme has to be compatible with the agreement.[41]

19.34 The other major point to note is that Westminster, but not the Oireachtas, described the provisions as amounting to an amnesty.

19.35 Section 2(1) of the United Kingdom act refers to 'the amnesty period' in a decommissioning scheme. This is 12 months from the passing of the act (27 February 1997), though the secretary of state may extend it for up to 12 months[42] (but not beyond five years – 26 February 2002 being a statutory deadline as regards amnesty in the United Kingdom). The possibility of an amnesty was allowed to lapse between 26 February 1998 and 24 March 1998, before the secretary of state extended the period by order.

37 Decommissioning scheme is defined in section 1(1) of the United Kingdom act: it is made by the secretary of state to facilitate decommissioning.

38 This function refers to any United Kingdom decommissioning schemes and to any Irish regulations or arrangements.

39 The word mechanism is used here, and in the fourth recital of the preamble.

40 Subsection (2)(a)–(f), dealing with the commission, plus subsection (2)(h) (any other matters at the discretion of the minister) seem not to have been included in the regulations. Functions (i)–(vi) may be related to article 4 of the international agreement.

41 The understanding of the IICD is that only the legislation and the decommissioning scheme/regulations matter: Annex to report of 2 July 1999.

42 Northern Ireland Arms Decommissioning Act 1997 (Amnesty Period) Order 1998, SI 1998/893 (amnesty period, 24 March 1998 to 26 February 1999); Northern Ireland Arms Decommissioning Act 1997 (Amnesty Period) Order 1999, SI 1999/454 (amnesty period, 26 February 1999 to 23 February 2000); Northern Ireland Arms Decommissioning Act 1997 (Amnesty Period) Order 2000, SI 2000/452 (amnesty period, 24 February 2000 to 22 May 2000); Northern Ireland Arms Decommissioning Act 1997 (Amnesty Period) (No. 2) Order 2000, SI 2000/1409 (amnesty period, 23 May 2000 to 19 May 2001).

19.36 Section 4 (amnesty) states that no proceedings may be brought for an offence listed in the schedule in respect of anything done in accordance with a decommissioning scheme. Section 5 prohibits a decommissioned article, or information derived from it, being admissible in evidence in criminal proceedings (except evidence adduced on behalf of the accused). Section 6 greatly restricts the testing of decommissioned articles. But section 11(2) – a saving – states that nothing in the act shall prejudice any power or discretion exercisable apart from the act in relation to the institution or conduct of criminal proceedings.

19.37 The Irish act contains only prohibitions. Section 5 prohibits proceedings against a person for an offence in relation to any particular arms if he is involved in decommissioning (as specified in the act). Section 6 prohibits forensic examination or testing, with a limited number of exceptions. The Irish regulations – made under the act – are stated to come into operation on 30 June 1998, and shall expire on 22 May 2000.[43] There is no reference to an amnesty period. However, under section 5(1)(c) of the Irish act, 30 June 1998 to 22 May 2000 is an amnesty period.

The work of the Independent International Commission on Decommissioning (24 September 1997–)

19.38 The only public source of information on the work of the IICD is the reports published, usually after presentation to the secretary of state and the minister for justice equality and law reform: a first report of 21 November 1997, to the liaison sub-committee on decommissioning set up within the multi-party negotiations; a second report of 2 July 1999, part of *The Way Forward* attempt of the same date to set up the executive; a third report of 15 November 1999, part of the process of agreement on establishing the executive; a fourth report of 10 December 1999, which followed devolution; a fifth report of 31 January 2000 (which was held back apparently at the insistence of the Irish government until 11 February 2000); and a sixth report of 11 February 2000, which came too late to prevent suspension of the institutions by the secretary of state.

19.39 After 24 September 1997, the IICD consulted with participants in the talks, and the security forces in the two jurisdictions, on the methods of decommissioning identified in the Mitchell report (namely, complete destruction as a result of transfer, discovery or depositing with the commission – or destruction by the parties).

19.40 On 21 November 1997, the commission reported to the liaison sub-committee on decommissioning set up within the talks process. The report covered their consultations, and proposals to the two governments for decommissioning schemes, and outlined a basic scenario for decommissioning.

19.41 Subsequently, the IICD decided upon discovery as a result of information provided by paramilitary groups, and self destruction.[44] (These – having been submitted on 15 January 1998 – were embodied eventually in the United Kingdom decommissioning scheme[45] and the Irish regulations.[46])

43 Regulation 2.
44 These had been provided for in section 3(1)(c) and (d) of the United Kingdom act.
45 Paragraph 2.
46 Regulation 4.

19.42 The commission had asked the paramilitary groups to nominate a representative or point of contact.[47] The Ulster Volunteer Force (UVF)[48] did so in October 1997. The Loyalist Volunteer Force (LVF) followed in June 1998 (though he resigned in June 1999). In September 1998, Sinn Féin nominated Martin McGuinness. The Ulster Defence Association (UDA)[49] did not, but there was contact with the appropriate paramilitary party. It was not until 2 December 1999 that the IRA announced it had appointed a representative to enter into discussions with the commission. The UDA[50] followed suit on 8 December 1999.

19.43 The first – and only – incident of decommissioning had taken place on 18 December 1998, by the LVF: it surrendered to the commission four sub-machine guns, two rifles, two pistols, a sawn-off shotgun, 348 rounds of ammunition, 31 shotgun shells, five detonators, two pipe bombs, two weapons stocks and five assorted magazines. It is not clear whether the LVF point of contact became a contact person under the decommissioning scheme and Irish regulations.[51]

19.44 The report of 2 July 1999 originated in a request from the two governments. An earlier draft – dated 29 June 1999 – was held back (in circumstances considered below), but it is possible to update events to 30 June 1999 from the text released.

19.45 The IICD stated that, since 30 June 1998, it had sought to put the methods of decommissioning into effect. However, neither the UDA nor the IRA had nominated a point of contact with the commission. 'No proposal to start actual decommissioning had been accepted by any paramilitary group except the LVF.'

19.46 Between 21 and 28 June 1999, the commission had met ten political parties, and posed three general questions. One, on the completion of decommissioning by 22 May 2000, some 'spoke more broadly of their support for decommissioning in the context of the demilitarisation of Northern Ireland'. Two, on what implementation might trigger decommissioning, 'most parties argued the need for full implementation of the Good Friday Agreement'. Three (a question addressed effectively to paramilitary parties), on 'a firm basis for expecting decommissioning' and a date for confirmation of practical modalities: 'It was hoped the question would elicit positive signals from the paramilitary groups themselves. There were no responses ... from either the IRA or the UDA by the 28 June deadline.'[52]

19.47 The third report of 15 November 1999 was part of the agreement which emerged from the Mitchell review of September to November 1999 (see further below). The commission stated (referring to the establishment of the institutions):

47 It is not clear whether the IICD is using this term as an equivalence to 'contact person' in the subordinate legislation.
48 Plus Red Hand Commandos.
49 Plus Ulster Freedom Fighters.
50 Referred to as the Ulster Freedom Fighters.
51 Respectively, paragraph 4(iii) and regulation 3(1).
52 'The UVF provided a response which emphasised the need for the Good Friday Agreement to be implemented in full and an acceptance by republicans that the Agreement is "the final settlement of the constitutional conflict".'

'The implementation of the Agreement in all its aspects will create a new context in which the situation will be transformed.' However, the commission explained that urgent progress was now needed, and it would play a more active role.

19.48 It was the announcements by the IRA and the UDA on, respectively, 2 and 8 December 1999, which led to the fourth – 'some progress. We expect more to follow' – report on 10 December 1999. 'These events', the commission said of devolution, 'provide the basis for an assessment that decommissioning will occur.' However, it also stated: 'the commission is prepared, if necessary, to state that actual decommissioning [wa]s to start within a specified period'.

19.49 The fifth report of 31 January 2000 – which had been signalled on 10 December 1999[53] – was not published at the time. 'While we believe that conclusion [that decommissioning would happen] was well founded', it read, 'we await further evidence to substantiate it.' No information had been received from the IRA as to when decommissioning would start. The two loyalist groups reiterated that they would only move when it was clear the IRA would. It was signalled that completion by 22 May 2000 would soon be logistically impossible; the IICD concluded that, if decommissioning was not to happen, it would recommend to the two governments that it be disbanded.

19.50 The sixth report of 11 February 2000, which failed to avert suspension in circumstances which remain confused (see further below), seemed to indicate transformation: 'We find particularly significant and view as valuable progress the assertion made to us by the IRA representative that the IRA will consider how to put arms and explosives beyond use, in the context of the full implementation of the Good Friday Agreement, and in the context of the removal of the causes of conflict.' Another paragraph stated that the representative had stated 'the context in which the IRA [would] initiate a comprehensive process to put arms beyond use, in a manner to ensure maximum public confidence'. The commission concluded that there was 'the real prospect of an agreement which would enable it to fulfil the substance of its mandate'.

What is the law on decommissioning?

19.51 This is a very simple legal question to answer, in both United Kingdom law and Irish law, even if decommissioning remains unresolved as a political issue.

19.52 At every moment from the relevant date of 15 December 1993 (the *Downing Street Declaration*), the IRA – and other republican and loyalist organizations – have been illegal.[54] (The IRA may be distinguished: with 18 Sinn Féin members of the assembly elected on 25 June 1998, it was the only paramilitary party bound to join the executive under the d'Hondt rules.) All the above have been proscribed organizations, specified in schedule 2 to the Northern Ireland (Emergency Provisions) Act 1996 (or earlier legislation), or they have been unlawful organizations in the Republic of Ireland, under the Offences against the State Act 1939. Their members have been at risk, upon

53 The report had referred twice to 'in January'.

54 The secretary of state moved promptly to rebut an allegation that she was about to legalize the IRA, by virtue of the concept of specified organization in the prisoners' bill: 6 June 1998, Northern Ireland Information Service: http://www.nio.gov.uk.

conviction in court, based upon evidence (including confessions) of serious legal penalties.[55]

19.53 Secondly, all their firearms, ammunition, explosives and explosive substances have been illegal arms, under most (not all) of the offences scheduled to the Northern Ireland Arms Decommissioning Act 1997, and the offence in relation to any particular arms specified in section 5(1) of the Decommissioning Act 1997 of the Republic of Ireland. Again, members of the illegal organizations, and others, have been at risk of serious legal penalties.

19.54 The only legality in connection with illegal arms belonging to illegal organizations has been in the context of decommissioning, as provided for in the legal texts discussed above (here, decommissioning becomes a term of art in United Kingdom and Irish law.) The mechanism has been amnesty; and it covers only the destruction of illegal arms facilitated by the IICD (or a designated person of the secretary of state or the Irish justice minister[56]). From 24 September 1997, the commission was able to function legally in both parts of Ireland. It was required to undertake such tasks that may have facilitated decommissioning[57] (in accordance with section 3 of the United Kingdom act). The amnesty – in United Kingdom law and in Irish law – bit on 30 June 1998. And the IICD (or a designated person in both jurisdictions), was able legally to verify collection for destruction, or destruction by persons in unlawful possession.

19.55 Refusal to decommission was not legal between 24 September 1997 and 30 June 1998. Members of paramilitary groups remained at risk, even while on ceasefire (and present in the multi-party negotiations), of being charged with membership and possession offences.

19.56 On 30 June 1998, the amnesty period began (alternatively,[58] it had begun in Northern Ireland on 27 February 1997,[59] lapsed on 26 February 1998,[60] and been restored on 24 March 1998[61]). It was renewed on 26 February 1999,[62] and 24 February 2000[63]). The amnesty was due to end on 22 May 2000. On 23 May 2000,[64] it was extended until 19 May 2001; it is not clear why it was not made for a full year. (In United Kingdom law, it may be extended to 26 February 2002; in Irish law, it could be extended by new regulations). The paramilitary parties were

55 This fact led a former Irish taoiseach, Dr Garret FitzGerald, to propose an ethical protocol for the Irish media in its handling of stories about republicans: a preface stating the interviewer was not going to ask a Sinn Féin interviewee about IRA membership (*Irish Times*, 17 July 1999).

56 Section 3(1)(a)–(c) of the United Kingdom act from 24 September 1997; and, from 30 June 1998, section 3(1)(c); section 1(1) of the Irish act throughout.

57 Article 4 of the international agreement.

58 Depending upon the construction of section 4(1) of the United Kingdom act.

59 Northern Ireland Arms Decommissioning Act 1997.

60 Northern Ireland Arms Decommissioning Act 1997 s 2(2)(a).

61 Northern Ireland Arms Decommissioning Act 1997 (Amnesty Period) Order 1998, SI 1998/893.

62 Northern Ireland Arms Decommissioning Act 1997 (Amnesty Period) Order 1999, SI 1999/454.

63 Northern Ireland Arms Decommissioning Act 1997 (Amnesty Period) Order 2000, SI 2000/452.

64 Northern Ireland Arms Decommissioning Act 1997 (Amnesty Period) (No. 2) Order 2000, SI 2000/1409.

given, on 30 June 1998, the opportunity to avail of the amnesty period (less than 23 months – there is no two-year time scale in this respect).

The negotiation of the Belfast Agreement

19.57 As heads of government, the prime minister and the taoiseach could not – and did not at any time – countenance illegal arms being held by illegal organizations in their respective jurisdictions. It would have been unconstitutional in, respectively, United Kingdom law and Irish law.[65] At no point during their time at Castle Buildings, did Tony Blair or Bertie Ahern ever suggest it was legal not to decommission (before a certain date or event); this is the meaning of the political slogan: decommissioning is not a precondition (in the context of illegal arms held by illegal organizations).

19.58 Decommissioning remained a condition precedent throughout, because, without it, the rule of law would have been suspended in Northern Ireland and in the Republic of Ireland. Nothing in the Belfast Agreement, in the other ten sections, much less the Decommissioning section, alters this position on illegality.[66]

19.59 A crucial piece of evidence is the letter of 10 April 1998, from the prime minister to David Trimble (which has been published by Senator Mitchell[67]). This is believed widely to have led finally to the MPA. Tony Blair (and Mo Mowlam) were two of the signatories of the Belfast Agreement. The letter was sent shortly before the final plenary (not afterwards as stated increasingly). And it is inconceivable that the other two signatories, Bertie Ahern and David Andrews, did not see it before signing the BIA (the Irish government has never claimed that it was unaware of the prime minister's undertaking).

19.60 It has a bearing on the meaning of the Belfast Agreement, in particular the Decommissioning section. Under article 31(1) of the 1969 Vienna convention on the law of treaties, the letter is arguably part of the context of the BIA for the purpose of interpretation. This may be established factually under article 31(2)(b). Alternatively – and here the letter is not so central – there should be taken into account, under article 31(3)(c), the principle of legality (by analogy with United Kingdom[68] law and Irish law[69]) in international law.[70] Thirdly, I submit that, under article 32, the letter may be part of the preparatory work of the treaty, and/

65 The taoiseach told the Seanad on 7 July 1999: 'There are still some voices ... who insinuate that we are appeasing terrorism and undermining democracy. The charge is totally unjustified ... I would like if some political leaders and commentators would give a little more credit to both Governments, for our total dedication to protecting the integrity of democracy and constitutional order.' (http://www.irlgov.ie/taoiseach/press/.

66 Thus the prime minister, in reply to a question in parliament, said on 23 June 1999: 'My view is that decommissioning should have happened two years ago. It should have been happening all the time. It should never have been the case that people had weapons in the first place.' (House of Commons, *Hansard*, 6th series, 333, 1163, 23 June 1999)

67 Mitchell, *Making Peace*, pp. 179–80. The letter was reported widely in the press, including (in part) in the *Irish Times* of 11 April 1998.

68 A.V. Dicey, *An Introduction to the Study of the Law of the Constitution*, 10th edn, 1965, pp. 202–3.

69 Articles 6.2, 15.2.1, 15.6.1–2, 28.3.1 & 3 of BNH.

70 Article 38(1)(c), Statute of the International Court of Justice: 'the general principles of law recognized by civilized nations'.

or the circumstances of its conclusion, and recourse may be had to it as a supplementary means of interpretation.

19.61 The prime minister wrote to the leader of the UUP: 'I understand your problem with paragraph 25 of Strand 1 [exclusion or removal from office] is that it requires decisions on those who should be excluded or removed from office in the Northern Ireland Executive to be taken on a cross-community basis.[71] [new paragraph] This letter is to let you know that if, during the course of the first six months of the shadow Assembly or the Assembly itself [that is, 1 July 1998 to 31 December], these provisions have been shown to be ineffective, we will support changes in these provisions to enable them to be made properly effective in preventing such people from holding office. [new paragraph] Furthermore, I confirm that in our view the effect of the decommissioning section of the agreement, with decommissioning schemes coming into effect in June, is that the process of decommissioning should begin straight away.'

19.62 The third, and last, paragraph (also sentence) is relevant to the meaning of the Decommissioning section. The sentence at first blush is illogical. It refers (indirectly) to the end of June 1998. It then goes on to say immediately (10 April 1998).

19.63 The resolution of this conundrum is simple: the prime minister was affirming the illegality of arms being held by paramilitary groups (there was no agreement to let them hold on to them, until some unspecified future event);[72] and he was referring to the point in the Belfast Agreement (paragraph 5 of the Decommissioning section), which signalled that an amnesty – which had been on the statute books in Dublin and London since 26/27 February 1997 – would come into force by the end of June 1998. The paramilitary groups were not told to wait until then; they were told to get on with the transition to legality, and the amnesty – all the protection they had sought and required – would be in place shortly after the assembly elections (and well before the likely nomination of ministers).[73]

19.64 Decommissioning (used colloquially) – in United Kingdom, Irish and international law – had been, and remained, a legal imperative. The Belfast Agreement, made in international law, did not in any way affect the law on decommissioning (as it was specified in two acts, one international agreement, and, shortly, a decommissioning scheme and regulations, plus appropriate orders). It simply contained a promise of the two governments to complete the process of providing for an amnesty; which was not of course – whatever of the politics – a condition precedent to the destruction of paramilitary arms.

The Belfast Agreement in general

19.65 Decommissioning is dealt with in six of the eleven sections of the Belfast Agreement. Given the political project launched by the two governments in December 1993 – to encourage terrorists to cross the bridge to democracy – it is

71 David Trimble was concerned presumably that the SDLP would not support the UUP against Sinn Féin.

72 He could, of course, do no other. And this stance served politically at the time to get agreement.

73 Paragraph 3 of Validation, Implementation and Review.

not surprising that an international agreement by two states parties should be infused with a rejection of political violence.

19.66 The five sections (other than that on Decommissioning) are:

- one, the Declaration of Support section: paragraph 1 refers to 'a new beginning'; paragraph 2 refers to 'a fresh start'; and paragraph 4 invokes the Mitchell principles in part: opposition to any use or threat of force by others for any political purpose; and total and absolute commitment to exclusively democratic and peaceful means of resolving differences on political issues;
- two, the Strand One, Democratic Institutions in Northern Ireland section: paragraph 25 on exclusion or removal from office; this includes the injunction that ministers should use only democratic, non-violent means; also, that those who do not should be excluded or removed from office under this paragraph; failure to meet ministerial responsibilities is the test; this includes responsibilities set out in the Pledge of Office; the mechanism is a loss of confidence vote, requiring cross-community support; paragraph 35, dealing with the transitional period, requires shadow ministers, including the First Minister and Deputy First Minister, to affirm opposition to any use or threat of force by others for political purposes, and commitment to non-violence and exclusively peaceful and democratic means; there is also a good faith requirement; and a requirement to observe the spirit of the Pledge of Office; the Pledge of Office is annexed: there is another good faith requirement in that pledge; it also includes a commitment to non-violence and exclusively peaceful and democratic means; there is also a requirement to comply with an (attached) Ministerial Code of Conduct;
- three, the Rights, Safeguards and Equality of Opportunity section: human rights is the first part; the first paragraph 1 refers to the civil rights and religious liberties of everyone in the community; the first paragraph 2 refers to the United Kingdom government completing incorporation of the 1950 Convention; the first paragraph 4 refers to a possible bill of rights for Northern Ireland; the first paragraph 9 refers to an equivalent level of protection of human rights in the Republic of Ireland; the post-Second World War concept of human rights is premissed on freedom and the rule of law;[74] human rights are incompatible with political violence; while terrorists cannot be denied their rights (*Lawless v Ireland (No. 3)* (1961) 1 EHRR 15, ECtHR), the Convention cannot be used by such groups to engage in any activity or perform any act aimed at the destruction of any of the rights and freedoms (article 17); the HRA 1998 will have an indirect horizontal effect in Northern Ireland law;
- four, the Security section: paragraph 1 refers to the development of a peaceful environment; paragraph 3 refers to any continuing paramilitary activity;
- five, the Prisoners section: paragraph 2 sets the condition precedent of a complete and unequivocal ceasefire before prisoners belonging to a paramilitary organization will be released.

74 Fourth recital to the 1950 Convention.

Moving goalposts

19.67 Decommissioning was implied from the time of the *Downing Street Declaration* (15 December 1993). Sinn Féin resisted IRA decommissioning before entry into talks. Its first victory was the Mitchell report of 22 January 1996, even though it went on to break its complete cessation (and did not renew it until 19 July 1997).

19.68 Sinn Féin then resisted IRA decommissioning during the multi-party negotiations, including after its entry on 9 September 1997. Its second victory was the manner of the establishment of the IICD on 24 September 1997, which took decommissioning out of the talks (while the amnesty provisions were not fully in force). They were not in place until 30 June 1998 – after the Belfast Agreement.

19.69 With the beginning of the transitional period the following day, Sinn Féin continued to resist IRA decommissioning on a number of old and new grounds: it did not speak for the IRA;[75] a condition precedent was the formation of the executive; a condition precedent was the full implementation of the Agreement (as defined by Sinn Féin); the requirements in the Decommissioning section applied to all parties, and amounted only to best endeavours; and latterly, the 22 May 2000 deadline could not be met (the implication being that Sinn Féin ministers were entitled to two years in office before IRA decommissioning).

19.70 Sinn Féin's third victory was the formation of the executive without IRA decommissioning on 2 December 1999, at the expense of the United Kingdom government maintaining the rule of law in part of its state. Other participants insist that the UUP's abandonment of no guns/no government was to get government followed by decommissioning, and that Sinn Féin had indicated in various ways that there would be a start to decommissioning before the de Chastelain January 2000 report (see further below).

19.71 This third victory was rendered Pyrrhic with suspension on 12 February 2000.

19.72 However, with restoration on 30 May 2000, without decommissioning, Sinn Féin secured a fourth victory. The price – which emerged – was inspection (see below). It remains to be seen whether decommissioning has given way to inspection. If so, it will have been game, set and match to Sinn Féin.

19.73 The most authoritative source on the possibility of the IRA decommissioning is Lord Dubs, a NIO minister from May 1997 to December 1999. On 9 February 2000, he told the house of lords: 'Personally, I believe that the leadership of Sinn Fein does want decommissioning; or at least I think that I believe that. I am not certain because we do not know. Such discussions are not held in public, unlike those of the other parties in Northern Ireland.'[76]

TITLE: DECOMMISSIONING

19.74 The word decommissioning came to dominate Northern Ireland politics in the 1990s. It was not used in paragraph 10 of the *Downing Street Declaration* of 15

75 On this, the prime minister has written: 'There are both loyalist parties, and Sinn Féin, who have a clear link to paramilitary groups. Sinn Féin and the IRA are part of the same movement. You can't have the political side in the tent, if the paramilitary side is outside and active.' (*The Times*, 25 June 1999)

76 House of Lords, *Hansard*, 5th series, 609, 694, 9 February 2000.

December 1993 (though it was implied). It certainly appeared in the Washington speech of the secretary of state of 7 March 1995, where three conditions precedent to participation in talks were spelt out: 'a willingness in principle to disarm progressively'; 'a common practical understanding of the modalities, that is to say, what decommissioning would actually entail'; 'in order to test the practical arrangements and to demonstrate good faith, the actual decommissioning of some arms as a tangible confidence building measure and to signal the start of the process'. Disarmament is the goal. Decommissioning would appear to have been coined to cover (as became clear in the Mitchell report) the option of destruction by the paramilitary groups of their own arms. Decommissioning did not become a legal term of art until 26/27 February 1997.

> 1. **[The p]Participants [agreed,]** ***recall their agreement*** **in the Procedural Motion adopted on 24 September 1997[,] "that the resolution of the decommissioning issue is an indispensable part of the process of negotiation"[.], [It is, therefore, an indispensable part of this agreement.]** ***and also recall the provisions of paragraph 25 of Strand 1 above.***

19.75 This paragraph suggests that decommissioning as an issue was settled in the multi-party negotiations. Further, that the sanction of ministerial exclusion or removal was the way to deal with a Sinn Féin (because only Sinn Féin among the paramilitary parties was a beneficiary of the d'Hondt provision) linked to a IRA continuing to refuse to decommission. The paragraph was strengthened at Castle Buildings. The original two sentences were illogical: the first referred historically to the negotiations; the second, to the result. The first implied that, with the successful end of negotiations, the decommissioning issue had been resolved (in the agreement). The loss of the second sentence improved the paragraph. The addition of the reference to paragraph 25 of Strand One brought in immediately the question of sanction.

19.76 The date 24 September 1997 was the day the IICD was established in Northern Ireland and the Republic of Ireland, through the international agreement entering into force.

19.77 On 15 September 1997, the prime minister and the taoiseach had issued a joint statement dealing mainly with decommissioning. The *Downing Street Declaration* was cited. On the main issue, they said: 'The two Governments see the resolution of the decommissioning issue as an indispensable part of the process of negotiation, alongside other confidence-building measures for all sides.' This was a reference to the republicans considering the unionist community, and the United Kingdom government responding to the minority. They affirmed total commitment to the Mitchell report, but noted: 'Successful decommissioning will depend on the co-operation of the paramilitary organisations themselves and cannot in practice be imposed on them as a precondition for successful negotiation or as an absolute obligation.'

19.78 At the plenary of the multi-party negotiations on 24 September 1997, the procedural motion[77] did inter alia three things. One, with the establishment of the IICD, it adjourned discussion of its proposals on decommissioning to a subsequent

77 The text to which it refers – Agenda for Remainder of the Opening Plenary – is reproduced in Mitchell, *Making Peace*, p. 84.

plenary. Two, it endorsed the 15 September 1997 statement: 'Plenary agrees that the resolution of the decommissioning issue is an indispensable part of the process of negotiation, alongside other confidence building measures; all delegations are hereby committed to work constructively and in good faith to secure the implementation of the compromise approach to decommissioning set out in the Report of the International Body.' Three, on the issue of mechanisms, it set up a liaison sub-committee on decommissioning (to assist as appropriate the implementation of all aspects of decommissioning as set out in the Report of the International Body), and another on confidence building measures (for those mentioned in the Mitchell report, and any others referred by the plenary). Sinn Féin voted against the decommissioning proposals, but, under the rules of procedure, was unable to prevent substantive negotiations proceeding on the basis of the procedural motion. (As noted in the Prologue, Sinn Féin did not vote for the Belfast Agreement on 10 April 1998, so it never had to recall the procedural motion to which it had been opposed.)

19.79 Paragraph 25 of Strand One is discussed above in Chapter 12.

> **2. *They* [Participants] note the progress made by the Independent International Commission on Decommissioning and the Governments in developing schemes which *can* represent a workable basis for achieving the decommissioning of illegally-held arms in the possession of paramilitary groups.**

19.80 The change to the MDP – the deletion of participants – was necessary because, while participants came to be used to mean political parties, under the *Ground Rules for Substantive All-Party Negotiations*, Cm 3232, 16 April 1996, the participants included the two governments (rule 10). The participants could not, therefore, note the progress of the two governments. (Possibly for the same reason, the definite article was dropped before participants in paragraph 1 above; alternatively, it was to get round the problem of Sinn Féin having voted against on 24 September 1997.)

19.81 The progress of the IICD, from its establishment on 24 September 1997, has been reviewed above. The only development of significance was the decision on a decommissioning scheme (to use United Kingdom legal language), which was submitted to the two governments on 15 January 1998.

19.82 The Irish act defined decommissioning as either the destruction of arms, or the transferring to or leading to the collection and destruction by the commission or a person designated by the secretary of state or the Irish justice minister. Destruction was defined as 'includ[ing] making permanently inaccessible or unusable'.[78] The United Kingdom act was drafted more clearly. Destruction was defined as 'includ[ing] making permanently inaccessible or permanently unusable'.[79] (It was only in late 1999/early 2000 that permanently inaccessible began to assume the meaning of bunkers under seemingly joint control.) Four methods of decommissioning were outlined in section 3 (though a decommissioning scheme could include more): one, transfer to the commission/a designated person for destruction; two, depositing for collection and destruction by the

78 Section 1(1).
79 Section 10(1).

commission/a designated person; three, provision of information for the purpose of collection and destruction by the commission/a designated person; and four, destruction by persons in unlawful possession.

19.83 The progress made by the IICD was to whittle these four methods down to two, the third and fourth. They were contained in the decommissioning scheme[80] and regulations[81] of 30 June 1998.

19.84 This paragraph, however, makes clear that decommissioning covers only illegally held arms in the possession of paramilitary groups.

> **3. All participants *accordingly* reaffirm their commitment to the total disarmament of all paramilitary organisations. *They also confirm* [and] their intention to continue to work constructively *and in good faith* with the Independent Commission [on Decommissioning to achieve this.]**
>
> **[4.] [All participants undertake to work constructively and in good faith with the Independent Commission], *and to use any influence they may have*, to achieve the decommissioning of all paramilitary arms within [a fixed and limited period of (X] two years following endorsement in referendums North and South of the *agreement* [overall settlement)] *and* in the context of the implementation of the overall settlement.**
>
> **[[Note from the Independent Chairmen: Remaining to be resolved is the time frame for decommissioning (paragraph 3 above).]]**

19.85 This is the most important paragraph of the section, dealing with the obligations under the Belfast Agreement of the paramilitary parties. There were originally two paragraphs – 3 and 4 – plus a note at the end from the independent chairmen in square brackets (it referred to paragraph 3 when it should have been paragraph 4). The text was amended considerably at Castle Buildings, and 'X years' was specified as two years from 22 May 1998.

19.86 The addition of the word 'accordingly' links this new paragraph 3 to paragraphs 1 and 2. The subject in all three is the 'participants', understood, in paragraph 2, as the political parties. Participants in paragraph 1 and here includes the political parties. 'reaffirm their commitment to the total disarmament of all paramilitary organisations' refers to the Mitchell principles. The second principle is: '[affirm their total and absolute commitment] To the total disarmament of all paramilitary organisations'. The political parties made their affirmations at the start of multi-party negotiations, on 12 June 1996. Sinn Féin did it on 9 September 1997 (only to have the IRA distance itself the following day – a distancing the United Kingdom and Irish governments refused to accept[82]). 'they also confirm' was reference to paragraph 1 and the procedural motion of 24 September 1997. This included: 'All delegations are committed to work constructively with the Independent Commission to enable it to carry out its role;'. (Role is specified in the international agreement, in articles 3 [objective] and 4 [functions].) However, Sinn Féin did not vote for this on 24 September 1997. It was therefore in no position to

80 Paragraph 2; though the designated person is not mentioned.

81 Regulation 4.

82 'As to the IRA's attitude to the Mitchell Principles per se, well, the IRA would have problems with sections of the Mitchell Principles. But then the IRA is not a participant in the talks.' (*An Phoblacht*, 11 September 1997); Mitchell, *Making Peace*, p. 115.

confirm on 10 April 1998. In good faith was added to the confirmation. Good faith is mentioned in paragraph 5 of the Declaration of Support. It is also contained in the Pledge of Office, annexed to Strand One.

19.87 'and to use any influence they may have' was added to the MDP. It has been used by Sinn Féin in 1998-2000 as the basis of its minimalist construction of its obligations under this section; that is, Sinn Féin and the IRA are separate, and it has little or no influence. Its addition did not weaken the obligations for two reasons.

19.88 One, the language of the Belfast Agreement is at times diplomatic and at other times rhetorical. Thus, new beginning and new start in the Declaration of Support. If the agreement marked a historical turning point, then it would have been undiplomatic in the extreme to have singled out the three paramilitary parties in the negotiations (Sinn Féin, the Progressive Unionist Party and the Ulster Democratic Party) in this section.[83] Two, the two governments, the signatories of the BIA (to which the MPA is Annex 1) had encouraged these three parties into the talks precisely because of their close connections with, respectively, the IRA, the UVF and the UDA. Ceasefires were a condition precedent for political participation. And the the UDP and Sinn Féin were suspended from the talks for actions of the UDA and the IRA. Those connections, and widespread perceptions that they exist, did not alter, even if 10 April 1998 represented a moment of hope. The spirit of the Belfast Agreement – exemplified most clearly in the release of terrorist prisoners – was that violence was a thing of the past; the paramilitary parties represented an irreversible transition from terrorism to democracy.

19.89 'to achieve the decommissioning of all paramilitary arms within two years following endorsement in referendums North and South of the agreement' is the goal of the paragraph, indeed of the section, and arguably of the Belfast Agreement. It is clear, again, that only paramilitary arms are being specified. To achieve suggests a general obligation on all participants, the two governments and the eight political parties. This is true, to some extent. The two governments have general legal obligations to do with the rule of law. Other political parties have foregrounded decommissioning; they can argue legitimately that they are fulfilling their obligations under this paragraph. But – I submit – this obligation relates most closely to the three paramilitary parties. The two heads of government, after all, had said on 15 September 1997: 'Successful decommissioning will depend on the co-operation of the paramilitary organisations themselves and cannot in practice be imposed on them as a pre-condition for succcessful negotiation or as an absolute obligation.' The date for the referendums of 22 May 1998 is given in paragraph 2 of the Validation, Implementation and Review section. This makes 22 May 2000 the deadline for Sinn Féin, the PUP and the UDP having achieved the decommissioning of all paramilitary arms (at least of the IRA, the UVF and the UDA).

19.90 'in the context of the implementation of the overall settlement' is an important phrase. Decommissioning is a condition precedent through the operation of general law. Within the terms of the Belfast Agreement, there are no

83 According to the Rt. Hon. John Taylor MP: 'If the detail of when and how decommissioning would take place was omitted, this was in recognition of the difficulty of the task facing republican leaders.' (*Irish Times*, 18 February 2000)

strict conditions precedent. The executive is not a condition precedent for decommissioning. Nor is it a condition precedent for the NSMC (as paragraphs 35 of Strand One and paragraph 7 of Strand Two read together indicate).

19.91 The spirit of the Belfast Agreement – as is clear from its legal structure in the BIA – is that all parties (plus the two governments) have to discharge their obligations side by side. It was only when that happened, that the BIA could enter into force (and devolution take place simultaneously). If was, of course, anticipated that devolution would take place before the completion of decommissioning, or the release of all the prisoners. There are few deadlines in the agreement (31 October 1998 is a target in paragraph 8 of Strand Two). However, there are two specific periods of time mentioned: two years for decommissioning in this paragraph; and two years for the final release of qualifying prisoners in paragraph 3 of the Prisoners section (which was also added to the MDP). It is difficult not to believe there is a relationship between prisoners and decommissioning in the agreement (as well as in politics). There is no start date for the release of prisoners, but late June 1998 is given as the earliest possible beginning. Similarly, no start date is given for decommissioning (aside from the illegality point, which is reason enough for not specify a start date). But, again, late June 1998 is specified, though this time for the decommissioning schemes (on which the amnesty rests).[84]

19.92 In the context of the implementation of the overall settlement means – I submit – that all parties and the two governments have to show good faith by doing what they are required to do under the agreement. Most work fell to the United Kingdom government. The Irish government's responsibility was commensurately less. Much of the responsibility for creating the institutions of government fell on the First Minister and Deputy First Minister from 1 July 1998. The only responsibility of the three paramilitary parties, other than participating in a preparatory assembly, was to complete the transition from terrorism to democracy by fulfilling the practical and symbolic task of decommissioning to the satisfaction of the IICD.

19.93 The parenthetical note from the independent chairmen in the MDP is further evidence of the objective of this paragraph: decommissioning pure and simple within a fixed time period from 22 May 1998.

> [5.] 4. **The Independent Commission will monitor, review and verify progress on decommissioning of illegal arms, and will report to both Governments at regular intervals.**

19.94 This paragraph is crucial to the status of the IICD. It makes clear that decommissioning is the responsibility of the two governments. They, after all, comprise the commission, and have ultimate responsibility for the rule of law. The objective of the IICD under article 3 of the international agreement is to facilitate

84 Lord Dubs, who helped take the NIA 1998 through the house of lords said: 'However, I say to the republicans in Northern Ireland that under the Good Friday Agreement there was no starting date for prisoner releases, no starting date for dealing with the question of the RUC, no starting date for reducing the number of troops in Northern Ireland and no starting date for the criminal justice review. We, The Government, started all that. Therefore, when they say that in the Good Friday agreement there was no starting date for decommissioning, certainly, there was not. However, in terms of good faith and building up trust, it was clear that there was a proper expectation, and we achieved many difficult things.' (House of Lords, *Hansard*, 5th series, 609, 695–6, 9 February 2000)

decommissioning. Functions are dealt with in article 4. The third function is to undertake such tasks that may be required. These include observing, monitoring and verifying. They are the three specified in this paragraph. This does not mean that the functions under the Belfast Agreement have been restricted. The phrase progress on decommissioning means it is a process, ending with complete disarmament. The term illegal arms resembles illegally-held arms in paragraph 2. Both confirm the point made about legality and general law. Reporting to both governments at regular intervals is provided for in article 4; function (d). There, the commission is to report periodically.

> **6. [sic] Both Governments will take all necessary steps to facilitate the decommissioning process** ***to include bringing the relevant schemes into force by the end of June.***

19.95 This paragraph is incorrectly numbered. The problem originated with this being paragraph 6 in the MDP. The merging of paragraphs 3 and 4 led to the renumbering; it should be paragraph 5. The correct number has been entered in Cm 4705 (and in the 1999 Irish version). The text was also amended. The version in the MDP made clear that decommissioning was the ultimate responsibility of the two governments. Their role is defined as facilitating, which is the same as the IICD. But the two governments established the commission, and, under article 12, may terminate the treaty by mutual agreement.

19.96 This remains the position, with the amendment in the FA. The relevant schemes are referred to in paragraph 2. The concept of schemes originated in the United Kingdom decommissioning act, which received the royal assent on 27 February 1997. A decommissioning scheme is defined in section 1(1) as made by the secretary of state. Relevant schemes in this section could arguably be a reference to section 1(1). However, the two governments here, and the IICD in paragraph 2, are operating in the context of an international agreement. I submit that schemes – in the plural – includes the regulations and arrangements defined in section 1(1) of the Irish decommissioning act, the relevant regulations being provided for in section 2.

19.97 On 29 June 1998, Adam Ingram, a junior NIO minister, for and on behalf of the secretary of state, issued the United Kingdom's decommissioning scheme (a booklet produced by the NIO), to come into force on the following day. Also on 29 June 1998, the Irish justice minister, John O'Donoghue, made the Decommissioning Act 1997 (Decommissioning) Regulations 1998, to come into operation on the following day.

Decommissioning since the Belfast Agreement

19.98 Since 10 April 1998, as is clear from the IICD report of 2 July 1999 (discussed above), there has been one instance of decommissioning. This was by the LVF on 18 December 1998. There has been no decommissioning by the IRA, the principal republican organization. Nor has there been any decommissioning by the UVF or UDA. No other smaller organizations have decommissioned.

19.99 This is in spite of the paramilitary groups having a central concern in securing the release of their prisoners, under the Prisoners section of the Belfast Agreement. The relationship between prisoner releases and decommissioning is considered in Chapter 22.

19.100 There have been four major attempts to secure decommissioning, both involving subsidiary political agreements. Three were negotiated by the prime minister and the taoiseach, and the third, by Senator George Mitchell. The first attempt was at Hillsborough Castle (outside Belfast) with a declaration on 1 April 1999 (the eve of Good Friday that year).[85] The second, with the joint statement, *The Way Forward*, was at Castle Buildings on 2 July 1999.[86] The third, also at Castle Buildings, the Mitchell review of September to November 1999 (which led to devolution on 2 December 1999), resulted in sequenced statements between 15 and 18 November 1999. The fourth attempt was arranged at Hillsborough Castle on 4 and 5 May 2000, and led to four sequenced documents, most especially a statement from the IRA.

19.101 On the first occasion, the two governments and all the other political parties were aligned against Sinn Féin. In the second, the UUP – isolated among the so-called pro-agreement parties – refused to assent; this led to the resignation of the Deputy First Minister on 15 July 1999 (a resignation subsequently not accepted by the assembly). On the third occasion, there was an understanding apparently between Sinn Féin and the UUP, and, when decommissioning did not result by 31 January 2000, the secretary of state moved to suspend the institutions on 12 February 2000. On the fourth occasion, the United Kingdom and Irish governments sponsored an apparent agreement between the UUP and Sinn Féin.

The Hillsborough declaration of 1 April 1999

19.102 This is a four-page text, described as a working draft.[87] It was the work of the prime minister and the taoiseach. Accompanying it was a set of additional standing orders (also dated 1 April 1999) – numbers 22–25 – with amendments underlined. The text contains statements about the position of various parties.

19.103 The prime minister also spoke on behalf of the two heads of government at a press conference at Hillsborough Castle. He referred to devolution 'within the next few weeks'. There was to be a pause for reflection – over Easter – until 13 April 1999, with a final round of meetings then. (This was because – according to the declaration – Sinn Féin, while acknowledging the obligation to decommission, was unable to indicate the timescale to the beginning.[88])

19.104 The declaration also defined the polar positions in the decommissioning debate: Sinn Féin 'do not regard the Agreement as imposing any requirement to make a start before the establishment of the new institutions'; 'the UUP do not wish to move to the establishment of the new institutions without some evident progress with decommissioning'.

85 Talks began on 29 March 1999.

86 Talks began on 28 June 1999. This was the title of part IV of the discussion paper, *The Future of Northern Ireland: a paper for discussion*, NIO 1972.

87 It was published in the *Irish Times* of 2 April 1999.

88 1 April 1999 also saw the publication of the IRA's Easter statement in *An Phoblacht*: 'We reaffirm our commitment to our objectives, a united and independent Ireland, a national democracy, the achievement of which offers, we believe, the best guarantee of the establishment of a just and lasting peace. The IRA wants to see a permanent peace in this country.'

19.105 In the declaration, the prime minister and the taoiseach used the phrase, of the Belfast Agreement, implementation in full. (This was to return.) They also stated that all parties agreed that decommissioning, while not a precondition, was 'an obligation deriving from their commitment in the Agreement'. This requires two comments: one, there is a condition precedent in general law, and, under the Belfast Agreement, a condition precedent can certainly be implied as the date of 22 May 2000 approaches;[89] two, the admission about an obligation does not preclude a further obligation in general law. Decommissioning was also to take place 'within the timescale' of the agreement. And it would be done 'through the efforts' of the IICD.

19.106 The Hillsborough declaration put forward a five-point plan sequenced as follows. One, on a date to be set, the running of d'Hondt to select shadow ministers. Two, on a date to be set by the IICD (not later than one month), a collective act of reconciliation. This would see some arms put beyond use on a voluntary basis, in a manner to be verified by the IICD, and further changes in security policy. There would be ceremonies of remembrance of all victims of violence. Three, around the time of the act of reconciliation, the devolution of powers to Northern Ireland, and the entry into force of the BIA. Four, one month after nomination date, an IICD report on progress. And five, if points two to four are not met, the nominations made under point one fail to be confirmed by the assembly.

19.107 This joint United Kingdom/Irish plan had the following characteristics.[90] First, there was a shadow period, as anticipated in paragraph 35 of Strand One (this was provided for in additional standing order 22(1) and (13).) Secondly, the time scale for aborting the exercise, at least in additional standing order 22(13), was 1 May 1999; entry was possible, because exit without damage was guaranteed. Thirdly, the IICD fixed the date for the collective act of reconciliation, which could not be later than its report on progress (it could be the same day). Fourthly, the collective act of reconciliation was a new creative idea, but the ceremonies of rememberance had not evidently been thought through.[91] Fifthly, the definition of arms put beyond use on a voluntary basis: put beyond use was new terminology; voluntary (decommissioning) recalled the joint statement of September 1997. This was, nevertheless, decommissioning as legally required by the IICD. Sixthly, the linkage with changes in security policy made express what was only implied in the Belfast Agreement. Seventhly, the relationship between decommissioning and devolution was obscured by 'around the time of the act of reconciliation'. However, since the act of reconciliation was decided by the IICD, and devolution by the secretary of state, and there was an effective failsafe of lapsing nominations, there was no risk of members of paramilitary parties acquiring ministerial powers. Eighthly, the IICD had to report on progress. Progress could only be decommissioning (even if not actual decommissioning). Ninthly, the nominations would fall automatically, unless confirmed by the assembly on a cross-community basis on a motion proposed by the First Minister and Deputy First Minister acting jointly.

89 Anthony Aust, *Modern Treaty Law and Practice*, Cambridge 2000, pp. 201–2.

90 The prime minister, on behalf of the two governments, outlined the plan differently.

91 The prime minister did not mention them in his summary.

The Way Forward *document of 2 July 1999*

19.108 This document was prefaced by events at Downing Street on Friday, 14 May 1999. By then, Sinn Féin had refused to accept the 1 April declaration. The Irish government, one party after another, and then the United Kingdom government, peeled away from the Hillsborough position. The UUP was left alone, faced with a – one-page – plan to let Sinn Féin into (initially shadow) positions without decommissioning; devolution was anticipated for 30 June 1999.[92]

19.109 *The Way Forward*[93] was based on a joint statement of principles of 25 June 1999: an inclusive executive exercising devolved powers; decommissioning of all paramilitary arms by May 2000; decommissioning to be carried out in a manner determined by the Independent International Commission on Decommissioning.[94]

19.110 The document – a joint statement by the United Kingdom and Irish governments – comprises another five-point plan in two pages of text.[95] One, a reaffirmation of the three principles of 25 June 1999. Two, the running of d'Hondt on 15 July 1999. Three, the devolution order (required by section 3 of the NIA 1998) to be laid before parliament on 16 July 1999, to take effect on (Sunday) 18 July 1999. Four, the IICD: to confirm the start of decommissioning 'within the period specified' by the commission; the commission to specify actual decommissioning 'is to start within a specified time'; progress reports in September 1999, December 1999 and May 2000. Five, a failsafe paragraph: legislation to provide for automatic suspension of the institutions, if commitments regarding decommissioning or devolution are not met, in accord with the review provisions of the Belfast Agreement. 'All sides have legislative safeguards to ensure that commitments entered into are met.'

19.111 This joint United Kingdom/Irish plan – with legislation at Westminster[96] – was notable for the following. First, in the three principles, a possible change to the objective of the IICD, with it determining the manner of decommissioning.[97] Secondly, the d'Hondt provision was as on 1 April 1999, but with the context removed. Thirdly, devolution was now inevitable, between 16 and 18 July 1999. Fourthly, the start to decommissioning, and actual decommissioning, was left entirely to the commission.[98] While the commission was to report on (at least)

92 *Irish Times*, 17 May 1999.

93 The origin of the phrase has been debated.

94 *Irish Times*, 26 June 1999. These three principles originated in the prime minister's comments to the press conference at Hillsborough on 1 April 1999, based upon the declaration. These principles are reiterated in *The Way Forward*.

95 The prime minister made a statement in the commons on the plan: House of Commons, *Hansard*, 6th series, 334, 639–53, 5 July 1999.

96 Lord Dubs told the House of Lords: 'We have kept [the Irish government] in touch with developments on this Bill and we continue to do so. We have not formally sought their agreement to it: we seek that only from Parliament.' (House of Lords, *Hansard*, 5th series, 604, 395, 14 July 1999.

97 See the reference to de Chastelain as arbiter in a report of the 14 May 1999 meeting in Downing Street: *Sunday Telegraph*, 27 June 1999.

98 General de Chastelain, in a statement of 2 July 1999, specified the former as 'literally a couple of days after devolution', and the latter 'within a few weeks of the start of the

three occasions, the failsafe required the IICD to declare a breach of its secret agreement with the paramilitary group (it was not automatic). Fifthly, there is no requirement for suspension in the review provisions of the Belfast Agreement. And the sanction appeared – but only appeared – to bite initially on the UUP if it should decline to participate in the running of d'Hondt on 15 July 1999.

19.112 Two texts help explain this plan: one headed, 'Breaking the impasse: A Sinn Féin declaration', released on 1 July 1999;[99] and the second, the 2 July 1999 report of General de Chastelain's commission.[100]

19.113 The Sinn Féin text was only to be issued following the establishment of the executive by 30 June 1999.[101] The declaration was not, therefore, made. It would have included the following paragraphs: 'Sinn Féin have long argued that it is only through the full implementation of the agreement, in particular the operation of its institutions and delivery of equality and justice, that the issue of arms will be finally and satisfactorily settled ... we believe that all of us, as participants acting in good faith, could succeed in persuading those with arms to decommission them in accordance with the agreement. We agree that this should be in the manner set down by the Independent Commission on Decommissioning within the terms of the Good Friday Agreement ... This reflects our conviction that through the overall implementation of the Good Friday Agreement we are working to remove the cause of conflict. Conflict must be finished forever – it must for all of us [be] a thing of the past.'[102]

19.114 Full implementation was inspired by the 1 April 1999 declaration. That is not what paragraph 3 of this section says. And the draft declaration makes clear Sinn Féin's maximalist interpretation of the agreement (which it has always portrayed as a transitional arrangement). Secondly, it is not admitted even implicitly that Sinn Féin has any responsibility for IRA arms. Thirdly, the key word is could – not would, or will. Fourthly, within the time frame of the agreement is not specified (and was subsequently rejected as not being possible).[103]

19.115 The IICD report of the following day relied entirely upon this text. To paragraph 10 of the draft report, General de Chastelain added: 'the Sinn Fein statement of 1 July offers promise that decommissioning by all paramilitary groups may now begin. The Commission expects that Sinn Fein's proposal will be endorsed by the IRA and reciprocated by loyalist and other republican paramilitary groups.' But paragraph 16 made clear the offer was highly conditional: 'In anticipation that this proposal may translate into a commitment to decommission paramilitary arms, the Commission believes that to complete its mandate by 22 May 2000, the process of decommissioning should begin as soon as possible.'[104]

decommissioning process'. These were quoted by Mo Mowlam, *Irish News*, 3 July 1999, and by the prime minister: House of Commons, *Hansard*, 6th series, 334, 640, 5 July 1999.

99 Published in the *Irish Times*, 2 July 1999.

100 Released with *The Way Forward*.

101 For what two Newry republicans say they were told by Sinn Féin leaders at Castle Buildings on 30 June 1999, see the *Daily Telegraph*, 5 and 6 July 1999. See also Gerry Adams' interview in *An Phoblacht*, 8 July 1999, and his article in the *Irish Times* and *Guardian* of 14 July 1999.

102 Annex 1. This text differs significantly from the paraphrasing earlier in the document.

103 This may have been inspired by paragraph 20 of the 1 July 1999 declaration by Sinn Féin.

104 See also paragraph 20 to similar effect.

19.116 Events turned to Westminster, where the Northern Ireland Bill had its first reading in the commons on Monday, 12 July 1999. Since suspension under clauses 1(1)(b) and 6(4) could operate only after devolution, there was no immediate sanction on the UUP; also, clause three allowed for two meetings of the assembly during this time. As for decommissioning, a new concept of commitment was introduced.[105] An unfavourable report from the IICD was a condition precedent for the secretary of state acting. The assembly and executive committee would be suspended.

19.117 A draft agreement between the two governments of 13 July 1999 (placed in the library of the house of commons)[106] also specified the impact on the international organizations: the BIC and NSMC would not meet (they could not in any case); however, the BIIC would continue;[107] also, the implementation bodies would continue for four months.

19.118 Second and third reading in the commons were on the Tuesday. The government refused all amendments, most from the opposition and UUP combined. On the Wednesday at question time, the prime minister promised amendments: one, the IICD's timetable;[108] two, automatic suspension for breach of the timetable; and three, identification of the defaulting parties in decommissioning or devolution. (The amendments were promised for the following day; as events transpired, they were never produced.) Their inspiration was attributed to the Rt. Hon. John Major MP and the Rt. Hon. David Trimble MP.[109] The bill had its first and second reading in the Lords the same day. That evening, the UUP reaffirmed its 'no guns, no government' position.

19.119 In order to prevent an anti-Sinn Féin debate, the party declined to attend the assembly the following morning, Thursday, 15 July 1999. The secretary of state, however, proceeded with the meeting of the assembly – which meant the running of d'Hondt.[110] There was, however, an emergency initial standing order – ISO 22(15) – which required, after the appointment of ten ministers, their immediate removal from office if there were not three designated unionists. A government for Northern Ireland of six SDLP and four Sinn Féin members existed – without powers – for some seconds.[111] Following this, the Deputy First Minister made a personal statement resigning his post (the initial presiding officer, contrary to the wishes of the secretary of state, allowed party leaders to reply).[112]

19.120 The secretary of state – announcing the resignation to the commons shortly afterwards (at 12.30) – stated that the bill would now not proceed on the emergency timetable in the lords (this was repeated by Lord Dubs at 15.44). There

105 Defined in clause 1(6) as 'a commitment arising under the Belfast Agreement or the Joint Statement'. The joint statement was *The Way Forward*. It was scheduled to the bill.

106 Under cover of a letter from Geoffrey Hoon, minister of state in the FCO, 13 July 1999.

107 There is an argument (under the second paragraph 7 of Strand Three, and section 54 of the NIA 1998) that the absence of Northern Ireland ministers – due to suspension – precludes the discussion of Northern Ireland non-devolved business.

108 General de Chastelain, however, had reported this was to be drawn up in negotiations with the paramilitary groups.

109 House of Lords, *Hansard*, 5th series, 604, 341, 14 July 1999.

110 Under ISO 22(1) of 8 July 1999.

111 New Northern Ireland Assembly, *Official Report*, vol. 2, p. 323, 15 July 1999.

112 New Northern Ireland Assembly, *Official Report*, vol. 2, pp. 324–37, 15 July 1999.

was no devolution order on Friday, 16 July 1999, and no devolution on 18 July 1999.

The outcome of the Mitchell review, 15–18 November 1999

19.121 The basis of the review was again the three principles of 25 June 1999: inclusiveness; decommissioning; the IICD. Senator Mitchell agreed in July 1999 to return to Northern Ireland. The review began on 6 September 1999. On 9 October 1999, David Trimble, at his party's annual conference, hinted at devolution followed by decommissioning.[113] Mo Mowlam was replaced as secretary of state by Peter Mandelson on 11 October 1999. Irish government officials also returned to Castle Buildings. But this time the two heads of government left it to Senator Mitchell. He worked with the parties, and to a lesser extent with the two governments (plus the United States), mainly at Castle Buildings in Belfast, but also crucially in London (at Winfield House, the residence of the United States ambassador).

19.122 The political agreement[114] – after eleven weeks – was based on a sequence of choreographed statements by the main players,[115] between Monday 15 November 1999 and Thursday 18 November 1999:[116]

- one, a statement by Senator Mitchell on the Monday, in which he said that 'the pro-Agreement parties and the governments share the view that devolution should occur and the institutions should be established at the earliest possible dates', and that 'it was also common ground that decommissioning should occur as quickly as possible and that the commission should play a central role in achieving this under the terms of the agreement';
- two, the assessment of the IICD requested on 2 November – the third de Chastelain report discussed above – also published on 15 November, in which the decommissioning commission referred to 'a new context in which the situation will be transformed', but stated urgent progress – in particular authorized representatives, and discussions about modalities – was now needed. A further report was promised within days of meetings with paramilitary representatives;
- three, a long statement by the UUP, at 10.35 on the Tuesday, which acknowledged the legitimacy of constitutional nationalism, and concluded: 'If, in our view, a genuine and meaningful response is forthcoming [to the IICD report], the way will then be clear for the establishment of the political institutions envisaged in the Belfast Agreement';

113 'To me the words "jump together", "choreography" and "sequencing" all refer to the same thing, namely the procedures by which we make sure that devolution is accompanied by decommissioning.' (*Irish Times*, 11 October 1999)

114 The secretary of state referred on 15 November 1999 to 'the parties' agreement'.

115 'The review has not produced a single text like the Good Friday agreement. Instead it has concentrated on building trust and confidence by means of a number of important steps forward rather than waiting for one giant leap that might never be made.' (Peter Mandelson, House of Commons, *Hansard*, 6th series, 339, 345, 22 November 1999)

116 All of which were accessed from the *Irish Times*' Breaking News service: http://www.ireland.com.

- four, a Sinn Féin statement later, at 12.10, which referred to almost four years of an IRA cessation: 'IRA guns are silent and the Sinn Fein leadership is confident that the IRA remains committed to the objective of a permanent peace.' The party reiterated essentially the Mitchell principles, and stated that the two Sinn Féin ministers would honour the pledge of office. It concluded: 'All sections of our people have suffered profoundly in this conflict. That suffering is a matter of deep regret but makes the difficult process of removing conflict all the more imperative. Sinn Fein wishes to work with, not against, the unionists and recognises this as yet another imperative';
- five, an IRA statement on the Wednesday, signed by P. O'Neill – hailed by the United Kingdom and Irish governments as a new development – which included: 'We acknowledge the leadership given by Sinn Fein throughout this process.' The IRA announced that, following the establishment of the institutions, it would appoint a representative 'to enter into discussions with' the IICD; and
- six, Senator Mitchell's concluding report of the review on the Thursday. 'Not long ago', he said, 'the Ulster Unionists and Sinn Fein did not speak directly. In the early weeks of the review, their exchanges were harsh and filled with recrimination. But gradually, as one of them put it, "trust crept in".' He concluded: 'I believe that a basis now exists for devolution to occur, for the institutions to be established, and for decommissioning to take place as soon as possible. Devolution should take effect, then the Executive should meet, and then the paramilitary groups should appoint their authorised representatives, all on the same day, in that order.'

19.123 These six statements together reveal the following: one, the role of the IICD was crucial (Mitchell, 15 November and 18 November); two, the de Chastelain commission requested authorized representatives, and discussions about modalities (IICD, 15 November); three, the UUP appeared to suggest that, if one or both happened, devolution would follow (UUP, 16 November); four, the republican movement indicated that, following devolution, an IRA representative would be appointed (Sinn Féin, 16 November; IRA, 17 November), five, Senator Mitchell confirmed the republican movement's version[117] (including a meeting of the executive), but he also referred to 'a basis now exist[ing] ... for decommissioning to take place as soon as possible'[118] (18 November).

19.124 Everything but decommissioning ensued: the secretary of state reported political progress to parliament on 22 November 1999;[119] the Ulster unionist council voted by 480 to 349 (58 per cent in favour) to enter government (and agreed to review the matter in February 2000); ministers were nominated in the assembly on 29 November 1999;[120] the devolution order was laid before parliament on 30 November 1999;[121] devolution took place on 2 December 1999 (and all the institutions were established); the IRA announced on 2 December

117 See also the statement of the secretary of state of 17 November 1999.

118 This was reiterated by the secretary of state on 20 November 1999.

119 House of Commons, *Hansard*, 6th series, 339, 345–59, 22 November 1999.

120 New Northern Ireland Assembly *Official Report*, vol. 3, no. 1, pp. 23–7, 29 November 1999.

121 House of Commons, *Hansard*, 6th series, 340, 253–76, 30 November 1999; Northern Ireland Act 1998 (Appointed Day) Order 1999, SI 1999/3208.

1999 appointment of a representative, and the UDA followed on 8 December 1999; in de Chastelain's fourth report of 10 December 1999, it was revealed that initial meetings had taken place.

19.125 No progress (as was to be revealed when the Irish government agreed to its release) was reported on 31 January 2000, in de Chastelain's fifth report; the secretary of state told the house of commons on 3 February 2000 there would be a suspension;[122] parliament debated the Northern Ireland Bill between 8 and 10 February 2000;[123] on 11 February 2000 – before the receipt of de Chastelain's sixth report – the secretary of state signed the suspension order;[124] this took effect on 12 February 2000, the day the Ulster unionist council met to review sharing power with Sinn Féin; under section 2 of the Northern Ireland Act 2000, a review under the Belfast Agreement was a condition precedent for the restoration of the institutions.

19.126 Considerable controversy was generated by the events of 11 February 2000. The legally significant points are: one, the idea for suspension came from London and Dublin in July 1999, as the solution to a default on devolution or decommissioning; two, this was reiterated by the secretary of state in the house of commons on 22 November 1999;[125] three, there is evidence that David Trimble only agreed to devolution because the secretary of state (and the Irish government) promised to suspend if there was no decommissioning by 31 January 2000;[126] four, there appears to have been an agreement, or at least understanding, between the UUP and Sinn Féin, on which Senator Mitchell could comment;[127] five, the IRA was under notice from 1 February 2000, and its offer of 11 February 2000 (as reported by the decommissioning commission) was either tactical[128] or, alternatively, substantive[129] and extracted under pressure; six, the secretary of state suspended the institutions to save David Trimble (from the UUP and the 29–29 unionist split in the assembly), using the argument of a loss of political confidence

122 House of Commons, *Hansard*, 6th series, 343, 1311–27, 3 February 2000.

123 House of Commons, *Hansard*, 6th series, 344, 121–220, 8 February 2000; House of Lords, 5th series, 609, 664–704, 9 February 2000 and 776–97, 843, 10 February 2000.

124 Northern Ireland Act 2000 (Commencement) Order 2000, SI 2000/396.

125 House of Commons, *Hansard*, 6th series, 339, 346, 349–50, 354, 358, 22 November 1999; statement of the taoiseach to Dáil Éireann, *Official Report*, 23 November 1999. See also the secretary of state's statement to parliament: House of Commons, *Hansard*, 6th series, 340, 256, 30 November 1999.

126 House of Commons, *Hansard*, 6th series, 344, 150, 8 February 2000.

127 'I accept that it was clearly understood during the course of the Mitchell review that, while no commitment or guarantee was given that decommissioning should happen in January, none the less it was equally clear throughout, among all those who were involved in the Mitchell review, that if there was no decommissioning by the end of January, the Ulster Unionists would be unable to sustain their involvement in the Executive in Northern Ireland. There was no ambiguity about that – no guarantee, but no ambiguity either.' (Secretary of state, House of Commons, *Hansard*, 6th series, 343, 1313, 3 February 1999); House of Commons, *Hansard*, 6th series, 344, 131–2 & 206, 8 February 2000; see also statement by secretary of state, 23 February 2000.

128 Rt. Hon. John Taylor MP, *Irish Times*, 18 February 2000; IRA statement, *Irish Times*, 23 February 2000.

129 'On that very day, there was a significant shift in position by the IRA. They began to address the question of whether decommissioning would happen, but not how or when' (Statement by secretary of state, 23 February 2000)

in the majority community, but fundamentally to prevent a collapse of devolution.[130]

The restoration of the institutions on 22 May 2000, following the Hillsborough accord of 5 May 2000

19.127 A major crisis in Anglo-Irish relations ensued after suspension on 12 February 2000. At some point, Dublin refocused on Sinn Féin (seemingly on the basis of the putative early offer). The secretary of state downplayed references to decommissioning as an obligation under the Belfast Agreement.[131] As early as 20 February 2000, he had trailed in a newspaper interview, concessions he was prepared apparently to make to the republicans, covering criminal justice, a bill of rights, demilitarization, prisoners and policing.[132]

19.128 The United Kingdom government prepared for Hillsborough on 4 and 5 May 2000.[133] The form of the gathering was a stock take of the full implementation of the Belfast Agreement. The deal announced late on the second day was contained in the following sequenced documents:

- one, a joint statement by the United Kingdom and Irish governments of 5 May 2000, announcing that London would restore the institutions on 22 May 2000. This was in the following context: 'that paramilitary organisations must now, for their part, urgently state that they will put their arms completely and verifiably beyond use';
- two, a joint letter by the two heads of government, also of 5 May 2000 (delivered the following day), to party leaders on full implementation of the Belfast Agreement by June 2001. This covered the following sections: Rights, Safeguards and Equality of Opportunity; Security; Policing and Justice; and Prisoners;
- three, an IRA statement of 6 May 2000, in which it stated that it would 'initiate a process that will completely and verifiably put IRA arms beyond use'. The IRA promised to resume contact with the IICD. It also agreed, as a confidence-building measure, inspection of a number of arms dumps by agreed third parties;
- four, a joint statement by the prime minister and taoiseach, also of 6 May 2000, dealing with the confidence-building measure. Following consultation with the IICD, the inspectors were announced as Martti Ahtisaari, the former president of Finland, and Cyril Ramaphosa, former secretary-general of the African National Congress, both now involved in the International Crisis Group. (They visited London, Belfast and Dublin on 15 May 2000 for discussions consequent upon their mandate.[134])

130 House of Commons, *Hansard*, 6th series, 339, 353, 22 November 1999.

131 On 6 April 2000, he said at a CBI Northern Ireland dinner: 'But we must all think hard about the implications of making decommissioning a condition for the revival of the institutions. What purpose has been served if, in trying to achieve both devolution *and* decommissioning, we end up with neither? (http://nio.gov.uk)

132 *Observer*, 20 February 2000.

133 It is believed that the prime minister had met Sinn Féin representatives the preceding weekend (*Irish Times*, 3 May 2000). There were also meetings at Downing Street on 2 May 2000.

134 'to inspect the contents of a number of IRA arms dumps and, having done so, to report on

19.129 This agreement would appear to have the following characteristics. One, no amendment of the Belfast Agreement, or the international and domestic provisions for the IICD (though the joint statement of 5 May 2000 envisages further decommissioning schemes). Two, no abrogation of the United Kingdom's power to revoke a restoration, as provided for in section 4 of the NIA 2000. This is in spite of paragraph 8 of the 5 May 2000 joint statement, which makes an express reference to the review provisions of the Belfast Agreement. Three, an ambiguity about the June 2001 deadline: does it refer to decommissioning, or only to the obligations of the two governments under the Belfast Agreement?[135] Four, the question of whether decommissioning has now been divorced from devolution, either by being kicked into the long grass or solved as a problem by dropping as an issue. On one interpretation, decommissioning has been replaced by putting arms beyond use (and, from 8 May 2000, by deactivation[136]) – which may approximate to inspection only. However, the obligation of the Belfast Agreement did not expire on 22 May 2000, and inspection relates only to confidence building, not putting arms beyond use (under any new decommissioning schemes).

The first inspection

19.130 The institutions were restored (not on 22 May 2000 as intended but) on Tuesday 30 May 2000.[137] The reason for the delay was the postponement by a week of the Ulster Unionist Council meeting; on 27 May 2000, it voted by 459 votes to 403 (53.24 per cent to 46.75 per cent) to test the IRA's 6 May statement by returning to the power-sharing executive.

19.131 Nothing ensued in the following four weeks. Then, on Sunday, 25 June 2000, the two inspectors reported from London to the IICD on their first inspection of IRA weapons dumps (they had arrived in the Republic of Ireland apparently on Wednesday, 21 June 2000, and the report was published on 26 June 2000): 'We inspected a number of arms dumps. The arms dumps held a substantial amount of military material, including explosives and related equipment, as well as weapons and other material. We observed that the weapons and explosives were safely and adequately stored. We have ensured that the weapons and explosives cannot be

this to the Independent International Commission on Decommissioning. We will regularly re-inspect these dumps to ensure that the weapons have remained secure'. (Northern Ireland Information Service statement) On 25 June 2000, the inspectors stated that they had accepted their appointments on the basis of the joint statement of 6 May 2000 plus the IRA statement of the same date.

135 In favour of the former interpretation is the sentence in the 5 May 2000 joint statement: 'The governments now believe that the remaining steps necessary to secure full implementation of the agreement can be achieved by June 2001, and commit themselves to that goal.' In favour of the latter is the sentence which follows: 'They have drawn up, and are communicating to the parties, an account of these steps.' The joint letter of 6 June 2000 makes no reference to decommissioning. Against this is the opening sentence of the joint letter: 'This sets out the Governments' proposals necessary to secure full implementation of the Agreement by June 2001, in addition to those already set out in our agreement.' Also against the latter interpretation is the fact that none of the deadlines specified in the joint letter is June 2001.

136 House of Commons, *Hansard*, 6th series, 349, 508–9, 8 May 2000.

137 Northern Ireland Act 2000 (Restoration of Devolved Government) Order 2000, SI 2000/1445. The Order was signed on Saturday, 27 May 2000. It was not laid before parliament until 5 June 2000.

used without our detection. We are satisfied with the cooperation extended to us by the IRA to ensure a credible and verifiable inspection. All our requests were satisfactorily met. We plan to re-inspect the arms dumps on a regular basis to ensure that the weapons have remained secure.'[138] This report deserves two comments. One, the inspectors, in quoting the IRA statement of 6 May 2000, referred to the IRA 'initiat[ing] a process that [would] completely and verifiably put IRA arms beyond use'. This was distinct from confidence building. Two, they referred to inspection – the confidence-building measure – as 'credible and verifiable'. Was decommissioning (putting arms beyond use) being replaced by inspection (with the inspectors guaranteeing that the 'weapons and explosives [could]not be used without [their] detection')?

19.132 The question was not answered on Monday, 26 June 2000 (when the story broke). An IRA statement announced that it was resuming contact with the IICD. There was a reference to the inspection. But not to putting arms beyond use. The inspectors visited the prime minister in Downing Street early that morning. Speaking to the press afterwards, the prime minister stated that inspection was 'not decommissioning itself, it is a step on the way'. The taoiseach, however, speaking in Oslo, said: 'I think that brings the decommissioning saga to, hopefully, a successful end.'[139] (He also met the inspectors at Dublin airport upon his return from Norway.)

138 Attachment to IICD report of 25 June 2000.
139 *Guardian*, 27 June 2000.

20

Security

20.1 This is another short section of the Belfast Agreement, also comprising five paragraphs. Security, however, was not a dominant issue between 1 July 1998 and 2 December 1999 (even in the form of demilitarization). Security is absolutely necessary for the success of the Belfast Agreement. This topic is not normally discussed in the public domain. And both the United Kingdom and Irish governments guard their powers and duties. The section is at page 21 of Cm 3883 and page 36 of Cm 4705 (page 30 of the 1999 Irish version). As with the Rights, etc., section, the Irish government also has obligations as regards security. The security in question is the internal security of the United Kingdom, plus that of the Republic of Ireland. I indicate [deletions] to the MDP, and *additions* thus.

20.2 Security is one of a quartet of related issues in the Belfast Agreement. Decommissioning is about terrorists[1] becoming democrats. Security is inter-related, representing the response of the state to a diminishing threat. Policing and Justice is about good government. The fourth section, Prisoners, demonstrates most clearly the truly historic opportunity for a new beginning (proclaimed in paragraph 1 of the Declaration of Support). This section promises a transition from counter-terrorism to normality – but on a basis of continuing threat assessment.

Security in the Northern Ireland troubles

20.3 This is not a summary history of security law and practice in Northern Ireland, and in the Republic of Ireland, over the last 30 years.[2] Rather, it is a short account of – domestic – security as an issue in international relations in Ireland. This approach follows from the legal nature of the Belfast Agreement.

20.4 The following topics dealing with political violence were mentioned in the 1973 Sunningdale communiqué (in the shadow of the council of Ireland): a United Kingdom/Irish law enforcement commission, to consider extradition and alternatives;[3] protection of human rights in both parts of Ireland; public support

1 Terrorism was defined first as regards Northern Ireland as 'the use of violence for political ends and includes any use of violence for the purpose of putting the public or any section of the public in fear' (Detention of Terrorists (Northern Ireland) Order 1972, SI 1972/1632, art 2(2)). It was redefined – as a result of Lord Lloyd of Berwick's report, *Inquiry into legislation against terrorism*, of October 1996, Cm 3420 – as: 'the use or threat, for the purpose of advancing a political, religious or ideological cause, of action which – (a) involves serious violence against any person or property, (b) endangers the life of any person, or (c) creates a serious risk to the health or safety of the public or a section of the public' (Terrorism bill, clause 1(1)). See now Terrorism Act 2000 S1(1).

2 A useful work, dealing with the position up until 29 July 1988, is Gerard Hogan and Clive Walker, *Political Violence and the Law in Ireland*, Manchester 1989.

3 *Report of the Law Enforcement Commission*, Cmnd 5627, May 1974.

for and identification with the police; suggestions of cooperation on security; devolution of policing to be considered after security problems were resolved; establishment of a police authority in the Republic to interrelate with that in Northern Ireland (established there in 1970); an all-party assembly committee on policing; the ending of detention when the security situation permits.[4]

20.5 On 8 December 1980, the prime minister and the taoiseach commissioned joint studies covering possible new institutional structures, citizenship rights, security matters, economic cooperation and measures to encourage mutual understanding 'in order to assist them in their special consideration of the totality of relationships within these islands'. The *Joint Report and Studies* of November 1981[5] was published, but without the section on security matters. The resulting Anglo-Irish intergovernmental council is unlikely to have addressed security considerations on any sort of continuing basis.

20.6 The 1983–84 new Ireland forum was established against 'a background of deep division, insecurity and violence'.[6] However, these problems were seen as disappearing with a unitary state (the first of three preferred solutions). The study by C.K. Boyle and D.S. Greer, *The Legal Systems: North and South* (1984), was cited to show purportedly that 'there would be no significant technical obstacle to the creation of a unified legal system'.[7] There would be a single police service, according to the new Ireland forum, 'so designed that both nationalists and unionists could identify with it on the basis of political consensus'.[8]

20.7 The 1985 Anglo-Irish Agreement was – in inspiration – partly an all-Ireland security accord.[9] The preamble referred to 'lasting peace and stability', and to the 'total rejection of any attempt to promote political objectives by violence or the threat of violence'.

20.8 The intergovernmental conference was to be a consultation body dealing with: political matters; security and related matters; legal matters including the administration of justice; and the promotion of cross-border cooperation (article 3).

20.9 Article 7 dealt with security and related matters, encompassing security policy, relations between the security forces and the community, and prisons policy. The security situation would be addressed at the regular meetings, including policy issues, serious incidents and forthcoming events. The second area related principally to making the security forces more readily acceptable to the nationalist community. As for prisons policy, individual cases could be raised as appropriate.

20.10 Article 8 (legal matters, including the administration of justice) mentioned a number of issues: possible harmonization of areas of the criminal law; public confidence in the administration of justice, including the possibility of mixed courts in both jurisdictions; the policy aspects of extradition and extra-territorial jurisdiction.

20.11 Article 9 on cross-border cooperation began with security (and was

4 Paragraphs 10–18.
5 Cmnd 8414.
6 *Report*, May 1984, p. 5.
7 *Report*, May 1984, p. 31.
8 *Report*, May 1984, p. 32.
9 See paragraphs 7–9 of the joint communiqué issued with the agreement.

followed by economic, social and cultural matters). This comprised largely a programme of work set for the chief constable of the RUC and the commissioner of the Garda Síochána. It was stressed that the conference would have no operational responsibilities.

20.12 In the joint communiqué, the taoiseach announced that the Republic of Ireland would accede to the 1977 European Convention on the Suppression of Terrorism.[10] This led to the Extradition (European Convention on the Suppression of Terrorism) Act 1987 and the Extradition (Amendment) Act 1987 (plus the Extradition (Amendment) Act 1994). However, while the Irish state signed the convention on 24 February 1986, it did not ratify it until 21 February 1989 (because of a case concerning a bilateral extradition agreement with the United States,[11] where the Irish Supreme Court held, on the basis of article 29.5.2 of the constitution, that the treaty was not binding upon the Irish state – surely only in Irish law? – because it had not received the prior approval of Dáil Éireann).

20.13 The intergovernmental conference from late 1985 did include a regular item on security. The nature of this work is not readily accessible.

20.14 The successor body – though in the new constitutional context of Strand Three of the Belfast Agreement – is the BIIC. The second paragraph 6 of that section envisages facilitation of cooperation in security matters. This is not specified further. However, the paragraph goes on to refer to rights, justice, prisons and policing in Northern Ireland (if not devolved) as being addressed in the BIIC, including all-island or cross-border aspects.

20.15 The Northern Ireland administration, under the second paragraph 7, has effectively a right of attendance (see Chapter 17). According to the memorandum on supplementary procedural arrangements, agreed at the inaugural meeting of the BIIC in London on 17 December 1999, meetings are to begin normally with a bilateral London-Dublin session. When security-related matters are under discussion, such meetings may include police and security advisors and may be in restricted format. Where appropriate, the two governments will subsequently give a short oral report at the outset of the plenary session.[12]

TITLE: SECURITY

20.16 While this section is headed security, it does not deal comprehensively with that issue – as it is transacted on the London-Dublin plane. The five paragraphs are about progressively ending emergency law and practice as the threat from republican and loyalist paramilitary groups diminishes.

1. **The Participants note that the development of a peaceful environment on the basis of this[A]*a*greement can and should mean a normalisation of security arrangements and practice.**

20.17 'The participants' follows the Decommissioning section. There, the problem in paragraphs 1–3 was whether the two governments were included; they were not, in paragraph 2. Under the *Ground Rules for Substantive All-Party Negotiations*, Cm 3232, 16 April 1996, rule 10, participants includes the two

10 Cmnd 7390, Treaty Series No. 93 (1978).

11 *The State (Gilliland) v Governor of Mountjoy Prison* [1987] IR 201.

12 Paragraph 4.4.

governments. However, the term tended to be used in the multi-party negotiations to mean the political parties. It is not clear in which sense it is used here. If it is used strictly, it means that the United Kingdom government, and indeed the Irish government, are committing themselves to a security response.

20.18 'the development of a peaceful environment' is not specified. By implication, it means the end of the terrorist violence of the previous 30 or so years. Environment does not appear to be a technical term. However, the phrase peaceful environment would seem to have been used as an alternative to peace. This would allow – as paragraph 3 makes clear – for some continuing paramilitary activity, not precluding the reduction of the state's response to political violence. 'on the basis of this agreement' was changed from upper to lower case, to stress the MPA rather than the BIA. The implication is that the Belfast Agreement will bring about a peaceful environment, if not peace. 'can and should mean' is not will or would. The two governments are not being bound. 'a normalisation of security arrangements and practices.' shows that the Belfast Agreement is not a complete concession to republican violence. It states clearly that there will be security, and that this will be normal for a peaceful society.

2. **The British Government will make progress towards the objective of as early a return as possible to normal security arrangements in Northern Ireland, consistent with the level of threat and with a published overall strategy, dealing with:**
   (i) **the reduction of the numbers and role of the Armed Forces deployed in Northern Ireland to levels compatible with a normal peaceful society;**
   (ii) **the removal of security installations;**
   (iii) **the removal of emergency powers in Northern Ireland;** ***and***
   (iv) **other [appropriate] measures [consistent]** ***appropriate to and compatible*** **with a [move to normalisation] normal peaceful society.**

20.19 This is the main paragraph of the section. It binds the United Kingdom government.

20.20 The term 'British Government' has been used throughout the MPA, and even the BIA. This is in spite of the name of the state being the United Kingdom of Great Britain and Northern Ireland, with United Kingdom an appropriate adjective (not least to cover Northern Ireland). The practice of using British government – a product of either Irish insistence or United Kingdom weakness, or both – represents a break with the 1985 Anglo-Irish Agreement. Yet the BIA was meant to see a maturing of relations in the international field. The United Kingdom, even given domestic law on the matter, has recognized the preferred name of the Irish state (Ireland) abroad. Éire/Ireland has not reciprocated.

20.21 The United Kingdom government has undertaken to make progress towards an objective. This is 'as early a return as possible to normal security arrangements in Northern Ireland'. Such an objective is dependent upon the level of threat reducing and disappearing. 'normal security arrangements' is not defined. Is this Northern Ireland before 1968? Or what might be considered normal in a European state, even though traditions and standards vary considerably? Nor is as early a return as possible defined. It is, however, related to the level of threat.

20.22 'and with a published overall strategy' is a specific commitment. The paragraph goes on to elaborate at length.

20.23 The question of a published overall strategy had been raised during the the first two attempts in 1999 to find a solution to the decommissioning problem; demilitarization was the political focus.

20.24 In the 1 April 1999 (Hillsborough) declaration, the prime minister stated that steps had been taken towards the normalisation of security arrangements and practices (using the language of paragraph 1 above). (He also mentioned the police review, the criminal justice review and – in a separate, unrelated paragraph – the release of prisoners.) Step two of the United Kingdom and Irish governments' plan was the collective act of reconciliation. In return for some (paramilitary) arms being put beyond use on a – verified – voluntary basis, there would be 'further moves on normalisation and demilitarisation in recognition of the changed situation on security'. (This was a rare government use of Sinn Féin terminology.) The two acts were treated as equivalent in the phrase: 'the arrangements in respect of military material'.[13]

20.25 There was no demilitarization provided for in *The Way Forward* document of 2 July 1999. However, in listing the features of the Belfast Agreement, the prime minister used the phrase: 'equality, justice, human rights, and the normalisation of Northern Ireland society'. In its document of 1 July 1999, Sinn Féin had urged: 'Human rights, justice and equality on political, economic, social and cultural matters are central requirements. Policing is a key issue. The impact of demilitarisation on the day-to-day lives of people would be widespread. The promised British government strategy to give effect to this, as required by the agreement, is yet to be produced.' In advocating *The Way Forward*, the prime minister argued, comparing it favourably with the 1 April declaration (which Sinn Féin had rejected), that that text had 'demanded equivalent acts of decommissioning from everyone else, including the British government'.[14]

20.26 On 22 December 1999, nearly three weeks after devolution, the United Kingdom government published its security strategy.[15] This effectively fulfilled its obligation under this paragraph. The government reiterated its commitment to a balanced approach: 'normalising security arrangements and practices as quickly as the current threat allows'. Strangely, it made no reference to the nature or degree of threat, other than: 'the difficulty in predicting the activities of those groups who continue to use or threaten violence', which 'prevent[ed the government] from establishing in advance a precise timetable or sequence of measures to achieve normalisation'.

20.27 The document discussed each of the four specific obligations in this paragraph, starting with what had already been done, and then outlining further steps to follow.

13 The prime minister did not refer to the act of his government when presenting the plan at the press conference. Instead, he made a separate point: 'we envisage further moves on normalisation and demilitarisation in recognition of the changed security situation'.

14 *Sunday Times*, 4 July 1999. This became: 'reciprocal steps by the British and Irish' in the house of commons: House of Commons, *Hansard*, 6th series, 334, 640, 5 July 1999.

15 It is headed: *Security: return to normality: the government's approach*: Northern Ireland Information Service: http://www.nio.gov.uk.

20.28 The first commitment is troop numbers. Since Northern Ireland is a part of the United Kingdom, it has always had a share of garrison troops. Since their introduction on to the streets on 14 August 1969 for security duty, the number of soldiers has fluctuated with the perceived threat. The security document of 22 December 1999 stated there had been 'significant reductions' to the level of 1970: under 15,000 personnel since January 1999 (except during the summer marching season). The police now operated mainly without army support. Further steps amounted to a continuing reduction in numbers, including possibly the progressive withdrawal of the three remaining battalions from Great Britain posted temporarily to Northern Ireland.

20.29 The second commitment refers to the network of temporary forts and watch towers, many of them dating from the early 1970s, across urban and rural Northern Ireland. A network along the border has been integral to security policy, given the IRA has used the Republic of Ireland as a base (despite being an unlawful organization there). There are also, under security installations, barriers, checkpoints and vehicle control zones. According to the security document of 22 December 1999, 26 army bases and installations had been closed since 1995 (including the six remaining patrol bases in Co. Fermanagh). A total of 102 cross-border roads had been reopened. Security barriers and checkpoints had been opened or stopped. And the great majority of the vehicle control zone orders rescinded. Under further steps to follow, it was stated that there was an existing review of installations throughout Northern Ireland, the first phase of which would be completed early in 2000.[16] 'Any changes', the document stated, '[would] of course depend on genuine cessations of violence and continued progress in the political process.'

20.30 The third commitment seems to be general. But does it mean all? This is unlikely, and would be inconsistent with the risk-assessment tone of this section. The paragraph below implies a continuing paramilitary threat, and that is realistic.

20.31 Northern Ireland had emergency powers from its establishment: the Civil Authorities (Special Powers) Act (Northern Ireland) 1922–43. The act was renewed annually by the Northern Ireland parliament: in 1928, this became for five years; in 1933, it was made permanent. It was accompanied by a system of special powers regulations. There was also the Public Order Act (Northern Ireland) 1951, and the Flags and Emblems (Display) Act (Northern Ireland) 1954.

20.32 The outbreak of the troubles produced further local legislation: the Protection of Persons and Property Act (Northern Ireland) 1969; the Public Order (Amendment) Acts (Northern Ireland) 1970–71; the Criminal Justice (Temporary Provisions) Act (Northern Ireland) 1970; the Prevention of Incitement to Hatred Act (Northern Ireland) 1970.

20.33 Direct rule from London in 1972 lead to a new apparatus of emergency legislation (applying uniquely to Northern Ireland): the Detention of Terrorists

16 According to the Irish government's defence white paper of 29 February 2000, this review was 'in consultation with the Irish government, the political parties and interested groups'. (para. 2.3.5) This is not the stated position of the United Kingdom government: on 3 December 1999, the secretary of state had announced that the chief constable and the general officer commanding would be participating; he invited members of the public to submit their views by 14 January 2000.

(Northern Ireland) Order 1972; the Northern Ireland (Emergency Provisions) Act 1973;[17] the Northern Ireland (Emergency Provisions) (Amendment) Act 1975;[18] the Northern Ireland (Emergency Provisions) Act 1977; the Northern Ireland (Emergency Provisions) Act 1978; the Northern Ireland (Emergency Provisions) Act 1987;[19] the Northern Ireland (Emergency Provisions) Act 1991; the Northern Ireland (Emergency Provisions) Act 1996;[20] and the Northern Ireland (Emergency Provisions) Act 1998 (this extended the emergency provisions legislation to 24 August 2000, and dispensed with the need for a continuance debate in 1998).[21]

In addition, United Kingdom-wide legislation also applies to Northern Ireland: the Prevention of Terrorism (Temporary Provisions) Act 1974;[22] the Prevention of Terrorism (Temporary Provisions) Act 1976; the Prevention of Terrorism (Temporary Provisions) Act 1984;[23] the Prevention of Terrorism (Temporary Provisions) Act 1989;[24] the Criminal Justice and Public Order Act 1994; the Prevention of Terrorism (Additional Powers) Act 1996.

20.35 The legislative framework for Northern Ireland until recently was the Northern Ireland (Emergency Provisions) Act 1996 (EPA), as amended by the 1998 act, and the Prevention of Terrorism (Emergency Provisions) Act 1989 (PTA). Emergency legislation has three main aspects: proscription by the secretary of state of terrorist organizations, with related crimes; specific offences connected with terrorism; and police powers.

20.36 To this must be added the Criminal Justice (Terrorism and Conspiracy) Act 1998 (passed on 4 September 1998).[25] This emergency legislation followed the Omagh bomb of 15 August 1998 (attributed to the Real IRA), in which 29 people were killed. There was similar – synchronized – emergency legislation in the Republic of Ireland (see below).

17 This followed a report by Lord Diplock. On 18 July 2000, in a written parliamentary answer, and following a civil service review established in December 1999, it was announced that the government had decided not to reinstate jury trials for terrorist suspects because of the threat of intimidation.

18 Following a report by Lord Gardiner.

19 Following a report by Sir George Baker.

20 John Rowe QC reported on the operation of the act in 1997, his report being published on 30 June 1998. The reviewer commented on possible incompatibility with Convention rights. This was his fifth annual report on the emergency legislation. He is the reviewer for 1998, including the provisions inserted by the Criminal Justice (Terrorism and Conspiracy) Act 1998.

21 Enacted 8 April 1998, it repealed the power of executive detention (internment). The act allowed the temporary provisions to continue in force until 15 June 1999. The Northern Ireland (Emergency and Prevention of Terrorism Provisions) (Continuance) Order 1999, SI 1999/1709, which came into force on 16 June 1999, extended the temporary provisions for a further 12 months.

22 This followed the Birmingham pub bombs.

23 Following a review by Lord Jellicoe.

24 Following a review by Lord Colville of Culross. The Northern Ireland (Emergency and Prevention of Terrorism Provisions) (Continuance) Order 1999, SI 1999/1709, which came into force on 16 June 1999, extended the temporary provisions for a further 12 months.

25 For an excellent published opinion, see Barry McDonald in SACHR, *Report for 1998–1999*, HC 256, pp. 77–100. The discussion of the European Convention on Human Rights, however, makes no reference to the important concept of margin of appreciation.

20.37 The United Kingdom act amended inter alia the PTA and the EPA as amended. The legislation was necessitated partly by the removal of internment from the Northern Ireland statute book on 8 April 1998. It made admissible in court – in Great Britain and in Northern Ireland – evidence of a police superintendent that an individual belonged to a proscribed organization (which was also specified[26]). It also allowed inferences from silence to be drawn. The act had retrospective effect as regards arrest and detention.[27] The secretary of state was to report to parliament every 12 months on the working of the act (as with the PTA, which required to be renewed annually). There were no convictions in connection with the new provisions – police officer's evidence, and inferences from silence – in United Kingdom courts in 1998 or in 1999.

20.38 On 17 February 2000, John Rowe QC – who had reported since 1993 on the working of the PTA, advising annual renewal[28] – submitted his report for 1999: this included reporting on section 1 of the 1998 act (which applied only to Great Britain: he is, however, also the reviewer for the EPA).[29] John Rowe QC concluded: 'I have two terms of reference: as to the past year, has the Act been used fairly and properly, and as to the future, is there a continuing need of it. As appears from my report, I am satisfied on both points – there has indeed been proper use, and there is still a need for the powers of the Act.'[30] He reported on the situation in Northern Ireland – this was for the year 1999, when the main ceasefires were deemed to be holding: 'first, paramilitary groups are still in existence, and they are known to have structure and organisation and they apply expertise to their planning and management'; 'Second, throughout 1999 there has been continuing incidents of deaths, injury, and damage to property, carried out by paramilitary groups'; 'There is evidence of weapons and arms training'; 'The paramilitary organisations exercise significant influences over certain sections of communities'; 'The paramilitaries have a continuing need for money, and there is plenty of evidence of extortion and counterfeiting. And armed robberies average 8 per week.'[31]

20.39 Following the election of the labour government in May 1997, there was an internal review of all emergency legislation (for Great Britain and Northern Ireland). The aim was new, permanent, counter-terrorism legislation. (This had been recommended by Lord Lloyd of Berwick in October 1996.[32]) A consultation paper, *Legislation against Terrorism*, Cm 4178, was published eventually in December 1998. It was presented to parliament by the home secretary and the secretary of state for Northern Ireland. The consultation paper distinguished Irish terrorism from international terrorism and domestic (i.e. Great Britain) terrorism.[33] The government continued with the PTA and the EPA as amended.

26 Under section 3(8) of the Northern Ireland (Sentences) Act 1998.

27 Section 3(2) read with the Prevention of Terrorism (Temporary Provisions) Act 1989 s 2A(12) and Northern Ireland (Emergency Provisions) Act 1996 s 30A(11).

28 His predecessor was His Honour Judge Viscount Colville of Culross QC. The post of reviewer was established in 1984.

29 *Report on the Operation in 1999 of the Prevention of Terrorism (Temporary Provisions) Act 1989*, Home Office, 2000.

30 Letter of 17 February 2000 accompanying the report.

31 Pages 12–13 of the *Report*.

32 *Inquiry into Legislation against Terrorism*, Cm 3420.

33 This was without apparent protest by the Irish government.

However, as the home secretary admitted to the house of commons on 23 June 1999, there was a problem with the 1998 and 1999 continuance orders relating to the former act; as a result of inadequate drafting by parliamentary counsel (a mistake accepted by the home secretary), sections 16A to D[34] – applying only to Great Britain – had been allowed to lapse from 22 March 1998 (the home secretary tabled a draft order to correct the position).[35]

20.40 The Terrorism bill – the responsibility of the home office and the NIO – was introduced finally in the house of commons on 2 December 1999. It repeals the PTA, reenacting and amending main provisions on a permanent basis. The EPA as amended was to be repealed on 24 August 2000, but part VII of the bill would reenact measures specific to Northern Ireland for a maximum of five years.[36] The bill will allow the United Kingdom to withdraw the 1988 derogation from the ECHR – concerning detention for up to seven days – because the government now accepts judicial oversight.[37] The definition of terrorism – first enacted as regards Northern Ireland in 1972 – was altered to: 'the use or threat, for the purposes of advancing a political, religious or ideological cause, of action which – (a) involves serious violence against any person or property, (b) endangers the life of any person, or (c) creates a serious risk to the health or safety of the public or a section of the public' (clause 1(1)). This was significantly amended.[38] Second reading of the Terrorism Bill was on 14 December 1999.[39] It was then referred to a standing committee.[40] It returned to the house of commons on 15 March 2000.[41] Royal assent was on 20 July 2000.

20.41 The security document of 22 December 1999 listed, under what had already been done: a considerable reduction in the use of emergency powers from 1994 (including the announced closure of the Castlereagh holding centre); the

34 Parts IVA and B plus schedule 6A. The powers dated from 1994 and 1996.

35 House of Commons, *Hansard*, 6th series, 333, 1171–8, 23 June 1999. The mistake came to light because of an article in *Criminal Law Week* of 24 May 1999. The order was made on 24 June 1999, and came into force the following day: Prevention of Terrorism (Temporary Provisions) Act 1989 (Revival of Parts IVA and IVB) Order 1999, SI 1999/1813.

36 Schedule 1 is intended to extent the EPA as amended on a temporary basis from 15 June 2000 until enactment.

37 As a result of *Brogan v United Kingdom* (1988) 11 EHRR 117. See schedule 3 of the HRA 1998. Detention is dealt with in clause 39 and schedule VII.

38 '1(1) In this Act "Terrorism" means the use or threat of action where – (a) the action falls within subsection (2), (b) the use or threat is designed to influence the government or to intimidate the public or a section of the public, and (c) the use or threat is made for the purpose of advancing a political, religious or ideological cause. (2) Action falls within this subsection if it – (a) involves serious violence against a person, (b) involves serious violence to property, (c) endangers a person's life, other than that of the person committing the action, (d) creates a serious risk to the health or safety of the public or a section of the public, or (e) is designed seriously to interfere with or seriously to disrupt an electronic system. (3) The use or threat of action falling within subsection (2) which involves the use of firearms or explosives is terrorism whether or not subsection (1)(b) is satisfied ... .' (section 1).

39 House of Commons, *Hansard*, 6th series, 341, 152–233.

40 Standing Committee D, 18, 20, 25 & 27 January and 1, 3 and 8 February 2000.

41 House of Commons, *Hansard*, 6th series, 346, 329–473, 15 March 2000. The PTA was renewed immediately after third reading: House of Commons, *Hansard*, 6th series, 346, 474–8 (Prevention of Terrorism (Temporary Provisions) Act 1989 (Continuance) Order 2000, SI 2000/835).

1998 terrorism and conspiracy act as a targeted, proportionate response to small unrepresentative groups not observing a full and unequivocal ceasefire; and the repositioning of – temporary – emergency Northern Ireland legislation in the permanent terrorism bill. Under further steps to follow, the document announced: the closure of the Gough Barracks and Strand Road holding centres as soon as practicable; an increase in the proportion of jury trials; and new United Kingdom-wide legislation, consistent with human rights obligations.[42]

20.42 The fourth and final commitment is a residual category. In the MDP, reference was made to a move to normalisation (as in paragraph 1 above). This has been altered to a normal peaceful society, the term used in commitment (i).

20.43 In the security document of 22 December 1999, the United Kingdom government referred, under what had been done already, to changes in policing: first, a reduction in policing using emergency powers; second, a number of changes consequent upon the Police (Northern Ireland) Act 1998, though the act was not mentioned. It is considered in Chapter 21. Under further steps to follow, the government announced: continued significant reductions in military support for the police; an end to all military operations in support of the police (except where specifically requested); a review of the use of plastic baton rounds; and the closure of HMP Maze by the end of 2000.

20.44 No time scale for demilitarization was evident in the 22 December 1999 document. This is because demilitarization (the word was not used) was related solely to the level of threat. However, in the wake of the suspension of the institutions on 12 February 2000, the secretary of state, in an interview in the *Observer*, was reported as willing to consider a time scale: 'I do not rule out attaching timeframes to demilitarisation, but that has to be in the context of the threat going away and politics working.'[43]

> 3. **The Secretary of State will consult regularly on progress, and the response to any continuing paramilitary activity, with the Irish Government and the political parties, as appropriate.**

20.45 This paragraph admits the possibility of continuing paramilitary activity. It is in keeping with the realistic tone of this section. The nature of the activity is not defined. It therefore means any activity of paramilitary groups, whether on behalf of republicanism or loyalism or some post-troubles criminal endeavour.

20.46 'The secretary of state will consult regularly on progress' is a reference to the progress of the United Kingdom government in normalizing security under paragraph 2. The inclusion of 'the response to any continuing paramilitary activity' allows for precisely what happened after Omagh on 15 August 1998. The consultation will be 'with the Irish government and the political parties'. This consultation, arguably, is only to take place after the BIA enters into force (if this section is to be given legal status). The paragraph therefore has to be read – as regards the Irish government – with the second paragraph 6 of Strand Three,

42 This was contested by the Northern Ireland Human Rights Commission: briefing papers for second reading, committee, third reading and report, available at: http://www.nihrc.org; see also, speech of Kevin McNamara MP: House of Commons, *Hansard*, 341, 175–6, 14 December 1999.

43 *Observer*, 20 February 2000.

dealing the BIIC. The 'as appropriate' refers mainly to the Irish government. The political parties are those in the assembly. This is an additional undertaking to consult, as appropriate, with inter alia the parties comprising the government of Northern Ireland – even though security is not a transferred matter under the NIA 1998.

4. The British Government will continue its consultation on firearms regulation and control on the basis of the document published on 2 April 1998.

20.47 This paragraph refers to legally held arms, by mainly civilians but also those involved in the Northern Ireland security forces. There are about 9,800 personal protection handguns in Northern Ireland, and approximately 2,000 target pistols. As of 31 October 1997, there were altogether around 83,500 certificates covering 138,727 legally held firearms (the vast majority being shotguns and airguns).

20.48 The general background was a review instigated in November 1995, of the Firearms (Northern Ireland) Order 1981, SI 1981/155 (based on the Firearms Act 1920). The order requires certificates, and regulates the 52 firearms clubs and 160 dealers. The review was published on 2 April 1998, as a NIO consultation document entitled *Control of Firearms: proposals for reform*. The document contained a list of 41 proposals for legislative and other reform, the last being a consultative firearms forum. The others covered the gamut of issues: deregulation, certificates, firearms clubs, dealers, police powers, guidance to the chief constable. Public safety was the principal consideration, and applicants for certificates were to show good reason. The consultation period was to end on 12 June 1998.

20.49 The immediate background was the killings at Dunblane in Scotland in 1996, and the subsequent report of the tribunal of enquiry headed by Lord Cullen.[44] This led to extensive handgun controls in Great Britain. Of Lord Cullen's 24 recommendations, all but one (crucially, the proscription of handguns) were either current practice in Northern Ireland, or had been accepted in principle. 'After much thought', the secretary of state said in response to a written parliamentary question, 'I am not persuaded of the need to prohibit the possession and use of target handguns in Northern Ireland. Nor do I believe that it would be appropriate to prohibit the possession of handguns, licensed by the Chief Constable, for the personal protection of those individuals under threat of attack and their families.'

20.50 This paragraph simply refers to the consultation begun on 2 April 1998, and due to end on 12 June 1998.[45]

5. The Irish Government will initiate a wide-ranging review of the Offences Against the State Acts 1939–85 with a view to both reform and dispensing with those elements no longer required as circumstances permit.

20.51 This is an obligation upon the Irish government, just as the first paragraph

44 Cm 3386.

45 The Irish government, however, in its defence white paper of 29 February 2000, takes this to be a continuing commitment (para. 2.3.5).

9 of the Rights, Safeguards and Equality of Opportunity section required comparable steps to be taken in Dublin.

20.52 The paragraph relates entirely to the Irish government's emergency legislation.

20.53 The Irish Free State, particularly in its early years, dealt with political violence in a number of ways. The Constitution (Amendment No. 17) Act 1931 was essentially a public safety measure. It inserted a new article 2A in the constitution, making the rest of the text subject to its provisions. These included a military tribunal, which could impose a death penalty from which there was no appeal. Its validity was upheld by the supreme court in December 1934.[46]

20.54 Bunreacht na hÉireann came into operation in Éire/Ireland on 29 December 1937. The Offences Against the State Act 1939 was passed in anticipation of the Second World War, and amended by the Offences Against the State (Amendment) Act 1940.[47] It provided for a special criminal court (which lasted until 1962, and was reactivated in 1972). The 1940 amended act allowed for internment. The declaration of emergency made in September 1939 – under article 28.3.3 of the constitution – continued until 1976.

20.55 The troubles in Northern Ireland had led to the Offences Against the State (Amendment) Act 1972. Section 3(2) provided that where a police chief superintendent gave evidence that he believed 'the accused was at a material time a member of an unlawful organisation, the statement [should] be evidence that he was such a member'.[48] The killing of the United Kingdom ambassador led to the Emergency Powers Act 1976;[49] it provided for seven days' detention following arrest for a scheduled offence. Forfeiture of bank accounts was permitted under the Offences Against the State (Amendment) Act 1985.

20.56 The Offences Against the State Acts 1939–85 have been characterized as a single, permanent, comprehensive code against political violence. 'It could not be said to be excessively harsh or draconian in its operation, especially in view of the circumstances prevailing at the time of its enactment.' While it contains safeguards, proposals for reform have been made.[50]

20.57 To the list of emergency legislation must be added the Offences Against the State (Amendment) Act 1998. It was the Irish government's response to the Omagh bombing of 15 August 1998. This was the first time the Irish state responded in such a manner to a terrorist event in Northern Ireland. The reason was its role in the achievement of the Belfast Agreement.[51] The bill was rushed through the Dáil and Seanad on 2 and 3 September 1998. The act includes

46 *The State (Ryan) v Lennon* [1935] IR 170.

47 This was referred by the president to the Supreme Court, which upheld its constitutionality. This means that internment is most unlikely to be challengeable as contrary to the constitution.

48 The special criminal court, however, acquitted if there was denial or controversion: *The People (Director of Public Prosecutions) v Ferguson*, unreported, 27 October 1975.

49 Its precursors were the Emergency Powers Act 1939 and the Emergency Powers (Amendment) (No. 2) Act 1940. It was referred by the president to the Supreme Court, which upheld its constitutionality.

50 Hogan and Walker, *Political Violence*, p. 182.

51 The taoiseach called it 'an indiscriminate attack on democracy and the British-Irish Agreement'. (Dáil Éireann, *Official Report*, 2 September 1998)

provisions dealing with membership of an unlawful organization, the right to silence, the creation of five new offences, increased powers of detention (up to four days), unlimited fines and the forfeiture of property. The minister for justice claimed that it was consistent with the constitution, and the state's international human rights obligations.[52] The act was to lapse on 30 June 2000. It was, however, renewed by the Oireachtas on 20 June 2000, and extended for a further year.[53] There were no court proceedings under the act between 3 September 1998 and 29 May 2000.

20.58 The Irish government was unable to use (or threaten) its internment powers under the 1940 act (because the United Kingdom had repealed its act).[54] These measures may be seen as providing legitimacy for the United Kingdom act passed on 4 September 1998.

20.59 This paragraph exists in the context of this section. Thus the phrase 'as circumstances permit' is used. It is similar to consistent with the level of threat in paragraph 2 above. The Irish government is referred to in the section in two ways: one, in paragraph 3 above, as the consultee of the secretary of state on progress being made in Northern Ireland on security normalization; two, in this paragraph, as moving events in the same direction in the Republic of Ireland.[55]

20.60 On 2 September 1998, the minister for justice, equality and law reform, introducing the Offences Against the State (Amendment) Bill in the Dáil, referred to this paragraph. He stated that the date in the bill of 31 December 2000 (when the act would have to be renewed) was fixed with reference to the commitment to carry out the Offences Against the State Acts 1939–85 review. But there is no time scale in this paragraph (he may have been referring to some understanding between the United Kingdom and Irish governments). The most that can be inferred is that progress in Northern Ireland, and in the Republic of Ireland, should be related; alternatively, that the level of threat should determine the pace in the former, and as circumstances permit in the latter. The minister went on to state that he would bring forward the date for review of the bill to 30 June 2000.

20.61 The minister stated he would honour the commitment in the paragraph. He would shortly establish a special committee, under independent chairmanship, and with the participation of both governments (meaning presumably also the United Kingdom government) and outside experts.

20.62 This accords with the wide-ranging review required by the paragraph. It specifies reform, meaning presumably the retention of the legal code, but also dispensing with those elements on longer required. On 2 September 1998, the minister said: 'I hope that, by [30 June 2000] ... violence for political ends will have ended completely and that it will be possible to reform the Offences against the

52 This seems not to have been ascertained by the time of the first Irish cabinet meeting on the crisis on Wednesday, 19 August 1998: *Sunday Times*, 23 August 1998.

53 Under section 37 of Criminal Justice Act 1999.

54 Gerard Hogan, *Irish Times*, 19 August 1998; Dr Garret FitzGerald, *Irish Times*, 22 August 1998; *Sunday Times*, 23 August 1998; Tony Blair, *Observer*, 23 August 1998; Vincent Browne, *Irish Times*, 2 September 1998.

55 The taoiseach said: 'Following the Agreement we would much prefer to be going in the opposite direction, removing emergency legislation we do not strictly need.' (*Dáil Éireann*, 2 September 1998)

State Acts and dispense with those elements no longer required, both generally and by reference to the provisions of this Bill. Much will depend on the decisions which those groups which have not yet renounced violence take. Only they can create the conditions whereby it will be possible to dispense with many of the powers which the ... Acts provide.'[56]

20.63 On 22 July 1999, the Irish government quietly began the review by appointing a committee.[57] Its chairman is The Hon. Mr Justice Anthony Hederman. No other participants were identified initially; subsequently, they were reported to include: Prof. William Binchy of Trinity College, Dublin; Dr Gerard Hogan SC; Eamonn Leahy SC; Pat O'Toole, the assistant Garda commissioner, plus officials from the taoiseach's and other departments.[58] The terms of reference of the committee are to examine all aspects of the Offences Against the State Acts 1939–98, taking into account (essentially) the Belfast Agreement; the threat posed by international terrorism and crime, and the state's obligations in international law. The committee was asked to report as soon as practicable with recommendations for reform. Confidential written submissions were invited by 3 September 1999, with the possibility of oral presentations later.[59] The committee was still in existence on 14 March 2000, but its secretary could not comment on when it might be reporting.[60] In June 2000, it was reported that the committee would run until the end of the year.[61]

20.64 Though the Irish government is only bound by this paragraph, its white paper on defence – the first in the history of the state – published on 29 February 2000, discusses security and defence in Ireland (sic) after the Belfast Agreement.[62]

20.65 'Ireland faces a generally benign security environment', concluded the government's current review in chapter 2.[63] There were no specific threats in the external security environment. The European Union defined the state's security obligations. As for 'the on-island security environment', it was 'being transformed through progress under the Good Friday Agreement. While some threats to peace remain, the Agreement proves the basis for a lasting peace.' The former chief of staff of the Irish defences forces, Lieut. Gen. Gerry McMahon, commented immediately and publicly: 'the White Paper [is] hopelessly optimistic on ... the internal security situation vis-à-vis Northern Ireland ...'.[64]

20.66 The question of Northern Ireland was addressed in paragraphs 2.3.1–11: on-island internal security environment. The points made are: for the last 30 years, internal security has been most important for the state, with the defence forces acting in aid to the civil power (the minister for justice, equality and law reform and the Garda Síochána) (2.3.1); the Good Friday Agreement had transformed the position (2.3.2); this was due to the ceasefires by the main republican and loyalist groups, and the beginning of the normalization of security arrangements (2.3.3);

56 Dáil Éireann, *Official Report*, 2 September 1998.
57 *Sunday Independent*, 1 August 1999.
58 *Irish Times*, 17 May 2000.
59 E-mail from Eamon Saunders, secretary to the committee, 25 August 1999.
60 E-mail from Eamon Saunders, secretary, 14 March 2000.
61 *Irish Times*, 21 June 2000.
62 Available: http://www.ireland.com.
63 Defence and Security Environment Assessment.
64 *Irish Times*, 1 March 2000.

the position rehearsed on decommissioning is that of 2 December 1999, and not after 12 February 2000 (2.3.4);[65] the United Kingdom government was bound by the security section of the Belfast Agreement, and reference was made to the security document of 22 December 1999 and the secretary of state's statement of 19 January 2000 on policing (2.3.5); the BIIC had a security reponsibility (2.3.6); 'the greater threat to the security of the State stems from the activities, and potential activities, of dissident republican paramilitary groups' (2.3.7); the dissident republicans were not an insurgency threat, and the loyalists could not reply upon support within the state (2.3.8–9); externally based subversive groups were not a threat, nor was there one from externally based organized crime (2.3.10–11).

20.67 As for defence policy and programmes (chapter 3[66]), the on-island context was considered in paragraphs 3.2.10–12. The points made are: internal security arrangements contribute to confidence in both parts of Ireland, and thus support 'the new political structures emanating from the peace process' (3.2.10); the defence forces would be required to act in aid to the civil power 'for the foreseeable future', in 'respond[ing] to paramilitary activity on either a localised or nation-wide basis' (3.2.11); 'security issues in the Border area will continue to be of importance, at least in the short term' (3.2.12).

65 This was not subject to comment on 24 February 2000, when the minister for defence reached an agreement with the existing chief of staff of the defence forces, on amendments to be added to the white paper subsequently.

66 Defence Policy and Programmes – Roles of the Defence Forces.

21

Policing and Justice

21.1 This section of the Belfast Agreement – with seven paragraphs and two annexes – is loosely drafted. It deals with two separate topics, policing and criminal justice. The United Kingdom government was committed substantively to two reviews (as is the Irish government in paragraph 5 of the Security section). The section is at pages 22–24 of Cm 3883 and pages 37–40 of Cm 4705 (pages 31–34 of the 1999 Irish version). It comprised pages 52–60 of the 65-page MDP (a striking 15 per cent of that text).[1] I indicate [deletions] to the MDP, and *additions* thus; however, since this section is eclipsed significantly by the reports on policing and criminal justice which were published respectively in September 1999 and March 2000, I have relegated Annexes A and B to the footnotes (the terms of reference are discussed under the reports which ensued).

21.2 The relevant reports are: *A New Beginning: policing in Northern Ireland*, the report of the independent commission on policing for Northern Ireland, published by the commission in Belfast on 9 September 1999 (and known after its chairman as the Patten report); and the *Review of the Criminal Justice System in Northern Ireland*, published by the Stationery Office Limited on 30 March 2000 (and referred to as the criminal justice review).[2]

21.3 Though each will be discussed separately below, the two reports have been contrasted: the first – which led to considerable political controversy – is intellectually ambitious, with little apparent grasp of policing theory and practice in the United Kingdom; the second is rooted evidently in Northern Ireland's criminal justice system (which does not mitigate its huge array of proposed recommendations), and its publication produced little political or other disagreement.

21.4 Policing and Justice is one of a quartet of related issues in the Belfast Agreement. Decommissioning is about terrorists[3] becoming democrats. Security

1 Strand One in contrast is pages 11–21 of the MDP.

2 The Patten report and the criminal justice review have the same legal status: the former is crown copyright, and reference is made to the copyright unit (p. 130); the latter acknowledges this is part of Her Majesty's Stationery Office, and the front of the report carries the coat of arms.

3 Terrorism was defined first as regards Northern Ireland as 'the use of violence for political ends and includes any use of violence for the purpose of putting the public or any section of the public in fear' (Detention of Terrorists (Northern Ireland) Order 1972, SI 1972/1632, art 2(2)). It was redefined – as a result of Lord Lloyd of Berwick's report, *Inquiry into legislation against terrorism*, of October 1996, Cm 3420 – as: 'the use or threat, for the purpose of advancing a political, religious or ideological cause, of action which – (a) involves serious violence against any person or property, (b) endangers the life of any person, or (c) creates a serious risk to the health or safety of the public or a section of the public.' (Terrorism bill, clause 1(1)). See now Terrorism Act 2000 s1(1).

is interrelated, representing the response of the state to a diminishing threat. Policing and Justice is about good government. The fourth section, Prisoners, demonstrates most clearly the truly historic opportunity for a new beginning (proclaimed in paragraph 1 of the Declaration of Support). This section promised reports on policing and criminal justice by the summer/autumn of 1999.

Policing and justice in the Northern Ireland troubles

21.5 This is not a summary history of policing by the Royal Ulster Constabulary (RUC), and of the criminal justice system in Northern Ireland, over the last 30 years. Rather, it is a short account of – domestic – policing and justice issues in international relations in Ireland. This approach follows from the legal nature of the Belfast Agreement.

21.6 Among the topics mentioned in the 1973 Sunningdale communiqué (in the shadow of the council of Ireland) were a United Kingdom/Irish law enforcement commission, to consider extradition and alternatives;[4] public support for and identification with the police; devolution of policing to be considered after security problems were resolved; establishment of a police authority in the Republic to interrelate with that in Northern Ireland (established there in 1970); and an all-party assembly committee on policing.[5]

21.7 On 8 December 1980, the prime minister and the taoiseach commissioned joint studies covering possible new institutional structures, citizenship rights, security matters, economic cooperation and measures to encourage mutual understanding 'in order to assist them in their special consideration of the totality of relationships within these islands'. The *Joint Report and Studies* of November 1981,[6] however, did not deal centrally with Northern Ireland. The resulting Anglo-Irish intergovernmental council is most unlikely to have had anything to do with policing and criminal justice there.

21.8 The 1983–84 new Ireland forum was established against 'a background of deep division, insecurity and violence'.[7] However, these problems were seen as disappearing with a unitary state (the first of three preferred solutions). The study by C.K. Boyle and D.S. Greer, *The Legal Systems: North and South* (1984), was cited to show purportedly that 'there would be no significant technical obstacle to the creation of a unified legal system'.[8] There would be a single police service, according to the new Ireland forum, 'so designed that both nationalists and unionists could identify with it on the basis of political consensus'.[9]

21.9 The 1985 Anglo-Irish Agreement was – in inspiration – partly an all-Ireland security accord.[10] The preamble referred to 'lasting peace and stability',

4 *Report of the Law Enforcement Commission*, Cmnd. 5627, May 1974.
5 Paragraphs 10–18.
6 Cmnd 8414.
7 *Report*, May 1984, p. 5.
8 *Report*, May 1984, p. 31.
9 *Report*, May 1984, p. 32.
10 See paragraphs 7 to 9 of the joint communiqué issued with the agreement.

and to the 'total rejection of any attempt to promote political objectives by violence or the threat of violence'.

21.10 The intergovernmental conference was to be a consultation body dealing with: political matters; security and related matters; legal matters including the administration of justice; and the promotion of cross-border co-operation (article 3).

21.11 Article 7 dealt with security and related matters, encompassing security policy, relations between the security forces and the community, and prisons policy. The security situation would be addressed at the regular meetings, including policy issues, serious incidents and forthcoming events. The second area related principally to making the security forces more readily acceptable to the nationalist community. Among special measures to be considered were: local consultative machinery; training in community relations, crime prevention schemes involving the community; improvements in arrangements for handling complaints; and actions to increase the proportion of members of the minority in the RUC. As for prisons policy, individual cases could be raised as appropriate.

21.12 Article 8 (legal matters, including the administration of justice) mentioned a number of issues: possible harmonization of areas of the criminal law; public confidence in the administration of justice, including the possibility of mixed courts in both jurisdictions; the policy aspects of extradition and extra-territorial jurisdiction.

21.13 Article 9 on cross-border cooperation began with security (and was followed by economic, social and cultural matters). This comprised largely a programme of work set for the chief constable of the RUC and the commissioner of the Garda Síochána. It was stressed that the conference would have no operational responsibilities.

21.14 In the joint communiqué, the taoiseach announced that the Republic of Ireland would accede to the 1977 European Convention on the Suppression of Terrorism.[11] This led to the Extradition (European Convention on the Suppression of Terrorism) Act 1987 and the Extradition (Amendment) Act 1987 (plus the Extradition (Amendment) Act 1994). However, while the Irish state signed the convention on 24 February 1986, it did not ratify it until 21 February 1989 (because of a case concerning a bilateral extradition agreement with the United States,[12] where the Supreme Court held, on the basis of article 29.5.2 of the constitution, that the treaty was not binding upon the Irish state – surely only in Irish law? – because it had not received the prior approval of Dáil Éireann).

21.15 The intergovernmental conference from late 1985 did include a regular item on security. The nature of this work is not readily accessible, though obviously the RUC and Northern Ireland's system of criminal justice were considered. In the initial meetings – according to the communiqué – Belfast and Dublin would concentrate upon relations between the security forces and the minority community; ways of enhancing security cooperation; and measures which would give substantial expression to the aim of underlining public confidence in the administration of justice.

11 Cmnd 7390, Treaty Series No. 93 (1978).

12 *The State (Gilliland) v Governor of Mountjoy Prison* [1987] IR 201.

21.16 The successor body – though in the new constitutional context of Strand Three of the Belfast Agreement – is the BIIC. The second paragraph 6 of that section envisages facilitation of cooperation in security matters. This is not specified further. However, the paragraph goes on to refer to rights, justice, prisons and policing in Northern Ireland (if not devolved) as being addressed in the BIIC, including all-island or cross-border aspects.

21.17 The Northern Ireland administration, under the second paragraph 7, has effectively a right of attendance (see Chapter 17). According to the memorandum on supplementary procedural arrangements, agreed at the inaugural meeting of the BIIC in London on 17 December 1999, meetings are to begin normally with a bilateral London-Dublin session. When security-related matters are under discussion, such meetings may include police and security advisers and may be in restricted format. Where appropriate, the two governments will subsequently give a short oral report at the outset of the plenary session.[13]

21.18 A great deal of work was done on policing from 1994, in Belfast and in London. This was outside the intergovernmental conference, and even the multi-party negotiations leading to the Belfast Agreement of 10 April 1998. There was evidently an internal reform agenda of the policing family. But this was to be eclipsed, in the autumn of 1999, by the politics of the Patten report, and, in particular, its attack upon RUC symbols.

21.19 First, the RUC. The most important piece of work remains: *A Fundamental Review of Policing* (1996), a 220-page report (plus appendices), containing 190 recommendations, by – as he then was – Deputy Chief Constable Ronnie Flanagan of the RUC. The fundamental review commenced after the ceasefires of August and October 1994, and was completed after the London Docklands bombing by the IRA in February 1996.

21.20 The chief constable's unpublished fundamental review of 1996 was the basis – though this is not acknowledged – of very many of the reforms proposed by the independent commission on policing for Northern Ireland in 1999 (see further below).[14]

21.21 Second, the United Kingdom government. The Police (Northern Ireland) Bill was introduced on 4 December 1997, while the parties were still meeting. Its inspiration was proposals of the then opposition of May 1996 (coinciding with a government white paper[15]), plus the Hayes report on reforming police complaints.[16] Principal provisions trailed were: the appointment of an independent police ombudsman; the removal of the reference to the queen in the oath of office; a new umbrella title, Northern Ireland police division, including the RUC, reservists, civilians[17] and traffic wardens; this was changed later to the Northern Ireland police service.

13 Paragraph 4.4.

14 See also *Policing: a new beginning*, the PANI submission of December 1998, containing 70 recommendations; *Submission by the Police Federation for Northern Ireland*, of 14 September 1998, containing 44 recommendations.

15 *Foundations for Policing*.

16 NIO, *A Police Ombudsman for Northern Ireland?: a review of the police complaints system in Northern Ireland by Dr Maurice Hayes*, London 1997.

17 3,500 civil servants work for the RUC.

21.22 The bill received the royal assent on 24 July 1998 (after the first meeting of the assembly). Parts of it came into force on 8 October 1998;[18] other commencement orders followed on 8 February 1999[19] and 30 March 1999.[20] Sections dealing with the police ombudsman remained to be brought into force in 2000.[21]

21.23 The first changes related to: police planning and accountability mechanisms; changes to the oath of office; and enhancement of the role of the police authority. The chief constable was required to publish an annual policing plan,[22] containing policy objectives set by the secretary of state[23] and the police authority. The oath of office of constable, with references to Almighty God and our Sovereign Lady the Queen,[24] had been replaced from 5 October 1998 – at the recommendation of the police authority – with a declaration similar to that used in Scotland.[25] As for the police authority, it was required to consult the community further, while district councils were given the right to question it about its role in policing.

21.24 The independent commission for policing in Northern Ireland (see further below) commented on the Police (Northern Ireland) Act 1998: '[it] contains labyrinthine provisions as to objectives, performance targets and policing plans, and the respective roles of Secretary of State, the Police Authority and the Chief Constable. We have found these confusing, both in the text and in the oral briefings we have received from government officials (and we are mystified as to why this legislation was put through parliament in the weeks following the establishment of this Commission, given that our terms of reference required us to take a new look at the subject).'[26]

21.25 Three, parliament. One of the select committees of the house of commons published a report on the RUC on 27 July 1998: the third report of the Northern Ireland affairs committee, on the composition, recruitment and training of the RUC, in two volumes.[27] The second volume contains minutes of evidence and

18 The Police (1998 Act) (Commencement No. 1) Order (Northern Ireland) 1998, SR 1998/346.
19 The Police (1998 Act) (Commencement No. 2) Order (Northern Ireland) 1999, SR 1999/48.
20 The Police (1998 Act) (Commencement No. 3) Order (Northern Ireland) 1999, SR 1999/176.
21 On 19 May 1999, Adam Ingram MP, the security minister, reopened the process to find a police ombudsman. The first attempt had not produced a suitable candidate. The target for filling the post was August/September 1999. On 11 October 1999, he announced the appointment of Nuala O'Loan as police ombudsman designate. The independent commission for police complaints was to continue, until the ombudsman establishes her office, expected to be in the summer of 2000.
22 The first was published on a non-statutory basis earlier in 1998. The second, under the act, on 25 March 1999.
23 On 24 March 1999, for the second year, the secretary of state set new objectives for policing: to counter the terrorist threat; to maintain public order; to reduce road traffic accidents; to target the supply of illegal drugs.
24 Constabulary Act (Northern Ireland) 1922, second schedule.
25 Police (Northern Ireland) Act 1998 s 24 & sch 2; Police (1998) Act (Commencement No. 1) Order (Northern Ireland) 1998, SR 1998/346.
26 *A New Beginning: policing in Northern Ireland*, 9 September 1999, para. 5.11.
27 Northern Ireland Affairs Committee, *Third Report: Composition, Recruitment and Training of*

appendices from inter alia the RUC, the Police Authority for Northern Ireland (PANI) and the Police Federation for Northern Ireland (PFNI).

21.26 In the government's response of 4 November 1998 to the Northern Ireland affairs committee, the secretary of state accepted some of the proposals: members of the loyal orders, the ancient order of hibernians and freemasons to register their membership, initially voluntarily; a more rigorous system for new recruits; registration on a private basis with RUC management, and perhaps with the independent commission for police complaints. The government rejected for the moment the proposal that membership should preclude recruitment, pending the report of the independent commission on policing for Northern Ireland. Another recommendation was accepted by the chief constable: the union flag would no longer be flown from police stations on 12 July.

21.27 The government restricted itself otherwise to diplomatic comments about the RUC while the independent commission on policing for Northern Ireland was sitting. 'The two extremes of no change and total disbandment of the RUC', Adam Ingram MP, the security minister, told the house of commons on 23 February 1999, 'are not likely to be on the Commission's agenda and they aren't on the Government's.'[28]

TITLE: POLICING AND JUSTICE

21.28 Paragraphs 1–3 of this section relate to policing. The first two are preambular, paragraph 3 containing the provision of an independent commission on policing. Paragraphs 4 and 5 relate to criminal justice, the latter containing the proposal for a criminal justice review. Paragraphs 6 and 7 deal with implementation and devolution.

1. **The [P]*p*articipants recognise that policing is a central issue in any society. They equally recognise that Northern Ireland's history of deep divisions have made it highly emotive, with great hurt suffered and sacrifices made by many individuals** ***and their families, including those in the RUC and other public servants. They believe that the agreement provides the opportunity for a new beginning to policing in Northern Ireland with a police service capable of attracting and sustaining support from the community as a whole.*** **They** ***also*** **believe that this [A]*a*greement offers a unique opportunity to bring about a new political dispensation which will recognise the full and equal legitimacy and worth of the identities, senses of allegiance and ethos of all sections of the community in Northern Ireland. They consider that this opportunity should inform and underpin the development of a police service representative in terms of the make-up of the community as a whole and which, in** ***a peaceful environment*** **[the absence of threats which require otherwise], should be routinely unarmed.**

21.29 This is the first of two long preambular paragraphs on future policing. Four sentences in the MDP were increased to five. The first sentence is anodyne. 'The participants' may here include the two governments. The second sentence was altered significantly. It is not clear who suffered the great hurt. The sacrifices

the RUC, volume I (Report and Proceedings of the Committee) and volume II (Minutes of Evidence and Appendices), London, ordered to be printed, 8 July 1998, 337-I and 337-II.

28 http://www.nio.gov.uk.

made by many individuals in the MDP may have been a reference to the 302 police officers killed and the thousands injured. However, the addition of 'including those in the RUC and other public servants', while recognizing these groups, makes the many individuals and their families universal terms. The third sentence is completely new. The reference to 'a new beginning' is evocative of paragraph 1 of the Declaration of Support. 'a police service capable of attracting and sustaining support from the community as a whole' is clearly the goal. It chimes with concepts of normalization of security arrangements and practices (paragraph 1 of the Security section). The fourth sentence is not relevant to the subject of policing. The idea of a new political dispensation could, and should, have been placed elsewhere; probably in the Declaration of Support. There is no reference to policing, in the context of 'full and equal legitimacy and worth', etc. The fifth and last sentence is aspirational. It contains two points: one, 'representative ... of the community as a whole' (only 8 per cent of the RUC is catholic); and two, an 'unarmed' police service, but only when there is a peaceful environment (the term used in paragraph 1 of the Security section).

2. **The participants believe it essential that policing structures and arrangements are such that the police service is professional, effective and efficient, fair and impartial, free from partisan political control; accountable, both under the law for its actions and to the community it serves; representative of the society it polices, and operates within a coherent and co-operative criminal justice system,** ***which conforms with human rights norms*****. The participants also believe that those structures and arrangements must be capable of maintaining law and order including responding effectively to crime and to any terrorist threat and to public order problems[,].** ***A*** **[as a] police service which cannot do so will fail to win public confidence and acceptance. They believe that any such structures and arrangements should be capable of delivering a police service, in constructive and inclusive partnerships with the community at all levels, and with** ***the maximum delegation of*** **authority and responsibility [exercised at the lowest level possible], consistent with the foregoing principles. These arrangements should be based on principles of protection of human rights and professional integrity and should be unambiguously accepted and actively supported by the entire community.**

21.30 The paragraph is again preambular, with another five – longer – sentences. The first sentence is probably the most crucial, containing what is described in paragraph 3 below as the agreed framework of principles. These can be summed up best as professional policing. Only three require comment. 'free from partisan political control' is strange. It is presumably a reference to unionist rule. However, under the Police Act (Northern Ireland) 1970, with the establishment of the PANI, political control of the RUC was weakened. Further, the RUC has been under United Kingdom government (based on single party) control since 1972. 'representative of the society it polices' is repetition of the point made in paragraph 1 above. 'a coherent and co-operative criminal justice system' is confusing. Justice is about decision-making, within a context of the rule of law; it involves at times legal deprivation of the liberties of the subject (to use the terminology of United Kingdom law). The second sentence recognizes the functions of policing; 'law and order'; 'responding effectively to crime', 'any terrorist threat', 'public order problems'. The third sentence was carved out of the second in the MDP. 'public confidence and acceptance' was based upon effective policing. It now reads to include the principles in the first sentence. The fourth sentence locates the police service in the Northern Ireland community. Authority and responsibility exercised at the lowest level possible has been altered to 'the maximum delegation of authority and responsibility'. Delegation does not mean autonomous, communal police forces. The fifth sentence does three things. It repeats a point about human rights (which was added above to the reference to criminal justice). It calls for professional integrity. And it enjoins acceptance and support from the community.

21.31 It is difficult to distil clear principles – as opposed to slogans – from these two paragraphs. They are drafted at a level of generality, but with hints of the particularity of Northern Ireland. Much of the rhetoric is the stuff of modern management science, though there are maximalist hints allowing for the continuing withholding of consent to any less than perfect police service.

> **3. An [I]independent Commission will be established to make recommendations for future policing arrangements in Northern Ireland** ***including means of encouraging widespread community support for these arrangements*** **within the agreed framework of principles reflected in the paragraphs above and in accordance with the terms of reference at Annex A. The Commission will be broadly representative with expert and international representation among its membership and will be asked to consult widely and to report no later than Summer 1999.**

21.32 This is the one substantive paragraph dealing with Policing. The first sentence binds the United Kingdom government to establish an independent commission. This is to make recommendations on future policing in Northern Ireland, to again the United Kingdom government. Added – crucially in this paragraph – is the phrase 'including means of encouraging widespread community support for these arrangements'. Arrangements refers to the recommendations of the commission. The new phrase therefore assumes the recommendations will be accepted. Means of encouraging widespread community support is a reference to the political selling of the commission's report.[29]

21.33 The commission is given terms of reference in Annex A. But it is also given the agreed framework of principles in paragraphs 1 and 2 above. In the MDP, the commission was also given four further relevant principles (already specified in paragraph 2 above). These were removed at Castle Buildings.[30] Nevertheless, the

29 This phrase was used in the background note, produced by the NIO, to the queen's speech of 17 November 1999.

30

ANNEX A

COMMISSION ON POLICING FOR NORTHERN IRELAND

[Relevant Principles

Policing Structures and arrangements should be such that:

- the police service is professional, effective and efficient, fair and impartial, free from partisan political control; accountable, both under the law for its actions and to the community it serves; representative of the society it polices and operates within a coherent and co-operative criminal justice system;

- they are capable of maintaining law and order including responding effectively to crime and to any terrorist threat, and to public order problems, as a police service which cannot do so will fail to win public confidence and acceptance;
- they are capable of delivering a police service, in constructive and inclusive partnerships with the community at all levels, and with authority and responsibility to be exercised at the lowest level consistent with the foregoing principles; and
- these arrangements should be based on principles of protection of human rights and professional integrity, and should be unambiguously accepted and actively supported by the entire community.]

Terms of Reference

Taking account of the[se] principles *on policing as set out in the agreement*, the Commission will inquire into policing in Northern Ireland and, on the basis of its findings, bring forward proposals for future policing structures and arrangements, *including means of encouraging widespread community support for those arrangements*.

Its proposals on policing should be designed to ensure that policing arrangements, including composition, recruitment, training, culture, ethos and symbols, are such that in a new approach Northern Ireland has a police service that can enjoy widespread support from, and is seen as an integral part of, the community as a whole.

Its proposals should include recommendations covering any issues [(]such as *re*-training, *job placement and educational and professional development* [and severance arrangements)] required in the transition to policing in a peaceful society.

Its proposals should also be designed to ensure that:

- the police service is structured, managed and resourced so that it can be effective in discharging its full range of functions (including proposals on any necessary arrangements for the transition to policing *in* a normal peaceful society);
- *the police service is delivered in constructive and inclusive partnerships with the community at all levels with the maximum delegation of authority and responsibility;*
- [that] the legislative and constitutional framework requires the impartial discharge of policing functions and conforms with internationally accepted norms in relation to policing standards;
- the police operate within a clear framework of accountability to the law and the community they serve, so:
  - they are constrained by, accountable to and act only within the law;
  - their powers and procedures, like the law they enforce, are clearly established and publicly available;
  - there are open, accessible and independent means of investigating and adjudicating upon complaints against the police;
  - there are clearl*y established* arrangements enabling local people, and their political representatives, to articulate *their views and* concerns about policing *and to establish publicly policing priorities and influence policing policies*, [(]subject to safeguards to ensure police impartiality and freedom from partisan political control[) and to establish publicly policing priorities and influencing policing decisions];
  - there are arrangements for accountability and for the effective, efficient and economic use of resources in achieving policing objectives;
  - there are means to ensure independent professional scrutiny and inspection of the police service to ensure that proper professional standards are maintained;
- the scope for structure co-operation with the Garda Siochana and other police forces is addressed; and
- the management of public order events which can impose exceptional demands on policing resources is also addressed.

The Commission should focus on policing issues, but if it identifies other aspects of the criminal justice system relevant to its work on policing, including the role of the police in prosecution, then it should draw the attention of the Government to those matters.

terms of reference of the independent commission are completely unlike those drafted normally by United Kingdom officials, when establishing enquiries and royal commissions. (The Patten report [see below] also handled its terms of reference in an unorthodox manner.[31])

21.34 The second sentence specifies the independent commission. It is to be 'broadly representative'. This is not the representative of the community in Northern Ireland in sections 68(3) and 73(4) of the NIA 1998. It does not preclude Northern Ireland participation. But it seems that the United Kingdom government was required to take an international perspective. Neverthless, broadly representative is still perplexing. 'international representation' further elaborates. And 'expert' representation suggests, if not police commanders, then criminologists with expertise in policing internationally. 'consult widely' is a clear requirement. As is 'report no later than summer 1999'. Summer is normally considered to be the months of June, July and August.

> The Commission should consult widely, including with non-governmental expert organisations, and through such focus groups as they consider it appropriate to establish.
> The Government proposes to establish the Commission as soon as possible, with the aim of it starting work as soon as possible and publishing its final report by Summer 1999.

31 Contrary to the tradition in the United Kingdom, the commission did not begin with its terms of reference. They are not mentioned until paragraph 1.9. There follows the sentence: 'These seek to direct our work towards implementing the principles set out in [the] paragraph [2].' But the work of the commission was to make recommendations. It was for the United Kingdom government – after consultation – to implement the recommendations it accepted. The terms of reference are then relegated to Annex 1 of the report (along side four other annexes of witnesses and meetings). Among the points made in the terms of reference are: (again) that the proposals shall include means of encouraging widespread community support for those arrangements; a police service that can enjoy widespread support from, and is seen as an integral part of, the community as a whole; the legislative and constitutional framework should conform with internationally accepted norms in relation to policing standards. Given that Patten did not lay out the terms of reference at the beginning of the report, it is not surprising that the commission did not do all it was asked by the participants in the multi-party negotiations. Patten does not even begin with the Policing and Justice section of the Belfast Agreement. While the third sentence of paragraph 1 (as noted above) is used as an epigraph to chapter 1 of the report, the first paragraph then goes on to quote the Declaration of Support (described inaccurately as a preamble) from the 10 April 1998 agreement. Paragraph 1.8 then discusses the sentence at the top of chapter 1. Paragraph 1.9 quotes extensively from paragraph 2 of the Policing and Justice section. And that is the introduction to the terms of reference in Annex 1. Paragraph 2 includes: 'The participants also believe that these structures and arrangements must be capable of maintaining law and order including responding effectively to crime and to any terrorist threat and to public order problems. A police service which cannot do so will fail to win public confidence and acceptance.' Paragraph 1.10 then claims that 'these principles [in paragraph 2] have provided the benchmark against which we have tested all our proposals.' But Patten has not included all the principles in paragraph 2. The report goes on to state its tests: '1. Does this proposal promote effective and efficient policing? 2. Will it deliver fair and impartial policing, free from partisan control? 3. Does it provide for accountability, both to the law and to the community? 4. Will it make the police more representative of the society they serve? 5. Does it protect and vindicate the human rights and human dignity of all?' These are derived only from the first sentence of paragraph 2. No reference is made to the second and third sentences. The fourth sentence refers to delivering a police service consistent with the foregoing principles. And the fifth (and last) sentence describes arrangements 'unambiguously accepted and actively supported by the entire community.'

21.35 The independent commission on policing was announced hurriedly by the secretary of state on Wednesday, 3 June 1998, after the referendums but before the assembly elections. The chairman was Chris Patten, most recently the last governor of Hong Kong but also a former NIO minister. There were also seven other members, mostly from outside Northern Ireland.

21.36 The first ranked were Sir John Smith, a former deputy commissioner of the metropolitan police in London, and Kathleen O'Toole, secretary for public safety in Boston, Massachusetts.[32] They were followed by Peter Smith QC, a Northern Ireland barrister, and Maurice Hayes, a former senior civil servant and ombudsman (who had recommended a police ombudsman[33]). Next, representing the academic world, were Professor Clifford Shearing, a South African working in Canada, and Dr Gerald Lynch, president of John Jay College in New York. The seventh member was Lucy Woods, chief executive of British Telecom in Northern Ireland.[34]

21.37 There are six men and two women, one of whom (O'Toole) is a former police officer. Northern Ireland has two local representatives, one from each tradition (Smith and Hayes), plus one of the women, working there (Woods). The other five are outsiders: the chairman, a former conservative cabinet minister; the two police officers, from the United Kingdom and the United States; and the two academics, from Canada and the United States. Most attention focused on Professor Shearing, reputed to be a radical advocate of community policing.[35]

21.38 According to this paragraph, the independent commission (a Strand One matter) is the responsibility of the United Kingdom government. This did not prevent the Irish government from seeking to influence the selection of commissioners.[36]

32 Later, an administrator at Boston College.

33 NIO, *A Police Ombudsman for Northern Ireland?: a review of the police complaints system in Northern Ireland by Dr Maurice Hayes*, London 1997.

34 This position was later relinquished.

35 See *Changing Paradigms in Policing: the significance of community policing for the governance of security*, Occasional Paper No. 34, August 1998: http://www.iss.co.za/Pubs. His model of community policing includes the following: 'strategies and institutions within communities that will ensure that communities, and not the police, do the bulk of the policing'. However, the prime minister, addressing RUC recruits in Northern Ireland on 6 May 1998, during the referendum campaign, had said: 'Occasionally I read things in the newspapers about, does the Agreement mean the RUC is to be disbanded – answer no. Do it mean that we are going to have gangs of former paramilitaries running local police – answer no.' (http://www.nio.gov.uk)

36 Ten names were submitted through the Maryfield secretariat, but only one – Gerald Lynch – was accepted eventually. A memorandum by the secretary of state's private secretary in Belfast of 4 June 1998 (leaked to the *Irish Times* of 9 June 1998), gives an important insight into the workings of government there; it details decision-making in the 24 hours to the announcement of the Patten commission. It is a unique document of contemporary history. It is impossible to say whether this was typical of decision-making in that phase of the NIO's governance of Northern Ireland. Among the events recounted are an assurance from the prime minister to the taoiseach on Monday, 1 June 1998, that he and the secretary of state would consider further Irish representations; the secretary of state (in response to reports of Irish alarm) telephones Dermot Gallagher, head of the Anglo-Irish division of the department of foreign affairs in Dublin, on Tuesday, 2 June 1998; Dermot Gallagher states that Sinn Féin and the SDLP would attack the membership of the commission: 'the Irish

21.39 The Patten report – with 175 recommendations – was published eventually on 9 September 1999.[37] It contained proposals for the transformation of the RUC.[38] There was no tribute to the 302 officers killed and almost 9,000 injured during the troubles. It is believed the chairman accepted recommendations on symbols (see below) as the price of not altering the structure of the RUC.[39] The chairman also showed a readiness to equate support for and opposition to the RUC as morally equivalent, with his notion of 'two stories' about policing in Northern Ireland.[40]

21.40 The report was accepted sight unseen by the then secretary of state on behalf of the United Kingdom government.[41] Paragraph 3 of this section ('recommendations') was ignored initially in favour of paragraph 6 ('implementation'). However, with a new secretary of state appointed on 11 October 1999, the idea of an implementation plan was revised. The deadline for consultation remained 30 November 1999. On 23 November 1999, the queen, on the advice of the United Kingdom government, decided to award the George Cross to the RUC (wartime Malta being the only precedent for such a collective honour). But the response of the policing family – despite the chief constable's reform agenda of 1996 – remained determined inordinately by paragraph 17.6, 97 words dealing with four recommendations: the end of the RUC name; a new badge and symbols; no union flag on police buildings; and a new police flag.[42]

were getting bad vibes from the States' about Kathleen O'Toole; 'a nationalist with street cred within Northern Ireland was essential', such as Angela Hegarty or Martin O'Brien; the secretary of state suggests Gerald Lynch might be included; Senator Edward Kennedy later calls the secretary of state 'describ[ing] Gerald Lynch as very good news and he also had no objections to the appointment of Kathleen O'Toole'; the secretary of state postpones the announcement on 3 June 1998, to allow Dermot Gallagher to contact the taoiseach; Dermot Gallagher reports 'he had taken a very emotional and angry telephone call from Rita O'Hare' of Sinn Féin; the secretary of state telephones Rita O'Hare and 'explain[s] ... the pressures which she was under [from the media]'; Seamus Mallon and Dr Hayes then telephone, the secretary of state 'suspect[ing] they may have been prompted (by the Irish?) to phone her'; both argued for 'a nationalist ... with street cred'; Dr Hayes 'said he was not prepared to be described ... as a representative of *any* community, let alone the nationalist community and insisted it be changed.'; the secretary of state telephones Dermot Gallagher at 13.25 'ask[ing] him to convey to the Taoiseach her apology for having to go public in this way.'

37 Its content had been anticipated by Chris Ryder, in his memorandum to the Northern Ireland affairs committee in January 1998: 'The best model is for a single police service, centrally commanded but with a high degree of local devolution. The arrangements outlined in the Fundamental Review ... are therefore eminently suitable. These provide for a new head-quarters, making policy, setting objectives and providing central and specialized support services to a new network of 24–26 police Areas, co-terminous with the district council areas.' (*Third Report: Composition, Recruitment and Training of the RUC*, volume II, 337-II, London 1998, p. 137)

38 Pargraph 2.6.

39 See the speech of Michael McGimpsey, later a minister, to the UUP annual conference on 9 October 1999, where he contrasted the report with the stated positions of Sinn Féin and the SDLP.

40 *Irish Times*, 10 September 1999; *Observer*, 12 September 1999 (Henry Patterson); *Irish Times*, 15 February 2000.

41 *Observer*, 5 September 1999; statement, 9 September 1999, Northern Ireland Information Service: http://www.nio.gov.uk.

42 Chris Patten referred after publication to a leading politician (known to be David Trimble, the First Minister designate) as having argued to him that, it didn't matter if the commission

21.41 On 19 January 2000, the United Kingdom government gave a considered response to the Patten report in a statement by the secretary of state to parliament.[43] It amounted to a significant modification of the tone, and even the substantive recommendations, of the Patten report. First, there was a tribute to the RUC during the troubles. Second, the secretary of state distinguished the Belfast Agreement and the Patten report: 'The talks which led to the Good Friday Agreement addressed but did not resolve [policing] problems.' Third, the need for security proofing of recommendations was conceded, with the chief constable the principal adviser. Legislation was promised – in accord with the queen's speech[44] – for later in the 1999–2000 session.

21.42 Among the points made by the secretary of state were: one, already attested officers would not have to take the new human rights oath, 'which would in any case raise significant legal difficulties';[45] two, a tribute to the contribution of PANI, two of whose members had been killed in the troubles;[46] three, no reference to the devolution of policing powers (which had been recommended by Patten 'as soon as possible'[47]); four, no special arrangements for Belfast (four sub-groups in the district policing partnership board, and four police district commands had been recommended[48]); five, no power for district councils to purchase policing from the private sector[49] (a matter being considered in the criminal justice review); six, though not in the 19 January 2000 statement, bringing the parades commission under the HRA 1998 before 2 October 2000 through amendments to the Public Processions (Northern Ireland) Act 1998;[50] seven, no merger of special branch and crime branch,[51] the reorganization of headquarters being a matter for the chief constable; and eight, on symbols, the policing board to consider the question of the badge (including seemingly the George Cross).[52]

21.43 The implementation of the Patten report, in whole or in part, against the background of the security situation, is not of central concern here. (On 5 May 2000, the prime minister, in his joint letter with the taoiseach, at the time of agreement on restoration of the institutions, stated that legislation would be enacted by November 2000. The new Policing Board would be appointed in

got the substance of police reform more or less right: 'What mattered was the symbols; if we touched those, we would have blown it.' (*The Times*, 10 September 1999) Repeating this in an interview with Frank Millar, Chris Patten commented: 'And I think that is an argument which a lot of people would think tested rationality close to destruction.' (*Irish Times*, 11 September 1999)

43 House of Commons, *Hansard*, 342, 845–64, 19 January 2000.

44 'A Bill will be presented to implement proposals from the Independent Commission on Policing, following the completion of consultation' (17 November 1999).

45 Contrary to para. 4.7. The secretary of state reiterated that the home secretary had been asked to consider a human rights oath for the rest of the United Kingdom.

46 There is no tribute in the Patten report.

47 In para. 6.15.

48 In paras. 6.27 & 12.4 (but not recommendation 94?).

49 Paragraph 6.33.

50 Paragraph 9.9 referred to a role for neighbourhoods in parades. On 8 October 1999, the secretary of state set up a review of the parades commission. The findings were announced on 16 February 2000. This foregrounded a rights approach: Northern Ireland Information Service: http://www.nio.gov.uk.

51 Implied by para. 12.12.

52 Contrary to para. 17.6.

January 2001, and assume responsibilities in April 2001. The first recruitment process would start in April 2001.) What is of interest are three legal/constitutional issues raised by the report consequent upon the Belfast Agreement.

21.44 One, the constitutional basis of the Belfast Agreement. This has been discussed extensively in Part 2 above. Those legal propositions will, undoubtedly, be subject to argument. However, the constitutional provisions of the Belfast Agreement have been subjected also to considerable ideological interpretation.

21.45 Judging by comments made after publication of the report, Chris Patten showed that he had absorbed unwittingly elements of one particular worldview.

21.46 In an interview with Frank Millar in the *Irish Times* the day after publication of the report, the chairman said: 'It seems to me what was settled in the agreement was that the constitutional position should be determined democratically. But in return for making that manifest, I'd understood nationalists and republicans were offered two things. First, parity of esteem and recognition that there are two traditions in Northern Ireland, and that one shouldn't be seen (whether it is a justified observation or not) to be lording it over the other. And secondly, specific institutions of government were created to reflect that, while nationalists and republicans under the agreement are obliged to demonstrate their commitment to the democratic process, they're not obliged to owe their primary loyalty to the institutions of the State. I don't understand what the agreement is about if it isn't about that.'[53]

21.47 The following comments may be made. One, the first sentence is correct. But Northern Ireland is part of the United Kingdom (unproblematically in United Kingdom, international and Irish law). Democracy relates to – a possible future – unity by consent. Two, parity of esteem appears only in article 1 of the BIA (plus the first paragraph 4 of the Rights, Safeguards and Equality of Opportunity section). It has no legal constitutional significance in domestic law. Three, the same comment applies to the two traditions (from paragraph 5 of the Declaration of Support). This in fact stems from the preamble to the 1985 Anglo-Irish Agreement. Four, the question of the perception of lording it over the other, relates to ideology and not to law. Five, nationalists and unionists are required equally to demonstrate their commitment to the democratic process.

21.48 Six, nothing can be inferred about allegiance from specific institutions of government – as Chris Patten does.

21.49 The – common law – duty of allegiance in the United Kingdom (which is associated with protection) is owed to the crown. It is probably only enforceable to the extent of obeying the law. This allegiance also applies to friendly aliens within the jurisdiction[54] (and alien enemies within the realm with the express or implied licence of the crown[55]).

21.50 The question of British or Irish nationality, under article 1(vi) of the British-Irish Agreement (plus Annex 2), is of no relevance to the question of allegiance. In Northern Ireland, Irish citizens (who are not aliens) – like United

53 *Irish Times*, 11 September 1999.

54 *R v Owen* (1615) 1 Roll Rep 185.

55 E.C.S. Wade & A.W. Bradley, *Constitutional and Administrative Law*, 11th edn, London 1993, p. 438.

Kingdom citizens (which they are in the eyes of domestic law) – are required effectively to obey the law. (In the Republic of Ireland, in contrast, Irish citizens – only – are required, under article 9.2 of BNH, to show 'fidelity to the nation and loyalty to the State a[s] fundamental political duties'. It is not clear – from the case law – whether this is one or two duties.)[56]

21.51 Two, the issue of symbols in the Belfast Agreement (which has been discussed above in Chapter 18). Symbols arise in connection with two of Patten's recommendations: a new badge 'entirely free from any association with either the British or Irish states'; and a new flag 'free from association with the British or Irish states'.[57] This is to suggest a certain equivalence between the United Kingdom and Irish states, which is not, as argued, characteristic of the Belfast Agreement. Further and particularly, there is no clear direction in the Policing and Justice section of the Belfast Agreement, to justify this treatment of symbols.

21.52 Paragraph 1 contains this phrase: ' ... a new political dispensation which will recognise the full and equal legitimacy and worth of the identities, senses of allegiance and ethos of all sections of the community in Northern Ireland'. That is not a reference to the police. Insofar as it has a bearing on policing, it is affirming of different identities – not repressive of symbols, including those of the United Kingdom state (which remains the only state from the point of view of the law on policing).

21.53 The second paragraph in the terms of reference refers to 'culture, ethos and symbols'. This does refer to policing arrangements. Here the requirement is to have 'a police service that can enjoy widespread support from, and is seen as an integral part of, the community as a whole'. This is not an argument for obliterating symbols, unless it can be proved that one community does not mind the loss while the other requires their destruction to win its assent to the report.

21.54 A more accurate interpretation is that questions of culture, ethos and symbols to do with policing have to be handled delicately to secure widespread support from the community as a whole, in accord with the second paragraph 5 of the Rights, Safeguards and Equality of Opportunity section.

21.55 Three, the relationship between the Belfast Agreement and the Patten report. Paragraph 3 (as noted) provides for an independent commission to make recommendations for future policing arrangements. And paragraph 6 (see below)

56 Chris Patten's post-publication views seem to have inspired Sean Farren, later a minister (writing on the report). He advanced the – erroneous – interpretation of the constitutional provisions of the Belfast Agreement as creating 'a new civic order in Northern Ireland': 'while not completely distinct from the constitutional framework that maintains Northern Ireland's link with the United Kingdom, the new civic order will be separate from it ... it does not follow that all of its people will be required to give allegiance to the United Kingdom'. (*Daily Telegraph*, 29 October 1999) This was criticized by Eric Waugh in the *Belfast Telegraph*, 6 November 1999: 'On Mr Farren's prospectus the outlook here is bleak. His conception is the favoured nationalist one of the 50–50 Northern Ireland, one half looking longingly to Dublin, the other to London; with a marching regime on the way here which will be as near to Joint Authority as makes no difference ... A divided territory, which Mr Farren seems indefinitely to take for granted and wishes further to institutionalise, will not make for contentment. Nor will it further Irish reunion. It will postpone it.' See also Máire Geoghegan-Quinn, *Irish Times*, 4 December 1999.

57 Paragraph 17.6.

requires the government to discuss implementation of the recommendations with the political parties and the Irish government. Implementation does not imply acceptance of all the recommendations. The government cannot – in public law – fetter its discretion vis a vis the report. And the reference to the parties and the Irish government (the other participants in the multi-party negotiations) does not preclude consultation with inter alia the RUC, the PANI and the PFNI.

21.56 The Patten report, therefore, is not part of the Belfast Agreement. When the latter was voted upon in Northern Ireland on 22 May 1998,[58] the commission had not even been established. This was done hurriedly – before the Northern Ireland assembly elections of 25 June 1998 – on 3 June 1998. The commission was only beginning its work when the assembly met first on 1 July 1998.

21.57 Patten accepts this disjuncture between the Belfast Agreement and the report. Paragraph 1.2 (as noted above) seeks to justify the relevance of the commission's work after July 1999. The first and third reasons have a bearing on Patten as a freestanding set of recommendations.

21.58 The first is: 'As part of any final agreement to establish the customary institutions of democracy in Northern Ireland in a peaceful, civil society, the deeply controversial matters that we address will need to be confronted and settled. It may in some respects be better or more helpful that, with the publication of our proposals, they will now have to be debated openly by those who are looked to by the community to agree the way forward.'

21.59 This is a clear statement that the recommendations were on offer to Northern Ireland's political leaders. It may even be construed as a suggestion that Patten should have been tabled at the Mitchell review (which began the week the report was published).

21.60 The third reason has been discussed above, namely that the commission had been appointed in the enthusiastic wake of the 22 May 1998 referendum: 'So one day – and we hope that day will come sooner rather than later – the issues raised in our report will be an integral part of the agenda for a Northern Ireland that runs most of its own affairs in a spirit of reconciliation and good faith ... We publish these proposals in the strong belief that they offer the people of Northern Ireland the chance of establishing an effective and widely accepted police service for which they are themselves responsible.'

4. **The participants believe that the aims of the criminal justice system are [should be designed] to:**
   - **deliver a fair and impartial system of justice to the community;**
   - **have the confidence of all parts of the community; and**
   - **deliver justice efficiently and effectively.**

21.61 This paragraph and paragraph 5 below deal with the criminal justice system. Paragraph 4 is again preambular, but considerably shorter than paragraphs 1 and 2 on policing. The changes in the opening sentence greatly shifted the emphasis from designing a new criminal justice system, to identifying existing aims. These are fourfold: the first is uncontroversial (but there is a hint that the community determines what justice is); the second is more arguable, precisely

58 Not 21 May 1998, as Patten has it: paragraph 1.1.

because the community is mentioned twice; the third and fourth are unremarkable.

> **5. There will be a parallel wide-ranging review of [those aspects of] criminal justice (other than policing and those aspects of the system relating to the emergency legislation) to be carried out by the British Government through a mechanism with an independent element, in consultation with the political parties and others. The review will commence as soon as possible, will include wide consultation, and a report will be made to the Secretary of State no later than Autumn 1999. Terms of Reference are attached at Annex B.**[59]

21.62 This paragraph is similar to paragraph 3 above. It promises a criminal justice review. 'There will be a parallel wide-ranging review' is a reference to paragraph 3 above. 'of those aspects of criminal justice (other than policing and those aspects of the system relating to the emergency legislation)' means, the

59 ANNEX B

REVIEW OF THE CRIMINAL JUSTICE SYSTEM

[Overview and Relevant Principles

The criminal justice system in Northern Ireland exists to uphold the rule of law. It is concerned with crime in all its elements and the process which brings offenders to account, but constitutes only a part of society's response to crime. It involves a number of publicly funded bodies, as well as professions, defendants, witnesses and victims. The criminal justice system should be such as to:

- deliver a fair and impartial system of justice to the community;
- be responsive to the community's concerns, and encourage community involvement where appropriate;
- have the confidence of all parts of the community;
- deliver justice efficiently and effectively.]

Terms of Reference

Taking account of the[se] *aims of the criminal justice system as set out in the Agreement* [points], the review will address the structure, management and resourcing of publicly funded elements of the criminal justice system and will bring forward proposals for future criminal justice arrangements (other than policing and those aspects of the system relating to emergency legislation, which the Government is considering separately) covering such issues as:

- the arrangements for making appointments to the judiciary and magistracy, and safeguards for protecting their independence;
- the arrangements for the organisation and supervision of the prosecution process, and for safeguarding its independence;
- measures to improve the responsiveness and accountability of, and any lay participation in the criminal justice system;
- mechanisms for addressing law reform;
- the scope for structured co-operation between the criminal justice agencies on both parts of the island; and
- the structure and organisation of criminal justice functions that might be devolved to an Assembly, including the possibility of establishing a Department of Justice, while safeguarding the essential independence of many of the key functions in this area.

The Government proposes to commence the review as soon as possible, consulting with the political parties and others, including non-governmental expert organisations. The review will be completed by Autumn 1999.

whole of criminal justice less that considered by the Patten commission and the emergency legislation discussed above in Chapter 18. (The terms of reference in Annex B indicate that emergency legislation was also being reviewed internally.) 'to be carried out by the British Government' means this is not an independent review. It was to be done by officials from the NIO. 'through a mechanism with an independent element' was not explained (what ensued is considered immediately below). 'in consultation with the political parties and others' is a normal consultation process for any internal government review. 'The review will commence as soon as possible': it was launched on 27 June 1998 (two days after the assembly elections). 'will include wide consultation' repeats a point just made. 'a report will be made to the Secretary of State' does not contain any element of promise to publish. 'no later than Autumn 1999' means that officials were given longer than Chris Patten's commissioners.

21.63 The criminal justice review group was established by the secretary of state on (as just noted) 27 June 1998. Interestingly, it was described on 30 March 2000 as representing the secretary of state, the lord chancellor and the attorney-general.[60] It comprised four senior officials: Jim Daniell, director of criminal justice at the NIO, as chairman of the criminal justice review group; Glenn Thompson, director of the Northern Ireland court service; David Seymour, legal secretary to the law officers; and Brian White, head of the criminal justice policy division at the NIO (who was not announced initially as a member[61]). Ian Maye, of the NIO, was secretary to the criminal justice review group.

21.64 The independent element was a number of assessors: Eugene Grant QC, Professor John Jackson of Queen's University, Belfast; Professor Joanna Shapland of Sheffield University, Dr Bill Lockhart, director of Extern; and His Honour John Gower, a retired English circuit judge.[62] The criminal justice review states that the 'independent members ... played a full part in all aspects of the review'.[63]

21.65 The criminal justice review group met first on 1 July 1998, and held more than 45 days of plenary meetings in the following 21 months. On 27 August 1998, the secretary of state published a consultation paper produced by the review.[64] Over 5,000 copies were distributed. It comprised nine chapters, including the following: an appropriate set of principles and values for the criminal justice system (chapter 2); accountability to the community (chapter 4); the appointment of judges and magistrates (chapter 7); law reform (chapter 8); structured cooperation between criminal justice agencies in Northern Ireland and the Republic of Ireland. Written comments were sought by 30 October 1998. Over 90

60 Criminal justice review, para. 1.5. There was a precedent for the criminal justice review in 1997–98, as part of the comprehensive spending review (note 9 to para. 3.14). This, however, was confined to the workings, effectiveness and value for money of the criminal justice system as a whole. The criminal justice review group adopted the criminal justice board's aims for 1999–2000.

61 He was not a member in August 1998.

62 The order of names in the criminal justice review is: Shapland, Jackson, Grant, Lockhart and Gower.

63 Paragraph 1.8.

64 Criminal Justice Review Group, *Review of the Criminal Justice System in Northern Ireland: a consultation paper*, August 1998, London The Stationery Office Limited. It had presumably been in preparation for some time.

such submissions were received.[65] A progress report was published in April 1999.[66] A series of nine seminars was arranged for Northern Ireland in May and June 1999, to which over 3,000 individuals, groups and organizations were invited; around 300 people attended.[67] The criminal justice review group also commissioned a series of research reports, and 18 separate studies were also published on 30 March 2000.

21.66 The criminal justice review – a 447-page report of 17 chapters – may be contrasted with the Patten report, discussed above. First, it has 294 recommendations to Patten's 175, covering mainly prosecution, the judiciary, courts, sentences and law reform. Second, while Patten refers to the transformation of the RUC, the criminal justice review took as 'the focus of [its] work ... a desire to propose practical confidence building measures for a fresh political climate'.[68] It is active, and comprehensive, reformism: 'a major, but measured, programme of change'.[69] Third, while Patten declined to acknowledge the sacrifice of police officers, the criminal justice review pays tribute to all those in the system, including the police and defence lawyers.[70] Fourth, the criminal justice review deals with substance, and not centrally with symbols. (It also interprets the Belfast Agreement rationally.) Fifth, there is no moral equivalence between being for or against the criminal justice system, or some particular aspect of it. The criminal justice review group, while it had over 70 meetings with interested groups, organizations and individuals, did not report there were 'two stories' in Northern Ireland. Sixth, while the then secretary of state accepted Patten sight unseen, the secretary of state on 30 March 2000 announced a consultation period of 6 months: 'the Government will keep an open mind on the proposals until this period of consultation has been completed.'[71] It is unlikely that there will be the necessity for something like the secretary of state's 19 January 2000 statement on Patten (see above).[72] (On 5 May 2000, the prime minister, in his joint letter with the taoiseach, at the time of agreement to restore the institutions, stated that the United Kingdom government would state its intentions in October 2000. Legislation would be published in April 2001.) Seventh, there is no equivalent of paragraph 17.6 in Patten, dealing with symbols. The criminal justice review, in fact, comes up with contrary proposals as regards courts and district policing partnership boards.[73]

65 Appendix A lists 88 political parties and others who gave written submission or position papers, or met the criminal justice review group. Sinn Féin's submission is dated 10 December 1998.

66 Criminal Justice Review Group, *Review of the Criminal Justice System in Northern Ireland: a progress report*, April 1999.

67 Appendix C.

68 Paragraph 1.11.

69 Paragraph 1.30.

70 Paragraph 1.21.

71 Northern Ireland Information Service, 30 March 2000: http://www.nio.gov.uk.

72 'We do believe ... that great care must be taken in implementing any package of agreed changes to ensure that the quality of justice and the efficiency of the system are maintained and enhanced, during the period of implementation and thereafter. Given the breadth and complexity of issues which we address, it is crucial that sufficient time is taken to consult with the criminal justice agencies and those who work within the system and to plan and conduct any process of change in a measured way.' (para. 1.12)

73 Paras. 8.62–3. However, the terms of reference did not include 'ethos of the courts' (unlike Patten's terms of reference). Paras. 11.61–2.

21.67 The response of the United Kingdom government on 30 March 2000, when it announced a six-month consultation period, was: 'A number of key principles have underpinned the work of the Review Group. For example, their recommendations demonstrate a commitment to maintaining human rights, to ensuring that the criminal justice system is open and accountable, protecting the independence of the judiciary and the prosecution, and ensuring that merit must continue to be the key criterion in determining judicial appointments. The government supports these principles on which the group's recommendations are based.'[74]

> 6. **Implementation of the recommendations arising from both reviews will be discussed with the political parties and with the Irish Government.**

21.68 This paragraph relates to both reviews. According to paragraph 3, the independent commission on policing was to make recommendations. These presumably were to go the secretary of state. The secretary of state's role as the recipient of the criminal justice report is express in paragraph 5. What happens to both reviews is a matter for the United Kingdom government. This paragraph states that the implementation of the recommendations (which does not exclude the government accepting some and rejecting others) will be discussed with the political parties and the Irish government. The political parties are, of course, from Northern Ireland, and are mainly present in the assembly. The role of the Irish government is express here. This means there was no role for it in the setting up of the Patten commission and the criminal justice review.

> 7. **The participants also [to] note that the British Government remains ready in principle, with the broad support of the political parties, and after consultation, as appropriate, with the Irish Government, in the context of ongoing implementation of the relevant recommendations, to devolve responsibility for policing and justice issues.**

21.69 This is a major provision of this section, the possible devolution of responsibility for policing and justice.

21.70 Since 1972, policing and justice issues have been the responsibility of London. In the NIA 1998, which incorporates the Strand One aspects of the Belfast Agreement into United Kingdom law, schedule 3 (reserved matters) includes the following: criminal justice (paragraph 9); public order (paragraph 10); the police (paragraph 11); firearms and explosives (paragraph 12); and the courts (less matters in paragraph 11 of schedule 2) (paragraph 15). Under section 4(2) to (5), reserved matters can be transferred (and vice versa). The trigger is a vote of the assembly, on a cross-community basis. The secretary of state then lays before parliament the draft of an order in council amending schedule 3.

21.71 'The participants' here must be only the political parties. 'the British Government remains ready in principle' is a clear statement of intent. It also reaffirms the point that Strand One is a matter for the United Kingdom government alone. 'with the broad support of the political parties' has been incorporated into United Kingdom law through section 4(3) of the NIA 1998: cross-community support. 'and after consultation, as appropriate, with the Irish Government,' does

74 Northern Ireland Information Service, 30 March 2000: http://www.nio.gov.uk.

not infringe the Strand One rule. Under the second paragraph 6 of Strand Three, the Irish government has a say in policing and justice as long as they are not devolved. 'in the context of ongoing implementation of the relevant recommendations' is a reference to the two reviews. This suggests that ongoing implementation might take some time; alternatively, that devolution might be a realistic proposition in a foreseeable time scale.

22

Prisoners

22.1 This is the last substantive section of the Belfast Agreement. It was the most important in the weeks immediately following 10 April 1998. It comprises only five paragraphs (like the section on Decommissioning). But these five paragraphs, in the context of the multi-party negotiations, mark the definitive end – at least in terms of intention – of political violence. They provide for the conditional release of all terrorist prisoners, republican and loyalist – effectively an amnesty, even though this was denied. The section binds the United Kingdom and Irish states, which have neighbouring responsibilities for internal security in Ireland. It is at page 25 of Cm 3883 and page 41 of Cm 4705 (page 35 of the 1999 Irish version). I indicate [deletions] to the MDP, and *additions* thus.

22.2 Also relevant are the Northern Ireland (Sentences) Act 1998 (the United Kingdom act), which received the royal assent on 28 July 1998 (it had been published on 5 June 1998); and the Criminal Justice (Release of Prisoners) Act 1998 (the Irish act), which had been promulgated on 13 July 1998 (having been published belatedly on 30 June 1998).

22.3 Prisoners is one of a quartet of related issues in the Belfast Agreement. Decommissioning is about terrorists[1] becoming democrats. Security is interrelated, representing the response of the state to a diminishing threat. Policing and Justice is about good government. The fourth section, Prisoners, demonstrates most clearly the truly historic opportunity for a new beginning (proclaimed in paragraph 1 of the Declaration of Support).

United Kingdom precedents for the release of terrorist prisoners

22.4 In 1983, the United Kingdom government had set up life-sentence release mechanisms; these allowed terrorist prisoners to be freed after a fixed number of years. By the time of the 1998 sentences bill (which became the United Kingdom act), almost 450 life prisoners had benefited from this scheme.[2] Only two had been recalled – their licences being revoked – as a result of further serious terrorist-type offences.

1 Terrorism was defined first as regards Northern Ireland as 'the use of violence for political ends and includes any use of violence for the purpose of putting the public or any section of the public in fear' (Detention of Terrorists (Northern Ireland) Order 1972, SI 1972/1632, art 2(2)). It was redefined – as a result of Lord Lloyd of Berwick's report, *Inquiry into legislation against terrorism*, of October 1996, Cm 3420 – as: 'the use or threat, for the purpose of advancing a political, religious or ideological cause, of action which – (a) involves serious violence against any person or property, (b) endangers the life of any person, or (c) creates a serious risk to the health or safety of the public or a section of the public.' (Terrorism bill, clause 1(1)) Section 1 of the Terrorism Act 2000 contains the new definition.

2 It is alluded to in section 7(1)(b).

22.5 In 1995 – during the first IRA ceasefire, and the loyalist ceasefires – a release scheme for fixed-sentence prisoners was enacted at Westminster: Northern Ireland (Remission of Sentences) Act 1995. It provided for automatic release at the half-way point in a sentence. (While this was presented as an early release scheme for Northern Ireland, it simply brought the province back into line with the rest of the United Kingdom.[3] Section 1 has the marginal note: release on licence of persons subject to restricted remission. Section 1(2) brought prison rules back into play.) More than 245 prisoners were to have been released by the time of the 1998 sentences bill. Two had to be recalled for breaching their licences. The Major government (a point made repeatedly by the Blair government) continued the releases even though the IRA broke its ceasefire in February 1996. About half the remaining prisoners – this is significant – would have been released in the following two years (1998–2000) under the existing scheme; 'in many respects', Adam Ingram MP told the house of commons on 10 June 1998, 'we are today considering building on that Conservative legislation'.[4]

22.6 Prisoner releases, then, had an administrative and legal history. It was not an innovation of the Belfast Agreement. But the question became an issue in the Northern Ireland referendum of 22 May 1998. I discuss this here, since it is not appropriate in the consideration below of paragraphs 1–4 of the section; the United Kingdom and Irish acts, however, are considered there, in terms of the incorporation of this section of the Belfast Agreement.

The United Kingdom government paper, 'Prisoners and the Political Settlement' (20 April 1998)

22.7 This briefing note was placed in the library of the house of commons ten days after the Belfast Agreement. It was an undertaking as to what the United Kingdom government would be prepared to do in the context of a peaceful and lasting settlement. It purported to be in part an interpretation of the Prisoners section of the Belfast Agreement, at the point at which this was presented to parliament as Cm 3883.[5]

22.8 Among the details of the proposed arrangement were:[6]

- no early release for prisoners affiliated to groups engaging in violence;[7]
- prisoners released on licence, subject to recall;[8]
- secretary of state to have the power to suspend the scheme;[9]
- protection of the public to be a criterion for life-sentence prisoners;[10]
- secretary of state to keep under review organizations excluded from the scheme;[11]

3 Section 14 of the Northern Ireland (Emergency Provisions) Act 1991 had restricted remission for persons sentenced for scheduled offences.

4 House of Commons, *Hansard*, 6th series, 313, 1163, 10 June 1998.

5 House of Commons, *Hansard*, 6th series, 310, 481, 20 April 1998.

6 Footnotes show what was finally arranged.

7 Section 3(4) and (8), but only with reference to specified – not proscribed – organizations engaging in violence.

8 Sections 4–9.

9 Section 16.

10 Section 3(6).

11 Section 3(10).

- power of secretary of state to refer back cases to the (three to five member) sentences review body (provided for in an annex);[12]
- no general amnesty for terrorist prisoners;[13]
- legislation introduced after the referendum by June 1998;[14]
- all applications to be considered by June 1999;[15]
- all eligible prisoners released within two years;[16]
- secretary of state to have the power to bring that date forward, or move it back.[17]

The prime minister's referendum pledges

22.9 The Belfast Agreement – promising peace – was signed by the prime minister of the United Kingdom on 10 April 1998. Initial suspicions on the part of mainly the majority community were addressed to the related issues of decommissioning and prisoner releases. Would the IRA refuse to decommission? Would Sinn Féin, nevertheless, be allowed to enter the regional government? Would its prisoners continue to benefit from the release provisions? And what was the significance of the common two-year periods? These were the principal questions debated in the campaign leading to the referendum of 22 May 1998.

22.10 The prime minister addressed these concerns in a speech at Balmoral in Belfast on 14 May 1998 (almost exactly a year after his speech there on his first visit out of London as prime minister):

> The problem is: I believe that most people would be ready to accept even the hardest parts of the Agreement if they had genuine confidence that the paramilitaries were really ready to give up violence for good ...
>
> ... How can we be sure that acceptance of the agreement by these parties will mean an end to violence and a genuine commitment to exclusively peaceful means, when we know that for example Sinn Fein and the IRA remain inextricably linked ...
>
> In particular, how do we test it, judge it, assess it to be real? It is here that people feel that sentiments or intentions are not enough.
>
> People want to know that if these parties are going to benefit from proposals in the Agreement such as accelerated prisoner releases and Ministerial posts, their commitment to democratic non-violent means must be established, in an objective, meaningful and verifiable way. Those who have used the twin tactics of ballot box and the gun must make a clear choice. There can be no fudge between democracy and terror.
>
> ... There are a range of factors to take into account:
>
> first and foremost, a clear and unequivocal commitment that there is an end to violence *for good* ... and that the so-called war is finished, done with, gone; ...
>
> that ... the ceasefires are indeed complete and unequivocal: an end to bombings, killings and beatings, claimed or unclaimed; an end to targeting and procurement of weapons, progressive abandonment and dismantling of paramilitary structures

12 Section 8; section 1 and schedules 1 and 2.
13 Sections 4–9.
14 The bill was published on 5 June 1998.
15 This is not provided for in the act, nor in the rules: Northern Ireland (Sentences) Act 1998 (Sentence Review Commissioners) Rules 1998, SI 1998/1859. These came into force on 31 July 1998.
16 Section 10.
17 Section 10(4).

> actively directing and promoting violence;
> full co-operation with the Independent Commission on decommissioning, to implement the provisions of the Agreement;
> and no other organisations being deliberately used as proxies for violence.
> These factors provide evidence upon which to base an overall judgement – a judgement which will necessarily become more rigorous over time. What is more I have decided that they must be given legislative expression directly and plainly ...
> We are not setting new preconditions or barriers.

22.11 The prime minister (a barrister by background) outlined an objective test, which would be imposed more rigorously over time (though it is not clear how this could happen). The key factors to be assessed were: one, a declaration that the war was over; two, complete and unequivocal ceasefires (these being defined further); three, full cooperation with the IICD; and four, no use of proxies.

22.12 On 20 May 1998, at the University of Ulster at Coleraine, the prime minister made a personal pledge to the people of Northern Ireland (written in his own hand on the whiteboard in the lecture theatre where he was speaking[18]). There were five points. The fourth and fifth are:

- Those who use or threaten violence excluded from the Government of Northern Ireland.
- Prisoners kept in unless violence is given up for good.

22.13 On 22 May 1998 – the day of the referendum – the prime minister published an article in the *Belfast Newsletter* and in the *Irish News*:

> ... how can people be sure that the present ceasefires are not merely tactical and that the terrorists will not reap the benefits of the agreement, while retaining the possibility of a return to violence?
> The agreement itself is specifically designed to prevent this happening – and I have made clear in the pledge I gave on Wednesday [20 May 1998] that I will make the agreement stick.
> There can be no accelerated prisoner releases unless the organisations and individuals concerned have clearly given up violence for good – and there is no amnesty in any event. Representatives of parties intimately linked to paramilitary groups can only be in a future Northern Ireland government if it is clear that there will be no more violence and the threat of violence has gone. That doesn't just mean decommissioning but all bombings, killings, beatings, and an end to targeting, recruiting and all the structures of terrorism. I have set out the tests for this. They will be enshrined in law and these tests will be applied more and more rigorously as time goes on.
> There can be no fudge between democracy and terror.
> ... I urge you to trust me, as your prime minister, to deliver what the agreement promises.

22.14 These undertakings have a legal significance (albeit different from the prime minister's letter of 10 April 1998 to David Trimble, discussed in Chapters 12 and 19): 'I have decided that [a range of factors] must be given legislative expression directly and plainly' (14 May 1998); '[The tests] will be enshrined in law' (22 May 1998). The words of the prime minister in Northern Ireland – one of the four signatories of the Belfast Agreement – formed part of the instructions to

18 *Irish News*, 21 May 1998. This idea appears to have been suggested by Philip Gould, and opposed strongly by the NIO (*Sunday Telegraph*, 30 July 2000).

United Kingdom parliamentary counsel. Whether they are admissible in a United Kingdom court is governed by *Pepper (Inspector of Taxes) v Hart* [1993] AC 593. Whether they were acted upon in full or not is considered below under paragraph 2, where I consider its meaning in terms of the implementation of the Belfast Agreement through the United Kingdom act.

The Northern Ireland (Sentences) Act 1998

22.15 The bill (as noted) had been published on 5 June 1998 (before the assembly elections). The second reading in the house of commons was on 10 June 1998. 343 voted for; 10 against (including the Rt. Hon. David Trimble MP). The committee stage followed on 15 and 17 June 1998; third reading was on 18 June 1998. It was dealt with in the house of lords from 29 June 1998. Royal assent followed – slowly – on 28 July 1998. The long title of this United Kingdom act is 'an act to make provision about the release on licence of certain persons serving sentences of imprisonment in Northern Ireland'.

22.16 Section 1 (and schedule 1) of the act provided for an unspecified number of sentence review commissioners, who, as a group, would command widespread acceptance throughout the community in Northern Ireland (subsection (3)).[19] They were nowhere defined as being independent. Section 2 provided inter alia for panels of commissioners, and decisions by a single commissioner (paragraph 2). Under paragraph 1 of schedule 2 (commissioners' procedure), the secretary of state was empowered to make rules. These were laid before parliament on 30 July 1998, and came into force the following day.[20]

22.17 Section 3 was crucial. It allowed the commissioners to declare that a prisoner was eligible for release. For a fixed-term prisoner, three conditions had to be met. Those sentenced to life imprisonment had to meet four conditions, the fourth being: not a danger to the public (subsections (2) and (6)).

22.18 The first common condition was a sentence passed in Northern Ireland for a qualifying offence – defined in subsection (7) as a scheduled offence,[21] committed before 10 April 1998[22] – and with a sentence of life imprisonment or a term of at least five years (subsection (3)). The second common condition was that the prisoner was not a supporter[23] of a specified organization (subsection (4)). And the third common condition was that, if the prisoner were released, he would not be likely to become a supporter of a specified organization, or become involved in Irish terrorist activity[24] (subsection (5)).

22.19 A specified organization was central to the operation of the act; it is mentioned in subsections (4) and (5). Under the Northern Ireland (Emergency Provisions) Act 1996, paramilitary organizations are proscribed there. The law on illegality did not change, as the government tried to attract Sinn Féin, and therefore

19 This contrasts with representative of the community in Northern Ireland in sections 68(3) and 73(4) of the NIA 1998.

20 The Northern Ireland (Sentences) Act 1998 (Sentence Review Commissioners) Rules 1998, SI 1998/1859.

21 Under the Northern Ireland (Emergency Provisions) Acts 1973, 1978, 1991 and 1996.

22 And was not certified by the attorney general for Northern Ireland as not to be treated as a scheduled offence.

23 Supporter is nowhere defined in the act; it includes member.

24 He could become involved in other terrorism.

the IRA, into the political process. Proscribed organizations were recognized to be observing ceasefires. An organization was specified by the secretary of state, if it was engaged in terrorism and was not on ceasefire (subsection (8)). The double condition – where the second was implied by the first – was essentially to allow proscription to be eclipsed by specification, illegality by a complete and unequivocal ceasefire (indicating greater tolerance of paramilitarism by the state). This can be seen in subsection (10), under which the secretary of state could specify or despecify an organization (specification being the development of proscription). It was easier for a proscribed organization to be despecified, under subsection (10)(a), than it was to have a paramilitary group specified under subsection (10)(b): in the former, it is (8)(a) or (b),[25] while in the latter it is (8)(a) and (b).[26]

22.20 (Subsection (9) – applying to subsection (8)(b), a complete and unequivocal ceasefire – is discussed below with reference to the prime minister's referendum pledges. Subsection (9) contains essentially four questions, the answers to which the secretary of state had to take into account.) The IRA has been a proscribed organization throughout the troubles; it was not specified under this act at any point from enactment on 28 July 1998.

22.21 If proscription was not relevant, decommissioning was. One of the four factors the secretary of state had to take into account, was whether the terrorist organization was cooperating fully with the de Chastelain commission: section 3(9)(d). Evidence that it was not would go to the assessment of whether the organization was maintaining a complete and unequivocal ceasefire. A negative judgment could lead to the organization being specified (if it was also concerned in terrorism), and therefore to a halt in prisoner releases.

22.22 Sections 4 and 5 dealt with fixed-term prisoners. Under the 1995 act, prisoners were eligible for release having served half their sentence (as in the rest of the United Kingdom). Under section 4(1), this was reduced to one third of the sentence. Section 4(4) provided that the licence lapsed at the point at which the prisoner would have been released on the ground of good conduct under prison rules.[27] Section 5 dealt with special cases.

22.23 Sections 6 and 7 dealt with life prisoners. Under section 6(2), the commissioners were required to specify a day about two thirds of the way through the period which the prisoner would have been likely to have spend in prison.[28]

22.24 The licence conditions were: one, not to become a supporter of a specified organization; two, not to become concerned in terrorism; and three, for life prisoners, not to become a danger to the public (section 9).

22.25 Section 10, however, provided for accelerated release; it required an accelerated release day (subsections (1) and (2)). This was the second anniversary of enactment (28 July 2000), under subsections (4) and (5). Subsection (6)

25 This would theoretically allow a paramilitary group to remain involved in terrorism, as long as it had (formally) established a ceasefire!

26 In this case, those opposed to terrorism had to prove that the paramilitary group, as well as not observing a (formal) ceasefire, was engaged in terrorism.

27 The first report of a licence being revoked was Geroid Mag Uaid: *Irish Times*, 21 March 2000.

28 This was to be assessed under section 7.

provided for two years from sentencing, or remand, where the prisoner was not in gaol on 28 July 1998. And subsection (7) stated that nothing in this section should permit a release before two years of a sentence had been served (allowing for periods of remand). However, subsections (4) to (7) were subject – under subsection (8) – to amendment by the secretary of state by order.

22.26 Under section 16, the secretary of state could suspend, and later revive, the scheme; this operated through sections 3 and 10. (This was a general power. The secretary of state could only target one particular paramilitary group by specifying it under section 3(10). Any prisoner who was judged by the sentence review commissioners to be a supporter of the specified organization would be ineligible for release under the second and third conditions (section 3(4) and (5))).

22.27 Schedule 3 applied the act to sentences passed outside Northern Ireland, in England and Wales or in Scotland (paragraph 1(1)).

22.28 On 28 July 1998, the draft Northern Ireland (Sentences) Act (Specified Organisations) Order 1998, was laid before both houses. It was debated in the commons on 29 July 1998, and in the lords the following day. It came into force on 31 July 1998.[29]

22.29 At that point, the list of organizations proscribed in Northern Ireland under section 30(3) of the Northern Ireland (Emergency Provisions) Act 1996 was: the IRA, the Irish National Liberation Army (INLA), the Continuity IRA, the Irish Peoples Liberation Organisation, Cumann na mBan, Fianna na hEireann, Saor Eire, Red Hand Commandos, the Ulster Freedom Fighters (UFF), the Ulster Volunteer Force (UVF), the Ulster Defence Association (UDA) and the Loyalist Volunteer Force (LVF).[30]

22.30 The list of specified organizations – not observing a ceasefire in the judgment of the secretary of state on 30 July 1998 – comprised the four following: the Continuity IRA, the LVF, the INLA and the Real IRA.

22.31 On 12 November 1998, the secretary of state announced the despecification of the LVF: 'On the basis of all the security information available to me, and taking into account all the factors set out in the legislation, I have decided, subject to approval by Parliament, to despecify the LVF.'[31] On 3 March 1999, it was announced that the secretary of state was despecifying the INLA.[32] (The Irish government, in contrast, had announced on 18 December 1998, that it was

29 The Northern Ireland (Sentences) Act 1998 (Specified Organisations) Order 1998, SI 1998/1882.

30 The Real IRA was proscribed after the Omagh bomb of 15 August 1998.

31 Northern Ireland (Sentences) Act 1998 (Specified Organisations) (No. 2) Order 1998, SI 1998/2869, made on 18 March 1999 and coming into force the following day. The mechanism was the respecification of the other three organizations, under section 3(8) of the act. The secretary of state gave the following reasons: the LVF had maintained a ceasefire from May 1998; and the significant contacts with the IICD: press release, Northern Ireland Information Service, 12 November 1998: http://www.nio.gov.uk/.

32 Northern Ireland (Sentences) Act 1998 (Specified Organisations) Order 1999, SI 1999/1152, made on 11 April 1999 and coming into force the following day. The mechanism was again the respecification of the original two organizations under section 3(8) of the act, plus the specification of the two additional organizations. The reason given was a six-months' ceasefire; the secretary of state called upon the organization to cooperate with the IICD.

treating INLA prisoners as qualifying prisoners under its act.[33])

22.32 The 3 March 1999 was the occasion on which the secretary of state announced that the Orange Volunteers (OV) and the Red Hand Defenders (RHD) would be proscribed from midnight. An order specifying the two organizations had also been laid before parliament.[34] The list of specified organizations was once again four strong.

22.33 The secretary of state had appointed ten sentence review commissioners on 30 July 1998. The joint chairmen were Sir John Blelloch (a former NIO senior official), and Brian Currin (a South African working in mediation and institutional transformation). The five Northern Ireland members were David Bolton (a qualified social worker);[35] Peter Curran (a consultant psychiatrist[36]), Mary Gilpin (a former probation officer, and prison visitor at the Maze); Clodagh McGrory (a human rights activist); and David Wall (a leading worker with offenders). Clodagh McGrory would appear to be the statutory United Kingdom lawyer, under section 1(2)(a) and (5).[37] The other three members were Silvia Casale (an independent criminologist, seemingly resident in Great Britain); Ian Dunbar CB (a former prison governor from Great Britain); and Dr Adrian Grounds (a Cambridge lecturer in forensic psychiatry). On 27 August 1998, the joint chairmen held a press conference to clear up misunderstandings about procedures.[38]

22.34 On 1 September 1998, the victims minister, Adam Ingram MP, announced details of the early release information scheme. Under section 15 of the sentences act (an amendment to the bill), victims or their families could request in writing a ministerial statement about a prisoner potentially eligible for release. The secretary of state was required not to provide a statement if he believed that it would create a danger to the safety of any person (including, therefore, the prisoner).

The Republic of Ireland

22.35 There were also prisoners in the Republic of Ireland, who had been sentenced for scheduled offences. Most of these had been transferred recently from the United Kingdom,[39] under the 1983 Convention on the Transfer of Sentenced Prisoners.[40] Under article 3(1)(f), it was for the sentencing and administering

33 Press release, Dept. of Justice, Equality and Law Reform: http://www.irlgov.ie/justice/Press.

34 Northern Ireland (Sentences) Act 1998 (Specified Organisations) Order 1999, SI 1999/1152, made on 11 April 1999 and coming into force the following day.

35 David Bolton resigned and was replaced on 9 September 1998 by Dr Duncan Morrow (a lecturer in politics).

36 Required under section 1(2)(b) of the act.

37 This amendment, which was accepted by the government, was moved by William Ross MP.

38 They made three points: one, the process emerged from the Belfast Agreement, the act and the rules; two, the same information was shared between the applicant, the respondents (the NIO) and the commissioners; and three, the timings were laid down mainly in the rules.

39 Prisoners had also been transferred from Great Britain to Northern Ireland following the 1992 Ferrers report: *Report of the Interdepartmental Working Group's Review of the Provisions for the Transfer of Prisoners between UK Jurisdictions* (unpublished).

40 Council of Europe, ETS No. 112. There is also an additional protocol of 1997, Council of Europe, ETS No. 167. As of 13 March 2000, this has not been signed by the United Kingdom or Irish states.

states to agree to a transfer. This instrument had been ratified by the United Kingdom on 30 April 1985. The Republic's decision to ratify belatedly on 31 July 1995 (plus the return of the Blair government), led to transfers in 1997–98.[41] Article 10 provided for continued enforcement of a sentence; but article 11 allowed for conversion of the sentence (and article 12 for either party granting pardon, amnesty or commutation in accord with its own constitution and laws).

22.36 United Kingdom prisoners were transferred on the basis that they would continue to serve their sentences in the Republic of Ireland. (Others may have been sentenced in the Republic of Ireland, for offences in Northern Ireland under the Criminal Law (Jurisdiction) Act 1976. There was also a third category: those sentenced for Irish scheduled offences in the Republic under the state's – domestic – emergency criminal law.) It is important to bear these three categories in mind, especially the prisoners transferred from Great Britain and those sentenced in the Republic for offences committed there.

22.37 Section 33 of the Offences against the State Act 1939 allows the Irish government – at its absolute discretion – to grant full early release to terrorist prisoners. It does this by remitting in whole or in part any punishment imposed by the special criminal court. This power was used after the first – temporary – IRA ceasefire of 31 August 1994; nine prisoners were released just before Christmas. There were further releases in 1995 (many of those sentenced for Irish scheduled offences, or under the Criminal Law (Jurisdiction) Act 1976, appear to have benefited).

22.38 The process, however, was halted, when the IRA resumed its military campaign in February 1996.

22.39 Following the Belfast Agreement, the Irish government announced on 14 April 1998 the full early release of nine prisoners under the 1939 act. (These had not been transferred from the United Kingdom.) Though the obligations under the Belfast Agreement applied equally to the Irish government, it took the view that it had sufficient powers for prisoner releases under existing legislation[42] – even though it had promised to legislate by the end of June 1998.

22.40 Section 33 of the Offences against the State Act 1939 allows the government to release prisoners sentenced in the jurisdiction. (The Criminal Justice Act 1951 allows the minister to exercise the power for remission, or commutation, of any punishment.) The Criminal Justice Act 1960 adds a provision for temporary release by the minister (section 2). The Irish government cannot release prisoners on licence; however, it may impose conditions under the 1939 act, such as keeping the peace (and the minister may also do this under the 1960 act). The justice minister undertook to use mainly the 1960 act, because the majority of prisoners had been repatriated from the United Kingdom.

22.41 However, on 30 June 1998, the Criminal Justice (Release of Prisoners) Bill 1998 was published. (Opposition parties had pressed for legislation, as this was

41 On 18 December 1998, five prisoners were transferred. The home secretary predicted there would only be one republican prisoner in Great Britain at the end of 1998 (Michael von Tangen Page, *Prisons, Peace and Terrorism: penal policy in the reduction of political violence in Northern Ireland, Italy and the Spanish Basque Country, 1968–97*, Basingstoke, Hampshire 1998, p. 84).

42 A review was carried out by the department of justice and the attorney general's office.

specified in the Belfast Agreement.) It was enacted quickly and promulgated, as noted, within two weeks.

22.42 The Irish act provided for a – independent – three-person release of prisoners commission in section 2; the chairperson was to be a practising lawyer, one of the ordinary members an officer of the minister's department, and the other a member of the probation and welfare service. Section 3 defined its function as being to advise on request the minister, with respect to the exercise of any power of release by reference to the Prisoners section of the Belfast Agreement (section 3(4)). (The commission did not specify the qualifying prisoners; the minister does.)

22.43 Section 4 required the minister, when exercising the powers of release, to have regard to the relevant provisions and the commission's advice.[43] During the passage of the bill, the justice minister expressed the view that he would refer each case to the commission. The act had – significantly – (for convenience of reference) scheduled to it the Prisoners section, described as: provisions of the agreement reached in the multi-party talks which appear under the heading 'Prisoners' (under section 1(1), however, the MPA is related to the BIA).

22.44 Nine eligible IRA prisoners in the Republic of Ireland were released from Castlerea prison in Co. Roscommon on 20 December 1999.[44] There remained, however, another five, four of whom were convicted of the manslaughter of Garda McCabe in the Republic (who are considered further below).

TITLE: PRISONERS

22.45 This section has a one-word title. It is, however, defined as qualifying prisoners in paragraph 1.

1. **Both Governments will put in place mechanisms to provide for an accelerated programme for the release of prisoners, including transferred prisoners, convicted of scheduled offences in Northern Ireland or, in the case of those sentenced outside Northern Ireland, similar offences (referred to hereafter as qualifying prisoners). Any such arrangements will protect the rights of individual prisoners under national and international law.**

22.46 'Both Governments will put in place mechanisms' bound the United Kingdom government and the Irish government. The word mechanisms was used of the 1983 United Kingdom life-sentence release provisions.[45] That was not a statutory scheme.[46] Under those mechanisms, the secretary of state exercised powers to release life prisoners on licence. Mechanisms may have been required to cover the different positions in London and Dublin. Westminster had to legislate: the Northern Ireland (Sentences) Act 1998; the Oireachtas (as noted) did not have to add to existing powers in the Offences against the State Act 1939 and the

43 This is unlikely to mean he has to accept the advice: *In re Gallagher's Application* [1996] 3 IR 10.

44 *Irish Independence*, 21 December 1999.

45 House of Commons, *Hansard*, 6th series, 313, 1163, 10 June 1998.

46 Von Tagen Page, *Prisons, Police and Terrorism*, pp. 73–5 (making reference to a 1985 NIO memorandum).

Criminal Justice Act 1960. The Criminal Justice (Release of Prisoners) Act 1998 added nothing; the minister – if he needed it – could have obtained the advice provided for administratively.

22.47 'to provide for an accelerated programme for the release of prisoners' was dealt with differently in the two jurisdictions. There were already in the United Kingdom: the 1983 life prisoners programme; and the 1995 statutory scheme for fixed-term prisoners. Section 33 of the Offences Against the State Act 1939 covered the release of domestic prisoners. And the Criminal Justice Act 1960 allowed for temporary release, and for repatriated prisoners. An accelerated programme meant faster than the 1995 and 1983 schemes applying to Northern Ireland. There was no baseline in the Republic of Ireland, though there have been prisoners releases since 1994. An accelerated programme there has to be defined in terms of the end point, discussed under paragraph 3.

22.48 'including transferred prisoners' refers to those sentenced in England and Wales or Scotland, and transferred to Northern Ireland under the 1992 Ferrers report, or to the Republic of Ireland under the Convention for the Transfer of Sentenced Prisoners. The definition of prisoners included transferred prisoners in both parts of Ireland. 'convicted of schedules offences in Northern Ireland' referred to offences under the Northern Ireland (Emergency Provisions) Acts 1973, 1978, 1991 or 1996, as specified in section 3(7)(b) of the United Kingdom act (and not certified by the attorney general of Northern Ireland under paragraph (c)). Note the reference to conviction (not sentence). 'or, in the case of those sentenced outside Northern Ireland,' referred to England and Wales or Scotland. It seems not to have been intended to cover the Republic of Ireland, because reference would surely have been made to scheduled offences there. However, it is possible to argue that the Republic was included, since it is outside Northern Ireland. Note the reference to sentence (not conviction). Prisoners sentenced in England and Wales or Scotland were provided for in section 17 of the United Kingdom act, which referred to schedule 3. Similar offences was dealt with in paragraph 1(2)(b) and (3)(a) (an offence equivalent to a qualifying offence[47]), paragraph 2 (equivalent offences, involving certification by an appropriate law officer) and paragraph 7 (dealing with information for victims).

22.49 '(referred to hereafter as qualifying prisoners)' was used below in paragraph 3. There was no concept of qualifying prisoners in the United Kingdom act. However, there was a concept of qualifying offence in section 3(3)(a) (the first condition), which was defined in section 3(7): before 10 April 1998; a scheduled offence; not certified by the attorney-general of Northern Ireland. The Irish act, in contrast, had a concept of qualifying prisoners. They were defined in section 1(1) by reference to section 3(2). In this subsection, the minister specified the qualifying prisoners. This was for the purposes of the relevant provisions, namely the Prisoners section of the Belfast Agreement (as defined in sections 1(1) and 3(4) plus the schedule). This would have a bearing on sentenced prisoners outside Northern Ireland: sentenced on 10 April 1998.

22.50 'Any such arrangements' must be a reference to mechanisms in the first sentence. 'will protect the rights of individual prisoners' was a guarantee that, in

47 Section 3(3)(a) and (7).

attempting to secure the accelerated release of terrorist prisoners in both parts of Ireland, neither they (nor other prisoners) would have their rights abused. These other prisoners, in Northern Ireland, were those not convicted of a qualifying offence there (under section 3(3)(a) and (7)), or of an equivalent offence under section 17 and schedule 3 (paragraphs 1(2)(b) and (3)(a), 2 and 7) in England and Wales or Scotland (and imprisoned in Northern Ireland). 'under national and international law' referred to the array of relevant criminal justice legislation, in the United Kingdom and in the Republic of Ireland, plus article 5 of the European Convention.

2. **Prisoners affiliated to organisations which have not established or are not maintaining a complete and unequivocal ceasefire will not benefit from the arrangements. The situation in this regard will be kept under review.**

22.51 This paragraph related the individual prisoners, who may have secured a declaration from commissioners of eligibility for release, with the paramilitary groups with which they were most likely associated (even if they were not convicted of membership). It – apparently – was the express condition precedent for the programme of accelerated releases, each individual case being judged in terms of the conduct of a relevant paramilitary organization. However, the United Kingdom act linked each potentially eligible prisoner with an organization only negatively, through the concept of specification. This did not mean – under the Belfast Agreement – that there were not implied conditions precedent to accelerated release by virtue of the following: paragraphs 1, 2 and 4 of the Declaration of Support; paragraphs 25 and 35 of Strand One, plus the Pledge of Office; the first paragraphs 1, 2, 4, and 9 of the Rights, Safeguards and Equality of Opportunity section; and paragraphs 1 and 3 of the Security Section.

22.52 The prime minister's pledges in the referendum campaign (discussed above) were translated into legislative form in the Northern Ireland (Sentences) Bill ('the Bill'), published on 5 June 1998 (during the assembly elections). Royal assent was on 28 July 1998. The relevant clause – later section – is 3(9) (amendments to the Bill are shown):

3.(9) In applying subsection (8)(b) [which specifies a complete and unequivocal ceasefire, the second part of the legislative test for specifying a proscribed organization] the Secretary of State shall in particular take into account whether an organisation –

(a) is committed to the use now and in the future of only democratic and peaceful means to achieve its objectives;

(b) has ceased to be involved in any acts of violence or of preparation for violence;

(c) is directing or promoting acts of violence [committed] by other organisations;

(d) is co-operating fully with any Commission of the kind referred to in section 7 of the Northern Ireland Arms Decommissioning Act 1997 *in implementing the Decommissioning section of the agreement reached at multi-party talks on Northern Ireland set out in Command Paper 3883.*

22.53 The prime minister's pledges – I submit – were not translated fully into legislation (even allowing for the need for legal language).[48] He was the principal

United Kingdom signatory of the Belfast Agreement. This was also legitimized in the 22 May 1998 referendum in Northern Ireland, during which he gave assurances. These appear to have been intended to be incorporated in legislation (and parliamentary counsel affirmed this was what he was doing). Ministers also cited the prime minister's words when taking the bill through parliament.

22.54 First, the prime minister's starting point was the terms and spirit of the Belfast Agreement as a whole (not the second part of the legislative test for specifying a proscribed organization in section 3(8)). There was no reference in clause 3(9) of 5 June 1998 to the Agreement, in particular the sections on Decommissioning and Prisoners (with the two-year time scales). The Decommissioning section was added as a government amendment to clause 3(9)(d), with reference only to the IICD (no reference being made to the international agreement establishing the commission).

22.55 Secondly, the concept of take into account has been transmogrified. In the prime minister's pledges, the starting point was an objective test (albeit imposed more rigorously over time). Judgments would be made on the basis of evidence, four factors in particular being taken into account; the operative word was evidence. In the Bill/Act, this became a matter of the secretary of state's discretion (about a complete and unequivocal ceasefire, in the context of specifying proscribed organizations). An exercise of ministerial discretion was not immune from judicial review, but the secretary of state had been able to turn a blind – Nelsonian – eye to acts by particularly the IRA without apparently risking a finding of legal irrationality.[49] Ministerial discretion, however, may not be fettered; it must be exercised: taking into account all relevant considerations; and without regard to an improper purpose.

22.56 Thirdly, the first factor – the clear and unequivocal commitment that the war was over – had been turned into: committed to the use now and in the future of only democratic and peaceful means (section 3(9)(a)). It required no declaration from the IRA, even if it may be said to have been a continuing requirement.

22.57 Fourthly, the second factor, complete and unequivocal ceasefires were defined by the prime minister on 20 and 22 May 1998. In the Bill/Act, they became: ceased to be involved in any acts of violence or of preparation for violence (section 3(9)(b)). The prime minister specified: bombings, killings and beatings (claimed or unclaimed); an end to targeting and procurement of weapons; and progressive abandonment and dismantling of paramilitary structures actively directing and promoting violence.

48 House of Commons, *Hansard*, 6th series, 313, 1083–4, 1087 (secretary of state), 10 June 1998; 1162–3 (Adam Ingram); House of Commons, *Hansard*, 6th series, 314, 541–4 (secretary of state), 18 June 1998; House of Lords, *Hansard*, 5th series, 0591, 438 (Lords Dubs), 29 June 1998.

49 The *Wednesbury* test of unreasonableness ('so unreasonable that no reasonable authority could ever have come to it': *Associated Provincial Picture Houses Ltd v Wednesbury Corp.* [1948] 1 KB 223; *Council of Civil Service Unions v Minister for the Civil Service* [1985] AC 374: 'a decision which is so outrageous in its defiance of logic or accepted moral standards that no sensible person who had applied his mind to the question to be decided could have arrived at it').

22.58 Fifthly, the third factor (as noted), fully cooperating with the IICD to implement the provisions of the Belfast Agreement was originally: cooperating fully with any commission of the kind referred to in the 1997 decommissioning act (section 3(9)(d)). This was amended.

22.59 Sixthly, the fourth factor, no other organizations being deliberately used as proxies was translated as: directing or promoting acts of violence by other organisations (section 3(9)(c)). The proxy point was about deniability; in the Bill/Act it became a question of other organizations (which would have to be, not just proscribed, but specified under the Act).

22.60 In conclusion on the four factors (which are not exhaustive[50]), the Bill of 5 June 1998 and the Act of 28 July 1998 (despite one amendment) legalized all four inadequately. This point is separate from the meaning of the Belfast Agreement in terms of the early release of terrorist prisoners, when the new beginning envisaged by paragraph 1 of the Declaration of Support had not commenced evidently.

22.61 'Prisoners affiliated to organisations' defines the relationship between prisoner and organization. The concept of affiliation was not used in the United Kingdom act. Instead, that of supporter was used in section 3(4)[51] (the second condition) and (5)(a) (the third condition). Supporter was not defined anywhere. This was theoretically a matter for the courts. However, it was unlikely to arise. This was because the prisoner, to be eligible, had not to be a supporter of a specified organization. Specified organization was the operative concept. This was provided for in section 3(8) and (10), as a matter for the secretary of state. Immediately after the enactment of the Northern Ireland (Sentences) Act 1998, the secretary of state specified the Continuity IRA, the Real IRA, the INLA and the LVF. The LVF, and then the INLA, were despecified later. Two new proscribed organizations, the Orange Volunteers and the Red Hand Defenders, were subsequently added to the list of specified organizations.

22.62 Specification had never arisen in the case of the IRA, the UDA or the UVF. Being a supporter of one of those organizations, even if the prisoner had been convicted of membership, was of no consequence under the United Kingdom act. The only conditions for release were effectively: the first (a qualifying offence, and life imprisonment or a five-year term); and the fourth – for life prisoners – not a danger to the public (sections 3(3)–(6)).

22.63 Prisoner releases – contrary to the 20 April 1998 briefing note – were not affected by them being 'affiliated to groups that are continuing to engage in violence ...'.

22.64 'which have not established or are not maintaining a complete and unequivocal ceasefire' is the express condition precedent.

22.65 The idea of a ceasefire may be traced from paragraph 10 of the Downing Street Declaration of 15 December 1993 (the starting point for the transition from terrorism to democracy): 'The British and Irish governments reiterate that the achievement of peace must involve a permanent end to the use of, and support for, paramilitary violence. They confirm that, in these circumstances, democratically

50 Mo Mowlam, House of Commons, *Hansard*, 6th series, 314, 73, 15 June 1999.
51 Adam Ingram, House of Commons, *Hansard*, 6th series, 314, 43, 15 June 1998.

mandated parties which establish a commitment to exclusively peaceful methods and which have shown that they abide by the democratic process, are free to participate fully in democratic politics and to join in dialogue in due course between the Governments and the political parties on the way ahead.' A permanent end to the use of and support for paramilitary violence is the first condition precedent for entry into talks. A democratically mandated party is a second. A commitment to exclusively peaceful means is the third; and having shown that they abide by the democratic process is the fourth.

22.66 The IRA's complete cessation of military operations followed on 31 August 1994. It refused to call it a permanent ceasefire, and resumed its military campaign on 9 February 1996. Thereafter, the call for a permanent ceasefire gave way to a demand for the restoration of the 1994 one (which, of course, had only been temporary).

22.67 In the communiqué of the two governments of 28 February 1996 (which set the start date for talks), the phrase unequivocal restoration of the ceasefire of August 1994 was used. This was a condition precedent for ministerial dialogue with Sinn Féin. It became rule 9 of the *Ground Rules for Substantive All-Party Negotiations*, Cm 3232, 16 April 1996. Rule 8 defined participation in terms of political parties which achieve representation through an elective process, and 'establish a commitment to exclusively peaceful methods and which have shown that they abide by the democratic process'.

22.68 Section 2(3) of the Northern Ireland (Entry to Negotiations) Act 1996 required the secretary of state to refrain from inviting nominations, and to exclude delegates already nominated from entering into the negotations, if and for so long as he considered that requirements set out in paragraphs 8 and 9 of the *Ground Rules for All-Party Negotiations*, Cm 3232, 16 April 1996 were not met in relation to the party.

22.69 Sinn Féin – significantly – was tarred with the IRA brush by the Westminster parliament. It was not just a matter of government opinion, albeit based on security advice. This law applies, of course, to the other – loyalist – paramilitary parties in the talks: the PUP and UDP.

22.70 Have not established refers to the ceasefires of 31 August 1994 and 13 October 1994. Or are not maintaining had to be added to preclude the IRA breaking its second ceasefire. A complete and unequivocal ceasefire is inspired partly by the IRA complete cessation of 31 August 1994 (where complete does not mean permanent[52]), and partly by the unequivocal restoration phrase used by the two governments in their 28 February 1996 communiqué. A complete and unequivocal ceasefire is not necessarily a permanent ceasefire.

22.71 Will not benefit from the arrangements is a reference to the Northern Ireland (Sentences) Act 1998, and to the second sentence in paragraph 1 above. In the 1998 act, the central concept was specified organization. This is defined in section 3(8): 'A specified organisation is an organisation specified by order of the Secretary of State; and he shall specify any organisation which he believes – (a) is concerned in terrorism connected with the affairs of Northern Ireland, or in promoting or encouraging it, and (b) has not established or is not maintaining a

52 It probably always meant all IRA units.

complete and unequivocal ceasefire.' Specification implied proscription (though there is no reference to it in section 3 of the act). Concerned in terrorism, or in promoting or encouraging it, was a phrase used in emergency legislation: the definition of a terrorist organization to be proscribed. Paragraph (b) – a complete and unequivocal ceasefire – was derived from this paragraph.

22.72 'The situation in this regard will be kept under review.' was a reference to specification. The secretary of state specified by order under section 3(8). The duty to keep the list under review was expressly stated in section 3(10). Specification and despecification by order took place under section 3(8); on the basis of the orders to date, the secretary of state simply despecified an organization by not including it in a new list.[53]

22.73 However, the test for adding a paramilitary group to the list (and thereby losing access to the prisoner release scheme) was tougher than the test for being despecified. For an organization – say the LVF or INLA – seeking despecification, they only had to succeed on paragraph (a) or (b) in section 3(10); that is, no longer concerned in terrorism, etc., or established a complete and unequivocal ceasefire. A ceasefire was not strictly necessary. However, as section 3(9) indicated, paragraph (b) was the important criterion. The secretary of state had to make a judgment about the ceasefire, in particular taking into account the four factors there listed (including cooperation with the IICD on decommissioning). In contrast, for those wishing to have the IRA, UDA or UVF specified, because of alleged concern in terrorism (as defined again in section 13 of the act), they had to persuade the secretary of state that paragraphs (a) and (b) applied. Paragraph (a) was a matter of fact, but also of security advice. Paragraph (b) was the difficult one. Even though violence went to a ceasefire not being maintained, the secretary of state – relying upon section 3(9), which only referred back to section 3(8)(b) – interpreted take into account to mean a judgment rooted less in fact and more in an interpretation of – confidential – security advice.[54]

22.74 Whether the paramilitary organizations, and in particular the IRA, maintained a complete and unequivocal ceasefire after 28 July 1998, became an issue in the Williamson case in 1999–2000. This is discussed below, under problems with prisoner releases.

22.75 However, a point may be made here about the IRA and the IICD, following devolution on 2 December 1999. There is a presumption that the IRA was cooperating fully with the de Chastelain commission, when Sinn Féin ministers were part of the executive. This is not borne out by the commission report of 31 January 2000. But, assuming that there had been full cooperation, then, following the IRA statement of 15 February 2000, in which the IRA ended its engagement with the IICD, and withdrew all propositions put since November 1999, it is clear that the IRA stopped cooperating fully with the de Chastelain commission. This is proof of a breach of section 3(9)(d) of the United Kingdom act, and evidence that the secretary of state should have – under administrative law – taken into account in applying subsection (8)(b): maintaining a complete and unequivocal ceasefire. The failure to decommission could have, in certain circumstances, including a

53 Query how a final listed organization would be despecified under section 3(8)?

54 See the debate on the opposition motion, Terrorist Mutilations (Northern Ireland), House of Commons, *Hansard*, 6th series, 324, 347–97, 27 January 1999.

finding that the IRA was no longer maintaining a complete and unequivocal ceasefire (as defined), led to a halt in the release of its prisoners.

3. **Both Governments will complete a review process within a fixed time frame and set progressive release dates for all qualifying prisoners. The [intention will be to]** ***review process would*** **provide for the advance of the release dates of qualifying prisoners while allowing account to be taken of the seriousness of the offences for which the person was convicted and the need to protect the community.** ***In addition, the intention would be that should the circumstances allow it, any qualifying prisoners who remained in custody two years after the commencement of the scheme would be released at that point.***

22.76 This is the most important paragraph of the section, given that a two-year time scale was added to the MDP. A similar provision was added also to the Decommissioning section in the last days in Castle Buildings.

22.77 'Both Governments will complete a review process within a fixed time frame' was not, of course, an agreement to do this jointly. The release of prisoners was a matter of domestic jurisdiction. The United Kingdom government acted on this undertaking by passing the Northern Ireland (Sentences) Act 1998 on 28 July 1998. The announcement of the sentence review commissioners followed on 30 July 1998, and the rules came into force the following day. As noted, the joint chairmen clarified on 27 August 1998 the procedure for the release of eligible prisoners. The Irish government took the view that it had adequate powers under section 33 of the Offences against the State Act 1939 and the Criminal Justice Act 1960. However, it enacted the Criminal Justice (Release of Prisoners) Act 1998, promulgated on 13 July 1998. The release of prisoners commission was asked by the minister to advise on the exercise of powers of release with reference to the Prisoners section of the Belfast Agreement.

22.78 'and set progressive release dates for all qualifying prisoners.' Qualifying prisoners was used in paragraph 1 above. As noted, it was not used in the United Kingdom act, though qualifying offences was the concept in sections 3(3)(a) and (7) and paragraphs 1(2)(b), 2(1) and 7 of schedule 3. Qualifying prisoners was used in sections 1(1) and 3(2) of the Irish act. Progressive release dates was the purpose of sections 4 and 6 of the United Kingdom act. Fixed-term prisoners were entitled to release after one third of the sentence had been served, under section 4(1)(a). Life prisoners were entitled to release after two thirds of the period they would have been likely to have spent in prison under the sentence, under section 6(1). However, both sets of provisions were overtaken by accelerated release under section 10 (the two-year rule). Prisoners in the Republic of Ireland were released by the minister for justice, equality and law reform. The release of prisoners commission was not involved in administering the process, though the minister stated during the passage of the bill that each case would be referred to the commission.

22.79 'The review process would provide for the advance of the release dates of qualifying prisoners'. The concept of a review process was again used, though it is not clear whether it was narrow (preparations for release of prisoners) or broad (the entire – statutory based – scheme). The latter was suggested by the terminology of the United Kingdom act: sentence review commissioners. The text of this paragraph was strengthened: from the intention will be; to the review process would. It is clear that the purpose in both jurisdictions was to advance the release date of qualifying prisoners (all of whom, unless detained at the secretary of state's pleasure, had a release date; life prisoners knew a date might be set).

22.80 'while allowing account to be taken of the seriousness of the offences for which the person was convicted and the need to protect the community.' was legislated *de novo* by the United Kingdom government. No account was taken of the seriousness of the offences in terms of accelerating the release date. No distinction was made between different qualifying offences under section 3(3)(a) and (7), nor between fixed-term prisoners and life prisoners. This was a lacuna in terms of implementing this paragraph. Section 3(2)(b) and (6) imposed a fourth condition for life prisoners only: not a danger to the public. This did not apply to fixed-term prisoners, and, in this respect, may be considered another lacuna. All prisoners had to meet a second condition, not a supporter of a specified organization, and a third condition, not likely to become a supporter, or to become concerned in the commission of acts of terrorism.

22.81 The third sentence – all qualifying prisoners out within two years – was added to the MDP. This was provided for in section 10 of the United Kingdom act (accelerated release). Subsection (2) stated that a prisoner – with a declaration under section 3, and a release date under either sections 4 or 6 – was entitled to be released under that section on the accelerated release date. Under subsection (4), for a sentence passed before 28 July 1998, the accelerated release date was 28 July 2000. In the case of a sentence passed after 28 July 2000, under subsection (5) the accelerated release date was two years from sentencing (or the start of the sentence, under subsection (6)). Subsection (7) stated that nothing in this section should permit the release of a prisoner following a declaration under section 3(1) before he had served two years of the sentence to which the declaration related. However, under subsection (8), the secretary of state could by order amend subsections (4) to (7). The secretary of state could shorten – or lengthen – the two-year period (for prisoners sentenced before and after 28 July 1998). On 5 May 2000, the prime minister, in his joint letter with the taoiseach, announced, as part of the restoration of the institutions after suspension, that 'all remaining prisoners qualifying for early release w[ould] be released by 28 July 2000.' This would appear to have included any prisoners sentenced after 28 July 2000. It required an order of the secretary of state.

22.82 It would appear to have been a matter of administrative action in the Republic of Ireland. The government was given powers under section 33 of the Offences against the State Act 1939, but only for domestic prisoners. The Criminal Justice Act 1960 allowed for temporary release. It could also be used by the minister. It had to be used for repatriated prisoners. Conditions on the release were possible under either act. The release of prisoners commission was to advise on the relevant provisions, the Prisoners section of the Belfast Agreement (under section 3(1)–(2) of the Criminal Justice (Release of Prisoners) Act 1998). This is where the two-year rule was located. However, the minister decided under section 3(1)–(2) whether to seek the advice of the commission, and it was a matter of his discretion whether he accepted advice offered. Section 4 required the minister, in considering whether to release qualifying prisoners, to have regard to the Belfast Agreement and to the advice of the commission; he did not have to accept it.

22.83 Decommissioning and prisoner releases were related in the Belfast Agreement, because paragraph 3 of the Decommissioning section was altered at Castle Buildings as follows: '[4.] ... [All participants undertake] *They also confirm their intention* to *continue to* work constructively and in good faith with the Independent Commission, *and to use any influence they may have,* to achieve the decommissioning of all paramilitary arms within [a fixed and limited period of [x] *two* years following endorsement in referendums North and South of the [overall settlement]] *agreement and* in the context of the *implementation of the* overall settlement ... [[Note from the Independent Chairmen: Remaining to be resolved is the time frame for decommissioning (paragraph 3[55] above).]]'

22.84 Two years was added to this paragraph at Castle Buildings, just as it had been added to paragraph 3 of the Decommissioning section. Two years was the only express time frame in the Belfast Agreement (though there was the 31 October 1998 target in paragraph 8 of Strand Two). In the context of paragraphs 1 and 2 of the Declaration of Support, it was envisaged that – with the implementation of the overall settlement (a process rather than a goal) – decommissioning, verified by the IICD, and the release of prisoners, through the sentence review commissioners in Northern Ireland, would be achieved between 22 May and (mainly) 28 July 2000. The two – two-year – time frames were the same, even though they ran from different starting points around June 1998. But this chronological lack of absolute precision was to reflect the process of implementation.

22.85 Decommissioning and prisoner releases were related in the prime minister's referendum pledges: 'I believe that most people would be ready to accept even the hardest parts of the Agreement [prisoner releases plus Sinn Féin in government] if they had genuine confidence that the paramilitaries were really ready to give up violence for good [decommissioning]' (14 May 1998); 'how can people be sure that the present ceasefires are not merely tactical and that the terrorists will not reap the benefits of the agreement [prisoner releases plus Sinn Féin in government], while retaining the possibility of a return to violence [no decommissioning]?' (22 May 1998). The prime minister expressly included decommissioning in the four factors in his Balmoral speech (used to judge acceptance of the agreement), and, in his referendum day article, even included decommissioning in his definition of a ceasefire (in the context of paramilitaries in government).

22.86 Section 3 of the Northern Ireland (Sentences) Act 1998, however, inadequately reflected the Belfast Agreement (as interpreted by the prime minister). Decommissioning – in the form of cooperating fully[56] with the IICD in implementing the Decommissioning section – was included as paragraph (d) in section 3(9), as one of the four factors to be taken into account. However, this went only to whether a complete and unequivocal ceasefire was being maintained (section 3(8)(b)) (not to being concerned in terrorism under section 3(8)(a)).

55 This should have been '4'.

56 Fully was added by the government at the request of the opposition: Andrew MacKay, House of Commons, *Hansard*, 6th series, 314, 52, 15 June 1998.

4. The Governments will *seek to enact* [introduce] the appropriate legislation to give effect to these arrangements by the end of June 1998.

22.87 This is the first reference to legislation. Paragraph 1 refers to mechanisms being put in place. That does not preclude legislation, but the section would have been clearer if legislation had been specified in paragraph 1. This paragraph bound both governments. The Irish government was, therefore, required to legislate. The Criminal Justice (Release of Prisoners) Act 1998 came about because of opposition pressure to accord with the Belfast Agreement (and the United Kingdom government). The Irish government already had all the powers it needed under section 33 of the Offences Against the State Act 1998, and the Criminal Justice Act 1960 (section 2). The paragraph was altered from introducing legislation by the end of June 1998 (also the date given for decommissioning schemes in paragraph 5 of the Decommissioning section), to seek to enact. The word seek suggests that, on 10 April 1998, either one or both governments knew they would have difficulty legislating in time. On 20 April 1998, in its briefing note, the NIO stated it would not legislate until after the referendum on 22 May 1998. The United Kingdom bill was published well before the deadline, on 5 June 1998. It also passed through parliament fairly promptly. Royal assent, however, was not until 28 July 1998. This may well have been to get the sentence review commissioners in place; they were announced on 30 July 1998 (though, on 27 August 1998, they were having to justify delays in releasing prisoners as being due to the Belfast Agreement, the act and the rules made under it). The Irish act – though it had no significance for prisoner releases in the Republic – was not published until 30 June 1998, just making the deadline under the paragraph in the MDP. Promulgation on 13 July 1998 came closer to meeting the requirement of this paragraph, certainly in comparison with the United Kingdom government.

5. The Governments continue to recognise the importance of measures to facilitate the reintegration of prisoners into the community by providing support both prior to and after release, including assistance directed towards availing of employment opportunities, retraining and/or re-skilling, and further education.

22.88 This paragraph contains no definite commitments; 'continue to recognise' suggests that the appropriate services were in place.

22.89 However, this paragraph has to be construed, at least as regards the United Kingdom government, by the report of the Northern Ireland victims commissioner, Sir Kenneth Bloomfield, *We will remember them*, NIO, May 1998 (which was accepted by the secretary of state): 'Many people made the point to me that there seems to be a stronger and more effective lobby operating in the interests of prisoners and ex-prisoners than there is in the interests of victims. I would not contest for a moment the desirability of ensuring that former prisoners are assisted to achieve a re-integration into normal society and in particular to resume gainful employment. It would, however, be quite unacceptable to provide services for the benefit of those convicted of serious offences which are not matched in dealing with the victims of such crimes, including in particular people placed in the path of danger by service to their community.'[57]

57 Paragraph 5.26.

Problems with prisoner releases

22.90 In the two-year period from 28 July 1998, a number of problems arose with the accelerated programme for the release of qualifying prisoners (none of these problems had anything to do with the failure of principally the IRA to decommission).

The problem of qualifying prisoners in the Republic of Ireland

22.91 To whom does the Prisoners section of the Belfast Agreement apply? This is not readily answerable, partly because the two governments wished to retain discretion in the handling of individual cases.

22.92 The concept of qualifying prisoners was advanced in paragraph 1, and deployed in paragraph 3. It is defined as: 'prisoners, including transferred prisoners, convicted of scheduled offences in Northern Ireland or, in the case of those sentenced outside Northern Ireland, similar offences'.

22.93 Prisoners convicted of scheduled offences in Northern Ireland were terrorist prisoners. Transferred prisoners include those transferred to Northern Ireland administratively from Great Britain, and those transferred from the United Kingdom to the Republic of Ireland under the 1983 convention. But did the transferred prisoners account for all those sentenced outside Northern Ireland? Did this refer to Great Britain only, or did it include the Republic of Ireland? In other words, were all the qualifying prisoners on 10 April 1998, in the Republic of Ireland, transferees from Great Britain, or were there some who had been sentenced there for Irish scheduled offences (if not under the Criminal Law (Jurisdiction) Act 1976 for offences committed in Northern Ireland)?

22.94 This raises the further problem of whether qualifying prisoners were: offenders on remand; or sentenced prisoners. There is yet a third problem: did the offences have to be committed before 10 April 1998, or was the Belfast Agreement intended to apply to all new offences? (the latter interpretation is most unlikely, since it would be waiving the rule of law as regards future offences[58]). Paragraph 1 certainly implies that the prisoners had to be convicted on 10 April 1998. This does not necessarily mean that they had to be sentenced prisoners at that point (though paragraph 3 implies this). However, it is possible to construe paragraph 1 as referring to convicted Northern Ireland prisoners, and sentenced Great Britain prisoners transferred to the Republic (there being no domestic Irish prisoners according to this interpretation).

22.95 It certainly seems that the United Kingdom officials were thinking of Northern Ireland principally, and the Irish officials of the Republic of Ireland (quite naturally). Subsequently, the questions were answered differently. From the point of view of the Belfast Agreement, the issue is what the shared intention of the United Kingdom and Irish states was, not what the Irish state may or may not have said to Sinn Féin. Did London, for example, agree to the release of police killers in Northern Ireland, and agree with the Republic of Ireland that the text of paragraph 1 did not cover police killers in the Republic of Ireland?

22.96 The Northern Ireland (Sentences) Act 1998 made clear, in defining a qualifying offence in section 3(7), that it had to be committed before 10 April 1998

58 Secretary of state, House of Commons, *Hansard*, 6th series, 310, 481 & 493, 20 April 1998.

(paragraph (a)). London and Dublin appear to have been ad idem on that. However, section 10 (accelerated release) casts doubt on the sentenced prisoners theory: subsection (4) refers to sentences passed before 28 July 1998 (which allows for post-10 April 1998 sentences); subsection (5) refers expressly to sentences passed after 28 July 1998. Convicted Northern Ireland prisoners may have been convicted before 10 April 1998, and sentenced afterwards. But section 10 suggests that the prisoners on 10 April 1998 (given the proximity between conviction and sentencing) may only have been on remand awaiting trial.

22.97 Irish officials appear to have assumed that they were dealing only with prisoners transferred from the United Kingdom. However, this was to reckon without the McCabe case, a detective garda killed by the IRA in 1996 in Adare, Co. Limerick.[59] Five members were on remand awaiting trial on 10 April 1998. In February 1999, four were convicted of manslaughter (having pleaded guilty), and sentenced to terms of penal servitude; a fifth was sentenced for a related firearms offence. (The taoiseach, and the justice minister, referred deliberately to the murder of Garda McCabe after the verdicts in the Special Criminal Court.)

22.98 If those IRA members had been convicted in Northern Ireland of killing a member of the RUC, they would most likely have been due for release on 28 July 2000: Northern Ireland (Sentences) Act 1998 s 10(5); alternatively, two years from sentencing less time spent on remand under subsection (7) (whichever was the longer). The secretary of state – by order under subsection (8) – could have lengthened or shortened either two-year period. They are most unlikely to have been refused declarations by the sentence review commissioners under section 3(6).

22.99 At Castle Buildings – according to the Irish justice minister subsequently – the Irish government insisted to Sinn Féin that these police killers (in custody awaiting trial in the Republic) would not benefit, if convicted and sentenced, from the accelerated release scheme.[60] (It is not clear whether other police killers already sentenced were eligible.[61]) The minister described this later as a political judgment in order to secure support in the Republic for the Belfast Agreement.[62] The stance was reiterated by the justice minister during the debate in Dáil Éireann on the Belfast Agreement.[63] 'Ireland owes a great debt of gratitude,' he said on 2 July 1998, during the debate on the Criminal Justice (Release of Prisoners) Bill, 'to the Garda Síochána who died on duty and who served the State so well'.[64]

22.100 There is a major legal issue here, to do with the partial incorporation of

59 It is thought that, in the history of the state, the IRA has been responsible for the deaths of 16 gardaí and five soldiers.

60 Address to the Garda Representation Association, Tralee, 12 May 1999 (*Irish Times*, 13 May 1999); see also letter to Dr Philip McGarry of the Alliance party quoted in the *Irish Times* of 16 April 1999. This was reiterated subsequently. It is believed Sinn Féin refused to have the McCabe case expressly excluded in the Prisoners section of the Belfast Agreement.

61 The minister for justice was asked this question by Senators Connor and Costello during passage of the legislation, but did not receive an answer: Seanad Éireann, *Official Report*, 3 July 1998.

62 Letter to Dr Philip McGarry of the Alliance party, quoted in *Irish Times*, 16 April 1999.

63 Dáil Éireann, *Official Report*, 21 April 1998.

64 Dáil Éireann, *Official Report*, 2 July 1998.

the Belfast Agreement in United Kingdom and Irish law. The BIA – an international agreement – entered into force with devolution on 2 December 1999. However, it had an effect from 10 April 1998 through the conditions precedent in article 4(12). Depending upon the meaning of article 2, the two governments were under a moral, alternatively legal, obligation to implement inter alia the Prisoners section. Whatever of the nature of the obligation, it is implied that the provisions in Northern Ireland and the Republic of Ireland would have a similar effect. That is the consequence of an agreement between two contracting states which does not specify otherwise. And it is implied by the subject – the governments – in paragraphs 1, 3, 4 and 5 of the Prisoners section.

22.101 Westminster chose not to incorporate the Prisoners section of the agreement, but to build on the Northern Ireland (Remission of Sentences) Act 1995. It produced a scheme based on qualifying offences (and not being a supporter of a specified organization). However, the Northern Ireland (Sentences) Act 1998 could, in the courts in Northern Ireland, in the case of ambiguity, be construed in terms of that section of the Belfast Agreement.[65]

22.102 The Oireachtas, in contrast, choice to schedule the Prisoners section to the Criminal Justice (Release of Prisoners) Act 1998. While section 3(4) might suggest there is no incorporation, the act, and statements of the minister during passage, indicate that the Irish government sought to operate its prisoner release scheme according to the Belfast Agreement. It had the powers. It needed to know how to use them. Section 4 required the minister to have regard to the Prisoners section, and to the advice from the release of prisoners commission (whose job is to interpret the relevant provisions).

22.103 It is not clear how a court in the Republic of Ireland would decide a case on the McCabe killers. David Gwynn Morgan has argued that, if they were to seek judicial review of a decision not to grant them early release, they would be unlikely to succeed.[66]

22.104 There are a number of counter-arguments to do with the international law character of the Belfast Agreement. One, if the Prisoners section of the Belfast Agreement has been incorporated (which seems most likely), then that is the domestic law on which the minister should have been instructing himself properly. Since it is certain that the McCabe killers would be released in Northern Ireland,[67] and an Irish court could look at a United Kingdom act as foreign law, the meaning of the Belfast Agreement would suggest early release under existing Irish law.

22.105 Alternatively, if the Prisoners section has not been incorporated, the court, in interpreting the Criminal Justice (Release of Prisoners) Act 1998, could look – through the common law (and the rule above in United Kingdom law) – to resolve any ambiguity by reference to the Belfast Agreement.

22.106 Further, if the Irish justice minister were to release a RUC (or British

65 *R v Secretary of State for the Home Department, ex parte Brind* [1991] 1 AC 696, 747–8 per Lord Bridge of Harwich, 760 per Lord Ackner.

66 *Irish Times*, 10 February 1999.

67 To say nothing of killers of policemen in Great Britain being released as transferred prisoners in the Republic of Ireland, or killers of the RUC being released there having been convicted under the Criminal Law (Jurisdiction) Act 1976.

police officer) killer, and not the killers of Garda McCabe, he would be at risk of judicial challenge for having made a decision arbitrarily.

22.107 The most likely answer is: in international law, the Irish state entered into a binding obligation (though 'allowing account to be taken of the seriousness of the offences for which the person was convicted and the need to protect the community' in paragraph 3 might allow for national autonomy); in domestic law, the question of prisoner releases remained a matter of ministerial discretion, subject to judicial review by the courts; the issue turns on the relationship between international and domestic law, in particular whether the Belfast Agreement can be used interpretatively in domestic law.

The home secretary's judicial review regarding prisoners transferred from Great Britain

22.108 The sentence review commissioners, appointed on 30 July 1998, worked out of the public gaze. Media attention focused on the successive release of groups of republican and loyalist prisoners (but interest waned after a time). Unbeknown to those outside government, a difference developed between the NIO and the home office. The latter had a continuing interest in the prisoners from Great Britain on so-called restricted transfer. Schedule 3 (sentences passed outside Northern Ireland) of the Northern Ireland (Sentences) Act 1998 provided for these prisoners.

22.109 Paragraphs 3, 4 and 6 of schedule 3 dealt with the calculation of release dates for fixed-term prisoners and life prisoners from Great Britain. For fixed-term prisoners, the rules were largely similar (one third of the sentence[68]). With life prisoners, section 6 (two thirds of the likely period in prison[69]) also applied. However, section 7 (life prisoners: specified dates) was substituted by paragraph 6 in the schedule. In Northern Ireland, the sentence review commissioners were required to follow the practice for those released on licence after 1982 and before 1999 (including their own decisions).[70] Under paragraph 6 dealing with transferred prisoners, commissioners were required to have regard to English and Scottish (whichever is relevant) sentencing law and practice, including 'any other information, whether relating to the prisoner's case or to other cases, which the Secretary of State submits'.[71] Secretary of state here meant the home secretary. It was normally the position that the actual sentence served in Great Britain by a life sentence prisoner was longer than in Northern Ireland.

22.110 On 22 March 1999, it emerged that the home secretary was seeking an urgent judicial review[72] of a decision by the commissioners, to release three life prisoners[73] the following day and a fourth (Paul Magee) on 22 June 1999.[74] Three had mandatory life sentences; the other, a discretionary life sentence. The tariff for the first three, set by the home secretary, was 50 years; that for the fourth prisoner

68 Section 4(1)(a).
69 Subsection (1).
70 Section 7.
71 Substitute section 7(e).
72 There has also been a second judicial review.
73 Paul Kavanagh, Thomas Quigley and Gerald McDonnell.
74 The commission had originally specified days which would have fallen after the accelerated release date.

(Gerald McDonnell), set by the judge, was 25 years. All four were on restricted transfer to Northern Ireland from Great Britain.

22.111 (An interim order appears to have been obtained on 22 March 1999.) The application was heard in the High Court in Belfast by Girvan J on 23 March 1999 (and judgment given apparently ex tempore).

22.112 The home secretary maintained that the commissioners had failed to take into account the differing tariffs in England and Wales.[75] The commissioners had in fact accepted the home office view initially and taken account of the tariffs. 'Subsequently after protracted and detailed oral and written submissions the Commissioners changed their mind.' One can only surmise that the NIO may have been involved. They estimated effective sentences of 21 years (out of 50), in the case of the first three, and 20 years (out of 25) in the case of the fourth prisoner. The home secretary also argued that the commissioners failed to explain their change of mind.

22.113 The home secretary lost. The High Court said that the wisdom or fairness of the 1998 act was not a matter for it: 'History will be the ultimate judge.' The commissioners' decision was 'closely reasoned and carefully formulated'. The case turned on section 6: 'a day which they believe marks the completion of about two thirds of the period which the prisoner would have been likely to spend under the sentence'. Counsel for the prisoners argued that the belief need not be held reasonably (citing by analogy a case on emergency legislation[76]). 'A belief based on wholly irrational grounds', said Girvan J, 'could ... still be challenged on the *Wednesbury* unreasonable ground but *Wednesbury* irrationality is a difficult thing to establish.' Further, in section 7, the phrase 'have regard to' did not mean take into acount: *R v CD* [1976] 1 NZLR 436, 437 per Somers J. 'The provisions of sections 6 and 7 do not point to an exercise of discretion on the part of the Commission but do point to an exercise requiring the Commissioners to arrive at an honest belief as to what the Commissioners consider to be a future likelihood.'

22.114 Three prisoners were released that evening shortly after 21.30 (and the fourth on 22 June 1999). 'We made it clear last night that we were seeking urgent clarification of the law ...', the home office said in a statement. 'That clarification has now been obtained and we accept the court's decision.'[77]

22.115 It would seem that the court took the view that, parliament having decided to release terrorist prisoners early, it would not have imposed a restrictive – or even normal – due process on the sentence review commissioners. If the United Kingdom government, for reasons of state, was prepared to waive the rule of law, then a Northern Ireland court – faced with a conflict between the NIO and the home office – was not going to resolve the matter in the latter's favour; the home office was only fighting for the difference between 23 March 1999 and 28 July 2000.

75 The home secretary also argued: the commissioners took into account irrelevant factors; and erroneously permitted political developments to colour their approach. The court rejected these points: 'The factors on which ... the Home Secretary relied as pointing to fallacious reasoning by the Commissioners are not, in the final analysis, so foreign to the Commissioners proper line of enquiry that they could be categorised as irrelevant considerations.'

76 *McKee v Chief Constable for Northern Ireland* [1985] 1 All ER 1.

77 *Irish Times*, 24 March 1999.

The first annual report of the sentence review commissioners

22.116 This was published on 20 July 1999. It revealed that there had been 558 applications for early release to 31 March 1999 (the total number of paramilitary prisoners being 579[?]). Of the applicants, 411 (74 per cent) had been given dates. Of the remaining 147 applications: 23 were still being processed; 123 prisoners had been turned down on the grounds that they were not eligible; and one had been refused. Of the 411 prisoners who had been given dates, 280 had been released (68 per cent). Of the released prisoners, 144 were republicans, 127 were loyalists, and nine were non-aligned.

22.117 By 17 March 2000, 320 had been released reportedly, leaving 120 to be released by 28 July 2000.[78] On 20 March 2000, the secretary of state suspended the licence of a former prisoner, Gearoid Mag Uaid, following his appearance in court on explosives charges (having been arrested near Hillsborough); the case was referred to the sentence review commissioners.[79]

The Williamson *case*

22.118 Michelle Williamson was an applicant in judicial review proceedings, whose parents were killed in the Shankill Road bomb in 1993. The terrorist convicted of their murder, Sean Kelly, was expected to be released under the Prisoners section of the Belfast Agreement. On 5 May 2000, Tony Blair and Bertie Ahern announced that all remaining prisoners qualifying for early release would be released by 28 July 2000.[80]

22.119 The occasion for her case was alleged breaches in 1999 by the IRA of its complete and unequivocal ceasefire, including: the killing of Charles Bennett in west Belfast on 30 July 1999; and the arrest, in the United States and in the Republic of Ireland earlier in the same month, of alleged members suspected of importing arms. Both led to court proceedings. Williamson would, of course, as noted above, have had to have shown under section 3(9)(a) and (b) of the United Kingdom act that the IRA was not maintaining a complete and unequivocal ceasefire: section 3(8)(b). Further, that it was concerned in terrorism, or in promoting or encouraging it: section 3(8)(a). Only then could the secretary of state have specified the IRA under the United Kingdom act, and prevented the release of IRA prisoners. And all this in the context of the supervisory jurisdiction which allows the courts to look at the alleged illegality, irrationality or procedural impropriety of an executive act or inaction.

22.120 On 26 August 1999, the secretary of state ruled that there had been no breach of the ceasefire. Information on previous breaches had not been of sufficient strength. 'But in this case', she announced, 'the information is already clear and indeed the Chief Constable has said that there is no doubt that the IRA were involved in the Bennett murder.[81] Information is also clear in relation to the arms importation.' The secretary of state continued: 'I have left Sinn Féin in no doubt that all violence ... is unacceptable, and have called on them to use their influence to ensure that there is no repetition.' She concluded – having taken

78 *Electronic Telegraph*, 17 March 2000.

79 Northern Ireland Information Services: http://www.nio.gov.uk.

80 Joint letter to party leaders issued in Belfast.

81 This was on 25 August 1999.

account of all the factors in section 3(9) of the United Kingdom act: 'I do not believe that there is a sufficient basis to conclude that the IRA ceasefire has broken down. Nor do I believe that it is disintegrating, or that these recent events represent a decision by the organisation to return to violence.' The secretary of state stated that she had come 'very close' to judging that the IRA ceasefire was no longer for real (her words). (She did not, however, refer to the meaning of a complete and unequivocal ceasefire: section 3(8)(b).)[82]

22.121 Proceedings were commenced on 20 September 1999. Leave was granted, but Kerr J held on 19 November 1999 that the secretary of state had acted lawfully. The applicant appealed to the Court of Appeal. On 6 April 2000, the decision was upheld. The applicant petitioned the House of Lords, but this was dismissed on 4 July 2000.

The release of all remaining prisoners by 28 July 2000

22.122 In the letter of the prime minister and the taoiseach, of 5 May 2000, to party leaders, the date of June 2001 was set for full implementation of the Belfast Agreement (by the United Kingdom and Irish governments). Under prisoners, it said: 'all remaining prisoners qualifying for early release will be released by 28 July 2000'.

22.123 On 28 July 2000, 78 prisoners were released from the Maze prison; seven were released from Maghaberry, and one from Magilligan prison. The 86 comprised 46 IRA, 15 UDA, 11 UVF, six LVF and one non-aligned. This brought the total released in 1998–2000 to 428, including 143 prisoners serving life sentences. Only 14 prisoners remained, awaiting transfer to Maghaberry prison.

22.124 Two of these were loyalists, who had been given life sentences in February 2000. While on temporary home leave in July 2000, they were arrested (with three others) for the attempted murder of a rival loyalist. They appeared in court on 7 July 2000. When they applied for bail on 21 July 2000, McLaughlin J was told that the secretary of state was applying to the sentence review commissioners for their early release to be revoked. The bail application was dismissed.

22.125 On 19 July 2000, Michael Stone, a loyalist prisoner, had applied for judicial review of his release date. The issue was the difference between Friday, 21 and Monday 24 July 2000. His release date was Saturday 22 July 2000. Under normal prison rules, and because there are no weekend releases, he would have been released on the Friday. However, under the legislation consequent upon the Belfast Agreement, weekend releases – it was argued – were to take place on the following Monday. However, this had not been followed in 1998–2000, and the legal position was only noticed in early July 2000. Coghlin J, who described the

82 Statement, Northern Ireland Information Service: http://www.nio.gov.uk. Also, *Daily Mirror*, 27 August 1999. An interesting aspect of this case was the role of the Irish government: claims by ministers that it was up to the two governments to determine whether there was no longer a complete and unequivocal ceasefire in Northern Ireland (*Irish Times*, 4 August 1999 & 27 August 1999); and an assertion on 23 August 1999 by the Irish foreign minister that he, and the secretary of state, had decided there was no breakdown (only to be contradicted in public by the secretary of state (*Irish Times*, 24 & 27 August 1999)).

prison's mistake as 'most regrettable', denied that Stone had had a legitimate expectation of release on Friday rather than Monday.

22.126 One of the IRA prisoners released on 28 July 2000, James McArdle, who had been sentenced in England to 25 years for the London Docklands bomb of February 1996, and then for a further offence in Northern Ireland in March 1999, was granted the royal prerogative of mercy. He was not due to be released until March 2001. This was reported on 27 July 2000, as was a claim by three INLA prisoners (who had been convicted of murder in December 1997) that they had also been given the same option: they declined on principle, choosing to await their early release in October 2000 under the legislation. The secretary of state justified the use of the royal prerogative in McArdle's case: some of his accomplices, sentenced with him in March 1999, had received longer sentences, but, since they had been held on remand on those offences, they could be released under the legislation on 28 July 2000.

22.127 In the Republic of Ireland, one prisoner, Padraig Steenson from Dublin, was released on 28 July 2000. Remaining were:

- the five IRA McCabe killers in Castlerea, Co. Roscommon;
- 17 Real IRA members in Portlaoise;
- three awaiting extradition to the United Kingdom or with outstanding charges.[83]

83 Brendan McFarlane, Angelo Fusco and Paul Dingus Magee, all from Belfast.

23

Validation, Implementation and Review

23.1 This is the last section of the Belfast Agreement. Here the MPA and the BIA relate. The section concludes the MPA; however, the political face of the Belfast Agreement does not require validation. It does refer immediately to the BIA in the first paragraph; and the section also concludes the legal face of the Belfast Agreement as a treaty between the United Kingdom and Irish states (though there is an Annex 2 to the BIA). It is divided into two parts (with paragraphs consecutively numbered). The first, Validation and Implementation,[1] is not strictly for the participants in the multi-party negotiations. The second, Review procedures following implementation (sic),[2] is not exclusively the preserve of the United Kingdom and Irish governments. The section is at pages 25–6 of Cm 3883 and pages 42–3 of Cm 4705 (pages 36–7 of the 1999 Irish version). I indicate [deletions] to the MDP, and *additions* thus.

23.2 Validation, Implementation and Review, however, appears to have been neglected at Castle Buildings. There are two major mistakes in the first part, to do with Irish constitutional changes. And the provisions for review – here and elsewhere in the MPA – are insufficiently precise.

TITLE: VALIDATION, IMPLEMENTATION AND REVIEW

23.3 The MDP, until this point, has been a political agreement between the political parties and, arguably, the two governments. That breaks down with this section. The concept of validation refers to turning a political text into a legal one. It is not the same as legitimization (a process the Belfast Agreement was also to undergo after 10 April 1998), and is provided for in paragraph 2 in the first part.

23.4 Implementation raises the question of an international agreement, which has not yet entered into force, but where the two contracting states have conditions precedent to fulfil before it may do so. Implementation shows that the Agreement had an effect from 10 April 1998, even if it is not strictly a legal one; without implementation, there would have been no Agreement entering into force on 2 December 1999 in international law.

23.5 The concept of review is not unusual in an international agreement. The 1985 Anglo-Irish Agreement had arrangements for review in article 11. However, there are also review provisions elsewhere in the Belfast Agreement.

Subtitle: Validation and Implementation

23.6 The distinction between the two parts would appear to be chronological: before and after 2 December 1999 (there is, in paragraph 4 of the first part, a

1 This was centred and capitalized in the version distributed in Northern Ireland after 10 April 1998. So also in Cm 4705. Cm 4705 has the title in lower case with two capital letters.

2 This was ranged left, and in lower case, with one capital letter in the version distributed in Northern Ireland after 10 April 1998. This was reproduced in Cm 3883 and Cm 4705.

provision for review during the transition). Validation and Implemention – though they have been combined – do not necessarily constitute a unity.

1. **The two Governments will as soon as possible sign a new British-Irish Agreement replacing the 1985 Anglo-Irish Agreement, embodying understandings on constitutional issues and affirming their solemn commitment to support and, where appropriate, implement the agreement reached by the participants in the negotiations which shall be annexed to the *British-Irish* Agreement.**

23.7 At this point, 'The two governments' sever themselves from the participants (as defined in the *Ground Rules for Substantive All-Party Negotiations*, Cm 3232, 16 April 1996[3]). The participants were the subjects in the Decommissioning, Security, and Policing and Justice sections; it was only in the Prisoners section that the two governments came to the fore.

23.8 'will as soon as possible sign a new British-Irish Agreement replacing the 1985 Anglo-Irish Agreement', happened at the final plenary at Castle Buildings on 10 April 1998. It is described in the Prologue. A new agreement had been mooted first in the 1995 *Framework Documents*.[4] In the 12 January 1998 Heads of Agreement, there was included: 'a new British-Irish Agreement to replace the existing Anglo-Irish Agreement'. Following contributions by party leaders on 10 April 1998, the prime minister and the taoiseach (plus the secretary of state and Irish foreign minister) signed the BIA. It would seem that they signed the short version of the BIA (as annexed to the MPA). References are made to a new agreement in the MPA: paragraph 1 of Constitutional Issues; paragraph 1 of Strand Two; the first and second paragraphs 1 of Strand Three. Under article 3 of the BIA, the 1985 Anglo-Irish Agreement, and the intergovernmental conference, were due to cease when the BIA of 10 April 1998 entered into force on 2 December 1999.

23.9 'embodying understandings on constitutional issues' is evocative of the subheading to part II of the 1995 *Framework Documents*: 'A shared understanding between the British and Irish governments'. The inspiration was, however, article 1 of the 1985 Anglo-Irish Agreement. The concept of understanding is nowhere present in article 1 of the BIA, which has six paragraphs. This agreement between the two governments has also been included in the MPA, as Constitutional Issues. That section has paragraph 1, endorsing the article 1 agreement. There follow the six paragraphs. However, while there is no reference to any qualification of paragraph 1(vi), it is, by virtue of article 1 of the BIA, subject to Annex 2 of that agreement. Paragraph 2 of Constitutional Issues refers to the political agreement of the two governments to seek constitutional changes; these are contained in Annexes A and B. Paragraph 2, however, is not part of the understanding referred to here.

23.10 'and affirming their solemn commitment to support and, where appropriate, implement the agreement reached by the participants in the negotiations' is the language of international agreement. It is repeated in article 2 of the BIA: 'The two Governments affirm their solemn commitment to support,

3 Rule 10.
4 Part I, Annex B, paragraph 1; part II, paragraph 39.

and where appropriate implement, the provisions of the Multi-Party Agreement.' Affirming their solemn commitment to support is the strongest statement a government may make, without the state entering into specific obligations in international law to act specifically (though it depends upon the text in question).

23.11 This point is elaborated in the following phrase: and, where appropriate, implement. This means that the MPA (as Annex 1 to the BIA) binds the two governments, but only to the extent that an obligation is imposed expressly or impliedly. In other words, there is material in the MPA which does not require the two governments to do anything (it may, however, bind an actual or potential office holder). This paragraph, and article 2 of the BIA, point to the difficulty of interpretation of the Belfast Agreement. The first question is: What sort of legal instrument is it? The second question is: What are the appropriate rules of interpretation? The third question is: What obligations in the MPA, read as Annex 1 of the BIA, apply to which state party? And the fourth question is: Does anything else in the MPA impose an obligation on any other actual or potential office holder in international law, before incorporation in United Kingdom or Irish law? Given that the Belfast Agreement is a bilateral instrument in international law, other legal principles – most notably legality – apply to some or all of the text.

23.12 'the agreement reached by the participants in the negotiations' is the MPA. However, there is an ambiguity about the participants, as to whether it includes the two governments, or simply refers to the political parties. Here, participants seems to mean the political parties. However, in article 2 of the BIA, where there is no reference to participants, it is clear that the two governments have obligations under the MPA. This is not by virtue of them being included as participants, but by virtue of the MPA being Annex 1 of the BIA.

23.13 'which shall be annexed to the British-Irish Agreement.' This was changed from the Agreement, since agreement is used throughout the MPA (and in this paragraph) to refer to what became Annex 1 of the BIA. The MPA is annexed to the BIA, not through this paragraph, but by virtue of the first recital of the preamble to the BIA (and by physical annexing) (see Chapter 24). There are two annexings, in respectively Cm 3883 and Cm 4705, and they are different. The political face of the Belfast Agreement is the MPA with the BIA annexed (this is specified on the contents page, and, in Cm 3883, pages 1–26 (the MPA) are followed by pages 27–30 (the BIA (including a space for Annex 1))). In contrast, the legal face of the Belfast Agreement is the BIA, with, at Annex 1, the MPA (under article 31(2) of the 1969 Vienna convention on the law of treaties, the preamble and annexes are part of the text). This is how it was done in Cm 4705 (where the MPA contents page refers back to pages 1–6 for the text of the BIA). It is not how it was done in the 1999 Irish version. This starts correctly, but the BIA remains as an annex to the MPA, which has already been annexed to the British-Irish Agreement.

2. **Each Government will organise a referendum on 22 May 1998. Subject to Parliamentary approval, a consultative referendum in Northern Ireland, organised under the terms of the Northern Ireland (Entry to Negotiations, etc.) Act 1996, will address the question: "Do you support the agreement reached in the multi-party talks on Northern Ireland and set out in Command Paper 3883?". The Irish Government will introduce and support in the Oireachtas a Bill to amend the Constitution as described in**

paragraph 2 of the section "Constitutional Issues" and in Annex B, as follows: (a) to amend Articles 2 and 3 as described in paragraph 8.1 in Annex B above and (b) to amend Article 29 to permit the Government to ratify the new British-Irish Agreement. On passage by the Oireachtas, the Bill will be put to referendum.

23.14 'Each Government will organise a referendum on 22 May 1998.' was mooted first in the 1995 *Framework Documents*, though a referendum in the Republic of Ireland was less definite.[5] Referendums were not mentioned in the 12 January 1998 Heads of Agreement. Since two states are involved, there was never any doubt that there would be two separate referendums. This is aside from any question about the issues being decided. The fact that some chose, after 22 May 1998, to treat the outcome as an all-Ireland plebiscite – despite the different questions, and the different constitutional meanings of referendum – is of no significance in Irish or United Kingdom law; this is almost certainly the position also in international law. The date, 22 May 1998, was exactly six weeks after 10 April 1998. This was chosen with two considerations in mind: one, the timescale for setting up the shadow assembly, in relation to the marching season and summer holidays in Northern Ireland; and two, the legal requirements in the Republic of Ireland for constitutional amendments. The day, Friday, is the customary day for general elections and referendums in the Republic. The United Kingdom presumably shifted from its Thursday custom in order to have simultaneous referendums (if only to preempt any negative political effect resulting from an earlier Northern Ireland poll).

23.15 The second sentence in the paragraph relates entirely to the Northern Ireland referendum. The Northern Ireland (Entry to Negotiations, etc) Act 1996, which is cited there, received the royal assent on 29 April 1996. Its primary purpose was to provide for elections in Northern Ireland (for delegates from among whom participants in negotiations would be drawn). The forum for political dialogue was the mechanism chosen. But section 4 provides for referendums. The secretary of state may from time to time by order direct the holding of a referendum (for the purpose of obtaining the views of the people on any matter relating to Northern Ireland (subsection (1))). Subsection (4) made clear such a referendum was not a border poll.[6] This had the effect in April 1996 that: the status of Northern Ireland as part of the United Kingdom could not be a part of the outcome of the negotiations, because it could not be included in a referendum under the 1996 act.

23.16 The 'Subject to Parliamentary approval' must be a reference to section 4(2) of the 1996 act. This required an order under subsection (1) to be made by statutory instrument, following the positive resolution procedure. It is not a reference to the presentation of *The Belfast Agreement: an agreement reached at the multi-party talks on Northern Ireland*, Cm 3883, to parliament on 20 April 1998. The secretary of state made a short statement at 15.31, followed by questions.[7] It was announced that an order was being laid that day setting 22 May 1998 as the

5 Foreword by prime minister; part I, annex A, paragraph 4, annex B, paragraph 1; part II, paragraphs 21 & 55.

6 Under section 1 and schedule 1 of the NICA 1973.

7 House of Commons, *Hansard*, 6th series, 310, 479–500, 20 April 1998.

date for the referendum.[8] The order was made on 24 April 1998, and came into force the following day.[9]

23.17 'a consultative referendum on Northern Ireland,' is interesting. The word consultative is not used in section 4 of the 1996 act. However, the purpose is: 'obtaining the views of the people of Northern Ireland on any matter relating to Northern Ireland'.[10] In the United Kingdom constitution proper, the people – the electors in a referendum – do not have the same status as they do under the representation of the people acts. Parliament remains sovereign, and a referendum result is constitutionally not binding on the executive (it is – almost certainly highly – politically persuasive).

23.18 The question, 'Do you support the agreement reached in the multi-party talks on Northern Ireland and set out in Command Paper 3883?', is provided for in article 3(1) and (3) and schedule 1 of the Northern Ireland Negotiations (Referendum) Order 1998, SI 1998/1126, which came into force on 25 April 1998. The number of the command paper (3883) was clearly reserved by the NIO even before there was an agreement. This preparedness contrasts with the way the Irish government handled its constitutional changes. The agreement delivered to all households in Northern Ireland by the post office at business rate was entitled: *The Agreement: agreement reached in the multi-party negotiations*. This 30 page document – with the coloured front cover – is not a command paper and has no number. (The document is not identified in any way.) However, the MPA was described in Annex 1 to the BIA as 'The Agreement Reached in the Multi-Party Talks'. This is the same phrase used in this paragraph. And the question as drafted in this paragraph passed into the 25 April 1998 order, and on to the ballot papers. Subsequently, Annex 1 was amended to read: 'Agreement Reached in the Multi-Party Negotiations'[11] (though not before multi-party talks was used for section 1(1) of the Northern Ireland (Elections) Act 1998, and the long title of the NIA 1998). Command Paper 3883 was the form in which the Belfast Agreement was presented to parliament by the secretary of state on 20 April 1998. The phrase Command Paper 3883 can have had no meaning for a voter in the referendum (even one with his copy of the Belfast Agreement – as delivered – opened at this paragraph).

23.19 The referendum was held in Northern Ireland on Friday 22 May 1998. The issue was the Belfast Agreement. Article 5(1) of the Northern Ireland Negotiations (Referendum) Order 1998, SI 1998/1126 made the chief electoral officer for Northern Ireland the counting officer.

23.20 Paragraph (4) required the counting officer to certify the total of the ballot papers counted, the votes cast for each answer (yes or no), and the number of rejected ballot papers under each head shown in the statement of rejected ballot papers, for the whole of Northern Ireland. In other words, a province-wide

8 House of Commons, *Hansard*, 6th series, 310, 482 & 496, 20 April 1998.

9 Article 3(1) of the Northern Ireland Negotations (Referendum) Order 1998, SI 1998/1126 (note the change in title from Northern Ireland (Entry to Negotations, etc.) Act 1996 (Referendum) Order: House of Commons, *Hansard*, 6th series, 310, 501, 20 April 1998).

10 See also article 3(1) of the Northern Ireland Negotiations (Referendum) Order 1998, SI 1998/1126.

11 Cm 4705, p. 7; 1999 Irish version, p. 1.

vote (presumbly, the chief electoral officer acquired data on turnout by electoral area).

23.21 There was a total poll of 953,583, representing 81.1 per cent of the electorate. The number of spoiled ballot papers was 1,738 (0.18 per cent). The votes cast for the Belfast Agreement were 676,966 (71.12 per cent); against, 274,879 (28.88 per cent).

23.22 The procedure in the Republic of Ireland was very different. There was no vote on the Belfast Agreement, as in Northern Ireland. There was a normal constitutional amendment, under articles 46 and 47.1 of BNH; a new section 7 was added to article 29 (international relations) of the constitution. Article 29.7.1 does not, as argued already in Chapter 11, incorporate the Belfast Agreement into the Irish constitution.

23.23 It is true that the *Agreement Reached in the Multi-Party Negotiations* (the MPA with the BIA annexed) was distributed to households.[12] It is also the case that the referendum commission in the Republic, in a booklet on the referendum on Northern Ireland, stated that 'the [proposed] constitutional amendment must be considered in the context of the agreement reached in the Multi-Party negotiations which has annexed to it the text of the British/Irish Agreement'.[13]

23.24 But all the referendum commission literature bore the legend: constitutional amendments to articles 2, 3 and 29. Strictly speaking, there was only an amendment to article 29. And it was the changes to articles 2 and 3 which dominated the referendum campaigns which took place.

23.25 On 21 April 1998, the Nineteenth Amendment of the Constitution Bill 1998 had its second stage in Dáil Éireann.[14] (The Belfast Agreement had been laid before both houses on 15 April 1998. It was approved by Dáil Éireann just before the adjournment debate on 21 April 1998,[15] and by Seanad Éireann on 22 April 1998.) The Nineteenth Amendment completed its remaining stages in the Dáil on 22 April 1998. It went through all its stages in the Seanad on the same day.

23.26 Section 1 of the Bill reads: 'Article 29 of the Constitution is hereby amended as follows:'. Paragraph (a) goes on to amend the Irish text in part I of the schedule (in English and in Irish); paragraph (b), the English text in part II (in English and in Irish). Part II is a new article 29.7.1–5 (in English). It contains, however, Irish and English text for new articles 2 and 3, and a new article 29.8. This has been discussed in Chapter 11 above.

23.27 The nineteenth amendment – expressed to be an act to amend the constitution – was then ready to be submitted by referendum to the decision of the people (in accord with article 46.2 of BNH). This was governed by the Referendum Acts 1994-98. The Oireachtas had also approved (in Irish and English[16]) a

12 The text of the Amsterdam treaty – on which there was also a referendum amendment – was not distributed.

13 Page 7.

14 It followed the Eighteenth Amendment of the Constitution Bill 1998, which had had its second reading in the Dáil on 3 March 1998. This dealt with the Amsterdam treaty.

15 The motion: 'That Dáil Éireann hereby welcomes and approves the terms of the Agreement reached in the Multi-Party Negotiations in Belfast on 10 April, 1998, copies of which were laid before Dáil Éireann on 15 April, 1998.'

statement for information of voters, and the Referendum (Ballot Paper) (No. 2) Order 1998.

23.28 The (bilingual) statement for information of voters (pursuant to section 23 of the Referendum Act 1994) reads in English: '1. The Nineteenth Amendment of the Constitution Bill, 1998, proposes to insert the following section after section 6 of Article 29 of the Constitution: [there follows the text of article 29.7 in English but including Irish versions of articles 2, 3 and 29.8]. 2. IF YOU APPROVE of the proposal, mark X opposite the word YES on the ballot paper. 3. IF YOU DO NOT APPROVE of the proposal, mark X opposite the word NO on the ballot paper. 4. A copy of the Bill can be inspected or obtained free of charge at any Post Office.'

23.29 The question on the ballot paper was: 'Do you approve of the proposal to amend the Constitution contained in the undermentioned Bill?'. There follows: 'Nineteenth Amendment of the Constitution Bill, 1998'.

23.30 The total poll in the Republic of Ireland was 1,545,395 (compared with 953,583 in Northern Ireland). This represented a turnout of 56.3 per cent of electors (compared with 81.1 per cent in Northern Ireland).[17] The number of spoiled ballot papers was 17,064 (1.10 per cent).[18] The total number voting yes was 1,442,583 (94.39 per cent); no, 85,748 (5.61 per cent).[19] Separate figures were given for each constituency. The highest percentages of no voters were in Cork North-Central and Kerry North (7.21 each). The lowest was Cork East (3.66 per cent). The distribution of no voters was extremely evenly spread throughout the 26 counties.

23.31 Returning to this paragraph, the Irish government did introduce and support a bill in the Oireachtas: the Nineteenth Amendment of the Constitution Bill 1998. Paragraph 2 of the Constitutional Issues section simply states that, in the context of this comprehensive political agreement (not the BIA), the Irish government had undertaken to propose and support changes in the constitution. There was no cross reference. Annex B contains the proposed constitutional amendments. It is headed: 'IRISH GOVERNMENT DRAFT LEGISLATION TO AMEND THE CONSTITUTION'. And it begins: Add to article 29 the following sections: sections is wrong. Only section 7 was being added. Annex B is specified in this paragraph as containing two different proposals. Proposal (a) is described as the amendments to articles 2 and 3 as described in paragraph 8.1 in Annex B above. In fact, they are in section 7.3 (the reference to paragraph 8.1 stemming from the mistakes in the MDP discussed above in Chapter 11). Proposal (b) is described as to amend article 29 to permit the government to ratify the British-Irish Agreement. (Again, this is a mistake, stemming from the MDP text.) Following amendments to Annex B at Castle Buildings, the third sentence of this paragraph should have been redrafted. It was not. 'On passage by the Oireachtas, the Bill will be put to referendum.' It was, on 22 May 1998, with the results discussed above.

23.32 Article 29.7.1 (from promulgation on 3 June 1998) reads: 'The State may

16 There is an error in the English text of article 29.7.4; it is in Irish: Dáil Éireann, *Official Report*, 22 April 1998.

17 The turnout on the simultaneous Amsterdam treaty referendum was 56.2 per cent.

18 The number of spoiled ballot papers in the simultaneous Amsterdam treaty referendum was 33,228.

19 The comparable figures in the simultaneous Amsterdam treaty referendum were 932,632 (61.74 per cent) and 578,070 (38.26 per cent).

consent to be bound by the British-Irish Agreement done at Belfast on the 10th day of April, 1998, hereinafter called the Agreement.' There have been suggestions that this means that the Belfast Agreement is a part of the Irish constitution, and that the people, by voting for the amendment to article 29, voted to approve it.[20] This has been discussed in Chapter 11. Subsection 1 has no legal meaning in Irish law. The state – in the form of the Irish government – consented to be bound in international law by the BIA on 10 April 1998, when the taoiseach and the foreign minister signed the document at Castle Buildings. The relevant provisions of the constitution are: article 29.4 (executive power exercised externally by the government); and article 29.5–6 (procedure for treaties, and incorporation into domestic law).

23.33 The Belfast Agreement did not become a part of Irish law, much less the constitution on 22 May 1998. It was only on 9 March 1999 that Dáil Éireann – under article 29.5.1–2 – approved the terms of the Belfast Agreement, it having been laid before the lower house the day before.

23.34 The people of Northern Ireland did not vote for the Belfast Agreement understood as a legal text (that was a matter for the two contracting states). They endorsed only the MPA, to which the BIA was annexed in Cm 3883 (without becoming part of the MPA). In a similar vein, the people of the Republic of Ireland did not give the Belfast Agreement constitutional – and therefore legal – effect in their state. They did not have the power, under BNH, to authorize the Irish government to consent to a bilateral agreement with the United Kingdom government, and article 29.7.1 could not, on 3 June 1998, domestically effect something which had taken place internationally on 10 April 1998.

> 3. **If majorities of those voting in each of the referendums support this agreement, the Governments will then introduce and support, in their respective Parliaments, such legislation as may be necessary to give effect to all aspects of this agreement, and will take whatever ancillary steps as may be required including the holding of elections on 25 June, subject to parliamentary approval, to the Assembly, which would meet initially in a "shadow" mode.** ***The establishment of the North-South Ministerial Council, implementation bodies, the British-Irish Council and the British-Irish Intergovernmental Conference and the assumption by the Assembly of its legislative and executive powers will take place at the same time on the entry into force of the British-Irish Agreement.*** **[When all arrangements are in place for the new institutions to assume their functions as set out in this agreement, the Governments will ratify the British-Irish Agreement. It is the intention of the Governments that this be achieved by no later than February 1999.]**

23.35 This long paragraph comprises only two sentences. The second was totally replaced by a new one.

23.36 The first sentence covers the complete implementation of the Belfast Agreement from 22 May 1998 (to what was originally conceived as ratification of the BIA in February 1999). 'If majorities of those voting in each of the referendums support this agreement' is wrong. This agreement is the MPA. It was

20 *Irish Times*, 18 April 1998.

approved by a majority in the referendum in Northern Ireland. This was not the case in the Republic of Ireland, as explained with reference to paragraph 2 above. The phrase is at best a political statement seeking to legitimize what is a political agreement involving the Northern Ireland parties, validated through an international agreement between the United Kingdom and Irish states. The Irish referendum result has no meaning in United Kingdom law, and the Northern Ireland one is equally meaningless in Irish law. It is most unlikely that international law would take a different view.

23.37 'the Governments will then introduce and support, in their respective Parliaments, such legislation as may be necessary to give effect to all aspects of this agreement' was an obligation almost entirely of the United Kingdom's. Since the Belfast Agreement was largely for devolution of powers to Northern Ireland, the perspective on 10 April 1998 was the need for – what was called then – a settlement bill (the Government of Wales bill and the Scotland bill were then going through parliament). The long title of the Northern Ireland Bill was: to 'make new provision for the government of Northern Ireland for the purpose of implementing the agreement reached at multi-party talks on Northern Ireland set out in Command Paper 3883'. Drafting on the bill had begun before the 22 May 1998 referendum and 25 June 1998 assembly elections had taken place. Second reading in the house of commons was on 20 July 1998. There were four committee days: 22–24 and 27 July. Remaining stages were on 30 and 31 July. Second reading in the house of lords was on 5 October 1998. There were four committee days: 19, 21, 26 and 27 October. Report stage was 10 and 11 November. And third reading, 17 November. Lords amendments were taken in the commons on 18 November. And royal assent was on 19 November 1998. It is believed the Irish government was consulted by London while the bill was passing though parliament.

23.38 The other main legislative responsibility was the Northern Ireland (Sentences) Act 1998. Dublin contributed with the Criminal Justice (Release of Prisoners) Act 1998.

23.39 The responses to the Omagh bomb of 15 August 1998 – the Criminal Justice (Terrorism and Conspiracy) Act 1998, and the Offences Against the State (Amendment) Act 1998 – were no part of the Belfast Agreement, though they affected paragraphs 2(iii) and 5 of the Security section.

23.40 Strands Two and Three of the Belfast Agreement were not generally provided for legislatively. However, the six implementation bodies in paragraph 9(ii) of Strand Two required secondary legislation under section 55 of the NIA 1998: North/South Co-operation (Implementation Bodies) (Northern Ireland) Order 1999, SI 1998/859. Dublin's contribution was the British-Irish Agreement Act 1999, promulgated on 22 March 1999, and a later British-Irish Agreement (Amendment) Act 1999.

23.41 'And will take whatever ancillary steps as may be required including the holding of elections on 25 June, subject to parliamentary approval, to the Assembly,' was again principally a United Kingdom responsibility.

23.42 Whatever ancillary steps, given the subject of this sentence is the two governments, might appear to be international agreements, though this was not clear on 10 April 1998. Then, it was thought that the implementation bodies would be created legislatively. They were created by treaty: *Agreement between the Government of the United Kingdom of Great Britain and Northern Ireland establishing Implementation Bodies*, Cm 4293, Dublin 8 March 1999. It was also thought on 10 April 1998 that article 2 of the BIA was sufficient to establish the NSMC, the BIC and the BIIC. These, however, were established by three supplementary agreements, also done at Dublin on 8 March 1999: respectively, Cm 4294, Cm 4296 and Cm 4295.

23.43 Whatever ancillary steps was probably a residual category, given that the only instance was the assembly elections. This was exclusively a United Kingdom responsibility. And the elections were subject to parliamentary approval. On 7 May 1998, the Northern Ireland (Elections) Act 1998 received the royal assent. It was the immediate legislative priority after 10 April 1998. It passed all stages in the house of commons on 22 April 1998 (followed at 23.24 with the draft Northern Ireland Negotiations (Referendum) Order 1998, SI 1998/1126[21]). The bill had its second reading in the lords on 6 May 1998. This was much more than an elections measure; it was effectively the constitutional act for the transition from the elections to full legislative and executive powers being transferred from London to Belfast.

23.44 The Northern Ireland (Elections) Act 1998 provided for the new Northern Ireland assembly. This was purely a transitional gathering. Section 1(1) defined its purpose: 'taking part in preparations to give effect to the agreement reached at the multi-party talks on Northern Ireland set out in Command Paper 3883'.

23.45 Section 1(2) allowed the secretary of state to refer to the assembly: specific matters arising from that agreement (paragraph (a)); and such other matters as he thinks fit (paragraph (b)). Sections 1(3) to (5) provided for a 108-member assembly, with six in each parliamentary constituency. (Sections 2–5 dealt with the elections and consequences.) Section 1(6) referred to the schedule of supplementary provisions for the assembly. In the schedule, paragraph 1 states that meetings shall be held at such times and places as the secretary of state directs. Paragraph 2 provides for standing orders, and, under paragraph 10, these are determined by the secretary of state from time to time. The secretary of state is also responsible for the presiding officer (paragraph 3).

23.46 'which would meet initially in a "shadow" mode'. This is precisely what the Northern Ireland (Elections) Act 1998 did by providing for the new Northern Ireland Assembly. The concept of transition can be traced through the MPA: paragraph 35 of Strand One (dealing with the assembly, where reference is made to a transitional period, and shadow ministers); paragraph 7 of Strand Two (meetings of the assembly, BIC and NSMC in their transitional forms); and paragraphs 8 and 9 of Strand Two (the work programme in the transitional NSMC).

23.47 The second sentence was replaced by an entirely new one. Looking at the deleted sentence, it contains the notion of ratifying the BIA. This was compatible with Annex B to Constitutional Issues in the MDP, and suggests that this paragraph (at least) was drafted by Irish officials. When Annex B was altered, this sentence was scrapped. It should have been accompanied by the removal of the reference to

21 Plus an order winding up the forum for political dialogue: draft Northern Ireland (Entry to Negotiations, etc.) Act 1996 (Cessation of Section 3) Order 1998.

ratification in paragraph 2 above. The original legal idea was that everything would take effect at the one point, this being ratification. But the bilateral BIA was to be signed on 10 April 1998, and entry into force was governed by article 4. Also scrapped was the target for devolution of February 1999. It is believed, however, that the two governments continued to work to this timescale – certainly until the end of 1998. The date then became 10 March 1999, which explains the four supplementary Belfast-Dublin agreements of 8 March 1999.

23.48 The new second sentence simply relates domestic United Kingdom and international law, in order to coordinate devolution and the establishment of other institutions: all to 'take place at the same time on the entry into force of the British-Irish Agreement'.

23.49 Under section 3 of the NIA 1998, a devolution order was to be laid before parliament, 'if it appears to the Secretary of State that sufficient progress had been made in implementing the Belfast Agreement' (subsection (1)). The Belfast Agreement is defined in section 98(1) as 'the agreement reached at multi-party talks on Northern Ireland set out in Command Paper 3883'. This is the MPA, to which is annexed the BIA. Sufficient progress related to the MPA, principally Strand One, but also the domestic law aspects of Strands Two and Three, the Rights etc. section and the four 'terrorism to democracy' issues. The Northern Ireland Act 1998 (Appointed Day) Order 1999, SI 1999/3208 was made on 1 December 1999. It came into force the following day (seemingly at midnight on 1 December[?]). This order made 2 December 1999 the appointed day for the commencement of parts II and III of the NIA 1998. Legislative and executive powers were transferred from London to Belfast.[22] Later on 2 December 1999, in Dublin, the secretary of state for Northern Ireland and the Irish foreign minister exchanged notifications of completion of the requirements for entry into force of the BIA under article 4(2). At that point (circa 09.00), the BIA entered into force. This also brought into force the four subsidiary agreements of 8 March 1999, covering the NSMC, the implementation bodies, the BIC and the BIIC.

23.50 If at the same time means 2 December 1999, then that happened. If it means literally at the same hour and minute, that did not happen. Devolution was at midnight on 1 December 1999. The other institutions were established around 09.00 on 2 December 1999 (followed closely by the Irish constitutional amendments). The sequence shows that devolution was entirely a matter for the United Kingdom government, within domestic law. The other institutions, established in international law, required agreement between two contracting states. This paragraph may be misleading, in that it suggests everything happened on the entry into force of the BIA.

23.51 The secretary of state for Northern Ireland was the key legal actor. He made the judgment on sufficient progress, under section 3 of the NIA 1998. This was a matter of domestic law. He also notified the Irish government that the United Kingdom had completed its requirements for entry into force, under article 4(1)(a) and (c) of the BIA. The BIA then entered into force in international law.

22 The Northern Ireland Act 1998 (Commencement No. 5) Order 1999, SI 1999/3209, made on 30 November 1999, brought into force on 2 December 1999 other sections and schedules of the devolution act.

4. **In the interim, aspects of the implementation of the *multi-party* agreement will be reviewed at meetings of those parties relevant in the particular case (taking into account, once Assembly elections have been held, the results of those elections) [in the particular case], under the chairmanship of the British Government or the two Governments, as may be appropriate; and representatives of the two Governments and all relevant parties may meet under [[I]*i*ndependent [C]*c*hairmanship[]] to review implementation of the agreement as a whole.**

23.52 This paragraph does not belong to Validation and Implementation. It is about review (but review before devolution, and the BIA entering into force). This explains why it has not been placed in the Review procedures following implementation part of this section.

23.53 'In the interim' is another way of referring to the transition. This is specified in paragraph 35 of Strand One, and paragraphs 7, 8 and 9 of Strand Two.

23.54 'aspects of the implementation of the multi-party agreement' defines the breadth of a possible review or reviews. Aspects suggests issue by issue, rather than a total review, which would be effectively a complete renegotiation. Implementation is the second topic of this section. It also appears in the first sentence of article 2 of the BIA. I submit that it has a broad meaning; anything in the Belfast Agreement that has to be done by anyone – government or political party or office holder – during the transition. Multi-party was added to agreement, no doubt to clarify that the BIA is not subject to review under this paragraph (it would not in any case have entered into force during the transition). 'at meetings of those parties relevant in the particular case' refers definitely to political parties. It means only some may be relevant. The parenthesis shifts from the multi-party negotiations to the Assembly. It states that, whatever legitimacy the delegates elected in 1996 might have had, this is eclipsed by the Assembly members elected on 25 June 1998.

23.55 The paragraph then goes on to the type of review. There are three. The first two relate to only relevant political parties. Either the United Kingdom government chairs, implying this is a Strand One matter, or the two governments chair, implying this is for Strands Two and Three matters. The 'as may be appropriate' does not grant Dublin a right to co-preside over a review during the transition. The third type of review is that involving 'independent chairmanship'. The changes to the MDP are interesting. The term was in square brackets, but the independent chairmen made no comment. It also had upper-case first letters. During the multi-party negotations, Senator Mitchell and his two colleagues were known as 'the Independent Chairmen'. In the FA, the upper-case letters have gone, but so also have the original square brackets. Independent chairmanship could have meant something completely new (as noted below, the person primarily responsible for the square brackets returned to help the process in July 1999). Two things are interesting about this third type of review: one, it does not necessarily involve all parties (the concept of relevant is used again); two, the review is of implementation of the agreement as a whole (not aspects as for the first two types).

23.56 It would seem therefore that, under this paragraph, a distinction is made between a partial and a total review. If the former, it is chaired by the United

Kingdom government (and the Irish government is involved only if it is Strands Two or Three). If the latter, the two governments are involved, there is independent chairmanship, and all relevant parties take part in a review of implementation as a whole.

23.57 This paragraph bit after the failure of *The Way Forward* plan of the prime minister and the taoiseach of 2 July 1999, to establish the executive committee on 15 July 1999 (see Chapter 19 above).

23.58 In a statement, the taoiseach said there would now be a paragraph 4 review (this casts an interesting light on the efficacy of the BIA before it had entered into force.) But he went on to refer to the two governments consulting.[23] And the taoiseach and prime minister were to meet Senator Mitchell at Downing Street on Tuesday 20 July 1999. (Since 10 April 1998, Belfast had allowed Dublin to effectively co-manage the political process. This cannot have been under the 1985 Anglo-Irish Agreement, which remained in force. Nor could it be under the rules for the talks; those had finished. It certainly could not be under the Belfast Agreement: one, it did not envisage such practical joint authority; and two, it was not yet in force.[24])

23.59 Senator Mitchell agreed to devote a couple of days from 20 July 1999, and to return to Belfast as a 'facilitator' on 6 September 1999. He seemed intent upon including the anti-agreement (unionist) parties. The Mitchell review – under this paragraph – should have involved representatives of the two governments and all relevant parties, 'to review implementation of the agreement as a whole'. This does not immediately accord with the announced 'tightly focused' review aimed at 'a speedy conclusion' – a third attempt to resolve the question of the executive and decommissioning.[25]

Subtitle: Review procedures following implementation

23.60 This part takes up the concept of implementation (rather than devolution). It deals with review generally after the BIA entered into force on 2 December 1999. It must be read along with paragraph 36 of Strand One, the first paragraph 12 and the second paragraphs 7 and 9 of Strand Three.

> 5. **Each institution may, at any time, review any problems that may arise in its operation and, where no other institution is affected, take remedial action in consultation as necessary with the relevant Government or Governments. It will be for each institution to determine its own procedures for review.**

23.61 'Each institution', I submit, means the assembly, the NSMC, the implementation bodies, the BIC and the BIIC. The word institutions was used in paragraph 3 above in the MDP; it was replaced by the Strands One, Two and Three

23 Press release, 15 July 1999: http://www.irlgov.ie/taoiseach/press. United Kingdom and Irish official met in Belfast on 16 July 1999 to discuss the review (*Irish Times*, 17 July 1999).

24 In an article published on 13 July 1999, the taoiseach wrote: 'The Irish Government is a co-guarantor of democratic government under the Good Friday agreement.' (*Irish Times*)

25 The prime minister used the phrases on 20 July 1999: *Daily Telegraph* and *Irish Times*, 21 July 1999. The three principles of 25 June 1999 were the intended basis of the review.

bodies just listed. This paragraph, and this part, cover all three strands (despite the absence of a review paragraph in the Strand Two section).

23.62 'may, at any time, review any problems that may arise in its operation' allows a review to be called. It is implied that this requires a consensus. If there is no agreement for a review, it is most unlikely to take place.

23.63 'and, where no other institution is affected, take remedial action' provides for complete autonomy of action. Given the interrelated character of the Belfast Agreement, it is difficult to envisage no other institution being unaffected. The NSMC (and indirectly the implementation bodies), the BIC and (I submit) the BIIC, would all be affected by a problem with the assembly. The assembly – being the heart of the Agreement – could, however, continue to function while problems were solved in the international organizations.

23.64 'in consultation as necessary with the relevant Government or Governments' is London asserting its primacy, certainly within the United Kingdom, while a role is acknowledged potentially for the Irish government (in the NSMC, BIC and BIIC).

23.65 'It will be for each institution to determine its own procedures for review.' reaffirms the autonomy of review processes. Again, the point needs to be made that, a consensus for reviewing is implied.

6. **If there are difficulties in the operation of a particular institution, which have implications for another institution, they may review their operations separately and jointly and agree on remedial action to be taken under their respective authorities.**

23.66 This paragraph develops the theme of paragraph 5 above. If, as is likely, a problem in an institution affects another, what happens? The answer is less than enlightening: 'they may review their operations separately and jointly'. This surely should be or. If they review separately, there would have to be agreement for that. It is not clear what 'respective authorities' means. Is it the institution or is it a government or governments?

7. **If difficulties arise which require remedial action across the range of institutions, or otherwise require[d] amendment of the British-Irish Agreement or relevant legislation, the process of review will fall to the two Governments in consultation with the parties in the [Northern Ireland] Assembly. Each Government will be responsible for action in its own jurisdiction.**

23.67 This paragraph takes the process a step further: where the remedy involves a number (range?) of institutions, or amendments to the BIA or legislation. The review is to be held by the two governments and the parties in the assembly (effectively, the participants in the multi-party negotiations plus anti-agreement unionists). This is reasonable if the BIA has to be amended. It is an international agreement between two states. But why are the two governments involved in possible legislative changes? Most of the legislation relates to devolution, and there was no formal role for the Irish government in that during the talks. In this paragraph, Dublin has secured a tactical gain. This is in spite of the second sentence affirming sovereignty in the diluted form of jurisdiction.

23.68 This part of this section came into play following the suspension of the institutions on 12 February 2000.

23.69 When the Northern Ireland Bill was introduced in the house of commons on 4 February 2000, it contained as clause 2(1): 'As soon as is reasonably practicable after section 1 comes into force [suspension], the Secretary of State must take steps to initiate a review under the Validation, Implementation and Review section of the Belfast Agreement.' Subclause (3) stated: 'Before making a restoration order, the Secretary of State must take into account the result of the review conducted as a result of subsection (1).' Both were enacted in the Northern Ireland Act 2000, the suspension act. They provide for duties which are imposed upon the secretary of state; while he retains considerable discretion under section 2, a review is essentially mandatory.

23.70 The review, and the suspension act, were occasioned by the failure of the IRA to decommission by 31 January 2000, while Sinn Féin had two ministries (though the reason given by the United Kingdom government was the absence of cross-community confidence). The problem related to the executive committee, not to the assembly (where Sinn Féin members are allowed to sit regardless of what the IRA does). The issue had been envisaged in the Belfast Agreement as one of exclusion from the executive committee.[26] Suspension was an alternative to exclusion, an idea of the two governments in July 1999, but it was essentially the assembly which was to be suspended.

23.71 In the explanatory notes issued by the NIO (which did not form part of the bill, and had not been endorsed by parliament), paragraph 7 of the Validation, Implementation and Review section of the Belfast Agreement was quoted under clause 2. This was confirmed by the secretary of state during the second reading.[27] However, it is not clear why a paragraph 5 review was not invoked, the institution being the assembly and the participants being the parties therein plus the United Kingdom government. No doubt it could be argued that 'where no other institution is affected' is essential for paragraph 5. But other institutions were only affected because of the United Kingdom government's degree of suspension. Most likely, paragraph 7 was preferred to paragraph 5, because it allowed for 'the two Governments in consultation with the parties in the Assembly'.[28] It is by no means certain that the conditions in paragraph 7 are satisfied here: 'remedial action across the range of institutions'; 'or otherwise require amendment of the [BIA] or relevant legislation'.

> **8. Notwithstanding the above, each institution will publish an annual report on its operations. In addition, the two Governments and the parties in the Assembly will convene a conference 4 years after the agreement comes into effect, to review and report on its operation.**

23.72 This paragraph is clear, and contains two provisions.

23.73 The first is an annual report by each institution. To what extent has this been implemented? As regards the assembly (performing legislative and executive

26 Paragraph 25 of Strand One.

27 House of Commons, *Hansard*, 344, 135, 8 February 2000.

28 House of Commons, *Hansard*, 344, 135, 8 February 2000.

functions), there is no provision for annual reports in the NIA 1998. Nor do Standing Orders so provide.[29] The supplementary agreements establishing the NSMC, BIC and BIIC are silent on the matter. However, under article 2 of each agreement, each body is required to operate in accordance with the provisions of the multi-party agreement. The agreement establishing the implementation bodies also contains a similar provision (article 3). It can, therefore, be argued, that, under the BIA (the MPA being Annex 1) in the case of Strand One, and the four supplementary agreements of 8 March 1999 in the case of Strands Two and Three, there is a requirement for annual reporting. But to whom? The answer can only be: publication.

23.74 The second provision is a conference after 4 years, essentially an interim review of the workings of the Belfast Agreement. But there is a problem: which agreement? Agreement with a lower-case first letter means in this section the MPA: it is so used in paragraphs 1, 3 and 4 above. So what does the MPA coming into effect mean? Legally, it is Annex 1 to the BIA, and it entered into force on 2 December 1999. It remained in force after suspension on 12 February 2000. But not everything in the MPA will have legal effect. That depends upon obligations which bind one or other or both states parties, and, consequently, other office holders. The wording of this second provision does not give a lead role to the two governments. They convene the conference along with the parties in the assembly.

The other review provisions

23.75 Paragraphs 5–8 above are general to the Belfast Agreement. The institutions covered are the Strands One, Two and Three governing entities. How do they relate to the other review provisions: paragraph 36 of Strand One; and the first paragraph 12 and second paragraphs 7 and 9 of Strand Three? These have been discussed above in Chapters 12, 16 and 17 respectively.

23.76 First, Strand One. Paragraph 36, with its own subheading, Review, is compatible with the Review part of this section. Both relate to after devolution. Paragraph 36, however, is mandatory, though the period is not specified. The scope of the review would appear to be the whole of Strand One. However, reference is made especially to: electoral arrangements (which is an excepted matter under paragraph 12 of schedule 2 of the NIA 1998); and the assembly's procedures (a matter for standing orders under section 41 of the NIA 1998). Paragraph 36 of Strand One fits with the permissive paragraph 5 above.

23.77 The first paragraph 12 of Strand Three concerns the BIC. This also is a mandatory provision, compatible with the permissive paragraph 5 above. However, it specifies a formal published review at an appropriate time. This is not inconsistent with the annual report in paragraph 8 above. There is also a mandatory provision: contributing to any review of the overall political agreement. This, of course, is provided for in paragraph 8 above, 4 years after the BIA enters into force.

23.78 The second paragraphs 7 and 9 of Strand Three relate to the BIIC. The second paragraph 7 states inter alia that Northern Ireland ministers will be involved in the second paragraph 9 reviews. This provides for a review of the BIA

29 Northern Ireland Assembly, *Standing Orders: ordered to be printed by the Assembly on 9th March 1999*, NNIA 10.

after three years, much as happened with the 1985 Anglo-Irish Agreement. Northern Ireland ministers are to be involved. (It should have been placed in the BIA proper.) This review is distinct from the Review part of this section, to which reference is also made. The BIIC is to contribute to the MPA review after four years (under paragraph 8 above). However, 'it will have no power to override the democratic arrangements set up by this Agreement'. This can only mean the assembly is immune from any action of the two governments during a MPA review after four years.

PART 5

THE BRITISH-IRISH AGREEMENT

The final part of this book deals with the Agreement between the Government of the United Kingdom of Great Britain and Northern Ireland and the Government of Ireland, done at Belfast on 10 April 1998.[1] It was signed by Tony Blair and Marjorie 'Mo' Mowlam, for the United Kingdom government, and Bertie Ahern and David Andrews, for the Irish government. This agreement was annexed to the Belfast Agreement (namely the MPA), in the versions distributed in Northern Ireland, and in the Republic of Ireland. It is the BIA which gives the Belfast Agreement legal effect (though aspects of the MPA are purely aspirational). In versions published in 1999 and 2000, the Belfast Agreement comprises the BIA, with, at Annex 1, the MPA.

1 The relevant page numbers are pp. 27–30 of Cm 3883; pp. 1–6 of Cm 4705 (and, in the 1999 Irish version, six unnumbered pages, plus pp. 38–42).

24

The British-Irish Agreement

24.1 The BIA is an international agreement between the United Kingdom and Irish states. It was done at Belfast on 10 April 1998 (thus, the Belfast Agreement). Its signatories were Tony Blair and Marjorie 'Mo' Mowlam, and Bertie Ahern and David Andrews. It entered into force on 2 December 1999. It is at pages 27–30 of Cm 3883, and pages 1–6 of Cm 4705 (and the first unnumbered six pages, and pages 38–41, of the 1999 Irish version). It was not included in the MDP, not being an integral part of the multi-party negotiations.[1] There is therefore no earlier text with which to compare the BIA of 10 April 1998 (though it is believed to have gone through at least 14 drafts).

24.2 This chapter involves cross-references to the chapters on the MPA, which make up the bulk of this book. I have followed the structure of the texts of the Belfast Agreement as distributed to households in Northern Ireland, and in the Republic of Ireland, in April and May 1998.

Precedents for the British-Irish Agreement

24.3 There is only one, the 1985 Anglo-Irish Agreement: *Agreement between the Government of the United Kingdom of Great Britain and Northern Ireland and the Government of the Republic of Ireland*, Cmnd. 9657, Republic of Ireland No. 1 (1985). It was signed by the two heads of government, Margaret Thatcher and Garret FitzGerald, at Hillsborough, outside Belfast on 15 November 1985. (The Irish version of the agreement had the title: *Agreement between the Government of Ireland and the Government of the United Kingdom*.)

24.4 This was an international agreement – or treaty – between the United Kingdom and Irish states, dealing with Northern Ireland. Article 2(b) concluded: 'There is no derogation from the sovereignty of either the United Kingdom Government [sic] or the Irish Government [sic], and each retains responsibility for the decision and administration of government within its own jurisdiction'.

24.5 The Anglo-Irish Agreement – the name stems from the accompanying joint communiqué – established an intergovernmental conference (within the framework of the Anglo-Irish intergovernmental council set up after the 6 November 1981 bilateral meeting[2]). The intergovernmental conference – as I have described it already – was a consultation plus body.

1 Rule 21 of the *Ground Rules on Substantive All-Party Negotiations*, Cm 3232, 16 April 1996, provided for the Strand Three negotiations. These were between the two governments. Regular briefing and consultation meetings with the political parties were envisaged. 'The outcome of Strand Three will be considered by all the participants alongside the outcome of the other two strands.'

2 There was no legally binding international agreement. The Anglo-Irish intergovernmental council emerged from the Anglo-Irish Joint Studies, *Joint Report and Studies*, Cmnd 8414 November 1981, pp. 4–5 & 8–13.

24.6 It was to be 'concerned with Northern Ireland and with relations between the two parts of the island of Ireland'. Four functions were listed in article 2(a): political matters; security and related matters; legal matters, including the administration of justice; and the promotion of cross-border co-operation. These were elaborated in articles 5–10. Article 2(b) read in part: 'The United Kingdom Government accept[3] that the Irish Government will put forward views and proposals on matters relating to Northern Ireland within the field of activity of the Conference in so far as those matters are not the responsibility of a devolved administration in Northern Ireland.'

24.7 The United Kingdom government, and the Irish government, affirmed a commitment to devolution. According to article 4(c), the conference would be a framework within which 'the Irish Government may put forward views and proposals on the modalities of bringing about devolution in Northern Ireland, in so far as they relate to the interests of the minority community'.[4] If it should have proved impossible to achieve and sustain devolution, then, under article 5(c), the conference would be 'a framework within which the Irish Government may, where the interests of the minority community are significantly or especially affected, put forward views on proposals for major legislation and on major policy issues'.

24.8 The 1985 Anglo-Irish Agreement (as argued in Chapter 18) was not prototypical of later European national minority agreements. Nor did it provide for a role for the Irish government, if devolution should be achieved and sustained.[5]

A new British-Irish agreement?

24.9 This was mooted in the – two-part – 1995 *Framework Documents*.

24.10 In the first, United Kingdom, part, in Annex B, London suggested: 'the Anglo-Irish Agreement would be replaced by a new *and more broadly based agreement* between the two Governments reflecting the totality of relationships, and with provision for bilateral liaison, through an Intergovernmental Council. There would be a formal Intergovernmental Conference, with suitable rights of attendance and consultation for appropriate representatives of the new Northern Ireland political institutions. There would be a Secretariat to support the Conference and provide a channel of communication. The new agreement would be arrived at through direct discussion between the two Governments and the other Talks participants, and Northern Ireland political representatives would play a greater part in it than at present.'[6]

24.11 The joint understanding between the United Kingdom and Irish governments – part II – contained, under East-West Structures, eleven relevant paragraphs.

24.12 The first referred to a new and more broadly based agreement. The second specified an intergovernmental conference, and permanent secretariat. The third described it as a forum for the pursuit of joint objectives, basically reconciliation

3 Why not 'agree'?
4 This may be the putative authorization for the Irish government's role between 10 April 1998 and 2 December 1999.
5 An apparent exception is article 10(c), dealing with cross-border practical cooperation in economic, social and cultural areas.
6 Paragraph 1.

between the people of the island of Ireland. The fourth characterized the conference as 'a continuing institutional expression for the Irish Government's recognised concern and role in relation to Northern Ireland'. Reference was made to 'an intensification of the co-operation and partnership between both Governments'.

24.13 The fifth paragraph alluded to east-west, bilateral cooperation, either through the 1981 council, the (new) conference or otherwise.[7] Among the remaining six paragraphs: the eighth referred to the two governments reviewing the working of the agreement (seemingly the overall settlement): the ninth – paragraph 47 – referred to continuing north-south cooperation if devolution failed (the so-called default mechanism); and the tenth grudgingly acknowledged a role for Northern Ireland.

24.14 There was clearly a difference between London and Dublin (the latter pushing for practical joint authority or at least its appearance). The United Kingdom view on Strand Three was to prevail (augmented by the unionists' idea for a council of the islands).

24.15 In the *Ground Rules for Substantive all-Party Negotiations*, Cm 3232, 16 April 1996, rule 4 reads: 'Both Governments, as signatories of the Anglo-Irish Agreement, reaffirm that they would be prepared to consider a new and more broadly based [agreement] if that can be achieved through direct discussion and negotiation between all the parties concerned. The two Governments, for their part, have described a shared understanding of the parameters of a possible outcome of the negotiations in [the 1995 *Framework Documents*].'

24.16 The BIA was foreshadowed in the 12 January 1998 Heads of Agreement. 'A new British-Irish agreement' was envisaged, 'to replace the existing Anglo-Irish Agreement and help establish close co-operation and enhance relationships'. It was to embrace: an intergovernmental council (later, the BIC); a North-South ministerial council (the NSMC); suitable implementation bodies and mechanisms; and standing intergovernmental machinery (later, the BIIC).

What is the Belfast Agreement?

24.17 This is discussed above in Chapter 1. The Belfast Agreement is the document distributed in Northern Ireland, and in the Republic of Ireland. The former 30-page document, with coloured front cover, is entitled: *The Agreement: agreement reached in the multi-party negotiations*. The latter 35-page document is simply entitled: *Agreement Reached in the Multi-Party Negotiations*.

24.18 The name, the Belfast Agreement, came from Cm 3883, by which the secretary of state presented it to parliament on 20 April 1998.[8] It was used subsequently in the NIA 1998, the principal legal vehicle for implementation of the Belfast Agreement.[9] The use of a place name is suggestive of its legal character as an international agreement or treaty.

24.19 I have referred already to the two faces of the Belfast Agreement (Chapter

7 Paragraphs 39–43.

8 *The Belfast Agreement: an agreement reached at the multi-party talks on Northern Ireland*. It was not used in the Northern Ireland (Elections) Act 1998.

9 It is defined in section 98(1).

1). The April/May 1998 copies comprise a MPA,[10] to which is annexed the BIA. This annexing has no substantive effect. The political face of the Belfast Agreement is the MPA tout court.

24.20 Subsequently – in March 1999 – the United Kingdom government, and the Irish government, repackaged the Belfast Agreement for publication as a treaty: *Agreement between the Government of the United Kingdom of Great Britain and Northern Ireland and the Government of Ireland*, Cm 4292, Ireland No. 1 (1999), March 1999 – called the BIA by the MPA; the Irish 1999 version also put the BIA first (six unnumbered pages), made the MPA Annex 1 (pages 1–37) (with Annex 2 on the last unnumbered page), but then kept the BIA annexed at the end at pages 38–42.

24.21 This structure had existed legally on 10 April 1998. Tony Blair and Bertie Ahern (plus Marjorie 'Mo' Mowlam and David Andrews) signed the BIA. This provided then for Annex 1: The Agreement Reached iin the Multi-Party Talks (later, Negotiations) – the MPA. However, it seems that only the shortened BIA was signed.

24.22 The legal face of the Belfast Agreement is the BIA, with the MPA annexed. And, because article 31(2) of the 1969 Vienna convention on the law of treaties provides for annexes being part of the text, the Belfast Agreement is the BIA tout court. The annexing gives legal form to the MPA, though the legal parties are the two contracting states and not the Northern Ireland political parties.

24.23 However, the Belfast Agreement has to be interpreted legally to distinguish: obligations on one or both contracting states; text which is not legally binding in international law (but may, once incorporated in United Kingdom and/ or Irish law, bind a government or actual or potential office holder); and general principles of international law, which operate upon the text to become implied in the Belfast Agreement.[11]

TITLE: AGREEMENT BETWEEN THE GOVERNMENT OF THE UNITED KINGDOM OF GREAT BRITAIN AND NORTHERN IRELAND AND THE GOVERNMENT OF IRELAND

24.24 This is a standard title for an international agreement between two contracting states, though it is the practice for each state to put itself first in its own version (held by the other contracting state). Reference is made to Chapter 7 above, where the international law and domestic law names of the United Kingdom and Irish states are discussed extensively.

24.25 The BIA annexed to the MPA, and distributed in Northern Ireland, and in

10 First recital in preamble, BIA; Annex 1.

11 As the Supreme Court of Canada said: 'The Constitution is more than a written text. It embraces the entire global system of rules and principles which govern the exercise of constitutional authority. A superficial reading of selected provisions of the written constitutional enactment, without more, may be misleading. It is necessary to make a more profound investigation of the underlying principles animating the whole of the Constitution, including the principles of federalism, democracy, constitutionalism and the rule of law, and respect for minorities. Those principles must inform our overall appreciation of the constitutional rights and obligations that would come into play in the event that a clear majority of Quebecers vote on a clear question in faviour of secession.' (*Reference re secession of Quebec* [1998] 2 SCR 217, 220)

the Republic of Ireland, was as above: the United Kingdom of Great Britain and Northern Ireland, followed by Ireland. However, the actual Irish text of the BIA of 10 April 1998, in accord with practice, had Ireland first followed by the United Kingdom of Great Britain and Northern Ireland (the taoiseach and foreign minister signed on the left, the prime minister and secretary of state on the right).[12]

24.26 The practice as regards international agreements in 1998 – on the part of London but also Dublin – had changed clearly from that in 1985 (the United Kingdom of Great Britain and Northern Ireland and the Republic of Ireland versus Ireland and the United Kingdom).

24.27 As discussed in Chapter 7, the United Kingdom-law name – due to the origins of the Irish state, but also because of the territorial claim in the 1937 constitution – was Éire (until 1981) or the Republic of Ireland. The latter was used in the United Kingdom version of the 1985 Anglo-Irish Agreement. Why the change in 1998 to Ireland? United Kingdom law had not changed. So why did the United Kingdom government adopt the putative Irish-law name of the neighbouring state? The answer – as it emerged subsequently – was that there was a (secret) agreement between the two contracting states at Castle Buildings.

24.28 The two contracting states now use each other's names (the United Kingdom of Great Britain and Northern Ireland and Ireland) – but only in the title of treaties, as part of practice in international law. They still have a United Kingdom version, and an Irish version, the only difference being the order of names. This has made no change to the domestic, United Kingdom, law name: the Republic of Ireland. Nor has the Irish-law name – Éire/Ireland – or the description, the Republic of Ireland, altered in that separate legal system, though the term government of Ireland has been used with renewed vigour by the Irish state since the end of the territorial claim.

24.29 However, while the United Kingdom has scrupulously used Ireland, and even tried to surreptiously change its domestic law, the Irish state has not been so punctilious. The United Kingdom of Great Britain and Northern Ireland has been used only in the title of the BIA (and the four supplementary agreements of 8 March 1999). It was not used within the text of the BIA (United Kingdom was changed to British in article 3(1)), nor in the MPA: paragraph 5 of the Declaration of Support and paragraph 2 of Constitutional Issues. Nor has it been used in domestic Irish law.

24.30 The title of this treaty, better description, is the British-Irish Agreement. It is given by the MPA: paragraph 1 of Constitutional Issues; paragraph 1 of Strand Two; the first paragraph 1 of Strand Three; the second paragraph 1 of Strand Three; and paragraph 1 of Validation, Implementation and Review.

Subtitle/Preamble: The British and Irish Governments:

24.31 Whatever of the secret agreement between the two governments, it was more honoured by one than the other in the text of the BIA, and in the MPA.

24.32 In the 1985 Anglo-Irish Agreement, the terms United Kingdom govern-

12 This was also followed in the 1999 published version and the four supplementary agreements of 8 March 1999.

ment and Irish government were used in the text: articles 2(b) and 4.[13] The preamble began (in the United Kingdom version): The Government of the United Kingdom of Great Britain and Northern Ireland and the Government of the Republic of Ireland. The Irish version (as noted) was: The Government of Ireland and the Government of the United Kingdom.

24.33 The United Kingdom has continued to use the term Irish government. This is acceptable, given that it is the only state wholly within Ireland. The Irish government, however, has not just eschewed the adjectival United Kingdom. It has continued to use the term British to qualify constitutional nouns. And the United Kingdom has acceded to this[14] (to the extent of rewriting the 1985 title in the 1998 agreement: article 3(1)).

24.34 Thus, this subtitle, which should use the term the United Kingdom government to accord with the title. As for the MPA, the Irish government used, and the United Kingdom government accepted: British Acts of Parliament (against the Constitution of Ireland[15]); and 'British legislation relating to the constitutional status of Northern Ireland' (against the Constitution of Ireland).[16]

24.35 Against this argument is: the British-Irish Agreement; and, following from that description/title, the British-Irish Council and British-Irish Intergovernmental Conference. But – countering this point – the names of the council and conference are to transcend the term Anglo-Irish. This does have an antiquated flavour (Anglo being associated with English), not just from the viewpoint of Britain but also from Ireland (where Anglo-Irish has an internal and external meaning[17]). The Anglo-Irish of 1981 and (impliedly) of 1985 was best left behind in 1998. For that reason alone, the term British-Irish Agreement is preferable. These islands are Great Britain and Ireland. A description of a treaty may be geographical, as long as constitutionally the title and text use appropriate state names and adjectives.

> **Welcoming the strong commitment to the Agreement reached on 10th April 1998 by themselves and other participants in the multi-party talks set out in Annex 1 to this Agreement (hereinafter "the Multi-Party Agreement");**

24.36 This is the first recital of the preamble of the BIA. After the adoption of the MPA in the final plenary of the talks by the two governments and seven political parties (Sinn Féin did not vote), the prime minister and taoiseach signed the BIA (being followed by the secretary of state and the Irish foreign minister). This was not part of the final plenary. 'Agreement' is used twice in the recital. The first is a

13 However, the United Kingdom also used inconsistently the adjective 'British' (article 3).

14 It even did so in the 1985 joint communiqué, referring to the British Parliament against Dail Eireann (paragraph 6). There is a domestic United Kingdom problem, which may be resolved with devolution all round. Historically, the state used the English adjective (causing offence to Scotland, Wales and Ireland). British proved less offensive, especially in Ireland (later Northern Ireland), but also Scotland and Wales. However, United Kingdom national (in European law) is more accurate than British citizen (in United Kingdom law).

15 Paragraph 5 of the Declaration of Support.

16 Paragraph 2 of Constitutional Issues.

17 And is still used by the department of foreign affairs, to refer to the division which deals with the United Kingdom, including Northern Ireland.

reference to the MPA, the second to the BIA. This recital also gives the final plenary document the title Multi-Party Agreement. The (unamended) document voted upon had appeared earlier that day, under cover of a memorandum from the independent chairmen describing it as 'Final Agreement'. The word processed MDP as amended, however, bore the title 'AGREEMENT REACHED IN THE MULTI-PARTY NEGOTIATIONS' (which was used in the versions distributed in Northern Ireland, and in the Republic of Ireland). This recital clarifies the point about participants: here, the two governments acknowledge they were participants along with the political parties. However, the phrase multi-party talks intruded here (and was used to describe the content of Annex 1).[18] It appeared subsequently in: the subtitle of the *Belfast Agreement* Command Paper 3883, presented to parliament on 20 April 1998; section 1(1) of the Northern Ireland (Elections) Act 1998; and the long title of the NIA 1998. Annex 1 was later redescribed as 'Agreement reached in the Multi-Party Negotiations': Cm 4292, March 1999; and the 1999 Irish version.[19]

24.37 This recital – plus physical annexing – has the effect of annexing the MPA to the BIA, making it a part of the text of the treaty.

> **Considering that the Multi-Party Agreement offers an opportunity for a new beginning in relationships within Northern Ireland, within the island of Ireland and between the peoples of these islands;**

24.38 'a new beginning' is affirmed. The phrase in paragraph 1 of the Declaration of Support was a truly historic opportunity for a new beginning. A fresh start is also used in paragraph 2 of that section. The relationships phrase (plus a new beginning) is taken from rule 1 (Basis) of the *Ground Rules for Substantive All-Party Negotiations*, Cm 3232, 16 April 1996. It has the virtue of being consistent conceptually as regards Northern Ireland and the island of Ireland. However, peoples is introduced when these islands appear. 'relationships within Northern Ireland' (as is clear from rule 2) does not address the constitutional relationship (there is no reference to the United Kingdom). 'within the island of Ireland' is the new rhetoric of the nation used since the 1985 Anglo-Irish Agreement (though island consciousness was associated originally with Great Britain after 1707). 'the peoples of these islands' at least acknowledges a plurality (but is it only the British people and the Irish people?). A more consistent phrase was used in paragraph 3 of the Declaration of Support: relationships within Northern Ireland, between North and South, and between these islands.

> **Wishing to develop still further the unique relationship between their peoples and the close co-operation between their countries as friendly neighbours and as partners in the European Union;**

24.39 This was adapted from the first recital to the 1985 Anglo-Irish Agreement. There are two changes: wishing further to develop becomes 'wishing to develop still further'; and European Community is changed to 'European Union'. The idea of 'the unique relationship' had been used first on 21 May and 8 December 1980, in the communiqués of the two Anglo-Irish summits which led to the Anglo-Irish intergovernmental council.[20]

18 It is believed it appeared only in the final draft.

19 Though this retains the original description, in the second inclusion of the BIA.

20 Anglo-Irish Joint Studies, *Joint Report and Studies*, Cmnd 8413, November 1981, pp. 4 & 8.

Reaffirming their total commitment to the principles of democracy and non-violence which have been fundamental to the multi-party talks;

24.40 This is a reference to the Mitchell principles of 22 January 1996. It is not clear that the two governments wished to move beyond the anti-political violence recital of the 1985 Anglo-Irish Agreement.[21] Senator Mitchell and his two colleagues – the independent chairmen in the negotiations – had recommended in their report six principles of democracy and non-violence: 'there must be commitment and adherence to fundamental principles of democracy and non-violence. Participants in all-party negotiations should affirm their commitment to such principles. Accordingly, we recommend that the parties to such negotiations affirm their total and absolute commitment [to ...]:'.[22] It was Senator Mitchell who ensured that all the parties in the all-party, later multi-party, negotiations did so affirm.[23] The six Mitchell principles – including the second on the total disarmament of all paramilitary organizations – are discussed above in Chapter 18. The two governments had accepted the Mitchell report after 22 January 1996 (not least because the principles allowed for Sinn Féin's entry into talks without prior decommissioning). The Mitchell principles were affirmed in the joint communiqué of 28 February 1996.[24] 'fundamental to the multi-party talks' is a reference to the affirmations made by the two governments and all the parties at the beginning of the negotiations; multi-party talks was used in the first recital above.

Reaffirming their commitment to the principles of partnership, equality and mutual respect and to the protection of civil, political, social, economic and cultural rights in their respective jurisdictions;

24.41 This recital deals with principles and the protection of rights.

24.42 The principles are similar to paragraph 3 of the Declaration of Support: 'We are committed to partnership, equality and mutual respect as the basis of relationships within Northern Ireland, between North and South, and between these islands.' However, partnership, equality and mutual respect are not described there as principles. What do they mean here? 'partnership' is a synonym for power-sharing, the 1970s' concept. It gave rise to the concept of an inclusive assembly in paragraph 1 of Strand One, but more particularly the idea of a First Minister and Deputy First Minister in paragraph 14 and the d'Hondt system in paragraph 16. 'equality' cannot, in the preamble of the BIA, mean equality of outcome. This is because a whole section of the MPA is devoted to Rights, Safeguards and Equality of Opportunity. Equality must be a reference to equality of opportunity, since protection of rights is the next aspect of this recital. 'mutual respect' also occurs in that section, as mutual understanding and respect between and within communities in the first paragraph 13. It also occurs in the second paragraph 5 with reference to symbols and emblems.

21 'Reaffirming their total rejection of any attempt to promote political objectives by violence or the threat of violence and their determination to work together to ensure that those who adopt or support such methods do not succeed.'

22 Paragraphs 19 and 20.

23 George Mitchell, *Making Peace*, London 1999, pp. 53–4 & 111.

24 'They recognise that confidence building measures will be necessary. As one such measure, all participants would need to make clear at the beginning of the discussions their total and absolute commitment to the principles of democracy and non-violence set out in the report of the International Body.'

24.43 Protection of rights is a major obligation of states. However, while the United Kingdom state and the Irish state have undertaken in international law to do this, the two governments – through their legislatures – insist upon incorporation in domestic law before such rights are justiciable; the position is the same in both states. This is because the United Kingdom observes the doctrine of parliamentary sovereignty, while Éire/Ireland has a written constitution which recognizes the idea of fundamental (domestic) rights. There is another interesting contrast. The HRA 1998 in the United Kingdom does not incorporate Convention rights; it does, however, make the remedies available at home as an alternative to Strasbourg. That is likely to be practically very significant. Éire/Ireland, in contrast, in its Human Rights Commission bill, published on 8 July 1999, defined human rights in two ways: in section 2, they were rights guaranteed by the constitution, plus any rights in any international agreement to which the state is a party; in section 11, dealing with legal proceedings, they were only the rights in the constitution. The list of rights given by the two governments is interesting. They are taken clearly from the two 1966 conventions: the international covenant on economic, social and cultural rights; and the international covenant on civil and political rights (the order in which they are presented in the international bill of rights). The United Kingdom ratified both conventions in 1976; Éire/Ireland in 1990. 'respective jurisdictions' is the correct term when it comes to the enforcement of individual rights. However, while it was used in the 1985 Anglo-Irish Agreement in association with sovereignty (article 2(b)), it came to be used in London-Dublin diplomacy to describe the two states. To say there are two jurisdictions in Ireland allows for continuing notions of the nation; while to describe Northern Ireland and Scotland as separate jurisdictions (correctly) does not detract from the existence of the United Kingdom state.

Have agreed as follows:

24.44 This phrase distinguishes the preamble from the terms of the international agreement. While, under article 31(2) of the Vienna convention on the law of treaties, the preamble (like annexes) is a part of the text, it is not binding on the contracting states as articles 1–4 below are.

Heading: ARTICLE 1

24.45 This international agreement comprises four articles. It is to be distinguished from the 1985 Anglo-Irish Agreement, which had 13 articles. The intention would appear to have been a more practical international instrument, governing the involvement of the two contracting states in a putative solution to the Northern Ireland problem.

The two Governments:

24.46 This same phrase was used in article 1 of the 1985 Anglo-Irish Agreement, on the status of Northern Ireland.

(i) **recognise the legitimacy of whatever choice is freely exercised by a majority of the people of Northern Ireland with regard to its status, whether they prefer to continue to support the Union with Great Britain or a sovereign united Ireland;**

(ii) **recognise that it is for the people of the island of Ireland alone, by agreement between the two parts respectively and without external**

impediment, to exercise their right of self-determination on the basis of consent, freely and concurrently given, North and South, to bring about a united Ireland, if that is their wish, accepting that this right must be achieved and exercised with and subject to the agreement and consent of a majority of the people of Northern Ireland;

(iii) **acknowledge that while a substantial section of the people of Northern Ireland share the legitimate wish of a majority of the people of the island of Ireland for a united Ireland, the present wish of a majority of the people of Northern Ireland, freely exercised and legitimate, is to maintain the Union and accordingly, that Northern Ireland's status as part of the United Kingdom reflects and relies upon that wish; and that it would be wrong to make any change in the status of Northern Ireland save with the consent of a majority of its people;**

(iv) **affirm that, if in the future, the people of the island of Ireland exercise their right of self-determination on the basis set out in sections (i) and (ii) above to bring about a united Ireland, it will be a binding obligation on both Governments to introduce and support in their respective Parliaments legislation to give effect to that wish;**

(v) **affirm that whatever choice is freely exercised by a majority of the people of Northern Ireland, the power of the sovereign government with jurisdiction there shall be exercised with rigorous impartiality on behalf of all the people in the diversity of their identities and traditions and shall be founded on the principles of full respect for, and equality of, civil, political, social and cultural rights, of freedom from discrimination for all citizens, and of parity of esteem and of just and equal treatment for the identity, ethos, and aspirations of both communities;**

(vi) **recognise the birthright of all the people of Northern Ireland to identify themselves and be accepted as Irish or British, or both, as they may so choose, and accordingly confirm that their right to hold British and Irish citizenship is accepted by both Governments and would not be affected by any future change in the status of Northern Ireland.**

24.47 Paragraphs (i)–(vi) of this article have been included in the MDP, in paragraph 1 of the Constitutional Issues section. They are therefore discussed above in Chapter 9. The meaning of the six paragraphs stems from article 1 of the BIA. They represent a common statement by the two contracting states. Paragraph 1 of Constitutional Issues is simply an endorsement by the political parties (and the two governments). Nevertheless, the substantive analysis above applies here and will not be repeated.

24.48 This article 1 was inspired by article 1 of the 1985 Anglo-Irish Agreement. That constitutional understanding allowed the Republic of Ireland to acknowledge consent, in international law. The concept of a constitutional understanding was developed in the 1993 *Downing Street Declaration*[25] and the 1995 *Framework Documents.*[26] The phrase understandings on constitutional issues is used in paragraph 1 of Validation, Implementation and Review. Here, the United

25 Paragraphs 4 and 5.

26 Part I, Annex B, paragraph 1; part II, paragraphs 14–21.

Kingdom appears to make concessions on self determination and citizenship – in international law. They are much less significant than the – domestic law – constitutional changes in Annex A of Constitutional Issues. And, as argued in Chapter 10, those changes represented only a modification of the United Kingdom law position of 1973 until (as transpired) 1999.

24.49 Paragraph (vi) has to be read with Annex 2 to the BIA. This is in spite of their being no reference to Annex 2 of the BIA, in or near paragraph 1(vi) of Constitutional Issues in the MPA.

> **ARTICLE 2**
>
> **The two Governments affirm their solemn commitment to support, and where appropriate implement, the provisions of the Multi-Party Agreement. In particular there shall be established in accordance with the provisions of the Multi-Party Agreement immediately on the entry into force of this Agreement, the following institutions:**
>
> **(i) a North/South Ministerial Council;**
>
> **(ii) the implementation bodies referred to in paragraph 9(ii) of the section entitled "Strand Two" of the Multi-Party Agreement;**
>
> **(iii) a British-Irish Council;**
>
> **(iv) a British-Irish Intergovernmental Conference.**

24.50 This article is undoubtedly the most important in the BIA. Article 1 was about a shared constitutional understanding, Articles 3 and 4 are procedural. This article actually binds the two contracting states to implement the Belfast Agreement. The legality of every provision (as distinct from aspiration) of the MPA flows from this article.

24.51 The article comprises two sentences.

24.52 The first contains an affirmation of solemn commitment by the two governments to support the MPA. The MPA was agreed by the political parties on 10 April 1998 (but the two governments were also participants). The sentence, with different punctuation, was used in paragraph 1 of the Validation, Implementation and Review section. The affirmation is an important undertaking in international law. Support, however, while demonstrable by the actions of the two governments, does not necessarily imply any binding commitments to act. Much more important is the phrase: 'and where appropriate implement'. The MPA as Annex 1 to the BIA is given effect in international law by this phrase. The two governments have varying obligations under the MPA. Most – including the entire responsibility for devolution – descended upon the United Kingdom state.

24.53 The second sentence is an 'In particular'. If it had not been included, the two governments would have had to have implemented paragraphs 1 and 10 of Strand Two, the first paragraph 1 of Strand Three and the second paragraph 1 of Strand Three. This could only be done by an international agreement or agreements.

24.54 However, paragraph 1 of Strand Two refers to the NSMC being established under the BIA, and (perplexingly) 'related legislation at Westminster and in the Oireachtas'. Paragraph 10 of Strand Two refers (equally perplexingly) to 'necessary legislative and other enabling preparations' to create the implementation bodies. Similarly, the first paragraph 1 of Strand Three, and the second paragraph 1 of Strand Three, refer to the BIC and the BIIC being established under the BIA.

24.55 This is what the second sentence purports to do. It was drafted to distinguish the international institutions of governance in Strands Two and Three from the domestic, United Kingdom ones (the assembly) plus arguably the Human Rights Commission and the Equality Commission (as bodies corporate). The former are treaty bodies; the latter, statutory bodies. The word institutions is not a term of art, and does not derive its meaning from this sentence. It is used generically to refer to government decision making.

24.56 However, the wording of the second sentence caused the Irish government concern subsequently. It is normal when creating an institution in international law to do so like this: there is hereby established ... . Here, the drafter provided for: there shall be established ... on the entry into force of this Agreement. The use of other than the present tense (note article 4(1)) appears to have been to disguise the fact that it was the United Kingdom government, along with the Irish government, which was creating, in particular, the NSMC (there was no problem about the implementation bodies). The NSMC had, as a member, the Northern Ireland administration from the moment of devolution, and not the United Kingdom government (though the NSMC, under paragraph 7 of Strand Two, was required to meet in transitional form). The reference to establishment at some point in the future, is dealt with normally in a treaty by establishment in the present tense with an article dealing with entry into force (such as article 4). The Irish government seemingly read there shall be established, not to mean automatic establishment under this article at the point of entry into force under article 4, but as requiring a supplementary treaty establishing each institution – even though this was contrary to, at least, paragraph 1 of Strand Two, the first paragraph 1 of Strand Three, and the second paragraph 1 of Strand Three. Thus the four supplementary agreements of 8 March 1999 – respectively Cm 4294, Cm 4293, Cm 4296 and Cm 4295 – which have been discussed above in Chapters 14, 15, 16 and 17. Article 1 (of the first, third and fourth agreements) reads: 'Under and in furtherance of Article 2 of the British-Irish Agreement, there is hereby established ...' (Cm 4293 reads: 'the following Bodies are hereby established').

24.57 It would have been better to have created bodies (i)–(iv) in this article by: there is hereby established; and have them enter into force under article 4. They are, after all, specified as a condition precedent in article 4(1)(c). There would, however, have been a need for a supplementary agreement for the implementation bodies. Article 2 refers back to paragraph 9(ii) of Strand Two, but that refers simply to a future agreement. This would have had to have been provided for in a further treaty (though there is no recognition of this in paragraph 11 of Strand Two).

24.58 Because a supplementary agreement was necessary for the implementation bodies, then, according to the Irish government apparently, there should also be new agreements for the NSMC, BIC and BIIC. This does not follow legally, but the United Kingdom goverrnment acceded evidently to the Irish request.

24.59 The best explanation for the drafting of the second sentence is Northern Ireland's subordinate position within the United Kingdom. Only London has the power, in domestic law, to make international agreements with Dublin. But the

NSMC was meant to be a ministerial council linking Belfast and Dublin. The United Kingdom drafter apparently did not want to embarrass the new Northern Ireland administration with its legal impotence internationally. Thus, 'there shall be established', without express reference to the United Kingdom and Irish governments – which had the consequences outlined above. On 1 December 1999, the NSMC met finally in shadow form at Parliament Buildings in Belfast. It simply adopted the 8 March 1999 international agreement. Further, 'the Council agreed that the functions and structure of the implementation bodies, and the common arrangements applying to them, should be as specified in the Agreement' of 8 March 1999.[27]

ARTICLE 3

(1) This Agreement shall replace the Agreement between the British and Irish governments done at Hillsborough on 15th November 1985 which shall cease to have effect on entry into force of this Agreement.

(2) The Intergovernmental Conference established by Article 2 of the aforementioned Agreement done on 15th November 1985 shall cease to exist on entry into force of this Agreement.

24.60 This article terminates the 1985 Anglo-Irish Agreement. It may not have been strictly necessary, since the BIA is between the same contracting states and deals with the same subject matter. Under article 59(1) of the 1969 Vienna convention on the law of treaties: 'A treaty shall be considered as terminated if all the parties to it conclude a later treaty relating to the same subject-matter and: (a) it appears from the later treaty or is otherwise established that the parties intended that the matter should be governed by that treaty; or (b) the provisions of the later treaty are so far incompatible with those of the earlier one that the two treaties are not capable of being applied at the same time.'

24.61 Article 3 may be considered as an avoidance of doubt provision; alternatively, as political reassurance to the majority community.

24.62 Article 3(1) states that the 1985 Anglo-Irish Agreement shall cease to have effect when the BIA enters into force. (Note the change in party name from United Kingdom government to British government.) This means that the 1985 Anglo-Irish Agreement continued in force after 10 April 1998. It was not terminated until 2 December 1999. The 1985 Anglo-Irish Agreement was the only basis – seemingly – on which the Irish government could play a role in Northern Ireland during the transition. But it envisaged an attempt to bring about devolution (article 4(c)) and the continuation of direct rule after such a failure (article 5(c). It did not provide for the situation where a successor agreement had been made, but has not yet entered into force (just as it did not provide for termination).

24.63 Article 3(2) could have been incorporated in article 3(1). And such an article 3 (a point made above) was probably unnecessary given the BIA; the intergovernmental conference was succeeded by the BIIC. This is stated in the second paragraph 1 of Strand Three (which also refers to the end of the 1981 Anglo-Irish intergovernmental council).

27 Press release: http://www.northernireland.gov.uk.

24.64 But what about the secretariat – located at Maryfield outside Belfast (beside Palace Barracks in Hollywood) – provided for in article 3 of the 1985 Anglo-Irish Agreement? That stated: 'A Secretariat shall be established by the two Governments to service the Conference on a continuing basis ... .' (This is not the same as the shall be established in article 2 above.) This secretariat did not have the same legal status in international law as the intergovernmental conference. It is also dependent upon the intergovernmental conference. The end of the intergovernmental conference – which followed from the express or implied termination of the 1985 Anglo-Irish Agreement – also meant the end of the secretariat.

24.65 Before the conclusion of the Belfast Agreement on 10 April 1998, the United Kingdom prime minister gave an undertaking that the Maryfield secretariat would close by the end of the year. The secretary of state made this public on 20 April 1998, while making the statement on the Belfast Agreement to the House of Commons.[28] Maryfield duly closed before the end of 1998. But the Anglo-Irish secretariat transferred to offices in central Belfast, Windsor House in Bedford Street. It remained the secretariat under the Anglo-Irish Agreement (in so far as there was a role for the Irish government under that instrument after the conclusion of the Belfast Agreement).

24.66 The inaugural meeting of the BIIC, following devolution, took place in London on 17 December 1999. It approved a memorandum of understanding on supplementary procedural arrangements, which would not be legally binding nor override the MPA. This document signalled the establishment of the Joint Secretariat '[to] operate in accordance with arrangements to be determined from time to time by the two Governments'. Contrary to the impression given in the second paragraph 8 of Strand Three (Chapter 17), 'the Secretariat will provide support for the Conference, as appropriate, across its full remit to enable the Conference to carry out its functions'. It is then stated that the secretariat will be based in Northern Ireland, but that the two governments will designate officials in London and Dublin 'to support the work of the Secretariat, co-ordinate arrangements for Summit level meetings of the Conference and promote bilateral co-operation at all levels on matters of mutual interest' (paragraph 6). According to an Irish government press release of 8 December 1999,[29] citing only the BIA, the Anglo-Irish secretariat had become the British-Irish intergovernmental secretariat, also at Windsor House, with devolution on 2 December 1999, with a responsibility for non-devolved Northern Ireland matters. The joint secretaries in charge initially were Peter Bell[30] (from London) and Donal Hamill (Dublin).

ARTICLE 4

(1) It shall be a requirement for entry into force of this Agreement that:

(a) British legislation shall have been enacted for the purpose of implementing the provisions of Annex A to the section entitled "Constitutional Issues" of the Multi-Party Agreement;

(b) the amendments to the Constitution of Ireland set out in Annex B to

28 House of Commons, *Hansard*, 6th series, 310, 480, 20 April 1998.

29 Department of Foreign Affairs: http://www.irlgov.ie/information.

30 Peter Bell retired early in 2000.

the section entitled "Constitutional Issues" of the Multi-Party Agreement shall have been approved by Referendum;

(c) such legislation shall have been enacted as may be required to establish the institutions referred to in Article 2 of this Agreement.

(2) Each Government shall notify the other in writing of the completion, so far as it is concerned, of the requirements for entry into force of this Agreement. This Agreement shall enter into force on the date of the receipt of the later of the two notifications.

(3) Immediately on entry into force of this Agreement, the Irish government shall ensure that the amendments to the Constitution of Ireland set out in Annex B to the section entitled "Constitutional Issues" of the Multi-Party Agreement take effect.

24.67 Article 4 deals with entry into force. Reference has been made already to this in articles 2 and 3 above. Article 4(1) deals with a number of requirements, or conditions precedent; article 4(2) provides for an exchange of notes; and article 4(3) with an effect of entry into force in Irish municipal law.

24.68 The concept of condition precedent may be explained with reference to United Kingdom (and Irish) private contract law. A contract is said to be subject to a condition precedent, when one or both of the parties becomes liable only after inter alia the occurrence of a future event. The failure of a condition precedent (including of one or both legal parties to perform according to a contract not yet binding) may have a number of effects. One, suspension of the rights and obligations of both parties. Two, one party may assume an immediate unilateral binding obligation, but the bilateral contract does not come into existence until the condition is fulfilled. Three, an immediately binding contract, but with the suspension of some or all of the obligations pending fufillment of the condition. 'These conditions precedent are, however, normally contingent and not promissory, and in such a case neither party will be liable to the other if the condition is not fulfilled.'[31]

24.69 Article 4(1) lists – in international law – the conditions precedent for the entry into force of the BIA. (A requirement – singular – is used because (a), (b) and (c) are listed without an 'and' between (b) and (c).) Left out of this framework is devolution, a matter solely for the United Kingdom state. But paragraph 3 of Validation, Implementation and Review links devolution and entry into force, and this is part of Annex 1 of the BIA. (Devolution, however, is not a condition precedent to the BIA. It would, theoretically, have been possible to bring the BIA into force without devolution, but, if power had not been devolved to the assembly, it would have been impossible for the NSMC, BIC and – arguably – the BIIC to function in other than shadow mode).

24.70 The first two conditions precedent relate respectively to Annexes A and B of Constitutional Issues. It was noted above in Chapter 9, that Annexes A and B were not strictly part of the MPA (and therefore of the BIA).[32] Both governments, separately but simultaneously, undertook, at the time of the MPA, to seek to change

31 *Chitty on Contracts: volume 1: general principles*, 27th edn, London 1994, paragraph 12-026.

32 Alternatively, they are part of the MPA, but have no legal effect as a result of annexing to the BIA.

their domestic constitution law. Article 4(1)(a) refers to Annex A, and changes in United Kingdom legislation. These were effected by sections 1 and 2 of the NIA 1998, which received the royal assent on 19 November 1998. Under section 101(3), the secretary of state could by order bring these sections into force. As noted in Chapter 10 above, the government announced it would do this to coincide with devolution. To fulfil condition precedent (a), sections 1 and 2 need only to have been enacted (on 19 November 1998). Sections 1 and 2 were brought into force on 2 December 1999: Northern Ireland Act 1998 (Commencement No 5) Order 1999, SI 1999/3209. Article 4(1)(b) refers to Annex B, and changes to BNH. These were effected by the referendum on 22 May 1998, on the Nineteenth Amendment to the Constitution Bill 1998. Promulgation by the president on 4 June 1998, while necessary in Irish law, was not strictly necessary in order to fulfil condition precedent (b) in international law.

24.71 Article 4(1)(c) is not clear. The point has been made already that devolution is left out of this article on entry into force of the BIA. (Constitutional amendments are included, because they were not part of the MPA.) Condition precedent (c) refers to the Strands Two and Three institutions listed in article 2: the NSMC, implementation bodies, BIC and BIIC. This is not a reference here to creating them in international law as a condition precedent. That is the function of the second sentence of article 2. This condition precedent refers entirely to legislation, to presumably paragraph 10 of Strand Two. Construing article 4(1)(c), the operative word is establish. The implementation bodies were established by international agreement on 8 March 1999. They could not have been established by legislation, as presumably envisaged here. Alternatively, if legislation is the operative word, then the condition precedent was fulfilled when Westminster and the Oireachtas legislated to transfer functions. But this interpretation would require establish to mean established in Northern Ireland law and Irish law (which is not specified).

24.72 The three requirements for entry into force then were achieved on, respectively, 19 November 1998, 22 May 1998, and 8 March 1999.

24.73 Article 4(2) is straightforward. The United Kingdom government has to notify the fulfilment of article 4(1)(a) and (c); the Irish government, article 4(1)(b) and (c). 'requirements' – plural – is used, because (a), (b) and (c) amount to three separate requirements by two contracting states. Exchange of notes is a formal diplomatic communication (it is provided for also in article 5 of the implementation bodies agreement of 8 March 1999).

24.74 As noted in Chapter 1, the exchange of notification took place at a televised ceremony in Iveagh House, Dublin, attended by the secretary of state for Northern Ireland and the Irish foreign minister, early on 2 December 1999. In his short address, the secretary of state referred to the new 'British-Irish Treaty'.[33] The secretary of state had fulfilled already his domestic law duty of transferring powers from London to Belfast, under section 3 of the NIA 1998 (the devolution order).

24.75 Article 4(3) has been discussed above in Chapter 11. The Irish state's obligation in international law (insofar as the BIA had effect), is contained in article 4(1)(b). The Irish government did not undertake to change its constitution: that was for the people (it may not even have undertaken to propose and support

33 *Irish Times*, 3 December 1999.

the amendment[34]). But a successful referendum was a condition precedent for the BIA entering into force. That was achieved on 22 May 1998. But the new article 29.7 did not enter the constitution until 4 June 1998. Article 29.7.3–5 deals with the so-called declaration necessary in Irish constitutional law, to take the conditional amendments out of article 29.7.3 and substitute them for existing articles 2 and 3 (plus a new article 29.8). In Irish constitutional law, once the BIA had entered into force, the government had the discretion to make the declaration. But, in international law, under article 4(3), the Irish government was required to effect the amendments (immediately on entry into force of the Agreement). Immediately following the entry into force of the BIA, as noted in Chapter 11, the taoiseach, on the advice of the attorney general, in another televised ceremony, signed the declaration as required by the constitution. The new articles 2 and 3 replaced the Irish territorial claim, and a new article 29.8 took its place in BNH with immediate effect.

In witness thereof the undersigned, being duly authorised thereto by the respective Governments, have signed this Agreement.

Done in two originals at Belfast on the 10th day of April 1998.

For the Government of the United Kingdom of Great Britain and Northern Ireland[35]	**For the Government of Ireland**

24.76 This is a normal ending to an international agreement. Treaties are made by states. Governments act on behalf of states. And, here, the signatories express their authorization to act on behalf of their governments. The signatories were Tony Blair and Marjorie 'Mo' Mowlam for the United Kingdom government, and Bertie Ahern and David Andrews for the Irish Government. This is the United Kingdom version. The Irish version had the signatories reversed, with the Irish on the left. The names of the states follow those in the title of the agreement.

ANNEX 1

The Agreement Reached in the Multi-Party Talks

24.77 This first annex appears below the signatures, but it is annexed by the first recital of the preamble. The phrase 'multi-party talks' is used in the first and fourth recitals. Agreement Reached in the Multi-Party Negotiations was the title of the Final Agreement voted upon at the final plenary of the multi-party negotiations on 10 April 1998. However, the BIA, and not the MPA, name was used for Annex 1. It was corrected subsequently, between Cm 3883 and Cm 4292 (and in the 1999 Irish version).

ANNEX 2

Declaration on the Provisions of Paragraph (vi) of Article 1 In Relationship to Citizenship

34 Depending upon the construction of paragraph 2 of Constitutional Issues.

35 The version of the Belfast Agreement distributed in Northern Ireland contained a typographical error: an additional 'of Ireland' listed below this line.

> **The British and Irish Governments declare that it is their joint understanding that the term "the people of Northern Ireland" in paragraph (vi) of Article 1 of this Agreement means, for the purposes of giving effect to this provision, all persons born in Northern Ireland and having, at the time of their birth, at least one parent who is a British citizen, an Irish citizen or is otherwise entitled to reside in Northern Ireland without any restriction on their period of residence.**

24.78 Annex 2 seriously qualifies paragraph (vi) of article 1 of the BIA. However, since this paragraph was discussed above, in Chapter 9, as part of the analysis of subparagraph (vi) of paragraph 1 of the Constitutional Issues section, I simply refer here to that discussion.

THE BELFAST AGREEMENT

An Agreement Reached at the Multi-Party Talks on Northern Ireland

The Belfast Agreement: An Agreement Reached at the Multi-Party Talks on Northern Ireland

Presented to Parliament
by the Secretary of State for Northern Ireland
by Command of Her Majesty
April 1998

Cm 3883

TABLE OF CONTENTS

DECLARATION OF SUPPORT

1 We, the participants in the multi-party negotiations, believe that the agreement we have negotiated offers a truly historic opportunity for a new beginning.

2 The tragedies of the past have left a deep and profoundly regrettable legacy of suffering. We must never forget those who have died or been injured, and their families. But we can best honour them through a fresh start, in which we firmly dedicate ourselves to the achievement of reconciliation, tolerance, and mutual trust, and to the protection and vindication of the human rights of all.

3 We are committed to partnership, equality and mutual respect as the basis of relationships within Northern Ireland, between North and South, and between these islands.

4 We reaffirm our total and absolute commitment to exclusively democratic and peaceful means of resolving differences on political issues, and our opposition to any use or threat of force by others for any political purpose, whether in regard to this agreement or otherwise.

5 We acknowledge the substantial differences between our continuing, and equally legitimate, political aspirations. However, we will endeavour to strive in every practical way towards reconciliation and rapprochement within the framework of democratic and agreed arrangements. We pledge that we will, in good faith, work to ensure the success of each and every one of the arrangements to be established under this agreement. It is accepted that all of the institutional and constitutional arrangements – an Assembly in Northern Ireland, a North/South Ministerial Council, implementation bodies, a British-Irish Council and a British-Irish Intergovernmental Conference and any amendments to British Acts of Parliament and the Constitution of Ireland – are interlocking and interdependent and that in particular the functioning of the Assembly and the North/South Council are so closely inter-related that the success of each depends on that of the other.

6 Accordingly, in a spirit of concord, we strongly commend this agreement to the people, North and South, for their approval.

CONSTITUTIONAL ISSUES

1 The participants endorse the commitment made by the British and Irish Governments that, in a new British-Irish Agreement replacing the Anglo-Irish Agreement, they will:

(i) recognise the legitimacy of whatever choice is freely exercised by a majority of the people of Northern Ireland with regard to its status, whether they prefer to continue to support the Union with Great Britain or a sovereign united Ireland;

(ii) recognise that it is for the people of the island of Ireland alone, by agreement between the two parts respectively and without external impediment, to exercise their right of self-determination on the basis of consent, freely and concurrently given, North and South, to bring about a united Ireland, if that is their wish, accepting that this right must be achieved and exercised with and subject to the agreement and consent of a majority of the people of Northern Ireland;

(iii) acknowledge that while a substantial section of the people in Northern Ireland share the legitimate wish of a majority of the people of the island of Ireland for a united Ireland, the present wish of a majority of the people of Northern Ireland, freely exercised and legitimate, is to maintain the Union and, accordingly, that Northern Ireland's status as part of the United Kingdom reflects and relies upon that wish; and that it would be wrong to make any change in the status of Northern Ireland save with the consent of a majority of its people;

(iv) affirm that if, in the future, the people of the island of Ireland exercise their right of self-determination on the basis set out in sections (i) and (ii) above to bring about a united Ireland, it will be a binding obligation on both Governments to introduce and support in their respective Parliaments legislation to give effect to that wish;

(v) affirm that whatever choice is freely exercised by a majority of the people of Northern Ireland, the power of the sovereign government with jurisdiction there shall be the diversity of their exercised with rigorous impartiality on behalf of all the people in the diversity of their identities and traditions and shall be founded on the principles of full respect for, and equality of, civil, political, social and cultural rights, of freedom from discrimination for all citizens, and of parity of esteem and of just and equal treatment for the identity, ethos, and aspirations of both communities;

(vi) recognise the birthright of all the people of Northern Ireland to identify themselves and be accepted as Irish or British, or both, as they may so choose, and accordingly confirm that their right to hold both British and Irish citizenship is accepted by both Governments and would not be affected by any future change in the status of Northern Ireland.

2 The participants also note that the two Governments have accordingly undertaken in the context of this comprehensive political agreement, to

propose and support changes in, respectively, the Constitution of Ireland and in British legislation relating to the constitutional status of Northern Ireland.

ANNEX A

DRAFT CLAUSES/SCHEDULES FOR INCORPORATION IN BRITISH LEGISLATION

1 (1) It is hereby declared that Northern Ireland in its entirety remains part of the United Kingdom and shall not cease to be so without the consent of a majority of the people of Northern Ireland voting in a poll held for the purposes of this section in accordance with Schedule 1.

(2) But if the wish expressed by a majority in such a poll is that Northern Ireland should cease to be part of the United Kingdom and form part of a united Ireland, the Secretary of State shall lay before Parliament such proposals to give effect to that wish as may be agreed between Her Majesty's Government in the United Kingdom and the Government of Ireland.

2 The Government of Ireland Act 1920 is repealed; and this Act shall have effect notwithstanding any other previous enactment.

SCHEDULE 1

POLLS FOR THE PURPOSE OF SECTION 1

1 The Secretary of State may by order direct the holding of a poll for the purposes of section 1 on a date specified in the order.

2 Subject to paragraph 3, the Secretary of State shall exercise the power under paragraph 1 if at any time it appears likely to him that a majority of those voting would express a wish that Northern Ireland should cease to be part of the United Kingdom and form part of a united Ireland.

3 The Secretary of State shall not make an order under paragraph 1 earlier than seven years after the holding of a previous poll under this Schedule.

4 (Remaining paragraphs along the lines of paragraphs 2 and 3 of existing Schedule 1 to 1973 Act.)

ANNEX B

IRISH GOVERNMENT DRAFT LEGISLATION TO AMEND THE CONSTITUTION

Add to Article 29 the following sections:

7

1 The State may consent to be bound by the British-Irish Agreement done at Belfast on the day of 1998, hereinafter called the Agreement.

2 Any institution established by or under the Agreement may exercise the powers and functions thereby conferred on it in respect of all or any part of the island of Ireland notwithstanding any other provision of this Constitution conferring a like power or function on any person or any organ of State appointed under or created or established by or under this Constitution. Any power or function conferred on such an institution in relation to the settlement or resolution of disputes or controversies may be in addition to or in substitution for any like power or function conferred by this Constitution on any such person or organ of State as aforesaid.

3 If the Government declare that the State has become obliged, pursuant to the Agreement, to give effect to the amendment of this Constitution referred to therein, then, notwithstanding Article 46 hereof, this Constitution shall be amended as follows:

i. the following Articles shall be substituted for Articles 2 and 3 of the Irish text:

"2. [Irish text to be inserted here]

3. [Irish text to be inserted here]"

ii. the following Articles shall be substituted for Articles 2 and 3 of the English text:

"Article 2

It is the entitlement and birthright of every person born in the island of Ireland, which includes its islands and seas, to be part of the Irish nation. That is also the entitlement of all persons otherwise qualified in accordance with law to be citizens of Ireland. Furthermore, the Irish nation cherishes its special affinity with people of Irish ancestry living abroad who share its cultural identity and heritage.

Article 3

1. It is the firm will of the Irish nation, in harmony and friendship to unite all the people who share the territory of the island of Ireland, in all the diversity of their identities and traditions, recognising that a united Ireland shall be brought about only by peaceful means in both jurisdictions with the consent of a majority of the people, democratically expressed, in both jurisdictions in the island. Until then, the laws enacted by the Parliament established by this Constitution shall have the like area and extent of application as the laws enacted by the Parliament that existed immediately before the coming into operation of this Constitution.

2. Institutions with executive powers and functions that are shared between those jurisdictions may be established by their respective responsible authorities for stated purposes and may exercise powers and functions in respect of all or any part of the island."

iii. the following section shall be added to the Irish text of this Article:

"8. [Irish text to be inserted here]"

and

iv. the following section shall be added to the English text of this Article:

"8. The State may exercise extra-territorial jurisdiction in accordance with the generally recognised principles of international law."

4 If a declaration under this section is made, this subsection and subsection 3, other than the amendment of this Constitution effected thereby, and subsection 5 of this section shall be omitted from every official text of this Constitution published thereafter, but notwithstanding such omission this section shall continue to have the force of law.

5 If such a declaration is not made within twelve months of this section being added to this Constitution or such longer period as may be provided for by law, this section shall cease to have effect and shall be omitted from every official text of this Constitution published thereafter.

STRAND ONE

DEMOCRATIC INSTITUTIONS IN NORTHERN IRELAND

1 This agreement provides for a democratically elected Assembly in Northern Ireland which is inclusive in its membership, capable of exercising executive and legislative authority, and subject to safeguards to protect the rights and interests of all sides of the community.

The Assembly

2 A 108-member Assembly will be elected by PR(STV) from existing Westminster constituencies.

3 The Assembly will exercise full legislative and executive authority in respect of those matters currently within the responsibility of the six Northern Ireland Government Departments, with the possibility of taking on responsibility for other matters as detailed elsewhere in this agreement.

4 The Assembly – operating where appropriate on a cross-community basis – will be the prime source of authority in respect of all devolved responsibilities.

Safeguards

5 There will be safeguards to ensure that all sections of the community can participate and work together successfully in the operation of these institutions and that all sections of the community are protected, including:

(a) allocations of Committee Chairs, Ministers and Committee membership in proportion to party strengths;

(b) the European Convention on Human Rights (ECHR) and any Bill of Rights for Northern Ireland supplementing it, which neither the Assembly nor public bodies can infringe, together with a Human Rights Commission;

(c) arrangements to provide that key decisions and legislation are proofed to ensure that they do not infringe the ECHR and any Bill of Rights for Northern Ireland;

(d) arrangements to ensure key decisions are taken on a cross-community basis;

(i) **either** parallel consent, i.e. a majority of those members present and voting, including a majority of the unionist and nationalist designations present and voting;

(ii) **or** a weighted majority (60%) of members present and voting, including at least 40% of each of the nationalist and unionist designations present and voting.

Key decisions requiring cross-community support will be designated in advance, including election of the Chair of the Assembly, the First Minister and Deputy First Minister, standing orders and budget allocations. In other cases such decisions could be triggered by a petition of concern brought by a significant minority of Assembly members (30/108).

(e) an Equality Commission to monitor a statutory obligation to promote equality of opportunity in specified areas and parity of esteem between the two main communities, and to investigate individual complaints against public bodies.

Operation of the Assembly

6 At their first meeting, members of the Assembly will register a designation of identity – nationalist, unionist or other – for the purposes of measuring cross-community support in Assembly votes under the relevant provisions above.

7 The Chair and Deputy Chair of the Assembly will be elected on a cross-community basis, as set out in paragraph 5(d) above.

8 There will be a Committee for each of the main executive functions of the Northern Ireland Administration. The Chairs and Deputy Chairs of the Assembly Committees will be allocated proportionally, using the d'Hondt system. Membership of the Committees will be in broad proportion to party strengths in the Assembly to ensure that the opportunity of Committee places is available to all members.

9 The Committees will have a scrutiny, policy development and consultation role with respect to the Department with which each is associated, and will have a role in initiation of legislation. They will have the power to:

- consider and advise on Departmental budgets and Annual Plans in the context of the overall budget allocation;
- approve relevant secondary legislation and take the Committee stage of relevant primary legislation;
- call for persons and papers;
- initiate enquiries and make reports;
- consider and advise on matters brought to the Committee by its Ministers.

10 Standing Committees other than Departmental Committees may be established as may be required from time to time.

11 The Assembly may appoint a special Committee to examine and report on whether a measure or proposal for legislation is in conformity with equality requirements, including the ECHR/Bill of Rights. The Committee shall have the power to call people and papers to assist in its consideration of the matter. The Assembly shall then consider the report of the Committee and can

determine the matter in accordance with the cross-community consent procedure.

12 The above special procedure shall be followed when requested by the Executive Committee, or by the relevant Departmental Committee, voting on a cross-community basis.

13 When there is a petition of concern as in 5(d) above, the Assembly shall vote to determine whether the measure may proceed without reference to this special procedure. If this fails to achieve support on a cross-community basis, as in 5(d)(i) above, the special procedure shall be followed.

Executive Authority

14 Executive authority to be discharged on behalf of the Assembly by a First Minister and Deputy First Minister and up to ten Ministers with Departmental responsibilities.

15 The First Minister and Deputy First Minister shall be jointly elected into office by the Assembly voting on a cross-community basis, according to 5(d)(i) above.

16 Following the election of the First Minister and Deputy First Minister, the posts of Ministers will be allocated to parties on the basis of the d'Hondt system by reference to the number of seats each party has in the Assembly.

17 The Ministers will constitute an Executive Committee, which will be convened, and presided over, by the First Minister and Deputy First Minister.

18 The duties of the First Minister and Deputy First Minister will include, inter alia, dealing with and co-ordinating the work of the Executive Committee and the response of the Northern Ireland administration to external relationships.

19 The Executive Committee will provide a forum for the discussion of, and agreement on, issues which cut across the responsibilities of two or more Ministers, for prioritising executive and legislative proposals and for recommending a common position where necessary (e.g. in dealing with external relationships).

20 The Executive Committee will seek to agree each year, and review as necessary, a programme incorporating an agreed budget linked to policies and programmes, subject to approval by the Assembly, after scrutiny in Assembly Committees, on a cross-community basis.

21 A party may decline the opportunity to nominate a person to serve as a Minister or may subsequently change its nominee.

22 All the Northern Ireland Departments will be headed by a Minister. All Ministers will liaise regularly with their respective Committee.

23 As a condition of appointment, Ministers, including the First Minister and Deputy First Minister, will affirm the terms of a Pledge of Office (Annex A) undertaking to discharge effectively and in good faith all the responsibilities attaching to their office.

24 Ministers will have full executive authority in their respective areas of responsibility, within any broad programme agreed by the Executive Committee and endorsed by the Assembly as a whole.

25 An individual may be removed from office following a decision of the Assembly taken on a cross-community basis, if (s)he loses the confidence of the Assembly, voting on a cross-community basis, for failure to meet his or her responsibilities including, inter alia, those set out in the Pledge of Office. Those who hold office should use only democratic, non-violent means, and those who do not should be excluded or removed from office under these provisions.

Legislation

26 The Assembly will have authority to pass primary legislation for Northern Ireland in devolved areas, subject to:

(a) the ECHR and any Bill of Rights for Northern Ireland supplementing it which, if the courts found to be breached, would render the relevant legislation null and void;

(b) decisions by simple majority of members voting, except when decision on a cross-community basis is required;

(c) detailed scrutiny and approval in the relevant Departmental Committee;

(d) mechanisms, based on arrangements proposed for the Scottish Parliament, to ensure suitable co-ordination, and avoid disputes, between the Assembly and the Westminster Parliament;

(e) option of the Assembly seeking to include Northern Ireland provisions in United Kingdom-wide legislation in the Westminster Parliament, especially on devolved issues where parity is normally maintained (e.g. social security, company law).

27 The Assembly will have authority to legislate in reserved areas with the approval of the Secretary of State and subject to Parliamentary control.

28 Disputes over legislative competence will be decided by the Courts.

29 Legislation could be initiated by an individual, a Committee or a Minister.

Relations with other institutions

30 Arrangements to represent the Assembly as a whole, at Summit level and in dealings with other institutions, will be in accordance with paragraph 18, and will be such as to ensure cross-community involvement.

31 Terms will be agreed between appropriate Assembly representatives and the Government of the United Kingdom to ensure effective co-ordination and input by Ministers to national policy-making, including on EU issues.

32 Role of Secretary of State:

(a) to remain responsible for NIO matters not devolved to the Assembly, subject to regular consultation with the Assembly and Ministers;

(b) to approve and lay before the Westminster Parliament any Assembly legislation on reserved matters;

(c) to represent Northern Ireland interests in the United Kingdom Cabinet;

(d) to have the right to attend the Assembly at their invitation.

33 The Westminster Parliament (whose power to make legislation for Northern Ireland would remain unaffected) will:

(a) legislate for non-devolved issues, other than where the Assembly legislates with the approval of the Secretary of State and subject to the control of Parliament;

(b) to legislate as necessary to ensure the United Kingdom's international obligations are met in respect of Northern Ireland;

(c) scrutinise, including through the Northern Ireland Grand and Select Committees, the responsibilities of the Secretary of State.

34 A consultative Civic Forum will be established. It will comprise representatives of the business, trade union and voluntary sectors, and such other sectors as agreed by the First Minister and the Deputy First Minister. It will act as a consultative mechanism on social, economic and cultural issues. The First Minister and the Deputy First Minister will by agreement provide administrative support for the Civic Forum and establish guidelines for the selection of representatives to the Civic Forum.

Transitional Arrangements

35 The Assembly will meet first for the purpose of organisation, without legislative or executive powers, to resolve its standing orders and working practices and make preparations for the effective functioning of the Assembly, the British-Irish Council and the North/South Ministerial Council and associated implementation bodies. In this transitional period, those members of the Assembly serving as shadow Ministers shall affirm their commitment to non-violence and exclusively peaceful and democratic means and their opposition to any use or threat of force by others for any political purpose; to work in good faith to bring the new arrangements into being; and to observe the spirit of the Pledge of Office applying to appointed Ministers.

Review

36 After a specified period there will be a review of these arrangements, including the details of electoral arrangements and of the Assembly's procedures, with a view to agreeing any adjustments necessary in the interests of efficiency and fairness.

ANNEX A

PLEDGE OF OFFICE

To pledge:

(a) to discharge in good faith all the duties of office;

(b) commitment to non-violence and exclusively peaceful and democratic means;

(c) to serve all the people of Northern Ireland equally, and to act in accordance with the general obligations on government to promote equality and prevent discrimination;

(d) to participate with colleagues in the preparation of a programme for government;

(e) to operate within the framework of that programme when agreed within the Executive Committee and endorsed by the Assembly;

(f) to support, and to act in accordance with, all decisions of the Executive Committee and Assembly;
(g) to comply with the Ministerial Code of Conduct.

CODE OF CONDUCT

Ministers must at all times:

- observe the highest standards of propriety and regularity involving impartiality, integrity and objectivity in relationship to the stewardship of public funds;
- be accountable to users of services, the community and, through the Assembly, for the activities within their responsibilities, their stewardship of public funds and the extent to which key performance targets and objectives have been met;
- ensure all reasonable requests for information from the Assembly, users of services and individual citizens are complied with; and that Departments and their staff conduct their dealings with the public in an open and responsible way;
- follow the seven principles of public life set out by the Committee on Standards in Public Life;
- comply with this code and with rules relating to the use of public funds;
- operate in a way conducive to promoting good community relations and equality of treatment;
- not use information gained in the course of their service for personal gain; nor seek to use the opportunity of public service to promote their private interests;
- ensure they comply with any rules on the acceptance of gifts and hospitality that might be offered;
- declare any personal or business interests which may conflict with their responsibilities. The Assembly will retain a Register of Interests. Individuals must ensure that any direct or indirect pecuniary interests which members of the public might reasonably think could influence their judgement are listed in the Register of Interests;

STRAND TWO

NORTH/SOUTH MINISTERIAL COUNCIL

1 Under a new British/Irish Agreement dealing with the totality of relationships, and related legislation at Westminster and in the Oireachtas, a North/South Ministerial Council to be established to bring together those with executive responsibilities in Northern Ireland and the Irish Government, to develop consultation, co-operation and action within the island of Ireland – including through implementation on an all-island and cross-border basis – on matters of mutual interest within the competence of the Administrations, North and South.

2 All Council decisions to be by agreement between the two sides. Northern Ireland to be represented by the First Minister, Deputy First Minister and any relevant Ministers, the Irish Government by the Taoiseach and relevant Ministers, all operating in accordance with the rules for democratic authority and accountability in force in the Northern Ireland Assembly and the Oireachtas respectively. Participation in the Council to be one of the essential responsibilities attaching to relevant posts in the two Administrations. If a holder of a relevant post will not participate normally in the Council, the Taoiseach in the case of the Irish Government and the First and Deputy First Minister in the case of the Northern Ireland Administration to be able to make alternative arrangements.

3 The Council to meet in different formats:

(i) in plenary format twice a year, with Northern Ireland representation led by the First Minister and Deputy First Minister and the Irish Government led by the Taoiseach;

(ii) in specific sectoral formats on a regular and frequent basis with each side represented by the appropriate Minister;

(iii) in an appropriate format to consider institutional or cross-sectoral matters (including in relation to the EU) and to resolve disagreement.

4 Agendas for all meetings to be settled by prior agreement between the two sides, but it will be open to either to propose any matter for consideration or action.

5 The Council:

(i) to exchange information, discuss and consult with a view to co-operating on matters of mutual interest within the competence of both Administrations, North and South;

(ii) to use best endeavours to reach agreement on the adoption of common policies, in areas where there is a mutual cross-border and all-island benefit, and which are within the competence of both Administrations, North and South, making determined efforts to overcome any disagreements;

(iii) to take decisions by agreement on policies for implementation separately in each jurisdiction, in relevant meaningful areas within the competence of both Administrations, North and South;

(iv) to take decisions by agreement on policies and action at an all-island and cross-border level to be implemented by the bodies to be established as set out in paragraphs 8 and 9 below.

6 Each side to be in a position to take decisions in the Council within the defined authority of those attending, through the arrangements in place for coordination of executive functions within each jurisdiction. Each side to remain accountable to the Assembly and Oireachtas respectively, whose approval, through the arrangements in place on either side, would be required for decisions beyond the defined authority of those attending.

7 As soon as practically possible after elections to the Northern Ireland Assembly, inaugural meetings will take place of the Assembly, the British/Irish Council and the North/South Ministerial Council in their transitional forms. All three institutions will meet regularly and frequently on this basis during the period between the elections to the Assembly, and the transfer of powers to the Assembly, in order to establish their modus operandi.

8 During the transitional period between the elections to the Northern Ireland Assembly and the transfer of power to it, representatives of the Northern Ireland transitional Administration and the Irish Government operating in the North/South Ministerial Council will undertake a work programme, in consultation with the British Government, covering at least 12 subject areas, with a view to identifying and agreeing by 31 October 1998 areas where co-operation and implementation for mutual benefit will take place. Such areas may include matters in the list set out in the Annex.

9 As part of the work programme, the Council will identify and agree at least 6 matters for co-operation and implementation in each of the following categories:

(i) Matters where existing bodies will be the appropriate mechanisms for co-operation in each separate jurisdiction;

(ii) Matters where the co-operation will take place through agreed implementation bodies on a cross-border or all-island level.

10 The two Governments will make necessary legislative and other enabling preparations to ensure, as an absolute commitment, that these bodies, which have been agreed as a result of the work programme, function at the time of the inception of the British-Irish Agreement and the transfer of powers, with legislative authority for these bodies transferred to the Assembly as soon as possible thereafter. Other arrangements for the agreed co-operation will also commence contemporaneously with the transfer of powers to the Assembly.

11 The implementation bodies will have a clear operational remit. They will implement on an all-island and cross-border basis policies agreed in the Council.

12 Any further development of these arrangements to be by agreement in the Council and with the specific endorsement of the Northern Ireland Assembly and Oireachtas, subject to the extent of the competences and responsibility of the two Administrations.

13 It is understood that the North/South Ministerial Council and the Northern Ireland Assembly are mutually inter-dependent, and that one cannot successfully function without the other.

14 Disagreements within the Council to be addressed in the format described at paragraph 3(iii) above or in the plenary format. By agreement between the two sides, appointed to consider a particular matter and report.

15 Funding to be provided by the two Administrations on the basis that the Council and the implementation bodies constitute a necessary public function.

16 The Council to be supported by a standing joint Secretariat, staffed by members of the Northern Ireland Civil Service and the Irish Civil Service.

17 The Council to consider the European Union dimension of relevant matters, including the implementation of EU policies and programmes and proposals under consideration in the EU framework. Arrangements to be made to ensure that the views of the Council are taken into account and represented appropriately at relevant EU meetings.

18 The Northern Ireland Assembly and the Oireachtas to consider developing a joint parliamentary forum, bringing together equal numbers from both institutions for discussion of matters of mutual interest and concern.

19 Consideration to be given to the establishment of an independent consultative forum appointed by the two Administrations, representative of civil society, comprising the social partners and other members with expertise in social, cultural, economic and other issues.

ANNEX

Areas for North/South co-operation and implementation may include the following:

1 Agriculture – animal and plant health.

2 Education – teacher qualifications and exchanges.

3 Transport – strategic transport planning.

4 Environment – environmental protection, pollution, water quality, and waste management.

5 Waterways – inland waterways.

6 Social Security/Social Welfare – entitlements of cross-border workers and fraud control.

7 Tourism – promotion, marketing, research, and product development.

8 Relevant EU Programmes such as SPPR, INTERREG, Leader II and their successors.

9 Inland Fisheries.

10 Aquaculture and marine matters.

11 Health: accident and emergency services and other related cross-border issues.

12 Urban and rural development.

Others to be considered by the shadow North/South Council.

STRAND THREE

BRITISH-IRISH COUNCIL

1 A British-Irish Council (BIC) will be established under a new British-Irish Agreement to promote the harmonious and mutually beneficial development of the totality of relationships among the peoples of these islands.

2 Membership of the BIC will comprise representatives of the British and Irish Governments, devolved institutions in Northern Ireland, Scotland and Wales, when established, and, if appropriate, elsewhere in the United Kingdom, together with representatives of the Isle of Man and the Channel Islands.

3 The BIC will meet in different formats: at summit level, twice per year; in specific sectoral formats on a regular basis, with each side represented by the appropriate Minister; in an appropriate format to consider cross-sectoral matters.

4 Representatives of members will operate in accordance with whatever procedures for democratic authority and accountability are in force in their respective elected institutions.

5 The BIC will exchange information, discuss, consult and use best endeavours to reach agreement on co-operation on matters of mutual interest within the competence of the relevant Administrations. Suitable issues for early discussion in the BIC could include transport links, agricultural issues, environmental issues, cultural issues, health issues, education issues and approaches to EU issues. Suitable arrangements to be made for practical co-operation on agreed policies.

6 It will be open to the BIC to agree common policies or common actions. Individual members may opt not to participate in such common policies and common action.

7 The BIC normally will operate by consensus. In relation to decisions on common policies or common actions, including their means of implementation, it will operate by agreement of all members participating in such policies or actions.

8 The members of the BIC, on a basis to be agreed between them, will provide such financial support as it may require.

9 A secretariat for the BIC will be provided by the British and Irish Governments in co-ordination with officials of each of the other members.

10 In addition to the structures provided for under this agreement, it will be open to two or more members to develop bilateral or multilateral arrangements between them. Such arrangements could include, subject to the agreement of the members concerned, mechanisms to enable consultation, co-operation and joint decision-making on matters of mutual interest; and mechanisms to implement any joint decisions they may reach. These arrangements will not require the prior approval of the BIC as a whole and will operate independently of it.

11 The elected institutions of the members will be encouraged to develop interparliamentary links, perhaps building on the British-Irish Interparliamentary Body.

12 The full membership of the BIC will keep under review the workings of the Council, including a formal published review at an appropriate time after the Agreement comes into effect, and will contribute as appropriate to any review of the overall political agreement arising from the multi-party negotiations.

BRITISH-IRISH INTERGOVERNMENTAL CONFERENCE

1 There will be a new British-Irish Agreement dealing with the totality of relationships. It will establish a standing British-Irish Intergovernmental Conference, which will subsume both the Anglo-Irish Intergovernmental Council and the Intergovernmental Conference established under the 1985 Agreement.

2 The Conference will bring together the British and Irish Governments to promote bilateral co-operation at all levels on all matters of mutual interest within the competence of both Governments.

3 The Conference will meet as required at Summit level (Prime Minister and Taoiseach). Otherwise, Governments will be represented by appropriate Ministers. Advisers, including police and security advisers, will attend as appropriate.

4 All decisions will be by agreement between both Governments. The Governments will make determined efforts to resolve disagreements between them. There will be no derogation from the sovereignty of either Government.

5 In recognition of the Irish Government's special interest in Northern Ireland and of the extent to which issues of mutual concern arise in relation to Northern Ireland, there will be regular and frequent meetings of the Conference concerned with non-devolved Northern Ireland matters, on which the Irish Government may put forward views and proposals. These meetings, to be co-chaired by the Minister for Foreign Affairs and the Secretary of State for Northern Ireland, would also deal with all-island and cross-border co-operation on non-devolved issues.

6 Co-operation within the framework of the Conference will include facilitation of co-operation in security matters. The Conference also will address, in particular, the areas of rights, justice, prisons and policing in Northern Ireland (unless and until responsibility is devolved to a Northern Ireland administration) and will intensify co-operation between the two Governments on the all-island or cross-border aspects of these matters.

7 Relevant executive members of the Northern Ireland Administration will be involved in meetings of the Conference, and in the reviews referred to in paragraph 9 below to discuss non-devolved Northern Ireland matters.

8 The Conference will be supported by officials of the British and Irish Governments, including by a standing joint Secretariat of officials dealing with non-devolved Northern Ireland matters.

9 The Conference will keep under review the workings of the new British-Irish

Agreement and the machinery and institutions established under it, including a formal published review three years after the Agreement comes into effect. Representatives of the Northern Ireland Administration will be invited to express views to the Conference in this context.

The Conference will contribute as appropriate to any review of the overall political agreement arising from the multi-party negotiations but will have no power to override the democratic arrangements set up by this Agreement.

RIGHTS, SAFEGUARDS AND EQUALITY OF OPPORTUNITY

HUMAN RIGHTS

1 The parties affirm their commitment to the mutual respect, the civil rights and the religious liberties of everyone in the community. Against the background of the recent history of communal conflict, the parties affirm in particular:

- the right of free political thought;
- the right to freedom and expression of religion;
- the right to pursue democratically national and political aspirations;
- the right to seek constitutional change by peaceful and legitimate means;
- the right to freely choose one's place of residence;
- the right to equal opportunity in all social and economic activity, regardless of class, creed, disability, gender or ethnicity;
- the right to freedom from sectarian harassment; and
- the right of women to full and equal political participation.

United Kingdom Legislation

2 The British Government will complete incorporation into Northern Ireland law of the European Convention on Human Rights (ECHR), with direct access to the courts, and remedies for breach of the Convention, including power for the courts to overrule Assembly legislation on grounds of inconsistency.

3 Subject to the outcome of public consultation underway, the British Government intends, as a particular priority, to create a statutory obligation on public authorities in Northern Ireland to carry out all their functions with due regard to the need to promote equality of opportunity in relation to religion and political opinion; gender; race; disability; age; marital status; dependants; and sexual orientation. Public bodies would be required to draw up statutory schemes showing how they would implement this obligation. Such schemes would cover arrangements for policy appraisal, including an assessment of impact on relevant categories, public consultation, public access to information and services, monitoring and timetables.

4 The new Northern Ireland Human Rights Commission (see paragraph 5 below) will be invited to consult and to advise on the scope for defining, in Westminster legislation, rights supplementary to those in the European Convention on Human Rights, to reflect the particular circumstances of Northern Ireland, drawing as appropriate on international instruments and

experience. These additional rights to reflect the principles of mutual respect for the identity and ethos of both communities and parity of esteem, and – taken together with the ECHR – to constitute a Bill of Rights for Northern Ireland. Among the issues for consideration by the Commission will be:

- the formulation of a general obligation on government and public bodies fully to respect, on the basis of equality of treatment, the identity and ethos of both communities in Northern Ireland; and
- a clear formulation of the rights not to be discriminated against and to equality of opportunity in both the public and private sectors.

New Institutions in Northern Ireland

5 A new Northern Ireland Human Rights Commission, with membership from Northern Ireland reflecting the community balance, will be established by Westminster legislation, independent of Government, with an extended and enhanced role beyond that currently exercised by the Standing Advisory Commission on Human Rights, to include keeping under review the adequacy and effectiveness of laws and practices, making recommendations to Government as necessary; providing information and promoting awareness of human rights; considering draft legislation referred to them by the new Assembly; and, in appropriate cases, bringing court proceedings or providing assistance to individuals doing so.

6 Subject to the outcome of public consultation currently underway, the British Government intends a new statutory Equality Commission to replace the Fair Employment Commission, the Equal Opportunities Commission (NI), the Commission for Racial Equality (NI) and the Disability Council. Such a unified Commission will advise on, validate and monitor the statutory obligation and will investigate complaints of default.

7 It would be open to a new Northern Ireland Assembly to consider bringing together its responsibilities for these matters into a dedicated Department of Equality.

8 These improvements will build on existing protections in Westminster legislation in respect of the judiciary, the system of justice and policing.

Comparable Steps by the Irish Government

9 The Irish Government will also take steps to further strengthen the protection of human rights in its jurisdiction. The Government will, taking account of the work of the All-Party Oireachtas Committee on the Constitution and the Report of the Constitution Review Group, bring forward measures to strengthen and underpin the constitutional protection of human rights. These proposals will draw on the European Convention on Human Rights and other international legal instruments in the field of human rights and the question of the incorporation of the ECHR will be further examined in this context. The measures brought forward would ensure at least an equivalent level of protection of human rights as will pertain in Northern Ireland. In addition, the Irish Government will:

- establish a Human Rights Commission with a mandate and remit equivalent to that within Northern Ireland;

- proceed with arrangements as quickly as possible to ratify the Council of Europe Framework Convention on National Minorities (already ratified by the UK);
- implement enhanced employment equality legislation;
- introduce equal status legislation; and
- continue to take further active steps to demonstrate its respect for the different traditions in the island of Ireland.

A Joint Committee

10 It is envisaged that there would be a joint committee of representatives of the two Human Rights Commissions, North and South, as a forum for consideration of human rights issues in the island of Ireland. The joint committee will consider, among other matters, the possibility of establishing a charter, open to signature by all democratic political parties, reflecting and endorsing agreed measures for the protection of the fundamental rights of everyone living in the island of Ireland.

Reconciliation and Victims of Violence

11 The participants believe that it is essential to acknowledge and address the suffering of the victims of violence as a necessary element of reconciliation. They look forward to the results of the work of the Northern Ireland Victims Commission.

12 It is recognised that victims have a right to remember as well as to contribute to a changed society. The achievement of a peaceful and just society would be the true memorial to the victims of violence. The participants particularly recognise that young people from areas affected by the troubles face particular difficulties and will support the development of special community-based initiatives based on international best practice. The provision of services that are supportive and sensitive to the needs of victims will also be a critical element and that support will need to be channelled through both statutory and community-based voluntary organisations facilitating locally-based self-help and support networks. This will require the allocation of sufficient resources, including statutory funding as necessary, to meet the needs of victims and to provide for community-based support programmes.

13 The participants recognise and value the work being done by many organisations to develop reconciliation and mutual understanding and respect between and within communities and traditions, in Northern Ireland and between North and South, and they see such work as having a vital role in consolidating peace and political agreement. Accordingly, they pledge their continuing support to such organisations and will positively examine the case for enhanced financial assistance for the work of reconciliation. An essential aspect of the reconciliation process is the promotion of a culture of tolerance at every level of society, including initiatives to facilitate and encourage integrated education and mixed housing.

RIGHTS, SAFEGUARDS AND EQUALITY OF OPPORTUNITY

ECONOMIC, SOCIAL AND CULTURAL ISSUES

1 Pending the devolution of powers to a new Northern Ireland Assembly, the British Government will pursue broad policies for sustained economic growth and stability in Northern Ireland and for promoting social inclusion, including in particular community development and the advancement of women in public life.

2 Subject to the public consultation currently under way, the British Government will make rapid progress with:

(i) a new regional development strategy for Northern Ireland, for consideration in due course by a the Assembly, tackling the problems of a divided society and social cohesion in urban, rural and border areas, protecting and enhancing the environment, producing new approaches to transport issues, strengthening the physical infrastructure of the region, developing the advantages and resources of rural areas and rejuvenating major urban centres;

(ii) a new economic development strategy for Northern Ireland, for consideration in due course by a the Assembly, which would provide for short and medium term economic planning linked as appropriate to the regional development strategy; and

(iii) measures on employment equality included in the recent White Paper ("Partnership for Equality") and covering the extension and strengthening of anti-discrimination legislation, a review of the national security aspects of the present fair employment legislation at the earliest possible time, a new more focused Targeting Social Need initiative and a range of measures aimed at combating unemployment and progressively eliminating the differential in unemployment rates between the two communities by targeting objective need.

3 All participants recognise the importance of respect, understanding and tolerance in relation to linguistic diversity, including in Northern Ireland, the Irish language, Ulster-Scots and the languages of the various ethnic communities, all of which are part of the cultural wealth of the island of Ireland.

4 In the context of active consideration currently being given to the UK signing the Council of Europe Charter for Regional or Minority Languages, the British Government will in particular in relation to the Irish language, where appropriate and where people so desire it:

- take resolute action to promote the language;
- facilitate and encourage the use of the language in speech and writing in public and private life where there is appropriate demand;

- seek to remove, where possible, restrictions which would discourage or work against the maintenance or development of the language;
- make provision for liaising with the Irish language community, representing their views to public authorities and investigating complaints;
- place a statutory duty on the Department of Education to encourage and facilitate Irish medium education in line with current provision for integrated education;
- explore urgently with the relevant British authorities, and in co-operation with the Irish broadcasting authorities, the scope for achieving more widespread availability of Teilifis na Gaeilige in Northern Ireland;
- seek more effective ways to encourage and provide financial support for Irish language film and television production in Northern Ireland; and
- encourage the parties to secure agreement that this commitment will be sustained by a new Assembly in a way which takes account of the desires and sensitivities of the community.

5 All participants acknowledge the sensitivity of the use of symbols and emblems for public purposes, and the need in particular in creating the new institutions to ensure that such symbols and emblems are used in a manner which promotes mutual respect rather than division. Arrangements will be made to monitor this issue and consider what action might be required.

DECOMMISSIONING

1 Participants recall their agreement in the Procedural Motion adopted on 24 September 1997 "that the resolution of the decommissioning issue is an indispensable part of the process of negotiation", and also recall the provisions of paragraph 25 of Strand 1 above.

2 They note the progress made by the Independent International Commission on Decommissioning and the Governments in developing schemes which can represent a workable basis for achieving the decommissioning of illegally-held arms in the possession of paramilitary groups.

3 All participants accordingly reaffirm their commitment to the total disarmament of all paramilitary organisations. They also confirm their intention to continue to work constructively and in good faith with the Independent Commission, and to use any influence they may have, to achieve the decommissioning of all paramilitary arms within two years following endorsement in referendums North and South of the agreement and in the context of the implementation of the overall settlement.

4 The Independent Commission will monitor, review and verify progress on decommissioning of illegal arms, and will report to both Governments at regular intervals.

6 Both Governments will take all necessary steps to facilitate the decommissioning process to include bringing the relevant schemes into force by the end of June.

SECURITY

1 The participants note that the development of a peaceful environment on the basis of this agreement can and should mean a normalisation of security arrangements and practices.

2 The British Government will make progress towards the objective of as early a return as possible to normal security arrangements in Northern Ireland, consistent with the level of threat and with a published overall strategy, dealing with:

(i) the reduction of the numbers and role of the Armed Forces deployed in Northern Ireland to levels compatible with a normal peaceful society;

(ii) the removal of security installations;

(iii) the removal of emergency powers in Northern Ireland; and

(iv) other measures appropriate to and compatible with a normal peaceful society.

3 The Secretary of State will consult regularly on progress, and the response to any continuing paramilitary activity, with the Irish Government and the political parties, as appropriate.

4 The British Government will continue its consultation on firearms regulation and control on the basis of the document published on 2 April 1998.

5 The Irish Government will initiate a wide-ranging review of the Offences Against the State Acts 1939–85 with a view to both reform and dispensing with those elements no longer required as circumstances permit.

POLICING AND JUSTICE

1 The participants recognise that policing is a central issue in any society. They equally recognise that Northern Ireland's history of deep divisions has made it highly emotive, with great hurt suffered and sacrifices made by many individuals and their families, including those in the RUC and other public servants. They believe that the agreement provides the opportunity for a new beginning to policing in Northern Ireland with a police service capable of attracting and sustaining support from the community as a whole. They also believe that this agreement offers a unique opportunity to bring about a new political dispensation which will recognise the full and equal legitimacy and worth of the identities, senses of allegiance and ethos of all sections of the community in Northern Ireland. They consider that this opportunity should inform and underpin the development of a police service representative in terms of the make-up of the community as a whole and which, in a peaceful environment, should be routinely unarmed.

2 The participants believe it essential that policing structures and arrangements are such that the police service is professional, effective and efficient, fair and impartial, free from partisan political control; accountable, both under the law for its actions and to the community it serves; representative of the society it polices, and operates within a coherent and co-operative criminal justice

system, which conforms with human rights norms. The participants also believe that those structures and arrangements must be capable of maintaining law and order including responding effectively to crime and to any terrorist threat and to public order problems. A police service which cannot do so will fail to win public confidence and acceptance. They believe that any such structures and arrangements should be capable of delivering a policing service, in constructive and inclusive partnerships with the community at all levels, and with the maximum delegation of authority and responsibility, consistent with the foregoing principles. These arrangements should be based on principles of protection of human rights and professional integrity and should be unambiguously accepted and actively supported by the entire community.

3 An independent Commission will be established to make recommendations for future policing arrangements in Northern Ireland including means of encouraging widespread community support for these arrangements within the agreed framework of principles reflected in the paragraphs above and in accordance with the terms of reference at Annex A. The Commission will be broadly representative with expert and international representation among its membership and will be asked to consult widely and to report no later than Summer 1999.

4 The participants believe that the aims of the criminal justice system are to:

- deliver a fair and impartial system of justice to the community;
- be responsive to the community's concerns, and encouraging community involvement where appropriate;
- have the confidence of all parts of the community; and
- deliver justice efficiently and effectively.

5 There will be a parallel wide-ranging review of criminal justice (other than policing and those aspects of the system relating to the emergency legislation) to be carried out by the British Government through a mechanism with an independent element, in consultation with the political parties and others. The review will commence as soon as possible, will include wide consultation, and a report will be made to the Secretary of State no later than Autumn 1999. Terms of Reference are attached at Annex B.

6 Implementation of the recommendations arising from both reviews will be discussed with the political parties and with the Irish Government.

7 The participants also note that the British Government remains ready in principle, with the broad support of the political parties, and after consultation, as appropriate, with the Irish Government, in the context of ongoing implementation of the relevant recommendations, to devolve responsibility for policing and justice issues.

ANNEX A

COMMISSION ON POLICING FOR NORTHERN IRELAND

Terms of Reference

Taking account of the principles on policing as set out in the agreement, the Commission will inquire into Northern Ireland and, on the basis of its findings, bring forward proposals for future policing including means of encouraging widespread community support for those arrangements.

Its proposals on policing should be designed to ensure that policing arrangements, including composition, recruitment, training, culture, ethos and symbols, are such that in a new approach Northern Ireland has a police service that can enjoy widespread support from, and is seen as an integral part of, the community as a whole.

Its proposals should include recommendations covering any issues such as re-training, job placement and educational and professional development required in the transition to policing in a peaceful society.

Its proposals should also be designed to ensure that:

- the police service is structured, managed and resourced so that it can be effective in discharging its full range of functions (including proposals on any necessary arrangements for the transition to policing in a normal peaceful society);
- the police service is delivered in constructive and inclusive partnerships with the community at all levels with the maximum delegation of authority and responsibility;
- the legislative and constitutional framework requires the impartial discharge of policing functions and conforms with internationally accepted norms in relation to policing standards;
- the police operate within a clear framework of accountability to the law and the community they serve, so:
    - they are constrained by, accountable to and act only within the law;
    - their powers and procedures, like the law they enforce, are clearly established and publicly available;
    - there are open, accessible and independent means of investigating and adjudicating upon complaints against the police;
    - there are clearly established arrangements enabling local people, and their political representatives, to articulate their views and concerns about policing and to establish publicly policing priorities and policing policies, subject to safeguards to ensure police impartiality and freedom from partisan political control;
    - there are arrangements for accountability and for the effective, efficient and economic use of resources in achieving policing objectives;
    - there are means to ensure independent professional scrutiny and inspection of the police service to ensure that proper professional standards are maintained;

- the scope for structured co-operation with the Garda Siochana and other police forces is addressed; and
- the management of public order events which can impose exceptional demands on policing resources is also addressed.

The Commission should focus on policing issues, but if it identifies other aspects of the criminal justice system relevant to its work on policing, including the role of the police in prosecution, then it should draw the attention of the Government to those matters.

The Commission should consult widely, including with non-governmental expert organisations, and through such focus groups as they consider it appropriate to establish.

The Government proposes to establish the Commission as soon as possible, with the aim of it starting work as soon as possible and publishing its final report by Summer 1999.

ANNEX B

REVIEW OF THE CRIMINAL JUSTICE SYSTEM

Terms of Reference

Taking account of the aims of the criminal justice system as set out in the Agreement, the review will address the structure, management and resourcing of publicly funded elements of the criminal justice system and will bring forward proposals for future criminal justice arrangements (other than policing and those aspects of the system relating to emergency legislation, which the Government is considering separately) covering such issues as:

- the arrangements for making appointments to the judiciary and magistracy, and safeguards for protecting their independence;
- the arrangements for the organisation and supervision of the prosecution process, and for safeguarding its independence;
- measures to improve the responsiveness and accountability of, and any lay participation in the criminal justice system;
- mechanisms for addressing law reform;
- the scope for structured co-operation between the criminal justice agencies on both parts of the island; and
- the structure and organisation of criminal justice functions that might be devolved to an Assembly, including the possibility of establishing a Department of Justice, while safeguarding the essential independence of many of the key functions in this area.

The Government proposes to commence the review as soon as possible, consulting with the political parties and others, including non-governmental expert organisations. The review will be completed by Autumn 1999.

PRISONERS

1 Both Governments will put in place mechanisms to provide for an accelerated programme for the release of prisoners, including transferred prisoners, convicted of scheduled offences in Northern Ireland or, in the case of those sentenced outside Northern Ireland, similar offences (referred to hereafter as qualifying prisoners). Any such arrangements will protect the rights of individual prisoners under national and international law.

2 Prisoners affiliated to organisations which have not established or are not maintaining a complete and unequivocal ceasefire will not benefit from the arrangements. The situation in this regard will be kept under review.

3 Both Governments will complete a review process within a fixed time frame and set prospective release dates for all qualifying prisoners. The review process would provide for the advance of the release dates of qualifying prisoners while allowing account to be taken of the seriousness of the offences for which the person was convicted and the need to protect the community. In addition, the intention would be that should the circumstances allow it, any qualifying prisoners who remained in custody two years after the commencement of the scheme would be released at that point.

4 The Governments will seek to enact the appropriate legislation to give effect to these arrangements by the end of June 1998.

5 The Governments continue to recognise the importance of measures to facilitate the reintegration of prisoners into the community by providing support both prior to and after release, including assistance directed towards availing of employment opportunities, retraining and/or re-skilling, and further education.

VALIDATION, IMPLEMENTATION AND REVIEW

VALIDATION AND IMPLEMENTATION

1 The two Governments will as soon as possible sign a new British-Irish Agreement replacing the 1985 Anglo-Irish Agreement, embodying understandings on constitutional issues and affirming their solemn commitment to support and, where appropriate, implement the agreement reached by the participants in the negotiations which shall be annexed to the British-Irish Agreement.

2 Each Government will organise a referendum on 22 May 1998. Subject to Parliamentary approval, a consultative referendum in Northern Ireland, organised under the terms of the Northern Ireland (Entry to Negotiations, etc.) Act 1996, will address the question: "Do you support the agreement reached in the multi-party talks on Northern Ireland and set out in Command Paper 3883?". The Irish Government will introduce and support in the Oireachtas a Bill to amend the Constitution as described in paragraph 2 of the section "Constitutional Issues" and in Annex B, as follows: (a) to amend

Articles 2 and 3 as described in paragraph 8.1 in Annex B above and (b) to amend Article 29 to permit the Government to ratify the new British-Irish Agreement. On passage by the Oireachtas, the Bill will be put to referendum.

3 If majorities of those voting in each of the referendums support this agreement, the Governments will then introduce and support, in their respective Parliaments, such legislation as may be necessary to give effect to all aspects of this agreement, and will take whatever ancillary steps as may be required including the holding of elections on 25 June, subject to parliamentary approval, to the Assembly which would meet initially in a "shadow" mode. The establishment of the North-South Ministerial Council, implementation bodies, the British-Irish Council and the British-Irish Intergovernmental Conference and the assumption by the Assembly of its legislative and executive powers will take place at the same time on the entry into force of the British-Irish Agreement.

4 In the interim, aspects of the implementation of the multi-party agreement will be reviewed at meetings of those parties relevant in the particular case (taking into account, once Assembly elections have been held, the results of those elections), under the chairmanship of the British Government or the two Governments, as may be appropriate; and representatives of the two Governments and all relevant parties may meet under independent chairmanship to review implementation of the agreement as a whole.

Review procedures following implementation

5 Each institution may, at any time, review any problems that may arise in its operation and, where no other institution is affected, take remedial action in consultation as necessary with the relevant Government or Governments. It will be for each institution to determine its own procedures for review.

6 If there are difficulties in the operation of a particular institution, which have implications for another institution, they may review their operations separately and jointly and agree on remedial action to be taken under their respective authorities.

7 If difficulties arise which require remedial action across the range of institutions, or otherwise require amendment of the British-Irish Agreement or relevant legislation, the process of review will fall to the two Governments in consultation with the parties in the Assembly. Each Government will be responsible for action in its own jurisdiction.

8 Notwithstanding the above, each institution will publish an annual report on its operations. In addition, the two Governments and the parties in the Assembly will convene a conference 4 years after the agreement comes into effect, to review and report on its operation.

AGREEMENT BETWEEN THE GOVERNMENT OF THE UNITED KINGDOM OF GREAT BRITAIN AND NORTHERN IRELAND AND THE GOVERNMENT OF IRELAND

The British and Irish Governments:

Welcoming the strong commitment to the Agreement reached on 10th April 1998 by themselves and other participants in the multi-party talks and set out in Annex 1 to this Agreement (hereinafter "the Multi-Party Agreement");

Considering that the Multi-Party Agreement offers an opportunity for a new beginning in relationships within Northern Ireland, within the island of Ireland and between the peoples of these islands;

Wishing to develop still further the unique relationship between their peoples and the close co-operation between their countries as friendly neighbours and as partners in the European Union;

Reaffirming their total commitment to the principles of democracy and non-violence which have been fundamental to the multi-party talks;

Reaffirming their commitment to the principles of partnership, equality and mutual respect and to the protection of civil, political, social, economic and cultural rights in their respective jurisdictions;

Have agreed as follows:

ARTICLE 1

The two Governments:

(i) recognise the legitimacy of whatever choice is freely exercised by a majority of the people of Northern Ireland with regard to its status, whether they prefer to continue to support the Union with Great Britain or a sovereign united Ireland;

(ii) recognise that it is for the people of the island of Ireland alone, by agreement between the two parts respectively and without external impediment, to exercise their right of self-determination on the basis of consent, freely and concurrently given, North and South, to bring about a united Ireland, if that is their wish, accepting that this right must be achieved and exercised with and subject to the agreement and consent of a majority of the people of Northern Ireland;

(iii) acknowledge that while a substantial section of the people in Northern Ireland share the legitimate wish of a majority of the people of the island of Ireland for a united Ireland, the present wish of a majority of the people of Northern Ireland, freely exercised and legitimate, is to maintain the Union and accordingly, that Northern Ireland's status as part of the United Kingdom reflects and relies upon that wish; and that it would be wrong to make any change in the status of Northern Ireland save with the consent of a majority of its people;

(iv) affirm that, if in the future, the people of the island of Ireland exercise their right of self-determination on the basis set out in sections (i) and (ii) above to bring about a united Ireland, it will be a binding obligation on both Governments to introduce and support in their respective Parliaments legislation to give effect to that wish;

(v) affirm that whatever choice is freely exercised by a majority of the people of Northern Ireland, the power of the sovereign government with jurisdiction there shall be exercised with rigorous impartiality on behalf of all the people in the diversity of their identities and traditions and shall be founded on the principles of full respect for, and equality of, civil, political, social and cultural rights, of freedom from discrimination for all citizens, and of parity of esteem and of just and equal treatment for the identity, ethos and aspirations of both communities;

(vi) recognise the birthright of all the people of Northern Ireland to identify themselves and be accepted as Irish or British, or both, as they may so choose, and accordingly confirm that their right to hold both British and Irish citizenship is accepted by both Governments and would not be affected by any future change in the status of Northern Ireland.

ARTICLE 2

The two Governments affirm their solemn commitment to support, and where appropriate implement, the provisions of the Multi-Party Agreement. In particular there shall be established in accordance with the provisions of the Multi-Party Agreement immediately on the entry into force of this Agreement, the following institutions:

(i) a North/South Ministerial Council;

(ii) the implementation bodies referred to in paragraph 9 (ii) of the section entitled "Strand Two" of the Multi-Party Agreement;

(iii) a British-Irish Council;

(iv) a British-Irish Intergovernmental Conference.

ARTICLE 3

(1) This Agreement shall replace the Agreement between the British and Irish Governments done at Hillsborough on 15th November 1985 which shall cease to have effect on entry into force of this Agreement.

(2) The Intergovernmental Conference established by Article 2 of the aforementioned Agreement done on 15th November 1985 shall cease to exist on entry into force of this Agreement.

ARTICLE 4

(1) It shall be a requirement for entry into force of this Agreement that:

(a) British legislation shall have been enacted for the purpose of implementing the provisions of Annex A to the section entitled "Constitutional Issues" of the Multi-Party Agreement;

(b) the amendments to the Constitution of Ireland set out in Annex B to the section entitled "Constitutional Issues" of the Multi-Party Agreement shall have been approved by Referendum;

(c) such legislation shall have been enacted as may be required to establish the institutions referred to in Article 2 of this Agreement.

(2) Each Government shall notify the other in writing of the completion, so far as it is concerned, of the requirements for entry into force of this Agreement. This Agreement shall enter into force on the date of the receipt of the later of the two notifications.

(3) Immediately on entry into force of this Agreement, the Irish Government shall ensure that the amendments to the Constitution of Ireland set out in Annex B to the section entitled "Constitutional Issues" of the Multi-Party Agreement take effect.

In witness thereof the undersigned, being duly authorised thereto by the respective Governments, have signed this Agreement.

Done in two originals at Belfast on the 10th day of April 1998.

For the Government of the United Kingdom of Great Britain and Northern Ireland

For the Government of Ireland

ANNEX 1

The Agreement Reached in the Multi-Party Talks

ANNEX 2

Declaration on the Provisions of Paragraph (vi) of Article 1 In Relationship to Citizenship

The British and Irish Governments declare that it is their joint understanding that the term "the people of Northern Ireland" in paragraph (vi) of Article 1 of this Agreement means, for the purposes of giving effect to this provision, all persons born in Northern Ireland and having, at the time of their birth, at least one parent who is a British citizen, an Irish citizen or is otherwise entitled to reside in Northern Ireland without any restriction on their period of residence.

Index

This is an index of individuals and organizations only, complementing the three Tables at the beginning of the book. Judges are referred to only in non-judicial capacities.